MOON

PACIFIC NORTHWEST

ALLISON WILLIAMS

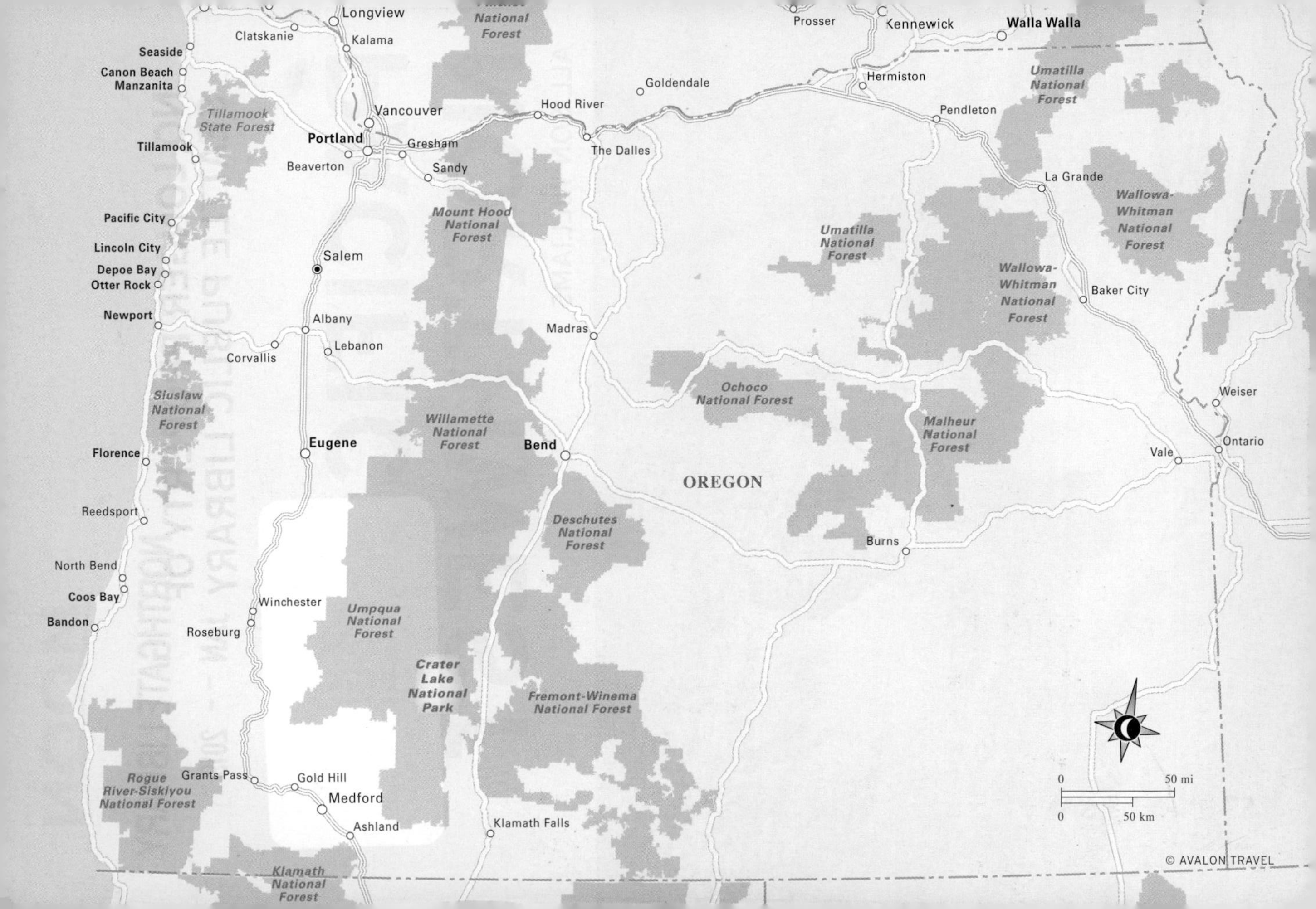
Longview
Clatskanie
Kalama
National Forest
Prosser
Kennewick
Walla Walla
Seaside
Canon Beach
Manzanita
Tillamook State Forest
Vancouver
Portland
Gresham
Tillamook
Beaverton
Sandy
Hermiston
Goldendale
Hood River
The Dalles
Pendleton
Umatilla National Forest
La Grande
Wallowa-Whitman National Forest
Pacific City
Lincoln City
Depoe Bay
Otter Rock
Newport
Mount Hood National Forest
Salem
Umatilla National Forest
Wallowa-Whitman National Forest
Baker City
Albany
Lebanon
Corvallis
Madras
Siuslaw National Forest
Ochoco National Forest
Weiser
Willamette National Forest
Malheur National Forest
Florence
Eugene
Bend
Ontario
Vale
OREGON
Reedsport
Deschutes National Forest
Burns
North Bend
Coos Bay
Bandon
Winchester
Roseburg
Umpqua National Forest
Crater Lake National Park
Fremont-Winema National Forest
Rogue River-Siskiyou National Forest
Grants Pass
Gold Hill
Medford
Ashland
Klamath Falls
Klamath National Forest
0
50 mi
0
50 km
© AVALON TRAVEL

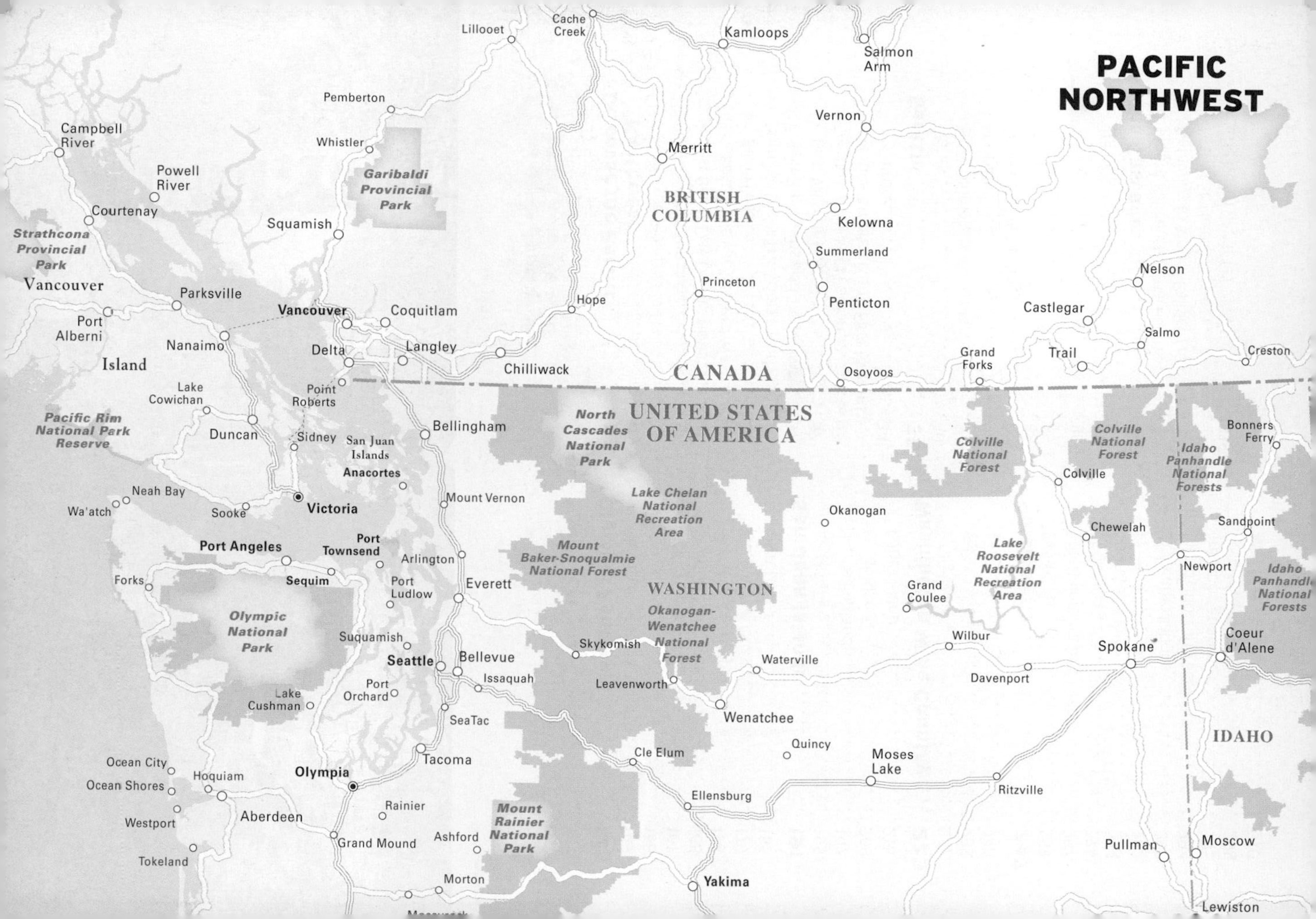
PACIFIC NORTHWEST
CANADA
BRITISH COLUMBIA
UNITED STATES OF AMERICA
WASHINGTON
IDAHO
Vancouver Island
Strathcona Provincial Park
Garibaldi Provincial Park
Pacific Rim National Park Reserve
Olympic National Park
North Cascades National Park
Lake Chelan National Recreation Area
Mount Baker-Snoqualmie National Forest
Okanogan-Wenatchee National Forest
Mount Rainier National Park
Colville National Forest
Lake Roosevelt National Recreation Area
Idaho Panhandle National Forests
Campbell River
Powell River
Courtenay
Vancouver
Parksville
Port Alberni
Nanaimo
Lake Cowichan
Duncan
Sidney
Victoria
Sooke
Neah Bay
Wa'atch
Lillooet
Cache Creek
Pemberton
Whistler
Squamish
Coquitlam
Delta
Langley
Point Roberts
Chilliwack
Hope
Kamloops
Salmon Arm
Vernon
Merritt
Kelowna
Summerland
Princeton
Penticton
Osoyoos
Nelson
Castlegar
Salmo
Trail
Grand Forks
Creston
Bellingham
San Juan Islands
Anacortes
Mount Vernon
Port Angeles
Port Townsend
Sequim
Arlington
Forks
Port Ludlow
Everett
Suquamish
Seattle
Bellevue
Issaquah
Port Orchard
Lake Cushman
SeaTac
Tacoma
Olympia
Ocean City
Ocean Shores
Hoquiam
Aberdeen
Westport
Tokeland
Rainier
Grand Mound
Ashford
Morton
Skykomish
Leavenworth
Wenatchee
Waterville
Cle Elum
Ellensburg
Quincy
Moses Lake
Yakima
Okanogan
Grand Coulee
Wilbur
Davenport
Ritzville
Spokane
Pullman
Colville
Chewelah
Newport
Sandpoint
Bonners Ferry
Coeur d'Alene
Moscow
Lewiston

Contents

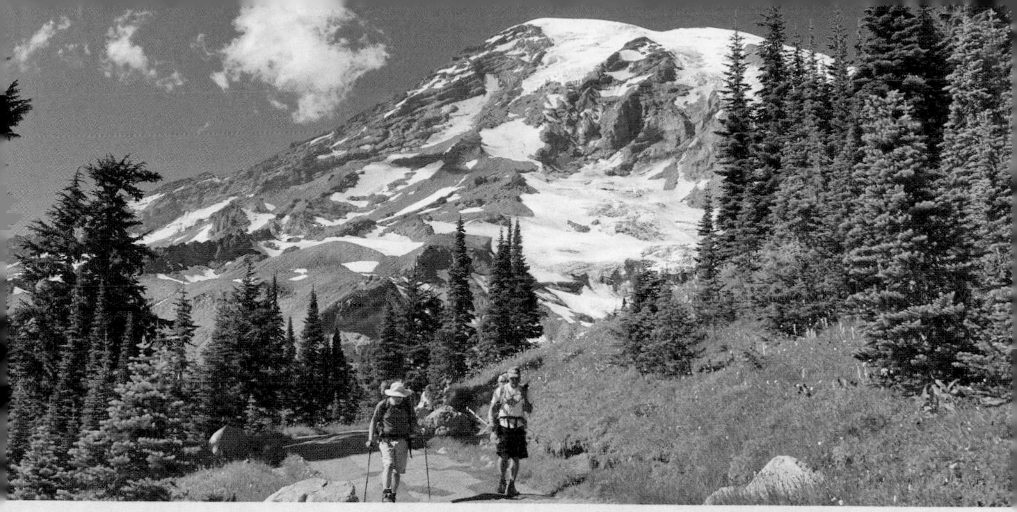

DISCOVER

the Pacific Northwest

It's not unusual to think of the Pacific Northwest as green and lush. But you must tour the entire region to truly appreciate how many shades of the color blanket this corner of the world.

There's the deep evergreen of Douglas fir trees and the dusty pale green of rainforest moss. The electric green of Seattle's hometown sports jerseys. A green ethos keeps Portland running on bicycle power and compost. And then there is all that green cash that companies like Starbucks, Nike, Microsoft, and others bring to the region. And envy? It seems like everyone's jealous of the great Pacific Northwest; population growth is off the charts. Between nature and culture, every possible shade of green appears here.

The best way to see the treasures of Washington, Oregon, and British Columbia is to follow the roads connecting vibrant cities like Seattle, Vancouver, and Portland with the wild green places in between—an untamed coast, a deep forest, and a legendary mountain (or two).

Clockwise from top left: Seattle Space Needle; Portland Farmers Market; Astoria-Megler Bridge; Vancouver; Olympic National Park; the Oregon Coast from Oswald West State Park.

12 TOP EXPERIENCES

1 **Wilderness Hiking:** From rainforests to high alpine meadows, you can explore the region's magnificent terrain by trail (page 27).

2 **Brewpubs and Taprooms:** Taste craft brews on their home turf (page 31). Most American beer hops are grown right here in the Pacific Northwest.

3 **Columbia River Gorge:** From rich evergreen forests to arid grasslands, with mountains and kiteboarders in between, this **National Scenic Area** offers an abundance of recreational options (page 298).

4 **Mountain Getaways:** Head to places like **Mount Rainier's Paradise Inn** (page 96) and **Mount Hood's Timberline Lodge** (page 310) for both relaxation and recreation at your doorstep.

5 Driving the Oregon Coast: Follow a highway that hugs the curves and coves of this wild, scenic coastline (page 374).

6 Pike Place Market: Fresh-caught fish fly through the air at this bustling marketplace, where you'll find everything from flower vendors to handmade crafts to heartsick buskers (page 40).

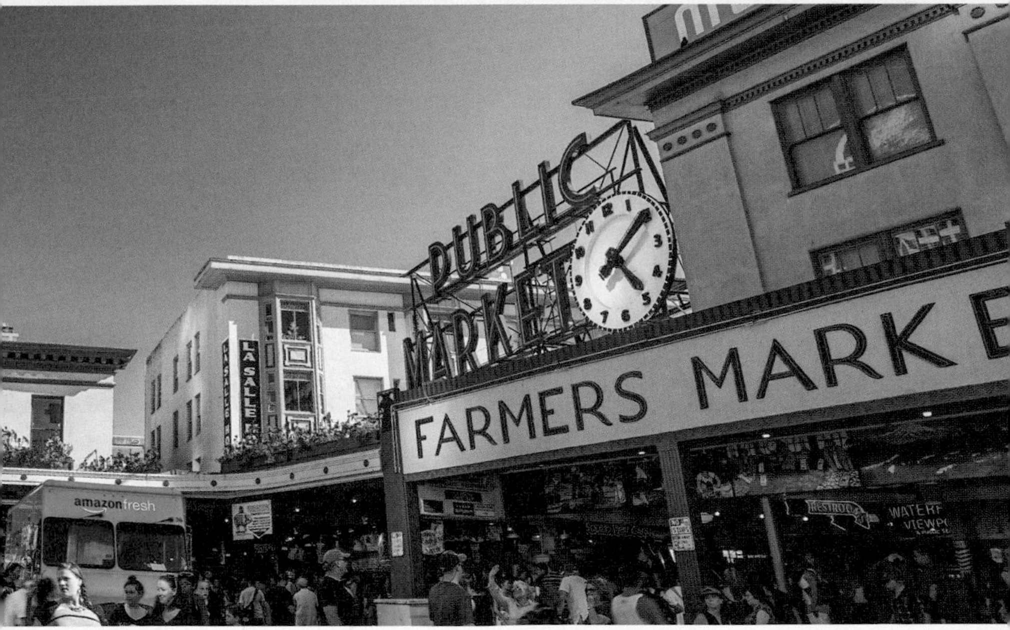
PUBLIC
MARKET
FARMERS MARKE
LA SALLE
amazonfresh
WATERF
VIEWP

^
^
^

7 **Wine Country:** Low-key, friendly winemakers take advantage of ideal climates in **Washington,** especially in **Walla Walla** (page 227), and **Oregon** (page 319).

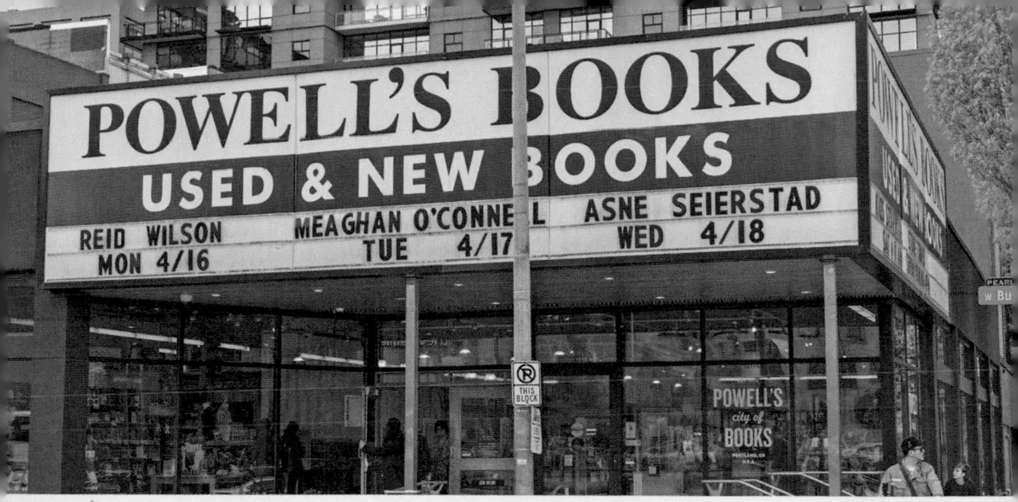

8 Powell's City of Books: Discover Portland in a nutshell at this storied store filled with books covering every quirky subject (page 258).

9 Whale-Watching from the San Juan Islands: You'll feel the true wonder of this archipelago when you spot some of its resident orcas (pages 201, 211, and 220).

^
^
^

10 Stanley Park: Enjoy Vancouver's waterfront from this picturesque peninsular park filled with beaches, trails, and an aquarium (page 445).

11 Oregon Shakespeare Festival: Bond with the Bard at this months-long festival in the charming town of Ashland (page 424).

12 Tea Time in Victoria: This refined city celebrates its British roots with elaborate afternoon teas served in classic style with scones and sandwiches (page 511).

Planning Your Trip

Where to Go

Seattle

The future is waiting around every corner of this waterfront city—from the towering **Space Needle** to the collection of spacecraft at the **Museum of Flight.** Wake early for the **Seattle Art Museum** and bustling **Pike Place Market,** but prepare to stay up late for farm-to-table **dining** and a diverse selection of **live music.**

The Cascades

When "The Mountain"—as **Mount Rainier** is known—is out, it's one of the most spectacular sights in the Northwest—a giant dotted with **glaciers** and flanked by **wildflower meadows.** Stop at the **Jackson Visitor Center** in the aptly named **Paradise,** or spend the night at the historical **Paradise Inn.** Add a side trip to **Mount St. Helens** and drive up to the **Johnston Ridge Observatory** for a firsthand look at where the mountain blew in 1980. Farther north, you'll find the Bavarian village of **Leavenworth;** the tiny town of **Chelan,** which affords access to the 50-mile **Lake Chelan;** and Wild West town **Winthrop,** gateway to **North Cascades National Park** and its remote, jagged peaks.

Olympic Peninsula

Washington's "green thumb" is a promontory of land rich in natural features. **Olympic National Park** is home to **Hurricane Ridge,** with its sweeping ridgetop vistas, and the verdant mists of the **Hoh Rain Forest.** The peninsula's **beaches and bays** stretch from the town of **Port Angeles** to **Neah Bay** and continue down the coast.

Olympic National Park

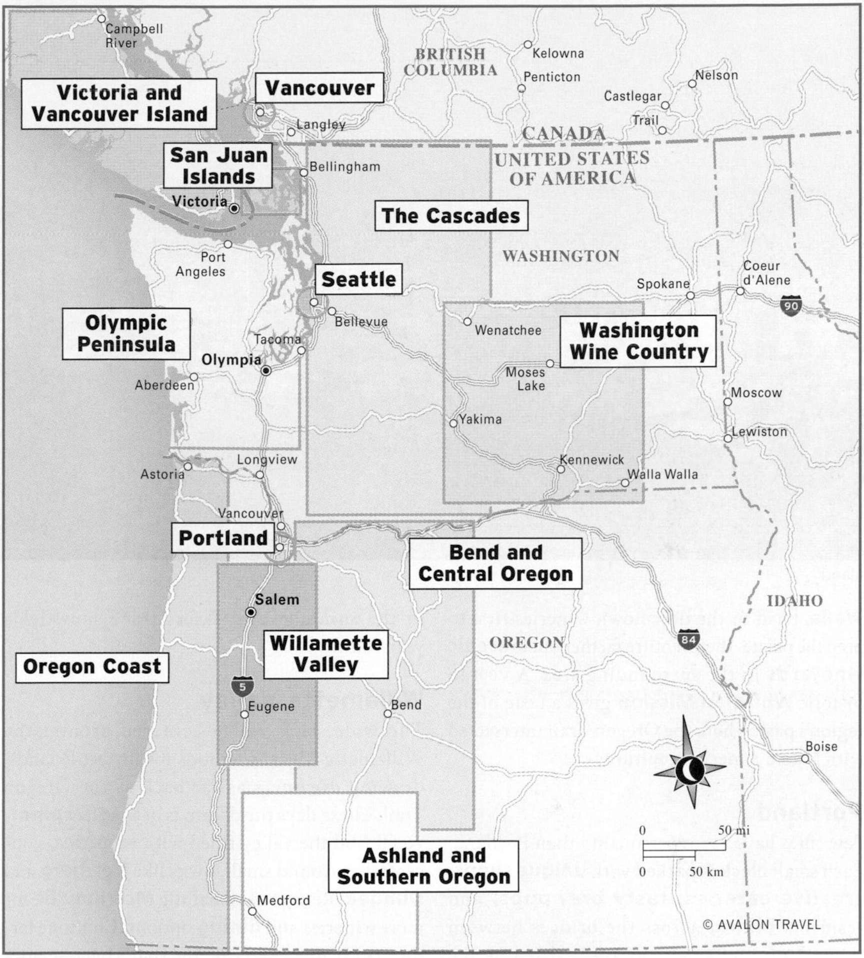

San Juan Islands

Accessible by ferry, the San Juan Islands just off the coast of Washington offer **bucolic getaways,** complete with opportunities for **whale-watching**—the San Juans have resident orca pods. Home to the quaint town of **Friday Harbor,** the historic **American Camp** and **English Camp,** and colorful **San Juan Islands Sculpture Park, San Juan Island** is the most bustling of the archipelago. Fun and funky **Orcas Island** and sleepy **Lopez Island** each have their own appeal, with hiking at **Mount Constitution** popular on the former and **biking** on the latter.

Washington Wine Country

Sit back and take in the rolling hills of eastern Washington with a glass of cabernet in hand. Wander through the **Yakima Valley** to small **wineries** and **breweries**—aside from its grapes, this region grows hops aplenty. Continue to the **Tri-Cities** to stroll along the Columbia River and visit the area's scattered wineries. In **Walla**

Portland

Walla, head to the downtown wineries first to prep the palate, then venture farther out to **scenic vineyards** in the surrounding area. A visit to historic **Whitman Mission** gives a taste of the region's past, where the Oregon Trail intersected with Native American culture.

Portland

Few cities have more personality than Portland. Each small block is packed with **unique shops, creative eateries, tasty brewpubs,** and residents **biking** across the bridges between them. Stop and smell the roses that line the **International Rose Test Garden** (one of the world's largest) in **Washington Park,** gaze in awe at the **Pittock Mansion**'s three-story staircase, and wander amid the giant playground that is the **Oregon Museum of Science and Industry.** Just outside the city are natural wonders to explore, including the **Columbia River Gorge,** cutting a chasm between forested hills and rocky bluffs lined with waterfalls, and **Mount Hood,** where majestic **Timberline Lodge** sits halfway up the volcano, hikers roam in the summer, and skiers trace snowfields year-round.

Willamette Valley

The wide, rich valley centered around the Willamette River is famous for its fertile lands, drawing dreamers as far back as the Oregon Trail. These days the dream is of a perfect **pinot;** you'll find the valley filled with **wineries,** concentrated around small towns like **Newberg** and **Dundee.** Retreat to charming **McMinnville** for more wineries and **dining** options. Continue farther south and you'll find the state's biggest cities after Portland, **state capital Salem** and hippie-inflected **Eugene,** home of the **University of Oregon.**

Bend and Central Oregon

Welcome to the high desert, where the air is dry, the sun shines, and the biggest decision of the day is what **outdoor adventure** to embark on and where to drink afterward. Hike, bike, or ski **Mount Bachelor,** float the **Deschutes River,** or head underground and explore the volcanic landscape at **Lava River Cave.** Leave plenty of

Best Rainy-Day Distractions

It doesn't rain *every* day in the Pacific Northwest, but it could. Fortunately there are plenty of ways to have fun indoors.

SEATTLE

- **Pike Place Market:** Seattle put its farmers market under a roof, so even the famous flying fish are covered (page 40).
- **Seattle Art Museum:** Several floors of galleries and free public tours offer shelter at this downtown museum (page 44).
- **Museum of History and Industry:** Follow Seattle's historic rise to tech giant, and then check the weather through the working periscope (page 51).

THE CASCADES

- **Paradise Inn:** The giant fireplaces inside this historical hotel provide plenty of warmth (page 96).

OLYMPIC PENINSULA

- **Northwest Maritime Center:** Watch craftspeople build wooden boats inside a warm boat shop (page 152).
- **Hoh Rain Forest:** Don't hide from the rain—embrace it in the thick forest of Olympic National Park (page 172).

PORTLAND

- **Pittock Mansion:** The historical home of a Portland luminary is crammed with beautiful antique furnishings (page 259).
- **Oregon Museum of Science and Industry:** Seek shelter inside a submarine that sits in the Willamette River (page 262).
- **Maryhill Museum of Art:** European treasures are artfully displayed in a mansion built on a lonely, scenic expanse of the Columbia River Gorge (page 309).

WILLAMETTE VALLEY

- **Evergreen Aviation & Space Museum:** Two giant hangars full of spacecraft and airplanes let in light but no weather (page 326).

BEND AND CENTRAL OREGON

- **High Desert Museum:** A 100-year-old sawmill still operates inside this museum devoted to the region's brushy, arid landscape (page 352).

OREGON COAST

- **Tillamook Cheese Factory:** How many cheese samples can you eat at once (page 388)?
- **Oregon Coast Aquarium:** There are plenty of creatures in the touch tanks to take up a whole afternoon (page 400).

VANCOUVER

- **Vancouver Police Museum:** A gray day sets the mood for murder exhibits in the city's old morgue (page 450).
- **University of British Columbia Museum of Anthropology:** Tall windows provide sanctuary in the museum's airy totem pole gallery (page 454).

VICTORIA AND VANCOUVER ISLAND

- **Fairmont Empress Hotel:** Warm up with the hotel's famous afternoon tea (page 499).

room for ales and meals to take advantage of Bend's vibrant **brewing** and **dining** scene. Also not to be missed is the rocky landscape of picturesque **Smith Rock State Park,** near the towns of **Redmond** and **Sisters.**

Oregon Coast

Driving down U.S. 101, it seems like the **beaches** of the Oregon Coast never end. Along the way, follow the footsteps of Lewis and Clark at **Fort Clatsop,** explore the tide pools at **Haystack**

Whistler

Rock, nibble bites of cheese at the **Tillamook Cheese Factory,** check out **lighthouses,** and discover local marinelife at the **Oregon Coast Aquarium.**

Ashland and Southern Oregon

If all the world's a stage, charming **Ashland** is the front row, host to the **Oregon Shakespeare Festival** and its months of plays and outdoor events. Find poetry in every form in the quiet paths of the town's **Lithia Park.** Then head north to magical **Crater Lake National Park,** the deepest lake in America, surrounded by scenic peaks and punctuated by **Wizard Island.**

Vancouver

Mountains tower over Vancouver, Canada—so close that **Grouse Mountain** skiers practically slide down next to the city's skyscrapers. Bike or walk around downtown's **Stanley Park**—home to the **Vancouver Aquarium**—browse the wares on offer at the **Granville Island Public Market,** and take in some **Olympic history** with a day trip or more to **Whistler.** At night, sample the myriad options on offer from Vancouver's **international culinary scene.**

Victoria and Vancouver Island

Victoria may be only a short ferry ride away, at the tip of Vancouver Island, but a visit here feels like crossing the pond to Britain. This is the **capital of British Columbia,** and a tour of the **British Columbia Parliament Buildings** provides a primer on the parliamentary system of government. Enjoy the delicate elegance of afternoon tea in the **Fairmont Empress Hotel** as it holds court over Victoria's Inner Harbour, and then visit **The Butchart Gardens,** a world-class garden housed in an old quarry. Far west across the wild island, **Tofino** is a **surf** town in a cold region, its wave-riders drawn to the crashing Pacific. Find more beaches at nearby **Pacific Rim National Park Reserve,** or warm up at **Hot Springs Cove.**

Know Before You Go

Seasons

If there's one thing you can depend on in the Pacific Northwest, it's that you *can't* depend on the weather. The region is known for **rain,** but it doesn't fall in regular intervals. **Summer** is the driest and sunniest season. Occasionally temperatures can soar above 90°F, and the lack of widespread air-conditioning can make it uncomfortable. **Fall** can vary between brisk, beautiful days and soggy, gray ones. **Winter** rarely brings much snow outside of the mountains and passes (but when it does snow in the city, stay off the streets). **Mountain roads,** such as those around Mount Rainier, are prone to **seasonal closures** and may require chains in winter months. **Spring** is often the rainiest time of year, but it doesn't tend to pour in the region—instead, expect drizzle with the occasional shower. (Sometimes it's even sunny!) In general, when the rain falls in the region it's of this gentler variety—which is why you'll notice the locals make do with hats and hoodies rather than umbrellas, and don't tend to let it stop them from getting out and about.

Passports and Visas

It's nice to leave room for the unexpected in a trip to the Pacific Northwest, but some things should be arranged in advance. International visitors will most likely need a visa, though Canadian neighbors can make due with only their **passport.** Residents of a country other than the United States or Canada should know in advance if they plan to **cross the border** on their trip. Most visitors will enter through the international airports in Seattle, Portland, or Vancouver; all have some form of public transportation running to the center of town, but not all run 24 hours.

Reservations

Hotels in big cities like Seattle and Portland can fill quickly during popular times: the middle of summer, winter holidays, and around

Vancouver Aquarium

beach on the Olympic Peninsula

Pike Place Market

big conventions and sporting events. Given the **limited accommodations in smaller towns** on the Olympic Peninsula and Oregon Coast, sellouts are possible. **Campgrounds** that take reservations are likely to fill up in advance during the summer, as are big national park or mountain lodges. Rental cars are less in danger of being completely out of stock, but **train and bus tickets** are best reserved in advance. **Ferry reservations** should be arranged as soon as travel plans are set; Washington State Ferry releases availability in batches for the San Juan Islands and Victoria trips.

As for attractions and dining, book ahead only if you need to ensure availability at a certain time, or have your heart set on a particular fine-dining restaurant. **Tickets for sporting events** like professional football and even soccer should also be scheduled in advance. Otherwise, once you've secured the bones of a Pacific Northwest trip, there's lots of room to explore, improvise, and discover things along the way.

The Best of the Pacific Northwest

Circle the Pacific Northwest in this **two-week drive.** Start in Seattle, Washington, and head north to Vancouver, British Columbia. After a brief stop in Victoria, ferry over to the Olympic Peninsula and drive down the Oregon Coast. Loop inland to Portland, and then head north with a stop at Mount Rainier before returning to Seattle. Alternatively, start in Portland or Vancouver and follow the loop from there.

Days 1-2

SEATTLE

Spend two days visiting the many sides of Seattle (see details and suggestions on page 41). Wander the city's bustling **downtown,** watch the fish fly at **Pike Place Market,** spot volcanoes from atop the **Space Needle,** and indulge in one of **Capitol Hill's restaurants.**

IF YOU HAVE MORE TIME

Add a day trip to the winemaking hub of **Woodinville.** Or head farther afield for an overnight in Washington wine country, which begins in the **Yakima Valley** and stretches east to **Walla Walla.** With 2-3 extra days, you can drive north to nearby Anacortes and hop a **ferry** to the **San Juan Islands** (see details and suggestions on page 33 under Days 2-3 of the *Seattle Loop*).

Days 3-5: Vancouver

SEATTLE TO VANCOUVER

141 MILES/227 KM (3 HOURS)

Head north on **I-5** to Vancouver, British Columbia. Leave plenty of time for delays at the **Peace Arch border crossing** between the United States and Canada because lanes back up on weekends and holidays.

Spend two days exploring downtown Vancouver (see details and suggestions on page

Seattle

444). Bike around sprawling **Stanley Park,** tour the city's **Olympic sights,** and drive north of the city to ride the tram up **Grouse Mountain.**

Include a day trip to **Whistler** for epic skiing in the winter and beautiful hiking or mountain biking in the summer.

Day 6: Victoria

VANCOUVER TO VICTORIA

70 MILES/113 KM (3 HOURS)

From Vancouver, drive 35 kilometers (22 miles) south on **Highway 99** to the **Tsawwassen ferry terminal** and board the **B.C. Ferry** to Victoria. The 90-minute boat trip arrives in **Swartz Bay.** Follow **Highway 17** for 32 kilometers (20 miles) south to Victoria. It's a quick trip into the city, though traffic can build in the early morning.

Explore Victoria's Inner Harbour (see details and suggestions on page 499). Reserve an afternoon tea at the **Fairmont Empress Hotel,** take the Harbour Ferry to **Fisherman's Wharf,** and cap the night in bustling **Chinatown** and its historical Fan Tan Alley.

IF YOU HAVE MORE TIME

Explore more of wild **Vancouver Island** with a two-day side trip to **Tofino** on the western coast (see details and suggestions for Victoria to Tofino on page 34 under the *Seattle Loop*).

Days 7-8: Olympic Peninsula

VICTORIA TO FORKS

80 MILES/129 KM (3 HOURS)

Take the **Black Ball Ferry Line** across the Strait of Juan de Fuca, arriving in **Port Angeles,** Washington. Follow **U.S. 101** west as it passes through **Olympic National Park** (see details and suggestions on page 149). Stop at **Hurricane Ridge Visitor Center** for sweeping views, and then spend the night at **Lake Crescent** or continue south to **Forks.**

Day two brings quick access to the crashing waves at **La Push,** or explore the park's **Hoh Rain Forest** and **Lake Quinault.**

Cannon Beach on the Oregon Coast

Oregon Museum of Science and Industry

Best Hikes

THE CASCADES

- **Skyline Trail:** Take the first steps up giant Mount Rainier through alpine meadows, with views of the peak's giant glaciers (page 97).
- **Grove of the Patriarchs:** A suspension bridge links sections of a flat and easy ramble through the Rainier area's biggest trees (page 99).
- **Eruption Trail:** The gaping crater of Mount St. Helens provides a backdrop to an educational walk through volcanic rock and wildflowers (page 116).

OLYMPIC PENINSULA

- **Mount Storm King:** Brave some elevation gain through Olympic forest to reach lookouts with Lake Crescent views (page 169).
- **Sol Duc Falls:** One of the classic waterfalls of the famously lush Olympic Peninsula is just a short loop from the trailhead (page 170).
- **Hoh River Trail to Glacier Meadows:** Charge into the rain forest on a flat route along one of the Pacific Northwest's most picturesque rivers (page 173).

WASHINGTON WINE COUNTRY

- **Cowiche Canyon Trail:** Sneak a wine tasting into a hike through the dry eastern Washington landscape (page 237).

PORTLAND

- **Dog Mountain:** In spring, this hike's hillsides break into colorful wildflowers, with views of the Columbia River Gorge below (page 303).

WILLAMETTE VALLEY

- **Trail of Ten Falls:** Hike a classic loop trail past 10 gorgeous waterfalls (page 333).

BEND AND CENTRAL OREGON

- **Todd Lake:** Catch views of Cascade volcanoes from a scenic lake in the warm Central Oregon forest (page 359).

Sol Duc Falls

OREGON COAST

- **Hobbit Trail:** Reach the sands of the Oregon coastline through a magical, short hike that recalls a fantasy landscape (page 406).
- **Devil's Churn:** The wild Pacific waves turn a section of Cape Perpetua into a frothing, active cauldron of seawater (page 406).

ASHLAND AND SOUTHERN OREGON

- **Wizard Island:** The climb atop a mini volcano in the middle of Crater Lake begins with a boat tour, making it a well-rounded nature day in the Pacific Northwest (page 434).

VANCOUVER

- **Grouse Grind:** The haul up Vancouver's ski mountain is a challenge but comes with plenty of summit rewards (page 468).

VICTORIA AND VANCOUVER ISLAND

- **Wild Pacific Trail:** Hike along the rocky coast near Tofino and enjoy crashing Pacific waves and a sense of remoteness (page 528).

Mount Hood

Day 9: Olympic Peninsula to the Oregon Coast

FORKS TO ASTORIA

185 MILES/298 KM (4 HOURS)

It's a long trip on **U.S. 101** from **Forks** down to **Astoria** on the Oregon Coast, so start early. Traffic is less likely to be an issue, but any small backup or accident on the road can cause problems. Plan to arrive in Astoria in time for a casual dinner in the industrial waterfront town.

Day 10: Oregon Coast

ASTORIA TO FLORENCE

183 MILES/295 KM (4.5 HOURS)

This simple drive down the Oregon Coast follows **U.S. 101** south, with worthwhile stops along the way (see details and suggestions on page 374). Stop for lunch on the sand in **Cannon Beach,** visit the aquarium in **Newport,** or take a sand dune tour in **Oregon Dunes National Recreation Area.**

IF YOU HAVE MORE TIME

If you're up for more driving and have time to spare, you can explore the **Three Capes Loop** from **Tillamook,** which adds 50 miles. Or keep heading south another 75 miles from Florence on U.S. 101 to see more of the rugged coastline and end at the charming town of **Bandon.**

Days 11-12: Portland

FLORENCE TO PORTLAND

173 MILES/278 KM (3 HOURS)

Leave Florence early, following **U.S. 126** east for 56 miles to I-5. Take **I-5** north for 115 miles to Portland. You'll roll into the city just after the morning traffic jams.

You can see a lot of Portland in two days (see details and suggestions on page 252). Spend one day exploring downtown sights such as **Powell's City of Books** and the **South Park Blocks.** On day two, cross the Willamette River to visit the southeast neighborhoods and the **Oregon Museum of Science and Industry.**

IF YOU HAVE MORE TIME

Add on a day trip to the **Columbia River Gorge** or **Mount Hood** for gorgeous scenery and outdoor recreation. Or head to **Willamette wine country** to taste some of Oregon's famous pinots.

With an extra couple of days, venture into central Oregon to explore **Bend** (see details and suggestions on page 351) and its many **breweries** and recreational opportunities.

Day 13: Mount Rainier

PORTLAND TO MOUNT RAINIER

137 MILES/220 KM (2.5 HOURS)

Leave Portland early (before rush-hour traffic). Head north on **I-5,** then take **U.S. 12** east for 30 miles. At Morton, follow **Highway 7** north for 15 miles to **Highway 706.** Turn east and take Highway 706 to Mount Rainier's **Nisqually Entrance.**

Spend the day hiking through wildflower meadows at **Paradise,** or enjoy a scenic drive through the national park to **Sunrise** (see details and suggestions on page 90).

Day 14: Return to Seattle

MOUNT RAINIER TO SEATTLE

86 MILES/138 KM (2 HOURS)

In summer, head north out of the national park on **Highway 410,** driving through Enumclaw back to Seattle. When the roads are closed, exit back through the Nisqually Entrance on **Highway 706** toward Ashford and circle back to **I-5** and Seattle.

IF YOU HAVE MORE TIME

Head into the **North Cascades** and spend a night in the charming **Bavarian-themed** town of **Leavenworth** to enjoy beers and brats before making your way back to Seattle.

Options for Shorter Trips

SEATTLE AND VANCOUVER

Hit the region's two biggest cities in a short road trip. Start in **Seattle** and spend two days exploring the downtown sights. Drive north on **I-5,** stopping in **Anacortes** or the tiny towns of Bow and Edison. Arrive in **Vancouver** and enjoy some outdoorsy side trips to the mountains north of the city or to **Whistler.**

PORTLAND AND THE OREGON COAST

An easy loop from Portland includes the best of both city and nature. Spend two days discovering **Portland**'s neighborhood gems, and then take **I-5** north into Washington and drive 44 miles to Longview. At Longview, jog west on **Highway 432** to **U.S. 30** and continue 45 miles to **Astoria** on the coast. Spend a day or two following **U.S. 101** south along the coast with stops to walk on the beach or watch whales. At Newport, take **U.S. 20** east for about 63 miles to the towns of Corvallis and Albany, where it meets up with I-5. From Albany, follow **I-5** north for 70 miles to return to Portland.

SEATTLE, PORTLAND, AND THE COASTAL NORTHWEST

To experience both Seattle and Portland, as well as their respective states' dramatic coastlines, start in **Seattle** and head west to the **Olympic Peninsula.** You can take a ferry or loop down and back up through Tacoma. Spend a couple of days making your way counterclockwise on the peninsula via **U.S. 101** and exploring **Olympic National Park.** Continue south on U.S. 101 to the **Oregon Coast,** budgeting 2-3 days to follow the rugged coastline. At **Florence,** head east on **Highway 26** to meet up with **I-5** in **Eugene** and loop back up north through **Portland.**

Portland Loop: The Foodie Northwest

This itinerary outlines a one-week trip starting and ending in Portland, but travelers can also fly into Bend and do this trip in the opposite direction.

Days 1-2: Portland

Explore Oregon's charming big city by kicking off the day with brunch at **Tasty N Alder.** Afterward, if it's a Saturday, wander the lively **Portland Farmers Market.** Continue to walk off your meal by ambling the aisles of the massive cookbook section, among others, at **Powell's City of Books.** Burn more calories by heading to the **International Rose Test Garden,** where you can enjoy copious flowers for free. Finish the day across the river at southeast Portland's **Pok Pok,** making sure to order the famous sticky chicken wings. Dessert is a scoop of ice cream from a nearby outpost of **Salt & Straw,** famed for its creative blends. Then stroll along the busy Division Street corridor to check out the vibe of its many other restaurants.

Start your next day at **Kenny and Zuke's Delicatessen** before devoting the day to Portland's signature beers. You might choose one neighborhood and hop around; **breweries** are everywhere. Good bets include **Lucky Labrador Brewing Company** and **BridgePort Brewpub.** If you need a quick snack at any point, check out one of the city's many **food cart** pods. Then spend some time ambling along the Willamette River at **Tom McCall Waterfront Park** before dinner at one of the city's preeminent dining spots like **Ava Gene's** for its handmade pastas and veggie dishes or **Han Oak** for its prix fixe.

Days 3-4: Willamette Wine Country

42 MILES/68 KM (1 HOUR)

Grab a gourmet doughnut at the renowned **Voodoo Doughnut** for breakfast, then hit the road, heading south on **I-5** to **Highway 99** and following it southwest to McMinnville, which will be your home base for a couple of days in **Willamette wine country.** Spend the day exploring the quaint downtown and indulge in your first wine tastings at spots like the **Willamette Valley Vineyards Tasting Room** and **The Eyrie Vineyards,** both known for **pinots.** For lunch, go for **Ribslayer BBQ to Go,** and for dinner, get a farm-to-table meal at **Thistle.**

On your second day in wine country, get coffee and pastries for the road, or have a sit-down breakfast, at the charming **Community Plate.** Then head about 15 miles northeast on Highway 99 to the **Newberg** and **Dundee** area to taste classic pinots at **Erath Winery** and bubblies at **Argyle Winery.** For lunch, head to **Red Hills Market** for fresh sandwiches and salads or wood-fired pizzas, or pick from its cheese and charcuterie selection and picnic at the outdoor patio of **Duck Pond Cellars.** Take a book-browsing or caffeine break at **Chapters Books and Coffee** before dinner at the **Painted Lady.**

Days 5-6: Bend

157 MILES/253 KM (3.25 HOURS)

From McMinnville, head south on **Highway 99** then east on **Highway 22,** taking it all the way to **U.S. 20,** which continues east to Bend. Eat an indulgent breakfast along the way in **Salem** at **Sassy Onion Grill.** Once you get to Bend, your first day is all about beer. Grab a map of the **Bend Ale Trail** and hit the best breweries in town, from **Crux Fermentation Project** to longtime standby **Deschutes Brewery Bend Public House,** where you can also eat a hearty, yummy lunch. Continue on the beer trail as you like, then, for dinner, choose between fried chicken at **Drake** or international street food at **Spork.**

Best Brewpubs and Taprooms

SEATTLE

- **Rhein Haus:** The bocce courts are always active and the beer steins overflowing at this Bavarian-themed beer garden (page 57).

THE CASCADES

- **Icicle Brewing:** Here in Leavenworth, the home of the Northwest's biggest Oktoberfest, a local brewer delivers ales that pair well with bratwurst (page 129).

OLYMPIC PENINSULA

- **Fish Tale Brewpub:** In Olympia, a town once synonymous with a cheap, fairly light beer, a new generation of thoughtful brewers is creating organic ales and creative ciders (page 188).

WASHINGTON WINE COUNTRY

- **Bale Breaker Brewing Company:** Tucked in the middle of hop fields, this brewery is a beer oasis in wine country (page 238).

PORTLAND

- **BridgePort Brewpub:** Hops are king at a classic Portland brewery known for IPAs, the region's hallmark beer (page 267).
- **Hopworks Urban Brewery:** Green practices and organic brewing give this bike-friendly beer spot an upbeat do-gooder vibe (page 268).
- **Double Mountain Brewery:** Hoppy beers flow at one of Hood River's big-name brewhouses (page 306).

BEND AND CENTRAL OREGON

- **Deschutes Brewery Bend Public House:** This two-story brewpub is the granddaddy of beer spots, with a line of pub-only beers and some of the best food in town (page 360).
- **Crux Fermentation Project:** With a giant lawn, food trucks, fire pits, and views of Mount Bachelor, you almost don't need Crux's excellent Bend beers to have a good time—but they help (page 360).

Rhein Haus

OREGON COAST

- **Fort George Brewery and Public House:** This brewer set up shop in an old service station, often hosts big public events, and likes to bring a sense of humor to brewpub decor and beer names (page 378).
- **Pelican Pub & Brewery:** Catch some salt air at this beachfront brewery in Pacific City, with a thorough menu of both pours and food options (page 391).
- **Rogue Ales Brewery:** One of Oregon's most popular beers is made here (page 400).

VANCOUVER

- **Granville Island Brewing:** Tucked into Vancouver's waterfront arts and culture hub, this brewery crafts one of British Columbia's most popular brands of beer (page 459).

VICTORIA AND VANCOUVER ISLAND

- **CANOE Brewpub:** This brewery offers waterfront views, hosts live music, and welcomes children much of the day in its historical brick building (page 505).

Best Wineries

WASHINGTON WINE COUNTRY

- **Mark Ryan Winery:** Drink award-winning syrah at this Walla Walla winery (page 227).
- **Amavi Cellars:** This traditional winemaker is known for classic reds like cabernet sauvignon and syrah (page 227).
- **Sleight of Hand Cellars:** The playful tasting room is full of records, and wines include approachable red blends (page 227).
- **L'Ecole No 41:** Try a bordeaux in a rural old schoolhouse from one of the best-regarded winemakers in the region (page 228).
- **Col Solare Winery:** Outside the Tri-Cities, locals partner with French winemakers for well-regarded cabernets (page 243).
- **Alexandria Nicole Cellars:** Beautiful acres of vineyards are a tranquil setting to try unusual wines like the winery's Marsanne (page 243).

Willamette Valley

WILLAMETTE VALLEY

- **Duck Pond Cellars:** Drink award-winning red and white pinots here for a good cause—some of this cellars' sales go toward supporting environmental issues (page 319).
- **Argyle Winery:** Head to a giant tasting room for sparkling wines that will make you forget the fuss over French champagne. (page 320).
- **Erath Winery:** Pinot gris shines at a sleek, unfussy tasting room in the heart of Oregon wine country (page 320).
- **Domaine Drouhin Oregon:** With roots in Burgundy, the winemakers here pull from tradition for classic chardonnays (page 320).
- **The Eyrie Vineyards:** A visit to this industrial tasting room is a salute to pinot history; its founding winemaker is credited with the region's pinot kick. (page 325).
- **King Estate Winery:** This winery is out of the way but worth finding for its excellent pinot gris (page 341).

On day two in Bend, grab a real boiled bagel and more at **Rockin' Dave's Bagel Bistro,** then head out to take advantage of the area's **outdoor recreation** possibilities, whether hiking or river floating in the summer or skiing in the winter. For dinner, go for a locally sourced tasting menu at **Ariana.**

Day 7: Back to Portland

177 MILES/285 KM (3.5 HOURS)

Head north 23 miles to **Sisters** via **U.S. 20** on the way back to Portland for takeout pastries at **Sisters Bakery** or a rich, homey sit-down breakfast at **Cottonwood Cafe.** Then hop back onto the highway, heading north and west on U.S. 20 and **Highway 22,** connecting with **I-5** back to Portland.

Seattle Loop: Island Edition

Seattle's prime coastal location makes it a perfect perch from which to explore nearby islands for rest and relaxation to balance the bustle of city life.

Day 1: Seattle

Enjoy a full day of activity in the city before embarking on your island itinerary. You'll feel like a local with coffee and a breakfast sandwich at **Cherry Street Coffee.** Make your way to the **Seattle Art Museum** to wander amid world-class art, or the **Seattle Center,** where you can take in city views from the **Space Needle.** For a different view, explore the city beneath the city on the 75-minute **Underground Tour.** Head to the market area for lunch at **The Pink Door** (the entrance is behind that namesake door), and let your belly settle while you peruse **Pike Place Market.** Next, for one of the city's best free lookouts, climb to the top of the **Seattle Central Library,** then find the speakeasy at the top of nearby **Smith Tower.** Enjoy dinner on the second-story **Matt's at the Market,** where windows overlook shoppers below. Finish the day at another speakeasy, the city's best, **Bathtub Gin and Co.** Stay at the original hipster gathering place, the tiny **Ace Hotel** in Belltown, or head farther afield to stay in a quaint neighborhood spot, **Ballard Inn.**

Days 2-3: San Juan Island

107 MILES/172 KM (3.25 HOURS)

Drive north on **I-5** to the town of Burlington, then head west on **Highway 20** to **Anacortes,** an 80-mile drive that takes about 1.5 hours. Hop on one of the day's earlier ferries to make the most of your time on San Juan Island, a rural retreat yet not far from Seattle; depending on whether the ferry stops at other islands along the way, the ride takes 1-1.5 hours. You'll disembark at the town of **Friday Harbor,** where you can enjoy a daily brunch at **The Restaurant at Friday Harbor House.** Walk around the quaint downtown area, enjoying its shops and relative bustle, or pop into **The Whale Museum** to see an intact orca skeleton. Head out of town for a scenic drive through San Juan's countryside, heading northwest on Roche Harbor Road. In a few miles, stop for a wine tasting at **San Juan Vineyards**—and wave at **Mona the Camel** across the street!—then head up the road another mile to **Lakedale Resort** and its canvas glamping tents under trees, your home for the next two nights. Enjoy dinner at **Duck Soup,** tucked into the forest across the road.

The next day, continue the counterclockwise loop, driving 5 miles to **Roche Harbor,** the island's other hub. Grab a bite to eat at **Lime Kiln Cafe** before or after visiting the nearby **San Juan Islands Sculpture Park.** Next, drive 10 miles south to the tiny lighthouse at **Lime Kiln State Park,** where you can **whale-watch** from shore. Complete the loop by driving 9 miles east to arrive back in Friday Harbor. Enjoy dinner at **Downriggers.**

Days 4-6: Victoria and Vancouver Island

VICTORIA

40 MILES/64 KM (2.5 HOURS)

Eat breakfast at **Rocky Bay Cafe,** then board the **ferry** at Friday Harbor to Sidney, B.C. The ferry ride, accounting for loading and unloading time, takes about two hours. It's a half-hour drive of about 27 kilometers (17 miles) south on **Highway 17** into Victoria, but pop by **The Butchart Gardens** on your way into town to stretch your legs amid its lush acres.

Check into the **Fairmont Empress Hotel,** located on Victoria's Inner Harbour. After a fancy **afternoon tea,** take off on foot to explore the little city's nooks and crannies. Don't miss **Fan Tan Alley,** the narrowest street in Canada, lined with shops. See if you can spot costumed actors sharing history at the **British Columbia Parliament**

Native American and First Nations Culture

Across the Pacific Northwest, museums and cultural centers salute the rich Native American and First Nations cultures of the region.

SEATTLE

- **Tillicum Village:** Local Native American dance and storytelling culture comes alive, complete with a salmon feast (page 44).

OLYMPIC PENINSULA

- **Makah Museum:** Long-buried treasures of the Makah people unearthed by archaeologists are on display in a far corner of the Olympic Peninsula (page 177).

WASHINGTON WINE COUNTRY

- **Whitman Mission:** A historic site explores the fraught history between Native Americans and early white settlers in Oregon (page 229).
- **Sacajawea State Park:** The culture of Lewis and Clark's Native American guide is celebrated with a Maya Lin-designed story circle installation (page 243).

VANCOUVER

- **University of British Columbia Museum of Anthropology:** Indoor totem poles and historical outdoor structures delve into Canada's native history (page 454).
- **Squamish Lil'wat Cultural Centre:** Whistler's sizable museum enlivens First Nations history through lively guides, exhibits, and experiences (page 485).

Buildings. For dinner, find uber-local produce on the plate at **10 Acres.**

VICTORIA TO TOFINO

197 MILES/317 KM (4.5 HOURS)

Have breakfast at the **Blue Fox Cafe** before heading out to explore more remote corners of Vancouver Island. Break up the long drive (via **Highways 1, 19,** and **4**) by stopping for lunch at **Nanaimo** or **Port Alberni** on the way. As you near the peninsular town of **Tofino,** where you'll spend the night, you'll pass scenic **Chesterman Beach;** stop and relax, watching the surfers or checking out the tide pools. Continue toward town and go for a short hike on the **Tonquin Beach Trail,** which leads to a beach that makes a great sunset spot. Finally, head into town proper for a drink at **The Hatch Waterfront Pub** followed by dinner at **Wolf in the Fog.** Stay at the quirky **Inn at Tough City,** or splash out for the **Wickaninnish Inn,** considered one of Canada's best hotels.

On day two, soak up the waterfront views with brunch at **The Pointe,** then start heading slowly back to Victoria, stopping about 17 kilometers (10.5 miles) into the drive for **Pacific Rim National Park Reserve.** Amble along the park's aptly named **Long Beach** for a stretch—it's 10 kilometers (6.2 miles) in length. Or, if you made an early start, head south 40 kilometers (25 miles) to Ucluelet for the rewarding 10 kilometer (6.2-mile) **Wild Pacific Trail.** Hop back in the car and make your way to Victoria in time for dinner at **Il Terrazzo Ristorante.** Follow it up with a drink and possibly live music at **Bard & Banker.**

Day 7: Back to Seattle

185 MILES/298 KM (5 HOURS)

Head north on **Highway 17** to **Swartz Bay** to catch a ferry to **Tsawwassen** on mainland B.C., which takes a little over an hour and a half. Then follow **Highway 99** to the border crossing at **Peace Arch,** getting on **I-5** to return to Seattle.

Seattle

Look for ★ to find recommended sights, activities, dining, and lodging.

Highlights

★ **Pike Place Market:** Fish are tossed through the air with the greatest of ease, but that's not this bustling farmers market's only famous seller—a little coffee shop called Starbucks started here in 1971 (page 40).

★ **Seattle Art Museum:** A 48-foot-tall *Hammering Man* sculpture stands at the entryway to this collection of world-class art. (page 44).

★ **Olympic Sculpture Park:** Giant art pieces by Alexander Calder and Richard Serra fit into the many terraces and levels of this waterfront space (page 48).

★ **Space Needle:** Seattle's retro landmark may date back to the city's 1962 World's Fair, but the views are timeless (page 49).

★ **Museum of History and Industry:** Ensconced in an old art deco armory building on Lake Union are city artifacts, a working periscope, and a flag made out of petticoats (page 51).

★ **Museum of Flight:** The giant building abuts an airfield and has planes of every type, including an old Air Force One and a space shuttle replica you can walk through—plus astronaut ice cream in the gift shop (page 54).

★ **Volunteer Park:** Designed by the same visionaries who laid out New York City's Central Park, the city's prettiest green space crams lawns, fountains, a conservatory, an art museum, and a tower into only 48.3 acres (page 65).

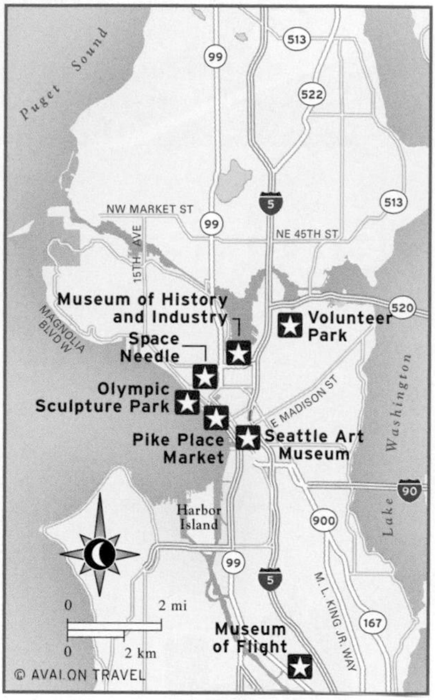

More than half a century has passed since a World's Fair transformed this Northwestern port into a global city. Just look at the Space Needle for evidence of Seattle's endless optimism and vision.

Built on a bumpy series of hills between a lake and a bay, Seattle has grown into a mature metropolis. The vibe is more about achievement than status; it's not cool to work so hard that you can't, say, kayak a little before dinner or jam with your folk rock quartet on the weekend. A healthy arts and music scene has grown beyond Seattle's rush of '90s grunge. But never fear—the city hasn't completely moved beyond its youthful exuberance. It's still the home of the bustling coffee shop and the ambitious start-up. Creative energy explodes from tech minds, performers, and chefs who, like the Space Needle, reach for the stars.

Evidence of past success is around every corner in Seattle. Starbucks, once a tiny coffee shop near Pike Place Market, occupies downtown with the same ubiquity it's achieved around the world. The online bookstore turned tech monolith, Amazon, has colonized the South Lake Union neighborhood and helped turn its forgotten blocks into a bustling cultural center. There are signs everywhere not only of Microsoft—it began here and is headquartered just outside town—but also of the entities it helped build, like the campus of the philanthropic Bill & Melinda Gates Foundation and Paul Allen's football stadium and music museum.

Most of the country lies to the east of Seattle, but the city faces west toward Puget Sound and the Pacific Ocean. With just enough history to build considerable civic pride, there's enough optimism to look to the horizon—or perhaps just to the sunsets that illuminate the Olympic Mountains on clear nights. Sure, it rains sometimes, but it makes the beautiful days all the sweeter.

PLANNING YOUR TIME

The Emerald City requires 2-3 days minimum to explore. Many of Seattle's sights are downtown or in the neighborhoods surrounding

Previous: monorail passing through the Museum of Pop Culture; Seattle waterfront. **Above:** flowers at Pike Place Market.

Seattle

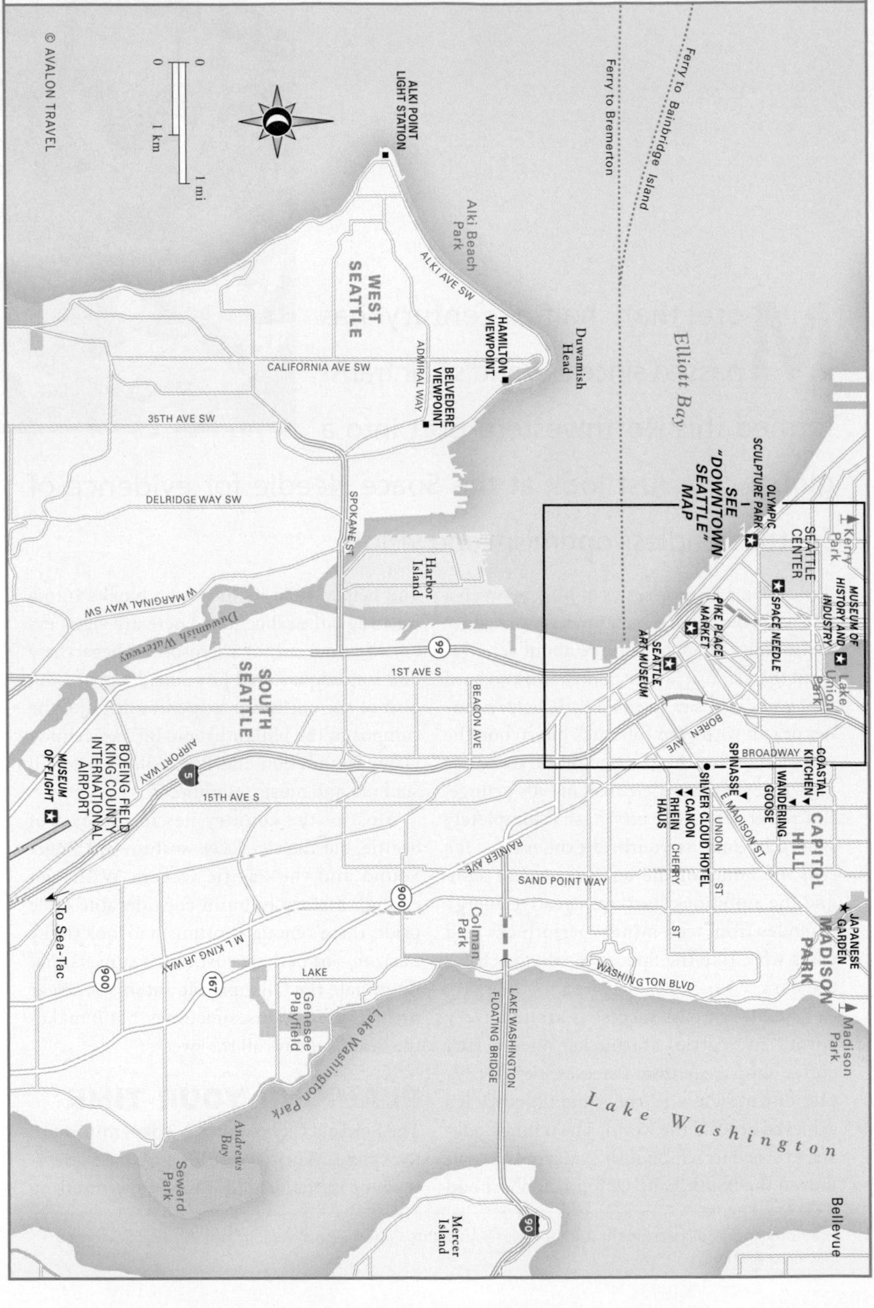
© AVALON TRAVEL
0
1 mi
0
1 km
ALKI POINT LIGHT STATION
Ferry to Bremerton
Ferry to Bainbridge Island
Alki Beach Park
ALKI AVE SW
WEST SEATTLE
HAMILTON VIEWPOINT
Duwamish Head
Elliott Bay
CALIFORNIA AVE SW
ADMIRAL WAY
BELVEDERE VIEWPOINT
35TH AVE SW
DELRIDGE WAY SW
SPOKANE ST
Harbor Island
W MARGINAL WAY SW
Duwamish Waterway
OLYMPIC SCULPTURE PARK
SEE "DOWNTOWN SEATTLE" MAP
SEATTLE CENTER
Kerry Park
MUSEUM OF HISTORY AND INDUSTRY
SPACE NEEDLE
PIKE PLACE MARKET
SEATTLE ART MUSEUM
Lake Union Park
99
1ST AVE S
SOUTH SEATTLE
BEACON AVE
BOREN AVE
BROADWAY
COASTAL KITCHEN
WANDERING GOOSE
SPINASSE
SILVER CLOUD HOTEL
CANON
RHEIN HAUS
E MADISON ST
UNION ST
CHERRY ST
CAPITOL HILL
AIRPORT WAY
5
BOEING FIELD KING COUNTY INTERNATIONAL AIRPORT
MUSEUM OF FLIGHT
15TH AVE S
RAINIER AVE
SAND POINT WAY
900
To Sea-Tac
Colman Park
JAPANESE GARDEN
MADISON PARK
Madison Park
WASHINGTON BLVD
M L KING JR WAY
167
LAKE
Genesee Playfield
Lake Washington Park
LAKE WASHINGTON FLOATING BRIDGE
Lake Washington
Andrews Bay
Seward Park
Mercer Island
90
Bellevue

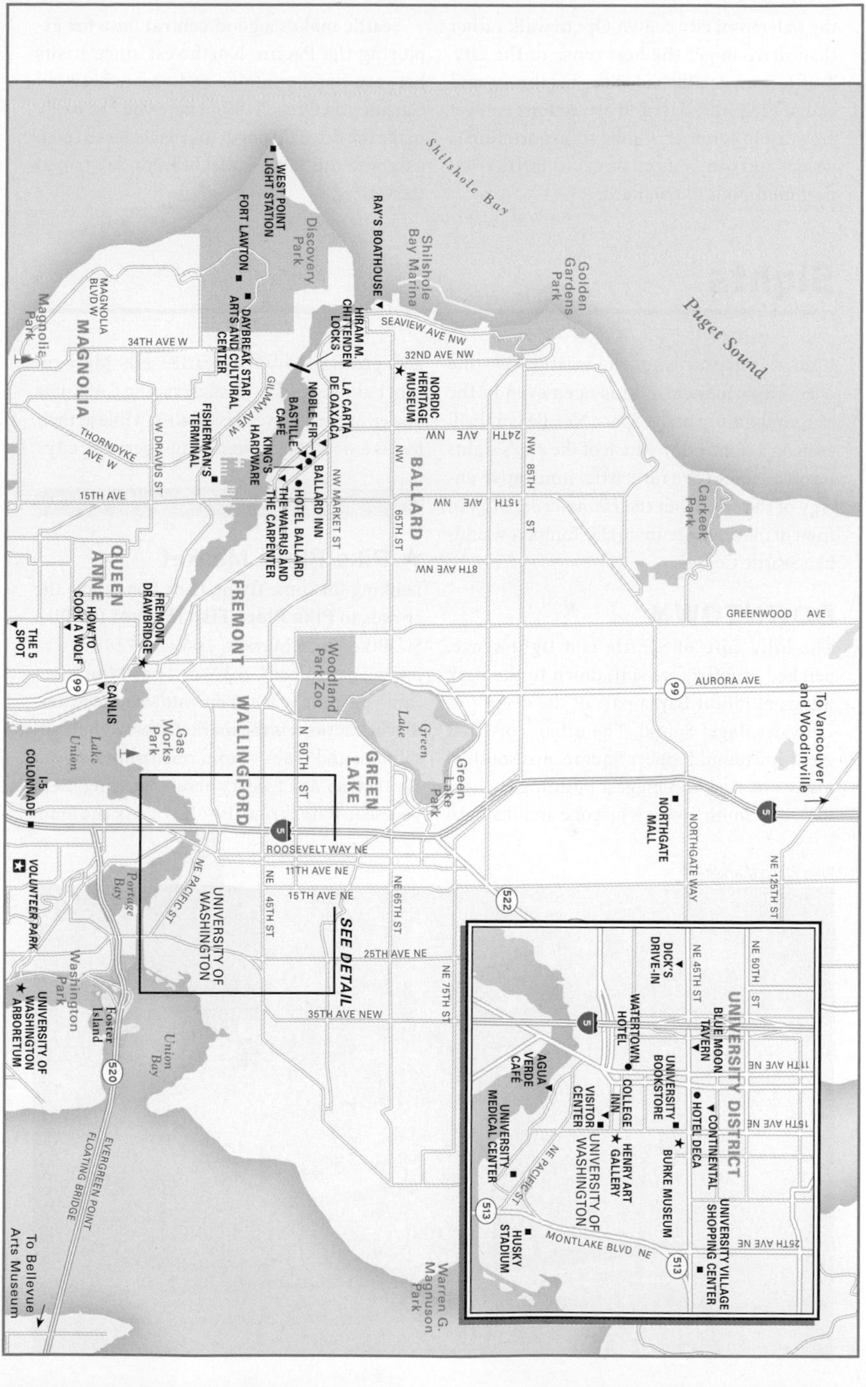
Puget Sound
Shilshole Bay
Shilshole Bay Marina
Golden Gardens Park
Carkeek Park
Discovery Park
WEST POINT LIGHT STATION
FORT LAWTON
DAYBREAK STAR ARTS AND CULTURAL CENTER
RAY'S BOATHOUSE
HIRAM M. CHITTENDEN LOCKS
NORDIC HERITAGE MUSEUM
LA CARTA DE OAXACA
NOBLE FIR
BASTILLE CAFE
KING'S HARDWARE
BALLARD INN
HOTEL BALLARD
THE WALRUS AND THE CARPENTER
FISHERMAN'S TERMINAL
SEAVIEW AVE NW
32ND AVE NW
24TH AVE NW
15TH AVE NW
8TH AVE NW
NW 85TH ST
NW 65TH ST
NW MARKET ST
34TH AVE W
GILMAN AVE W
W DRAVUS ST
THORNDYKE AVE W
15TH AVE
MAGNOLIA BLVD W
Magnolia Park
MAGNOLIA
BALLARD
QUEEN ANNE
FREMONT
FREMONT DRAWBRIDGE
HOW TO COOK A WOLF
THE 5 SPOT
CANLIS
99
Woodland Park Zoo
WALLINGFORD
Gas Works Park
Lake Union
I-5 COLONNADE
Green Lake
Green Lake Park
GREEN LAKE
GREENWOOD AVE
AURORA AVE
To Vancouver and Woodinville
N 50TH ST
NORTHGATE MALL
NORTHGATE WAY
NE 125TH ST
5
ROOSEVELT WAY NE
11TH AVE NE
15TH AVE NE
NE 65TH ST
NE 45TH ST
NE PACIFIC ST
UNIVERSITY OF WASHINGTON
Portage Bay
VOLUNTEER PARK
522
SEE DETAIL
25TH AVE NE
NE 75TH ST
35TH AVE NEW
Washington Park
Foster Island
Union Bay
UNIVERSITY OF WASHINGTON ARBORETUM
520
EVERGREEN POINT FLOATING BRIDGE
To Bellevue Arts Museum
Warren G. Magnuson Park
NE 50TH ST
NE 45TH ST
11TH AVE NE
15TH AVE NE
25TH AVE NE
UNIVERSITY DISTRICT
DICK'S DRIVE-IN
BLUE MOON TAVERN
WATERTOWN HOTEL
UNIVERSITY BOOKSTORE
CONTINENTAL
HOTEL DECA
BURKE MUSEUM
UNIVERSITY VILLAGE SHOPPING CENTER
AGUA VERDE CAFE
COLLEGE INN
VISITOR CENTER
HENRY ART GALLERY
UNIVERSITY OF WASHINGTON
UNIVERSITY MEDICAL CENTER
NE PACIFIC ST
513
HUSKY STADIUM
MONTLAKE BLVD NE

the waterfront city center. Opt to walk rather than drive to get the best sense of the city. Traffic is especially bad at the beginning and end of each workday, and attractions can get crowded in summer. Public transportation is decent and can be used to get to farther-out neighborhoods like Ballard.

Seattle makes a good central base for exploring the Pacific Northwest since it sits between the mountains and ocean, between Canada and Oregon. From here you can easily make the drive up north to Anacortes to catch a ferry to the San Juan Islands, or day-trip to the Cascades.

Sights

It doesn't matter what the weather is—the open-air farmers market is open even in the rain, and the top of the Space Needle is a thrill even on a cloudy day. Much of the city's sights revolve around the futuristic, innovative energy of the city, from the *Hammering Man* in front of the art museum to the Tomorrowland-like Seattle Center.

DOWNTOWN

The hilly core of Seattle is a tight space, perched on hills that spill down to the dark waters of Elliott Bay, a part of the deep V of saltwater Puget Sound. The urban core first grew up around Pioneer Square, just south of today's busiest and biggest buildings, where the white Smith Tower is just one architectural gem preserved from an earlier era. More recent buildings, like the skyscraping Columbia Tower, are reflective glass giants, while at their feet is a walkable, if sometimes vertical, city.

TOP EXPERIENCE

★ Pike Place Market

Looking for some flying fish? Just follow the crowds to **Pike Place Fish Market** (86 Pike St., Pike Place Market, 206/682-7181, www.pikeplacefish.com, 6:30am-6pm Mon.-Sat., 7am-5pm Sun.). One of downtown's most popular attractions is the market's tossed halibut, salmon, and crabs—from one fishmonger to another, so don't worry about catching them yourself. Why throw fish? If you ask the loud,

Pike Place Market

Two Days in Seattle

Seattle is an international city with arts, food, science, and the outdoors to explore. To get the most in a short trip, focus first on the city's core, and then venture out onto the water or to one of the city's parks.

DAY 1

Start the day like any other day—at **Starbucks.** The location in Pike Place Market isn't quite as "original" as the T-shirts and mugs would have you believe, but it's an interesting reminder that the chain used to be just another local coffee stand. Java in hand, explore **Pike Place Market** and its long rows of craft and food stands. Watch fish fly at **Pike Place Fish Market,** and venture past the **Gum Wall.**

Walk two blocks south along 1st Avenue to the *Hammering Man* at the **Seattle Art Museum,** and venture inside for one of the West Coast's best art collections. From there it's only three blocks down University Street to the waterfront—just head for the big, round **Seattle Great Wheel.** Take a boat ride on **Argosy Cruises** or hop a big white **Washington State Ferry.**

Once you're back on dry land, take a cab to the **Seattle Center.** You're probably starving, and the Armory hosts small outlets of some of the city's best cheap eats. The Seattle Center alone contains enough entertainment for a week, so pick your (fun, cool) poison: science at the **Pacific Science Center** or rock and roll and pop culture at the **Museum of Pop Culture.** Topping either one will take something big—like, say, the **Space Needle.** Travel to the observation deck at the top and catch views in every direction.

For dinner, head to Belltown and hit up one of the city's memorable restaurants: **El Gaucho** is known for steak, while **Six Seven** earns acclaim for both seafood and its waterfront location. If you still have energy, return downtown for a symphony show at **Benaroya Hall** or rock at the **Showbox.**

DAY 2

Start the day with French toast and the breakfast toppings bar at **Portage Bay Café** in South Lake Union. Walk 0.5 mile east on Harrison Street and then turn right on Yale Avenue for some quick shopping at **REI.** Or simply follow Terry Avenue north to Lake Union Park and the **Museum of History and Industry** to learn the story of Seattle and its high-flying, computer-inventing ways. Before you leave South Lake Union, head back down Terry Avenue and grab a massive meal at **Lunchbox Laboratory.**

Drive northwest to **Discovery Park** and ramble out to the beach. Enjoy your lunch and explore the tide pools and historical lighthouse. The former fort is big enough that you'll forget you're in the middle of the Northwest's biggest city.

Reenter civilization by driving north on 15th Avenue West and across one of the city's many drawbridges to reach Ballard, a former fishing center. Turn west on NW Market Street to reach the **Hiram M. Chittenden Locks.** The locks are more than an engineering marvel, though it's fun to watch the gates open and the locks fill as boats move in and out. But there's also a fish ladder with underground viewing windows and a botanical garden.

Before leaving Ballard, try some of the neighborhood's fine dining. Back on NW Market Street, turn south on 22nd Avenue to reach Ballard Avenue and the French fare at **Bastille Café.** Or wait for the city's best oyster bar at the superb **The Walrus and the Carpenter,** a mere three blocks away. Bars in Ballard are among the city's best, so stay on Ballard Avenue and take a tipple at **Noble Fir** or **King's Hardware,** and drink as the anglers once did on these very streets. Finish the night in Capitol Hill—dancing at **Q** and drinks at the bustling **Quinn's Pub** go late.

Downtown Seattle

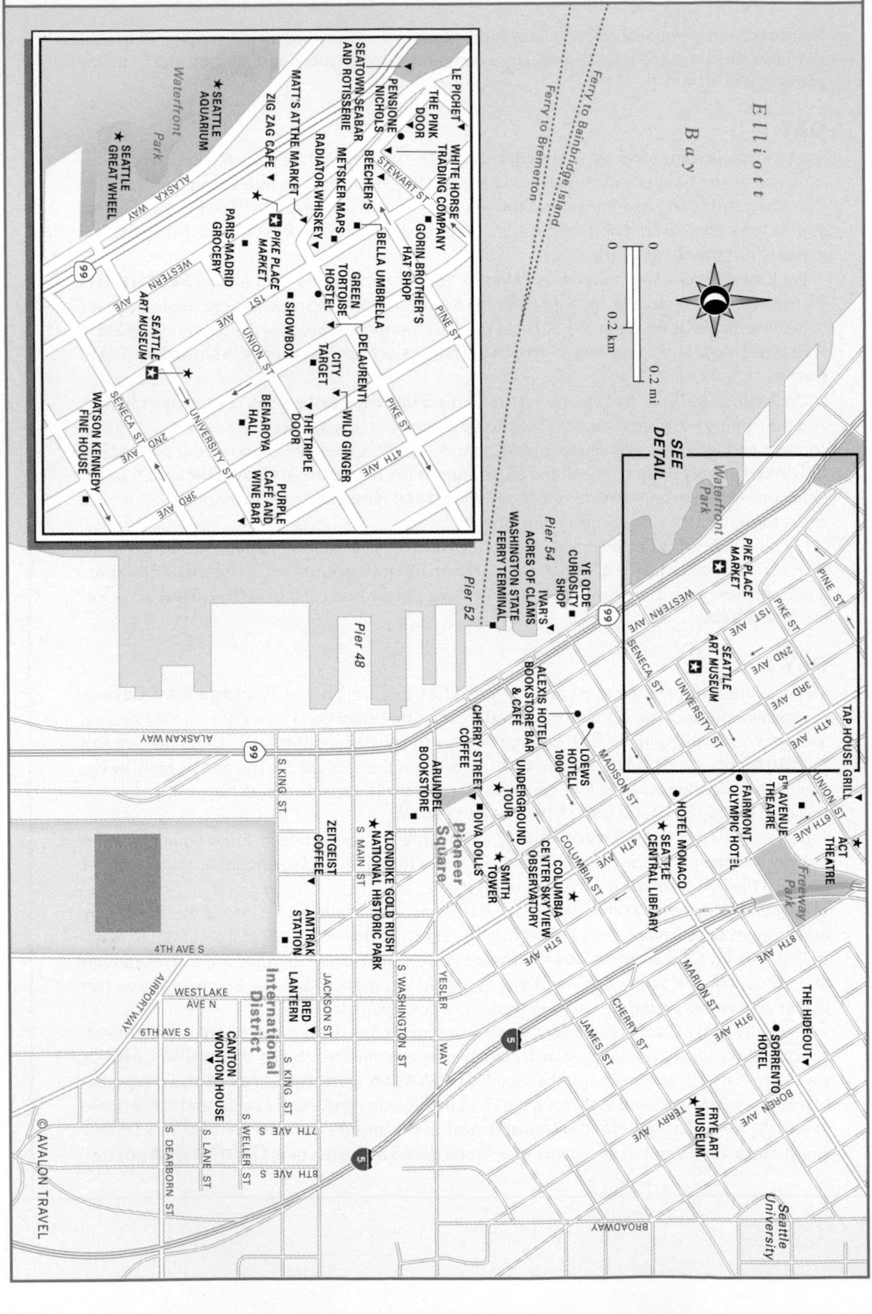

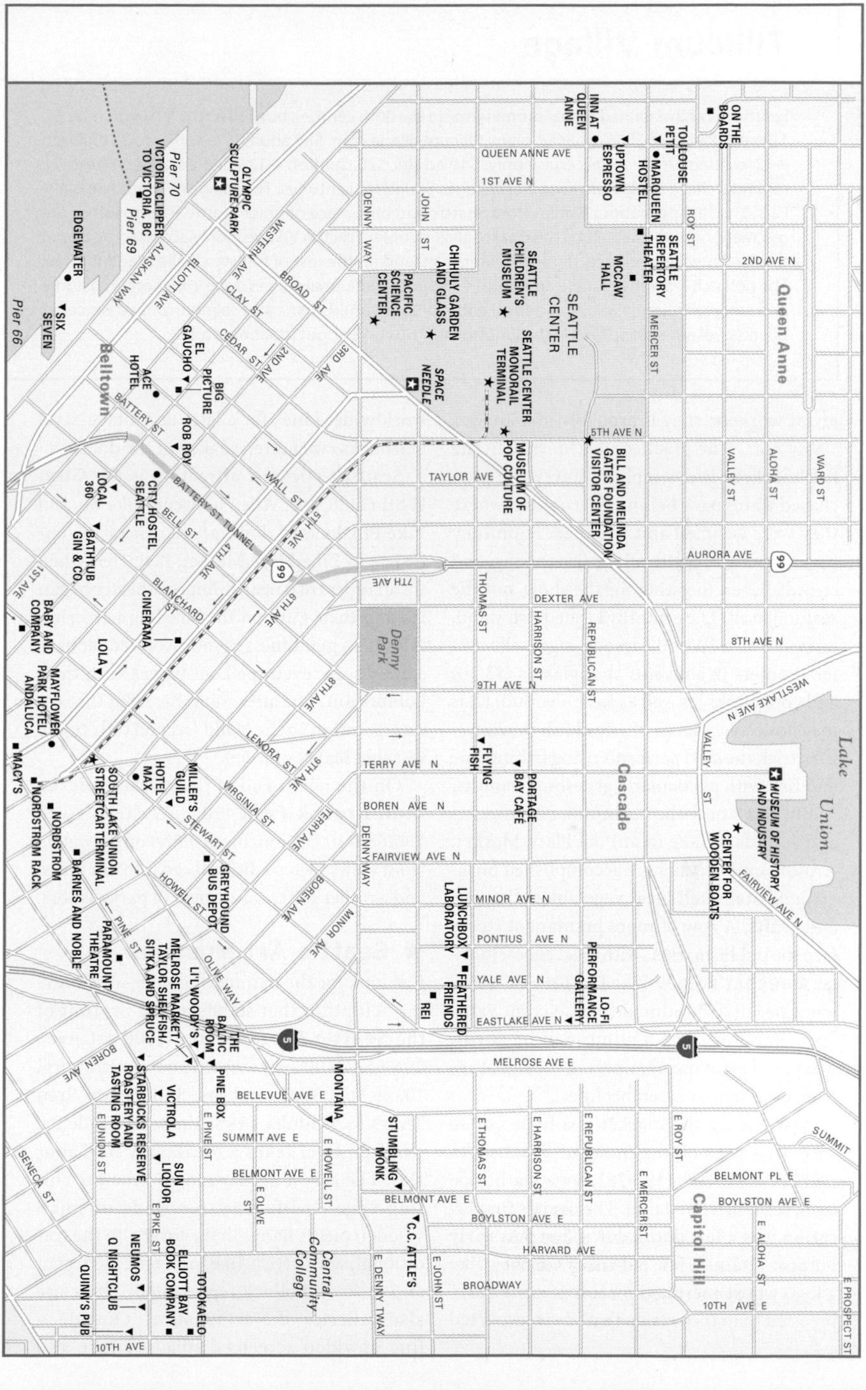
Queen Anne
Seattle Center
Belltown
Cascade
Capitol Hill
Lake Union
Denny Park
Central Community College
Pier 70
Pier 69
Pier 66
ON THE BOARDS
TOULOUSE PETIT
MARQUEEN HOSTEL
UPTOWN ESPRESSO
INN AT QUEEN ANNE
OLYMPIC SCULPTURE PARK
VICTORIA CLIPPER TO VICTORIA, BC
EDGEWATER
SIX SEVEN
SEATTLE REPERTORY THEATER
MCCAW HALL
SEATTLE CHILDREN'S MUSEUM
CHIHULY GARDEN AND GLASS
PACIFIC SCIENCE CENTER
SEATTLE CENTER MONORAIL TERMINAL
SPACE NEEDLE
MUSEUM OF POP CULTURE
BILL AND MELINDA GATES FOUNDATION VISITOR CENTER
EL GAUCHO
BIG PICTURE
ACE HOTEL
ROB ROY
CITY HOSTEL SEATTLE
LOCAL 360
BATHTUB GIN & CO.
CINERAMA
BABY AND COMPANY
LOLA
MAYFLOWER PARK HOTEL/ ANDALUCA
MACY'S
NORDSTROM RACK
NORDSTROM
SOUTH LAKE UNION STREETCAR TERMINAL
HOTEL MAX
MILLER'S GUILD
GREYHOUND BUS DEPOT
BARNES AND NOBLE
PARAMOUNT THEATRE
MELROSE MARKET/ TAYLOR SHELLFISH/ SITKA AND SPRUCE
LI'L WOODY'S
THE BALTIC ROOM
PINE BOX
STARBUCKS RESERVE ROASTERY AND TASTING ROOM
VICTROLA
SUN LIQUOR
NEUMOS
ELLIOTT BAY BOOK COMPANY
TOTOKAELO
Q NIGHTCLUB
QUIN'S PUB
MONTANA
STUMBLING MONK
C.C. ATTLE'S
LUNCHBOX LABORATORY
FEATHERED FRIENDS
REI
LO-FI PERFORMANCE GALLERY
FLYING FISH
PORTAGE BAY CAFÉ
MUSEUM OF HISTORY AND INDUSTRY
CENTER FOR WOODEN BOATS
QUEEN ANNE AVE
1ST AVE N
2ND AVE N
5TH AVE N
ROY ST
MERCER ST
VALLEY ST
ALOHA ST
WARD ST
TAYLOR AVE
AURORA AVE
DEXTER AVE
8TH AVE N
9TH AVE N
WESTLAKE AVE N
TERRY AVE N
BOREN AVE N
FAIRVIEW AVE N
MINOR AVE N
PONTIUS AVE N
YALE AVE N
EASTLAKE AVE N
MELROSE AVE E
BELLEVUE AVE E
SUMMIT AVE E
BELMONT AVE E
BELMONT PL E
BOYLSTON AVE E
HARVARD AVE
BROADWAY
10TH AVE E
10TH AVE
SUMMIT
E PROSPECT ST
E ALOHA ST
E ROY ST
E MERCER ST
E REPUBLICAN ST
E HARRISON ST
E THOMAS ST
E JOHN ST
E DENNY WAY
E HOWELL ST
E OLIVE ST
E PINE ST
E PIKE ST
E UNION ST
SENECA ST
BOREN AVE
OLIVE WAY
PINE ST
HOWELL ST
STEWART ST
VIRGINIA ST
LENORA ST
BLANCHARD ST
BELL ST
BATTERY ST
BATTERY ST TUNNEL
WALL ST
CEDAR ST
CLAY ST
BROAD ST
DENNY WAY
JOHN ST
THOMAS ST
HARRISON ST
REPUBLICAN ST
WESTERN AVE
ELLIOTT AVE
ALASKAN WAY
1ST AVE
2ND AVE
3RD AVE
4TH AVE
5TH AVE
6TH AVE
7TH AVE
8TH AVE
9TH AVE
TERRY AVE
MINOR AVE
99
5

Tillicum Village

Seattle may have gained global prominence in the 20th century, but **Tillicum Village** (Pier 55, 1101 Alaskan Way, 206/622-8687, www.tillicumvillage.com, $84 adults, $75 seniors, $32 children 4-12, children under 4 free; cruise only: $40 adults, $20 children 4-12, children under 4 free) is a reminder that people have lived along Puget Sound for centuries. The village is located on Blake Island, a state park about 8 miles from Seattle and birthplace of Chief Seattle. The buildings are re-creations of those built by the Coast Salish people. Tillicum Village is only accessed by a boat tour and meal experience, though boaters can land on the rest of forested Blake Island for free. The potlatch—a Native American festival—includes traditional dances done in elaborate costume and storytelling by a native of a local tribe, plus steamed clams and salmon cooked on cedar planks over alderwood fires in the longhouse. Trips take about four hours total.

jovial workers, they'll probably just answer "Why not?" The practice started early in the fish market's life, simply to hurry the purchased wares back behind the counter, where they were weighed and wrapped. Soon they began having fun with all the fish tossing, and crowds began to gather for the show, not the seafood itself. The centrally located fish stand, topped with a "World Famous" sign, sells oyster shooters in souvenir shot glasses ($3.50) and cookbooks, as well as fresh seafood. Kids may notice the mouth of a dead fish moving—it's a trick the staff performs using fishing line and fish with particularly gruesome mouths.

But that's only the beginning of the sights and sounds to take in at Pike Place Market. Around every corner are accomplished buskers, and stalls sell local vegetables, flowers, and crafts. A row of more permanent stores face the public market, with local cheesemonger **Beecher's** (1600 Pike Pl., 206/956-1964, www.beechershandmadecheese.com, 9am-7pm daily) offering a glimpse of its curds, whey, and giant metal mixers in the signature Flagship cheddar assembly line.

Also facing the market is a little coffee shop that goes by the name of **Starbucks** (1912 Pike Pl., 206/448-8762, www.starbucks.com, 6:30am-9pm daily). The chain's first location was a few doors down, but this early outpost retains a few old-timey touches, like a logo whose mermaid mascot is more bare-breasted than the version that's been exported worldwide. Lines for a latte or vintage-style Starbucks swag often snake out the door.

Seattle's stickiest attraction is the **Gum Wall** (1428 Post Alley between Pike St. and Pike Pl.), located down an alley near the entrance to Pike Place Market. It started when theatergoers of a nearby improv theater began leaving their gum on the building's exterior. Now it's a giant mess of multicolored blobs—some people even spell out names with their bubblegum. The attraction was rated the second-germiest in the world (second only to the kissable Blarney Stone).

On the north end of the market, **Victor Steinbrueck Park** (2001 Western Ave., 206/684-4075, 6am-10pm daily) offers waterfront views, two traditional cedar totem poles, and a rather gritty assortment of park visitors.

★ Seattle Art Museum

Just look for the hammering man—the moving sculpture that stands guard in front of the **Seattle Art Museum** (1300 1st Ave., 206/654-3100, www.seattleartmuseum.org, 10am-5pm Wed. and Fri.-Sun., 10am-9pm Thurs., $20 adults, $18 seniors, $13 students, children free) takes a break only on Labor Day. The art on display ranges from the cutting edge—a life-size tree made of small wooden pieces hangs in the foyer—to the traditional, with artists like John Singer Sargent and Jackson Pollock represented. There are also galleries of Northwest art: Outside, a line of video screens displays nature and

Seattle Art Museum

city images, and occasionally even live shots from below the museum. Admission is free the first Thursday of the month, and periodic SAM Remix events open the galleries extra late on Friday nights and feature a raucous dance party.

Seattle Aquarium

From its spot on two piers, **Seattle Aquarium** (1483 Alaskan Way, 206/386-4300, www.seattleaquarium.org, 9:30am-5pm daily, $29.95 adults, $19.95 children 4-12, children under 4 free) dangles over the waters it celebrates. In the lobby a giant Window on Washington Waters tank is filled with local fish, and throughout the day divers pop inside to show off its inhabitants. Look for the mottled orange of the rockfish, which can live up to 100 years but develops eye problems in captivity. The Seattle Aquarium's vet has done extensive work on eye surgery and even hopes to provide prosthetic eyes for the creatures. The aquarium has touch tide pools and bird exhibits, plus weird-looking sea creatures like the octopus and hundreds of jellyfish. Larger habitats house sea and river otters, and a new amphitheater-style area holds three harbor seals. Check at the front desk for the schedule of daily animal feedings. The café has pizzas, sandwiches, some seafood entrées (sustainable ones only, of course), and microbrews, and the outdoor balcony is open on days with decent weather.

Seattle Great Wheel

When the **Seattle Great Wheel** (1301 Alaskan Way, 206/623-8600, www.seattlegreatwheel.com, 10am-11pm Sun.-Thurs., 10am-midnight Fri.-Sat., shorter hours in winter, $14 adults, $12 seniors, $9 children 4-11, children under 4 free) popped up on Seattle's waterfront in 2012, it took the city by surprise—but it carried a million riders in its first year. The 175-foot ride is the tallest of its kind on the West Coast, and the enclosed cars can hold eight people each. From inside each gondola, the views shift from downtown Seattle to Elliott Bay and the Olympic Mountains across Puget Sound, and the Ferris wheel's end-of-the-pier location means that you'll dangle over the dark blue water. One of the cars is not like the others: The VIP gondola has leather seats and a glass floor, and a ride inside ($50) comes with a champagne toast, free T-shirt, and the ability to skip the line.

Ye Olde Curiosity Shop

Ye Olde Curiosity Shop (1001 Alaskan Way, 206/682-5844, www.yeoldecuriosityshop.com, 9am-9pm daily summer; 10am-6pm Sun.-Thurs., 9am-9pm Fri.-Sat. winter) is indeed a shop, but it's also a historical Seattle attraction. In 1899 it opened as the Free Museum and Curio, mainly showing off artifacts from Alaska that gold rushers had brought back. The preserved mummy named Sylvester is the shop's biggest attraction; the body was supposedly dug from the Arizona desert in 1895 and may have been mummified by natural dehydration, though a CT scan revealed the bullet that killed him. There's also a large collection of shrunken human heads, Siamese cow bodies, walrus tusks, and the Lord's Prayer engraved on a single grain of rice. The wares for sale are a little less exotic—souvenirs, porcelain collectibles, and saltwater taffy, plus Northwest Native American totem poles and masks. You can also buy a shrunken head replica made of goat hide.

Seattle Central Library

There are a million books inside **Seattle Central Library** (1000 4th Ave., 206/386-4636, www.spl.org, 10am-8pm Mon.-Thurs., 10am-6pm Fri.-Sat., noon-6pm Sun., free) and nearly as many glass panels on the unusual exterior. Being inside is something like visiting a greenhouse, but one that grows books. The windowed building was designed by Dutch architect Rem Koolhaas and has enough glass to cover more than five football fields. Groups of five or larger can book free tours of the space, but everyone can wander for free and access the cell phone tour (206/686-8564). Readings and events occur daily in the library's auditorium and other meeting spaces, and the expansive 3rd floor has a café, reading areas, and computers with Internet access. For the best views in the building, head to level 10, the Betty Jane Narver Reading Room.

Columbia Center Sky View Observatory

How high do you want to go? Visit **Columbia Center Sky View Observatory** (701 5th Ave., 206/386-5564, www.skyviewobservatory.com, 8am-11pm daily, $14.95 adults, $9.75 seniors, students, and children 6-12, children under 6 free) for the absolute tallest observation point in the city (yes, taller than the Space Needle). The view at 902 feet off the ground makes it the highest publicly accessible spot west of the Mississippi. On the way up, visit the 40th-floor Starbucks, the chain's highest outpost in the world.

Frye Art Museum

The charming **Frye Art Museum** (704 Terry Ave., 206/622-9250, www.fryemuseum.org, 11am-5pm Tues.-Wed. and Fri.-Sun., 11am-7pm Thurs., free) isn't too far from downtown, tucked away among the hospitals of First Hill, but it has a quieter vibe (and free parking). The Fryes, a Seattle couple who lived in the early 20th century, left a collection of European paintings, and the museum has since taken on a collection of contemporary art and hosting of temporary exhibits as well. The Fryes stipulated that their art be shown for free and in particular arrangements; the

Seattle Central Library

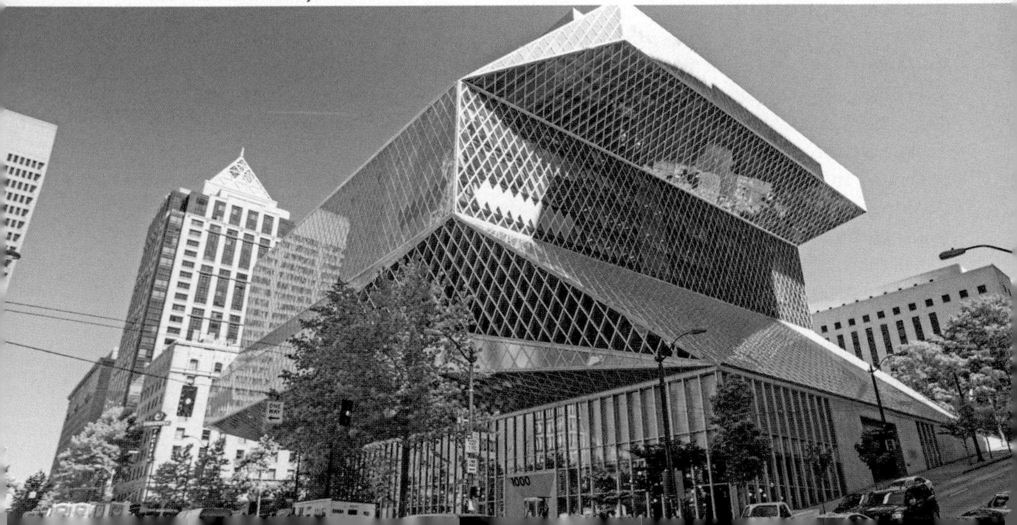

building was designed by modernist architect Paul Thiry and is made up of large concrete forms and sharp right angles. Free public tours are given daily at 1pm, and the museum also houses a café.

PIONEER SQUARE

Pioneer Square (Yesler Way and 1st Ave., www.pioneersquare.org), located on the south end of downtown, is the city's oldest neighborhood. Much of the architecture is classic Victorian and Edwardian styles, built on fill that buried the first story of many of the town's buildings after a fire ravaged the area. During the Klondike gold rush, the Pioneer Square neighborhood was full of outfitters and saloons where prospectors would prepare for the trip to Alaska. During the Great Depression, a shantytown emerged and the area fell into disrepair. Since the 1960s, the Pioneer Square buildings have been preserved and protected. Although the whole neighborhood carries the name, Pioneer Square itself is at the corner of Yesler Way and 1st Avenue, a relatively small patch of grass and an ornate pergola that dates back to the 1909 Alaska-Yukon-Pacific Exposition.

Klondike Gold Rush National Historical Park

When you think "gold rush," you probably either picture California or Alaska, not Seattle. But the **Klondike Gold Rush National Historical Park** (319 2nd Ave. S, 206/220-4240, www.nps.gov/klse, 9am-5pm daily summer, 10am-5pm daily winter, free), run by the National Park Service, is located in the middle of the Pioneer Square neighborhood. The museum tells the story of how Seattle served as the gateway to the Klondike. Old newspaper reports reveal the great excitement that arose in 1897 when gold from the Klondike River in Alaska and Canada arrived via steamship at the American ports. Prospectors came to Seattle to be outfitted for the trip north—even Seattle's own mayor quit to join the stampede. The Canadian Mounties, worried that all those people were going to starve in the wilderness, began requiring that each person bring a year's worth of food. Fun hands-on exhibits and gold-panning demonstrations show how the Seattle economy grew from that gold rush—and how poorly most prospectors fared.

Underground Tour

If someone tells you a separate city exists underneath the streets of Seattle, they're not pulling your leg (probably). The **Underground Tour** (608 1st Ave., 206/682-4646, www.undergroundtour.com, 9am-7pm daily summer, 10am-6pm daily winter, $22 adults, $20 seniors and students, $10 children 7-12, children under 7 free) began in the 1960s when renovation of the Pioneer Square area reminded locals that the original first story of many buildings had been buried with dirt to stabilize the marshy tidal area. A *Seattle Times* reporter began leading people down dark stairways to the buried sidewalks and edifices. Now the 75-minute tour is incredibly popular and even has an occasional adult-oriented version that points out old opium dens and red-light districts. The walking tour is fascinating, even if the underground spaces are a bit more cramped than one would imagine when they hear the phrase "buried city."

Smith Tower

The Space Needle is weirder and the Columbia Tower is taller, but the **Smith Tower** (506 2nd Ave., 206/622-4004, www.smithtower.com, 10am-9pm daily, $19 adults, $15 seniors, students, and children 6-12, children under 6 free) is a beautiful historical building that used to be the tallest in the West. Built in 1914, the pointy white tower was long a symbol for the city. On the 35th floor—reached on an original Otis elevator with operator—an observation deck offers a 360-degree view of the city, waterfront, and distant mountains. The outdoor viewing deck is surrounding by ornate white gates, and the room is a lovely destination with breathtaking views. Though it once held Chinese artifacts, it's now part of

Seattle's World's Fair

Even Elvis discovered Seattle in 1962 when the Century 21 Exposition put the city on the map. The World's Fair was meant to show off Washington State as the center of jet-age progress, proving it was more than an out-of-the-way region often confused with Washington, D.C.

Over breakfast meetings in the city's finest hotel, the Olympic, a group of businessmen dreamed up the infrastructure that would become Seattle's icons—the Seattle Center, the monorail, the Space Needle. In the middle of the space race against the Soviet Union, the home of Boeing had to show off its science and technology above all. A giant replica of a dam had water falling down six spillways, and a giant glass elevator called the Bubbleator took riders through a World of Tomorrow exhibit. There was even a visit from a famous cosmonaut, Gherman Titov, but his notoriety was religious, not technological—at his World's Fair press conference, he proclaimed, "I don't believe in God. I believe in man." Four days later, U.S. astronaut John Glenn agreed that he didn't see God in space, but only because God was too big for such an appearance.

For all the showing off, the fair was mostly about fun. The country tasted its first Belgian waffles in a popular stand on the outdoor area called the Gayway. Rides and games for the kiddies were out front, but an observant visitor could find Show Street, where the bawdy Gracie Hanson hosted a topless girlie show.

The Shah of Iran, a British prince, Bob Hope, and Lassie all popped by the six-month fair, but of the almost 10 million visitors, none was more adored than Elvis Presley. He shot the film *It Happened at the World's Fair* and, in his off hours, avoided crowds by going on double dates with a production assistant—one was even to see an Elvis movie.

When the Century 21 Exposition finally closed in October 1962, its most anticipated guest, President John F. Kennedy, bowed out, claiming a cold. The festivities went on without him, and a few days later it was revealed that the Cuban Missile Crisis, not congestion, had kept JFK away.

a larger historical tour and experience, with a bar that serves retro speakeasy-style cocktails.

BELLTOWN

★ Olympic Sculpture Park

An oil company's waterfront land was reborn as **Olympic Sculpture Park** (2901 Western Ave., 206/654-3100, www.seattleartmuseum.org, sunrise-sunset daily; pavilion: 10am-5pm Tues.-Sun. summer, 10am-4pm Tues.-Sun. winter, free), a series of zigzagging green spaces that hold massive works of art. The centerpiece is Alexander Calder's *The Eagle*, a twisted figure in red visible to the ferries that cross Elliott Bay. A glass bridge is decorated with images of the skyline, and the piece *Love & Loss* has a prominent ampersand on a tall spike. A Z-shaped path crosses the green space as it leads down to the water. The vivarium, a narrow building with a 60-foot nurse log inside, showcases an intersection of art and nature—illustrating how a dying tree serves as an incubator for new plants. Outside, the sculpture park includes ginkgo and dawn redwood trees, plus meadow grasses and a shoreline often visited by seals. A pavilion holds restrooms and offices, plus a large space for events.

QUEEN ANNE

Seattle Center

Born as the fairgrounds of the 1962 World's Fair, the **Seattle Center** (305 Harrison St., 206/684-7200, www.seattlecenter.com) is a giant play space, workshop, stage, and meeting spot. Beyond its signature tall white arches—part of the Pacific Science Center, designed by the same architect that designed New York City's World Trade Center—is the domed International fountain and 74 acres of performance spaces, museums, and parks. The Seattle Center serves as the city's collective backyard, or perhaps its welcoming parlor, as a number of festivals take place on the grounds celebrating music, art, and culture. One lawn has a giant, multicolored outdoor

The Eagle by Alexander Calder at Olympic Sculpture Park

glass mosaic by Paul Horiuchi, and a pagoda made of Japanese cypress wood houses a bell that was given to the city by its sister city, Kobe, Japan.

★ SPACE NEEDLE

The city's retro icon was born as a sketch on a cocktail napkin by one of the 1962 World's Fair planners, but the 605-foot **Space Needle** (400 Broad St., 206/905-2100, www.spaceneedle.com) was built in less than a year. During the World's Fair, the space-age elevators were operated by pretty young women; today the operators (of both genders) tell a quick story of the tower during the trip to the top. At 520 feet, the **Observation Deck** (10am-11pm Mon.-Thurs., 9:30am-11:30am Fri.-Sat., 9:30am-11pm Sun., $19-29 adults, $16-22 seniors, $13-18 youth 4-12, children 3 and under free) features indoor and outdoor binoculars and information on what you can see (or what you'd see if the clouds would clear); a snack bar and gift shop are located inside. Timed tickets can be purchased in advance; lines often wrap the Space Needle base, so plan ahead. The revolving **SkyCity Restaurant** is undergoing renovations but will eventually feature a glass floor.

PACIFIC SCIENCE CENTER

Life-size dinosaurs and bigger-than-life IMAX films live at the kid-friendly **Pacific Science Center** (200 2nd Ave. N, 206/443-2001, www.pacificsciencecenter.org, 10am-5pm Mon. and Wed.-Fri., 10am-6pm Sat.-Sun., $19.75 adults, $17.75 seniors, $14.75 children 6-15, $11.75 children 3-5, children under 3 free). During the 1962 World's Fair, this was the U.S. Science Pavilion, and there's a retro midcentury feel to the outdoor pools and boxy buildings. The exhibits inside are much more up to date, featuring a live-weather globe and interactive health displays. Warm and humid, the Tropical Butterfly House is filled with 500 tropical butterflies every week; animal exhibits, such as the East African naked mole rat, include residents known to be a little less glamorous. Outside, the *Sonic Bloom*'s sculptured flowers show off the power of solar radiation by glowing with solar-powered energy. Laser shows take place regularly, arranged to pop or psychedelic tunes, and large visiting history and art exhibitions come to the newly renovated gallery space. Two IMAX theaters show nature films and popular cinema (shows and special exhibitions require additional tickets).

SEATTLE CHILDREN'S MUSEUM

Located downstairs in the Armory, the **Seattle Children's Museum** (305 Harrison St., 206/441-1768, www.thechildrensmuseum.org, 10am-5pm Mon.-Fri., 10am-6pm Sat.-Sun., $11.50 adults and children, $10.50 seniors, children under 1 free) appeals to tots 10 and younger—in fact, you have to have a kid of that age to enter. Exhibits are hands on and image based, like the Global Village where the dresser drawers and table are filled with clothing and food from around the world. There is a construction zone, play bus, and a big art studio.

Although the building has had many uses both during and after the World's Fair, today the Armory serves as a pavilion boasting a truly gourmet food court. Some of Seattle's most popular restaurants have outposts here, including Skillet Street Food, Mod Pizza, Bigfood BBQ, and Eltana Wood-Fired Bagels. Order from the counter and then head outside if the weather's good; public bathrooms are also available in the building.

CHIHULY GARDEN AND GLASS

You can't go far in the Northwest without seeing some spectacular glass art. **Chihuly Garden and Glass** (305 Harrison St., 206/753-4940, www.chihulygardenandglass.com, 11am-8pm Sun.-Thurs., 11am-9pm Fri.-Sat., $29 adults, $22 seniors, $18 children 5-12, children under 5 free) celebrates the country's most famous glassblower, Dale Chihuly, with a gallery of his works and a fanciful garden of glass flowers and sculpture. Prepare to feel like Alice wandering around Wonderland. Chihuly's signature bulbs are lit creatively inside. One room consists of a glass ceiling overflowing with anemone-like works, while another turns the pieces into a light installation. The attached Collections Café reflects Chihuly's penchant for collections—each table center has handfuls of his tin toys, or accordions, or carnival masks, or other items housed under glass.

MUSEUM OF POP CULTURE

What would you do with a billion dollars? Microsoft cofounder Paul Allen started, among other things, the Experience Music Project in honor of Jimi Hendrix and his hometown's musical heritage, and the Frank Gehry-designed building morphed into the EMP Museum and now the **Museum of Pop Culture** (325 5th Ave. N, 206/770-2700, www.mopop.org, 10am-7pm daily summer, 10am-5pm daily winter, $33 adults, $30 seniors and students, $24 children 5-17, children under 5 free), dedicated to pop culture. Outside the museum's guitar tower are interactive booths for trying out keyboards or turntables. Downstairs an animatronic dragon overlooks a fantasy exhibit (pull his tail—he'll move), which also has a giant magical tree and interactive exhibits about fantasy archetypes. Also downstairs, a science fiction exhibit includes a *Star Trek* captain's chair and *Doctor Who* props.

Space Needle

Seattle Center Monorail

The lumbering old metal **Seattle Center Monorail** (Harrison and Broad Sts., 206/905-2600, www.seattlemonorail.com, 7:30am-11pm Mon.-Fri., 8:30am-11pm Sat.-Sun. summer; 7:30am-9pm Mon.-Thurs., 7:30am-11pm Fri., 8:30am-11pm Sat., 8:30am-9pm Sun. winter, $2.25 adults, $1 seniors and children 5-12, children under 5 free) skates down a mile-long track to the center of downtown, a reminder of the city's once-extensive plans for public transportation. The trip is great fun for transportation junkies or tourists looking to see the city from a few stories up, but it's not much of a commuter time-saver, running from the Seattle Center to the Westlake Mall. Still, the train rumbling above 5th Avenue or through the Experience Museum Project, which was built around it, remains one of the enduring sights of Seattle.

Bill & Melinda Gates Foundation Visitor Center

Although Bill Gates first made his mark as the founder of Microsoft, he's now trying to solve the world's biggest problems of health and extreme poverty through his foundation. The **Bill & Melinda Gates Foundation Visitor Center** (440 5th Ave. N, 206/709-3100, www.gatesfoundation.org, 10am-5pm daily, free) is a chance to highlight for visitors what the foundation does. The ash and apple wood displays explain how the Gates' money helps smaller organizations deliver health care and crop assistance. A giant interactive wall offers a timeline of the Gates family and the group itself. But perhaps the biggest emphasis is on toilets: In an effort to bring sustainable sanitation to people living in unhygienic conditions, the foundation's Reinvent the Toilet Challenge produced a waterless solar-powered toilet prototype that now stands in the lobby.

SOUTH LAKE UNION

★ Museum of History and Industry

When the **Museum of History and Industry** (860 Terry Ave. N, 206/324-1126, www.mohai.org, 10am-5pm Fri.-Wed., 10am-8pm Thurs. summer; 10am-5pm daily winter, $19.95 adults, $15.95 seniors, $13.95 students, children free) moved to this waterfront ex-armory building in 2012, it spurred a renewed interest in the museum's mix of artifacts, hands-on exhibits, and curiosities. The working World War II-era periscope offers a chance to peek out onto Lake Union, and displays explain the impact of events like the Great Seattle Fire of 1889 and the 1962 World's Fair. An old notepad bears the scribbling of a young Bill Gates, and the city's preeminent beer sign, from the old Rainier brewery, gets center stage. Outside are several historical ships and tugboats and a small pond with model sailboat rentals.

South Lake Union Streetcar

The city of Seattle has almost as many forms of transportation as it has hills. The **South Lake Union Streetcar** (206/553-3060, www.seattlestreetcar.org, 6am-9pm Mon.-Thurs., 6am-11pm Fri.-Sat., 10am-7pm Sun., $2.25

Museum of Pop Culture

adults, $1 seniors, $1.50 children 6-17, children under 6 free) begins at Stewart Street and Fifth Avenue and travels through the South Lake Union neighborhood and up the east side of Lake Union. The neighborhood has quickly become home to new restaurants and stores in recent years, thanks to the relocation of the Amazon campus to the once-sleepy neighborhood.

CAPITOL HILL

Seattle Asian Art Museum

The **Seattle Asian Art Museum** (1400 E Prospect St., 206/654-3100, www.seattleartmuseum.org) is operated by the Seattle Art Museum, but is located in the middle of Volunteer Park in a beautiful 1933 building that once housed the entire SAM collection, with pieces of Chinese, Indian, Korean, Japanese, and Southeast Asian origin. Replicas of Ming dynasty camel statues sit outside among well-kept flower beds, perfect as props in a photo. The museum is currently closed for renovations but anticipates reopening in 2019.

UNIVERSITY DISTRICT

Locals say "UW" or the shorter "U-Dub" when they're talking about the sprawling **University of Washington** (1401 NE Campus Pkwy., 206/543-9686, www.washington.edu). The campus was first a fairground, host to the 1909 Alaska-Yukon-Pacific Exposition. Students crowd the central Red Square between classes or relax on grassy quads, but the busiest gathering space on game days is the rebuilt Husky Stadium on Lake Washington.

Burke Museum of Natural History and Culture

What's cooler than dinosaur skeletons? How about the bones of a giant sloth, remains that were found at Seattle-Tacoma airport and delivered to the **Burke Museum of Natural History and Culture** (17th Ave. NE and NE 45th St., 206/543-5590, www.burkemuseum.org, 10am-5pm daily, $10 adults, $8 seniors, $7.50 students and children 5 and older, children under 4 free) at the University of Washington. The fossils of a mastodon and stegosaurus are even more massive, and the museum holds treasures that didn't come out of the dirt as well. A survey of the Pacific cultures that influenced the Northwest includes exhibits from Japan, Korea, China, and Hawaii. A new building opens in 2019, and throughout the move the old building will

Museum of History and Industry

show the behind-the-scenes work of moving specimens to the new space.

Henry Art Gallery

The University of Washington's **Henry Art Gallery** (15th Ave. NE at NE 41st St., 206/543-2280, www.henryart.org, 11am-4pm Wed. and Fri.-Sun., 11am-9am Thurs., $10 adults, $6 seniors, students and children under 14 free) is not only a repository for art, it's one of the university's hubs for arts and cultural events. Originally founded by a local philanthropist as the first public art museum in the state, it started with 19th- and 20th-century paintings but later grew to have a substantial photography collection and new-media installations. There are also textiles from around the world, including rugs from Central Asia and costumes from Eastern Europe. The gallery's café (8am-4pm Tues.-Fri., 10:30am-2pm Sat.-Sun.) has salads, sandwiches, and coffee, plus pastries and wraps.

BALLARD

Nordic Museum

Although much of the Northwest can trace some roots to Scandinavia, Ballard in particular was founded by people of Northern Europe. So it's no wonder the **Nordic Museum** (2655 NW Market St., 206/789-5707, www.nordicmuseum.org, 10am-5pm Tues.-Wed. and Fri-Sun., 10am-8pm Thurs., $15 adults, $12 seniors, $10 students and youth, free for children under 5) is located in Ballard. A new building was erected in 2018, right where the working waterfront meets the neighborhood. Its exhibits show off photos and artifacts that tell the story of Nordic immigrants to the United States in the 19th century, especially their work in the fishing and lumber industries. The Folk Art Galleries have costumes, textiles, and furniture with roots in the Nordic countries: Denmark, Finland, Iceland, Norway, and Sweden. Visiting exhibitions explore specific artists or themes.

GREATER SEATTLE

Discovery Park

The large waterfront **Discovery Park** (3801 Discovery Park Blvd., 206/386-4236, www.seattle.gov, park: 4am-11pm daily, cultural center: 8:30am-5pm Tues.-Sun., free), near the Seattle neighborhood of Magnolia, used to be a military installation called Fort Lawton, though the army presence there was never very large. In World War II it served as a POW camp for Germans and Italians, and some of the latter were allowed to socialize

Seattle Asian Art Museum

with Seattle residents. More than 500 acres became Discovery Park in the 1970s, named for George Vancouver's ship, including areas around the 1881 West Point Lighthouse on Puget Sound. The park has more than 2 miles of beaches, plus wooded bluffs and meadows with great views. Trails cross the park; it's a 1.5-mile walk to the beach from the parking lots, passing some old military buildings and a radar that serves as backup for the Seattle-Tacoma airport. There are tennis courts and a playground, and tide pools are visible during low tides on the north beach. The visitors center at the main entrance has park staff and limited exhibits.

Woodland Park Zoo

The 92 acres of **Woodland Park Zoo** (550 Phiney Ave. N, Green Lake, 206/548-2500, www.zoo.org, 9:30am-6pm daily spring-summer, $20.95 adults, $18.95 seniors, $12.95 children 3-12, children under 3 free; 9:30am-4pm daily fall-winter, $14.95 adults, $12.95 seniors, $9.95 children 3-12, children under 3 free) hold more than 1,000 animals of more than 300 species, many of which are endangered. Nearly a million people visit the zoo every year, so it's one of the city's busiest attractions. An African Savanna area has giraffes, hippos, gazelles, and zebras, and the Tropical Asia exhibit has orangutans. Keepers give demonstrations with different raptor species, and grizzly bears are fed salmon every day even though their exhibit has a stream stocked with fish. Ask about when the gorillas get their afternoon snack packs filled with food and toys. The zoo gives discounts for taking public transportation; check the website before going.

University of Washington Arboretum

The **University of Washington Arboretum** (2300 Arboretum Dr. E, Madison Park, 206/543-8800, http://depts.washington.edu, visitors center 9am-5pm daily, free) is more than a simple garden, it's a tree sanctuary that holds more than 20,000 of them over 230 acres, including well-regarded collections of maple, pine, oak, and mountain ash. Trails circle the park, and yes, there are plenty of flowers, too. Wetlands on Lake Washington are especially populated with waterfowl.

The nearby **Japanese Garden** (1075 Lake Washington Blvd. E, 206/684-4725, www.seattle.gov/parks, noon-5pm Mon., 10am-5pm Tues.-Sun. Mar. and Oct.; noon-7pm Mon., 10am-7pm Tues.-Sun Apr. and Aug.; noon-8pm Mon., 10am-8pm Tues.-Sun. May-July; noon-6pm Mon., 10am-6pm Tues.-Sun. Sept.; 10am-4pm Tues.-Sun. Nov., $6 adults, $4 seniors, students, and children 6-17, children under 6 free) is operated by the city, not the university, so there's a fee to enter. The garden is especially popular when the cherry blossom trees bloom. Tea ceremonies are held occasionally, and a community center inside the formal Japanese garden has periodic art displays.

Bellevue Arts Museum

Who says Seattle has all the culture? Across Lake Washington in the posh city of Bellevue is the **Bellevue Arts Museum** (510 Bellevue Way NE, Bellevue, 425/519-0770, www.bellevuearts.org, 11am-5pm Wed.-Sun., $12 adults, $10 seniors and students, children under 6 free). It focuses on Northwest creations, with an emphasis that puts crafts and design works next to paintings and sculptures.

★ Museum of Flight

You might think you like airplanes, but until you've been to the **Museum of Flight** (9404 E Marginal Way, South Seattle, 206/764-5720, www.museumofflight.org, 10am-5pm daily, $23 adults, $19 seniors, $14 children 5-17, children under 5 free), you don't really understand what it means to be obsessed with flight. The building is located next to Boeing Field, an airstrip used by Boeing and private aircraft, whose tarmac is often lined with new and experimental aircraft. The museum has 150 planes and flying machines, many hanging in a giant glass pavilion—there's the Mach 3 Blackbird, the fastest plane ever built, and early airmail biplanes, a sailplane, WWI fighters, and a Huey helicopter. A big red barn—the original Boeing airplane factory—traces the history of flight and the Boeing industry in Seattle. Outdoors is a kind of parking lot for cool old airplanes, including a supersonic Concorde jet and the first jet to serve as Air Force One—you can walk through the 707 and see where President Kennedy sat on his flights. The 3-D theater and flight simulators let you feel like you got off the ground.

One of the most exciting parts of the Museum of Flight is the space exhibits, including a full-size replica of an International Space Station lab and a Soyuz module used by Charles Simonyi, a billionaire who used his Microsoft money to visit space (and built the gallery that houses many of the museum's space artifacts). In the center of the room is the giant Space Shuttle Trainer, a full-scale replica of the now retired spacecraft. It never went to space, but every shuttle astronaut trained on it. **Tours** ($20-25, reservations recommended) are available for a peek inside the crew compartment, though any museum visitor can look inside the cargo bay—Queen Elizabeth once dined inside it when she visited NASA in Houston, Texas.

SIGHTSEEING TOURS

When is a bus like a boat? When you're riding one of the amphibious craft at **Ride the Ducks** (516 Broad St., 206/441-3825, www.ridetheducksofseattle.com, 10am-4pm Mon.-Fri., 9:30am-4pm Sat.-Sun., $35 adults, $32 seniors, $20 children 4-12, $5 children under 2). These vehicles were originally used in World War II, but now they're rollicking tour vessels that show off Seattle by land and sea. Tours begin with goofy introductions by the driver, who'll likely wear a silly hat the entire trip. Expect a little bit of history and a lot of loud music and games, like screaming "ka-ching" every time you pass a Starbucks, and the humming of duck-shaped kazoos that some riders purchase. After a loop through the downtown streets, the Duck open-air vehicles travel to the north end of Lake Union, where they head into the water and become boats. The water tour passes Gasworks Park and the floating homes that were popularized in the movie *Sleepless in Seattle*.

Not only does **Argosy Cruises** (Pier 55, 1101 Alaskan Way, 888/623-1445, www.argosycruises.com, $27-84 adults, $22-75 seniors, $13-32 children 4-12, children under 4 free) run the Tillicum Village experience, it also has a whole slate of boat tours

Museum of Flight

Day Trip to Woodinville Wine Country

Most of Washington's famed wine-making takes place east of Seattle, across the mountains. But go just a little east of the city for a town that's become a kind of emissary for the far-off vineyards. **Woodinville** is just 30 miles from the Space Needle but can feel like a different world, one with a slower pace and finer appreciation for sitting around and sipping spirits.

In the center is **Chateau Ste. Michelle** (14111 NE 145th St., 425/488-1133, www.ste-michelle.com, tastings and tours 10am–5pm daily, free), a French-style behemoth that should look utterly out of place in rural Washington. Instead the quaint shutters and giant wooden doors on the estate are welcoming, if a bit weird, and the winery gives tastings and hosts summer concerts on its well-trimmed lawns.

Besides the big French castle, dozens of other establishments have tasting rooms around Woodinville, and two-thirds of the 99 wineries in town actually produce wine here. Nearly half produce fewer than 2,000 cases, compared to Chateau Ste. Michelle's more than two million. It's possible to wander on foot between tasting rooms in the industrial part of town, or simply stop at one of the larger establishments for a snack and a lengthy tasting.

Drinks may be taken care of, but there's always dinner to consider, and the town has a clear favorite dining spot in **The Herbfarm** (14590 NE 145th St., 425/485-5300, http://theherbfarm.com, seatings at 4:30pm or 7pm, $205-265). Originally home to an educational meal on the site of a small local farm, now it's relocated to a flowery spot across the street from Ste. Michelle. Meals are a single-seating, nine-course affair preceded by a garden tour and introduction to swine named Basil and Borage—they're pets, not future pork dishes. As befits the wine-loving town, the restaurant chooses pairings from a 26,000-bottle cellar.

around Puget Sound and Lake Washington. The harbor cruise, a narrated one-hour experience, visits the city's industrial waterfront and shipping terminal, providing water views of the Space Needle. The Locks Cruise (2.5 hours) includes a trip through the Ballard Locks and peeks at the houseboats on Lake Union. Other tours that visit Lake Washington—with its floating bridges, waterfront mansions, and stadium views—leave from marinas in South Lake Union or Kirkland. Dining and murder-mystery-game cruises are scheduled regularly, and in the winter the Christmas Ship, decked in white lights, travels to 45 different waterfront communities and broadcasts the caroling performance of the onboard choir. The tradition reaches back more than 60 years, and once the schedule is posted, the residents of each Seattle waterfront community make a point of greeting the ship as it passes. Tickets can be booked on both the Christmas Ship with its choir or the Parade Boat that follows it.

Entertainment and Events

It's been a long time since the city was just known for grunge music. Culture in Seattle ranges from a strong jazz tradition to thriving independent movie theaters. Cocktail culture is nationally recognized, but the city's quirky sensibilities are still found in watering holes, clubs, and music venues.

NIGHTLIFE

Brewpubs and Taprooms

DOWNTOWN

There are bars with impressive beer selections, and then there's the **Tap House Grill** (1506 6th Ave, 206/816-3314, http://taphousegrill.com, 11am-1am Sun.-Thurs., 11am-2am Fri.-Sat.) A curved wall behind the bar has 160 taps, claimed to be the largest selection in the region. The Tap House Grill carries international styles like Belgians and bitters, but, this being the hoppy Pacific Northwest, more than two dozen IPAs are featured. Almost all local breweries are represented, and bartenders offer tastes to help customers find the perfect choice. The basement space is a large, corporate-style restaurant, but happy hour flatbreads topped with chicken sausage or bacon and pineapple are a great deal. The rest of the menu is broad, encompassing nearly as many food styles as beer varieties: jambalaya, prime rib, pad Thai, and more.

CAPITOL HILL

The barn-like **Rhein Haus** (912 12th Ave., 206/325-5409, www.rheinhausseattle.com, 3pm-2am Mon.-Fri., 10am-2am Sat.-Sun.) is a German theme park unto itself, with multiple bars, indoor bocce courts, a fireplace, and long beer-hall tables popular with students from Seattle University across the street. Beer comes in glasses that range from a two-ounce taste to a full-liter mug, and most pours hail from Germany and Austria. A special machine spirals potatoes thin, so they can be fried on a stick like a never-ending potato chip.

The idea of a beer bar in a mortuary sounds grim, but in practice at **Pine Box** (1600 Melrose Ave., 206/588-0375, www.pineboxbar.com, 3pm-2am Mon.-Fri., 11am-2am Sat.-Sun.) it's a perfect fit. With its giant curved windows and high molded ceilings, the space feels like a warm church dedicated to the worship of beer and hanging out. The bar has a few dozen beers on tap, and the food menu is split between "less," "more," and pizza dishes, all the kind of spicy, saucy eats that pair well with a high-alcohol specialty beer. For all the grandeur of the former place of mourning, including a loft overlooking the whole space, it's a loud and crowded beer hall.

Local beer is crucial to the Northwest drinking scene; since most of the nation's hops are grown here, the bitter IPA practically flows from the water taps, and every week there's a new brewery putting out IBUs from a suburban garage or Ballard bike shed. **Stumbling Monk** (1635 E Olive Way, 206/860-0916, 6pm-2am daily), a fixture that sits between two busy hubs of Capitol Hill, takes a different approach to beer appreciation by specializing in Belgians and other imports. It's as dark as a European pub, with high-backed booths and wooden tables that look like they have as much history as the Habsburgs. Though the bottle menu attracts aficionados, the selection of board games is a clear sign that the joint isn't about beer snobbery.

Bars and Clubs

DOWNTOWN

Down the stairs from Pike Place Market is the quintessential Seattle cocktail bar, **Zig Zag Café** (1501 Western Ave., No. 202, 206/625-1146, www.zigzagseattle.com, 5pm-2am daily). Bartenders in neat black vests take pride in crafting memorable cocktails and remembering customer's faces, making it a local's favorite even as tourists wander up the steps outside. Stroll down the alley that runs just uphill from the market and look for a half-open Dutch door; that's **White Horse Trading Company** (1908 Post Alley, 206/441-7767, 4pm-midnight Mon.-Thurs., 4pm-2am Fri.-Sat.), a snug British drinkery crowded with old-timey golf clubs, bookshelves, and paintings of red-coated fox hunters. Besides British ales, the bar serves Pimm's Cup highballs, a drink that's to Brits at Wimbledon what a mint julep is to Southerners at the Kentucky Derby.

For an even more literate quaff, **Bookstore Bar & Café** (Alexis Hotel, 1007 1st Ave., 206/624-3646, www.bookstorebar.com, 7am-10pm Mon.-Fri., 8am-10pm Sat.-Sun.) sits under rows of books for sale. Any tome is $5, and dishes at happy hour (3pm-6pm daily) aren't much more. The best reading in the house, however, is the menu of 70 single-malt Scotch whiskeys and almost as many American whiskeys.

To call **The Hideout** (1005 Boren Ave., 206/903-8480, www.hideoutseattle.com, 4pm-2am Mon.-Fri., 6pm-2am Sat.-Sun.) an art bar is a vast understatement—nearly every inch of the 16-foot-high walls are plastered with canvases, a thoughtful still life next to a frantic modern collage. The signage outside is modest, perhaps to best fit in with the surrounding hospitals in First Hill, or "Pill Hill." Be sure to swing by the art vending machine in the bar's dark corner before ordering from the bar. You can get a beer, a decent cocktail, or an artwork price list and flashlight to shop the gallery around you.

BELLTOWN

Peek down an alleyway and look for a metal placard noting the entrance to neo-speakeasy **Bathtub Gin and Co.** (2205 2nd Ave., 206/728-6069, www.bathtubginseattle.com, 5pm-2am daily), a thin, multilevel establishment that does more than trade on its twee theme. Great dates take place in the bar's intimate nooks, but sit at the small bar to have the talented bartenders create original cocktails.

White Horse Trading Company

When it comes time to pay, request a receipt—they'll usually handwrite one, complete with doodles of beer bottles or cocktail glasses.

For cocktails just as fancy but easier to find, **Rob Roy** (2332 2nd Ave., 206/956-8423, www.robroyseattle.com, 4pm-2am daily) isn't far away. Even classic cocktails here are on the obscure side (ever heard of a Jungle Bird?), and if you're lucky, ice will be chopped by hand to fit the glass. Original creations are even more eyebrow raising—the Gunpowder Punch includes rum, gin, spices, and actual gunpowder. Just a little, though.

SOUTH LAKE UNION

Despite its location as a lonely club on a somewhat quiet street, **Lo-Fi Performance Gallery** (429 Eastlake Ave., 206/254-2824, www.thelofi.net, hours vary) is definitely best known as a dance club, especially on its most popular theme nights. A '60s soul night steers away from overplayed hits, while the massively popular monthly '90s dance party is full of chart toppers.

CAPITOL HILL

The area's cocktail cathedral is the prim and proper **Canon** (928 12th Ave., 206/552-9755, www.canonseattle.com, 5pm-2am daily), where bartenders, whiskeys, and bitters are the stars. No one is let inside unless a seat is available, so there's no throwing elbows to reach the bar. Not that there isn't a sense of humor here—page 63 of the massive menu is labeled "hardcore porn" for bottles like a $1,225 Canoe Club whiskey from 1898 or a Maker's Mark named for the Triple Crown-winning horse Seattle Slew.

As the home of the city's party scene, Capitol Hill isn't all good behavior. There's an obvious Western theme at **Montana** (1506 E Olive Way, 206/422-4647, www.montanainseattle.com, 4pm-2am daily), where specials are scrawled on a blackboard. Bearded young men in flannel shirts fill the wooden booths, and even the women here are likely to be wearing plaid.

Every other pattern under the sun is represented at **The Unicorn** (1118 E Pike St., 206/325-6492, www.unicornseattle.com, noon-2am Mon.-Fri., 11am-2am Sat.-Sun.), a veritable assault on the senses. Decorated like a circus seen through an acid trip, it even has horned beasts mounted on the walls—real taxidermy ones, not unicorns. Downstairs is even wilder: a basement bar called the Narwhal, named for the unicorns of the sea. Pinball machines, a photo booth, and sticky floors are a good match for the cheap cocktails and bowls of popcorn.

Though located in Capitol Hill, **The Baltic Room** (1207 Pine St., 206/625-4444, www.balticroom.com, 10pm-2am Mon.-Sat.) is just a bridge away from downtown, so it pulls scenesters from both neighborhoods. It hosts a wide range of DJs and the usual mix of pop, R&B, and house-music nights, but you can also find odder things taking place on the dance floor, like a live art painting event while speakers thump dance music around the artists.

BALLARD

The spacious **King's Hardware** (5225 Ballard Ave. NW, 206/782-0027, www.kingsballard.com, 3pm-2am Mon.-Fri., noon-2am Sat.-Sun.) isn't the only bar in Seattle with Skee-Ball, but it's probably the best. Linda Dershang, Seattle's expert on great casual hangouts, helped create the bar in an old hardware space, taking care to include must-haves like an outdoor patio, a vintage Donkey Kong game, burgers, and a jukebox.

Slightly more upscale is the nearby **Noble Fir** (5316 Ballard Ave. NW, 206/420-7425, www.thenoblefir.com, 4pm-midnight Tues.-Thurs., 4pm-1am Fri.-Sat., 1pm-9pm Sun.), a sleek establishment that gets more natural light than most firs in the forest. The beer menu shows evidence of fastidious selection, and one corner has a hiking and travel book library nook.

Gay and Lesbian

With its white walls and floor, sleek surfaces, and high-concept lighting, **Q** (1426 Broadway, www.qnightclub.com, 9pm-2am Wed.-Thurs., 10am-3am Fri.-Sat.) can feel more like an Apple Store than a dance club. But then the music kicks up and drinks start flowing, featuring house-made infused vodkas in Hickory Bacon or Chocomint flavors.

While it's common to find a mixed crowd on Q's dance floor, **The Cuff** (1533 13th Ave., 206/323-1525, www.cuffcomplex.com, 2pm-2am daily) is unapologetically a gay bar. It's popular among the leather, bear, and fetish crowds, but the dance floor draws a diverse mix of men, and the spot's disco ball has hung in local gay bars since the 1970s. It's a more chill scene at **C.C. Attle's** (1701 E Olive Way, 206/726-0565, www.ccattles.net, 3pm-2am Mon.-Fri., 2pm-2am Sat.-Sun.), a bear bar with pool and more sunlight than many drinking holes on the Hill.

Live Music

The art deco styling of the downtown **Showbox** (1426 1st Ave., 206/628-3151, www.showboxpresents.com) doesn't lie. The theater has been around since the 1930s and once hosted burlesque superstar Gypsy Rose Lee in her hometown. Today the space creates intimacy with the audience spread over several levels, making it a popular stop for rock, indie, and R&B acts.

Born as a Beaux-Arts vaudeville and movie theater in the 1920s, the **Paramount Theatre** (911 Pine St., 206/902-5500, www.stgpresents.org/paramount) now welcomes traveling Broadway shows, big headlining musicians, and massive political rallies. The old dame of a theater was renovated in the 1990s by a Microsoft executive with a flair for the dramatic; she donated the theater to a nonprofit group to manage it.

More intimate performances take place at downtown's **The Triple Door** (216 Union St., 206/838-4333, www.thetripledoor.net), with plush booth seating and an Asian fusion menu. The stage at **Dimitriou's Jazz Alley** (2033 6th Ave., 206/441-9729, www.jazzalley.com) is surrounded by two levels of tables and upscale diners.

Neumos (925 E Pike St., 206/709-9442, www.neumos.com) got its name because it's the "New Moe's," the resurrection of a '90s club that welcomed Radiohead, Pearl Jam, and Neil Young; even President Bill Clinton popped in for a show when he was in town. Today the performance space is the center of a complex that includes a fish fry eatery, a casual bar, and a more-intimate stage.

Paramount Theatre

THE ARTS

Theater

It may be more than 3,000 miles from **5th Avenue Theatre** (1308 5th Ave., 206/625-1900, www.5thavenue.org) to Broadway, but the trip feels quicker for the musicals produced here that have gone on to successful Broadway runs—including two Tony Award winners for Best Musical. Besides future blockbusters like *Memphis* and *Hairspray,* the theater hosts touring productions.

Seattle Repertory Theatre (155 Mercer St., 206/443-2222, www.seattlerep.org) dates back to the arts enthusiasm that arose after the 1962 World's Fair left the city with a number of performance spaces. The group has premiered plays by big-name playwrights like August Wilson and Neil Simon, and its theater in the Seattle Center is recognized as the city's foremost nonmusical theater stage. The downtown **ACT Theatre** (700 Union St., 206/292-7660, www.acttheatre.org) specializes in contemporary productions and commissions new works from up-and-coming playwrights.

Classical Music, Opera, and Dance

As the home of the Seattle Symphony, **Benaroya Hall** (200 University St., 206/215-4800, www.seattlesymphony.org/benaroya) performances are most often under the direction of electric conductor Ludovic Morlot, though the stage also hosts talks and even film events. A giant Dale Chihuly sculpture decorates the main hall, and giant glass windows open to a downtown view. **McCaw Hall** (321 Mercer St., 206/733-9725, www.

mccawhall.com) in Seattle Center shares its stage with **Seattle Opera** (www.seattleopera.org) and **Pacific Northwest Ballet** (www.pnb.org), the latter a nationally recognized dance troupe.

Modern dance works are a highlight of the Queen Anne-based **On the Boards** (100 W Roy St., 206/217-9886, www.ontheboards.org), whose summer NW New Works Festival encourages artists to take big risks in theater performances.

CINEMA

The giant 70-foot curved screen of **Cinerama** (2100 4th Ave., 206/448-6680, www.cinerama.com) harks back to an earlier era when movies had intermissions and IMAX didn't exist. The retro theater hosts first-run movies, classic movie nights, and special events, and even the popcorn is special—coated in chocolate.

The menu's much broader at **Big Picture** (2505 1st Ave., 206/256-0566, www.thebigpicture.net), a small basement theater with a full bar outside. Order a drink before the lights dim to get in-seat delivery in the middle of the flick.

FESTIVALS AND EVENTS

Wintergrass (Bellevue, www.acousticsound.org, Feb.) is an annual bluegrass music event that draws banjo players and fiddle masters just east of Seattle every winter. Hotel ballrooms fill with music performances, but the hallways and sidewalks are just as likely to be packed with folk tunes as musicians gather and jam.

Seattle is known as a nerd town, so it's no wonder that the **Emerald City ComicCon** (www.emeraldcitycomicon.com, Mar.) has grown into a giant festival of comic books, superheroes, and fantasy. Actor appearances, book signings, and film screenings draw attendees, and thousands of people don costumes for the event.

Seattle's annual **Pride Parade** (www.seattlepride.org, June) now celebrates the legalization of same-sex marriage in Washington. The parade usually starts at 11am and runs north down 4th Avenue to Denny Way. Billed as the largest free Pride festival in the country, Seattle **PrideFest** (www.seattlepridefest.org, June) fills Seattle Center (305 Harrison St., 206/684-7200, www.seattlecenter.com) with vendors and performers.

Things go fast at **Seafair** (www.seafair.com, June-Aug.), the city's annual summer festival that stretches from June to August. Hydroplanes race around Lake Washington at more than 150 miles per hour, and fighter jets turn loops above a boat flotilla that forms on the lake. But not everything is in a rush—the annual Torchlight Parade and Parade of Ships are no faster than a mosey.

Once an upstart neighborhood event, the **Capitol Hill Block Party** (www.capitolhillblockparty.com, July) has grown into a raucous July weekend party. Independent musicians appear on stages throughout the hipster enclave of South Capitol Hill, though the festival's growth has meant more and more recognizable names on the bill.

Even before Washington legalized recreational marijuana use in 2012, **Hempfest** (www.hempfest.org, Aug.) has been the largest pot-themed gathering in the world. Bands, bong sales, and activist work fill the now three-day festival held the third weekend in August, always free and always 100 percent volunteer run.

The city's biggest music festival is named for something locals are proud to do without—umbrellas, or in British slang, **Bumbershoot** (www.bumbershoot.org, Sept.). Every Labor Day weekend, the Seattle Center grounds fill with arts of every stripe, from headlining bands playing Key Arena to art shows and poetry readings.

Shopping

Who says Seattle doesn't have style? It's a common joke, what with all the polar fleece and hiking boots worn on the street. But there is also a quirky sophistication on display, with local designers often incorporating outdoorsiness into attractive and, dare we say it, refined clothes and home decor.

DOWNTOWN

Books

The downtown **Barnes and Noble** (600 Pine St., 206/264-0156, www.barnesandnoble.com, 9am-10pm Mon.-Thurs., 9am-11pm Fri.-Sun.) doesn't look too big on the street level—just magazines, a few shelves of books, and some checkout stands. Go down the escalators for the full store with a children's section, travel section, Starbucks, and DVD shelves. The basement store opens to the lower lobby of the Pacific Place shopping center and parking garage.

The charming **Arundel Bookstore** (214 1st Ave. S, 206/624-4442, www.arundelbookstores.com, 11am-6pm daily) is a sweet store in Pioneer Square that is dedicated to the printed word. It specializes in art and rare books and also runs a publishing operation so small that it uses a hand-cranked press.

Clothing and Shoes

Downtown boutique **Baby & Company** (1936 1st Ave., 206/448-4077, www.babyandco.us, 10am-6pm Mon.-Sat., noon-5pm Sun.) has carried the torch for Seattle fashion since the 1970s, carrying quirky brands that defy the city's fleece-and-hiking boots reputation. The feel is one part Bohemian, one part urban chic, in a glistening white space decorated with palm fronds.

There may not be many Seattle occasions for a fancy chapeau from **Goorin Brothers Hat Shop** (1610 1st Ave., 206/443-8082, www.goorin.com, 10am-7pm Mon.-Thurs., 10am-8pm Fri.-Sat., 11am-7pm Sun.), but the staff specializes in personal service and fittings. Learn the difference between a cloche and a fedora, or pick up feathered pings to decorate your own grubby ball cap. **Diva Dollz** (624 1st Ave., 206/652-2299, www.divadollz.com, noon-6pm daily), in Pioneer Square, is a different kind of throwback, where pinup and rockabilly-style dresses create '60s silhouettes. It's not hard to imagine Bettie Page rocking these frocks—when she wore clothes at all, that is.

Department Stores

The downtown **Nordstrom** (500 Pine St., 206/628-2111, http://shop.nordstrom.com, 9:30am-9pm Mon.-Sat., 10am-7pm Sun.) serves as both the shopping chain's flagship and the city's retail anchor. The store's roots are in shoe sales, but the giant has since grown to include high-end clothing, jewelry, and makeup. Some days a piano player serenades shoppers as they glide up and down the store's escalators. But anyone priced out of the main store can head underground next door to **Nordstrom Rack** (400 Pine St., 206/448-8522, http://shop.nordstrom.com, 9:30am-9pm Mon.-Sat., 10am-7pm Sun.). The outlet for the department chain has heavily discounted high fashion and rows of shoes on sale.

The nearby **Macy's** (300 Pine St., 206/506-6000, www.macys.com, 10am-8pm Mon.-Wed., 10am-9pm Thurs., 10am-10pm Fri.-Sat., 11am-7pm Sun.) takes a slightly broader approach, carrying more housewares, furniture, and linens. Seattle was one of three cities to first receive **City Target** (1401 2nd Ave., 206/494-3250, www.target.com, 7am-11pm daily), a slightly smaller version of the cheap big-box retailer meant for the urban dweller. There are fewer large items for sale in the three-floor store, and food selections include ready-made lunches.

Metsker Maps

Gift and Home

Go ahead, let locals claim they don't carry an umbrella. That pride has probably meant a miserable walk or two, and they're missing the plethora of bumbershoots at **Bella Umbrella** (1535 1st Ave., 206/297-1540, www.bellaumbrella.com, 10am-6pm Mon.-Sat., 11am-5pm Sun.). Besides selling and renting a variety of styles (the latter for large events, not an unexpected downpour), the proprietor shows off selections from her own vintage collection.

It's worth getting lost in **Metsker Maps** (1511 1st Ave., 206/623-8747, www.metskers.com, 9am-8pm Mon.-Fri., 10am-8pm Sat., 10am-6pm Sun.), a travel store with enough inspiration for several trips around the world. Besides a selection of travel books and folded maps of every corner of the globe, the store specializes in map art, including gorgeous woodcut charts of the Salish Sea. There are gifts galore in **Watson Kennedy Fine Home** (1022 1st Ave., 206/652-8350, www.watsonkennedy.com, 10am-6pm Mon.-Sat., noon-5pm Sun.), but you'll likely be tempted to shop for yourself among the vintage-style glassware, framed art, and fine treats. Local touches can be seen in the Fran's chocolates (a Seattle brand favored by President Obama) and weathered signs listing ferry destinations around Puget Sound.

Gourmet Goodies

As one corner of the mighty Pike Place Market, **DeLaurenti** (1435 1st Ave., 206/622-0141, www.delaurenti.com, 9am-6pm Mon.-Sat., 10am-5pm Sun.) has a prime location for its fine-food wares. A long cheese and meat counter sits toward the back, while prepared deli foods up front cause out-the-door lines to form at lunchtime. Head up the steps to a wine room that hosts tastings.

Not everything from **Paris-Madrid Grocery** (1418 Western Ave., 206/682-2827, www.spanishtable.com, 10am-6pm Mon.-Sat., 11am-5pm Sun.) hails from France and Spain, but most of it does—there's also quite a bit from Portugal. A cheese counter doles out Manchego and pâté, and a selection of cookbooks provides instruction on how to achieve Iberian flavors.

SOUTH LAKE UNION

Outdoor Equipment

Outdoor store **REI** (222 Yale Ave. N, 206/223-1944, www.rei.com, 9am-9pm Mon.-Sat., 10am-7pm Sun.) is still the same co-op it was when it was founded by a group of Seattle hikers, only supersized. The flagship's rock climbing wall, stone fireplace, indoor hiking trail, and outdoor bike route allow customers to really try out the merchandise, and the rental counter downstairs loans out snowshoes, sleeping bags, and tents. The focus is cozier at the nearby **Feathered Friends** (263 Yale Ave. N, 206/292-2210, www.featheredfriends.com, 10am-8pm Mon.-Fri., 10am-6pm Sat., 11am-5pm Sun.), a fluffy foundry of down everything—coats, booties, sleeping bags, and featherbeds. The store also carries a smaller selection of the same outdoor gear found at REI, but the staff is more reliably knowledgeable.

Gallery Hopping

Pioneer Square is home to many of the city's art galleries. The area is centered on the intersection of Washington Street and 3rd Avenue South and is a good destination on the first Thursday of every month, when the **First Thursday Seattle Art Walk** (www.firstthursdayseattle.com, noon-8pm) keeps galleries open. **Foster/White Gallery** (220 3rd Ave. S, 206/622-2833, www.fosterwhite.com, 10am-6pm Tues.-Sat.) is Northwest-artist focused, and next door is the **Greg Kucera Gallery** (212 3rd Ave. S, 206/624-0770, www.gregkucera.com, 10:30am-5:30pm Tues.-Sat.), known for contemporary paintings, prints, and sculptures, often highlighting works with a political focus.

Located downtown, close to the Seattle Art Museum, **Patricia Rovzar Gallery** (1111 1st Ave., 206/223-0273, www.rovzargallery.com, 11am-5pm daily) has bright contemporary works. **Sisko Gallery** (3126 Elliott Ave., 206/283-2998, www.siskogallery.com, 11am-5pm Fri.-Sun.), near the Olympic Sculpture Park, displays contemporary work and hosts a reservation-only life-drawing club on Sunday.

Capitol Hill's art scene tends to be looser, younger, and less expensive. **Vermillion** (1508 11th Ave., 206/709-9797, 4pm-midnight Tues.-Thurs., 4pm-1am Fri.-Sat., 4pm-11pm Sun.) is an art gallery with a fantastic secret—a bar behind the display space. The funky space has a good-sized serving area, a blackboard displaying food items, a good wine list, exposed brick walls, and friendly bartenders.

CAPITOL HILL

Books

In literate Seattle, **Elliott Bay Book Company** (1521 10th Ave., 206/624-6600, www.elliottbaybook.com, 10am-10pm Mon.-Thurs., 10am-11pm Fri.-Sat., 11am-7pm Sun.) is practically a church. Readers gather among bookshelves, in the café, or in a basement reading room that fills almost daily for names big and small. This is the kind of indie bookstore where the staff recommendations are spot-on and the café seats are a hot commodity.

Clothing and Shoes

In a city this fanatical about recycling, it's unsurprising that we'd have a shop like **NuBE Green** (1527 10th Ave., 206/402-4515, www.nubegreen.com, 11am-6pm Mon.-Thurs, 10am-6pm Fri.-Sat., 10am-5pm Sun.), where home decor and fashion meet sustainability. The in-house line remakes pieces using vintage and thrift goods, and everything sold is in some way U.S. made or recycled.

In a stylish, vast space, the wares of **Totokaelo** (1523 10th Ave., 206/623-3582, www.totokaelo.com, 11am-7pm Mon.-Sat., 11am-6pm Sun.) get a chance to breathe. The menswear, women's wear, and home furnishings are so fashionable that the local store has more customers in New York City than in Seattle.

Gourmet Goodies

There are two options at **Melrose Market** (1501-1535 Melrose Ave., 206/568-2666, www.melrosemarketseattle.com): Buy meats and cheeses for a meal at home, or indulge in the handful of restaurants that sit around the two stands. The indoor gourmet market is abutted by **Taylor Shellfish Farms** (1521 Melrose Ave., 206/501-4321, www.taylorshellfishfarms.com, 11am-9pm Sun.-Thurs., 11am-11pm Fri.-Sat.), where local oysters and mussels are ready to be slurped and steamed.

UNIVERSITY DISTRICT

Books

Not only does the **University Book Store** (4326 University Way NE, 206/634-3400, www.bookstore.washington.edu, 9am-8pm Mon.-Fri., 10am-7pm Sat., noon-5pm Sun.) carry many of the Northwest authors that are taught at the University of Washington next door, but there's also every kind of Husky shirt, bag, sticker, and flag imaginable. The large store often holds events with visiting writers.

GREATER SEATTLE

Books

The first place is home and the second place is work. **Third Place Books** (6504 20th Ave. NE, 206/525-2347, www.thirdplacebooks.com, 8am-9pm Sun.-Thurs., 8am-10pm Fri.-Sat.) is meant to be a third important part of a Seattle resident's life, and sells new and used books in two locations in the city. (This is the Ravenna spot, closest to downtown.) The downstairs **Pub at Third Place** (206/523-0217, 3pm-11pm Mon.-Thurs., 3pm-midnight Fri.-Sat., 3pm-10pm Sun.) features 18 beer taps, most with local brews, and an international selection of wine. On-site **Vios Café** (206/525-5701, 8am-9pm daily) offers Greek-inspired menus.

Sports and Recreation

PARKS

★ Volunteer Park

Green space impresarios the Olmstead Brothers (who designed Central Park, among other spaces) designed Capitol Hill's **Volunteer Park** (1247 15th Ave. E, 206/684-4075, www.seattle.gov/parks, 6am-10pm daily)—less than 50 acres, but with a little bit of everything. A stately brick water tower offers panoramic views from the top, and a glass conservatory blooms even when the weather's at its worst outside. Lawns dot the space around the Seattle Asian Art Museum, guarded by twin camel statues, and the Isamu Noguchi sculpture *Black Sun* has a keyhole view of the Space Needle.

Kerry Park

For the absolute best view of the Space Needle, head to **Kerry Park** (211 W Highland Dr., 206/684-4075, www.seattle.gov/parks) on Queen Anne Hill. This tiny space is known primarily for how it looms over the landmark. It fills quickly on New Year's Eve, when fireworks shoot from the top of the tower.

Volunteer Park

Green Lake

The very urban **Green Lake** (7201 E Green Lake Dr. N, 206/684-4075, www.seattle.gov) is one busy oasis. A walking and biking trail surrounds the lake that's about 3 miles around, and a swimming beach is available (though the lake sometimes closes for algae blooms). The calm waters are perfect for beginning kayakers and stand-up paddleboarders, and an impressive old bleacher stand faces the water near a boathouse. The 3-mile loop is popular for families, dog walkers, and inline skaters, and the fields around the lake fill with sports team. Boat rentals are available at **Green Lake Boat Rental** (7351 E Green Lake Dr. N, 206/527-0171, www.greenlakeboatrentals.net, 9am-7pm daily spring-fall, $22-30 per hour), including sailboats and paddleboats. Next to the lake, the **Green Lake Pitch & Putt** (5701 E Green Lake Way N, 206/632-2280, www.seattle.gov/parks, 9am-dusk Mar.-Oct., $7) is a nine-hole, par-three golf course.

Gasworks Park

There's something beautiful about the industrial ruins in **Gasworks Park** (2101 N Northlake Way, 206/684-4075, www.seattle.gov/parks, 6am-10pm daily), even if state ecologists are still testing the metal refineries and tanks for pollution. No swimming is allowed in the waterfront park because of contaminants, but the city views—and the kite-flying—are perfect from atop the park's biggest hill.

Hiram M. Chittenden Locks

For the mechanically minded, there's nothing like an afternoon watching the **Hiram M. Chittenden Locks** (3015 54th St. NW, 206/783-7059, www.nws.usace.army.mil), operated by the U.S. Army Corps of Engineers and opened almost a century ago. On a scenic stretch of the ship canal in Ballard, next to a manicured botanical garden, the water elevator lets boats come and go. An underground passage shows off the fish ladder that allows the fish to do the same.

BEACHES

Don't laugh. There really is sand on **Alki Beach Park** (1702 Alki Ave. SW, 206/684-4075, www.seattle.gov/parks, 4am-11:30pm daily), in West Seattle on a peninsula that protrudes farther into Puget Sound than downtown. Even when it isn't all that sunny, locals toss Frisbees, bike along the sandy stretch, or warm themselves around fire pits.

Gasworks Park

Center for Wooden Boats

Located north of the city, **Golden Gardens Park** (8498 Seaview Pl. NW, 206/684-4075, www.seattle.gov/parks, 6am-11:30pm daily) is barbecue central, with room for a volleyball net and an off-leash area for pets. The view of Salmon Bay feels hopelessly far from downtown Seattle.

In a beach that's more about being seen than swimming, **Madison Park** (E Madison St. and E Howe St., 206/684-4075, www.seattle.gov/parks, 4am-11:30pm daily) buzzes with chatter, stereos playing, and even some splashing on summer afternoons. Lifeguards overlook the swimmers in the Lake Washington waters, more bearable than the chilly Puget Sound.

BIKING

Cars have the freeway, bikes have the lengthy **Burke-Gilman Trail** (206/684-7583, www.seattle.gov/parks), which stretches almost 19 miles from Ballard to Bothell. Enter the trailhead at NW 45th Street and 11th Avenue NW; the trail turns into the Sammamish River Trail around NE Bothell Way and 73rd Avenue NE, in Bothell. Hardy cyclists can pedal all the way to the wineries of Woodinville. Commuting bikers are known to buzz the more leisurely walkers on the path if they don't pay attention to lane markings.

It's impossible to get lost on the **Green Lake Trail** (7201 E Green Lake Dr. N, 206/684-4075, www.seattle.gov/parks), a biking and running route around one of the city's more residential lakes. Pass swimming spots, roller skaters, dog parks, an amphitheater, and sports fields in the 3-mile loop.

Bike Rentals

Downtown's **Bicycle Repair Shop** (68 Madison St., 206/682-7057, www.thebicyclerepairshop.com, 8am-6pm Mon.-Fri, 10am-6pm Sat., noon-6pm Sun.) is right on the waterfront, offering hybrid and road bikes ($9-15 per hour) from a spot near the Great Wheel and ferry dock. Self-guided tour maps are free. Seattle has a mandatory helmet law, so all bike rentals come with free headwear.

BOATING

You have two choices: Rent a kayak or stand-up paddleboard at **Agua Verde Café and Paddle Club** (1303 NE Boat St., University District, 206/545-8570, www.aguaverde.com, $18-24 per hour) *before* you try the fresh Mexican quesadillas and margaritas, or *after*. The latter allows you to work off the calories you gained, but you might lose the willpower to paddle up the ship canal to Lake Washington or even peek at the nearby houseboats on Lake Union.

As an organization, **Center for Wooden Boats** (1010 Valley St., 206/382-2628, www.cwb.org, 12:30pm-5pm or dusk Sat.-Sun., $30-60 per hour), on the south end of Lake Union, promotes shipbuilding and sailing. On a clear day, they do so by renting rowboats, pedal boats, or sailboats. For those nervous about their seafaring skills, there's no shame in picking up a model version for use on a nearby pond.

HIKING

Although it begins south of downtown near the stadiums, the best place to hop on the **Elliott Bay Trail** (www.mtsgreenway.org) is in the Olympic Sculpture Park. Look for the trail running along Puget Sound; as the trail heads north, it passes a rose garden, rocky beaches, and picturesque (really!) waterfront grain elevators. The route travels from Myrtle Edwards Park at Alaskan Way and Broad Street to Smith Cove Park at 23rd Avenue West and West Marina Place in Magnolia.

Food

Of course there's seafood here. We can practically fish mussels and salmon right from Seattle's downtown piers. But the city is also becoming world-renowned—think James Beard Award-winning chefs—for its local sourcing. And then there's the Asian influence in the thriving International District and in popular fusion restaurants across town. There's even a place for classics like the Canlis salad, a high-end dish that hasn't changed in 50 years.

DOWNTOWN

Pacific Northwest

The beloved ★ **Matt's at the Market** (94 Pike St., No. 32, 206/467-7909, www.mattsinthemarket.com, 11:30am-2:30pm and 5:30pm-10pm Mon.-Sat., lunch $10-16, dinner $28-34) started as a tiny 23-seat eatery and is not that much bigger now. The 2nd-story location keeps it feeling like something of a secret, even though the big curved windows look directly at the iconic Pike Place Market sign. Chefs shop the market daily to create their menus, usually a short list of seafood or other meat dishes and simple, fresh salads.

Seafood

It's no wonder that **Six Seven** (2411 Alaskan Way, 206/269-4575, www.edgewaterhotel.com, 6:30am-9pm Sun.-Thurs., 6:30am-9:30pm Fri.-Sat., lunch $10-16, dinner $29-48), located in the pier-built Edgewater Hotel, specializes in seafood—it's practically in Puget Sound. The jazzy atmosphere and killer western views (try to make it here for sunset) almost overshadow the delicate preparations, which are careful not to overpower the halibut, scallops, or salmon. There are also a number of meat dishes, but they're clearly not the stars of the show. The dessert menu includes a thick, delicious honey lavender crème brûlée. The outdoor deck opens when weather permits, seating diners mere feet from the dark waters of Elliott Bay.

The **Seatown Seabar and Rotisserie** (2010 Western Ave., 206/436-0390, www.tomdouglas.com, 11am-9pm Mon.-Thurs., 11am-10pm Fri., 9am-10pm Sat., 9am-9pm Sun., breakfast $8.50-15.50, lunch $10.50-25, dinner $10.50-28.50), located right next to Pike Place Market, is restaurateur Tom Douglas's most direct take on seafood. Oysters are popular with the after-work crowd, when the long bar fills quickly. There are also several kinds of Alaskan crab on the menu, plus rotisserie chicken. The Rub with Love Shack next door sells the spices and rubs used at the Tom Douglas restaurants in town.

The popular **Ivar's Acres of Clams** (1001 Alaskan Way, 206/624-6852, www.ivars.com, 11am-10pm Mon.-Thurs., 11am-11pm Fri.-Sat., $10-32) is Seattle's iconic, signature fast food. Locations are throughout the region, but the downtown waterfront spot is the most popular. Ivar Haglund, a colorful Seattle character, opened the chowder and fish-and-chips spot in 1938, bringing in crowds not only with food but also with octopus wrestling and eating contests. The Pier 54 spot has a regular dining room and dockside fast food. It offers both white and red clam chowder, so chowder purists can argue over which is best. Fish-and-chips are made with Alaskan cod and Ivar's tartar sauce. Ivar's own motto was "keep clam," and a statue commemorating him stands near the restaurant.

American

Located across from Matt's at the Market and also featuring curved windows, **Radiator Whiskey** (94 Pike St., No. 30, 206/467-4268, www.radiatorwhiskey.com, 4pm-midnight Mon.-Sat., $14-22) has a completely different feel. This is a hangout joint, one where not only the kitchen is open but the shelves are stacked with dishes and napkins. The menu is scrawled across a blackboard, and there are barrels behind the bar. Those barrels hold special whiskeys and barrel-aged cocktails, none of which come cheap; the lengthy whiskey menu is also easy to get lost in. Despite being in the middle of a tourist favorite, on the 2nd floor of a market location, the bar draws locals and restaurant industry folk with a happy hour menu of tot-chos—nachos made with tater tots—and a "dirty" sandwich that comes with a side of a Rainier tall boy and a shot of whiskey. Regular dinner still feels like a happy hour thanks to the crowds and buzz of the joint, though meat dishes like a lamb neck sloppy Joe and beef brisket are certainly substantial enough. A smoked half-pig head ($60) will feed the whole table but must be ordered in advance.

The grill is the thing at meat-centric **Miller's Guild** (612 Stewart St, 206/443-3663, http://millersguild.com, 7am-10pm daily, $25-54), attached to Hotel Max. The wood-fired grill in the restaurant cooks beef that was dry-aged for 75 days, plus a daily selection that can include Wagyu ribeye and lamp chops; look to the handwritten "From the Inferno" menu. The nose-to-tail butchery is taken seriously, and even the morning breakfast is hearty, drawing on foraged mushrooms for the frittata. The modern interior keeps it from feeling like an old-fashioned steak house; seats at the bar are the best way to get a look at the monster grill.

You almost have to lean back to see the top of the wine tower in the two-story **Purple Café and Wine Bar** (1225 4th Ave., 206/829-2280, www.thepurplecafe.com, 11am-11pm Mon.-Thurs., 11am-midnight Fri., noon-midnight Sat., noon-11pm Sun., $13-35). The cavernous space fills with diners during happy hour and on weeknights, feeding as many business diners as theater patrons. The menu is filled with the kind of rich bites that pair well with wines—wild boar rillettes and cheese flights, plus a killer braised bacon

Ivar's Acres of Clams

poutine. It's almost overkill, what with the sandwiches, pizzas, pastas, and other entrées fighting for attention, but the wine list has international scope and wit—the madeira varietal, for example, is described as "the Chuck Norris of wine."

Coffee

In a town that seems to have a Starbucks on every corner, **Cherry Street Coffee** (103 Cherry St., 206/621-9372, www.cherrystreetcoffee.com, 6:30am-5pm Mon.-Fri., 8am-3pm Sat.-Sun., $4.50-9.50) is a nice combination of independent coffee spot and consistent chain, with eight locations downtown. Each location features local artists, and the Cherry Street flagship has an underground seating area with an antique bank vault. Besides a wide array of coffee drinks with their own blends, the café serves sandwiches, salads, and quiches. Because most locations have large seating areas, any Cherry Street Coffee is a good place to sit a spell and soak in the so-called "coffee culture" of Seattle.

Pioneer Square's artsiest coffee stop, **Zeitgeist Coffee** (171 S Jackson St., 206/583-0497, http://zeitgeistcoffee.com, 6am-7pm Mon.-Fri., 7am-7pm Sat., 8am-6pm Sun., $5-9), dates to the 1990s, when coffee culture became a defining characteristic of the city. The decor, however, feels very of-the-moment, as the name implies: There's exposed brick, exposed ducts hanging from tall ceilings, and warm blond wood panels on the wall. Art is the shop's secondary calling, with original pieces on the wall and large gatherings on First Thursday Seattle Art Walk nights. The written word gets its share of the space, with newspaper racks and a dictionary on display. There's breathing room and a number of tables to enjoy the lattes topped with delicate foam art, plus a sandwich if you want to linger over the dictionary.

Asian

Considering Seattle's spot on the Pacific Rim, it's no surprise that an Asian fusion restaurant like **Wild Ginger** (1401 3rd Ave., 206/623-4450, www.wildginger.net, 11:30am-3pm and 5pm-11pm Mon.-Fri., 11:30am-3pm and 4:30pm-11pm Sat., 4pm-9pm Sun., lunch $7-22, dinner $13-33) would do so well for so long. Inspirations come from throughout Asia, particularly Malaysia, Indonesia, China, and Vietnam. Pad Thai shares the menu with satay and grilled boar. There's a special vegan menu and a live tank supplying clams and mussels. The restaurant's signature dish is the fragrant duck, served with puffy white steamed buns and plum sauce. The quarter-duck size probably isn't big enough for your table, unless you're dining alone—it's that good. The large restaurant is across from Benaroya Hall, so the staff is adept at getting diners out in time for shows and concerts.

You don't go to **Canton Wonton House** (608 S Weller St., 206/682-5080, 11am-11pm Tues.-Thurs. and Sun., 11am-midnight Fri.-Sat, $4-7, cash only), in the International District, for the fancy digs. The storefront is plain, and the tables are the plain Formica found in cafeterias and company lunchrooms. You come for the steaming dishes: Find all sorts of varieties of noodle soup, noodles with meat and vegetables, and congee. The restaurant is family run, and customers are firm devotees of their favorite variety of wonton soup. The spot has the hole-in-the-wall feel that makes fancier furniture—or a floor that's not linoleum—unnecessary.

Many of the International District eateries sacrifice ambience in favor of flavor and flavor only, but **Red Lantern** (520 S Jackson St., 206/682-7211, www.redlanternseattle.com, 11am-2:30pm and 5pm-9:30pm Mon.-Sat., lunch $8-12, dinner $9-16) manages to deliver both in a space that stays simple but nevertheless decorates with wood tables and sleek red light fixtures. The food hails from northern China and Korea, which means both familiar bites like pot stickers and sweet-and-sour beef, plus brown-braised pig feet and duck cooked in shaoxing wine. Certain house specialties, like Sichuan peppercorn crab and steamed ginger fish, require calling ahead. The dessert menu has red tea tiramisu and black tea crème brûlée.

French

The small ★ **Le Pichet** (1933 1st Ave., 206/256-1499, www.lepichetseattle.com, 8am-midnight daily, lunch $10-12, dinner $10-20) is a taste of France in the middle of downtown Seattle, complete with sidewalk café, mirrors on the walls, and white-tile floors. The menu is so French it's actually written in the language (with translations), but the most important thing to know is that the roasted whole chicken for two people takes an hour to cook. Good thing there are plenty of drinks and charcuterie selections to keep you occupied—it's worth the wait. For all the French quality, there's nothing fussy about the restaurant. In fact, it's been voted both "Best Hangover Meal" and "Best Ambiance" in the city.

Italian

The Pink Door (1919 Post Alley, 206/443-3241, www.thepinkdoor.net, 11:30am-11:30pm Mon.-Thurs., 11:30am-1am Fri.-Sat., 4pm-10pm Sun., lunch $11-22, dinner $16-26) is a strange combination of restaurants. The outdoor patio, overlooking the waterfront and Pike Place Market, is a casual dining spot, but inside is a candlelit dining room where the Italian menu is served under hoops and swings used by occasional cabaret and trapeze performers. Still, the reliable and large saucy dishes are local favorites, and shows (with cover) can include burlesque performers and a balloon artist. The restaurant is indeed behind a pink door located on Post Alley, but it's much less hidden than it sounds. Look for a hanging pointed finger directing the way.

BELLTOWN

Pacific Northwest

Imagine Seattle in the middle of a circle with a radius of 360 miles. At ★ **Local 360** (2234 1st Ave., 206/441-9360, www.local360.org, 9am-10pm Sun.-Thurs., 9am-11pm Fri,-Sat., brunch $5-15, lunch $8-18, dinner $9-26), almost every ingredient comes from within that circle, including the lengthy spirits list. The restaurant goes for a funky feel, what with the rough-hewn wood walls, candlesticks, and peanut-butter-and-jelly bonbons on the menu (they come with a shot of milk, naturally). The young crowd comes here for snacks to go with their cocktails, or perhaps even a whole meal with fried chicken or a pork shank. A slight touch of a Southern influence is evident from the grits, collard greens, and tasting flight of locally brewed moonshines.

American

A gaucho is a South American cowboy, but there's nothing rough-and-tumble about **El Gaucho** (2505 1st Ave., 206/728-1337, www.elgaucho.com, 4pm-10pm Sun.-Thurs., 4pm-midnight Fri.-Sat., $37-78). The steak house has restaurants in Seattle, Portland, Tacoma, and across the lake in Bellevue. If you close your eyes, you can almost imagine you're back in the swinging '50s—indeed, it was inspired by a supper club of that era. It's almost dinner theater: An open charcoal grill isn't far from patrons dressed to the nines, and a Bananas Foster is set aflame as it's served at a leather banquette. Lobster tail and diver sea scallops are on the menu, but it's a shame to order anything but a dry-aged steak or perhaps the Chateaubriand tenderloin, carved tableside.

Mediterranean

Although Tom Douglas has fun with his restaurant themes, **Lola** (2000 4th Ave., 206/441-1430, www.tomdouglas.com, 6am-midnight Mon.-Thurs., 6am-2am Fri., 7am-2am Sat., 7am-1am Sun., $17-39) is refreshingly grown up. The Mediterranean- and North African-inspired menu makes use of local seafood and lots of Greek favorites, pita, tagines, and lamb in a number of forms—the lamb burger comes with chickpea fries. Daily brunch is popular, especially the made-to-order doughnuts. The ceiling is hung with orange wire light fixtures, and the restaurant is decorated in warm oranges and yellows. The round bar is a good, social spot for a drink, but in the dining room the booths block the bustle well.

QUEEN ANNE

Pacific Northwest

To be precise, ★ **Canlis** (2576 Aurora Ave. N, 206/283-3313, www.canlis.com, 5:30pm-9:30pm Mon.-Thurs., 5:30pm-10pm Fri., 5pm-10pm Sat., $85-125) isn't exactly a restaurant—it's more of an experience, a destination, a landmark. It was opened in 1950 by Peter Canlis and is run today by his grandsons in a beautiful midcentury building with a stone fireplace and angled windows overlooking Lake Union. Its signature service is all about personal touches, like the valet that doesn't take a name or offer a ticket, just remembers each driver's face and delivers the car as if by magic (the coat check works the same way). Meals come in a variety of tasting menus, but the Canlis salad is a must-try: greens and a dressing made of lemon, olive oil, and coddled egg prepared tableside. Main dishes are simple, well-prepared classics: grilled sea bass, slow-roasted chicken that takes an hour to prepare, and Muscovy duck breast for two. Dining at Canlis is an all-evening affair, and men are required to wear a suit or sport coat.

Sorry, but there's no wolf on the menu at **How to Cook a Wolf** (2208 Queen Anne Ave. N, 206/838-8090, www.ethanstowellrestaurants.com, 5pm-11pm daily, $14-24). The name comes from a book by midcentury food writer M. F. K. Fisher. The eatery does have endless fresh and finely crafted dishes, so it's just as well. Situated in the local's neighborhood on the top of Queen Anne, it's more regularly visited by discerning Seattle diners, not tourists. Dishes are simple and rustic, drawing from Italian inspiration. The short menu usually has a handful of pastas and several small, sharable appetizers like chicken liver mousse or black bass. Order several of each to fill up, but expect a few extra tastes here and there from the kitchen.

American

What kind of restaurant is **The 5 Spot** (1502 Queen Anne Ave. N, 206/285-7768, www.chowfoods.com, 8:30am-midnight Mon.-Fri., 8:30am-3pm and 5pm-midnight Sat.-Sun., breakfast $8-11, lunch $9-13, dinner $12-20)? It's a diner, plus a Florida seafood joint. Or a New Mexico cantina. Or a Texas barbecue restaurant. The menu has a stable half and a changing half, and goofy decor rotates with the theme. (The artwork is often connected to the door; look to see what changes when the front door swings.) Not every American cuisine tackled here is perfectly realized, but no one can say the cooks are unadventurous. The comfy diner has a signpost noting all the places the menu has been, plus a cheap late-night menu and a hearty breakfast. It's where to go when you're fine with ending up just about anywhere.

Coffee

Part of a local chain, **Uptown Espresso** (525 Queen Anne Ave. N, 206/285-3757, www.velvetfoam.com, 5am-10pm Mon.-Thurs., 5am-11pm Fri., 6am-11pm Sat., 6am-10pm Sun.) earns character points with its collection of dining room tables and walls laden with a hodgepodge of mirrors, framed oil paintings, and historical photographs. It's a quiet respite on a busy block of Queen Anne, where students hunker down with laptops or chat in small groups. The house coffee is known as Velvet Foam, a roast almost as creamy as the hot chocolate topped with whipped cream.

Southern

Very little is small about the New Orleans-themed ★ **Toulouse Petit** (601 Queen Anne Ave. N, 206/432-9069, www.toulousepetit.com, 8am-2am daily, breakfast $8-25, lunch $9-22, dinner $14-42). Located a 10-minute walk from Belltown or the Seattle Center, the restaurant is crowded on weekend nights with flirty young professionals enjoying the late-night happy hour and tossing back sweet cocktails. Some ornate furnishings, as might befit the French Quarter, hang over booths and tables. The endless menu has appetizers, entrées, salads, seafood, charcuterie, "curiosities," oysters, pastas, steaks, and a prix fixe option—if you can't find something to eat at Toulouse Petit, you must really not like food.

Some but not all dishes have a Louisiana twist, and there is plenty of shrimp and spicy sausage. At brunch the party continues, this time with mimosas flowing freely and house-made fried beignets served with a chicory crème anglaise. The generous hash will sop up any mistakes you made the night before.

SOUTH LAKE UNION

Seafood

While the raw halibut soar through the air at Pike Place Market, the dishes at **Flying Fish** (300 Westlake Ave. N, 206/728-8595, www.flyingfishrestaurant.com, 11:30am-2pm and 4pm-10pm Mon.-Thurs., 11:30am-2pm and 4pm-11pm Fri., 4pm-11pm Sat., 4pm-10pm Sun., $23-32) arrive in a much calmer fashion. Seafood-first restaurants should be a dime a dozen in Seattle, but they're really not. This is one of the few in the neighborhood that is unapologetically fishy. But that's not its only claim to fame. After 18 years, a neighborhood move, and numerous accolades, the chef sold to a Chinese restaurant group and started incorporating Asian flavors into the menu—Thai crab cakes, cod served with Sichuan broth, and mussels with chili-lime dipping sauce. But the menu still emphasizes organic, wild ingredients, and the space has the same happy din. The colors are bright, with none of the all-shades-of-blue cliché found in so many sea-themed eateries.

American

The mad scientist who came up with **Lunchbox Laboratory** (1253 Thomas St., 206/621-1090, www.lunchboxlaboratory.com, 11am-11pm daily, $11-14) had some strange experiments—how else do you explain burgers made of churken (chicken and turkey), a lamb patty topped with feta, or a dork (duck and pork) concoction? For all the strange combos, the upbeat burger joint is a cheery and tasty joint, and each offering is almost big enough to split. They do homage to the Dick's burger, a cheap drive-in Seattle classic, and plenty of normal combinations as well. Sweet potato fries are the best side dish (then come skinny fries, homemade chips, and tater tots), and the milkshakes come either with alcohol or not. Weekly specials are billed as experiments and are even crazier than the regular menu. The brightly colored spot is close to REI and, like the outdoor store, is a whimsical destination for grown-ups.

Breakfast

When it's time for brunch, the lines form at ★ **Portage Bay Café** (391 Terry Ave. N, 206/462-6400, www.portagebaycafe.com, 7:30am-2:30pm daily, breakfast $8.50-16, lunch $11.50-15). The South Lake Union location is one of three around the city, but this location has two big rooms of seating. In the center is the breakfast bar filled with seasonal fruits, nuts, and organic maple syrup. Choose from the five French toast or five pancake options, then top it from the breakfast bar. The menu has many vegan and vegetarian options, and most of the French toasts can be made gluten-free. Rowing sculls hang from the ceiling inside, and during weekend brunches the waiting crowd outside is its own social scene.

CAPITOL HILL

Pacific Northwest

The crown jewel of Melrose Market, a collection of food-based shops and eateries in Capitol Hill, is ★ **Sitka and Spruce** (1531 Melrose Ave., 206/324-0662, www.sitkaandspruce.com, 11:30am-2pm Mon., 11:30am-2pm and 5:30pm-10pm Tues.-Thurs., 11:30am-2pm and 5:30pm-11pm Fri., 10am-2pm and 5:30pm-11pm Sat., 10am-2pm and 4:30pm-9pm Sun., $10-29). The restaurant excels at local cuisine, headed up by rising-star chef Matthew Dillon. The kitchen isn't just open—it's an equal part of the small space, with cooks bustling around the chopping blocks and stoves with bundles of greenery. Diners sit at the windows, at small tables, or at a large, blocky communal table. Seasonal veggies are served without unnecessary fanfare, and diners share flavorful chicken, salmon, chanterelles, mussels, or whatever's freshest that day. The menu is short but aggressively local. On Mondays the restaurant serves a special menu inspired by Mexican cuisine, for a very different feel from the rest of the week but prepared with the same exacting standards.

Seafood

You're always at the coast at **Coastal Kitchen** (429 15th Ave. E, 206/322-1145, www.coastalkitchenseattle.com, 8am-midnight daily, $13-28), even though the location of the coast changes. The seafood restaurant has a rotating focus that shifts every three months. The destinations are specific, like Veracruz, Mexico, or New Orleans, Louisiana. The regular menu includes seafood standbys, like fish-and-chips, oysters, and calamari, plus a few entrées other than seafood. The space is open late and has $5 drinks at the three "Don't Judge Me" happy hours (one's from 8am-10am). Art pieces on the wall rotate with the changing menu, and humorous language lessons play in the bathroom. The large restaurant has several counters and bars, plus tables and a garage door that's open on nice days. On Mondays the restaurant hosts jazz performances.

American

Only one thing at **Li'l Woody's** (1211 Pine St., 206/457-4148, www.lilwoodys.com, 11am-11pm Mon.-Thurs., 11am-3am Fri.-Sat., 11am-10pm Sun., $4.50-8) is "li'l"—the quarter-pound burger that comes with Tillamook cheese and basic toppings. The rest of the burgers are a third of a pound and loaded with bacon and horseradish, or green chiles, or pickled figs with gorgonzola cheese. You can even load a burger with peanut butter. Skinny skin-on fries come plain, with house-made cheese, or with "crack," a small bowl of milkshake for dipping. With a few local beers on tap, a loft seating area, and a window-front counter, the small restaurant manages to be an eat-in joint, not just a burger counter. The location is in Capitol Hill, but on the edge, just across the freeway from the convention center, making it the best burger close to downtown.

Everybody goes to **Quinn's Pub** (1001 E Pike St., 206/325-7711, www.quinnspubseattle.com, 3pm-1am daily, $8-24), a two-story restaurant that occupies a prime location on one of Capitol Hill's busiest streets. It's nice enough for a business meal (well, a casual, impress-with-the-food kind of business meal), dim enough for a date, rowdy enough for dinner with friends, and flavorful enough for a special occasion. The burger is one of the most popular menu items, but it's no burger joint; the bistro fare includes a Scotch egg and grilled Vermont quail. Desserts are small and, at $3 each, meant to be ordered in multiples. The bar, with access to the knowledgeable bartenders pouring Trappist ales, is prime seating but hard to score. Upstairs tables have less ambience, which can mean more elbow room. Besides the 14 beer taps, the alcohol offerings lean toward bourbons and whiskeys.

Coffee

Capitol Hill was once known for its coffee shops, but many have been forced out in recent years, unable to keep up with skyrocketing rents in the hip neighborhood. One survivor is **Victrola** (411 15th Ave. E, 206/325-6520, www.victrolacoffee.com, 6am-10pm Mon.-Sat., 6am-9pm Sun.), where the usual bustle of baristas and students hums under a kind of art gallery for local artists. The space has hosted radio events, movie nights, and even an insect safari. It also serves up more pedestrian fare like sandwiches and salads. The company's second café is located farther down Capitol Hill (310 E Pike St.), with free educational coffee tastings on Wednesdays at 11am; Victrola does its roasting at this building in Capitol Hill's old auto row.

Starbucks began as a modest coffee shop near Pike Place Market, and it has grown to include outposts on nearly every Seattle corner, plus a global headquarters south of the stadiums. But its pinnacle might be Capitol Hill's **Starbucks Reserve Roastery and Tasting Room** (1124 Pike St., 206/624-0173, http://roastery.starbucks.com, 6:30am-11pm daily), an airy space meant to show off the company's claim to high-end coffee mastery.

It doesn't serve the normal Starbucks menu, but rather its limited Reserve line roasted here and brewed in a variety of methods—pour-over, Clover, French press, and more. The coffee show happens in a room filled with copper pipes and beans running through pneumatic tubes, so it's meant to be appreciated by the coffee lover.

Asian

The cheery **Poppy** (622 Broadway E, 206/324-1108, www.poppyseattle.com, 5:30pm-11pm Sun.-Thurs., 5:30pm-midnight Fri.-Sat., $11-27) is a less common take on Indian dining. The menu is based around *thali* platters of many small dishes, using local ingredients and traditional Indian spices. The *thalis,* which might include soup, salad, nigella-poppy naan, some kind of pickle, and a braised meat or fresh fish, change daily. The cocktails use fresh juices and flavors that match the complex *thalis.* The small garden out back has both outdoor seating and the restaurant's herb garden. Inside it's all exposed brick and bright orange design accents.

Italian

In a city where new American pub cuisine and creative seafood concepts get all the attention, **Spinasse** (1531 14th Ave., 206/251-7673, www.spinasse.com, 5pm-10pm Sun.-Thurs., 5pm-11pm Fri.-Sat., $12-32) excels at Italian fare and a sophisticated atmosphere. The food is from Northern Italy and relies on local ingredients and handmade pastas. Salads, antipasti, and meaty rabbit or pork belly are all delicious, but the *tajarin*—egg pasta served with ragu or butter—is the simple, delectable standout. It may be one of the best single dishes in Seattle, so splurge for the bigger portion. If the table doesn't devour the shareable plates, it makes for killer leftovers. Some seats face the open kitchen. The sister bar next door, Artusi, also has small Italian bites, plus expert bartenders and a sunny, modern space.

Southern

The ★ **Wandering Goose** (403 15th Ave. E, 206/323-9938, www.thewanderinggoose.com, 7am-4pm daily, $5-13) sounds like a fairy tale character, and indeed the owner has written a children's book. The restaurant itself is sweet and comfortable, with counter service and wooden chairs at little wooden tables. The food is Southern and breakfast-inspired: biscuits, grits, ham, gravy, plus some salads for lunch and baked goods. The honey is house-made and sourced from beehives on the roof. On Fridays, a special fried-chicken meal is served at 5pm: three pieces of buttermilk chicken, a biscuit, and three sides, like collard greens or coleslaw. If a farmhouse café was neatly blended with a Southern diner, it would look and feel—and luckily taste—something like this.

UNIVERSITY DISTRICT

Mexican

You have two choices at **Agua Verde Cafe** (1303 NE Boat St., 206/545-8570, www.aguaverde.com, 11am-9pm Mon.-Sat., $7-15), located on Portage Bay between Lake Washington and Lake Union: Eat Mexican food and then rent a kayak, or kayak first and then bliss out on tacos, Mexican beer, and margaritas. Well of course you can skip the boat rentals altogether, but the view and proximity are very tempting. The restaurant has dishes with a Baja California vibe—empanadas, enchiladas, and open-face tacos, ordered from a counter and then served in a funky, beachy space. The attached **Agua Verde Paddle Club** (206/545-8570, $18-24) rents single and double kayaks and stand-up paddleboards. Routes go to Lake Washington or to Lake Union for views of downtown and Gasworks Park. Occasional tours lead kayakers to the University of Washington Arboretum or on moonlit paddles.

BALLARD

Seafood

Both stories of **Ray's Boathouse** (6049 Seaview Ave. NW, 206/789-3770, www.rays.com, 5pm-9:30pm daily, $13-39) have views of Shilshole Bay and the distant peaks of the

Olympics. The pier-side restaurant serves seafood specialties, some local as well as Maine lobster and Gulf prawns. The café upstairs is more casual, but the downstairs bar faces the water and is topped with blown-glass light fixtures.

An oyster bar named for the poem in *Alice in Wonderland,* ★ **The Walrus and the Carpenter** (4743 Ballard Ave. NW, 206/395-9227, www.thewalrusbar.com, 4pm-10pm Sun.-Thurs., 4pm-11pm Sat.-Sun., $8-12) has wait times that are hard to believe—up to or even surpassing two hours, even on a weeknight. The small space has a handful of tables and a bar, and all the seafood is locally sourced. A handful of veggie dishes complement the oysters and shellfish, especially the fried Brussels sprouts. Steak tartare and cheese plates complete the menu, but the spot isn't a good bet for anyone hoping to avoid seafood. And yes, the wait is worth it for a table in the sparkling white space and handfuls of shareable plates. To ease the pain of the line, leave a phone number at the door and head to another bar on Ballard Avenue for a drink—they'll call when you're next up for oysters.

French

The French ★ **Bastille Café** (5307 Ballard Ave. NW, 206/453-5014, www.bastilleseattle.com, 5:30pm-midnight Mon.-Thurs., 5:30pm-1am Fri.-Sat., 10am-3pm and 5:30pm-midnight Sun., brunch $9-15, dinner $11-26) is a lovely, adult addition to a bar-heavy neighborhood that's matured in recent years. The walls are rustic exposed brick and gleaming white tiles, and menus are scrawled on mirrors; chandeliers hang from exposed beams. The outdoor patio and indoor fire hearth fill for weekend brunches and casual dinners. Sconces and other touches try to evoke a hip French bistro (or maybe a very fancy metro station). Honey is sourced from 50,000 honeybees living on hives up on the roof.

Mexican

It's a long way from Seattle to the Mexican border, but **La Carta de Oaxaca** (5431 Ballard Ave. NW, 206/782-8722, www.lacartadeoaxaca.com, 5pm-11pm Mon., 11:30am-3pm and 5pm-11pm Tues.-Thurs., 11:30am-3pm and 5pm-midnight Fri.-Sat., $6-17) serves authentic Mexican fare in a small, crowded space. The guacamole is made by hand, and the open kitchen proves that the mole is made here. A wall of framed photographs lightens the restaurant, but everyone is concentrating on shoveling in tortillas, tostadas, and *entomatadas*. Reservations are not accepted, and the spot's quality is well known, so expect a wait.

GREATER SEATTLE

American

Although Bellevue doesn't have the range of dining options that Seattle does, it does have **Bis on Main** (10213 Main St., Bellevue, 425/455-2033, www.bisonmain.com, 11:30am-11pm Mon.-Thurs., 11:30am-midnight Fri., 5:30pm-midnight Sat., 5pm-9pm Sun., $23-49). There's free valet parking on most nights. The restaurant is a stellar example of how the area's second city is no slouch. The menu has straightforward American classics like filet mignon and maple leaf duck breast but also includes a touch of luxury in truffle French fries and a $60 special rack of lamb. The unassuming class of the space makes it popular for business dinners—the 300-bottle wine list probably doesn't hurt—and service is friendly.

Asian

You'll travel to the 2nd floor of a mall building to find **Din Tai Fung Dumpling House** (700 Bellevue Way NE #280, Bellevue, 425/698-1095, www.dintaifungusa.com, 11am-10pm Mon.-Fri., 10am-10pm Sat.-Sun., $3.50-8), but lines often form for the giant space—in fact they were over three hours long when the spot opened. The chain originated in Taiwan and has locations around the world, including in Seattle's downtown and University District—but the Bellevue location was the first in the area. Specialties include soft buns filled with pork, vegetables, or pastes, and steamed soup dumplings (a.k.a. *xiao long bao*) that are delicate and flavorful. (And hot! Take care with your chopsticks or spoon.) Folks with ties to Asia often flock to Din Tai Fung for a taste of home; besides the food, there are Asian beers. Windows in front show the staff folding the buns.

Italian

Café Juanita (9702 NE 120th Pl., Bellevue, 425/823-1505, www.cafejuanita.com, 5pm-9pm Tues.-Thurs., 5pm-10pm Fri.-Sat., $16-55) isn't really near anything of note in a quiet neighborhood north of Lake Washington, and it's hard to find. But the Italian restaurant has a great reputation (they've racked up awards) and ardent fans. The Northern Italian fare includes homemade pastas and rich dishes like braised rabbit. Even though it's tucked away, the refined food and classy setting give it a sense of occasion.

Accommodations

Being a well-appointed hotel in Seattle is not enough—you have to have a personality. Often that's expressed in art collections and modern decor, but it's also manifested in views, in-house dining, and programming for locals and visitors alike.

DOWNTOWN

Under $150

Few properties in the city can boast a location more convenient than that of the **Green Tortoise Hostel** (105 Pike St., 206/340-1222, www.greentortoise.net, $38-65 dorms), across the street from Pike Place Market and within walking distance of downtown, Pioneer Square, Belltown, and, with a little trek, the Seattle Center. The hostel has bunk beds with private lights, fans, and power outlets, plus curtains for a small amount of privacy. Some bunk beds are doubles. There's free wireless Internet and continental breakfast, and three times a week the hostel serves free dinner.

$150-250

The homey **Pensione Nichols** (1923 1st Ave., 206/441-7125, www.pensionenichols.com, $180-300 shared bath) is a bed-and-breakfast with killer views of Elliott Bay and an unbeatable location next to Pike Place Market. The antique furnishings lean slightly toward the grandmother's-living-room aesthetic, but the house dogs are plenty welcoming.

Over $250

Every door in ★ **Hotel Max** (620 Stewart St., 206/728-6299, www.hotelmaxseattle.com, $340-450) is covered in local artwork, and each floor has a theme. Bold colors and mature art give the property an adult vibe, and meaty dishes from the wood-fired grill in the restaurant next door can be sent up as room service 24 hours a day.

The more traditional **Mayflower Park Hotel** (405 Olive Way, 206/623-8700, www.mayflowerpark.com, $278-323) is decked out in Queen Anne style, complete with chandeliers and brass knobs, a mark of its 85-year history. The central location is between downtown and Belltown, with the Mediterranean eatery **Andaluca** (6:30am-11am Mon., 6:30am-11am and 5pm-9pm Tues.-Fri., 7am-noon and 5pm-10pm Sat.,7am-noon and 5pm-9pm Sun.) just downstairs.

The electric colors of **Hotel Monaco** (1101 4th Ave., 206/621-1770, www.monaco-seattle.com, $310-385) start in the lobby—where walls are blue and patterns are bright—and continue in guest rooms, where even the bathrobes are vivid in animal prints. The downtown location is close to the Seattle Central Library and walkable to major attractions. Despite all the design pizzazz, the staff wants you to feel at home—so much so that you can get a complimentary loaner goldfish to act as your pet while you're there. The nearly 200 rooms are modern and equipped with high-end electronics, furniture, and linens.

While there's a bookish theme to the **Alexis Hotel** (1007 1st Ave., 206/624-4844, www.alexishotel.com, $405-485), the very modern decor in the lobby is less reminiscent of a library, though rooms have intricate headboards and classic furnishings. The hotel has bikes available for guest use, and there's a free wine reception in the lobby every evening. Valet parking is $42 per night, but hybrid vehicles get it at half price. The cozy **Bookstore Bar & Café** (7am-10pm Mon.-Fri., 8am-10pm Sat.-Sun.) sells tomes ($5) along with whiskeys and salads.

The Beatles stayed at the waterfront ★ **Edgewater** (2411 Alaskan Way, 206/728-7000, www.edgewaterhotel.com, $409-629) when they came to town, famously posing with fishing poles out their window. The chic Northwest decor includes gas fireplaces and stuffed footstools shaped like brown bears.

When presidents like John F. Kennedy visited Seattle, they stayed in the historical rooms of the **Fairmont Olympic Hotel** (411 University St., 206/621-1700, www.fairmont.com, $373-529). Not only was it the site of the original University of Washington, this long-time landmark was also the site of much planning for the city's World's Fair. Its rooms are decked in pale luxury, with classic Victorian-inspired furniture and gray marble in the bathrooms. The large lobby is home to 2nd-floor interior balconies, red-carpeted stairs, and potted palms, while a tucked-away swimming pool sits inside a glass solarium, perfect for Seattle's not-so-warm days.

The luxe **Loews Hotel 1000** (1000 1st Ave., 206/957-1000, www.hotel1000seattle.com, $401-520) is a boutique property with easy access to downtown, the waterfront, and Pioneer Square. Bathrooms are large and include bathtubs whose faucets are on the ceiling. The rooms have creative but tasteful decor and fine linens. The basement spa (206/357-9490) offers a variety of treatments, while the virtual Golf Club (8am-10pm daily) brings the links of the world to a small room. The hotel also has a restaurant.

BELLTOWN

Under $150

Don't be fooled by the beautiful building that looks more like an embassy than a cheap place to crash. **City Hostel Seattle** (2327 2nd Ave., 206/706-3255, www.hostelseattle.com, $38-40 dorms, $99-120 private rooms) is indeed a hostel. The property has breakfast and free luggage storage, plus kitchens and an outdoor grill for guest use. Most rooms use shared hall bathrooms. Each room is decorated with a different kind of mural or painting, many with glaringly bright colors, and the hostel also has a 20-seat movie theater.

In an old boardinghouse, a collective of creative entrepreneurs opened the ★ **Ace Hotel** (2423 1st Ave., 206/448-4721, www.acehotel.com/seattle, $129-219), putting turntables and reclaimed wood furniture in every room. Some rooms share hall bathrooms, and some rooms have original wood floors. Original art in the rooms comes from the likes of Shepard Fairey. A large black table sits in the lobby, and a breakfast room serves waffles and coffee in the morning.

QUEEN ANNE

$150-250

Billed as a historical property, the **Inn at Queen Anne** (505 1st Ave. N, 206/282-7357, www.innatqueenanne.com, $179-199) definitely has the dark corners of an older property. Rooms are simple, but all have private bathrooms and some have stoves, and the Seattle Center is right across the street.

The age of the nearby **MarQueen Hotel** (600 Queen Anne Ave. N, 206/282-7407, www.marqueen.com, $239-339) manages to convey a bit more luxury, with beveled glass doors and Alaskan marble in the floors. Some rooms have awkwardly placed but charming sitting parlors.

CAPITOL HILL

Over $250

As one of the only hotels in Capitol Hill, **Silver Cloud Hotel** (1100 Broadway, 206/325-1400, www.silvercloud.com, $289-359) earns cool points just for being so close to the city's best restaurant and bar scene. Otherwise the chain is standard but well appointed, with an indoor pool and in-room refrigerators and microwaves. The artsy vibe is meant to echo the apartments on trendy Capitol Hill.

The ★ **Sorrento Hotel** (900 Madison St., 206/622-6400, www.hotelsorrento.com, $259-379) is like an Italian transplant next to the city's collection of world-class hospitals. It features the crooked, charming rooms of a historical building. The cozy Fireside Room hosts a monthly silent reading party.

UNIVERSITY DISTRICT

$150-250

The **Watertown Hotel** (4242 Roosevelt Way NE, 206/826-4242, www.watertownseattle.com, $209-309) is owned by the Pineapple Hospitality Group, a fact only notable because the lobby is stocked with pineapple cupcakes; otherwise there's nothing tropical about the hotel. The location is a few blocks from the university, and the hotel offers free bike rentals. Free daily shuttles go to downtown Seattle, and there is a free laundry machine for guest use. A related property down the street has an outdoor pool that guests can use. Some rooms have downtown views.

Over $250

The name of the **Hotel Deca** (4507 Brooklyn Ave. NE, 206/634-2000, www.hoteldeca.com, $309-329) refers to the art deco aesthetic that inspired the hotel, and in fact the property dates back to art deco's heyday in the 1930s. Rooms are more modern and some have great views. There's also an in-house restaurant, the **District Lounge** (6:30am-2pm and 5pm-10pm Mon.-Fri., 7:30am-noon and 5pm-10pm Sat.-Sun.), and a coffee shop. The street is a busy one, especially on weekend nights, but the building is tall enough that most disturbances are minimized. It's one of the few properties walkable to the main part of the University of Washington campus.

BALLARD

$150-250

Ballard Inn (5300 Ballard Ave. NW, 206/789-5011, www.ballardinnseattle.com, $189-239) has the same owners as the Hotel Ballard, which is right next door, but a cozier feel. Many rooms share hall baths, and all are smaller than those in its sister property.

Over $250

The ★ **Hotel Ballard** (5214 Ballard Ave. NW, 206/789-5011, www.hotelballardseattle.com, $399-499) is unusual in that it's an upscale boutique Seattle hotel, but isn't in downtown. It sits on Ballard's busiest street, right across from the buzziest bars, restaurants, and performance spaces, and above the high-end Olympic Athletic Club—sharing access to the club's giant saltwater pool. The top-floor open-air patio has a view of Ballard's industrial waterfront. Rooms are luxe and decorated in a modern European style, and the bathtubs are sizable. The downstairs restaurant specializes in wood-fired pizzas.

GREATER SEATTLE

Over $250

In the Bellevue suburb of Kirkland, the luxury **Heathman Hotel** (220 Kirkland Ave., Kirkland, 425/284-5800, www.heathmankirkland.com, $309-409) makes the most of quiet streets next to the shores of Lake Washington. Northwest farm-to-table cuisine is top rate at the in-house Trellis restaurant, and rooms are spacious and filled with the kind of linens that makes you want to steal. Even farther from the center of Kirkland, **Woodmark Hotel** (1200 Carillon Point, Kirkland, 425/822-3700, www.thewoodmark.com, $299-459) is a calming spot next to a marina and flanked by two good dining spots, ideal for a city getaway that almost feels remote.

Information and Services

This is a tech-heavy city, and it's not afraid to show off how much information it has. Look around Pike Place Market or the Convention Center area for tourist info, and head to the Central Library for the glass cathedral full of books and free Internet access.

VISITOR INFORMATION

To obtain maps, book tours, and get information, head to one of downtown's two visitors centers operated by the city. **Seattle Visitor Center and Concierge Services** (Washington State Convention Center, 7th Ave. and Pike St., 866/732-2695, www.visitseattle.org, 9am-5pm daily summer, 9am-5pm Mon.-Fri. rest of the year) is on the uphill end of downtown, while the **Market Information Center** (Pike Place Market's southwest corner, First Ave. and Pike St., 866/732-2695, www.visitseattle.org, 10am-6pm daily) is closer to the waterfront.

Though nowhere near as comprehensive, **Travel Gay Seattle** (614 Broadway Ave. E, 206/363-9188, www.travelgayseattle.com, 9am-5pm Mon.-Thurs., 9am-6pm Fri., 10am-2pm Sat.) is a visitor information booth located in a 1st Security Bank branch in Capitol Hill, traditionally the city's most LGBT-friendly area. They have maps showing businesses that specifically support the city's growing gay and lesbian travel industry.

MEDIA AND COMMUNICATIONS

For a long time Seattle was a two-daily town, but when the *Seattle Post-Intelligencer* newspaper folded its print operation, the older ***The Seattle Times*** (www.seattletimes.com) became the only major paper in town. The *Times* is printed seven days a week and is available at newsstands, in newspaper boxes, and at many cafés and delis. It has local and international news, business, sports, and lifestyle coverage.

The ***Seattle Weekly*** (www.seattleweekly.com) has long provided independent weekly coverage, including music performance information and news and political reporting. The slightly, well, stranger weekly in town is ***The Stranger*** (www.thestranger.com), published biweekly in Capitol Hill and featuring

King Street Station

sex-advice columnist Dan Savage. It also has news and culture reporting as well as performance listings. Both are distributed for free in newspaper boxes, and both have websites with much of the same information.

SERVICES

The central **Seattle Post Office** (301 Union St., 206/748-5417, www.usps.com, 8:30am-5:30pm Mon.-Fri.) branch is in the middle of downtown. A small stand in the lobby sells packing materials while the official desk has national and international shipping options. Look for the automated postage machine in the lobby for faster service.

Seattle's train station and Amtrak depot, the 1906 **King Street Station** (303 S Jackson St., 206/296-0100, www.amtrak.com, 6am-11pm daily) is a real beauty. Its signature 12-story brick tower, modeled after the famous San Marco bell tower in Venice, is visible from around the south side of downtown. A renovation finished in 2013 fixed the historical plasterwork and cleaned up the shiny white interior. However, the station still doesn't have many eateries, but there is **luggage storage** for a fee.

For urgent but not emergency cases of medical need, try one of the city's many urgent care clinics, like **ZoomCare** (531 Broadway, 206/971-3728, www.zoomcare.com/clinic/capitol-hill, 8am-midnight Mon.-Fri., 9am-6pm Sat.-Sun.). Appointments can be booked online or over the phone, and doctors can treat minor injuries and illnesses. The city's major emergency room is at **Harborview Medical Center** (325 9th Ave., 206/744-3300, www.uwmedicine.org/harborview), where helicopters often land carrying trauma patients from around the Northwest.

Transportation

GETTING THERE

Air

Sea-Tac International Airport (SEA, 17801 International Blvd., 206/787-5388 or 800/544-1965, www.portseattle.org/sea-tac) is located 15 miles south of downtown Seattle. From I-5, follow Highway 518 about 1 mile west. The airport is a busy terminus that receives both domestic and international flights. At its center is a large glass atrium lined with rocking chairs and outposts of local restaurants. Parking ($3-4 per hour), car rentals (3150 S. 160th St.), and public transportation are available.

A taxi from the airport to the downtown core costs a flat rate of $40. The **Central Link light rail** (www.soundtransit.org, 5am-1am Mon.-Sat., 6am-midnight Sun., $3) traces a 40-minute ride through Seattle's southern neighborhoods before stopping in the downtown underground transit tunnel. The **Downtown Airporter** (425/981-7000, http://downtownairporter.hudsonltd.net) provides shuttle service from the airport to select hotels downtown.

Train

Amtrak (800/872-7245, www.amtrak.com) trains arrive and depart daily from Seattle's King Street Station (303 S Jackson St.), located near Pioneer Square just south of downtown. The Cascades route travels from Vancouver, BC, to Eugene, Oregon, with stops in Tacoma, Portland, and Salem; the Empire Builder route runs east all the way to Chicago; and the Coast Starlight travels south from Seattle with stops in Portland, Oregon, and throughout California.

Car

The 141-mile drive from **Vancouver** to Seattle takes about 3 hours, though border delays can vary. Leave downtown Vancouver by taking Granville Street south over Granville Bridge. Continue south on **Highway 99** through the residential neighborhoods of greater Vancouver. Despite the frequent stoplights, traffic moves quickly outside of rush hours. Follow Highway 99 south as it turns left on Park Drive and then south on Oak Street. Highway 99 crosses the Oak Street Bridge to become the Vancouver-Blaine Highway through the Richmond suburbs. Speeds slow at the Canada-U.S. border, and cars are directed into waiting lanes to be questioned by border control agents. Once clear of customs, pass the massive white Peace Arch monument, which claims to be the first monument built and dedicated to world peace. The route is now called **I-5,** a freeway that runs from the Canadian border to Tijuana, Mexico. Follow I-5 south through the town of **Bellingham,** Washington, and the expansive Skagit Valley, home of a spring tulip festival. Freeway traffic may start to slow around **Everett,** an industrial hub 30 miles north of Seattle and home to some of Boeing's largest airplane factories and runways. Express lanes, which change direction depending on time of day, may be open about 8 miles north of downtown Seattle. They are often faster than the freeway, but offer fewer off-ramps. The multilane I-5 narrows as it enters downtown Seattle, where the freeway darts through tunnels and under buildings, with exits springing both left and right.

Seattle is 175 miles north of **Portland** along I-5, about 2.75 hours without traffic; with traffic the drive can take closer to 3-3.5 hours. Exit central Portland on **I-405** North, which crosses the Willamette River over the arch of the Fremont Bridge. Join **I-5** North, which runs through residential Portland before crossing the wide Columbia River and entering Washington. After traversing the city of Vancouver, Washington (not to be confused with Vancouver, British Columbia), I-5 runs north through rural farmland and along the Columbia River, past the small cities of Kelso, Longview, Chehalis, and Centralia. The state capitol dome is visible from the freeway as I-5 turns northeast in **Olympia;** the scenic view of the Nisqually National Wildlife Refuge marks your last stretch of uninterrupted greenery. Traffic can get thick through the Joint Base Lewis-McChord and the industrial city of **Tacoma,** about 35 miles south of Seattle. As you follow I-5 North into downtown Seattle, the freeway narrows and passes through several short tunnels.

GETTING AROUND

San Francisco may be known as the hilliest West Coast city, but Seattle makes its case for steep slopes. While a grid governs most of central and north Seattle, the many hills and waterways make for some confusing routes—and traffic is no joke around rush hour.

Car

Seattle is not an easy city to navigate by car because the downtown neighborhood is hilly and filled with one-way streets, and the traffic is notorious. **Rush hour** is far longer than an hour (7am-9am and 4pm-6pm), and the I-5 freeway through the city is often clogged with cars. The I-90 freeway, Highway 99, and surface streets are also known for rush-hour jams. A car isn't needed if staying in a downtown hotel. Most attractions are within walking distance, and cabs frequent the area.

The only **toll road** in Seattle is the bridge that crosses Lake Washington on Highway 520. It has no toll booths, but cameras will capture license plates and mail bills to drivers without a prepaid sticker. Rates range from $3.25 to $5.40, with free periods in the middle of the night.

Parking in downtown Seattle is in street parking or private lots. Meters for street parking accept credit cards, and rates range $1-4 per hour; hours are generally 8am-8pm.

To rent a car in downtown Seattle, look to **Hertz** (1501 8th Ave., 206/903-6260, www.hertz.com, 7:30am-6pm Mon.-Fri., 8am-2pm Sat., 9am-2pm Sun.), **Budget** (801 4th Ave., 206/682-8989, http://locations.budget.com, 7am-6pm Mon.-Fri., 8am-4pm Sat.-Sun.), or **Avis** (1919 5th Ave., 206/448-1700, http://locations.avis.com, 7am-7pm Mon.-Fri., 8am-5pm Sat.-Sun.). All the major car rental chains have desks in Sea-Tac Airport's car rental facility.

Seattle is also covered in **car2go** (877/488-4224, http://seattle.car2go.com) SmartCar rentals, where very small cars are rented by the minute, gas included, and can be picked up on the street around the city or at the airport. Advance registration is required because users get a card that opens and activates their rental car.

Taxi

To hail a taxi in Seattle, try **Yellow Cab** (253/872-5600, www.yellowtaxi.net) or hail one on the street in the downtown core. Taxi rates in Seattle are $2.70 per mile with an initial charge of $2.50.

Ride-hailing companies including **Uber** (www.uber.com) and **Lyft** (www.lyft.com) operate in Seattle.

Ferry

The iconic green and white **Washington State Ferry** (Pier 52, 801 Alaskan Way, 888/808-7977, www.wsdot.wa.gov/ferries, $8 adults, $4 seniors and children) boats are constantly crossing Puget Sound in front of downtown. They allow commuters to travel to islands around Puget Sound and from the Olympic Peninsula on a daily basis, but can also be a fun, cheap ride for tourists. Walk on to a Bainbridge-bound ferry to get the great views in both directions. Check the schedule ahead of time, or head to the terminal to catch the next boat (but prepare to wait). Tickets can be purchased from machines in the terminal lobby. On the Bainbridge side, walk to the nearby **Bainbridge Island Museum of Art** (550 Winslow Way E, 206/842-4451, www.biartmuseum.org, 10am-6pm daily, free), grab a bite of poutine at the English-inspired **Harbour Public House** (231 Parfitt Way SW, 206/842-0969, www.harbourpub.com, 11am-midnight daily, $10-16), a 10-minute walk away, or just ride the boat back.

The **King County Water Taxi** (Pier 50, 801 Alaskan Way, www.kingcounty.gov, $5.25 adults and children 6-18, $2.25 seniors, children under 6 free) is a shorter ride on a smaller boat but offers many of the same breathtaking downtown views. It travels to West Seattle, and despite it being a long walk from that dock to Alki Beach, there is a waterfront trail and the Hawaiian-inspired food at **Marination Ma Kai** (1660 Harbor Ave. SW, 206/328-8226, www.marinationmobile.com/ma-kai, 9am-8pm Tues.-Thurs. and Sun., 9am-9pm Fri.-Sat., $3-10.50). Inspired by a local food truck, this great spot on the water has outdoor tables and a small bar.

RV

Renting an RV in Seattle is not easy because companies are based in Everett, about 28 miles north of the city, or in southern suburbs. Those flying into Sea-Tac Airport can look to **Five Corners RV** (16068 Ambaum Blvd. S, 206/241-6111, www.fivecornersrv.com, 8:30am-4pm Mon.-Fri.), located very close to the airport.

To park an RV in Seattle, look east to **Issaquah Valley RV Park** (650 1st Ave. NE, Issaquah, 425/392-9233, www.ivrvpark.com, $44-50). Although it's located very close to I-90, about 16 miles from downtown Seattle, it's also very close to the area's great outdoor recreation and is a neat, well-run facility. The **Vasa Park Resort** (3560 E. Lake Sammamish Pkwy., Bellevue, 425/746-3260, www.vasaparkresort.com, $32-40), also in the suburbs east of Seattle, is on the shores of Lake Sammamish and has a boat launch and swimming beach.

Public Transit

The Seattle city bus system, **King County Metro Transit** (206/553-3000, http://metro.kingcounty.gov, $2.50-3.25 adults, $1 seniors, $1.50 children 6-17, children under 6 free) has an extensive web of routes all over the city, including bus tunnels that run under downtown and subway-like stations. Drivers only accept exact change, but the downtown underground bus stations have vending machines for ORCA cards, which can hold a balance for bus fare. Bikes can be loaded onto bike racks on the front of most buses.

ORCA cards are also accepted on the

water taxis (206/553-3000, http://metro.kingcounty.gov/tops/watertaxi, $5.25 adults, $2-2.50 seniors, $3-5.50 children 6-17, children under 6 free) that travel from downtown Seattle at 801 Alaskan Way, south of the ferry docks, to Vashon Island and West Seattle. The former is mostly a commuter route, but the latter ends at a dock with a beautiful view of the city and an eatery.

Though only useful for travelers on a very specific route, **South Lake Union Streetcar** (206/553-3060, www.seattlestreetcar.org, 6am-9pm Mon.-Thurs., 6am-11pm Fri.-Sat., 10am-7pm Sun., $2.25 adults, $1 seniors, $1.50 children 6-17, children under 6 free) could be the future of Seattle transit. It goes from a stop behind Westlake Center, at 5th Avenue and Olive Way, to the Eastlake neighborhood. Station platforms have ticket machines, and cash is accepted on board. It's most useful for tourists looking to go from downtown to Lake Union, where the Museum of History and Industry and the Center for Wooden Boats are located.

South Lake Union Streetcar

The Cascades

Look for ★ to find recommended sights, activities, dining, and lodging.

Highlights

★ **Paradise Inn:** The massive fireplaces and log ceiling in this historical hotel are worth a look even if you're not staying overnight (page 96).

★ **Skyline Trail:** This route along the flank of Mount Rainier offers up-close views of the state's massive peak, plus a sweat-inducing climb through meadows and volcanic rock (page 97).

★ **Crystal Mountain:** Ride in style to a killer viewpoint that just happens to have a gourmet restaurant (page 103).

★ **Johnston Ridge Observatory:** From this spot overlooking the crater of Mount St. Helens, it's possible to imagine the catastrophic 1980 eruption that changed this wilderness forever (page 115).

★ **Diablo Lake Boat Tours:** Take an educational and scenic boat ride on a brilliant blue body of water (page 122).

★ **Leavenworth's Oktoberfest:** You'll feel like you're in Germany at this Bavarian-style town's classic beer festival, complete with live brass band and dancers in lederhosen (page 129).

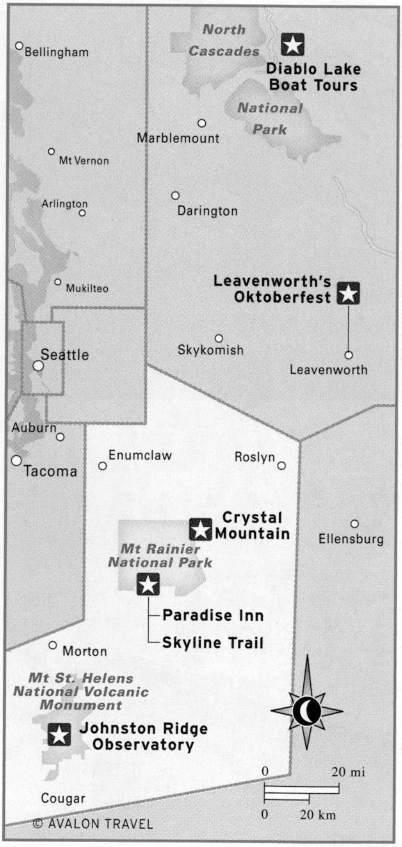

The Cascade Mountains split Washington like a spine. This range of volcanoes, with its jagged ridges, hidden lakes, and rolling hills, holds some of the region's best outdoor recreation.

Running from Canada in the north and through Oregon into California in the south, the Cascades separate the Pacific Northwest into its lusher, greener western side and sunnier prairie- and ponderosa pine-dotted eastern side. Though the range boast numerous tall peaks covered year-round in snow, some prominent mountains serve as landmarks. At the center of the north-south line is Mount Rainier, the grande dame of the Washington skyline. Down south is the volcanic wonderland of famously explosive Mount St. Helens. And up north near Washington's border with Canada, you'll find the remote wilderness of North Cascades National Park, as well as small-town charm in Bavarian-styled Leavenworth, lakeside Chelan, and Old West-themed Winthrop.

You'll find all manner of active options here, from summer hiking and mountain biking to winter skiing. For a mix of recreational energy and rural calm, it doesn't get any better.

PLANNING YOUR TIME

When exploring the Cascades, keep in mind that attractions and recreation sites may be scattered miles apart, separated by small, winding roads, so it's wise to take at least two days to appreciate the scenery. The beautiful mountain drives between the small towns are an attraction in themselves.

Mount Rainier National Park can be explored as a day trip from Seattle, or stay overnight at Paradise Inn. For the North Cascades, you might base yourself in Leavenworth or Chelan and take day trips to other spots. Alternatively, make Winthrop your hub to explore North Cascades National Park in depth. Mount St. Helens is a good lengthy detour on a drive between Seattle and Portland; it actually makes more sense as a day trip from Portland.

Avoid winter travel if you aren't interested

Previous: North Cascades; Leavenworth. **Above:** a float plane on Lake Chelan.

Mount Rainier and Vicinity

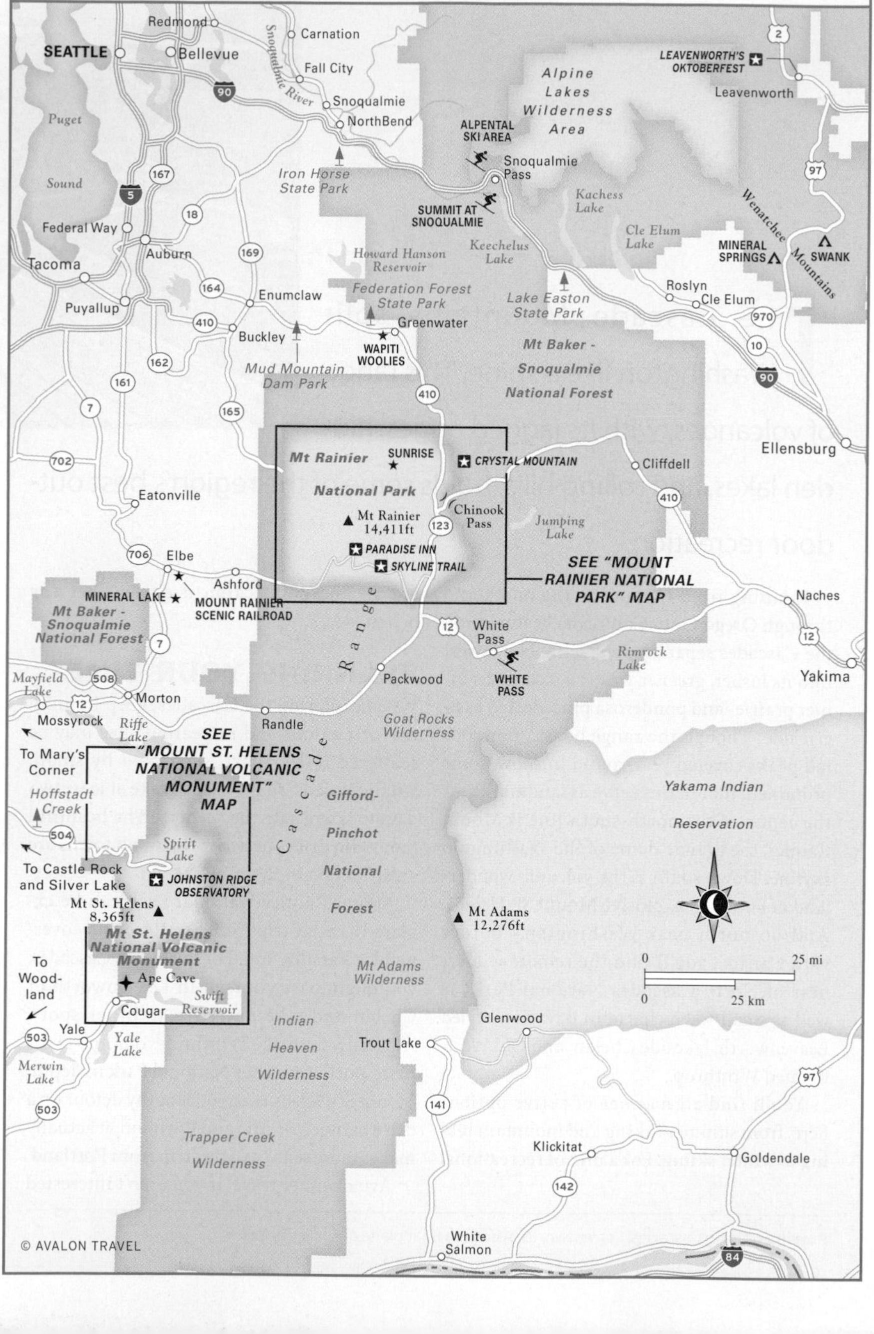
Redmond
SEATTLE
Bellevue
Carnation
Snoqualmie River
Fall City
Snoqualmie
NorthBend
Puget Sound
Iron Horse State Park
Federal Way
Auburn
Tacoma
Puyallup
Enumclaw
Buckley
Mud Mountain Dam Park
Howard Hanson Reservoir
Federation Forest State Park
Greenwater
WAPITI WOOLIES
Alpine Lakes Wilderness Area
ALPENTAL SKI AREA
Snoqualmie Pass
SUMMIT AT SNOQUALMIE
Keechelus Lake
Kachess Lake
Cle Elum Lake
Lake Easton State Park
LEAVENWORTH'S OKTOBERFEST
Leavenworth
Wenatchee Mountains
MINERAL SPRINGS
SWANK
Roslyn
Cle Elum
Mt Baker - Snoqualmie National Forest
Ellensburg
Mt Rainier National Park
SUNRISE
CRYSTAL MOUNTAIN
Cliffdell
Mt Rainier 14,411ft
Chinook Pass
Jumping Lake
PARADISE INN
SKYLINE TRAIL
SEE "MOUNT RAINIER NATIONAL PARK" MAP
Eatonville
Elbe
Ashford
MINERAL LAKE
MOUNT RAINIER SCENIC RAILROAD
Mt Baker - Snoqualmie National Forest
Naches
White Pass
WHITE PASS
Rimrock Lake
Yakima
Cascade Range
Packwood
Mayfield Lake
Morton
Mossyrock
Riffe Lake
Randle
Goat Rocks Wilderness
To Mary's Corner
SEE "MOUNT ST. HELENS NATIONAL VOLCANIC MONUMENT" MAP
Hoffstadt Creek
Gifford-Pinchot National Forest
Yakama Indian Reservation
Spirit Lake
To Castle Rock and Silver Lake
JOHNSTON RIDGE OBSERVATORY
Mt St. Helens 8,365ft
Mt St. Helens National Volcanic Monument
Mt Adams 12,276ft
To Wood-land
Ape Cave
Mt Adams Wilderness
Cougar
Swift Reservoir
Yale
Yale Lake
Merwin Lake
Indian Heaven Wilderness
Trout Lake
Glenwood
Trapper Creek Wilderness
Klickitat
Goldendale
White Salmon
0 25 mi
0 25 km
2 97 90 167 5 18 169 164 410 162 161 7 165 702 706 123 12 508 504 503 141 142 970 10 84
© AVALON TRAVEL

in the area's seasonal activities and sports; the icy roads aren't worth the bother, and the fall and winter crowds in Leavenworth—book accommodations at least six months in advance if you plan to visit during the town's Oktoberfest or Christmas Lighting Festival—ease in early spring. Few major roads run through the Cascades, but the east-west I-90 and U.S. 2 are useful thoroughfares. They stay open year-round, but in winter may have short closures for avalanche control, severe snow, or accidents. Access to the North Cascades is very limited in winter, as Highway 20, the North Cascades Highway, closes every year between mileposts 134 and 171 when snows start to fall. The closure typically lasts mid-November-mid-April.

Mount Rainier National Park

Massive Mount Rainier is on Washington's license plates, on its state quarter, and in all of its prettiest pictures. But "The Mountain" is more than the state's mascot or backdrop. Mount Rainier is an active volcano beloved by outdoor enthusiasts, naturalists, and sightseers.

This behemoth has more glaciers than any other spot in the contiguous United States; mountain climbers claim that it has everything Mount Everest does, save the altitude. The peak is about 75 miles from Seattle so it can be visited as a day trip, but the problem is that on a pretty day it's hard to tear yourself away from the subalpine meadows and colossal glaciers. Stop by a visitors center for a quick view, but try to schedule an hour for a flat nature walk, an afternoon for a gondola ride or hike, or even a night to camp under the canopy of old-growth forest.

Mount Rainier is protected in a national park, and the forests that surround it are a patchwork of national forest, designated wilderness, logging land, and private holdings. The small towns support small fishing and recreation communities, but dining options—not to mention gas stations—are limited, though there are a number of fine, if rustic, hotels and cabins.

Although the mountain has been an icon

Mount Rainier from Paradise

One Day in Mount Rainier

A visit to Mount Rainier National Park is best enjoyed in summer, when the park roads are open and free of snow. Start by enjoying the drive to the Nisqually Entrance and grabbing breakfast at the café at **Whittaker's Motel and Historic Bunkhouse.** Once inside the park, drive the 6.5 miles to Longmire slowly, both to appreciate the thick forest and to take care on the road's tight turns. In Longmire, pop into the **Longmire Museum** to learn about the family that once settled here, or walk the short **Trail of the Shadows** through the meadows. Back on the road, drive 11 miles to Paradise as Mount Rainier looms larger. Grab lunch at the deli inside the **Jackson Visitor Center,** and then hit the trail to climb the **Skyline Trail** to Panorama Point. The uphill hike is exhausting, but it's the best way to wander the Paradise meadows and Rainier's rocky flank.

Back at Paradise, check in to the **Paradise Inn** and enjoy dinner in the lofty dining room. Curl up with a book in front of one of the lobby's giant wood-burning fireplaces before hitting the hay.

IF YOU HAVE TIME

After breakfast, take **Paradise Valley Road** to Stevens Canyon Road and turn left. Drive 19 miles to Highway 123, stopping along the way for a picture at Reflection Lakes, just 3 miles after the turn. At the junction with Highway 123, turn left and continue 11 miles as the road becomes Highway 410, and in 3.5 miles turn left onto Sunrise Park Road and drive 15.5 miles to **Sunrise.** A burger from the snack stand is best enjoyed outside before hitting the 2-mile **Silver Forest Trail** to the Emmons Glacier Overlook or a more ambitious hike on the **Burroughs Mountain Trail** among the marmots.

Return to Highway 410 via Sunrise Park Road and turn left to exit the park in 4.5 miles. Turn right onto Crystal Mountain Boulevard and drive 8 miles to the ski resort of **Crystal Mountain.** Grab dinner at the **Snorting Elk Cellar** or, if it's open, the **Summit House** on top of the gondola.

To return to Seattle, drive the 8 miles back to Highway 410 and turn right. Follow Highway 410 north for 32.5 miles to Enumclaw, then continue west on Highway 410 for another 15 miles. At Sumner, take Highway 167 north for just under 20 miles to I-405. Follow I-405 south for 2 miles, and then take I-5 north for 10 miles to Seattle.

for centuries, it didn't become a national park until 1899. Naturalist John Muir visited the area and sang its praises, wowed by the wildflower meadows that surround it like a floral skirt. Today hundreds of climbers pay homage to the park's first champion at a camp halfway up the mountain named Camp Muir.

VISITING THE PARK

Mount Rainier National Park (360/569-2211, www.nps.gov/mora, $30 entrance fee per car) consists of five main regions: Longmire, Paradise, Ohanapecosh, Sunrise, and the remote Carbon and Mowich area. Even though the park is open year-round, **summer** is by far its most popular season. Snowdrifts can linger in Paradise well into the summer, and the Sunrise visitors center doesn't generally open until July. August weekends are the most crowded in the national park, when wildflowers are at their peak and sunny days are more common.

Snowflakes begin falling in **September** or **October** and lead to serious accumulation—for many years the mountain held a world record for the most snowfall in a year, a record only broken by nearby Mount Baker. As thick snow blankets the park in **winter,** the narrow (but plowed) roads make for slow going and cars need chains, though the only attractions open are the Jackson Visitor Center (on weekends) and the National Park Inn.

Entrances

The park has two major entrances. The southwest Nisqually Entrance goes to the largest visitor destination at Paradise but first passes through the Longmire encampment. The northeast White River/Sunrise entrance (May-Nov.) leads to the visitors center at Sunrise. Entrance stations charge $30 per car, $25 per motorcycle, and $15 for bike- or walk-ins, good for up to seven days. Seniors age 62 and over can score a lifetime pass for $80, or an annual pass for $55.

The **Nisqually Entrance** is located in the southwest section of the park on Highway 706 approximately 6 miles from Ashford. The road from the entrance to Longmire stays open year-round (weather permitting) and provides the only winter access to the park. November 1-May 1 a gate closes the road from Longmire to Paradise (nightly at 5pm Mon.-Fri. and 7pm Sat.-Sun.) and may stay closed longer if snow builds up. All cars, including those with four-wheel drive, are required to carry chains November-May. From Seattle, drive south on I-5 for 10 miles, and then turn east to follow I-405 north for 2 miles. Take exit 2 for Highway 167 South and continue driving south for about 20 miles. Near Puyallup, Highway 167 merges with Highway 512 for about 3 miles. Where Highway 512 continues west, take the Highway 161 exit south toward Eatonville. Highway 161 ends at Eatonville in 23 miles. Turn left onto Center Street; after 0.5 mile, Center Street becomes the Alder Cutoff Road. Follow Alder Cutoff Road for 6.5 miles and then take a left onto Highway 7 (the National Park Highway). Highway 7 eventually becomes Highway 706, and after about 13 miles, you will arrive at the Nisqually Entrance. The 80-mile drive from Seattle to the Nisqually Entrance takes about 1.75 hours.

Sunrise and **White River** form the northeast entrance to the park. This entrance is accessed via Highway 410, 13.5 miles south of Greenwater; this road into the park is only open May-November; through access from Ohanapecosh and Longmire is available seasonally. The road from the White River Entrance station to Sunrise is open early July-October (weather permitting) and closes nightly from its junction with the White River Campground (open seasonally), reopening in the morning. From Seattle, drive south on I-5 for 10 miles, and then turn east to follow I-405 north for 2 miles. Take exit 2 for Highway 167 South. Drive south for a little less than 20 miles and take the exit for Highway 410 East. Follow Highway 410 east for 50 miles, through the town of Enumclaw and the small community of Greenwater, to the national park entrance. Continue 5 miles and turn right to reach the White River Entrance and pay the fee to Sunrise. When that section of road is closed, you can drive through the national park without a fee, exiting on Highway 123 near Packwood.

Other park entrances include the **Ohanapecosh Entrance,** the southeast entrance to the park. Packwood, 11 miles southwest, is the nearest gateway. Highway 123 from U.S. 12 is open May-November; this entrance is inaccessible the rest of the year.

Carbon River is the northwest entrance to the park; vehicles are not permitted past the entrance station. The Mowich Lake hike-in campground lies south of the Carbon River entrance, at the end of an unpaved road (mid-July to mid-Oct.) that may be difficult for some cars to navigate. A machine near the park entrance collects the entry fee.

Visitors Centers

Henry M. Jackson Memorial Visitor Center (360/569-6571, 10am-7pm daily June-Sept., 10am-4:30pm Sat.-Sun. Oct.-May) is located in Paradise and is the largest of the visitors centers in the area. It's always crowded on sunny summer days.

Other area visitors centers also have maps and rangers available to answer questions, as well as educational placards about wildlife. The **Longmire Information Center** (360/569-6575, 9am-5pm daily June-Sept., 9am-4:30pm daily Oct.-May) is located in the Longmire Museum and offers general visitor information. In the summer the **Longmire Wilderness Information Center** (360/569-6650, 7:30am-5pm daily mid-May-mid-Oct.) can also help with general

Mount Rainier National Park

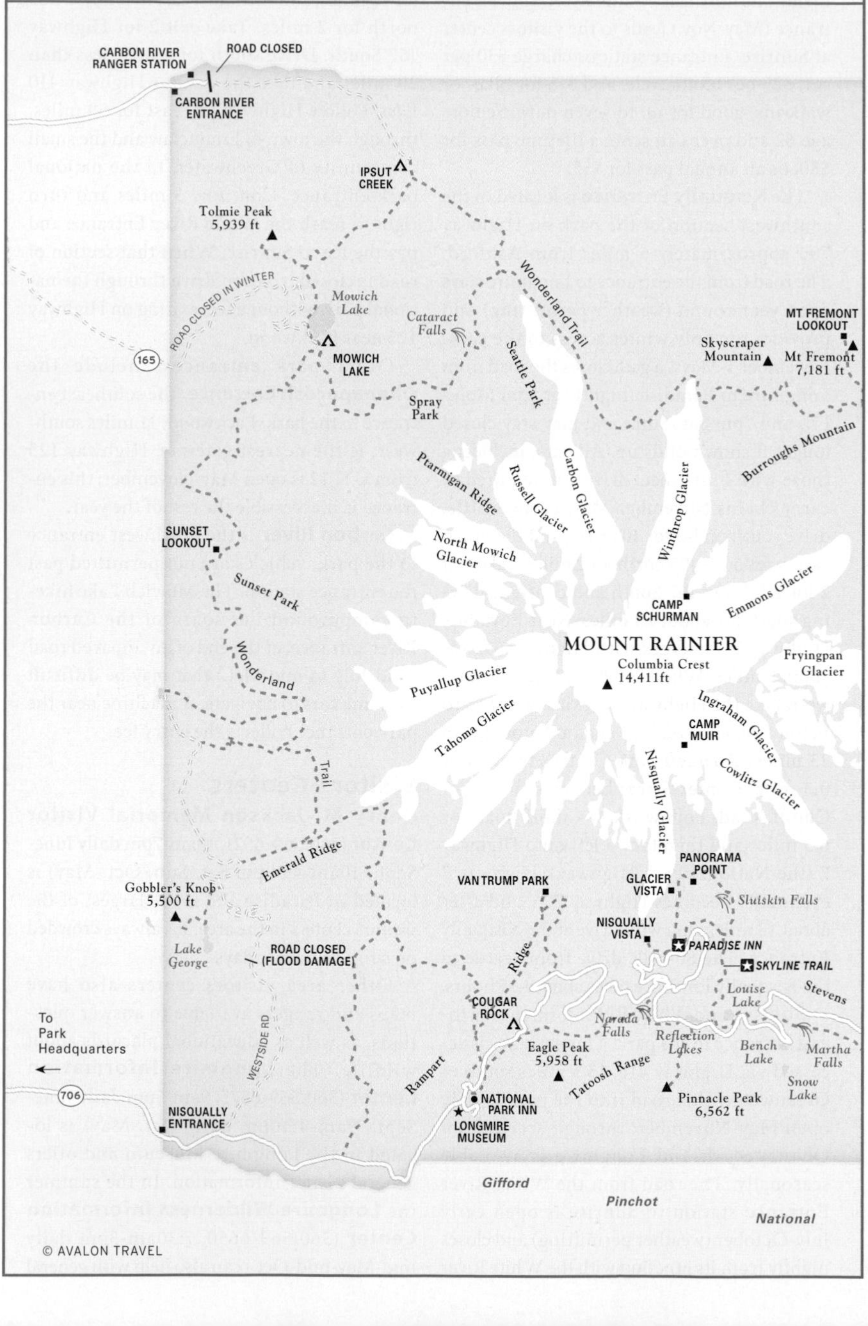
CARBON RIVER RANGER STATION
ROAD CLOSED
CARBON RIVER ENTRANCE
IPSUT CREEK
Tolmie Peak 5,939 ft
ROAD CLOSED IN WINTER
Mowich Lake
Cataract Falls
MOWICH LAKE
165
Wonderland Trail
Seattle Park
Spray Park
MT FREMONT LOOKOUT
Skyscraper Mountain
Mt Fremont 7,181 ft
Burroughs Mountain
Ptarmigan Ridge
Russell Glacier
Carbon Glacier
Winthrop Glacier
SUNSET LOOKOUT
North Mowich Glacier
Sunset Park
Emmons Glacier
CAMP SCHURMAN
MOUNT RAINIER
Columbia Crest 14,411ft
Fryingpan Glacier
Wonderland
Puyallup Glacier
Tahoma Glacier
Ingraham Glacier
CAMP MUIR
Nisqually Glacier
Cowlitz Glacier
Trail
Emerald Ridge
PANORAMA POINT
VAN TRUMP PARK
GLACIER VISTA
Slutskin Falls
Gobbler's Knob 5,500 ft
NISQUALLY VISTA
PARADISE INN
SKYLINE TRAIL
Lake George
ROAD CLOSED (FLOOD DAMAGE)
Ridge
Louise Lake
Stevens
COUGAR ROCK
Narada Falls
Reflection Lakes
To Park Headquarters
WESTSIDE RD
Eagle Peak 5,958 ft
Bench Lake
Martha Falls
Rampart
Tatoosh Range
Snow Lake
706
NATIONAL PARK INN
Pinnacle Peak 6,562 ft
NISQUALLY ENTRANCE
LONGMIRE MUSEUM
Gifford
Pinchot
National
© AVALON TRAVEL

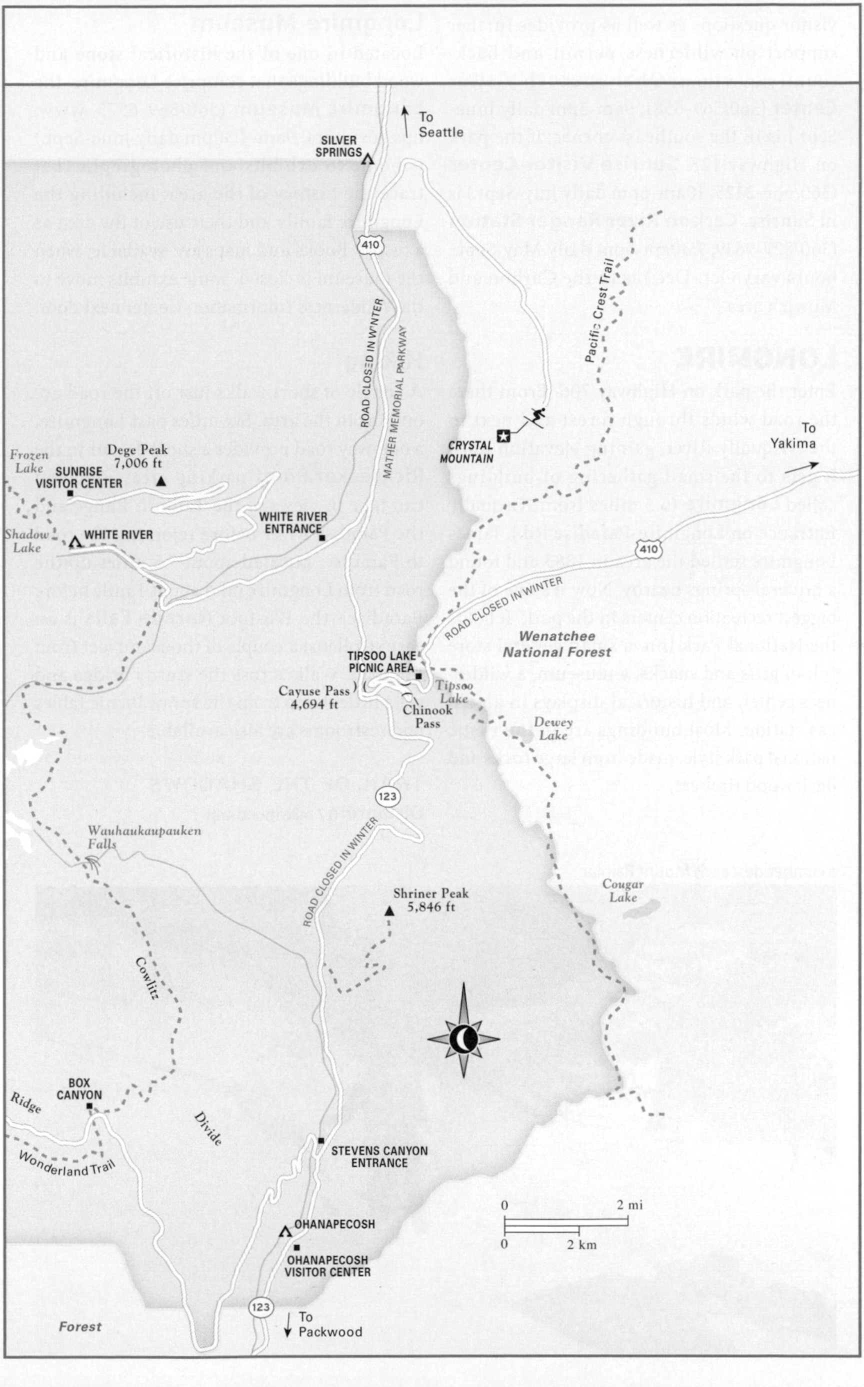
To Seattle
SILVER SPRINGS
410
ROAD CLOSED IN WINTER
MATHER MEMORIAL PARKWAY
Pacific Crest Trail
CRYSTAL MOUNTAIN
To Yakima
Frozen Lake
Dege Peak 7,006 ft
SUNRISE VISITOR CENTER
WHITE RIVER ENTRANCE
Shadow Lake
WHITE RIVER
410
ROAD CLOSED IN WINTER
Wenatchee National Forest
TIPSOO LAKE PICNIC AREA
Cayuse Pass 4,694 ft
Tipsoo Lake
Chinook Pass
Dewey Lake
123
ROAD CLOSED IN WINTER
Wauhaukaupauken Falls
Shriner Peak 5,846 ft
Cougar Lake
Cowlitz
BOX CANYON
Ridge
Divide
Wonderland Trail
STEVENS CANYON ENTRANCE
0
2 mi
0
2 km
OHANAPECOSH
OHANAPECOSH VISITOR CENTER
123
To Packwood
Forest

visitor questions as well as provides further support on wilderness permit and backcountry questions. **Ohanapecosh Visitor Center** (360/569-6581, 9am-5pm daily June-Sept.) is in the southeast corner of the park on Highway 123. **Sunrise Visitor Center** (360/663-2425, 10am-6pm daily July-Sept.) is in Sunrise. **Carbon River Ranger Station** (360/829-9639, 7:30am-5pm daily May-Sept., hours vary Oct.-Dec.) is in the Carbon and Mowich area.

LONGMIRE

Enter the park on Highway 706. From there the road winds through forest and next to the Nisqually River, gaining elevation until it gets to the small gathering of buildings called **Longmire** (6.5 miles from Nisqually Entrance on Longmire-Paradise Rd.). James Longmire settled the area in 1883 and found a mineral springs nearby. Now it's one of the biggest recreation centers in the park. It holds the National Park Inn, a small general store full of gifts and snacks, a museum, a wilderness center, and historical displays in an old gas station. Most buildings are in the rustic national park style, made from large rocks and dark wood timbers.

Longmire Museum

Located in one of the historical stone and wood buildings that comprise Longmire, the **Longmire Museum** (360/569-6575, www.nps.gov/mora, 9am-4:30pm daily June-Sept.) is home to exhibits and photographs that trace the history of the area, including the Longmire family and their use of the area as a resort. Books and maps are available; when the museum is closed, some exhibits move to the Wilderness Information Center next door.

Hiking

A couple of short walks just off the road are options in the area. Six miles past Longmire, a one-way road provides a short detour to the **Ricksecker Point** parking area. Here you can take in views of the Tatoosh Range and the Paradise River before rejoining the road to Paradise. Located about 7.5 miles up the road from Longmire (and about 1 mile before Paradise), the 176-foot **Narada Falls** is an easy stroll just a couple of thousand feet from the road. Walk across the sturdy bridge and get a little damp from the spray. Picnic tables and restrooms are also available.

TRAIL OF THE SHADOWS

Distance: 0.7 mile round-trip

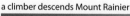

a climber descends Mount Rainier

Duration: 30 minutes
Elevation gain: none
Effort: easy
Trailhead: across the street from the National Park Inn in Longmire

The Trail of the Shadows skirts one of the Longmire family's old cabins—it's actually a replica—and the mineral springs. Bear right after 0.5 mile. The first springs is ringed in rocks, and the second has a rusty color thanks to iron in the water. Look for placards explaining some of the natural history of the area. Complete the loop by taking a right at the last junction.

RAMPART RIDGE TRAIL

Distance: 4.5 miles round-trip
Duration: 2-3 hours
Elevation gain: 1,300 feet
Effort: moderate
Trailhead: across the street from the National Park Inn in Longmire

Start on the Trail of the Shadows, moving clockwise, but head left when you reach the intersection after 0.5 mile; it's marked with a small wooden sign. You'll head uphill through thick forest, hiking up switchbacks on a well-maintained dirt trail. Eventually the trail flattens out and heads north. Stop for a long snack or lunch break when Mount Rainier rises above you like a sentinel, its glaciers in full view. Continue on the loop until it bends down to Longmire again. Intersections are well signed.

TWIN FIRS TRAIL

Distance: 0.5 mile round-trip
Duration: 20 minutes
Elevation gain: 50 feet
Effort: easy
Trailhead: two miles west of Longmire, on the north side of the road

This loop travels through old-growth timber, including the namesake twin Douglas fir trees and cedar trees. Some of the greenery is giant, while others are small due to the floods and mudslides that can scour the meadows regularly. Kautz Creek burbles nearby, and the meadows burst with trillium when the snow melts. It's an easy ramble for kids or anyone who forgot to wear more than flip-flops.

Food and Accommodations

The **National Park Inn** (Paradise-Longmire Rd., 6 miles from Nisqually Entrance, 360/569-2275, www.mtrainierguestservices.com, $126-177 shared bath, $177-263 private bath, open daily year-round) in Longmire is less grand than its Paradise cousin, but it has a cozier charm—plus it's open year-round. It has only 25 rooms in a building constructed in 1910 and has both a stone fireplace indoors and a long porch outside, lined with chairs for relaxing with ice cream or a hot chocolate (or beer). Rooms are simple, small, and not particularly modern, but rooms with a shared bath come with robes and slippers for trips through the hallway.

The casual **National Park Inn Dining Room** (7am-11am, 11:30am-4:30pm, and 5pm-7pm Sun.-Thurs., open until 8pm Fri.-Sat. year-round) serves straightforward hearty meals for lunch ($12-16) and dinner ($19-34) like pot roast, beef chili, and grilled cheese sandwiches, but the sweets—including blackberry cobbler and hot chocolate—are the best. Breakfasts ($9-14) include pancakes, biscuits and gravy, and eggs Benedict made with grilled portobello mushrooms.

Camping

Located just a couple miles past Longmire, **Cougar Rock Campground** (2 miles past Longmire on the Longmire-Paradise Rd., www.recreation.gov, May-Sept., $20) is one of the most popular places to camp in the state because of its proximity to Paradise. The 173 sites have access to flush toilets and an RV dump station, and five group sites ($60) can hold up to 40 people and five cars. There are no hookups, and RVs with generators must observe quiet hours. Across the road, a trail leads down to the Nisqually River, and a bridge crosses it to lead to a trail to Carter Falls. Ranger programs, sharing historical and natural information about the area, are held at a central amphitheater. Reservations are required in the busy summer months.

Information and Services

Longmire Information Center (360/569-6575, www.nps.gov/mora, 9am-5pm daily June-Sept., 9am-4:30pm daily Oct.-May), in the Longmire Museum, is the main visitor information center in the Longmire area.

In summer, the **Longmire Wilderness Information Center** (360/569-6650, www.nps.gov/mora, 7:30am-5pm daily mid-May-mid-Oct.) can answer a lot of the same questions as the Longmire Information Center, but it can also provide more technical information pertaining to wilderness permits and backcountry questions.

PARADISE

From Longmire, **Paradise Road** continues to climb and crosses the Nisqually River; pull over at the **Christine Falls** parking lot to see a dramatic two-tiered waterfall and charming stone bridge. After 11 miles, the road approaches the tree line and you'll see lush subalpine meadows—this is Paradise, home to a hotel, visitors center, and climbing center.

During the approach from Longmire, keep to the left and follow signs for access to Paradise (the road runs both directions until Paradise). After passing the parking lots, the road becomes **Paradise Valley Road** and continues one-way in a scenic five-minute loop. It runs under Mazama Ridge before meeting up again with the main Paradise-Longmire Road and Stevens Canyon Road, which continues east into the park.

Continue driving past Paradise and stop at **Inspiration Point.** The pullout and viewpoint is located on Stevens Canyon Road (just past where it meets the Paradise-Longmire Road and Paradise Valley Road outlet). The views here stretch up Paradise Valley and across the Tatoosh Range. Continue along Stevens Canyon Road to Reflection Lakes, 3 miles from Paradise. These subalpine lakes are accessible from the roadside and are famous sites for photographers to capture Mount Rainier reflected in the icy-cold water.

Jackson Visitor Center

At the center of Paradise is the steep peaked roof of the **Henry M. Jackson Memorial Visitor Center** (Paradise Rd. E, 360/569-6571, www.nps.gov/mora, 10am-7pm daily June-Sept., 10am-4:30pm Sat.-Sun. Oct.-May), shaped so it doesn't hold the snow during the winter and an ideal refuge when the weather turns cold or windy. It has a theater showing a short history film and displays about the area's natural history, plus a café and gift shop. Look for a relief map of the entire park, where you can see how the folds of smaller mountains surround Mount Rainier; the route mountaineers take to the top; and how little Tahoma, a side peak, manages to be dwarfed by its big sister even though it's one of the tallest points in the state. Note in the historical displays how the Paradise area has changed over the years; the meadows weren't always pristine, so it's important to observe posted signs when you wander outside. Even if you don't plan to hike, the visitors center—and, mostly, the view outside it—is worth a visit: Mount Rainier seems to rise right from the Paradise parking lot

TOP EXPERIENCE

★ Paradise Inn

Regardless of whether you're staying the night, the lobby of the **Paradise Inn** (98368 Paradise-Longmire Rd., 360/569-2275, www.mtrainierguestservices.com, May-Sept.) is a must-see. The long room, anchored by massive stone fireplaces at each end, is marked by regular exposed log beams. It's decorated with a 14-foot grandfather clock, built by the same German carpenter, and a piano, played by President Harry Truman during a visit. Couches and long wooden tables dot the lobby, often filled with as many recovering hikers and climbers—planning their next trek, or recounting their last one—as hotel guests, and you can enjoy drinks and food from the nearby snack bar. When the air turns chilly—that is, on all but the sunniest of summer days—the crackling fireplaces offer a chance to warm wind-scoured hands.

Hiking

ALTA VISTA TRAIL

Distance: 1.75 miles round-trip
Duration: 1.25 hours
Elevation gain: 600 feet
Effort: easy
Trailhead: lower or upper parking lot

Paradise's real treasures are outside. The short Alta Vista Trail that begins near the parking lot (look for trails branching uphill next to the Henry M. Jackson Memorial Visitor Center) is mostly paved to help preserve the fragile landscape of subalpine meadows, which burst in summer with purple lupine and orange-red Indian paintbrush. Follow the small signs as the trail heads subtly up toward Rainier, and don't step off the path. The Alta Vista Trail ends at a scenic overlook, after which you can turn around and return the way you came, but you can also add to the journey by taking the tiny spur paths that follow the meadows over small knolls and give slightly different views of Rainier's flanks. The trails here are a tangle of routes, so it's easy—and advisable—to wander on your return, provided the weather is clear enough to make your way back to the Paradise center by sight. Although Alta Vista might be a starting point, the pleasure of these paths is largely in the opportunities they offer for interesting meandering.

★ SKYLINE TRAIL

Distance: 4-5.5 miles round-trip
Duration: 2.5-4 hours
Elevation gain: 1,700 feet
Effort: strenuous
Trailhead: north side of the upper parking lot

Skyline is a comprehensive trail that includes the best meadows of Paradise, but climbs high enough for wider views of the entire park, plus closer looks at the vast snowfields and cracked glaciers on Rainier. The whole loop is well signed and has some of the best views of Mount Rainier and the jagged Tatoosh Range to the south. It starts at the same trailhead as Alta Vista, but most of the paved paths that lead uphill from the Paradise parking lot eventually funnel into Skyline; follow the small signs that sit at most trail intersections. The trail gradually inches higher along the flanks of the mountain, then gets steeper while the trees get less common, and finally tops out at Panorama Point (look for a bathroom that's been built into the rock

Paradise Inn

here). It then heads east before swinging back to Paradise. Summit-bound climbers may pass by with large packs and ice axes. Be sure not to feed any wildlife, including chipmunks and the furry marmots that sun themselves on the large boulders of the mountainside. The entire 5.5-mile loop returns to Paradise via Sluiskin Falls, but there's a cutoff just past Panorama Point that will shorten the loop length to just 4 miles total (though you won't knock off any elevation gain). The cutoff and main route join again at roaring Myrtle Falls just above Paradise Inn.

PINNACLE PEAK

Distance: 3 miles round-trip
Duration: 3 hours
Elevation gain: 1,150 feet
Effort: strenuous
Trailhead: across the road from Reflection Lakes
Directions: Take the Paradise-Longmire Road or the Paradise Valley Road to Stevens Canyon Road for three miles.

Escape some of the crowds by heading up a trail that gains some elevation, moving south of the road into the Tatoosh Range. It ends at the rocky Pinnacle Saddle and offers a spectacular view of Mount Rainier; climbing any farther requires scrambling experience and is not advised.

BENCH AND SNOW LAKES

Distance: 2.5 miles round-trip
Duration: 2 hours
Elevation gain: 700 feet
Effort: moderate
Trailhead: 1.5 miles east of Paradise down Stevens Canyon Road

This is one of the most beautiful of the park's easier trails. You'll sometimes traverse wooden boardwalks over wet grass, as well as walk through wildflower meadows and eventually gain some elevation and skirt Bench Lake. Keep going until the trail ends at Snow Lake, fed by Unicorn Creek, about 1.25 miles from the trailhead, where there's a small backpacking campground. The trail is snow-covered at the start of summer and muddy until midsummer. The area is also popular with black bears—stay mindful and don't try to feed them.

Food and Accommodations

The stately old **Paradise Inn** (98368 Paradise-Longmire Rd., 360/569-2275, www.mtrainierguestservices.com, May-Sept., $119-155 shared bath) is one of the country's

Skyline Trail

most distinguished national park lodges, built in 1916 and decorated with rustic woodwork by a German carpenter who wanted to evoke alpine styles. Many of the cedar logs were from a grove nearby that had been decimated in a fire. The original space had only a few dozen rooms, which today have shared hall bathrooms and cozy shapes under the steep roof. An annex built in 1920 added four floors of rooms, all of which have private bathrooms, though these are undergoing renovations through 2018; the main lodge rooms with shared bath will still be available during this time.

The attached **Paradise Inn Dining Room** (7am-9:30am, noon-2pm, and 5:30pm-8pm daily May-Sept., $17-35) is impressive in its elegant, rustic style. While it serves a wide array of seafood, small plates, steak, and a bourbon-buffalo meatloaf, the decor is more impressive than the flavors.

The **Paradise Camp Deli** (10am-6:45pm daily June-Sept., 11am-4pm Sat.-Sun. Oct.-May), in the Jackson Visitor Center, is a fast-service restaurant serving salads, pizzas, and soft drinks. Enjoy soft-serve ice cream or coffee outside, or eat inside when the weather's bad.

Information and Services

The **Paradise Climbing Information Center** (360/569-6641, 7am-4pm daily May-Sept.), located in the historical Guide House, provides climbing permits for those attempting to summit Mount Rainier as well as backcountry hiking and camping permits. For information on day hiking or less advanced outdoor activities, visit the Jackson Visitor Center.

OHANAPECOSH

The southeastern corner of the park is known as Ohanapecosh, named for a settlement of the Upper Cowlitz tribe. Ohanapecosh is located at an elevation of 2,000 feet, much lower than other areas in the park, and the old-growth forest here is likely to be free of rain when Paradise or Longmire are wet and soggy. The **Ohanapecosh Visitor Center** (360/569-6581, www.nps.gov/mora, 9am-5pm daily June-Sept.) provides services to the area. The Ohanapecosh Campground (the park's largest) operates May-October and provides picnic tables and bathrooms for visitors.

Ohanapecosh is located about 11.5 miles north of Packwood on U.S. 12 and is most accessible from Portland and points south. May-November, Ohanapecosh is accessible via a 19-mile drive from Paradise or a gorgeous 14-mile drive south of the White River Entrance. The park roads from Paradise and White River are closed in winter.

Hiking

GROVE OF THE PATRIARCHS

Distance: 1.3 miles round-trip
Duration: 1 hour
Elevation gain: 100 feet
Effort: easy
Trailhead: 0.25 mile past the Stevens Canyon Entrance on Stevens Canyon Road

Sometimes you don't want a visitors center, or even an overwhelming view of the mountain—or maybe it's too cloudy to see the mountain anyway. In that case, the Grove of the Patriarchs Trail is an excellent way to get a taste of the wilderness in a short, flat, and very easy hike through old-growth forest. Signs point out cedar, western hemlock, and Douglas fir trees. Cross a suspension footbridge (*one at a time,* the sign warns) to gaze up at 300-foot-tall trees more than 1,000 years old—which means that they sprouted in the time of Saint Francis of Assisi and Genghis Khan.

SILVER FALLS LOOP

Distance: 3.8 miles round-trip
Duration: 2 hours
Elevation gain: 300 feet
Effort: easy
Trailhead: just north of the Stevens Canyon Entrance on Stevens Canyon Road, across from the Grove of the Patriarchs trailhead

This trail leads to a waterfall on the Ohanapecosh River that flows with glacial water; the name is a Native American one, from the groups who lived here long before the national park was formed. Start by moving south through the trees, reaching the falls in 0.5 mile. Anglers sometimes frequent the river, and woodpeckers are numerous in the area. Continue on the route south to Ohanapecosh Campground where, in the 1920s, a resort stood. None of those buildings remain, but the hot springs (not big enough for soaking) that first drew tourists here can still be seen along the Hot Springs Nature Trail, an easy 0.3-mile spur marked with interpretive signs that begins behind the old visitors center building at the campground and rejoins the Silver Falls Loop as it moves north.

Camping

Ohanapecosh Campground (Stevens Canyon Rd. near the intersection of Hwy. 123, www.recreation.gov, May-Oct., $20) is the largest of the park's campgrounds, with 188 sites, including two group spots ($60) and 10 walk-in campsites. The campground is set at 1,914 feet, a lower elevation than Cougar Rock or White River, and is more sheltered by trees. Amenities include water, flush toilets, and a dump station. There are no hookups, and RVs must observe quiet hours. Reservations are required in the busy summer months.

SUNRISE

The park's Sunrise area got its name the obvious way—by offering a spectacular view of the mountain when the sun first emerges from the east. Located on the northeast side of the park and situated at the high elevation of 6,400 feet, Sunrise is covered in snow most of the year. This region is less developed than the west side of the mountain, with only a small visitors center, a nearby campground, picnic facilities, and limited food options. Sunrise Road stretches from the White River Entrance station to the Sunrise Visitor Center, and the road is usually open by mid-July and closes by October. Overnight visitors may camp at White River Campground, but are not permitted at Sunrise. The road between the visitors center and the campground closes nightly.

Sunrise is accessible via Highway 410. The region is about 50 miles (1.5 hours) south of the town of Enumclaw and is a two-hour drive from Paradise when the park road is open.

Sunrise Visitor Center

The **Sunrise Visitor Center** (Sunrise Rd., 360/663-2425, www.nps.gov/mora, 10am-6pm daily July-Sept.), on the northeast corner of the park, is even higher than Paradise, with views of the Emmons Glacier side of the peak,

Sunrise Visitor Center

the White River Valley below, and Mount Baker and Glacier Peak up north. It's particularly spectacular at—what else—sunrise, especially from the **Sunrise Point** overlook on the road that approaches the wood-sided visitors center. Inside are more exhibits about the mountain and its history, and rangers lead programs and hikes. Services are less extensive than at Paradise, with only a snack bar and small bookstore.

Sights

As Highway 410 enters the national park, it becomes Mather Memorial Parkway. In 8 more miles, Mather Memorial Parkway meets Highway 123 at Cayuse Pass (elevation 4,694 feet). Head east to continue along Mather Memorial Parkway for 3 miles to **Tipsoo Lake.** The lake is surrounded by glorious mountain meadows, and picnic tables offer a spot to sit and soak in the views.

Hiking

Hikes around Sunrise lead through the Yakima Park meadows and rocky expanses inhabited by mountain marmots and fuzzy white mountain goats.

SILVER FOREST TRAIL

Distance: 2 miles round-trip
Duration: 1 hour
Elevation gain: 150 feet
Effort: easy
Trailhead: south end of the Sunrise parking lot

At the Emmons Vista Overlook near the visitors center, look on the south side of the parking lot for the trailhead to the Silver Forest Trail, which offers great views with little elevation gain. In late summer, the meadows explode with wildflowers, including purple lupine and Indian paintbrush.

BURROUGHS MOUNTAIN TRAIL

Distance: 6 miles round-trip
Duration: 3 hours
Elevation gain: 1,200 feet
Effort: strenuous
Trailhead: south end of the Sunrise parking lot

From the same trailhead as the Silver Forest Trail, head west through meadows toward Frozen Lake, then turn at a large, well-signed intersection for the Burroughs Mountain Trail. With massive Rainier still looming in front, the rocky Burroughs mountains present a challenge of their own, mostly exposed to the hot sun as you climb their flanks. Reach the top of First Burroughs about three-quarters of a mile past Frozen Lake, then the even higher Second Burroughs a little more than a half mile past that. Turn here and return the way you came for the 6-mile hike, though the trail itself continues on for 2.2 miles (and loses a lot of elevation) to Glacier Basin Camp. Keep your eyes and ears peeled for the marmots that live in the area, who whistle to each other as they hide in the nooks between big boulders.

SOURDOUGH RIDGE

Distance: 3 miles round-trip
Duration: 1.5 hour
Elevation gain: 500 feet
Effort: moderate
Trailhead: north side of the Sunrise parking lot

Take a quick loop up a ridge above Sunrise with views of the mountains north of Rainier, such as Glacier Peak and Mount Baker. The trail splits less than a quarter mile from the trailhead and you can go in either direction. Explore the ridge, which offers opportunities to spot marmots, elk, mountain goats, and more.

GLACIER BASIN

Distance: 6.5 miles round-trip
Duration: 3 hours
Elevation gain: 1,700 feet
Effort: strenuous
Trailhead: White River Campground, in Loop D

The first part of this route is on an old mining road, but the wide, easy ramble quickly narrows to a conventional trail. The forest is home to a number of bears (give them space if you spot one), and at about 3 miles in, hikers can spot the rusty remnants of an old mine. Head just past the backcountry campsites to take in Glacier Basin, and see if you can spot climbers heading up the Interglacier at the end of the valley—they're likely heading to Camp Schurman, one of the two most popular base camps for Rainier summiters (the other is Camp Muir above Paradise).

NACHES PEAK LOOP

Distance: 3.4 miles round-trip
Duration: 2.5 hours
Elevation gain: 600 feet
Effort: moderate
Trailhead: three miles south of the White River Entrance Station
Directions: Follow Highway 410 east for Tipsoo Lake and a parking lot.

Though only partially in the national park, this loop boasts big open alpine meadows, mountain views, and fewer hikers than routes out of Sunrise or Paradise. Don't expect to have the trail entirely to yourself, though, especially during wildflower season in late summer. You can hike in either direction, but a clockwise route provides the best vistas.

Food

The **Sunrise Day Lodge** (www.mtrainierguestservices.com, 10am-7pm daily June-Sept.) includes a small snack bar that serves grilled burgers and hot dogs, sandwiches, and soft-serve ice cream. Although there's space to eat inside, the view from the picnic tables outside overlooks the subalpine meadows that skirt Mount Rainier. An attached gift shop sells books and small souvenirs. The snack bar provides the only food service in the area and can open as late as July in especially snowy years.

Camping

The 112-site **White River Campground** (360/569-2211, www.nps.gov/mora, June-Sept., $20) lies 3 miles from Sunrise at 4,400 feet, a higher elevation than the other two major campgrounds in the park. A few of the 112 sites have prime locations next to the White River. Look for a historical patrol cabin located between two of the campsite loops to hear about the area's history at ranger programs by a campfire circle. Amenities include water and flush toilets, but no RV dump station (though RVs are allowed). Reservations are not accepted, so this is one of the few places you can still score a drive-up spot.

Though located outside the national park, the **Silver Springs Campground** (Highway 410, www.recreation.gov, May-Sept., $20-32) is just a mile west of the White River Entrance—useful when the White River Campground sites are all full. The forest here is full of old-growth cedar and western hemlock, and a small river flows through the 55 sites. Amenities include water, flush and vault toilets, and picnic tables; no electrical hookups are available.

Information and Services

The **White River Wilderness Information Center** (White River Entrance Station, 360/569-6670, 7:30am-5pm May-Oct.) can provide permit information for backcountry hikers and campers on the mountain's north side. Climbers attempting to summit Mount Rainier from the north side must register here.

The **Silver Creek Visitor Information Center** (69211 Hwy. 410 E, 360/663-2284, www.fs.usda.gov) is a classic log-cabin structure located about 1.5 miles north of the national park boundary. It's operated seasonally by the Snoqualmie Ranger District, with national forest rangers who can offer advice on recreation and informational materials.

CARBON AND MOWICH

The northwest corner of the park is the least accessible area of Mount Rainier National Park—except for the miles and miles of wilderness, of course. Highway 165 leaves Highway 410 west of Enumclaw in the town of Buckley and winds its way through rural landscape for 10.5 miles before Carbon River Road even begins. Then it's another 5.5 miles to the park entrance and the end of the road. The **Carbon River Ranger Station** (360/829-9639, www.nps.gov/mora, 7:30am-5pm daily

May-Sept., hours vary Oct.-Dec.) operates seasonally.

The road from the entrance station into the park washed out in a flood, so visitors must park and hike or bike 4 miles to the picnic area on the Carbon River. It's another mile to **Ipsut Creek Campground** (backcountry permits required).

Mowich Lake Campground (first-come, first-served, mid-July to mid-Oct., free) is located on the park's deepest lake, accessed by staying on Highway 165 for an additional 17 miles after the Carbon River Road cutoff. The road is open in summer only, and many sections are unpaved or difficult for small vehicles. The campground has 10 primitive, tent-only sites; there is no water, and campfires are prohibited.

★ CRYSTAL MOUNTAIN

Sprawling **Crystal Mountain Resort** (33914 Crystal Mountain Blvd., 360/663-2265, www.crystalmountainresort.com, $74 adults, $50 seniors and children 11-17, children under 11 free, $8 for gondola) is the biggest ski resort in the state and has Washington's only gondola. It has bunny hills, new chairlifts, and backcountry skiing. The jib park is for trick skiers and snowboarders and has a giant airbag for aerial tricks ($5-25)—though anyone attempting to flip onto the cushion has to sign a waiver and wear a helmet. Rent ski equipment at the base ($45 adults, $35 children), or visit a dedicated boot shop for fittings and adjustment.

Non-skiers can do more than just sip hot chocolate at the base lodge: **Snowshoe tours** ($65) include equipment rental and a cheese fondue dinner, plus a guide for the trek along a ridge near the summit. Scenic rides on the **Mount Rainier Gondola** (10am-5pm Sun.-Fri., 10am-7pm Sat., closed fall and spring, $23 adults, $18 seniors, $12 children 4-12, children under 3 free) allow anyone to see the top, with a climb of 2,500 feet in less than 10 minutes in an enclosed car—but be warned that in winter the wind up top can be unforgiving.

Even though Crystal Mountain Resort is best known as a ski destination, the gondola runs during summer to carry hikers and sightseers up the hill. Guided hikes (11am and 1 pm Fri.-Sun. summer, weather permitting) with a U.S. Forest Service ranger are free with a gondola ticket, as are wildflower hikes with naturalists; head to the top of the gondola and look for a meetup sign. A disc golf course is free, at least if you're willing to hike uphill to hit all 27 baskets (otherwise buy

Crystal Mountain

a gondola ticket and work your way down). The **Mountain Shop,** at the base, rents lawn games like bocce and croquet, and a taco truck is parked outside on weekends. Find maps of hikes at the Mountain Shop as well; unsurprisingly, they're all downhill from the top of the lifts.

If you're not looking to walk yourself, **Chinook Pass Outfitters** (800/726-3631, www.crystalmountainoutfitters.com, 8am-6pm daily in season, $35-180) leads horseback riding trips from parking lot C. Overnight and fishing trips are also available.

Food

The Austrian theme of the Alpine Inn at Crystal Mountain extends to the in-house restaurant, the **Snorting Elk Cellar** (33818 Crystal Mountain Blvd., 888/754-6400, www.crystalhotels.com, 11am-10pm daily summer; 11am-10pm Sun.-Thurs, 11am-midnight Fri.-Sat. winter, $11-30). Low arched ceilings cover a fireplace and walls painted in floral designs that wouldn't be out of place at any Oktoberfest. Seattle brewery Elysian creates the bar's namesake beer, but there are plenty of other taps for après-ski or après-hike visits. The menu leans toward hearty fare like stone-fired pizzas and thick sandwiches. The hot-drinks menu includes a hot toddy, hot buttered rum, hot spiced wine, and a drink called the Face Plant—imagine a rummy hot chocolate with peppermint schnapps and whipped cream.

You can't get much higher than the **Summit House** (33914 Crystal Mountain Blvd., 360/663-3085, www.crystalmountainresort.com, 10:30am-4:30pm Sun.-Fri. and 10:30am-6:30pm Sat. summer, 10:30am-2:45pm daily weather permitting winter, $18-32) and still get waiter service—from 6,872 feet at the top of Crystal Mountain, Summit House claims to be Washington's highest restaurant (and no one's arguing). Located at the top of the Mount Rainier Gondola, it's a meal that requires serious planning. Skiers swarm the area during winter months, and the wind is significant. Even in summer, clouds can obscure the spectacular Mount Rainier view, and sunset dinners mean a flashlight-led walk back to the gondola. Still, the wood-trimmed dining room with stone fireplace and antler chandeliers is worth the trip, and the menu includes gourmet fondue, fish specials, and filet mignon. Reservations and a gondola ticket are required. Hours can vary from year to year, so it's a good idea to check the Crystal Mountain website for the most up-to-date hours.

Accommodations

Of the three hotels at the base of the Crystal Mountain ski area, **Alpine Inn** (33818 Crystal Mountain Blvd., 360/663-2262, www.crystalhotels.com, $145-290) has the most charm. The exterior is all Bavarian, complete with bright green shutters and a large porch, and the hotel itself is located across the creek from the parking lot. Inside, a small fireplace anchors the lobby, and the hallways are lined with vintage black-and-white photos of skiers with wooden equipment and jaunty old ski outfits. Rooms are small but come in combinations with a sleeper sofa or bunk beds to accommodate families. Most don't have a TV or phone—the mountain is your entertainment.

The simpler **Village Inn** (33818 Crystal Mountain Blvd., 360/663-2262, www.crystalhotels.com, $205-240), just across the parking lot, has rooms only with a queen bed or two twins. Headboards are made of thick wooden logs, and rooms have balconies facing the ski mountain. Rooms come with refrigerators and, unlike the Alpine Inn across the way, a TV. But like the Alpine Inn, it's a short walk to the Mount Rainier Gondola.

The **Alta Crystal Resort** (68317 Hwy. 410, 360/663-2500, www.altacrystalresort.com, $299-350) isn't at Crystal at all, but rather down the road a few miles. It's a small complex of suites, some two stories with two bedrooms. All have wood-burning fireplaces and either a kitchenette or full kitchen, and rooms aren't cramped. A large honeymoon cabin is on a creek and located away from the rest of the buildings. Steam rises from the hot tub and heated pool (set to 90°F in the winter), and a recreation lodge holds board games and a foosball table. Unlike some cabins in the area, the hotel has indoor distractions like wireless Internet and cable television, plus movie rentals and meals to cook in the room, but also holds campfires, s'more making, and other evening activities during weekends, holidays, and summer months.

Gateways to Mount Rainier

ASHFORD

Don't be fooled by its tiny size, or even the fact that there's no "town" of Ashford at all, just a loose string of business and houses stretched over a few miles of highway. It's the last chance for food and hotels outside Mount Rainier National Park's southwest **Nisqually Entrance,** and the entire area has art, culinary, and outdoor surprises.

Ashford sits in the Nisqually River Valley, anchored by the river that begins on a glacier on Mount Rainier and travels to Puget Sound near Olympia. It's home to two of the three companies that offer guided climbs of Mount Rainier, and it's not unusual to see crowds of mountaineers loading into vans for the drive up to Paradise.

Recycled Spirits of Iron

The **Recycled Spirits of Iron** (Hwy. 706, 4 miles west of Ashford, www.danielklennert.com, hours vary, free) is a singular attraction, one that represents the artistic output of sculptor Dan Klennert. Klennert calls his home collection Ex Nihilo, or "something out of nothing." His works appear throughout the state, but Klennert's home is his greatest accomplishment—the junk he collects in scrap yards and industrial sites has become a lawn of strange animals and dancing figures: a giant seahorse created out of horseshoes and deer and dinosaurs made from salvaged metal and wood. He'll use an animal skull in one sculpture, then take his blowtorch to a rusty old sprocket for another. Entrance to see the approximately 50 sculptures is free, though donation boxes are posted (separate ones for Democrats and Republicans). Opening hours are irregular, mostly when Klennert is around to open the front gates.

Entertainment and Events

The **Rainier Mountain Festival** (30027 Hwy. 706 E, Ashford, 800/238-5756) takes place at "Rainier Base Camp" at Whittaker's Bunkhouse over a weekend in the middle of September, combining a trail run with films, music performances, food, and a gear sale as the guide outfit unloads the stuff it rented to clients all summer. Famous alpine climbers, including the Whittaker brothers, sign books and take photos. You don't have to be a climber to enjoy the festival, but kids can get the mountain bug by ascending the rock wall for free.

It's not all climbing ropes and ice axes in Ashford. The early winter **Mount Rainier Fall Wine Festival** (Mt. Rainier Lions Grand Tasting Hall, 27726 Hwy. 706 E, Ashford, 877/617-9951, www.road-to-paradise.com, Nov. or Dec., $25) celebrates the finer side of mountain life, highlighting Washington wines and microbrews. Entrance to the indoor event comes with a wine glass and tickets for 10 tastes. Children are welcome (to attend, not to drink), and rooms booked in the area during the festival weekend come with one free entry.

Shopping

If you forgot anything important for a hiking trip, like sunglasses or a headlamp, **Whittaker Mountaineering** (30027 Hwy. 706 E, Ashford, 800/238-5756, 7am-8pm Wed.-Mon., 7am-6pm Tues. summer, 9am-5pm daily winter) rents and sells trail gear. But don't be scared off by all the hardcore climbers about the place—they can give advice on taking a small stroll in the Rainier area.

The little red **Painter Art Beads** (30517 Hwy. 706 E, Ashford, 360/569-2644, www.painterartbeads.com) is open irregular hours but has a quirky combination of wares: lots of beads, some crystals, original art by proprietor Joan Painter, and some jewelry—plus a beaded tapestry and the cast of a Bigfoot footprint.

The building that houses **Ashford Creek Pottery** (30510 Hwy. 706 E, Ashford, 360/569-1000, www.ashfordcreekpottery.com, 10am-6pm daily summer, 10am-6pm Sat.-Sun. winter) was once a snowplow shed, but it now holds the works of local potters and painters. One, Dee Molenaar, is a local legend, having penned a well-read history of Rainier and worked as a local guide; his paintings and maps grace many National Park Service brochures and signs. Also find books about the region (sometimes signed when the authors are local), a book room with author portraits, and stained-glass artwork.

Food

The menu at **Copper Creek Restaurant** (35707 Hwy. 706, Ashford, 360/569-2799, www.coppercreekinn.com, 8am-9pm Mon.-Thurs., 7am-9pm Sat.-Sun. summer; 11am-7pm Mon.-Fri., 8am-8pm Sat., 8am-7pm Sun. spring and fall; 11am-7pm Mon. and Thurs.-Fri., 8am-8pm Sat., 8am-7pm Sun. winter, $12-28) has two parts—the part that's blackberry pie, and the part that isn't. The fare is varied, with veggie burgers, biscuits, and gravy to feed hungry hikers, and lemon chicken. The bright red spot, complete with white shutters, first began as a gas station in the 1920s and has been a restaurant since the 1940s, but now its blackberry pies take top billing. They sit on cooling racks near the counter, demanding to be served a la mode. Sure, there are plenty of sweet options, including cinnamon rolls and blackberry butter for the rolls, and the gift shop is full of blackberry syrup and local gifts. But leaving without a slice of pie just seems wrong.

Is it odd to find a Nepali restaurant like **Wildberry** (37718 Hwy. 706, Ashford, 360/569-2277, www.rainierwildberry.com, 11am-8pm daily, $11-30) in the middle of rural Washington State? Not if you consider that Mount Rainier is a training ground for climbers heading to Mount Everest, K2, and other famous climbs in Nepal—and Everest climbing sherpas are known to serve as Rainier mountaineering guides. The fare resembles Indian food in its curries, but with slightly different spices: Sherpa Stew is a thick, meaty concoction with dumplings, and Sherpa Tea is flavored with cardamom and cinnamon. The owners had a restaurant near Mount Everest Base Camp, and they enjoy putting yak on the menu next to American options like burgers and fish. But it's the *thali*-style meals—served on a tray with veggies, rice, a naan-like bread, soup, and other dishes—that warm the belly on a windy Rainier day.

At the Whittaker Motel and Historic Bunkhouse, the **Rainier BaseCamp Grill** (30205 Hwy. 706, Ashford, 360/569-2439, www.whittakersbunkhouse.com, 11am-8pm daily summer only, $7-21) has hardier fare like burgers, pizzas, and beers.

Accommodations

The **Whittaker's Motel and Historic Bunkhouse** (30205 Hwy. 706, Ashford, 360/569-2439, www.whittakersbunkhouse.com, $35 dorms, $90-145 private rooms) is the closest thing to a center of town in Ashford. The complex is made up of several buildings next to "Rainier Base Camp," home base for the climbing guide company Rainier Mountaineering, Inc., started by Lou Whittaker in 1969. He and his wife bought a 1908 bunkhouse used by loggers and millworkers in National, a town three miles away, and moved it to its current location. The bunkhouse beds are popular with Rainier climbers preparing for their ascent and have no bedding, but the other rooms have private baths and normal hotel amenities. The hot tub can help relax post-hike muscles, and the **Whittaker Café** (6:45am-8pm daily summer,

8am-6pm Fri.-Sun. winter) sells coffee and snacks. The national park is just up the road, and several hidden gems are around the property. A tall sculpture, much like a totem pole, towers over the bunkhouse in front, and from a trail behind the parking lot, visitors can reach a tranquil reflecting pool and a memorial to fallen mountain guides made from old ice axes. Follow a trail up the hill about a half mile. It leads to a bench—actually a salvaged ski-mountain chair—overlooking the valley.

The rooms at **Copper Creek Inn** (35707 Hwy. 706 E, Ashford, 360/569-2799, www.coppercreekinn.com, $89-295) have even more to offer than proximity to their restaurant's specialty blackberry pie. One cabin behind the diner is directly on Copper Creek, with two acres of land and no other buildings within sight. Several other cabins have private hot tubs, and some are big enough to sleep 12; other tiny cabins sleep 3 but have detached bathrooms. An art studio cabin even comes with an easel and art supplies, as it was once the studio of a local artist. The cabins are best for couples looking for privacy since there's little to tie the separate buildings together. Suites in the restaurant building itself feel more like a hotel.

When hobbits vacation, they probably go to a place like **Wellspring** (54922 Kernahan Rd. E, Ashford, 360/569-2514, www.wellspringspa.com, $95-195), a collection of cabins in the woods. The dwellings have feather beds and fireplaces, some with lofts and hammocks, and either a full kitchen or kitchenette. It gets even more creative: The Trail's End tent is next to a nature trail (but has a woodstove inside—this isn't roughing it), and the Timbuktu hut is decorated in an African safari theme. The Treehouse is what it sounds like, located 15 feet above the ground and containing a queen bed. Below it is a little patio and private bathroom, but for all its charm, only adults are allowed up.

Wellspring also includes a spa, two outdoor hot tubs, and a sauna (and one guest room that gets exclusive access to a hot tub after dark). A gazebo and wood-fired grill is available for guests hoping to cook dinner outside. A small info board next to the garden out front includes instructions for checking in—and finding the staff around the spacious grounds.

Camping

Campers with reservations make a beeline into the national park for sites at one of its three car campgrounds, but outside the boundaries, other options may be less crowded. The **Big Creek Campground** (Skate Creek Rd., 5 miles south of Hwy. 706, 541/338-7869, www.reserveamerica.com, May-Sept., $18-30) takes reservations and has three pull-through sites for RVs under 22 feet. Located in the Gifford Pinchot National Forest, the campground has thick trees, and some sites abut the burbling Big Creek. Look for the start of the Osbourne Mountain Trail, a route that heads steeply uphill for views of Mount Rainier and the Nisqually Valley.

Getting There

Ashford is 80 miles south of Seattle. From Seattle, take I-5 south for 10 miles and exit onto I-405 North. Once on I-405, take exit 2 onto Highway 167 South. Drive south for a little more than 20 miles, and then take Highway 512 west for 3 miles. Take the Highway 161 exit toward Eatonville; you'll reach that small town in about 23 miles. From Eatonville, turn left onto Center Street, which becomes Alder Cutoff Road. Follow Alder Cutoff Road for 6.5 miles to its junction with Highway 7. Turn left onto Highway 7, which becomes the National Park Highway. In 4.5 miles is the small settlement of Elbe; stay east onto Highway 706 and continue 8 more miles to Ashford.

ELBE

Just a few miles up the road, west of Ashford and the park's **Nisqually Entrance,** is the tiny town of Elbe, good for a coffee stop, train ride, or one of the **last gas stations** before the park.

Mineral Lake Resort

Nearby Mineral Lake is billed as the "Home

of the 10-pound trout" and hosts a popular fishing derby every April. The **Mineral Lake Resort** (148 Mineral Hill Rd., Mineral, 360/492-5367, www.minerallakeresort.com) offers boat rentals ($20-120) and dock fishing, including pole or crayfish pot rental ($5). A bait and tackle shop on the resort's dock also sells snacks and ice. The lake is well stocked with rainbow and steelhead trout, among others, and crayfish are plentiful when the weather is warm. The resort has cabins ($88-108) that come without amenities like bedding or Wi-Fi.

Mount Rainier Scenic Railroad

Mount Rainier Scenic Railroad (54124 Mountain Hwy. E, Elbe, www.mrsr.com, 888/783-2611, $41-54 adults, $21-34 children 4-12, children under 4 free) is a bit of a misnomer. The rails don't get much closer to the peak itself than the actual depot in Elbe. But the "scenic" part of the moniker is no lie. The route to Mineral has views of Rainier, or the closer forested hills when the clouds get in the way. The trip is along a section once used by the Chicago, Milwaukee, St. Paul & Pacific Railroad, and is about 40 minutes each way. You're pulled along by vintage steam locomotives and sit on wood benches in open-air cars when the weather allows. (But this is Washington, after all, so there is an enclosed coach car for the inevitable days of drizzle.) There are also regular themed rides, including a Christmas trip and Civil War history trip. Bring a picnic for the break between the ride to Mineral and back, or indulge your inner rail buff at the train and logging museum, where admission is included for the price of the ticket. It includes an engine you can climb inside and a look at the locomotive restoration being done by the volunteers who largely operate the railway, plus dioramas and tools.

Accommodations

The Ritz it's not. The rooms of the **Hobo Inn** (54106 Hwy. 7, Elbe, 360/569-2500, www.rrdiner.com, $115) are actually individual train cabooses, parked next to the Mount Rainier Scenic Railroad in the whistle-stop town of Elbe. The whimsical little hotel has loads of vintage charm, and you can climb up to look out the cupola lookouts on top of some of the cabooses. But despite some funky touches, inside the rooms can be musty and they have small bathrooms. Breakfast is included—in the dining car, obviously. Skip the dinner here and try something up the road in Ashford.

The **Mineral Lake Lodge** (195 Mineral Hill Rd., Mineral, 360/492-5253, http://minerallakelodge.com, $119-145 shared bath, $157 private bath, no children under 12) is off the beaten path, a three-story hotel built by a Scandinavian out of cedar in 1906. It has served as both sanitarium and gambling hall (and maybe even brothel) in the years when logging, mines, and lumber mills supported the area. Rooms are bed-and-breakfast style, with quilts on the beds and bric-a-brac on the walls. Half have their own bathrooms, and half share the hall bathrooms. Mount Rainier is visible across the lake from the hotel's wraparound porch or fire pit, and a cedar sauna sits out back. The private waterfront and dock are for the hotel, though boat rentals are just down the shore at the public beach. Just across the street is the smallest post office in the continental United States, or what used to be. The wooden structure was built in the 19th century and is little bigger than an outhouse; attached to the now-empty building is a white sign nearly half its size, describing the post office's history.

EATONVILLE

Alder Lake Park

Between Eatonville and Elbe, **Alder Lake Park** (50324 School Rd., Eatonville, 360/569-2778, www.mytpu.org, parking $5 summer) offers water recreation like fishing and boating, plus picnic areas and camping on the seven-mile-long Alder Lake. The giant concrete Alder Dam forms the reservoir, and at 330 feet high, the dam was one of the tallest in the world when it was constructed in 1945. Its turbine generators create electricity for

Tacoma Power. Drive to the end of the road inside the main entrance for a view of the dam. Before that you'll pass almost 50 picnic sites, a playground, a day-use shower house, and a swimming beach (but remember that these waters come from a glacier and certainly are not warm). Boat launches are at this main area and at the Rocky Point Campground, accessed four miles east on Highway 7. The park includes a day-use area at the summer-only Sunny Beach Point, about half a mile south on the highway, with a swimming beach, picnic tables, and grills. The park boasts four **campgrounds** (888/226-7688, $23-33) with a total of 173 sites.

Alder Lake is stocked with kokanee, a kind of sockeye salmon, but also has varieties of crappie, bass, and catfish. Of course, the glacial silt in the lake can complicate things, so plan lures accordingly. Find bait at **Elbe Mall and Sporting Goods** (54011 Hwy. 7 E, Elbe, 360/569-2772, 5am-8pm daily).

Northwest Trek Wildlife Park

Plenty of wild animals roam the Rainier area, but nowhere are they more concentrated than at **Northwest Trek Wildlife Park** (11610 Trek Dr. E, Eatonville, 360/832-6117, www.nwtrek.org, 9:30am-4pm Mon.-Fri., 9:30am-5pm Sat.-Sun. mid-Mar. to June and Sept.-Oct., 9:30am-3pm Fri.-Sun. Nov.-Mar., $22.25 adults, $20.25 seniors, $14.25 children 5-12, $10.25 children 3-4, children under 3 free). The county-run property is dedicated to wildlife conservation through education and, in certain cases, raising animals for release into the wild. Trams drive through a free-range area of almost 500 acres, where bison, mountain goats, elk, and other animals wander freely. The 50-minute ride includes a tour guide, and it's rather like a safari, Washington-style.

Other enclosures dedicated to bears, bobcats, and wolves are viewed from a footpath. Naturalists bring animals out onto three stages for short educational sessions, and a family discovery center provides sheltered exhibits and activities. An old trapper cabin teaches kids about all aspects of wildlife research with computer models and binoculars. A zip line and high-ropes course is strung above the park but requires a reservation and special ticket ($21-70).

Pioneer Farm Museum

The **Pioneer Farm Museum** (7716 Ohop Valley Rd. E, Eatonville, 360/832-6300, www.pioneerfarmmuseum.org, 11:15am-4pm daily mid-June to early Sept., 11:15am-4pm Sat.-Sun. Mar. to mid-June and late Sept.-Nov., $11 adults, $10 seniors and children) promises a "hands-on homestead" that teaches kids about 19th-century settlers' life in the Ohop Valley and the Coast Salish culture that was already well established in the area. Experience the outdoor space through a 90-minute farm tour, and try your hand at working in a blacksmith shop or barn. The 90-minute Ohop Indian Village tour has activities—like bow-and-arrow shooting, dressing up, and jewelry making—for every season of life among the Coast Salish people. The gift shop is in the original 1887 log cabin homestead, but no food is for sale.

GREENWATER AND ENUMCLAW

It's a stretch to call Greenwater a town, with only a handful of buildings visible from the road, plus many more houses and cabins hidden from sight. But it's the only real stop on Highway 140 between the town of Enumclaw and the **White River/Sunrise Entrance** on the northeast side of Mount Rainier National Park. Mountain stops along the way include Crystal Mountain Resort, just outside the park, and Sunrise Visitor Center in the national park proper. Despite its name, Greenwater sits on the White River, which braids through gravel and rock with milky, glacial water. What's green is the forest, which slowly changes from regularly logged parcels to dappled, preserved acres as you approach the national park.

To rent equipment before you hit Crystal Mountain, try **Greenwater Skis** (58703 Hwy.

410 E, Greenwater, 360/663-2235, www.greenwaterskis.com, 8:30am-5pm Mon.-Thurs., 8am-6pm Fri., 7am-6pm Sat.-Sun., $35-50).

Federation Forest State Park

The 619 acres of the **Federation Forest State Park** (Hwy. 410 near milepost 41, 360/902-8844, www.parks.wa.gov, 8am-dusk daily summer, closed winter) are some of the best places to see classic old-growth Washington forest, thick with Douglas firs, western hemlock, and western red cedar. The park was protected with help from the General Federation of Women's Clubs in the mid-1940s. Nature trails leave from the interpretive center, and a picnic area sits next to the White River. On the Hobbit Trail or Naches Trail, find the **Hobbit House,** remnants of a tiny children's village, complete with a small mailbox and little fences. (It's not easy to find, located on a poorly maintained trail, so keep your eyes peeled.) The park is located on Highway 410, about 16 miles east of Enumclaw.

Suntop Lookout

The **Suntop Lookout** (Mount Baker-Snoqualmie National Forest, Forest Road 7315, near milepost 49 on Highway 410, parking $5) is no easy viewpoint—it's a 10-mile drive up to a point more than 5,000 feet in elevation, just 10 miles from Mount Rainier. The structure was built in the early 1930s and has a picnic area adjacent to it. On a clear day, you can see the Olympic Mountains and Mount Baker near the Canadian border. Just don't look down because the drop off one side is about 3,000 feet. Suntop is one of the few fire lookouts that can be reached by car, but only in the summer—once the road closes in winter, you'll need snowshoes or cross-country skis.

Mountain Biking

The rough terrain around Mount Rainier provides plenty of challenge to any level of biker. Rent wheels at **Enumclaw Ski and Mountain Sports** (240 Roosevelt Ave. E, Enumclaw, 360/825-6910, http://skiandbicycle.com, 10am-6pm Mon.-Fri., 9am-4pm Sat., 10am-3pm Sun. summer, 7:30am-6pm Mon.-Fri., 7am-6pm Sat.-Sun. winter, $35-55 per day). Then head to **Mud Mountain Dam Park** (Mud Mountain Rd., www.nws.usace.army.mil, 9am-4pm Mon.-Fri.), a recreational area with a rim trail popular with experienced bikers. Bikes can roll down the ski trails on Crystal Mountain during the summer but aren't allowed on the gondola, so bikers must earn the downhill trip with a serious pedal up.

Wapiti Woolies

Just try walking out of **Wapiti Woolies** (58414 Hwy. 410, Greenwater, 360/663-2268, www.wapitiwoolies.com, 9am-6pm Mon.-Fri., 8am-7pm Sat.-Sun.) without a hat. The store used to make its own custom hats and still carries some headwear under its own name, but now it carries racks of hats from many brands, many in the ear-flap style reminiscent of Scandinavia. Look for pictures on the wall of mountain climbers and professional skiers who have worn Wapiti creations on ascents in the Himalayas or Alaska. The store also carries other outdoor wear, including sweaters, and has a café in back serving coffee and ice cream.

Getting There

Enumclaw lies 40 miles southeast of Seattle. From Seattle, take I-5 South for 10 miles to I-405 North and continue 2 miles. Exit onto Highway 167 South and continue south for a little less than 20 miles. Take the Highway 410 East exit, and stay on Highway 410 for 15 miles to reach Enumclaw. Greenwater is 21 miles farther south on Highway 410.

From Sunrise, Greenwater is about 13 miles north of the national park exit, and Enumclaw lies another 21 miles farther north. From Sunrise, follow Highway 410 West out of the park; the road from Sunrise to the park boundary is only open May-November. Highway 410 from the park boundary north is open year-round and is usually in good condition, since skiers make their way to nearby Crystal Mountain even during the biggest snows.

PACKWOOD

There's absolutely nothing fancy about Packwood, but it serves as an entry point to all kinds of recreation—skiing, hunting, fishing, and hiking—at the southeast **Ohanapecosh Entrance** to the park. The town was named for William Packwood, one of the first Caucasian people in the area, who came with James Longmire to trace a wagon road across the Cascade Mountains. The area is known for its communities of elk, which graze around town. A large flea market takes place every Labor Day all around town.

White Pass Country Museum

The **White Pass Country Museum** (12990 Hwy. 12, 360/494-4422, Packwood, www.whitepasscountrymuseum.org, noon-5pm Thurs.-Sat. summer, noon-4pm Sat. winter, $2 adults, $1 children) has small-town charm but is little more than a repository for a handful of local artifacts. But the story pole outside is a lovely artwork made by a local chainsaw artist, topped with a snow goose to represent a local Native American elder who lived to be 115 years old. Look for a bearded man, meant to be the town's namesake.

White Pass Ski Area

Originally a small family mountain, the **White Pass Ski Area** (48935 Hwy. 12, Naches, 509/672-3100, www.skiwhitepass.com, $63 adults, $43 children 7-15, $5 children under 7 and seniors over 73) was expanded in late 2010, making it one of the state's bigger ski destinations. The resort has a terrain park, night skiing, and ski rentals ($32 adults, $22 seniors and children). Directly across the highway is a network of 11 miles of groomed Nordic trails ($15), departing on the side of Leech Lake (prettier than it sounds). Rent skis or snowshoes ($14-19 adults, $14 seniors and children), take a lesson ($45 including rental), and get trail information at the yurt near the parking lot.

Morton Logging Jubilee

The early August **Morton Logging Jubilee** (451 Knittles Way, Morton, 360/523-4049, www.loggersjubilee.com) is billed as "The Granddaddy of All Logging Shows." It began in the 1930s, celebrating the area's biggest industry. It kicks off with the coronation of the Queen and then has a 10K run, bed races, a grand parade, and a street dance. The festival includes lawnmower races through a track lined with hay bales, a tradition that's decades old—the event actually includes time trials, and according to the official rules, "brakes are legal, but not mandatory." And, of course, there is the logging show, with speed climbing, tree topping, logrolling, axe throwing, and more.

Food

In the small town of Packwood, **Blue Spruce Saloon** (13019 Hwy. 12, Packwood, 360/494-5605, 11am-midnight Mon.-Thurs., 6am-2am Fri.-Sat., 6am-midnight Sun., $9-12) is the destination for anyone in desperate need of straightforward burgers, beer, or both. The jukebox plays classics, the liquor pours are generous, and the special sauce on the burgers elevates the grub just above normal dive-bar status (but don't try the Bigfoot one-pound burger unless you're really, really hungry). The joint serves breakfast on weekend mornings, but for the best ambience, try to hit it on a karaoke night.

The pies are straightforward at **Cruiser's Pizza** (13028 Hwy. 12, Packwood, 360/494-5400, www.eatcruiserspizza.com, 9am-9pm Mon.-Fri., 8am-10pm Sat., 8am-9pm Sun., $10-26)—though the cashews on the Packwood Special is a bit unusual, and the restaurant itself is pretty bare, with counter service and arcade games. The rest of the menu includes everything from a fishwich to gizzards, but stick with a burger or pizza.

A good coffee joint like **Mountain Goat Coffee Company** (105 E Main St., Packwood, 360/494-5600, 7am-5pm daily, $1-4) is essential in any mountain town, but this hometown joint also delivers creative savory scones and fresh muffins baked on-site, and sells local crafts that hang on the walls. A long wooden bench sits outside, near where a farm stand sets up in the warm months.

Accommodations

Built in 1912, the **Hotel Packwood** (104 Main St., Packwood, 360/494-5431, www.packwoodwa.com, $29-49 shared bath, $49 private bath) has all the trappings of a vintage property—wraparound veranda, wood siding, and mostly shared bathrooms. Rooms are very sparse, but the iron beds add a tiny touch of charm, and elk are known to wander through the parking lot.

The **Cowlitz River Lodge** (13069 Hwy. 12, Packwood, 360/494-4444, www.escapetothemountains.com, $90-130) excels in straightforward motel style: basic rooms and adequate service. A fireplace in the lobby spruces up the place, and the location is just removed enough from the road that you don't quite feel like you're sleeping on the highway. The hotel has wireless Internet and laundry facilities.

With pillars made from river rock out front, the **Crest Trail Lodge** (12729 Hwy. 12, Packwood, 800-477-5339, http://whitepasstravel.com/cresttrail, $129-139) is a cheery addition to the small town of Packwood. Free breakfast includes waffles, biscuits and gravy, and other hot offerings, and complimentary nightcaps are poured in the evening.

Camping

Although the name of the **1896 Homestead** (U.S. 12 and Huntington Rd., 360/496-8283, www.packwoodonline.com, $15) sounds pastoral, it's a sparse parking spot for RVs, but elk sometimes wander the area. Flea markets crowd the site on Memorial Day and Labor Day weekends. Some parking spots are directly next to the (very tiny) Packwood Airport.

La Wis Wis Campground (U.S. 12, 5 miles east of Packwood and right before the national park entrance, 541/338-7869, www.reserveamerica.com, May-Sept., $20-38) has a whopping 122 sites, including a few walk-in tent sites away from the fray. The narrow parking spots and lack of hookups discourage most RV drivers, so the campground is largely tent campers. The most popular sites are those directly on the Ohanapecosh River. Reservations can be made online.

Getting There

Packwood lies almost 12 miles south of the Ohanapecosh Entrance on U.S. 12. To reach the entrance, take U.S. 12 north for 7.5 miles and turn left onto Highway 123 (road closed Nov.-May). Follow Highway 123 north for 3.5 miles to the turnoff for Ohanapecosh Campground.

To reach Packwood from Portland (70 miles) or Seattle (97 miles), take I-5 to exit 68 and follow U.S. 12 east for 64.5 miles to Packwood.

Mount St. Helens

Mount Rainier is no simple lump of rock. It's an active volcano, one of the largest in the country. What does that mean? Just ask any local about May 18, 1980, when nearby Mount St. Helens erupted—and consider that Mount Rainier could do the same.

Mount St. Helens is located 35 miles south of Mount Rainier and is a somewhat smaller 8,365 feet to Rainier's 14,410 feet. In March 1980, steam and ash started spitting out the peak of St. Helens, and a bulge—signifying an upcoming eruption—formed on the side. On May 18 the hot magma erupted out of the mountain, along with hot gas and rock. Trees for 6 miles were flattened like dominos, and an ash cloud traveled 15 miles up. Ash fell like snow all over the state (and as far east as the Great Plains), and lahars—volcanic mudslides—rushed down river valleys. The resulting landscape looked something like the surface of the moon, and St. Helens went from a pointy peak to a wide, flat crater.

Although 57 people were killed by the eruption, the most famous casualty was Harry Truman (no relation to the 33rd U.S. president). Truman was a cantankerous 83-year-old who refused to leave his lodge (or his 16 cats) at Spirit Lake, near the base of the volcano. He gave a number of interviews in the months before the eruption as experts begged him to leave, but his responses were mostly too laden with profanity to print or air.

Today Mount St. Helens is a **National Volcanic Monument** (www.fs.usda.gov/mountsthelens) administered by the forest service. There's no fee to access the area.

WEST SIDE

Highway 504 (Spirit Lake Highway) runs more than 50 miles from I-5 to the base of Mount St. Helens near Spirit Lake, and is the most popular route into the monument. The road was reconstructed after the eruption, and moved farther off the valley floor in order to avoid destruction in case of a future event. The route from I-5 runs mostly through the rural countryside and over bridges that cross the Toutle River. Approximately 25 miles from I-5, the volcano appears. Notice how smaller trees and a land shaped by mudflows show evidence of the 1980 blast zone.

In 20 miles, the road passes Coldwater Lake and begins to climb amid the rocky hillsides. It ends more than 4,200 feet above sea level at Johnston Ridge. From this viewpoint, you can see not just the outer profile of the mountain, but the crater that formed in the middle, 5 miles away.

In winter, Highway 504 closes after Coldwater Lake, near milepost 45.

Visitors Centers

A visit to Mount St. Helens National Volcanic Monument today shows just how much the landscape has recovered in the last few decades and how the land also still holds scars. The **Weyerhaeuser Forest Learning Center** (Milepost 33, Hwy. 504, www.weyerhaeuser.com, 10am-4pm Fri.-Wed. May-Sept., free) was opened by the Weyerhaeuser logging company to highlight the company's replanting efforts, and is a good spot for viewing elk. With the closing of a county-owned visitors center in 2017, the best stop is the state-run **Mount St. Helens Visitor Center** (3029 Spirit Lake Hwy.,

Mount St. Helens

Mount St. Helens National Volcanic Monument

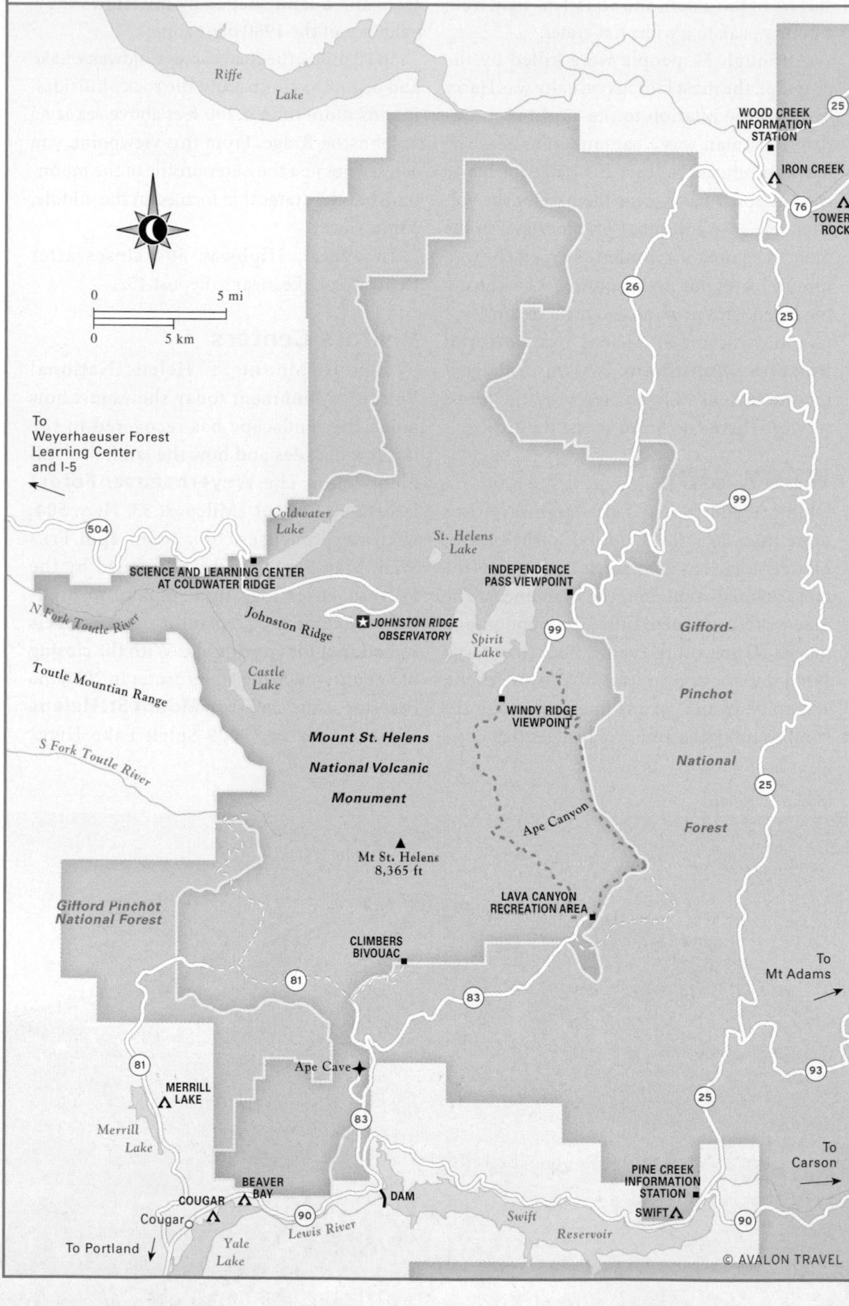
Riffe
Lake
WOOD CREEK
INFORMATION
STATION
IRON CREEK
TOWER
ROCK
25
76
26
0
5 mi
0
5 km
To
Weyerhaeuser Forest
Learning Center
and I-5
504
Coldwater
Lake
St. Helens
Lake
99
SCIENCE AND LEARNING CENTER
AT COLDWATER RIDGE
INDEPENDENCE
PASS VIEWPOINT
N Fork Toutle River
Johnston Ridge
JOHNSTON RIDGE
OBSERVATORY
Spirit
Lake
Gifford-
Castle
Lake
Toutle Mountian Range
WINDY RIDGE
VIEWPOINT
Pinchot
Mount St. Helens
National Volcanic
Monument
S Fork Toutle River
National
Ape Canyon
Forest
Mt St. Helens
8,365 ft
Gifford Pinchot
National Forest
LAVA CANYON
RECREATION AREA
CLIMBERS
BIVOUAC
81
83
To
Mt Adams
Ape Cave
93
MERRILL
LAKE
Merrill
Lake
To
Carson
BEAVER
BAY
PINE CREEK
INFORMATION
STATION
COUGAR
DAM
Cougar
90
Swift
SWIFT
Reservoir
Lewis River
To Portland
Yale
Lake
© AVALON TRAVEL

Castle Rock, 360/274-0962, http://parks.state.wa.us/245/Mount-St-Helens, 9am-4pm daily Mar. 1-May 15 and Sept. 16-Oct. 31, 9am-5pm daily May 16-Sept. 15, 9am-4pm Thurs.-Mon. Nov. 1-Feb. 28, $5 adults, $2.50 children 7-17, children under 7 free) in Silver Lake, which has a seismograph and step-in model of the volcano.

Coldwater Lake

Anglers and kayakers dot the surface of Coldwater Lake (Hwy. 504, 45 miles east of I-5). The lake was created when the eruption reshaped the Washington topography. To understand the process that created the lake, walk along the **Birth of a Lake Interpretive Trail,** a brief 0.5 mile with illustrated signs.

Access to the trails, picnic area, and lake is $8 per person per day. Fishing for rainbow trout is restricted to anglers with single barbless hooks and in boats without gasoline motors, and limited to only one fish more than 16 inches long. A state license is required.

Mount St. Helens Science and Learning Center

The **Mount St. Helens Science and Learning Center** (19000 Spirit Lake Hwy., 360/274-2114, www.mshslc.org, 10am-6pm Sat.-Sun. mid-May to Nov., 10am-4pm Sat.-Sun. winter, weather permitting) at Coldwater is mostly used for education programs and private events, but there is an information desk in the building and picnic areas outside. The center is located at milepost 43 on Highway 504. Snowfall may close the road, but Highway 504 is usually open as far as Coldwater Lake.

★ Johnston Ridge Observatory

At the very end of Spirit Lake Highway is the site where USGS volcanologist David Johnston was camping when Mount St. Helens blew its top. The **Johnston Ridge Observatory** (24000 Spirit Lake Hwy., 360/274-2140, www.fs.usda.gov, 10am-6pm daily mid-May to Oct., $8 adults, children under 15 free) has videos about the eruption and a giant viewing deck where you can see the lava dome and crater (pay your entrance fee before you start snapping photos). A light-up model of the mountain shows where and how the lava flowed, and some displays focus on the serious and catastrophic loss of life in the area. Outside, an amphitheater with fantastic views holds summer music concerts.

Johnston Ridge Observatory

Hiking

HUMMOCKS TRAIL

Distance: 2.4 miles round-trip
Duration: 1.5 hours
Elevation gain: 100 feet
Effort: easy
Trailhead: 2.2 miles past the Mount St. Helens Science and Learning Center

Named for the steep hills and mounds formed by the debris as it moved through the valley after the eruption, the Hummocks Trail is a popular loop route for kids who need a break on the long drive to the mountain. There are interpretive signs along the first 0.25 mile, and then the trail winds through ponds and wetlands—and the hummocks. Look for elk and birds on the trail.

ERUPTION TRAIL

Distance: 0.5 mile round-trip
Duration: 0.5 hour
Elevation gain: 25 feet
Effort: easy
Trailhead: main parking lot at Johnston Ridge Observatory

This paved trail from the end-of-the-road visitors center shows off not only the lava dome and crater, but the plain of pumice (or volcanic rock) that formed from the eruption, as well as the landslides. Look for informational placards and a memorial to those who died in the blast, as well as wildflowers in the dry, ashy dirt.

Getting There

Access to the west side of Mount St. Helens is from I-5, 57 miles north of Portland and 116 miles south of Seattle. From I-5, take exit 49 to the town of Castle Rock, and then follow Highway 504 east for approximately 50 miles to the Johnson Ridge Observatory.

To reach the Johnston Ridge Observatory area on the west side of Mount St. Helens from Mount Rainier, exit the national park through the Nisqually Entrance and follow Highway 706 for 10 miles to the town of Elbe. Turn left onto Highway 7 and follow it south for 17 miles to U.S. 12, then drive 31 miles west to I-5 South. Stay on the interstate for only one exit, exiting 5 miles south at Highway 505. Follow Highway 505 and signs for 16 miles to Highway 504, then turn left and take winding Highway 504 for 37 miles to the Johnston Ridge Observatory. The drive takes about three hours without traffic.

SOUTH SIDE

Highway 503 offers access to recreational activities on the south side of Mount St. Helens. The town of **Cougar,** about 30 miles east of I-5 on Highway 503, serves as a base for trips to Lava Canyon and the Ape Caves, plus has permits and access for climbers attempting to summit Mount St. Helens.

Visitors Centers

The **Pine Creek Information Station** (15311 Forest Rd. 90, Cougar, 9am-6pm daily May-Sept.) is a summer-only stop located about 18 miles east of Cougar. Volunteers offer maps and guidance for visiting the south side of Mount St. Helens, and picnic areas and restrooms are available (only open seasonally), as well as a spot to buy bottled water. Some trails in the area require recreation passes, which can be obtained here as well.

Ape Cave

The **Ape Cave Lava Tube** (Forest Rd. 8303, www.fs.usda.gov/mountsthelens, 10am-5pm daily June-Sept., $5 parking, $5 lantern rental) is the third-longest lava tube in North America. A trip here offers evidence that lava has been carving up this landscape for almost 2,000 years.

Inside the cave, unaccompanied visitors usually walk the muddy floor of the **Lower Cave Trail** (1.6 miles round-trip). The more difficult **Upper Ape Cave Trail** (3 miles round-trip) includes an eight-foot lava fall and a "skylight" hole that opens to the surface.

A light source is required for trips into the cave, so visitors should bring one flashlight per person (rangers suggest two) or rent a lantern during summer. It gets cold underground, so wear layers and sturdy shoes.

To prevent the spread of white-nose syndrome (a bat disease), rangers are on hand to encourage visitors to decontaminate their shoes and clothing.

To reach Ape Cave from Cougar, follow Forest Road 90 east for 3 miles. Turn left onto Forest Road 83 and continue approximately 1.5 miles to Forest Road 8303. Turn left and drive 1 mile to the Ape Cave entrance. In winter, cars must park at the Trail of Two Forests trailhead and hike 1 mile to the cave.

Lava Canyon

Lava Canyon operates as a trailhead and interpretive site, with a viewpoint that overlooks Mount St. Helens, a canyon, and a waterfall. From the viewing platform, look for the layers of lava from an ancient eruption. It's a steep walk back up the paved trail to the parking lot.

To reach Lava Canyon from Cougar, follow Forest Road 90 east for 3 miles. Turn left onto Forest Road 83 and continue for 15 miles. The last 15 minutes of this drive can take the better part of an hour because of the small wilderness roads. A recreation pass is required to park here.

Hiking

TRAIL OF TWO FORESTS

Distance: 0.25 mile round-trip
Duration: 20 minutes
Elevation gain: none
Effort: easy
Trailhead: one mile before Ape Cave, right at the intersection of Forest Roads 83 and 8303

While visiting the Ape Cave Lava Tube, add a boardwalk stroll along the Trail of Two Forests. The short trail shows off the old-growth Douglas fir forest as well as the recovering forest that grew after the 1980 eruption. The parking lot is open year-round and serves as the trailhead to the Ape Cave in the winter. A parking fee or recreation pass is required.

JUNE LAKE

Distance: 2.8 miles round-trip
Duration: 2 hours
Elevation gain: 450 feet
Effort: moderate
Trailhead: Forest Road 83, about 10 miles from its junction with Forest Road 90

There's little elevation gain to June Lake, but it passes through forests and lava flows. A 70-foot waterfall tumbles into the lake at about 1.3 miles into the hike. Unlike many stops in the area, access here does not require a parking pass.

Climbing

How do you summit a mountain that no longer has a summit? Thousands of people do it every year at Mount St. Helens, ascending to the crater rim at 8,365 feet. The climb itself is nontechnical, but it's a strenuous trip that can take anywhere from 7-12 hours. In winter, the snow cornices around the crater are very dangerous, and anyone in the area should be prepared for ash fall.

Permits ($22 Apr.-Oct., free Nov.-Mar.) are required for every climb above 4,800 feet and can be purchased online from the **Mount St. Helens Institute** (http://mshinstitute.org), which also offers guided climbs ($225-300). For climbing April-October, permits must be secured in advance; permits typically go on sale in February and sell out. If you're lucky enough to score one, you can pick up your permit at **Lone Fir Resort** (16806 Lewis River Rd., Cougar, 360/238-5210, www.lonefirresort.com). In winter, self-registration is required.

Those attempting a climb in the summer start their trek at the **Climbers Bivouac Trailhead.** To reach the trailhead from I-5, take Highway 503/Lewis River Road east for 31 miles, then turn onto Forest Road 90 and continue 3.5 miles. Turn left onto Forest Road 83 and drive 3 miles, turning left onto Forest Road 81. Continue 1.7 miles, then turn onto the gravel Forest Road 830 and look for the trailhead sign 2.5 miles farther. Note that some roads close in winter.

Camping

There is no camping within the Mount St. Helens National Volcanic Monument, which encompasses the mountain, Spirit Lake, and much of the surrounding area to the north, including Coldwater Lake. Most area camping is found outside the monument borders on the South Side. Privately managed **Cougar Park & Campground** (reservations accepted at 360/238-5251, www.pacificorp.com, Memorial Day-Labor Day, $21) has 45 sites for tents or RVs and one group site, as well as showers, a boat ramp, and a swimming area in the Yale Reservoir. **Beaver Bay Camp** (503/813-6666, www.pacificorp.com, late Apr.-Sept., $21) has 63 tent sites and one group site, as well as a swimming area and showers. All sites are first-come, first-served. Both camps are located on Highway 503/Lewis River Road about 34 miles east of I-5, just past the town of Cougar. Alcohol is not permitted at either location.

Merrill Lake Campground (www.dnr.wa.gov, spring-fall) is located in the town of Ariel, north of Cougar. This walk-in campground has nine tent sites and a day-use area with a boat launch and picnic area. All sites are first-come, first-served, and there is no drinking water. From the town of Cougar, follow Forest Road 81 north for almost 6 miles to the Merrill Lake Campground. A state recreation pass (866/320-9933, www.discoverpass.wa.gov, $10 one day, $30 annual) is required.

Getting There

Mount St. Helens and the town of Cougar, Washington, are approximately 50 miles northeast of Portland, Oregon. From Portland, take I-5 north for 29 miles to Woodland, Washington. Take exit 21 for Highway 503 (or Lewis River Road) and follow it as it heads east along the Lewis River, passing Lake Merwin and Yale Lake before reaching the small town of Cougar in 28 miles.

To reach the south side of Mount St. Helens from Mount Rainier, exit the national park through the Nisqually Entrance and follow Highway 706 for 10 miles to the town of Elbe. Turn left onto Highway 7 and follow it south for 17 miles to U.S. 12, then drive 31 miles west to I-5 South. Stay on the interstate for 45 miles heading south to the town of Woodland, taking exit 22 for the Old Pacific Highway and driving west for 1 mile. Turn left on East Scott Avenue, and then immediately take a left on Lewis River Road, also known as Highway 503. Follow it for 27.5 miles to the town of Cougar. Without traffic, it takes about 2.5 hours to reach Cougar from the edge of Mount Rainier National Park.

At one point, Highway 503 bends south, but signed traffic toward Mount St. Helens continues straight on Lewis River Road. Lewis River Road becomes Forest Road 90 just past Cougar; 3 miles farther, Forest Road 83 breaks left and heads north toward the mountain. Forest Road 90 is plowed and remains open well past the Forest Road 83 cutoff (to around Pine Creek Information Center) in winter, but big snows can affect access. Forest Road 83 is open to past Ape Cave year-round and provides access to sno-parks, but often closes before the June Lake trailhead.

The North Cascades

North of U.S. 2 and upward toward Washington's border with Canada you'll discover the wild region known as the North Cascades. More difficult to access, it rewards adventurous travelers with the remote wonders of North Cascades National Park, as well as charming mountain towns, scenic lakes, and the recreational paradise of the Methow Valley.

NORTH CASCADES NATIONAL PARK

Of Washington State's three national parks, the North Cascades is the newest and wildest. Incorporated in 1968, it's made up of more than half a million acres at the top of the state's Cascade mountain range, with two protected recreation areas, Ross Lake and Lake Chelan, on either side. More than 300 glaciers are tucked into its remote spaces, but only a few trails and buildings. This is the wild West.

Up here, the mountains are tall, jagged peaks lined with thick forests of evergreen, but the east and west sides feel distinct. On the west the park is lush and damp, while the east side has a dry, sunny feel. A highway runs through the park, but most of its miles of forest are inaccessible to most people, though the drive itself, looking over crystal-blue lakes and up at snowcapped peaks, is a destination.

But don't let the rugged nature of North Cascades National Park intimidate you. With far fewer visitors than Mount Rainier or Olympic National Parks, it gives curious comers access to the great outdoors with few or no crowds.

Visiting the Park

North Cascades National Park sprawls over the north-central section of the state and is best understood by the road that runs through it—**Highway 20,** also known as the **North Cascades Highway,** which cuts east-west through the park—and the two long and skinny bodies of water that stick out above and below, lakes Ross and Chelan. Though the **Ross Lake National Recreation Area** and **Lake Chelan National Recreation Area**

the North Cascades

The North Cascades

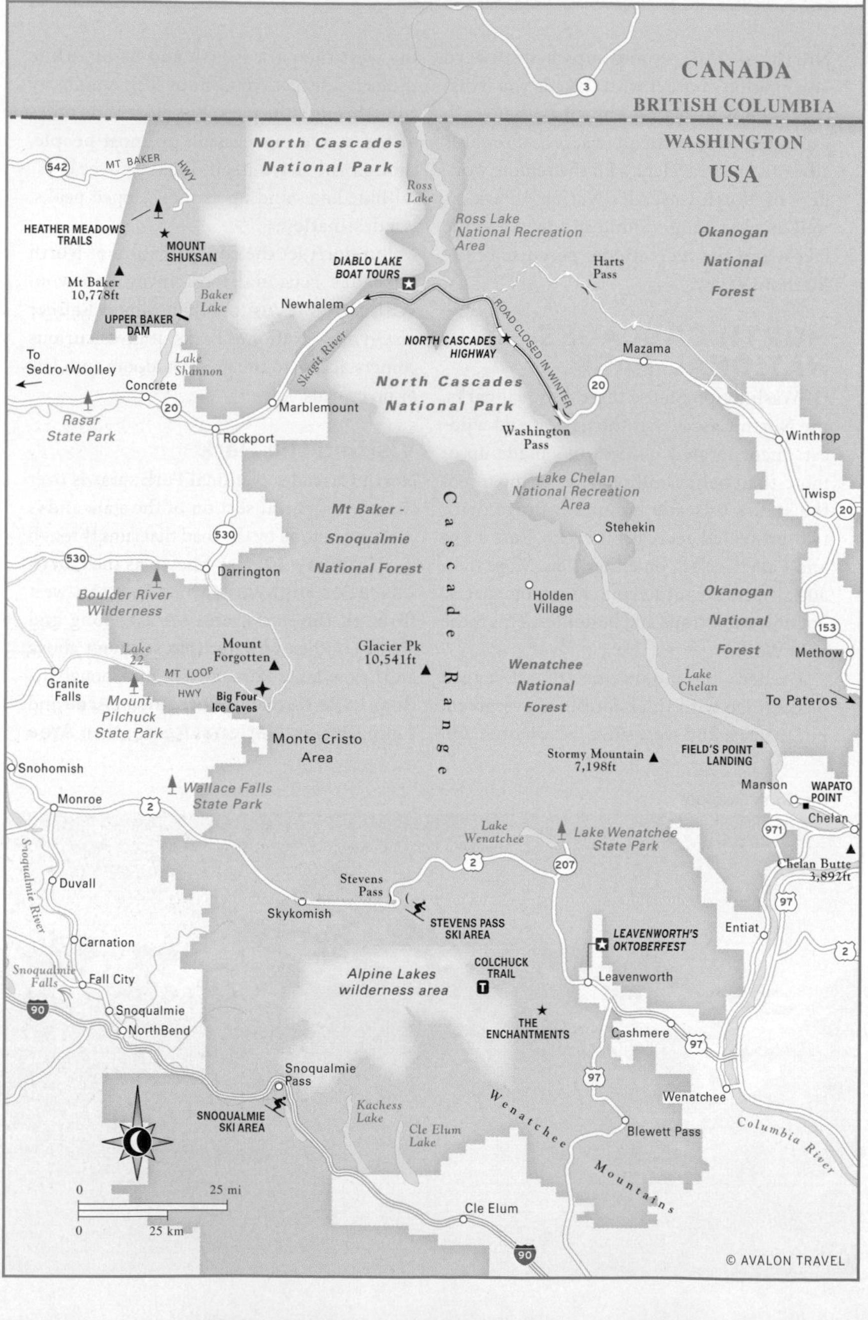
CANADA
BRITISH COLUMBIA
WASHINGTON
USA
North Cascades National Park
Ross Lake
Ross Lake National Recreation Area
Okanogan National Forest
MT BAKER HWY
HEATHER MEADOWS TRAILS
MOUNT SHUKSAN
Mt Baker 10,778ft
Baker Lake
UPPER BAKER DAM
DIABLO LAKE BOAT TOURS
Newhalem
Harts Pass
ROAD CLOSED IN WINTER
NORTH CASCADES HIGHWAY
Mazama
To Sedro-Woolley
Lake Shannon
Skagit River
Concrete
Rasar State Park
Marblemount
Rockport
North Cascades National Park
Washington Pass
Winthrop
Lake Chelan National Recreation Area
Twisp
Mt Baker - Snoqualmie National Forest
Cascade Range
Stehekin
Darrington
Boulder River Wilderness
Holden Village
Okanogan National Forest
Methow
Mount Forgotten
Glacier Pk 10,541ft
Wenatchee National Forest
Lake 22
MT LOOP HWY
Granite Falls
Mount Pilchuck State Park
Big Four Ice Caves
Lake Chelan
To Pateros
Monte Cristo Area
Stormy Mountain 7,198ft
FIELD'S POINT LANDING
Snohomish
Wallace Falls State Park
Manson
WAPATO POINT
Monroe
Chelan
Lake Wenatchee
Lake Wenatchee State Park
Chelan Butte 3,892ft
Snoqualmie River
Duvall
Stevens Pass
Skykomish
STEVENS PASS SKI AREA
Entiat
Carnation
LEAVENWORTH'S OKTOBERFEST
COLCHUCK TRAIL
Leavenworth
Snoqualmie Falls
Fall City
Alpine Lakes wilderness area
Snoqualmie
NorthBend
THE ENCHANTMENTS
Cashmere
Snoqualmie Pass
Wenatchee
SNOQUALMIE SKI AREA
Kachess Lake
Cle Elum Lake
Wenatchee Mountains
Blewett Pass
Columbia River
0 25 mi
0 25 km
Cle Elum
© AVALON TRAVEL

have slightly different rules and protections, they are functionally part of North Cascades National Park to the casual visitor (perhaps the biggest distinction is that dogs are allowed on trails in some of the recreation areas). Unlike, say, Mount Rainier National Park, there's no obvious center or signature section of the park; every corner has its own wonder and appeal, though sections off Highway 20 are the most accessible.

Access to the North Cascades is very limited in winter. Highway 20 closes every year from milepost 134-171 when snows start to fall; the danger of avalanches and heavy snowfall aren't compatible with winter drivers. The closure usually lasts from mid-November-mid-April, though dates can vary drastically depending on snowfall. Updates on opening progress are posted on the **Department of Transportation website** (www.wsdot.wa.gov).

VISITORS CENTERS

The biggest visitors center in the park is the **North Cascades Visitor Center** (Hwy. 20 near milepost 120, 206/386-4495, www.nps.gov/noca, 9am-5pm daily mid-May-Sept., 9am-5pm Sat.-Sun. Mar.-mid-May), near the small town of Newhalem. It's right off the highway but you'll drive across the Skagit River to reach it; a one-way bridge is controlled by a traffic light. Inside, you can learn about the park via nature exhibits and videos, and rangers can also give advice. A relief map provides a 3D look at the park.

Other North Cascades visitors centers are on the fringes of the park or in very remote locations, largely serving as permit and information stations for serious backcountry trekkers.

ENTRANCE STATIONS

Highway 20 cuts east-west through the park, allowing the easiest access into it. There are no entrance stations at North Cascades National park, as it's free to enter. However, note that parking in some of the regions surrounding the park, like national forests or state parks, may require permits or day-use fees.

Highway 20 (North Cascades Highway)

Also known as the North Cascades Highway, Highway 20 is one of the most gorgeous in the western United States, and driving it is an attraction in itself. The 88-mile, two-lane drive from **Marblemount** on the western side of the Cascades to **Winthrop** on the eastern side takes you through lush greenery, up narrow mountain passes, and past glistening Diablo and Ross Lakes before descending into the scenic Methow Valley. It takes about two hours to drive without stops, but you'll definitely want to stop—on a clear day, the photogenic landscape is impossible to deny. At any rate, it's a scenic treat and, with hairpin turns and winding sections, it's best to take it slowly. About 57 miles in, be sure to stop at the overlook at **Washington Pass,** where the road takes a sharp turn and the eastern slopes of the Cascades open to a spectacular view, including classic mountains like Early Winter Spire and Liberty Bell.

Newhalem Dam Tours

Newhalem is a company town created by Seattle City Light to oversee the dams built here on the Skagit River to harness the power of glacial meltwater as it tumbles downhill, west to Puget Sound. It's home to the **Gorge Powerhouse,** a stately building with giant windows looming over the river. You can find information at the **Gorge Powerhouse Visitor Gallery** (9am-4pm daily May-Sept.), on the east end of town by the bridge park. Short trails circle the garden area outside the powerhouse, one with a view of Ladder Creek Falls. At night an LED light show illuminates the falls (dusk-11pm summer).

Powerhouse Insider tours (360/854-2589, www.seattle.gov/light/damtours, 10am daily late June-early Sept., $20 adults, $18 seniors, $15 children 10-12) offer a guided peek around town and into the generator floor of the power plant, with lunch included afterward. Reservations are required, and note that children under 10 aren't allowed. Or take the **Dam Good Chicken Dinner and Ladder Creek Falls by Night tour** (www.seattle.gov/light/damtours, 7pm-10pm Thurs.-Fri. late June-early Sept., $19 adults, $14 children 6-12, $5 children under 6) for a meal in Newhalem followed by a slideshow presentation on the growth of hydroelectric power and then a guided ramble to the waterfalls. Reserve in advance online or at the **Skagit Information Center** (360/854-2589, www.seattle.gov/light/damtours/local.asp, 9am-5pm Fri.-Sun. June and Sept., 9am-5pm daily July-Aug.). You can also skip the dinner and just join the slideshow and tour for free.

Ross Lake and Diablo Lake

The two central bodies of water in the far North Cascades, Diablo Lake and Ross Lake, seem to brim with natural beauty. But the lakes are reservoirs formed by two Skagit River dams, one named for each lake. Still, they're lovely to look at. Both are part of the Ross Lake National Recreation Area, operated by North Cascades National Park and functionally part of the park.

Diablo Lake's water shines a brilliant turquoise in sunlight, and its shoreline is publicly accessible at **Colonial Creek Campground** (Hwy. 20 at milepost 130), where there's a dock and boat launch. But note that even in the height of summer, the lake's waters are incredibly cold.

Ross Lake, just northeast, is much larger, a skinny body of water 23 miles long stretching past Highway 20 up to the Canadian border. The waterway is known for boating. **Ross Lake Resort** (Hwy. 20 near milepost 127, 206/386-4437, www.rosslakeresort.com, June-Oct.) rents motorboats, canoes, and kayaks to explore the lake ($40-125 per day) as well as fishing rods and tackle ($20 per day). Reservations are recommended for day users looking to rent equipment, about a week in advance for most weekend days.

★ DIABLO LAKE BOAT TOURS

Seattle City Light offers **Diablo Lake Boat Tours** (360/854-2589, www.seattle.gov/light/damtours/diablotours.asp) on the *Alice Ross IV*, which has both indoor and outdoor seating and cruises in leisurely fashion around the lake. While the tour includes plenty of stories about the area's crucial industry, consider this primarily a nature-viewing boat tour with some cool dam views and stories thrown in. You'll learn, for instance, how

Ross Lake

Diablo Lake

the giant hydroelectric project came to be, about colorful project founder J. D. Ross, and how Monkey Island in the middle of Diablo Lake got its name (hint: Ross borrowed a few creatures from a zoo to keep him company). But more importantly you'll gain a special vantage from the scenic lake, surrounded by thick forest populated with wildlife—like deer, bald eagles, sometimes even bears—including glimpses of hidden waterfalls and vistas.

Morning cruises (10:30am Thurs.-Mon. late June-mid-Sept., 10:30am Sat.-Sun. mid-Sept.-late Sept., $42 adults, $40 seniors, $21 children 3-12, free for children under 3), which include lunch, last 3.25 hours. **Afternoon cruises** (1:30pm Fri.-Sun. late June-early Sept., $30 adults, $28 seniors, $15 children 3-12, free for children under 3) last 2.25 hours. Reservations are required, and tours meet at the **North Cascades Environmental Learning Center** (1940 Diablo Dam Rd.).

Hiking

Day hikes described below are accessible off Highway 20 and ordered from west to east.

CASCADE PASS

Distance: 7 miles round-trip
Duration: 4 hours
Elevation gain: 1,800 feet
Effort: moderate
Trailhead: Cascade Pass parking lot
Directions: From Marblemount on Highway 20, take a right on Cascade River Road and drive 23 miles. The road is partly unpaved but well-maintained, and closes during heavy snows.

Welcome to one of the most beautiful spots in the state, a saddle that sits between the towering peaks of the North Cascades. Views here are hard earned; the out-and-back trail immediately starts ascending through the trees, with regular switchbacks. The last mile angles up to the pass, where you can see Sahale and Johannesburg Peaks, as well as glaciers and the Stehekin Valley below. The beautiful vista draws lots of hikers in the summer, but the wide saddle provides plenty of room for everyone to eat lunch and enjoy the scenery. Note the trail is likely snow-covered October-mid-June.

SOURDOUGH MOUNTAIN

Distance: 10.5 miles round-trip
Duration: 5-7 hours
Elevation gain: 4,870 feet
Effort: strenuous
Trailhead: Near milepost 126 on Highway 20, turn at the sign for Diablo and park next to the domed swimming pool building.

Who's ready for a workout? The steep out-and-back trail that leads to Sourdough is one of the hardest hikes available to day hikers in the national park, but the payoff is huge. For several miles the trail switchbacks through the forest, gaining 3,200 feet in the first two miles alone. You'll cross a creek after four miles and enter a subalpine zone with rocky expanses and wildflower meadows. At last, you'll reach the Sourdough Mountain Lookout, one of the

U.S. Forest Service's first lookouts. Back in the 1960s, the Beat poets got jobs as fire lookout staffers, writing during their off hours. Poets Gary Snyder and Philip Whalen staffed this one, while Jack Kerouac manned Desolation Peak's lookout farther up Ross Lake. Though the historical building has been restored, it's locked. But you'll still be able to catch 360-degree views of Cascade mountaintops and into remote valleys from the summit's sizable plateau; there's a reason they put a firewatcher here—you can survey for miles. The mountaintop meadows burst with flowers in mid-summer.

PYRAMID LAKE

Distance: 4.2 miles round-trip
Duration: 2-3 hours
Elevation gain: 1,500 feet
Effort: moderate
Trailhead: Just before milepost 127 on Highway 20 (look for signs for the Pyramid Creek Trailhead)

Wander past Douglas fir and lodgepole pine trees on this out-and-back forest trail, looking for signs of the wildfires that regularly tear through the region. The area is chock-full of wildlife, including woodpeckers, thrush, and other noisy birds. After about two miles, you'll reach a mountain lake teeming with newts, giant floating logs, and insects; don't forget bug spray while you take a gander at the peaks above before heading back. Expect to see climbers beginning their trek to the tops of Colonial, Pyramid, and Snowfield Peaks beyond the lake.

THUNDER KNOB

Distance: 3.6 miles round-trip
Duration: 2 hours
Elevation gain: 425 feet
Effort: easy
Trailhead: at Colonial Creek Campground near Diablo Lake on the north side of the highway (look for footbridges at the trailhead)

Pass through a creek bed and into the dense forest in the center of the North Cascades, slowly heading uphill at a gentle grade. There's a viewpoint and bench about a mile in with views of Colonial Peak before the final stretch past a pond and to viewpoints of Diablo Dam and Lake. Catch views of Sourdough Mountain and Jack Mountain before returning the way you came.

MAPLE PASS LOOP

Distance: 7.5 miles round-trip
Duration: 4-5 hours
Elevation gain: 2,000 feet
Effort: moderate
Trailhead: a parking lot on the southwest side of Highway 20 near milepost 158

Though not a grueling hike in elevation gain, Maple Pass Loop is long enough—and its trailhead far enough from most camping or lodging—that it makes for an all-day affair. Technically located in the Okanogan National Forest, most of the amazing views earned will be of the national park. Unlike most trails in the area, it's a loop. Travel counterclockwise by first hiking 1.25 miles to the Lake Ann cutoff; you'll be able to see the body of water from above as you continue on the trail (there's also an 0.5-mile detour to the lake itself). The trail climbs to Heather Pass, where high alpine meadows fill with wildflowers in midsummer. Continue on a ridgeline to Maple Pass and you'll see a row of peaks, including Black Peak and Liberty Bell, a favorite for rock climbers. Eventually the trail dips back into the trees before returning again to the parking lot.

Food and Accommodations

Newhalem's Skagit General Store (502 Newhalem St., 206/386-4489, 10am-5pm daily) sells snacks, a few cheap sandwiches, pizza, and its famed homemade fudge.

To overnight in style in the middle of the North Cascades, head to **Ross Lake Resort** (Hwy. 20 near milepost 127, 206/386-4437, www.rosslakeresort.com, June-Oct., $195-370). It's no easy task, though; the series of a dozen cabins may have amazing views of Ross Lake, electricity, hot water, and small kitchens, but there's no way to drive directly there. Originally built in 1950, the entire thing is on log floats on Ross Lake, connected by docks. Consult the hotel's website for options on how to best reach the resort. You can drive across Diablo Dam and be picked up by a Seattle City Light boat, then carried by a resort truck to the cabins ($28 pp round-trip), or drive to milepost 125 and hike a mile down to the lakeshore and pay $2 for a speedboat to carry you across the foot of Ross Lake. The resort rents fishing rods and tackle, motorboats, canoes, and kayaks to explore the lake ($20-125 per day). Book far in advance to stay overnight; reservations become available a year in advance and fill up about nine months in advance, though cancellations for the summer ahead are sometimes available mid-spring.

Camping

Campsites in the area are typically open May-September, though some may be available without services (water, bathrooms) the rest of the year.

North Cascades National Park (877/444-6777, www.nps.gov/noca) operates two campgrounds near the Skagit River just west of the town of Newhalem. Look for signs at the North Cascades Visitor Center. **Newhalem Creek** ($16) has 111 sites, including large RV sites but no hookups, and takes reservations (www.recreation.gov) for most sites. The much smaller **Goodell Creek** ($16) has 19 sites for tents and small RVs and is first-come, first-served only. It may be open in winter months, weather-dependent (but likely with no water or other services). The most popular spot in the national park is **Colonial Creek Campground** (Hwy. 20 at milepost 130, $16) on Diablo Lake. It has campground loops both north and south of the highway, with a dock and lake access on the southern side. The southern loop's 100 sites are reservable (www.recreation.gov), while the northern loop's 42 campsites are first-come, first-served and fill up on midsummer weekends. Note that large RVs will not fit here. Some campsites are walk-in, a short ramble from the car. Campsites may also be available off-season without services.

Outside the national park's boundaries are several campgrounds run by the U.S. Forest Service (www.fs.usda.gov). **Marble Creek Campground** (Cascade River Rd., $14-20), eight miles east of Marblemount, offers about two dozen sites but no water service. Past the eastern border of the national park, **Lone Fir Campground** (Hwy. 20, past milepost 168, $12) sits on Early

trail in the North Cascades

Winters Creek. Its 27 sites are first-come, first-served, but may not have water available until midsummer.

LEAVENWORTH

You didn't take a wrong turn into Germany, but it sure feels like it here—this Washington mountain town, with the roaring Wenatchee River running through it, is Bavarian-themed, with every commercial building in town sporting some kind of bric-a-brac, wooden shutter, or delicately painted flower, including the McDonald's and the grocery store. What started as an attempt to draw tourists has grown into the town's identity. Leavenworth hosts wildly popular Oktoberfest and Christmas lights festivals, and bratwurst is available every day of the year. But the towering mountains surrounding town aren't just a Heidelberg-style backdrop. You'll find every form of hiking, rafting, and skiing around Leavenworth. Whether you want to hold a beer stein or a paddle, you'll be comfortable here.

Sights

NUTCRACKER MUSEUM

Nothing says Christmas quite like a nutcracker, the German-inspired kitchen tool-turned-decorative piece. But at the **Nutcracker Museum** (735 Front St., 509/548-4573, www.nutcrackermuseum.com, 1pm-5pm daily, $5 adults, $3.50 seniors, $2 children 6-16, free for children under 6), the figures are a year-round attraction. Up a steep staircase, you'll find gallery walls lined with nutcrackers in every incarnation—from the traditional toy soldier to varieties resembling Joan of Arc or Mickey Mouse. Ask for scavenger hunts for children, who can browse the more than 6,000 crackers to find those on their list. Some are also for sale, and be assured that a single nutcracker is much less creepy than dozens and dozens of them staring at you at once.

WINERIES AND TASTING ROOMS

Leavenworth is one of the gateways to eastern Washington, where grapes grow better than on the damp, western side of the mountains. Fittingly, there are a number of wine-tasting spots in and around town. A few miles southeast of town via U.S. 2 you'll find a trio of spots. **Silvara Vineyards** (77 Stage Rd., 509/548-1000, www.silvarawine.com, noon-5pm Thurs.-Mon. Jan.-Apr., noon-6pm daily May-Dec., $10 tasting fee) is one of the grandest local wineries, situated on a hill. You can

Leavenworth

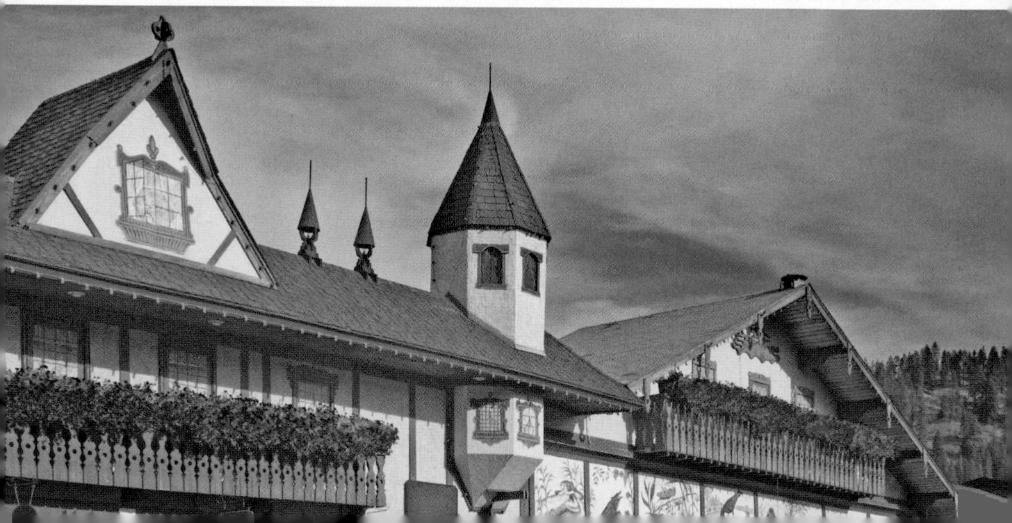

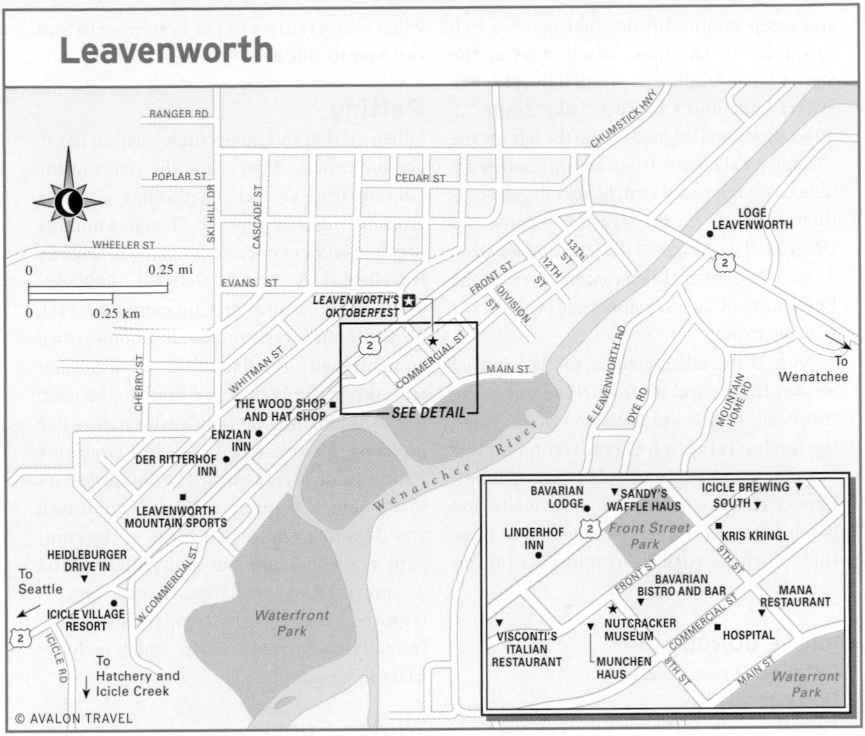

appreciate its beautiful landscaping from the tasting room's large windows. **Icicle Ridge Winery** (8977 North Rd., Peshastin, 509/548-6156, http://icicleridgewinery.com, 11am-5pm Fri.-Sat., noon-5pm Sun.-Thurs., $10 tasting fee) has a tasting room downtown, but its main winery is in a sprawling log cabin. Taste some wines, but also leave time to sit by the massive fireplace. At the smaller **Wedge Mountain Winery** (9534 Saunders Rd., 509/548-7068, www.wedgemountainwinery.com, 10am-5pm Fri.-Mon., $10 tasting fee), the owner personally fills every bottle of wine produced. He also drives wine tasters around the property in a tractor (seating is on hay bales), and tastings are done in an underground cave.

Hiking

With more regular sunshine than the western side of the state—but no shortage of snow—the Leavenworth area is a popular hiking destination.

COLCHUCK LAKE

Distance: 8 miles round-trip
Duration: 5 hours
Elevation gain: 2,280 feet
Effort: strenuous
Trailhead: Stuart Lake Trailhead (annual Northwest Forest Pass or $5 day-use pass purchasable at the kiosk required to park)
Directions: From Leavenworth, drive southwest via U.S. 2, turning off and heading south on Icicle Creek Road for 8.5 miles. Turn left onto Forest Road 7601, driving the dirt road 3.7 miles uphill.

Above Leavenworth is a series of high alpine lakes and peaks known as The Enchantments, so popular with backpackers that a lottery is held annually for permits to camp there. But day hikers can get close at Colchuck Lake, a circular body of water surrounded by trees and steep mountainsides that glows a rich turquoise in summer. You'll start at the Stuart Lake Trailhead. A junction splits the Stuart Lake and Colchuck Lake Trails 2.5 miles in; it's well signed—take the left for the Colchuck Lake Trail. Continue up another 1.5 miles through rocky switchbacks to your destination. Look for the jagged Colchuck and Dragontail Peaks across the lake, and for steep Asgard Pass, where hikers ascend to reach the Enchantment Lakes, before heading back the way you came.

Note that a self-issued permit is required for day hikers and must be filled out at the trailhead; this is not the same as the parking fee, but rather a free registration for day use that every party member must fill out. Expect rangers to ask for your self-issued day-hiker permit when passing and to issue fines to those with overnight gear but no overnight paperwork.

ICICLE GORGE LOOP

Distance: 4.5 miles round-trip
Duration: 2-3 hours
Elevation gain: 150 feet
Effort: moderate
Trailhead: on the river side of the parking lot about a half mile past the Chatter Creek Guard Station (annual Northwest Forest Pass or $5 day-use pass purchasable at the kiosk required to park)
Directions: From Leavenworth, drive southwest via U.S. 2, turning off and heading southwest on Icicle Creek Road (which becomes Forest Rd. 7600) for 15.5 miles, the last few of which are gravel.

You can hike this loop in a clockwise or counterclockwise direction—either is enjoyable and makes for a gentle ramble near Icicle Creek, a roaring waterway that feeds into the Wenatchee River. Take a map at the trailhead kiosk, then head a few hundred feet to the junction; turn left or right to enter the loop. You'll pass interpretive signs explaining the wildlife and ecology of the area, plus a few benches for rest. Since the trail stays in the trees, the shady hike is ideal in midsummer when temperatures in the Leavenworth area can soar to 100°F.

Rafting

When all that mountain snow melts, it has to go somewhere. That's why the rivers of the Leavenworth area are so glorious, and why river rafting is so popular. Though a number of guide services operate out of town, **Osprey Rafting** (U.S. 2 and Icicle Rd., 509/548-6800, http://ospreyrafting.com, $79-111), on the town's western end, is a homegrown company with regular full-day white-water trips down the Wenatchee River to the town of Cashmere, hitting rapids with names like Bad Boy, Drunkard's Drop, and Grannie's Pantie's (don't freak out at The Suffocator; it's just a name). With up to 15 miles of travel, you'll paddle and earn a break at the company's personal take-out spot, with food and live music on weekend trips. No experience is required except for the company's more extreme High Adventure trip, which includes Class IV rapids.

Winter Sports

With mountains this steep and snow this heavy, it's no wonder skiing is a popular activity come winter in the Leavenworth area. Just 35 miles west of town, a 45-minute drive, the **Stevens Pass Ski Area** (U.S. 2, 206/812-4510, www.stevenspass.com, $89 adults, $20 seniors 70 and over, $60 children 7-15) has terrain for skiers from beginner to expert, plus Nordic ($14-22) and snowshoe trails ($13). Note that lifts get crowded on weekends, since it's the closest large ski mountain to Seattle. Heavy snows can close U.S. 2 when road crews clear snow and blast for avalanches.

Closer to town, **Leavenworth Ski Hill** (10701 Ski Hill Dr., 509/548-6975, http://skileavenworth.com, $19 adults, $15 children 6-17 and seniors 75 and over, free for children under 6) is a locals' hill, equipped with a rope tow, for beginners. Sledding ($5), tubing

($20), snowshoeing ($10), and fat biking ($10) are also possible here.

Entertainment and Events

NIGHTLIFE

Though the town may be Bavarian at heart, **Icicle Brewing** (935 Front St., 509/548-2739, http://iciclebrewing.com, noon-10pm Mon.-Wed., 11am-10pm Thurs., 11am-11pm Fri.-Sat., 11am-10pm Sun.) is a Northwest brewery. Anchored by the Bootjack IPA and its local Yakima hops, the brewery also offers a raspberry wheat, pilsner, amber, and more in a space decorated with plenty of log beams. The outdoor seating fills quickly on weekends throughout the year, and Bavarian pretzels and meat plates are served. Free tours take place at 11am and 1pm on weekends. Expect live music (and crowds) on weekends and occasional weekdays. This is an all-ages venue until 10pm.

Forget the Bavarian schtick at **The Loft** (843 Front St., 509/888-0231, noon-2am daily), a 2nd-floor bar that, antique skis mounted above the bar notwithstanding, could be located just about anywhere. Food is fried, and the fries are loaded with cheese, and if the game isn't playing on the TV, you can start your own foosball championship. Some windows look down on the decorated streets and tourists below, but the joint is more for drinkers looking to relax and maybe join in on the occasional pub trivia night.

★ OKTOBERFEST

This town doesn't just look like Bavaria; it drinks like it too. The annual **Oktoberfest** (Leavenworth Festhalle, 1001 Front St., www.leavenworthoktoberfest.com, 6pm-midnight Fri. and noon-1am Sat. Sept.-Oct., $10 Fri., $20 Sat., free for children under 12), usually spread across three weekends in the fall, is the town's biggest party. Multiple beer tents pour dozens of different beers, and the autumn mountain breeze is no match for the throngs that come clad in lederhosen. Free shuttles run around downtown Leavenworth and to the town of Wenatchee, about 22 miles southeast, so there's no need to drive after a stein or three. Every Saturday during the festival at 1pm the mayor does a ceremonial keg tapping, followed by oom-pah music from the town band, the Musikkapelle Leavenworth. All ages are allowed until 9pm.

CHRISTMAS LIGHTING FESTIVAL

Second only to Oktoberfest, the Christmas season is a wildly popular time in Leavenworth.

Oktoberfest in Leavenworth

The **Christmas Lighting Festival** (Front Street Gazebo, 820 Front St., Sat.-Sun. Nov.-Dec., free) feels like a loose city-wide Christmas party, but on weekends leading up to December 25, Santa arrives at downtown's central gazebo at noon on Saturdays and Sundays, and live music from carolers and bell choirs fills the streets. Holiday lights are turned on at 4:30pm in a small public ceremony each Saturday and Sunday, but the lights themselves twinkle November-February. All told, about a half million tiny lights illuminate the buildings and trees of Leavenworth during the holiday season.

Shopping

Christmas ornaments in May? Why not. **Kris Kringl** (907 Front St., 509/548-6867, www.kkringl.com, 10am-6pm daily) is open and decorated in holiday decor year-round—mostly from the yuletide but also celebrating other holidays like Easter and Halloween. Browse the aisles for cheer any time, or get your Christmas shopping done really early. Open for almost three decades, the store is staffed with experts who know just about every kind and brand of Christmas ornament.

The side-by-side **The Wood Shop and Hat Shop** (719 Front St., 509/548-4442, http://hatshopwoodshop.com, 10am-6pm daily), their doors under a shared mural of a snowy alpine scene, offer more than just what's indicated by their names. The former has wooden toys, including beautiful handmade pieces, plus Legos, board games, dolls, and more. Its twin shop has goofy novelty and play hats, along with some more subtle everyday headwear. Both are toy shops of a kind, ideal for browsing and gift-buying.

When preparing for the great outdoors, **Leavenworth Mountain Sports** (220 U.S. 2, 509/548-7864, www.leavenworthmtnsports.com, 10am-6pm Mon.-Fri., 9am-6pm Sat.-Sun.) has everything you need to stay cool, stay warm, stay on your feet, or keep the bugs away. The shop offers the kind of small-town friendliness and useful advice that make a great outdoor store. Find backpacks and clothing, plus ski, snowshoe, ice axe, paddleboard, climbing shoe, and wetsuit rentals.

Food

GERMAN

A must-stop for the true Leavenworth Bavarian experience, ★ **Munchen Haus** (709 Front St., 509/548-1158, www.munchenhaus.com, 11am-9pm Sun.-Thurs., 11am-10pm Fri. -Sat., $5-7) is an outdoor, counter-service stop for bratwurst and beer, with tables, some with fire pits, in a sunny courtyard. The many kinds of German sausage—pork, beef, chicken, and veggie varieties are on offer—can be topped off with sauerkraut simmered in apple cider and doused with a slew of mustards, from spicy to sweet. Each brat is a meal unto itself, so save it for a reward after skiing or hiking, or just wandering through every quaint shop in the village.

When you need to sit down for some serious German eats, **Bavarian Bistro and Bar** (801 Front St., 509/548-5074, http://bavarianbistrobar.com, 11am-10pm Mon.-Wed., 11am-11pm Fri., 11am-midnight Sat.-Sun., $11-22) has everything from spaetzle to schnitzel to knackwurst. Burgers are available for anyone needing a break from the ultra-European menus, and the bar also serves Olympia oysters and Baja-style rockfish. The cheery interior has low ceilings slung with exposed wooden beams and windows complete with carved shutters. Between the beer, the food, and the decor, it's impossible not to feel cozy inside.

PACIFIC NORTHWEST

Located in the Sleeping Lady Resort a few miles south of town on Icicle Road, **Kingfisher Restaurant and Wine Bar** (7375 Icicle Rd., 509/548-6344, www.sleepinglady.com/kingfisher-restaurant-wine-bar.php, 7:30am-9am and 5:30pm-8pm Mon.-Thurs., 7:30am-9am and 5:30pm-8:30pm Fri., 7:30am-10am and 5:30pm-8:30pm Sat., 7:30am-10am and 5:30pm-8pm Sun., $42) is a beguiling combination of buffet and high-end dining. This is no droopy salad bar; options available for the single-price meal include pork shoulder or line-caught swordfish, with a variety of side dishes. Seating is under the exposed beams of a large dining room, sometimes bustling with the resort's many guests. The rustic theme can be a nice break from the kitsch of Leavenworth's Bavarian decor.

On the delicate end of the scale, **Mana Restaurant** (1033 Commercial St., 509/548-1662, www.manamountain.com, 6:30pm Fri.-Sun., $65-85) does a single seating on its few open nights, preparing an eight-course prix fixe menu of locally sourced foods; ingredients are organic and sustainable. Sunday dinner is a bit less formal (only five courses) and is probably the only meal appropriate for kids. Dinners take up to three hours and are an event unto themselves in the farmhouse-style yellow house, with reservations required.

AMERICAN

It's got a great pun and offers a great burger: **Heidleburger Drive In** (12708 U.S. 2, 509/548-5471, http://heidleburger.com, 11am-9pm daily, $4-6) is a cheery little cabin with outdoor picnic tables as well as indoor seating, with every basic burger joint option on the menu, plus fried clams, fried chicken, tater tots, and fried mushrooms. Expect simple fare that's fast and filling and locals waiting in line alongside you.

Head 15 minutes or so southwest of town for **Country Boys BBQ** (400 Aplets Way, Cashmere, 509/782-7427, www.countryboysbbq.com, 11am-8pm Tues.-Sat., $12-18), located in the small riverfront town of Cashmere. Everything here is simple and classic, from the wood-paneled walls to the meat-heavy menu. Decide between baby back ribs, pulled pork, barbecue chicken, and beef brisket, plus potato salad, coleslaw, and bean sides. The ribs are particularly rich, overwhelming the red-and-white-checkered paper that lines the serving baskets, and ribbon fries are more like potato chips, thin and with a bit of crunch. Sit outside in summer or take your food to go and sit by the river somewhere.

BREAKFAST

Breakfasts at **Sandy's Waffle Haus** (894 U.S. 2, 509/548-6779, 7am-2pm daily, $7-14) include eggy burritos and thick German sausages, but the waffles are the obvious draw, topped with piles of fruit and mounds of whipped cream. Ask for a Belgian-style waffle for a thick disc; the buckwheat or plain waffle is of a thinner style. With a simple diner-like interior, there's little fuss inside, but the appeal of fried potatoes and waffles brings throngs on weekend mornings.

ITALIAN

When it's time for a proper sit-down meal in Leavenworth, **Visconti's Italian Restaurant** (636 Front St., 509/548-1213, www.viscontis.com, 11am-9:30pm Sun.-Thurs., 11am-10pm Fri.-Sat., $19-44) offers classic pasta and salads in a low-lit environment—not formal, exactly, but calmer than a beer garden. Pastas are made in house and meats are cured here as well, with rich entrées like lemon crab linguine and veal saltimbocca. Tables are on the 2nd floor and have views of the well-lit central square. A gelato stand on the ground floor makes for a perfect dessert spot any time of year.

LATIN

Latin food may seem like an odd juxtaposition with the snowy landscape and nutcracker decor outside but, thanks to its filling dishes, **South** (913 Front St., 509/888-4328, www.southrestaurants.com,11:30am-9pm Mon.-Thurs., 11:30am-11pm Fri., 11am-11pm Sat., 11am-9pm Sun., $12-18) is one of the most popular stops for hikers and skiers returning through Leavenworth after a hard day's play. Enchiladas meet poblano chicken or Argentine steak, and the sampler of three kinds of pork tacos delivers spicy and sweet on the same plate. It can be hard to make it to dessert still hungry, but both the *tres leche* vanilla sponge cake and flan are tasty. Indoor seating can be dim, though the walls are painted in bright colors, and outdoor tables have both heaters for the winter and draped sunshades for the summer.

Accommodations

Note that due to Leavenworth's two very popular seasons—fall Oktoberfest and the ramp-up to Christmas in December—hotels book out far in advance and may have minimum-stay requirements. Book up to a year in advance if you're planning on visiting during these periods.

UNDER $150

Located a few miles southeast of town, **River's Edge Lodge** (8401 U.S. 2, 509/548-7612www.riversedgelodgewa.com, $99-159) has some of the cheapest rates in town. The phone isn't always answered in the off-season, and rooms have a simple but clean motel feel. Some rooms have kitchens and the property is right on the rushing Wenatchee River, so it's a step up from the usual roadside spot.

$150-250

From the wooden slats of the balconies to the scalloped edges of its decor, **Bavarian Lodge** (810 U.S. 2, 888/717-7878, www.bavarianlodge.com, $214-264) lives up to its name with German-first touches inside and out. In winter, it's lit up like a Christmas tree with tiny lights dripping from every roof and entryway. Inside you'll find fairly conventional hotel rooms with a few woodsy touches, plus pillow-top beds. A hot breakfast is included, and the 90-room lodge has two hot tubs and a pool that's heated year-round. Walkability is a big draw; it's across U.S. 2 from the center of downtown.

With more than 100 rooms and tons of Bavarian flair, like window flower boxes and chalet-style roofs, the **Enzian Inn** (590 U.S. 2, 800/223-8511, http://enzianinn.com, $205-355) is one of the anchoring hotels of Leavenworth. Rooms have hand-painted floral patterns on the walls and hand-carved Austrian furniture pieces, and like many local hotels, a hot breakfast is included with your stay. The hot tub outside is shaped like alpine flowers, and guests can play the nearby Enzian Falls Championship Putting Course—18 holes of miniature golf—for free. Mountain goats hang out next to the course.

Right next door to the Enzian Inn, the relatively small **Linderhof Inn** (690 U.S. 2, 509/828-5680, http://linderhof.com, $180-205) has only 33 rooms, but still offers many of the same amenities as its bigger brethren, including a hot tub and free hot breakfast. It also offers free access to the nearby Enzian Falls Championship Putting Course. Rooms are small and relatively simple, but some have jetted tubs in the room. In winter, the hotel offers free cross-country ski equipment rentals. The location is fairly central and sometimes has cheap deals midweek and in the off-season.

A block farther west from downtown than the Enzian Inn, **Der Ritterhof Inn** (190 U.S. 2, 509/548-5845, www.derritterhof.com, $239-259) is a smaller, more hotel-style property guarded by a giant 25-foot knight statue made from steel and old car parts—worth a double-take while driving by. The squat buildings and seasonal pool (no hot tub) make for a quieter stay than some of the bigger hotels, and the 51 rooms are a bit dated. Still, the addition of laundry and grills for guest use makes it an ideal stop for road-trippers looking for a quiet night or two.

The large **Icicle Village Resort** (505 U.S. 2, 509/548-7000, www.iciclevillage.com, $155-249 rooms, $279-459 suites and condos) is a 15-minute walk west from downtown. Accommodations range from simple hotel rooms to 1- to 3-bedroom condos, all newly updated. Many have great views of the mountains. The property boasts a full spa and year-round swimming pool, plus the Icicle Junction Activity Center, which has sports gear rentals, couches, and an indoor game room and arcade, plus a miniature golf course.

With an emphasis on building community, **Loge Leavenworth** (11798 U.S. 2, 509/690-4106, www.logecamps.com/leavenworth-wa, $175-275) encourages guests staying in its handful of cabins to share fire pits and meet each other. The cabins feature modern rustic decor, and the property caters to serious outdoors enthusiasts with a mountain bike gear center, an avalanche gear demo center, and dog-friendliness. As part of a growing collection of similar properties, Loge is trying to update old accommodations in a hip style. Young, active travelers will feel right at home. It's located about a 10-minute walk east of downtown, across the river.

OVER $250

The sprawling ★ **Sleeping Lady Resort** (7375 Icicle Rd., 509/548-6344, www.sleepinglady.com, $293-375) feels like a perfect fit with Leavenworth and somehow also a world away—largely because it's outside the zone wherein Bavarian trim is required by town codes. Rooms are mostly in connected buildings but feel like private cabins. "Alcove" rooms have beds with hand-hewn headboards centrally located under exposed wooden beams, plus twin beds tucked into specially built alcoves, ideal for children or groups. Other rooms have lofts. Walkways wander through tall trees and green landscaping so thick it can be hard to get a sense of how big the 67-acre property actually is. The outdoor hot tub and pool are more like rocky quarries, complete with waterfalls, and there is an indoor library and a playroom for when the weather gets intense.

CAMPING

There are several campgrounds sprinkled along Icicle Road, and rock climbers tend to pull over and turn empty spots along the gravel into impromptu campsites. **Eightmile Campground** (Icicle Creek Rd., 877/444-6777, www.recreation.gov, $22-44)—about eight miles southwest of town—has 26 sites and pit toilets. Open April-October, it offers a trail down to the river and reservable sites appropriate for tents or RVs, though there are no electric hookups. A few sites have river views.

Given the popularity of Leavenworth, campsites don't come cheap at **Leavenworth/ Pine Village KOA** (11401 River Bend Dr., 509/548-7709, http://koa.com), just across the Wenatchee River from downtown. Still, the property has many amenities, including a pool open seasonally, a hot tub, a dog park, bike rentals, and a free shuttle into town. During summer the campground hosts outdoor movie nights, tie-dye craft days, and the occasional bounce house. In addition to tent ($38-50) and RV sites with hookups ($74-89), there's a series of cute cabins ($112-131), some with bunk beds and full kitchens.

Information and Services

Leavenworth's chamber of commerce has a **visitors center** (940 U.S. 2, Ste. B, 509/548-5807, http://leavenworth.org, 8am-6pm Mon.-Fri., 8am-8pm Sat., 8am-4pm Sun.) with maps and travel ideas. Find the **post office** next door (960 U.S. 2, 800/275-8777, 8am-5pm Mon.-Fri, 9am-1pm Sat.).

Getting There

From Seattle, head north on I-5 for 27 miles to Everett, then take exit 194 to get on U.S. 2 East. The road passes through rural towns and then the Cascade Mountains. Snow is common in winter; be prepared with chains as they may be required. You'll drive about 100 miles east on U.S. 2 to Leavenworth. The drive is about 130 miles total and takes 2.5 hours. Alternatively, take I-90 from Seattle east to the town of Cle Elum, about 83 miles away. Take exit 85 to get on Highway 970, which will become U.S. 97 after about 10 miles, as it exits rural farmland and climbs into the forest around Blewett Pass; this area can be dangerous during winter months. Carry snow chains and leave lots of distance between cars, as accidents caused by cars sliding on frozen roads are common. After 35 miles, turn left on U.S. 2. You'll enter the town of Leavenworth about 4 miles later. This drive is about 135 miles total and takes just under 2.5 hours.

CHELAN

Chelan sits at the southern foot of Lake Chelan, the state's biggest lake and the third deepest in the entire country. The lake is an impressive sight from town, with cold, clear blue water shimmering under the rounded brown hills. The thin, 50-mile snake of a lake winds from this spot in warm, dry central Washington all the way north to North

Cascades National Park. With reliable sunshine and a small-town pace—Chelan has small, walkable blocks, and there's also the tinier town of Manson eight miles west—this is a region permanently on vacation. Wineries are tucked into the low hills surrounding the lake, and water sports and recreation rule here; the flat lake's surface is dotted with Jet Skis and motorboats from spring to fall.

Wineries and Tasting Rooms

Like much of central Washington, Chelan is surrounded by vineyards and winemakers, so wine tasting is a popular activity here.

Four miles west of town, **Nefarious Cellars** (495 S Lakeshore Rd., 509/682-9505, www.nefariouscellars.com, noon-5pm Sat.-Sun. Apr.-May, 2pm-5pm Wed.-Sun. June, 11am-5pm daily July-Sept., noon-5pm Wed.-Sun. Oct., $10 tasting fee) has a beautiful view from its red barn tasting room on the west side of Lake Chelan, plus a full slate of red and white wines. At **Karma Vineyards** (1681 S Lakeshore Rd., 509/682-5538, www.goodkarmawines.com, 11am-5pm Thurs.-Sun., $5-20 tasting fee), located a mile farther up the lakefront road, the specialty is sparkling wine, all *méthode champenoise*—made in the same style as French champagne. Tastings at its 18 Brix restaurant come with small bits of bread.

On the northern side of the lake near Manson, **Hard Row to Hoe Vineyards** (300 Ivan Morse Rd., Manson, 509/687-3000, www.hardrow.com, noon-5pm daily, $12 tasting fee) has a slightly different vibe. It's named for the rowboat ride early miners had to take to a brothel located up the lake. The selection is wide, and wines have funny names like Shameless Hussy and Nauti Buoy. The small hillside tasting room is open year-round and makes for a fun drive into the hills above the lake.

Sports and Recreation

WATER SPORTS

The wide, flat Lake Chelan is perfect for Jet Skiing; expect to see the roaring machines cross the lake all summer. Rent one at **Jet Skis Ahoy** (1320 W Woodin Ave., 509/682-5125, www.jetskisahoy.com, $45-200 Jet Ski, $165-450 boat), which offers three-seater machines and will patiently show newbies how to use them. Motorboats are available as well and range in size up to a 14-person pontoon. Rent on weekdays for a discount.

What's even more intense than motoring down the lake? Doing it in the air.

Lake Chelan

Chelan

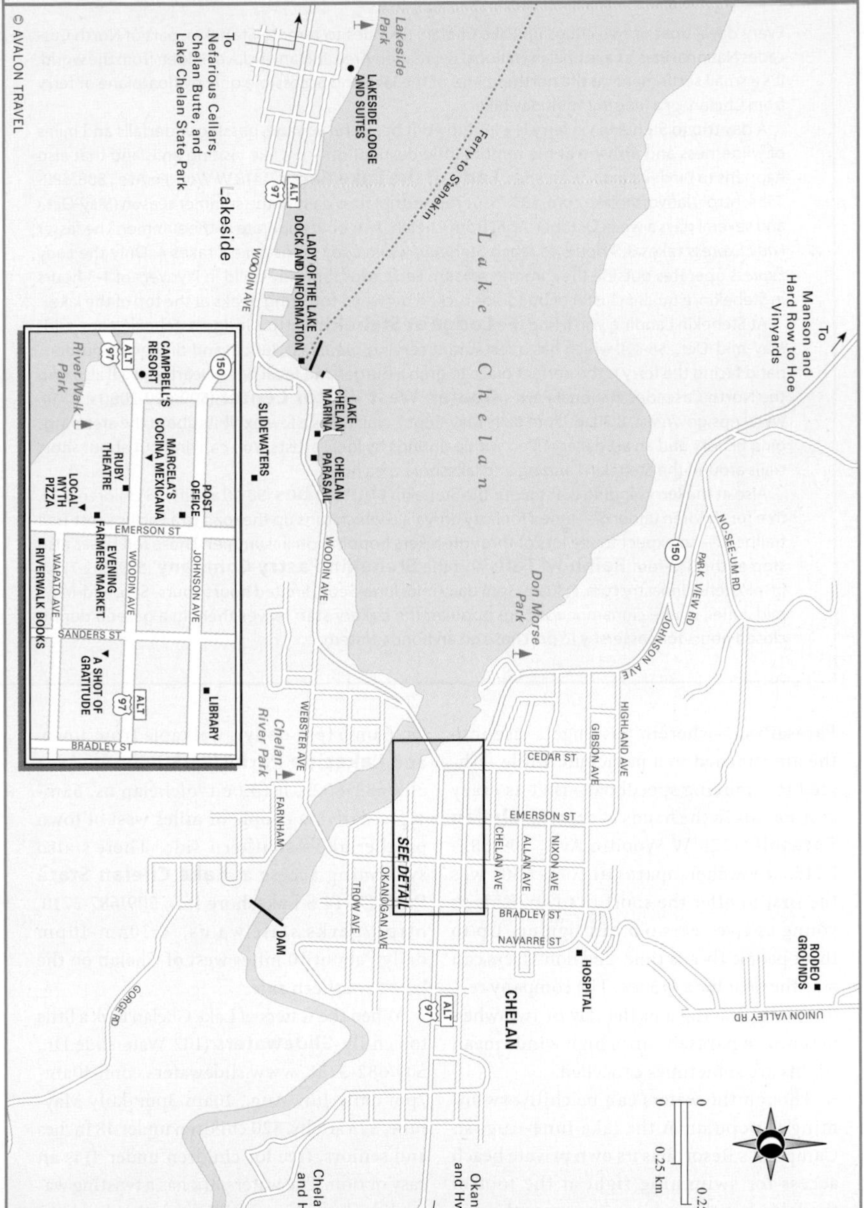
To Nefarious Cellars, Chelan Butte, and Lake Chelan State Park
LAKESIDE LODGE AND SUITES
Lakeside Park
Ferry to Stehekin
Lakeside
WOODIN AVE
ALT 97
LADY OF THE LAKE DOCK AND INFORMATION
Lake Chelan
To Manson and Hard Row to Hoe Vineyards
LAKE CHELAN MARINA
SLIDEWATERS
CHELAN PARASAIL
WOODIN AVE
Don Morse Park
150
NO-SEE-UM RD
PARK VIEW RD
JOHNSON AVE
HIGHLAND AVE
GIBSON AVE
CEDAR ST
EMERSON ST
CHELAN AVE
ALLAN AVE
NIXON AVE
BRADLEY ST
NAVARRE ST
HOSPITAL
RODEO GROUNDS
UNION VALLEY RD
CHELAN
SEE DETAIL
WEBSTER AVE
FARNHAM
Chelan River Park
TROW AVE
OKANOGAN AVE
DAM
GORGE RD
To Okanogan and Hwy 97
To Chelan Falls and Hwy 97
0 0.25 mi
0 0.25 km
CAMPBELL'S RESORT
River Walk Park
MARCELA'S COCINA MEXICANA
POST OFFICE
RUBY THEATRE
LOCAL MYTH PIZZA
EVENING FARMERS MARKET
RIVERWALK BOOKS
WAPATO AVE
WOODIN AVE
JOHNSON AVE
SANDERS ST
A SHOT OF GRATITUDE
LIBRARY
BRADLEY ST
© AVALON TRAVEL

Day Trip to Stehekin

Every day a boat or two chugs up Lake Chelan, 50 miles to remote Stehekin, part of North Cascades National Park's Lake Chelan National Recreation Area and an enclave hidden from the world. It's a small settlement on the northern end of the lake and accessible only by floatplane or ferry from Chelan, or a lengthy, multiday hike.

A day trip to Stehekin via ferry is a lengthy but beautiful voyage, passing waterfalls and miles of wilderness and arriving at the remote little destination—it's like visiting an island that also happens to be deep in the Cascades. **Lady of the Lake Ferry** (1418 W Woodin Ave., 888/682-4584, http://ladyofthelake.com, $33.75-61 round-trip) runs daily in the summer season (May-Oct.) and several days a week October-April from Chelan. Two boats operate in the summer: The faster *Lady Express* takes 2.5 hours to reach Stehekin while *Lady of the Lake II* takes 4. Only the *Lady Express* operates outside the summer season. Ferry trips typically build in layovers of 1-3 hours in Stehekin, a quaint cluster of buildings tucked between towering peaks at the top of the lake.

At Stehekin Landing you'll find the **Lodge at Stehekin** (http://lodgeatstehekin.com, mid-May-mid-Oct., $8-11), which has a restaurant serving breakfast, lunch, and dinner; its outdoor patio facing the ferry is the perfect place to grab a burger and local beer. Nearby, you'll also find the North Cascades National Park's **Golden West Visitor Center** (509/699-2080 ext. 14, www.nps.gov/noca, 8:30am-5pm daily May-Sept.), which has a few exhibits about the area's logging history and an art gallery filled with paintings by local artists. You can find out about short trails around the Stehekin Landing and lakeshore area here.

Also at the ferry landing is a stop for the Stehekin **shuttle bus** ($8-10 adults, $5 children 6-12, free for children under 6)—timed for ferry arrivals—which runs up the road to a Pacific Crest Trail trailhead—so expect to see lots of through-hikers hopping on in summer. These red buses also stop at the 312-foot **Rainbow Falls** and the **Stehekin Pastry Company** (509/682-7742, http://stehekinpastry.com, 7:30am-5pm daily mid-June-Sept., limited hours Thurs.-Sun. mid-May-mid-June), where cinnamon rolls are popular; the bakery staff leaves them in a gazebo during closed hours for passersby to purchase on an honor system.

Parasailing—wherein passengers rise into the air attached to a parachute while tethered to a moving speedboat—isn't as crazy as it sounds in the hands of experts. **Chelan Parasail** (1228 W Woodin Ave., 509/682-7245, www.chelanparasail.com, $60) was the first to offer the sport in town. Kids as young as five years old can sign up. Up to three people fly at a time, and non-flyers can ride the boat for a $15 fee. The company recommends leaving a buffer day or two when planning a parasail, since high winds mean flights are sometimes cancelled.

Though the waters can be chilly, swimming is popular in the lake June-August. Campbell's Resort has its own private beach access for swimming right at the foot of the lake, but the public can access the waters at **Don Morse Park** (485 W Manson Hwy., 509/682-8023, http://cityofchelan.us, 6am-11pm daily), walkable from town, and **Lakeside Park** (105 E Johnson Ave., 509/682-8023, http://cityofchelan.us, 6am-11pm daily), a couple of miles west of town on the lake's southern side. There's also swimming access at **Lake Chelan State Park** (7544 S Lakeshore Rd., 509/687-3710, http://parks.state.wa.us, 6:30am-10pm daily), about 10 miles west of Chelan on the lake's southern side.

When the waters of Lake Chelan look a little too chilly, **Slidewaters** (102 Waterslide Dr., 509/682-5751, www.slidewaters.com, 10am-7pm daily July-Aug., 10am-3pm daily May-June, $25 adults, $20 children under 48 inches and seniors, free for children under 4) is an easy option. The water park has a twisting waterslide, lazy river, and hot tub that holds 60 people. Attractions are appropriate for every age of kid all the way up to adult, from wading pool to a 400-foot slide in the dark.

WINTER SPORTS

Though the mountains are low around Chelan, **Echo Valley Ski Area** (1700 Cooper Gulch Rd., Manson, 509/687-3167, www.echovalley.org, $15-25) is a small locals' ski hill with rope tows and a surface lift, plus tubing and cross-country skiing options. Ideal for a kid's play day in the snow, it's run by volunteers and is tucked into the forests above Manson.

ZIP-LINING

Though this part of Washington is known for its water sports, zip-lining has become a popular way to zoom over the landscape. **Tunnel Ziplines** (19840 U.S. Hwy. 97A, 509/682-0151, www.tunnelziplines.com, $75) offers rides on a series of lines over the vineyards and rocky cliffs above the lake, with the longest ride more than 800 feet long.

Entertainment and Events

NIGHTLIFE

You don't have to drink straight alcohol at **A Shot of Gratitude** (312 E Woodin Ave., 509/682-7100, noon-9pm Mon. and Thurs.-Fri., 9am-9pm Sat.-Sun.). The giant "righteous" Bloody Marys are probably more popular. With a menu that ranges from brunch items to tacos and hot dogs, it has much to offer as a restaurant but still has the feel of a local's bar, with beer signs everywhere and mismatched furniture. The outdoor patio and fire pit are a welcome place to hang out on summer evenings.

Sunset Bar and Grill (76 W Wapato Way, Manson, 509/687-7000, www.sunsetbargrill.com, 7am-2am daily) in nearby Manson has a warm, relaxed feel, like the place isn't trying too hard. There's an antique sled on one wall and soccer paraphernalia on another, a short line of taps, and a long bar. Twice-a-day happy hours bring the price of Rainier beer under $2, and the joint slings food from breakfast to dinner. Right at the intersection of family restaurant and drinking hole, it's a solid local's joint for a small town.

THE ARTS

The century-old **Ruby Theatre** (135 E Woodin Ave., 509/682-5016, http://rubytheatre.com, $10 adults, $9 seniors and children 13-17, $12 children under 13) has its original balcony and tin ceiling, and still shows movies like it was built to do in 1914. It claims to be the oldest continuously running movie house in the state. The restored theater, sitting in the middle of Chelan's downtown, plays recent first-run releases.

FESTIVALS AND EVENTS

Though the lake is always a party in summer, winter brings the **Lake Chelan Winterfest** (www.lakechelan.com/winterfest, Jan., $5-30), a 30-year tradition held over two weekends in January. The center of town erupts into celebration, with ice sculptures and polar bear swims, all with live music and lots of wine tastings, plus a free beach bonfire.

It's hard to think of a body of water less suited to pirates than Lake Chelan, but the **Lake Chelan Pirate Fest** (Chelan High School, 215 Webster Ave., www.lakechelanpiratefest.com, June-July) has become a funky annual tradition, with a carnival ($20), fun run, and live events around the Fourth of July. You don't have to dress up like a pirate, but why wouldn't you?

Shopping

Though shopping is limited in downtown Chelan—besides swimwear shops and a few clothing boutiques—**Riverwalk Books** (116 E Woodin Ave., 509/682-8901, www.riverwalkbooks.com, 10am-6pm Mon.-Sat.) is a solid two-story bookstore with a crowded children's section and beautiful wood bookcases.

Located inside a winery, **Lake Chelan Cheese** (Lake Chelan Winery, 3519 SR 150, Manson, 509/888-0268, www.lakechelancheese.com, 11am-5pm Sun.-Thurs., 11am-7pm Fri.-Sat.) makes a case for cheese being the signature food of the area. Try a free cheese tasting and shop from among dozens of cow, sheep, and goat cheeses, plus a few cured meats. It makes for a perfect lakeshore or on-deck snack.

Food

A joint like **Local Myth Pizza** (122 S Emerson St., 509/682-2914, http://localmyth-pizza.com, 11:30am-8pm Tues.-Thurs., 11:30am-9pm Fri.-Sat., $8-18) could only exist in a small town like this. A light fixture is made of kitchen equipment (is that a colander?), booths are painted in bright colors, and locals abound. One of the salads is served in what looks like a cocktail glass. But the pizza has a nice thick crust.

Located in the fields above Manson, **Blueberry Hills** (1315 Washington St., Manson, 509/687-2379, http://wildaboutberries.com, 8am-3pm daily summer, 8am-3pm Wed.-Sun. winter, $9-13) is as much farm as restaurant, with 10 acres of you-pick berry fields and a homey eatery serving a serious breakfast and a decent lunch. Waffles come with blueberry pie filling on top. The restaurant is filled with knickknacks like music records hanging from the ceiling.

Cozy **Marcela's Cocina Mexicana** (119 E Woodin Ave., 509/682-4754, http://marcelascocinamexicana.com, 11am-10pm daily, $8-17) offers the best from-scratch margaritas for miles, plus an impressive menu of Mexican classics of the big and saucy variety. It's hard to walk away hungry, and the bright colors inside give it a bit of neon glow. After a long day on the lake, it's a simple destination.

Unlike some fresh markets, there's no reason to get up early for Chelan's **Evening Farmer's Market** (S Emerson and Wapato Sts., www.chelanfarmersmarket.org, 4pm-7pm Thurs. May-Sept.), held in the town's Riverwalk Park. Produce from the rich fields around the area is on sale alongside fresh pastries and locally made goat cheese, and the market hosts live entertainment and story time.

Accommodations

$150-250

With 93 rooms, **Lakeside Lodge and Suites** (2312 W Woodin Ave., 509/769-3195, http://lakesidelodgeandsuites.com, $219-309), sitting on the southern side of the lake, has a similar feel to the town's defining hotel, Campbell's Resort, though perhaps slightly less impressive views; indoor and outdoor pools and hot tubs, however, up the ante. Some rooms have kitchenettes but all come with a hot breakfast, and furnishings are unfussy but in good condition.

OVER $250

For more than a century, the name Campbell has been almost synonymous with the lake. The family's ancestor staked a claim here in 1901, and now **Campbell's Resort** (104 W Woodin Ave., 509/682-2561, http://campbellsresort.com, $299-389) anchors the southern tip of Lake Chelan with 170 rooms on eight acres, including a private beach. Rooms are impressively updated, with whimsical but sophisticated decor—and every single one has a lake view and either a balcony or deck. The attached Campbell's Pub and Veranda has lovely outdoor dining, if not particularly memorable food, and fire pits line the waterfront.

Located in nearby Manson, **Wapato Point Resort** (1 Wapato Point Pkwy., Manson, 888/768-9511, www.wapatopoint.com, $275-445) has 116 acres and a full mile and a half of waterfront. Condo-style units with fireplaces, ranging in size from a studio to a three-bedroom, mean full kitchens and a barbecue for each unit. Pools, hot tubs, and tennis courts are spread throughout the property, and many rentals—for boats, paddleboards, bikes, and more—can be had right here. There's even a stocked fishing pond in the summer. It's a resort for families or groups who want a stable home base.

CAMPING

With waterfront on a less-busy stretch of lake, about 10 miles from Chelan on the southern side, **Lake Chelan State Park** (7544 S

Lakeshore Rd., 509/687-3710, http://parks.state.wa.us, $12-45) is a beautiful piece of public real estate with a public boat-launching dock and more than 100 campsites, 39 with partial or full hookups. There's also running water and showers, plus a roped-off swimming area and a snack stand. It's a popular spot, and sites can and should be booked in advance; reservations are accepted up to nine months ahead.

Information and Services

For information on the area, visit downtown Chelan's **Lake Chelan Chamber of Commerce and Visitor Center** (216 E Woodin Ave., 509/682-3503, www.lakechelan.com, 9am-6pm Mon.-Sat., 10am-5pm Sun.), where maps as well as advice on wine tasting, adventure sports, or visiting Stehekin are available. Look for the **post office** (144 E Johnson Ave., 800/275-8777, 8:30am-5pm Mon.-Fri.) downtown as well.

Getting There

To reach Chelan from Seattle, take I-90 east to the town of Cle Elum, about 83 miles away. Take exit 85 to get on Highway 970, which will become U.S. 97 after about 10 miles, as it exits rural farmland and climbs into the forest around Blewett Pass; this area can be dangerous during winter months. Carry snow chains and leave lots of distance between cars, as accidents caused by cars sliding on frozen roads are common. After 35 miles, turn right on U.S. 2 and head about 14 miles southeast to the town of Wenatchee, taking the exit for U.S. 97 North Alternate; look for signs for Chelan. U.S. 97 North Alternate runs along the west side of the Columbia River for 33 miles, climbing above the river in the last few miles to reach the town of Chelan. The total distance is about 180 miles and takes just over three hours.

From Leavenworth, Chelan is about 55 miles northeast via U.S. 2 and U.S. 97 North Alternate, making for a drive of just over an hour.

WINTHROP

Just like Leavenworth is a trip to Bavaria, Winthrop is a trip back in time to the Old West. Located in the middle of the beautiful, remote Methow Valley, the town committed to an old-timey theme in the 1970s, on the site of what was once a real frontier town. Now modern buildings have clapboard facades and wooden sidewalks, hand-painted signs, and hitching posts. The Methow and Chewuch

the Old West town of Winthrop

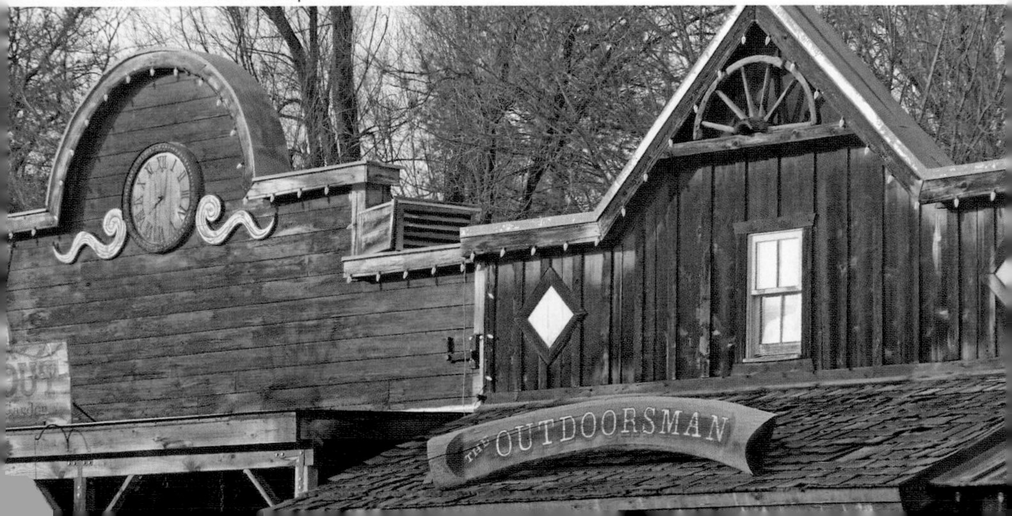

Rivers run through town, making for some beautiful patio settings. Beyond, the outdoor mecca of the Methow Valley stretches in every direction. The region has become a favorite for cross-country skiers, hikers, and second-home buyers.

Sights

Though re-created history is on display all over town, the **Shafer Historical Museum** (285 Castle Ave., 509/996-2712, http://shafermuseum.com, 10am-5pm daily summer, admission by donation) has the real thing, or rather exhibits about it. Some of the many buildings on-site are original 19th-century structures that have been moved to the museum. Inside are printing presses and household items, mining equipment, and old photos. Open only in summer, the tree-shaded spot makes a nice in-town detour.

And now for something completely different: The **North Cascade Smokejumper Base** (23 Intercity Airport Rd., 509/997-2031, www.northcascadessmokejumperbase.com, 10am-5pm daily June-Oct., free) is the gathering spot for the firefighters who parachute into the scene of a wildfire. Smokejumping is a dangerous profession, and one that dates back to 1939—this is where it was developed. The crew offers free tours of the red barn where they're based, about five miles south of Winthrop. You'll learn about the job of smokejumpers, how they have to be ready to take off in just two minutes when a fire call is heard, and how they use chainsaws and hand tools to fight the fire once they land. In a region particularly susceptible to forest fires, the job is a crucial and fascinating one.

Hiking

In summer, there are miles of trails to explore. **Methow Trails** (309 Riverside Ave., 509/996-3287, www.methowtrails.org, 8:30am-3:30pm Mon.-Fri.), a nonprofit that manages a system of trails in the area, offers maps useful for finding hiking options and opens its skiing trails to hikers for free in the summer. Or head to **Winthrop Mountain Sports** (257 Riverside Ave., 509/996-2886, www.winthropmountainsports.com, 9:30am-6pm Mon.-Fri, 9am-6pm Sat., 9am-5pm Sun.) for books with more detailed hike information.

PATTERSON MOUNTAIN

Distance: 3.7 miles round-trip
Duration: 2-3 hours
Elevation gain: 1,000 feet
Effort: moderate
Trailhead: parking lot on Patterson Lake Road
Directions: Head east out of Winthrop and turn right onto Twin Lakes Road after about a half mile. Follow Twin Lakes Road for three miles and turn right on Patterson Lake Road, continuing for four miles.

Though very exposed to sunshine in the middle of the Methow Valley's hot summer, Patterson Mountain has glorious views. In spring it boasts fields of wildflowers, and in fall the aspen trees turn yellow. The trail splits as it starts to climb, signed as the Northern Loop and Southern Loop Trails. Either work; they meet again about a half mile before the summit, and you can take one to the summit then the other back. Note that the Northern Loop section has steps over a barbed wire fence. The rocky summit area affords the best vistas, but the entire route through brushy, open hills affords beautiful views of the green Methow Valley and a few snow-topped mountains beyond.

GOAT PEAK LOOKOUT

Distance: 5 mlles round-trip
Duration: 3-4 hours
Elevation gain: 1,400 feet
Effort: strenuous
Trailhead: parking lot on Forest Road 200
Directions: From Winthrop, head northwest on Highway 20 for 8 miles and turn right on Goat Creek Road. Follow Goat Creek Road for 4.8 miles and turn right on Forest Road 52. After 2.5 miles, turn left on Forest Road 5225. Drive 6.2 miles and turn right on Forest Road 5225-200, continuing for 2.9 miles.

Taking you up to a height of 7,000 feet, this out-and-back trail is steep at first through the forest, then eventually levels out before a final rise to the top, every break in the trees revealing views down into the valley below. On top is a historical lookout, no longer regularly staffed but once locally famous for its "Lightning Bill" firewatcher. Peer across to the Pasayten Wilderness and the peaks of the North Cascades, and keep your eyes peeled for mountain goats; they're occasionally spotted here. Note that the steep trail can be rough going in the midsummer heat.

Mountain Biking

The sunny Methow is ideal for mountain biking, and the valley boasts dozens of trails from easy to difficult. Find updates on what's open—these hillsides can be covered in snow well into early summer—and route descriptions at the website of **Methow Cycle and Sport** (29 Hwy. 20, 509/996-3645, www.methowcyclesport.com, 9am-6pm Mon.-Sat., 9am-5pm Sun.), which also offers bike rentals ($20-50 per day) in the area. **Methow Trails** (309 Riverside Ave., 509/996-3287, www.methowtrails.org) opens up some of its trails to mountain bikers in the summer.

Winter Sports

Though at one time the Methow was eyed for a giant downhill ski area the size of Whistler, plans fell through and it remained a sleepy gem rather than a bustling destination resort. Now the region is known for its Nordic skiing, particularly on the stellar **Methow Trails** (309 Riverside Ave., 509/996-3287, www.methowtrails.org, $24 adults, free for children under 18) that loop through the entire valley—more than 120 miles of trail, much of it groomed regularly from about December to April, weather dependent. Trails wind past rivers and into the forests above the valley, past million dollar homes and small farms. Passes are required to ski on the trails, with extra charges for dogs ($20). Snowshoers can access the routes for $5, while fat bikers pay $10. Be sure to check which routes are open to non-skiers. Get a map or pass at the Methow Trails office or at many of the cafés and shops around town. The easiest place to access the system is at the **Winthrop Trailhead** (208 White Ave.), but there is access throughout the valley.

Entertainment and Events

NIGHTLIFE

What's an Old West town without a saloon? The **Three Fingered Jack Saloon** (176 Riverside Ave., 509/996-2411, www.3fingeredjacks.com, 7am-midnight

Patterson Mountain

daily) is the oldest legal saloon in the state, it claims, and it's named after a local man who had a bad accident while cutting meat—not the happiest story in town. It has pool tables and booths, wall-mounted antlers, plastic tablecloths, and enough beer on tap to please any Northwesterner.

A delicate, well-designed cocktail bar with modernized rustic decor in the middle of a small mountain town, **Copper Glance** (134A Riverside Ave., www.copperglancewinthrop.com, 4pm-11pm Tues.-Thurs. and Sun., 4pm-1am Fri.-Sat.) makes the juxtaposition between Winthrop's Old West sidewalks and its white-tiled bar backsplash seem natural. Well-blended craft cocktails, many with simple but Instagram-ready garnishes, are served alongside small plates, and the bar sometimes hosts live music.

FESTIVALS AND EVENTS

Although March is a bit of an in-between season for the region, the **Winthrop Balloon Festival** (http://winthropwashington.com, Mar.) lights up the sky with hot-air balloons, more than a dozen, over the course of one weekend. Spectators are invited to come watch the inflations and launches for free. There are morning launches Friday-Sunday at the **Winthrop Inn** (960 Hwy. 20), and on Saturday evening there's an additional launch downtown, near sunset. You can also hop in a hot-air balloon during the festival for $225-250 per person. Reservations are recommended at least a month in advance.

Cowboys come to town during **Winthrop '49er Days** (downtown and at Winthrop Barn, 51 Hwy. 20, http://winthropwashington.com, May), a festival that's been held for more than 70 years. The event, which takes place over a weekend, starts off with a horse-packing trip that local riders take through the mountains, a kind of wagon train without the wagons. When the line of horses comes back into town, the festival begins. A parade, cowboy poetry night, and country-western dance follow. Most events are free, while others are ticketed and run $7-25.

Once a year, the town becomes music central when the giant (for the Methow Valley) **Winthrop Rhythm and Blues Festival** (19190 Hwy. 20, 509/997-3837, http://winthropbluesfestival.com, July, $110 admission, $45 camping, $10-15 parking) takes over. Held over a three-day weekend, the event includes a large outdoor stage at the Blues Ranch a mile outside town, with tunes going until 2am.

Shopping

If you're driving to Winthrop from the north, one of the first businesses you'll see after crossing the North Cascades Highway is the **Mazama Store** (50 Lost River Rd., Mazama, 509/996-2855, www.themazamastore.com, 7am-6pm daily), a proper introduction to the Methow Valley and about 15 miles north of Winthrop. The general store has high-end groceries, gifts and housewares, plus a coffee stand and pastries alongside a few premade sandwiches. The outdoor tables are a pleasant place to rest after a long drive, and don't be surprised to see Pacific Crest Trail hikers here in the late summer, making their last stop before completing a total thru-hike; their final destination of Canada is only about a week's hike north.

Indie book shop **Trail's End Bookstore** (241 Riverside Ave., 509/996-2345, www.trailsendbookstore.com, 10am-6pm Mon.-Thurs., 10am-7pm Fri., 9am-8pm Sat., 9am-6pm Sun.) has a cozy window reading spot with views of the river outside, plus a great selection of outdoor and hiking books. The store also hosts readings and poetry nights.

If you need it for the outdoors—or own it, but forgot it—**Winthrop Mountain Sports** (257 Riverside Ave., 509/996-2886, www.winthropmountainsports.com, 9:30am-6pm Mon.-Fri, 9am-6pm Sat., 9am-5pm Sun.) has it. Hiking clothes, bandannas, sunscreen, trekking poles, and winter gear, including Nordic skis, are on the shelves. This is also a great stop for hiking books and maps of the area.

Food

The cheery **Old Schoolhouse Brewery** (155 Riverside Ave., 509/996-3183, www.oldschoolhousebrewery.com, $10-14) is a brewpub with a sense of community, where bar patrons share a raised counter and locals chat as they're waiting for a table. Burgers are sizable and satisfying, if not particularly memorable, and the housemade beer can stand up to more famous varieties brewed around the state. The stage inside, hosting regular live music, is called the Log Jam.

Though the food isn't particularly noteworthy, the back patio at **Carlos1800 Mexican Bar and Grill** (149 Riverside Ave., 509/996-2245, http://carlos1800.com, 11am-8pm Mon.-Thurs., 11am-10pm Fri., 11am-11pm Sat., 11am-9pm Sun. summer, 3pm-8pm Fri., noon-8pm Sat.-Sun. winter, $13-19), plus its extended opening hours, make it a solid addition to the Old West stretch of downtown Winthrop. Enjoy giant margaritas on the deck overlooking the Methow River after a long hike, or down some enchiladas after an exhausting ski.

The charming **Rocking Horse Bakery** (265 Riverside Ave., 509/996-4241, www.rockinghorsebakery.com, $3-9) has a boat, bicycle, and skeleton, along with the signature wooden horse, hanging from its ceiling, plus cross-country skis and snowshoes on the wall. The wood-sided café, which has a back porch and multiple rooms with tables, is a cozy spot for good coffee, rich pastries, and a few pizza options by the slice. The shop also sells passes to the Methow Trails system.

As one of the only local restaurants that can claim to offer something close to fine dining, **Arrowleaf Bistro** (207 White Ave., 509/996-3919, www.arrowleafbistro.com, 5pm-9pm Wed.-Sun., $25-36) cares about presentation along with taste. Not to say that the interior is formal; rather the simple dining room uses muted colors to allow the well-plated food to shine. Dishes are based on local ingredients, including a boeuf bourguignon made from cows raised in the Methow Valley and salads sourced from a nearby farm's produce.

Accommodations

UNDER $150

You haven't seen this before: The **Rolling Huts** (18381 W Hwy. 20, 509/996-4442, http://rollinghuts.com, $145), about nine miles north of town, are cabins designed by one of Seattle's most famous architects, Tom Kundig, and placed on rolling tractor trailer bases. The six structures sit facing an open field and are called the "herd," though they don't actually move much. Don't picture a log cabin; these ultra-modern units have straight lines and modular furniture and a sleeping platform. Bathrooms are separate but not far, including private toilets for each cabin. Picture camping, but nowhere near as hard. It's a taste of tiny-house life without committing to getting rid of all your possessions.

$150-250

Don't fear that Winthrop's old-timey facade means old-fashioned interiors. The cabins at **River's Edge Resort** (115 Riverside Ave., 509/996-8000, www.riversedgewinthrop.com, $160-245) have full kitchens and private hot tubs. With a central location, the cabins still manage to feel peaceful from their perch on the Chewuch River.

OVER $250

The large **Sun Mountain Lodge** (604 Patterson Lake Rd., 509/996-2211, www.sunmountainlodge.com $307-387) is an old-fashioned mountain hotel, complete with stone fireplaces and rough-hewn furniture, but with careful updates and good consistency throughout its 112 rooms. Rooms may have exposed wooden beams or rustic quilts, but beds are modern and comfortable. Outside you'll find one of the best hot tubs in the valley, with beautiful views of the valley below. The property also has two restaurants, a gym, ski rentals, and a great spa. Up in the mountains about 10 miles from Winthrop, it boasts more of a resort feel.

CAMPING

Located about five miles east of town, **Pearrygin Lake State Park** (561 Bear Creek Rd., 509/996-2370, http://parks.state.wa.us, $12-45) offers 76 regular sites and just as many hookup sites, plus 11,000 feet of waterfront access and more than six miles of hiking trails. The lake is a placid one, good for fishing, and day visitors flock here even in winter, when snowshoeing and fat-tire biking are popular. There's a swimming area and campfire programs on Tuesday and Thursday evenings in summer.

The very active **Winthrop/North Cascades National Park KOA** (1114 Hwy. 20, 509/996-2258, http://koa.com, $43-55), a couple of miles south of town, has a heated swimming pool and a playground with as many Western touches as the town of Winthrop itself. There are a few rustic cabins, and some sites are basically riverfront, tucked between trees.

Information and Services

Even the Winthrop **post office** (1110 Hwy. 20, 509/996-2282, 9am-4:30pm Mon.-Fri.) has Old West siding; find it just southeast of town on Highway 20. The **Methow Valley Ranger Station** (Methow Valley Ranger District, 24 W Chewuch Rd., 509/996-4003, www.fs.usda.gov, 7:45am-4:30pm Mon.-Fri.), staffed by U.S. Forest Service rangers, has some maps and information about local hikes and recreation.

Getting There

Reaching Winthrop means a beautiful drive but possibly a long one. From Seattle, it's most easily reached by Highway 20 through North Cascades National Park, which closes in early winter and does not reopen until late spring. When it's open, head north from Seattle via I-5 for 65 miles to exit 230. Turn right onto Highway 20 and follow it for about 125 miles over the Cascades to reach Winthrop. The entire trip takes about 3.75 hours.

When the North Cascades Highway is closed, take I-90 from Seattle east to the town of Cle Elum, about 83 miles away. Take exit 85 to get on Highway 970, which will become U.S. 97 after about 10 miles, as it exits rural farmland and climbs into the forest around Blewett Pass; this area can be dangerous during winter months. Carry snow chains and leave lots of distance between cars, as accidents caused by cars sliding on frozen roads are common. After 35 miles, turn right on U.S. 2 and head about 14 miles southeast to the town of Wenatchee, then follow signs to stay on U.S. 2/U.S. 97. Continue on, heading north for about 54 miles, hugging the Columbia River until the town of Pateros. There, turn left on Highway 153 and follow it north for 31 miles as it becomes Highway 20. Follow it for 11 miles into Winthrop. This route takes about 4.25 hours from Seattle.

From Chelan, Winthrop is about 60 miles north via U.S. 97 North Alternate and U.S. 97, Highway 153, and Highway 20, making for a drive of 1.25 hours.

Olympic Peninsula

Look for ★ to find recommended sights, activities, dining, and lodging.

Highlights

★ **Fort Worden State Park:** This military campus turned state park boasts beaches, a lighthouse, old battlements, and historical houses (page 150).

★ **Northwest Maritime Center:** All things boat-related are taught, made, and celebrated at the home of the Wooden Boat Festival (page 152).

★ **Hurricane Ridge:** This alpine meadow overlooking the Olympic Mountains is a celebrated cornerstone of Olympic National Park (page 167).

★ **Hoh Rain Forest:** More than 12 feet of rain fall on this stretch of old-growth forest, home to herds of Roosevelt elk (page 172).

★ **Cape Flattery:** Welcome to the edge of the world, where a rugged point of land meets the Pacific Ocean (page 177).

Just across the water from Seattle, the remote Olympic Peninsula has its own mystique, with a thick rain forest, a wild coast, and gritty towns.

You can't drive across the Olympic Peninsula—a mountain range is in the way. Here the route circles instead, caught between the shoreline and the slopes. The rectangular peninsula is more than just trees and shore. Historical Port Townsend has a preserved military base with killer views and a Victorian downtown embellished with art galleries. In industrial Port Angeles, ships come from faraway ports, making their first stops on the continent in a harbor hugged by the delicate sand spit of Ediz Hook.

Past the sparkling waters of Lake Crescent is an area that survived the *Twilight* boom. Anglers and loggers share their modest little town of Forks with vampire fans and werewolf groupies. And just off the main roads, each separated by pristine, wild beaches, the Native American reservations of the Makah, Quileute, Hoh, and Quinault tribes marry ancient tradition with modern economies.

At the tip of the Olympic Peninsula sits Cape Flattery, the very corner of the country and the most northwestern point of the contiguous United States. Stand above the craggy cliffs, where the brutal waves of the Pacific roll in endlessly from the mist.

A temperate rain forest and herds of elk are even farther south, as is the gritty hometown of grunge legend Kurt Cobain, where he wrote songs under a grotty bridge. Take your time on the peninsula's large loop, and don't forget to stop for the hot springs, the majestic old hotels, and—if you see him—Bigfoot.

PLANNING YOUR TIME

Because this corner of Washington State is so decentralized, it's best to budget at least two days' exploration. No one town makes a perfect base for the Olympic Peninsula, so moving from Port Townsend west to Forks or Lake Quinault allows for a more thorough experience of the region.

Although the out-of-the-way peninsula is a destination that requires intention, once here, you'll find it's fairly relaxing. Crowds are fortunately minimal, though Olympic National Park sites can get popular in the midsummer,

Previous: Hurricane Ridge; Cape Flattery. **Above:** Kalaloch.

Olympic Peninsula

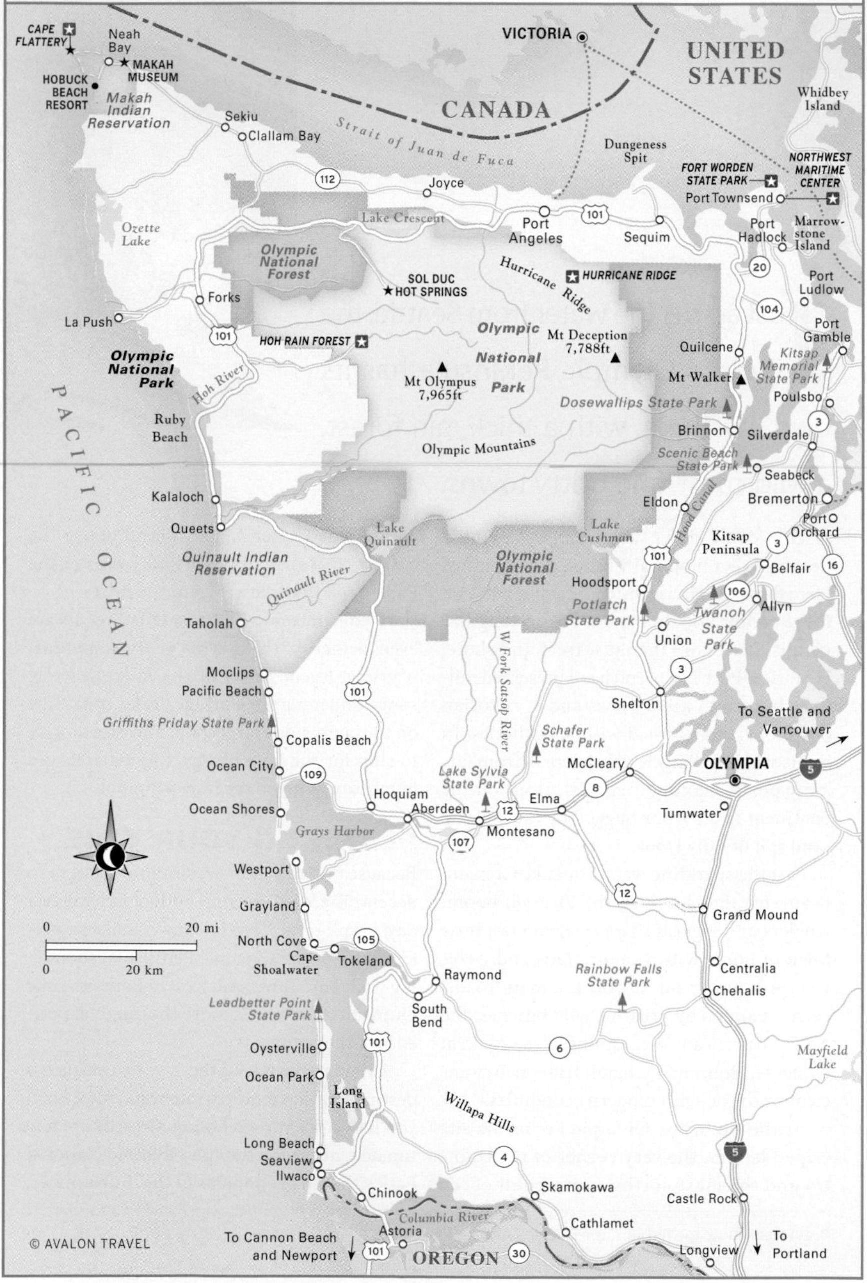
CAPE FLATTERY
Neah Bay
MAKAH MUSEUM
HOBUCK BEACH RESORT
Makah Indian Reservation
VICTORIA
UNITED STATES
CANADA
Whidbey Island
Sekiu
Clallam Bay
Strait of Juan de Fuca
Dungeness Spit
FORT WORDEN STATE PARK
NORTHWEST MARITIME CENTER
Port Townsend
Joyce
112
101
Lake Crescent
Port Angeles
Sequim
Port Hadlock
Marrowstone Island
Ozette Lake
Olympic National Forest
SOL DUC HOT SPRINGS
Hurricane Ridge
HURRICANE RIDGE
20
Port Ludlow
Forks
104
La Push
Port Gamble
HOH RAIN FOREST
Olympic National Park
Mt Deception 7,788ft
Quilcene
Kitsap Memorial State Park
Mt Olympus 7,965ft
Mt Walker
Poulsbo
Hoh River
Dosewallips State Park
3
Ruby Beach
Brinnon
Silverdale
PACIFIC OCEAN
Olympic Mountains
Scenic Beach State Park
Seabeck
Kalaloch
Eldon
Bremerton
Hood Canal
Port Orchard
Queets
Lake Quinault
Lake Cushman
Kitsap Peninsula
16
Quinault Indian Reservation
Belfair
Quinault River
Hoodsport
106
Allyn
Potlatch State Park
Twanoh State Park
Taholah
Union
W Fork Satsop River
Moclips
Shelton
Pacific Beach
To Seattle and Vancouver
Griffiths Priday State Park
Schafer State Park
Copalis Beach
McCleary
OLYMPIA
5
Ocean City
109
Lake Sylvia State Park
8
Hoquiam
Elma
Aberdeen
12
Tumwater
Ocean Shores
Montesano
Grays Harbor
107
Westport
Grayland
Grand Mound
0
20 mi
20 km
North Cove
105
Cape Shoalwater
Tokeland
Raymond
Centralia
Rainbow Falls State Park
Chehalis
Leadbetter Point State Park
South Bend
Oysterville
6
Mayfield Lake
Ocean Park
Long Island
Willapa Hills
Long Beach
Seaview
4
Ilwaco
Chinook
Skamokawa
Castle Rock
Columbia River
Cathlamet
To Cannon Beach and Newport
Astoria
OREGON
30
Longview
To Portland
© AVALON TRAVEL

Two Days on the Olympic Peninsula

If you're taking the ferry from Seattle, start this itinerary in Port Townsend. Ferrying from Victoria, the trip picks up in Port Angeles (a one-hour drive west of Port Townsend).

DAY 1

In **Port Townsend,** start with breakfast at **The Blue Moose Café.** Afterward, it's just a short drive east on Sims Way to downtown. Appreciate the Victorian architecture and then tour the wooden boats at the **Northwest Maritime Center.** Drive 2 miles north on Jackson Street to **Fort Worden State Park** and explore the former military site's abandoned old battlements.

From Port Townsend, it's an hour drive west on Highway 20 to U.S. 101 and the coastal city of **Port Angeles.** The Victoria ferry lands here, and the town is a suitable gateway for excursions into the Hurricane Ridge area of **Olympic National Park.** Chow down at **Next Door Gastropub,** and then drive 17 miles south on Heart O' the Hills Road to the **Hurricane Ridge Visitor Center.** Enjoy a short hike before driving back to Port Angeles; turn east on U.S. 101 to Lake Crescent and spend the night at the park's **Lake Crescent Lodge.**

DAY 2

From Lake Crescent Drive, it's a 40-minute drive south on U.S. 101 to Forks. Grab a coffee or a sack lunch at **Forks Coffee Shop** and follow La Push Road 15 miles west to the town of the same name. Hike the **Second Beach Trail** and enjoy your lunch with views of the sea stacks.

Return to Forks and head 30 miles south on U.S. 101 to explore the southern sections of Olympic National Park. Turn east on Upper Hoh Road to reach the **Hoh Rain Forest Visitor Center,** home to the famous Olympic rain forest. Or stay on U.S. 101 and drive 68 miles south to **Lake Quinault** for nature walks and epic trees. **Kalaloch,** 30 miles south of Forks, provides a nice beach detour along the way.

From Lake Quinault, it's a straight shot south on U.S. 101 for 44 miles to **Aberdeen.** In Aberdeen, you have two options: Head inland via Highway 8 for 50 miles to Olympia and I-5, returning to either **Seattle** or **Portland;** or continue 70 miles south on U.S. 101 to Astoria, Oregon, and explore the **Oregon Coast.**

especially ocean beaches. It's relatively easy, if slow, to get around by car, but public transportation is very minimal. U.S. 101, which makes a giant circle around the peninsula, is the main route and generally stays snow-free the entire year.

Port Townsend

The Victorian seaport of Port Townsend is pretty as a picture, with a waterfront central street stacked with ornate, historical buildings. Ferries glide into a dock that bookends one end of town, while a massive wooden boat center stands on the other. The town was founded before Seattle. Its location on the northeast corner of the peninsula was considered key, and at one point it was expected to become the state capital. (It didn't, losing out to Olympia.)

The thriving port was busy with the timber trade, and the U.S. military built fortifications, which they called Fort Worden, at the nearby point. But the town became known for something else in the early 20th century—it was one of the biggest centers for shanghaied sailors on the West Coast, where inebriated crewmen could wake up to find themselves on a slow boat to anywhere in the world.

Although the town suffered in the Great Depression, the pulp and paper mill just south of the city helped sustain the area. The smell of pulp is still in the air as you approach the city of almost 10,000.

SIGHTS

★ Fort Worden State Park

At one time the parade grounds of **Fort Worden** (200 Battery Way, 360/344-4400, www.parks.wa.gov/fortworden, 8:30am-dusk, $10 parking) were used by marching soldiers; now they're perfect kite-flying fields. The 434-acre state park includes rows of old military housing, now used as conference buildings and vacation rentals.

Two miles of shore line the park, with the red-roofed **Port Wilson Lighthouse** located among the driftwood. The **Port Townsend Marine Science Center** (360/385-5582, www.ptmsc.org, 11am-5pm Wed.-Mon. summer, noon-5pm Fri.-Sun. fall-spring, $5 adults, $3 children 6-17, children 5 and under free) sits on a pier among the waves, with a natural history offshoot back on shore. Although trails cross parts of the park, the old battlements are the most exciting places to wander. The concrete **Battery Kinzie** held two 12-inch disappearing guns 1910-1943, ready for a possible attack from the west. Plenty of metal ladders, short tunnels, and dark bunkers remain. The **Commanding Officer's Quarters** (noon-5pm daily May-Sept., noon-5pm Sat.-Sun. Oct.-Nov. and Mar.-Apr., $6 adults, $5 seniors, $1 children 3-12) is a museum that focuses on the military history of the area, as well as the creation of the nearby national park.

Even though Fort Worden never saw military action, its claim to fame came later when the film *An Officer and a Gentleman* starring Richard Gere was largely filmed on its grounds in 1981.

Jefferson County Historical Society

The Jefferson County Historical Society runs several historical sites around town. Right on the town's main street, in the old city hall built in 1892, is the **Jefferson Museum of Art and History** (540 Water St., 360/385-1003, www.jchsmuseum.org, 11am-4pm daily, $6 adults, $5 seniors, $1 children), which uses the courtroom and fire hall spaces. It's a classic small-town history museum, with a nine-minute video introduction to the area and

Port Townsend

Port Townsend

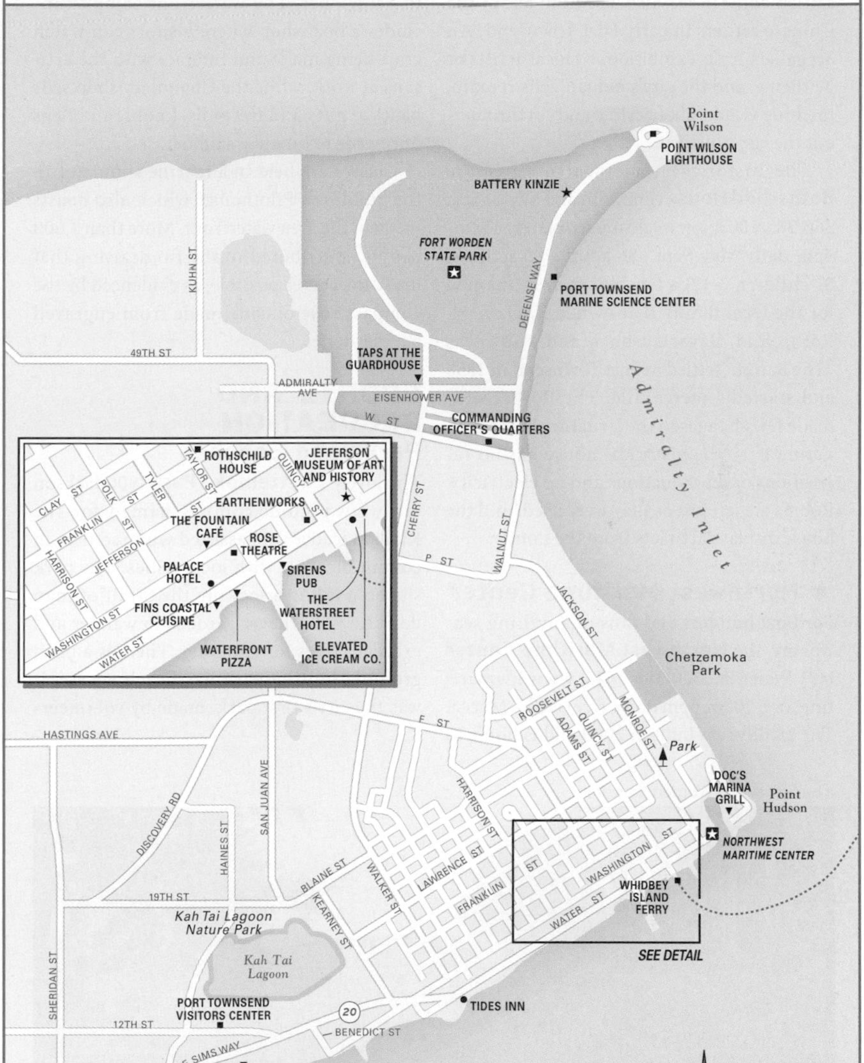
Point Wilson
POINT WILSON LIGHTHOUSE
BATTERY KINZIE
FORT WORDEN STATE PARK
DEFENSE WAY
PORT TOWNSEND MARINE SCIENCE CENTER
KUHN ST
49TH ST
TAPS AT THE GUARDHOUSE
ADMIRALTY AVE
EISENHOWER AVE
W ST
COMMANDING OFFICER'S QUARTERS
Admiralty Inlet
CHERRY ST
WALNUT ST
P ST
JACKSON ST
Chetzemoka Park
ROOSEVELT ST
MONROE ST
ADAMS ST
QUINCY ST
F ST
Park
HASTINGS AVE
DOC'S MARINA GRILL
Point Hudson
NORTHWEST MARITIME CENTER
HARRISON ST
DISCOVERY RD
HAINES ST
SAN JUAN AVE
BLAINE ST
WALKER ST
LAWRENCE ST
WASHINGTON ST
WHIDBEY ISLAND FERRY
FRANKLIN ST
WATER ST
KEARNEY ST
19TH ST
Kah Tai Lagoon Nature Park
Kah Tai Lagoon
SEE DETAIL
SHERIDAN ST
PORT TOWNSEND VISITORS CENTER
20
TIDES INN
12TH ST
BENEDICT ST
E SIMS WAY
THE BLUE MOOSE CAFÉ
10TH ST
7TH ST
MANRESA CASTLE
Port Townsend
To Old Fort Townsend State Park
0 0.25 mi
0 0.25 km
ROTHSCHILD HOUSE
TAYLOR ST
QUINCY ST
JEFFERSON MUSEUM OF ART AND HISTORY
CLAY ST
POLK ST
TYLER ST
EARTHENWORKS
FRANKLIN ST
THE FOUNTAIN CAFÉ
ROSE THEATRE
HARRISON ST
JEFFERSON ST
PALACE HOTEL
SIRENS PUB
THE WATERSTREET HOTEL
FINS COASTAL CUISINE
WASHINGTON ST
WATER ST
WATERFRONT PIZZA
ELEVATED ICE CREAM CO.

exhibits that represent both the peninsula's Native American history and its more recent settlement. There's also a section about the Chinese settlers in early Port Townsend. An art gallery hosts exhibitions by local artists or by theme, and the city's old jail cells remain, teaching visitors about crime and sin throughout the city's history.

The historical society also runs the **Rothschild House** (Franklin and Taylor Sts., 360/385-1003, www.jchsmuseum.org, 11am-4pm daily May-Sept., $6 adults, $5 seniors, $1 children 3-12) a few blocks away, named for the local family that owned it. D. C. H. Rothschild, Bavarian-born and known as "The Baron," settled in Port Townsend in 1858 and started a mercantile. The Rothschilds made few changes to the structure before donating it, so the historical house has no recreations or reproductions and no electricity. Rooms are left just as they were used, and the house displays artifacts from the family.

★ Northwest Maritime Center

For boat builders and fans of anything seaworthy, the **Northwest Maritime Center** (431 Water St., 360/385-3628, www.nwmaritime.org, 10am-5pm daily, free) is like Mecca. The facility was built in 2009 and is home to the Wooden Boat Foundation, which runs the hugely popular annual Wooden Boat Festival in September. The waterfront complex includes a boat shop where visitors can watch craft being made and interact with the artisans at work, while the Chandlery shop sells nautical gifts and the pulls, knobs, and flags one needs to kit out a sailboat.

Classes are held in a marine simulator in the building's Pilothouse, which also boasts views of the area waterfront. More than 1,600 people contributed to the fundraising that made the center possible, as evidenced by the compass rose outside made from engraved paving stones.

SPORTS AND RECREATION

Parks and Beaches

The lovely **Chetzemoka Park** (900 Jackson St., www.ptguide.com) is named for the Klallam leader who assisted white settlers in communicating with local tribes. The park sits on a hill overlooking the Strait of Juan de Fuca, with flower gardens to wander and excellent trees for climbing. There is a playground, and the park has beach access. It was the city's first park, made by volunteers

a bunker at Fort Worden State Park

in 1904. Hop on a swing for one of the best views in town.

Biking

The best-known bike trail in town is the **Larry Scott Memorial Trail** (www.ptguide.com), which travels from Port Townsend to the Four Corners area near Discover Bay. It is also the first section of the still-evolving **Olympic Discovery Trail** (www.olympicdiscovery-trail.com), which winds 130 miles from Port Townsend to the Pacific Ocean, crossing the entire peninsula. (For now about half of the trail miles are completed, with the rest on the busy highway.) The **Larry Scott Trail** is about 8 miles long and begins at the Boat Haven Marina (2601 Washington St.). Park near the restroom in the boat yard, or find more parking across the main road at a park-and-ride lot near the Safeway. The paved trail goes along the waterfront and then west; after 4 miles it turns south at Cape George Trailhead (Cape George and Crutcher Rd.). The next several miles of trail, to Four Corners, are still under construction.

There are also 12 miles of bike trails in **Fort Worden** (200 Battery Way, 360/344-4400, www.parks.wa.gov/fortworden), which make for an easy mountain-biking day. Park at the parade grounds and bike west, looking for dirt roads that head right from the main road.

The downtown **PT Cyclery** (252 Tyler St., 360/385-6470, www.ptcyclery.com, 9am-6pm Mon.-Sat. summer, noon-6pm Tues.-Sat. winter) rents mountain and road bikes ($7 per hour), plus tandem bikes and child trailers. They have maps and information about local mountain biking.

The Broken Spoke (630 Water St., 360/379-1295, http://thebrokenspokept.blogspot.com, 9am-6pm Mon.-Sat., 11am-4pm Sun. summer; 10am-6pm Mon.-Sat., 11am-4pm Sun. winter) also does rentals (half day $20-35) and has a repair shop in case you actually end up with a broken spoke. Both stores offer free lock and helmet rental with their bikes.

Kayaking

Located near the water inside Fort Worden, **Port Townsend Paddlesports** (Harbor Defense Way, Fort Worden State Park, 360/379-3608, www.ptpaddlesports.com, 9am-5pm daily June-Sept.) rents kayaks and stand-up paddleboards ($35-45 per two hours), as well as bikes. It also has wetsuit rentals for the very cold days. Reservations are

Northwest Maritime Center

recommended, but walk-up rentals are also available noon-4pm. It also leads kayak tours ($50-110 adults, $39-69 children) of the waterfront area near Fort Worden or beyond to North Beach and Bird Island; specialty tours require a reservation.

ENTERTAINMENT AND EVENTS

Nightlife

Sirens Pub (823 Water St., 360/379-1100, www.sirenspub.com, noon-2am daily) has 11 microbrews on tap, but the beer isn't usually the most interesting draw at this downtown bar. Live music takes the form of a Tuesday bluegrass night, an open mic night, karaoke, and dance music following live shows on weekends. A deck out back overlooks the water and ferry dock, while brick walls and dark trim dim the interior. Food features a local twist on pub fare—fried oysters, crab cakes, and steamed clams, plus burgers, pasta, and pizzas. Look for the bar's sign on the main drag, Water Street, then head up a long staircase to this locals' hangout.

Don't be alarmed by the jail cells at Fort Worden's **Taps at the Guardhouse** (300 Eisenhower Ave., 360/344-4400, fortworden.org/eat-here, 1pm-10pm daily): You haven't had so much to drink that you ended up in the pokey. This was formerly used by military law enforcement, and the historical aspects are well preserved. The bar's menu features hearty bites that go well with local beers and nicely crafted cocktails. Sit outside to get a view of the bustle of the fort, but leave time to explore the interior that dates back to 1904.

Though the small town of Chimacum used to be little more than a crossroads on the way to Port Townsend, a slew of new attractions has made it worth stopping for. **Finnriver Cidery** (124 Center Rd, 360/339-8478, www.finnriver.com, Mon.-Thurs. noon-6pm, Fri.-Sat. noon-9pm, Sun. 10am-9pm), built on the site of an old dairy, has a tasting room featuring a wide selection of apple-based drinks, including habanero cider and a dry-hopped favorite. A wood-fired oven bakes pizzas for the long tables of drinkers, and orchard views and horseshoes make it feel more like a family picnic spot.

Cinema

Only a few drive-in movie theaters are left in the state, making the **Wheel-In Motor Movie** (210 Theatre Rd., 360/385-0859, 7:45pm Wed.-Sun., $9 adults, $7 children 6-12, children 5 and under free), in operation since 1953, a special place to see a flick. A sign out front reads "Howdy Pardner"; drive in and park on the open field. The screen is surrounded by a thick forest of evergreen trees, which means double features are uninterrupted by excess light. A snack bar serves the requisite hot dogs and nachos.

The historical **Rose Theatre** (235 Taylor St., 360/385-1089, http://rosetheatre.com) was originally a vaudeville house in 1908 until it closed. It was then a variety of stores before reopening in 1992, when the original murals and tin-tile ceiling were restored. Now it's a cinema showing independent movies, filmed arts performances, and cult classic films. The **Starlight Room** (http://rosetheatre.com), above the Silverwater Café next door, has cocktails, beer, wine, antipasti, desserts, and popcorn.

Festivals and Events

The **Strange Brewfest** (American Legion Hall, 209 Monroe St., 360/385-3454, www.strangebrewfestpt.com, Jan.) is dedicated to all the weird ways you can make beer—with fruit, chocolate, coffee, and even odder ingredients. Many beers are specially made for the event, and winners can be picks like a tomato beer, peanut butter beer, or a salami beer. Entertainment during the event includes costume contests and circus performers. It's also a music festival with an eclectic lineup of funk and soul music.

Centrum (223 Battery Way, Fort Worden State Park, 360/385-3102, www.centrum.org), an arts organization based in Fort Worden, hosts the **Festival of American Fiddle Tunes and Jazz Port Townsend** (July),

Port Townsend Acoustic Blues Festival (Aug.), and **Olympic Music Festival** (Aug.-Sept.)

The **Wooden Boat Festival** (360/385-3628, www.woodenboat.org, Sept.) is a Port Townsend tradition that stretches back more than 40 years. The festival, centered at the Northwest Maritime Center (431 Water St.), includes demonstrations and hundreds of wooden boats on display—this is where boat enthusiasts come to celebrate their craft. Guests can buy single-day or multiday tickets. Boats are open for tours, and boat builders demonstrate everything from caulking to decorating to how to hold a chef's dinner at sea; other talks are about the history and nature of local waterways. Posters for the annual festival are a popular collector's item, so expect to see past versions around town.

The **Great Port Townsend Kinetic Sculpture Race** (www.ptkineticrace.org, Oct.) is something between an art festival and a drag race. Entrants make bizarre moving structures that are human-powered, then drivers (called "kineticnauts") race them on a course over road, water, sand, mud, or other surfaces. Bribes are encouraged in the voting process—one motto is "cheating is not a right, but a privilege." The biggest winner is the Mediocrity Award, for the vehicle that scores right in the middle. The races are held all over, but Port Townsend's version is one of the wildest, and organizers are proud of its grassroots, noncorporate history. The race begins at City Hall (250 Madison St.).

SHOPPING

The Northwest Man (901 Water St., 360/385-6734, http://theclotheshorseporttownsend.wordpress.com, 10am-5:30pm daily) is an emporium of all things manly, at least the flannel stuff. Besides shirts and hats, the best finds are Pendleton blankets made of stiff, durable wool woven in patterns inspired by Native American designs (they've been made in the Northwest for more than 100 years).

When you're ready to dress like a pirate, head to **World's End** (1020 Water St., 360/379-6906, www.worldsendporttownsend.com, 10am-6pm daily), where almost every piece of clothing for sale is in black-and-white stripes. Steampunk-style jewelry and frilly cuffs complete the nautical look, and there's even a photo of Johnny Depp from the *Pirates of the Caribbean* movies for inspiration.

In a town of galleries, **Earthenworks** (702 Water St., 360/385-0328, www.earthenworks-gallery.com, 10am-5:30pm daily) is both the best known and arguably the best. The airy store displays Northwest arts and crafts, including metalwork, ceramics, wood pieces, and paintings.

Chefs or anyone who has fun in the kitchen will find treasures at home decor store **The Green Eyeshade** (720 Water St., 360/385-3838, 10am-6pm daily), which specializes in gifts to be given with a chuckle: a mason jar cocktail shaker, or a weathered wall sign that reads "I Love You More Than Cheese."

FOOD

The menu at **The Fountain Café** (920 Washington St., 360/385-1364, hwww.fountaincafept.com, 11:30am-3pm and 5pm-9pm Sun.-Thurs., 11:30am-3pm and 5pm-9:30pm Fri.-Sat., $15-36) includes touches of Italian pastas and Moroccan chicken, but the saffron-yellow walls and red stools suggest a Southwestern cheeriness. In a small space that exudes Boho chic, the eatery draws locals as much as tourists willing to make the very small detour off the main drag.

Finding **The Blue Moose Café** (311 Haines Pl., 360/385-7339, 6:30am-2pm Mon.-Fri., 7am-2pm Sat.-Sun., $8-15, cash only) means venturing into Port Townsend's busy marina, where fishing boats are being cleaned and sailboats are lifted into dry docks by giant hoists. Inside the cramped quarters are mostly locals, happy to share a table when the breakfast crowd overwhelms the tiny establishment. A breakfast burrito is enough for two meals, but that could be the friendly chatter that fills you up, too.

Classic country diner ★ **Chimacum Café**

(9253 Rhody Dr., Chimacum, 360/732-4631, 6am-8pm Sun.-Thurs., 6am-9pm Fri.-Sat., $6-12) is a great place to stop just outside of Port Townsend—just look at the back of the menu: There you'll find a long list of homemade pies. If the café has the seasonal wild blackberry, it's a can't-miss—a sweet dream served a la mode.

At one time **Doc's Marina Grill** (141 Hudson St., 360/344-3627, http://docsgrill.com, 11am-11pm daily, $13-32) housed nurses on Point Hudson, the very end of town and right on the waterfront. Now the restaurant dishes up halibut, rockfish tacos, and half-pound burgers and has plenty of outdoor seating. It's a bit of an awkward walk from downtown, as you'll stroll through parking lots around the harbor, though it's physically not far; there are plenty of sailboat docks to pass along the way.

Pick your (tasty) poison: Downstairs at **Waterfront Pizza** (951 Water St., 360/385-6629, 11am-8pm daily, $8.50-32) is a crowded counter selling slices loaded with toppings, easy to carry out to the piers that extend into Puget Sound nearby. As befits a small-town pizzeria, the staff is jovial, if perhaps raucous at times. Up a narrow staircase on the 2nd floor is the pizzeria's full-service restaurant, where the sourdough-crust pizzas can be topped with homemade Italian sausage.

Where there are piers, sailboats, and a parade of tourists, there will be an old-fashioned ice cream parlor. Fortunately, ★ **Elevated Ice Cream Co.** (631 Water St., 360/385-1156, www.elevatedicecream.com, 10am-9pm Sun.-Thurs., 10am-10pm Fri.-Sat., $4) is as uplifting as it was when it began in the 1970s in an antique elevator. Homemade flavors like cardamom and maple walnut are served by the ounce, not by the scoop. Request "jimmies," a house specialty: The scooper will dunk your cone in sprinkles before handing it over.

ACCOMMODATIONS

Under $150

The ★ **Palace Hotel** (1004 Water St., 360/385-0773, www.palacehotelpt.com, $99-159) is every bit the dollhouse inside that it

Chimacum Café

looks to be from the street. The most convenient hotel in town is a block from the ferry terminal and right on the main drag, in a building constructed in 1889 by a retired sea captain. Both inside and out, it's decorated in bright, sometimes clashing colors—perhaps a nod to its life as a brothel in the early 20th century. Rooms are more sedate, with wrought-iron beds, and guests share bathrooms with claw-foot tubs. Plenty of froufrou decorates the hotel, but it doesn't get too precious. Thank the endless staircases and landings, hallway turns, and chandeliers—one almost suspects a secret passageway could be found in the old hotel's bones.

Head inside the Pacific Traditions Gallery to find **The Waterstreet Hotel** (635 Water St., 360/385-5467, www.waterstreethotelporttownsend.com, $50-175). The inn's front desk is within the art space, with the well-hidden rooms in the two floors above. Smaller rooms share baths, while suites have full kitchens, and one suite can sleep up to six. The vibe is much of the same Victorian hodgepodge that's everywhere in Port Townsend, but the unlabeled location helps it feel calmer, and some rooms have water views.

If you're looking to stay in a castle, you won't find many opportunities beyond **Manresa Castle** (651 Cleveland St., 360/385-5750, www.manresacastle.com, $101-245) in this corner of the world. The cream stone and pointed tower are Prussian in style, after the birthplace of the building's first owner and the town's first mayor. It sits atop a hill south of town, less out of place than it would be in any other Northwest town. Each hotel room has Victorian touches like a brass bedframe or highly ornate living room furniture. A chapel, which dates back to when Jesuits owned the property, is now a café that serves breakfast.

$150-200

How proud is **Tides Inn** (1807 Water St., 360/385-0595, www.tides-inn.com, $109-299) of its scene in the 1980s flick *An Officer and a Gentleman*? Very—the movie poster is still above the reception desk, even though the place barely resembles the roadside motel it was 30 years ago. Now, larger suites make up most of the inn, with balconies that face the very top of Puget Sound and a rocky beach. Inside furnishings are either plain or oddly ornate (and really quite ugly), but the sprinkling of private whirlpool tubs in select rooms forgives all manner of sins.

Over $250

There's hardly any town to speak of around **Inn at Port Ludlow** (1 Heron Rd., Port Ludlow, 360/437-7000, www.portludlowresort.com/inn, $260-350), though the rural area is certainly populated. The small bay is a popular boat harbor at the tip of Hood Canal, and the resort itself is connected to an 18-hole golf course. The Fireside restaurant in the hotel's base is centered around a large stone hearth, but all rooms have gas fireplaces of their own—not to mention whirlpool tubs.

Almost every type of accommodation is available at **Fort Worden** (200 Battery Way, 360/344-4434, www.parks.wa.gov/fortworden). The Officer's Row ($449-849) houses many duplexes with servant's quarters and fireplaces; rentable units have as many as six bedrooms, and kitchens are fully stocked. Also all built before 1915, the Non-Commissioned Officer houses ($249-370) have full kitchens and 2-4 bedrooms. Then there are more unusual rentals, like Alexander's Castle ($359), a Scottish-style brick tower from 1883 that's now a one-bedroom rental. Blissful Vista house ($359) has two bedrooms, a fireplace, and a remote location with a view.

Camping

Fort Worden (360/344-4431, www.parks.wa.gov, open year-round) has two campgrounds. The **Beach Campground** ($31-39) is near the old battery ruins and the Port Townsend Marine Science Center; it has 50 full-service RV sites in an open field. The **Upper Campground** ($29-35), with only 30 water and electric sites, is in a forested area. Reservations are recommended for both. There are also five walk-in primitive sites ($12) and one for boat-in campers ($12).

INFORMATION AND SERVICES

The **Port Townsend Visitors Center** (2409 Jefferson St., 360/385-2722, www.visitjeffersoncountywa.com, 9am-5pm Mon.-Fri., 10am-4pm Sat.-Sun.) has brochures and maps of Port Townsend, as well as information on the entire Quimper Peninsula, this particular bump of the larger Olympic Peninsula.

GETTING THERE

Port Townsend sits on the northeast tip of the Olympic Peninsula, abutting Puget Sound. It is 47 miles east of Port Angeles (and the ferry to Victoria, BC) via U.S. 101 and a three-hour drive (with no ferry crossings) west from Seattle via I-5 and U.S. 101. Olympia lies 98 miles directly south on U.S. 101.

You can cross Puget Sound by ferry at Edmonds, about 15 miles north of downtown Seattle. Take I-5 north to exit 177, following

Island Hopping

TO WHIDBEY ISLAND

The **Washington State Ferry** (206/464-6400, www.wsdot.wa.gov, $3.25 adults, $1.60 seniors and youth, $0.50 bicycle surcharge, $13.40 cars) boats, with their signature white-and-green color scheme, are a common and picturesque sight on the Port Townsend waterfront. The ferry leaves from the downtown terminal (1301 Water St.) and travels a short 30 minutes to Keystone (1400 Hwy. 20, Coupeville) on Whidbey Island. RVs and trailers must have reservations for the ferry, and it's recommended for cars.

On Whidbey, the terminal is close to **Fort Casey** (S Engle Rd., 360/678-4519, www.parks.wa.gov/parks, $10 parking), a park with concrete ruins, trails, the 1903 Admiralty Head Lighthouse, and guided tours of the gun batteries on weekends in summer. There is also a **campground** (888/226-7688, http://washington.goingtocamp.com) with 21 tent sites ($12-31) and 14 RV sites ($30-42).

TO SAN JUAN ISLAND

The passenger boat **Puget Sound Express** (227 Jackson St., 360/385-5288, www.pugetsoundexpress.com, $103.50 adults, $65 children 2-10, $15 bicycles) is a kind of private ferry service between Port Townsend and Friday Harbor on San Juan Island. The once-daily service leaves at 9am and returns at 5pm (May-Sept. only) and includes the boat ride and two hours in the quaint town of Friday Harbor. The company also runs a four-hour **whale-watching tour** ($95 adults, $65 children 2-10) from Port Townsend, multiday tours, and special Christmas trips to Seattle.

Highway 104 and signs for the Kingston ferry. Check departure times for the **Washington State Ferry** (888/808-7977, www.wsdot.wa.gov, $8.20 adults, $4.10 children 6-18, children 5 and under free, $18.20 for car and driver). Plan to arrive a half hour or even a full hour early—long lines lead to lengthy waits, especially on summer weekends. After the 30-minute crossing, continue west on Highway 104 across the Hood Canal Bridge, and then turn right on Highway 19 through Beaver Valley. The road merges into Highway 20 right before reaching Port Townsend. Without traffic on the Hood Canal Bridge, it's about a 35-mile, 50-minute drive from the ferry dock to Port Townsend.

Sequim

Sequim (pronounced "skwim") sits almost halfway between Port Townsend and Port Angeles and is a mostly residential area. It's notable for its acres of lavender fields and the long Dungeness Spit reaching out into the Strait of Juan de Fuca.

DUNGENESS NATIONAL WILDLIFE REFUGE

The Dungeness Spit is a 5.5-mile stretch of sand that reaches out into the Strait of Juan de Fuca; it's been part of the **Dungeness National Wildlife Refuge** (Voice of America Rd. and Park Rd., 360/457-8451, www.fws.gov/washingtonmaritime/dungeness, $3 parking) since 1915. The beach here doesn't allow pets, Frisbees, or kites because they disturb the birds and harbor seals protected here. Fish, migrating birds, shellfish, and seals can be found throughout the protected area, and the black brant bird is present in especially high numbers in April. The spit itself grows every year due to sand build-up and is the longest of its kind in the country.

It's possible to hike the spit out to near the end where the **New Dungeness Lightstation** (http://dungeness.com/lighthouse) alerts passing boats. The 11-mile round-trip hike should be carefully planned with tides, though it's always passable. Daily tours of the lighthouse are available.

The nearby county park, **Dungeness Recreation Area** (554 Voice of America Rd. W, 360/683-5847, www.clallam.net), has a one-mile bluff hiking trail, picnic areas, and **camping** in 64 sites (tents $25, hike-in/bike-in $7). There are no utility hookups, but there are showers.

LAVENDER FARMS

Sequim calls itself the lavender capital of the world because the plant grows almost as well here as it does in the south of France. A number of farms offer tours, you-pick gathering, plant sales, and lavender products. **Oliver's Lavender Farm** (82 Cameron Acres Ln., 360/681-3789, www.oliverslavender.com, 10am-5pm daily June-Sept.) has manicured gardens and a quaint gazebo. **CreekSide Lavender Farm** (1141 Cays Rd., 888/881-6055, www.lavenderconnection.com, summer only) sells lavender essential oil and other bath and home products. **Nelson's Duck Pond and Lavender Farm** (73 Humble Hill Rd., 360/681-7727, www.nelsonsduckpond.com, 10am-5pm Thurs.-Sun. May-Sept., 10am-5pm Thurs.-Mon. Oct.-Apr.) has a small pond and a wide selection of lavender products. The **Lavender Festival** (www.lavenderfestival.com, July) takes place in town with a street fair and farm tours. A cycling event, the **Tour de Lavender** (http://tourdelavender.wordpress.com, Aug.) encourages visitors to bike between farms; a more intense long-distance ride is from the Kingston ferry terminal.

FOOD

A plate of Dungeness silver oysters feels like the most appropriate dish at **Dockside Grill** (2577 W Sequim Bay Rd., 360/683-7510, www.docksidegrill-sequim.com, 11:30am-3pm and 4pm-9pm Wed.-Sun. Apr.-Oct., 11:30am-3pm and 4pm-8pm Wed.-Sun. Nov.-Mar, $17-24), given that the windows face the marina and gray-blue waters of Sequim Bay. The seafood is local, including halibut and salmon, and dishes are classic—shrimp and grits, prawns in white wine and butter. A surprising number of vegan options are also on offer. Reservations might be helpful when the warm summer evenings fill the small dining room.

Get ready to confess at **Blondie's Plate**

the Olympic Mountains and Dungeness Spit from the air

(134 S 2nd Ave., 360/683-2233, www.blondies-plate.com, 4pm-9pm Sun.-Thurs., 4pm-10pm Fri.-Sat., $11-40), an eatery that occupies an 1896 Episcopalian church. The arched windows may scream sermon, but the interior feels more like an upscale diner, with midcentury accents and striking light fixtures. The menu leans heavily on local clams, market vegetables, and salmon. Dishes tend toward the hearty and warm, including risotto and buttermilk fried chicken, and there are significant discounts during happy hour (4pm-5pm). Many items are vegetarian, gluten-free, or dairy-free.

Everything on the menu at **Nourish Sequim** (101 Provence View Ln., 360/797-1480, www.nourishsequim.com, 11:30am-9pm Wed.-Sat., 11am-9pm Sun., $16-28) is gluten-free, and everything down to the condiments is made in-house to ensure there's no contamination. Flavors in the seasonal menu tend to be lighter, with a number of salads on offer and pastas paired with local fish—though there is a tasty burger, too. Brunch includes garbanzo flour crepes and farm-egg Benedicts. The restaurant is located on a farm that dates back to 1880; many of the herbs and produce are grown just feet away. Guests are invited to walk the gardens, including the lavender patch—the spot claims to be the oldest herb farm in the state.

ACCOMMODATIONS

Although part of a chain, the **Holiday Inn Express Hotel and Suites** (1441 E Washington St., 877/859-5095, www.ihg.com, $258-296) has neat, modern rooms, some with kitchenettes. There's a pool and free access to the hot breakfast bar. The rooftop is lined with solar panels, and the outdoor patio has tables, strings of lights, and a nice view of the hillside.

The **Juan de Fuca Cottages** (182 Marine Dr., 360/683-4433, www.juandefuca.com, rooms $210-350, cottages $300-360) are located right on the Strait of Juan de Fuca, and some units have views of the Dungeness Spit and its lighthouse. Kayaks, bicycles, and snowshoes are available to rent. Rooms in the main beach house have fold-out sleeper sofas and one has a rock fireplace, plus they're close to the beach. The Dungeness Bay Lodge rooms are slightly farther inland and have whirlpool tubs and electric fireplaces. Cottages are scattered around the property, and some have outdoor patios. Most units have kitchens, though a few just have mini-fridges and microwaves.

Nelson's Duck Pond and Lavender Farm (73 Humble Hill Rd., 360/681-7727, www.nelsonsduckpond.com, $225-275 for two nights) also has a rental cabin in a red barn that sleeps four, with a full bath, kitchen, and access to the you-pick lavender field. Check-in comes with a lemon lavender pound cake.

GETTING THERE

Sequim is located on U.S. 101 about 17 miles east of Port Angeles; it is a 31-mile drive from Port Townsend. Take Highway 20 for 13 miles from Port Townsend to Discovery Bay, where it meets U.S. 101. Take U.S. 101 west for 18 miles to Sequim.

Port Angeles

If Port Townsend is a Victorian dollhouse turned into a town, then Port Angeles is the backyard tool house reimagined as a small coastal city. The long Ediz Hook protects a harbor that was a center of business long before Europeans settled here—Klallam tribes have used it for thousands of years. The peninsula's booming logging trade led to shipping facilities and pulp mills near the harbor, though recent years have seen a decline in the city's industrial health.

But still, everything in town has a job to do: The Coho ferry departs for Victoria in Canada, and signs in downtown stores welcome the crews of large barges by name. The town is also home to the headquarters for Olympic National Park, and the road that leads to its largest visitors center, at Hurricane Ridge, starts in the middle of the gritty downtown.

SIGHTS

Ediz Hook

Accessing the three-mile **Ediz Hook** means a trip through the downtown lumber mills, which have seen a flurry of sales and management changes in recent decades. The public is allowed to drive about two-thirds of the way out, but the U.S. Coast Guard lays claim to the end of the spit. Like the Dungeness Spit in Sequim, the Ediz Hook is a narrow path into the massive waterway that borders the top of the Olympic Peninsula, though here you get a much better glimpse of the region's industrial life. The rocks and driftwood that made up the edges of the hook make a good platform for shore-based whale-watching or simply counting the ships that pass through the Strait of Juan de Fuca. At dusk, look back at land to see the lights of Port Angeles reflected in the water, a sharp contrast to the Olympic Mountains that rise steeply behind them.

Feiro Marine Life Center

Located next to Hollywood Beach on the Port Angeles waterfront, **Feiro Marine Life Center** (315 N Lincoln St., 360/417-6254, www.feiromarinelifecenter.org, 10am-5pm daily summer, noon-4pm daily winter, $5 adults, $3 children 3-17, children under 3 free)

Port Angeles

Port Angeles

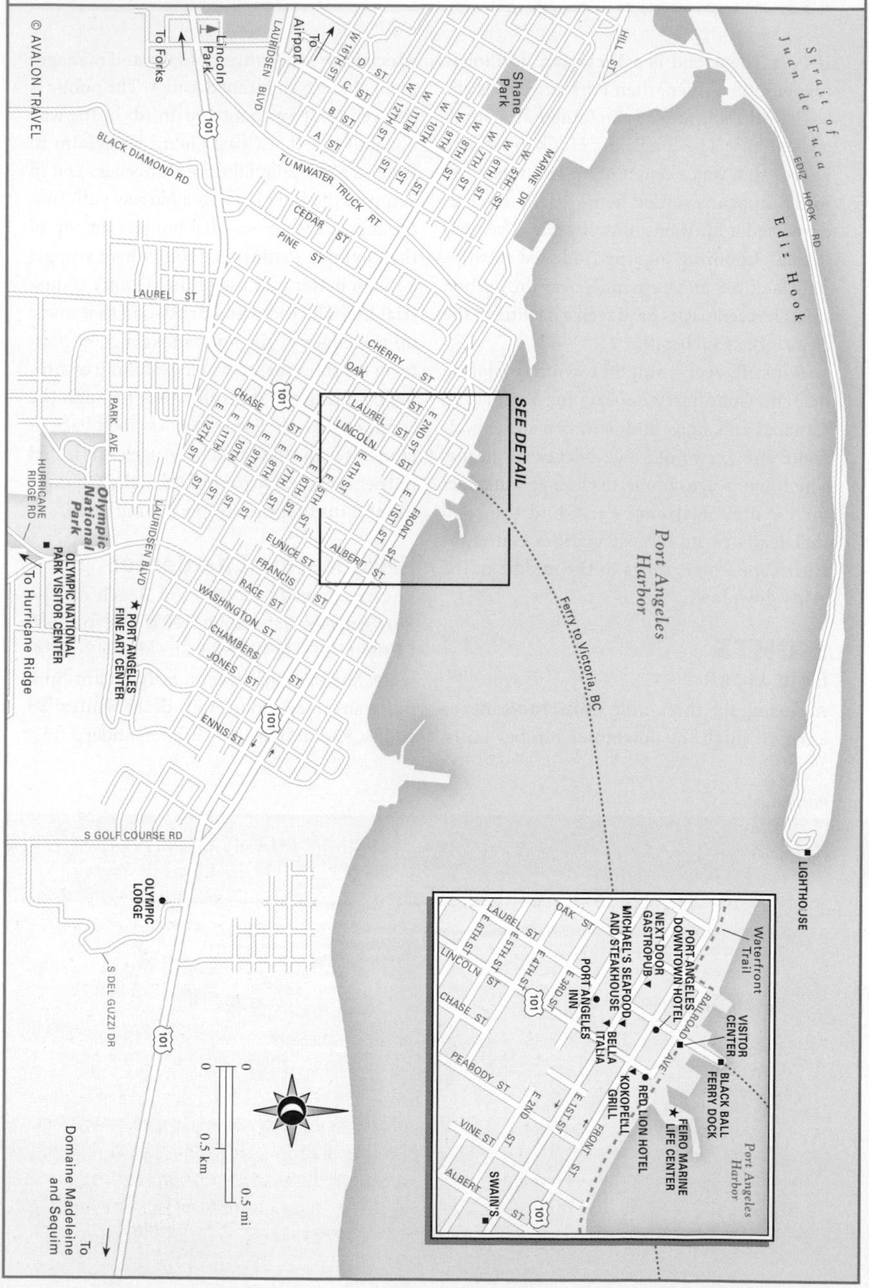
Strait of Juan de Fuca
Ediz Hook
EDIZ HOOK RD
LIGHTHOUSE
Port Angeles Harbor
Ferry to Victoria, BC
SEE DETAIL
Shane Park
Lincoln Park
To Forks
To Airport
LAURIDSEN BLVD
BLACK DIAMOND RD
TUMWATER TRUCK RT
CEDAR ST
PINE ST
LAUREL ST
CHERRY ST
OAK ST
MARINE DR
HILL ST
W 5TH ST
W 6TH ST
W 7TH ST
W 8TH ST
W 9TH ST
W 10TH ST
W 11TH ST
W 12TH ST
W 16TH ST
D ST
C ST
B ST
A ST
CHASE ST
LINCOLN ST
E 2ND ST
E 4TH ST
E 5TH ST
E 6TH ST
E 7TH ST
E 8TH ST
E 9TH ST
E 10TH ST
E 11TH ST
E 12TH ST
E 1ST ST
FRONT ST
ALBERT ST
EUNICE ST
FRANCIS ST
RACE ST
WASHINGTON ST
CHAMBERS ST
JONES ST
ENNIS ST
PARK AVE
HURRICANE RIDGE RD
Olympic National Park
OLYMPIC NATIONAL PARK VISITOR CENTER
To Hurricane Ridge
PORT ANGELES FINE ART CENTER
S GOLF COURSE RD
OLYMPIC LODGE
S DEL GUZZI DR
To Domaine Madeleine and Sequim
0 0.5 mi
0 0.5 km
101
Waterfront Trail
VISITOR CENTER
BLACK BALL FERRY DOCK
FEIRO MARINE LIFE CENTER
RED LION HOTEL
KOKOPELLI GRILL
BELLA ITALIA
PORT ANGELES INN
MICHAEL'S SEAFOOD AND STEAKHOUSE
NEXT DOOR GASTROPUB
PORT ANGELES DOWNTOWN HOTEL
RAILROAD AVE
E 3RD ST
PEABODY ST
VINE ST
SWAIN'S
© AVALON TRAVEL

has touch tanks full of marine critters and staff to show you how to touch an anemone or starfish without causing any damage. But it's not just about the colorful sea creatures—there are also wet and dry displays about the very important plant life from the area and microscopes to view slides. Small children will enjoy getting the tide pool experience without having to balance on slippery rocks.

Port Angeles Fine Arts Center

The **Port Angeles Fine Arts Center** (1203 E Lauridsen Blvd., 360/457-3532, www.pafac.org, 11am-5pm Thurs.-Sun. spring-fall, 10am-4pm Thurs.-Sun. winter, free) is a small contemporary art museum started by a painter and philanthropist married to a newspaper publisher. It's located in a midcentury house with a curved side that sits on a hill in Port Angeles, giving visitors great views from the gallery. The Webster's Woods area outside includes a five-acre sculpture park with works by dozens of Northwest artists carefully placed within the trees.

SHOPPING

If you can't find it at **Swain's** (602 E 1st St., 360/452-2357, www.swainsinc.com, 8am-9pm Mon.-Sat., 9am-6pm Sun.), you probably don't need it in Port Angeles. The general store is a hometown staple, the kind of place where high school students sell cookies as a fundraiser out front. Aisles upon aisles stock piles of blue jeans, rolls of socks, and home goods—think of this as the local, proto-Wal-Mart. Local salmon and halibut catches are listed near the hunting bow displays, and there's plenty of camo, but the shoe selection also includes practical, high-end styles alongside hip waders and hiking boots. The store also has an extensive gardening section.

FOOD

The Southwestern influence at **Kokopelli Grill** (203 E Front St., 360/457-6040, www.kokopelli-grill.com, 11am-9pm Mon.-Thurs, 11am-10pm Fri.-Sat., 2pm-8pm Sun., $15-35) isn't overwhelming, as the menu still features dishes decidedly not desertlike, such as smoked salmon chowder and Louisiana bayou shrimp and grits. The wall of wine racks and the purple walls, on the other hand, seem to suggest an Italian vineyard theme. But the restaurant is a well-decorated dinner spot that doesn't skimp on portion size—burgers are a real two-handed workout.

The all-underground **Michael's Seafood and Steakhouse** (117B E 1st St., 360/417-6929, www.michaelsdining.com, 4pm-10pm daily, $25-50) has the feel of a wine cellar—which would make its patrons, sitting in quiet booths celebrating big events, the shelved wine. But it's very happy wine in the town's only fine-dining location. Chef's specials include a ceviche made of bay shrimp and geoduck (pronounced "gooey duck"), a giant local mollusk that can live more than 150 years.

Even though the town has its share of grubby taverns, ★ **Next Door Gastropub** (113 W 1st St., Ste. A, 360/504-2613, www.nextdoorgastropub.com, 11am-11pm Mon.-Thurs., 11am-midnight Fri.-Sat., 10am-10pm Sun., $9-30) is a bar with a restaurant feel. A blackboard lists microbrew specials, there's a small outdoor patio, and Sundays feature live music. A night-owl menu includes a build-your-own-french-fries platter.

Downtown's **Bella Italia** (118 E 1st St., 360/457-5442, www.bellaitaliapa.com, 4pm-9pm Sun.-Thurs., 4pm-10pm Fri.-Sat., $10-25) features a spread of fresh Italian dishes; some incorporate local Dungeness crab or clams, halibut caught in Neah Bay, or mushrooms from the forests around the Olympic Mountains. Otherwise, the menu covers the Italian basics—veal parmigiana, chicken saltimbocca, and a slate of pizzas and pastas. The wine list has more than 500 wines, including a special house blend of sangiovese. Despite the overwhelming selection, the restaurant still has a family-dining vibe. The logo in the window is a big, bright tomato, which matches the bright red walls inside and the red exterior door.

ACCOMMODATIONS

Colette's Bed and Breakfast (339 Finn Hall Rd., 360/457-9197, www.colettes.com, $195-375) has 10 acres of beautiful gardens that overlook the Strait of Juan de Fuca. The rhododendron plants, when they bloom, are multicolored, and the grounds also include purple thistles and stately cedar trees. The five rooms have water views and private patios, plus jetted tubs and fireplaces. The decor is right between modern and homey, and rooms are fully equipped with modern conveniences (TVs with cable, wireless Internet, and coffeemakers). There are also pillow and blanket menus. The common room has a fireplace and a 40-foot wall of windows. A small fire pit is outdoors. The extensive breakfasts make use of local ingredients whenever possible.

Despite its name, the **Olympic Lodge** (140 S Del Guzzi Dr., 800/600-2993, www.olympiclodge.com, $179-259) isn't a national park property, or even particularly wilderness-like. Located just off U.S. 101, its backside has the best view, facing a golf course. Still, it's the nicest digs in town, with a light-filled lobby with a wood-burning fireplace and an outdoor pool. Rooms are large and decked out in generic but classy suburban hotel style. Some rooms have patios—fortunately facing the links, not the road.

Port Angeles' only large waterfront hotel, the **Red Lion Hotel** (221 N Lincoln St., 360/452-9215, www.redlion.com, $199-239) has retro appeal. The accordion roof and long hallways have a 1970s vibe, though rooms feel more updated and many face Hollywood Beach and the water. With 186 rooms, meeting space, and an outdoor pool, the hotel has a sprawling, substantial feel.

The colorful paintings on the walls of the **Port Angeles Downtown Hotel** (101 E Front St., 360/565-1125, www.portangelesdowntownhotel.com, $60-120) are done by the manager, and the whole property has a European, hostel feel. Rooms are sparsely appointed, most sharing hall bathrooms, located on the 2nd and 3rd floors of a downtown building. A kitchenette apartment is a little larger, while the apartment suite (which tops out at $120 per night in the high season) boasts two queen beds, a bathroom, and a full kitchen, plus enough living-room space to hold a small dance party.

The **Port Angeles Inn** (111 E 2nd St., 360/452-9285, www.portangelesinn.com, $160-195) is a hardy motel just uphill from the town's two main streets, with lattice balconies, striped awnings, and small windows overlooking the water. For all its homeyness—and the flower baskets do have a comfy charm—it's no backup hotel. Rooms book up for summer weekends, with regular customers planning ahead to get their favorite views.

INFORMATION AND SERVICES

The website for the **Port Angeles Regional Chamber of Commerce and Visitor Center** (121 E Railroad Ave., 360/452-2363, www.portangeles.org) has useful area information on transportation, lodging, and weather. **Port Angeles Underground and Heritage Tours** (360/460-1001, http://portangelesheritagetours.com, 10am and 2pm Mon.-Sat. May-Sept., 10am and 2pm daily Oct.-Apr., $15 adults, $12 seniors and students, $8 children 6-12, children under 6 free) leave from the office. The website for the **Olympic Peninsula Tourism Commission** (www.olympicpeninsula.org/destinations/port-angeles) also has useful information like festival listings and suggested itineraries. The **Olympic National Park Visitor Center** (3002 Mount Angeles Rd., 360/565-3130, www.nps.gov/olym, open daily but hours vary) has information about activities throughout the entire peninsula.

GETTING THERE

Port Angeles is about an hour's drive from Port Townsend. Take Highway 20 about 13 miles southeast to the bottom of Discovery Bay, where it dead-ends. Then turn right onto U.S. 101 and follow it 34 miles to Port Angeles, where the major highway splits into two one-way streets in town. From Forks, take U.S. 101 about 57 miles northeast, winding through a section of Olympic National Park and around Lake Crescent.

The **Black Ball Ferry Line** (www.cohoferry.com, $18.50 adults, $9.25 children 5-11, children 4 and under free, $64 for car and driver, $11-16 reservation fee) departs Victoria Harbor 2-4 times daily. (Ferry reservations are available online.) The 90-minute cruise crosses the Strait of Juan de Fuca arriving in Port Angeles.

Olympic National Park

The highest peak on the peninsula is called Mount Olympus, the mythic home of the gods, and so the mountain range and landmass itself have a mythic name. But Olympic National Park, the approximately one million protected acres that make up much of the peninsula's northern end, contains treasures of an earthly variety. Its three million annual visitors make it one of the top five most-trafficked national parks, coming in just behind big names like Yellowstone and Yosemite.

It took two Roosevelts to make the park: First, Teddy protected lands as a national monument in one of his last acts as president, then Franklin D. Roosevelt began the push to make it a proper park. It's no wonder the elk that roam the lands in herds are known as Roosevelt elk, and the area was almost given the moniker "Elk National Park."

The heart of the mountain range is accessed only by the hardiest of backpackers and climbers, but the periphery offers plenty of wild experiences, from hiking among marmots at Hurricane Ridge to watching waves crash on the remote beaches.

VISITING THE PARK

The Olympics owe their mossy, green feel to the rain that gathers here, up to 14 feet a year on the western side. Precipitation is always a possibility, though chances of the sun breaking out are best in July, August, and September. Hurricane Ridge is snow covered through the winter and early spring months yet is often still accessible to brave drivers on weekends.

Visitors Centers

The **Olympic National Park Visitor Center** (3002 Mount Angeles Rd., 360/565-3130, www.nps.gov/olym, open daily but hours vary by season) in Port Angeles is a kind of gateway to the national park, and a good place to stop whether you're going straight up the hills to Hurricane Ridge or continuing on U.S. 101 to one of the other national park locations. The center has videos and exhibits about the area's natural history and early settlers. There are two short nature trails next to the center, and rangers are available to plan hikes or other activities.

Entrances

Olympic National Park has two major components. The Olympic Mountain range and its surrounding foothills make up a giant circle in the heart of the Olympic Peninsula. The second section of the park is a narrow strip along the west coast of the Olympic Peninsula, reaching from Ozette Lake past Kalaloch. The two pieces don't touch, and it's difficult to visit multiple parts of the park in a single day.

The hugely popular **Hurricane Ridge** area, with its visitors center and trailheads, is 17 miles south of Port Angeles and has the most activities. Cars must carry chains on the road to Hurricane Ridge November 15-April 1, and the road can close in bad weather. The visitors center (360/565-3130, www.nps.gov/olym, free) is open daily in summer, but weekends only the rest of the year and when the road isn't closed to snow.

West of Port Angeles, the area's main thoroughfare, U.S. 101, goes directly along the

Olympic National Park

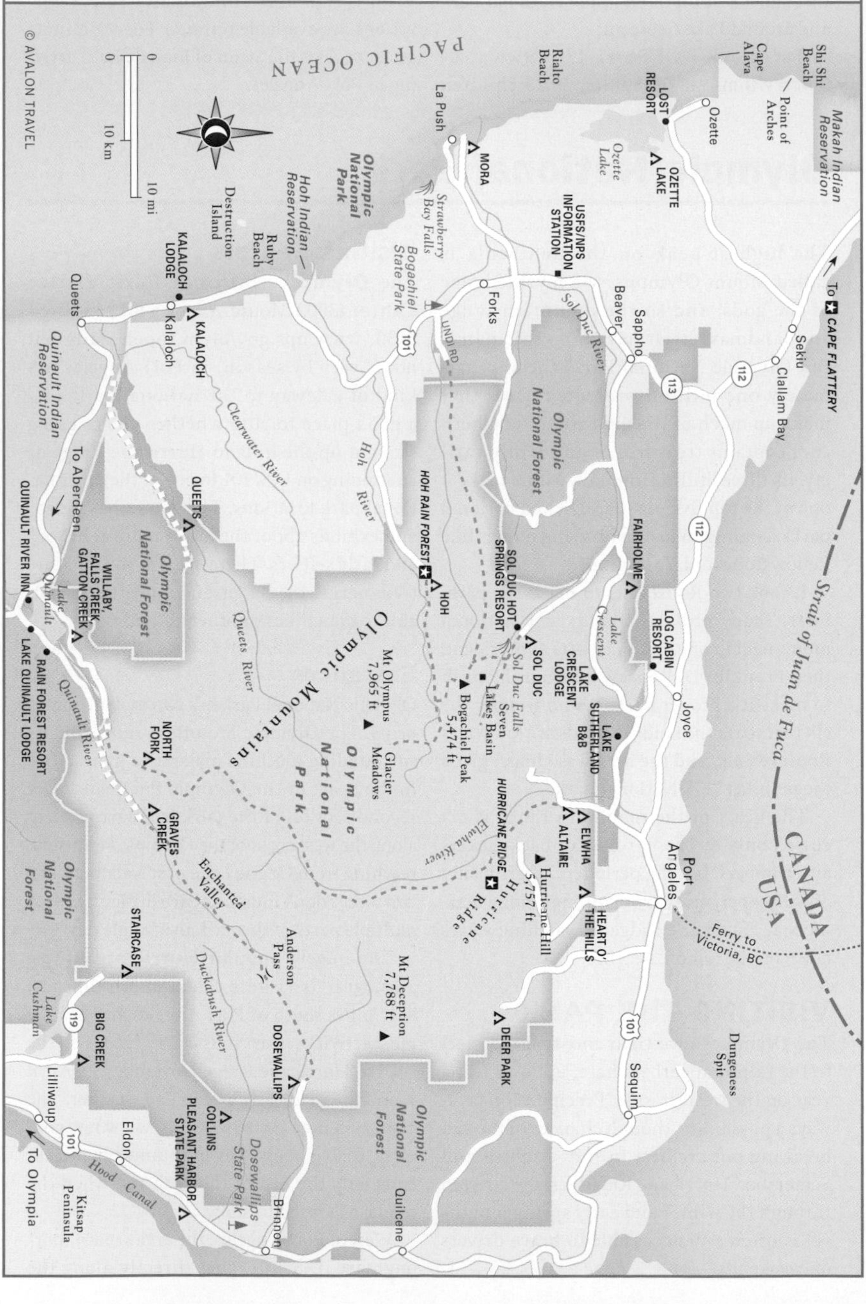
PACIFIC OCEAN
Shi Shi Beach
Cape Alava
Point of Arches
Makah Indian Reservation
Ozette
LOST RESORT
OZETTE LAKE
Ozette Lake
Rialto Beach
La Push
MORA
Olympic National Park
Strawberry Bay Falls
Bogachiel State Park
USFS/NPS INFORMATION STATION
Forks
Beaver
Sappho
Sol Duc River
To CAPE FLATTERY
Sekiu
Clallam Bay
Hoh Indian Reservation
Ruby Beach
Destruction Island
KALALOCH LODGE
KALALOCH
Kalaloch
Queets
UNDI RD
Olympic National Forest
Clearwater River
Hoh River
HOH RAIN FOREST
HOH
FAIRHOLME
SOL DUC HOT SPRINGS RESORT
Quinault Indian Reservation
To Aberdeen
QUEETS
WILLABY, FALLS CREEK, GATTON CREEK
QUINAULT RIVER INN
RAIN FOREST RESORT
LAKE QUINAULT LODGE
Lake Quinault
Quinault River
Queets River
Olympic Mountains
Mt Olympus 7,965 ft
Glacier Meadows
Bogachiel Peak 5,474 ft
Seven Lakes Basin
Sol Duc Falls
SOL DUC
LAKE CRESCENT LODGE
Lake Crescent
LOG CABIN RESORT
Joyce
LAKE SUTHERLAND B&B
Strait of Juan de Fuca
CANADA
USA
NORTH FORK
GRAVES CREEK
Enchanted Valley
Olympic National Park
Elwha River
HURRICANE RIDGE
Hurricane Ridge
ELWHA
ALTAIRE
Hurricane Hill 5,757 ft
HEART O' THE HILLS
Port Angeles
Ferry to Victoria, BC
Olympic National Forest
STAIRCASE
Anderson Pass
Mt Deception 7,788 ft
DEER PARK
Duckabush River
Lake Cushman
BIG CREEK
DOSEWALLIPS
Dungeness Spit
Sequim
Lilliwaup
Eldon
COLLINS
PLEASANT HARBOR STATE PARK
Dosewallips State Park
Brinnon
Quilcene
Hood Canal
To Olympia
Kitsap Peninsula
0 10 mi
0 10 km
© AVALON TRAVEL

shores of Lake Crescent and past the **Storm King Ranger Station** (summer only). This is the easiest national park area to visit without going off the main road, though with fewer activities and vistas here. U.S. 101 is open year-round. The Sol Duc area is a 14-mile drive off U.S. 101. The road leaves the highway west of Lake Crescent and is open year-round when there isn't too much snow.

The **Hoh Rain Forest Visitor Center** is southeast of Forks, about an hour's drive from the small town. It is about 18 miles east of U.S. 101, and the road is open year-round. Farther south, Lake Quinault almost touches U.S. 101, about 43 miles north of Aberdeen. Like Lake Crescent, it is very accessible from the main road but doesn't get as deep into the protected lands and mountains; the road is open year-round.

Fee **entrance stations** ($30 per car, $25 per motorcycle, $15 per person on foot or bicycle) are on the roads to Hurricane Ridge, the Hoh Rain Forest, and Sol Duc. The fee is good for seven days at any Olympic National Park entrance. If roads are open but fee stations are unstaffed, payment is still required at the self-pay stations. No entrance fee is required at Lake Crescent or to drive U.S. 101 through the national park.

★ HURRICANE RIDGE

The vista from Hurricane Ridge, on clear days, is a breathtaking one, with peaks and deep valleys crowding the panorama. The Olympic Mountain range isn't tall, by most standards, topping off just under 8,000 feet, but the uneven terrain makes the center of the mountain clump hard to access. This area comes by its name honestly—winds in the exposed meadow near its visitors center top 75 miles per hour, sculpting the snow in the winter and blowing off ball caps in the summer. Numerous trails are accessible from here.

The Hurricane Ridge area is located 17 miles south of Port Angeles on Hurricane Ridge Road. From U.S. 101 in downtown Port Angeles, turn south (away from the water) onto Race Street, which becomes Hurricane Ridge Road. The mountain road is plowed of snow on winter weekends.

Hurricane Ridge Visitor Center

The **Hurricane Ridge Visitor Center** (360/565-3130, www.nps.gov/olym, open year-round, hours vary seasonally) houses exhibits (including a 20-minute orientation film) and a limited snack bar and a gift shop on the lowest level. But the real draw is outdoors, where

Hurricane Ridge in winter

wildflowers bloom in the alpine meadows in the summer. In their signature wide-brimmed hats, park rangers—part police force, part naturalists, part tour guides—give guided walks and talks about the area.

Hiking

HURRICANE HILL

Distance: 3 miles round-trip
Duration: 1.5 hours
Elevation gain: 650 feet
Effort: moderate
Trailhead: Hurricane Ridge Visitor Center

Views of the area get even better from the top of Hurricane Hill, a peak more than 5,700 feet high. From here you can see the broad Strait of Juan de Fuca and the full spread of the Olympic peaks. The entire route is paved, but only the first section is wheelchair accessible.

BIG MEADOW TRAIL

Distance: 0.5 mile round-trip
Duration: 20 minutes
Elevation gain: none
Effort: easy
Trailhead: Hurricane Ridge Visitor Center

The gentle Big Meadow Trail crosses the high-alpine meadows on a paved route. Though it doesn't climb above the parking area, it allows for some new views of the Strait of Juan de Fuca below.

HIGH RIDGE TRAIL

Distance: 0.5 mile round-trip
Duration: 20 minutes
Elevation gain: 200 feet
Effort: easy
Trailhead: Hurricane Ridge Visitor Center

The High Ridge is partially paved, but there's slight elevation gain and a short spur to a viewpoint, where the jagged peaks of the Olympics to the south are visible in sharp relief to the deep valleys that separate them, the bottoms of the deep Vs often lost in thick green trees.

KLAHHANE RIDGE

Distance: 7.6 miles round-trip
Duration: 3 hours
Elevation gain: 1,700 feet
Effort: moderate
Trailhead: Hurricane Ridge Visitor Center

Klahhane Ridge is a more challenging route. Climb 2.8 miles to the Klahhane Switchback Trail, then follow it for 1 mile to Klahhane Ridge. Switchbacks climb through meadows and forest, and even on temperate days can exhaust hikers who don't bring plenty of water. Once on Klahhane Ridge, follow the Lake Angeles Trail for as long as you're comfortable, taking care with the steep drop-offs and taking in views of towering Mount Angeles. Look for maps in the visitors center, since the many trail connections in the area can be confusing.

Winter Sports

In winter, the Hurricane Ridge area is popular with the local crowd, with an average snowfall that tops 400 inches. Skiers from Port Angeles come up on weekends to use **Hurricane Ridge Ski and Snowboard Area** (360/565-3131, www.hurricaneridge.com, $34), one of only three downhill ski areas located in a national park. Two rope tows and one surface lift operate on weekends, with a separate area just for tubing. Downhill and cross-country skis, as well as snowshoes, are available for rent in the visitors center.

Camping

Camping is available in the **Heart O' the Hills** campground (Hurricane Ridge Rd., www.nps.gov/olym, first-come, first-served, $20, year-round), home to 105 sites in old-growth forest and located on the road to Hurricane Ridge. The campground has running water and flush toilets, but no hookups. In summer, rangers lead campfire programs in the amphitheater. When heavy snows hit, campers may have to walk, rather than drive, to campsites. It's located just past the Heart O' the Hills entrance station, about 5 miles from Port Angeles and about 12 miles from the Hurricane Ridge area.

Lake Crescent

LAKE CRESCENT

It's shocking how close the highway gets to the waters of Lake Crescent. It feels like a twitch on the steering wheel would put your car right in the middle of the deep blue, glacier-carved lake. The lake is popular with boaters and divers. This body of water is so deep that measurements are hard to make, but a wrecked 1927 Chevrolet is at the bottom (it takes an experienced diver to go down that far). The lake also has a unique kind of trout, which was isolated in the lake when a landslide blocked it from a nearby lake 7,000 years ago.

Lake Crescent is located right on U.S. 101 about 18 miles west of Port Angeles and about 34 miles east of Forks. The road is on the lake's south shore, passing the Lake Crescent Lodge area, the Storm King Ranger Station, and a boat launch and campground at Fairholme. The Log Cabin Resort is on the north shore.

Storm King Ranger Station

The **Storm King Ranger Station** (www.nps.gov/olym, summer only, hours and days vary) is next to the Lake Crescent Lodge on the lake's south shore, the first right after the highway turnoff and next to the boat launch. It has accessible bathrooms and ranger assistance when open. When it's closed, the front desk at the Lake Crescent Lodge may have useful maps and directions.

Hiking

MARYMERE FALLS NATURE TRAIL

Distance: 1.8 miles round -trip
Duration: 1 hour
Elevation gain: 400 feet
Effort: easy
Trailhead: Storm King Ranger Station next to Lake Crescent

The route travels under U.S. 101 before curving up into old-growth forest. Several other trails branch off from the main route, but junctions are well signed. Just 0.9 mile from the trailhead, it reaches Marymere Falls, a 90-foot drop that can be viewed from below or from the stairs to the right of the falls. The trail has little elevation gain in the ascent and is one of the easiest, quickest, and most popular day trips in the area. No park fee payment is required.

MOUNT STORM KING

Distance: 4.5 miles round-trip
Duration: 2.5 hours
Elevation gain: 2,000 feet
Effort: moderate
Trailhead: Storm King Ranger Station next to Lake Crescent

This trail begins on the same route as Marymere Falls, then veers east after the trail goes under U.S. 101 and steeply switchbacks up the mountain. The work is worth it; during breaks you can enjoy the lush smell of the damp Olympic greenery. The trail gains a moderate amount of elevation on the grind up, and with exposed ledges, it's not a hike for those new to the outdoors. Two lookouts are near the top, the first with a spectacular view of Lake Crescent.

SOL DUC FALLS

Distance: 1.6 miles round-trip
Duration: 1 hour
Elevation gain: 200 feet
Effort: easy
Trailhead: Sol Duc Trailhead at the very end of Sol Duc Hot Springs Road, about a mile past the Sol Duc Hot Springs Resort and the ranger station

The Sol Duc Valley is best known for its hot springs, but the trail to Sol Duc Falls is almost as popular. It's a mostly flat route to the falls, which are wide with many fingers rather than one tall pillar. There are viewing areas and an old shelter. It's a quick walk but a significant 12-mile drive from the highway and requires a park entrance fee. A longer loop can be made by starting at the Sol Duc Hot Springs Resort and taking the Lover's Lane Trail along the Sol Duc River to the Sol Duc Falls, then crossing at the bridge there and returning along the north side of the river for a 6-mile loop.

Boating

The 5,000-acre Lake Crescent—so deep it was once fabled to be bottomless—is popular with boaters. It's not unusual to see sailboats next to kayaks and even motorboats. There are boat ramps at Storm King Ranger Station in the middle of the lake, as well as at Fairholme on the west end, and East Beach and Log Cabin Resort on the east end. **Lake Crescent Lodge** (416 Lake Crescent Rd., 360/928-3211, www.olympicnationalparks.com, 9am-4pm daily May-Oct. weather permitting), next to Storm King Ranger Station, rents canoes, single and double kayaks, and rowboats ($20 per hour, $60 per day). **Log Cabin Resort** (3183 East Beach Rd., 888/896-3818, www.olympicnationalparks.com, 8am-7pm daily May-Sept. weather permitting) rents stand-up paddleboards, single and double kayaks, paddleboats, and canoes ($20 per hour, $60 per day). The **Fairholme Store** on the west end of the lake, just off U.S. 101, rents kayaks, canoes, and rowboats ($10 per hour).

Fishing

Fishing in Lake Crescent is catch-and-release, with a season that lasts June 1-October 31. The lake is home to Beardslee and coastal cutthroat trout. In the 20th century, more than 14.5 million fish were planted in this lake. No license is required, and anglers must use artificial lures with single, barbless hooks. Motorboats are also allowed on the lake. Lake Crescent no longer rents fishing equipment, so guests need to bring their own or stock up in Port Angeles; **Swain's** (602 E 1st St., 360/452-2357, www.swainsinc.com, 8am-9pm Mon.-Sat., 9am-6pm Sun.) is a good resource for outdoor gear.

Food

The **Lake Crescent Lodge Restaurant** (416 Lake Crescent Rd., 360/928-3211, www.olympicnationalparks.com, 7am-10:30am, 11am-2:30pm, and 5pm-9pm daily May-Jan., $15-40) has windows that overlook Lake Crescent. It specializes in fine Washington wines and has dozens of Washington and Oregon vintages on the menu. Dinner entrées include a bison burger and wild salmon cooked on cedar planks. The lavender lemonade is homemade, and desserts use local marionberries.

Because the hot pools are a dozen miles from the main highway and even farther from other restaurants, the **Springs Restaurant** (12076 Sol Duc Hot Springs Rd., 360/327-3583, www.olympicnationalparks.com, 7am-10:30am and 5pm-9pm daily Mar.-Oct., $15-35), at Sol Duc Hot Springs Resort, is popular with both hotel guests and campers. It serves both breakfast and dinner, but a deli out by the hot springs pools has sandwiches, snacks, beer, and wine at lunchtime, and also sells boxed lunches. The restaurant's breakfast features pancakes, omelets, and other hearty dishes, including a Dungeness crab cake Benedict, and dinner includes fresh fish, pork ribs, and a rotating mac-and-cheese special.

Accommodations

Guests gather around the lobby's stone fireplace at ★ **Lake Crescent Lodge** (416 Lake Crescent Rd., 360/928-3211, www.

Waterfall Wanders

Where there's a rain forest and mountains, there are waterfalls. Hundreds of water features are scattered throughout the peninsula. Some are located near the road, while others are accessible only to the hardiest hikers. Of the 23 waterfalls in the greater Olympic Peninsula, the following provide a nice detour on your road trip. Visit www.olympicpeninsulawaterfalltrail.com/map for a complete map and details.

LAKE CRESCENT

- **Marymere Falls:** Just 0.9 mile down the Marymere Falls Nature Trail (page 169), this 90-foot drop can be viewed from below or from the stairs to the right of the falls.
- **Sol Duc Falls:** It's a 12-mile drive to the trail to Sol Duc Falls (page 170), a 0.8-mile walk to a cascading waterfall.

NEAH BAY AND OZETTE LAKE

- **Beaver Falls:** This block of falls, about 20 feet wide, is just a few feet off the road on Highway 113 (2 miles from Sappho) heading south on the way to Forks.

HOH RAIN FOREST

- **Mineral Creek Falls:** The Hoh River Trail (page 173) starts at the Hoh Rain Forest Visitor Center and runs a full 18 miles to the Blue Glacier. This tall, skinny waterfall is only 2.8 miles from the trailhead, on the left side of the trail.

LAKE QUINAULT

- **Willaby Creek Falls:** The short Quinault Rain Forest Nature Trail (page 175) includes a footbridge across Willaby Creek for a view of the small, multitiered falls.
- **Merriman Falls:** This 40-foot waterfall is just off South Shore Road, 3.5 miles from Gatton Creek Campground (page 175).
- **Bunch Creek Falls:** The 60-foot-long Bunch Creek Falls doesn't fall straight but rather meanders down between rocks. It's just next to Lake Quinault's South Shore Road, 12 miles from where it leaves U.S. 101.

FORKS AND LA PUSH

- **Strawberry Bay Falls:** On a hike to Third Beach (page 181), turn left once you reach the sand. The 100-foot, very thin stream of water—so small it can disappear completely in summer—is a little more than half a mile south on the beach.

olympicnationalparks.com, rooms $123-238, cottages $292-328), even if they're staying in one of the hotel's cottages. The building was erected in 1916 and is a light gray, wood-paneled building—not a heavy log or stone lodge. A glassed-in sun porch faces the crescent-shaped lake. Some rooms in the historical building share bathrooms, but others have private baths in the Storm King, Marymere, and Pyramid Mountain buildings. None have TVs, all the better to focus on nature. One- and two-bedroom cottages have little porches with wicker chairs, but are lined up in a row—they're private but not secluded. The Roosevelt Fireplace Cabins have fireplaces but still no TVs or telephone. All rooms and cabins are simply decorated, and although many materials are worn, the hotel has a shabby charm.

Across the lake from Lake Crescent Lodge, the **Log Cabin Resort** (3183 East Beach Rd., 888/896-3818, www.olympicnationalparks.com, May-Sept., rooms $164-191, cabins $111-205) is a calmer destination, off the beaten path of U.S. 101. Hotels have been in the spot since 1895, though the current building dates back only to the 1950s. Lodge rooms have private bathrooms and a small outdoor patio, all facing the water (and the mountains beyond). A-frame chalets sleep up to six, while the rougher camper cabins share communal bath facilities but do have electricity. Other rustic cabins date back to the 1920s and have lake views as well as private bathrooms, and some have kitchens. A small general store sells some food, beer and wine, and candy. A restaurant, the **Sunnyside Cafe,** has a breakfast buffet ($13.75 adults, $8.75 children 5-12, children under 5 free), and a lakeside deli offers sandwiches and pizzas, plus laundry facilities.

The heated pools of **Sol Duc Hot Springs Resort** (12076 Sol Duc Hot Springs Rd., 360/327-3583, www.olympicnationalparks.com, Mar.-Oct., $208-287) are its biggest draw, bringing people up a 12-mile road that traces the Sol Duc River in the north end of the national park. The mineral waters are pumped into round pools used by cabin guests and fee-paying walk-ins; there are also massage services. Besides the natural hot tubs, the accommodations are rather bare, and the "deluxe-style" cabins have dated furniture. The river suite has three bedrooms and better decor. The area waterfalls are noted for their misty beauty, and coho salmon clog the river when they spawn. Several trails leave from the resort area.

Camping

Fairholme Campground (U.S. 101, 27 miles west of Port Angeles, www.nps.gov/olym, May-Sept., $20) is located on the westernmost point of Lake Crescent. The campground has 88 sites and flush toilets but no hookups or showers, and all sites are first-come, first-served. A boat launch is here, and a general store sells snacks and candy and rents boats.

The **Sol Duc Campground** (Sol Duc Hot Springs Rd., 12.5 miles from U.S. 101, www.nps.gov/olym, year-round, $21-24) is helpful because it's close to the hot springs pools. It offers 82 reservable sites, many along the Sol Duc River, with running water in summer. There are no hookups or showers. In winter, there is no water and only pit toilets, and the road may close in bad weather.

The **Sol Duc Hot Springs Resort Campground** (12076 Sol Duc Hot Springs Rd., 360/327-3583, www.olympicnationalparks.com, Mar.-Oct., $21-40) is about a quarter mile from Sol Duc Hot Springs Resort. It has 17 sites with water and electric, and the campground accepts reservations.

★ HOH RAIN FOREST

Unlike other Olympic National Park spots, there are no sweeping vistas of peaks or the ocean here. The real draw is the trees—many Sitka spruce—and thick forest. The 12-14 feet of rain that falls here annually is the reason the forest feels so rich. When trees die and fall, they become nurse logs to new plants, so it's rare to find any surface that isn't coated in mossy life. Sometimes trees grow in a line, evidence that they all began on the same nurse log.

Come to see one of the most spectacular temperate rain forests in the world and more shades of green than you thought existed. Most travelers stop at the visitors center before hitting the trails or seeing the rushing Hoh River. Keep an eye out for Roosevelt elk, birds, and black bears; about one-tenth of the park's elk live in this river valley.

Located on the western edge of the park, the Hoh Rain Forest is accessible via Upper Hoh Road heading east from U.S. 101. Take U.S. 101 for 13 miles south from Forks and look for national park signs. At the end of the 18-mile road is an 88-site year-round campground, located on the banks of the Hoh River.

Hoh Rain Forest Visitor Center

In the **Hoh Rain Forest Visitor Center** (Upper Hoh Rd., 18 miles from U.S. 101, 360/374-6925, www.nps.gov, daily June-Sept., Fri.-Tues. May-June, hours vary) exhibits explain the complexities of the temperate rain forest, and self-guided nature trails leave from the central location. A small gift shop is here, but no food is sold; picnic tables are outside. The small, low building blends into the thick forest, and even the phone booth is layered with moss and lichen. Cars pass through a fee station before reaching the visitors center.

Hiking

HALL OF THE MOSSES

Distance: 0.8 mile round-trip
Duration: 30 minutes
Elevation gain: 100 feet
Effort: easy
Trailhead: Hoh Rain Forest Visitor Center

Look for information plaques along this short, informational trail, which winds through the giant, moss-covered trees that Olympic National Park is famous for. Elk graze nearby, and the signage tells the story of the forest's complex ecosystem.

SPRUCE NATURE TRAIL

Distance: 1.2 miles round-trip
Duration: 45 minutes
Elevation gain: 250 feet
Effort: easy
Trailhead: Hoh Rain Forest Visitor Center

Like the Hall of the Mosses trail, this is a short, family-friendly wander through the woods, though it also goes to the Hoh River, an ideal spot to stop for a snack. Wildlife in the area includes bears, but rangers keep tabs on dangerous animals, so it's a safe area.

HOH RIVER TRAIL TO GLACIER MEADOWS

Distance: up to 35 miles round-trip
Duration: 1 hour-multiple days
Elevation gain: 300-3,700 feet
Effort: moderate
Trailhead: Hoh Rain Forest Visitor Center

This more intense hike goes along the Hoh River all the way to the base of Mount Olympus. Climbers hoping to scale the Olympics' tallest peak often begin here. It's 17.3 miles to Glacier Meadows below the mountain, which is about as far as casual backpackers should go (past that point, special equipment is necessary to go up the Blue Glacier to the summit). Day hikers can follow

Hoh Rain Forest

the trail as far out as they like before turning back. The river is visible after 1 mile, the Mount Tom Creek campsite is 2.3 miles out, and **Mineral Creek Falls** is 2.8 miles out. Five Mile Island, in the Hoh River, is about 5.3 miles from the visitors center, and a picnic shelter is 0.5 mile farther, a good place to turn around for an intense, nearly 12-mile day hike. Fortunately, there's little elevation gain in the first 10 or so miles from the Hoh Rain Forest Visitor Center, so hikers can appreciate the burbling river and giant trees.

Boating

Located outside the national park, **Rainforest Paddlers** (4883 Upper Hoh Rd., 360/374-5254, www.rainforestpaddlers.com, May-Oct., $44-79) offers river rafting and kayak trips on the Hoh River. The Hoh is mostly serene, never more than Class II rapids, and guides talk about the area's natural and human history during half- or full-day trips. Wetsuit, helmet, and life jacket rentals are included. They also have kayak rentals ($11 per hour, $29 per day), but customers must have kayak experience. The store is almost 5 miles up Upper Hoh Road, on the way to the Hoh Rain Forest Visitor Center. A shuttle will take renters within 10 miles for $10 per group.

Camping

Right before the visitors center is the **Hoh Campground** (Upper Hoh Rd., 18 miles from U.S. 101, www.nps.gov/olym, $20, year-round) with three loops of 88 sites with no hookups. Sites are in the old-growth forest next to the Hoh River. There's a dumpsite, running water, and storage lockers to keep animals out of food. Like most Olympic National Park campgrounds, reservations are not accepted as sites are first-come, first-served.

LAKE QUINAULT

Located on the edge of Olympic National Park, Lake Quinault is at the intersection of public recreational use, protected forest, and Native American reservation land. The lake sits near where two forks of the Quinault River combine, at the base of the Quinault Valley. It makes a great base for exploring the national park's forests. You can camp anywhere, from a remote, small campground to a lakeside site with amenities and easy access to restaurants. Short trails wind near the lake, and longer day hikes leave farther up the valley. And best of all, you're never far from U.S. 101.

Lake Quinault is within the lands of the Quinault Indian Nation, which regulates boating and fishing access; the lake has a limited trout fishing season. Permits are required, and the front desk of the Lake Quinault Lodge has more information on what's required at any given time. Swimming is permitted.

Information Stations

Two offices have visitor information on Lake Quinault. On the north side of the lake, the **Quinault Rain Forest Ranger Station** (North Shore Rd., 4 miles from U.S. 101, www.nps.gov/olym, Thurs.-Mon. June-Sept., hours vary) on Kestner Creek has bathrooms, picnic tables, and a ranger available to answer questions. Short interpretive trails leave from the parking lot, including Kestner Homestead Trail and Maple Glade Trail.

On the south shore of the lake is the **Pacific Ranger District-Quinault office** (353 South Shore Rd., 360/288-2525, www.fs.usda.gov, 8am-4:30pm Mon.-Fri., 9am-4pm Sat.-Sun. summer; 8am-4:30pm Mon.-Fri. winter). It's operated by the U.S. Forest Service, not the national park, but staff can answer many questions about driving and hiking in the area.

Hiking

KESTNER HOMESTEAD TRAIL

Distance: 1.5 miles round-trip
Duration: 1 hour
Elevation gain: none
Effort: easy
Trailhead: Quinault Rain Forest Ranger Station on North Shore Road

On the north end of the lake, this trail heads up Kestner Creek before reaching the site of the 1889 Kestner-Higley Homestead, where a barn and house still stand. Interpretive signs along the route explain homesteading and pioneer life in the valley. The short hike is rewarding for those who've tired of the endless lush greenery and need a little human history.

QUINAULT LOOP TRAIL

Distance: 4 miles round-trip
Duration: 2 hours
Elevation gain: 500 feet
Effort: moderate
Trailhead: Rainforest Trail Loop trailhead, 1.3 miles up South Shore Road

Stop in the ranger station for a map of the trails from this trailhead as they can be combined in a number of ways. For a moderate stretch of the legs, go up into the forest past a cedar bog, then back down to the lakeside, past Lake Quinault Lodge, and along the shore back to where you started.

QUINAULT RAIN FOREST NATURE TRAIL

Distance: 0.5 mile
Duration: 20 minutes
Elevation gain: 50 feet
Effort: easy
Trailhead: Rainforest Trail Loop trailhead, 1.3 miles up South Shore Road

The trail gives a quick peek into the woods; some, but not all, of the short loop is wheelchair accessible. Walk past the old-growth conifer forest and thick ground cover of ferns that define this part of the Olympics. As you pass the bridge over the South Shore Road, look underneath to where Willaby Creek heads toward the lake. A footbridge across the creek has a view of **Willaby Creek Falls.**

GRAVES CREEK TRAIL

Distance: 7 miles round-trip
Duration: 3 hours
Elevation gain: 1,500 feet
Effort: moderate
Trailhead: at the end of South Shore Road, past where it turns to gravel (6.2 miles past the bridge that links the North and South Shore Roads)

Get away from the bustle of the lake by heading up the Quinault Valley and along Graves Creek. Switchbacks help make the elevation gain bearable, and a number of (easy) creek crossings keep the path interesting. When the trail dead-ends into the rushing waterway at 3.5 miles, turn around and head back the way you came.

To skip hiking altogether, head to **Merriman Falls,** a 40-foot waterfall a few feet off the road. It's about 3.5 miles from Gatton Creek Campground on South Shore Road and on the way to the Graves Creek Trailhead.

Accommodations

A rain gauge is painted on the chimney exterior at ★ **Lake Quinault Lodge** (345 South Shore Rd., Quinault, 360/288-2900, www.olympicnationalparks.com, $229-364), its rainbow hues cheerfully marking how many feet of water fell in the previous year. The original 1926 building has steep roofs and Catskill resort charm, with Adirondack chairs dotting the lawn that slopes down to Lake Quinault. An indoor pool and game room entertain guests during real downpours, because the original guest rooms are small. The decor in the main building matches the rustic lodge style of the structure—wood furniture and delicate light fixtures, and some rooms have claw-foot tubs. Fireside, Lakeside, and Boathouse rooms in other buildings have various combinations of views, decks, fireplaces, and more modern furnishings. The **dining room** (www.olympicnationalparks.com, 7:30am-3pm and 5pm-9pm daily spring-summer, 7:30am-11am, 11:30am-2pm, and 5pm-8pm daily fall-winter, $12-36) is named for its most famous guest, Franklin Delano Roosevelt, who dined here less than a year before proposing the lands become a national park. Coincidence? Perhaps it was the lovely view. Today the restaurant serves omelets that use Olympic Mountain mushrooms, hearty burgers, and some seafood dishes.

The Quinault area has several other accommodations that are not national park concessions. The **Quinault River Inn** (8 River Dr., 360/288-2237, www.quinaultriverinn.

com, $159) is just off U.S. 101, right where the Quinault River leaves Lake Quinault. Some rooms have wood-paneled walls and balconies overlooking the river. Most are decorated with vintage-style photography. There is a campfire circle outside, a small fitness center, and an RV campground ($29) that takes reservations.

On the south shore, **Rain Forest Resort** (516 South Shore Rd., 360/288-2535, www.rainforestresort.com, rooms $145-189, cabins $179-245) sits right on the lake with two small buildings with hotel rooms, all with simple furnishings and private bathrooms. Cabins have fireplaces, and some have kitchens as well. The RV campground has 31 sites ($30) with water and electrical hookups, but it does not accept reservations.

Camping

Two campgrounds are located within the Olympic National Park, past Lake Quinault and up the Quinault Valley. **Graves Creek Campground** (South Shore Rd., 19 miles from U.S. 101, www.nps.gov/olym, $20, year-round) is located in temperate rain forest on the South Fork of the Quinault River. The 30 primitive sites (no hookups) are quiet, with restrooms in summer, but no water and only pit toilets in winter. The road to the campground is gravel for the last dozen miles.

North Fork Campground (North Shore Rd., 17 miles from U.S. 101, www.nps.gov/olym, $10, open seasonally) has only 9 sites, no water, and only pit toilets. When it's open, it's a very remote camping spot. The road in is narrow and not recommended for RVs.

Three national forest campgrounds are located on the south shore of Lake Quinault, all about 1 mile from each other. **Willaby Campground** (South Shore Rd., 1.5 miles from U.S. 101, www.fs.usda.gov, $25), **Falls Creek Campground** (South Shore Rd., 3 miles from U.S. 101, www.fs.usda.gov, $25), and **Gatton Creek Campground** (South Shore Rd., 3.5 miles from U.S. 101, www.fs.usda.gov, $20) are all close to area trails and the lakeshore. Willaby and Falls Creek sites have flush toilets, while Gatton Creek has only pit toilets. Combined they offer 50 RV sites (no hookups) and 17 walk-in tent sites. Reservations are not accepted.

Getting There

Lake Quinault is next to U.S. 101, 63 miles south of Forks and 42.5 miles north of Aberdeen. The North Shore Road, which heads east from U.S. 101, leads to the Quinault Rain Forest Ranger Station and then continues on to the North Fork campgrounds in the Quinault Valley via a gravel road. The South Shore Road, which also heads east from U.S. 101 about 2 miles south of North Shore Road, leads to Lake Quinault Lodge and the Olympic National Forest park information station, and then becomes a gravel road that leads up to the Graves Creek Campground. There is a bridge across the Quinault River past where both become gravel roads.

Northwestern Peninsula

NEAH BAY

The community of Neah Bay is so isolated, it's unsurprising that the Makah Indian Reservation town flew under the radar for so long. Situated on a small bay at the state's—and the country's—very northwest tip, this is home to fewer than 1,000 people and was best known to anglers who came to reach the halibut that live just off the coast. But in the late 1990s, the Makah petitioned the U.S. government and International Whaling Commission to allow them to partake in their treaty-granted whaling rights.

When the Makah hunted a gray whale in 1999, their first in 70 years, it became an internationally followed incident, with protesters making the long trek to Neah Bay. The hunt used a combination of traditional

Cape Flattery

methods—including using almost every part of the whale's blubber, oil, and meat—and modern techniques intended to more humanely kill the whale. Despite the attention and legal struggle, the Makah haven't hunted a whale since, outside of a kill not sanctioned by the tribe in 2007.

Besides tribal buildings, the village is home to a U.S. Coast Guard station and a tugboat tasked specifically to respond to oil spills in the remote but crowded shipping lane.

Sights

MAKAH MUSEUM

Two giant statues welcome visitors to Neah Bay and the Makah Cultural and Research Center. The complex is home to the **Makah Museum** (1880 Bayview Ave., 360/645-2711, http://makahmuseum.com, 10am-5pm daily, $5 adults, $4 students, children 5 and under free), which is home to many of the artifacts discovered at the Lake Ozette site that yielded an archaeological bonanza in 1970. A botanical garden outside grows native plants. The museum store sells crafts from Makah artists as well as the recreation permit ($10) needed to park in any reservation trailhead or beach.

★ CAPE FLATTERY

Just past Neah Bay and up a few miles from the last signs of civilization is the trailhead for **Cape Flattery,** a jagged point where the Pacific Ocean meats the Strait of Juan de Fuca. The 0.75-mile trail is well maintained, with boardwalks and steps over the muddy terrain. Several viewing platforms face the tiny coves and massive sea stacks that make up the point, with the biggest facing Tatoosh Island. The small island just off the coast was once a Makah whaling camp and now has the unmanned Cape Flattery lighthouse, built in 1857. Although wind, rain, and furious waves are common, on clear days whales and otters can be seen in the dark waters.

Food and Accommodations

Even though dining options in Neah Bay are scarce, the **Warm House Restaurant** (900-1099 Bayview Ave., 360/645-2077, 7am-7pm Sun.-Thurs., 7am-8pm Fri.-Sat, $8-15) has harbor and marina views and staples like halibut and burgers. Service is known to be slow, but there aren't many reasons to hurry in this out-of-the-way town.

★ **Hobuck Beach Resort** (2726 Makah Passage, 360/645-2339, www.hobuckbeachresort.com, cabins $150-200) has campsites and RV hookups, but once you've made it to this far-off corner of the world, it's worth staying in the waterfront cabins. Small but solid, some have beautiful views and are fully furnished, all with stoves and fridges. Most have twin bunks or a sleeping loft in addition to a master bedroom. Follow signs from Neah Bay, leaving the main road before it heads out to Cape Flattery. Beach access requires a $15 daily pass.

Getting There

Neah Bay is located at the end of Highway 112, about 71 miles northwest of Port Angeles. From Port Angeles, take U.S. 101 west for about 5 miles to Highway 112 and turn right.

Follow Highway 112 west for 65 miles to the small town of Neah Bay. From Forks, drive north on U.S. 101 for about 12 miles, then turn left onto Highway 113. Head north on Highway 113 for 10 miles to where it meets Highway 112; stay straight to follow Highway 112 west for 26.5 miles to Neah Bay.

OZETTE LAKE

There's a serenity to Ozette Lake, located near the north end of Olympic National Park's coastal strip. The lake is only barely inland, reached by a 21-mile road from Seiku on Highway 112—but the expanse takes well over an hour to travel as it follows a series of rivers toward the ocean. Though remote, the area was once populated by homesteaders, who left traces of buildings that stood more than a century ago. Native American petroglyphs are older signs of civilization. Continue all the way to **Ozette Ranger Station** (Hoko-Ozette Rd., 206/963-2725, www.nps.gov/olym, hours vary but usually daily June-Sept.), 21 miles from Highway 112. The ranger station has bathrooms and picnic areas, and there's a national park fee station.

Hiking

OZETTE TRIANGLE/ CAPE ALAVA LOOP

Distance: 9.5 miles round-trip
Duration: 4.5 hours
Elevation gain: 100 feet
Effort: moderate
Trailhead: Ozette Ranger Station

Though the hike from Ozette to the ocean is time-consuming, it's one of the state's most classic hikes. Before you begin, ask for a handout at the Ozette Ranger Station to spot the Makah petroglyphs on Wedding Rock, and to consult tide charts to avoid being trapped during high tides. Hike three miles on a boardwalk trail (which can be slippery when wet) that hovers above the delicate forest, eventually reaching a wet prairie at a little over two miles; it was once a farm but shows little evidence. Continue to the beach and the roaring Pacific, where at low tide the tide pools teem with life, and sea otters can be spotted in the ocean. Turn left and make your way to Wedding Rock and the Cape Alava archaeological site. A 300-year-old village was unearthed by archaeologists, who found more than 50,000 artifacts, among them longhouses that had been buried in mudslides. A small replica longhouse stands at the site, but most of what was recovered is in the Makah Museum in Neah Bay. Return via the Sand Point Trail, marked on the beach with a large disc.

Fishing

A license is not required to fish in Ozette Lake, but you can only keep yellow perch, largemouth bass, pikeminnow, and bullhead (with no limits) from the last Saturday in April to October 31. Only artificial lures and barbless single-point hooks are permitted. Other fish are catch-and-release. Check the Olympic National Park's fishing regulations (www.nps.gov/olym/fishregs.htm) for any updates and consumption advisories. Boat launches are next to the Ozette Ranger Station and about a mile south of Lost Resort on Hoko-Ozette Road. However, there are no spots to rent fishing gear or boats.

Camping

The national park campground on **Ozette Lake** (Hoko-Ozette Rd., 21 miles from Highway 112, $20, year-round) has only 15 sites and limited bathroom facilities. Spots fill quickly in summer, and some campsites close when water levels rise. It has limited drinking water access and only pit toilets; no RV hookups. All sites are first-come, first-served.

Lost Resort (208660 Hoko-Ozette Rd., 360/963-2899, www.lostresort.net, Feb. 15-Nov. 15, campsites $20, cabins $85), just outside the national park boundary, has more campsites and sells essentials like espresso and breakfast. Cabins are rustic, each with a double bed and bunk bed, linens, and electric stove; showers and bathrooms are attached to the store. The owners claim to have never filled the campground or been forced to turn away campers.

Getting There

Lake Ozette is one of the most remote parts of Olympic National Park. From Port Angeles, it's a two-hour drive. Go west on U.S. 101 for 4.5 miles, then turn right onto Highway 112 West. Follow it for 48.5 miles, sometimes winding along the coast, through the towns of Clallam Bay and Sekiu; 2.3 miles after Sekiu, turn left onto Hoko-Ozette Road and follow it 21 miles to Ozette Lake.

From Forks, take U.S. 101 north 10 miles and turn left onto Highway 113. Go 10 miles north to where it meets and becomes Highway 112. Stay straight and follow Highway 112 for 10.5 miles to Hoko-Ozette Road; follow it 21 miles to Ozette Lake. For both routes, the last gas station is in Clallam Bay, about 40 miles from Ozette Lake.

Washington Coast

FORKS

Once upon a time, there was a tiny town that wasn't really on the road to anywhere. It was best known to anglers, campers, and anyone making the full loop of the Olympic Peninsula. Then a tiny book called *Twilight* happened to Forks—the teen vampire romance is set here—and the one-time timber town became the destination for vampire fans the world over.

Twilight mania has largely faded in Forks since the release of the last movie—the films weren't shot here, and you're more likely to see fishing puns on motel reader boards than vampire references. The town remains a useful fuel stop and home base for trips to Neah Bay, La Push, or the western end of the national park.

Sights

Even though mania over Stephenie Meyer's blockbuster book series has mostly died down, its impact on Forks was notable. The town's chamber of commerce website (http://forkswa.com) has an entire section devoted to the phenomenon, including the annual celebration in September, Forever Twilight; head to **Rainforest Arts Center** (11 N. Forks Ave., 360/374-2531, limited hours) for a gallery of costumes and props from the movie, including a motorcycle. Tours used to be offered by various locals, but as the phenomenon has died down, they've ceased. A vacation rental on the road to La Push has billed itself as the home of a book character, and drivers stop to photograph the red house and prominent sign. Just before the edge of Forks on U.S. 101 is an outdoor firewood stand hawking "Twilight firewood," which, at $5 per bundle, appears to be indistinguishable from other firewood sold at local on-your-honor roadside stands.

Food

The prices at **Sully's Drive-In** (220 S Forks Ave., 360/374-5075, 10:30am-10pm Mon.-Sat., $4) are a throwback to another era, when a deluxe burger could actually come in under $3. The menu is a gut-busting array of chili dogs, fish-and-chips, burgers, and delicious milkshakes, but it's not actually a drive-in, so at least you'll get a few steps of exercise on the way in.

The **Forks Coffee Shop** (241 S Forks Ave., 360/374-6769, www.forkscoffeeshop.com, 5:30am-8pm daily, $5-18) is a basic diner, albeit one with an 18-point stuffed elk head as decor. It has booths and a long lunch counter, and the menu is the kind that calls pancakes "hotcakes." Burgers are only $2.50, and the kitchen will pack sack lunches with sandwiches, fruit, pastries, chips, and candy.

The bright yellow building that houses **Taqueria Santa Ana** (80 Calawah Way, 360/374-3339, 7am-9pm Mon.-Sat., 7am-8pm Sun., $7-15) is a welcoming sight in an often drizzly town, and the no-frills Mexican joint dishes equally bright meals. Breakfasts include loaded Mexican omelets and, sometimes, cinnamon toast specials, while the dinner menu is a broad selection of tacos, tortas, and burritos. Order at the counter and pick a glass-bottled drink to enjoy while you wait.

Head to **Blakeslee's Bar and Grille** (1222 S Forks Ave., 360/374-5003, 11am-11pm Sun.-Thurs, 11am-2am Fri.-Sat., $10-27) on the north end of town for drinks and something fried, but don't expect frills. The building is somewhat blank and overlarge, inside and out, but the place attracts locals who appreciate the full bar, pool table, and social atmosphere.

Accommodations

There's a certain simplicity to the **Forks Motel** (351 S Forks Ave., 360/374-6243, www.forksmotel.com, $95-175). Rooms are small and the TVs are tiny, and the beds aren't winning any comfort awards. But rooms are cheap and plentiful in the property, and some have lovely exposed-beam ceilings. The motel even has an outdoor pool for the rare warm, sunny days in Forks.

"Edward Cullen didn't sleep here" reads one of the slogans on the sign for **Olympic Suites Inn** (800 Olympic Dr., 800/262-3433, www.olympicsuitesinn.com, $104-119). (For the uninitiated, he's the *Twilight* vampire.) The collection of suites feels more like a neighborhood apartment complex than a hotel, nestled in thick fir trees just outside Forks. The suites come in one- and two-bedroom sizes and have full kitchens and living rooms. Signs remind guests not to gut fish in the recently renovated units.

The three-story 1916 house that holds the **Miller Tree Inn Bed and Breakfast** (654 E Division St., 360/374-6806, www.millertreeinn.com, $215-275) has a large wraparound porch and a white picket fence. This is the classic bed-and-breakfast experience. Some rooms have gas fireplaces or jetted tubs, and all have TVs. Some rooms have quilts on the wall and some bric-a-brac, but most are more understated. The house has a cat, which is kept out of guest rooms. Although the inn is close to the middle of town, the views are mostly of hillsides and an old barn.

The **Pacific Inn Motel** (352 S Forks Ave., 360/374-9400, www.pacificinnmotel.com, $104-199) is, for the most part, a basic motel in the middle of Forks. Rooms have standard motel furnishings, air-conditioning, wireless Internet, and flat-screen TVs, and there are on-site laundry facilities. A larger suite has a gas fireplace and a washer and dryer in the room. The motel does have a few *Twilight*-themed rooms with posters, dark linens, and embroidered towels.

Information and Services

The **Forks NPS/USFS Recreation Information Center** (551 S Forks Ave./U.S. 101, 360/374-5877, www.nps.gov/olym, hours vary, closed in winter) has maps and a few exhibits about the local wilderness and the ocean coast. Rangers can answer questions about hikes in the area.

Getting There

Forks is located on U.S. 101, 56.5 miles west of Port Angeles and 107 miles north of Aberdeen.

LA PUSH

West of Forks, the Quileute Indian Reservation at La Push is a very small settlement built at the end of the Quillayute River. The beaches west of Forks may not be named with any imagination, but the stretches of First, Second, and Third Beaches are rugged and beautiful. First Beach is the beach within the town of La Push, and a good viewing spot for drive-up whale-watching. Second and Third Beaches require flat hikes on boardwalk trails to reach secluded shorelines surrounded by headlands and natural rock arches.

Hiking

The epic waves, stately sea stacks, and sandy stretches of La Push's best beaches are accessible only by short hikes.

SECOND BEACH TRAIL

Distance: 1.4 miles round-trip
Duration: 1 hour
Elevation gain: none
Effort: easy
Trailhead: a small parking lot on La Push Road about 0.75 mile from where the road ends in La Push (past Quileute tribal administration buildings)

Take an easy ramble through the seaside woods to reach the ocean; you'll hear and smell it well before you see the sand. Second Beach is a mile wide with natural rock arches and views of sea stacks inhabited by birds. The walk isn't too taxing, but don't try to cross the headlands to the beaches on either side; tides and crumbling, steep coastline can be dangerous. Instead, return the way you came.

THIRD BEACH TRAIL

Distance: 3.6 miles round-trip
Duration: 2 hours
Elevation gain: 300 feet
Effort: moderate
Trailhead: 3.8 miles west of where Mora Road branches off La Push Road

A walk on a wide forest trail eventually becomes a careful descent down to the crashing waves; the trail isn't too difficult thanks to roots and rocks that serve as steps, but be ready to have your hands available for balance. The route ends at the mile-long beach between two headlands, covered in driftwood that visitors often pile into forts or makeshift benches. If you'd like to possibly catch a glimpse of small **Strawberry Bay Falls**—so thin it sometimes disappears completely in summer—turn left once you hit the sand; it's a little more than half a mile south on the beach. Swimming isn't recommended on these beaches, where currents can be strong and the waters of the Pacific Ocean are very cold. Expert surfers and sea kayakers take to the waves, but most visitors enjoy the wild views from the sandy and rocky shore.

Surfing

The waves in the entire northwest corner of the state are intense, and the surfing out here isn't anything like the chill, crowded scene on California or Hawaiian beaches. **North By Northwest Surf Company** (902 S Lincoln St., Port Angeles, 360/452-5144, www.nxnwsurf.com, noon-6pm Tues.-Fri., 9am-6pm Sat.-Sun.) is headquartered in Port Angeles but has a summer outpost in La Push, where it offers one-day surf lessons ($70-80 with equipment) along what it calls "the last remaining stretch of true wilderness in the

La Push

continental U.S." The company also rent surfboards, wetsuits, and other gear ($15-30 per day).

Food and Accommodations

There's not much to the **River's Edge Restaurant** (41 Main St., 360/374-0777, 8am-7pm daily, $10-13) in La Push, but there are generous portions of simple salads, salmon dishes, and steaks. Look for the multicolored totem pole outside. The views are much more spectacular than the food, with windows facing the ocean, sea stacks, and marina.

Even though there's little for tourists in La Push, the **Quileute Oceanside Resort** (330 Ocean Dr., 360/374-5267, www.quileuteoceanside.com, $20 camping, $40 RV sites, $134-189 rooms, $99-299 cabins) has been built into quite the complex, with hotel rooms and cabins just outside the town proper. The 33 deluxe waterfront cabins are the most impressive, with fireplaces, kitchens, and large jetted tubs, some with beach views. The hotel rooms have kitchens or kitchenettes.

The **Mora Campground** (Mora Rd., 3.6 miles from La Push Rd., www.nps.gov/olym, $20), run by Olympic National Park, is just across the Quillayute River mouth, but getting there from La Push means driving 6 miles back up La Push Road to where it meets Mora Road and following that 3 miles to the campground. It has 94 first-come, first-served sites in the forest, some with river views. The campground has an RV dump station (but no hookups) and flush toilets. A ranger station is open intermittently in summer. Rialto Beach is 2 miles farther down Mora Road and just 200 feet from the road via an accessible path. The Hole-in-the-Wall arched rock formation is 1.5 miles north on the beach. Always check tide tables before hiking on the beach so as not to get trapped at high tide.

Getting There

From Forks, head north on U.S. 101 for 1.5 miles and turn left onto La Push Road/Highway 110. Follow La Push Road/Highway 110 for just under 8 miles. Where Mora Road splits from the main road, stay on La Push Road for another 6 miles. The road ends in the small settlement of La Push. First Beach is located at the end of the road at a large parking area.

RUBY BEACH

Scenic **Ruby Beach** (U.S. 101, 27 miles south of Forks and 19.5 miles north of Kalaloch) has a free parking area just off the highway and requires a short 300-foot walk down to the shore. With tide pools and many rock formations and sea stacks, it's one of the most picturesque beaches on the coast and makes for a quick stop. The sand is somewhat red in places, but the stretch is breathtaking even without the beach's namesake shade. You can hike 3 miles north along the water to where the Hoh River empties into the ocean.

KALALOCH

Kalaloch, a Quinault word for "good place to land," is a small stop along a long stretch of U.S. 101 that sticks close to the beach. **Kalaloch Ranger Station** (U.S. 101, 34.5 miles south of Forks) is on the inland side of the highway and has a few exhibits about shore wildlife, as well as rangers with area maps and advice about hiking along the beach.

Food

The **Kalaloch Creekside Restaurant** (157151 U.S. 101, 360/962-2271, www.thekalalochlodge.com, 7am-9pm daily, $16-38) in the Kalaloch Lodge has an outdoor patio and views of where Kalaloch Creek meets the Pacific Ocean amid a mess of driftwood. The menu has egg and pancake dishes for breakfast, a salmon burger and flatbread pizzas for lunch, and dinner entrées like Pacific lingcod and grilled salmon with a marionberry port sauce.

Accommodations and Camping

The ★ **Kalaloch Lodge** (157151 U.S. 101, 360/962-2271, www.thekalalochlodge.com, $195-311 rooms, $246-350 cabins)—pronounce it "klay-lock"—sits on a pristine stretch of Pacific coastline, nestled in a small cove. The main lodge has beds with Pendleton blankets, and some have lovely views of Kalaloch Creek and the ocean; others are above the kitchen and face U.S. 101. The larger Becker's Room has a wood-burning fireplace that comes with a bundle of wood. Ten more rooms in the Seacrest Building (located with the property's cabins closer to the bluff above the beach) have private balconies or patios, and some have fireplaces. In between are 40 cabins in two lines on a beachfront bluff. The weathered wood that makes up each cabin's exterior belies the cozy, well-appointed rooms within. Wood fires are stocked with firewood, and each cabin has a kitchenette or kitchen and breakfast table. Neither cabins nor rooms have wireless Internet, TVs, or phones. A single group campsite can hold three small RVs or six tents and has no hookups.

Less than a mile north of the lodge is **Kalaloch Campground** (U.S. 101, 34 miles south of Forks, 877/444-6777, www.recreation.gov, $14-18), one of only two campgrounds in Olympic National Park that takes reservations for summer months (the other is in Sol Duc). Most sites are in the trees close to the beach, but some sites are right up against the bluff. This campground has 170 sites and running water year-round, but no RV hookups.

Getting There

Kalaloch is located right on U.S. 101, 34.5 miles south of Forks and 73 miles north of Aberdeen. Services are few and far between on the western side of the Olympic Peninsula (the gas station here closed in 2013). The nearest gas station is in Queets, 7 miles south on U.S. 101.

ABERDEEN

The twin industrial towns of Aberdeen and Hoquiam sit at the inside tip of Grays Harbor, a bay near Washington's southwestern corner. At one time the Hoquiam River was thick with timber coming to the mills, ships, and trains in the two towns. Now both have seen depressed economic growth, though yacht building in the Westport Shipyards and biodiesel manufacturing still buoy the area.

Sights

ABERDEEN MUSEUM OF HISTORY

There's more to the region than just the roots of Nirvana, according to the **Aberdeen**

the beach at Kalaloch

Museum of History (111 E 3rd St., 360/533-1976, www.aberdeen-museum.org, 10am-5pm Tues.-Sat., noon-4pm Sun., suggested donation $2 adults, $1 students and seniors). Located in an old armory from 1922, the museum has a replica blacksmith shop, a re-created general store, and a museum shop with, yes, Kurt Cobain action figures.

KURT COBAIN LANDING

Before fronting Nirvana during the birth of grunge, and long before his suicide rocked the '90s music scene, Kurt Cobain was just a teenager writing lyrics under a Wishkah River bridge in his hometown of Aberdeen. Now the area is a small park known as **Kurt Cobain Landing,** with a guitar sculpture and a sign explaining the site's impact on Cobain and the band—Nirvana's last album is named for the river, where some of the late singer's ashes were spread. There's little parking for the site, which sits at the end of East 2nd Street northeast of downtown, but it's a pleasantly serene site in the middle of the industrial city.

For more memories of the area's most famous son, see the Aberdeen Museum of History's **Walking Tour of Kurt Cobain's Aberdeen** (www.aberdeen-museum.org/kurt.htm), a self-guided route described online. They note the addresses of where Cobain lived as a baby, where his uncle bought him his first electric guitar, and where a teenaged Kurt Cobain vandalized an alley and got arrested. Most sites don't commemorate Cobain in any way, but the modest buildings are a reminder of how unglamorous the rock star's life was before he hit it big.

LADY WASHINGTON

The replica *Lady Washington* is based on a 1787 vessel, the first American ship to land on the West Coast and the first American-flagged vessel to travel to Japan, Hong Kong, and Honolulu. The 1989 version was built in Aberdeen and docks at the **Grays Harbor Historical Seaport Landing** (320 S Newell St., 360/532-8611, www.historicalseaport.org, 4pm-5pm Tues.-Fri, 10am-1pm Sat.-Sun., hours vary seasonally, $3 or by donation) when it isn't out sailing the world—which is often. The 72-foot ship appears in movies and on TV, most notably in *Pirates of the Caribbean* and in a Macklemore video. The ship, along with the similar *Hawaiian Chieftain*, travels around the western coast doing educational programs, scenic sails, and walk-on tours. When the ship is in town, it is also open for walk-on tours.

the bridge over the Wishkah River once frequented by Kurt Cobain

Food and Accommodations

With few tourist attractions or notable dining options, Aberdeen is likely only an overnight stop for those too tired to make it to Seattle or Tacoma after a Peninsula trip. There's absolutely no pretense in this rough, industrial town, and **Billy's Bar & Grill** (322 Heron St., 360/533-7144, www.billysaberdeen.com, 8am-11pm Mon.-Sat., 7am-9pm Sun., $9-23) is a straightforward eatery with big burgers, a prime rib dinner, and a busy bar. It's located on a corner in downtown and has a neon "Cocktails" sign outside. The bar is allegedly named for a local serial killer who used to capture naval officers and dispose of their bodies out a chute in the restaurant in the early 1900s. Still, children are welcome during daytime hours.

The **GuestHouse Inn & Suites** (616 W Heron, 360/533-4200, www.guesthouseintl.com, $96-147) is a serviceable hotel that sits right where the Wishkah River meets the bigger Chehalis River—and next to a Wal-Mart. Wi-fi is free, and the inn has a heated indoor pool and hot tub.

A Harbor View Inn (111 W 11th St., 360/533-0433, www.aharborview.com, $139-169) is a bed-and-breakfast in a house built in 1905 that was, before being broken up and enduring a fire, a 30-room palace. It was restored in the 1920s and has since been largely unchanged. Because it's located on a hillside overlooking the Wishkah and Chehalis Rivers, every room has a water view. The five guestrooms also have private baths, TVs, and wireless Internet. Many of the furnishings are antiques, and one room has a claw-foot tub. A sunroom overlooks Grays Harbor where breakfast is served.

Getting There

Aberdeen is located on Grays Harbor, where U.S. 101 meets Highway 12. From Kalaloch, follow U.S. 101 south for 73 miles.

To continue south on the Oregon Coast, stay on U.S. 101 South as it brushes past Willapa Bay. At 54.6 miles after leaving Aberdeen, take a left on Highway 4. Follow Highway 4 south about 5 miles and take a right on Highway 401, which travels 12 miles south to the Astoria Megler Bridge. Take a left to rejoin U.S. 101 south and cross the bridge to Astoria, Oregon. The drive takes about 1.75 hours.

Olympia

Though not the biggest city in Washington—it's much smaller than Seattle—Olympia wields some power as the state capital. Located at the base of the V-shaped Puget Sound, Olympia has the reputation for being a funky little city. The local Evergreen State College promotes alternative education, and signs around town still have the Olympia Beer motto, "It's the Water," even though the brewery has been closed for years.

The town has a sprawling Capitol campus with historical buildings and manicured grounds, a thriving farmers market, and several blocks of downtown shops. The I-5 freeway runs through town, making Olympia a way station between Seattle and Portland.

SIGHTS

Artesian Well

Olympia's offbeat vibe is best captured at the **Artesian Well** (4th Ave. E between Adams St. SE and Jefferson St. SE, www.olympiawa.gov), where water bubbles up from 90 feet underground. For a long time the well was just a metal pipe in a downtown parking lot, and locals stopped by to fill jugs with the crisp, pure water. The flow of water never stops—10 gallons per minute, all free to anyone who wants it. Recently an artist decorated the pipe with a large mosaic and mural, turning it into a piece of art. In 2013 the city council voted to make the spot, now a parking lot between

Olympia

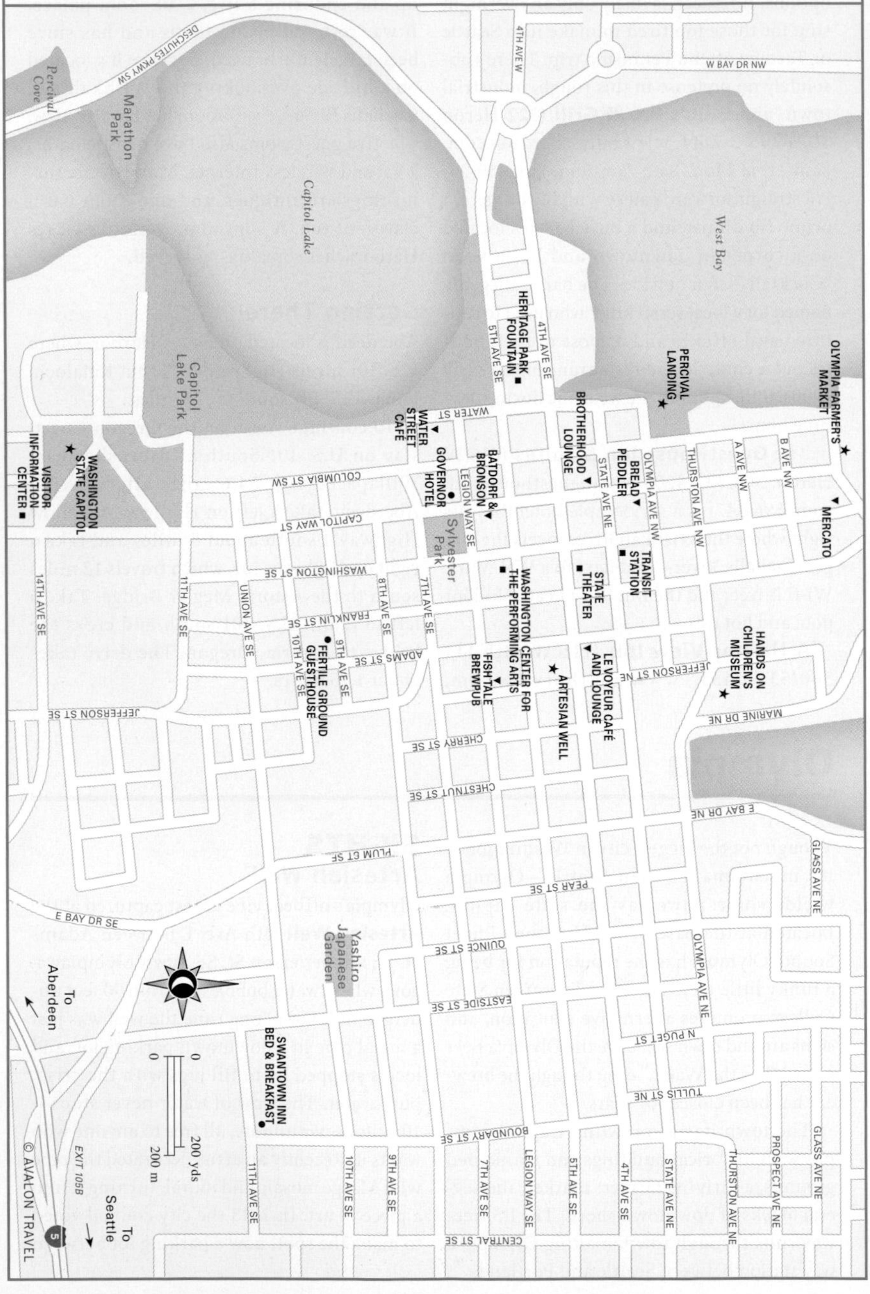
DESCHUTES PKWY SW
Percival Cove
Marathon Park
Capitol Lake
4TH AVE W
W BAY DR NW
West Bay
Capitol Lake Park
HERITAGE PARK FOUNTAIN
4TH AVE SE
5TH AVE SE
PERCIVAL LANDING
OLYMPIA FARMER'S MARKET
WATER ST
WATER STREET CAFE
BROTHERHOOD LOUNGE
STATE AVE NE
OLYMPIA AVE NW
THURSTON AVE NW
A AVE NW
B AVE NW
WASHINGTON STATE CAPITOL
VISITOR INFORMATION CENTER
GOVERNOR HOTEL
BATDORF & BRONSON
BREAD PEDDLER
MERCATO
COLUMBIA ST SW
LEGION WAY SE
CAPITOL WAY ST
Sylvester Park
TRANSIT STATION
WASHINGTON ST SE
WASHINGTON CENTER FOR THE PERFORMING ARTS
STATE THEATER
14TH AVE SE
11TH AVE SE
UNION AVE SE
8TH AVE SE
7TH AVE SE
FRANKLIN ST SE
HANDS ON CHILDREN'S MUSEUM
ADAMS ST SE
9TH AVE SE
10TH AVE SE
FERTILE GROUND GUESTHOUSE
FISH TALE BREWPUB
ARTESIAN WELL
LE VOYEUR CAFÉ AND LOUNGE
JEFFERSON ST NE
JEFFERSON ST SE
MARINE DR NE
CHERRY ST SE
CHESTNUT ST SE
E BAY DR NE
GLASS AVE NE
PLUM ST SE
PEAR ST SE
E BAY DR SE
Yashiro Japanese Garden
QUINCE ST SE
OLYMPIA AVE NE
To Aberdeen
EASTSIDE ST SE
N PUGET ST
SWANTOWN INN BED & BREAKFAST
0
200 yds
0
200 m
TULLIS ST NE
BOUNDARY ST SE
EXIT 105B
11TH AVE SE
10TH AVE SE
9TH AVE SE
7TH AVE SE
LEGION WAY SE
5TH AVE SE
4TH AVE SE
STATE AVE NE
THURSTON AVE NE
PROSPECT AVE NE
GLASS AVE NE
To Seattle
5
CENTRAL ST SE
© AVALON TRAVEL

downtown buildings, a city park with bathroom facilities and space for food-truck parking.

Hands On Children's Museum

The **Hands On Children's Museum** (414 Jefferson St. NE, 360/956-0818, www.hocm.org, 10am-5pm Tues.-Sat., 11am-5pm Sun.-Mon., $12.95 adults, $10.95 seniors, children under 2 free), located near the marinas on the northeastern corner of downtown, has play spaces for very young children, each dedicated to nature, construction, arts and crafts, or the ever-exciting emergency vehicles. The Puget Sound display has a microscope and moving crane, and the nature area has a two-story slide. There's also a museum café.

Olympia Farmers Market

The covered **Olympia Farmers Market** (700 N Capitol Way, 360/352-9096, www.olympiafarmersmarket.com, 10am-3pm Thurs.-Sun. Apr.-Oct., 10am-3pm Sat.-Sun. Nov.-Dec.) has rows of stalls selling produce, flowers, and meat, plus crafts and baked goods. Outside, a stage is used for daily performances in summer, and food stands sell prepared goods. Close to half a million visitors come to the market every year, and in summer the parking lot gets very crowded.

Percival Landing

Percival Landing (Olympia Ave. NW and Columbia St. NW, www.olympiawa.gov) is a waterfront park named for the old commercial wharf and the family that ran it. Today it has boat docks, a playground, picnic areas, and a boardwalk with benches. The nearly mile-long boardwalk follows the marina to where the industrial port begins. Right before it ends, a viewing tower sits near the Olympia Farmers Market.

Washington State Capitol

The dome of the **Washington State Capitol** (Cherry Lane SW and Sid Snyder Ave. SW, 360/902-8880, www.des.wa.gov) is visible from I-5 and much of downtown since it towers above the rest of the city on a hill. The dome was finished in 1928 and is one of the biggest masonry domes in the world, coming in after the likes of St. Peter's Cathedral and the Florence Duomo. A Tiffany chandelier under the dome's rotunda has 438 pieces and is the largest in the world—weighing in at 10,000 pounds.

Free guided tours begin hourly at the

Washington State Capitol

Tour Information Desk, just inside the main entrance doors of the domed Legislative Building. The **Visitor Information Center** (103 Sid Snyder Ave., 360/704-7544, www.visitolympia.com, 10am-5pm Mon.-Fri., summer only 10am-4pm Sat., free) has maps and tourist information.

The campus around the dome includes a sunken garden and a 50-foot Tivoli Fountain, a replica of the famous one in Copenhagen, Denmark. Sculptures and memorials populate the grounds, and a trail leads down a steep hill to Capitol Lake and downtown. The trail circles 1.5 miles around Capitol Lake, and it's a short walk to the **Heritage Park Fountain** (330 5th Ave. SW) with jets erupting from the ground.

Parking is available along Water St. SW, along the diagonal roads that cross the main lawn, or in lots throughout the campus.

ENTERTAINMENT AND EVENTS

The **State Theater** (202 4th Ave. E, 360/786-0151, www.harlequinproductions.org) was once a grand downtown movie theater. But it was an abandoned dollar-movie house when Harlequin Productions (a local theater troupe) bought it and restored it to former glory. The group puts on original plays and classic theater pieces, plus an annual 1940s- or 1950s-themed Christmas show and the occasional rock musical version of a Shakespeare play.

Downtown's biggest performance venue is the **Washington Center for the Performing Arts** (512 Washington St. SE, 360/753-8585, www.washingtoncenter.org), which has a facade with 1924 pieces but an all-modern interior. It hosts visiting classical, jazz, blues, and pop musical acts, along with comedy shows, lecturers, and film screenings.

The **Brotherhood Lounge** (119 Capitol Way N, 360/352-4153, www.thebrotherhoodlounge.com, 3pm-2am daily, cash only) is so named because the space used to be home to labor unions. A large sign still reads "Labor Temple" outside. Now the popular bar has shuffleboard and pool, an outdoor patio, and a photo booth. Draft beers are mostly local. Sometimes aerialists and trapeze artists perform, other times a movie is playing in the bar, and DJs play on some weekend nights.

Once upon a time, the city was known for Olympia Beer (which is still produced, but brewed elsewhere); now the city's biggest beer export is Fish Tale organic ales from Fish Brewing, located in an old knitting factory with a brightly painted mural on its facade. Across the street is its **Fish Tale Brewpub** (515 Jefferson St. SE, 360/943-3650, www.fishbrewing.com, 11am-10pm Mon.-Thurs., 11am-midnight Fri., 9am-midnight Sat., 9am-10pm Sun.), also with murals on the exterior, and with 14 beer and cider taps plus a menu of oyster shooters, fish-and-chips, burgers, salads, and desserts. It has outdoor seating in the summer and occasional live music performances.

The menu at **Le Voyeur Café and Lounge** (404 E 4th Ave., 360/943-5710, www.voyeurolympia.com, 11am-2am daily) is a double of itself, because every sandwich, salad, and entrée has a vegan counterpart. Bottled beers come from around the world. The space has red walls and funky, colorful decor. Most nights it hosts live music, often without a cover.

FOOD

The **McMenamins Spar Café** (114 4th Ave. E, 360/357-6444, www.mcmenamins.com/spar, 7am-midnight Sun.-Thurs., 7am-1am Fri. Sat., $12-25) was a classic downtown diner with logging paraphernalia on the walls until it was purchased by the McMenamins, a Portland-based company known for historical restoration. What was once a cigar counter is now a large seating area, but its history remains on the walls. The beer brewed on-site uses artesian well water, and the menu boasts pub classics like burgers, pizza, and salads.

The ★ **Bread Peddler** (222 Capitol Way N, 360/352-1175, www.breadpeddler.com, 7am-5pm daily, $8-12) opened in Olympia when a French chef decided the town needed a bakery like those in his home country—and he wasn't afraid to write the menu in French. Patrons order at a counter before sitting with a croque Madame, salad, cheese puff, or other delectable pastry. The café is sunny and busy, with just a few chairs next to the bakery counter, but expands into adjacent spaces that include a bistro section with more and bigger tables for breakfast and lunch, and a white-walled creperie next door.

Although the coffee roastery for **Batdorf & Bronson** (516 S Capitol Way, 360/786-6717, www.batdorfcoffee.com, 6:30am-6pm Mon.-Fri., 7am-6pm Sat.-Sun.) is next to the farmers market and offers tasting tours, the homegrown company sells its drinks at a coffeehouse downtown. There's a fireplace and couches, plus free wireless Internet. The vibe is more personable than a chain coffeehouse, but more adult than a college meet-up spot.

An old American Legion hall next to Capitol Lake is now ★ **Waterstreet Café** (610 Water St. SW, 360/709-9090, www.waterstreetcafeandbar.com, 10:30am-2pm and 4:30pm-9pm Sun.-Thurs., 10:30am-2pm and 4:30pm-midnight Fri.-Sat., $16-30), an Italian restaurant with some of the finest plates in town. The menu includes fish dishes, chutneys, and combinations like scallops with pulled pork. Brunch is daily. The restaurant is dark inside, despite the fireplace and light touch to the furniture and art pieces, but a large outdoor patio has views of the lake.

The feel of **Gardner's** (111 Thurston Ave. NW, 360/786-8466, gardnersrestaurant.com, 5pm-10pm daily, $22-36) is so classic it's strange that it only dates to the 1980s, not the establishment of statehood. It offers fine dining, complete with scallop dishes and a daily rack of lamb preparation. Even the cocktails are classics, from martinis to Manhattans, and the dark wood ceilings give the space the proper solemnity.

Since the fresh vegetable stands of the farmers market are just across the street from **Mercato** (111 Market St., 360/528-3663, http://ramblinrestaurants.com, 11am-9pm daily, $14-26), it's no wonder so many of its Italian dishes feature fresh produce. The menu is filled with accessible but well-crafted pastas and pizzas, and weekdays feature a special three-course chef's menu. Outdoor seating is popular in the summer, but the large interior keeps wait times down.

ACCOMMODATIONS

The downtown **Governor Hotel** (621 Capitol Way S, 360/352-7700, www.olympiagovernorhotel.com, $119-219) is located between the commercial district and the Capitol campus and easily walkable to both. Long a serviceable if unflashy hotel, it recently was reborn as a boutique-style property with modern and retro-style furnishings, bold flashes of color, large flat-screen TVs, and luxury down comforters and showerheads. The hotel hasn't completely shaken its dated exterior, but the location is very convenient, and some rooms overlook Capitol Lake and have private balconies.

The **Swantown Inn Bed & Breakfast** (1431 11th Ave. SE, 877/753-9123, www.swantowninn.com, $179-249) is located in a bold Victorian house east of downtown. It's not within walking distance of shops and restaurants but is in a quiet residential neighborhood. The 1887 mansion has four guest rooms decorated in dark, ornate wallpapers and draperies and all with private baths. One room has a two-person jetted tub. A day spa in the attic offers massages and antique foot soak tubs.

More than a bed-and-breakfast, **Fertile Ground Guesthouse** (311 9th Ave. SE, 360/352-2428, www.fertileground.org, $95-110) is a garden and tool-share site and a place for chickens to hang out in a coop next to rows of vegetables. A sauna handmade from cedar and redwood sits next to the 100-year-old house located downtown. A shared bathroom has wood floors, claw-foot tubs, and bubble bath. One of the three rooms has a private bath, while a dormitory room offers three beds and a bathroom. Room rentals come with breakfast.

GETTING THERE

To reach Olympia from Aberdeen, take U.S. 12 (which crosses U.S. 101 in downtown Aberdeen) east for 21.5 miles until it becomes Highway 8 in Elma (no turns necessary). Follow Highway 8 east for 23 miles where it again changes names (no turns), becoming U.S. 101. From this point, continue 7.5 miles east on U.S. 101 to I-5; take I-5 North and exit almost immediately at exit 105 and follow signs for Olympia. The drive takes about an hour when there's no traffic coming into Olympia.

The local **Amtrak** station (6600 Yelm Hwy. SE, www.amtrak.com, 8:15am-9:30pm daily) isn't actually in Olympia; it's outside the suburb of Lacey on Yelm Highway. There's no ticket office, just a kiosk and an enclosed waiting area. Six trains depart daily for Seattle ($14-44) and six trains daily for Portland ($20-61). **Intercity Transit** bus route 64 (Olympia Transit Center, 222 State Ave. NE, 360/786-1881, www.intercitytransit.com, $1.25 adults and children 6-18, children under 6 free) goes from downtown Olympia to the Amtrak station, a 42-minute trip.

San Juan Islands

Look for ★ to find recommended sights, activities, dining, and lodging.

Highlights

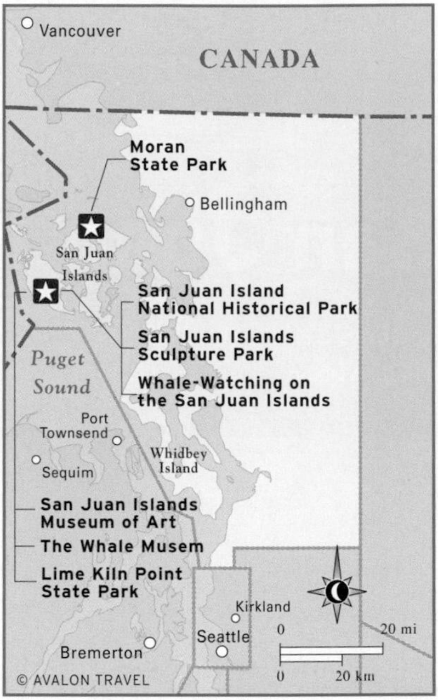

★ **The Whale Museum:** Orcas, the wildlife stars of the San Juans, get their own dedicated education center (page 197).

★ **San Juan Islands Museum of Art:** This venue grows the island's cultural scene and showcases local artists (page 197).

★ **San Juan Islands Sculpture Park:** Wander through gardens filled with kooky, beautiful artworks (page 199).

★ **San Juan Island National Historical Park:** Learn about the strange history of the islands at two separate military sites (page 199).

★ **Lime Kiln Point State Park:** Come for the waterfront trails and stay for the land-based whale-watching (page 200).

★ **Whale-Watching on the San Juan Islands:** Spot the archipelago's resident orcas, whether by land or sea (pages 201, 211, and 220).

★ **Moran State Park:** Here you'll find lakes, trails, and a sublime mountaintop view (page 209).

Sprinkled in the Puget Sound like breadcrumbs, the San Juan Islands are somehow remote and nearby all at once. The quaint islands offer an escape from urbanity and a sampling of charming rural Washington.

Though there are more than a hundred islands in the chain, only four of the San Juans can be reached by major ferries: San Juan, Orcas, Lopez, and Shaw. Big white-and-green boats shepherd passengers and their vehicles to the main isles.

Life is slow on the bucolic islands, with a vibe that reminds some of rural, maritime New England—think narrow roads that wind between small pastures and grassy fields, and sailboats lining the shore. Although there's a second-home contingent here, the San Juans don't feel like a resort. Each island has the feel of a small town, supportive of its independent businesses and culture. Locals wear casual clothes and beat-up sneakers even if they own a million-dollar waterfront house.

Here you'll find charming hubs with surprisingly good dining, as well as outdoor recreation opportunities aplenty, from hiking to kayaking to biking. Gorgeous viewpoints are possible from the islands' vantages. And in the waters surrounding the islands, resident orcas breach, adding an even more magical layer to the environs.

PLANNING YOUR TIME

For a first visit to the San Juan Islands, it's hard to pass up a day or two in Friday Harbor on San Juan Island. It's the archipelago's biggest town, has a number of good shops, and whale-watching boats leave regularly. From there, you can explore the rest of San Juan Island, including the charming Roche Harbor Resort, the anchor of the island's northwest side, and the historic American and English Camps. Free spirits may prefer horseshoe-shaped Orcas Island, where there are fewer restaurants in its central hub of Eastsound but lots of ways to play in kayaks or in a funky little brewery. Cyclists and those needing peace and quiet can head to Lopez Island, a rural spot with few amenities—most centered in a cluster known as Lopez Village—but plenty of

Previous: San Juan Islands' resident orcas; Lime Kiln State Park. **Above:** Rosario Resort on Orcas Island.

San Juan Islands

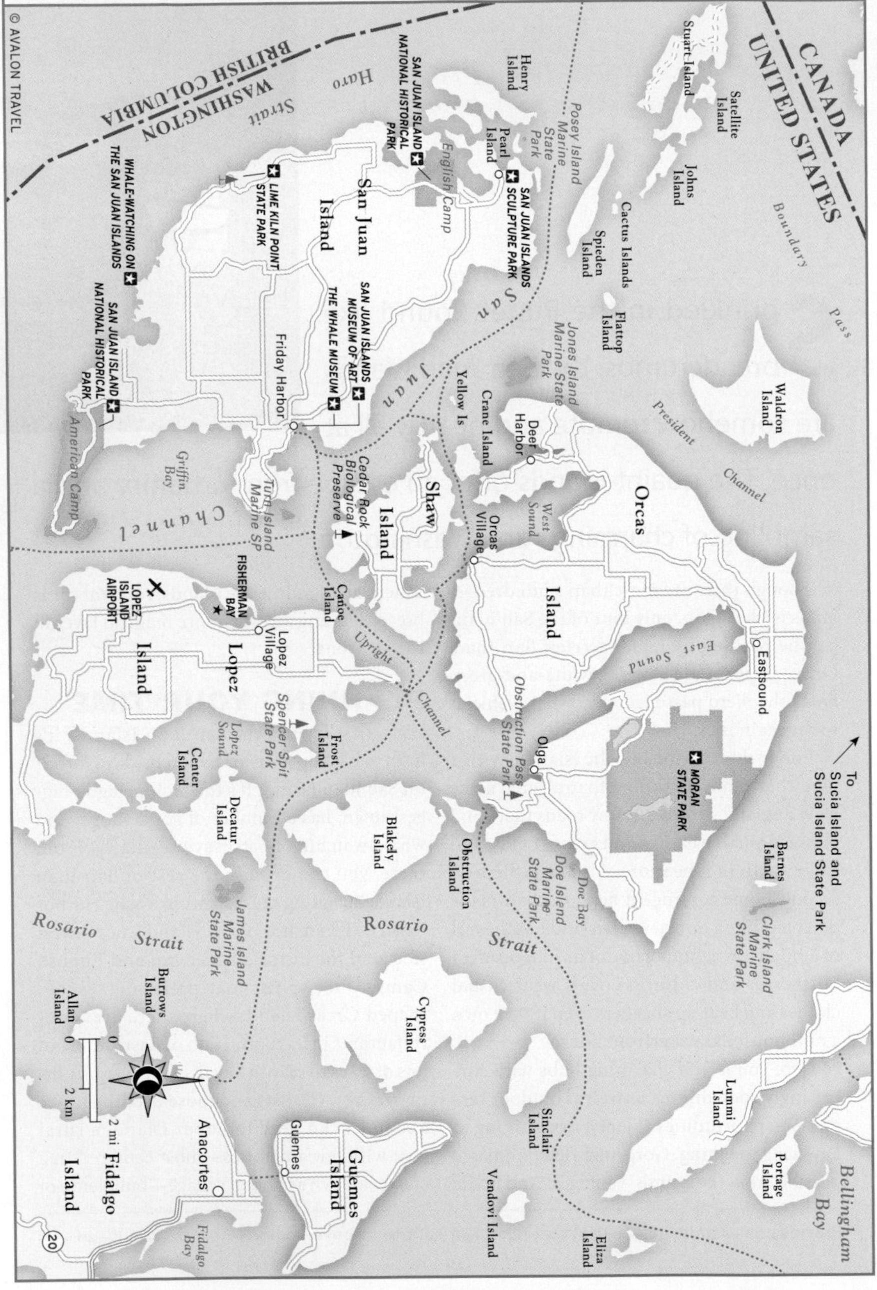

© AVALON TRAVEL
BRITISH COLUMBIA
WASHINGTON
CANADA
UNITED STATES
Haro Strait
Boundary Pass
President Channel
San Juan Channel
Upright Channel
Rosario Strait
Stuart Island
Satellite Island
Johns Island
Cactus Islands
Spieden Island
Flattop Island
Waldron Island
Henry Island
Pearl Island
Posey Island Marine State Park
Jones Island Marine State Park
Yellow Is
Crane Island
Deer Harbor
West Sound
Orcas Village
Orcas Island
East Sound
Eastsound
Olga
Obstruction Pass State Park
MORAN STATE PARK
To Sucia Island and Sucia Island State Park
Barnes Island
Clark Island Marine State Park
Doe Bay
Doe Island Marine State Park
Obstruction Island
Blakely Island
San Juan Island
SAN JUAN ISLAND NATIONAL HISTORICAL PARK
English Camp
SAN JUAN ISLANDS SCULPTURE PARK
LIME KILN POINT STATE PARK
WHALE-WATCHING ON THE SAN JUAN ISLANDS
SAN JUAN ISLANDS MUSEUM OF ART
THE WHALE MUSEUM
Friday Harbor
American Camp
Griffin Bay
Turn Island Marine SP
Cedar Rock Biological Preserve
Shaw Island
Canoe Island
LOPEZ ISLAND AIRPORT
FISHERMAN BAY
Lopez Village
Lopez Island
Lopez Sound
Spencer Spit State Park
Frost Island
Center Island
Decatur Island
James Island Marine State Park
Burrows Island
Allan Island
Cypress Island
Sinclair Island
Vendovi Island
Eliza Island
Lummi Island
Portage Island
Bellingham Bay
Guemes Island
Guemes
Anacortes
Fidalgo Island
Fidalgo Bay
20
0 2 mi
0 2 km

friendliness. Whale-watching is possible from all three islands, but the most outfitters are available on San Juan Island.

Many people pick one island at a time to focus on in the San Juans; 2-3 days is the minimum amount of time you'd want to budget for a trip given the time-consuming logistics of ferry travel. There is an interisland ferry, so you can island-hop if you choose—but don't try to hit up more than one island unless you have 3-4 days at least.

If you're planning on bringing your car—which many do, as a private vehicle is the best way to get around the islands—it's best to snag a ferry reservation as soon as you know your travel dates, especially in summer. The Washington State Ferry releases a third of each sailing's reservable vehicle spots at the beginning of each season. Another third becomes available two weeks before each sailing date, and the final third two days in advance. Ten percent of every sailing's trips are held for standby vehicles, so if you don't score a ferry reservation, you might get lucky on standby—but expect to linger at the ferry dock for several hours at least. There are no limits for walk-on passengers.

The high season in the San Juans is summer, when it's not too chilly to kayak (but still, it can get brisk!). But thanks to a mild climate, it's a destination year-round. Some smaller shops and restaurants close or have limited hours in the winter, but Friday Harbor and Eastsound stay humming, albeit mostly on weekends. Lopez Island, notably, is a very sleepy island outside of the summer. Whale-watching boat trips are active year-round, but whales are more regularly spotted in the summer months.

Anacortes

The town of Anacortes is the gateway to the San Juan Islands, and it's actually on an island of its own, Fidalgo Island—but thanks to a large bridge over a narrow strait, access is much easier. With marinas filled with boats around practically every corner, it's definitely a seafaring town, but there's little here to warrant an extended stay. Still, sometimes ferry schedules to the San Juans necessitate an overnight here, and there are ample services in that event.

SIGHTS

Deception Pass State Park

Deception Pass State Park (41020 Rte. 20, 360/675-3767, http://parks.state.wa.us, 6:30am-dusk daily mid-May-early Sept., 8am-dusk daily early Sept.-mid-May, $10 parking) spans Fidalgo Island, on which Anacortes is located, and Whidbey Island, just to the south. It's Washington's most visited state park thanks to its beachfront, trails through old-growth forest, tide pools, and a small museum (10am-6pm daily mid-May-early Sept., free) dedicated to the Civilian Conservation Corps, the workforce that built many of the country's parks during the Depression. Don't be surprised if you hear fighter jets roaring above; a naval air station is based on Whidbey Island. The much-photographed Deception Pass Bridge links Fidalgo and Whidbey Islands; you can take in the view from overlooks with parking lots on either side, as well as on tiny Pass Island in between the two larger islands. A pedestrian path next to the car lanes also allows you to walk the entire span. Deception Pass State Park is about a nine-mile, 15-minute drive south of Anacortes on Highway 20.

Anacortes Museum

Originally built as a library, the **Anacortes Museum** (1305 8th St., 360/293-1915, www.cityofanacortes.org, 10am-4pm Tues.-Sat., 1pm-4pm Sun., free) has displayed local history and artifacts since 1968. An Anacortes collector named Wallie Funk amassed almost

100,000 photographs of life in the area from 1880 through the 21st century. Operating under the same umbrella is the **Maritime Heritage Center** (703 R Ave., www.cityofanacortes.org, 10am-4pm Tues.-Sat., 11am-4pm Sun., free), which has seagoing artifacts on display. Next door, the *W.T. Preston,* a stern-wheeler steamboat from 1939, is open for tours ($5 adults, $4 seniors, $3 children 5-16, free for children under 5).

FOOD

Dining is mostly casual in Anacortes, and **Adrift** (510 Commercial Ave., 360/588-0653, www.adriftrestaurant.com, 8am-9pm Mon.-Thurs., 8am-10pm Fri.-Sat., 8am-2pm Sun., $10-29) is the best of the lot. It's a seafood joint better known for its wide variety of burgers and ice cream floats made with stout or champagne. Top a burger with pan-fried oysters, or dig into a big pancake or French toast at brunch.

Try the barbecue and biscuits at **Dad's Diner** (906 Commercial Ave., 360/899-5269, 7am-4pm Tues.-Thurs. and Sat.-Sun., 7am-9pm Fri., $8-20). A chalkboard menu lists the hearty breakfasts of the day, sandwiches, salads, and burgers. Service is friendly but not necessarily fast; if you have a ferry to catch, ask for the food to go—it'll taste even better from takeout containers in the ferry line.

No matter what time you arrive in Anacortes, there's a fresh treat waiting at **Donut House** (2719 Commercial Ave., 360/293-4053, 24 hours daily, $1-4.50), which never closes. The eatery is bare-bones, but it has fritters as well as crème-filled and flavored old-fashioned doughnuts whenever the craving hits.

ACCOMMODATIONS

The **Nantucket Inn** (3402 Commercial Ave., 360/333-5282, www.nantucketinnanacortes.com, $129-219) is a bed-and-breakfast offering a decidedly homey experience with its backyard fire pit and breakfasts served in a comfy nook. All rooms have private baths, and some have a twin-sized bed tucked under a window, ideal for children.

Taking an early ferry? **Ship Harbor Inn** (5316 Ferry Terminal Rd., 360/293-5177, www.shipharborinn.com, $169-249) is about a 15-minute walk from the ferry terminal, and the motel offers even more charm than it needs to given its convenient location. The white walls and red roof are easy to spot, and some rooms have kitchenettes, fireplaces, and jetted tubs. Watch the boats inch across Puget

Deception Pass State Park

Sound from Adirondack chairs perched on a hill above the hotel.

Located near the restaurants of downtown Anacortes, ★ **Majestic Inn and Spa** (419 Commercial Ave., 360/299-1400 www.majesticinnandspa.com, $241-323) is one of the nicest places to stay for miles around. The historical property, in a building originally erected in 1890, has been completely redone to include a rooftop lounge with a fire pit, and there's a newer second building. Rooms have a modern flair and high-end linens, even in the historical wings. The spa is an ideal escape when coastal weather hits Anacortes.

GETTING THERE

To reach Anacortes from Seattle, head north on I-5 for about 65 miles, taking exit 230 in Burlington for Highway 20. Look for signs for the San Juan Islands. Follow Highway 20 west for about 15 miles through open fields and past industrial shipyards, remaining on it as it becomes Commercial Drive in Anacortes. Without traffic, it takes about 1.5 hours to drive from Seattle to Anacortes.

San Juan Island

San Juan is the busiest of the island chain named after it, and the town of Friday Harbor on the eastern shore is the center of the action. Ferries arrive a mere block from town, making it the most walkable area in the archipelago with its many nearby museums, restaurants, and shops. The island's other hub, on the western side, is Roche Harbor, where a small resort sits on the bay along with a café, with the San Juan Islands Sculpture Park just outside. Country roads crisscross the island, most lined with farmhouses and residences.

SIGHTS

★ The Whale Museum

Orcas are more than the most popular attraction in the San Juan Islands; they're part of the ecological and human history of the region. The adorable two-story **Whale Museum** (62 1st St., 360/378-4710, http://whalemuseum.org, 9am-6pm daily, $6 adults, $5 seniors, $3 students and children 5-18, free for children under 5), with its photo-ready exterior murals, is an educational primer on how orcas live in the changing oceans. Most of the exhibits in the museum are locally focused on the three resident orca pods, so familiar to locals that each whale has a name; look for the family tree that lays out their names and relationships. Here you'll find a refabricated skeleton of an orca that died mysteriously on local shores hanging from the ceiling, along with displays on how Native Americans viewed orcas and the ways plastics in the water are affecting the species. The museum gift shop offers an "adopt an orca" program ($35-70) so visitors can sponsor one of the 70-something killer whales that remain in Puget Sound; it comes with a photo of the whale, stickers, monthly updates on the whale, and a museum membership.

★ San Juan Islands Museum of Art

The **San Juan Islands Museum of Art** (540 Spring St., 360/370-5050, http://sjima.org, 11am-5pm Thurs.-Mon. May-Sept., 11am-5pm Fri.-Mon. Oct.-Apr., $10 adults, free for children under 18) was built in an old ambulance garage, and a giant glass atrium was added to the front of the one-story building. It makes a sunny space for art exhibits and, along with two more galleries inside the building, showcases artists from around the globe in traveling exhibits, from quilt shows from the American South to photography from the Middle East—but care is always taken to link the themes to the Salish Sea, the body of water that encompasses Puget Sound and the waterways around it. Local artists are regularly

San Juan Island

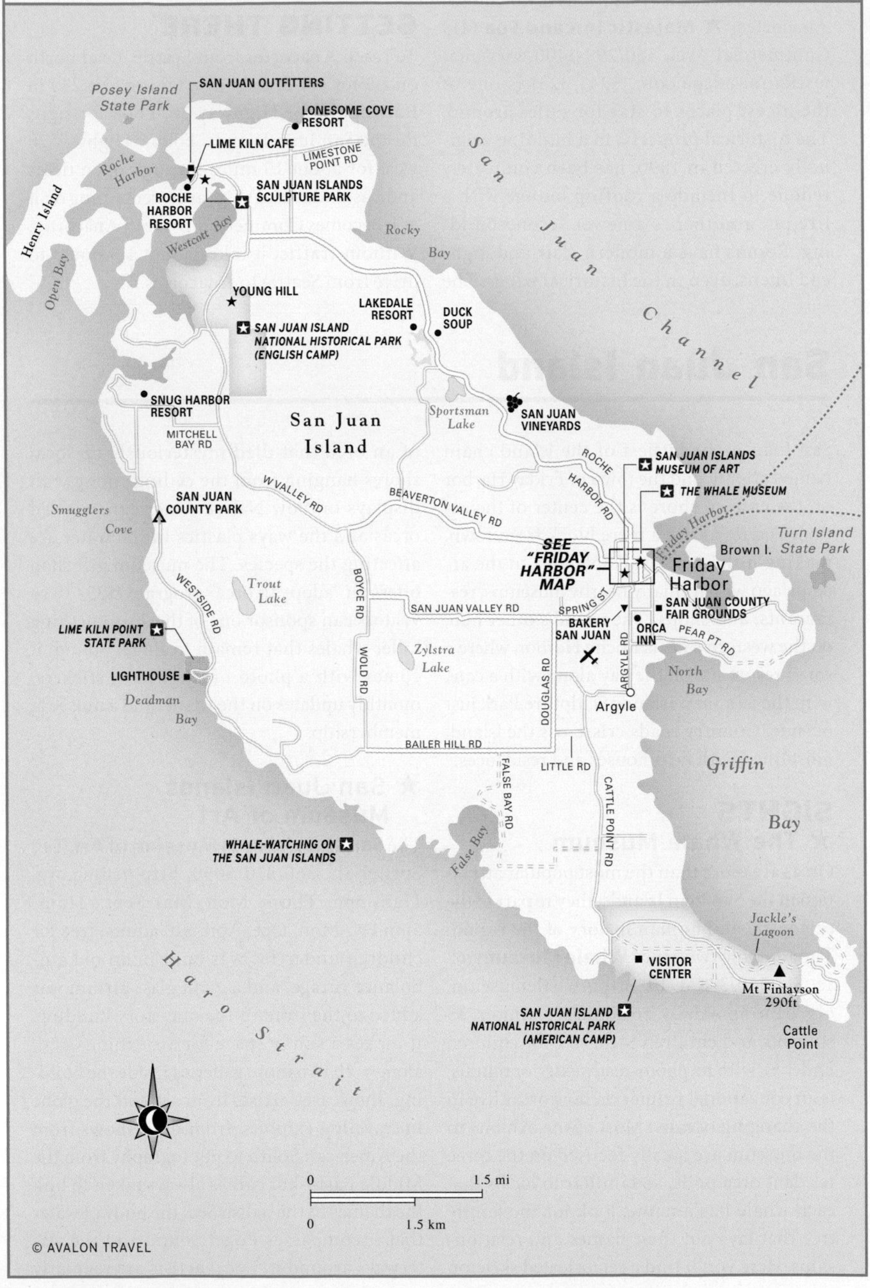
SAN JUAN OUTFITTERS
Posey Island State Park
LONESOME COVE RESORT
LIME KILN CAFE
LIMESTONE POINT RD
Roche Harbor
ROCHE HARBOR RESORT
SAN JUAN ISLANDS SCULPTURE PARK
Henry Island
Westcott Bay
Rocky Bay
Open Bay
San Juan Channel
YOUNG HILL
LAKEDALE RESORT
DUCK SOUP
SAN JUAN ISLAND NATIONAL HISTORICAL PARK (ENGLISH CAMP)
SNUG HARBOR RESORT
Sportsman Lake
SAN JUAN VINEYARDS
San Juan Island
MITCHELL BAY RD
ROCHE HARBOR RD
SAN JUAN ISLANDS MUSEUM OF ART
W VALLEY RD
BEAVERTON VALLEY RD
THE WHALE MUSEUM
Smugglers Cove
SAN JUAN COUNTY PARK
Friday Harbor
Turn Island State Park
Brown I.
SEE "FRIDAY HARBOR" MAP
Friday Harbor
WESTSIDE RD
BOYCE RD
Trout Lake
SAN JUAN VALLEY RD
SPRING ST
SAN JUAN COUNTY FAIR GROUNDS
LIME KILN POINT STATE PARK
BAKERY SAN JUAN
ORCA INN
PEAR PT RD
ARGYLE RD
WOLD RD
Zylstra Lake
North Bay
LIGHTHOUSE
DOUGLAS RD
Argyle
Deadman Bay
BAILER HILL RD
LITTLE RD
Griffin Bay
FALSE BAY RD
CATTLE POINT RD
WHALE-WATCHING ON THE SAN JUAN ISLANDS
False Bay
Haro Strait
Jackle's Lagoon
VISITOR CENTER
Mt Finlayson 290ft
SAN JUAN ISLAND NATIONAL HISTORICAL PARK (AMERICAN CAMP)
Cattle Point
0
1.5 mi
0
1.5 km
© AVALON TRAVEL

featured. The space is also a gathering place for community events, like a weekly Saturday arts and crafts event (10am, free with donations encouraged) that focuses on, for instance, building kaleidoscopes or exploring topography by making maps. Guest artists teach workshops, and experts come in for lectures a few times a year.

San Juan Historical Museum

The small **San Juan Historical Museum** (405 Price St., 360/378-3949, www.sjmuseum.org, 10am-2pm Thurs.-Sat. June, 10am-2pm Tues.-Sat. July-Sept., by appointment Oct.-May, $6) hosts summer concerts and events at its downtown Friday Harbor location, and it's a good stop when you're wandering town and waiting for the ferry. Exhibits mostly explore 19th- and 20th-century life on the island.

San Juan Vineyards

The tasting room for **San Juan Vineyards** (3136 Roche Harbor Rd., 360/378-9463, www.sanjuanvineyards.com, 11am-5pm daily summer, $5 tasting fee) is located in a white 19th-century schoolhouse. While grapes grown here are used in the wine, many come from the drier Yakima Valley and Horse Heaven Hills region in eastern Washington. The winery focuses on more obscure white wines made from Madeleine Angevine and Siegerrebe grapes, both of which pair well with seafood, as well as has some reds and rosés. Sometimes a tasting room-only wine named for Mona the Camel, just across the street, is offered.

★ San Juan Islands Sculpture Park

Located on the west side of the island, near Roche Harbor, the **San Juan Islands Sculpture Park** (9083 Roche Harbor Rd., 360/370-0035, http://sjisculpturepark.com, dawn-dusk daily, free) is a serene 20-acre field filled with audacious sculptures—for instance, a horse and whale made from scrap metal, a bizarre seated figure on a tree stump, and a massive puzzle piece—more than 150 are scattered across the manicured gardens. The park dates back to 1998 when it was developed to illustrate art and nature in harmony. Works stay on display for about two years before being sold, and sculptures come from around the world. Walking paths weave around the sculptures and a small pond, and a starfish-shaped sand pit encourages visitors to make their own creations.

If you cross Roche Harbor Road and walk a few yards up Afterglow Drive, you'll find a walking trail. Follow it about a hundred yards to the **McMillin Mausoleum** (free). It's not formally part of the sculpture park, more of a historical relic that happens to be near the collection of artwork, and technically part of a nearby cemetery. It salutes the family of John McMillin, a lime works owner who once hosted Teddy Roosevelt on the island. The mausoleum is an open-air rotunda made of Greek pillars, with a stone table at the center—it's beautiful and a little spooky.

★ San Juan Island National Historical Park

There's only one place to see where the United States and Great Britain fought each other on the West Coast—in a battle over a pig. In the 18th century both countries claimed the San Juan Islands, coming to a head when an American farmer shot an English-owned pig on the island in 1859. The ensuing, infamous Pig War (no one died but the pig) approached being a serious conflict but was eventually resolved, and the United States got full control of the islands in the 1870s. The 2,000-acre **San Juan Island National Historical Park** (360/378-2240 www.nps.gov/sajh, grounds dawn-11pm daily, free) encompasses the American Camp and the English Camp. Both are historical sites of military encampments, today holding swaths of green fields, trails, and scenic views of the landscape. Although each has distinct artifacts, you might just choose one camp to focus on.

English Camp (3905 W Valley Rd.) sits on the northwest side of the island, not far from Roche Harbor. Here you'll find the **English Camp Visitor Center** (9am-5pm daily

June-Sept.), a formal garden of hedges and manicured flower beds, plus an old commissary building and barracks. There are several trails, most of which go inland, with Bell Point Trail heading to the water.

The **American Camp** (4668 Cattle Point Rd.) is on the southern end of the island. It has parade grounds overlooking the water and restored officers' quarters. The Redoubt, a raised section of prairie land, is one of the best-preserved fortifications of its kind in the country. The **American Camp Visitor Center** (8:30am-5pm daily June-Aug., 8:30am-4:30pm Wed.-Sun. Sept.-Feb., 8:30am-4:30pm daily Mar.-May) is open year-round.

★ Lime Kiln Point State Park

Waterfront **Lime Kiln Point State Park** (1567 Westside Rd., 360/378-2044, http://parks.state.wa.us, 8am-dusk daily, $10 parking), on the island's west side, has natural beauty in spades, occupying 40 acres of rocky shoreline topped off with forest. Trails wind through the park, offering plenty of beautiful views of Vancouver Island. Limestone was once dug here, and you can peek in the old stone kiln that remains. The park also happens to be a stellar land-based spot to view killer whales surfacing in the waves of Haro Strait, the waterway that separates San Juan Island from Vancouver Island. In summer, be sure to visit the tiny 1919 lighthouse on the grounds, where a college professor sets up his annual whale count to keep tabs on the resident orcas. You can peer from the windows of the lighthouse for a decent chance of spotting a black fin, or peruse the nearby **interpretive center** (11am-4pm daily May-Sept.) to learn more about the marine life spotted here. Year-round, seal and various bird sightings are possible. May-September, free lighthouse tours take place on Thursday and Saturday evenings, and free whale talks from the professor happen on Friday and Saturday at 3pm.

Pelindaba Lavender Farm

Can you get lost in a field of lavender? Find out at **Pelindaba Lavender Farm** (45 Hawthorne Ln., 866/819-1911, www.pelindabalavender.com, 9:30am-5:30pm daily May-Sept., 9:30am-5:30pm Wed.-Sun. Apr. and Oct., free), where the signature flower appears in every form imaginable. First there are the fields of live plants, which spread around a central building open to visitors April-October, along with picnic areas. You can also see different lavender varieties in

San Juan Island National Historical Park

the Demonstration Garden, and a distillery shows how the essential oil is extracted from the plant. At the height of the purple flower bloom, the owner gives tours (July-Labor Day). The Gatehouse Farm Store has more than 200 products made from lavender for sale, from soaps to wreaths to dog biscuits, and you can also cut your own lavender here in the farm's Cutting Field. November-March, you're welcome to walk the fields, but all other facilities are closed.

Other Sights

Of all the sights in the San Juans, none is quite as strange as **Mona the Camel** (Roche Harbor Rd. across from San Juan Vineyards). She arrived on a farm here in 2005 as a pet. Her pasture is visible from the road, and tourists often pull over to take a look or feed her; obey the signs about human food (forbidden since it makes her sick) and look for her companion llamas in the same field. She even has her own Facebook page. But she's not the island's only mascot; down in Friday Harbor, near where the ferry arrives, **Popeye the Harbor Seal** has been hanging out for decades. Blind in one eye—hence the name—she has been known to bite tourists who feed her.

SPORTS AND RECREATION

TOP EXPERIENCE

★ Whale-Watching

Whale-watching is perhaps the most popular activity on the island chain. While orcas can be spotted from land anywhere where there's a vista of the waters of Puget Sound, **Lime Kiln Point State Park** (1567 Westside Rd., 360/378-2044, http://parks.state.wa.us, 8am-dusk daily) is your best bet for land-based whale-watching. In summer, it hosts a college professor who sets up a whale count near the lighthouse and provides free lectures.

To get closer to the creatures, you can take a boat tour. Frequent San Juan Island tours load up with a few dozen passengers and head out to spot harbor seals, sea lions, and, of course, orcas. Captains from various companies stay in touch to keep track of where the resident killer whale pods are hanging out, so tours have a high success rate of spotting the big animals—most advertise that more than 90 percent of their trips find them. Strict laws keep whale-watching boats from getting too close to whales, and generally all the local outfitters respect that distance. Most companies advertise membership in various whale-watch associations or have naturalist certification through a local group.

San Juan Safaris (10 Front St., 800/450-6858, www.sanjuansafaris.com, $99 adults, $69 children 2-12) is one of the most popular outfitters, though most companies offer similar trips. On a three- to four-hour trip, San Juan Safaris takes a route through the local waterways in search of wildlife. Like most whale-watching expeditions, San Juan Safaris staffs its boats with a naturalist who shares information about the whales and their habitat. There is one midday departure daily March-October, a sunset trip daily mid-May-mid-August, and a few weekend trips in February and November. A smaller boat—with no more than 22 people—travels at higher speeds for a more adventuresome outing twice daily mid-May-mid-September ($119, adults only).

San Juan Excursions (10 Front St., Ste. 101, 360/378-6636, www.watchwhales.com, $99 adults, $69 children 3-12) also offers whale-watching boat trips—with a guarantee to see whales or else receive a voucher for a free trip. Like San Juan Safaris, trips last 3-4 hours. They take place on a 65-foot former naval vessel that holds up to 80 people. Tours run April-October with one departure per day except for July and August weekends, when there are two. San Juan Excursions boats carry a naturalist and have indoor seating and a hydrophone that picks up the sounds of the whales underwater.

Hiking

BELL POINT

Distance: 1.5 miles round-trip

Duration: 0.5-1 hour
Elevation gain: 50 feet
Effort: easy
Trailhead: English Camp Visitor Center

From the center of English Camp, head toward the Formal Gardens to see a meticulous, European-style collection of shrubs and flowers. Continue past the old blockhouse, commissary, and hospital buildings as you walk up the bluffs over the water, taking time to stop in the historical buildings. Past the commissary, look for a trail between the bathroom building and shoreline, and follow it up along the water, through madrone trees, to scenic Bell Point. Stop here, less than a mile in, for views of wildlife like waterfowl and deer. Continue on the loop as it traces the bottom of Westcott Bay, and find an area of picnic tables, an ideal spot to rest for lunch. Finish the loop near the bathroom building, and either walk back through the historical section or take an old service road back to the parking lot.

SOUTH BEACH

Distance: 2 miles round-trip
Duration: 1 hour
Elevation gain: 200 feet
Effort: easy
Trailhead: American Camp Visitor Center

Pass the parade grounds on the way to the Redoubt; it's well signed. Once past the Redoubt, you'll pass a trail that bisects yours; continue about a quarter mile to just where the bluffs sit over the Strait of Juan de Fuca. Turn left at a trail intersection and follow it east along the water for about half a mile; small spurs lead even farther out over the bluffs. Continue to slowly descend to South Beach, a long sandy stretch littered with driftwood. To finish the loop and return, look for a trail that leads straight up into the grasslands; follow it north as it gradually bends back west toward the visitors center. The trail will connect near the Redoubt.

MOUNT FINLAYSON

Distance: 3.2 miles round-trip
Duration: 1.5-2 hours
Elevation gain: 350 feet
Effort: moderate
Trailhead: parking lot labeled "Jakle's Lagoon
Directions: From the American Camp Visitor Center, head to Cattle Point Road and turn right, following the road for about 1.5 miles.

Mount Finlayson is only a few hundred feet tall, but its trail offers a nice walk through the parklands for views of the island. Enter the trail from the parking lot and stay right as it goes through grasslands parallel to the road. At about half a mile in, keep right again at an intersection as the trail begins to climb through the trees. You'll reach the summit about a mile in, gaining views of the lighthouse at Cattle Point and possibly whales out in the strait. Continue east on the trail past the summit, then take the first left. Descend through the fir trees to a lagoon, taking another left about a quarter mile later. Follow the trail—a wide old road at this point—as it carves the bluffs over Griffin Bay, eventually passing a second body of water, Jakle's Lagoon. Just past Jakle's, take either trail, straight or left—both return to the parking lot in about the same distance, with little difference in elevation.

Kayaking

A number of companies offer kayak trips into the waters around San Juan Island, which can be a great way to combine wildlife-watching with exercise. **San Juan Outfitters** (248 Reuben Memorial Dr., Friday Harbor, 866/810-1483, www.sanjuanislandoutfitters.com, 8am-6pm daily summer, 9am-5pm daily winter) offers three- and six-hour guided sea kayaking tours ($99-125) April-October. You'll explore the island's coastline and often run into marinelife. No experience is necessary but bring warm layers. It also rents both kayaks and stand-up paddleboards ($25-30). Kayak rentals are only available to professionals with specific BCU certifications and after direct conversation with staff; no company on the island will rent sea kayaks without some kind of evidence of prior experience, since the open waters can be tough for beginners

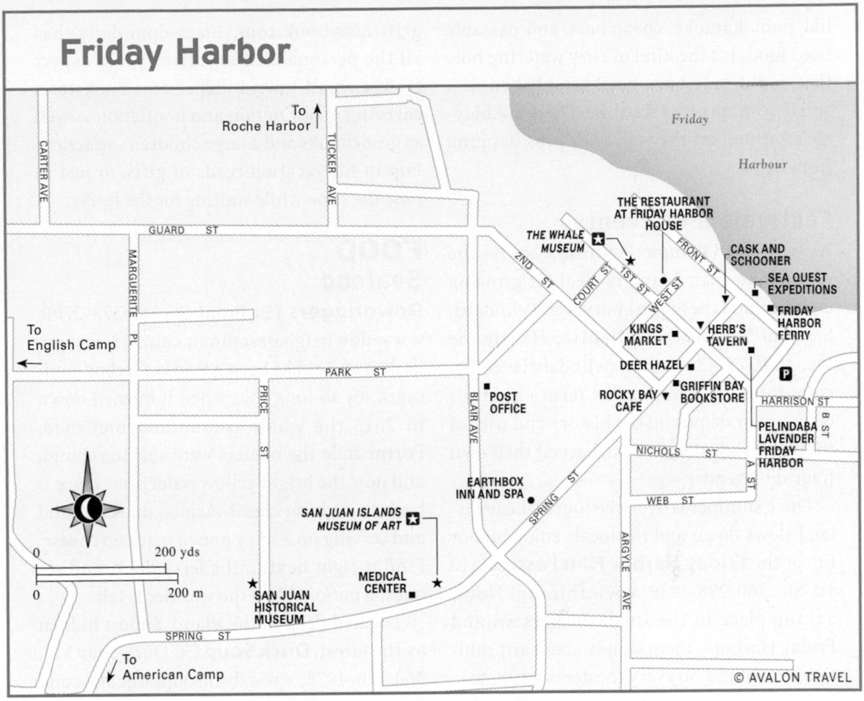

to navigate without a guide. **Sea Quest Expeditions** (2 Front St., Friday Harbor, 360/378-5767, www.sea-quest-kayak.com, 8am-7pm daily summer, 10am-4pm Mon.-Fri. winter, $89-109 per day), for example, requires a thorough accounting of your experience, itinerary, and proof of self-rescue training from a school.

Biking

San Juan Island's rural roads don't have much elevation gain and so are popular with cyclists. Bike rentals are available at a number of outfitters in Friday Harbor, including **Discovery Adventure Tours** (260 Spring St., Friday Harbor, 360/378-2559, www.discoveryadventuretours.com, 8am-5:30pm daily Apr.-Sept.), which specializes in road bikes ($35-50 per day) and electric-assist bikes ($55 per day). While local drivers are adept at driving slow and avoiding cyclists on the shared roads—there are no bike lanes to speak of—tourists may whip around road curves more quickly, so some experience in road cycling is advised.

ENTERTAINMENT AND EVENTS

Nightlife

Located in bustling downtown Friday Harbor, **Cask and Schooner** (1 Front St., 360/378-2922, www.caskandschooner.com, noon-9pm Mon.-Fri., 11am-9pm Sat., 11am-8pm Sun.) is an English pub serving the warm comfort food that designation suggests, including plenty of seafood. English bottled beers and cider are a nice change from all the local beers you'll find elsewhere (and on tap here too), and the bar mixes classic cocktails. The interior has exposed brick walls and a nautical theme, unsurprisingly, and there's a giant model ship in the middle of the dining area.

The oldest tavern on the island is the plain, no-frills **Herb's Tavern** (80 1st St., 360/378-7076, 11am-2am Mon.-Fri., 8am-2am Sat., 8am-midnight Sun.), which has bar staples like pool, karaoke, cheap beer, and passable fried food. It's the kind of cozy watering hole that could only have been established in a small community like this. There's a bicycle mounted on the wall with bras hanging from it.

Festivals and Events

As with the Olympic Peninsula across the sound, San Juan Island is ideal for growing lavender, and the biggest purveyor, Pelindaba, hosts the **Lavender Festival** (45 Hawthorne Ln., 360/378-4248, www.pelindabalavender.com, July) in summer. The farm's grounds open up for demos on the history and uses of the plant, and attendees can harvest their own fragrant lavender.

Once summer is over, the tourist-heavy island slows down and the locals enjoy indoor fun at the **Friday Harbor Film Festival** (10 1st St., 360/298-1939, www.fhff.org, Nov.). Taking place in the small theaters around Friday Harbor—there simply aren't any multiplexes around, so every theater is intimate—the festival highlights documentary films that entertain and inspire.

SHOPPING

The streets of Friday Harbor are lined with boutiques and gift stores, none more fun than **Deer Hazel** (165 Spring St., 360/370-5180, 10:30am-5pm Mon.-Thurs., 10:30am-5:30pm Fri.-Sun.). It carries sophisticated women's clothing as well as graphic pieces with a sense of humor, plus a few men's pieces and a smattering of gifts. There's nothing cheesy here; the wares make for good souvenirs of a trip to a cool island.

Pelindaba Lavender Friday Harbor (150 1st St., 866/819-1911, www.pelindabalavender.com, 9:30am-5pm daily) is the lavender farm's outpost in downtown Friday Harbor, a one-stop shop for lavender bath products, oils, honey, and more. The fragrant plant is thought to help foster relaxation and sleep, and Pelindaba's wares make for ideal gifts.

The quaint **Griffin Bay Bookstore** (155 Spring St., 360/378-5511, www.griffinbaybook.com, 10am-6pm daily) has all the personalized selections you'd expect from a small-town independent bookstore, carrying major fiction and nonfiction as well as guidebooks and a large children's selection. Pop in for vacation reads or gifts, or just to pass the time while waiting for the ferry.

FOOD

Seafood

Downriggers (10 Front St, 360/378-2700, www.downriggerssanjuan.com, 11am-9pm daily, $14-34) has been a Friday Harbor landmark for so long that when it burned down in 2013 the whole community mourned. Fortunately the owners were able to rebuild, and now the bright yellow waterfront space is back to dishing clams farmed on the island and serving up a spicy prawn mac and cheese. Find it right next to the ferry dock, and request a patio table if the weather is fair.

Located deep in the island, almost hidden by the forest, **Duck Soup** (50 Duck Soup Ln., 360/378-4878, www.ducksoupsanjuans.com, 5pm-9pm Wed.-Sun. June-Sept., 5pm-9pm Thurs.-Sun May and Oct., 5pm-9pm Fri.-Sat. Feb.-Apr. and Nov.-Dec., $31-39) is a fine-dining restaurant hidden inside a rustic cottage. Food here comes almost entirely from local purveyors. Shellfish figures largely on the menu, and there's almost always duck confit in a salute to the restaurant's name. Make reservations in advance, since the charming spot is as small as it looks.

American

With a patio and windows facing the picturesque harbor, it's hard to focus on the local-first menu at ★ **The Restaurant at Friday Harbor House** (130 West St. #101, 360/378-8455, http://fridayharborhouse.com/dining.php, 7:30am-11am and 5pm-9pm Mon.-Tues. and Thurs.-Fri., 7:30am-11am Wed., 8am-1pm and 5pm-9pm. Sat.-Sun., $17-38). But it's worth appreciating, especially the indulgent daily brunch and appetizers that range from veal sweetbreads to caramelized brussels sprouts.

Though it's tucked a bit far from the hustle and bustle of downtown Friday Harbor, **Bakery San Juan** (775 Mullis St., 360/378-5810, www.bakerysanjuan.com, 8am-6pm Mon.-Sat. summer, 8am-5pm Mon.-Fri. fall, winter, and spring, $3-6), only a few blocks farther into the island, is deservedly famous for its pizza. Don't wait too long to grab a lunch slice; the delectable pepperoni and rich potato pizza go quickly. Pair with a pastry or a hearty cookie; there are tables outside for an impromptu picnic.

When on the west side of the island near Roche Harbor, **Lime Kiln Cafe** (248 Reuben Memorial Dr., 360/378-9892, www.rocheharbor.com/dining/lime-kiln, 7am-3pm daily, $12-16) on the waterfront is one of the only places for a hot, cheap lunch. Doughnuts are made here every morning, and smashed burgers—wherein the patty is smashed while cooked on the griddle—are a lunch feature next to soups and hot sandwiches.

Breakfast

It used to be a tradition for locals and visitors alike: Park the car in the ferry line to secure a spot, then go have breakfast at **Rocky Bay Cafe** (225 Spring St., 360/378-5051, 7am-2pm daily, $9-13). Now that the ferry accepts reservations, Rocky Bay is a casual destination anyway, with beef hash and pancakes dished under mural-painted walls. On an expensive island, it's the rare place that feels like a deal.

Markets

In a town without chain stores, **Kings Market** (160 Spring St., 360/378-4505, www.kings-market.com, 7:30am-9pm daily) is a necessity. The grocery store has lots of fresh produce and all the usual food staples, as well as a nice wine and beer selection. While prices can be a bit higher than in the chain stores back in Anacortes, it's a lively and friendly central shop that feels like a throwback to a time when general stores were the center of town life.

The Friday Harbor **Farmers Market** (150 Nichols St, http://sjifarmersmarket.com, 10am-1pm Sat. Apr.-Oct., some Saturdays in winter) has been around for decades, but until recent years it was held in a parking lot. Now the historical Brickworks building, walking distance from the downtown core of Friday Harbor, hosts the market, with more than 50 vendors selling produce, crafts, and more.

ACCOMMODATIONS

Under $150

It'll never win any luxury awards, but **Orca**

breakfast at The Restaurant at Friday Harbor House

Inn (770 Mullis St., 360/378-2724, www.orcainnwa.com, $90-130) is an efficient and cheap little motel on an island full of high-end resorts. Rooms are tiny and, with their wood-paneled walls and tiny bathrooms, feel more like ship berths than suites. But it's one of the most affordable options in all of the San Juans, boasts friendly management, and is located right across from the equally budget-friendly Bakery San Juan.

$150-250

Roche Harbor Resort (248 Reuben Memorial Dr., 800/451-8910, www.rocheharbor.com, $255-295, shared bath $165-185) comprises house and condo rentals as well as the charming old Hotel de Haro. The latter is the state's oldest hotel, operating since 1886 but recently renovated, though most rooms have shared baths. Some cottages are more than 100 years old. They all surround a busy marina and a beautiful manicured garden.

Quieter than nearby Roche Harbor, **Snug Harbor Resort** (1997 Mitchell Bay Rd., 360/378-4762, www.snugresort.com, $199-299) is a collection of fairly new wooden cabins overlooking the water. Since cabins have full kitchens and there are few restaurants nearby, be sure to stop in Friday Harbor for groceries first. It's a family-friendly destination that gives discounts to schoolteachers and has free kayak and paddleboard rentals for guests.

Over $250

Located smack dab in the middle of the island, amid a series of small lakes, ★ **Lakedale Resort** (4313 Roche Harbor Rd., 360/378-2350, www.lakedale.com) boasts a beautiful lodge ($300-310), a few cabins ($469-645), and several glamping tents ($189-289) that put high-end beds and furniture behind canvas walls (with access to a nice bathhouse), as well as campsites ($40-67). You can canoe, fish, and play lawn games here, and the Duck Soup restaurant is right across the street.

From its position on a bluff overlooking the ferry terminal, **Friday Harbor House** (130 West St., 360/378-8455, www.fridayharborhouse.com, $389-499) is a small but well-known high-end hotel. It's a getaway that feels like it's in the heart of everything. Rooms are well appointed and have terrific waterfront views, but there isn't a lot of elbow room in the hotel. Some rooms have balconies.

The **Earthbox Inn and Spa** (410 Spring St., 360/378-4000, www.earthboxinn.com, $225-295, two-night minimum) is slightly

Lakedale Resort

farther inland than most of Friday Harbor's hotels, but it makes for a quiet, peaceful retreat. It has an indoor pool and free bike usage for guests, plus one of the best spas on the islands. Some rooms have kitchenettes, but the hotel is close enough to Friday Harbor restaurants that you needn't cook for yourself if you don't want to.

Camping

Lakedale Resort has a number of campsites, some of which are appropriate for groups or RVs. Elsewhere, there is RV camping at **San Juan County Fairground** (846 Argyle Ave., 360/378-8420, www.sanjuanco.com/473/RV-Camping, $35), walkable to downtown. Tent campers and RV campers alike are welcome at **San Juan County Park** (15 San Juan Park Rd., 360/378-8420, www.sanjuanco.com/921/San-Juan-Island, $32-45), on the west side of the island. Note that there are size restrictions on RVs, and big vehicles may need to go to the San Juan County Fairground for accommodations.

INFORMATION AND SERVICES

The San Juan Islands Chamber of Commerce has a useful **visitors center** (640 Mullins St., Ste. 210, 360/378-9551, www.visitsanjuans.com, 8:30am-5pm Mon.-Fri.) with maps, brochures, and someone to answer questions about exploring the island.

TRANSPORTATION

Getting There

FERRY

The most popular way to reach San Juan Island, or any of the commonly visited islands, is by **Washington State Ferry** (888/808-7977, www.wsdot.wa.gov/ferries, round-trip $13.50 adults, $6.70 seniors and children 6-18, free for children under 6, $65.60 standard-size vehicle and driver) from Anacortes. Car-and-passenger ferries depart Anacortes for San Juan, Orcas, Shaw, and Lopez Islands as well as Sidney, B.C. on Vancouver Island. The trip to Friday Harbor has 6-8 departures daily and takes 1-1.5 hours. Reservations are highly recommended for all vehicle traffic and are available by phone or online. In summer, the reservations are snatched up quickly, and only 10 percent of the ferry car spaces are held for walk-ups and emergency vehicles. One option is to leave a car in Anacortes and walk on the ferry; Friday Harbor on San Juan Island especially is highly walkable. Keep in mind taxi service is rare or even unavailable on many islands, where hitchhiking is common.

The islands are also accessible by passenger ferry from downtown Seattle. The **Victoria Clipper** (800/888-2535, www.clippervacations.com, $55 adults, $27.50 children under 12) operates late April-mid-October and takes 3-3.5 hours to reach Friday Harbor on a once-a-day schedule.

AIR

Floatplanes from **Kenmore Air** (866/435-9524, www.kenmoreair.com), which depart from Lake Union in Seattle, take a mere 45 minutes to reach the islands and can land at a number of resorts and ports around the San Juans, including islands not serviced by the ferry. Trips from Boeing Field to one of the islands' land airports are also available. The trip is as much an adventure and sightseeing excursion as it is transportation. Floatplane and wheeled-plane trips to San Juan Island cost about $159-169 but can vary, in the case of floatplane trips, by destination.

Getting Around

CAR

Most visitors to the San Juan Islands bring a car, as it's the most convenient way to travel. If you're only planning to visit Friday Harbor, it's unnecessary, but if you want to see some of the rest of the island, wheels are necessary.

There is one car-rental company in Friday Harbor, **M&W Auto** (725 Spring St., 360/378-2886, www.sanjuanauto.com). It has small two-door cars, average-size sedans, and vans, with prices ranging $58-80 per day; slightly cheaper rates are available for half-day rentals. Vehicles are limited, so reserve in advance

Working the Washington State Ferry System

The San Juan Islands are magical. Getting there, however, isn't always quite so wonderful. Limited space on the **Washington State Ferry** (www.wsdot.wa.gov/ferries) has long meant hours-long waits for each sailing, with lines of cars backing up on weekends in the summer. In recent years, the system instituted **reservations** for some sailings, requiring reservation holders to arrive 30-90 minutes before the boat departs. Check the website to find out exactly when reservations will be released for a particular sailing—a third of the tickets for a day's sailing are released at the beginning of each season, the next third become available two weeks before, and the final third are released two days before the ferry's departure. Only 10 percent of a ferry's vehicle spots are held for **drive-up passengers.** Book in advance, online or by phone, as far ahead as possible. Expect weekend departures in the summer to sell out within minutes of becoming available online.

Leaving a car in Anacortes and walking on the ferry is one way to guarantee passage as there's no limit to walk-on passengers, but know you'll be at the mercy of cabs or, more commonly, hitchhiking once you arrive on the islands. **Long-term parking lots** are available near the Anacortes ferry terminal ($10 per day), and some local businesses offer overnight parking at varying rates. Lots fill to capacity only during weekends in the middle of summer. Do not try to park on the nearby residential streets of Anacortes; they are signed to prohibit visitor parking and cars left there will be ticketed or towed. It's also possible to **rent cars** on San Juan Island and Orcas Island, which may eliminate some hassle, but note it's not economical if you're staying more than day.

The white-and-green ferries also travel between the four main San Juan Islands. There are 3-6 departures daily on the **interisland ferry** serving San Juan, Orcas, Lopez, and Shaw. Fares are collected for cars on interisland trips traveling west ($23 per vehicle)—from Lopez to Orcas, or Orcas to Friday Harbor, for example—but not from Friday Harbor going east. Passengers on the interisland ferry always ride free. Reservations aren't available or necessary for interisland trips. Still, expect to arrive at the ferry terminal about an hour before the sailing to be ensured a spot. Rides take about 30-75 minutes, depending on which islands you're traveling between.

during the summer. If you plan to stay more than a day, it isn't cost-effective to walk on to the ferry and rent in Friday Harbor, but visitors who arrive via airplane may appreciate the option. Note that the small local company is not a national chain, and vehicles may not be as new as visitors expect from large airport car-rental agencies.

TAXI

To travel around San Juan Island by cab, try **Bob's Taxi and Tours** (360/378-6777, http://bobs-taxi.com), a longtime operator in Friday Harbor. The company has a fleet of vans, ideal for large groups and luggage. To travel from Friday Harbor to Roche Harbor, expect to pay about $25. Book about half an hour in advance in the off-season and as much as a few days in advance during the height of summer.

SHUTTLE BUS

Limited bus service is available on San Juan Island via **San Juan Transit** (360/378-8887, www.sanjuantransit.com, $5 adults, $3 children under 13), which runs one route in the shoulder seasons and two routes in summer, including stops at locations such as Roche Harbor, Lime Kiln State Park, English Camp, and Pelindaba Lavender Farm. Carry exact change and pay the driver.

INTERISLAND FERRY

To travel to one of the other islands in the archipelago via ferry, consult the **Washington State Ferry** (888/808-7977, www.wsdot.wa.gov/ferries) schedule; many shops and restaurants in Friday Harbor will have it posted in a window or by a sales register. During peak season there are about five interisland ferries per day, with fewer in the other seasons, but note that schedules often change on Sunday. Interisland ferries typically head east from Friday Harbor to Orcas Island (1 hour), Shaw Island (1.25 hours), then Lopez Island (1.5 hours), or stop in Lopez Island before heading to the mainland. A staffer (often wearing a reflective vest) at the ferry terminal will direct cars as they approach the lineup; be prepared to tell them where you're headed, and note that you can't change your destination once your car is in a waiting line for the ferry. Neither walk-on passengers nor drivers with vehicles pay a fare for interisland travel out of Friday Harbor.

Orcas Island

Orcas, funky and fun, is named for a viceroy who launched an expedition to the region, not for the killer whales that circle it. It's a little less crowded than San Juan Island, with fewer attractions and amenities, but still more than enough to fill an exciting few days, especially thanks to the recreation options of Mount Constitution. The island is shaped like a horseshoe, with the town of Eastsound at the center, a collection of walkable blocks with bakeries, restaurants, and shops. In summer months, traffic moves slowly through this dense little town—not that it moves much faster on the rest of the island, thanks to low speed limits. From Eastsound, it's no more than a 20-minute drive to nearly all the island's attractions.

SIGHTS

Orcas Island Historical Museum

Located in downtown Eastsound, **Orcas Island Historical Museum** (181 N Beach Rd., 360/376-4849, www.orcasmuseums.org, 11am-4pm Wed.-Sat. May-Sept., free) is a modest series of historical cabins, rebuilt and linked together, that shows off the history of this quirky little island. Besides photographs of early settlers and artifacts from when the cabins were first in use, the museum explores Native American history on the island.

SPORTS AND RECREATION

Parks and Beaches

CRESCENT BEACH PRESERVE

Just east of Eastsound, the 135-acre **Crescent Beach Preserve** (http://sjclandbank.org) has wetlands as well as over 1,000 feet of waterfront on Ship Bay including, yes, a crescent-shaped beach. Three parking areas are located on Crescent Beach Drive between Harrison Point Lane, right where the town of Eastsound ends, and gas stations near the intersection with Olga Road. Cross the street to wander the beach, home to oyster farms—look for the small structures on the tidal flats at low tide—and wildlife, including geese and loons. Kayak rentals are available across the street from Crescent Beach.

★ MORAN STATE PARK

Lovely **Moran State Park** (3572 Olga Rd., 360/376-2326, http://moranstatepark.com, 6:30am-10pm daily mid-May-mid-Sept., 8am-dusk daily mid-Sept.-mid-May, $10 parking) takes up a large chunk—5,000 forested acres—of Orcas Island's eastern side, and the island's main road winds right through it, under a curved entry arch. The park contains five lakes, including Cascade Lake, which has boat ramps and is a popular spot for water sports. Nearly 40 miles of trails also wind through the park, accessible to hikers, with some open to mountain bikers as well. Also here is towering

Orcas Island

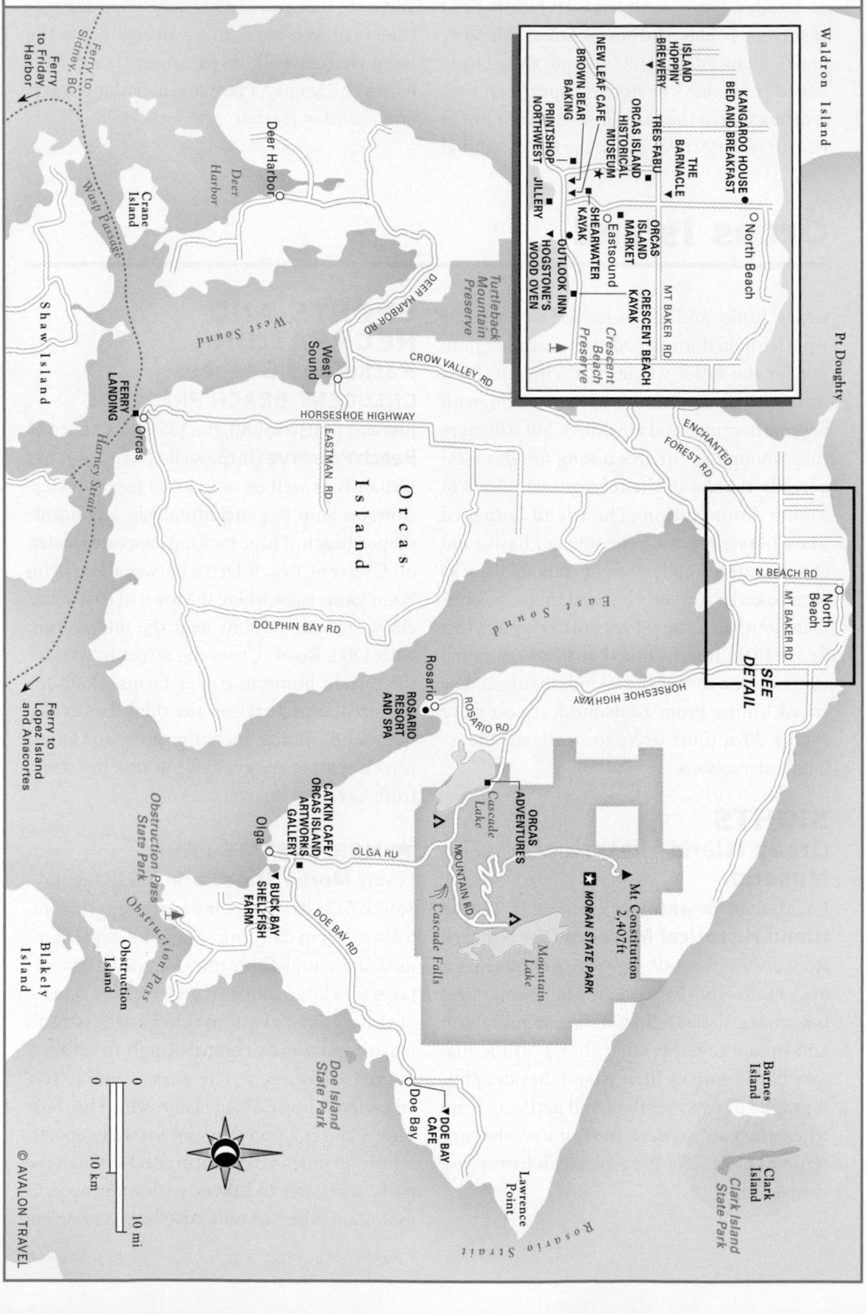
Waldron Island
Pt Doughty
KANGAROO HOUSE BED AND BREAKFAST
North Beach
ISLAND HOPPIN BREWERY
THE BARNACLE
TRES FABU
ORCAS ISLAND HISTORICAL MUSEUM
NEW LEAF CAFE
BROWN BEAR BAKING
PRINTSHOP NORTHWEST
JILLERY
ORCAS ISLAND MARKET
Eastsound
SHEARWATER KAYAK
OUTLOOK INN
HOGSTONE'S WOOD OVEN
CRESCENT BEACH KAYAK
MT BAKER RD
CRESCENT BEACH
Crescent Beach Preserve
Turtleback Mountain Preserve
DEER HARBOR RD
CROW VALLEY RD
Ferry to Sidney, BC
Ferry to Friday Harbor
Deer Harbor
Deer Harbor
Crane Island
Wasp Passage
Shaw Island
West Sound
West Sound
FERRY LANDING
Orcas
Harney Strait
HORSESHOE HIGHWAY
EASTMAN RD
Orcas Island
ENCHANTED FOREST RD
N BEACH RD
North Beach
MT BAKER RD
SEE DETAIL
East Sound
DOLPHIN BAY RD
Rosario
ROSARIO RESORT AND SPA
ROSARIO RD
Ferry to Lopez Island and Anacortes
ORCAS ADVENTURES
Cascade Lake
Mt Constitution 2,407ft
MORAN STATE PARK
MOUNTAIN RD
Mountain Lake
Cascade Falls
CATKIN CAFE/ ORCAS ISLAND ARTWORKS GALLERY
Olga
OLGA RD
BUCK BAY SHELLFISH FARM
DOE BAY RD
Obstruction Pass State Park
Obstruction Pass
Obstruction Island
Blakely Island
Barnes Island
Clark Island
Clark Island State Park
Doe Island State Park
DOE BAY CAFE
Doe Bay
Lawrence Point
Rosario Strait
0
10 mi
0
10 km
© AVALON TRAVEL

The Nuns of Shaw Island

The Washington State Ferry visits four islands. San Juan, Orcas, and Lopez have accommodations and restaurants. What about the fourth island? Shaw Island, located right next to Orcas Island, is a residential, quiet bit of land. There are no services besides a very small general store near the ferry terminal. But in the middle of the island, **Our Lady of the Rock Benedictine Monastery** (360/468-2321, http://olrmonastery.org) is home to a small collection of Catholic nuns. They run a farm, raising sheep, llamas, alpacas, and more, and sell products including raw milk cheese and Cotswold yarn at local farmers markets and the general store at the ferry terminal. The women welcome visitors in the spirit of their Benedictine practices, asking only for donations in exchange for lodging in their modest retreat house. But it's no vacation spot; the retreat house is meant for those wishing to explore their spiritual life and contribute to the farm work. Those wishing to visit the monastery need to call well in advance, at least a month ahead in summer. Check the website for the island life blog by Mother Hildegard.

Mount Constitution—hike or drive up to its summit for views from the stone watchtower on top, which takes in the surrounding Puget Sound, Mount Baker on the mainland, and Canada in the distance. Trails may be snow-covered in winter, but the drive can be made any time of year.

OBSTRUCTION PASS STATE PARK

Just south of Moran State Park, **Obstruction Pass State Park** (860 Trailhead Rd., 360/902-8844, http://parks.state.wa.us, 6:30am-dusk daily mid-May-mid-Sept., 8am-dusk daily mid-Sept.-mid-May, $10 parking) is a small 80-acre park on the southern end of this half of the island "horseshoe." Only a small corner of the park is accessible by vehicle, but it has a mile of shoreline, accessible by walking the short Obstruction Pass Beach Trail. There is no potable water available here, though there are restrooms.

TURTLEBACK MOUNTAIN PRESERVE

In sharp contrast to busy and popular Moran State Park across the island, **Turtleback Mountain Preserve** (Wildrose Ln. near Deer Harbor Rd., 360/378-4402, http://sjclandbank.org) is a quiet slice of the San Juans. A high ridge rises from the sea-level road below, with thick woods and grassy meadows. The 1,700-acre preserve isn't particularly developed, but there are two main trailheads, a southern and northern one, both accessible to hikers, and the latter is open to cyclists on even days and equestrians on odd days as well.

TOP EXPERIENCE

★ Whale-Watching

While whale-watching outfits aren't nearly as plentiful on Orcas Island as they are in nearby San Juan, **Outer Island Excursions** (54 Hunt Rd., 360/376-3711, http://outerislandx.com, daily Mar.-Sept., $69 adults, $89 seniors, $79 children 12-17, $59 children under 12) offers a similar experience as you'll find there—a trip to see the orcas with a naturalist on board. Excursions take a half day, or about 3-4 hours, with 1-2 departures per day. Boats hold around 30 people, and you're guaranteed a whale sighting—or every passenger receives a voucher to return on another trip for free.

Whales are often spotted off the coast of Orcas Island from land, but it's unlikely to see them in the shallow bays of East Sound, West Sound, or Ship's Bay. You can head to the outer rim of the island, for instance the point at Doe Bay, for a better chance of a land-based sighting.

Water Sports

When driving by the long, rocky Crescent Beach near Eastsound, your eyes will be drawn to the multicolored boats at **Crescent Beach Kayaks** (239 Crescent Beach Dr., 360/376-2464, http://crescentbeachkayaks.com, 9am-6pm daily), just across the street from the water. You can rent kayaks for an easy paddle through Orcas's protected waters here, but don't forget to take the tide into consideration; a little wind and current can also make the return trip harder than expected. Rentals are $18 per person per hour, $50 per person for a half day.

Shearwater Kayaks (138 N Beach Rd., 360/376-4699, http://shearwaterkayaks.com, Apr.-Sept., $85-120 adults, $55 for children under 15), leads kayak tours around the island, some to a state park on nearby Sucia Island. Experience isn't necessary, and trips range from a three-hour paddle to all-day or sunset trips. Minimum age for trips varies, ranging from 5-15 years old. There are usually a few departures per day from various locations around the island.

Moran State Park (3572 Olga Rd., 360/376-2326, http://moranstatepark.com, 6:30am-10pm daily mid-May-mid-Sept., 8am-dusk daily mid-Sept.-mid-May, $10 parking) offers boat rentals through **Orcas Adventures** (www.orcasadventures.com, noon-4pm Fri., 10am-5pm Sat. and 10am-3pm Sun. Apr.-May, 10am-5pm daily June-Aug.), which has a location in the park at Cascade Lake, which boasts even calmer waters than the protected bays elsewhere on Orcas. Everything is first-come, first-served, from rowboats and canoes ($20 per hour, $55 half-day, $75 full-day) to paddleboards ($25 per hour) to kayaks ($15-20 per hour, $55 half-day, $75 full-day) to pedal boats ($20 per hour). Orcas Adventures also offers limited rental options for Mountain Lake, the other large lake in the park, all arranged out of the Cascade Lake office.

Hiking

CRESCENT BEACH PRESERVE

Distance: 1.4 miles round-trip
Duration: 1 hour
Elevation gain: 50 feet
Effort: easy
Trailhead: Crescent Beach Preserve parking lot to the east of the beach

This wide, well-signed, and well-maintained trail in this wooded preserve starts on shore and quickly disappears into trees as you head inland, passing marshland along the way. Look for birds like loons and herons here, and note how the trees get larger the farther you get from Ship Bay. After 0.7 mile, you'll reach another parking area. Turn here and return the way you came.

MOUNT CONSTITUTION

Distance: 8.6 miles round-trip
Duration: 3-4 hours
Elevation gain: 2,400 feet
Effort: strenuous
Trailhead: Moran State Park day-use area next to Cascade Lake (cross Olga Road to find the trailhead)

Down in the middle of Moran State Park's busy center, you're almost at sea level. From here you'll hike through old-growth evergreens and start climbing on switchbacks; this early climb makes up the bulk of the extreme elevation gain. After 1.5 miles, stay right at an intersection; in another 0.7 mile pass the Cold Springs shelter, parking lot, and picnic tables and cross Mount Constitution Road. Try not to envy the people making the drive to the summit! Continue past the road through the trees and turn left at the junction after 0.3 mile. Pass the tip of Summit Lake and, after 1 mile, finally reach the mountain's summit mile. Climb the observation tower built in the 1930s to take in views of Puget Sound and the Cascade Mountains, and pat yourself on the back for being one of the few to make it up on foot rather than by car. Return the way you came.

OBSTRUCTION PASS BEACH

Distance: 1.2 miles round-trip
Duration: 1 hour
Elevation gain: 100 feet
Effort: easy
Trailhead: at the end of the road at the far end of the parking lot loop in Obstruction Pass State Park

You'll take an immediate right at a four-way

intersection at the start of this trail before descending slightly through the woods for about a quarter mile and emerging at an overlook on East Sound, where there are several picnic tables down by the water. Look for interpretive signs with information on the natural history and wildlife of the area. Continue through the calm, quiet woods to another intersection; go right to reach the south end of the park and sandy Obstruction Pass Beach in about another quarter mile. A few primitive campsites sit here among madrone trees, and a privy perches above the beach. See if you can spot an unmarked trail that heads west a hundred yards or so to Picnic Rock, which has great views of the rocky coast and other islands. From the beach, head back the way you came until you reach the second intersection; either return the way you came (taking a left) or go straight for an even more direct route back to the parking lot.

TURTLEBACK MOUNTAIN PRESERVE

Distance: 3 miles round-trip
Duration: 2 hours
Elevation gain: 850 feet
Effort: moderate
Trailhead: From the ferry terminal, head north for 2.5 miles and turn left on Deer Harbor Road. After 2.2 miles, turn right onto Wildrose Lane.

From the southern trailhead in the preserve, head down into a ravine and through the forest for less than 0.5 mile to a junction; turn right and 0.5 mile later reach another junction. Go left and climb to an overlook at 760 feet, a good place to rest. Look down on West Sound and the east side of Orcas Island. The trail gets steeper here and goes in and out of grassy meadows to the Ship Peak overlook, just off the trail, with some classic views of the entire San Juan Islands archipelago. Take time to relax before returning to the trail and continuing on, descending through forest 0.3 mile. Turn left to stay on the Lost Oak Trail. Enjoy brief breaks in the forested cover before reaching the first junction of the trip and completing the loop. Turn right and hike just under 0.5 mile back to the parking lot.

Biking

Rent wheels to explore the island at **Wildlife Cycles** (350 N Beach Rd., 360/376-4708, http://wildlifecycles.com, 9:30am-5:30pm Mon.-Sat., 10am-4pm Sun. May-Sept., limited hours Oct.-Apr., $9-15 per hour), but be prepared for roads without much of a shoulder; locals know to drive slow, but tourists can take the winding corners quickly. The shop has suggestions on good routes and info on what you'll need to tackle the island's toughest and most rewarding challenge—a pedal up Mount Constitution. There are also some mountain bike trails in Turtleback Mountain Preserve and Moran State Park.

Skateboarding

While much of Orcas Island's recreation is based around nature, the **Orcas Island Skatepark** (600 Mt. Baker Rd., www.orcasparkandrec.org/parks/skate-park, sunrise-sunset daily) is all about concrete. With 12,000 square feet of space, it's a popular destination for skaters.

ENTERTAINMENT AND EVENTS

Nightlife

The Barnacle (46 Prune Alley, 360/622-2675, 5pm-11pm Mon. and Wed.-Thurs., 5pm-midnight Fri., noon-midnight Sat., noon-5pm Sun.), a tiny, precious bar in Eastsound, has a polished bar made from a jagged piece of wood and shelves full of elixirs and house-infused spirits. It serves a few small plates of food, but the carefully crafted cocktails are the real draw.

Located near the island's little-used landing strip, **Island Hoppin' Brewery** (33 Hope Ln., 360/376-6079, www.islandhoppinbrewery.com, noon-9pm daily) actually does get hopping when its outdoor tables fill with beer fans. The brewery crafts a number of beer varieties, and the space is welcoming. It's one of the only places on Orcas where you can find Wi-Fi after 7pm.

Festivals and Events

The **Orcas Island Chamber Music Festival** (360/376-2281, http://oicmf.org, Aug., $10-40) comprises a series of small-group instrumental concerts over the first few weeks of August—though performances outside the busy summer season are also programmed—often featuring well-known classical pieces alongside modern or more obscure works. Venues vary, with some medium-sized spaces as well as small salon-style ones; guests must call the festival office to join the guest list for the ultra-intimate concerts, which only have space for 35-60 audience members.

The Doe Bay Resort holds the Doe Bay Fest, an early August music festival and one of the island's biggest events—but the popular festival sells out early and limits tickets primarily to locals or past guests of the resort; very limited tickets are available to the public online. But its **Imagine Festival** (http://imagine-orcasisland.com, Sept., $160-225 adults, $50 children 13-18 and seniors, free for children under 13)—a four-day music and arts festival with a psychedelic bent—is much easier to access. Attendees stay in Doe Bay cabins or camp on the resort grounds.

SHOPPING

This small store in Eastsound run by jewelry maker Jill Curtiss is appropriately named **Jillery** (310 Main St., 360/376-5522, www.jilleryonorcas.com, 10am-5pm daily). She sells chunky and delicate silver accessories as well as larger gifts like glass garden blooms and other sculptures.

The artsy silk-screen designs at **Printshop Northwest** (109 N Beach Rd., 360/622-6277, http://printshopnorthwest.com, 10am-8pm daily) are quintessentially San Juan, featuring whales, ferryboats, tractors, and the occasional Bigfoot. Purchase a shirt or bag with your choice of design printed on it, or emblazon your own shirt with one of the images. The graphic studio is ideal for gift shopping for those family members and friends unlucky enough to miss exploring the San Juans.

Though it looks like a funky house from the outside, **Tres Fabu** (238 N Beach Rd., 360/376-7673, 11am-5pm Mon.-Sat. summer) is a clothing store with little rooms and nooks filled with racks. The style is a bit hippie, as befits the island, and it's a pleasant spot to browse.

Island Hoppin' Brewery

Located in the same building as the Catkin Cafe, a 1938 building used in packaging strawberries, the **Orcas Island Artworks Gallery** (11 Point Lawrence Rd., 360/376-4408, http://orcasartworks.com, 10am-5pm daily mid-Feb.-Dec.) celebrates local artists and craftspeople in a beautiful, open space. Locally made jewelry, paintings, sculpture, and lots of pottery and glass adorn the shelves and walls, and the gallery's collective-style format means it's run by the artists themselves.

FOOD

Seafood

Tiny **Buck Bay Shellfish Farm** (117 E J Young Rd., 360/376-5280, www.buckbayshellfishfarm.com, 11am-6pm Mon.-Sat., noon-5pm Sun. Apr.-Oct.) may sound familiar if you've looked at menus around western Washington; the farm supplies many restaurants with oysters and other seafood. When open in season, you can pick out fresh oysters, and staff will shuck them for you. Bring additional picnic foodstuffs to supplement the oysters and enjoy at the tables overlooking the oyster beds. Hours can be variable at the family-run farm, so it never hurts to call ahead.

American

The bright **New Leaf Cafe** (171 Main St., 360/376-2200, www.outlookinn.com, 8am-11:30am and 5pm-9pm Sun.-Mon. and Thurs., 8am-11:30am and 5pm-9:30pm Fri., 8am-12:30pm and 5pm-9:30pm Sat.), located in the Outlook Inn in the middle of Eastsound, feels closer to a normal-sized restaurant than most of the small eateries on the rest of the island. Brunches are especially good, and dishes are sometimes inspired by the chef's French heritage.

Tiny **Hogstone's Wood Oven** (460 Main St., 360/376-4647, www.hogstone.com, 5:30pm-9pm Fri.-Mon.) in Eastsound has a giant oven outside that produces pizzas with outsized flavors. During the summer, Hogstone only has outdoor seating, and its indoor space is reserved for a different restaurant under the same management called Aelder, which is newer and offers fine dining with a prix fixe. But in the winter indoor seating is for both restaurants, with both menus served. The dual concept is a little confusing, but the staff is friendly and happy to explain. Reservations are recommended.

Located in the free-spirited resort of the same name, the **Doe Bay Cafe** (107 Doe Bay Rd., Olga, 360/376-8059, http://doebay.com, 5pm-10pm Thurs., 8am-2pm and 5pm-9pm Fri.-Mon. Apr.-Oct., 5pm-9pm Fri.-Sat. Nov.-Mar., $21-32) is a veggie and seafood eatery on the resort's wooded grounds that manages to do a lot with the produce grown in its own sprawling garden. Tables almost all have views of tiny Doe Bay, and the bar makes creative cocktails with house-made syrups. Don't skip dessert. In winter, it's a good idea to call ahead and confirm hours.

Breakfast

Lines often wind out the door at **Brown Bear Baking** (29 N Beach Rd., 360/855-7456, 8am-4pm Thurs.-Mon.), as locals and tourists alike stock up on baked goods and coffee. Open for only a few years, it already feels like a mainstay, especially since it's located at the intersection of Eastsound's two biggest streets. The couple that owns the bakery got some blowback—and an overwhelming push of public support—when they decided to hang a pride flag on the pole outside; for some time, people would come take their photos with the flag.

Little **Catkin Cafe** (11 Point Lawrence Rd., 360/376-3242, www.catkincafe.com, 9am-3pm Wed.-Sun., $10-15), 7.5 miles south of Eastsound via Olga Road, has both breakfast and lunch on its all-day menu, a grand total of less than a dozen options. But each one is full of fresh island produce and rich sauces. After dining, wander through the other half of the building, home of the Orcas Island Artworks Gallery.

Markets

Located in the middle of Eastsound, **Orcas Island Market** (469 Market St.,

360/376-6000, http://orcasislandmarket.com, 7am-9pm Mon.-Sat., 8am-8pm Sun.) is the biggest grocery store on the island and has operated in some form for more than a century. It's locally owned and still retains the charm of the island.

ACCOMMODATIONS

$150-250

Kooky, free-spirited ★ **Doe Bay Resort** (107 Doe Bay Rd., Olga, 360/376-2291, http://doebay.com, two-night minimum) is known for its cabins ($173-250), arts and music festivals, and general hippie vibe. The cabins dot the 38-acre property, some tucked back into the trees. Most have full amenities and kitchens, but some have merely woodstoves and access to a shared bathhouse. The resort also has yurts ($133) and campsites ($51-77), located in an even more wooded section of the property, next to the tiny Doe Bay waters themselves. A tiny general store sits next to the restaurant, and a shed rents kayaks and paddleboards. This central area is walkable from all the accommodations and serves as a gathering and hangout spot. The best amenities are the clothing-optional soaking pools and sauna, perched on an outdoor deck overlooking the bay.

Located in the middle of Eastsound, the stately white **Outlook Inn** (171 Main St., 360/376-2200, www.outlookinn.com, $199-289) looks like it belongs in a New England fishing town. The sheer walkability to all of Eastsound is a huge bonus. Just outside is a small island in the bay, accessible by foot when the tide is out. Historical rooms ($109) have a shared bath.

No, there are no Australian animals at **Kangaroo House Bed and Breakfast** (1459 N Beach Rd., 360/376-2175, www.kangaroohouse.com, $195-240), a 1907 Craftsman house-turned-bed-and-breakfast, perhaps the oldest on the island. It's located about a mile north of town, and rooms are named after birds and have flowered quilts and stained-glass windows. Request the Nuthatch Room for a unique enclosed bed with its own chandelier.

Over $250

It's no surprise that **Rosario Resort and Spa** (1400 Rosario Rd., 360/376-2222, http://rosarioresort.com, $269-419, two-night minimum) was once the home of a wealthy resident; it feels like visiting Daddy Warbucks's island home. The waterfront resort comprises the historical main mansion building and hosts

Orcas Island waterfront

a restaurant, museum, and basement swimming pool. The rest of the resort is newer and features water-facing suites and more swimming pools. The mansion was built by a Seattle industrialist who struck it big during the Yukon gold rush—supplying gold hunters, not finding it himself—and then building ships. History is baked into the entire estate, and it's open to the public for self-guided tours and a Saturday afternoon concert on a unique pipe organ.

Camping

Besides the campsites at Doe Bay Resort, there is camping at **Moran State Park** (888/226-7688, $12-45). Three camp locations surround Cascade Lake near the road, and one more primitive collection of sites is at more remote Mountain Lake. Only some can accommodate RVs. Reservations are available and recommended.

INFORMATION AND SERVICES

The **Orcas Island Chamber of Commerce** (65 N Beach Rd., 360/376-2273, http://orcasislandchamber.com, 10am-3pm Mon.-Sat.) has a small visitor information center with brochures and maps in Eastsound.

TRANSPORTATION

Getting There

FERRY

You can reach Orcas Island via the car-and-passenger **Washington State Ferry** (888/808-7977, www.wsdot.wa.gov/ferries, round-trip $13.50 adults, $6.70 seniors and children 6-18, free for children under 6, $46 standard-size vehicle and driver) from Anacortes. There are about 7-8 departures from Anacortes to Orcas Island daily in the summer, with fewer daily departures outside this peak season, and trips take just under an hour.

AIR

Floatplanes from **Kenmore Air** (866/435-9524, www.kenmoreair.com) depart from Lake Union in Seattle and take about 45 minutes to reach the islands. Flights cost around $159-169 depending on drop-off location on Orcas Island.

Getting Around

CAR

Like all the San Juan Islands, Orcas is best explored by private vehicle. If you didn't bring your own, **Orcas Island Shuttle** (360/376-7433, www.orcasislandshuttle.com) rents used cars starting at $65 per day, which includes pick-up and drop-off at the ferry if reservations are made 24 hours in advance.

TAXI

Orcas Island Taxi Service (360/376-8294, http://orcasislandtaxi.com) services the island. Note that fares incur a $5 per person charge after the first two people and may also add a surcharge midnight-5:30am. Call in advance for reservations, especially in the middle of summer. A cab from the ferry terminal to Eastsound is $27 and to Doe Bay $60.

SHUTTLE BUS

San Juan Transit (360/378-8887, www.sanjuantransit.com, $5 adults, $3 children under 13) operates a shuttle bus Friday-Sunday late June-Labor Day. Stops include the ferry landing, Eastsound at Orcas Island Market, and Moran State Park, with about five trips in each direction (eastbound and westbound) per day. Bring exact fare in cash.

INTERISLAND FERRY

Consult the **Washington State Ferry** (888/808-7977, www.wsdot.wa.gov/ferries) for interisland ferry schedules. In summer, there are about four departures from Orcas Island to Lopez (30-45 minutes), four to Shaw (20 minutes), and six to Friday Harbor (45-60 minutes). Only cars on ferries headed westbound, to Friday Harbor, pay a fare ($28.65 standard vehicle and driver). Pedestrian passengers ride free.

Lummi Island

Though it's only a few miles away, Lummi Island isn't often grouped with the rest of the San Juans—that's probably because it's not accessible by the Washington State Ferry but by a small **county-run ferry** (360/778-5000, www.co.whatcom.wa.us/382/ferry, $13 vehicle and driver, $7 adult passengers, cash or check only) based near the town of Bellingham in Washington. The ferry ride only takes about five minutes, and fares are only collected on the way to the island. The ferry runs about every 20 minutes from early in the morning to often past midnight, and there are no reservations accepted. Lummi is home to one of the Northwest's—and the country's—best restaurants, **Willows Inn** (2579 W Shore Dr., 360/758-2620, www.willows-inn.com, $195 dinner, $175-450 rooms), which has received national acclaim from newspapers and magazines. A young chef, Blaine Wetzel, put the sleepy island and its quiet beaches on the map with his cooking, and now the multi-course prix fixes are a destination unto themselves. Many people stay at the restaurant's attached inn after partaking in the meal of locally sourced, fine-crafted dishes. Hotel guests are given the opportunity to book dinner reservations in advance—plan to book at least two months ahead. Those not staying at the inn can only make dinner reservations within two weeks of the dining date, but reservations are often already sold out before that window opens.

Lopez Island

Don't be surprised when everyone on Lopez Island waves to you, even if they don't know you; on an island this small, everyone is friendly. Lopez is largely popular with cyclists, given its very flat and rural roads, or those seeking rest and relaxation amid the farmland, as there's less to see and do here, making it much less crowded than Orcas and San Juan. The tiny's island's sleepy hub is Lopez Village, a small collection of shops. Remember not to rush; people refer to the island as "Slowpez."

SIGHTS

Lopez Island Vineyards (724 Fisherman Bay Rd., 360/468-3644, http://lopezisland-vineyards.com, call or check website for hours) has a tasting room that opens for limited hours to pour wines, including ones made from Siegerrebe and Madeline Angevine grapes grown on the island.

SPORTS AND RECREATION

Parks and Beaches

SPENCER SPIT STATE PARK

Spencer Spit State Park (521 A. Bakerview Rd., 888/226-7688, http://parks.state.wa.us, 8am-dusk daily Mar.-Oct., $10 parking) occupies 200 waterfront acres on the island's northeast corner. It offers Junior Ranger programs in the summer and access to clamming and crabbing along a long sandy spit, which forms a kind of triangle with a lagoon inside. Shorebirds are prevalent here, and driftwood gathers along the sandy shore. Kayak, bike, and stand-up paddleboard rentals are available.

SHARK REEF SANCTUARY

Shark Reef Sanctuary (Shark Reef Rd. and Burt Rd., www.lopezisland.com/parks) was once used as a military post and is now a 40-acre county park, named for a nearby reef. A short 0.5-mile walk through Douglas fir trees brings you to the shoreline and a lookout point, next to gnarled trees and a few feet of sandy beach, offering lovely views directly

Lopez Island

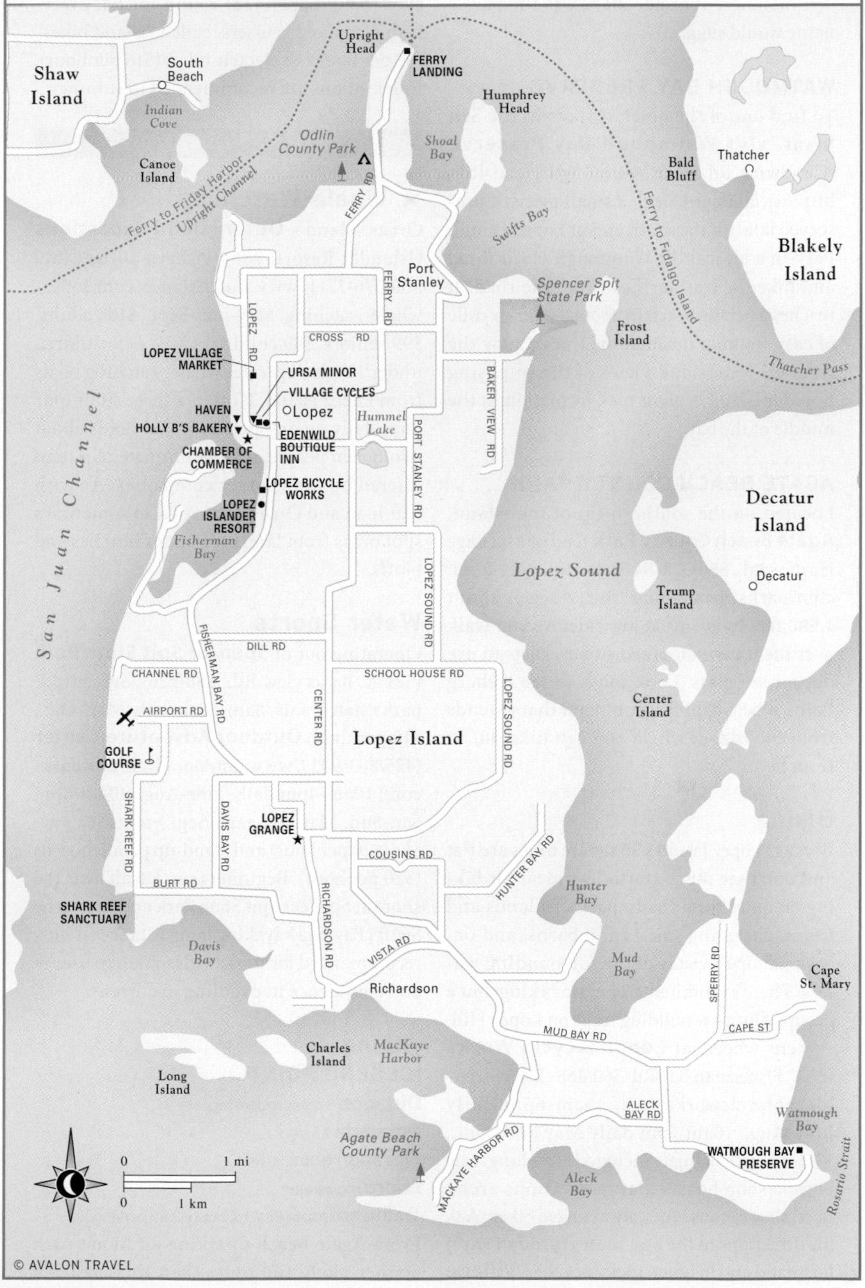
Upright Head
FERRY LANDING
Shaw Island
South Beach
Indian Cove
Humphrey Head
Odlin County Park
Shoal Bay
Canoe Island
Bald Bluff
Thatcher
Ferry to Friday Harbor
Upright Channel
FERRY RD
Swifts Bay
Ferry to Fidalgo Island
Blakely Island
Port Stanley
Spencer Spit State Park
Frost Island
CROSS RD
LOPEZ RD
FERRY RD
Thatcher Pass
LOPEZ VILLAGE MARKET
URSA MINOR
VILLAGE CYCLES
HAVEN
Lopez
Hummel Lake
HOLLY B'S BAKERY
EDENWILD BOUTIQUE INN
CHAMBER OF COMMERCE
BAKER VIEW RD
PORT STANLEY RD
LOPEZ BICYCLE WORKS
LOPEZ ISLANDER RESORT
Decatur Island
San Juan Channel
Fisherman Bay
Lopez Sound
Decatur
Trump Island
LOPEZ SOUND RD
DILL RD
FISHERMAN BAY RD
CHANNEL RD
SCHOOL HOUSE RD
Center Island
AIRPORT RD
CENTER RD
LOPEZ SOUND RD
Lopez Island
GOLF COURSE
SHARK REEF RD
DAVIS BAY RD
LOPEZ GRANGE
COUSINS RD
HUNTER BAY RD
Hunter Bay
BURT RD
RICHARDSON RD
SHARK REEF SANCTUARY
Davis Bay
VISTA RD
Mud Bay
SPERRY RD
Cape St. Mary
Richardson
MUD BAY RD
CAPE ST
Charles Island
MacKaye Harbor
Long Island
ALECK BAY RD
Watmough Bay
Agate Beach County Park
MACKAYE HARBOR RD
WATMOUGH BAY PRESERVE
0
1 mi
0
1 km
Aleck Bay
Rosario Strait
© AVALON TRAVEL

across Cattle Pass to San Juan Island, as well of the Olympic Mountains. Seal spottings are common here (but not sharks, as the park's name would suggest).

WATMOUGH BAY PRESERVE

To find one of the quietest spots in the San Juans, visit **Watmough Bay Preserve** (Chadwick Rd. near Watmough Head Rd., http://sjclandbank.org), a small piece of preserved land on the south end of Lopez Island. Park in a lot just off Watmough Head Road and hike the trail farthest from the road. It reaches a pebbly beach in about a quarter mile of easy walking through the trees. Enjoy the tranquil waters and views of the imposing Boulder Island, a giant rock formation in the middle of the bay.

AGATE BEACH COUNTY PARK

Located on the southern tip of the island, **Agate Beach County Park** (end of Mackaye Harbor Rd., 360/378-8420, www.lopezisland.com/parks) has a long, rocky beach about 1,500 feet in length at low tide. As you walk over the water-smoothed stones, keep an eye out for sea glass. Look south to see Iceberg Point, a beautiful finger of land that extends from the island, which you can hike out to from here.

Biking

Because Lopez Island's 30 square miles are flat and don't see much traffic, it's ideal for biking on quiet rural roads, past farmlands and forest, charming small rural barns, and occasional open vistas of the surrounding waters. There's is limited mountain biking, but a group of locals is building trails on Lopez Hill.

Rent wheels at **Lopez Bicycle Works** (2847 Fisherman Bay Rd. 360/468-2847, http://lopezbicycleworks.com, 10am-6pm daily June-Aug., 10am-5pm daily May and Sept., $7 per hour), helmets included. The longtime bicycle shop boasts that reservations aren't necessary because they always have bikes. Ask for directions to the best routes through rural farmland and to quiet, rocky beaches. **Village Cycles** (214 Lopez Rd., 360/468-4013, http://villagecycles.net/bicycle-rentals, 10am-4pm Wed.-Sat.) is open year-round and has everything from old cruisers, called "island bikes" ($7 per hour), to electric bikes ($16 per hour). Reservations are recommended in summer.

TOP EXPERIENCE

★ Whale-Watching

Orcas Island's **Outer Island Excursions** (Islander Resort, 2864 Fisherman Bay Rd., 360/376-3711, www.outerislandx.com/lopez-whale-watching, May-mid-Sept., $109 adults, $99 seniors, $89 children 12-17, $69 children under 12) also operates whale-watching boats from Lopez Island. It offers a three-hour tour once daily on an open boat that holds about two dozen people, a more intimate trip than offered by some larger companies. As with San Juan and Orcas, you can also sometimes spot orcas from land off Lopez's beaches and bluffs.

Water Sports

Operating out of **Spencer Spit State Park** (521 A. Bakerview Rd., 888/226-7688, http://parks.state.wa.us, 8am-dusk daily Mar.-Oct., $10 parking), **Outdoor Adventure Center** (425/883-9039, www.outdooradventurecenter.com, 10am-4pm daily June-Aug., 10am-4pm Sat.-Sun. May and early Sept.) rents sea kayaks ($20 per hour) and stand up paddleboards ($20 per hour). Beginners can kayak near the shore at Spencer Spit State Park and in nearby Swifts Bay. Sea kayaking long distances is only recommended for those with some experience and confidence in paddling in currents.

Hiking

ICEBERG POINT

Distance: 3 miles round-trip
Duration: 1.5 hours
Elevation gain: 50 feet
Effort: moderate
Trailhead: Agate Beach County Park parking lot

From Agate Beach's parking lot (don't park farther along the route than this, as it's a

Ursa Minor

private road), walk south along Mackaye Harbor Road and look for a right turn onto a gravel road, marked by signs in creative forms ("Iceberg Point" painted on an old saw nailed to a post, another painted on driftwood). If you see even bigger "No Parking" signs, you're going the right way. Follow the gravel road for about a mile and a half, taking care to keep dogs leashed and not moving beyond the road; it's all private property. Emerge from the shaded road and reach the open end of the finger of land jutting out into the water for spectacular views, which may include wildlife, such as seals and seabirds, and wildflowers along rocky bluffs. Return the way you came.

ENTERTAINMENT AND EVENTS

It's appropriate that the biggest event on Lopez Island is a bike race—and a noncompetitive one at that. The **Tour de Lopez** (www.lopez-island.com/tourdelopez.htm, Apr., $50 adults, $30 children 6-12), a local fundraiser, brings cyclists together for a massive one-day ride through scenic Lopez. Participants choose from four routes, ranging 5-31 miles. The ride ends with lunch, a beer garden, and musical performances.

FOOD

Nothing is too fancy on Lopez, but **Haven** (9 Old Post Rd., 360/468-3272, www.lopezhaven.com, noon-3pm and 5pm-8pm Wed.-Sat., $13-34) offers a nice sit-down meal with everything from a filet mignon to copious vegetarian options. With waterfront views and a bar serving creative cocktails, it's a breezy, comfortable dinner option.

When **Ursa Minor** (210 Lopez Rd., 360/622-2730, 5pm-9pm Fri.-Mon. Mar.-Dec., $19-31) opened in 2017, it seemed like Lopez Island would finally get a destination dining spot. Like so many well-regarded eateries in the area, it focuses on local dishes, foraged nettles, and seafood harvested just down the road—and the chef takes care to elevate those ingredients. Though there are some small plates, the prix fixe presentation ($65) of six courses is the best way to experience the unique flavors. Like many places on Lopez Island, the eatery closes for long periods in the winter and may have limited hours in the late fall and early spring.

The cookbook from the owners of **Holly B's Bakery** (165 Cherry Tree Ln., 360/468-2133, www.hollybsbakery.com, 7am-4pm Fri.-Sun.) is called *With Love and Butter,* and both are evident at the bakery. Giant cinnamon rolls are a regular favorite, but the glass cases also hold cookies and freshly baked breads.

Charming **Lopez Village Market** (162 Weeks Rd., 360/468-2266, http://lopezvillagemarket.com, 7:30am-7pm daily) sits next to a small tower topped with a weathervane. It has produce, a few housewares, a deli, bulk foods, and beer and wine.

ACCOMMODATIONS

Most visitors to Lopez stay in house rentals through AirBnB or VRBO, but there are a couple of small accommodation options.

The **Edenwild Boutique Inn** (132 Lopez

Rd., 360/468-3238, http://theedenwild.com, $228-300) is family run with bed-and-breakfast-style rooms, each one unique and some with fireplaces, porches, and soaking tubs. The decor isn't fussy, and there are fresh pastries waiting every morning.

The **Lopez Islander Resort** (2864 Fisherman Bay Rd., 360/468-2233, www.lopezfun.com, $159-219) is perhaps the only traditional hotel on the island, featuring standard and well-appointed rooms with a patio or deck, some with a fireplace. Located next to a marina and with a waterfront restaurant and tiki lounge, it's a good place for visitors who are looking for activity more than seclusion. There's a swimming pool, hot tub, and lawn game area.

Camping

Lopez Islander Resort offers campsites ($28-38) for both tents and RVs. **Spencer Spit State Park** (521 A. Bakerview Rd., 888/226-7688, http://parks.state.wa.us, $12-35) has 37 sites but no hookups for RVs.

INFORMATION AND SERVICES

You can find Wi-Fi at the **Lopez Library** (2225 Fisherman Bay Rd., 360/468-2265, http://lopezlibrary.org, 10am-5pm Mon. and Sat., 10am-6pm Tues. and Thurs.-Fri., 10am-9pm Wed.), a bright red building that's also a kind of community center. You can also find maps of Lopez Island at the ferry terminal and at the **Lopez Chamber of Commerce** (265 Lopez Rd., www.lopezisland.com, 10am-4pm Tues.-Sat.).

TRANSPORTATION

Getting There

FERRY

The **Washington State Ferry** (888/808-7977, www.wsdot.wa.gov/ferries, round-trip $13.50 adults, $6.70 seniors and children 6-18, free for children under 6, $46 standard-size vehicle and driver, $4 bicycle surcharge) runs car-and-passenger services from Anacortes. The ferry from Anacortes to Lopez Island takes about 50 minutes, and there are about six departures daily.

AIR

Floatplanes from **Kenmore Air** (866/435-9524, www.kenmoreair.com) depart from Lake Union in Seattle and take about 45 minutes to reach the islands. Flights to Lopez Island cost about $159-169.

Getting Around

No car rentals or taxi services are available on Lopez Island.

SHUTTLE BUS

San Juan Transit (360/378-8887, www.sanjuantransit.com, $5 adults, $3 children under 13) operates a shuttle Friday-Sunday late June-Labor Day, with about five departures per day in each direction, northbound and southbound, including stops at the ferry terminal, Shark Reef Sanctuary, and Spencer Spit State Park, among others. Carry exact change for your fare.

INTERISLAND FERRY

Washington State Ferry (888/808-7977, www.wsdot.wa.gov/ferries) runs interisland ferry services from Lopez Island west to Orcas Island (20 minutes), Shaw Island (20-40 minutes), and San Juan Island (1.25 hours). The cost for westbound travel on the interisland ferry from Lopez is $28.65 for a standard vehicle and driver. Walk-on passengers and cyclists ride free. During peak season, there are about five interisland ferry departures per day.

Washington Wine Country

Look for ★ to find recommended sights, activities, dining, and lodging.

Highlights

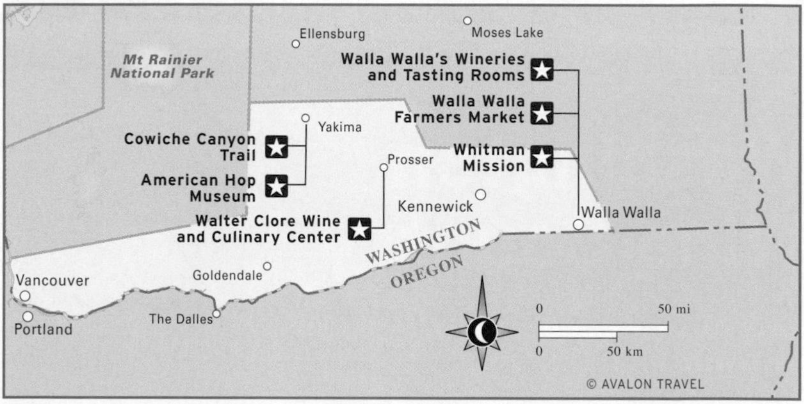

★ **Walla Walla's Wineries and Tasting Rooms:** Explore the abundant tasting rooms downtown and wineries in the surrounding countryside (page 227).

★ **Walla Walla Farmers Market:** Don't forget to grab an onion—the local variety are sweet enough to be eaten like an apple—at this lively produce market (page 229).

★ **Whitman Mission:** Site of an infamous attack, this national historic site offers a peek into encounters between some of the first white settlers in the West and local Native Americans (page 229).

★ **American Hop Museum:** Beer would be boring without hops. This funky old museum has the whole story about how Yakima became the hops capital of the world (page 236).

★ **Cowiche Canyon Trail:** Hike between sagebrush and basalt columns, then follow a spur trail leading to a winery (page 237).

★ **Walter Clore Wine and Culinary Center:** Learn about Washington's viticulture in a modern visitors center offering wine tastings and good views (page 242).

East of the Cascade Mountains, Washington's signature evergreen forests and jagged peaks give way to rolling hills, rocky soil, sunny skies, and miles of agricultural land where grapes thrive.

Although European immigrants were planting grapes in the region in the 19th century, it wasn't until the 1970s that southeast Washington began to grow a reputation for premium vintages, exploding into one of the biggest viticultural scenes in the country. Washington's wines, notably its robust reds—cabs and merlots—are known to stand up against California's best. Think of it as a mini Napa Valley, without the exorbitant prices and elite clientele.

Washington's wine country stretches east from the Yakima Valley, home to not only grape growers but hop fields fueling the craft beer movement, to the Tri-Cities, a trio of towns with wineries on their outskirts, and farther east to the center of Washington's wine country in Walla Walla, a breezy town bursting at the seams with tasting rooms and great dining options.

Don't pack anything fancy for a trip to Washington wine country, just sunglasses year-round (this ain't the rainy side of the state) and a willingness to hang with the people who create some of the best bottles in the country.

PLANNING YOUR TIME

Wine country in Washington begins with Walla Walla—for pure beauty, concentration of wine attractions, and stellar dining, it can't be beat. The town merits at least a two- to three-day stay. Most people stay in the walkable downtown for access to restaurants and tasting rooms, making excursions into the surrounding countryside to visit a few wineries.

Yakima Valley is more agricultural and the Tri-Cities more residential. Both are closer to Seattle and would make good stopovers on a road trip from the big city to Walla Walla—consider visiting one on the way to, and one on the way back—as each has its own collection of wineries and tasting rooms, as well as

Previous: a vineyard near the Tri-Cities; The Inn at Abeja winery. **Above:** wine grapes in Yakima Valley.

Washington Wine Country

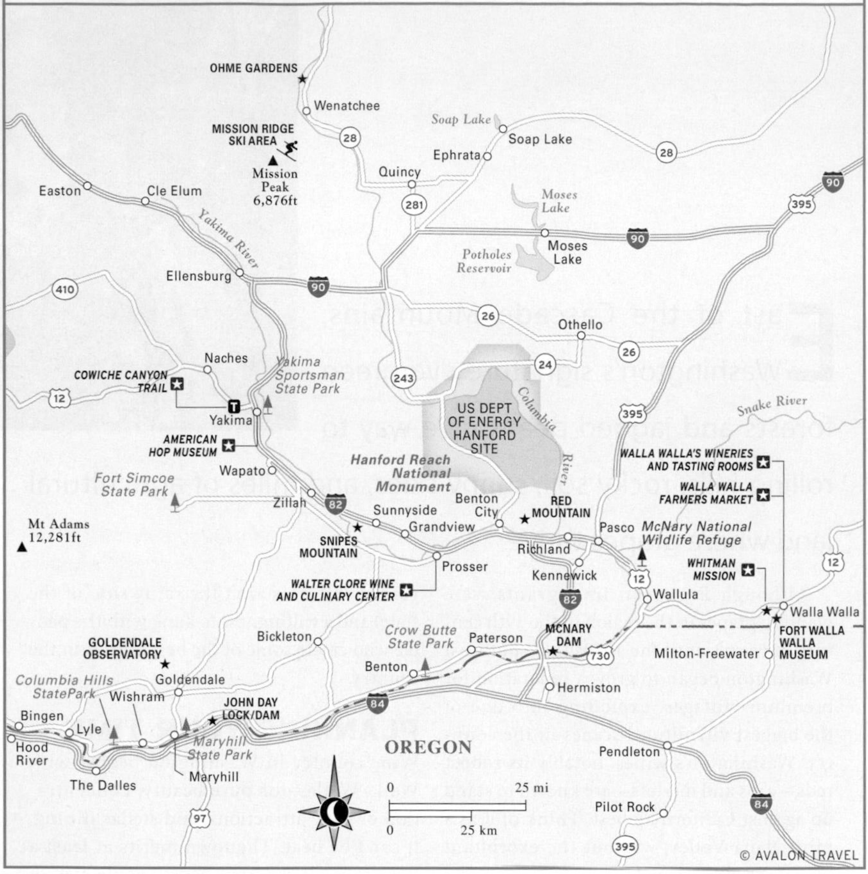

some diverting attractions of the natural, historical, and quirky roadside variety.

Washington wine country is popular year-round, but the high season in Walla Walla begins in May, with the area receiving a steady stream of visitors through summer and the fall harvest. Spring is ideal for shoulder season travelers, with sunshine and mild temperatures, though wineries in the Yakima Valley and Tri-Cities have more limited hours during this season. January-February tend to be the quietest months in wine country here.

Walla Walla

TOP EXPERIENCE

Walla Walla, the town so nice they named it twice, gets its name from a Native American word that means "running waters"; the Walla Walla River runs southwest of town. Some of the first white settlers off the Oregon Trail ended up here, and the agricultural region eventually became known for the sweet Walla Walla onion—at least until wine came along. Note the T-shirt you'll see in some shops around town: "Walla Walla for my wine, Napa for my auto parts."

Downtown Walla Walla surrounds the towering Marcus Whitman Hotel. Blocks are short and walkable, with boutiques and restaurants mixed in with winery tasting rooms. Many buildings date back to the 19th century and feature Victorian-era moldings and flair. Whitman College, a small but highly regarded liberal arts school, sits just east of downtown; with about 1,500 students it's not big enough to make as big an impact on the town as its wining and dining scene, but its stately clock tower and academic reputation lend prestige.

★ WINERIES AND TASTING ROOMS

Walla Walla is the beating heart of Washington wine country. Set amid grassy farmlands and low hills, it hosts an abundance of tasting rooms in both its downtown as well as surrounding countryside, typically off U.S. 12 to the east and west of town and off Highway 125 to the south, right near the Oregon border.

It's easy to create a do-it-yourself wine-tasting itinerary in Walla Walla. Expect to pay about $10 per tasting, though most wineries waive fees if you purchase bottles. Some wineries serve food, but most downtown don't.

Downtown

You'll find plenty of style at **Maison Bleue Winery** (20 N 2nd Ave., 509/525-9084, www.mbwinery.com, 11am-5pm Wed.-Mon., $10 tasting fee), which boasts a blue couch and blue walls, a solid contrast to the winery's bold whites and reds.

Trust Cellars (14 N 2nd Ave., 509/529-4511, www.trustcellars.com, 11am-5pm Sun. and Thurs.-Fri., 11am-6pm Sat. summer, $10 tasting fee) goes for a hipster look with exposed pipes and a vintage cycle parked inside. It's especially known for its well-balanced syrah.

Mark Ryan Winery (26 E Main St., 509/876-4577, www.markryanwinery.com, 11am-5pm Sun.-Thurs., 11am-8pm Fri., 11am-6pm Sat., $10 tasting fee) displays a motorcycle in the window and also serves up a floral and fruity syrah.

Airport Area

About five miles east of downtown is an industrial area near the Walla Walla Regional Airport that hosts numerous wineries, many in remodeled World War II-era military buildings. **Dunham Cellars** (150 E Boeing Ave., 509/529-4685, www.dunhamcellars.com, 11am-4pm daily, $10 tasting fee) is in an old airplane hangar. Its tasting room is cheerfully decorated—it has a "tree" made of wine bottles—and one of the winery's best (and affordable) wines is a rich red blend named for its late three-legged dog.

Southside

Just south of town you'll find many more tasting rooms, sometimes next to rolling vineyards.

Amavi Cellars (3796 Peppers Bridge Rd., 509/525-3541, www.amavicellars.com, 10am-4pm daily, $10 tasting fee) feels traditional, with a patio opening up to views of vineyards and hills. But there's also often a food truck parked out back. Try an earthy syrah or cabernet sauvignon here.

Sleight of Hand Cellars (1959 J B George Rd., 509/525-3661, www.sofhcellars.com, 11am-5pm Sat.-Thurs., 11am-6pm Fri., $10 tasting fee) is reliable fun. It puts magicians on

Walla Walla

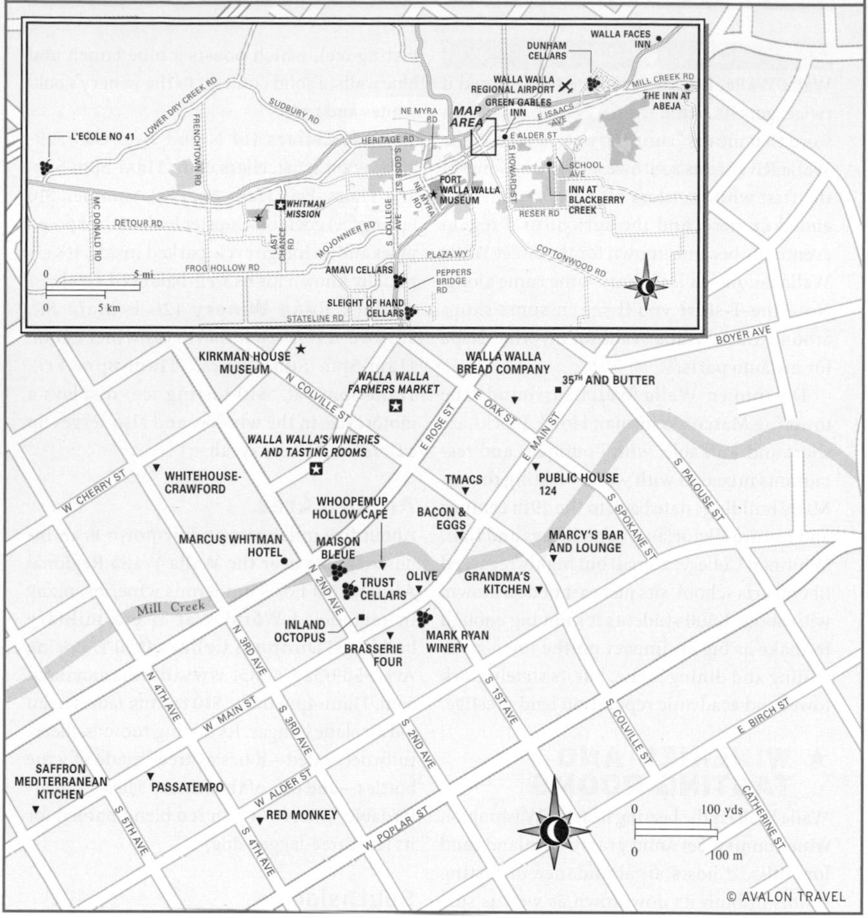

its labels, and the tasting room is lined with vinyl records; pick anything you want as a tasting soundtrack. A few rows of vines are here, but its popular, accessible wines are mostly made from vineyards spread across the region.

Westside

L'Ecole No 41 (41 Lowden School Rd., Lowden, 509/525-0940, www.lecole.com, 11am-5pm daily, $10 tasting fee), about a 20-minute drive west of downtown, is a well-established winery that just happens to be inside an old schoolhouse. Take the time to wander the charming building. Its bordeaux blend is a stand-out, made from one of its highest-elevation vineyards

Wine Tours

Sticking to downtown tasting rooms makes for an easy way to avoid driving, but to fully appreciate the region and enjoy the sprawling vineyards, you'll need to venture outside of town. You can go with a touring service like **Tesla Winery Tours** (253/797-6596, www.

teslawinerytours.com, $90 per hour for up to six people, four-hour minimum) which shuttles tasters around in a fancy Tesla car.

SIGHTS

★ Walla Walla Farmers Market

Eastern Washington is one of the Northwest's agricultural hubs, so it's no surprise that the seasonal, weekly **Walla Walla Farmers Market** (Main St. and 4th Ave., 509/520-3647, www.wallawalla.org, 9am-1pm Sat. May-Oct.) offers bundles of rich produce and, of course, plenty of the sweet onions for which the region is known, sometimes even including a caramel version that resembles a candy apple. Expect lots of melon varieties, as well as potatoes. You'll also find ready-to-eat foods like salads, sandwiches, and cheeses, as well as artisan crafts including jewelry and ceramics. It's all held under a glass pagoda downtown, not more than a block in size—a small but mighty farmers market.

Kirkman House Museum

When Walla Walla grew in the late 19th century, many stately mansions were built, including the one that became the **Kirkman House Museum** (214 N Colville St., 509/529-4373, www.kirkmanhousemuseum.org, 10am-4pm Wed.-Sat., 10am-2pm Sun., $7), an example of Victorian Italianate architecture. Today the house hosts traveling exhibits and permanent displays about the history of Walla Walla, once the biggest town in the Washington Territory. There's also a weaver's cottage dedicated to the history of traditional textile making.

Fort Walla Walla Museum

Located on the grounds of a 19th-century fort about a mile southwest of downtown, **Fort Walla Walla Museum** (755 NE Myra Rd., 509/525-7703, www.fwwm.org, 10am-5pm daily Mar.-Oct., 10am-4pm daily Nov.-Feb., $8 adults, $7 seniors and students, $3 children 6-12, free for children under 6) traces the region's history from its Native American roots through Lewis and Clark's journey to the site's time as a military outpost. Made up of 15 acres, the grounds once held a substantial fort, and today host 17 historical buildings—including a blacksmith shop and school—gathered into a small pioneer village. All were moved here to preserve them, with some dating back to the 19th century. Inside the museum's modern buildings, five exhibit halls display items such as horse-powered agricultural equipment and military artifacts. Kids will enjoy the blend of topics and seeing a past era come to life in the pioneer village, while military buffs will enjoy the eras covered; anyone else may not find much engaging here. You can also cross the road to see a cemetery and several military memorials, which don't require an admission fee to access.

★ Whitman Mission

From Walla Walla's signature hotel to Whitman College, you'll find a lot around town named for Marcus and Narcissa Whitman. They founded the **Whitman Mission** (328 Whitman Mission Rd., 509/522-6360, www.nps.gov/whmi, 9am-4pm daily June-Sept., 9am-4pm Wed.-Sun. Feb.-May and Oct.-Nov., free), about eight miles west of downtown via U.S. 12 and now a National Historic Site, and were some of the first white settlers (and Narcissa perhaps the first white woman) in the state. The site of their Christian outpost became a rest stop along the Oregon Trail and is famous for dark reasons; the couple and other white settlers were killed by local Cayuse Indians in 1847, who blamed the Whitmans for bringing infectious disease to the region—a measles outbreak killed many Cayuse Indians. Here you'll find an exhibit hall examining the circumstances and cultural differences leading up to the contentious event that became known as the Whitman Massacre, a major turning point in the American West that some credit with motivating Congress to declare Oregon a U.S. territory. No original buildings from the rustic mission remain, but the exhibit hall is surrounded by grassy fields, short walking trails with interpretive signs, a cemetery and memorial, and a hilltop lookout. It's a beautiful site to wander and learn about the region's history that touches on both its Native American and Oregon Trail roots.

ENTERTAINMENT AND EVENTS

Nightlife

Red Monkey (6721 Greenwood Ave. N, 206/619-5794, http://redmonkeydowntown.com, 11am-midnight daily) offers a nice mix: The chill bar has stone pillars inside, a slew of beer and wine on tap, and a menu ranging from edamame to french fries and drumsticks. Its lack of pretension is manifest in its juxtaposition of a disco ball hanging from the ceiling and a big-screen TV typically showing sports games. And the bartenders can offer great local tips.

The exterior of **Marcy's Bar and Lounge** (35 S Colville St., 509/525-7482, www.marcysbarandlounge.com, 3pm-2am daily) is one of its biggest draws; the old art deco building used to be a gas station but passes for something with much more style. Indoors the bartenders are advanced mixologists using bitters and house-made syrups, and the lounge's classic Moscow mule with house-made ginger soda is a refreshing tipple in midsummer. The crisp, uncluttered interior fills with live music some nights.

At **Public House 124** (124 E Main St., 509/876-4511, www.ph124.com, 3pm-11pm Tues.-Sat.), the drinks are the stars of the show, including cocktails, signature margaritas, and sangria. A food menu includes appropriate side bites like truffle fries. Exposed brick and dim lighting can make the place feel more serious than it actually is.

Festivals and Events

Walla Walla's **Spring Release Weekend** (www.wallawallawine.com/spring-release-weekend, May) in the beginning of May, sees many wineries hosting winemaker dinners, special tastings, and other events. Fees vary by event.

The Walla Walla onion's sweetness is attributable to low sulfur levels in the local soil—which, incidentally, also helps grow great wine grapes. The annual **Sweet Onion Festival** (3rd and Main St., 509/525-1031, http://sweetonions.org/festival, July), a town staple for more than 30 years, celebrates this onion so sweet you can eat it raw, like an apple. The weekend-long festival offers tons of fried and raw eats, as well as events like onion bowling and a contest to see whose bald head most resembles one of the veggies. The festival is free except for food and some activities like the fun run.

Walla Walla Wine Walk (http://servefirst.

Whitman Mission

Joining the Harvest

While summer is the most popular tourism season in Washington wine country, fall is something special, as the weather cools, grapes are harvested, and winemakers celebrate with crush events and other happenings. Plan to hit up one of the larger festivals or special food events like pairing dinners, or check out individual wineries for live music.

WALLA WALLA

During the fall harvest, Canoe Ridge Vineyard hosts a **Grape Stomp & Lunch** (1102 W Cherry St., 509/525-1843, http://canoeridgevineyard.com, Sept., $10 tasting fee, $75 event fee), a traditional grape-crushing event (take off your shoes!) followed by a picnic. The **Walla Walla Wine Walk** (http://servefirst.org/event/wine-walk, Sept., $25) is a single-day tasting event that routes through downtown, benefiting local charities. There's often a $20 wine stomp on Main Street, then live music at a venue like **Plumb Cellars** (39 E Main St., 509/529-9463), also the registration site. But to mingle with the biggest wine fans in the state, attend the **Walla Walla Fall Release Weekend** (www.wallawallawine.com/fall-tasting, Nov.), the celebratory event capping off the season. Purveyors break out new releases, host live music and dinners, and otherwise toast the end of a season. Admission fees vary as each winery does something different, but events might include, for instance, special flight tastings or cheese pairings.

YAKIMA VALLEY

For one weekend in mid-October, wineries around the Yakima River throw parties for **Catch the Crush** (509/965-5201, http://wineyakimavalley.org, Oct.). The region's wine organization collects a list of events happening at each winery that weekend, including live music performances, fall releases, and grape-stomping events. A Premier Pass ($30-35) waives tasting fees that weekend at 40-plus wineries throughout the region. Pass holders also get perks like winery tours and access to grape-stomping events, maybe even a chance to take home grape samples. Free tastings extend down to the Red Mountain and Prosser wineries, though not all waive fees; some offer discounts, bottle specials, or food. The festival advises you to bring your own wine glass, as these small operations have trouble keeping enough on hand during the event.

TRI-CITIES

The **Tri-Cities Wine Festival** (Three Rivers Convention Center, 7016 W Grandridge Blvd., Kennewick, 509/737-3700, www.tricitieswinesociety.com, Nov.) takes place on a single Saturday evening at a convention center in Kennewick. Up to 100 wineries attend the indoor event, pouring about 400 wines. Attendees pay a single price to enter ($60-65), which covers all wine, plus food bites from more than a dozen food purveyors. The local wine society holds a competition, one of the oldest in the Northwest.

org/event/wine-walk, Sept., $25) is a single-day tasting event that goes through downtown.

During **Walla Walla Fall Release Weekend** (www.wallawallawine.com/fall-tasting, Nov.), wineries break out new releases and host dinners, live music, and, sometimes, grape stomps. Fees vary by event.

SHOPPING

Look for the big purple cephalopod to find downtown's **Inland Octopus** (7 E Main St., 509/526-0115, www.inlandoctopus.com, 10am-6pm daily), everything a toy store should be. Inside you'll find an eclectic and whimsical selection, including plenty of stuffed animals, boxed Lego toys, gumballs, and dolls, plus adorable and weird kids' clothing

There's no food at **35th and Butter** (205 E Main St., 509/876-1514, 10am-5:30pm Mon.-Tues. and Thurs.-Sat., 10am-4pm Sun.), but plenty of delectable, colorful jewelry that looks good enough to eat. The shop also carries a few home goods, but the focus is on signature women's jewelry—bangles, earrings, chokers—that makes an impact.

FOOD

American

While the restaurant scene in town has grown up in recent years, **Whitehouse-Crawford** (55 W Cherry St., 509/525-2222, http://whitehousecrawford.com, 5pm-9pm Wed.-Mon., $27-44) has been the standard bearer for fine dining in Walla Walla since 2000. Located inside a renovated mill, the cavernous space has high windows and exposed beams, but the venerable restaurant manages to stay relevant; white-tablecloth aesthetics aside, the food is creative and tasty, especially a pork belly steamed bun appetizer that could serve as a meal if you order enough of them.

While the baked-in-house loaves get center stage at **Walla Walla Bread Company** (201 E Main St., 509/522-8422, www.w2breadco.com, 8am-8pm daily, $7-16), the popular joint also offers pizzas, salads, and pastas. Small tables and a casual vibe make it feel more like a café than a full restaurant—though there's also a dedicated bar section and cocktails are served—and the open views to the baking pans help blur the line between bakers and diners.

Breakfast

Fortunately, there's more than the titular breakfast on offer at **Bacon & Eggs** (503 E Main St., 509/876-4553, www.baconandeggswallawalla.com, 8am-2pm Thurs.-Tues., $7-12); even better, the bacon and eggs are delicious. Crowded during brunch thanks to its huevos rancheros, omelets, and biscuits and gravy, the multiroom space happily takes advantage of many counters and long shared tables to get diners seated. Look for the wall of hot sauces near the bathroom; it's enough to make even the most seasoned spice-lover cry.

French

Rotating artwork changes up the look of **Brasserie Four** (4 E Main St., 509/529-2011, http://brasseriefour.com, 5pm-9pm Tues.-Thurs., noon-9pm Fri.-Sat., $11-29), its white molded ceiling and wood tables offering a simple backdrop. The refreshingly warm and low-key French eatery sticks to classics like moules frites, steak frites, and a rich French onion soup made with local Walla Wallas.

Italian

When a well-known chef in Seattle helped launch the Italian **Passatempo** (215 W Main St., 509/876-8822, www.passatempowallawalla.com, 3-10pm Thurs.-Mon., 5-11pm Fri.-Sat., $16-32) in Walla Walla in 2016, it drew notice; when the handmade pastas were finally tasted, it earned its fame. The taverna specializes in dishes that pair particularly well with wine, such as rustic Italian entrées like grilled lamb and gnocchi with roast chicken. Be sure to ask for the house focaccia.

Walla Walla regulars might not recognize this longtime downtown staple until they realize it's the nickname for the restaurant formerly called T. Maccarone's. That did sound more like an old Italian joint with checkered tablecloths and saucy pastas. But longtime fans needn't worry; only the name made a major change. Now **TMACS** (4 N Colville St., 509/522-4776, http://tmacsww.com, 11am-9:30pm Tues.-Sat., $12-19), the name fits the bistro's more casual vibe and mixed menu of just a few pastas—Bolognese with a pork and beef ragu, agnolotti with mushrooms—plus some steaks and chicken. The dark wood interior casts a solemn vibe, which the colorful dishes help counteract.

Mediterranean

Though Walla Walla is far from the warm shores of the Mediterranean, **Saffron Mediterranean Kitchen** (330 W Main St., 509/525-2112, www.saffronmediterraneankitchen.com, 2pm-9pm Tues.-Sun., $14-42) offers a taste of the great flavors of that region in dishes like Valencian paella and grilled lamb with spiced lentils; it's meant to feel like the intersection of Italy and Spain. Once in a tiny space overwhelmed by its popularity, it's now in a larger 1909 brick building.

Mexican

Sometimes you need a big plate of fresh Mexican tacos or handmade guacamole after a day of fine sipping. **Grandma's Kitchen** (36 S Colville St., 509/301-4565, 11am-3pm and 5pm-9pm Mon.-Thurs., 11am-3pm and 5pm-10pm Fri., 1pm-10pm Sat., 3pm-8pm Sun., $5-9) keeps it simple with a number of fillings and a few forms they can take—in addition to tacos, think burritos, tostadas, and tortas. Order at the counter and appreciate that the vinyl tablecloths will catch any drippings.

Southern

Go ahead and make noise for the **Whoopemup Hollow Cafe** (13 E Main St., 509/525-5000, www.whoopemuphollowcafe.com, 11:30am-3pm and 5pm-10pm Tues.-Sat., $16-38), a name that's as fun to say as the eatery's food is fun to eat. This Walla Walla outpost of a popular New Orleans-themed café in a rural town nearby means now there's gumbo and crawfish pie right next to the city's tasting rooms. The tight interior is cheery despite little natural light, and there are a few small tables outside. Save room for the Mississippi Mud Pie.

ACCOMMODATIONS

$150-250

Downtown's tallest building—it's only about a dozen stories high, but it towers over everything else—and Walla Walla's signature, the ★ **Marcus Whitman Hotel** (6 W Rose St., 509/525-2200, http://marcuswhitmanhotel.com, $184-269 rooms, $269-339 suites) has a 1928 edifice impossible to miss. Inside, the lobby has southern European charm, down to the green ferns unfurling out of giant vases. The 133 rooms have been updated three times this century; these are some of the nicest accommodations in Washington east of the Columbia River. It's hard to go wrong in this hotel synonymous with the town, especially when the area's great dining is just steps outside the door.

The connection between the name of this 1909 bed-and-breakfast and *Anne of Green Gables* is not accidental; most of the six rooms have labels that hark back to the children's book. **Green Gables Inn** (922 Bonsella St., 509/876-4373, www.greengablesinn.com, $219-279) is decorated in florals, but the rich colors keep it from feeling like a grandmother's pincushion. The Craftsman-style home has plenty of dark brown leather couches and dark wood trim. Some rooms have patio access and walk-in showers. It's several blocks

the Marcus Whitman Hotel

east of downtown, near Whitman College and about a 20-minute walk to most central tasting rooms and restaurants.

A couple of miles east of busy downtown in a residential neighborhood next to a burbling stream, the **Inn at Blackberry Creek** (1126 Pleasant St., 509/522-5233, www.innatblackberrycreek.com, $203-215) is a bed-and-breakfast that knows you might need a mini-fridge in your room to chill the chardonnay you just picked up. The intimate 1905 farmhouse has just three rooms, and the four-poster (or in one case, two-poster) beds have romantic charm. Sit on the porch, pet the resident cat, and move at a slower pace.

Over $250

With just seven rooms (plus a giant farmhouse that rents separately), **The Inn at Abeja** (2014 Mill Creek Rd., 509/522-1234, www.abeja.net/inn, $359-499) is a quiet set of accommodations at a well-regarded winery, some with full kitchens. Some suites are in an old carriage barn, another in an old hayloft, but it's not rustic; picture French doors, antique armoires, spa tubs, and views for days. Breakfasts made with farm-fresh eggs and house-made apple sausage are served in a farmhouse dining room, a patio, or in your suite. The winery isn't open to the public, but guests get special access to wine tastings. The inn is located about seven miles east of town.

The four rooms at **Walla Faces Inn at the Vineyard** (254 Wheat Ridge Ln., 877/301-1181, www.wallafaces.com/hotels, $195-395), overlooking vineyards not far from the winery, have clean, modern lines. Some have kitchen facilities. An outdoor swimming pool is available for guest use only and has views out to the vineyards and mountains beyond. About eight miles east of town, it's perfect for those who want privacy and quiet.

Camping

Located between downtown Walla Walla and the Oregon border that lies not far south, **RV Resort Four Seasons** (1440 Dalles Military Rd., 509/529-6072, www.rvresortfourseasons.com, $42) offers close access to the county fairgrounds, a disc golf course, a grocery store, and a dog park. The campground is decorated with little more than various plastic animal figurines and is for RVs only, with 90 sites, some pull-through.

INFORMATION AND SERVICES

In downtown Walla Walla, head to the **visitor information kiosk** (26 E Main St., 509/525-8799, www.wallawalla.org, 10am-5pm daily summer, 10am-4pm Fri., 10am-5pm Sat. winter) near the Mark Ryan Winery, where a staffer sits inside a window to offer assistance and hand out maps, pamphlets, and some coupons for local services. You'll find the **post office** (128 N 2nd Ave., 800/275-8777, http://usps.com) across from the Marcus Whitman Hotel.

GETTING THERE

Walla Walla Regional Airport (ALW, 45 Terminal Loop, 509/525-3100, www.wallawallaairport.com), located about five miles east of town, has flights from Seattle 2-3 times daily. The flight takes about an hour.

In total, it's about 265 miles southeast, a 4.5-hour drive, from Seattle to Walla Walla. To reach Walla Walla from Seattle, head east on I-90 for 135 miles to just past where it crosses the Columbia River. Take exit 137 to get on Highway 26 East briefly; after about a mile, stay right to get onto Highway 243. Follow this south and then east for 28 miles, then stay right for Highway 24 and cross the Columbia River again. Continue on Highway 24 for 5.5 miles; it'll become Highway 240 East, which you'll follow for 29 miles southeast, passing the broad expanse of the Hanford Reach to your left. Turn right to stay on Highway 240, and four miles later take the right-hand ramp onto I-182 East to Pasco/Kennewick. After 10 miles, continue on as the road becomes U.S. 12. Stay on U.S. 12 for about 47 miles into Walla Walla.

Yakima Valley

On a clear day Mount Adams is visible in the hills above Yakima. A large, hand-painted sign greets drivers to the central Washington city, "Welcome to Yakima, The Palm Springs of Washington." While that may not be entirely true (there's plenty of sunshine but few golf courses and even less stylish architecture to be found), the hub of this agricultural region has slowly been moving beyond fast food and rundown motels, and the valley that heads southeast from town, toward the Tri-Cities, is increasingly full of wineries. What's more, the region grows most of the hops fueling the country's craft beer explosion.

WINERIES AND TASTING ROOMS

Wineries are more scattered in the Yakima Valley than in Walla Walla or the outskirts of the Tri-Cities, but you'll find a number of great tasting rooms, a few loosely off U.S. 12 to the north of Yakima and I-82 to the south.

Yakima Area

Gilbert Cellars (5 N Front St., Yakima, 509/249-9049, www.gilbertcellars.com, 1pm-7pm Mon.-Thurs., 1pm-9pm Fri.-Sat., 1pm-6pm Sun., $6 tasting fee) has a tasting room downtown. The owners pour 10 wines in this sunny space. If you'd like to try the offerings among the vineyards, you can make a tasting appointment at the **winery** (2620 Draper Rd., Yakima, 509/249-9049 ext. 7), in an agrarian setting with beautiful sunsets located about 10 miles southwest of downtown.

About eight miles west of town, **Wilridge Winery** (250 Ehler Rd., Yakima, 509/966-0686, www.wilridgewinery.com, 11am-7pm daily summer, call for winter hours, $5 tasting fee) was originally based in Seattle—and is still the city's oldest winery—and planted vineyards in Yakima in 2007. Here, the winery serves a full slate of whites, rosés, and reds, from rieslings to malbecs. It also operates a distillery that makes brandy from the fruit grown in the orchards here.

About eight miles south of Yakima you'll find **Owen Roe** (309 Gangl Rd., Wapato, 509/877-0454, www.owenroe.com, 11am-4pm daily, $10 tasting fee). The producer got into the Northwest wine scene before it was cool, back in 1999. The winery has a tasting patio and a big lawn for picnics. You can also request a private tasting ($30) in the barrel room. Just down the road, closer to the freeway, is **Treveri Cellars** (71 Gangl Rd., Wapato, 509/877-0925, www.trevericellars.com, noon-5pm Mon.-Thurs., noon-6pm Fri.-Sat., noon-4pm Sun., $5 tasting fee), which makes a series of sparkling wines from riesling, syrah, and more at its winery on a hill overlooking the interstate. Treveri's wine has even been poured at the White House.

Rattlesnake Hills

Named for the snakes that travel this dry landscape (don't worry, bites aren't common), the Rattlesnake Hills AVA is a wine region just southeast of Yakima. The rolling hills rising above the Yakima River are dotted with wineries. Most winemakers here run small operations, few of which tend to make a splash statewide; instead, their charms lie in immediacy—there's a good chance the winemaker him- or herself will be the one performing the tastings.

Located near the town of Zillah, **Dineen Vineyards** (2980 Gilbert Rd., Zillah, 206/276-4287, www.dineenvineyards.com, noon-5pm Fri.-Sun. Apr.-Oct., $5 tasting fee) has more than 70 acres of vineyards and a view of Mount Rainier. It makes a cabernet sauvignon and rich heritage red wine blend. On some Saturdays the tasting room also sells wood-fired pizza.

Small, scenic **Bonair Winery and Vineyards** (500 S Bonair Rd., Zillah,

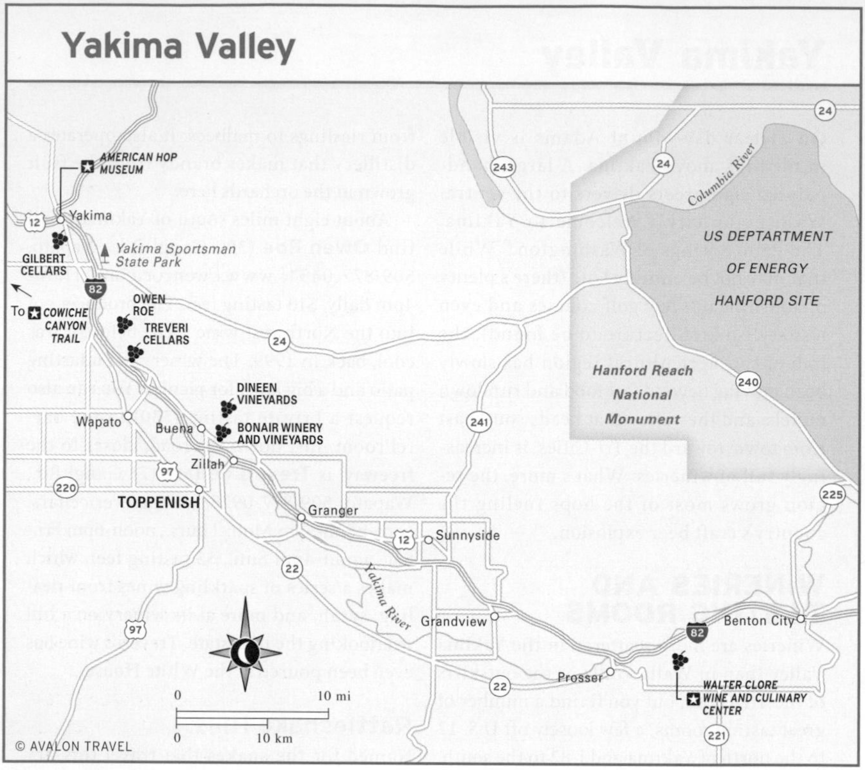

509/829-6027, www.bonairwine.com, 11am-4pm daily Apr.-Oct., $5 tasting fee) is proud of its estate wine status; here you can taste the chardonnays, merlots, and malbecs made from the vineyards right outside. Tours are also available and by reservation only; the winery tour ($10) takes you through the barrel rooms and steel vats, while the vineyard tour ($20) is a 1.5-hour trip in a 4x4 through the estate's 35 acres of grapes.

SIGHTS

★ American Hop Museum

Where would we be without hops? The recent IPA craze would look a lot different. But the charming **American Hop Museum** (22 S B St., Toppenish, 509/865-4677, http://americanhopmuseum.org, 10am-4pm Wed.-Sun., $5 adults, $3 children 6-12, free for children under 6) is a reminder that the crop isn't a brand-new addition to the landscape. Start with the 10-minute video, which will give you an endless appreciation for wet-hopped beers, then follow a small indoor path through the slightly dusty displays—the museum compellingly looks like it was imagined in the 1950s, eschewing the current hipness of hops. Picture vintage-style exhibits showing farmers shipping hops east as early as the 1870s, mannequins wearing old farm clothes, baskets of hops everywhere, and artfully displayed old tractors and harvesters outside. Located in Toppenish, about 20 miles south of Yakima, the building itself is beautiful, adorned with some of the landscape murals that appear all over the small town. There are no hoppy beers to drink on-site, but the gift shop has plenty of beer-themed gifts.

Teapot Dome Service Station

There's always time for some random roadside attractions. The **Teapot Dome Service Station** (117 1st Ave., Zillah, www.cityofzillah.us/teapot.html), about 20 miles southeast of Yakima off I-82 in the town of Zillah, was built in 1922 as a gas station, a reference to the Harding administration's bribery scandal involving secretly leased oil reserves in Teapot Dome, Wyoming. It's simply a building shaped like a teapot—and listed on the National Register of Historic Places—but makes for fun photos. There's parking and a bathroom, and inside the teapot you'll find brochures for local attractions and other tourist information.

Fort Simcoe Historical State Park

Located a 45-minute drive, about 36 miles, southwest of Yakima, on the Yakama Indian Reservation that takes up much of this corner of the state, the **Fort Simcoe Historical State Park** (5150 Fort Simcoe Rd., White Swan, 509/874-2372, http://parks.state.wa.us, 8am-dusk Wed.-Sun. Apr.-Oct., $5 parking) offers enough to make the drive worthwhile. The fort predates the Civil War, and rangers tell of how it morphed from military installation to a boarding school where Native Americans were forced to send their children. You'll see barracks and lookouts here, and you'll also find day-use facilities including a playground and picnic tables for relaxing. Birders also enjoy the area.

SPORTS AND RECREATION

Hiking

The 5,000 acres of central Washington landscape east of Yakima known as **Cowiche Canyon** (www.cowichecanyon.org) are filled with 30 miles of trails and an old jeep track. It offers one of the prettiest hikes close to Yakima and is easy enough for beginners looking to stretch their legs.

★ COWICHE CANYON TRAIL

Distance: 6-7.6 miles round-trip
Duration: 3-4 hours
Elevation gain: 100-300 feet
Effort: moderate
Trailhead: Cowiche Canyon Road
Directions: From Yakima, head west on U.S. 12 for 3.5 miles. Turn left on Ackley Road and left again on West Powerhouse Road. After 0.25 mile, turn right on Cowiche Canyon Road and drive 2.5 miles.

Walk along Cowiche Creek from the trailhead, taking in the sage-covered grasslands. You'll cross the creek three times and then reach a turnoff to a winery on the right; continue straight ahead, hopping back and forth over the creek under beautiful cliffs and impressive basalt column formations. Keep an eye out for birds; everything from robins to turkey vultures are seen here regularly. Rattlesnakes are also common in the area, so avoid leaving trail to where they're less visible in the brush. Turn back when you reach the Cowiche Canyon West Trailhead and return the way you came.

On your way back, you can pop up to the **Wilridge Winery** (250 Ehler Rd., Yakima, 509/966-0686, www.wilridgewinery.com, 11am-7pm daily summer, call for winter hours, $5 tasting fee), via the spur trail previously passed, and reward yourself with a tasting or glass of wine. It's an extra 1.6 miles total.

ENTERTAINMENT AND EVENTS

Nightlife

In the middle of town, **Hop Nation Brewing** (31 N 1st Ave., Yakima, 509/367-6552, www.hopnation.us, 4pm-9pm Mon. and Wed.-Fri., noon-10pm Sat.-Sun.) provides plenty of the bitter brew. Located in a 100-year-old fruit-packing warehouse that, oh yeah, once stored hops, the brewery's beers draw on its location's abundance: lots of hop-heavy ESBs and IPAs. The tasting room also offers a German-style Hefeweizen and bratwurst, as well as American-style brisket and barbecue chicken. It hosts live music every Friday at 5pm.

One family looked at their hop fields and realized a brewery would fit nicely right in the middle. **Bale Breaker Brewing Company** (1801 Birchfield Rd., Yakima, 509/424-4000, www.balebreaker.com, 3pm-8pm Tues.-Thurs., noon-9pm Fri.-Sat., noon-5pm Sun.), about five miles east of downtown, fittingly makes hop-forward beers in its big red brewery, and the cheery tasting room has a large patio, surrounded by hops. In summer you'll often find live music here and a food truck parked nearby.

Though the outside of this tasting room looks industrial, the woodsy interior of **Tieton Cider Works** (619 W J St., Yakima, 509/571-1430, http://tietonciderworks.com, 2pm-8pm Mon. and Wed.-Thurs., noon-9pm Fri.-Sat., noon-6pm Sun.), a couple of miles north of town, fits the rustic vibe of the drink. The cidery's bar has picnic tables outside and a few snacks for sale to balance the alcoholic apple beverages.

Attached to the Cowiche Canyon Kitchen, **Ice House Bar** (202 E Yakima Ave., Yakima, 509/457-2007, www.cowichecanyon.com, 11am-10pm Sun.-Mon., 11am-11pm Tues.-Wed., 11am-midnight Thurs.-Sat.) offers festive cocktails in downtown Yakima. Designed by high-end Seattle architects, the space is lean and angular, with wood beams that end abruptly and skinny pedestal lights. The drinks themselves are made from cold-pressed, house-made juices and other small-batch ingredients; many are cocktail classics with pedigree, like the corpse reviver and Bobby Burns drink. It's also the best place in town to get a good glass (or bottle) of wine.

Though it sounds like a gym, **Yakima Sports Center** (214 E Yakima Ave., Yakima, 509/453-4647, www.sportscenteryakima.com, 11am-midnight daily) is actually the city's fun dive bar. With a long line of taps, a giant neon sign outdoors and more neon signs indoors, and live music, it's a no-fuss hangout, dimly lit and with loud tunes. The food menu offers seared ahi poke and steamed clams, but this is really a place for big burgers topped with chili or a sandwich called The Great Rubenski, stacked high with house-made corned beef.

Festivals and Events

In a salute to an ingredient that put the region on the map, the **Fresh Hop Ale Festival** (Millennium Plaza, 22 S 3rd St., Yakima, 509/823-4174, http://freshhopalefestival.com, Sept., $45-85) is a beer party with pours from more than 50 breweries, plus beer

Cowiche Canyon Trail

competitions for brews that went from vine to stein in less than 24 hours. Children are not admitted.

During **Catch the Crush** (509/965-5201, http://wineyakimavalley.org, Oct., $30-35), wineries around the Yakima River throw parties over the course of a weekend celebrating the harvest season, including tastings and live music, a grape stomp, and fall release events.

FOOD

With its skinny fries and Dungeness crab Thai rice bowls, **Cowiche Canyon Kitchen** (202 E Yakima Ave., Yakima, 509/457-2007, www.cowichecanyon.com, 11am-9pm Sun.-Mon., 11am-10pm Tues.-Thurs., 11am-11pm Fri.-Sat., $15-37), along with its Ice House Bar, changed the whole tenor of downtown Yakima when it opened in 2014. The beautiful space, with windows that look out on two sides, polished wood everywhere, and an open kitchen, is casual but still feels special. Many dishes have gimmicks to make them stick out, like chicken cooked under a brick and made-to-order egg drop soup, but meals are classic and comfortable.

A former opera house was reborn as **Carousel Restaurant and Bistro** (25 N Front St. No. 6, Yakima, 509/248-6720, www.carouselfrenchcuisine.com, 4:30pm-9pm Tues.-Thurs., 4:30pm-10pm Fri.-Sat., 10am-2pm Sun., $29-38), a French bistro with fine dining. Classics like rabbit seared in wine béchamel and coq au vin are served in an intimate space with exposed brick and candlelight. Most dramatic is the cherries jubilee dessert, flambéed tableside.

With an informal vibe and large menu that pleases everyone from salad fans to hamburger lovers, **Second Street Grill** (28 N 2nd St., Yakima, 509/469-1486, www.secondstreetgrill.com, 11am-midnight Mon.-Sat., 10am-midnight Sun.) is a comfortable staple in downtown Yakima. While the interior is decorated in vintage photos, exposed brick, and black wood, the eatery's nowhere near as serious as that makes it sound. When the weather's nice, windows open onto the patio tables outside. Pizzas are a solid bet.

North Town Coffee House (32 N Front St., Yakima, 509/895-7600, www.northtowncoffee.com, 6am-midnight Mon.-Fri., 7am-midnight Sat.-Sun., $2-6) is located in a 1919 building that used to be Yakima's train depot. More spacious than most coffee joints, it's well suited as a gathering spot, with Stumptown coffee and comfy couches under tiled walls next to vintage-style globe lamps.

For years unassuming ★ **Los Hernandez Tamales** (3706 Main St., Union Gap, 509/457-6003, 11am-6pm Sun.-Fri., 10am-7pm Sat.), about four miles south of downtown Yakima, was a local's secret. In 2018, the James Beard Foundation noticed, giving the eatery its Classics award. Here you can eat a hot tamale or two before taking a half dozen or more home ($16-23 per dozen). In spring, asparagus tamales, made with sharp pepper jack cheese, are delightful. Likely the national recognition will make the treats even harder to come by—tamales often sell out during asparagus time—but somehow the staff always manages to find an extra package when you're really desperate. Los Hernandez is not just a Yakima treasure but a state treasure, too.

ACCOMMODATIONS

The **Rosedell Bed and Breakfast** (1811 W Yakima Ave., Yakima, 509/961-2964, www.rosedellbb.com, $125-160) sits on an acre and a half of land just west of downtown Yakima and looks like a castle, its stone neoclassical structure a strange contrast to most of the local architecture; the bathroom in one of the rooms is in a rounded turret. Four rooms are available, and beds are king-sized. Some rooms have private decks.

Hotel Maison (321 E Yakima Ave., Yakima, 509/571-1900, http://thehotelmaison.com, $199-209 rooms, suites $249) turned an old Mason's lodge downtown into a boutique hotel with 36 rooms, preserving many of the historical Freemason architectural elements and symbols. The earthy browns of the rooms' interiors can feel severe, but the large walk-in showers and sizable TVs feel as up to date as anything else for miles.

Halfway between the cities of Yakima and Ellensburg, along the winding Yakima River Canyon, ★ **Canyon River Ranch** (14700 Canyon Rd., Ellensburg, 509/933-2100, www.canyonriverranch.net, $299-349) is a fishing retreat in a beautiful setting. The canyon's steep brown hills rise behind a wood lodge-style hotel, the only one of its kind in the entire region. The 10 rooms are condo-style with multiple bedrooms and full kitchens, and the pool out back sits between trees, the lodge, and the roaring river. Canvas-wall tents are available in the summer ($59-79) but have no linens, just empty cots (it's camping, not glamping). With few dining options nearby, it's best to bring groceries. The fly shop on property also runs guided fly-fishing trips down the Yakima River.

Camping

With plenty of trees, **Yakima Sportsman State Park** (904 University Pkwy., Yakima, 509/575-2774, http://parks.state.wa.us/278/Yakima-Sportsman, $12-45) offers both some shade and good birding close to downtown. The 30 tent sites and 37 RV sites can be reserved.

INFORMATION AND SERVICES

Teapot Dome Service Station (117 1st Ave., Zillah, www.cityofzillah.us/teapot.html) serves as a basic info center; it's not manned, but there are attraction brochures and maps handy. Otherwise, try the **Yakima Valley Visitor Center** (101 N Fair Ave., Yakima, 509/573-3388, www.visityakima.com, 9am-4pm Mon.-Fri., may close earlier in winter) in the middle of town. Besides brochures there's a gift shop and sometimes even wine tastings.

GETTING THERE

Four daily flights go between Sea-Tac and **Yakima Air Terminal** (YKM, McAllister Field, 2406 W Washington Ave., 509/575-6149, http://flyykm.com). The flight takes about 45 minutes.

To reach Yakima from Seattle by car, head east on I-90 for about 105 miles, taking exit 110 in Ellensburg to get on I-82 East. Follow it for 30 miles south to reach Yakima. The drive takes about 2.5 hours without traffic or weather slowdowns over Snoqualmie Pass.

Tri-Cities

The three proximate cities comprising the Tri-Cities are Kennewick, Richland, and Pasco, and together they make up a surprisingly large urban area in south-central Washington, a sprawl of residential areas at the confluence of the Columbia, Snake, and Yakima Rivers. The towns themselves are quite indistinct, bleeding into one another; chain restaurants and wide multilane roads define the area. Of the three, Kennewick may be the best place to stay, with lots of riverside parkland and a central location and access to the freeways. It has a short two blocks of a historic downtown that many locals are trying to revitalize with more shops and restaurants, though it doesn't yet have a dynamic feel.

The big industry here comes from the Hanford Nuclear Reservation to the west, a giant piece of land that once held nuclear power stations and, before that, the plutonium reactor that made the Nagasaki bomb as part of the Manhattan Project in World War II. Now the region is generally devoted to cleanup—there's a lot of toxic waste to be dealt with—and science; some of the Hanford acres now house cutting-edge laboratories. And just to the west of the Tri-Cities, off I-82, the Benton City and

Tri-Cities

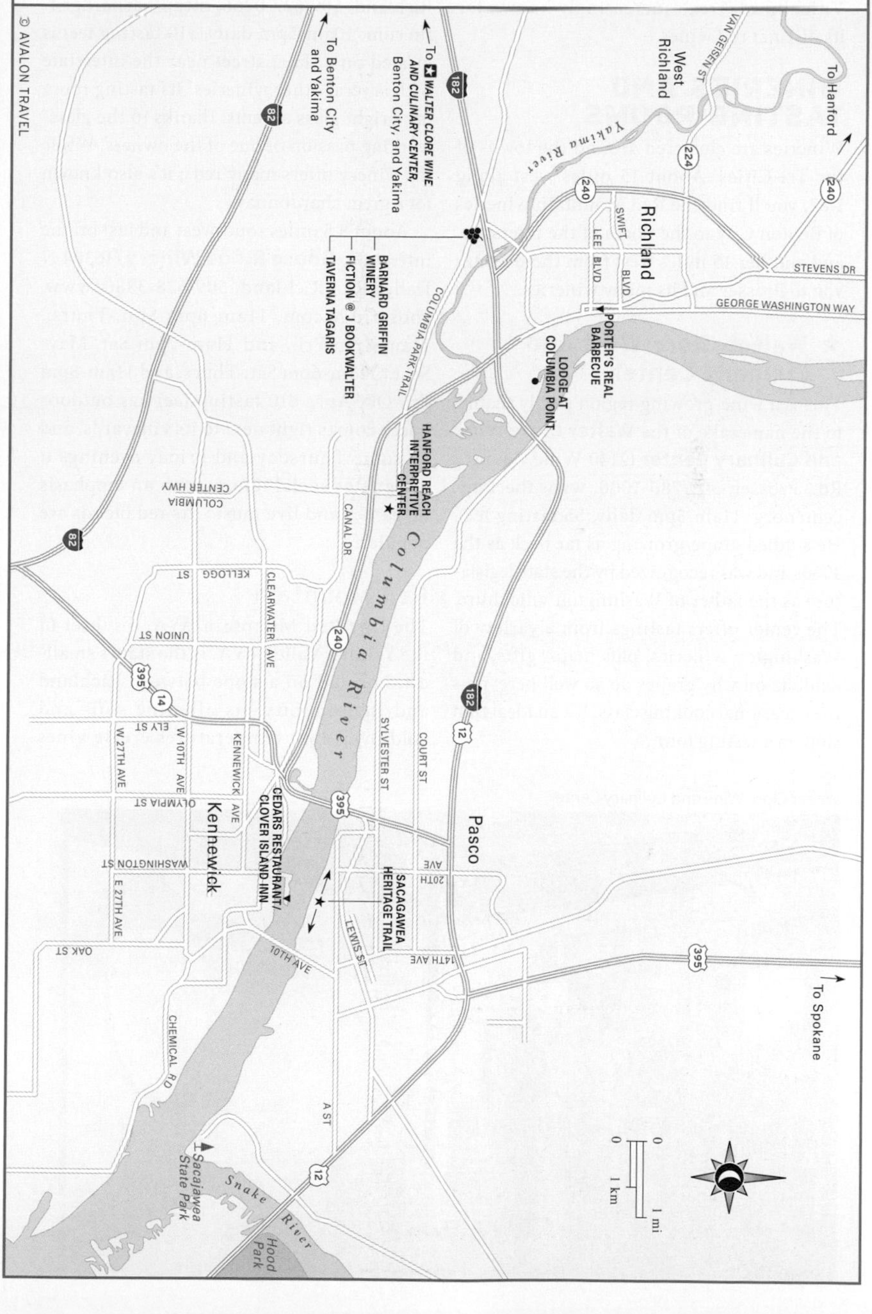
To Hanford
West Richland
VAN GEISEN ST
Yakima River
224
240
Richland
SWIFT BLVD
LEE BLVD
STEVENS DR
GEORGE WASHINGTON WAY
PORTER'S REAL BARBECUE
LODGE AT COLUMBIA POINT
182
To WALTER CLORE WINE AND CULINARY CENTER, Benton City, and Yakima
BARNARD GRIFFIN WINERY
FICTION @ J BOOKWALTER
TAVERNA TAGARIS
COLUMBIA PARK TRAIL
To Benton City and Yakima
82
HANFORD REACH INTERPRETIVE CENTER
COLUMBIA CENTER HWY
CANAL DR
Columbia River
KELLOGG ST
CLEARWATER AVE
UNION ST
395
14
12
ELY ST
W 10TH AVE
W 27TH AVE
KENNEWICK AVE
SYLVESTER ST
COURT ST
OLYMPIA ST
Kennewick
CEDARS RESTAURANT
CLOVER ISLAND INN
Pasco
WASHINGTON ST
20TH AVE
SACAGAWEA HERITAGE TRAIL
E 27TH AVE
LEWIS ST
OAK ST
10TH AVE
14TH AVE
To Spokane
CHEMICAL RD
A ST
Sacajawea State Park
Snake River
Hood Park
0 1 mi
0 1 km
© AVALON TRAVEL

Prosser areas are a burgeoning wine region thanks to the Red Mountain AVA (American Viticultural Area), increasingly known for its distinct red wines.

WINERIES AND TASTING ROOMS

Wineries are clustered around the towns of the Tri-Cities. About 15 miles west along I-82, you'll find the Red Mountain wineries of Benton City to the north of the interstate, and another 15 miles west from there brings you to Prosser and its many wineries.

★ Walter Clore Wine and Culinary Center

This is a wine-growing region partly thanks to the namesake of the **Walter Clore Wine and Culinary Center** (2140 Wine Country Rd., Prosser, 509/786-1000, www.theclore-center.org, 11am-5pm daily, $5 tasting fee). He studied grape-growing as far back as the 1930s and was recognized by the state legislature as the father of Washington viticulture. The center offers tastings from a variety of Washington wineries, plus maps, gifts, and exhibits on why grapes do so well here, plus the occasional cooking class. It's an ideal first stop on a tasting tour.

Richland

Barnard Griffin Winery (878 Tulip Ln., Richland, 509/627-0266, http://barnardgriffin.com, 10am-5pm daily, $10 tasting fee) is located on a short street near the interstate with several other wineries. Its tasting room has bright glass accents, thanks to the glass-working passion of one of the owners. While the winery offers many reds, it's also known for a great chardonnay.

About 8.5 miles southwest and just off the interstate, **Goose Ridge Winery** (16304 N Dallas Rd., Richland, 509/628-3880, www.gooseridge.com, 11am-6pm Sun.-Thurs., 11am-8pm Fri., and 11am-7pm Sat. May-Sept., 11am-6pm Sat.-Thurs. and 11am-8pm Fri. Oct-Apr., $10 tasting fee) has outdoor bocce courts right next to its vineyards, and on some Thursday and Friday evenings it designates social hours, with an emphasis on games and live music. Its red blends are popular.

Red Mountain

The tiny Red Mountain AVA, a subset of the Yakima Valley AVA, is the state's smallest. Located on a slope between Richland and Benton City, its alkaline soils and cold overnight temperatures create vines

Walter Clore Wine and Culinary Center

that produce excellent grapes. **Col Solare Winery** (50207 Antinori Rd., Benton City, 509/588-6806, www.colsolare.com, 11am-5pm Wed.-Sun., tours 2pm Sun., $17 tasting fee) bridges Northwest and European winemaking traditions in a partnership between the state's biggest winery, Chateau Ste. Michelle, and an Italian winemaker to create well-regarded wines like their cabernet sauvignon. The low-slung winery, painted an earthy yellow, almost disappears into the landscape.

Prosser

14 Hands Winery (660 Frontier Rd., Prosser, 509/786-5514, www.14hands.com, 10am-5pm daily, $10 tasting fee) takes its name from the way equine heights are measured (by hand widths)—the region used to be full of wild horses. The winery's tasting room has wood siding on every surface and giant windows that look out on the nearby Horse Heaven Hills. Though its cheaper wines are available around the state, here 14 Hands serves estate wines with more complex blends and memorable flavors.

Alexandria Nicole Cellars (2880 Lee Rd., Ste. D, Prosser, 509/786-3497, www.alexandrianicolecellars.com, 11am-5pm Mon.-Sat., noon-5pm Sun., $10-20 tasting fee) offers a regular and reserve tasting. The latter might include one of its award winners, like the lesser known marsanne.

SIGHTS

Sacajawea State Park

The mighty Columbia River defines the Tri-Cities, cutting between the separate towns and providing miles of waterfront in the otherwise arid region. **Sacajawea State Park** (2503 Sacajawea Park Rd., Pasco, 509/545-2361, http://parks.state.wa.us, 8am-dusk daily Apr.-Oct., $5 parking) is a great place to encounter the river. The park is named for the Native American woman who traveled this area on the Lewis and Clark Expedition more than 200 years go; it sits where the Snake and Columbia Rivers meet—and where the expedition once paused. An interpretive center explains how the native tribes in the area lived and how drastically the rivers changed once they were dammed to create electricity. Also on the grounds is *Story Circles*, an outdoor installation by renowned artist Maya Lin focused on the area's natural and human history. There is also a boat launch and small swimming area in the park.

14 Hands Winery

Hanford Reach Interpretive Center

The Hanford Reach, a 50-mile section of the Columbia River, and Hanford Nuclear Reservation, the abutting area of more than 500 square miles and former site of a nuclear production complex, are so massive that it takes the **Hanford Reach Interpretive Center** (1943 Columbia Park Trail, Richland, 509/943-4100, www.visitthereach.org, 10am-4:30pm Tues.-Sat. and noon-4:30pm Sun. June-Aug., 10am-4:30pm Tues.-Sat. Sept.-May, $10 adults, $6 students and seniors, free for children under 6), also known as the REACH, to put the whole region in perspective. Here you'll find four permanent exhibits, including one covering the Manhattan Project and the role the Hanford Site, as the nuclear reservation is also called, played in it—sobering, if a bit more focused on the scientific advances of the plutonium bomb's creation than the effect it had when dropped on Japan—as well as displays on the natural and human history of the area, and an outdoor gallery including vintage vehicles.

SPORTS AND RECREATION

Biking

The largely flat Tri-Cities area is perfect for bicycling. The **Sacagawea Heritage Trail** is a 23-mile paved bike- and pedestrian-only path that loops around both sides of the Columbia River. The southern trailhead is at **Sacajawea State Park** (2503 Sacajawea Park Rd., Pasco, 509/545-2361, http://parks.state.wa.us, $5 parking), but you can access it along the riverfront in Pasco, Richland, or Kennewick.

Don't have wheels? **Greenie's** (701 George Washington Way, Richland, 509/946-3787, www.greenielife.com, 10am-6pm Mon.-Sat., rentals $20-70) offers rentals of road and mountain bikes, plus tandems and trailers. It's not directly on the heritage trail, but staff can direct you to it.

ENTERTAINMENT AND EVENTS

If you've never heard of hydroplane races, you will if you're in town when they take to the Columbia waters—they're boats that speed like NASCAR cars and they are loud. The annual **Tri-City Water Follies** (5111 Columbia Park Trail, Kennewick, 509/783-4675, http://waterfollies.com, July, admission $15-25 adults, $5-10 children 6-12, free for children under 6, $5-10 parking, $10 pit access) is a three-day festival, the main focus of which is the Columbia Cup Race, a hydroplane race on the river that has been held for more than half a century. There are multiple viewing spots for the races, including the heats and qualifiers, not to mention practice runs, and it's an all-day affair watching 30-foot boats getting up to 200 miles per hour. The hydroplane circuit has fierce competition, but it's charming that a coveted parking spot under a specific tree for the following year is one of the prizes—the biggest star in the sport used to claim the spot every year, and it's now awarded in his honor.

Spend a Saturday evening at the **Tri-Cities Wine Festival** (Three Rivers Convention Center, 7016 W Grandridge Blvd., Kennewick, 509/737-3700, www.tricitieswinesociety.com, Nov., $60-65) where up to 100 wineries pour about 400 wines. Admission includes all tastings plus food bites.

FOOD

On the busiest block in Richland—this row has some of the best dining around—you'll find **Fiction @ J Bookwalter** (894 Tulip Ln., Richland, 509/627-5000, www.jbookwalterfiction.com, noon-9pm Mon.-Thurs., noon-10pm Fri.-Sat., 10am-8pm Sun., $17-35). Here you'll find a $10 half-sandwich-and-soup lunch special (the pastrami and roast pork are substantial) and great salads at dinner, including one with Columbia River steelhead. Pizzas are topped with fresh ingredients and ideal for eating on the outdoor patio while the sun is setting. Another foodie destination on Tulip Lane is **Taverna Tagaris** (844 Tulip Ln.,

Richland, 509/628-0020, www.tagariswines.com, 11am-9pm Mon.-Sat., 11am-3pm Sun.). It focuses on fresh produce and local meats. It also has a tapas menu, and flatbread is made in-house daily, then topped with seasonal ingredients. The interior is sleek and sophisticated, with dark wood tables and a deep red ceiling. Both restaurants are connected to wineries, but shine for their cuisine.

At **Porter's Real Barbecue** (705 The Parkway, Richland, 509/942-9590, 11am-7pm Mon.-Sat., $8-15) the counter dishes brisket, pulled pork, and a hogzilla sandwich made of pork, sausage, and bacon—at least until it's gone. Dessert is banana pudding or molasses bars. What started as a food truck serving Southern-style meat has grown into a busy restaurant where bottles of barbecue sauce and paper towel rolls crowd the small tables, and sides are still served in Styrofoam.

Located out on an island in the river accessible by car, near Port of Kennewick industrial areas, **Cedars Restaurant** (355 N Clover Island Dr., Kennewick, 509/582-2143, www.cedarskennewick.com, 4pm-10pm daily, $29-46) is a classic; it's been around since the 1970s. Think seafood fettucine and Chicken Oscar, and any cut of steak you can imagine, with a baked potato on the side. Lovely river views and soaring wood beams above give the whole place a solid, comfortable feel.

ACCOMMODATIONS

Under $150

Though the **Clover Island Inn** (435 N Clover Island Dr., Kennewick, 509/586-0541, http://cloverislandinn.com, $84-104 rooms, $199-349 suites) can feel a bit dated, it is so in a charming way. The property sits on a car-accessible island in the river, along with the Cedars Restaurant, and has a swimming pool overlooking the water and soaring bridge that crosses the Columbia. With 150 rooms it's a sizable property, and linen and furniture updates do what they can to make the blocky, mid-century-style building feel fresh. There's a free hot breakfast and free bike rentals for use on the Sacajawea Heritage Trail that passes nearby.

$150-250

A series of waterfront hotels are the nicest lodgings in the Tri-Cities, and the **Lodge at Columbia Point** (530 Columbia Point Dr., Richland, 509/713-7423, http://lodgeatcolumbiapoint.com, $199-329) is perhaps the most appealing thanks to modern architecture, in-room fireplaces, and an outdoor but covered pool and patio with views of the river. Some bathrooms have walk-in showers, and the public spaces use exposed wood beams to good effect. Some of the 82 rooms have elegant patios ideal for sipping wine, and a shared fire pit works for everyone else.

Over $250

If you really want to stay where the wine is, the Desert Wind Winery's **Inn at Desert Wind** (2258 Wine Country Rd., Prosser, 509/786-7277, $295), delivers, though strangely it's located right next to the interstate, about 30 miles west of the Tri-Cities in Prosser. Four guest rooms in the adobe winery building manage to feel world's away thanks to fireplaces, balconies, and jetted tubs. On-site spa rooms don't hurt either. Each room is named for a member of the Lewis and Clark party.

Camping

Located on the south end of the Tri-Cities next to the freeway, **Columbia Sun RV Resort** (103907 Wiser Pkwy., Kennewick, 509/420-4880, http://columbiasunrvresort.com, $47-59) has 145 total sites, with plenty for large RVs. With no trees, it's an open, exposed site, but all spots have full hookups and the property boasts a swimming pool, dog park, fitness center, game room, and sports equipment.

INFORMATION AND SERVICES

Local information can be found at the **Hanford Reach Interpretive Center** (1943 Columbia Park Trail, Richland, 509/943-4100, www.visitthereach.org, 10am-4:30pm Tues.-Sat. and noon-4:30pm Sun. June-Aug., 10am-4:30pm Tues.-Sat. Sept.-May). The **Walter Clore Wine and Culinary Center** (2140 Wine Country Rd., Prosser, 509/786-1000, www.theclorecenter.org, 11am-5pm daily) serves as home base for wine tourism. There's also the **Visit Tri-Cities Center** (7130 W Grandridge Blvd., Ste. B, Kennewick, www.visittri-cities.com, 8am-5pm daily June-Aug., 8am-5pm Mon.-Fri. Sept.-May).

GETTING THERE

From Seattle, the Tri-Cities are about 205 miles southeast, a 3.25-hour drive. To reach the Tri-Cities from Seattle, head east on I-90 for 135 miles to just past where it crosses the Columbia River. Take exit 137 to get on Highway 26 East briefly; after about a mile, stay right to get onto Highway 243. Follow this south and then east for 28 miles, then stay right for Highway 24 and cross the Columbia River again. Continue on Highway 24 for 5.5 miles; it'll become Highway 240 East, which you'll follow for 29 miles southeast, passing the broad expanse of the Hanford Reach to your left. Turn right to stay on Highway 240 and continue into Richland, the first of the three towns you'll encounter of the Tri-Cities when heading here from the west.

Portland

Look for ★ to find recommended sights, activities, dining, and lodging.

Highlights

★ **Portland Farmers Market:** Get overwhelmed by endless fresh produce, high-quality crafts, and ready-to-eat meals (page 253).

★ **Portland Art Museum:** This expansive yet accessible art collection emphasizes Native American and Northwest art (page 256).

★ **Powell's City of Books:** Portland's renowned bookstore fills a city block with more than a million volumes of new and used books (page 258).

★ **Pittock Mansion:** One of the city's best views comes from a stately old home with one very weird and wondrous shower (page 259).

★ **International Rose Test Garden:** The acres of roses astound even those without green thumbs. The grassy amphitheater is an ideal resting spot after a busy day on Portland streets (page 261).

★ **Oregon Museum of Science and Industry:** This hands-on science museum and its submarine aren't just for kids, though you'll feel like one by the end of a day here (page 262).

★ **Brewpubs and Taprooms:** Beer is the signature quaff of Portland, arguably the country's capital of craft brewing (page 267).

★ **Forest Park:** More than 80 miles of trails await in one of the largest city forests in the country (page 278).

★ **Biking:** Human-powered propulsion is encouraged and celebrated in this city where two-wheeled activity is as popular with locals as visitors (page 280).

★ **Timberline Lodge:** One of America's great mountain lodges offers a slice of scary-movie history and access to a towering volcanic mountain (page 310).

It's easy to be charmed by Portland's relaxed and idiosyncratic vibe, with its elaborate doughnuts, waterfront parks, endless bike lanes, and ecofriendly practices.

Portland redefines what a city in America can look like with its devotion to all things local and artisanal.

Downtown is crowded with food carts, independent boutiques and restaurants, and live music venues, and the small blocks make the streets highly walkable. Driving alternatives—from streetcars to bicycles to aerial tram—can be found everywhere.

Other Portland neighborhoods are equally welcoming. Out on Alberta, Belmont, Hawthorne, or Division streets, you'll find more of the indie eateries, bars, and stores that give the city its reputation for great finds. Locals are friendly and, more often than not, transplants themselves—visitors who came to Portland, loved the way of life here, and never left.

The home of Nike and Intel's biggest campus also offers a wealth of nature. Located on the Willamette River, it hosts Forest Park, one of the largest urban forests in the country, as well as cinder cone volcanoes. And just a short drive east, the Columbia River Gorge and Mount Hood offer a dizzying array of ways to play outdoors.

The city doesn't want for nicknames: Rose City, Stumptown, Portlandia (the city where "hipsters go to retire"). Sure, everyone teases the city for its earnest, hipster weirdness—but to tease Portland is to love it.

PLANNING YOUR TIME

Though a smaller city than Seattle, Portland's excellent culture, shopping, and dining beg for at least two days, hopefully more. It's an easily walkable city, and public transportation is strong. Navigating Portland isn't difficult, even though there seem to be bridges everywhere. The Willamette River separates the east from the west side, and Burnside Street divides the city into its south and north sides, while North Williams Avenue separates north from northeast Portland. While the west side of the river holds the city's compact downtown and northwest neighborhoods like the Pearl District, neighborhoods are more dispersed on the east side, where businesses tend to be

Previous: Columbia River Gorge; iconic Portland sign. **Above:** Arlene Schnitzer Concert Hall.

Portland

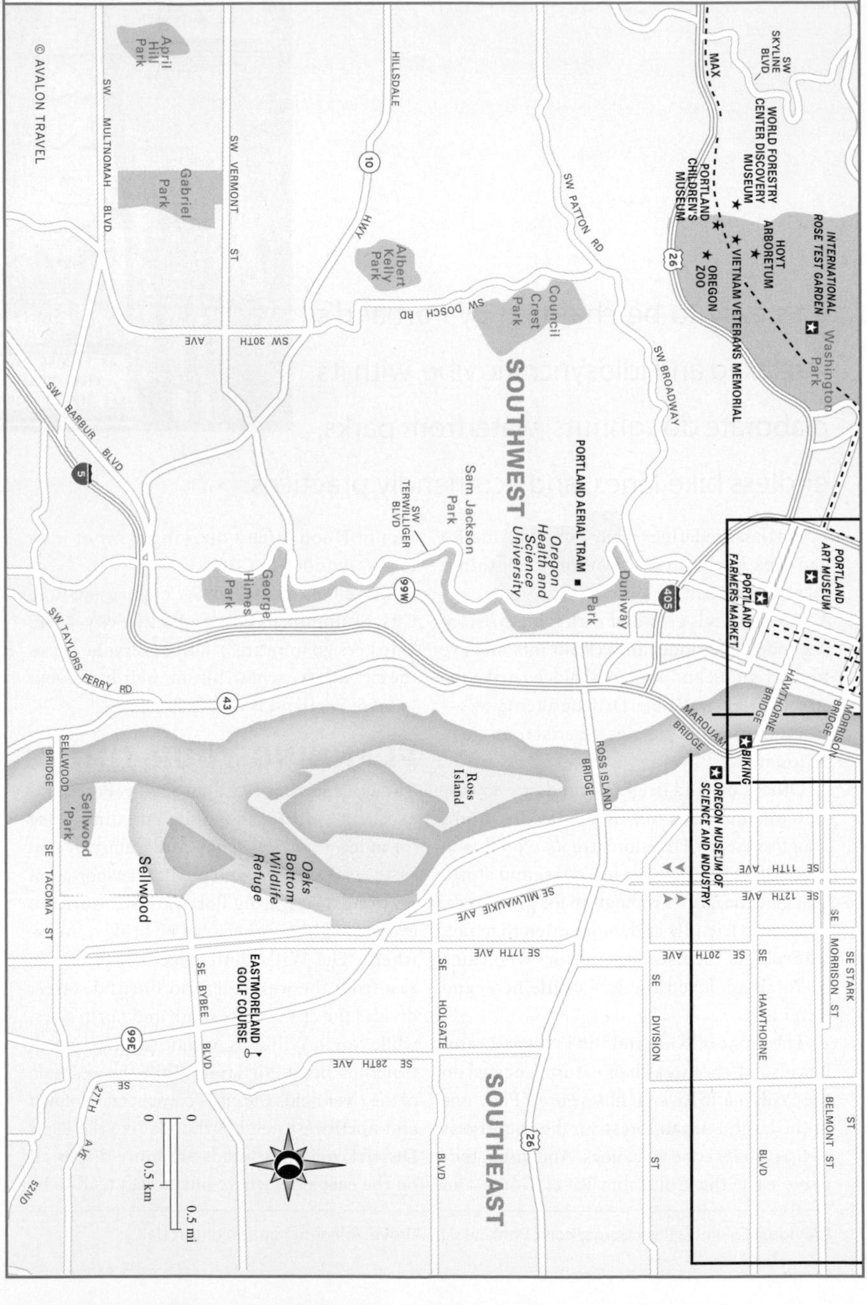

© AVALON TRAVEL
April Hill Park
Gabriel Park
SW MULTNOMAH BLVD
SW VERMONT ST
HILLSDALE
10
HWY
Albert Kelly Park
SW PATTON RD
26
SW DOSCH RD
Council Crest Park
SW 30TH AVE
SW BROADWAY
SOUTHWEST
SW BARBUR BLVD
5
PORTLAND AERIAL TRAM
Oregon Health and Science University
Sam Jackson Park
SW TERWILLIGER BLVD
George Himes Park
99W
Duniway Park
405
SW TAYLORS FERRY RD
43
SW SKYLINE BLVD
MAX
WORLD FORESTRY CENTER DISCOVERY MUSEUM
PORTLAND CHILDREN'S MUSEUM
INTERNATIONAL ROSE TEST GARDEN
HOYT ARBORETUM
VIETNAM VETERANS MEMORIAL
OREGON ZOO
Washington Park
PORTLAND ART MUSEUM
PORTLAND FARMERS MARKET
HAWTHORNE BRIDGE
MORRISON BRIDGE
MARQUAM BRIDGE
BIKING
OREGON MUSEUM OF SCIENCE AND INDUSTRY
ROSS ISLAND BRIDGE
Ross Island
Oaks Bottom Wildlife Refuge
SELLWOOD BRIDGE
Sellwood Park
Sellwood
SE TACOMA ST
SE 11TH AVE
SE 12TH AVE
SE MILWAUKIE AVE
SE 17TH AVE
SE 20TH AVE
SE MORRISON ST
SE STARK
SE HAWTHORNE BLVD
SE DIVISION ST
SE HOLGATE BLVD
SE BYBEE BLVD
EASTMORELAND GOLF COURSE
99E
SE 28TH AVE
SE 27TH AVE
52ND
SOUTHEAST
BELMONT ST
26
0
0.5 mi
0
0.5 km

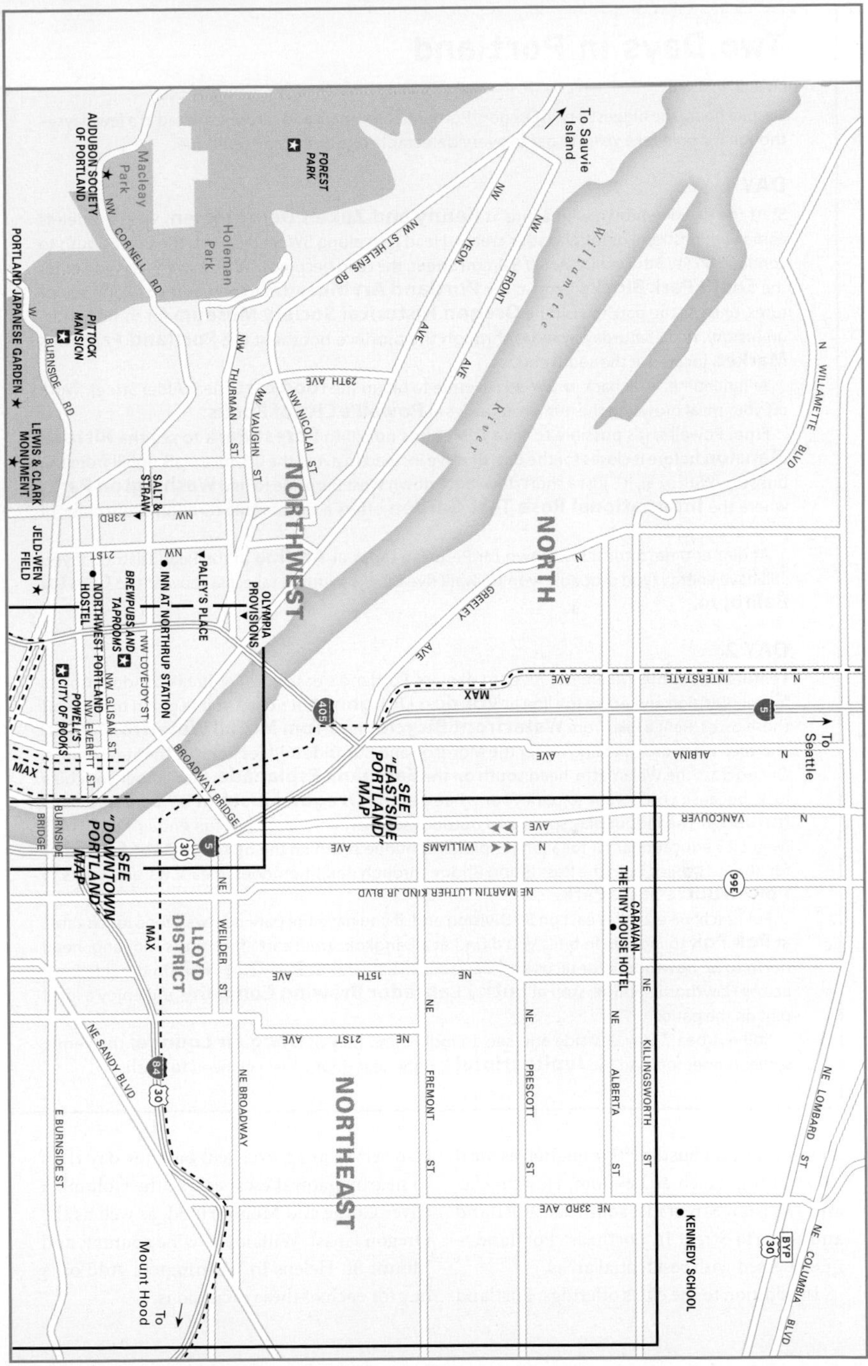
To Sauvie Island
FOREST PARK
AUDUBON SOCIETY OF PORTLAND
Macleay Park
NW CORNELL RD
Holeman Park
NW ST HELENS RD
NW YEON AVE
NW FRONT AVE
Willamette River
PITTOCK MANSION
W BURNSIDE RD
PORTLAND JAPANESE GARDEN
LEWIS & CLARK MONUMENT
NW THURMAN ST
NW VAUGHN ST
NW NICOLAI ST
29TH AVE
NORTHWEST
SALT & STRAW
NW 23RD
21ST
JELD-WEN FIELD
NORTHWEST PORTLAND HOSTEL
NW 21ST
INN AT NORTHRUP STATION
PALEY'S PLACE
OLYMPIA PROVISIONS
BREWPUBS AND TAPROOMS
NW NORTHRUP ST
NW LOVEJOY ST
POWELL'S CITY OF BOOKS
NW GLISAN ST
NW EVERETT ST
MAX
BURNSIDE BRIDGE
BROADWAY BRIDGE
SEE "DOWNTOWN PORTLAND" MAP
NORTH
N GREELEY AVE
N WILLAMETTE BLVD
N INTERSTATE AVE
MAX
405
5
To Seattle
N ALBINA AVE
SEE "EASTSIDE PORTLAND" MAP
N VANCOUVER AVE
N WILLIAMS AVE
5
30
99E
NE MARTIN LUTHER KING JR BLVD
CARAVAN-THE TINY HOUSE HOTEL
LLOYD DISTRICT
NE WEIDLER ST
MAX
NE 15TH AVE
NE 21ST AVE
NE KILLINGSWORTH ST
NE ALBERTA ST
NE PRESCOTT ST
NE FREMONT ST
NE BROADWAY
NORTHEAST
NE SANDY BLVD
84
30
E BURNSIDE ST
NE 33RD AVE
KENNEDY SCHOOL
NE LOMBARD ST
BYP 30
NE COLUMBIA BLVD
To Mount Hood

Two Days in Portland

Despite being the biggest city in Oregon, Portland is compact and can be explored in a few days—though it would take years to get to every delectable bite, brew, and boutique.

DAY 1

Start the day downtown with a bite at **Kenny and Zuke's Delicatessen,** where omelets come with pastrami or lox and sour cream. Head east along SW Stark Street, then turn south to continue on SW 9th Avenue. At SW Salmon Street, the road becomes SW Park Avenue as you enter the **South Park Blocks.** Stop at the **Portland Art Museum** to peruse the striking sculptures, or cross the park to visit the **Oregon Historical Society Museum** for some hands-on history. If it's Saturday, wander through the produce booths at the **Portland Farmers Market,** located at the south end.

At lunchtime, walk back up SW 9th Avenue to hit up the **food carts** near Alder Street. Work off your meal browsing the numerous aisles at **Powell's City of Books.**

From Powell's, it's possible to take TriMet bus no. 20 to **Forest Park** to see the **Pittock Mansion** before it closes for the day, or drive instead to avoid the 0.5-mile walk uphill from the bus stop. With a car, it's just a short drive back down West Burnside to find **Washington Park,** where the **International Rose Test Garden** offers a free ramble through every color of petal imaginable.

At dinner time, return downtown for Peruvian tapas at **Andina** in the Pearl District. If you still have energy (you probably won't!), walk five blocks south to take in a show at the **Crystal Ballroom.**

DAY 2

Venture across the Willamette River to explore Portland's east side. For breakfast downtown, forget nutrition and brave the line at **Voodoo Doughnut;** it's okay, you're going to work off those carbs. Rent a bike from **Waterfront Bicycles** near **Tom McCall Waterfront Park,** and then ride north, passing under the Morrison and Burnside Bridges, to cross the Steel Bridge. Once across the Willamette, head south on the **Eastbank Esplanade.** Remember your bike lock, because you'll want to park your wheels at the **Oregon Museum of Science and Industry.** The indoor play space and outdoor submarine tour are just fun enough that you'll forget it's educational. Or for a longer pedal, continue south on the **Springwater Corridor** for about 12 miles from the Ross Island Bridge through neighborhoods, meadows, and parks to **Powell Butte State Park.**

For lunch, bike 2 miles east on SE Division and, if you have the patience, wait for a lunch table at **Pok Pok** to indulge in bites you'd find at a Bangkok street cart. If the line's too long, head north to SE Hawthorne for tacos and delicious margaritas at **Por Que No?** On the ride back across Hawthorne Bridge, stop at **Lucky Labrador Brewing Company** and enjoy a local pint on the patio.

Still not beat? Stay eastside and see an indie band play at **Doug Fir Lounge;** the venue serves dinner too, and the **Jupiter Hotel** is right next door when you need to crash.

concentrated on bustling thoroughfares ideal for strolling—such as Belmont, Hawthorne, and Division Streets in southeast Portland and Alberta Street in northeast Portland—interspersed with residential areas.

In addition to the city's offerings, Portland also serves as an excellent base for day trips to nearby natural escapes like the Columbia River Gorge and Mount Hood, as well as the Oregon Coast, Willamette wine country, and Mount St. Helens in Washington. Add on a day for each of these excursions.

Sights

The people-watching on the streets of Portland is almost enough entertainment for a weekend trip—you'll see tattoos, outlandish outfits, and perhaps a double-decker unicycle if you hang outside Powell's long enough. But for all its street theater, the city doesn't skimp on organized, institutionalized culture. Its museums are robust, and its gardens show off Portland's international sides, right down to its forest of roses.

DOWNTOWN

The city's densest area of activity is located south of West Burnside Street, a major thoroughfare that nevertheless is lined with restaurants and small shops. One-way streets are the norm, with many of the area's tiny blocks dedicated to parks (or food trucks). Park once and wander on foot. It's much easier to enjoy downtown's quaint bustle when you're not worried about driving the wrong way.

South Park Blocks

The **South Park Blocks** (SW Park Ave. from Salmon St. to Jackson St., www.portlandoregon.gov) is a long promenade with sculptures, lampposts, trees, and small gardens that leads right through downtown. Major attractions like the Portland Art Museum and the Oregon Historical Society Museum now face the park, and the large Portland Farmers Market is held at the south end, close to Portland State University. The park is 12 blocks long, and artwork includes a peace memorial made of granite pillars and a bronze statue of Theodore Roosevelt on horseback, decked out as he was when he charged San Juan Hill. The Portland Parks department has a walking tour of the blocks on their website (www.portlandoregon.gov), along with a map of all the trees.

★ Portland Farmers Market

Forget what you think you know about farmers markets. The **Portland Farmers Market** (SW Park Ave. and SW Montgomery St., 503/241-0032, www.portlandfarmersmarket.org, 8:30am-2pm Sat. Mar.-Oct., 9am-2pm Sat. Nov.-Dec.) is bigger, greener, and busier than what you've experienced before. Blocks

Portland Farmers Market

Downtown Portland

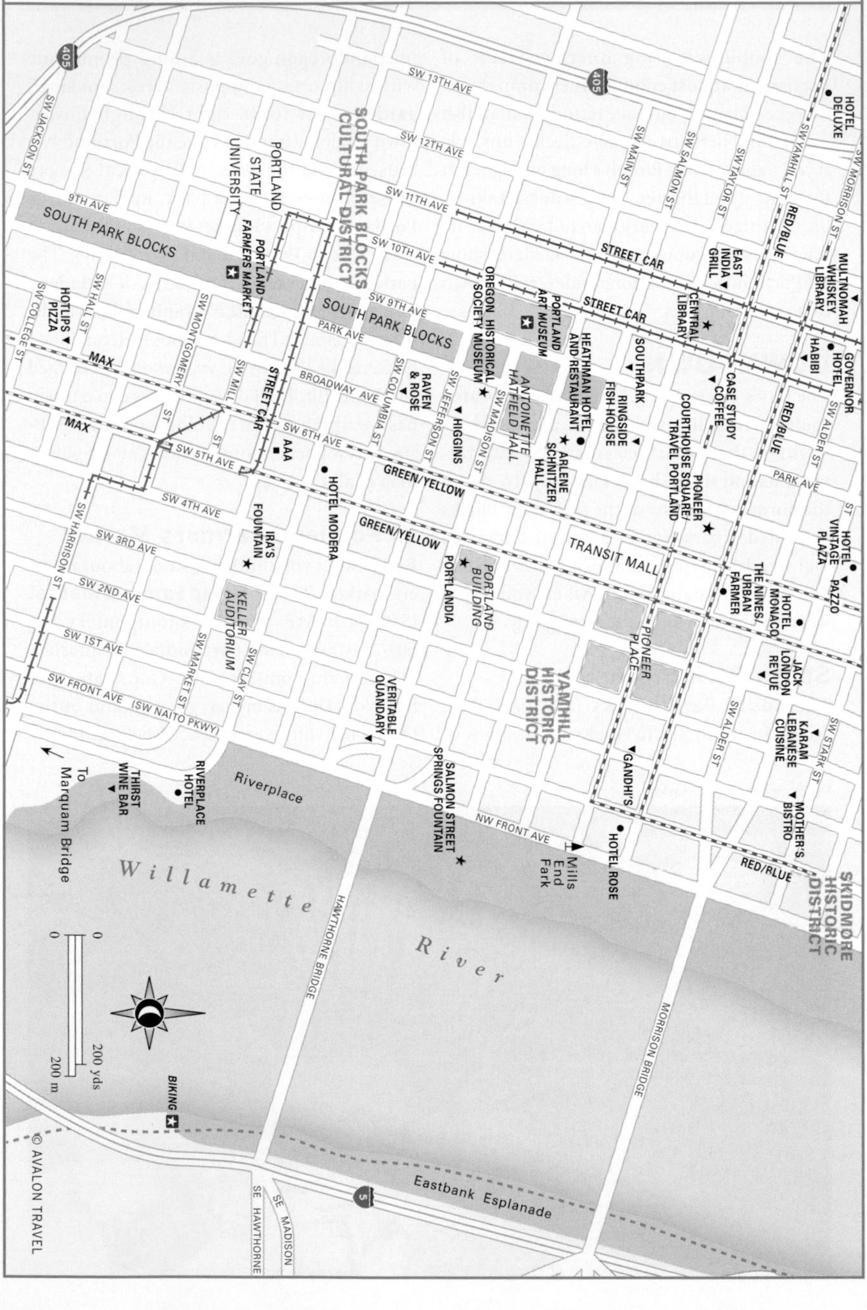

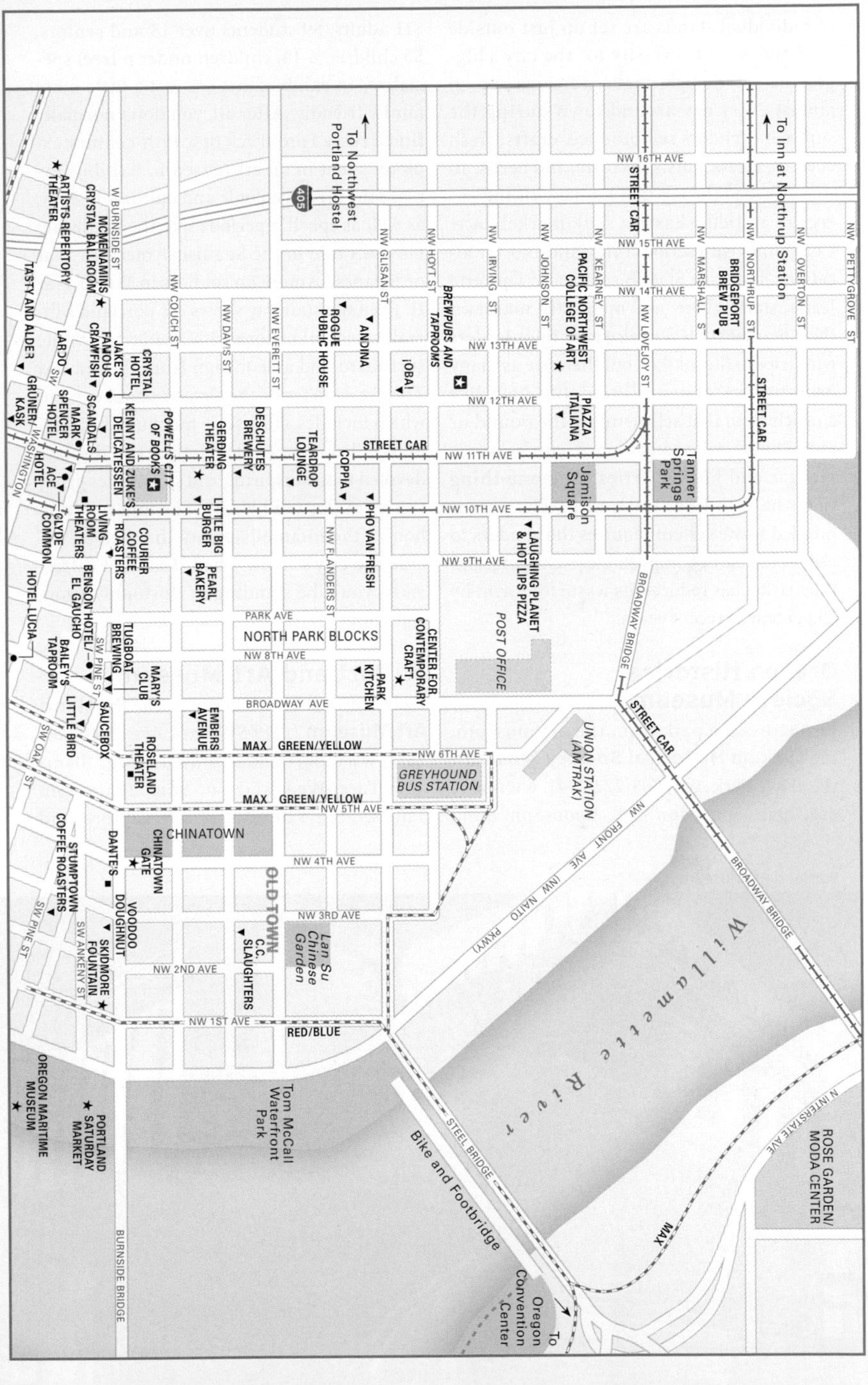
To Inn at Northrup Station
To Northwest Portland Hostel
405
NW 16TH AVE
NW 15TH AVE
NW 14TH AVE
NW 13TH AVE
NW 12TH AVE
NW 11TH AVE
NW 10TH AVE
NW 9TH AVE
PARK AVE
NW 8TH AVE
BROADWAY AVE
NW 6TH AVE
NW 5TH AVE
NW 4TH AVE
NW 3RD AVE
NW 2ND AVE
NW 1ST AVE
NW PETTYGROVE ST
NW OVERTON ST
NW NORTHRUP ST
NW MARSHALL ST
NW LOVEJOY ST
NW KEARNEY ST
NW JOHNSON ST
NW IRVING ST
NW HOYT ST
NW GLISAN ST
NW FLANDERS ST
NW EVERETT ST
NW DAVIS ST
NW COUCH ST
W BURNSIDE ST
SW WASHINGTON
SW PINE ST
SW OAK ST
SW ANKENY ST
STREET CAR
MAX GREEN/YELLOW
RED/BLUE
MAX
BRIDGEPORT BREW PUB
PACIFIC NORTHWEST COLLEGE OF ART
PIAZZA ITALIANA
Tanner Springs Park
Jamison Square
BREWPUBS AND TAPROOMS
¡OBA!
ANDINA
ROGUE PUBLIC HOUSE
TEARDROP LOUNGE
COPPIA
PHO VAN FRESH
LAUGHING PLANET & HOT LIPS PIZZA
DESCHUTES BREWERY
GERDING THEATER
POWELL'S CITY OF BOOKS
CRYSTAL HOTEL
KENNY AND ZUKE'S DELICATESSEN
LITTLE BIG BURGER
COURIER COFFEE ROASTERS
PEARL BAKERY
JAKE'S FAMOUS CRAWFISH
SCANDALS
MCMENAMINS CRYSTAL BALLROOM
ARTISTS REPERTORY THEATER
LARDO
MARK SPENCER HOTEL
TASTY AND ALDER
GRÜNER
KASK
ACE HOTEL
CLYDE COMMON
LIVING ROOM THEATERS
BENSON HOTEL/EL GAUCHO
HOTEL LUCIA
BAILEY'S TAPROOM
TUGBOAT BREWING
MARY'S CLUB
SAUCEBOX
LITTLE BIRD
NORTH PARK BLOCKS
CENTER FOR CONTEMPORARY CRAFT
PARK KITCHEN
POST OFFICE
EMBERS AVENUE
ROSELAND THEATER
GREYHOUND BUS STATION
UNION STATION (AMTRAK)
CHINATOWN
CHINATOWN GATE
DANTE'S
STUMPTOWN COFFEE ROASTERS
VOODOO DOUGHNUT
SKIDMORE FOUNTAIN
OLD TOWN
C.C. SLAUGHTERS
Lan Su Chinese Garden
NW FRONT AVE (NW NAITO PKWY)
BROADWAY BRIDGE
Willamette River
STEEL BRIDGE
Bike and Footbridge
Tom McCall Waterfront Park
PORTLAND SATURDAY MARKET
OREGON MARITIME MUSEUM
BURNSIDE BRIDGE
N INTERSTATE AVE
ROSE GARDEN/MODA CENTER
To Oregon Convention Center

of individual stands are set up just outside Portland State University for the city's biggest market, though smaller versions pop up almost every day around town during the summer. Vendors sell produce, crafts, fresh cheeses, meats, nuts, chocolate, and herbs, all in a crowded throng that hums with the energy of a Middle Eastern souk marketplace. Companies with serious brick-and-mortar locations, like Pine State Biscuits and Lauretta Jean's, started here, and many still maintain their market stalls. Locals stock their larders with trips to the market, but there are as many opportunities for immediate gratification, like a peach farm that sells fruit by the pound or individually grilled and topped with balsamic vinegar and huckleberries. The one thing that's hard to find: trash cans. The green-minded waste system requires the venders to use recyclable or compostable packaging, and the market has reduced its waste footprint by 75 percent in recent years.

Oregon Historical Society Museum

Just across the park from the art museum, the **Oregon Historical Society Museum** (1200 SW Park Ave., 503/222-1741, www.ohs.org, 10am-5pm Mon.-Sat., noon-5pm Sun., $11 adults, $9 students over 18 and seniors, $5 children 6-18, children under 6 free) specializes in exhibits that are just a little more family friendly. After all, you don't normally find a rusty Ford truck or a 19th-century explorer's tent in an art museum. Exhibits explore the area's geologic and cultural history, as well as specific periods like the battleship *Oregon*'s role in the Spanish-American War or Japanese American soldiers in World War II. Even the stairway shows off Portland's literally colorful history with a pink-and-white surfboard and a neon sign from the old Fox Theatre. Don't miss the *Oregon Voices* exhibit, which includes a full-scale mockup of a MAX light rail car and endless interactive displays devoted to the inspiring and sometimes gritty stories of Portland locals. The museum also houses the infamous penny that helped decide the city's name—had it landed differently, you'd be standing in Boston, Oregon, right now.

★ Portland Art Museum

Founded in the 19th century, the **Portland Art Museum** (1219 SW Park Ave., 503/226-2811, www.portlandartmuseum.org, 10am-5pm Tues.-Wed. and Sat.-Sun., 10am-8pm Thurs.-Fri., $20 adults, $17 seniors and

Portland Art Museum

college students, children under 17 free) claims to be the oldest museum in the Pacific Northwest—one of the oldest in the country even. Although it has traveling exhibits, like a roomful of bicycles hung like sculptures or art from the Louvre, it dedicates 90 percent of its gallery space to the permanent collection. That includes a Vincent van Gogh painting and more than 5,000 prehistoric and historical Native American objects. The complex includes a modern and contemporary art center and a film center, which shows festival, student, and art films. And the art isn't kept from the elements—besides the outdoor sculptures, the 4th-floor gallery is dotted with skylights to show off contemporary works by artists that hail from the Northwest. On most days, including twice on Saturdays, a curator or special guest leads tours of the museum (free with museum admission).

Central Library

For a gallery of exhibits about the city, visit the **Central Library** (801 SW 10th Ave., 503/988-5123, www.multcolib.org, 10am-8pm Mon., noon-8pm Tues.-Wed., 10am-6pm Thurs.-Sat., 10am-5pm Sun.). Part of the Multnomah County Library system, this 1913 building holds three floors of books, including the Beverly Cleary Children's Library and a garden eco-roof, visible on free 20-minute tours booked at the front desk.

Pioneer Courthouse Square

If Portland has a central meeting place, it's probably **Pioneer Courthouse Square** (701 SW 6th Ave., 503/223-1613, www.thesquarepdx.org). The plaza sits on a block originally purchased by a shoemaker in 1849—he paid just $24 and a pair of boots for the land. It later held a schoolhouse and the Portland Hotel. Then eventually it was donated by the Meier & Frank Company to become a public square and was named for the courthouse on one side. The square now holds a fountain and sculptures of horses and a man holding an umbrella, and a signpost points the way to Mecca, Times Square, and other far-off destinations. Brick steps provide plenty of seating in the square. The Weather Machine is a doohickey on a post that, every noon, predicts the weather by presenting small figurines out of the top and playing a musical fanfare. The square is also home to a number of concerts, and on Mondays in summer it hosts a branch of the Portland Farmers Market.

Portland Building

The 15-story **Portland Building** (1120 SW 5th Ave., 503/823-4000) is a simple municipal office building, but its striking architecture has made it notable since it opened in 1982. The architect is Michael Graves, now more famous than he was when he won the design competition for the project. The boxy building, with its small square windows, blue glass, and stark color combinations, is known as one of the first postmodern buildings in the country. Which is not to say that it's a beloved structure—it has been named one of the "World's Ugliest Buildings" by *Travel + Leisure* magazine and is generally hated.

Mill Ends Park

Before you get lost in the giant forest preserve of Forest Park (or in the blocks of shopping downtown), visit tiny, ridiculous **Mill Ends Park** (SW Naito Pkwy. and Taylor St., www.portlandoregon.gov). It's only two feet in diameter, located in a concrete median on SW Naito Parkway near the waterfront. The park was started by Dick Fagan, a journalist at the *Oregon Journal,* who could see the hole from his office window back in the 1940s. In his column, he called it the world's smallest park (and claimed leprechauns lived there); it became an official city park on St. Patrick's Day in 1976. The small circle of dirt is usually home to a small clump of greenery, but it has been known to feature a miniature swimming pool and little statues. At one point a tiny Ferris wheel was installed—using a full-size crane.

Oregon Maritime Museum

The **Oregon Maritime Museum** (SW Naito Pkwy. at Pine St., 503/224-7724, www.oregonmaritimemuseum.org, 11am-4pm Wed. and Fri.-Sat., $7 adults, $5 seniors, $4 students 13-18, $3 children 6-12, children under 6 free) is located on the river on the sternwheeler tug *Portland* moored next to Tom McCall Waterfront Park. The boat has a giant paddlewheel and looks something like a Mississippi riverboat. The last of its kind still operating in the country, it's been the home of the museum for more than a decade. Sometimes it even takes cruises for special events, traveling to the mouth of the Columbia. Museum visitors should explore the boat first and then check out the exhibits that touch on Oregon shipbuilding, the warships that have visited the area, and local underwater diving. The boat also holds a library of maritime history and a gift store. It's moored on the river at the foot of Pine Street. Look for a ramp with a blue awning.

Portland Saturday Market

Less overwhelming than the farmers market—but only slightly—the **Portland Saturday Market** (2 SW Naito Pkwy., 503/241-4188, www.portlandsaturdaymarket.com, 10am-5pm Sat., 11am-4:30pm Sun. Mar.-Dec.) is an open-air collection of artisans and craftspeople, billed as the biggest such market in the world. Located in Tom McCall Waterfront Park on the Willamette River, just south of the Burnside Bridge and Ankeny Plaza across the road, it hosts 750,000 shoppers every year. Jewelry, clothing, and woodworks are popular crafts, but the market's directory includes a whole host of crafts that defy categorization, like a fire-starting survival tool and kinetic sculptures. Folk, jazz, and international music acts perform, and the info booth will issue parking validation or a free TriMet transit ticket for purchases over $25. (Oh, and yes, it's open on Sundays despite its name.)

PEARL DISTRICT AND NORTHWEST

Once a gritty industrial area, the Pearl District got its moniker only recently, when a local business owner wanted to convey the hip reinvention that had taken over the old warehouses and railroad yard. Sitting just north of the downtown core, it has become known for its art galleries and cobblestone streets, with breweries and restaurants tucked into old warehouses. Gus Van Sant used the neighborhood as a gritty backdrop for his 1989 indie flick *Drugstore Cowboy*. Now it's home to Powell's Books and high-end shopping.

Even though the Northwest District is best known for its residential blocks and shopping along NW 23rd Avenue, it is also the gateway to the city's wildest quarter and legendary parks. Besides a startling amount of natural beauty, the area also has a singular pop culture claim to fame—the creator of *The Simpsons*, Matt Groening, is a Portland native who named many of his characters after street names in the area, such as Flanders, Quimby, and Kearney.

TOP EXPERIENCE

★ Powell's City of Books

If you think you've seen big bookstores before, you haven't traveled the byways of **Powell's City of Books** (1005 W Burnside St., 800/878-7323, www.powells.com, 9am-11pm daily). More than a million volumes fill the store, which takes up an entire block on the site of an old car-repair shop. It's open every day of the year, and color-coded signs direct newbies through the rooms and rooms of tall bookshelves. New and used books share shelf space, along with some branded T-shirts and small gifts. A café sits near the romance section (grab a coffee, sneak a peek).

Powell's buys used books and offers cash or store credit. At one time the bookstore bought 7,000 volumes from author Anne Rice's personal library, some signed or with personal annotations; they're marked as such but sold like any other. Readings and other events occur daily, often one after another, and feature major writers passing through Portland.

Center for Contemporary Art and Culture

When the Museum of Contemporary Craft in the Pearl District closed in 2016, it was a major blow to Portland's vibrant art scene; it had been one of the oldest museums of its kind. Fortunately, the **Center for Contemporary Art and Culture** (511 NW Broadway, 503/226-4391, http://ccac.pnca.edu, 11am-6pm Thurs.-Sun., free) at the nearby Pacific Northwest College of Art took over the collection, and now plans a digitization project for all the holdings. The center has regular exhibits focusing on Northwest art, and one major exhibition in 2018 will cover the cataloging process of the old museum's artifacts.

Lan Su Chinese Garden

The Ming Dynasty gets a showpiece in the middle of the Pearl District at the **Lan Su Chinese Garden** (239 NW Everett St., 503/228-8131, www.lansugarden.org, 10am-7pm daily Mar.-Oct., 10am-4pm daily Nov.-Feb., $10 adults, $9 seniors, $7 college students and youth 6-18, children under 6 free), built by designers from Suzhou, Portland's Chinese sister city, in 2000. The walled botanic garden surrounds pavilions and an artificial lake, and often hosts Chinese holiday celebrations. Plants are mostly native to China, including collections of magnolia, rhododendron, and bamboo. Tea is almost as prevalent as the greenery, with a teahouse located in the central Tower of Cosmic Reflections run by the Portland-based company The Tao of Tea. Events around the history of tea, or its connection to poetry or meditation, are held regularly, along with free sessions of tai chi, qigong, and calligraphy.

Chinatown Gate

The **Chinatown Gate** (NW 4th Ave. and Burnside St.) marks the entrance to Portland's Chinatown, even though the neighborhood isn't the bustling center of Chinese culture it once was. The gate was built in the 1980s, has three levels, and is guarded by two lion statues.

★ Pittock Mansion

Although accessed by driving through a residential neighborhood of perfectly normal-sized houses, the **Pittock Mansion** (3229 NW Pittock Dr., 503/823-3623, www.

Pittock Mansion

pittockmansion.org, 10am-5pm daily July-Sept., 10am-4pm daily Feb.-June and Sept.-Jan., $10 adults, $9 seniors, $7 children 6-18, children under 6 free) lives up to its name with twenty-something rooms and a view to die for. Located on a hill inside a 46-acre park, the house was the brainchild of businessman and newspaper owner Henry Pittock, who got modern comforts like intercoms and a central vacuum system when the house was completed in 1914. Henry and his wife only got to live in the estate for a few years, and by the 1950s the family had to put it on the market; the city purchased the house and turned it into a landmark. The three-story staircase at the center is the house's most arresting feature—oh, to take a ride on those gleaming wooden bannisters—but it's hardly the only spectacle. Henry's shower is a wonder of hydraulics, with multiple sprays located at various heights (why don't we have a "liver spray" these days?) and a toe tester to gauge the temperature.

Besides the gift shop located in the former garage, the Pittock grounds include several benches and a green lawn overlooking downtown Portland. Walks around the castle are free and worth the trek even when the house itself is closed.

Washington Park

Washington Park (head of SW Park Pl., http://washingtonparkpdx.org, 5am-10pm daily) makes up for its small size with tons of activities and attractions. It contains the International Rose Test Garden and Japanese Garden, Vietnam Veterans' and Holocaust memorials, and the **Hoyt Arboretum** (4000 SW Fairview Blvd., 503/865-8733, www.hoytarboretum.org, visitors center 9am-4pm Mon.-Fri., 11am-3pm Sat.-Sun., grounds 5am-9:30pm daily, free), a tree sanctuary and outdoor laboratory that offers 90-minute guided tours ($3) through the collections.

The **Children's Park,** located near the International Rose Test Garden, is a maze of brightly colored play sculptures. The **Washington Park and Zoo Railway** (10:30am-4pm daily, train $4, carousel $3) dates back to the 1950s when it was paid for using the proceeds of a children's book and by children selling "shares." The park begins in the **Oregon Zoo** (4001 SW Canyon Rd., 503/226-1561, www.oregonzoo.org, 9am-6pm daily June-Aug., 9am-4pm daily Sept.-Dec. and Mar.-May, 10am-4pm daily Jan.-Feb., $11.50 adults and children over 12, $10 seniors, $8.50 children 3-11, children under 3 free), Portland's first zoo, which started when

Portland Japanese Garden

International Rose Test Garden

a pharmacist bought two pet bears in the 1880s. Today it houses elephants, penguins, polar bears, and orangutans.

The **Portland Children's Museum** (4015 SW Canyon Rd., 503/223-6500, www.portlandcm.org, 9am-5pm daily, $10.75 adults and children, $9.75 seniors, children under 1 free) is full of hands-on exhibits for tots, like a Building Bridgetown area with tools and a clay studio for art projects. Because it's Portland, one area is for ecofriendly art projects and a tree house. The pet hospital exhibit has fake pets, but the water wheels run on real water. The museum is best for small tikes; once they're tall enough to see over the Zany Maze, it's less exciting. There are visiting exhibits as well, and a café with sandwiches, make-your-own salads, and a kids' menu with peanut butter-and-jelly sandwiches and macaroni.

When it's too wet outside to enjoy Washington Park's trees and gardens, the **World Forestry Center Discovery Museum** (4033 SW Canyon Rd., 503/228-1367, www.worldforestry.org, 10am-5pm daily Memorial Day-Labor Day, 10am-5pm Thurs.-Mon. Labor Day-Memorial Day, $7 adults, $6 seniors, $5 children 3-18, children under 3 free) is one way to experience the outdoors while inside. The museum, built in 1971, has exhibits on local and worldwide forests. A canopy lift ride ($4) offers a mini chairlift to show off what lives above the forest floor, and simulators show off what smoke jumping and timber harvesting are like. There's also a 1909 locomotive that was used to move timber hauls around the Pacific Northwest, and a petrified stump from a giant sequoia tree that's 5 million years old and weighs 10,000 pounds.

★ INTERNATIONAL ROSE TEST GARDEN

Although its name has a whiff of science, the **International Rose Test Garden** (850 SW Rose Garden Way, 503/227-7033, www.rosegardenstore.org, 7:30am-9pm daily, free) is a lush bacchanalia of roses, a hillside of thorns and blooms that's every bit as romantic as a rose garden should be. The Shakespeare Garden includes varieties mentioned in his works, as well as strains named for Shakespearean characters, and a giant grassy amphitheater hosts music concerts and plays. But the garden's name means something else—the 7,000 roses in 500 different varieties represent "the best and newest roses," many of which will bloom in early summer, just in time for the city's Rose Festival.

PORTLAND JAPANESE GARDEN

The 5.5-acre **Portland Japanese Garden** (611 SW Kingston Ave., 503/223-1321, www.japanesegarden.com, noon-7pm Mon., 10am-7pm Tues.-Sun. spring-summer; noon-4pm Mon., 10am-4pm Tues.-Sun. fall-winter; $14.95 adults, $12.95 seniors, $11.95 students, $10.45 children 6-17, children under 6 free) shows off five styles of Japanese gardens, including the Flat Garden, with a raised porch for viewing, and the Sand and Stone Garden, made from a type of raked sand often found in Zen monasteries. Reach the garden from the parking lot in two ways: Ride a free shuttle up a short road (daily in summer, weekends the rest of the year), or climb a short trail through a Japanese gate before making a few switchbacks on the way to the entrance.

SOUTHEAST

★ Oregon Museum of Science and Industry

Its proper name is the **Oregon Museum of Science and Industry** (1945 SE Water Ave., 503/797-4000, www.omsi.edu, 9:30am-5:30pm daily, $14 adults, $10.75 seniors, $9.75 children 3-13, children under 3 free, parking $5), but the active center just across the river from downtown is always called **OMSI.** With a mission to teach and inspire through science, OMSI is disguised as a giant playground, especially *Turbine Hall* with its industrial remnants, suspension bridge, ball room, robotic arm, and earthquake house. Large visiting exhibitions take up one wing of the museum, and a theater shows IMAX films. Just outside, the USS *Blueback,* a U.S. Navy submarine that appeared in *The Hunt for Red October,* is open for tours ($6.75).

NORTHEAST/NORTH

Rose Quarter

Unlike the rose garden in Washington Park, the **Rose Garden Arena** (1 N Center Court St., 503/235-8771, www.rosequarter.com) isn't pretty or delicate. Instead, it's a major arena that hosts the **Portland Trail Blazers** basketball team (www.nba.com/blazers) and the **Winterhawks** (www.winterhawks.com), a junior hockey team. It also serves as a performance space for some of the biggest arena music acts that travel to Portland. (As of 2013, the venue is technically called the Moda Center, though locals still call it the Rose Garden.)

Oregon Convention Center

The two glass spires of the **Oregon Convention Center** (777 NE Martin Luther King Jr. Blvd., 503/235-7575, www.oregoncc.org) almost look like they belong on a church, but the building is actually the largest convention center in the region. It holds travel, entertainment, and industry conventions throughout the year in a number of different spaces, including the Yard, Garden, and Patio Show in late winter and the Portland International Auto Show in February. The building also holds a number of art pieces,

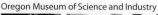

Oregon Museum of Science and Industry

The McMenamins and Portland History

When visiting Portland hotels, bars, and concert halls, one name keeps coming up: McMenamins. The company owns 30 pubs around the city, but it's not a chain, exactly. It all started with two brothers, Mike and Brian McMenamin, who had a passion for saving historical buildings and businesses. They opened their first pub in 1983, and they're now the fourth-largest producer of microbrews thanks to the 24 breweries they've purchased. They own hotels and restaurants throughout the Northwest, but most of their holdings are in Portland.

Not all McMenamins properties are historical, but many are. In Portland alone, they own **McMenamins Tavern & Pool** (1716 NW 23rd Ave., 503/227-0929, www.mcmenamins.com/tavern, 11am-11pm Mon.-Tues., 11am-midnight Wed.-Thurs., 11am-1am Fri.-Sat., noon-11pm Sun.), with two shuffleboard tables and a woodstove, and **Greater Trumps** (1520 SE 37th Ave., 503/235-4530, www.mcmenamins.com/greatertrumps, 3pm-midnight Mon.-Thurs., noon-1am Fri.-Sat., noon-midnight Sun.), a cigar bar next to its **Bagdad Theater** (page 272). The **Barley Mill Pub** (1629 SE Hawthorne Ave., 503/231-1492, www.mcmenamins.com/barleymill, 11am-midnight Mon.-Thurs., 11am-1am Fri.-Sat., noon-11pm Sun.), the brothers' first venture, is decorated in Grateful Dead paraphernalia and pinball machines.

Most hotels owned by the McMenamins are unusual in some way. The **Kennedy School** (page 263) used to be an elementary school and has blackboards in its guest rooms and a bar in the old boiler room. The **Crystal Hotel** (page 290) has a colorful past; the building was once a racketeering hub and, later, a gay bathhouse. Rooms are inspired by performances at the **Crystal Ballroom** (page 270), the live music venue across the street and also a McMenamins property. Don't miss the soaking pool in the hotel's basement, in a cozy bamboo-walled space. **Edgefield** (2126 SW Halsey St., Troutdale, 503/669-8610, www.mcmenamins.com/edgefield, $30 hostel, $50-115 shared bath, $155-175 private bath), located about 20 minutes east of downtown Portland, is a former farm that now has a hotel, hostel, garden, glassblowing studio, brewery, distillery, movie theater, golf course, music venue, and more. McMenamins properties are usually a mix of historical, artistic, and quixotic elements, and no two are exactly alike.

including one called *Ode to a Women's Restroom, Ode to a Men's Restroom* (guess where you go to find that), a 40-foot dragon boat, and a giant Foucault pendulum.

Kennedy School

Ready to go back to school? Even if you're not staying the night, you can play for the day at the **Kennedy School** (5736 NE 33rd Ave., 503/249-7474, www.mcmenamins.com), a former elementary school transformed by the McMenamins into a hotel-playground to which even the locals flock. The hallways lead to a campus of fun spots, including an outdoor **soaking pool** (adults Mon.-Sun. 10am-8pm, minors 10am-6pm, $5)—bring your own towel—and the multistory **Boiler Room Bar** (Mon.-Thurs. 4pm-1am, Fri. 2pm-2:30am, Sat. noon-2:30am, Sun. noon-1am). Other smaller bars include the **Detention Bar** (Mon.-Thurs. 5pm-10pm, Fri. 5pm-midnight, Sat. 1pm-midnight, Sun. 1pm-10pm), which also sells cigars; **Honors Bar** (Mon.-Thurs. 5pm-10pm, Fri. 5pm-midnight, Sat. 1pm-midnight, Sun. 1pm-10pm), playing classical music; and the reggae-themed **Cypress Room** (Mon.-Thurs. 4pm-midnight, Fri. 3pm-1am, Sat. 1pm-1am, Sun. 1pm-midnight). **The Courtyard Restaurant** (7am-1am daily, $13-26) serves American fare, convenient if not particularly noteworthy—though it sometimes incorporates produce from the school's garden, and cinnamon rolls and breads are baked on the premises. Beers are from the Concordia Brewery in the building. Also on the property is a **movie theater** ($4 adults, $2 children 3-11, children under 3 free) in the school's old auditorium, where patrons sit on

Eastside Portland

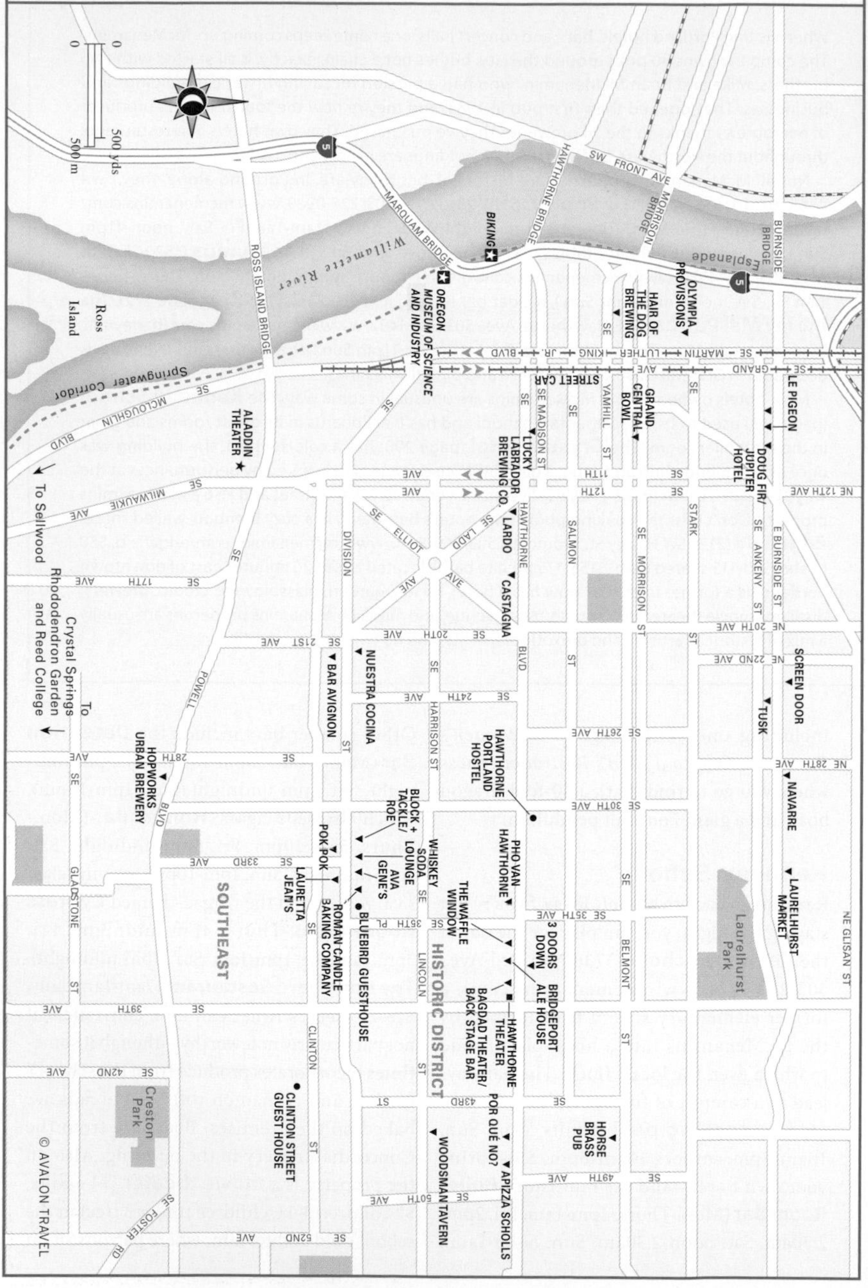

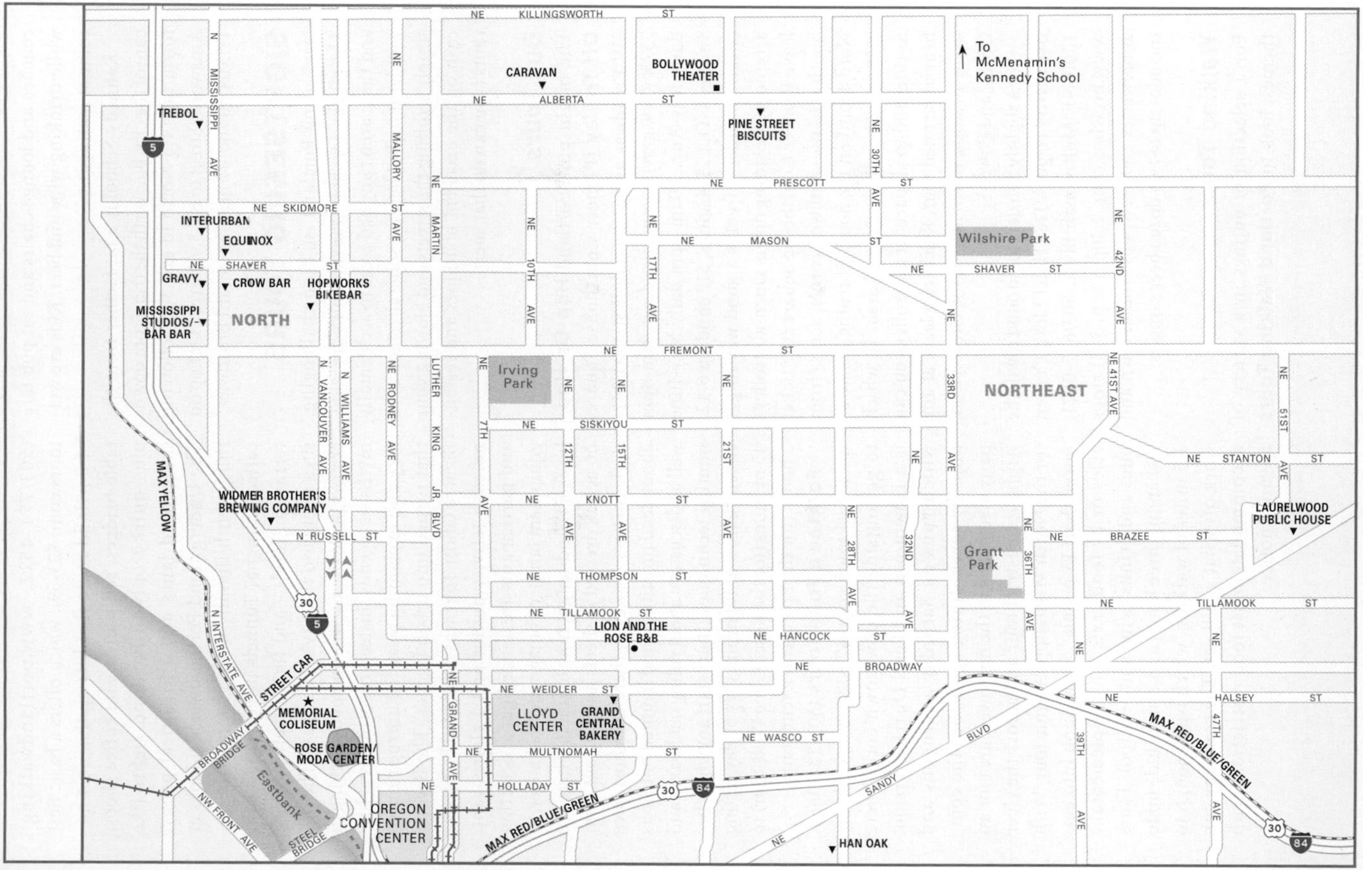
To McMenamin's Kennedy School
CARAVAN
BOLLYWOOD THEATER
PINE STREET BISCUITS
TREBOL
INTERURBAN
EQUINOX
GRAVY
CROW BAR
HOPWORKS BIKEBAR
MISSISSIPPI STUDIOS/BAR BAR
NORTH
NORTHEAST
Irving Park
Wilshire Park
Grant Park
WIDMER BROTHER'S BREWING COMPANY
LAURELWOOD PUBLIC HOUSE
LION AND THE ROSE B&B
MEMORIAL COLISEUM
ROSE GARDEN/MODA CENTER
LLOYD CENTER
GRAND CENTRAL BAKERY
OREGON CONVENTION CENTER
HAN OAK
MAX YELLOW
MAX RED/BLUE/GREEN
STREET CAR
Eastbank
BROADWAY BRIDGE
STEEL BRIDGE
NW FRONT AVE
N INTERSTATE AVE
NE KILLINGSWORTH ST
NE ALBERTA ST
NE PRESCOTT ST
NE SKIDMORE ST
NE MASON ST
NE SHAVER ST
NE FREMONT ST
NE SISKIYOU ST
NE KNOTT ST
N RUSSELL ST
NE THOMPSON ST
NE TILLAMOOK ST
NE HANCOCK ST
NE BROADWAY
NE WEIDLER ST
NE HALSEY ST
NE WASCO ST
NE MULTNOMAH ST
NE HOLLADAY ST
NE STANTON ST
NE BRAZEE ST
NE SANDY BLVD
N MISSISSIPPI AVE
N VANCOUVER AVE
N WILLIAMS AVE
NE RODNEY AVE
NE MALLORY AVE
NE MARTIN LUTHER KING JR. BLVD
NE GRAND AVE
NE 7TH AVE
NE 10TH AVE
NE 12TH AVE
NE 15TH AVE
NE 17TH AVE
NE 21ST AVE
NE 28TH AVE
NE 30TH AVE
NE 32ND AVE
NE 33RD AVE
NE 36TH AVE
NE 39TH AVE
NE 41ST AVE
NE 42ND AVE
NE 47TH AVE
NE 51ST AVE
5
30
84

couches and lounge chairs and eat pub fare while drinking wine and beer. Kids are welcome at matinees.

Kennedy School is a bit farther from the core of the city, but worth the trip. From downtown, take I-5 North to exit 303, following Ainsworth Street to NE 33rd Street. Or hop on TriMet bus no. 17 heading toward Broadway.

SIGHTSEEING TOURS

Navigating Portland isn't too challenging. The blocks are short, the sidewalks are wide, and there aren't any bad areas to accidentally wander into. But here are some alternatives to simply strolling the streets and blowing your cash on the excellent boutiques and restaurants (you can do that later).

Bus Tours

The bright pink Portland **Hop-On Hop-Off Trolley** (Pioneer Courthouse Square, SW Broadway and SW Yamhill St., 503/241-7373, www.graylineofportland.net, 9am-4pm daily July-Aug., 10am-4pm daily May-June and Sept.-Oct., $34 adults, $17 children 6-12, children under 6 free) is a good way to get around while sitting down. Open-air trolleys leave Pioneer Courthouse Square (the ticket booth is in the southwest corner, across from Nordstrom) on the hour, returning as late as 5:20pm. There are enclosed areas in which to ride, and in all parts of the trolley you can hear a narrated tour. Riders can leave at any of the 10 stops, which include the Oregon Zoo, OMSI, and Powell's.

For a slightly boozier ride around town, the **Brew Bus** (DoubleTree Hotel Lloyd Center, 1000 NE Multnomah Blvd., 503/647-0021, www.brewbus.com, 1:30pm Sat., $45) stops at breweries and brewpubs around town and includes up to two dozen beer samples.

Walking Tours

For a selection of outings in a variety of themes, look to **Portland Walking Tours** (503/774-4522, www.portlandwalkingtours.com, $23-59), which offers a basic Best of Portland route that hits up the most notable bridges, sculptures, and coffee shops, plus quirky only-in-Portland sights like skateboard lanes and a historical penny. The Underground Portland version looks at things both literally underground—the so-called Shanghai Tunnels in Portland's subterranean levels—and figuratively so, with sites related to the city's illicit past. The operators pride themselves on not trafficking in myths or legends, instead reporting real history and explaining away the untrue rumors that turned into urban legends. The Beyond Bizarre Ghost Tour was developed by a paranormal activity author and a clairvoyant, and participants are handed ghost detection equipment (an electromagnetic field meter, to be exact) and taught how to use it. There are no actors dressed in sheets jumping out from dark corners; however, there are ghost tales about dead prostitutes and haunted hotels, as well as discussion about ruling out hoaxes and hunting techniques. Tours start anywhere between 10am and 10pm and vary by day, lasting 45 minutes (for the Roses Gone Wild Tour) to 3 hours (for the Epicurean Excursion).

Forktown Food Tours (503/234-3663, www.forktown.com, $75-89) is a good way to get outside the downtown core. There is a Downtown and Pearl District version, which runs on Saturday afternoons and pops by seven dining spots. But the company also heads to the northwest area for an Alphabet District tour and across the river for the North Mississippi Avenue tour. With fewer than 15 people, groups pop into eateries or by food carts for complementary bites and drinks (wine and beer too). Tours last about three hours and can include up to 1.5 miles of walking, which isn't enough to work off what you'll eat. The company can accommodate most food restrictions with advance notice.

Entertainment and Events

NIGHTLIFE

★ Brewpubs and Taprooms

Portland won't drink just anything; one of its nicknames is Beervana for a reason. The city has an affinity for craft beer—generally beer made by smaller breweries—and more than 15 percent of the ale poured in the state was made in state. In fact, the state has the second most breweries per capita in the United States. Two of the oldest, Widmer Brothers Brewing and BridgePort Brewing, started in the 1980s, though Henry Weinhard began brewing here back in 1862. More hops, a major ingredient in beer, are grown in Washington and Oregon than anywhere else in the country, so that's one reason why home brewing and microbreweries are so popular here.

It's easy to create your own self-guided itinerary, but for tours check out **Brewvana** (pickups at DoubleTree Portland, 1000 NE Multnomah St., 503/729-6804, www.experiencebrewvana.com, $65-79), which uses small buses equipped with mini fridges and beer murals to give brewery tours around the city.

DOWNTOWN

At **Bailey's Taproom** (213 SW Broadway, 503/295-1004, www.baileystaproom.com, noon-midnight daily), the beers have a certain clean organization, with the tidy row of 24 taps and a giant TV of beer offerings with place of origin and alcohol content. Many are from Oregon and Washington, and almost a hundred more are available by the bottle. Old board games like hangman, Connect Four, and backgammon are available, but beer nerds will be busy enough tasting, judging, and tasting again. There's a good amount of seating under the exposed brick walls, but it gets loud in the evening.

PEARL DISTRICT AND NORTHWEST

Perhaps Oregon's most well-known beer comes from **Deschutes Brewery** (210 NW 11th Ave., 503/296-4906, www.deschutesbrewery.com, 11am-11pm Sun.-Thurs., 11am-midnight Fri.-Sat.) in Bend, but it has a sizable brewpub in the Pearl District. The giant space has room to sell T-shirts and bike jerseys with the Black Butte Porter or Mirror Pond Pale Ale logos. The booths, tables, outdoor seating, and waiting areas can get packed. The 18 taps include variations on Deschutes classics and seasonal favorites. Northwesterners mark the change of season when the Deschutes Jubelale comes back every year. Food is hearty fare like a pretzel with porter-spiked mustard and flatbreads, but there's also an entire gluten-free menu.

The rotating taps at **BridgePort Brewpub** (1313 NW Marshall St., 503/241-3612, www.bridgeportbrew.com, 11:30am-11pm Tues.-Thurs., 11:30am-midnight Fri.-Sat., 11:30am-10pm Sun.-Mon.) offer the brewery's own wares, like the triple-hopped Kingpin and a floral IPA. They really like hops in this joint: Hop Czar is a favorite, and seasonal beers often get hop heavy. The brewpub serves salads, pizzas, and hot, meaty entrées, and also displays local art on the walls.

SOUTHEAST

The British-style **Horse Brass Pub** (4534 SE Belmont St., 503/232-2202, www.horsebrass.com, 11:30am-2:30am daily) prides itself on its Imperial pints (that's 20 ounces) and English pub fare. It pours beers from around Portland and the world—with 59 taps, it's quite the spread—and also always has regular and cask-conditioned William Younger's Special Bitter from Rogue Ales, named for the pub owner's late brother. Food includes freshly made meat pies, Scotch eggs, and of course, fish-and-chips.

The tasting room at **Hair of the Dog Brewing** (61 SE Yamhill St., 503/232-6585, www.hairofthedog.com, 11:30am-10pm Fri.-Sat., 11:30am-8pm Sun.) is simple, with large wooden tables and a garage door that opens in good weather. The brewery specializes in bottle-conditioned beers that have a high alcohol content and can age like wine. There are also usually seven or eight beers on tap, plus a food menu that includes pan-roasted Brussels sprouts and Chuck Norris duck wings ("with a solid punch and a nice kick").

Sustainability is no joke at **Hopworks Urban Brewery** (2944 SE Powell Blvd., 503/232-4677, www.hopworksbeer.com, 11am-11pm Sun.-Thurs., 11am-midnight Fri.-Sat.). The beers are organic, and the brewery/brewpub composts and is completely powered by renewable energy sources. But for all the ecofriendliness, the beers pack a punch, particularly the popular IPA and Abominable Winter Ale (a.k.a. "The Beast").

With four locations around the city, **Lucky Labrador Brewing Company** (915 SE Hawthorne Blvd., 503/236-3555, www.luckylab.com, 11am-midnight Mon.-Sat., noon-10pm Sun.) is a standby local beer pub for much of Portland. The Hawthorne location is where it all started in 1994, in an old warehouse space that now serves sandwiches and bento boxes, plus a house peanut curry. It has 12 taps of beer. With a name like Lucky Lab, it's no surprise the brewpub has a pet-friendly patio.

NORTHEAST/NORTH

Since Portland is a town that loves its two-wheeling, it's no wonder **Hopworks BikeBar** (3947 N Williams Ave., 503/287-6258, hopworksbeer.com/eat/bikebar, 11am-11pm Sun.-Thurs., 11am-midnight Fri.-Sat.), an outpost of Hopworks Urban Brewery, exists. The BikeBar serves creative beers, like one featuring oyster flavors, and is so family friendly it features a kids' menu and both an indoor play area and outdoor playground. Along with bike directions on the website and plenty of bike parking, you'll find bike frames decorating the ceiling, bike tools, and bike takeout (specially packaged to be taken home by bicycle).

In a town of microbreweries, **Widmer Brothers Brewing Company** (929 N Russell St., 503/281-2437, www.widmerbrothers.com, 11am-10pm Sun.-Thurs., 11am-11pm Fri.-Sat.) is one of the best known and most successful—so much so that it's now part of the Craft Beer Alliance partially owned by Anheuser-Busch. Started in 1979 as soon as home brewing became legal in the state, Kurt and Rob Widmer managed to open a brewery only five years later. An experiment with leaving their Weizenbier unfiltered led to the first American-style *hefeweizen*. The brothers also claim to be the first American brewery to have a four-season beer list. They also launched the Oregon Brewer's Festival, making them something of godfathers among the Portland brewing scene. Free tours are available of the brewery, but the pub has more than a dozen varieties on tap, including the brewery's first beer and, of course, their flagship *hefeweizen*.

Deschutes Brewery

Bars and Clubs

DOWNTOWN

The bar **Kask** (527 SW 12th Ave., 503/241-7163, www.grunerpdx.com/kask, 4pm-11pm

daily) is adjacent to the alpine-themed Grüner restaurant (owned by a James Beard Award-winning chef), but has its own menu of cured meats and small plates. Despite the names and a small, well-curated beer and wine selection, the highlights aren't drinks that come in casks: The cocktail menu is extensive, divided by spirit, and experienced bartenders take their time with creations served on a bar made of a giant pile of rocks, next to walls lined with vintage chalkboards.

The **Multnomah Whiskey Library** (1124 SW Alder St., 503/954-1381, http://mwlpdx.com, 4pm-midnight Mon.-Thurs., 4pm-1am Fri.-Sat.) might be the hardest library to access on the entire West Coast; members are the only ones who can make reservations, and the rest of us have to wait on a walk-up basis (which can mean very long waits on the ground floor under the main bar, in a separate bar called the Green Room). Oh, and there's a waitlist for memberships. But the special "hall pass" is a one-time reservation for $25, worth it if you have a single day and want to experience the 1,500-plus spirits and impeccable speakeasy decor. Bartenders can help select a whiskey you've never heard of that will become your new favorite.

Portland is known for its strip clubs (there's even one that serves vegan food), but none is more famous than **Mary's Club** (129 SW Broadway, 503/227-3023, www.marysclub.com, 11am-2:30am daily, $2 cover on weekends), where Courtney Love danced back in the 1980s. Mary's is more than 50 years old, claiming to be Portland's first topless joint. Its proprietor, who passed at the age of 90, is still memorialized on the readerboard out front. Look for its trademark retro neon-and-stars sign out front.

Although the pan-Asian cuisine at **Saucebox** (214 SW Broadway, 503/241-3393, www.saucebox.com, 4:30pm-midnight Tues.-Thurs., 4:30pm-2am Fri., 5pm-2am Sat.) is one of its calling cards, its cocktail program is the true highlight. It's so humble that one of its signature tipples is called "the best drink"—gin with mint and ginger brew. It infuses vodkas and gins in-house with Thai chili, watermelon, and kaffir lime, and bartenders will mix with any spirit from whiskey to sake. The ambience is calm and candlelit, but DJs spin in the space regularly.

PEARL DISTRICT AND NORTHWEST

The **Teardrop Cocktail Lounge** (1015 NW Everett St., 503/445-8109, www.teardroplounge.com, 4pm-12:30am Sun.-Thurs., 4pm-2am Fri.-Sat.) doesn't skimp on naming drinks ($10-14). There's the Misspent Youth with vodka and pear cider, or the Heartbreak Kid with herbaceous lemon vodka, black tea, and Lillet Blanc. They also borrow concoctions from bar books that date back to the 1860s. The round bar puts the bartenders on display as they carefully pound, chip, peel, crush, and pour while constructing the drinks. A brief menu of bites ($7-16) includes a pretzel baguette with bacon-mustard sauce and sweet-and-sour pork belly to pad your stomach, so the tipples don't make you tip over.

SOUTHEAST

Holocene (1001 SE Morrison St., 503/239-7639, www.holocene.org, hours vary) is located in an old warehouse space and is part music venue, part nightclub. Many nights have dance parties, others host music acts and multimedia art events. There's a regular '90s dance night that's been around for more than 10 years—so longer than the 1990s themselves—and led by a DJ with a PhD.

NORTHEAST/NORTH

Describing itself as a "new American saloon," **Interurban** (4057 N Mississippi Ave., 503/284-6669, www.interurbanpdx.com, 3pm-2:30am Mon.-Fri., 10am-2:30am Sat.-Sun.) combines cocktail culture with a relaxed neighborhood bar, more upscale than the owner's other joint in the neighborhood, the German **Prost!** (4237 N Mississippi Ave., 503/954-2674, http://prostportland.com, 11:30am-2:30am Mon.-Thurs., 11am-2:30am Fri.-Sun.). Tables are tiny, meant to fit drinks and only a few of the small bites from the menu, like bacon-wrapped shrimp cocktail and steak tartare. The back patio fills on sunny days, but the bar itself is the most social spot. Chat with the bartenders about the worldly beer and wine list, or consider a cocktail Jello shot, a strange combination of quality ingredients that is a college-party tradition. Children are allowed inside before 8pm.

The repetitively named **Bar Bar** (3939 N Mississippi Ave., 503/288-3895, www.mississippistudios.com, noon-2am daily) is part of Mississippi Studios, a live music venue, but still has a neighborhood bar aspect. Big windows open to the street, generally where a steady throng of concertgoers moves through. There are two outdoor patios, and a "secret garden" with a fire pit out back.

In a neighborhood that's becoming increasingly popular and polished, **Crow Bar** (3954 N Mississippi Ave., 503/280-7099, www.crowbarpdx.com, 3pm-2am daily) shows off some simple watering hole pleasures: pinball games, a jukebox, and specials for employees of other bars and restaurants. It even offers margaritas on tap. Works from local artists hang on the walls, elevating the bar well above a dive.

Gay and Lesbian

It's billed as the city's premier gay nightclub, but **C.C. Slaughters** (219 NW Davis St., 503/248-9135, www.ccslaughterspdx.com, 3pm-2am daily) in the Pearl District is the place for everyone to dance. It was originally a gay country-western bar and named for the first male born in the Republic of Texas (and a man rumored to be gay). Now it plays dance music and has Sunday-night drag shows. There's no regular cover, and a system allows dancers to text song requests directly to the DJ.

Scandals (1125 SW Stark St., 503/227-5887, www.scandalspdx.com, noon-2:30am daily) likes to call itself Portland's gay *Cheers* bar, and it has a history stretching back to 1979. It hosts karaoke nights, bands, and DJs and is generally known for its male crowd but is usually welcoming to women. Go for cheap drinks and the company, but not for the food. Sometimes there's dancing, but there's always pool to be played. Patio seating is available out front, and students get a food discount in the afternoons.

The **Embers Avenue** (110 NW Broadway, 503/222-3082, 11am-2am daily) is a show and dance club that often hosts drag shows and leather bingo. The hosts have monikers like Onalicious Mercury and Onyx Lynn. The bar has grubby corners, but service is generally good, and a fish tank (yes, full of fish) is under the bar. The back bar, the Avenue, opens at 9pm.

Live Music

The retro, mod **Doug Fir Lounge** (830 E Burnside St., 503/231-9663, www.dougfirlounge.com, 7am-2:30am daily) recalls Los Angeles or Palm Springs in the 1960s, but blended with a log cabin. The performance space holds only a few hundred people, so concerts stay intimate, and the bill usually features local singer-songwriters and indie bands. Though not in downtown, the attached Jupiter Hotel helps feed the busy restaurant, bar, and patio.

The **Mississippi Studios** (3939 N Mississippi Ave., 503/288-3895, www.mississippistudios.com, noon-2am daily) was, once upon a time, a Baptist church, but now it worships at the secular church of rock, pop, and indie hip-hop. The venue is small but flat, so the best viewpoints are up front or on a small balcony, which has a few chairs.

The long and storied history of the **Crystal Ballroom** (1332 W Burnside St., 503/225-0047, www.crystalballroompdx.com) includes a century of Beat poets and police raids, Grateful Dead concerts, and Ike and Tina Turner shows. It has a unique "mechanical" dance floor and ornate curved windows, but you won't notice them or the chandeliers when the live music starts. Performing acts tend to be indie rock bands and singer-songwriters, but tribute shows to major bands and swing dances are also held in the space.

A number of bands have recorded live albums at **Roseland Theater** (8 NW 6th Ave., 971/230-0033, www.roselandpdx.com), which sits right between downtown and the Pearl District. Most concerts are standing room only, with limited seating on a balcony.

Graced with a giant vertical "Portland" marquee, the **Arlene Schnitzer Concert Hall** (1037 SW Broadway, 503/248-4335, www.portland5.com) sits in a 1928 building that once housed the Portland Public Theater, built in rococo revival style. Now the space hosts classical and jazz concerts, major lectures, visiting dance companies, the occasional ski flick, and big-name popular music acts. The Artbar & Bistro restaurant serves cocktails and a Northwest-inspired dinner menu before shows.

There's an intimate feel to the smallish **Hawthorne Theatre** (1507 SE 39th Ave., 503/233-7100, www.hawthornetheatre.com), but nothing delicate or precious. Smaller indie, punk, metal, and pop bands share nightly bills with DJs, and the space is just dark, hot, and sticky enough to earn a real rock 'n roll reputation.

The acts on stage at **Dante's** (350 W Burnside St., 503/345-7892, www.danteslive.com, 11am-2:30am daily) range from rock to cabaret and burlesque, making it one of the more eclectic live destinations in the city. Occasionally there's karaoke on stage with a band—called Karaoke from Hell—and it serves pizza by the slice.

When Portland's quintessential jazz club, Jimmy Mak's, closed in 2017 in the wake of the death of local legend Jimmy Makarounis, the city's music scene was in shock until the owners of Dante's opened a new venue called **Jack London Revue** (529 SW 4th Ave., 866/777-8932, http://jacklondonrevue.com). Located in the basement of the Rialto Poolroom Bar & Cafe, which boasts a poker lounge and an off-track gambling parlor, the Jack London Revue incorporates many of the musicians who were left without a stage when the old club closed. There are also new groups appearing regularly, not just jazz but indie rock and experimental and everything in between.

THE ARTS

The **Portland Center Stage** (Gerding Theater at the Armory, 128 NW 11th Ave., 503/445-3700, www.pcs.org) is a theater group that produces new and well-known plays and musicals and also hosts an annual playwriting festival. It performs in the Gerding Theater at the Armory, which gives public tours (503/445-3727) of the space that was built in 1891 and has served all number of functions since.

Unlike some of the city's older institutions, **Oregon Ballet Theatre** (Keller Auditorium, 222 SW Clay St., or Newmark Theatre, 1111 SW Broadway, 503/227-0977, www.obt.org) is fairly new, formed only in 1989. Still, the company has established itself in the city and performs classics like George Balanchine's *Nutcracker* along with premieres choreographed by the artist director. Dancers represent Portland's diversity, and the company performs at several spots around town, including the Tony Keller Auditorium and intimate Newmark Theatre.

The **Oregon Symphony** (Arlene Schnitzer Concert Hall, 1037 SW Broadway, 503/228-1353, www.orsymphony.org) was established more than 120 years ago—it's the oldest orchestra west of the Mississippi—and performs both classical symphony works and pops concerts, often performing with visiting pop singers. The symphony cares about reaching out—it offers $5 tickets to locals who receive state food assistance (as do other arts organizations in town). Students can get $10 tickets.

The **Portland Opera** (Keller Auditorium, 222 SW Clay St., 503/241-1802, www.portlandopera.org) starts its season with a Big Night concert, staging some of opera's biggest hits. The group tries to make its performances accessible, hosting Q&A sessions with the general director after every performance and prepping audiences with pre-curtain talks an hour before the show. Subtitles—or rather supertitles, as they're properly called—are projected above the stage.

CINEMA

The **Living Room Theaters** (341 SW 10th Ave., 971/222-2010, www.livingroomtheaters.com, $11 adults, $9 matinees, $8 students and seniors, $6 Mon.-Tues.) plays first-run movies, but tends toward the artsy and documentary type, not the blockbusters, though it's not unheard of for a comic book film to pay. The building has a sleek wooden style inside and out, with a bar serving a cheese plate and chicken skewers, plus drinks, which can be taken into the theaters. Seats have small tables and are large and comfortable, though screens are small, as befits an art house cinema. The café also has outdoor seating.

No, it's not a typo. **Bagdad Theater** (3702 SE Hawthorne Blvd., 503/236-9234, www.mcmenamins.com, $9.50 adults, $8 matinees, $6.50 children under 13) is spelled differently from the city in the Middle East. The theater was a former movie palace, built in 1927. (It once hosted the premiere of *One Flew Over the Cuckoo's Nest.*) Now renovated by the McMenamins group, the theater shows new-release movies amid its Arabian-style interior. The neon sign outside is one of the city's most striking marquees.

Unlike the theaters that have been used as such for decades, **Mission Theater** (1624 NW Glisan St., 503/223-4527, www.mcmenamins.com, $4 adults, $3 children, $2 matinees) was a former evangelical mission and a Longshoremen's union. The space now has a pulpit, screen, and balcony and hosts new movies as well as readings, lectures, a jazz series, and other performances. Sometimes the big screen shows live sporting events like *Monday Night Football* or Trailblazers basketball games. The attached pub serves McMenamins beers, and children aren't permitted at movies that begin after 6pm.

FESTIVALS AND EVENTS

Despite the name, the **Fertile Ground Festival** (www.fertilegroundpdx.org) in January isn't about farming, but art. The focus is on local artists and their latest creations, including new plays, films, and pieces of music. Recent years have seen more than 100 premieres across the city; passes good for all 11 days run about $50.

In the City of Roses, the **Portland Rose Festival** (503/227-2681, www.rosefestival.org, June) is a central event that's more than 100 years old. It takes place in early June, right about when the area's roses are in bloom (if the weather cooperates, that is). The Grand Floral Parade features marching bands, horseback riders, vintage cars, and dancers, plus floats made out of roses. It begins at Veterans Memorial Coliseum (300 N Winning Way), crosses the river at the Burnside Bridge, and zigzags around downtown before ending at Lincoln High School near SW Salmon Street and SW 14th Avenue. There's also dragon boat races, a Rose Festival Fleet Week featuring visiting naval and coast guard vessels, and a Starlight Parade the week before the Grand Floral Parade, plus an annual Spring Rose Show at the Lloyd Center Ice Rink (953 Lloyd Center, 503/777-4311, www.portlandrosesociety.org, $3).

The **World Naked Bike Ride** (South Park Blocks, SW Park Ave. from Salmon St. to Jackson St., www.pdxwnbr.org, June) takes place all around the world, but the Portland version is usually the biggest, with thousands of riders. Not everyone is fully nude, but some folks are. The theme is "bare as you dare," and cameras are banned at the start and end points. People ride to promote cycling, protest the country's dependence on oil, celebrate the nude lifestyle, and just for silly fun. It takes place at night, and a body-painting area usually operates near the start. One year the Portland Art Museum even opened up for participants, charging them a dollar for every piece of clothing they wore. A marching band kicks off the ride, and after parties continue into the night at the end. The ride is the signature event of the monthlong **Pedalpalooza** (www.shift2bikes.org/pedalpalooza) in June, a series of mostly free bike-related events that incorporate everything from political protest to drinks and food to costumes and kazoos.

The annual **Portland Pride** (Waterfront Park, Naito Pkwy. between SW Harrison St. and NW Glisan St., 503/296-9788, www.pridenw.org, June) weekend celebrates local LGBTQ culture with a parade and festival on the waterfront, featuring live music and comedy performances.

One of the biggest blues festival in the country, the **Waterfront Blues Festival** (Waterfront Park, Naito Pkwy. between SW Harrison St. and NW Glisan St., 503/275-9750, www.waterfrontbluesfest.com, July) began as a concert to support Portland's homeless. Most of the festival can be accessed with a cheap ticket and two cans of food. The Oregon Potters Association sells handmade bowls to symbolize hunger, raising more money for food banks. It always occurs around the Fourth of July and includes the biggest fireworks show in the state, held over the Willamette River.

The **Oregon Brewers Festival** (Naito Pkwy. between SW Harrison St. and NW Glisan St., www.oregonbrewfest.com, admission free, tasting $7 plus $1 tokens) in July is one of the largest outdoor festivals on the West Coast, bringing more than 80,000 to Tom McCall Waterfront Park in late July for five days of craft beer tastings.

The giant food fest **Bite of Oregon** (Waterfront Park, Naito Pkwy. between SW Harrison St. and NW Glisan St., 503/248-0600, www.biteoforegon.com, Aug.) raises money for Special Olympics Oregon by selling tastes of Oregon food and drink. Restaurants from around the state bring more than a hundred dishes, and dozens of Oregon wineries and breweries pour tasting sizes. There's an Iron Chef Oregon competition and two stages of entertainment. Just remember to bring cash.

MusicFest NW (www.musicfestnw.com, Aug. or Sept.) is like a Northwest version of Austin's South by Southwest, with shows around the city in a variety of venues. The fest scores big names in the rock and pop worlds, and recent years have seen the addition of outdoor concerts in downtown's Pioneer Courthouse Square. A technology version of the festival, **TechFestNW** (www.techfestnw.com), held in March, has speakers, competitions, and panels about start-ups, media, and online design.

Labor Day weekend's **Art in the Pearl** (NW 8th Ave. between W Burnside and NW Glisan, 503/722-9017, www.artinthepearl.com, Sept.) includes rows of booths in the middle of the North Park Blocks in the Pearl District, featuring the work from more than a hundred artists, plus a World Music Stage with performances and a kids' pavilion. There's a food row for snacks, and a demonstration where groups show off wood carving, metalwork, digital painting, papermaking, and more.

The annual **Feast Portland** (http://feastportland.com, Sept.) is a culinary festival held over four days and replete with chef dinners and demonstrations, classes, and drinks events. The main events involve food tents set up in central Portland locations, with individual restaurants or chefs serving bites and drinks—admission fees cover all food costs inside. The annual festival often brings in notable guest chefs and highlights regional cuisine and trends.

The **Time-Based Art Festival** (503/242-1419, http://pica.org/programs/tba-festival, Sept.), also known as TBA, is run by the Portland Institute for Contemporary Art. The mid-September event includes visual art exhibits that run for weeks, but most of the festival revolves around contemporary performances and installations in theaters, galleries, and public spaces, plus lectures and workshops. It might include a cabaret singer with the Oregon Symphony one night and a laser multimedia show the next.

Shopping

"Independent" is the watchword of Portland shops, which also tend to sell local and sustainable items. Clothing styles tend to have a vintage touch, while housewares are quirky and artsy. The lack of sales tax in Oregon makes it a shopping mecca. Look for Washington residents who've come down for a trip just to peruse the town's many fabulous boutiques.

DOWNTOWN

Clothing and Shoes

Steven Alan (1029 SW Stark St., 971/277-9585, www.stevenalan.com, 11am-7pm Mon.-Sat., 11am-6pm Sun.) isn't headquartered in Portland but has prime placement across from the Ace Hotel, in a pedestrian alleyway mall of stores known as the Union Way. The exposed roof trusses and skylights are a good match for Steven Alan's clean lines for men and expensive leather accessories. Head to the back for a wall of shirts whose patterns just bridge the line between hipster chic and practical style.

Also in the Union Way mall is **Will Leather Goods** (1022 W Burnside St., Unit N, 971/279-4698, www.willleathergoods.com, 11am-7pm daily), where the wares are new but the store is made from old mid-20th-century gym bleachers from a Portland-area college, an old Smokey the Bear sign, and an artfully rusty vintage cash register (a sign reminds shoppers that everything inside is indeed for sale; inquire about prices for the decor). There are belts and leather portfolios, as well as thick aprons appropriate for the avid chef or hardy backyard griller.

Animal Traffic (429 SW 10th Ave., 503/241-5427, www.animaltrafficpdx.com, 11am-6pm daily) first opened in the Mississippi district, selling outdoorsy sweaters and thick Western shirts, particularly brands like Pendleton and Minnetonka. Eventually it opened this downtown outpost, decorated with barn doors and wood beams from farm buildings. Besides the canvas knapsacks, men's coats, and women's vintage-style dresses, there's a spot to get measured for made-to-order White's Boots (a century-old company based in Spokane that once made rugged footwear for Northwest loggers).

With its headquarters just one town away in Beaverton, the flagship store for **Nike** (638 SW 5th Ave., 503/221-6453, www.nike.com, 10am-8pm Mon.-Sat., 11am-6pm Sun.) has to be impressive—appropriately, a gray statue of Michael Jordan making a dunk hangs from the ceiling. Walls of multicolored Nike sneakers surround racks of workout wear, and fancy display boxes explain the various technological wonders of particular lines of shoes in the three-store space.

In a town known for its vintage shopping, **Fat Fancy** (1013 SW Morrison St., 503/445-4353, www.fatfancyfashions.com, 11am-6pm Mon.-Fri., 11am-7pm Sat., noon-6pm Sun.) has a special niche: plus-size women. The proprietor was so passionate about the shop that she first started it in her studio apartment, inviting friends and acquaintances to shop next to her bed and other furniture, before moving to a basement space. Beth Ditto, fashion icon and singer in the Olympia band The Gossip, became a loyal customer, eventually making the real storefront possible. The new and vintage clothing represents a wide range of sizes and styles, from rockabilly chic to office wear; they've begun carrying plus-size men's clothing as well, along with shoes and accessories.

Radish Underground (414 SW 10th Ave., 503/928-6435, www.radishunderground.com, 11am-7pm Mon.-Sat., noon-6pm Sun.) is quintessential Portland shopping, combining a whimsical name with women's clothing from independent designers, many of them local, in a space decorated with a distressed floor and artful light fixtures. Styles are mostly clean and modern, and a handful of pieces—socks, T-shirts, some etched wooden cuff links—appeal to men as well.

Gift and Home

In a town full of tony home stores, **Canoe** (1136 SW Alder, 503/889-8545, www.canoeonline.net, 10am-6pm Tues.-Sat., 11am-5pm Sun.) is one of the best. The airy white store is flooded with daylight, and even the wood floor is pale and spotless. Most pieces could be either artworks or useful items. It's no wonder the store often pops up in national design and travel magazines. Locally made articles are highlighted, like the Eena canvas bags from Beckel Canvas that the store sells exclusively; they're trimmed with leather and visible stitching. Linen tea towels with special wood-grain designs are almost too pretty to use on kitchen spills.

Tender Loving Empire (412 SW 10th Ave., 503/243-5859, www.tenderlovingempire.com, 11am-7pm daily) is more than a shop—it's a record label and screen-printing studio, and owners started it hoping to preserve a sense of community in Portland's bustling downtown. Murals by local artists are all over the store walls, and art pieces in the gallery are sold on consignment. Also find a selection of gifts like engraved spoons, scarves knitted to look like a fox, and screen-printed Onesies.

You could think of **Crafty Wonderland** (808 SW 10th Ave., 503/224-9097, www.craftywonderland.com, 10am-6pm Mon.-Sat., 11am-6pm Sun.) as a gift store, but one with a decidedly Portland bent. Find drinking glasses printed with mustaches and prints of the Oregon state shape. The greeting card selection is good but pricey, and a different local is highlighted in the "Artist of the Month" corner.

It might cost a lot to ship something home from **The Joinery** (922 SW Yamhill St, 800/259-6762, thejoinery.com, 10am-6pm Mon.-Sat., 11am-5pm Sun.), but the handcrafted furniture is the kind of piece that you'll hand down to your grandchildren one day. The wood pieces evoke the Pacific Northwest without feeling like Paul Bunyon's dorm furnishings.

Outdoor Gear

The two-story climbing rock at the Portland **REI** (1405 NW Johnson St., 503/221-1938, www.rei.com, 10am-9pm Mon.- Sat., 10am-7pm Sun.) is visible from the street and from both floors of retail space. The building boasts an ecofriendly design that made it one of the first retail spaces in the country to get a LEED Gold award. The store carries all the jackets, sleeping bags, hiking boots, and kayaks one would ever need on an outdoor excursion, and regular classes show off how to use the equipment. The store has a famously generous return policy, accepting any unsatisfactory gear for return or exchange within a year of purchase.

Though not a chain like REI, **U.S. Outdoor Store** (219 SW Broadway, 503/223-5937, www.usoutdoor.com, 9am-8pm Mon.-Fri., 10am-6pm Sat., 11am-5pm Sun.) carries nearly as many kinds of outdoor gear. A signpost on the ground level directs shoppers up or down to find snowboards, climbing gear, and rainproof everything.

Portland Outdoor Store (304 SW 3rd Ave., 503/222-1051, 9:30am-5:30pm Mon.-Sat.) bursts with personality, including a giant neon sign with a bucking cowboy on it. "Outdoor" has a different definition here—a western supply store with boots and saddles, plus Filson bags and Western shirts for anyone without a horse. The shop includes used gear, and clerks are chatty.

PEARL DISTRICT AND NORTHWEST

Clothing and Shoes

The **Keen Garage** (505 NW 13th Ave., 971/200-4040, www.keenfootwear.com, 10am-7pm Mon.-Sat., 11am-5pm Sun.) is the flagship store for a local brand that makes hardy, weather-ready shoes and hiking boots. The warehouse space has polished wood floors, hanging blackboards, and display racks that move on pulleys and wheels. Best of all is the metal chute that emerges from the upstairs storage space, so boxes fly through the store on their way down to the cash register.

Sloan (738 NW 23rd Ave., 503/222-6666, www.sloanpdx.com, 11am-7pm Mon.-Fri., 10am-7pm Sat., 11am-6pm Sun.) is a boutique with women's clothing especially popular with the younger set. The shoe store next store is an extension of Sloan and offers contemporary styles.

Gift and Home

There's a little bit of everything in the giant former tire factory that is now **Cargo** (380 NW 13th, 503/209-8349, www.cargoimportspdx.com, 11am-6pm daily). It has wooden furniture, paper lanterns, jewelry, fans, Chinese socks, wooden hand models, play masks, wind-up toys of a duck riding a tricycle—and so much more. The importer prides itself on bringing the entire globe to Portland, and one can spend hours in the crowded aisles, always finding a new basket of treasure.

Gourmet Goodies

The European-style **City Market Northwest** (735 NW 21st Ave., 503/221-3007, 9:30am-7pm daily) sells produce, wines, fresh pastas, and gourmet foodstuffs, all in a bright, cheery market. The people working the meat and cheese counters know what they're talking about.

SOUTHEAST

Clothing and Shoes

The jewel box of **Xtabay** (2515 SE Clinton St., 503/230-2899, www.xtabayvintage.blogspot.com, 11am-6pm daily) is a lovely salon of vintage women's wear, sorted by color and carefully tagged. Formal dresses are protected by plastic covers, and a separate bridal shop sells vintage wedding gowns. Hats and shoes from a dressier era line both sides of the small store. It's where to go for a *Mad Men* style fix, or just to remember how flattering the various styles of the past could be.

From the suit jackets to the snazzy shoes, **Wildfang** (1230 SE Grand Ave., 503/208-3631, www.wildfang.com, noon-6pm daily) is all about the tomboy look, dressing Portland's women in traditional male styles but with fun touches like Beyoncé prints and bright patterns. An exposed-wood space serves as a stage for hoodies, graphic T-shirts, and a very feminist jacket that announces "slay the patriarchy."

Gourmet Goodies

Even though the **Woodsman Tavern Market** (4529 SE Division St., 971/373-8267, www.woodsmantavern.com, 9am-7pm daily) is right next to the polished eatery with which it shares ownership, it's a much more casual shop, selling vinegars, oils, pastas, and jarred pickles, plus literary food journals. The space is small and lined with white tile, but it fits a butcher's counter, with cheeses and many meats smoked or cured locally, and a rotating selection of fish, sausage, and burgers. Sandwiches, salads, and soups are available to go.

NORTHEAST/NORTH

Books

In Other Words (14 NE Killingsworth St., 503/232-6003, www.inotherwords.org, noon-7pm Tues.-Sat., 1pm-7pm Sun.) is more than just a sketch on *Portlandia*. It's a feminist community center and bookstore, hosting events like reading groups that focus on feminist and queer science fiction, craft nights, yoga, dream discussion nights, and open mic nights. The lending library gathers radical books and feminist zines, and the store sells books on feminist issues as well as health, religion, gardening, and craft titles.

The small, independent **Broadway Books** (1714 NE Broadway, 503/284-1726, www.broadwaybooks.net, 10am-7pm Mon.-Sat., noon-5pm Sun.) has survived for more than 20 years, selling new and used books along with gifts, games, and journals. Compared to the cavernous Powell's, this shop is personal, cheerful, and happy to gift wrap for free. Staff recommendations are carefully selected, and locals enjoy a frequent buyer card that earns them a free book for every 12 they buy. Readings are held regularly.

Portlandia Keeps Portland Weird

Portland has been known for many things—bridges, roses, lumber—but since 2011 it has been known by a new nickname: Portlandia. The comedy TV show *Portlandia* riffs on the city's indie and alternative scene, ecofriendliness, and bike culture, calling it "the city where young people go to retire."

The show is a modest hit, but it's referenced often. The boutique **Land Gallery** (3925 N Mississippi Ave., 503/451-0689, www.landpdx.com, 10am-7pm daily) became famous as the site of the show's "Put a Bird on It" sketch, and the "Women & Women First" feminist bookstore is actually **In Other Words** (14 NE Killingsworth St., 503/232-6003, www.inotherwords.org, noon-7pm Tues.-Sat., 1pm-7pm Sun.).

The **Secrets of Portlandia Walking Tour** (SW 6th Ave. between SW Morrison St. and SW Yamhill St., 503/703-4282, www.secretsofportlandia.com, 11am daily May-Oct., free) is a free daily excursion that runs spring-fall, covering quirky attractions representative of Portland—like food cart pods, the Weather Machine (a public art piece that tells the weather), Mill Ends Park (the world's smallest park), and more. It passes the ***"Keep Portland Weird"*** sign that's painted on a building at 3158 East Burnside Street (the phrase is also on a lot of T-shirts and bumper stickers). The tours, done by Portland locals only for tips, are not directly affiliated with the show, but claim to reveal "Portland's obsession with beer, bikes, and beards."

Though recently popularized, the moniker "Portlandia" comes from a 1985 sculpture of a woman holding a trident, crouching down, and reaching out. It's located on the **Portland Building** designed by Michael Graves (SW 5th Ave. between SW Madison and SW Main St.) and is the second-largest copper statue of its kind in the United States—right behind the Statue of Liberty. Look up a few stories to see her. And when touring the city, any time you see a tattooed cyclist, an organic garden on a roof, or a random street performance by steampunk clowns, don't be surprised if someone says, "That's so *Portlandia*."

Clothing and Shoes

The boutique **Flutter** (3948 N Mississippi Ave., 503/288-1649, www.flutterclutter.com, 11am-6pm Sun.-Wed, 11am-7pm Thurs.-Sat.) gets its name from "found objects and clutter," which it displays in a space with bright turquoise walls and chandeliers. There are vintage dresses and lots of jewelry, old mannequins artfully arranged, plus paper goods and pillows. It's all a little crammed together, as the name suggests. That sound in the back? Finches—yes, live birds—tweeting the day away in a big French birdcage.

Gift and Home

Land Gallery (3925 N Mississippi Ave., 503/451-0689, www.landpdx.com, 10am-7pm daily) will go down in history as the shop from the *Portlandia* sketch "Put a Bird on It," where the TV show's stars parodied the hipster practice of decorating housewares, tote bags, and clothing. And yes, the store does carry cute paper goods, socks, and T-shirts (most without birds on them), but it also has a gallery space that displays the works of independent Northwest artists.

Gourmet Goodies

Even though the neighborhood has good bars and breweries, **Bridgetown Beerhouse** (915 N Shaver St., 503/477-8763, noon-10pm Mon.-Thurs., noon-11pm Fri.-Sat., noon-8pm Sun.) simply offers bottled and canned beer, plus five taps for filling growlers. The craft beers they carry are carefully selected (but they admit to having cheap Pabst Blue Ribbon, too), and they care for the ales by filtering the UV light in the space, rotating the beers in the front of the case, and keeping them all at 38°F. It's also a pub with a simple wooden counter and a few wooden tables, so you can drink on-site.

Sports and Recreation

PARKS

★ Forest Park

There's no singular entrance to **Forest Park** (NW 29th Ave. and Upshur St. to Newberry Rd., 503/223-5449, www.forestparkconservancy.org, 5am-10pm daily), and no one way to enjoy what is one of the largest city forests in the country. The 5,100 acres make up a chunk of wildness 30 miles long, one end only a few miles from downtown. Trails wind through the space partly designed by the famous Olmstead Brothers, land that was once surveyed by the Lewis and Clark expedition back in 1806. Dozens of mammals and birds live among the Douglas fir and maples trees, including deer, bobcats, woodpeckers, and coyotes, even migratory elk—and bear scat has even been sighted.

Despite plenty of space for stationary meditation in the thick forest, the trails are the rock stars of Forest Park. More than 80 miles, including old roads and fire lanes, are open to runners and hikers, with many accessible to bikers and equestrians. Dogs must be leashed. The **Wildwood Trail** alone is 30 miles long and passes the Stone House, a Works Progress Administration cabin from the 1930s, now gutted and used solely for scenic purposes. For a quick visit to the park, try the trail leaving from the **Audubon Society of Portland's Bird Sanctuary** (5151 NW Cornell Rd., 503/292-6855, www.audubonportland.org, 9am-5pm Mon.-Sat., 10am-5pm Sun.); the Pittock Mansion is a short hike downhill on the Wildwood Trail.

Director Park

In a city with nature-focused parks in the trees and on the river, **Director Park** (815 SW Park Ave., 503/823-8087, www.portlandoregon.gov, 5am-midnight daily) is a decidedly city spot, located right in the middle of downtown and featuring a large plaza with benches, as well as tables outside the **Elephants in the Park Café** (877 SW Taylor St., 503/937-1073, www.elephantsdeli.com, 11am-8pm daily, $7-13). A giant chess game has movable pawns and rooks the size of preschoolers. The terrace is covered by a tall glass roof, and the flat

Forest Park

Tom McCall Waterfront Park

Teacher's Fountain area has arching jets popular with kids.

Tom McCall Waterfront Park

Located right on the Willamette River, the 30-acre **Tom McCall Waterfront Park** (Naito Pkwy. between SW Harrison St. and NW Glisan St., www.portlandoregon.gov, 5am-midnight daily) has views of the bridges that give Portland one of its nicknames. The site used to be Harbor Drive until former governor Tom McCall led a charge to remove the road and add a park in the 1970s. It has an esplanade walkway and a large lawn, which fills with spectators during the annual dragon boat races. Ornamental cherry trees, known for their annual burst into pink bloom, grow next to a sculpture that commemorates Portland's sister city in Japan.

Park highlights include the **Salmon Street Springs** water fountain, which shoots almost 5,000 gallons of water per minute (the springs' water patterns are controlled by computer), and the **Japanese American Historical Plaza.** The plaza is dedicated to the people who were put in internment camps during World War II, when the U.S. government decreed that everyone of Japanese descent, including American citizens, could be forced from their homes and into prison-like camps for security reasons (the government issued apologies and compensation in 1988). The plaza includes a sculpture called *Songs of Innocence, Songs of Experience* and a memorial garden.

Across the Willamette River from Tom McCall Waterfront Park, the east side of Portland gets a riverfront public space of its own in the **Eastbank Esplanade** (www.portlandoregon.gov). The path starts at the Steel Bridge, near where NE Oregon Street meets NE Lloyd Boulevard, and goes south past the Burnside Bridge, the Morrison Bridge, and the Hawthorne Bridge, ending south of OMSI where SE Caruthers Street meets SE Water Avenue. Along the 1.5-mile pedestrian and bike path are 22 interpretive panels and several pieces of public art, including one meant to represent the Shanghai tunnels that were once used to kidnap sailors and deliver them to waiting ships. Part is a floating walkway, the longest of its kind, with a public dock.

Mount Tabor Park

There's a volcanic cinder cone in the city of Portland at the east side's **Mount Tabor Park** (SE 60th Ave. and Salmon St., 503/823-2525, www.portlandoregon.gov, 5am-midnight daily), named for a mountain in Israel. This isn't to say that it looks like a volcano. The hill is now home to water reservoirs and a park with sparkling views. The nearly 200 acres contain playgrounds, a horseshoe pit, a stage, and tennis courts. The large statue is of Harvey W. Scott, an editor of the *Oregonian* in the 19th century, and made by the same man who carved Mount Rushmore. As for the volcanic cone underground, Mount Tabor is two million years old and hasn't erupted for at least 300,000 years—and isn't expected to do so again soon.

★ BIKING

When someone lists the best U.S. cities for biking—*Bicycling* magazine, for instance—Portland always comes up at the very top of the list. By their count, in 2012 Portland had more cyclists per capita than anywhere else in America, and the city has dedicated bike lanes, bike parking everywhere from coffee shops to the airport, and its annual Naked Bike Ride is usually the best attended nude pedal in the world.

For easy cruises from downtown, depart from **Tom McCall Waterfront Park** (also the location of a number of bike-rental spots). Head north along the water, under the Morrison and Burnside Bridges, then cross the Steel Bridge to reach the **Eastbank Esplanade** heading south. Cross the river again at Hawthorne Bridge for a 3-mile total loop.

For a longer ride, before crossing the Hawthorne Bridge continue south to pass OMSI, ending up at the Ross Island Bridge, the start of the **Springwater Corridor** (www.portlandoregon.gov), a former rail line. It's now a bike trail that goes all the way to the town of Boring, though a short section is on streets around Umatilla Boulevard. The first major stop on the route is **Oaks Bottom Wildlife Refuge** (SE 7th Ave. and Sellwood Blvd., www.portlandoregon.gov), a meadows and wetlands park on the river. Ride all the way to **Powell Butte State Park** (16160 SE Powell Blvd., www.portlandoregon.gov), an extinct cinder cone volcano with hiking trails, picnic areas, and restrooms. It's about 13 miles east of downtown via U.S. 26.

Really want to escape the cars? Within Forest Park, you're protected from everything gas-powered. **Leif Erikson Drive** (Thurman park entrance: NW Thurman St. and NW Aspen Ave.) is an 11-mile dirt trail with forest views and just a taste of mountain biking's hard work—some rocks, some climbs.

The city is bike friendly, but cars can still present danger, and light rail trains and streetcars can catch pedalers unaware. Riding on sidewalks isn't allowed in downtown Portland, and bikes must yield to pedestrians on walkways like the Eastbank Esplanade. Helmets are required for riders under 16 but are recommended for everyone. Bikes can go on buses or MAX trains, but never leave one unattended without locking it up first. Bike maps are available on the city's website (www.portlandoregon.gov).

Bike Rentals

To rent a bicycle in Tom McCall Waterfront Park, look next to the Salmon Street Springs fountain for **Kerr Bikes** (1020 SW Naito Pkwy., 503/808-9955, www.albertinakerr.org, 11am-5pm daily Mar., 11am-5pm Mon.-Fri. and 11am-7pm Sat.-Sun. Apr., 9am-7pm Mon.-Fri. and 8am-7pm Sat.-Sun. May-June, 8am-8pm Mon.-Fri. and 8am-9pm Sat.-Sun. Jul.-Aug., 9am-7pm daily Sept., 11am-5pm Sat.-Sun. Oct., 9am-5pm Wed.-Sun. Nov.-Feb., bikes $10-16 per hour, surreys $25-35 per hour). It has regular, tandem, and kids' bikes, plus car-like four-seater surreys, trailers, and scooters. The "U-Fix-It" station has tools, lifts, and pumps for repairs to any cycle. All proceeds from the rentals support the Albertina Kerr group, a local nonprofit that benefits people with mental development disabilities, and folks from the foundation often work the bike rental kiosk. It's a good starting place for a gentle pedal around the waterfront, so ask about maps to gentle routes that stick to bike paths.

The city's biggest bike rental shop is **Waterfront Bicycles** (10 SW Ash St., 503/227-1719, www.waterfrontbikes.com, 10am-6pm Mon.-Fri., 9am-6pm Sat.-Sun., rentals $9-15 per hour, $30-100 per day), located just across from Tom McCall Waterfront Park. It has more than 100 cycles in its rental fleet, including three-speed cruisers with wicker baskets and ultralight road bikes (men's and women's models). It also offers a number of children's accessories like trailers, bike extensions, and child seats. Reserve online more than two days before rental or call within 48 hours.

At **Everybody's Bike Rentals & Tours**

(305 NE Wygant St., 503/358-0152, www.pdxbikerentals.com, 10am-5pm daily May-Oct.), the bikes ($8-15 per hour) are notably light and easy to move up curbs or into one of the city's many bike parking spots. There are even vintage road bikes and fixies available so you don't stick out in the cool bike crowds of Portland. Tours ($39-59) come with a free 24-hour rental, making them an ideal starting point for wannabe city cyclists.

Bike Tours

You can tour the city with **Cycle Portland Bike Tours** (117 NW 2nd Ave., 503/902-5035, www.portlandbicycletours.com, $39-49 including bike rental). An Essential Portland Tour hits up the Park Blocks, the Pearl District, and Waterfront Park in an easy two-hour pedal, so you needn't be a seasoned road warrior, just comfortable cruising slowly near cars. The Bike-O-Rama! takes a more creative look at the city, focusing on bike culture itself. The bike-enthusiast guides show off the varieties of bike lanes and greenways and then discuss the various non-car transportation options in the city. And, of course, there's a brewery tour by bike.

Pedal Bike Tours (133 SW 2nd Ave., 503/243-2453, www.pedalbiketours.com, $59-99) does offer downtown and brewery tours, but its more exciting options include a Lava Tour to Mount Tabor, an extinct volcano that's actually within the city limits. The 20-plus-mile route and hills require you to be at least an intermediate cyclist.

SPECTATOR SPORTS

Basketball

When Seattle lost its NBA franchise in 2008, the Portland **Trail Blazers** (Moda Center, 1 N Center Court St., 503/797-9619, www.nba.com/blazers, $11-220) became the only professional basketball team in the Northwest. They play in the building once known as the Rose Garden—now the Moda Center—and games often sell out. Although the team hasn't appeared in the NBA finals in decades, it has a fervent following.

Hockey

It has no NHL team, but the city is home to the Portland **Winterhawks** (503/236-4295, www.winterhawks.com, $15-55), a junior league team in the Western Hockey League that plays teams from Seattle, Spokane, Victoria, and elsewhere in games that go August-May. They split their home games between the **Moda Center** (1 N Center Court St.) and **Veterans Memorial Coliseum** (www.rosequarter.com) directly next door.

Roller Derby

The **Rose City Rollers** (www.rosecityrollers.com, $16-22) is a female flat-track roller derby league in Portland, made up of skaters known by nicknames like Nacho Lucky Day and Scald Eagle. Teams compete with each other or visiting roller derby teams at bouts year-round held at **Memorial Stadium** (300 N. Winning Way) and The Hanger at **Oaks Amusement Park** (7805 SE Oaks Park Way).

Soccer

Although the Portland **Timbers** (Jeld-Wen Field, 1844 SW Morrison St., 503/553-5400, www.portlandtimbers.com) have only been a Major League Soccer team since 2011, the team is part of a soccer renaissance in the Pacific Northwest. There's a healthy rivalry with the Seattle Sounders FC and Vancouver Whitecaps FC (and if you ask a rabid fan, particularly with the former). The organized Timber Army cheering section, filled with fans in green-and-white scarves, is raucous. The season begins in March and ends in October, but preseason matches can start in January.

Food

What is the quintessential Portland meal? It's not of a particular cuisine, but it's probably locally and sustainably sourced, and it might even be served from the side of a food truck or from a counter. One of the most popular joints in town is a Thai restaurant that re-creates the street food of Bangkok, while the longest lines are at Salt & Straw ice cream on a hot summer day. (Seriously, you'll wait forever.) Great food isn't necessarily expensive in Portland, even though pricey tasting menus and fine French fare do exist here.

DOWNTOWN

Seafood

It's not a typo—**Jake's Famous Crawfish** (401 SW 12th Ave., 503/226-1419, www.mccormickandschmicks.com, 11:30am-11pm Mon.-Thurs., 11:30am-midnight Fri.-Sat., 3pm-10pm Sun., $20-47) has been around "since 1892" serving cedar plank salmon and steaks. The fish on the menu hails from Alaska, Hawaii, Washington, and of course, British Columbia, though the lobster tails do come all the way from Maine. Not a lot of crawfish on the menu, but you'll find them in the étouffée. The desserts—cobblers, truffle cake, and the decadent "chocolate bag" full of mousse—are just as rich. The sign outside is old-fashioned neon, and inside is a classic dining room with wood accents and stained glass.

American

In a city devoted to quirk and vintage style, **Higgins Restaurant** (1239 SW Broadway, 503/222-9070, www.higginsportland.com, 11:30am-midnight Mon.-Fri., 4pm-midnight Sat.-Sun., $25-40) is a refreshingly straightforward restaurant painted in soothing neutral tones—no antlers on the wall, no taxidermy by the door. The country-style menu is farm fare gone high end: a summer vegetable sandwich with sheep's milk feta, or risotto with chanterelles and squash, or a "whole pig plate" that includes sausage, roast loin, belly, and ribs. It's a grown-up's dinner out.

The building that holds **Raven & Rose** (1331 SW Broadway, 503/222-7673, www.ravenandrosepdx.com, 11:30am-2pm and 5pm-10pm Mon.-Fri., 10am-2pm and 5pm-10pm Sat., 10am-2pm and 4pm-9pm Sun., $12-36) used to be the carriage house for the Ladd Estate that stood in the middle of today's downtown Portland, but at three stories and with ornate exterior decorations in the English Stick style, it hardly looks like the garage. The 1st floor's main restaurant has regular seating, a stately bar, and four seats right at the kitchen where you can see chefs prepare the flatbread, meatballs, and mussels in the wood oven. Meals are simple but rich: buttermilk-fried rabbit, salmon with succotash, and beef short ribs with mashed potatoes and Yorkshire pudding. Try the Caesar salad, served with pieces of rabbit. Upstairs in the Rookery is another bar in a giant loft with exposed wooden beams, leather seating, and a pool table, which serves small bites from the kitchen.

Lines form to fill the metal chairs and reclaimed wood benches at ★ **Tasty N Alder** (580 SW 12th Ave., 503/621-9251, www.tastynalder.com, 9am-10pm Sun.-Thurs., 9am-11pm Fri.-Sat., $14-35) before it even opens for brunch (which it serves daily). Entrées include Korean fried chicken with house kimchi and Indonesian short rib, drawing from exotic influences but giving them a decidedly Portland, homegrown spin. Fries are fried in *washimi wagyu* beef tallow, and the burger comes with a hazelnut *romesco*. Decorations, besides the rustic light fixtures, are few, but the service is prompt.

Clyde Common (1014 SW Stark St., 503/228-3333, www.clydecommon.com, 3pm-12:45am daily, $14-29) is located right next to the lobby of the Ace Hotel, and it shares some of that joint's indie, hip feel. Decorated in rough-hewn wood and canvas, it nevertheless has an upscale, not outdoorsy feel. The liquor menu is mostly whiskeys and bourbon—what more do you need?—plus a little absinthe. Try snacks like truffle popcorn or roasted beets, or attack a full meal of ravioli or steak. But do speak up, as the din inside the busy joint fills with Ace guests, locals, and other very loud, very chatty young folks.

The green-sounding **Urban Farmer** (525 SW Morrison St., 8th Floor, 503/222-4900, www.urbanfarmerportland.com, 6:30am-3pm and 5pm-10pm Sun.-Thurs., 6:30am-3pm and 5pm-11pm Fri.-Sat., $29-80) is actually an "urban steakhouse" specializing in farmhouse fare like brioche French toast and duck breast. And then, of course, there's the steak, broken down by cut and origin, and each selection notes how the cows were fed: on Oregon grass for the 14-ounce rib eye, or on corn in California for the 14-ounce New York. The creamy spinach gratin makes the best pair for steak. The wine list has 350 bottles (many of them local), beers come from within Portland, and cocktails are made from Oregon spirits, plus the weekend brunch has a Bloody Mary bar. It's located in the Nines Hotel, on the 8th floor of a downtown building, in what feels like an outdoor patio that's actually surrounded by floors of hotel room windows.

If you miss mom's cooking while on the road, **Mother's Bistro** (212 SW Stark St., 503/464-1122, www.mothersbistro.com, 7am-9pm Tues.-Thurs., 7am-10pm Fri., 8am-10pm Sat., 8am-2:30pm Sun., $11-20) just makes sense—it serves traditional dishes you'd find at home, provided your home supper consisted of pork loin medallions with beer and caramelized onions or steak *frites.* Every month the restaurant features a different mother and her favorite dishes, done in her style. The Mother of the Month menus are often seasonal and hail from around the globe, and diners nominate favorite moms on the restaurant's website. The space, too, is probably a little fancier than what you get at home—chandeliers hang over a bright, airy space on one side, and exposed brick walls face the bar on the Velvet Lounge side. There' a small play area for children—doesn't every home kitchen have one?

All the deli classics are at **Kenny and Zuke's Delicatessen** (1038 SW Stark St., 503/222-3354, www.kennyandzukes.com, 7am-8pm Mon.-Thurs., 7am-9pm Fri., 8am-9pm Sat., 8am-8pm Sun., $11-18)—pastrami, chopped liver, cheese blintzes, and big Reuben sandwiches. The owner's pastrami, sold at a farmers market, was so popular he eventually opened a whole collection of Kenny and Zuke's spots around the city. Here all-day breakfast is served in the big corner space. Sit down to read the blackboards, or take an order at the counter to go, grabbing a bagel with a schmear for the road.

Coffee

Stumptown Coffee Roasters (128 SW 3rd Ave., 503/295-6144, www.stumptowncoffee.com, 6am-7pm Mon.-Fri., 7am-7pm Sat.-Sun.) used to be a small coffee roaster on Division Street when it opened in 1999, named for the logging industry. Founder Duane Sorenson delivered coffee to wholesale customers out of his own Ford Pinto. The company supported sustainable growth and trade practices—Sorenson became known for paying the highest per-pound price ever for beans in some Latin American countries. Eventually it became popular enough to open outposts around Portland, and then in cities like Seattle and New York, and in California. In 2015 the company was sold to the Peet's coffee chain, leading to some disappointment among those who liked the independent backstory. The 3rd Avenue space was the first Stumptown in the downtown area and epitomizes the chain's rustic aesthetic with exposed brick walls and wood counters, plus taps for their cold brew. Sit at the wall of magazines and stools where you can watch the baristas work.

Unlike the very hip Stumptown, **Case Study Coffee** (802 SW 10th Ave., 503/475-3979, www.casestudycoffee.com, 7am-6pm Mon.-Fri., 8am-6pm Sat.-Sun.) is more about

Food Cart Revolution

some of Portland's many food carts

Almost every city has some kind of street food—hot dog stands, halal carts, ice cream trucks. But Portland takes it to another level, with more than 500 food carts around the city. Many are grouped in pods, which can have anywhere from three to dozens of different options. How do you know what's good? You wander, you look—and you just try something, since most food options are under $7.

The biggest food cart pod is the block between **SW 9th and SW 10th Avenues, and SW Alder and SW Washington Streets.** More than 60 food purveyors park here, making it the biggest single concentration of street food vendors in the country. Office workers fill the square at lunchtime, and while some carts open on weekends, not all will. If you don't want to eat while walking, head across the street to **O'Bryant Square** (SW Park Ave. and Washington St., www.portlandoregon.gov/parks). The brick half acre is not the lushest of city parks, but there are ledges to sit on while you wolf down a panini or bowl of pho. Another pod, at SW 3rd Avenue between SW Washington and Stark Streets, is close to Tom McCall Waterfront Park.

A **website** (www.foodcartsportland.com) lists the location of carts and pods, along with a link to a phone app that maps the locations. The host of the website leads 90-minute **tours** (www.foodcartsportland.com, tours@foodcartsportland.com, $50, children under 12 free) Monday-Saturday around lunchtime, giving visitors a history of the food cart movement and tastes from a few carts.

the café vibe, with just two locations in the city and only this one in the downtown core. The wood coffee bar sits under a retro-futuristic light fixture, but everything else is sleek. It has all the chai lattes and cappuccinos and ice-brewed varieties we've come to expect from coffee shops, but a mug of house coffee starts at just $2.50. Food is just pastries, bagels, and granola.

The small **Courier Coffee Roasters** (923 SW Oak, 503/545-6444, www.couriercoffeeroasters.com, 7am-6pm Mon.-Fri., 9am-5pm Sat.-Sun.) is a small shop that is everything Starbucks isn't—local, friendly, and unusual. Drinks are served in mason jars, and labels are hand stamped. You'll want to chat with the barista before you choose from the beans on hand. Coffee is made using reusable filters that are plated with 23-karat gold. Pastries and homemade granola bars are all made from locally sourced ingredients.

Dessert

It's a good thing ★ **Voodoo Doughnut** (22 SW 3rd Ave., 503/241-4704, www.voodoo-doughnut.com, 24 hours daily, $1-4) never closes, because people are always looking for its signature weird doughnuts—maple bars with a strip of bacon on top, or treats topped with breakfast cereal or M&Ms. If you're looking for more than a sugar rush, order a wedding—they start at $35 for a nonlegal vow renewal ceremony (with no free treats) and go up to $325 for a legal ceremony and doughnuts for six people. Look for a brick building and a line outside. Cash only.

French

As the little sister restaurant to the fancier Le Pigeon, **Little Bird** (219 SW 6th Ave., 503/688-5952, www.littlebirdbistro.com, 11:30am-midnight Mon.-Fri., 5pm-midnight Sat.-Sun., $13-45) is allowed to be a little looser, so antlers hang on the walls across from deep red banquettes. Lunch includes casual French munchies like an oyster po'boy and *moules-frites,* and drinks come in half sizes—can you stop at just a half martini? Dinner features cassoulet of duck leg, pork belly, and sausage, and a chicken-fried trout, plus the burger off the Le Pigeon menu.

PEARL DISTRICT AND NORTHWEST

Pacific Northwest

Paley's Place (1204 NW 21st Ave., 503/243-2403, www.paleysplace.net, 5:30pm-10pm Mon.-Thurs., 5pm-11pm Fri.-Sat., 5pm-10pm Sun., $15-30) doesn't look much like a restaurant at first glance, hidden behind trees in a Victorian building with a long porch. The chef has garnered attention from everyone from the James Beard Foundation to *Bon Appétit,* but the restaurant is still a sedate 50-seater that focuses on Pacific Northwest ingredients like wild salmon, potatoes, halibut, and mushrooms. The restaurant will serve half portions of main entrées so that tables can enjoy a greater selection of the menu.

American

Ready to experience the entire menu at **Little Big Burger** (122 NW 10th Ave., 503/274-9008, www.littlebigburger.com, 11am-10pm daily, $4.75)? It's cheeseburgers, hamburgers, veggie burgers, fries, sodas, and floats. That's it—so let's hope you were craving something on a bun. The burgers are a quarter pound and served on a brioche bun, a tiny, vertical mound that looks something like an overgrown slider (but not quite a grown-up burger). Fries are served with white truffle oil, a flavor some people love but others could do without, so make sure you know your position before you indulge. Fry sauce and ketchup are homemade, and floats are a combination of Tillamook ice cream and root beer.

Asian

Though the spot was once an upscale Vietnamese restaurant named Silk, it was rebranded and reopened as **Pho Van Fresh** (1012 NW Glisan St., 503/248-2172, www.phovanfresh.com, 11am-10pm Mon.-Sat., $6-13); there are still a few old Silk favorites like the hoisin ribs on the menu. Like its predecessor, the new fast-casual eatery aims for authenticity, but leans heavily toward crowd favorites like fried Brussels sprouts and pork belly steamed buns—the banh mi are also popular. Pho, a Vietnamese rice noodle soup with vegetables, beef, or chicken, is the centerpiece, and the bar serves cocktails inspired by Asian flavors. Pho Van's original location is in southeast Portland, but this more central outpost pairs more easily with a day of downtown exploration.

Dessert

The ice cream empire of **Salt & Straw** (838 NW 23rd Ave., 971/271-8168, www.saltandstraw.com, 11am-11pm daily, $3.75-6.50) started as an ice cream pushcart, but since the owner had begun her career working at

Fortune 500 businesses, it was no surprise that it quickly grew to a string of stores in Portland, including outposts on Division and Alberta Streets, as well as San Francisco and Seattle. Flavors combine the savory and sweet—the strawberry has balsamic vinegar in it, and the coffee flavor comes with bourbon. Try the pear with blue cheese or the sea salt ice cream with caramel ribbon for the classic flavor profile, or try a special flavor, developed with seasonal ingredients, sometimes by local chefs. There are sundaes and floats, but the scoops themselves are plenty complex; even if you're just getting chocolate, you can top your cone with finishing salt for an extra $0.50.

European

Olympia Provisions (1632 NW Thurman St., 503/894-8136, www.olympiaprovisions.com, 11am-10pm Mon.-Fri., 9am-10pm Sat.-Sun., $22-34) started as a meat maker, curing salami and winning awards for its European-style chorizo, *soppressata,* and other varieties. Now it has two restaurants whose menus go far beyond meat, with roasted veggies, crispy salmon, and gnocchi (don't worry—plenty of meat comes with the plate of bratwurst, kielbasa, and ham, and there's an entire charcuterie menu). The smaller, original location sits across the river, but this sunny space has more seating and lots of light, and the chef did a stint at Bouchon with Thomas Keller.

Peruvian

The multilevel **Andina** (1314 NW Glisan St., 503/228-9535, www.andinarestaurant.com, 11:30am-2:30pm and 4pm-9:30pm Sun.-Fri., 11:30am-2:30pm and 5pm-10:30pm. Sat., $21-40) feels smaller than it is once you sit down, more like a neighborhood tapas bar than the bustling warehouse restaurant it is. The Peruvian fare includes tapas and "novo-Andean" main courses like diver scallops, a quinoa dish that resembles risotto, slow-cooked lamb shank, and pork loin. Vegetarian, vegan, and gluten-free menus are also served. The bar has Latin-inspired live music performances, including a jazz trio, gypsy swing, and guitar-playing singer-songwriters.

SOUTHEAST

Pacific Northwest

The very modern, upscale ★ **Castagna** (1752 SE Hawthorne Blvd., 503/231-7373, www.castagnarestaurant.com, 5:30pm-10pm Wed.-Sat., $100-165) makes Pacific Northwest food artful and exciting. Menus are prix fixe, either a standard dinner of appetizer, salad, entrée, and dessert, or a chef's tasting menu of nine small courses—plan on several hours, as many as four, for that option. Wine pairings are extra. The chef, Justin Woodward, won the Rising Star Chef prize from the James Beard Foundation and is known for presenting his food with artistic and elaborate care. It is as fine a dining experience as you can find in town. Reservations are recommended, though the related ★ **Café Castagna** (503/231-9959, 5pm-10pm Tues.-Thurs., 5pm-11pm Fri.-Sat., 5pm-9:30pm Sun., $12-30) next door is more likely to handle walk-ins, and is overseen by the same star chef.

American

Stumptown founder Duane Sorenson turned to food and hard drink for **The Woodsman Tavern** (4537 SE Division St., 971/373-8264, www.woodsmantavern.com, 5pm-10pm Mon.-Fri., 9am-10pm Sat.-Sun, $16-60), a restaurant-bar on a quiet stretch of Division. Although meant to pay tribute to the logging industry, the space is more defined by its oysters on ice and retro light fixtures than the woodsy landscape paintings crowding the walls. Main courses are heavy on the meat—pork shoulder, meatloaf sandwich—though starters are smaller and lighter. Fried chicken comes in a bucket with honey, and a special Oyster Hour is 5pm-6pm. The bar has 14 beers on taps and cocktails that seem high end, even when they're not—like the $7 Pickleback (Irish whiskey with a dram of pickle juice).

The **Roman Candle Baking Company** (3377 SE Division St., 971/302-6605, www.romancandlebaking.com, 7am-4pm daily) bakery smells faintly of flour, thanks to the pastries and breads ($4-9) cooked here. The space used to be a coffee processing site for Stumptown Coffee and has white tile walls and exposed wood beams. For a full meal turn to the pizza Bianca ($4-6 per slice, $28-44 per slab), a flatbread pizza made in a wood-fired oven and topped with locally sourced veggies and meats. Drinks include Italian sodas, wines, and coffee made in an elaborate espresso machine made of glass and copper tubes.

The small **Lauretta Jean's** (3402 SE Division St., 503/235-3119, www.laurettajean.com, 8am-10pm Sun.-Thurs., 8am-11pm Fri.-Sat., $7-11) serves pies and parfaits, plus craft cocktails in a sweet shop with pastel walls and small tables. Pies are shown off at the big glass case under the counter, but the menu has egg scrambles, biscuit sandwiches, and quiches in the morning and sandwiches and salads for lunch and dinner.

The treats at **The Waffle Window** (3610 SE Hawthorne Blvd., 971/255-0501, www.wafflewindow.com, 8am-6pm Sun.-Thurs., 8am-9pm Fri.-Sat., $3-8) aren't exactly breakfast or lunch on their own, which may only prompt you to rejoin the line after eating so that you can order again. It is indeed a window, located on the side of the Bread and Ink Café (with indoor seating there), and a covered outdoor seating area is right around the corner. The Liege sugar waffles are covered in sugar, dipped in dark chocolate, or topped with savory combos like mushroom and spinach or bacon and brie. For the spicy fans, the spicy bacon cheddar jalapeño waffle, topped with avocado-tomatillo salsa, is heavenly.

Asian

The chef behind Thai outpost ★ **Pok Pok** (3226 SE Division St., 503/232-1387, www.pokpokpdx.com, 11:30am-10pm daily, $11-19) is so well regarded, he won a James Beard award and opened three related branches in Portland and three in New York City. The original location has covered outdoor seating with colored lights, plus an upstairs dining room. The Southeast Asian food is meant to reflect the street and home cooking of Thailand, and many dishes are meant to be shared. It's not the pad Thai you may be used to; instead you'll find marinated baby back ribs, Chiang Mai sausage, and wild-caught prawns cooked with pork belly. Besides an extensive whiskey list and cocktail menu (including a Korean yuzu-honey hot toddy), there are nonalcoholic drinking vinegars, which are seasonal flavors mixed with soda water. Even the table water has flavor, that of the pandanus leaf. Reservations are only taken for groups larger than five, but if the wait is long, you can sneak in a drink at the related **Whiskey Soda Lounge** (3131 SE Division St., 503/232-0102, www.whiskeysodalounge.com, 4pm-midnight Sun.-Thurs., 4pm-1am Fri.-Sat.) across the street.

French

The French **Le Pigeon** (738 E Burnside St., 503/546-8796, www.lepigeon.com, 5pm-10pm daily, $24-35) has a short but impeccable menu, served as a five-course chef's tasting menu for $85. Starters include the likes of foie gras, glazed eel, and clam flatbread, with entrées of beef cheek bourguignon and rabbit blanquette. The unassuming small restaurant has bright white curtains and exposed brick walls for an intimate farmhouse feel, and some tables are communal.

Italian

Although **Apizza Scholls** (4741 SE Hawthorne Blvd., 503/233-1286, www.apizzascholls.com, 5pm-9:30pm Mon.-Fri., 11:30am-2:30pm and 5pm-9:30pm Sat.-Sun., $19-26) serves pizza, don't think of it as a greasy pizza joint. Pies are made from dough that's handmade each day, which keeps the small restaurant from opening for lunch—when they run out of dough, they're done for the day. There's often a line, and servers ask how many pizzas you'll order when they add your name to the waiting list, but drinks, salads, and seating are available to patrons waiting for a table. The pizzas themselves have a ciabatta-like crust, so delicate the kitchen limits toppings to three per pie, and no more than two meats. House combinations include a margherita with anchovies or cured pork shoulder, cheese with truffle oil and sea salt, and a cheesy, sauceless concoction with house-cured bacon.

The charming ★ **Ava Gene's** (3377 SE Division St, 971/229-0571, avagenes.com, 5pm-10pm Mon-Thurs., 5pm-11pm Fri., 4:30pm-11pm Sat., 4:30pm-10pm Sun., $19-36) quickly gained a reputation as one of Portland's best restaurants. Its produce-minded Roman menu is served in a rather casual setting, and handmade pastas and mouthwatering vegetable dishes are the highlight. One of the restaurant's local purveyors is usually highlighted on each day's menu. Family-style dining is available if the whole table buys in ($75 pp). Pay attention to what the waitstaff highlights as the day's specials, since the seasonal nature of the menu means there are always surprises.

Mexican

Taco joint ★ **Por Que No?** (4635 SE Hawthorne Blvd., 503/954-3138, www.porquenotacos.com, 11am-10pm Mon.-Sat., 11am-9:30pm Sun., $5-13) is a prime example of the kind of eatery taking Portland by storm—you order at the counter, pay for your food and drinks, then find a table and wait for your food. But the Mexican restaurant is not merely fast-casual; the red-walled space is crammed with old paintings and funky decor, and meals are served with real silverware and in solid bowls and baskets. The tacos are made with house-made corn tortillas, and it's hard to pick one variety, or even three, but the *al pastor,* carnitas, and *pollo asada* are among the best. That and the line-caught cod *pescado* tacos are, or maybe the calamari ones. Bigger plates have tamales and salads, and you can start with flautas or fresh guacamole and house-made chips. Margaritas come in classic and pomegranate flavors.

Middle Eastern

The inside of beloved ★ **Tusk** (2448 E Burnside St., 503/894-8082, tuskpdx.com, 5pm-10pm Mon.-Wed., 5pm-midnight Thurs.-Fri., 10am-2pm and 5pm-midnight Sat., 10am-2pm and 5pm-10pm Sun., $15-40) is bright white, though the dishes themselves are filled with the colors of Middle Eastern cuisine and local produce. A new favorite regularly hailed as the best dinner in Portland, it's run by the same team behind Ava Gene's, and the two restaurants share an "aggressively

Por Que No? taco joint

seasonal" philosophy. Get several meat skewers or a big pork chop with veggies on the side, or simply sign up for the $50-per-plate chef's menu, called a "magic carpet ride."

NORTHEAST/NORTH

American

Almost all the produce served at **Navarre** (10 NE 28th Ave., 503/232-3555, http://navarre-portland.blogspot.com, 4:30pm-10:30pm Mon.-Thurs., 4:30pm-11:30pm Fri., 9:30am-11:30pm Sat., 9:30am-10:30pm Sun., $23-35) is local—and when they say local, they mean fruits and vegetables grown within Portland's city limits. The wine list is crammed with Oregon vintages. For all the local sourcing, however, the menu has European inspirations, and they serve an excellent breakfast in the narrow space.

The **Laurelhurst Market** (3155 E Burnside St., 503/206-3097, www.laurelhurstmarket.com, 10am-10pm daily, $14-39) is a neighborhood brasserie, crowded with tables and serving a huge variety of steaks, salads, and sides. But it's also a butcher shop that sells hormone- and antibiotic-free meats and house-made sausages. Even if you're not looking to get your ham hocks to go, it's nice to know that your restaurant's kitchen has the very best cuts. The large modern space is a destination for meat eaters—salads and sides are on the menu, but nearly everything green is cooked with or topped with bacon.

At **Pine State Biscuits** (2204 NE Alberta St., 503/477-6605, www.pinestatebiscuits.com, 7am-3pm daily, $4-8), what started as a modest farmers market stand is now a sizable counter-service restaurant devoted to the biscuit. The buttermilk concoctions are served with sausage or mushroom gravy, and as any kind of sandwich you could want—fried chicken, steak club, pulled pork, or with egg. A few other Southern touches, like blueberry cornmeal pancakes and grits, round out the menu. Iron stools line a counter next to the open kitchen, and lights above look like mason jars, completing the homey look.

Asian

Getting into the delicious **Han Oak** (511 NE 24th Ave., http://hanoakpdx.com, 5:30pm-9pm Fri.-Sat., 5pm-10pm Sun.-Mon., $10-19) is a trial, but the lucky few can score reservations to the Friday and Saturday night prix fixe ($45), which is the primary way of dining here, full of whipped tofu, noodles, and pork belly—or maybe fried chicken or barbecue—from the Korean jewel. Leave time to find it; it's tucked into a courtyard like a secret hideaway. On Sundays and Mondays it serves dumplings a la carte, but the weekend dinners often change at the whim of the chef and owner.

Breakfast

★ **Gravy** (3957 N Mississippi Ave., 503/287-8800, www.gravyrestaurant.com, 7:30am-3pm daily, $8-13) is so popular the lines get intense. Portions are massive, with hash made from corned beef, roast beef, and smoked salmon, and a Monte Cristo sandwich made on French toast. The hash browns are cooked into thick, crispy disks. Good luck finding the biscuit itself in the sea of sausage gravy. Grab coffee while you wait and expect to leave with a to-go box.

Indian

The counter-service, bustling **Bollywood Theater** (2039 NE Alberta St., 971/200-4711, www.bollywoodtheaterpdx.com, 11am-10pm daily, $5-19) is Indian food inspired by Bombay street stands, right down to the steel cups and steel plates. It's so popular the line is usually out the door (though it moves quickly, as do most of the hip new restaurants of this type in Portland). The menu has samosas and curry *thali* meals similar to what you'd find in other Indian takeout joints, while the Goan-style shrimp has curry leaves and chiles, and the *kati* rolls are like Indian burritos, with chicken, cheese, or beef wrapped in Indian flatbread with green chutney. Drinks include local beers, Indian beer on tap, and a Pimm's Cup cocktail.

Southern

Screen Door (2337 E Burnside St., 503/542-0880, www.screendoorrestaurant.com, 8am-2pm and 5:30pm-10pm Mon.-Fri, 9am-2:30pm and 5:30pm-10pm Sat., 9am-2:30pm and 5:30pm-9pm Sun., $12-18) serves cuisine inspired by the South, specifically the soul food traditions of the South Carolina Lowcountry, along with the Creole cuisine of New Orleans. Hushpuppies come with a pepper jelly dipping sauce, and fried okra plus mouthwatering buttermilk-fried chicken are also on the menu. The vegetarian sides include grits and sweet potato fries, but the collard greens? They're definitely not vegetarian—they're cooked with bacon and ham hocks. The restaurant is as casual as you'd expect from a place that serves pulled pork sandwiches, with boards on the walls and bright blue booths.

Accommodations

Most hotels in Portland try to show off some kind of character—a rock-and-roll aesthetic, or a fine-arts look complete with artwork in every room. Some cheaper hotels offer shared-bath accommodations, but they're not dingy rooming houses with crowded locker rooms—most patrons barely notice that their single-occupant bathroom is across the hall instead of across the room. Because parking is limited in the downtown core, most hotels charge steep prices for valet parking.

DOWNTOWN

Under $150

In case you forget what **Ace Hotel** (1022 SW Stark St., 503/228-2277, www.acehotel.com/portland, $125-195 shared bath, $175-345 private bath) is, giant distressed metal letters spell out HOTEL in the wood-paneled lobby. There's a cooler-than-thou vibe to the place, with record players in each room and handmade bikes available to rent. Low beds in white-walled rooms are covered with special wool Pendleton blankets that you'll be tempted to steal (but don't, they're for sale online). Some rooms share single hallway baths, while others have their own shower or claw-foot tub; all have TVs.

$150-250

The somewhat trippy ★ **Crystal Hotel** (303 SW 12th Ave., 503/972-2670, www.mcmenamins.com/crystalhotel, $155 shared bath, $215-235 private bath), part of the McMenamins empire, has mural-painted headboards on each bed, walls in dark colors, and thick black curtains—and each room is named for a band or performance from the live music venue Crystal Ballroom across the street, like songs by James Brown and the Flaming Lips. The 1911 building was once called the Majestic Hotel, which housed a rowdy gambling and drinking establishment, then a nightclub. Hall bathrooms are plentiful, so the European-style shared-bath rooms are a good bargain. There are reserved tickets for whatever's playing at the Crystal Ballroom; call ahead to score some for the night of your stay. Downstairs in a low-ceilinged room with bamboo walls is a soaking pool shaped like a big amoeba.

The artsy ★ **Hotel Lucia** (400 SW Broadway, 503/225-1717, www.hotellucia.com, $199-369) has a long, modern lobby with sculptures and framed photography on the walls; the hotel owns the world's largest collection of works by Pulitzer Prize-winning photographer David Hume Kennerly (he's also a Portland local). Rooms are generally modest but decorated in somber dark mahogany and black oak, and beds have pillow-top mattresses and come with a pillow menu. The location on Broadway is central but still fairly quiet. Attached to the hotel are two food spots: The upscale **Imperial** (410 SW Broadway, 503/228-7222, www.imperialpdx.

com, 6:30am-2pm Mon.-Wed., 6:30am-2pm and 5pm-10pm Thurs., 6:30am-2pm and 5pm-11pm Fri., 8am-2pm and 5pm-11pm Sat., 8am-2pm and 5pm-10pm Sun.) has a large wood-fired grill and serves rib eyes, pork chops, and chanterelles cooked with bone marrow.

Over $250

Enter **The Benson** (309 SW Broadway, 503/228-2000, www.coasthotels.com, $198-450), and you'll be greeted by tall wooden pillars and a classic, marble-floored hotel lobby, so it's easy to see the century-old roots in the hotel. Rooms feature deluxe striped curtains and plush linens and bathrobes, and it's not unusual to see personal touches from the staff, like towels folded into the shapes of animals. The **Palm Court** (6:30am-close daily) in the lobby has live jazz music for much of the week and serves breakfast, lunch, and dinner and hosts two daily happy hours. Next door, **El Gaucho** (319 Broadway, 503/227-8794, 4:30pm-1am Mon.-Sat., 4pm-11pm Sun.) is an old-world steakhouse with a cigar room.

Hotel Rose (50 SW Morrison St., 866/866-7977, www.hotelroseportland.com, $179-389) has a mid-20th-century feel in the lobby, but purely modern rooms with large showers and memory-foam mattresses. Free bicycle rentals and gold umbrellas are also available. Its location on the east side of downtown, near the river, yields waterfront and cityscape views. The eatery downstairs, **Bottle + Kitchen** (503/484-1415, www.bottlekitchen.com, 6:30am-midnight Sun.-Thurs., 7am-noon Fri.-Sat.), features a New Zealand chef cooking globally inspired food with a local ethos.

The charming **Mark Spencer** (409 SW 11th Ave., 503/224-3293, www.markspencer.com, $289-329) is just a block away from the hipper Ace but has a more traditional vibe. The stately old building has rooms with exposed brick walls, and larger suites have fully equipped kitchens for longer stays. The overall vibe is not one of extravagance, but rooms are simple and comfortable. Swing by the lobby for free afternoon tea and cookies, then evening wine and cheese. Hybrid cars can park for half price. You can even bid for a room at a lower price online; enter your credit card information and propose a rate for a room, then wait for a response. If it's accepted, the card will be charged and the reservation is nonrefundable. Bid too low or for a booked night and you'll receive alternate suggestions.

The **Hotel Modera** (515 SW Clay St., 503/484-1084, www.hotelmodera.com, $279-319) claims to have more than 500 pieces of local art on its walls, and that's not counting the hotel itself, with its white mod lobby chairs and open fireplaces in the Nel Centro restaurant. Although billed as a boutique hotel, it has almost 175 rooms, all with Italian marble in the bathrooms and bath products made from Italian olive oils. Like most city hotels it doesn't have a swimming pool, but guests get free passes to the gym a block away. The **Nel Centro** (1408 SW 6th Ave., 503/484-1099, www.nelcentro.com, 6:30am-10:30am, 11:30am-2pm, and 5pm-9pm Mon.-Thurs., 6:30am-10:30am, 11:30am-2pm, and 5pm-10pm Fri., 7:30am-11:30am and 5pm-10pm Sat., 8am-2pm and 5pm-9pm Sun.) restaurant serves a menu inspired by the French and Italian Riviera, and has a large outdoor patio.

Walk into the **Sentinel Hotel** (614 SW 11th Ave., 503/224-3400, www.sentinelhotel.com, $209-429) and then look up—the hotel was built in 1909, and the intricate designs and glasswork on the ceiling are beautiful. Outside, art deco ornamentations adorn the building's exterior (though some think they look like robots). Rooms are done in calming neutrals with a few classic touches, like fireplaces and wood wardrobes, but mostly have modern amenities. Off the lobby, **Jake's Grill** (611 SW 10th Ave., 503/220-1850, www.mccormickandschmicks.com, 7am-11pm Mon.-Thurs., 7am-midnight Fri., 7:30am-midnight Sat., 7:30am-11pm Sun.) has basic grill fare and a bar, plus a giant mural that traces the history of the Lewis and Clark expedition. Lobby bar **Jackknife** (3pm-2am daily) serves champagne with a straw and a small menu of salads and sandwiches.

The name of the **Hotel deLuxe** (729 SW 15th Ave., 503/219-2094, www.hoteldeluxe-portland.com, $189-359) isn't just about the fine amenities—though rooms are very nice—but rather the Hollywood color lab Deluxe, which is why the rooms and hallways feature black-and-white classic movie images. In the room are a number of menus—a pillow menu, a spiritual book menu, an iPod menu (borrow one with music from a particular genre), and even a pet spiritual menu, full of books on pet massage and psychology. The Pop-Up Cinema series screens classic films in a private screening room with historical touches and only 36 seats. Restaurants include the sedate **Gracie's** (503/222-2171, 6:30am-2pm and 5pm-9pm Mon.-Thurs., 6:30am-2pm and 5pm-10pm Fri., 8am-2pm and 5pm-10pm Sat., 8am-2pm and 5pm-9pm Sun.) and the hip **Driftwood Room** (503/820-2076, 2pm-11:30pm Sun.-Thurs., 2pm-12:30am Fri., noon-12:30am Sat.), which recalls a cocktail bar in the 1950s. For all the black-and-white glamour, rooms are bright and modern.

The stately **Hotel Vintage Plaza** (422 SW Broadway, 503/228-1212, www.vintage-plaza.com, $166-401) is a solid combination of boutique property and chain hotel. Rooms are decorated in upscale linens and furniture with plush animal-print robes, but there's a personal touch with yoga mats in the rooms and daily wine hours in the lobby. Parking is $37 for valet service, but hybrid cars get 50 percent off. The Italian **Pazzo Ristorante** (627 SW Washington, 503/228-1515, www.pazzo.com, 7am-10:30am, 11:30am-2:30pm, and 5pm-9:30pm Mon.-Thurs., 7am-10:30am, 11:30am-2:30pm, and 5pm-10pm Fri., 8am-2pm and 5pm-10pm Sat., 8am-2pm and 5pm-9pm Sun.) is attached to the hotel.

Outside the ★ **Heathman Hotel** (1001 SW Broadway, 503/241-4100, http://portland.heathmanhotel.com, $170-408), the bellhop can't be missed—he is dressed in an elaborate orange getup that wouldn't look out of place on a Vatican guard. The boutique hotel is resolutely memorable, including a lending library with a catalog and more than 2,000 books, some first editions. Beds feature tentacle headboards that look either like the rising sun or a giant octopus, depending on your point of view, and you can select a bed type: featherbed, pillow top, or Tempur-Pedic. Signature suites are decorated in arts, literature, or symphony motifs, and a portion of the hotel's revenue goes to support a Portland arts organization.

The chic **Hotel Monaco** (506 SW Washington St., 503/222-0001, www.monaco-portland.com, $151-405) is almost aggressively hip—the walls are everything from dark red to wallpapered in whimsical bird patterns, and you can get a pet goldfish to stay in your room while you're there. (You even get to name him or her.) There are free loaner bicycles and a wine and microbrew hour every day at 5pm with free drinks. Most rooms have city views, and the hotel location is convenient for downtown dining and shopping. The in-house restaurant, the **Red Star Tavern** (503 SW Alder St., 503/222-0005, 6:30am-11am, 11:30am-2pm, and 5pm-10pm Mon.-Fri., 8am-2pm and 5pm-10pm Sat., 8am-2pm and 5pm-9pm Sun.) serves casual American cuisine and has a long whiskey and bourbon list.

Nearly every room at the **RiverPlace Hotel** (1510 SW Harbor Way, 503/228-3233, www.riverplacehotel.com, $175-421) has a spectacular city, waterfront, or park view. Rooms are on the luxury end, with soft beds and softer bathrobes; even the smallest single rooms are sizable. Free bicycles are available in the lobby, and yoga mats are included in every room. Valet tickets include a free drink at the downstairs **Three Degrees Waterfront Bar and Grill** (503/295-6166, www.threedegrees-portland.com, 7am-10:30am, 11:30am-2pm, and 5pm-9pm Mon.-Fri., 8am-2pm and 5pm-9pm Sat.-Sun.).

The rooms at **The Nines** (525 SW Morrison St., 877/229-9995, www.thenines.com, $373-411) start on, yes, the 9th floor of a downtown building that was once the headquarters of department store Meier & Frank. Striking art pieces mark the way from the elevator to the front desk. Rooms are decked with velvet couches, marble vanities, and rainforest showers—but they don't come cheap. The cozy library features billiards and a giant antler chandelier. Dining options include **Urban Farmer** (503/222-4900, www.urbanfarmerportland.com, 6:30am-3pm and 5pm-10pm Sun.-Thurs., 6:30am-3pm and 5pm-11pm Fri.-Sat.), a high-end steakhouse, while **Departure**'s (503/802-5370, http://departureportland.com, 4pm-midnight Sun.-Thurs., 4pm-1am Fri.-Sat.) Asian fusion menu and extensive sake offerings are served on two outdoor decks.

PEARL DISTRICT AND NORTHWEST

Under $150

The **Northwest Portland Hostel** (425 NW 18th Ave., 503/241-2783, www.nwportlandhostel.com, $25-39 dorms, $69-88 private rooms without bathrooms) is actually four buildings with traditional hostel rooms and guesthouse rooms that more closely resemble a bed-and-breakfast. The Victorian main building is listed on the National Register of Historic Places and has both types of rooms, and smaller houses next door have more guesthouse rooms. The property boasts no curfew, free Wi-Fi, bike rentals, and an outdoor garden with a grill for guest use. The residential block is only a few blocks from the Pearl District, and the shopping and dining streets of Nob Hill are in the other direction.

Over $250

The **Inn at Northrup Station** (2025 NW Northrup St., 503/224-0543, www.northrupstation.com, $309-339) looks more like a condo development than a hotel from the outside with its balconies and palm-tree landscaping. The colors inside are brighter than a Miami dance party, with walls painted yellow and bedspreads a bright orange. An outdoor patio has the same tangerine and lime colors represented in the patio furniture. All rooms are suites with kitchens and dishwashers, some with ranges and full-size fridges. The sofas fold out to beds, adding more room in the sizable suites. The area is somewhat residential but close to a streetcar line and within walking distance of Northwest District restaurants and the Pearl District.

SOUTHEAST

Under $150

The **Hawthorne Portland Hostel** (3031 SE Hawthorne Blvd., 503/236-3380, www.portlandhostel.org, $28-37 dorms, $66-74 private rooms) has a calmer vibe than downtown hostels and is located in a 1909 house with a funky gazebo out front. There's a full kitchen, a few private rooms, and several dorm rooms. Meals on Sundays are potlucks for guests, and the hostel organizes pub crawls, travel talks, and garden work parties. Bikes are available to rent, and cyclists who ride their bikes into town get a $5 discount every night.

The charming **Bluebird Guesthouse** (3517 SE Division St., 503/238-4333, www.bluebirdguesthouse.com, $95-115 shared bath, $135-192 private bath) is the anti-hotel, with just seven rooms located in a 1910 house built in the Arts and Crafts style, complete with a porch out front. It offers free Wi-Fi and computer use, free parking, laundry, and a full kitchen available for guests. Social rooms are all painted a different bright, cheery color, and the guest rooms are named for authors like Gabriel García Márquez and Sherman Alexie. Some rooms have claw-foot tubs, and all feature antique furniture. Not all have private baths though, and basement rooms are located on a different floor from the shared baths.

$150-250

The motel bones underneath the heavily renovated ★ **Jupiter Hotel** (800 E Burnside St., 503/230-9200, www.jupiterhotel.com, $169-209) are visible, but they're overlaid with heavy layers of party chic. Room doors are blackboards that can be decorated (or used as message boards for the cleaning crew). Ask for the "chill" side if you want quiet because the two floors of rooms on the "bar patio" side get more noise from the attached Doug Fir Lounge, a busy live music venue. Rooms come with low-to-the-ground beds and wall murals—and complementary condoms instead of pillow chocolates. The area is nevertheless much quieter than the middle of downtown, and the hotel is also located a block from famed Le Pigeon restaurant. Reaching other parts of the city from here requires a little more walking, or the hotel has bikes and two ZipCars on-site for rent.

NORTHEAST/NORTH

$150-250

★ **Kennedy School** (5736 NE 33rd Ave., 503/249-3983, www.mcmenamins.com/kennedyschool, $155-225), run by the fun-loving McMenamins company, is housed in an actual elementary school built in 1915 that closed in 1997. Classrooms were split in two to create 57 guest rooms, and some rooms have chalkboards still inside, which are low to the ground, of course, to accommodate elementary-aged students. Others have author themes, like the Ramona room and Sometimes a Great Notion room in tribute to local writers Beverly Cleary and Ken Kesey. Although the neighborhood around the school is pretty residential, there's plenty to do on campus. The building contains multiple bars; a restaurant serving breakfast, lunch, and dinner; an outdoor soaking pool (free for overnight guests); and a movie theater that plays second-run films, with old couches, cushy armchairs, and tables—the theater bar serves liquor and pub food.

Caravan-The Tiny House Hotel (5009 NE 11th Ave., 503/288-5225, www.tinyhousehotel.com, $165) is less a hotel than a tiny, impermanent commune, made up of small dwellings on wheels that range 100-200 square feet in size. Each has a bathroom with a shower and kitchenette, and all come with loft beds (some have a second sleeping surface below). The hotel is located in a small circle in a quiet area near Alberta Avenue, located behind a gate and wire fence; it used to be a parking lot for repossessed cars. Adirondack chairs are set up in the middle around a fire pit. The owners call the lot a kind of "urban campground" and hope to show off to visitors that caravan living in such small places is possible.

Lion and the Rose Victorian Bed & Breakfast (1810 NE 15th Ave., 800/955-1647, www.lionrose.com, $125-210 shared bath, $140-250 private bath) is located inside a 1906 Queen Anne mansion topped with a turret and decorated with intricate columns. Inside it's no less detailed, with parlors that live up to the name—think furniture you can't put your feet on. Breakfast is complementary, and free parking is generally easy to find in this residential neighborhood. Rooms have four-poster beds or decorative headboards, and most have floral wallpaper and antique furnishings. Some rooms have Jacuzzi tubs, and all have cable TV and wireless Internet access.

Information and Services

VISITOR INFORMATION

Located in the middle of Pioneer Courthouse Square, **Travel Portland Visitor Information Center** (701 SW 6th Ave., 877/678-5263, www.travelportland.com, 8:30am-5:30pm Mon.-Fri., 10am-4pm Sat., 10am-2pm Sun. summer only) has maps and brochures, along with a window that vends tickets for the bus, MAX light rail, and streetcar.

MEDIA AND COMMUNICATIONS

The city's daily newspaper is ***The Oregonian*** (www.oregonlive.com), one of the 25 biggest papers in the country. It has won five Pulitzer Prizes and is generally recognized as the area's newspaper of record, sold in newsstands and in newspaper boxes. However, those looking for information on a night out are better off scouring the streets for a box offering the free ***Willamette Week*** (www.wweek.com), an indie weekly that has covered local news and politics since 1974, but also has a hefty section on arts and music, including listings for the week's shows. Its website is also useful for planning a night out. The main newspaper's rival, ***The Portland Mercury*** (www.portlandmercury.com), has similar coverage and is a sister paper to Seattle's ***The Stranger.*** For a periodical with more feature stories and lengthier (though fewer) reviews, find ***Portland Monthly*** (www.portlandmonthlymag.com), a magazine, at newsstands and bookstores. The magazine's website also has collections of best-of lists and event picks.

SERVICES

The lobby of the **Portland Post Office** (715 NW Hoyt St., 503/294-2399, www.usps.com) in the Pearl District is open 24 hours, but they sell stamps only 8am-6:30pm Monday-Friday and 8:30am-5pm Saturday.

As one of several urgent care centers in the city, **ZoomCare** (900 SW 5th Ave., 503/608-3082, www.zoomcare.com, 8am-6pm Mon.-Fri.) has outposts throughout the city, including downtown; other locations are open on weekends. You can book a same-day appointment, get lab tests or a prescription, and even receive stitches and simple burn care. You pay a flat rate whether you bill to insurance or not (around $100 per visit). To treat more urgent and serious ailments, an emergency room is at **Providence Portland Medical Center** (4805 NE Glisan St., 503/215-1111, www.providence.org), but it's a few miles from downtown, so call 911 in an emergency rather than try to navigate the bus system.

Transportation

GETTING THERE

Air

The city is served by the **Portland International Airport** (PDX, 7000 NE Airport Way, 503/460-4234, www.pdx.com). A flight from **Seattle-Tacoma International Airport** (SEA, 17801 International Blvd., 206/787-5388 or 800/544-1965, www.portseattle.org/sea-tac) is only about 45 minutes long, so you'll spend more time at the airport than in the air. United Airlines (www.united.com) and Alaska Airlines (www.alaskaair.com) have several daily departures.

The Portland airport is located in the northeast corner of the city. Make your way downtown by taxi (about $36), or take the **MAX Light Rail** (503/238-7433, www.trimet.org, $2.50 adults), a trip that's less than 40 minutes.

Train

Amtrak (800/872-7245, www.amtrak.com, $26-54) has five departures to Portland daily, with most trips just under four hours. The Cascades route departs King Street Station (303 S Jackson St.) in Seattle's Pioneer Square neighborhood and stops near Sea-Tac Airport (SEA, 17801 International Blvd., 206/787-5388 or 800/544-1965, www.portseattle.org/sea-tac). The route continues through Tacoma, Olympia, Centralia, Kelso-Longview, and Vancouver (Washington, just across the river from Portland) on its way to **Portland's Union Station** (800 NW 6th Ave.). Train cars have wireless Internet access available, and a snack bar sells sandwiches and snacks. You can check baggage as well. Reservations are required.

Bus

BoltBus (877/265-8287, www.boltbus.com) offers service between Seattle and Portland, with up to eight trips daily, each lasting about 3.5 hours. Prices range $17-28 for a one-way trip ($1 fares are advertised but only a few are available each trip). Wireless Internet access is available. Buses depart the Seattle station (5th Ave. S at S King St.) and arrive in Portland at SW Salmon Street between 5th and 6th Avenues. Advance online reservations are highly encouraged.

Bus service is also available through **Greyhound Lines** (800/231-2222, www.greyhound.com), which offers about three departures daily and costs $19-36. The Seattle station is at 503 S Royal Brougham Way (206/628-5526, 7am-12:30am), and the Portland station is at 550 NW 6th Avenue (503/243-2361, 5:45am-11pm).

Car

From Seattle, **I-5** travels southbound directly to Portland, but that doesn't mean it's a quick trip. The 175-mile journey on I-5 can be driven in just under 3 hours when there isn't traffic, but that occurrence is rare. Usually you can expect a crowded freeway, which can make for a drive closer to 3-3.5 hours, especially during weekday rush hours (7:30am-9am and 3:30pm-6:30pm). Other sticky sections include I-5 through Tacoma (35 miles south) and near Joint Base Lewis-McChord (15 miles south of Tacoma), where thousands of military personnel commute to work. Past Olympia (about 20 miles farther south), traffic tends to thin, as do roadside services, though you're never more than a few exits from a gas station. From Centralia, I-5 passes the Cowlitz River and the towns of Kelso and Longview before sliding up to the Columbia River, which marks the border between Washington and Oregon. Once the freeway crosses the Columbia River, the city of Portland emerges immediately on the Oregon side, and downtown is another eight miles south on I-5. To reach downtown Portland, take exit 300 B and follow signs for Morrison Street. You'll cross the Morrison Bridge, ending up on Washington Street, a one-way street that heads west through downtown

GETTING AROUND

Car

Car rentals are available from major vendors (Enterprise, Hertz, Avis, and more) at the Portland International Airport, but two options allow for short-term car rentals. **Car2Go**

Portland Streetcar

(1100 NW Glisan, 877/488-4224, www.car2go.com/en/portland, 9:30am-5:30pm Mon.-Fri., 10am-3pm Sat.) has tiny two-person Smart cars parked all around the city. Register at the Pearl District office or online in advance. You'll then receive a card that unlocks any vacant car2go and get billed by the minute (just $0.38 if below 150 miles in a single rental period) until you leave it anywhere within the zones. **Parking** is free in legal street spots. Find the empty cars via the company's app or website. It's an easy way to do a one-way trip, but the cars don't hold much luggage when a passenger sits in the front seat.

Taxi

With lots of one-way streets, streetcars, and pedestrian crossings, hiring a taxi doesn't guarantee a quick trip through downtown. However, when stranded in one of the westside parks, or eager to get to an eastside restaurant, they're much faster than the bus. Don't wait to flag one down on the street; call **Broadway Cab** (503/333-3333, www.broadwaycab.com), which also can be hailed online via its app, or by text at 571/309-5276. Or try **Radio Cab** (503/227-1212, www.radiocab.net), which also has text (777222) and app options on its website.

Ride-hailing companies including **Uber** (www.uber.com) and **Lyft** (www.lyft.com) also operate in Portland.

Public Transit

The **TriMet** (503/238-7433, www.trimet.org) handles the bus, light rail, and commuter rail in Portland, and provides information on the Portland Streetcar (operated separately). Tickets ($2.50 adults, $1.25 seniors, $1.25 children 7-15, children under 7 free) are good for two hours of travel and work on any combination of vehicles. For anything over a single return trip, a one-day pass ($5 adults, $2.50 seniors, $2.50 children 7-15, children under 7 free) is worthwhile. Visitors with longer stays can invest in a seven-day pass ($26 adults, $7 seniors, $8 children 7-15, children under 7 free). Buses have the most reach, while the MAX (a light rail system that stands for Metropolitan Area Express) has four lines that go to the airport, the nearby towns of Beaverton, Hillsboro, and Gresham, and the Expo Center. All lines go through the Rose Quarter and Pioneer Square, and trains generally come about every 15 minutes, though they're less frequent at night.

The **Portland Streetcar** is more useful for travel in the city core. The North/South line goes from the waterfront through the city center and the Pearl District to the Northwest District. The Central Loop line heads from the city center across the river to the Convention Center and OMSI.

Although Portland is a fairly flat city, it has one way to travel by air—the **Portland Aerial Tram** (3303 SW Bond Ave., 503/865-8726, www.gobytram.com, 5:30am-9:30pm Mon.-Fri., 9am-5pm Sat., 1pm-5pm Sun. summer only, $4.70 adults round-trip, children under 7 free), which leaves every six minutes. However, its path isn't one usually frequented by tourists, from the waterfront south of downtown to the Oregon Health and Science University area. On a rainy day, however, it can be worth a ride for a dry look at the city.

Columbia River Gorge

TOP EXPERIENCE

The Columbia River Gorge is a wide canyon that forms much of the state border between Oregon and Washington. It's a National Scenic Area, and it's easy to see why—the Gorge's beauty is dramatic, the water flowing between steep mountains on either side, heavily wooded and lush on the western end before transitioning to flat-topped buttes and brown grasslands east of the Cascades. Both sides have a distinct beauty. The section that stretches east from Portland is the most traveled. Small towns dot both the Washington and Oregon sides, but the latter's Hood River is the biggest tourist hub, home to kiteboarders and breweries. The sleepy little communities in between also add charm.

Each side of the river has a roadway close to the bank, running east-west along the Gorge, like mirror images. The I-84 freeway is on the Oregon side and Highway 14 is on the Washington side; the former has multiple lanes and moves much faster than the Washington road, which has more turns, fewer lanes, and more stoplights. To reach a spot on the Washington side from Portland, it's often fastest to travel east-west through Oregon and then take the Bridge of the Gods or Hood River Bridge to reach your destination across the Columbia River. Note that high winds and winter weather can slow or stop traffic on both thoroughfares.

The devastating Eagle Creek Fire in 2017 ravaged the Oregon side of the Gorge, mostly west of Cascade Locks, touching more than 50,000 acres. While the landscape is still beautiful and mostly intact as seen from the waterfront, the fires affected higher elevations. As a result, many trails are closed as authorities slowly measure the effects. You can check for area closures on the **U.S. Forest Service website** (http://www.fs.usda.gov/recmain/crgnsa/recreation).

HISTORIC COLUMBIA RIVER HIGHWAY

The 70-mile **Historic Columbia River Highway (U.S. 30)** runs next to I-84 along the Gorge, but offers a beautiful byway experience—it was the country's first designated

wildflowers near the eastern edge of the Columbia River Gorge

Multnomah Falls

scenic highway. You can hop onto it from I-84 at Troutdale (exit 17) or Corbett (exit 22).

Damage from the Eagle Creek Fire means that some sections of the historic highway are currently closed, but the scenic stretch from Troutdale to Bridal Veil Falls, on the way to Multnomah Falls, is open. State officials hope to reopen the rest of the road once cleared for stability; the most up-to-date road information is on the state's **TripCheck website** (http://tripcheck.com).

Viewpoints

Your first major scenic viewpoint is at the **Women's Forum Overlook,** about a mile and a half from Corbett. It offers a sweeping perspective of the Columbia River Gorge.

A mile later, you'll come upon the **Vista House** (40700 E Historic Columbia River Hwy., 503/595-2230, www.vistahouse.com, 9am-6pm daily, free), a small museum housed in a historical building that stands sentinel over the Columbia River below, offering another epic vantage point.

Bridal Veil Falls

Along this stretch of the historic highway, you'll pass multiple waterfall options. Five miles from the Vista House, you could stop for a short 0.25-mile ramble on a paved and gravel walkway to the two-tiered **Bridal Veil Falls.**

Multnomah Falls

Though the entire Pacific Northwest is draped in waterfalls—thanks, rain!—Multnomah Falls, boasting a picturesque pillar of water and easy accessibility from Portland, is the area's most popular. The triple-decker falls, the longest of which is more than 500 feet, offer a prime photo op. Also here is the **Multnomah Falls Lodge** (53000 Historic Columbia River Hwy., 503/695-2376, www.multnomahfallslodge.com), a 1925 building that holds a restaurant and small **Forest Service visitors center** (9am-5pm daily). The Eagle Creek Fire came close to the area, but the well-loved site was spared thanks to the diligent work of firefighters.

GETTING THERE

To get to Multnomah Falls from downtown Portland, head east on I-84 and take the left-hand exit 31. When traffic doesn't clog the interstate, it takes about 45 minutes. Note the parking lot at Multnomah Falls can be difficult to navigate, since drivers are coming from both directions and the falls are such an attraction. If you'd like to avoid it, an express shuttle called the **Columbia Gorge Express** (http://columbiagorgeexpress.com, $5 round-trip) offers round-trip service 10 times a day Friday-Sunday in the summer from **Gateway Transit Center** (9900 NE Multnomah Ave.).

CASCADE LOCKS, OR

Cascade Locks is a small town that enjoys a scenic perch on the river. Also here is one of the links between Oregon and Washington over the Columbia River, the **Bridge of the Gods.** Named for a rock formation, the bridge garnered widespread attention, twice—first when Charles Lindberg flew

Columbia River Gorge and Mount Hood

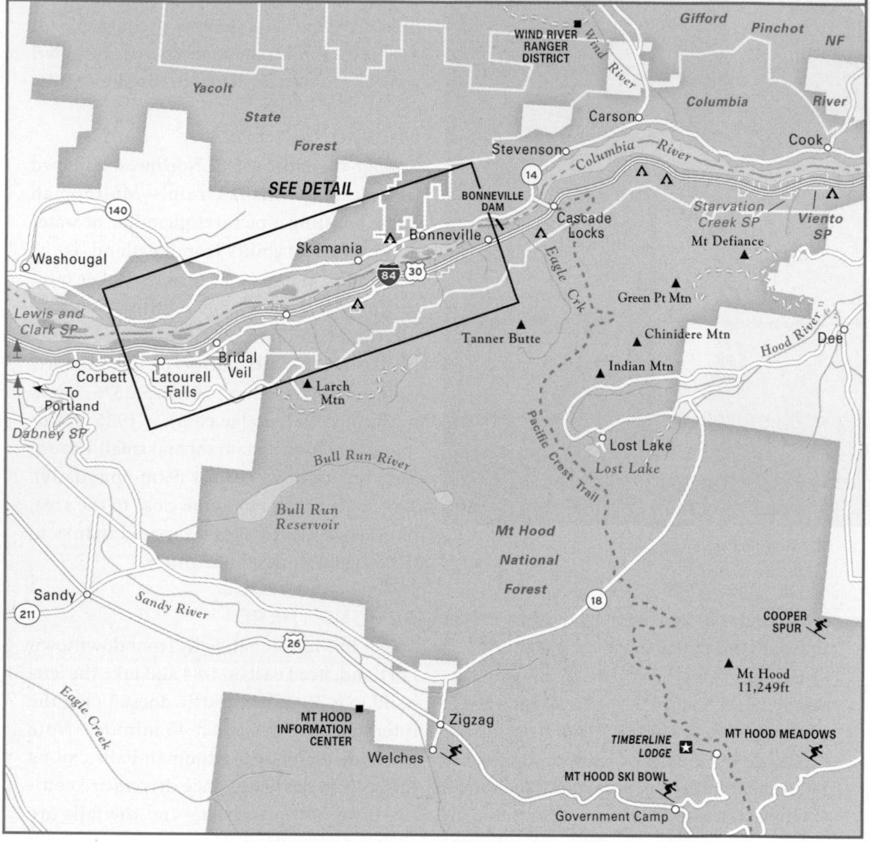

his *Spirit of St. Louis* plane low over, then under (reportedly), the then-new bridge in the 1920s, and then in 2014 when the movie *Wild,* which was based on Cheryl Strayed's 2012 memoir and filmed a climactic scene here, was released. The famous Pacific Crest Trail (PCT), which runs from Mexico to Canada, passes through Cascade Locks, and so the town sees many thru-hikers. The 2017 Eagle Creek Fire damaged the trail enough for a lengthy closure of the section, but PCT hikers will likely continue to detour through town to pay homage to the bridge, a famous landmark of the 2,659-mile route even before it showed up in *Wild.*

Sights and Recreation

BONNEVILLE DAM OREGON VISITORS CENTER

The Bonneville Dam has come to define this stretch of the river; it produces hydroelectric power by harnessing the flowing river. It has accessible features on either side of the Gorge; pick whichever one is more convenient to you, as there's no need to visit both. On the Oregon side, five miles south of Cascade Locks, is the **Bradford Island Visitor Center** (exit 40, 541/374-8820, www.nwp.usace.army.mil/bonneville, 9am-5pm daily, free), which sits on an island in the middle of the river. Powerhouse tours (10:30am, 1:30pm, and

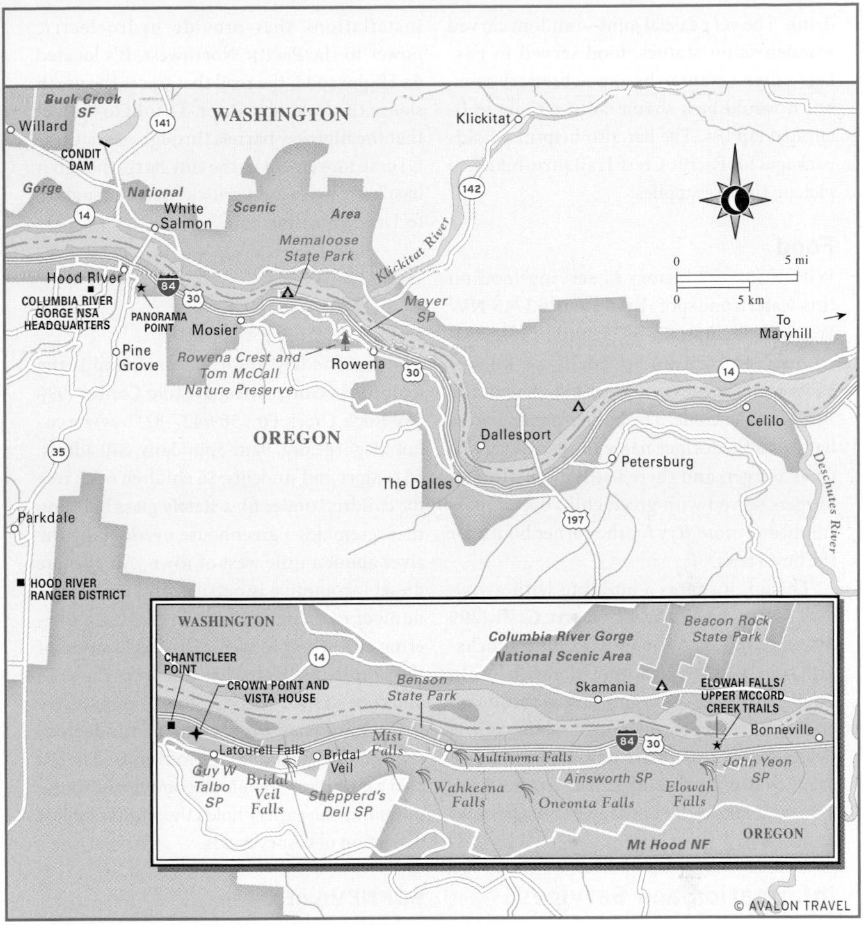

3:30pm Sat.-Sun.) are free and first-come, first-served. The building also has underwater windows from which you can see migrating salmon and Pacific lamprey moving through the fish ladder, an underground passage created for the animals to bypass the dam. Up top a rooftop deck takes in Gorge views, and interior exhibits lay out the life cycle of salmon and the history of dam construction.

RIVER CRUISES

To get out on the water without getting wet, book a tour on the **Columbia Gorge Sternwheeler** (www.portlandspirit.com/sternwheeler.php, May-Oct., $30-94 adults, $20-51 children), which offers lunch, dinner, history-minded, and sightseeing trips along the waterway in a three-story paddle wheel boat. You'll see Native American fishing platforms, kiteboarders, dams, and historical buildings from a spacious boat, ideal for taking in the whole region without much physical exertion.

Entertainment and Events

With 10 rotating taps and an outdoor patio, **Cascade Locks Ale House** (500 Wa Na Pa St., 541/374-9310, http://cascadelocksalehouse.com, 11am-9pm Wed.-Mon., $9-17) is a popular place to relax with pizza and a drink. The very casual joint—random carved wooden sailor statues, food served in baskets—says it plans to become a brewery soon, but it would be a shame to lose their well-curated tap list. The bar also helpfully holds packages for Pacific Crest Trail thru-hikers to pick up their resupplies.

Food

With a 50-year history of serving food on this waterfront spot, **Bridgeside** (745 NW Wa Na Pa St., 541/374-8477, http://bridgesidedining.com, 6:30am-9pm daily, $7-13) has, as its name suggests, a great big view of the Bridge of the Gods. The burger menu gives a hat tip to the former name of the eatery, the Char Burger, and there's still a long line of burgers served with green chili, bacon, pastrami, and more. Try for the corner booth for the best views.

Though it shares a building with a visitors center, **Locks Waterfront Grill** (299 SW Portage Rd., 541/645-0372, http://locksgrill.com, $8-12) is plenty popular with locals. Food is simple—fish-and-chips and burgers—but the exposed wooden beam ceiling over a collection of wire tables makes it feel as much like a gathering hall as a restaurant. Take a drink to the outdoor patio for views of the river.

Information and Services

A visitor center in **Marine Park** (299 SW Portage Rd., 10:30am-4pm daily May-Oct., 10:30am-4pm Fri.-Mon. Nov.-Apr.) offers maps and local information; it's right next to the Locks Waterfront Grill.

Getting There

From Portland, head east on I-84 for about 42 miles to Cascade Locks. Take exit 44 and continue on Wa Na Pa Street, which goes through the center of town. The drive takes about 45 minutes.

STEVENSON, WA

The small town of Stevenson sits near the Bonneville Dam, one of the many river installations that provide hydroelectric power to the Pacific Northwest. It's located on Highway 14, the road that traces the north side of the Columbia River. Thanks to the fact that the highway barrels through town, there is some movement in the tiny burg, though it hasn't quite reached critical mass enough to feel like a bustling hub.

Sights

COLUMBIA GORGE INTERPRETIVE CENTER

The region's best informational stop is the **Columbia Gorge Interpretive Center** (990 SW Rock Creek Dr., 509/427-8211, www.columbiagorge.org, 9am-5pm daily, $10 adults, $8 seniors and students, $6 children 6-12, free for children under 6), a stately glass building that resembles a greenhouse overlooking the river about a mile west of town. An antique diesel locomotive is outside, and there are a number of exhibits inside, including a towering fish wheel as well as an exploration of the Bonneville Dam that discusses the pros and cons of hydroelectric power, an industry that's dominated the region and fundamentally changed its fishing traditions. There's also an unlikely religious component to the museum; one gallery holds the world's largest collection of rosary beads.

BONNEVILLE DAM WASHINGTON VISITORS CENTER

On the Washington side, five miles south of Stevenson, is the **Washington Shore Visitor Complex** (Hwy. 14 at Dam Access Rd. near milepost 38.5, 541/374-8820, www.nwp.usace.army.mil/bonneville, 9am-5pm daily, free), which has exhibits on salmon and hydroelectricity, as well as free powerhouse tours (10:30am, 1:30pm, and 3:30pm Sat.-Sun.) on a first-come, first-served basis.

BEACON ROCK STATE PARK

Protecting a giant basalt column that serves as one of the landmarks along the river, **Beacon Rock State Park** (34841 Hwy. 14, 509/427-8265, http://parks.state.wa.us, 8am-dusk daily) stretches up into the hills away from the water. Hiking to the top of the titular rock, which affords spectacular views of the Gorge, is the primary activity here. Camping, as well as other trails and picnic facilities, is also available. The state park is about 10 miles west of Stevenson.

Hiking

BEACON ROCK

Distance: 2 miles round-trip
Duration: 1-2 hours
Elevation gain: 800 feet
Effort: moderate
Trailhead: parking lot ($5 parking fee) on the south side of Highway 14 across from the park headquarters building

The good news is that the climb to the top of this massive basalt monolith is only 800 feet; the bad news is that it all comes in about a mile. From the trailhead, enjoy the gradual ascent as the trail corkscrews around the giant rock for the first half. Eventually the trail turns to boardwalk with handrails, topping out after a whopping 52 switchbacks. Up top are views of the Gorge, including Bonneville Dam. Stop to read the interpretive panels on the way up as a break; your walk back down goes relatively quickly.

DOG MOUNTAIN

Distance: 6 miles round-trip
Duration: 3-4 hours
Elevation gain: 2,800 feet
Effort: moderate
Trailhead: parking lot on the non-river side of Highway 14 near milepost 53, about 10 miles east of Stevenson

There are two reasons to make a spring trek to Dog Mountain: views and wildflowers—and given the trail's popularity during this season, note that a **hiking permit** (www.recreation.gov, Sat.-Sun. Apr.-Oct., $1.50) is necessary on weekends. You ascend through the forest on switchbacks, gaining elevation quickly. Take a right at the junction after a half mile and continue until the trail opens onto wide, angled meadows that, in spring, erupt into color with yellow balsamroot, orange Indian paintbrush, and blue lupine. The switchbacks are long and leisurely at this point. About a half mile before the top, you'll reach a flat lookout spot known as Puppy Point, the site of a former fire lookout. The views are probably the best here, but it's worth continuing the last half mile to claim the summit. Return the way you came.

Entertainment and Events

Named for the two explorers who came up this way in the early 1800s, **Clark & Lewie's Travelers Rest Saloon & Grill** (130 SW Cascade Ave., 509/219-0097, www.clarkandlewies.com, 11:30am-8pm Wed.-Thurs., 11:30am-8:30pm Fri., 10am-8:30pm Sat.) goes all-out with the gimmick by labeling dishes after members of the exploration party (Sacagawea Wings, Charbonneau Onion Rings). The outdoor deck overlooking the river is an ideal spot for a post-adventure drink. Clark & Lewie's website even has a live camera of the patio so you can judge the crowds and weather in advance.

Walking Man Brewing (240 1st St., 509/427-5520, www.walkingmanbeer.com, 4pm-9pm Sun. and Wed.-Fri., 3pm-9pm Sat., $8-15) has long been unafraid of going big on hops, and its IPAs are legion—expect a half-dozen or so on tap—and pair well with the fat pub fries and banh mi burger made with a hemp-based patty. The two-floor brewery and pub has a nice outdoor garden and an overall farmhouse feel.

Food

With giant plates of pasta and hearty burgers, **Big River Grill** (192 2nd St., 509/ 427-4888, www.thebigrivergrill.com, 11am-9pm Mon.-Thurs., 11am-9:30pm Fri., 8am-9:30pm Sat., 8am-9pm Sun., $14-17) is a roadhouse in spirit, a place to rest on a drive and get a helping of food and local character. Sit under a mermaid mural or a collection of license plates. The eatery reaches a dull roar during summer weekends but maintains a nice buzz the rest of the time.

Located inside the substantial Skamania

Lodge Resort, about a mile and a half west of town, the **Cascade Dining Room** (1131 SW Skamania Lodge Way, 800/221-7117, www.destinationhotels.com/skamania, 7am-1pm and 5pm-9pm Mon.-Sat., 9am-1pm Sun., $27-49) boasts a wood-fired oven and a repurposed wood floor that dates back centuries. Though inspired by the national park inn style, the menu leans toward more delicate preparations, like short ribs topped with forest mushrooms and steelhead with spaetzle. Reservations are recommended.

Accommodations

With riverfront balconies for its eight rooms—each half of a log cabin—**Columbia Gorge Riverside Lodge** (200 SW Cascade Ave., 509/427-5650, www.cgriversidelodge.com, $109-229), kitchens in each one, and forested surroundings, this is (mostly) a quiet retreat in town. The decor is rustic but the amenities are quite nice, and there are private and shared hot tubs by the river. The one caveat: A nearby railway means occasional nighttime train sounds, though in 2016 they ceased blowing their whistles. Still, earplugs are provided.

The region's only sizable resort-style accommodations, **Skamania Lodge** (1131 SW Skamania Lodge Way, 509/314-4177, www.destinationhotels.com/skamania, $299-409 rooms, $599-649 tree houses) sits a bit up from the river, about a mile and a half west of town, nicely hugged by the forest. Some of the 250-plus rooms have calm but unremarkable views of the trees, while others have more open vistas of the river and Gorge. The high-end tree houses are more like cabins that happen to be sitting off the ground; some have private outdoor fire pits. The resort also has a good spa and a golf course.

Step back in time at **Carson Hot Springs** (St. Martins Springs Rd., Carson, 509/427-8296, http://carsonhotspringresort.com, $149-219 rooms, $250-339 suites), tucked high above the river (but without views of the Gorge) about six miles east of Stevenson. It includes a building that dates back to 1901 bearing its original name, Hotel St. Martin. The resort's 28 rooms are in more modern buildings and are simple, some with hot tubs outside. It also boasts access to a nearby golf course, but the real star is the vintage bathhouse, offering a classic treatment ($30-35): Soak in mineral waters in a clawfoot tub, then get wrapped in linens like a burrito, a soothing experience. It feels more like a 1930s sanitarium than a modern spa, but it's a fun blast from the past.

CAMPING

Find RV parking at **Lewis & Clark Campground & RV Park** (355 Evergreen Dr., North Bonneville, 509/427-5559, www.lewisandclarkcampground.com, $25-30), about eight miles southwest of town. It feels uncrowded and is surrounded by trees. Bookings must be made by phone.

Located in the trees north of the actual rock, the main campground at **Beacon Rock State Park** (34841 Hwy. 14, 509/427-8265, http://parks.state.wa.us, $20-30) has 26 tent campsites. The **Woodward Creek Campground,** also within the park but close to the river on the south side of the highway, has five spots ($25-40) suited to RVs.

Information and Services

You can find some informational items in the lobby of the **Columbia Gorge Interpretive Center** (990 SW Rock Creek Dr., 509/427-8211, www.columbiagorge.org, 9am-5pm daily), no admission necessary.

Getting There

Stevenson is just across the river from Cascade Locks. From Portland, head east on I-84 for about 42 miles to Cascade Locks. Take exit 44 to cross the **Bridge of the Gods** ($2 toll, credit cards accepted for an extra fee) across the Columbia River. After crossing, turn right on Highway 14 and follow it 3 miles to Stevenson. The drive takes about 50 minutes.

HOOD RIVER, OR AND WHITE SALMON, WA

The biggest tourist draw on this section of the Gorge is the town of Hood River, a small but bustling city on the banks of the Columbia River on the Oregon side and well known for its water sports and breweries. Just across the river via the Hood River Bridge, Washington's White Salmon is a sleepier town with a better view of Mount Hood rising in the distance. Its main street is set back a bit from the river, with a short greenbelt separating it from the water.

Sights

FRUIT LOOP

Hood River is situated in one of the richest agricultural regions of the state, and you can experience it on a drive known as the **Fruit Loop** (www.hoodriverfruitloop.com), a 35-mile route. The do-it-yourself drive starts in Hood River, heads south on Highway 35, then loops around through the town of Parkdale and back north via Highway 281. One of the best places to visit on the route is **The Gorge White House** (2265 Hwy. 35, Hood River, 541/386-2828, http://thegorgewhitehouse.com, 10am-6pm daily June-Sept., 10am-6pm Fri.-Mon. Apr.-May and Oct.), comprising a Dutch colonial farmhouse that dates back to 1908 and farmlands. The property, about five miles south of Hood River, has beer and cider tastings, a snack bar, fresh fruit for sale, and a dahlia garden with more than 50 varieties. You can clip your own dahlias, lilies, daffodils, and more at its U-pick flower fields.

MOUNT HOOD RAILROAD

Take a 22-mile ride on the **Mount Hood Railroad** (110 Mt. Hood Railroad, 800/872-4661, www.mthoodrr.com, $35-65 adults, $30-60 children), heading south from Hood River to Parkdale on a route that resembles the Fruit Loop's highway drive. In spring, the Fruit Blossom Special (Sun. Apr.-May) comes with gift bags that include local fruit to eat as you pass the beautiful flowering trees in the fields. Other trips feature pure sightseeing (select days May-Oct.) or a Western robbery theme (select Sat. July-Sept.). Several different classes of service are available, and the 4.5-hour rides include a 1-hour layover at the Parkdale terminus to the south, then return to Hood River. Bring a picnic to enjoy outdoors at the break.

Water Sports

Winds whip up the Columbia River, making it a world-famous windsurfing and kiteboarding location. The former sport caught on first, and launch points for both forms of river play are still marked by a windsurfer icon sign. But kiteboarding, with its more flexible equipment, has caught on in recent years. Users don a snowboard-like board and use a parachute to propel themselves across the water. Though not a simple sport, it's possible to learn through a number of providers, including **Cascade Kiteboarding** (216 Cascade Ave., Hood River, 541/392-1212, www.cascadekiteboarding.com, $217 adults, $149 children). To simply watch the flyers, some of whom can do tricks and flips while zooming across the water, head to Hood River's **Waterfront Park** (650 Portway Ave., Hood River, 541/387-5201, http://hoodriverwaterfront.org) for excellent views.

On the White Salmon side of the river, a churning river flows south from the snow-covered slopes of Mount Adams toward the Columbia River. White-water rafting is popular on the waterway, and one of the longest-running outfitters is **Zoller's Outdoor Odysseys** (1248 Hwy. 141, White Salmon, 509/493-2641, www.zooraft.com, $70-110 adults, $55 children under 12). With launch sites for three different sections of the river, excursions range from a low-key, float-like experience to a wilder white-water trip that requires aggressive paddling and some guts.

Hiking

TAMANAWAS FALLS

Distance: 3.6 miles round-trip
Duration: 2 hours
Elevation gain: 600 feet

Effort: easy
Trailhead: From Hood River, take Highway 35 to milepost 72, about 25 miles south; look for the signed trailhead.

This simple hike heads to a beautiful waterfall you can walk behind. From the parking lot, cross the creek on a log bridge and turn right onto the East Fork Trail. After the trail climbs through the forest, head left when it splits and cross Cold Springs Creek on a bridge. Stay on the main trail as it rises above the creek and finally opens onto a rocky area where Tamanawas Falls tumbles over a 150-foot lava cliff. If venturing behind the falls, take care on the slippery rocks.

COYOTE WALL

Distance: 3.8 miles round-trip
Duration: 2.5 hours
Elevation gain: 850 feet
Effort: moderate
Trailhead: From White Salmon, head 3 miles east on Highway 14, turning left onto Courtney Road and right onto Old Highway 8.

Start by hiking along a wide road—Old Highway 8—then turn left on the signed Little Moab Trail. Follow it as it rises up, staying left at two junctions, then pass the Coyote Wall, a towering cliff of river-facing basalt. Past the wall, turn right at a junction to traverse east, staying straight on the Little Maui Trail, which descends back to the river through open grasslands and past a stream. You'll be facing the river as you come down. Wildflowers bloom along the trail in late spring, turning the fields into a riot of purple and yellow. When you reach the old highway, turn right to return to the trailhead.

Entertainment and Events

NIGHTLIFE

The Gorge's most famous beer maker boasts a substantial tasting room and brewpub at **Full Sail Brewing Company** (506 Columbia St., Hood River, 541/386-2247, http://fullsailbrewing.com, 11am-9pm daily). Take a free tour (1pm, 2pm, 3pm, and 4pm Fri.-Sun.) of the facility and try $2.50 tasters after, or settle down in the brewpub for whole pints of Full Sail's classic amber and IPA, plus barrel-aged beers and creative selections only found in its pub.

Double Mountain Brewery (8 4th St., Hood River, 541/387-0042, www.doublemountainbrewery.com, 11am-10pm Sun.-Thurs., 11am-11pm Fri.-Sat.) has growing reach around the Pacific Northwest; the brand pops up on taps from Bend to Seattle. Free tours are offered on Saturday at noon, and there's often live music in the evenings in the taproom. The Hop Lion and Hop Lava beers make it clear—they're all about the hop flavor here. Beers pair well with the brick-oven pizzas served.

Pfriem Family Brewers (707 Portway Ave., Ste. 101, Hood River, 541/321-0490, www.pfriembeer.com, 11:30am-9pm daily) is probably the chicest beer spot in town. It's located across from the waterfront parkland, and its menu boasts snacks like mussels served with a saffron cream sauce and roasted beet salad. The beer list is extensive, reaching from the usual varieties—pale ales, stouts—to German styles and sours. Barrel-aged specials appeal to the beer nerd who likes to dive deep.

In a town known for its breweries, **River City Saloon** (207 Cascade Ave., Hood River, 541/387-2583, 4pm-2:30am Mon.-Fri, noon-2:30am Sat., 9:30am-2:30am Sun.) is a place to catch the game while scoring a Coors Light or a selection from a number of brewers and cider-makers. With dim lighting and pool tables, it's a relaxed hangout.

FESTIVALS AND EVENTS

With such rich agricultural industry, the **Hood River Harvest Fest** (Hood River Event Site, Portway Ave. and N 1st St., 541/386-2000, www.hoodriver.org/harvest-fest, Oct., $6 adults, $3 seniors on Fri., free for children under 12) has lots to show off over the course of three days, from fresh apples and pumpkins to crafts and live music. Expect a large showing by pears, the region's signature fruit.

Food

HOOD RIVER

Located opposite a long expanse of riverfront park, ★ **Solstice Wood Fire Pizza** (501 Portway Ave., 541/436-0800, http://solsticewoodfirecafe.com, 11am-8:30pm Sun.-Thurs., 11am-9pm Fri.-Sat. summer, 11am-8:30pm Sun.-Mon. and Wed.-Thurs., 11am-9pm Fri.-Sat. winter, $13-21) has excellent views and even better food; the wood-fired pizzas are some of the very best meals in town. A large covered outdoor patio makes up about a third of the seating, but be warned that it can be windy outside even with the protection.

Gleaming **Celilo** (16 Oak St., 541/386-5710, www.celilorestaurant.com, 5pm-10pm Mon.-Thurs., 11:30am-3pm and 5pm-10pm Fri.-Sun., $19-32) does a modern take on rustic interiors, with wood pillars, black ceilings, and sparse decor. The farm-to-table entrées are simple—pork shoulder, salmon—but emphasize fresh ingredients. Service is friendly and efficient. As casual as Hood River is, it's a solid dining-out experience.

Bette's Place (416 Oak St., 541/386-1880, www.bettesplace.com, 5:30am-3pm daily, $9-13), a straightforward diner, may not have the flash of a brewpub or sleek restaurant, but it does classics extremely well—and has since 1975. It's best known for its breakfast, including a dense, softball-sized cinnamon roll and hearty Benedicts. The lunch menu has basics like burgers and sandwiches, but the morning meals are enough to feed you for most of the day.

WHITE SALMON

The most popular stop on White Salmon's main street, ★ **Everybody's Brewing** (151 E Jewett Blvd., 509/637-2774, http://everybodysbrewing.com, 11:30am-9:30pm Sun.-Thurs., 11:30am-10pm Fri.-Sat., $10-16) draws locals and tourists together in a buzzy restaurant that specializes in substantial salads and sandwiches, plus creative burritos. Come for the outdoor patio and atmosphere, with Everybody's beers—less well known than Hood River's blockbuster brews—and regular live music.

Ideal after a rafting, kiteboarding, or hiking adventure, **Pioneer Pizza Kitchen** (216 E Jewett Blvd., 509/493-0028, www.pioneerpizzakitchen.com, 4pm-9pm Mon.-Thurs., 11:30am-9pm Fri.-Sun., $11-24) has thick, lightly browned crust pies topped with a variety of classic and creative combinations. The kitchen slathers pizzas with ghee or mole, and will put butternut squash on top right next to the usual toppings. Pizzas can take a while to cook, so settle in with a beer or visit the arcade corner after ordering.

Accommodations

HOOD RIVER

The most spectacular hotel building on the river belongs to ★ **Columbia Gorge Hotel and Spa** (4000 Westcliff Dr., 541/386-5566, www.columbiagorgehotel.com, $289-319), a mission-style building that would fit in in Los Angeles. Located a couple of miles west of downtown and overlooking the river, it's definitely historical—narrow hallways, small rooms—but was renovated in 2012 and has hosted a number of famous guests from Hollywood over the years. The 40 rooms have four-poster beds and vintage-style touches, like in-room sinks and standing mirrors, and some have river views. The attached spa and outdoor gardens help make it a relaxing spot, even though it's crammed between the freeway and river.

Dating back to 1911, the **Hood River Hotel** (102 Oak St., 541/386-1900, http://hoodriverhotel.com, $109-289) has 40 rooms, some with river views and some more affordable ones without. Thoughtful refurbishing has retained much of the character of the downtown hotel, with modern rustic decor and hipster-cool touches like retro wool blankets and giant art pieces. Weekend bookings may have minimum stay requirements, and some rooms may get train noise from the railway.

Tucked next to where the Hood River Bridge soars across the Columbia to White

Mount Hood Scenic Loop

From Portland, you can drive a scenic loop that links the **Columbia River Gorge** and Mount Hood. Drive east on I-84 from Portland (detouring to the **Historic Columbia River Highway** if you like), passing **Multnomah Falls** along the way, to **Hood River.** From here, head south toward Mount Hood on U.S. 35 until it intersects with U.S. 26. You can take a short detour from here to **Timberline Lodge,** or start heading back west through **Government Camp** to SE Burnside and NE Hogan Roads before meeting up with I-84 back to Portland. Without stops, the 162-mile drive takes about 3 hours and 20 minutes in summer, longer when icy roads slow traffic speeds in winter.

Salmon, the **Best Western Plus Hood River Inn** (1108 E Marina Dr., 541/386-2200, www.hoodriverinn.com, $150-250 rooms, $225-420 suites) is on the waterfront and close to town, though not ideal for pedestrian travel into downtown. Waterfront rooms have patios or balconies, and the outdoor pool and hot tub have beautiful views of the river and hills. Rooms don't feel too business-like, even though it's a chain; they're sizable and decorated with wood paneling or art. The hotel's Riverside restaurant boasts the only true riverfront restaurant in Hood River.

WHITE SALMON

Located in a beautiful, low-slung brick building on the Washington side of the river, **Inn of the White Salmon** (172 W Jewett Blvd., 509/493-2335, www.innofthewhitesalmon.com, $129-159) goes for a sleek, eco-conscious look. With just 22 rooms, it has a boutique hotel feel, with wooden headboards in guest rooms, works by local artists in the hallway, and a backyard seating area near the garden. The prices make it one of the best deals on the entire Gorge, and it's right on White Salmon's main street.

CAMPING

For RV camping, head to **Bridge RV Park and Campground** (65271 Hwy. 14, White Salmon, 509/493-1111, $30-55), located between the highway and the river (but thanks to railroad tracks and trees, no water views). Tent spots are on a shaded lawn, and RV sites are dotted with trees.

Head east from Hood River on I-84 for 17 miles, about 20 minutes, to find **Memaloose State Park** (exit 76, 800/452-5687, http://oregonstateparks.org), located on the riverside near where Chinook Indian tribes once performed burial rites. There are 66 tent sites ($19) and 43 hookup sites ($31) for RVs, plus hot showers, as well as beautiful views of the river and the tree-dotted hills rising on the other side of the Gorge.

Information and Services

There's a small **Hood River County Visitors Center** (Port Marina Park, 720 E Port Marina Dr., Hood River, 503/386-2000, http://hoodriver.org, 9am-5pm Mon.-Fri., 10am-4pm Sat.-Sun.) located in its chamber of commerce. Tiny but better staffed is White Salmon's **Mt. Adams Chamber of Commerce tourist information desk** (1 Heritage Plaza, Hwy. 14, 509/493-3630, www.mtadamschamber.com, 10am-5pm daily), located with bathrooms in a highway pull-off.

Getting There

To reach Hood River from Portland, head east on I-84 for 61 miles. The drive takes about 1.5 hours. Hood River is about 20 miles east of Cascade Locks via I-84.

To reach White Salmon, take exit 64 on I-84 to cross the Hood River Bridge ($2 toll, cash only without a preregistered account), across the Columbia River to Highway 14.

Turn left on the highway and then take the first right onto Rock Grade Road. It swings uphill for about a mile before dead-ending. Turn left to follow Jewett Boulevard into downtown. White Salmon is about 24 miles east of Stevenson on Highway 14.

MARYHILL, WA AND VICINITY

The Maryhill area was built around land owned by Sam Hill, an entrepreneur who settled in Washington in the early 20th century. Although he's responsible for improvements to road systems across the state, his planned settlement here never came to much, with the area encompassing little more than his spectacular old home, now a thoughtful art museum, standing alone on an empty, scenic stretch of the Gorge, with a few houses, a fruit stand, and small farms and vineyards sloping gently down toward the river. The larger town of Goldendale, 13 miles up the road, is known for its observatory.

Maryhill Museum of Art

Built by entrepreneur Sam Hill and named for his daughter, the **Maryhill Museum of Art** (35 Maryhill Museum Dr., 509/773-3733, www.maryhillmuseum.org, 10am-5pm daily mid-Mar.-mid-Nov., $12 adults, $10 seniors, $9 students, $5 children 7-18) is a beautiful place in an otherwise quiet, relatively unoccupied section of the Gorge. The stately mansion looks like it belongs on an English estate, its grand three-story facade backed by the brown bluffs characteristic of the Gorge's eastern side. Its permanent and traveling exhibits salute American art and Hill's global reach; he had friends among the European art world and royalty. The museum's collection includes Russian icons given to Hill by Queen Marie of Romania, memorabilia from dancer Loie Fuller, and Auguste Rodin sculptures.

Stonehenge Memorial

A few miles east of the mansion, another hillside sight draws plenty of eyes: a semi-replica of the famous British monument, the **Stonehenge Memorial** (87 Stonehenge Dr., www.maryhillmuseum.org, 7am-dusk, free). Another of Sam Hill's visions, this version is the same size as the original but built of bricks in a tidy circle. It was erected as a World War I memorial and sits next to the Klickitat County Veterans' Memorial. Beautiful views of the Gorge are afforded from this vantage.

Goldendale Observatory

Goldendale Observatory (1602 Observatory Dr., Goldendale, 509/773-3141, www.goldendaleobservatory.com) is part of a state park and open to all comers who want to learn about stars and peek into a powerful telescope—one of the country's largest publicly accessible telescopes. While the observatory closed in spring 2018 in anticipation of upgrades, a new facility is expected to open in June 2019. Until then, the observatory is holding regular solar and dark sky interpretive programs at the nearby **Stonehenge Memorial** (87 Stonehenge Dr., 1pm-11:30pm Thurs.-Sun., http://parks.state.wa.us), which is about 14 miles south.

Getting There

Maryhill's about 40 miles east of White Salmon via Highway 14. To reach Maryhill from Portland, head east on I-84 for about 101 miles to Biggs Junction. Take exit 104 to cross the river on U.S. 97, and once on the Washington side follow the road uphill about a mile and a half. Turn left on Highway 14; the museum is about 2.5 miles west on Highway 14, on the left. The drive takes about an hour and 50 minutes. To reach Goldendale from Maryhill, return to U.S. 97 and drive north about 10 miles.

Mount Hood

It looks like the platonic ideal of a mountain: triangle-shaped, with snow on top year-round. Mount Hood is actually a volcano, and still active, located about 50 miles east of Portland—visible from the city on a clear day—and one of the city's favorite playgrounds. Hike, ski (year-round!), and explore the wild areas, but be ready for two things: crowds and bad weather. Snow can make the highways dangerous, and the region's popularity and proximity make for lots of fellow visitors. Still, between the towering mountain and a classic lodge atop, it's an unbeatable destination.

At its base, Government Camp, a small town on U.S. 26, serves as a gateway, with services including restaurants and hotels. It was named after an army regiment holed up there for the winter. Attempts to change the name to "Pompeii" failed, perhaps because it called to mind the Italian city leveled by an ancient volcanic eruption.

SIGHTS

TOP EXPERIENCE

★ Timberline Lodge

If Mount Hood is a classic mountain, the **Timberline Lodge** (27500 E Timberline Rd., Government Camp, 503/272-3311, www.timberlinelodge.com) is the traditional mountain hotel, with a steep roof (so snow doesn't collect), a tall chimney, and walls made with smooth rock. Look familiar? It served as the exterior for the creepy hotel in Stanley Kubrick's *The Shining.* As its name suggests, the hotel sits right at the timberline, where the treeless alpine section of the mountain begins and snow touches down. Even if you're not staying overnight, visit the atmospheric round lobby—it has a fireplace—or have a hot chocolate or something stronger at the **Ram's Head Bar** (2pm-11pm Mon.-Thurs., 11:30am-11pm Fri.-Sun., adults only), a few stories above on a balcony overlooking the stone chimney—a great respite after a day of skiing or hiking.

Timberline Lodge

Mount Hood

Mount Hood Cultural Center and Museum

Down in Government Camp, the **Mount Hood Cultural Center and Museum** (88900 Government Camp Loop, Government Camp, 503/272-3301, http://mthoodmuseum.org, 9am-5pm daily, free) digs into the history and culture of the area, with exhibits on the region's natural history, the Barlow Road section of the Oregon Trail, and vintage skis and sleds.

SPORTS AND RECREATION

Hiking

TRILLIUM LAKE LOOP

Distance: 1.9 miles round-trip
Duration: 1-1.5 hours
Elevation gain: 50 feet
Effort: easy
Trailhead: From Government Camp, take U.S. 26 east about a mile and turn right for Trillium Lake. After 0.5 mile, stay left on the paved road, then 1.2 miles later turn right for day-use parking, past a campground entrance.

A scenic lake located near Mount Hood, Trillium Lake boasts a trail that goes all the way around with almost no elevation gain. The lake is popular with kayakers and canoers, and from some angles Mount Hood rises above like it's posing for a postcard. Follow the trail clockwise or counterclockwise around the lake, sometimes over boardwalks and hidden in the spruce trees, other times on the lakeshore dotted with lily pads and water lilies. Look for beaver lodges—piles of sticks built by the animals, which enter and escape underwater. Note that much of the water's edges are boggy—this is a lake formed after a dam was built—but the day-use area has a good boat put-in spot.

MOUNTAINEER TRAIL LOOP

Distance: 2.8 miles round-trip
Duration: 2 hours
Elevation gain: 1,100 feet
Effort: moderate
Trailhead: At Timberline Lodge, head up the steps across from the parking lot and turn right, then right again a few yards later; you'll see signs for the Mountaineer Trail.

Mount Hood feels so close you can touch it—and from Timberline Lodge, you can and should. This loop travels up the alpine slopes of the mountain to the Silcox Hut, a cabin positioned between the ski area's top two chairlifts. Follow the trail as it heads through mountain hemlock at the tree line; at a four-way junction, keep straight. The trail becomes a road that heads up to Silcox, with some of the best views of Hood's rocky features along the way. On a clear day, you can see down Oregon's line of volcanoes to Mount Jefferson and the Three Sisters. From the hut, your high point at 7,000 feet, go west and down the road to find where the trail picks up again, heading downhill. As you get close to tree line again, head straight through a junction and past the ruins of an old cabin. Pass under ski lifts to reach the lodge. Remember that traveling uphill is harder than usual at this altitude, and bring plenty of water in the summer.

PARADISE PARK

Distance: 11.3 miles round-trip
Duration: 6 hours
Elevation gain: 2,300 feet
Effort: strenuous
Trailhead: Timberline Lodge

The Paradise Park out-and-back trail offers classic views of Hood. From the lodge, follow the Pacific Crest Trail west, skirting the slopes of the mountain, for 2.9 miles. You'll head into the trees, then emerge again for views up to the summit. Turn right and descend into Zigzag Canyon and then climb back out of it over the course of a mile, which makes for much of the hike's elevation change. You'll cross wildflower meadows to reach a shelter at Paradise Park. Retrace your steps back to Timberline Lodge.

Skiing

The Mount Hood area is awash in ski lifts, all with their own specialty. **Mount Hood Meadows** (14040 Hwy. 35, 503/337-2222, www.skihood.com, $82 adults, $59 seniors, $49 children 7-14, $12 children under 7, $69 beginners) is the biggest, with the most terrain and a very traditional ski area. Find legitimate double-black, advanced runs, as well as terrain parks. Check the website for opening times as hours are highly variable. The **Nordic Center** ($21 adults, $18 seniors, $16 children under 13) at Mount Hood Meadows has 15 kilometers of groomed trails for cross-country aficionados, accommodating both skate- and traditional-style skiers. Rentals ($32) and lessons are available, and the trails are generally open December-March.

Mount Hood Ski Bowl (87000 Hwy. 26, 503/272-3206, www.skibowl.com/winter, skiing 3pm-10pm Mon.-Thurs., 9am-11pm Fri.-Sun. winter, snow tubing 5pm-11:30pm Fri., 9:45am-11:30pm Sat., 9:45am-9:15pm Sun. winter, skiing $70-76 adults, $40-44 seniors and children 7-12, free for children under 7 and seniors over 71, tubing $26-30 adults, $20-24 children under 48 inches tall) rises on a peak next to Hood, though its base is in Government Camp; there are only a few lifts but lots of varied terrain and the most night skiing acreage in North America. It also offers day and night snow tubing.

Timberline Ski Area (27500 E Timberline Rd., Government Camp, 503/272-3158, www.timberlinelodge.com, $71-76 adults, $61-63 children 15-17, $47 children 7-14 and seniors, $37-39 beginners) is a mid-size ski area whose base is at Timberline Lodge; both the bottoms and tops of different chairlifts converge here. Its highest lifts often traverse snow year-round—yes, Timberline offers year-round skiing (depending, of course, on how much snow falls in a year). Ski hours vary by season, and current lift opening hours are best checked on the website (www.timberlinelodge.com/conditions).

Snowshoeing

You can snowshoe on most trails in the area that are open to hiking in the summer. The route up to the Silcox Hut on the Mountaineer Trail is popular in winter. Be sure to stay clear of the ski boundary. **Timberline Lodge** (503/272-3409, www.timberlinelodge.com, $20) has limited rentals.

FOOD

Cozy **Mount Hood Brewing Company** (87304 Government Camp Loop, Government Camp, 503/272-3172, www.mthoodbrewing.com, 11am-9pm daily, $14-24) is one of the more bustling spots in Government Camp, with pizzas and nachos to go with the locally made beer. There's an outdoor deck for sunny days.

The wood-walled interior of **Charlie's Mountain View** (88462 Government Camp Loop, Government Camp, 503/272-3333, www.charliesmountainview.com, 11am-2am Mon.-Fri., 8am-2am Sat.-Sun., $10-21) is plastered with ski stickers and photos, and the bar-like interior is low-key. Burgers are as tall as they are wide, and weekend breakfasts are dense. The prime rib is also served as a rich French dip sandwich.

Glacier Haus Bistro (88817 Government Camp Loop, Government Camp, 503/272-3471, www.glacierhaus.com, noon-9pm Thurs.-Sun., $12-20) has a European alpine feel, from the international flags outside to the steins of beer inside. The comfort food here includes time-tested classics: Hungarian goulash, wiener schnitzel, Bavarian sausage.

The Timberline Lodge's **Cascade Dining Room** (27500 E Timberline Rd., Government Camp, 503/272-3104, www.timberlinelodge.com, 7:30am-10am, 11:30am-2pm, 6pm-8pm Mon.-Fri., 7:30am-10:30am, 11:30am-3pm, 5:30pm-8pm Sat., 7:30am-10:30am, 11:30am-3pm, 6pm-8pm Sun., $26-39) has a classic lodge feel: the requisite exposed wooden beams, a central fireplace, and curtains that recall classic striped wool blankets. It was even dedicated in 1937 by President Roosevelt. Entrées are also classics—steak, salmon—but expensive.

ACCOMMODATIONS

Staying at the **Timberline Lodge** (27500 E Timberline Rd., Government Camp, 503/272-3311, www.timberlinelodge.com, $255-360 rooms, $150-210 bunk-bed-only rooms) is a memorable experience. Besides having the best location for skiing or hiking, there's an outdoor hot tub and access to all of the building's classic corners. While the lodge may be historical, its 70 rooms are well renovated. Some have extra beds or bunk beds, and there are even bunk-bed-only rooms for groups. Pet-friendly rooms are also available.

Charming **Huckleberry Inn** (88611 Government Camp Loop, Government Camp, 503/272-3325, http://huckleberry-inn.com, $115-160) hasn't even reached the era of online booking; call to book rooms, which range from small and simple to slightly larger with trundle beds. There are also a few two-room suites, plus a dorm room that sleeps 10 that's rented as a single unit. With a few dozen rooms, attached laundromat, and old but rustic furnishings, it feels dated but warm.

When Government Camp fills up, **The Resort at the Mountain** (68010 E Fairway Ave., Welches, 503/622-3101, www.mthood-resort.com, $249-309), about 12 miles west down the highway from Government Camp, is a workable alternative. With more than 150 rooms, two restaurants, a golf course, and an outdoor pool, it's a busier property and one suited to lowland activities like biking and golfing. Rooms are sizable and beds are soft, and the attached spa has a beautiful relaxation room and tea garden for before and after treatments.

Camping

A couple of miles east of Government Camp and the closest campsite to Timberline Lodge, **Still Creek Campground** (E Perry Vickers Rd., www.fs.usda.gov, late May-early Sept., $22) has 27 sites in the trees, some of which are on the creek itself. Reservations are available online (www.recreation.gov) and recommended at least a few weeks in advance for summer weekends. A primitive hiking trail travels a mile to Government Camp.

Trillium Lake Campground (877/444-6777, www.fs.usda.gov, late May-late Sept., $22-45) offers some lakefront sites. The campground has 54 sites, most of which include RV hookups, and some back up to the 63-acre lake. Reservations (www.recreation.gov) are recommended as much as a month in advance for most dates at this campsite, farther out for weekends, though some sites are available on a first-come, first-served basis. To get there, take U.S. 26 about a mile east of Government Camp and turn onto Trillium Lake Road. After 0.5 mile, stay left on the paved road, and 1 mile later turn right for the campground entrance.

GETTING THERE

Government Camp is a near-straight shot south of Hood River via Highway 35, connecting to U.S. 26. The 43-mile drive takes just under an hour.

To reach Government Camp from Portland, head east on I-84 for 13 miles to exit 16. Head south on NE 238th Drive through the suburb of Gresham. Stay on the main route as it changes names to 242nd Drive, then NE Hogan Drive. About three miles later, turn left on NE Burnside Road, which quickly merges with U.S. 26. Follow U.S. 26 east for 38 miles to Government Camp. The drive takes about an hour and 20 minutes. For Timberline Lodge, you'll turn left just past Government Camp onto Timberline Highway and follow it about six miles up the mountain, keeping right at a junction.

Willamette Valley

Look for ★ to find recommended sights, activities, dining, and lodging.

Highlights

★ **Newberg and Dundee's Wineries and Tasting Rooms:** Big names in Oregon wine can be found in these tiny towns and their surrounding hills (page 319).

★ **McMinnville:** A classic little burg crowded with shops, restaurants, and tasting rooms, this is a picturesque example of small-town Oregon (page 325).

★ **Evergreen Aviation & Space Museum:** Here you'll find a giant collection of airplanes centered around the biggest one of all—the massive, wooden Spruce Goose built by Howard Hughes (page 326).

★ **Oregon State Capitol:** Salem's art deco statehouse has style and substance aplenty, free to discover on a guided or DIY tour (page 329).

★ **Trail of Ten Falls:** Experience nature at its finest by hiking this loop lined with 10 magical waterfalls (page 333).

★ **Alton Baker Park:** Eugene's riverfront park holds hundreds of acres ripe for exploration, including a trail in honor of the city's most famous son (page 341).

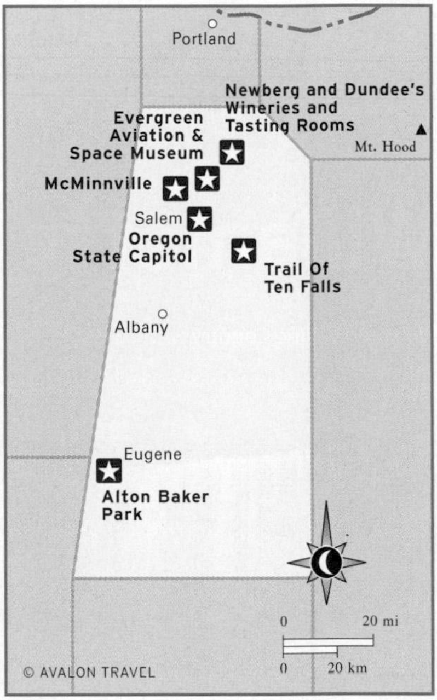

The Oregon Trail ended here for a reason. Located just south of Portland, the Willamette Valley is a lush region of farms, wineries, and small towns, where life moves at a slow, welcoming pace.

This is Oregon wine country, where the state has turned pinots into a blockbuster varietal. Wineries are wedged into every corner of the farmland here, and undulating fields of vineyards pop up behind cow pastures and big red barns. In wine country's tiny towns of Newberg, Dundee, and McMinnville, it seems like tasting rooms make up half of each downtown block. Don't expect the glamour of Napa Valley, but rather the cheerful welcome of a rural region that's found its calling.

A bit further south along I-5, you'll find Oregon's second- and third-largest cities, Salem and Eugene, respectively. They're almost the same size in terms of population but have distinct vibes. Salem is the state capital, centered around a manicured campus of government buildings. Surrounding the capitol buildings are museums and a handful of homey local eateries, with the Willamette River forming the west border of town. The Willamette River also runs through Eugene, which is defined by its world-class public university with 23,600 students and vibrant college-town atmosphere—with a hippie bent—to match. The city sits in a green plain between the Cascade foothills, and residents tend to be active and young—or at least young at heart—with an environmental ethos.

PLANNING YOUR TIME

The Willamette Valley traces the same route that I-5 runs today, south from the city of Portland. For wine country, you'll veer off to the west on Highway 99. Newberg is the first of the towns you'll hit on your way south, at around 25 miles away, a 50-minute drive from Portland, followed a few miles later by Dundee, and then, heading off onto Highway 18, McMinnville, about 40 miles from Portland. Given their proximity, you can easily visit on a day trip from Portland. For a more relaxed experience, 2-3

Previous: Willamette Valley vineyard; on the Trail of Ten Falls. **Above:** Oregon State Capitol park.

Willamette Valley

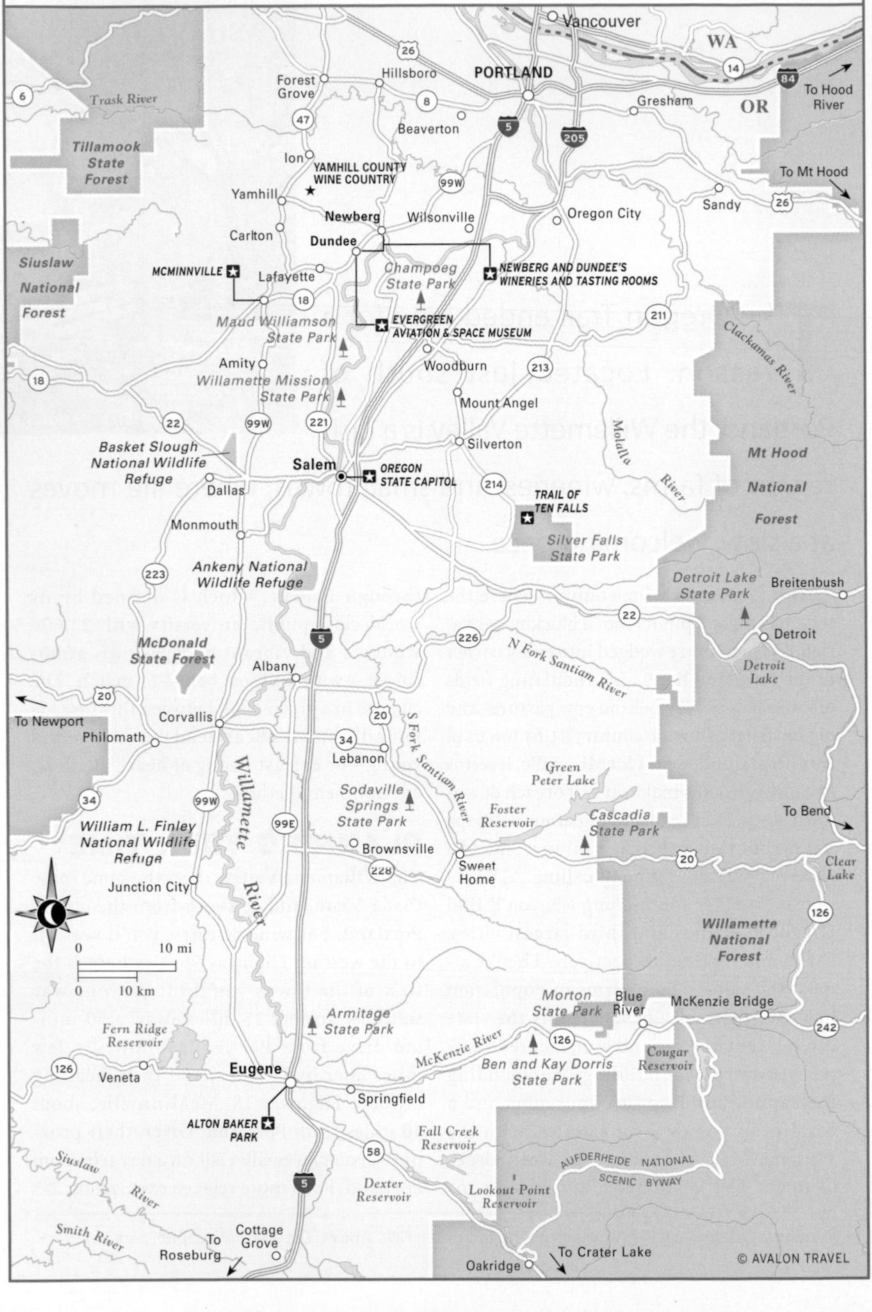

days is a nice amount of time to spend in wine country. McMinnville is a good place to base yourself.

For Salem and Eugene, you could budget an extra 1-2 days. These larger cities also make good places to stop and break up a drive if you're on a longer trip. Salem offers convenient access to the coast, and Eugene is only about 2.5 hours from Bend and 3 hours from Ashland.

Willamette Wine Country

TOP EXPERIENCE

The small towns of Newberg, Dundee, and McMinnville are hubs for the Willamette Valley's wine country, with the greatest concentration of notable, award-winning wineries. When Oregon wines appear on store shelves and restaurant menus outside the state, this is likely where they came from. Wineries and tasting rooms can be found in the downtown areas as well as just off the highways in the surrounding hills.

NEWBERG AND DUNDEE

The twin tiny towns of Newberg and Dundee sit less than three miles apart on Highway 99 and are somewhat nondescript. The latter is basically just a single-road town, while the former has a whopping two main streets (one going in each direction). But this is the heart of Oregon wine country. Enjoy close proximity to some of the best-known wineries in the state in Dundee, and don't miss the excellent dining in Newberg, which has a slightly more centralized downtown and yet more wineries.

★ Wineries and Tasting Rooms

One of few tasting rooms located in Newberg proper, **Chehalem Winery** (106 S Center St., Newberg, 503/538-4700, www.chehalemwines.com, 11am-5pm daily, $20 tasting fee) has a stately space with rustic-chic exposed brick, barrel tables, and artful hanging lightbulbs. Some evenings the tasting room becomes more of a wine bar with flights and cheese plates, even live music.

Like many local wineries, **Duck Pond Cellars** (23145 Hwy. 99W, Dundee,

a vineyard in Dundee

503/538-3199, www.duckpondcellars.com, 11am-5pm daily, $10 tasting fee, $35 tasting and tour) specializes in pinots; some of its sales specifically support environmental causes like wildlife protection. The pinot gris and pinot noir have each won a slew of awards. The low-slung white tasting room also has an outdoor patio. Advanced reservations are required for tours, which include a walk through the vineyards.

Famous for its bubblies, **Argyle Winery** (691 Hwy. 99W, Dundee, 503/538-8520, http://argylewinery.com, 11am-5pm daily, $20 tasting fee) pours all kinds of varietals at its new tasting room, a grand edifice on its winery property that feels like it should host more music and gathering events than it does, but it allows for the most elbow room in the county. These are the kinds of wines you'll want to take home for special occasions.

Charming **Erath Winery** (9409 NE Worden Hill Rd., Dundee, 503/538-3318, www.erath.com, 11am-5pm daily, $10 tasting fee) is an expert at pinots, both gris and noir, and its sleek farmyard tasting room feels a bit like a wood-walled sauna (though at a comfortable temperature). Enjoy the unfussy tasting room only a few miles into the hills from Dundee's main drag.

Though Oregon prides itself on its local wine, **Domaine Drouhin Oregon** (6750 NE Breyman Orchards Rd., Dayton, 503/864-2700, www.domainedrouhin.com, 11am-4pm daily, $10 tasting fee, $40 tasting and tour) reaches across the oceans to link this rural region with France. The winery, located far in the hills off the highway, is owned by a Burgundy family, and the pinot noirs and chardonnays are overseen by a fourth-generation winemaker. The tour takes in the entire estate and includes a seated tasting; reservations are required.

The family behind **Stoller Family Estate** (16161 NE McDougall Rd., Dayton, 503/864-3404, www.stollerfamilyestate.com, 11am-5pm daily, $20 tasting fee) takes sustainability seriously: It was the first winery in the world to be certified LEED gold, a measurement of green practices. The slanted roof of the tasting room and towering windows facing the vineyards let sunlight into the space; the rest of the electricity comes from solar panels. The estate's pinot noir has been listed by wine publications as one of the best in Oregon.

WINE TOURS

If you'd like to avoid driving between Newberg and Dundee, **The Trolley** (503/437-5969, www.the-trolley.com, $95 pp), an old-fashioned bus driven by "conductors" in vests and hats, usually visits three wineries and a restaurant for a large lunch.

To explore the area by bike with a guide and wine tastings, try **Pedal Bike Tours** (133 SW 2nd Ave., Portland, 503/243-2453, http://pedalbiketours.com, $99) out of Portland. It provides bikes and van transportation to the Newberg area, with 10 miles of cycling in five hours, including several winery stops. Groups are no larger than four.

You can see the vineyards from a new angle at **Vista Balloon Adventures** (1050 Commerce Pkwy., Newberg, http://vistaballoon.com, $220 pp), which gives hot-air balloon rides over the rural miles comprising Oregon's wine country and offers a brunch option. On a clear day you'll see the line of Cascade volcanoes running from Oregon to Washington, their white peaks lined up like pearls on a necklace. Flights start at dawn and generally run April-October, weather permitting.

Sights and Recreation

CHAMPOEG STATE HERITAGE AREA

Champoeg State Heritage Area (Champoeg Rd. NE and French Prairie Rd. NE, St. Paul, 800/551-6949, www.oregonstateparks.org, $5 parking) was, in the 18th century, where Oregon's first provisional government was formed. Today it has a **visitors center** (9am-5pm daily May-Sept., 11am-4pm daily Oct.-Apr.), log cabin museum, and historical house, plus a historical garden outside. The on-site store is the oldest

Wine-Country Weekend

Close proximity to Portland means it's easy to make a quick escape south for a weekend to relax in the region's wine country.

FRIDAY

Make the short (just under an hour) drive southwest from Portland via I-5 and Highway 99 to Newberg in time to catch dinner. A number of great places to dine are here, but the **Painted Lady** is one of the region's best. Go for the prix fixe tasting with wine pairings. Drive three miles northeast and check into **The Allison Inn and Spa** for a very comfortable overnight.

SATURDAY

Start the day very early with a hot-air balloon ride over the region's vineyards via **Vista Balloon Adventures,** or sleep in before finding breakfast at **Babica Hen Café,** just off Highway 99 in Dundee. Then hit some of the best-known wineries in the area: **Argyle Winery** is just north of Babica Hen on the highway, and **Erath Winery** and **Domaine Drouhin Oregon** are in the hills to the west.

Continue south on Highway 99 for about 10 miles: It's time to move on to McMinnville. Check into the **Atticus Hotel** for sumptuous accommodations right downtown and in walking distance to everything, or **The Vintages Trailer Resort,** off Highway 203 and on the way from Dundee to McMinnville, if you feel like going more rustic. **Ribslayer BBQ to Go** downtown makes for a quick, hearty lunch before walking around and wine tasting at spots like the **Willamette Valley Vineyards Tasting Room,** just a few blocks away, and **The Eyrie Vineyards,** just over a half mile northeast. All the ambling will prepare you for dinner at **Bistro Maison,** on the 3rd Street thoroughfare, where French classics pair with local wines. If you're up for more after dinner, pop by the **Gem Creole Saloon,** just a handful of blocks west down the street, for a subdued cocktail.

SUNDAY

In the morning, go to **Community Plate** on 3rd Street, an airy café with light breakfasts and good coffee. Before heading back to Portland, check out the **Evergreen Aviation & Space Museum,** about a 10-minute drive east via Three Mile Lane and Highway 18, to see Howard Hughes's Spruce Goose. Have a designated driver? You can make plenty more winery stops while returning to Portland through Dundee and Newberg.

continuously operating shop in the state. Rangers give occasional tours to talk about the history of the site, but it's a bird-watcher's haven year-round. From Newberg, the park is about 6.5 miles southeast via Highway 219, a 10-minute drive.

BIKING

The **Willamette Valley Scenic Bikeway,** a 135-mile route long on rural roads, cuts a north-south path to the city of Eugene and has its northern trailhead in the **Champoeg State Heritage Area** (Champoeg Rd. NE and French Prairie Rd. NE, St. Paul, 800/551-6949, www.oregonstateparks.org, $5 parking). There aren't many bike rental stores on the north end of the Willamette Valley, though, so you may need to rent wheels in Portland.

Entertainment and Events

With 16 taps pouring beers from around the West Coast, **Barley and Vine Tavern** (408 E 1st St., Newberg, 503/554-1704, www.barleyandvinetavern.com, 2pm-11pm Mon.-Thurs, noon-11pm Fri.-Sun.) is a good reminder that not everything in town needs to be served in a stemmed glass—although of course there's an excellent list of wines by the glass as well, but mostly global in origin rather than local. The upscale bar is decorated in chrome and exposed concrete, with snacks of the artisanal pretzel variety.

Wolves and People Brewing (30203 NE Benjamin Rd., Newberg, 503/487-6873, www.wolvesandpeople.com, 4pm-8pm Fri., noon-8pm Sat., noon-6pm Sun.), a farmhouse brewery just outside Newberg, offers tastings in its old wooden barn on weekends, often with a food truck parked outside. The farm uses its own fruit in making the beer, though many of the ingredients and styles also have European roots.

The **Newberg Old Fashioned Festival** (Memorial Park, S Blaine St. at E 5th St., Newberg, www.newbergoldfashionedfestival.org, July) is an annual multiday celebration of old-timey costumes and games, and includes a 5K run/walk, parades, a carnival, and a car show. If there was ever a time to dig out your stovepipe hat, this is it. Entry is free, though rides and 5K registration have fees.

Shopping

The half-bookstore, half-café space of the brick-fronted **Chapters Books and Coffee** (701 E 1st St., Newberg, 503/554-0206, www.chaptersbooksandcoffee.com, 6am-7pm Mon.-Fri., 8am-7pm Sat.-Sun.) feels like a perfect balance, with shelves of well-curated used and new books and coffee shop tables in a spacious setting.

Made from fresh goat milk, the cheeses at **Briar Rose Creamery** (19231 NE Fairview Dr., Dundee, 503/538-4848, www.briarrosecreamery.com, noon-5pm Fri.-Sat., by appointment only Mon.-Thurs.) are rich and smooth. The creamery is known for its Lorelei, a square-shaped, beer-washed goat cheese. It also specializes in chèvre and crumbly feta. Visit the tiny farm store to taste the handmade creations.

Food

Rudick/Wood (720 E 1st St., Newberg, 503/487-6133, http://ruddickwood.com, 11:30am-3pm and 5pm-9pm Tues.-Sun., $21-29), a restaurant in a converted 1920s garage, has an open kitchen serving homey bistro meals and a warm, inviting atmosphere. Expect hearty meat cuts, including pork chops and leg of lamb, but the fresh, local produce accompaniments are the real standout.

The elegant ★ **Painted Lady** (201 S College St., Newberg, 503/538-3850, http://thepaintedladyrestaurant.com, 5pm-10pm Wed.-Sun., $85-110) sits a couple of blocks away from Newberg's small main streets. It offers fine, prix-fixe dining, where a five- or nine-course meal comes with the option of specialized wine pairings. Intended for special events and unhurried diners, the local-ingredient dishes are served in the rooms of a Victorian house with simple, sophisticated decor.

With lots of small colleges in the area, it's no wonder there's a place for food that's quick, hot, and cheap. **Ixtapa** (307 E 1st St., Newberg, 503/538-5956, 11am-9:30pm Mon.-Thurs., 11am-10:30pm Fri.-Sat., 11am-9pm Sun., $9-17) and its saucy Mexican food delivers. It's the place to go for big, salted margaritas and baskets of chips.

Jory Restaurant (2525 Allison Ln., Newberg, 503/554-2526, 6:30am-10:30am, 11:30am-2pm, and 5:30pm-9pm Mon.-Fri., 9am-2pm and 5:30pm-9pm Sat.-Sun, $38-52)—named for a type of soil—is a fine-dining standout in the region. The farm-to-table eatery carefully presents dishes and uses fresh, organic ingredients like Northwest razor clams. Like The Allison Inn and Spa, in which it's located a few miles northeast of town, the restaurant has understated high-end style. Its dining room, even when full, is always at a low, respectful murmur.

Red Hills Market (155 SW 7th St., Dundee, 971/832-8414, www.redhillsmarket.com, 7am-8pm daily, $9-18), just off the highway, is an enclosed market with wines, cheeses, and gourmet snacks that also serves sandwiches, pizzas, and salads in its general store-style interior. One of its wood-fired ovens is in a vintage truck outside. Order at the counter and grab a place to sit, or simply pop in to shop for fresh local cheeses and pastries for your picnic basket.

In a minimalist dining room inside the Inn at Red Hills, **Babica Hen Cafe** (1410 Hwy. 99W, Dundee, 503/538-7970, www.babicahencafe.com, 8am-8pm daily, $12-21), offers comfort food like mashed potatoes, short rib stroganoff, and meatloaf. It has a long counter inside and a patio outside for warm weather.

Accommodations

$150-250

Located on a hill outside Newberg, **Chehalem Ridge Bed and Breakfast** (28700 NE Mountain Top Rd., Newberg, 503/538-3474, http://chehalemridge.com, $175-325) is at a peaceful remove from the crowds of wine tasters. From its balcony, you can look out on the entire valley. The bed-and-breakfast's five rooms have farmhouse chic—one has a picket-fence headboard—and some have jetted or clawfoot tubs. All but one have divine views, and some have fireplaces.

When arriving from the south, **Inn at Red Hills** (1410 N Hwy. 99W, Dundee, 503/538-7666, www.innatredhills.com, $219-259) is one of the first things you see in Dundee proper, and it's a lovely greeting. Most of the 20 rooms have at least a small couch, some with large windows stretching up to the ceilings. The on-site restaurant, Babica Hen Cafe, is conveniently close dining.

The English-style **La Bastide Bed and Breakfast** (21150 NE Niederberger Rd., Dundee, 503/351-4239, www.labastidebandb.com, $170-230) looks like it belongs on a continental estate, thanks to white pillars and a large green lawn, though it's located not far off Highway 99. Its seven rooms have hillside or vineyards views, and a two-course breakfast is included in your stay. With contemporary decor, it feels more like a classy friend's guest room than an overfussy bed-and-breakfast.

OVER $250

★ **The Allison Inn and Spa** (2525 Allison Ln., Newberg, 503/554-2525, www.theallison.com, $435-445) is the only hotel of its kind in the region, more of a large resort with 85 rooms and a wonderful attached spa. Rooms all have gas fireplaces and terraces, with high-end linens and original artwork. Though far from most of the action, located a few miles northeast of Newberg, the hotel has an indoor pool and the acclaimed Jory Restaurant on-site, so it's not hard to pass the time. A two-night minimum stay is required.

The Allison Inn and Spa

Oregon Pinots

You don't need to know a lot about wine to drink in Oregon, but you should know one word: pinot. The pinot grape—all the rage here and nearly synonymous with the region—is notoriously difficult to cultivate but when done correctly produces medium-bodied and complex wines. Vineyards in the Willamette Valley date back to when the Oregon Trail deposited settlers in the rich, fertile region, but it wasn't until the mid-20th century that growers realized that since the valley is at the same latitude as key French and Italian regions—look for signs along the road noting you're passing the 45th parallel—it would make an ideal place for pinot noir. Competition wins against European wineries in the 1970s and 1980s by David Lett of The Eyrie Vineyards gave Oregon wines some street cred, and in the decades since, the region's reputation has only grown. While pinot noirs receive the most attention and acclaim, pinot gris (derived from a related grape) is a fast-growing favorite.

WHERE TO GO FOR PINOT NOIR:

- **Domaine Drouhin Oregon:** Owned by a French family and harnessing the knowledge of a fourth-generation winemaker, this winery produces notable pinot noirs.
- **Willamette Valley Vineyards Tasting Room:** Head to this convenient McMinnville outpost to taste offerings from the leading producer of pinot noir in Oregon.
- **The Eyrie Vineyards:** The late David Lett, pinot pioneer, made his wine here, and his son continues to make pinots today.

WHERE TO GO FOR PINOT GRIS:

- **Duck Pond Cellars:** Dundee's environmentally minded winery has won awards for its well-crafted pinot gris.
- **Erath Winery:** Erath's pinot gris is a well-loved, affordable classic throughout Oregon.
- **King Estate Winery:** Located farther south near Eugene, this winery produces a standout pinot gris that appears on fine-dining menus around the Northwest.

CAMPING

In between all the historical buildings of **Champoeg State Heritage Area** (Champoeg Rd. NE and French Prairie Rd. NE, St. Paul, 800/551-6949, www.oregonstateparks.org) are 75 RV sites ($31) and six tent sites ($19), plus six rustic cabins ($43-53) and six yurts ($43-53). The park also has a disc golf course and a dock on the Willamette River.

Information and Services

Find information and maps on the region at the **Oregon Wine and Hospitality Information Center** (2119 Portland Rd., Newberg, 503/538-2014, http://visit.chehalemvalley.org, 9am-5pm Mon.-Fri., 10:30am-3pm Sat.-Sun. June-fall) inside the Chehalem Valley Chamber of Commerce.

Getting There

To reach Newberg from Portland, head south on I-5 to exit 289 in Tualatin. Turn right to take Tualatin-Sherwood Road and stay on it for about 4.5 miles, keeping left for Highway 99 West and following it for 8.5 miles. The drive is about 25 miles and takes 50 minutes total without traffic, but note that it's rare to escape backups on this route.

To continue to Dundee, stay on Highway 99 West for 2.5 more miles.

McMinnville

★ MCMINNVILLE

This is the Platonic ideal of a wine country town: historical buildings—many dating back to the 19th century—packed together into a walkable downtown lined with trees as well as independent shops, restaurants, and tasting rooms. Despite the Victorian touches on some old buildings, this isn't an overly fussy or cutesy town, but a functional and winning one. Cars stop for pedestrians. Locals are friendly and glad to give directions. And a small industrial district lies about a 15-minute walk away from the 3rd Street core, home to several more wineries, with residential blocks filling the spaces between.

Wineries and Tasting Rooms

Many of the makers in this region are mom-and-pop operations with sweetly rustic vibes, but downtown's **Naked Winery** (211 NE 3rd St., 541/386-3700, www.nakedwinery.com, noon-7pm Mon.-Thurs., noon-8pm Fri.-Sat., noon-6pm Sun, $15 tasting fee) is a whole other ballgame. With wines named after naughty puns (Foreplay Chardonnay, Booty Call Sweet Blush), and tasting rooms across Oregon, the winery is less about authenticity and more about fun. On Sundays, add a mimosa to your spread at the brightly colored tasting room.

The very classic **Willamette Valley Vineyards Tasting Room** (300 NE 3rd St., 503/883-9013, www.wvv.com, $10-15 tasting fee) is the leading producer of pinot noir in Oregon, and it has an outpost in downtown McMinnville. With couches, side tables made of barrels, and earth tones everywhere, it's a tasting room by the book.

Also downtown, **R Stuart and Co Wine Bar** (528 NE 3rd St., 503/472-4477, www.rstuartandco.com, noon-6pm Sun.-Tues., noon-8pm Wed.-Sat., $12-15 tasting fee) feels a bit more like a bar than a tasting room, and indeed you can buy wine by the glass as well as by the flight. Rather than hovering over a counter, you can relax at small tables that can hold plenty of pinot noirs and still leave room for a cheese plate.

A collection of wineries, informally called the Granary District, can be found in old industrial buildings a few blocks off McMinnville's downtown strip. **The Eyrie Vineyards** (935 NE 10th Ave., 503/472-6315, www.eyrievineyards.com, noon-5pm daily, $10-20 tasting fee) is one of the most notable in the area thanks to late winemaker David Lett, who helped pioneer pinot craftsmanship and won awards for his work. Today his son holds the reins at the winery and its intimate tasting room.

WINE TOURS

Pick up a wine map in almost any downtown McMinnville store or restaurant to plan your route through the area's wineries. Downtown tasting rooms are easily walkable, but if you'd like to head farther afield and have someone else take the wheel, try **Oregon Select Wine Tours** (971/404-5178, http://oregonselectwinetours.com/tours, $75 per hour) for a driver who'll pick you up in an SUV and may be able to arrange private or reserve tastings.

Want an even more extreme wine country experience? **Equestrian Wine Tours** (6325 NE Abbey Rd., Carlton, 503/864-2336, www.equestrianwinetours.com, $150) puts you atop a Tennessee Walking Horse or in a horse-drawn carriage to get between wineries.

Sights and Recreation

★ EVERGREEN AVIATION & SPACE MUSEUM

You can't miss the **Evergreen Aviation & Space Museum** (500 NE Captain Michael King Smith Way, 503/434-4185, www.evergreenmuseum.org, 9am-5pm daily, $27 adults, $24 seniors, $19 children 5-16, free for children under 5), about 3.5 miles east of McMinnville via Highway 18—you'll see it coming a mile away, comprised as it is of three giant buildings with airliners parked outside. Drive down an old runway to reach the museum and enter the largest building (it's well signed) to find a massive window-lined hanger filled with airplanes old and new, military and pleasure craft. Another building holds a massive theater—be sure to catch a screening of one of the nature documentaries or 3D flight movies. The third building holds space exploration vehicles and artifacts.

The star attraction here is the massive Spruce Goose, a wooden airplane built by eccentric millionaire Howard Hughes during World War II. With the biggest wingspan of any plane, ever, it makes even sizable fighter jets look tiny by comparison. Regular museum admission allows you access to the cargo hold, but if you want to get into the cockpit, you'll have to take a tour ($25-50), which includes peeks down the inside of the plane's massive wingspan and a chance to sit in Hughes's seat. Even casual aviation fans will be entranced.

WINGS AND WAVES WATERPARK

Located next to the Evergreen Aviation & Space Museum, **Wings and Waves Waterpark** (460 NE Captain Michael King Smith Way, 503/687-3390, http://wingsandwaveswaterpark.com, 10am-6pm Sat.-Thurs., 11am-7pm Fri. summer, winter hours vary, $29 over 42 inches tall, $20 under 42 inches tall, $10 nonswimmers) gets in on the plane theme with a 747 airliner parked on the roof—one of the waterslides actually starts inside it. With slides appropriate for every age, plus splash pools and sprinklers, it's a family-minded destination.

Evergreen Aviation & Space Museum

ERRATIC ROCK STATE NATURAL SITE

The name sounds a bit more exciting than the state park really is. **Erratic Rock State Natural Site** (800/551-6949, www.oregonstateparks.org, free) doesn't showcase, say, a rock acting in bizarre ways. It's named for a geology term describing a stone that's out of place with its surroundings; here it's a 90-ton rock that moved over 500 miles some 12,000 years ago—all the way from the Rocky Mountains. The park has sweeping views of the Willamette Valley and makes for a peaceful stop after a busy day of planes or pinots. It's located 7.5 miles southwest of town via Highway 18.

Entertainment and Events

NIGHTLIFE

There's a warm breeze that runs through **Gem Creole Saloon** (236 NE 3rd St., 503/883-9194, www.mcminnvillegem.com, 11:30am-2:30pm and 4pm-9pm Sun.-Thurs., 11:30am-2:30pm and 4pm-10pm Fri.-Sat.), making it feel a little more like New Orleans than old Oregon. Deep purple walls and brass instruments on the wall give it a strong Mardi Gras theme, but the scene at the bar and small tables is no bacchanal. Good times do roll, though, with crawfish étouffée, oyster po'boys, and tall mixed hurricanes or a "hoochie momma" punch. The saloon also has a solid list of local wines by the glass.

Although **The Oak** (326 NE Davis St., 503/857-0577, www.theoakmac.com, 3pm-midnight Mon.-Wed., 3pm-1am Thurs.-Sat., 3pm-2:30am Sun.) is sedate in the afternoons and early evenings, it's up to something most nights—karaoke, trivia, live music, pool, etc. It lives up to its name with wood floors, long wooden tables, and a smooth wood bar, and the mix of artisanal cocktails, rotating bar taps, and local bottles of wine also lends a refined feel.

FESTIVALS AND EVENTS

A town this devoted to wine needs a festival to celebrate it, and the annual **Sip McMinnville Food and Wine Classic** (500 NE Captain Michael King Smith Way, http://sipclassic.org, Mar., $17-36), held under the airplanes at the Evergreen Aviation & Space Museum for a quarter century, delivers dozens of wines, plus small bites and art booths.

Bumper stickers may plead that we "Keep Portland Weird," but the **McMenamins UFO Festival** (310 NE Evans St., http://ufofest.com, May), held at its Hotel Oregon, is doing its part to make McMinnville an oddity as well. Held for 20 years, the multiday event combines serious speakers on Area 51 and UFO phenomena with a parade, fun run, and alien pet costume contest. Some events are free, while speaker events tend to run $20-40. The truth is out here, somewhere.

Shopping

Want to dress like a local? Try **Yamhill Valley Dry Goods** (416 NE 3rd St., 503/883-0019, http://yamhillvalleydrygoods.squarespace.com, 10am-6pm Mon.-Sat., 11am-4pm Sun.), where the puffy vests and upscale outdoorsy gear endemic to the population is sold. It isn't cheap to wear funky clogs, but necklaces with wire pendants in the shape of Oregon are hard to resist.

Anchoring McMinnville's main drag, **Third Street Books** (320 NE 3rd St., 503/472-7786, www.thirdstreetbooks.com, 10am-6pm Mon.-Sat., 10am-4pm Sun.) offers new and used tomes, curated recommendations, and a kids' section with giant papier-mâché animals atop the shelves.

Sometimes you want to see all the wines at once. **Woodard Wines** (323 NE Davis St., 971/237-2502, www.woodardwines.com, 11am-6pm Mon.-Sat.), a shop just off the town's main street, always carries a selection of local bottles and features occasional tastings as well. Talk to owner Jeff Woodard for suggestions or join his pinot club, which mails his picks to participants several times a year.

Food

The only thing wrong with ★ **Community Plate** (315 NE 3rd St., 503/687-1902, www.communityplate.com, 7:30am-3pm daily,

$7-14) is that the airy café isn't open all the time. The light-filled space has a few touches of vintage hardware, clocks, and mounted antlers, a small counter, veggie-heavy scrambles, hearty salads, breakfast cocktails, and coffee. Tea comes in a vintage teapot.

Named for the boulevard in the heart of Barcelona, **La Rambla** (238 NE 3rd St., 503/435-2126, www.laramblaonthird.com, 11:30am-2:30pm and 4pm-8pm Mon.-Thurs., 11:30am-2:30pm and 4pm-10pm Fri., 11:30am-10pm Sat., 11:30am-8pm Sun., $13-25) salutes Spain with paella and tapas. The 350-bottle wine list, of course, includes both Spanish and Oregonian selections.

Look for the little house on main street with a small fence and gate to find **Bistro Maison** (729 NE 3rd St., 503/474-1888, www.bistromaison.com, 11:30am-2pm and 6pm-9pm Wed.-Thurs., 11:30am-2pm and 5pm-9pm Fri., 5pm-9pm Sat., noon-2pm and 3pm-6:30pm Sun., $21-33). French classics like confit de canard and coq au vin—as well as a truffle fondue that brings together two local delicacies, Oregon white truffles and Oregon cheddar cheese—are served in the house's small rooms.

When you're tired of red wines and cheese plates, **Golden Valley Brewery** (980 E 4th St., 503/472-2739, www.goldenvalleybrewery.com, 11am-10pm Mon.-Thurs., 11am-11pm Fri.-Sat., 11am-9pm Sun., $12-36) offers a refreshing antidote: grass-fed beef and a blonde ale made with local hops, served in a cozy pub environment with wood-paneled walls and snug booths. Pick between ribeye, filet, or a New York cut and add Gorgonzola potatoes.

Delicate **Thistle** (228 NE Evans St., 503/472-9623, http://thistlerestaurant.com, 5:30pm-10pm Tues.-Sat., $24-27) is nowhere near as prickly as its namesake. The small dining room is crowded with mason jars, garden-scene wallpaper, and hanging bulbs. Here the idea is "nose-to-tail, farm-to-fork" dining, meaning ingredients are local and may include, say, duck liver, beef cheek, or lamb tongue. Seasonal menus mean the small and medium plates change up regularly.

It's easy to stumble upon **Ribslayer BBQ to Go** (575 NE 2nd St., 503/472-1309, www.ribslayer.com, 11am-7pm Tues.-Sat., $10-17), or rather the giant 25-foot smoker that sits outside the alley-entry hole-in-the-wall. The smell of brisket or pork wafts through downtown's streets. Pork is bundled halfway through the smoking process to retain the flavor, and all the meat offerings are rich and saucy. Despite the name, there are indeed several tables in the tiny joint for eat-in meals, plus a picnic table outside with a perfect view of the 9,000-pound smoker.

Accommodations

UNDER $150

Never has a row of trailers looked more like an Instagram post than at ★ **The Vintages Trailer Resort** (16205 SE Kreder Rd., Dayton, 800/844-1492, www.the-vintages.com, $115-175), about seven miles east of town. The 14-acre RV campground abuts two lines of rentable trailers, most with included cruiser cycles parked out front. The trailers, Airstreams and similar, date back to the 1940s and 1950s and have been renovated or refurbished—but a stay here still feels a bit like roughing it. Some look out onto empty farmland, while others face a hedge that separates the rentables from the RVs. They book up fast.

$150-250

The 42-room **McMenamins Hotel Oregon** (310 NE Evans St., 503/472-8427, www.mcmenamins.com/hotel-oregon, $135-165 shared bath, $175-200 private bath) is a classic McMenamins property: It's a 1905 building that was a bus depot, soda fountain, and beauty parlor before it became one of their signature hotels, where some rooms share bathrooms (there's rarely a wait) and all have hand-painted walls. The downtown building boasts a 4th-floor rooftop bar.

There's nothing very Italian about **A'Tuscan Estate** (809 NE Evans St.,

503/434-9016, http://a-tuscanestate.com, $172-256 rooms, $269-275 suites or apartment), though perhaps the twin lion statues guarding the porch have an old-world flair. The bed-and-breakfast is in a colonial-style house downtown, and its three rooms and three suites boast four-poster beds and elegant furnishings. Suites also have full kitchens. It's in an ideal location downtown.

OVER $250

Atticus Hotel (375 NE Ford St., 503/472-1975, http://atticushotel.com, $300-490) is trying something new for downtown McMinnville. The city's classic Oddfellows hall is now a high-end property, which feels a little out of place in low-key McMinnville—but fortunately it's designed with subtle, if refined, charm. The hotel's four stories include 36 studios boasting luxury amenities like Pendleton bathrobes and Internet-enabled TVs. Valet parking, yoga classes, a glass of sparkling wine—it's all included, and the property is staffed by a concierge. The penthouse even has a butler's pantry.

CAMPING

Located near the Evergreen Aviation & Space Museum east of town, **Olde Stone Village** (4155 NE Three Mile Ln., 503/472-4315, www.oldestonevillage.com, $46) is a step above most RV parks, thanks to very green lawns, a seasonal pool, and tennis courts. More than 70 sites are on the tree-lined streets.

Getting There

To reach McMinnville from Portland, head south on I-5 to exit 289 in Tualatin. Turn right to take Tualatin-Sherwood Road and stay on it for about 4.5 miles, keeping left for Highway 99 West and following it for 15 miles. Bear left when it splits for Highway 18. Continue on for 8 miles, following signs into downtown. The drive is just over 40 miles and takes about one hour and ten minutes total.

Salem

Welcome to the center of Oregon, its state capitol, and a city that seems an equal distance from the ocean beaches, dry high desert, city life, and rural farmland. It offers a little bit of everything, with a smattering of sights, museums, and parks. It's also home to Willamette University. Originally called Chemeketa in the local Santiam language, it was likely named after Salem, Massachusetts. Government and college buildings form the core of the town's center, with the Willamette River outlining the western border. This is a workaday city, with busy locals, students focusing on classes, and small businesses serving their neighbors. Wine culture is fully on the fringes of town, though diners can expect a good local wine or two on every drink menu.

SIGHTS

★ Oregon State Capitol

Located in the middle of a well-manicured campus, the **Oregon State Capitol** (900 Court St. NE, 503/986-1388, www.oregonlegislature.gov, 8am-5pm Mon.-Fri., free) is a striking building from the 1930s that evokes the art deco era, with a crimped tower at its center, unusual among America's statehouses. The capitol building is open year-round for the public to explore, with sculptures depicting Oregon Trail history, a rotunda nine stories tall inside, a collection of Oregon rocks and minerals, and numerous statues. Oregon's history fills the murals that appear all over the campus. Free guided tours are available at 10:30am, 11:30am, 1:30pm, and 2:30pm Monday-Friday and take about 45 minutes.

In the summer (June-Sept.), these can be combined with tours of the tower—taking you up 121 steps to see the bronze Oregon Pioneer sculpture that stands atop it—which take place at 10am, 11am, 1pm, and 2pm. At the top, see if you can spot the Cascades through the clouds.

Hallie Ford Museum of Art

As part of Willamette University, **Hallie Ford Museum of Art** (700 State St., 503/370-6855, http://willamette.edu/arts/hfma, 10am-5pm Tues.-Sat., 1pm-5pm Sun., $6 adults, $4 seniors, $3 college students, free for children under 18) doesn't have a flashy entrance, but its galleries go on farther than you'd expect for a museum in a small city, stretching over two floors. Art from nearby Native American tribes is represented, and exhibits push the envelope with thoughtful and mixed-media pieces.

Gilbert House Children's Museum

Gilbert House Children's Museum (116 Marion St. NE, 503/371-3631, http://acgilbert.org, 10am-5pm daily summer, 10am-5pm Tues.-Sun. fall-spring, $8 adults, $7 seniors, free for children under 1) feels like a small town made just for kids—obviously children would prefer a town that's one-third playground, which this is. Named for the local figure who also invented Erector Sets, it has a play structure that looks like the famous toy. Farm and Victorian houses—three historical buildings in all, plus newer structures mixed in—host hands-on exhibits and toys, and outside there's a model paddle wheeler and ridable train. Small folk can spend hours here and burn off energy. Adults without children may be let in with admission, but they'll likely get a suspicious eye and find little to entertain themselves.

Willamette Heritage Center

An old mill was reborn as the **Willamette Heritage Center** (1313 Mill St. SE, 503/585-7012, www.willametteheritage.org, 10am-5pm Mon.-Sat., $8 adults, $7 seniors, $5 college students, $4 children 6-17, free for children under 6), now a small campus that joins together small shops and historical exhibits. Pay admission inside the main, cherry-red building to get a self-guided tour of the old mill structures, leading visitors through more than a half-dozen buildings spread over five acres. They contain artifacts from the once-mighty industry, plus re-creations of 19th-century homes

Oregon State Capitol

Salem

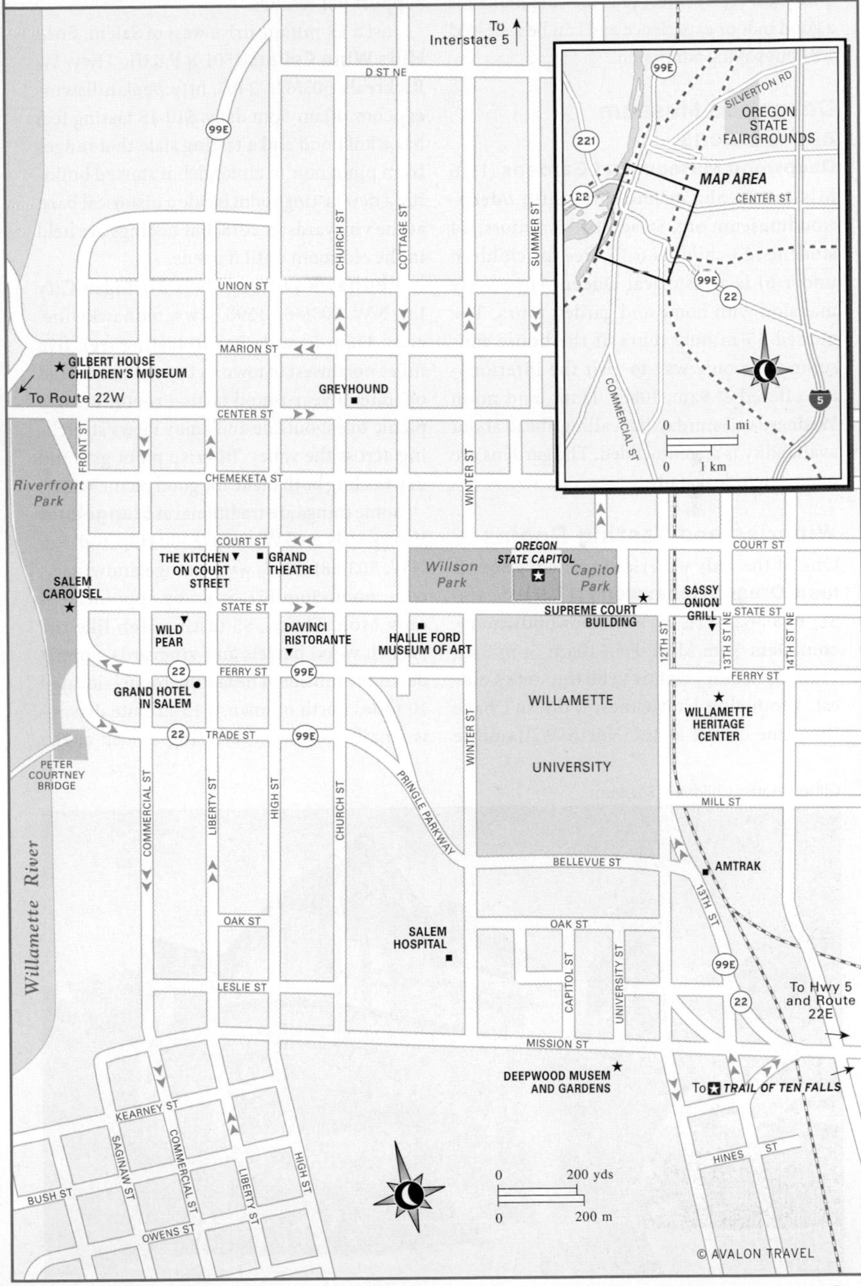
To Interstate 5
D ST NE
99E
UNION ST
MARION ST
GILBERT HOUSE CHILDREN'S MUSEUM
To Route 22W
GREYHOUND
CENTER ST
FRONT ST
CHURCH ST
COTTAGE ST
SUMMER ST
Riverfront Park
CHEMEKETA ST
WINTER ST
COURT ST
THE KITCHEN ON COURT STREET
GRAND THEATRE
OREGON STATE CAPITOL
Willson Park
Capitol Park
SALEM CAROUSEL
STATE ST
SUPREME COURT BUILDING
SASSY ONION GRILL
WILD PEAR
DAVINCI RISTORANTE
HALLIE FORD MUSEUM OF ART
12TH ST
13TH ST NE
14TH ST NE
22
FERRY ST
GRAND HOTEL IN SALEM
WILLAMETTE
WILLAMETTE HERITAGE CENTER
TRADE ST
PETER COURTNEY BRIDGE
UNIVERSITY
COMMERCIAL ST
LIBERTY ST
HIGH ST
PRINGLE PARKWAY
MILL ST
Willamette River
BELLEVUE ST
AMTRAK
13TH ST
OAK ST
SALEM HOSPITAL
CAPITOL ST
UNIVERSITY ST
LESLIE ST
To Hwy 5 and Route 22E
MISSION ST
DEEPWOOD MUSEM AND GARDENS
To TRAIL OF TEN FALLS
KEARNEY ST
SAGINAW ST
HINES ST
BUSH ST
OWENS ST
0 200 yds
0 200 m
© AVALON TRAVEL
SILVERTON RD
OREGON STATE FAIRGROUNDS
221
MAP AREA
CENTER ST
5
0 mi
0 1 km

that used to stand nearby. The self-guided tour takes about an hour. The shops, with art and gifts most represented, plus the café make for a good indoor experience and can be accessed without paying admission.

Deepwood Museum and Gardens

Deepwood Museum and Gardens (1116 Mission St. SE, 503/363-1825, http://deepwoodmuseum.org, $6 adults, $5 seniors, $4 students, $3 children 6-15, free for children under 6) is a historical Queen Anne-style mansion with home and garden tours. The guided 45-minute tours of the house museum—the only way to visit the interior—are offered at 9am, 10am, 11am, and noon Wednesday-Saturday, but calling ahead about availability is recommended. The gardens are open dawn-dusk daily.

Wineries and Tasting Rooms

One of the only wineries in Salem's downtown, **Oregon Honeywood** (1350 Hines St. SE, 503/362-4111, www.honeywoodwinery.com, 9am-5pm Mon.-Fri., 10am-5pm Sat., 11am-5pm Sun.) claims to be the state's oldest. Producing fruit wines, it doesn't have the same cachet as the North Willamette Valley's pinot growers, but it's an unpretentious little shop. Wines named after dogs support pet rescues.

Just a 15-minute drive west of Salem, **Eola Hills Wine Cellars** (501 S Pacific Hwy. W, Rickreall, 503/623-2405, http://eolahillswinery.com, 10am-5pm daily, $10-15 tasting fee) has a koi pond and a tasting slate that ranges from pinot noir to zinfandel. It started building a new tasting room inside a historical barn at the vineyards in 2018, but tastings are held in the old room until it opens.

Redhawk Winery (2995 Michigan City Ln. NW, 503/362-1596, www.redhawkwine.com, 11am-5pm daily, $10 tasting fee), five miles northwest of town, is family-owned and operates a year-round tasting room. Bring a picnic to eat outside and enjoy views stretching across the valley. Its crisp pinot gris and dry riesling both make for good picnic wines.

Some things are traditional at **Stangeland Vineyards and Winery** (8500 Hopewell Rd. NW, 503/581-0355, www.stangelandwinery.com, noon-5pm Fri.-Sun., by appointment only Mon.-Thurs., $5 tasting fee), like the French wood barrels and vineyards sloping down the hillside. The tasting room—located 10 miles north of town, a 15-minute drive—is small but homey, offering a peek at the

Gilbert House Children's Museum

barreled wine and opening out right onto the vineyards. Remember that it's not *strange*land.

WINE TOURS

Imagine a taxi just for wine tasting, only you provide the taxi. **Main Street Drivers** (888/327-4460 www.mainstreetdrivers.com, $35 per hour) is the designated driver who shows up, drives your car around while you taste wines, then drops you back at your hotel. The cheap price and familiar comfort make it a good choice for visitors who don't want a tour guide but also don't want to drink and drive.

For an active look at the rural vineyards outside of Salem, take an Eola Hills Winery **bike tour** (501 S Pacific Hwy. W, Rickreall, 503/623-2405, http://eolahillswinery.com, $79). Tours occur on select days throughout the summer, so check the website for dates—there are discounts for reserving early.

SPORTS AND RECREATION

Silver Falls State Park

About 25 miles east of Salem, a 45-minute drive, is **Silver Falls State Park** (20024 Silver Falls Hwy. SE, Sublimity, 503/873-8681, www.oregonstateparks.org, 8am-5pm daily Nov.-Jan., 8am-6pm daily Feb., 8am-8pm daily Mar., 7am-9pm daily Apr.-Aug., 7am-8pm daily Sept., 8am-7pm daily Oct., $5 parking), one of the region's top attractions. It's the largest state park and Oregon's most famous, with 9,200 acres. More than 35 miles of trails for hiking, biking, and horseback riding are spread throughout the park, but it's well-known for one in particular: the Trail of Ten Falls. Those not interested in a long trek can still visit some of the waterfalls, such as South Falls and Winter Falls, via short paved walks from parking areas. Other activities in the park include picnicking, and there's an off-leash area for dogs and a playground with horseshoe pits. A café is located inside the central historical building, **Silver Falls Lodge** (9am-4pm daily Memorial Day-Labor Day and 9am-4pm Sat.-Sun. Labor Day-Memorial Day, $8-14), which offers sandwiches and burgers perfect for a post-hike snack.

★ TRAIL OF TEN FALLS

Distance: 7.3 miles round-trip
Duration: 3-4 hours
Elevation gain: 800 feet
Effort: moderate
Trailhead: South Falls Day Use Area

Can one ever tire of waterfalls? On this trail,

Trail of Ten Falls

one of Oregon's signature hikes, you'll pass, yes, 10 cascades of up to 178 feet tall—four of them even allow you to walk behind them. You can start the loop at any of the park's four trailheads, but if you begin from the South Falls Day Use Area and walk clockwise, downstream to Silver Falls Lodge, your first waterfall will be South Falls, one of the biggest, to start you off with a bang.

If you just want to check out South Falls, it's a one-mile round-trip walk, all on paved paths—you can make a quick loop back to the parking lot in about 30 minutes with about 280 feet of elevation gain.

Continuing on, you'll soon hit unpaved trail, heading down switchbacks into the thick green forest and past Lower South Falls. At a junction, head straight to Lower North Falls, over a footbridge to Double Falls, and past Drake and Middle North Falls. At the next junction, go left to amble past Twin and North Falls; just past the latter, take an 0.3-mile spur trail to Upper North Falls, then return to the main trail to finally head back past Winter Falls and return to the parking lot.

Other Parks

On the banks of the Willamette River, Salem's **Riverfront Park** (200 Water St. NE, 503/588-6261, www.cityofsalem.net/riverfront-park, 5am-midnight daily) occupies 26 acres. It has open grassy areas, an amphitheater, and a pavilion. Many town festivities, such as outdoor summer movie screenings, take place here. Also on the park grounds is the **Riverfront Carousel** (101 Front St. NE, 503/540-0374, http://salemcarousel.wixsite.com/salemcarousel, 10am-7pm Mon.-Sat. and 11am-6pm Sun. June-Aug., 10am-6pm Mon.-Thurs., 10am-7pm Fri.-Sat., and 10am-5pm Sun. Sept.-May, $1.50), a classic ride in an indoor space with all the brightly painted animals you could ask for. It's a conveniently short walk from here to the Gilbert House Children's Museum.

Located in the city center, **Bush's Pasture Park** (890 Mission St. SE, 503/588-6336, www.cityofsalem.net/bushs-pasture-park, 5am-midnight daily) has 90 acres of greenery, including playgrounds and a rhododendron garden. Jogging trails run through the park. Also in the park, on the western side, is the **Bush Barn Art Center** (600 Mission St., 503/581-2228, http://salemart.org/programs/bush-barn-art-center, 10am-5pm Tues.-Fri., noon-5pm Sat.-Sun., free), which has three galleries of local art.

About 15 miles east of Salem, across the wide Willamette Valley, the town of Silverton holds the sprawling **Oregon Garden** (879 W Main St., Silverton, 503/874-8100, www.oregongarden.org, 9am-6pm daily May-Sept., 10am-4pm daily Oct.-Apr., $8-14 adults, $6-12 seniors, $5-11 children 12-17, $2-8 children 5-11, free for children under 5) with 80 acres of botanical splendor. Dozens of specialty gardens feature conifers, water features, and medicinal plants, and pets are allowed.

ENTERTAINMENT AND EVENTS

Nightlife

It's all a game at **Coin Jam** (439 Court St. NE, 503/363-8209, www.thecoinjam.com, 11am-11:30pm Mon.-Thurs., 11am-1:30am Fri.-Sat., 11am-9pm Sun.), an arcade bar in downtown Salem. There's a row of classics like Pac-Man, and wall decor includes a re-creation of a frozen Han Solo from *Star Wars.* The goofy, childlike vibe is countered by the bar pushing pints.

Venti's Café and Basement Bar (325 Court St. NE, 503/399-8733, http://ventiscafe.com, 11am-9pm Mon.-Sat., 11am-8pm Sun., basement bar 4pm-10pm Mon.-Tues., 4pm-11pm Wed.-Thurs., 4pm-midnight Fri.-Sat., 4pm-8pm Sun.) is a cheery café and eatery (tacos, rice bowls, etc.) that also serves beer from 32 taps, one of them a nitro tap. But down a steep stairway is a second drinking hole, the dark Basement Bar with art on the walls and a crowded, elbow-to-elbow feel. It's a student favorite.

The Arts

Downtown's **Grand Theatre** (191 High St. NE, 503/362-9185, http://salemshg.com) is more than 100 years old and was once owned by the Oddfellows, a fraternal organization that had a strong presence in this part of Oregon. It now hosts local theater productions, and its marquee lights the block.

Festivals and Events

Held for almost 70 years in a row, the **Salem Art Fair and Festival** (Bush's Pasture Park, 600 Mission St. SE, 503/581-2228, http://salemart.org/art-fair, July, $5-10, $3 students on Sat., free for children under 12) is a staple of the region, an outdoor three-day weekend event with live music, food, beer and wine gardens, and, of course, art, with more than 200 artists represented. Admission prices support local art education.

When you need something fried but can't decide what, it's time for a state fair. The annual **Oregon State Fair** (2330 17th St. NE, http://oregonstatefair.org, Aug.-Sept., $6-8 adults, $5-6 children 6-11, $1 seniors, free for children under 6) is held in north Salem, as it has been for well over a century. Expect games, carnival rides, live music, and livestock shows.

SHOPPING

Once a performing arts space—a theater that closed in 1900—now a shopping destination, **Reed Opera House** (189 Liberty St. NE, www.reedoperahouse.com) houses everything from a cannoli bakery to a soap shop. The indoor corridors of the old theater now link shops and eateries. Hours vary by venue.

Drive past the cows as they stare at you from their barn to arrive at the **Willamette Valley Cheese Company** (8105 Wallace Rd. NW, 503/399-9806, www.wvcheeseco.com, 10am-5pm Tues.-Sun.), nine miles north of town. This tiny cheesemaker has dozens of types of Havarti, cheddar, and other cheese, and the generous tastings at the little shop might encourage a purchase for your picnic basket.

FOOD

Lunch items can be found on the menu at ★ **Sassy Onion Grill** (1244 State St., 503/378-9180, http://sassyonion.com, 6am-3pm Mon.-Fri., 7am-3pm Sat.-Sun., $8-15), but that's not the point. This eatery is famous for its rich mascarpone and berry-filled French toast—and that's not even the most indulgent thing on the menu. Try French toast made from two bear claw pastries and sprinkled with bacon bits. Spacious booths line the restaurant, sitting under photographs of food that looks healthier than the delectable meals coming from the kitchen.

The two sisters who run **Wild Pear** (372 State St., 503/378-7515, www.wildpearcatering.com/downtown/downtown.html, 10:30am-6:30pm Mon.-Sat., $11-16) were called the "wild pair," giving the restaurant its name. They serve some Vietnamese-inspired salads and soups, and a standout banh mi. Also on the menu are pizzas and truffle fries. The space is small but has cheery red booths and brick walls.

Neither a greasy spoon nor a dive bar, **The Kitchen on Court Street** (466 Court St. NE, 971/701-6902, www.thekitchenoncourtstreet.com, 24 hours daily, $9-15) nevertheless stays open all night and into the morning. Students make up the bulk of the clientele in the darkest hours, but during the day the Creole-inspired menu—served around the clock—draws all ages with its prawns and grits and crawfish Benedict.

Longtime Salem staple **DaVinci Ristorante** (180 High St. SE, 503/399-1413, http://davincisofsalem.com, 5pm-9pm Mon.-Thurs., 5pm-10pm Fri.-Sat., $18-32) offers dining on two levels, with the open loft overlooking the 1st floor and art hung high on the exposed brick walls. A quarter-moon-shaped bar and diners enjoying hot flatbread, classic pastas, and substantial meat dishes lend the place a warm buzz.

Entering **Roger That BBQ** (1492 Brush College Rd. NW, 503/363-6716, www.rogerthatbbq.com, 4pm-9pm Thurs.-Fri., noon-6pm Sat.-Sun., $10-24), located a few miles north of town, you may feel like you're walking into an old suburban dentist's office rather than a restaurant. But the meats here are so popular they often sell out. Go for the hearty ribs and pulled pork, and eat at one of the picnic tables outside.

Located among miles of rich agricultural farmland, it's no wonder that Salem has **farmers markets** all week. The two biggest are the **Saturday market** (865 Marion St. NE, www.salemsaturdaymarket.com, 9am-3pm Sat. Apr.-Oct.), with 150 vendors and music, and the **Wednesday market** (530 Chemeketa St. NE, www.salemsaturdaymarket.com/wednesday-market.html, 10am-2pm Wed. May-Sept.), with about half as many food sellers, just a block away.

ACCOMMODATIONS

Salem doesn't offer much in the way of non-chain accommodations for a town of this size, but there are some options nearby. On the other hand: Looking for a chain hotel? You'll find plenty here, clustered around exit 256 on I-5, plus a few around exit 253 on I-5 near where it intersects with Highway 22.

Downtown's only major accommodations are at **Grand Hotel in Salem** (201 Liberty St. SE, 503/540-7800, http://grandhotelsalem.com, $189-249), attached to the city's convention center. The entrance is large and the effect is impressive, though inside the decor is a bit dated; the water feature with changing colored neon lights has a distinct 20th-century feel. The nearly 200 guestrooms span the entire block, up four stories above the lobby. Rooms have a small separate living or seating area, and while the color scheme makes it feel like the business hotel it is, the central location and quality make it a useful visitors' hub.

The **Hopewell Bed and Breakfast** (22350 Hopewell Rd. NW, Hopewell, 503/868-7848, www.hopewellbb.com, $179-199), located on a rural highway about 12.5 miles north of town, is a sunny yellow bed-and-breakfast with two rooms, both with outdoor patio areas overlooking a small pond. Rooms have kitchenettes and access to a barbecue grill.

The intimate **Edward Adams House Bed and Breakfast** (729 S Water St., Silverton, 503/873-8868, www.edwardadamshousebandb.com, $170-190) in nearby Silverton, about 15 miles east of Salem, has just three rooms in a Queen Anne Victorian house, complete with delicate decorations on its wraparound porch. Rooms are decorated with just a touch of Victorian style, like floral wallpaper or a fainting couch. The parlor has a piano and a pump organ, with settees in front of the wood-burning fireplace.

Camping

On the north end of Salem, about three miles east of town, **Phoenix RV Park** (4130 Silverton Rd. NE, 503/581-2497, http://phoenixrvpark.com, $48) has carefully tended green lawns and trees planted between its more than 100 sites.

Camp close to the waterfalls at **Silver Falls State Park** (20024 Silver Falls Hwy. SE, Sublimity, 503/873-8681, www.oregonstateparks.org) with about a hundred sites, half of them for tents ($19) and half for RVs ($29). Some are on the South Fork of Silver Creek, and there are 14 cabins ($43-53) on the other side of the creek.

INFORMATION AND SERVICES

For maps and brochures, visit the **Travel Salem Visitors Center** (181 High St. NE, 503/581-4325, www.travelsalem.com, 9am-5pm Mon.-Fri., 10am-4pm Sat.), which has a seating area and free Wi-Fi.

Or get your information from a local. Salem residents volunteer to give **Salem Greeters Tours** (www.travelsalem.com/node/11081, free), which last 1-2 hours. These tour guides give their own peek into the city for free, but tours must be reserved at least a week in advance.

GETTING THERE

To reach Salem from Portland, head south on I-5 for 47 miles, taking exit 256. To reach downtown, turn right onto Market Street NE for about 2 miles, then turn left onto Commercial Street. The drive takes about an hour.

Eugene

You've arrived at what might be the greenest part of Oregon. No, we're not talking about the landscape, though the tree-filled city does sit in a basin of evergreens, its deciduous trees turning a brilliant gold in fall. Eugene is green with environmentalists, eco-friendly businesses, and earth-minded people. Its vibe is akin to Portland's hippie, alternative spirit but subtracts the urban bustle. It's also green thanks to the University of Oregon's green and yellow logo, which blankets the region.

The Willamette River runs through walkable Eugene, with the downtown and university areas side by side south of it. Just west of downtown is Whiteaker, a more working-class neighborhood that's quickly becoming a center for young people.

SIGHTS

University of Oregon

The state's biggest center of higher learning, the **University of Oregon** (1585 E 13th Ave., 541/346-1000, www.uoregon.edu), is home to more than 20,000 students and a well-regarded football team that plays in the country's top division. Its logo, a big yellow O on a green background, is ubiquitous, as are images of its duck mascot. The sizable campus is as tree-laden as the rest of town, centered around a large quadrangle called **Memorial Quad** (University St. and E 15th Ave.). **Hayward Field** isn't far from this central lawn, and it's probably the best-known running circle in the country; the school's track and field program produced both Steve Prefontaine, a famous runner and Olympic athlete who died in the early 1970s, and Phil Knight who, along with the track coach, developed the modern running shoe, then founded Nike. On the first and third Friday of the month at 8:30am, a student leads a 3.7-mile running tour of trails around the campus, stopping to share the track and field history of U of O. General tours of the campus start at the **Ford Alumni Center** (1720 E 13th Ave.) 3-5 times a day Monday-Saturday, and the free 90-minute tour is preceded by an admissions presentation. Book online for either tour (http://visit.uoregon.edu).

University of Oregon

Eugene

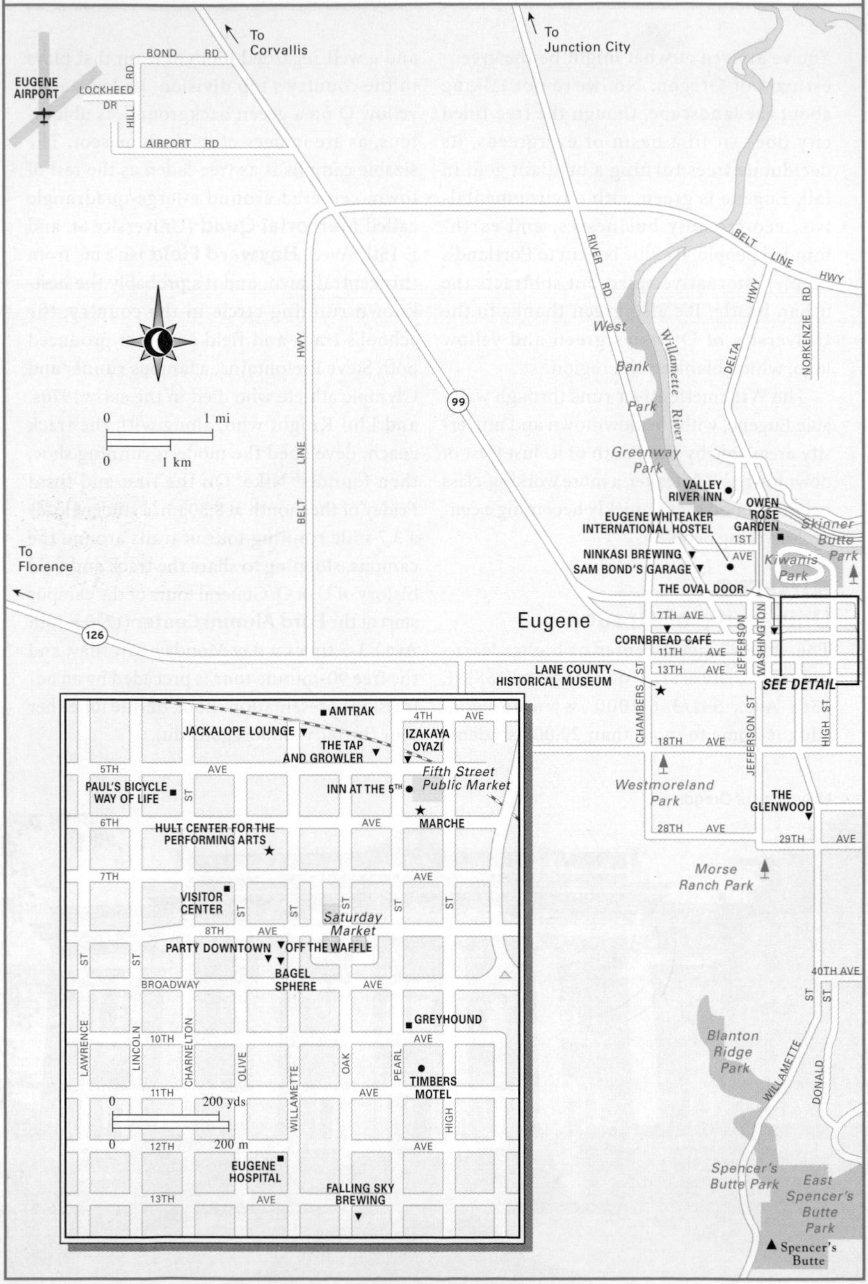
To Corvallis
To Junction City
BOND RD
EUGENE AIRPORT
LOCKHEED DR
HILL RD
AIRPORT RD
BELT LINE HWY
RIVER RD
DELTA HWY
NORKENZIE RD
West Bank Park
Willamette River
99
0 1 mi
0 1 km
BELT LINE HWY
Greenway Park
VALLEY RIVER INN
OWEN ROSE GARDEN
EUGENE WHITEAKER INTERNATIONAL HOSTEL
Skinner Butte Park
1ST AVE
NINKASI BREWING
SAM BOND'S GARAGE
Kiwanis Park
To Florence
THE OVAL DOOR
Eugene
7TH AVE
CORNBREAD CAFÉ
11TH AVE
13TH AVE
JEFFERSON
WASHINGTON
126
LANE COUNTY HISTORICAL MUSEUM
CHAMBERS ST
SEE DETAIL
18TH AVE
JEFFERSON ST
HIGH ST
Westmoreland Park
THE GLENWOOD
28TH AVE
29TH AVE
Morse Ranch Park
40TH AVE
ST
ST
Blanton Ridge Park
WILLAMETTE
DONALD
Spencer's Butte Park
East Spencer's Butte Park
Spencer's Butte
AMTRAK
4TH AVE
JACKALOPE LOUNGE
IZAKAYA OYAZI
THE TAP AND GROWLER
5TH AVE
Fifth Street Public Market
PAUL'S BICYCLE WAY OF LIFE
INN AT THE 5TH
6TH AVE
MARCHE
HULT CENTER FOR THE PERFORMING ARTS
7TH AVE
VISITOR CENTER
Saturday Market
8TH AVE
PARTY DOWNTOWN
OFF THE WAFFLE
BAGEL SPHERE
BROADWAY AVE
GREYHOUND
10TH AVE
LAWRENCE
LINCOLN
CHARNELTON
OLIVE
WILLAMETTE
OAK
PEARL
HIGH
TIMBERS MOTEL
11TH AVE
0 200 yds
0 200 m
12TH AVE
EUGENE HOSPITAL
FALLING SKY BREWING
13TH AVE

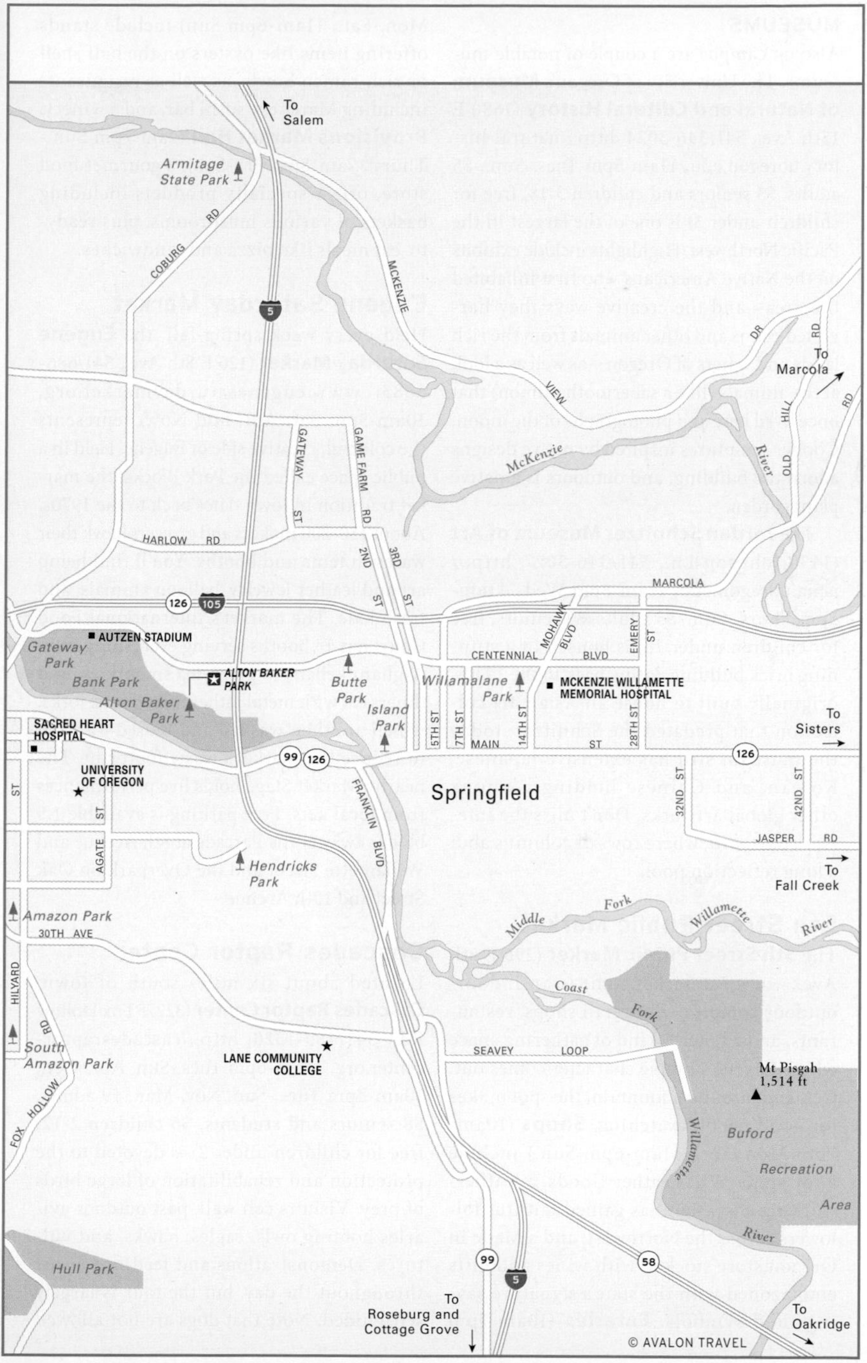
To
Salem
Armitage
State Park
COBURG RD
5
MCKENZIE
DR
HILL RD
To
Marcola
VIEW
OLD
RD
River
McKenzie
GATEWAY
GAME FARM
RD
ST
2ND
3RD
ST
ST
HARLOW RD
MARCOLA
MOHAWK
BLVD
EMERY
ST
126
105
AUTZEN STADIUM
Gateway
Park
CENTENNIAL BLVD
Bank Park
ALTON BAKER
PARK
Butte
Park
Willamalane
Park
MCKENZIE WILLAMETTE
MEMORIAL HOSPITAL
Alton Baker
Park
Island
Park
SACRED HEART
HOSPITAL
5TH ST
7TH ST
14TH ST
28TH ST
To
Sisters
MAIN ST
99
126
126
UNIVERSITY
OF OREGON
FRANKLIN BLVD
Springfield
ST
ST
AGATE
32ND ST
42ND ST
JASPER RD
Hendricks
Park
To
Fall Creek
Amazon Park
30TH AVE
Middle Fork Willamette River
Coast Fork
HILYARD
RD
South
Amazon Park
LANE COMMUNITY
COLLEGE
SEAVEY LOOP
Mt Pisgah
1,514 ft
FOX HOLLOW
Willamette
Buford
Recreation
Area
River
Hull Park
99
58
5
To
Roseburg and
Cottage Grove
To
Oakridge
© AVALON TRAVEL

MUSEUMS

Also on campus are a couple of notable museums. The University of Oregon's **Museum of Natural and Cultural History** (1680 E 15th Ave., 541/346-3024, http://natural-history.uoregon.edu, 11am-5pm Tues.-Sun., $5 adults, $3 seniors and children 3-18, free for children under 3) is one of the largest in the Pacific Northwest. Highlights include exhibits on the Native Americans who first inhabited the area—and the creative ways they harvested clams and other animals from the rich lands and waters of Oregon—as well as a look at the animals (like a sabertooth salmon) that once lived here and photographs of the moon. Copper sculptures inspired by native designs adorn the building, and outdoors is a native plant garden.

The **Jordan Schnitzer Museum of Art** (1430 Johnson Ln., 541/346-3027, http://jsma.uoregon.edu, 11am-8pm Wed., 11am-5pm Thurs.-Sun., $5 adults, $3 seniors, free for children under 18) is housed in a stunning brick building dating back to the 1930s, originally built to house an Asian art collection that predated the Schnitzer; today the museum still has extensive Japanese, Korean, and Chinese holdings, among other global artworks. Don't miss the interior courtyard, where rows of columns abut a long reflection pool.

5th Street Public Market

The **5th Street Public Market** (296 E 5th Ave., www.5stmarket.com) is an indoor/outdoor complex with retail shops, restaurants, and a hotel, a kind of gathering space where Eugene's hippie character comes out. Centered around a fountain, the spot makes for good people-watching. **Shops** (10am-7pm Mon.-Sat., 11am-6pm Sun.) include a toy store; Will Leather Goods, a leather-working shop that has gained faithful followers across the Northwest; and a Made in Oregon store stocked with wines and gifts emblazoned with the state's signature sayings and symbols. **Eateries** (10am-7pm Mon.-Sat., 11am-6pm Sun) include stands offering items like oysters on the half shell or rich ramen bowls, as well as restaurants including Marche, a sushi bar, and a winery. **Provisions Market Hall** (7am-7pm Sun.-Thurs., 7am-8pm Fri.-Sat.), a gourmet food store, offers specialty products including baskets of various mushrooms, plus ready-to-eat meals like pizza and sandwiches.

Eugene Saturday Market

Held every week spring-fall, the **Eugene Saturday Market** (126 E 8th Ave., 541/686-8885, www.eugenesaturdaymarket.org, 10am-5pm Sat. Apr.-mid-Nov.) represents the colorful, creative side of Eugene. Held in a public space called the Park Blocks, the market tradition in town dates back to the 1970s. About 150-200 makers and growers hawk their wares in tents and booths. You'll find hemp art and leather jewelry, balloon animals, and fresh kale. The market's International Food Court has 15 booths serving everything from Afghani kebabs to green tea smoothies, and diners eat with metal rather than plastic forks, which are then washed and reused—a push to reduce the market's waste footprint. The nearby Market Stage holds live performances from local acts. Free parking is available 1.5 blocks away at the Parcade at 8th Avenue and Willamette Street and the Overpark on Oak Street and 10th Avenue.

Cascades Raptor Center

Located about six miles south of town, **Cascades Raptor Center** (32275 Fox Hollow Rd., 541/485-1320, http://cascadesraptorcenter.org, 10am-6pm Tues.-Sun. Apr.-Oct., 10am-4pm Tues.-Sun. Nov.-Mar., $9 adults, $8 seniors and students, $6 children 2-12, free for children under 2) is devoted to the protection and rehabilitation of large birds of prey. Visitors can walk past outdoor aviaries holding owls, eagles, hawks, and vultures. Demonstrations and feedings occur throughout the day, but the tour is largely self-guided. Note that dogs are not allowed on-site, not even in parked cars (service animals excepted).

Wineries and Tasting Rooms

Though not at the center of wine country, Eugene boasts one of the state's most popular winemakers, **King Estate Winery** (80854 Territorial Hwy., 541/685-5189, www.kingestate.com, 11am-4pm Mon.-Tues., 11am-8pm Wed.-Thurs., 11am-9pm Fri., 10am-9pm Sat., 10am-4pm Sun., $15 tasting fee). Known for its pinot noir and especially its crisp pinot gris, the winery is located about a half-hour's drive southwest of downtown, deep in rural country. Housed in an Italian-style building, the winery holds a restaurant with an outdoor patio and a tasting room clad in rich red wood. Winery tours are held on the hour until 4pm.

Located about nine miles north of King Estate, **Silvan Ridge Winery** (27012 Briggs Hill Rd., 541/345-1945, http://silvanridge.com, noon-5pm daily, $2 per taste) has a more playful feel. It was the region's first winery (though it's been renamed since), opened in 1979, and is known for its summer music series and running events including a 5K and marathon. A large outdoor lawn is as inviting as the tasting room.

SPORTS AND RECREATION

★ Alton Baker Park

Located just north of the Willamette River across from downtown, **Alton Baker Park** (200 Day Island Rd., www.eugene-or.gov/altonbakerpark, 6am-11pm daily) is connected to the rest of Eugene by three pedestrian bridges. Its 373 acres encompass trails, a disc golf course, a dog park, and picnic spaces, plus the Cuthbert Amphitheater, used for outdoor performances. A Nobel Peace garden recognizes winners of the prize with plaques.

Also here is the 4.07-mile Pre's Trail, built in Olympian Steve Prefontaine's honor after his early death from a car accident—he liked to run in this park and pushed for a European-style dirt running trail to be built here. The trail has three loops and is best accessed from the parking area on Leo Harris Parkway, across from Autzen Stadium (other parking is available on Day Island Road near Club Road). Head west for a 1.36-mile loop past a tree garden and the amphitheater. Go east for a small 0.63-mile loop that leads to a pond and then a larger 1.59-mile loop with sections on the Willamette. The trail, largely made up of wood chips but also some dirt and gravel, is used by both walkers and runners. Today

Alton Baker Park

people call the trail (and Eugene) "Track Town USA," a salute to Pre's legacy and the fact that athletic giant Nike began here as a running-shoe company.

Biking

The city of Eugene, with few steep hills and a reputation for environmentalism, is a big biking city, with more than a hundred miles of roads with bike paths here. There's also the **Ruth Bascom Riverbank Path** (www.eugene-or.gov), about 14 miles of path on both sides of the Willamette River that passes ponds and bridges, gardens, and boat launches. Pedestrian/bike bridges make it easy to form a loop, and visible mile markers show progress, with "0" at **Maurie Jacobs Park** (Fir Ln. near River Rd., 541/682-4800, www.eugene-or.gov, 7am-11pm daily), a good place to park and start a loop. Head north on West Bank Path for 2.1 miles and then cross the waterway on the Owosso Pedestrian Bridge. Head south on the other side of the Willamette for about 1.9 miles on the East Bank Path, past the bird-filled Delta Ponds, to the Greenway Pedestrian Bridge that crosses back to Maurie Jacobs Park. It's a quieter, less populated option. Or, from the same starting point at Maurie Jacobs Park, head south on the South Bank Path, passing a slew of sights, from a rose garden to playgrounds to historical homes. At 2.75 miles, at the Autzen Pedestrian Bridge, cross the river to reach Alton Baker Park. Close your loop by heading north on the North Bank Path and following it back 2.5 miles to the Greenway Pedestrian Bridge that crosses back to Maurie Jacobs Park. Don't forget you're sharing these paths with pedestrians and strollers; it's all about the slow cruise, not re-creating the Tour de France.

To rent a bike in Eugene, head to **Paul's Bicycle Way of Life** (556 Charnelton St., 541/344-4105, http://bicycleway.com, 10am-6pm Mon.-Fri., 10am-5pm Sat.-Sun.), only about a three-minute ride from access to the Ruth Bascom Riverbank Path, near Alton Baker Park. The shop rents cruisers ($24 per day) and road bikes ($48 per day), plus trailers ($24 per day) and car racks ($5-21 per day). Subsequent day rentals are much cheaper. All bikes come with helmets and locks. It takes reservations and recommends them for summer weekend days.

Hiking

SPENCER BUTTE

Distance: 1.7-2.2 miles round-trip
Duration: 1-1.5 hours
Elevation gain: 700 feet
Effort: moderate
Trailhead: 85385 S Willamette Street, about six miles south of Eugene

The 2,000-foot Spencer Butte rises just south of the city, a rounded hill with several trails. Start at the South Willamette Trailhead and be faced with an immediate decision: take the long way up or down? Unless you're looking for a harder workout, go right for the Main Trail, ignoring signs for the West Trail—you'll hike down that way. Follow the Main Trail as it slowly ascends the butte, moving east through the tree cover. At 0.6 mile you'll reach a trail junction; turn left and the trail will start to get steeper. Reach the summit 0.5 mile later and take a break to enjoy the views; you can see the Three Sisters volcanoes near Bend on a clear day, plus the verdant Willamette Valley. Make a loop by taking the West Trail down, the steeper route that heads 0.6 mile directly back to the parking lot. To spare creaky knees, return the way you came instead, taking a right at the junction halfway down.

Spectator Sports

FOOTBALL

Though its history may be steeped in track and field, the University of Oregon is famous for its football. Games are held on Saturdays in the late summer-fall at **Autzen Stadium** (2700 MLK Jr. Blvd., http://goducks.com), on the north side of the Willamette River, which holds more than 50,000 fans. Attending one of the seven or so annual games is no easy task; season ticket holders get most of the seats, and even U of O students don't all get to go;

only about 20 percent of enrolled students can buy tickets at a discounted price. Single-game tickets ($50 and up) go on sale to the general public in early July for the entire season and sell out quickly.

ENTERTAINMENT AND EVENTS

Nightlife

For a wide tasting selection, look to **The Tap and Growler** (207 E 5th Ave., 541/505-9751, www.tapandgrowler.com, 11:30am-10pm Sun.-Thurs., 11:30am-11pm Fri.-Sat.), where 81 taps offer local beers, not-so-local beers, ciders, mead, soda, and kombucha. Some wines are also on tap, pouring an extensive selection of local pinots. Food options include a wide array of sandwiches and salads. Located near the 5th Street Public Market, it's well positioned.

The corner **Jackalope Lounge** (453 Willamette St., 541/485-1519, http://jackalopelounge.com, 11am-2am daily) is a relaxed dive with a row of taps (featuring Ninkasi, of course), pinball, pool tables, and cheesy nachos. The sports bar is usually playing whatever big game is on, and is always full on Oregon Ducks football days—it opens an hour early on Saturdays and Sundays during the football season.

Eugene's sake bar **Izakaya Oyazi** (259 E 5th Ave., 458/201-7433, http://izakayaoyazi.com, 5pm-midnight daily) has creative sushi rolls to go with its curated selection of Japanese liquors and cocktails crafted with house-made ingredients. Downstairs is a cozy space with occasional live music. Look closely at some of the wall decorations and you'll find *Star Wars* images reworked in Japanese style.

At **Falling Sky Brewing House and Pub** (1334 Oak Alley, 541/505-7096, http://fallingskybrewing.com, 11am-11pm Mon.-Thurs., 11am-midnight Fri., 10am-midnight Sat., 10am-11pm Sun.), on the south end of downtown, expect a long list of creative brews, from a Scotch ale to sours, even a lager made with Japanese rice. Generous daily specials give discounts for things like riding a bike to the brewpub or being a grad student. Long tables indoors and out get crowded with beer fans. You'll also find a menu of pub favorites like tacos and burgers here.

Ninkasi Brewing (272 Van Buren St., 541/344-2739, www.ninkasibrewing.com, noon-9pm Sun.-Wed., noon-10pm Thurs.-Sat.) is one of the state's signature brewers, and the Total Domination IPA is seen on taps around the Pacific Northwest. Located in the scruffy Whiteaker neighborhood west of downtown, the tasting room is an industrial-style space and decorated with works from local artists; food trucks park outside. Nearby, it's always a party at **Sam Bond's Garage** (407 Blair Blvd., 541/431-6603, www.sambonds.com, 4pm-1am daily). The crowded joint hosts live music every night, with a weekly Tuesday bluegrass jam and Irish music open mic on Sundays. Other days, local folk, rock, blues, and comedy acts take the stage. It also has its own brews, sandwiches and dips, and a full bar.

The Arts

Silva Concert Hall is located within the larger **Hult Center for the Performing Arts** (1 Eugene Center, 541/682-5000, www.hultcenter.org), a glassy, dramatic building downtown. It hosts touring musical theater, large dance performances, and Eugene's resident opera, ballet, and symphony companies.

Located in Alton Baker Park, the **Cuthbert Amphitheater** (2300 Leo Harris Pkwy., 541/762-8099, www.thecuthbert.com) is a beautiful outdoor lawn with a bandshell and some chair seating. Large pop, rock, and hip-hop shows are held in the space, mostly in warmer months, and with lawn seating the venue can hold 5,000 people.

Festivals and Events

Few people realize that Oregon is a hot spot for truffle mushrooms, but the annual **Oregon Truffle Festival** (http://oregontrufflefestival.org, Jan.-Feb.) is a celebration of the hard-to-find treasures. Although some varieties are cultivated and grown here, aficionados gather to celebrate the hunt for wild truffles: The annual Joriad is a truffle-hunting dog competition, and a two-day clinic teaches newcomers how to get their own pups to seek them out. Other festival events include chef demos and truffle meals. The two-weekend event starts in Eugene but finishes up north in wine country.

Held in performing halls around town, including the stunning Silva Concert Hall at the town's central Hult Center for the Performing Arts, the **Oregon Bach Festival** (http://oregonbachfestival.org, June-July) is a series of concerts, lectures, and even winery excursions, many of which reflect on the famous classical composer. Past guest artists have included Philip Glass, Yo-Yo Ma, and Joshua Bell.

The **Oregon Country Fair** (4207 Hwy. 126, Veneta, 541/343-4298, www.oregoncountryfair.org, July, $29-36 adults, $24-31 seniors, free for children under 11) is held the second weekend of July in the small town of Veneta, about 12 miles west of Eugene. The three-day festival focuses on community and artfulness and evokes the feel of a 1960s commune. There are more than 700 craft makers selling their wares; more than 75 food booths, arranged in long, meandering "roads" that wind next to the Long Tom River; and 12 stages for live music and performance at the wooded site. Costumes, creativity, and a hippie spirit are encouraged. The festival is more about wandering around wearing butterfly wings and catching bits of music than shopping.

FOOD

Taking its inspiration from Southern cuisine, ★ **Party Downtown** (64 W 8th Alley, 541/345-8228, http://partyeugene.com, 5pm-9pm Sun. and Tues.-Thurs., 5pm-10pm Fri.-Sat., $11-22) offers inventive spins like fried green tomatoes in the style of the Indian snack *pakora*, deep-fried with a mix of veggies. Also on its menu are items like zucchini noodles, burgers, and salads. A chef's special menu is available for just $35 per person and includes a series of small dishes and tastings from across and off the menu. The small space isn't very party-themed but more of a small, relaxed café.

Off the Waffle (840 Willamette St., 541/632-4225, http://offthewaffle.com, 8am-2pm daily, $4-10) has an outpost in Portland, but the original is here in the center of downtown Eugene. The eatery's Belgian liege waffles are known for their slightly crisp, sweet texture. Waffles come plain or topped with an array of sweet and savory items, from basil chiffonade to brie with a balsamic glaze. Order at the counter before finding a seat.

Bagel Sphere (810 Willamette St., 541/341-1335, http://bagelsphere.com, 7am-5pm Mon.-Fri., 8am-5pm Sat., 8am-4pm Sun., $4-8) makes bagels the right way: boiled and then baked in a stone hearth for a crisp exterior and chewy interior. And you can top them with flavored cream cheeses made in house, eggs, or lunch meats.

Marche (296 E 5th Ave., 541/743-0660, http://marcherestaurant.com, 8am-11pm Sun.-Thurs., 8am-midnight Fri.-Sat., $22-30) serves food so local, it can point to where much of it came from. Styled as a French bistro with white tablecloths and, of course, mirrors on the walls, the restaurant serves steak frites and cassoulet under red-painted ceilings. The restaurant is located in the 5th Street Public Market space.

With two locations in town, **The Glenwood** (1340 Alder St., 541/687-0355, www.glenwoodrestaurants.com, 7am-9pm daily, $8-14) at its university-adjacent location offers the kinds of breakfast you wait in line for: waffles, French toast made with brioche, and eggs scrambled with every ingredient you can imagine. It's comfort food in a comfortable house-like setting, a combo that more than just college students can love.

West of downtown, the **Cornbread Cafe** (1290 W 7th Ave., 541/505-9175, www.cornbreadcafe.com, 9am-9pm Mon.-Sat., 9am-3pm Sun., $8-12) features an entirely vegan menu, but there's so much flavor even meat-eaters will be satisfied. Names of dishes are a little cheesy (neatloaf, mac uncheese), but the sandwich made with a fried tofu patty is a sublime blend of textures. Rainbow-bright shades on the walls, booths, and a checkered floor make the space look like a Southern diner in Technicolor.

ACCOMMODATIONS

Under $150

The brightly painted **Eugene Whiteaker International Hostel** (970 W 3rd Ave., 541/343-3335, www.eugenehostel.org, 7am-10pm, $35-45 dorms, $50 private rooms) is a classic hostel, from the prayer flags to the potluck dinners. It's located in the Whiteaker neighborhood, west of downtown. Dorm rooms manage to avoid feeling sterile, thanks to murals and funky art on the walls. Private rooms also used shared bathrooms.

$150-250

The very retro **Timbers Motel** (1015 Pearl St., 541/343-3345, www.timbersmotel.net, $99-229) used to feel very 1978, but recent renovations ran with the theme and added modern decor with a mid-century bent to the 40-plus rooms. Rooms are still small, but the funky space makes up for it with character. The lobby has a few taps of local beers, of course. It's located between the 5th Street Public Market area and the university, near the Saturday Market.

The massive **Valley River Inn** (1000 Valley River Way, 541/743-1000, www.valleyriverinn.com, $159-219) has more than 250 rooms in its large complex, many of them overlooking the Willamette River. Located across from downtown, it isn't walkable to much except the bike path along the river, but rooms are large and all have a private patio or balcony. There's an indoor pool and outdoor hot tub, plus an on-site restaurant with a riverfront deck.

Enter **The Oval Door** (988 Lawrence St., 541/683-3160, http://ovaldoor.com, $135-185) through a regular-shaped entrance (the door's window is oval) to find a six-room bed-and-breakfast, located on the west end of downtown. Some rooms have four-poster beds, and all have themes that tie into the artwork displayed. The hosts serve complimentary wine and cookies in the library, and breakfasts are rich and include several options.

Over $250

★ **Inn at the 5th** (205 E 6th Ave., 541/743-4099, www.innat5th.com, $261-274 rooms, $360-702 suites) has ultramodern rooms and large suites. It has the feel of a boutique hotel though it has almost 70 rooms. Located in the large 5th Street Public Market complex, it's easily walkable to many shops and restaurants and is a comfortable place to stay.

Camping

About five miles north of town, **Armitage Park Campground** (90064 Coburg Rd., 541/682-2000, http://reservations.lanecounty.org, $30-43) offers tent and RV camping in a 57-acre county park. There are 32 RV sites and four tent sites, and the campground is close to a dog park and the McKenzie River.

INFORMATION AND SERVICES

The **Eugene, Cascades & Coast Visitor Information and Adventure Center** (3312 Gateway St., Springfield, 541/484-5307, 9am-6pm daily) is the region's main info stop. Maps and guides are here, and the staff can help with forest and recreation passes and use their 3D map to assist you in planning adventures. Grab coffee and shop for Oregon souvenirs. There's also the **Downtown Eugene Visitor Center** (754 Olive St., 541/484-5307, www.eugenecascadescoast.org/eugene, 9am-5pm Mon., 8am-5pm Tues.-Fri.), which has more limited resources. Also look for a mobile visitors services desk, a blue cargo bike ridden by a visitors information staff member who has maps, guides, and advice.

GETTING THERE

To drive to Eugene from Portland, head south on I-5 for 105 miles to exit 194B, where you'll hop on I-105. Take the first exit, Coburg Road, and follow it south one mile into downtown; the trip takes a little under two hours.

Amtrak (www.amtrak.com) runs three

trains a day (about a 2.5-hour trip) from Portland's Union Station to the **Eugene Amtrak Station** (433 Willamette St., 800/872-7245), a restored 1908 depot. Tickets run about $28-36. It's just about as fast to take the **BoltBus** (877/265-8287, www.boltbus.com), a line that runs between Seattle and Eugene. From Portland, trips are about 2.5 hours and costs run $8-13, with a few very cheap fares ($1) available if you book far in advance. Buses have Wi-Fi and reserved seating, and there are usually 2-4 departures per day, leaving from Portland at NW Everett St. between NW Broadway and NW 8th Ave. in the Pearl District and arriving at Eugene at the 5th Street Public Market.

Flights into the region go to **Eugene Airport** (EUG, 28801 Douglas Dr., 541/682-5544, www.flyeug.com), including direct flights from Seattle (70 minutes, 6-8 flights per day) and Portland (35 minutes, 3 flights per day).

Bend and Central Oregon

Look for ★ to find recommended sights, activities, dining, and lodging.

Highlights

★ **High Desert Museum:** Explore the region's landscape via exhibits devoted to history and nature, complete with live raptors and a working sawmill (page 352).

★ **Lava River Cave:** Nothing's cooler on a hot day than a trip through this natural tunnel carved by a long-ago lava flow (page 354).

★ **Mount Bachelor:** Ski around the top of a volcano at this resort known for sunny days and fluffy snow (page 355).

★ **Deschutes River:** These mountain-fed waters host tubers, stand-up paddlers, kayakers, and more (page 356).

★ **Bend Ale Trail:** Experience Bend's booming craft beer scene by hopping among some of its 16 breweries (page 359).

★ **Dee Wright Observatory:** A mountaintop observatory made of lava rocks rises from the highway as it crosses the crest of the Cascades (page 367).

★ **Smith Rock State Park:** This rock-climbing mecca contains some of central Oregon's most stunning landscapes (page 367).

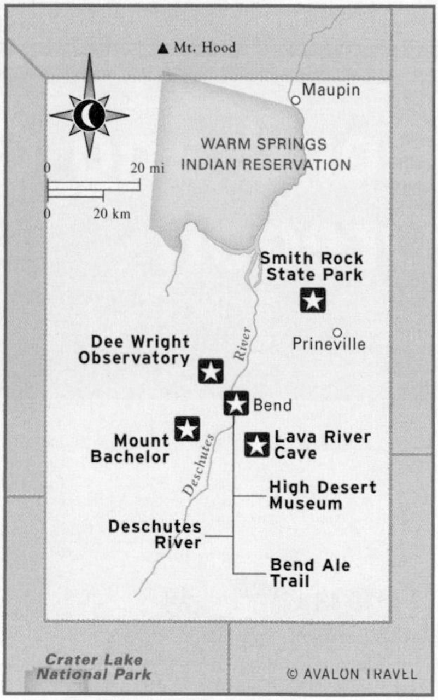

Located in a high desert on the east side of the Cascades, Bend is named for a turn in the Deschutes River, a cool run of mountain water that snakes through the town and region, which boasts more than 300 days of sunshine a year.

The town has grown by leaps and bounds since the timber industry here folded in the 1980s. Bend is all about recreation these days, serving as central Oregon's hub for all things outdoorsy. Active engagement in this juniper- and ponderosa pine-dotted landscape, riddled with lava-formed landscapes and mountain peaks, is simple no matter the season. Summer finds the Deschutes River crowded with floaters and paddleboarders and is the season of exploration for those interested in the area's volcanic attractions, while winter sees skiers and fat bikers abound at Mount Bachelor. Bend also has a strong second- and vacation-home community, though the streets still bustle with locals.

Just north, the small towns of Sisters and Redmond offer easy access to rock-climbing mecca Smith Rock State Park.

Between all this, not to mention the region's abundant golf courses and craft beer, there's always a way to vacation in central Oregon.

PLANNING YOUR TIME

No visit to central Oregon is complete without outdoor recreation, but that means you should be prepared to travel from mountain to river, from rock formation to outdoor rock concert. While most attractions are fairly close together, within about a half-hour drive from Bend, they spread in every direction from town. A minimum of 2-3 days is recommended here, but there will still be much left to explore.

There isn't really a low season in Bend, as it makes a great year-round outdoor destination, but spring and fall, outside of holidays, will likely see the most hotel availability and fewest crowds. Snow closes some roads in the area in winter, so access to many of the Newberry Volcanic National Monument

Previous: Mount Bachelor; Smith Rock State Park. **Above:** Dee Wright Observatory.

Bend and Central Oregon

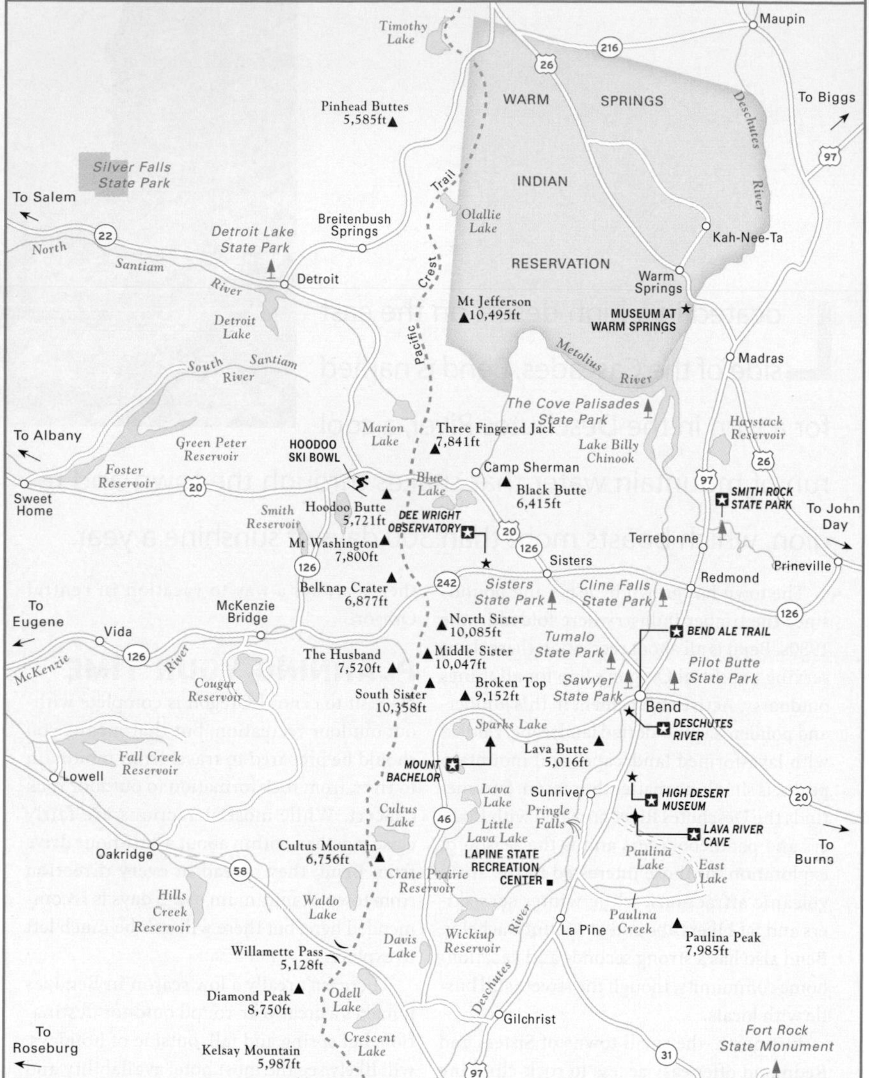
Timothy Lake
Maupin
216
26
WARM
SPRINGS
Deschutes River
To Biggs
97
Pinhead Buttes 5,585ft
Silver Falls State Park
To Salem
Trail
INDIAN
Olallie Lake
Breitenbush Springs
Kah-Nee-Ta
Detroit Lake State Park
North
22
Santiam
River
Detroit
Crest
RESERVATION
Warm Springs
Mt Jefferson 10,495ft
MUSEUM AT WARM SPRINGS
Detroit Lake
Pacific
Madras
South Santiam River
Metolius River
The Cove Palisades State Park
Haystack Reservoir
Marion Lake
Three Fingered Jack 7,841ft
Lake Billy Chinook
To Albany
Green Peter Reservoir
HOODOO SKI BOWL
Camp Sherman
26
Foster Reservoir
20
Blue Lake
Black Butte 6,415ft
97
SMITH ROCK STATE PARK
Sweet Home
Hoodoo Butte 5,721ft
Smith Reservoir
DEE WRIGHT OBSERVATORY
20
To John Day
Mt Washington 7,800ft
126
Terrebonne
126
Sisters
Prineville
Belknap Crater 6,877ft
242
Sisters State Park
Cline Falls State Park
Redmond
To Eugene
McKenzie Bridge
126
North Sister 10,085ft
BEND ALE TRAIL
Vida
Tumalo State Park
126
McKenzie River
The Husband 7,520ft
Middle Sister 10,047ft
Pilot Butte State Park
Cougar Reservoir
South Sister 10,358ft
Broken Top 9,152ft
Sawyer State Park
Bend
Sparks Lake
DESCHUTES RIVER
Fall Creek Reservoir
Lava Butte 5,016ft
Lowell
MOUNT BACHELOR
Lava Lake
Sunriver
HIGH DESERT MUSEUM
20
Cultus Lake
46
Little Lava Lake
Pringle Falls
LAVA RIVER CAVE
Oakridge
Cultus Mountain 6,756ft
LAPINE STATE RECREATION CENTER
Paulina Lake
East Lake
To Burns
58
Crane Prairie Reservoir
Hills Creek Reservoir
Waldo Lake
Paulina Creek
Davis Lake
Wickiup Reservoir
River
La Pine
Paulina Peak 7,985ft
Willamette Pass 5,128ft
Deschutes
Diamond Peak 8,750ft
Odell Lake
Gilchrist
To Roseburg
Crescent Lake
Fort Rock State Monument
Kelsay Mountain 5,987ft
31
97
Steamboat
Toketee Lake
138
Lemolo Lake
Fort Rock
North Umpqua River
Howlock 8,351ft
Lookout Mountain 5,015ft
Diamond Lake
Clearwater River
Mt Thielsen 9,182ft
Mt Bailey 8,363ft
To Lakeview
0
10 mi
138
0
10 km
Red Cone 7,372ft
Crater Lake National Park
230
© AVALON TRAVEL
Silver Lake

Two Days in Central Oregon

DAY 1

Start the day with a bagel at **Rockin' Dave's Bagel Bistro** in downtown Bend.

If it's summer, begin your day one adventure at the **Lava Lands Visitor Center,** about a 20-minute drive south of town on U.S. 97. Learn about the area's giant volcanic systems (one is the size of Rhode Island) and take in views of the surrounding volcanic rock plains. Then head south 1.4 miles on the highway to **Lava River Cave** for a cool 2.2-mile walk through the lava tube.

In the winter, or if you'd prefer to do more learning about the region's natural and human history instead of spelunking, head instead to the **High Desert Museum,** about a 15-minute drive south of Bend on U.S. 97.

Swing back north through Bend for a quick lunch at **Spork,** which serves tasty international street food. Then head west toward Mount Bachelor, about a 30-minnute drive away and a year-round destination. Whether you're hiking in the summer—try a loop around **Todd Lake**—or snowshoeing in the winter, the often clear, sunny weather allows for beautiful views.

Finish the day with a ramble through downtown Bend. Grab dinner at the **Drake,** then top off the night at **Dogwood Cocktail Cabin,** which looks like Bend distilled to its essence: woodsy whimsy. Retire for the night at a charming accommodation like the **Riverhouse Hotel** or **McMenamins Old St. Francis School**—the latter at which you can end the night with a soak in an indoor pool.

DAY 2

On day two for summer vacationers, it's time to hit the water out in the wild. Rent an inner tube or stand-up paddleboard in **Riverbend Park,** less than a 10-minute drive from downtown, where you can play on the **Deschutes River;** remember to pay for your shuttle bus ride before you start floating.

If you're here in the winter, day two should be spent skiing on **Mount Bachelor.**

In either season, you can fill out your day on the infamous **Bend Ale Trail,** on which you can brewery hop and get a stamp in your "passport" for each stop—if you hit 10, the **Bend Visitor Center** will give you a special souvenir gift. Don't forget you can also have bites to eat on your brewpub crawl; most stops serve food. If you can, try to make it to **Crux Fermentation Project** by sunset; fire pits blaze across the brewery's lawn as the sun goes down and the stars emerge in the clear, crisp central Oregon night.

sights, as well as Dee Wright Observatory, are limited to summer

Ski rentals should be arranged at least the night before, and golf tee times should be booked a few weeks in advance, at least. Reservations are recommended at downtown Bend restaurants, but are not taken at most brewpubs, which also serve food.

The towns of Sisters and Redmond are a short drive from Bend, but note that at rush hour the small highways can get crowded with locals commuting. Smith Rock State Park gets crowded on summer weekends, with overflow parking lining the roads near the park entrance.

Bend

For all its small-town charm, Bend is a sizable city with a population of over 100,000—but it has taken real care to keep a distinct, casual vibe at its core. Its young and active population are often dressed in outdoor gear (even to work!), the Deschutes River snakes scenically through town, and the walkable downtown is packed with independent bars, breweries, shops, and restaurants; the latter includes a nice mix of fine dining (but nothing too fancy!) and low-key options. And just south of downtown is the Old Mill District, a shopping and dining complex that reinvents the area's old mills.

SIGHTS AND RECREATION

Pilot Butte State Scenic Viewpoint

Rising right next to downtown Bend, **Pilot Butte State Scenic Viewpoint** (NE Greenwood Ave. near NE 12th St., 541/388-6055, www.oregonstateparks.org, 10am-10pm daily May-Nov., 10am-8pm daily Dec.-Apr.,) is one of many cinder cones that dot the region, and one of the most accessible. A road winds around the butte—which is just tall enough that it was once used as a marker for wagon trains—and takes you to the top (note the road closes Dec.-Apr. though the park remains open). Or if you'd prefer the more active option, a trail corkscrews to the summit after passing through sagebrush. It's a mile to the top with about 450 feet of gain, about an hour's hike. On a clear day you can spot Mount Bachelor in the distance and other cinder cones, like Black Butte and Lava Butte, plus miles of the scrubby high desert outside Bend's ever-growing city limits.

★ High Desert Museum

The central Oregon landscape isn't the kind of desert most people imagine—cacti and sand—but a complex terrain of buttes and bushy expanses. The **High Desert Museum** (59800 U.S. 97, 541/382-4754, www.highdesertmuseum.org, 9am-5pm daily Apr.-Oct., 10am-4pm daily Nov.-Mar., $12-15 adults, $10-12 seniors and students, $7-9 children 5-12, free for children under 5) fittingly sits

High Desert Museum

Bend

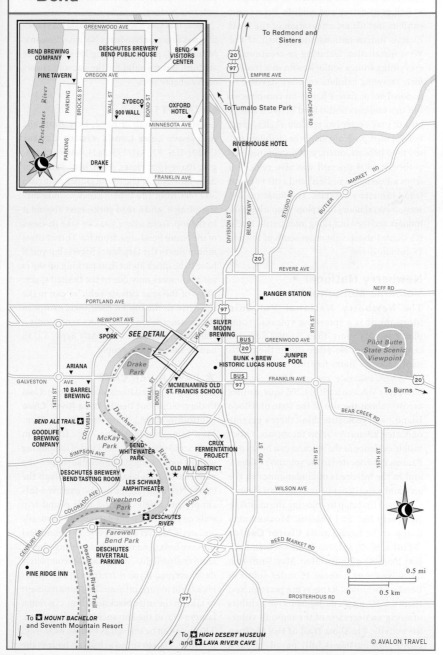

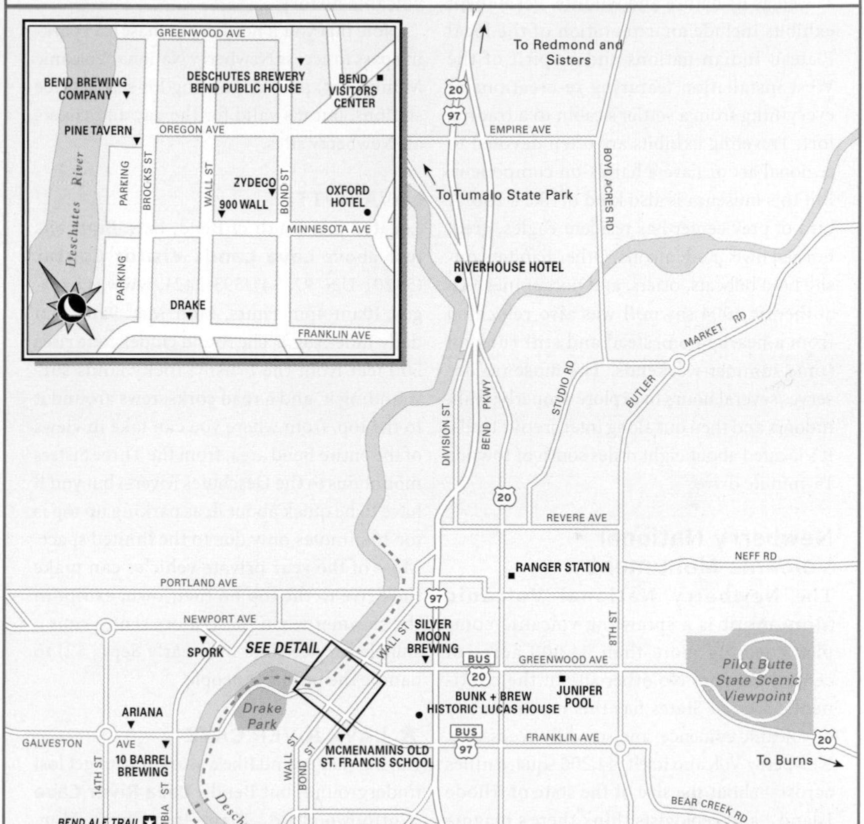
GREENWOOD AVE
BEND BREWING COMPANY
DESCHUTES BREWERY BEND PUBLIC HOUSE
BEND VISITORS CENTER
PINE TAVERN
OREGON AVE
Deschutes River
PARKING
BROCKS ST
WALL ST
BOND ST
ZYDECO
900 WALL
OXFORD HOTEL
MINNESOTA AVE
DRAKE
FRANKLIN AVE
To Redmond and Sisters
20
97
EMPIRE AVE
BOYD ACRES RD
To Tumalo State Park
RIVERHOUSE HOTEL
MARKET RD
BUTLER
STUDIO RD
DIVISION ST
BEND PKWY
REVERE AVE
NEFF RD
RANGER STATION
PORTLAND AVE
NEWPORT AVE
SPORK
SEE DETAIL
SILVER MOON BREWING
WALL ST
BUS
GREENWOOD AVE
BUNK + BREW HISTORIC LUCAS HOUSE
JUNIPER POOL
8TH ST
Pilot Butte State Scenic Viewpoint
ARIANA
Drake Park
GALVESTON
AVE
10 BARREL BREWING
14TH ST
BOND ST
MCMENAMINS OLD ST. FRANCIS SCHOOL
FRANKLIN AVE
To Burns
BEAR CREEK RD
BEND ALE TRAIL
COLUMBIA ST
Deschutes
GOODLIFE BREWING COMPANY
McKay Park
BEND WHITEWATER PARK
CRUX FERMENTATION PROJECT
SIMPSON AVE
River
3RD ST
9TH ST
15TH ST
DESCHUTES BREWERY BEND TASTING ROOM
OLD MILL DISTRICT
LES SCHWAB AMPHITHEATER
COLORADO AVE
Riverbend Park
WILSON AVE
DESCHUTES RIVER
Farewell Bend Park
CENTURY DR
REED MARKET RD
DESCHUTES RIVER TRAIL PARKING
Deschutes River Trail
PINE RIDGE INN
0
0.5 mi
0.5 km
BROSTERHOUS RD
To MOUNT BACHELOR and Seventh Mountain Resort
To HIGH DESERT MUSEUM and LAVA RIVER CAVE
© AVALON TRAVEL

on 135 acres of high desert, and its galleries showcase historical artifacts of the region as well as its nature and wildlife. Permanent exhibits include an exploration of the local Plateau Indian nations and a Spirit of the West installation featuring re-creations of everything from a settler's cabin to a trading fort. Traveling exhibits are often devoted to regional art or have a hands-on component. But this museum is also kind of like a zoo. A bird of prey center has resident eagles, great horned owls, and falcons. Other habitats on-site hold bobcats, otters, and porcupines. An authentic 1904 sawmill was also relocated from a nearby homestead and still runs on some summer weekends. The museum deserves several hours to explore properly; walk indoors and then out along interpretive trails. It's located about eight miles south of town, a 15-minute drive.

Newberry National Volcanic Monument

The **Newberry National Volcanic Monument** is a sprawling volcanic complex covering more than 54,000 acres of central Oregon. No other site in the continental United States has this much variety of volcanic evidence, and so easily accessible. Newberry Volcano itself is 1,200 square miles across—about the size of the state of Rhode Island—and geologists think there's magma only a few kilometers below the surface. Other visible evidence of the volcano can be seen at Paulina Lake, located in the volcano's caldera, and in the hundreds of cinder cones in the area and miles of basalt and obsidian flows.

A good first step to enjoying the multisite Newberry National Volcanic Monument is a stop at the **Lava Lands Visitor Center** (58201 U.S. 97, 541/593-2421, www.fs.usda.gov, 10am-4pm Thurs.-Mon. May, 9am-4pm daily June-Aug.), about 15 miles south of Bend's downtown. Rangers are present, and there's a 3D map and interpretive exhibits offering an overview of the region's volcanic activity. The short **Trail of the Molten Land** path outside is fully paved, about a mile's journey through the basalt flows and past interpretive signs covering the area's volcanic history.

Note that you'll need to purchase a $5 parking pass to access Newberry National Volcanic Monument, paid at parking lot self-service stations, but it's valid for the day and covers all Newberry sites.

LAVA BUTTE

Located just south of Bend, Lava Butte sits just above **Lava Lands Visitor Center** (58201 U.S. 97, 541/593-2421, www.fs.usda.gov, 10am-4pm Thurs.-Mon. May, 9am-4pm daily June-Aug.). The round cinder cone rises 500 feet from the brushy, rocky lands surrounding it, and a road corkscrews around it to the top, from where you can take in views of the entire Bend area, from the Three Sisters mountains to the Deschutes River—but you'll have to be quick about it, as parking up top is for 10 minutes only due to the limited space. Most of the year private vehicles can make the drive to the top on their own, except in the summer when the visitors center runs a shuttle service (late May-early Sept., $2) to handle the influx of people.

★ LAVA RIVER CAVE

Caving may sound like a scary way to get lost underground, but Bend's **Lava River Cave** (Cottonwood Rd., 10am-4pm Thurs.-Mon. May, 9am-4pm daily June-Aug., 10am-4pm daily Sept.) offers a simpler kind of spelunking with its long, straight, tunnel-like shape—the path that molten lava once took through the earth. Not many caves can be explored this simply and safely. The 2.2-mile round-trip walkway is periodically marked by handrails and steps. Marvel at how perfectly cylindrical the cave feels. And remember to bring a headlamp or flashlight—it is, of course, completely dark here, and if you're far from other visitors it's a thrill to turn off your light for a moment to take in the utter blackness. You can rent a lantern ($5) at the entrance if you forget one. The floor can be uneven as well, so wear solid footwear. Plan to spend at least an hour in the

Land of Volcanoes: DIY Discovery Tour

While there are volcanoes throughout the Cascades from California to the Canadian border, central Oregon has one of the highest concentrations of volcanic activity in the country. Between major volcanoes like the Three Sisters (all part of one complex volcano) and the Newberry Volcano, there are lava caves, craters, and cinder cones scattered throughout this high desert. Although there are no active lava flows such as what you'd find in Hawaii, there's plenty to explore. Don't be surprised to see pumice, volcanic rock with holes like a sponge, all around the area. Given seasonal closures, it's best to take this tour in the summer.

Start a DIY volcano tour at **Pilot Butte State Scenic Viewpoint** in downtown Bend, a cinder cone dotted with juniper. Hike the one mile to the summit, or drive the road to the top.

Next head to **Newberry National Volcanic Monument,** which encompasses more than 54,000 acres. Get your bearings at the **Lava Lands Visitor Center,** about 15 miles south of Pilot Butte on U.S. 97, a 20-minute drive; it's a good place to learn about the surrounding lava fields. From here you're right next to **Lava Butte.** Drive up (or take the shuttle in summer) to its concave little crater at the top.

Continue your exploration of the national volcanic monument by going for a 2.2-mile round-trip walk in the **Lava River Cave,** about 1.5 miles south of the visitors center on Cottonwood Road. Or head farther afield to **Paulina Lake,** at the center of the massive shield volcano's caldera. You can explore the basalt and obsidian around Paulina Lake on the **Big Obsidian Flow** trail, a short 0.6-mile loop that begins near the visitors center. To get here from the Lava Lands Visitor Center, head south on U.S. 97 for about 11 miles, then turn left onto Road 21 and stay on it for about 15 miles. It's a 40-minute drive to the **Paulina Visitor Center.**

Still itching for more volcanic beauty? Make the trip an all-day affair by heading back north on U.S. 97 toward Bend, then heading northwest on U.S. 20 to Sisters, about an hour and 20 minutes total. You might stop for a bite at the **Cottonwood Cafe** or **The Porch.** From Sisters take Highway 242 west for 15 miles to reach the **Dee Wright Observatory,** which sits in the middle of black lava rock that looks so much like the moon that NASA once used it for astronaut training.

cave; you can turn around at any point. Lava River Cave remains chilly even in the height of summer, so it's a good destination on central Oregon's hottest summer days. To get here from Bend, take exit 151 off U.S. 97. It's about a 20-minute, 13-mile drive south of town.

PAULINA LAKE

Newberry Volcano's caldera is five miles across and hosts two lakes. One of them, **Paulina Lake** (Road 21), is a favorite hiking destination, a vast area laced with trails. It has waterfalls, beaches, and an obsidian lava flow—picture a slope of black, glassy rock—that you can see on an easy jaunt via the 0.6-mile **Big Obsidian Flow** trail that starts just past the visitors center parking area. Anglers also come here in hopes of scoring a big catch—several record-setting fish have been caught in the lake. The **Paulina Visitor Center** (541/383-5700, www.fs.usda.gov, 10am-4pm Sat.-Sun. late May-early June, 9am-5pm daily early June-Aug., 10am-4pm daily Sept.), has an information desk, trail maps, and a few small exhibits about the volcano. It's located on the west shore of Paulina Lake next to picnic facilities and a boat ramp. From Lava Lands Visitor Center, head south on U.S. 97 for about 11 miles, then turn left onto Road 21 for about 15 miles. It's a 40-minute drive to the Paulina Visitor Center parking lot. This area only opens to cars in the summer, when you can drive along the southern shore of Paulina Lake and up to its twin, **East Lake.**

★ Mount Bachelor

Meet the city's playground. Known for its sunny days and dry snow, **Mount Bachelor**

(13000 SW Century Dr., 541/382-1709, www.mtbachelor.com, 9am-4pm daily Nov.-May, $96 adults, $78 children 13-18 and seniors, $54 children 6-12, free for children under 6) is the most popular ski destination in central Oregon. Just over 9,000 feet high, this is a volcano with a ski resort, including 10 chairlifts and several day lodges spread at the base and one halfway up the mountain (worth noting is that the latter offers dining and a solid selection of local beers on tap). Mount Bachelor's name comes from the fact that it's next to the Three Sisters, a trio of mountains that make for a beautiful vista from the ski area. In addition to skiing, showshoeing the snowy forest from the **Nordic Center** on the east side of the main Mount Bachelor parking lot is popular. Note that some trails are groomed and marked as official Nordic ski trails, open only to those with a pass purchased at the center ($20 adults, $13 youth and seniors, free for children under 6); other routes—or tromping through the woods off-trail—is free.

In summer, some hikers climb Mount Bachelor from the ski area parking lot. Several trails cross through the ski runs, which may not be free of snow until well into summer. Hikers can also take the **chairlift** (11am-5pm daily June-early Sept., $19 adults, $16 seniors, $13 children 6-12, free for children under 6) to the mid-mountain lodge. The **Downhill Bike Park** (11am-5pm daily June-early Sept., $19 adults, $16 seniors, $13 children 6-12, free for children under 6) allows riders to take their bikes up two lifts and ride down, and more play areas are located at the base of the mountain with jumps, hills, and other features for creative bike riding, some very small and simple for beginner riders.

Mount Bachelor is a 30-minute drive, 22 miles, south of Bend via SW Century Drive/Cascade Lakes National Scenic Byway.

★ Deschutes River

The Deschutes River, which flows north from its headwaters just south of Bend to the Columbia River, gives the town its name (it's named for a bend in the river), and in many ways its character too. The river infuses the area with beauty and outdoor recreation opportunities galore. It cuts through town, and walking paths on both banks of the river, plus frequent bridges, make it easy to wander up and down the Deschutes right in Bend.

Mount Bachelor

PARKS

If you just want to spend some time lazing near the Deschutes River, **Miller's Landing Park** (80 NW Riverside Blvd., 541/389-7275, www.bendparksandrec.org, 5am-10pm daily), near the Old Mill District, has open green space alongside it. Downtown's **Drake Park** (777 NW Riverside Blvd., 541/389-7275, www.bendparksandrec.org, 5am-10pm daily) faces Mirror Pond, a wide spot in the river so famous it has a Deschutes Brewery beer named after it.

WATER SPORTS

One of the best places to access the Deschutes River's glories are at **Riverbend Park** (799 SW Columbia St., www.bendparksandrec.org), a couple of miles south of downtown.

It boasts playgrounds, lots of picnic spaces, green lawns, and, in the summer, a stand-up paddleboard and tube rental shop, **Sun Country Tours** (http://suncountrytours.com, May 27-Labor Day, $10-20). A city-run shuttle ($3) brings floaters back to their starting place after a river trip, with pickup at Drake Park.

Tumalo Creek Kayak and Canoe (805 SW Industrial Way, 541/317-9407, http://tumalocreek.com), in the Old Mill District, rents kayaks ($40-70 for two hours) and leads half-day guided kayak tours (9am Tues. and Fri. June-Aug., 10am Tues. and Fri. Apr.-May and Sept.-Oct., $75) up to Benham Falls, an easy paddle through some placid stretches of the Deschutes.

Just north of the Old Mill District, where SW Colorado Avenue crosses the river, **Bend Whitewater Park** (541/388-5435, 5am-10pm daily, free) has man-made river rapids. A series of dirt berms separates the waterway, with one channel for tubers, who can take a fairly calm trip through, and one for swiftly churning water that allows white-water kayakers to noodle around in their boats.

If you're looking for real white water, you'll need to head a bit farther out of town. **Sun Country Tours** (531 SW 13th St., 541/382-1709, http://suncountrytours.com), the same company that rents equipment in Riverbend Park, also leads a three-mile trip (Apr.-Sept., $59 adults, $49 children 6-12) to the Big Eddy rapid, a Class 3 section of river that gives a bumpy ride, but nothing too scary. Multiple departures a day leave from Bend (two hours round-trip) and Sunriver (three hours round-trip). A full-day trip (Apr.-Sept., $108 adults, $98 children 6-12) covers 13 river miles and includes a stop for lunch and beach volleyball, exploring a section of the river far north of Bend. Guides will let you float through one gentle rapid by yourself, outside the boat—while wearing a lifejacket, of course.

FISHING

Fishing is also a popular activity on the Deschutes. There are even a few spots to practice casting around the Old Mill District; think of it as mini-golf for fly fishers. To take a guided trip, have **Deep Canyon Outfitters** (541/323-3007, www.deepcanyonoutfitters.com, $325-400 for 1-2 people) arrange a half-day excursion on the Crooked River or Upper Deschutes to go after the area's famous trout.

Golf

The reliable sunshine and dry air of the high desert make it a favorite golf destination; more

Deschutes River

than a dozen courses sit like green islands between the junipers of central Oregon. This includes public and private options, as well as some resort-based options that allow overnight guests to play.

River's Edge Golf Course (400 NW Pro Shop Dr., 541/389-2828, http://riversedgegolfbend.com, $39-59) is an affordable year-round public course close to downtown Bend, with views of the Three Sisters mountains and Deschutes River.

Widgi Creek Golf Club (18707 SW Century Dr., 541/382-4449, www.widgi.com, Apr.-Nov., $29-89), located on the road that winds west to Mount Bachelor, is a public course and home to one of the longest par 5 holes in the country: 653 yards from tee to green.

Just south of town, **Sunriver Resort Woodlands Golf Course** (17890 W Core Rd., 541/593-4402, www.destinationhotels.com/sunriver-resort, mid.-May-mid.-Sept., $50-70) is one of four golf courses at the Sunriver Resort. Designed by Robert Trent Jones, Jr., a famous course mastermind, it has both water features and the occasional lava rock sticking out of the ground (albeit not in the fairway). It's a good introduction to Sunriver's thriving golf community and is open to the public as well as resort guests.

Hiking

DESCHUTES RIVER TRAIL

Distance: 3 miles round-trip
Duration: 1-1.5 hours
Elevation gain: 100 feet
Effort: easy
Trailhead: Farewell Bend Park (1000 SW Reed Market Rd.), near the Old Mill District

The Deschutes River Trail runs more than 10 miles through the city, most of it next to the river. Hop on the riverside walkway for a jaunt and head away from the Old Mill smokestacks, upriver. Continue along the river as houses fall away and the dirt trail passes through brushy ponderosa pine; it can be hard to remember you're in the city. After about 1.5 miles, you'll reach a footbridge over the Deschutes River. Head across and then follow the trail back downstream to complete the loop.

If you want to add mileage at the end, keep going past Farewell Bend Park to add a wander through the Old Mill District and the Les Schwab Amphitheater, which sit on either side of the river; here the trail is paved and busier with urban pedestrians. Several bridges cross the river around the Old Mill, so you can turn around at various points. At the height of summer, be prepared for mosquitoes; many outdoor and convenience stores in the area sell insect repellent.

RILEY RANCH

Distance: 0.7-1.25 miles round-trip
Duration: 0.5-1 hour
Elevation gain: 0-150 feet
Effort: easy
Trailhead: Riley Ranch Nature Preserve (19975 Glen Vista Rd.)

Riley Ranch Nature Preserve was formed from 184 acres of private ranch land, a brushy mix of pine, juniper, and exposed lava rock with the Deschutes River slowly passing through. Some of the trails are paved but most are dirt. Two short nature walks, Juniper Loop (0.7 mile) and Sage Flat Loop (0.9 mile), head out in either direction; combine them to get a sense of the entire preserve. For a little more movement, traipse the 1.25-mile Canyon Loop, which dips down from the upper meadow to where the river has cut its path. Parking is limited, so arriving before 10am on weekends is advisable.

TUMALO FALLS

Distance: 2 miles round-trip
Duration: 1 hour
Elevation gain: 250 feet
Effort: easy
Trailhead: Tumalo Falls Day Use Area
Directions: From Bend, take NW Galveston Avenue, which becomes Skyliners Road, for 11.5 miles, then turn right onto Tumalo Falls Road, also called Forest Road 4603. Follow the unimproved dirt road for 2.5 miles.

Drive right up to the first waterfall of this hike, 90-foot Tumalo Falls (the last few miles of the drive here are harder than the walk from car to waterfall, which is just a few dozen feet). These tumbling falls are one of the region's most striking. Look left of the falls for the trail that continues up the North Fork Tumalo Creek, staying on the west side of the water. It's an easy ramble through the Oregon forest, and you'll reach Double Falls in about a mile. Though smaller than Tumalo Falls, the double drop is a good spot for a picnic. Return the way you came. Note that dogs are not allowed.

TUMALO MOUNTAIN

Distance: 4 miles round-trip
Duration: 3 hours
Elevation gain: 1,300 feet
Effort: moderate
Trailhead: northern end of Dutchman Flat Sno-Park
Directions: From Bend, take Century Drive for 21 miles toward Mount Bachelor.

Climb this small mountain next to towering Mount Bachelor for great views; the incline on this trail will get your blood pumping. You'll pass through pine, lava rocks, and wildflowers (in the summer) before you reach the large, flat top of Tumalo. From this open viewpoint, you'll be able to see the Three Sisters, Broken Top, Mount Bachelor, and beyond on a clear day; turn east to look back to Bend.

TODD LAKE

Distance: 1.7 miles round-trip
Duration: 1.5-2 hours
Elevation gain: 100 feet
Effort: easy
Trailhead: Todd Lake Day Use Area
Directions: From Bend, drive 24 miles southeast on Century Drive. Turn right onto Forest Road 4600-370. The parking lot is in 0.5 mile.

This hike is in the Cascade Lakes area, which—especially between Mount Bachelor and the Three Sisters—is overrun with trails, many of which have stunning views and beautiful mountain lakes. Todd Lake is one of the easiest ways to access this forest; the southern end of the lake, nearest the parking lot, has pit toilets and picnic tables, and the trail traces a path around the lake in a 1.7-mile loop. The best views of Broken Top, a nearby volcano, are at the start of the hike. Travel in either direction, and note that dogs are only allowed in summer.

Mountain Biking

Exploring the outdoors by bike is one of the region's biggest pastimes. Most ski shops become mountain bike shops in the summer. Local biking organization **Bend Trails** (http://bendtrails.org) provides maps and ideas on where to ride, with many suggestions grouped around Century Drive—the road that goes from Bend to Mount Bachelor) and Skyliners Road, just north of it. Rent mountain bikes at **Hutch's Bicycles** (725 NW Columbia St., 541/382-9253, http://hutchsbicycles.com, 9am-6pm Mon.-Sat., 11am-4pm Sun.), the region's largest outfitter. Reservations are recommended but not required. Rates range $20-55 per day and $65 for pedal-assisted e-bikes for road travel. Bikes come with locks and helmets. Note that since the region gets a lot of snow in the winter, mountain bike trails are only reliably open late spring-mid-fall.

When the snow does fall, there is still a way to pedal. Fat tire snow bikes are available for rent at **Mountain Water Snow** (170 Scalehouse Loop, 541/633-7694, http://mountainwatersnow.com, 10am-7pm Mon.-Sat., 10am-5pm Sun.) in the Old Mill District for $60 per day. **Cog Wild Tours** (255 SW Century Dr., 541/385-7002, www.cogwild.com) offers half-day fat tire snow bike tours, including hot chocolate (spiked with local liquor or not) at the ride's conclusion, for $110 per person.

ENTERTAINMENT AND EVENTS

Nightlife

★ BEND ALE TRAIL

All of Oregon may be known for beer, but Bend vies with Portland for the title of capital of the craft revolution: The state has the highest breweries per capita in the country, but while Portland has more breweries overall,

Bend has slightly more per capita. Breweries are very much part of the chill, congenial culture of central Oregon, and while almost every variety is represented, the IPA is a clear favorite. Beer is everywhere in Bend; even some gas stations have taps for growler fills.

The **Bend Ale Trail** entices you to explore the town's 16 breweries. Start by picking up a map and "passport" at the **Bend Visitor Center** (www.visitbend.com) or participating brewery, or download a free app from the visitors center website. Then hop among the breweries and collect stamps (no purchase necessary) in your passport. If you get stamped at 10 breweries over any amount of time, you'll earn a souvenir beer glass, which you can claim at the visitors center.

Some of Bend's breweries are within walkable distance, so you can do-it-yourself safely, but others may require wheels. The **Bend Brew Bus** (61535 S U.S. 97, 541/389-8359, www.bendbrewbus.com, $75) offers half-day tours by van, with free pickup at local hotels and nearby residences. The bus visits four breweries for included tastings, with appetizers at one of them. Otherwise, call a cab for easy transportation between drinking spots.

Most of the more popular breweries in town offer a restaurant/pub experience, but a few have tastings only. Each brewery has its own personality. Here are some of the most notable of the town's 16 breweries.

Nobody's bigger than Deschutes in Bend, one of the oldest local makers (they started way back in 1988!). Varieties like Mirror Pond and Black Butte Porter were part of the first wave of the craft beer explosion, but locals dig the Bachelor Bitter you can only get in its pubs like **Deschutes Brewery Bend Public House** (1044 NW Bond St., 541/382-9242, www.deschutesbrewery.com, 11am-10pm Sun.-Thurs., 11am-11pm Fri.-Sat.). The multilevel restaurant is perpetually busy, and the hot pretzel served with beer cheese and mustard is a good side for a tasting flight. Visit the **Deschutes Brewery Bend Tasting Room** (901 SW Simpson Ave., 541/385-8606, noon-7pm daily) nearby for a more technical tasting experience.

Crux Fermentation Project (50 SW Division St., 541/385-3333, www.cruxfermentation.com, 4pm-9pm Mon., 11:30am-9pm Sun. and Tues.-Thurs., 11:30am-10pm Fri.-Sat.) has a block party atmosphere in an industrial area, its grounds dotted with wood-burning fire pits and bean-bag games, and the lawn crowded with dogs and kids year-round. It's the perfect spot to watch the sun set behind Mount Bachelor while enjoying a fruit-tinged IPA. Its most popular bears are the Farmhouse saison and Crux Pilz pilsner, but the brewery taps always include some fun, unusual flavors.

Worthy Brewing (495 NE Bellevue Dr., 541/639-4776, www.worthybrewing.com, 11:30am-9pm Sun.-Thurs., 11:30am-10pm Fri.-Sat.) set up shop in a more locals-heavy neighborhood, eschewing the tourist crowds of downtown, but is still hopping. The well-manicured patio has gas fireplaces, and the food is a cut above most brewpubs. The brewery's signature IPA is made with five Northwest hops, and the stout has Madagascar vanilla beans for flavor.

One of the most successful Bend breweries, **10 Barrel Brewing** (1135 NW Galveston Ave., 541/678-5228, http://10barrel.com, 11am-11pm Sun.-Thurs., 11am-midnight Fri.-Sat.) has grown exponentially since it began—it sold to beer conglomerate Anheuser-Busch in 2014, earning criticism from the craft beer community—but the original Bend pub, and its outdoor fireplace, is really the heart of the enterprise and remains a busy and popular spot.

GoodLife Brewing Company (70 SW Century Dr., 541/728-0749, www.goodlife-brewing.com, noon-10pm daily) has long been a local's favorite for its Sweet As Pacific Ale and Descender IPA, among others. Expect hoppy, classic flavors and names that evoke the Bend lifestyle, like Puffy Coat Porter. The tasting room is moderately sized, but the outdoor area, open June-October, has lawn games and occasional live music.

BARS AND CLUBS

One of two Bend spots with a tree trunk inside—though this one isn't living, unlike the Pine Tavern's—**Dogwood Cocktail Cabin** (147 NW Minnesota Ave., 541/706-9949, www.thedogwoodcocktailcabin.com, 5pm-midnight Tues.-Sun.) feels like the inside of an eclectic mountain man's party hideout. From its animal mural to a ship's repurposed lights hanging over the bar to that tree trunk—a supportive column for the two-story bar—this spot is quirky and fun. Creative cocktails can be on the sweet side, but the bartenders are talented, the whiskey selection is strong, and the bacon-and-cheese topped brussels sprouts make a good side dish. DJs spin on the top balcony some nights.

Though the wooden walls and antler chandelier in the two-story **Velvet Lounge** (805 NW Wall St., 541/728-0303, www.velvetbend.com, 5pm-1:30am daily) give it an outdoorsy vibe—Bend's signature look—the art hanging on the walls makes the biggest statement at this downtown cocktail joint. Drinks are served in mason jars, and most concoctions have an herbal twist; the old-fashioned is made with cardamom and local blueberries, and there's an entire yerba mate section on the cocktail menu. Drinks are surprisingly cheap for a bar with this much style.

In a town that practically bleeds beer, **Stihl Whiskey Bar** (550 NW Franklin Ave., 541/383-8182, www.thestihl.com, 5pm-midnight Mon.-Thurs., 5pm-1am Fri.-Sat., 6pm-11pm Sun.) offers much-needed diversity to the scene with its more than 200 varieties of whiskey, hailing from Japan, Scotland, Kentucky, and beyond. Unlike most downtown bars, the vibe is modern, not woodsy, and the menu includes creative small plates, like shrimp baked in a bourbon sauce and a grilled cheese on thick Texas toast.

The ultra-chill **Brother Jon's Public House** (1227 NW Galveston Ave., 541/306-3321, www.brotherjonspublichouse.com, 11am-11pm Mon.-Sat., 8:30am-10pm Sun.) is inside a house-like building with lots of small rooms and a back porch that might as well be a neighbor's patio; there's no pretension in this spot that piles a single order of buffalo macaroni and cheese so high it's practically a family-style dish. Bartenders are familiar with the area beers and don't mind offering tastes so you can find your favorite, but it's less of a tasting spot (there are so many in town) and more a relaxed pub to stop thinking about

Crux Fermentation Project

craft beer intricacies and just sit back and enjoy a pint.

On big sports days—any football Sunday, basically—downtown's **Sidelines Sports Bar and Grill** (1020 NW Wall St., 541/385-8898, http://sidelines-bend.com, 8am-1am Mon.-Sat., 8am-11pm Sun.) is packed to the brim, the row of TVs behind the bar blaring. It can get a bit rowdy, and it's pretty far from the urban-minded beer meccas that surround it, but it does pour a number of quality local beers. This is the place to yell at the screen along with all the other sports fans. Thank the dim lighting that you don't have to dwell on who's elbowing you or spilling a drink at the next table.

Festivals and Events

Even in winter, the region is sunny and active, so **Bend Winterfest** (http://bendoregonfestivals.com/winterfest, Feb.) is less an escape from the season than a celebration of it. The Old Mill District hosts three days of music, food and wine events, ice sculpting, road running races, sports demos, and craft shopping. The road races and wine events require registration and a fee, but the festival is otherwise free.

Bend is so sporty that its signature event doesn't just have one discipline, it has four: skiing, cycling, running, and kayaking. Teams compete in the relay **Pole Pedal and Paddle** (541/388-0002, www.pppbend.com, May) while there's still snow on Mount Bachelor, but by the time contestants reach the boating leg on the Deschutes, it feels like summer. The single-day event is a large undertaking, and you can see competitors on the final leg at Riverbend Park.

In the summer, the **Les Schwab Amphitheater** (344 SW Shevlin Hixon Dr., www.bendconcerts.com), holds outdoor concerts that can be heard all around town. Performances are held Memorial Day-September, and tickets for shows—typically pop, rock, and soul—generally run $40-90, though prices can double that for A-list acts. Michael Franti and Dave Matthews Band make frequent appearances.

Held for more than 35 years, the **Cascade Cycling Classic** (www.cascade-classic.org, June or July) is the longest consecutively held stage cycling race in the country, and people from around the region watch this Oregon version of the Tour de France as teams of pros whisk through the dry high desert on bikes.

Does Bend have a beer festival, or is the town really just holding a year-round, non-stop beer festival? Both, really, though the summer **Bend Beer Fest** (Les Schwab Amphitheater, 344 SW Shevlin Hixon Dr., http://bendbrewfest.com, Aug.) is a giant celebration of the region's signature tipple. Attendees to the event buy a single mug and multiple tasting tokens, then get to explore offerings from more than 80 breweries. Kids are welcome during the day but will likely be unenthused by the beer-first mentality.

The Oxford Hotel hosts a popular jazz series, **Jazz at the Oxford** (10 NW Minnesota Ave., 503/432-9477, www.jazzattheoxford.com, $45-50), through the fall and winter. Most shows sell out, so book at least a week in advance.

SHOPPING

Though located in a mostly residential neighborhood west of downtown, **Roundabout Books** (900 NW Mount Washington Dr. #110, 541/306-6564, www.roundaboutbookshop.com, 9am-7pm Mon.-Fri., 10am-6pm Sat.-Sun.) is a destination-worthy stop for readers. Shelves are packed with a carefully curated selection, and the staff is knowledgeable and friendly. The sales counter doubles as a small coffee bar, and the children's section is small but lovingly presented.

Downtown's best book stop, **Dudley's Bookstore and Cafe** (135 NW Minnesota Ave., 541/749-2010, www.dudleysbookshopcafe.com, 9am-5:30pm Mon. and Wed., 8:30am-5:30pm Tues., 9am-7pm Thurs., 9am-6pm Fri., 10am-6pm Sat., 11am-5:30pm Sun.) feels mostly like a café at first, but upstairs are more shelves of guidebooks, history, fantasy, and fiction. New hardbacks are always discounted, used books are sold as well, and the couch makes for a comfortable spot to dive into a new purchase right away.

The throwback **Goody's** (957 NW Wall St., 541/389-5185, http://goodyschocolates.com, 10am-9pm Sun.-Thurs., 10am-10pm Fri.-Sat.) is a candy store from another era, with colorful sweets lined up in glass jars and a soda fountain counter in the back. Snag a pound of electric green gummies or gumballs for later. The smell of freshly molded waffle cones will compel you to walk out with the shop's own locally made ice cream.

Though hard to pronounce, **Skjersaa's** (345 SW Century Dr. #100, 541/382-2154, www.skibend.com, 8am-6pm daily) is as homey as a ski shop can be. The main floor has a nice selection of winter sports gear, and the shop also has ski waxes and ski and snowboard rentals. Up front is a small bar with a few beer taps, where the discussion is usually about the snow situation on the mountain.

Not everyone in town wears hiking boots and puffy jackets everywhere. **Hot Box Betty** (903 NW Wall St. #100, 541/383-0050, www.hotboxbetty.com, 10am-6pm daily) is where the town's stylish set shops for clothes. Many pieces have a casual but chic cut, and the staff shows off the minimalist style. Shoppers will also find shoes, jewelry, and purses that elevate Bend's fashion quotient one accessory at a time.

Bend is a popular second-home community, and **Lark Mountain Modern** (831 NW Wall St., 541/797-2099, www.larkmountainmodern.com, 10am-6pm Mon.-Sat., 11am-5pm Sun.) is the kind of store where new owners can decorate their dream vacation home. Most products, from table lamps to bedding, have an upscale cabin vibe, like tumblers shaped like mountains and wool blankets with a big Swiss cross in the center. It's also a great store to visit if you're looking for gifts.

Before the town was an outdoor enthusiast's dream, it was a timber town. Two of the area's now-defunct mills were reworked in the mid-1990s to become the **Old Mill District** (450 SW Powerhouse Dr., 541/312-0131, www.oldmilldistrict.com), a shopping mall. The three smokestacks that marked the mills are still visible from across town. Shops and restaurants are scattered in separate buildings. You'll find stores like REI and lululemon here. The Deschutes River makes up one border of the district; look along the river and you may glimpse some fly fishers practicing their casting.

FOOD

American

There's something refreshing about the **Drake** (801 NW Wall St., 541/306-3366, http://drakebend.com, 11am-9:30pm Sun.-Thurs., 11am-10:30pm Fri.-Sat., $15-32), with its clean lines, white tile floor, and long, thin dining area and counter that feels almost like a railway car. The menu at the bistro changes with the seasons but focuses on fresh American fare, with items like a red snapper sandwich or steak frites. The fried chicken is a standout. Reservations are recommended for dinner.

Yes, there's a tree in the middle of **Pine Tavern** (967 NW Brooks St., 541/382-5581, http://pinetavern.com, 11:30am-9pm daily, $14-40)—a real live ponderosa pine. The back dining room is built around the trunk, and the top shoots through the ceiling. But the longtime Bend favorite, dating back to 1936, is a go-to for other reasons, too, like hot scones served with honey butter before meals. Come for classics like beef stroganoff, meatloaf, pork chops, and solid, uncomplicated rib eye and filet mignon steaks. Out back, tables sit under yet more trees by the riverside.

The stately **900 Wall** (900 NW Wall St., 541/323-6295, www.900wall.com, 3pm-10pm daily, $15-34) uses its two levels to full advantage, the upstairs balcony seating providing lofty views of the exposed wooden beams and bustling dining floor below. Bottles line the exposed brick walls over the bar, and tables start filling up during happy hour. The menu features beef tartare and beef carpaccio, duck confit, and steak frites. Pizzas, made in a stone oven, have a sourdough crust and are a popular draw.

Sometimes you just need a simple burger. **Pilot Butte Drive-In** (917 NE Greenwood Ave., 541/382-2972, 7am-7pm daily, $9-14) dates back to 1983 but feels older and retro-charming with its booths and simple offerings, like a cheeseburger, patty melt, and Reuben sandwich. The 18-ounce Pilot Butte Cheese Burger should be shared with a friend.

One of Bend's more upscale restaurants, ★ **Ariana** (1304 NW Galveston Ave., 541/330-5539, www.arianarestaurantbend.com, 5pm-10pm Tues.-Sat., $27-37) is inside a Craftsman house, and its wood floors and white tablecloths brighten a small dining room. The menu pulls from local produce like Oregon wild mushrooms and rabbit cooked in local sunchokes. A tasting menu of five courses is $65.

Blacksmith (211 NW Greenwood Ave., 541/318-0588, www.bendblacksmith.com, 4pm-10pm Mon.-Tues., 4pm-midnight Fri.-Sat., 4pm-9pm Sun., $29-40) is, fittingly, in an old 1923 blacksmith shop, though the sophisticated steakhouse and lounge is now outfitted with black leather booths and a long white marble bar backed by illuminated bottles. Its menu is straightforward, with classics like surf and turf and salmon. The signature Tomahawk steak ($72) is 24 ounces of meat, bacon glazed and served with fried bacon brussels sprouts. You'll also find live music here twice a week, on Tuesdays and Fridays (7pm-9pm, free).

Asian

Born as a food truck, ★ **Spork** (937 NW Newport Ave., 541/390-0946, www.sporkbend.com, 11am-9pm Sun.-Thurs., 11am-10pm Fri.-Sat., $9-14) is now a brick-and-mortar hotspot. The global street food menu includes everything from chilaquiles to a West African peanut curry and Burmese fried cheese. The colorful, festive interior is almost always busy, but service is efficient. Heck, even the beer list saves time by calling its IPA variety "who cares, you're going to drink it anyway."

Breakfast

Drive across town for a morning bite? It's worth it for ★ **Rockin' Dave's Bagel Bistro** (661 NE Greenwood Ave., 541/318-8177, http://rockindaves.com, 7am-2pm Mon.-Sat., 9am-2pm Sun., $4-10), where mornings are always hopping. Real boiled bagels are topped with eggs and hash browns or lox and cream cheese. House-smoked pastrami rules at lunchtime. Order at the counter and leave the name of your favorite band, then sit and wait to hear the staff call it out when your order is ready. There's also a bar and lounge attached that hosts live music at night.

Mediterranean

Find a taste of the Mediterranean at **Joolz** (916 NW Wall St., 541/388-5094, www.joolzbend.com, 4pm-9pm daily, $18-31), where, they say, "the mezze meets the mesa." With warm tones and draped fabric, the interior conjures the Middle East, and the menu is dotted with classic hummus, harissa clams, and seafood tagine. But there are plenty of surprises from the Lebanese chef too, like elk chili. Order the fried cauliflower with tahini dipping sauce to start.

Southern

Find a taste of the South at downtown's **Zydeco Kitchen and Cocktails** (919 NW Bond St., 541/312-2899, www.zydecokitchen.com, 11:30am-2:30pm and 5pm-10pm Mon.-Fri., 5pm-10pm Sat.-Sun., $12-38), a sleek eatery decked out in dark wood and mirrors. Dishes are on the small side but packed with flavor, like shrimp andouille and crawfish jambalaya served with homemade cornbread. Ask for a free homemade dog biscuit at the end of the meal to share the love with Fido.

ACCOMMODATIONS

Under $150

Though most budget accommodations in Bend are of the chain variety, **Bunk + Brew**

Historic Lucas House (42 NW Hawthorne Ave., 458/202-1090, www.bunkandbrew.com, $45 dorms, $119-150 private rooms) is a charming hostel-style spot inside a 1910 brick house that caters to the adventure-loving crowd. True to its name, you'll get a free beer at check-in. Dorm rooms are simple bunks, and private rooms have the feel of a relative's guest room. The hostel provides a free light breakfast, an outdoor fire pit and grill, and a sense of community. Its downtown location is prime, and the hostel runs a free "Dirtbag Express" van to Mount Bachelor and Smith Rock.

$150-250

Riverhouse Hotel (3075 N Hwy. 97, 844/854-8179, www.riverhouse.com, $219-269), not far from the center of town, straddles the Deschutes River, with some rooms on either bank, linked by a footbridge. Rooms have microwaves and Keurig coffeemakers, and some include fireplaces and river views. The pet-friendly hotel also has a gas fire pit out by the river and hosts regular jazz concerts throughout the winter, and there's a pool and spa outside.

Part of a regional chain that reworks old buildings into bars, restaurants, and hotels, **McMenamins Old St. Francis School** (700 NW Bond St., 541/382-5174, www.mcmenamins.com, $210-260) inhabits a complex of buildings in downtown Bend, including a former Catholic schoolhouse from 1936. The property also includes a movie theater, a live music space, a pub, and an indoor soaking pool with a central fountain and mosaic walls, the latter of which the public can access for $5 per person. Rooms have wood-paneled walls and signature McMenamins hand-painted headboards.

Though it calls itself a motel and has the general appearance of one, **Wall Street Suites** (1430 NW Wall St., 541/706-9006, www.wallstreetsuitesbend.com, $185-240) is a midrange accommodation near downtown with some wonderful style, including natural stone showers, granite and custom wood decor, and an outdoor common space and fire pit for hanging with fellow guests and their pets (who enjoy an on-site dog park). The 17 rooms all have kitchens and dining tables, and free bike rentals are available. Minimum stays may apply.

Though its exterior has a bit of a dated 1980s sheen, **Pine Ridge Inn** (1200 SW Mount Bachelor Dr., 541/389-6137, www.pineridgeinn.com, $149-299) is updated on the inside and offers great perks like freshly baked goods and a full-time concierge. The location near the Old Mill District is ideal for access to both downtown and Mount Bachelor. Most rooms have a view of the Deschutes River, and the hotel offers free beer or wine at check-in. Some rooms have fireplaces and Jacuzzi tubs.

There's no lodging at Mount Bachelor, so the **Seventh Mountain Resort** (18575 SW Century Dr., 541/382-8711, http://seventhmountain.com, $174-334) is as close as you can get. The complex, nestled into acres that back up onto the Deschutes National Forest, includes hotel rooms and more expansive suites with kitchens and living rooms, some with as many as three bedrooms. In winter the complex has an ice skating rink, and the Widgi Creek Golf Course is right next to it. Minimum stays may apply.

Over $250

Bend's fanciest digs are at downtown's ★ **Oxford Hotel** (10 NW Minnesota Ave., 541/382-8436, www.oxfordhotelbend.com, $449-479), a boutique property with 59 sizable rooms with ultramodern decor, all with high-end linens and soaking tubs. The hotel offers a complimentary local shuttle to any destination within five miles and Breedlove Guitars to borrow, as well as a sauna, steam room, and hot tub. Its 10below Restaurant, located on the 1st floor, serves breakfast, lunch, and dinner. The Oxford Hotel also hosts a popular, ticketed jazz series in fall and winter.

Although it's a chain hotel, **SpringHill Suites Bend** (551 SW Industrial Way, 541/382-5075, www.marriott.com, $299-329) benefits from a great location—walking distance to the Old Mill District, the Deschutes River, Crux Fermentation Project, and downtown, plus close to the road to Mount Bachelor, making it easy to get a jump on traffic on weekends. Rooms have seating areas with sofa beds, microwaves, and mini-fridges, and a small workstation.

Located about 15 miles south of Bend on the Deschutes River, **Sunriver Resort** (17600 Center Dr., Sunriver, 855/420-8206, www.destinationhotels.com/sunriver-resort, $299-419) is more like a town than a simple resort; it has four golf courses, a spa, miles and miles of accommodations, and a central shopping area with restaurants. Since the entire area is laced with paved bike trails, it's a favorite family vacation destination. The resort's numerous lodging options range from guest rooms decorated in rustic mountain style, to multi-room accommodations featuring amenities like private decks and stone fireplaces, to vacation rentals and condos.

Camping

With so much beautiful natural scenery around, it makes sense to stay as close to it as possible. **Tumalo State Park** (64170 O. B. Riley Rd., 541/388-6055, www.oregonstateparks.org) is open year-round and has a variety of options, with RV ($33) and tent ($21) campsites, as well as yurts ($46-56). With 330 acres on the Deschutes River, it's an ideal place to camp and then wade into the cool water on a hot summer day. Some yurts are pet-friendly and some are disability accessible.

INFORMATION AND SERVICES

The **Bend Visitor Center** (750 NW Lava Rd., Ste. 160, 877/245-8484, www.visitbend.com, 9am-5pm Mon.-Fri., 10am-4pm Sat.-Sun.) has maps of town, sure, but also so much more—the large welcome center offers numerous magazines and brochures for local activities, including information on the Bend Ale Trail, and sells local crafts and products. It's one of the more up-to-date and useful visitors centers in the state.

GETTING THERE

Air

The closest airport to Bend is **Roberts Field, the Redmond Municipal Airport** (RDM, 2522 SE Jesse Butler Circle, Redmond, 541/548-0646, www.flyrdm.com); commercial flights from Portland, Seattle, Denver, Salt Lake City, Los Angeles, and more land here, on four major airlines. Car rental services are available at the terminal from six major car rental companies.

A cab from **Bend Cab Company** (541/389-8090, http://bendcab.com) from RDM to the center of Bend will cost $28-35.

Car

The fastest route to Bend from the north is via U.S. 26 East from Portland, following it for about 105 miles through the town of Madras, where it merges with U.S. 97 South. Continue on for about 40 miles to Bend, passing the town of Redmond along the way. The drive takes about 3.25 hours.

Alternately, take I-5 South from Portland for about 50 miles to the town of Salem, then take the exit for Highway 22 East (Santiam Highway). Follow Highway 22 for 80 miles, over Santiam Pass, until it merges with U.S. 20 East. Follow U.S. 20 for another 50 miles to reach Bend. This drive takes around 3.5 hours.

Reaching Bend from Portland means braving at least one mountain pass, so driving can be difficult in winter when ice and snow slow traffic. Check current conditions with the **Oregon Department of Transportation** (www.tripcheck.com), which operates a number of cameras along major routes. In winter, roads on the U.S. 26-U.S. 97 route tend to be in better shape since they are plowed regularly.

Sisters and Redmond

Sisters and Redmond make up the other two points of central Oregon's triangle of destinations. Bend may be the most popular with tourists, but these towns each have their own appeal. Sisters is a quaint little mountain town closer to the Cascades. With brightly painted storefronts and an annual rodeo, it's cornered the local market on charm, plus offers views of its namesake, the Three Sisters volcanoes. Redmond is set in the open, flat high desert and, with a cheaper cost of living, has fewer second homes and more year-round locals. It also offers easy access to Smith Rock. Just next to that rock climbing mecca is the small settlement of Terrebonne, more of a bump in the road than a full town but with some nice draws.

The towns are just north of Bend, with Sisters and Redmond, to its east, about 20 miles apart on Highway 126, while Terrebonne's about 6 miles north of Redmond on U.S. 97.

SIGHTS

★ Dee Wright Observatory

McKenzie Pass on Highway 242 spurs off from U.S. 20, just 15 miles west of Sisters. While the pass may be the highest point on this road, at 5,325 feet, the area you'll want to pause at is a few hundred yards east. Here at the top of the Cascades rib that separates Bend from western Oregon, **Dee Wright Observatory** (www.fs.fed.us, free) appears as if a castle made by a volcano. The stone structure was built in 1935 atop lava flows, from eruptions 2,700 years ago, by the Civilian Conservation Corps during the Great Depression. It seems like you're on the surface of the moon from this lookout, with the dark, rocky landscape variously jagged and smooth surrounding you. You'll find pieces of pumice formed by eruptions here. The miles of volcanic rock come from Belknap Crater, a shield volcano whose top pops up about two miles away—it's amazing that such a modest-looking hill could have produced such power. Bronze panels describe the other impressive volcanoes visible from the observatory: Mount Hood, Mount Jefferson, Mount Washington, the Three Sisters, and more.

Note that McKenzie Pass closes late fall-early or even midsummer, with snow keeping it inaccessible as late as July. The structure (with a parking lot) is accessible any time the road is open.

SPORTS AND RECREATION

★ Smith Rock State Park

The topography at **Smith Rock State Park** (NE Crooked River Dr., Terrebonne, 541/548-7501, www.oregonstateparks.org, dawn-dusk daily, $5 per vehicle) is so stunning it's no wonder the rocky towers and winding Crooked River have been used in film shoots—its most recent blockbuster appearance was in *Wild*. While jagged spires rise from an earthy brown landscape, down by the river it's green and lush, with mule deer along the banks and sometimes otters in the river. Smith Rock offers some of the Pacific Northwest's best climbing in its 650 acres, but even if you're not a climber, you can enjoy wandering the landscape and trails—about 20 miles worth—that wind through the park. The park is less than 10 miles north of Redmond via U.S. 97, about a 15-minute drive.

ROCK CLIMBING

Climbing enthusiasts flock to the difficult routes in the park, notably a tower that looks like a monkey's head viewed from the right angle. Less experienced rock climbers can hire a guide to literally show them the ropes; several companies operate in and around Smith Rock, including **Smith Rock Climbing School** (19437 Kemple Dr., Bend, 541/633-7450, www.smithrockclimbing.com, $85-285 pp depending on group size), which has accredited guides who can lead new, or experienced, rock hounds through the climbing mecca to find an appropriate route for everyone in the group; guides even know when spots get hit by sun so you can minimize your time in the blazing heat.

MOUNTAIN BIKING

Mountain biking is allowed on the park's riverside trails. Bike rentals are available in Redmond at **Hutch's Bicycles** (827 SW 7th St., Redmond, 541/548-8200, http://hutchsbicycles.com, 9am-6pm Mon.-Sat., 11am-5pm Sun., $30-45).

Golf

Eagle Crest Resort (1522 Cline Falls Rd., Redmond, 541/923-2453, www.eagle-crest.com, $34-76) has three courses relatively close to Redmond. Its Ridge Course, with scenic views of Smith Rock State Park, and beginner-friendly Challenge Course, 18 holes each, are open year-round to the public. The Resort Course's 18 holes, many of which require tricky shots that attract experts, are open March-mid-November. Resort guests get a discount on greens fees.

Located about 8.5 miles northwest of Sisters, **Black Butte Ranch** (13020 Hawks Beard Rd., 541/595-1500, www.blackbutteranch.com/golf, Apr.-Oct., $49-79) has two courses located close to the prominent butte. Big Meadow has a famous 14th hole, with beautiful views of the Three Fingered Jack volcano, and Glaze Meadow has rolling fairways and tees suitable for every level of player.

ENTERTAINMENT AND EVENTS

Nightlife

Though Sisters is a cozy little town, that doesn't mean it doesn't have sophistication. **The Open Door** (303 W Hood Ave., Sisters, 541/549-6076, www.opendoorwinebar.com, 11:30am-10pm Mon.-Sat.) is a wine bar that also serves delicate Italian dishes and rich desserts. The space is intimate and includes an art gallery that features Western art, and it regularly hosts live music as well.

Monkey Face Rock in Smith Rock State Park

Three Creeks Brewing Brewpub (721 Desperado Ct, Sisters, 541/549-1963, www.threecreeksbrewing.com, 11:30am-9pm Sun.-Thurs., 11:30am-10pm Fri.-Sat.) is a strong entry into the regional beer game for a town as small as Sisters. While the nearby **brewery** (265 E Barclay Dr., 3pm-7pm Fri.-Sat.) offers some on-site tastings June-September for $5, the brewpub has much more to offer: six-beer flights for $10, pitchers, pizzas made with beer-infused dough, and a happy hour, all in a log cabin-style home.

Redmond's **Smith Rock Brewing Company** (546 NW 7th St., Redmond, 541/279-7005, www.smithrockbrewing.beer, 11:30am-2pm and 5pm-7:45pm Tues.-Thurs., 11:30am-2pm and 5pm-8:45pm Fri, noon-2:30pm and 5pm-8:45pm Sat.) is a small brewpub that feels more like a winery—with a stone fireplace, tall tables, and walls painted in earth tones. Beers on tap include a cream ale and porter as well as, of course, several IPAs.

Festivals and Events

For almost 80 years, the **Sisters Rodeo** (67637 U.S. 20, Sisters, 541/549-0121, www.sistersrodeo.com, June), dubbed "The biggest little show in the world," has been the most exciting weekend in this small Cascades community. Prizes awarded for rodeo events like bull riding, roping, and barrel racing are among the highest in the nation, and the weekend still includes longtime traditions like a rodeo parade through downtown Sisters and a cowboy church service.

SHOPPING

Set on a farm, the Crescent Moon Ranch's **Alpaca Boutique** (7566 U.S. 97, Terrebonne, 541/923-2285, www.crescentmoonranch.com, 9am-5pm daily summer, 10am-4pm daily winter) harvests fibers from its alpacas to create sweaters, socks, and scarves. Alpaca fiber, like wool, is very warm but softer and hypoallergenic. The shop also sells alpaca products from around the world, and even has feed bags for sale so kids (or adults) can interact with the long-necked creatures.

FOOD

Make sure you have cash handy for ★ **Sisters Bakery** (251 E Cascade Ave., Sisters, 541/549-0361, www.sistersbakery.com, 6am-5pm daily), which doesn't take credit cards but has a delectable range of doughnuts, breads, and pies for sale. Breakfast croissants go quickly. The smell of the fresh-baked goods will convince you to buy more than you'd planned.

Welcome home to a cozy house that just happens to hold a quaint eatery, the **Cottonwood Cafe** (403 E Hood Ave., Sisters, 541/549-2699, www.cottonwoodinsisters.com, 8am-3pm daily summer, 8am-3pm Thurs.-Tues. fall-spring, $10-13). As sweet as Sisters is small, the side-street café is surrounded by a picket fence. Its menu includes breakfast and lunch, but the former is the real star, offering rich Benedicts, farmhouse hash, and a very rich bread pudding, among other options. What is it with homey restaurants in Sisters? Like the Cottonwood Cafe, **The Porch** (243 N Elm St., Sisters, 541/549-3287, www.theporchsisters.com, 5pm-9pm Wed.-Sun., $12-28) is in an old residential space, front porch included. It's a dinner-only destination with classic American fare inspired by what's locally available, plus a generous helping of seafood dishes, lots of green produce, and a popular shrimp curry. This is a relaxed dining spot that stays relatively quiet even during the busiest tourist season.

Diego's Spirited Kitchen (447 SW 6th St., Redmond, 541/316-2002, www.diegosspiritedkitchen.com, 11am-10pm daily, $9-25) has gained a following for its Latin-themed dishes and friendly service. Waiters dish chicken mole and burgers alike, plus a dozen different salads, and prepare guacamole frescoes tableside. The restaurant's red-painted walls impart a serious vibe, but the well-seasoned food is nothing but fun.

Terrebonne Depot (400 NW Smith Rock Way, Terrebonne, 541/548-5030, 11:30am-8:30pm Mon. and Wed.-Thurs., 11:30am-9:30pm Fri-Sat., 11:30am-9pm Sun., $11-20) is a casual restaurant in a sunny yellow old train depot. Food is simple—cheeseburgers, tacos, good soups—but a solid stop on the way to or from Bend, or after an active day at Smith Rock. The patio opens in nice weather.

Don't worry if you can't see the crust on a 16-inch large pie at **Base Camp Pizza** (8060 11th St., Terrebonne, 541/526-1181, www.bcamppizza.com, 11am-9pm daily, $16-22); it's there, just under a pile of toppings. Many combos are named for the rock climbing at nearby Smith Rock (you deserve a Free Climb pile-on after a big ascent), and there's a gluten-free crust option. Fare is simple, but the sauce and dough are made fresh daily, and outdoor seating is available in summer.

ACCOMMODATIONS

$150-250

Despite its name, **Sisters Motor Lodge** (511 W Cascade Ave., Sisters, 541/549-2551, www.sistersmotorlodge.com, $179-199) is no rundown motel. This charming boutique property dates back to the 1930s. The decor is cluttered but welcoming—think wicker rocking chairs and flowered pillows—and the grounds have a patio and hot tub. The 11 rooms have names like "Granny's Cozy Little Cottage" and "Picket Fences," and the monikers fit. Some rooms come with kitchens.

FivePine Lodge (1021 E Desperado Trail, Sisters, 541/549-5900, http://fivepinelodge.com) has the large, wood-sided exterior of a classic forest lodge, but it's comfortably located close to the highway between Sisters and Bend (yet not so close to the road as to cause annoyance). It has 32 rooms ($219-241) and cabins ($263-318) sprinkled around the property. Decor is classic with clean wood lines and stone accents. Outside is a heated pool, and there's a nightly wine and beer reception, lawn games, and free bike rentals. Minimum stays may apply.

Though Redmond is mostly populated with serviceable chain hotels—most of which make for a comfortable if anonymous overnight—**Eagle Crest Resort** (1522 Cline Falls Rd., Redmond, 541/923-2453, www.eagle-crest.com, $199-241) just east of town has a little more character. The large golf development is a little less woodsy than most other local resorts, but it has a placid lake and outdoor swimming pool, over 1,700 acres, and the Three Sisters looming on the horizon. Its spa boasts an indoor swimming pool topped with exposed wooden beams and a number of treatment rooms for when golfing, hiking, or just vacationing takes its toll on the body. The resort has rooms with private balconies overlooking the links, and most rooms have a separate lounge/sitting area.

Over $250

Like a woodsy Instagram post come to life, ★ **Suttle Lodge** (13300 U.S. 20, Sisters, 541/638-7001, www.thesuttlelodge.com) overlooks placid Suttle Lake to the east of Sisters and boasts adorable cabins, both rustic ($135) and not ($431), along with a big wood lodge with sizable rooms ($297-323). In summer the waterfront boathouse serves delicious fish sandwiches in a bright counter-service space, and the modest bar in the main lodge serves particularly delicious cracker-crust pizzas year-round.

Camping

Located just outside Sisters, **Creekside Campground** (504 S Locust St., Sisters, 541/323-5218, www.ci.sisters.or.us/creekside-campground, Apr.-Nov.) is one of the most convenient spots to set up a tent ($5-20) or camper ($20-45) in the region. The more than 60 sites include both full- and limited-service options, some along Whychus Creek. With its generous tree cover and creek footbridge, the camp feels foresty and lovely despite its closeness to town. In April, the campground operates as first-come, first-served, but reservations can be made over the phone or on the website for other open months.

GETTING THERE

To reach Redmond by car from Bend, take U.S. 97 north for 18 miles. It's a quick drive, just under 30 minutes, thanks to the double lanes and intermittent freeway-style exits that keep traffic moving. To reach Sisters from Bend, take U.S. 20 northwest for 25 miles. The drive takes about 30 minutes.

Roberts Field, the Redmond Municipal Airport (RDM, 2522 SE Jesse Butler Circle, Redmond, 541/548-0646, www.flyrdm.com) serves the area. Car rental services are available at the terminal from six major car rental companies. **Bend Cab Company** (541/389-8090, http://bendcab.com) can take you from the airport to Sisters for $35. Rates from the Redmond airport to destinations in Redmond will vary but should be around $10-15.

Oregon Coast

Look for ★ to find recommended sights, activities, dining, and lodging.

Highlights

★ **Fort Clatsop:** Lewis and Clark finished their epic journey here, where they were greeted by local Native Americans (page 376).

★ **Haystack Rock:** The unofficial symbol of the Oregon Coast is at Cannon Beach, where this photogenic rock also serves as a bird sanctuary (page 381).

★ **Tillamook Cheese Factory:** This warehouse offers views of giant cheese-making and packaging floors, plus endless free samples (page 388).

★ **Oregon Coast Aquarium:** Local sea life is represented well in this giant park with touch tanks and feeding shows (page 400).

★ **Yaquina Head Lighthouse:** Oregon's tallest lighthouse sits nestled within a protected wildlife area (page 400).

★ **Heceta Head Lighthouse:** One of the prettiest lighthouses on the Oregon Coast has something most don't—a bed-and-breakfast inside the keeper's house (page 405).

★ **Hobbit Trail:** A short, magical little hike goes through a charming forest before reaching a stretch of beach that feels blessedly removed from the highway (page 406).

★ **Oregon Dunes National Recreation Area:** The sandy hills that guard Oregon's beaches also serve as an outdoor playground for dune buggies (page 408).

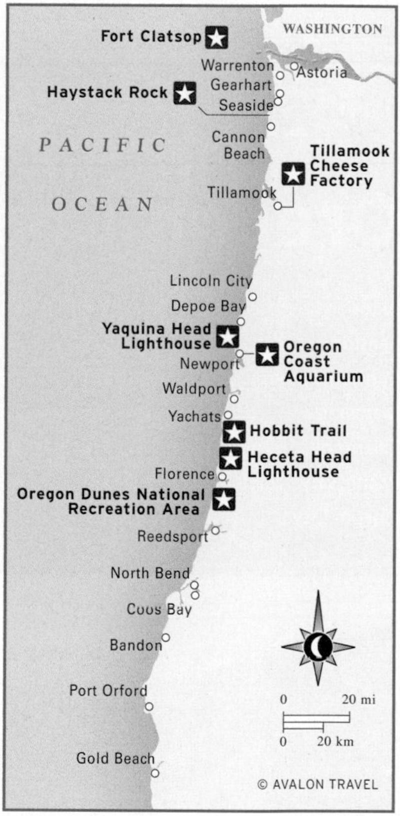

The Oregon Coast is a local point of pride. Its long, moody beaches are open to everyone, so no private landowner can hoard the savage beauty of the Pacific.

Every town dotting the waterfront along U.S. 101, which traces Oregon's coastline from its border with Washington to its border with California, holds its own distinct charm. In historical Astoria at the mouth of the Columbia River, barges still inch up the waterway. Seaside is the carnival town with the beachside promenade, whereas Cannon Beach is a laid-back sandcastle-on-the-beach area. Manzanita is cute and quirky, and Tillamook is the inland town with the great cheese tradition. Pacific City is an out-of-the-way hamlet with an oversized brewery, and Lincoln City has hotels and the world's shortest river. Tiny Depoe Bay is so close to the ocean it almost falls in. That's one reason it sees the most whales. Newport is a big town with big lighthouses, a working waterfront, and a renowned aquarium. Yachats is an unassuming bend in the road, while Florence is a genteel little town near the rolling coastal dunes. Further south there's calm Coos Bay and charming Bandon By the Sea, as it's known.

Of course, there are constants along the Oregon Coast—you'll find saltwater taffy and clam chowder almost everywhere, and wildlife pops up in tide pools and along sandstone cliffs. Lighthouses out here are hardy and necessary—shipwrecks still dot the coastline. You'll want to stay inside for storm-watching in the windy winter months, but that's why they made fireplaces, hot tubs, and chowder. Come summer, kites come out and sandcastles emerge.

PLANNING YOUR TIME

U.S. 101 stretches along Oregon's coast, only rarely wandering a few miles inland, and serves as the major artery of the region. While Cannon Beach or Astoria can be day trips from Portland, to see and experience more of this stretch of rugged coast you'll need at least two days.

It's best to travel the coast in a single direction, north or south. Most attractions are within a mile of the highway. Traffic can clog U.S. 101 during the summer, so it's best to not

Previous: Heceta Head Lighthouse; Haystack Rock; **Above:** Hobbit Trail.

TOP EXPERIENCE

One Day Driving the Oregon Coast

Start the day early in Astoria, at the end of the Columbia River and among classic Victorian houses. Wake up at the **Cannery Pier Hotel** under the **Astoria-Megler Bridge.** Learn a little about the area's history at the **Columbia River Maritime Museum** or the **Flavel House Museum,** or just start driving south on U.S. 101 to hit the beaches.

No shore visit is complete without a stop to see **Haystack Rock,** and the best place to park is in Cannon Beach, just south at **Tolovana Beach Recreation Site.** After poking through some tide pools, hop back on U.S. 101 and continue driving 40 miles south past **Oswald West State Park** and on to Tillamook for a stop at the **Tillamook Cheese Factory.** Those cheese samples will have to tide you over until lunch at **Pelican Pub & Brewery** in Pacific City, 25 miles south.

Back on U.S. 101, drive south for 35 miles through Lincoln City. Then slow down in Depoe Bay to see the smallest harbor in the world. In 10 miles, exit U.S. 101 at NW Lighthouse Drive (north of Newport) and follow it west to see **Yaquina Head Lighthouse,** the tallest lighthouse in the state.

It's only 5 more miles to Newport, where you can visit the **Oregon Coast Aquarium** to see a giant Pacific octopus and puffins.

From Newport, it's 50 miles south on U.S. 101 to Florence to watch the sun set from **Oregon Dunes National Recreation Area.** End the day with a drink at **Waterfront Depot** before heading to a bed at the **River House Inn,** located a short walk away under Florence's bridge. Or if you'd like to make your way further south from the dunes, continue another 50 miles to the charming town of Bandon for dinner at **Edgewaters** and a night at the cozy **Bandon Inn.**

be in a hurry, or to pop east to the Willamette wine country if the roads get too choked for travel. Sunshine is never reliable out here, but snow is almost nonexistent, and winter squalls make for good indoor storm-watching. Ocean views are most plentiful in summer, when the coast is least likely to get socked in. Take care while on bluffs over the beach and climbing rocks along the coast, as surfaces can be slippery and unstable.

Astoria

Sitting at the meeting point between a mighty river and a massive ocean, this historical little town lives and breathes its seagoing heritage. It was named for John Jacob Astor, the fur-trading magnate, whose company founded Fort Astoria only a few years after the Lewis and Clark Expedition hit the Pacific Ocean at nearby Fort Clatsop. Today the town retains many of its early 20th-century buildings and sits as an anchor at the top of the Oregon Coast.

SIGHTS

Astoria Column

From its position at Astoria's highest point, Coxcomb Hill, the 125-foot **Astoria Column** (1 Coxcomb Dr., 503/325-2963, www.astoriacolumn.org, dawn-dusk, $5 per vehicle) has the best view in the city. An Italian American artist was hired to mimic an Italian bas-relief technique that matches the column's inspiration, Trajan's Column in Rome. Images of the area's history spiral the pillar, starting with early Native American settlements and ending with the arrival of the railroad

Oregon Coast

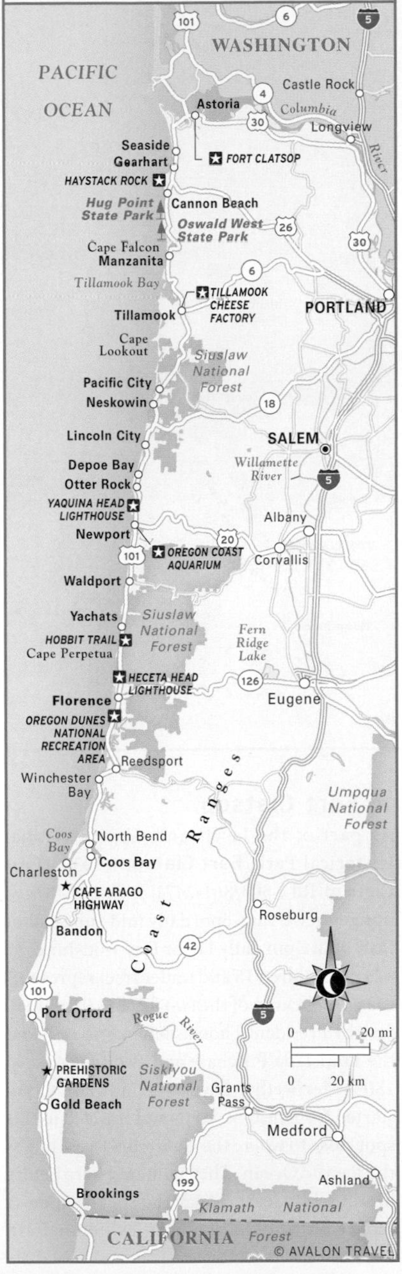

to Astoria. During World War II, the site was a base for a blimp squadron. The sea air is rough on the mural, but a major restoration, costing almost a million dollars, was completed in 2015. Today visitors can climb to a viewing platform at its top to see the Astoria-Megler Bridge, Cape Disappointment, and the Pacific Ocean—if the weather is clear enough, of course.

Astoria-Megler Bridge

At just over 4 miles long, the **Astoria-Megler Bridge** is an impressive expanse. It carries U.S. 101 from Oregon to Washington at the mouth of the Columbia and was the last link completed of the first California-to-Washington route. Winds at the mouth of the Columbia can get as high as 150 miles per hour during storms, but the views from the middle are well worth the pummeling felt by cars and cyclists (no pedestrians allowed).

Columbia River Maritime Museum

The **Columbia River Maritime Museum** (1792 Marine Dr., 503/325-2323, www.crmm.org, 9:30am-5pm daily, $14 adults, $12 seniors, $5 children, children under 6 free) preserves the seagoing and river travel history of Astoria with a museum and research library. Pilot boats and relics from area shipwrecks are a reminder of just how deadly the Columbia Bar has been to sailors. Out back, tethered to a dock, is the lightship ***Columbia,*** the last of five ships with that name to serve as a floating lighthouse. Climb aboard to see the officer's quarters and radio room, and the mess hall where off-duty crew hung out while stationed just five miles off the mouth of the river. Inside, films play at the museum's 3D digital theater. Next door is the **Barbey Maritime Center,** housed in a renovated 1925 railroad depot, offering wooden boat building classes and workshops in nature illustration.

Flavel House Museum

Being a bar pilot, or a captain who guides ships across the mouth of the Columbia River, has

Astoria and Vicinity

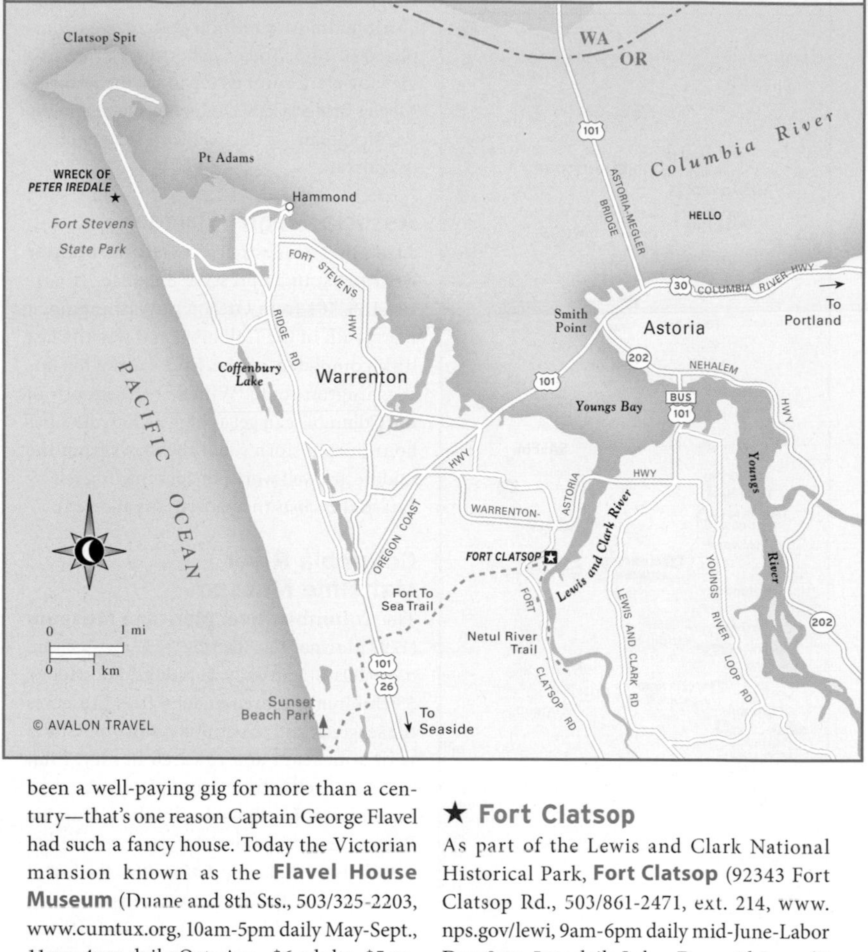

been a well-paying gig for more than a century—that's one reason Captain George Flavel had such a fancy house. Today the Victorian mansion known as the **Flavel House Museum** (Duane and 8th Sts., 503/325-2203, www.cumtux.org, 10am-5pm daily May-Sept., 11am-4pm daily Oct.-Apr., $6 adults, $5 seniors and students, $2 children 6-17, children under 6 free) is part of the Clatsop County Historical Society. The steep roof, wraparound porch, and octagonal tower—so Captain Flavel could keep an eye on boat traffic—are all touches from the Queen Anne architectural style. The roof and verandas still have original wrought-iron casting. Tours include the six fireplaces, music room, library, housekeeping areas, and the carriage house.

★ Fort Clatsop

As part of the Lewis and Clark National Historical Park, **Fort Clatsop** (92343 Fort Clatsop Rd., 503/861-2471, ext. 214, www.nps.gov/lewi, 9am-6pm daily mid-June-Labor Day, 9am-5pm daily Labor Day-mid-June, $5 adults, children 15 and under free) represents the winter camp of the two famous explorers. Sent by President Thomas Jefferson to explore the Louisiana Purchase and Pacific Coast in 1804, Meriwether Lewis and William Clark started from near St. Louis and traveled to this spot close to where the Columbia River meets the Pacific Ocean. They wintered here before heading back east. Today the spot includes a replica of the old fort and an exhibit hall. In the summer season (mid-June-Labor Day), ranger-led programs and costumed rangers bring the old Oregon to life on a daily basis.

From Astoria, drive 3.5 miles south on U.S. 101. Turn left onto Marllin Drive (or U.S. 101 Business) and follow Marllin Drive for about 0.5 mile. When the road dead-ends, turn left and stay on U.S. 101 Business for 2 miles. Turn right onto Fort Clatsop Road to reach the park.

PARKS AND BEACHES

Fort Stevens State Park

In the past, the head of the Columbia River was an important military center. Today **Fort Stevens State Park** (100 Peter Iredale Rd., Hammond, 503/861-1671, www.oregonstate-parks.org, $5 per vehicle) is a recreational area that embraces evidence of its past. It has overgrown military structures, miles of beach (including the wreck of the steel ship ***Peter Iredale***), and swimming areas and picnic tables at Coffenbury Lake.

To reach the park from Astoria, take U.S. 101 for 4.5 miles south, and then turn right on East Harbor Street. After a little more than a mile, turn left onto SW 9th Street in Warrenton. Drive 1 mile and turn right into NW Ridge Road. Follow NW Ridge Road for 2 miles, then turn left into the park.

Cape Disappointment State Park

Despite the name, **Cape Disappointment State Park** (Robert Gray Dr., Ilwaco, 360/642-3029, www.parks.wa.gov/parks, 6:30am-dusk daily, $10 parking) is hardly a letdown. The dramatic piece of land juts into the Pacific Ocean at the mouth of the Columbia River on the Washington side, across from Astoria. A lighthouse that dates back to 1856 is one hardworking beacon of light because the river bar is a hairy point along a coastal stretch known as the Graveyard of the Pacific. A second tower, the North Head Lighthouse, is also within the park.

FOOD

Like the Cannery Pier Hotel next door, the **Bridgewater Bistro** (20 Basin St., 503/325-6777, www.bridgewaterbistro.com, 11:30am-11pm Mon.-Sat., 10:30am-11pm Sun., $15-35) makes the most of its waterfront location in an old boatyard—most tables have river views. The fare is definitely inspired by the water, with salmon, oysters, and fish-and-chips, but includes plenty of steak, duck, and chicken for stubborn landlubbers. Gluten-free options abound, and live jazz bands play on weekend nights.

Fort Clatsop

Plenty of humor is on tap at **Fort George Brewery and Public House** (1483 Duane St., 503/325-7468, www.fortgeorgebrewery.com, 11am-11pm Mon.-Thurs., 11am-midnight Fri.-Sat., noon-11pm Sun., $10-18). They claim the coffee-flavored Working Girl Porter was brewed because the brewers were "looking for a good reason to drink beer in the morning." The public house sits in an old service station building and offers a variety of regular and seasonal beers on tap. Big baskets of fries—made from organic potatoes, of course—and house-made sausages are popular favorites. On weekends be sure to take a tour (1pm or 4pm) of the brewery either before or after eating.

The bar at **Silver Salmon Grille** (1105 Commercial St., 503/338-6640, http://silversalmongrille.com, 11am-10pm daily, $10-20 lunch, $19-33 dinner) is more than 130 years old and made from Scottish wood that had to be shipped on a boat around the world. The restaurant serves well-prepared seafood, oysters, and clam chowder.

The **Columbian Cafe** (1114 Marine Dr., 503/325-2233, www.columbianvoodoo.com, 8am-2pm Mon.-Fri, 9am-2pm Sat.-Sun., $15-20, cash only) is more than just an eatery, though there's plenty of vegetarian fare and seafood in the funky red café. The Voodoo Room event space is known for readings and music performances, while the Columbian Theater movie house, run by the same company, makes it an action-filled stop.

Just across the street from the Columbia River Maritime Museum, **Bowpicker Fish & Chips** (1634 Duane St., 503/791-2942, www.bowpicker.com, 11am-6pm Wed.-Sun. weather permitting, $9-11, cash only) is run out of a red-and-white gillnet boat called the *Columbia*. Lines stretch down the platform built next to the boat, now on a trailer in a gravel parking lot. You come here for one thing—the albacore tuna, fried to a delicate crisp, and a pile of steak fries. About the only choice you have is between tartar sauce and vinegar, or whether you want to split with a friend.

ACCOMMODATIONS

Under $150

The lobby of the renovated **Commodore Hotel** (258 14th St., 503/325-4747, www.commodoreastoria.com, $88-208) is a little bit hip, with a painted-on fireplace and sleek benches, and a little bit maritime in its braided-rope hangings. The building began its hotel history in the 1920s but then closed in the 1960s before reopening in the 21st century. Even where space is tight in the guest rooms, there's design—wall-to-ceiling modernist paintings over the beds stand in for headboards and canopies. Cabin rooms share the hall bathrooms, but rooms are stocked with flashlights for midnight walks to the facilities; suites have their own bathrooms.

Fort Stevens State Park (100 Peter Iredale Rd., Hammond, 503/861-1671, www.oregonstateparks.org, $56 yurts, $100 cabins) offers yurts and cabins for rent.

Cape Disappointment State Park (Robert Gray Dr., Ilwaco, 360/642-3029, www.parks.wa.gov/parks, 6:30am-dusk daily, $10 parking), across the Columbia River on the Washington side, offers yurts and cabins for rent ($69). The lighthouse keeper residence includes a two-story Victorian house ($308-437), complete with library. The seaside rental feels ghostly on the foggy, wet nights that are so common on the Pacific coast.

$150-250

The **Astoria Riverwalk Inn** (400 Industry St., 503/325-2013, http://riverwalkastoria.com, $158-194) is located near the Cannery Pier and Astoria-Megler Bridge. This straightforward hotel may have older furnishings, but the waffle bar and balconies overlooking the water make up for it.

A relic of the 1920s is **Hotel Elliot** (357 12th St., 503/325-2222, www.hotelelliott.com, $189-289), whose 32 rooms include a variety of suites. Many rooms have fireplaces, and all have goose down pillows and heated bathroom floor tiles. In the suites, amenities include Jacuzzi tubs and, in the presidential suite, a two-story apartment with full kitchen and piano. The rooftop terrace has a view of the Columbia River and is accessible to all guests whenever it isn't booked for private events.

Over $250

The **Cannery Pier Hotel** (10 Basin St., 503/325-4996, www.cannerypierhotel.com, $309-399) isn't exactly ostentatious, but its position under the Astoria-Megler Bridge, right on the Columbia River, makes it an oft-photographed site. The industrial shape evokes the cannery that once stood on these pilings, but guests don't rough it—every room has a balcony with a river view, a fireplace, and a dining table, and wine and lox are served every evening in the lobby. Retro bicycles are free for guests to use along the riverfront.

GETTING THERE

From downtown Portland, head west on U.S. 26, also known as the Sunset Highway. U.S. 26 intersects U.S. 101 in about 75 miles, between Cannon Beach and Seaside. Follow U.S. 101 north for 20 miles to reach Astoria. The last mile includes a beautiful drive across Youngs Bay, with views of the Columbia River. Alternately, take I-5 north for 46 miles to Longview, and then follow U.S. 30 west for 50 miles to Astoria. Both routes take just under 2 hours.

From Forks on the Olympic Peninsula, U.S. 101 continues south for 185 miles through rural southwest Washington to Astoria; the drive takes about 3.5 hours. It's 77 miles from Aberdeen to Astoria. The road sideswipes Willapa Bay, known for its oysters, and the long, skinny Long Beach Peninsula, which is dotted with the beach towns of Seaview, Long Beach, and Ocean Park.

Greyhound (800/231-2222, www.greyhound.com) runs bus service on some sections of U.S. 101, such as between Astoria (900 Marine Dr., 503/861-7433, 7:30am-6pm Mon.-Fri., 7am-6pm Sat.-Sun.) to Cannon Beach (187 E Madison St., 503/436-2623).

Seaside

While Astoria is crammed with history and Cannon Beach has amazing beaches, Seaside is a quintessential beach town. This is where you find saltwater taffy and arcade games and a history of beauty pageants (the Miss Oregon Pageant happens here). It may not be the fanciest stop on the coast, but Seaside still has classic appeal.

SIGHTS

Promenade

The seaside **Promenade** (Ave. U to 12th Ave.) is a century-old, 8,000-foot-long boardwalk right on Seaside Beach—that's 1.5 miles of flat, paved walking surface. At a turnaround at the end of Broadway is a Lewis and Clark memorial. In August, the Hood to Coast relay ends here. The 200-mile race begins in the mountains and is the longest relay race in the world.

Seaside Carousel

The **Seaside Carousel** (300 Broadway St., 503/738-6728, www.seasidecarouselmall.com, 9am-9:30pm daily summer, hours vary fall, winter, and spring, $2.50) isn't quite as old as it looks. It has a classic carnival look but was built in 1990. Many of the seats are made to resemble animals like rabbits, cats, and bears. The mall that surrounds the indoor carousel was built on the site of an old dance hall. Shops include a hat store and a candy spot, one of many places to find bin after bin of saltwater taffy.

For something more historical, try the bumper cars at **Interstate Amusement** (110 Broadway St., $0.50-1.25), where you can ride in the classic cars, play 10 holes of putt-putt golf, and eat a corndog. It's "open whenever there is a crowd."

SHOPPING

Saltwater taffy is sold everywhere on the Oregon Coast, but **Phillip's Candies** (217 Broadway St., 503/738-5402, www.phillipscandies.com, 10am-9pm Sun.-Thurs., 10am-10pm Fri.-Sat.) has a particularly delicious array, including a lime saltwater variety alongside the usual vanilla, strawberry, and peppermint. The store has been around since the 19th century, and there's a classic simplicity to the fudge flavors and lollipops.

FOOD

Tsunami Sandwich Company (11 Broadway St., 503/738-5427, opens 11am "most days," www.tsunamisandwiches.com, $8-14) is close to the beach and an easy place to grab food for a picnic. Tsunami bypasses the Oregon chowder competition by serving Ivar's clam chowder from Seattle, but the chili is homemade, and the ice cream is from Tillamook. Be forewarned when asking for extra meat—the MegaTsunami uses a full pound of pastrami. The store has a corner marked "Tsunami Info Zone" with maps of evacuation zones and a mural of the Lewis and Clark memorial just outside being dwarfed by a giant wave. Ask about the storm-watching tours led by the store's owner.

ACCOMMODATIONS

Some rooms at the **Sandy Cove Inn** (241 Ave. U, 503/738-7473, www.sandycoveinn.net, $169-199) have special themes—a Monopoly room has a game board painted on the wall, and a vintage game room has classic games as decor. The inn is a few blocks from the south end of the Promenade in a fairly residential neighborhood, a good 10 minutes by foot to Broadway. But the cozy motel shows off a calmer side of Seaside, and service is attentive.

True to its name, **The Inn at the Prom** (341 S Promenade, 800/507-2714, www.innatprom.com, $169-249) is right on the beach so waterfront rooms have an unobstructed view of the water. Rooms have two-person jetted tubs and fireplaces, while others have full kitchens or kitchenettes; some rooms can feel crowded with the giant pillow-top beds and foldout sofas. The small hotel is dwarfed by some of the bigger properties nearby, but the property is updated and has nice amenities. A gas barbecue is available for guest use along with chairs and beach toys outside.

Seaside Carousel

GETTING THERE

Seaside is about 17 miles south of Astoria on U.S. 101. From U.S. 101, take a right on Broadway, and then cross the Necanicum River to immediately reach downtown and the Promenade (watch for one-way streets). From the south, Seaside is 9 miles from Cannon Beach. From Portland, take U.S. 26 (a.k.a. the Sunset Highway) east from Portland. Turn right when U.S. 26 dead-ends into U.S. 101, 4 miles south of Seaside.

Cannon Beach

The big rock in the middle of this sandy stretch is one of the most photographed landmarks in the state. This is the kind of beach Oregon has become famous for, with soft, dense sand, scattered rocks, and enough wind for a good kite flight. Inches inland is shopping, a thriving small-town theater, and fine seafood dining.

SIGHTS

★ Haystack Rock

Guess what shape **Haystack Rock** (near S Hemlock and Pacific Sts.) is? Yep, the 235-foot basalt monolith is wide at the bottom and slightly pointed on top, one of the biggest and most recognizable rocks on Oregon's coast. If you visit just one section of the state's stretches of coastal sand, this should be it; the photo opportunities are classics. Tide pools around its base teem with sand dollars and anemones. When the tide is at its lowest, beach access to the rock is possible; however, would-be climbers should stay off the nesting refuge, populated by tufted puffins and other birds (and high tides still sometimes strand people on the rock). Around sunset, groups often make beach fires from piles of driftwood to stay warm in the chilly maritime air.

SPORTS AND RECREATION

Parks and Beaches

These parks—listed from north to south along U.S. 101—are the best places to access the beach.

ECOLA STATE PARK

On Tillamook Head between Cannon Beach and Seaside is **Ecola State Park** (Ecola State Park Rd., 503/436-2844, www.oregonstateparks.org, $5 per vehicle), protecting a bluff with killer views and picnic spots. William Clark, of the Lewis and Clark Expedition, sang its praises in his journal when he passed the area while looking for a beached whale. Trails wind through the waterfront area, and you can see the ghostly, abandoned Tillamook Rock Light just offshore. Just over a mile away on a small basalt rock, it got the nickname "Terrible Tilly"—not only was it incredibly

Cannon Beach

difficult to build, but an English vessel was shipwrecked right next to the lighthouse just days before it was lit for the first time. The expensive lighthouse was deactivated in the 1950s, and it is now privately owned as a repository for human ashes.

HAYSTACK HILL STATE PARK

Haystack Rock is one of the coast's most popular destinations, but **Haystack Hill State Park** (E Chena St. and S Hemlock St.) is seldom visited, even by locals. The state park is located between U.S. 101 and the beach, right across from Haystack Rock. Trails lead to an excellent viewpoint, the trees are thick, and it can feel like you've found an island of wilderness in the middle of residential Cannon Beach.

TOLOVANA BEACH RECREATION SITE

Tolovana Beach Recreation Site (W Warren Way and S Hemlock St., 503/436-2844, www.oregonstateparks.org) is the best place to access the sand in Cannon Beach. Less than a mile south of Haystack Rock, the wayside offers lots of parking—though hardly enough on busy summer weekends—and a ramp down the short bluff to the beach. It also has a bathroom and a small playground. **Mo's** (195 W Warren Way, 503/436-1111, www.moschowder.com, 11am-8pm Sun.-Thurs., 11am-9pm Fri.-Sat., $7-17), across the parking lot, is good for meals, but most of the other businesses here are hotels. On the beach, look for tufted puffins, a common sight since they nest on Haystack Rock. Several of the streets between Tolovana and Haystack Rock are named for Alaskan Rivers—Matanuska, Susitna, Chisana—but Tolovana gets its name from a hot springs in the Alaskan interior.

ARCADIA BEACH STATE RECREATION SITE

South of Tolovana Beach is **Arcadia Beach State Recreation Site** (U.S. 101 near S Park Ave., 503/368-3575, www.oregonstateparks.org), with access to a mile-long beach between Hug Point and Humbug Point. At low tide, you can pass Humbug Point and continue another 0.5 mile north to Silver Point. There are sandstone cliffs to the east. The parking area has picnic tables and bathrooms.

HUG POINT STATE RECREATION SITE

At **Hug Point State Recreation Site** (U.S. 101 near Hug Point Rd., 503/368-3575,

Ecola State Park

Cannon Beach

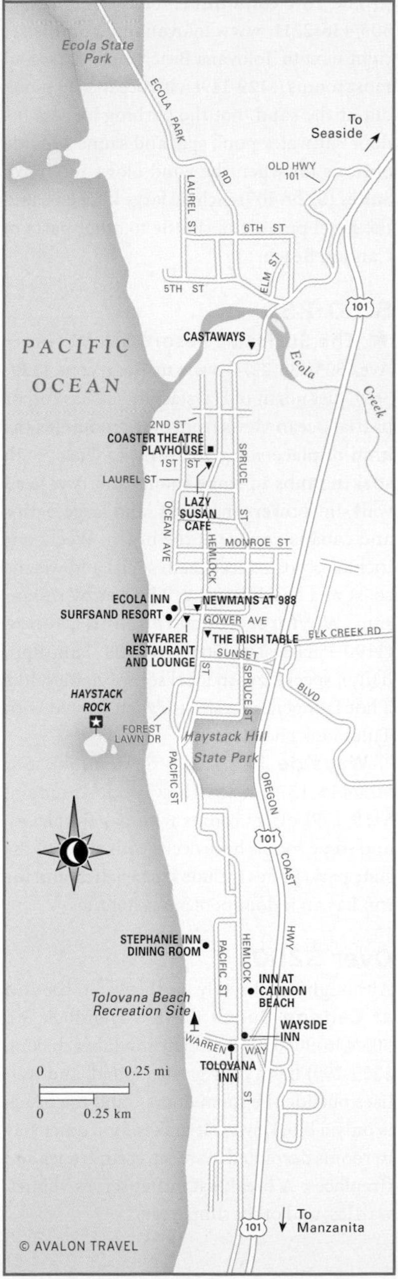

www.oregonstateparks.org) are traces of the old stagecoach road that followed the Oregon Coast. The area is named for the point where the trail hugged the rocks to get around a headland. The beach has access to sandstone cliffs, small caves, and a waterfall. There are picnic tables and a bathroom at the parking lot.

ENTERTAINMENT AND EVENTS

Although the town is chock-full of second homes and vacation rentals, a small-town theater scene is thriving at the **Coaster Theatre Playhouse** (108 N Hemlock St., 503/436-1242, www.coastertheatre.com, $20-25). The onetime roller rink now has a stage for classic musicals and popular Christmas shows, a warm entertainment option on the common rainy days on the Oregon Coast.

FOOD

Sure, the decor at **Lazy Susan Café** (126 N Hemlock St., 503/436-2816, www.lazy-susan-cafe.com, 8am-3pm Wed.-Mon. spring-summer, 8am-2:30pm Wed.-Mon. fall-winter, $7-14) is warm, with antiques on shelves, wood-paneled walls, and laminated tablecloths, but one sign does read, "Be Nice or Leave." The breakfast and lunch spot specializes in quiches and salads, but most exciting are the marionberry scones that are bigger than the plates.

Located in a swanky hotel on a quiet strip of beach, ★ **Stephanie Inn Dining Room** (2740 S Pacific St., 503/436-2221, www.stephanie-inn.com, 5:30pm-9pm daily, $33-50) goes for the immersive dining experience. Unlike most of the hotel rooms in the building, the dining room doesn't even face the ocean. The focus instead is the four-course menu that changes each night, often featuring local seafood paired with Washington and Oregon wines. Reservations are required, and meals aren't rushed.

Despite being just feet from the Pacific Ocean, ★ **Newmans at 988** (988 S Hemlock

St., 503/436-1151, www.newmansat988.com, 5pm-9pm daily July-Oct., 5pm-9pm Tues.-Sun. Oct.-June, $24-39) specializes in French-Italian cuisine, most notably food from the Piedmont and Genoa areas—like lobster ravioli, chicken marsala pasta, and duck breast. White tablecloths and fresh single roses add elegance to the small space, which is decorated with stained-glass pieces. Reservations are necessary because there are only a handful of tables and the chef-owner boasts a good local reputation, with multiple James Beard House appearances to his name.

Although the cuisine at **The Irish Table** (1235 S Hemlock St., 503/436-0708, www.theirishtablerestaurant.com, 5:30pm-9pm Fri.-Tues., $15-37) is appropriately inspired by the Emerald Isle, it isn't soda bread and potatoes—think lamb stew or chicken pasties, plus mussels, a cheese board, and salads. The beer and whiskey selection may be the most Irish thing about the spot. The space is a café and coffee roaster during the day, and it gets crowded at night; call ahead to get on the waitlist.

With a menu crammed with jambalaya and jerk chicken, **Castaways** (316 Fir St., 503/436-4444, 5pm-9pm Wed.-Sun., $20-33) evokes beach cultures around the world, not just Oregon's cold and windy ones. Cajun flavors meet popular mai tais, but yes—there is also a rich seafood chowder. The bright walls compete with the colors on the plate.

ACCOMMODATIONS

Under $150

The simplest rooms at **Ecola Inn** (1164 Ecola Ct., 503/436-2457, www.ecolainn.com, $127-145) have little more than standard beds and a few seaside decorations—paintings of seashells and such—but the waterfront location in front of Haystack Rock is the real appeal. The property is family run and almost 75 years old with 13 rooms; all have full kitchens, and some have fireplaces. The hotel closes in the dead of winter, save a short holiday season. Rooms rent by the night and week, and it's rare for any to be available in the summer season, but the hotel posts cancellations online.

The **Tolovana Inn** (3400 S Hemlock St., 503/436-2211, www.tolovanainn.com) is set right next to Tolovana Beach State Park, and most rooms ($129-149) with ocean views look out at the sand, not the parking lot. An indoor saltwater pool, spa, and sauna provide options for when the wind blows too hard. Suites ($229-409) include large kitchens, and the hotel provides a shuttle to other parts of Cannon Beach.

$150-250

★ **The Surfsand Resort** (148 W Gower Ave., 503/436-2274, www.surfsand.com, $129-369), just north of Haystack Rock, has full or partial ocean views from every room. It's the kind of place you don't want to leave, with soaking tubs in some rooms and two-head walk-in showers in others, and large patios and cabana service at the beach. Weekends include a hosted ice cream social and weenie roast at a beach bonfire. The nearby restaurant, **Wayfarer Restaurant and Lounge** (1190 Pacific Dr., 503/436-1108, 8am-9pm daily), specializes in local sea specialties, like a hot Dungeness crab sandwich topped with Tillamook cheddar.

Wayside Inn (3339 S Hemlock St., 503/436-1577, www.thewayside-inn.com, $159-259) offers rooms with gas fireplaces, and some rooms have decks with views of the state park. Suites include kitchenettes, and the inn has an indoor pool and a hot tub.

Over $250

Although not directly on the water, the **Inn at Cannon Beach** (3215 S Hemlock St., 503/436-9085, www.innatcannonbeach.com, $259-299) has a cozy garden, pond, and trellises outside the room doors—and the beach is only a block away. It makes for a quiet stay in rooms decorated in warm, earthy tones and fireplaces. A breakfast buffet serves yogurt, waffles, and other simple eats.

GETTING THERE

Cannon Beach is a short drive from Seaside, only 9 miles south on U.S. 101. Elin Avenue "exits" off 101 lead to Cannon Beach: The Sunset Boulevard turnoff goes to the more commercial north end of town, and Warren Beach Road heads straight to Tolovana Beach south of Haystack Rock. From the south, reach Cannon Beach by following U.S. 101 for 14.5 miles from Manzanita.

To reach Cannon Beach from Portland, take U.S. 26, also called the Sunset Highway, east from downtown Portland. U.S. 26 hits U.S. 101 about 4 miles north of Cannon Beach; take a left and start looking for Cannon Beach signs.

Greyhound (800/231-2222, www.greyhound.com) runs bus service on some sections of U.S. 101, such as between Astoria (900 Marine Dr., 503/861-7433, 7:30am-6pm Mon.-Fri., 7am-6pm Sat.-Sun.) to Cannon Beach (187 E Madison St., 503/436-2623).

Manzanita

The small town of Manzanita may be the most casually chic town on the Oregon Coast, its small commercial area dotted with boutiques and higher-end hotels. And yet the dining, while good, is mostly casual. The town is sandwiched between Neahkahnie Mountain and Nehalem Bay and is a favorite site for posh second homes. Of course, it's still the Oregon Coast, so the town is quaint and fairly unassuming. U.S. 101 only brushes the side of the town, so don't miss the turnoff, right next to a tight bend in the highway.

SPORTS AND RECREATION

Parks and Beaches

The 4-mile sand spit of **Nehalem Bay State Park** (9500 Sandpiper Ln., 503/986-0707, www.oregonstateparks.org, $5 per vehicle) keeps the park isolated. The dunes and shore pines—planted to secure the sand—surround day-use areas, a playground, and a campground. The beaches are popular for people hunting for washed-up treasure from cargo ships and from the area's former beeswax industry.

Oswald West State Park (U.S. 101 near milepost 39, 503/368-3575, www.oregonstateparks.org, free) is located about 4.5 miles north of Manzanita. U.S. 101 cuts right through it, and there are a few parking areas directly on the main road. It's a heavily wooded park but with beach access, about a half mile from the road, that's very popular with surfers. A bridge crosses Short Sand Creek just before the beach. The park protects 13 miles of coastline and many groves of western red cedar, western hemlock, and Sitka spruce trees. Recent tree falls, including one tree 11 feet in diameter, worried officials enough that overnight camping is no longer permitted in the park.

Hiking

NEAHKAHNIE MOUNTAIN TRAIL

Distance: 3 miles round-trip
Duration: 2 hours
Elevation gain: 900 feet
Effort: moderate
Trailhead: Use the South Neahkahnie Mountain Trailhead, located up a short road between mileposts 41 and 42 on U.S. 101.

The Neahkahnie Mountain Trail, just north of Manzanita and inside Oswald West State Park, is one of the most popular on the Oregon Coast, with views of headlands and the waves far below. From the southern trailhead, you'll hike up switchbacks and past a radio facility to the top of Neahkahnie Mountain, at 1,600 feet, and find breathtaking vistas. Keep an eye peeled, as rumor has it Spanish sailors stashed riches nearby (but don't dig—the rumors are persistent enough that digging for treasure is prohibited in the area). From the summit, return the way you came; though the trail does continue, it ends up at the North Neahkahnie Mountain Trailhead, and you'd need to walk south on U.S. 101 for a mile, a hazardous proposition, to reach your starting point.

SHOPPING

The beach may require nothing more than a bathing suit and a warm sweatshirt, but **Syzygy** (447 Laneda Ave., 503/368-7573, www.syzygymanzanita.com, 10am-5pm daily) can outfit shoppers for most occasions. The walls of this small-town boutique are different vivid colors. Their clothes are just as bright, and many are the kind of funky pieces that serve as both wardrobe staple and vacation souvenir. There are also high-end rain boots and raincoats. Home decor, while limited, is rarely along the beachy, seashell-and-anchor spectrum, tending more toward cheery paintings and mirrors.

Salt and Paper (411 Laneda Ave., 503/368-7887, 9am-6pm daily) is located in a house with worn wooden siding and behind a picket fence and vine-covered arbor—about as charming as a seaside cottage gets. The wares for sale have just as much charm. The front porch is crowded with flowerpots and hanging decorations, birdbaths and patio furniture. Inside are stationery and art supplies, plus the ubiquitous saltwater taffy.

Dogs are popular companions along the Oregon Coast. Many hotels accommodate pooches and even shower them with special gifts. The store **Four Paws on the Beach** (144 Laneda Ave., 503/368-3436, www.fourpawsonthebeach.com, 10am-5pm daily) specializes in spoiling canines and sells organic and specialty dog food, collars and leashes, plus gifts for pet owners. And, even more a gift for humans are the doggie costumes with skirts and headpieces. Better in concept, perhaps, than execution.

FOOD

Manzanita's central **Manzanita Coffee Co.** (60 Laneda Ave., 503/368-2233, 7am-9pm daily) serves the only thing better than a beach latte—doughnuts and ice cream. The doughnuts, croissants, and apple fritters are big and doughy, and the Tillamook ice cream case is a popular destination on sunny beach days. The bench outside is helpful because lines go out the door on weekends and in summer.

Only the **San Dune Pub** (127 Laneda Ave., 503/368-5080, www.sandunepub.com, 11:30am-10pm Mon.-Sat., 11:30am-9pm Sun., $7-16) would describe its location in relation to the nearest popular surf spot (Oswald West State Park, 10 miles away), rather than the town of Manzanita. The redbrick pub has 17 beers on tap and TVs playing big sports games. There's an outdoor patio for when it's warm and a wood-burning fireplace indoors for when it's not. More than a dozen kinds of burgers are on the menu, and fries can be covered in Tillamook cheese. Food is simple but well prepared—solid pub fare. The pub hosts live music on weekends, and it's popular with locals, surfer or not.

The small dining area at **Marzano's Pizza** (60 Laneda Ave., 503/368-3663, www.marzanospizza.com, 4pm-8:30pm Sun.-Tues. and Thurs., 4pm-9pm Fri.-Sat., $12-29) is nowhere near big enough for all the people who come for its bubbly pizza. The offerings are straightforward—pizza, calzones, and salads—and toppings are the usual combination of vegetables and meat, though the restaurant does make its own sausage. The most popular pizza is a roasted vegetable concoction, served only until they run out of fresh veggies. No alcohol is served in the restaurant, but it is available to go, and many families come for the takeout.

The ★ **Big Wave Cafe** (822 Laneda Ave., 503/368-9283, www.oregonsbigwavecafe.com, 8am-8pm Sun.-Thurs., 8am-9pm Fri.-Sat., $8-21) is a casual restaurant specializing in simple seafood preparations. A blackboard notes where every kind of seafood was caught.

Salads, burgers, and gourmet sandwiches round out the menu. And since the chef's wife is a pastry chef, desserts are house-made; the manager is their son. The interior is casual but the food is some of the best in town.

ACCOMMODATIONS

Under $150

Spindrift Inn (114 Laneda Ave., 503/368-1001, www.spindrift-inn.com, $109-225) is a cheery motel in the middle of Manzanita, its yellow shingle sides complementing white brick and blue trim. It was built in 1946, and though the interiors used to have all the lace touches and flowered bedspreads of eras past, recent renovations have added solid-color palettes and updated window treatments to the TVs and wireless Internet. Some rooms have kitchenettes and a sleeper sofa. The location is convenient, only a few blocks from the ocean but close to Manzanita's eateries. It doesn't offer late check-in, so get to the front desk by 8pm. Some rooms are pet friendly, and the inn has an interior flower garden.

The name doesn't lie—the **Sunset Surf Motel** (248 Ocean Rd., 503/368-5224, www.sunsetsurfocean.com, $85-169) gets a dead-on view of both the waves and the sunsets, though a road does pass between the motel and the beach. Still, the lawn and picnic tables and heated outdoor pool pretty up the view. Balconies run along the waterfront side of the motel, but you can still see the water from most rooms. Some rooms have gas fireplaces or nearly full kitchens. The 40 rooms are newly updated but still have a small-town charm. It's as nice as motels get.

It's not a misspelling: It's the **San Dune Inn** (428 Dorcas Ln., 503/368-5163, www.sandune-inn-manzanita.com, $135-155), not the Sand Dune Inn. Located just a block off the main street in Manzanita, the 14-room hotel is run by a British hotelier at a laid-back pace. About half the rooms are simple one-room units, while the others have separate bedrooms and full kitchens. The amenities are pretty bare bones, with no fancy TVs or DVD players, but there is a guest grilling area and beach chairs for the short walk to the sand—plus Frisbees, volleyballs, and bikes. Many rooms are pet friendly. Even though the rooms have some head-scratching design combinations, the service is friendly and personal.

$150-250

The ★ **Inn at Manzanita** (67 Laneda Ave., 503/368-6754, www.innatmanzanita.com, $179-225) is less a hotel than a collection of 13 small getaways. Each room has a private deck, double jetted tub, and fireplace, and the grounds are carefully maintained to give a sense of privacy between the trees and shrubbery. Many rooms have vaulted ceilings and hardwood floors. Although at one time the hotel only accepted families with children in certain rooms, policies have changed—but it still has the feel of a romantic retreat. (Walkways and trails on the hotel grounds are a little too delicate for rowdy children.) The beach is only a block away, and the stores and restaurants of Manzanita are right across the street.

Over $250

Despite just six units at **Coast Cabins** (635 Laneda Ave., 800/435-1269, www.coastcabins.com, $225-495), four have hot tubs and all have full kitchens or kitchenettes. Some have personal dry saunas and steam showers, and some have private barbecues. All are close to the cozy communal fire pit. A gym is on the property, and the **Spa Manzanita** (144 Laneda Ave., 503/368-4777, www.spamanzanita.com) is nearby, offering face and body treatments. The complex also includes an art gallery, which features contemporary art from Northwest artists. There are plenty of luxury touches, from granite countertops to featherbeds to teak lounge chairs, and lots of privacy.

Camping

The large campground at **Nehalem Bay State Park** (9500 Sandpiper Ln., 503/986-0707, www.oregonstateparks.org) includes 265 electrical and water sites ($29), 18 rentable yurts ($45-55), walk-in sites for hikers and bikers ($6), and hot showers. Got a private plane and no place to pitch a tent? There is also a 2,400-foot airstrip and dedicated fly-in sites ($11).

GETTING THERE

Manzanita is situated on U.S. 101, 15 miles south of Cannon Beach and 27 miles north of Tillamook.

Tillamook

The name is synonymous with cheese, and the rich countryside is a peek at the rich farming heritage of the state. The town is also home to the biggest wooden structure in the world, which was constructed to hold blimps in World War II. What's striking about Tillamook is how different it feels from the wind-blown seaside towns to the north and south. It's only just inland, on sloughs at the base of Tillamook Bay, but it might as well be the center of Oregon.

SIGHTS

Tillamook Air Museum

The wooden hangar that holds the **Tillamook Air Museum** (6030 Hangar Rd., 503/842-1130, www.tillamookair.com, 10am-5pm daily, $9.75 adults, $8.75 seniors, $6.50 children 6-17, $2.50 children under 6) is gargantuan for a reason—it was built to hold a fleet of blimps for the U.S. Navy in World War II. The space encloses seven acres, and the ceiling is 15 stories high. Inside are flight and war artifacts, rooms devoted to helium and engines, and dozens of aircraft. The Mini-Guppy parked outside, a fat plane built by Boeing, once carried NASA spacecraft. Even with enough exhibits to fill a few hours, the museum only takes up a small part of its massive hangar home.

★ Tillamook Cheese Factory

A million people every year trek to the **Tillamook Cheese Factory** (4175 U.S. 101, 503/815-1300, www.tillamook.com, 8am-6pm daily Labor Day to mid-June, 8am-8pm daily mid-June to Labor Day, free), drawn from all corners with the promise of free cheese.

Tillamook Cheese Factory

Tillamook Air Museum

Samples include small bits of Tillamook's signature cheddar and varieties like pepper jack, plus squeaky cheese curds. Just as popular an attraction is the ice cream stand selling cheap scoops of Tillamook ice cream. The factory also has views of the cheese production floors and the bright copper and silver equipment where production lines run around the clock. The most famous business on the coast, Tillamook is actually a cooperative; Tillamook County Creamery Association is owned by the farmers that provide the cream for cheese making, and has been for more than 100 years. Its famous blue-and-white building underwent recent renovations, reopening in 2018 with a new visitor center and tasting room.

Tillamook County Pioneer Museum

The **Tillamook County Pioneer Museum** (2106 2nd St., 503/842-4553, www.tcpm.org, 10am-4pm Tues.-Sun., $4 adults, $3 seniors, $1 children 10-17, children under 10 free) endeavors to preserve the area's history beyond its cheese accomplishments. It's located in an old courthouse downtown, a dignified building in a rather well-worn town. The museum's 45,000-item collection includes remnants from prehistoric times, relics from when Tillamook tribes lived in the area, and thousands of photographs of the farming and tourism roots of the area. The place has an old-timey feel to it, and exhibits are quaint but fascinating—stuffed and mounted animals on one floor and Civil War artifacts on the next. A case shows off the glass floats that sometimes appear on Oregon beaches, some from the other side of the Pacific.

FOOD AND ACCOMMODATIONS

The specials at **Blue Moon Café** (2014 2nd St., 503/354-5444, 9:30am-3:30pm Mon.-Fri., $10-14) are scrawled on a whiteboard—burgers, pizzas, and various shrimp and oyster dishes. The baked goods at the small eatery include homemade scones and pies, often using local marionberries and huckleberries. Greasy, hot sandwiches come with chips and a friendly attitude. It's also a good coffee shop with various mixed beverages and espresso milkshakes. The smell of grease hangs in the air, but at least it's tasty grease.

The town isn't known for luxury accommodations, but the **Ashley Inn of Tillamook** (1722 Makinster Rd., 503/842-7599, www.ashleyinntillamook.com, $125-170) has some of the best rooms available. There's an indoor saltwater pool, a hot tub, and a sauna, and the complimentary breakfast includes hot entrées. Some rooms have sofa beds, and all regular beds have memory-foam mattresses. The location is convenient, and the RV parking lot has 20 water and electrical hookups.

The **Shilo Inn Suites Hotel** (2515 N Main St., 503/842-7971, www.shiloinns.com, $134-164), located on the Wilson River in the middle of town, is a straightforward hotel with a small indoor swimming pool, steam room, and hot tub. Some rooms have

Side Trip: Three Capes Loop

The 50-mile Three Capes Loop is a scenic detour with stops at particularly beautiful points on the coast.

START: TILLAMOOK, INLAND ON U.S. 101

Cape Meares: 14 miles

In Tillamook, drive west on Highway 131 (this is called 3rd Street in town) and follow it northwest for 13.5 miles to **Cape Meares Lighthouse** (503/842-2244, Cape Meares, www.capemeares-lighthouse.org, 11am-4pm Mon.-Thurs., 11am-6pm Fri.-Sun., closed 2pm-2:30pm daily, May-Sept., free). The short, squat lighthouse was built in 1889 and features a Fresnel lens. A short trail passes by interpretive signs, viewpoints, and the Octopus Tree, a 250-year-old Sitka spruce with limbs that bend at right angles.

Leaving the park, follow Bayshore Drive south for 2.5 miles to Oceanside, where the road becomes Cape Meares Loop. Turn right on Pacific Avenue and stop for a snack at **Roseanna's Café** (1490 Pacific Ave. NW, 503/842-7351, http://roseannascafe.com, 11am-8pm Mon. and Thurs.-Fri., 10am-8pm Sat.-Sun., $9-32), located in a century-old wooden building, with plenty of seafood to match the waterfront location. After lunch, continue walking north along Pacific Avenue to explore **Oceanside Beach State Recreation Site** (1790-1798 Rosenberg Loop, 503/842-3182, www.oregonstateparks.org, year-round). Walk up the beach and look for a tunnel in the rocks that leads to the next beach, the aptly named Tunnel Beach (only accessible at low tide).

Cape Lookout: 8 miles

From Oceanside, follow Highway 131 south for 2.5 miles to the town of Netarts. Turn right on Netarts Bay Drive and follow it for 8 miles to **Cape Lookout State Park** (11645 Whiskey Creek Rd., 503/842-4981, www.oregonstateparks.org, $5 per vehicle). The park lies on a sand spit with quick beach access and more than 8 miles of trails as well as yurts ($44), a cabin ($88), and campsites ($21-29).

Cape Kiwanda: 12 miles

Leaving Netarts, follow Cape Lookout Road south for a little more than 3 miles. Turn right onto Sandlake Road and drive 8 miles to **Cape Kiwanda State Natural Area** (Hungry Harbor Rd. and McPhillips Dr., 503/842-3182, www.oregonstateparks.org), where **Pelican Pub & Brewery** (33180 Cape Kiwanda Dr., 503/965-7007, pelicanbrewing.com, 8am-10pm Sun.-Thurs., 8am-11pm Fri.-Sat., $12-24) marks your final stop on this detour. Grab a cream ale or an IPA and enjoy it on one of the patio tables outside. The microbrewery also serves yummy burgers, seafood, and pizza (in case your lunch has worn off).

END: TILLAMOOK (25 MILES) OR LINCOLN CITY (20 MILES)

To complete the loop, return to U.S. 101 by taking Cape Kiwanda Drive south for 1 mile. Turn left onto Pacific Avenue, and then make an immediate right onto Brooten Road, just after the bridge. Follow Brooten Road for 2.5 miles to U.S. 101. Take U.S. 101 north for 25 miles back to Tillamook, or drive south for 20 miles to Lincoln City to continue exploring the coast.

kitchenettes, and all are good-sized, but the furniture hasn't been updated in a while. Still, it's a decent stopping place. The attached restaurant is a greasy spoon with a bacon-wrapped hot dog and deep-fried onion rings on the menu.

GETTING THERE

Tillamook is located on U.S. 101, about 40 miles south of Cannon Beach and 44 miles north of Lincoln City. To venture inland, take Highway 6 east from Tillamook to where it intersects with U.S. 26 to reach Portland.

Pacific City

Tucked away off the main road, Pacific City is a nice place to take it slow. The town's biggest attraction is a pub and brewery, plus the beach that's just steps away.

SIGHTS

Cape Kiwanda

Call it the second most famous big rock on the Oregon Coast. Of course, the giant formation is called Haystack Rock, just like the one in Cannon Beach, so the area is better known as **Cape Kiwanda State Natural Area** (Hungry Harbor Rd. and McPhillips Dr., 503/842-3182, www.oregonstateparks.org, free). This rock is removed from the coast, but the cape has a large beach and is close to where small boats head into the Pacific to fish. It's a good beach for kite flying and beach walks. North past the headland, the beach quickly peters out at high tide, so head south for a long walk since the sand continues all the way down to Bob Straub State Park, where the Nestucca River empties into the Pacific.

SHOPPING

Pacific City Gallery (35350 Brooten Rd., 503/965-7181, 11am-4pm Thurs.-Sun.) isn't on the beach but across the river near the Pacific City Inn. The building has a wide porch that faces the highway. Inside it has, unsurprisingly, seascapes and glass-float art, plus woodcarvings, glass sculptures, and jewelry. The walls are crowded with pieces by Pacific Northwest artists. They also sell prints.

FOOD

The ★ **Pelican Pub & Brewery** (33180 Cape Kiwanda Dr., 503/965-7007, pelicanbrewing.com, 8am-10pm Sun.-Thurs., 8am-11pm Fri.-Sat., $12-24) is the real reason to leave the main road to travel up to Pacific City. It's so close to the beach that the outdoor patio tables are practically in the surf. The microbrewery was opened in 1996 and has a full slate of beers—a cream ale, an IPA, and the Imperial Pelican Ale. Four rounds of seasonal beers rotate through. The pub serves seafood entrées, burgers, and pizzas loaded with local shrimp, cheese, and veggies. The menus point out beer pairings, and a number of dishes actually use the beer itself to batter the onion rings or flavor the brownie sundae.

The other beach food in town is at **Doryland Pizza** (33315 Cape Kiwanda Dr., 503/965-6299, www.capekiwandarvresort.com, 11:30am-9pm daily, $8-10), next to and owned by an RV park. The dining room is crowded and lines form at the order window. The pizza is thick, cheesy, and bubbly, and the menu also has sandwiches, pasta, and a salad bar; there's a long line of local beer taps. Kids kill time waiting for pizza with arcade games.

ACCOMMODATIONS

The simple, small **Pacific City Inn** (35280 Brooten Rd., 503/965-6464, www.pacificcityinn.com, $117-195) has only 16 rooms, but it's a friendly little motel in a very quiet town. It even has a bistro with a wine and martini bar and room service. Some rooms have kitchenettes, and laundry is on the premises. The rooms have the kind of dated motel style one would expect from an out-of-the-way motel—some rooms even have fold-down Murphy beds. The cheery bistro has white tablecloths and a farmhouse vibe. The gardens behind the hotel have picnic tables and well-tended flowerbeds.

The massive **Inn at Cape Kiwanda** (33105 Cape Kiwanda Dr., 888/965-7001, www.yourlittlebeachtown.com/inn, $349-389) is a big building for modest Pacific City—all its rooms (most with balconies) face the ocean across the street and the Pelican Pub. The rooms have cushy-bed, leather-furniture luxury, even though the views of the ocean also include the Pelican parking lot. The lobby has a fireplace and comfy chairs, and the hotel has a mini spa. Bike rentals are available, and it's a good area for safe cycling. Some rooms have two-person jetted tubs, and all have gas fireplaces.

Camping

The **Cape Kiwanda RV Resort** (33305 Cape Kiwanda Dr., 503/965-6230, www.capekiwandarvresort.com, $37 tent sites, $51-55 RV sites, $77-175 cabins) is across the street from the Cape Kiwanda beach and has more amenities than the usual RV spot. It's been around since 1969 and eventually took over a nearby Doryman's Fish Company building. There are 107 sites with full hookups as well as two dozen cabins and cottages, though only the deluxe cabins come with linens. There are also 10 tent sites next to the trees. The complex has an indoor clubhouse with a heated pool, spa, and exercise room. The Marketplace near the road has a deli with hot prepared meals and a grocery store. The seafood market has fresh fish from the Pacific City dory fleet, and they smoke their own fish and oysters. The gift shop sells bathing suits. Outdoors is a playground and horseshoe pit. This really isn't roughing it—free wireless Internet is available. Reservations are recommended.

GETTING THERE

Unlike most towns on the Oregon Coast, Pacific City isn't on U.S. 101. Reach the small town by leaving U.S. 101 at 25 miles south of Tillamook or 20 miles north of Lincoln City. Take a left on Brooten Road and follow it 2.5 miles to the town of Pacific City. To reach the beach and Pelican Pub, keep going across the Nestucca River and take the first right onto Cape Kiwanda Drive. Cape Kiwanda State Natural Area is about a mile ahead on the left.

Lincoln City

Lincoln City is one of the biggest cities on this stretch of coast. It has hotels and restaurants for visitors, plus some of the bigger collections of fast-food restaurants and outlet stores. The town stretches down the coast, past the inland water bodies of Siletz Bay and Devil's Lake, because it was once a collection of smaller towns: Taft, Oceanlake, Delake, Nelscott, and Cutler City. They voted to become Lincoln City by a very small margin, and the resulting town was almost called Surfland. Wave riders do come to the area, but it's a cold, rough ocean out there—more visitors appreciate the coast by crabbing, building bonfires on the beach, or flying a kite.

SPORTS AND RECREATION

Parks and Beaches

DEVIL'S LAKE STATE RECREATION AREA

The **Devil's Lake State Recreation Area** (1452 NE 6th Dr., 541/994-2002, www.oregonstateparks.org) is nearly in the middle of downtown Lincoln City and has some of the most accessible green and camping space on the coast. The park stretches over both the northwest and southwest sides of the lake, with lots of residences lining its shores, but it's also home to birds like loons, cormorants, and even bald eagles.

D RIVER STATE PARK

The Pacific Ocean is a nearly endless body of water, but the **D River State Park** (SE 1st St. and U.S. 101, 541/994-7341, www.oregonstateparks.org), which connects Devils Lake to the Pacific, is a mere 120 feet long at high tide. It has appeared in the *Guinness Book of World Records* as the shortest river in the world. A group in Great Falls, Montana, started a competition with Oregon, claiming their river was the shortest, and eventually *Guinness* stopped listing the record. The four-acre park—basically just a parking lot next to the mini waterway—is the base for some of Lincoln City's kite festivals.

LINCOLN CITY BEACH

There are a number of spots to access the **Lincoln City Beach,** a stretch with a good amount of driftwood. Try the end of NW 26th Street, near NW Inlet Avenue, next to the Pelican Shores Inn. There's a bathroom and steps down to the beach, plus a handful of parking spots next to a stone wall. To drive on the sand itself, follow NE 15th Street to the end.

GLENEDEN BEACH STATE RECREATION SITE

Even though much of the waterfront south of Lincoln City has steep bluffs, **Gleneden Beach State Recreation Site** (Wesler St. and Raymond Ave., 541/265-4560, www.oregonstateparks.org, free) has a paved walkway down to the sand. The surfing spot is also popular with seals, which pop up among the waves. The beach entrance includes picnic tables and a bathroom.

Hiking

DRIFT CREEK SUSPENSION BRIDGE

Distance: 3 miles round-trip
Duration: 1.5 hours
Elevation gain: 550 feet
Effort: moderate
Trailhead: Forest Road 17
Directions: Take Drift Creek Road east off U.S. 101, then make a right on South Drift Creek Road and a left on Forest Road 17, continuing for about 10 miles.

It's only a short hike to the Drift Creek Suspension Bridge (www.fs.usda.gov), a 240-foot-long bridge that passes over 75-foot Drift Creek Falls. The materials had to be brought to the site via helicopter, and the bridge crosses about 100 feet above the creek and waterfall below. The hike goes downhill in the first half, then back uphill. A picnic table is near the bridge for a forest lunch, a perfect stop before returning the way you came.

ENTERTAINMENT AND EVENTS

The local **Theatre West** (3536 SE U.S. 101, 541/994-5663, www.theatrewest.com, $8-12) turned an old auditorium into a warm community theater, and since the 1980s it has brought in locals onstage, some with experience on Broadway. Productions tend toward comedy, and many are original productions. The low building right on U.S. 101 has a bright blue roof. Reservations must be made by phone.

The brisk winds on the Oregon Coast mean it's not the best for sunbathing, but it's one of the best kite-flying spots in the world. Lincoln City hosts one of the biggest Northwest kite events. The **Summer Kite Festival** (D River State Park, www.oregoncoast.org/summer-kite-festival) is held on the beach in June; the **Fall Kite Festival** (D River State Park, www.oregoncoast.org/fall-kite-festival) is in October. Performers launch show kites and do tricks, sometimes with dozens of kites tied together. They also include kite-making clinics and kids' parades, and an open area is for free kite flying—if you can handle the possible line tangles.

FOOD

There's a whole dog pound at the **Beach Dog Café** (6042 U.S. 101, 541/996-3647, 7am-2:30pm Wed.-Sun., $7-13, cash only), framed in pictures on the wall—row after row after row of illustrations and photos of pooches. The restaurant serves breakfast and lunch, but the first meal of the day gets the most play here, including French toast, pancakes, elaborate eggs, and potato dishes. More than a dozen hot dogs are on the menu, from a Chicago dog with mustard and relish to a "hot diggity dog" with sriracha sauce. Waits can get lengthy for the homey spot since it has few tables and is the go-to joint for many of the city's tourists—for good reason.

The windows at **The Bay House** (5911 SW U.S. 101, 541/996-3222, www.thebayhouse.org, 5:30pm-10pm Wed.-Sun., $26-44) face the water, in a building that's housed one eatery or another since 1937. It's now one of the finer dining establishments in town, serving dinner only in careful, artistic preparations. The menu is short, with a handful of fish, pasta, and meat entrées, but the tasting menu ($79) is a good mix of locally sourced bites, paired with Oregon wines ($29). Sunsets from the dining room are gorgeous.

The breaded and fried cod with fries at **J's Fish and Chips** (1800 SW U.S. 101, 541/994-4445, 11:30am-7pm Mon.-Thurs., 11:30am-9pm Fri.-Sat. 11:30am-4:30pm Sun., $7-12) is the star, but the restaurant's fish tacos are also popular—plus the halibut, prawns, rockfish, and other sea creatures listed on the blackboard. Order at the counter when you come in, then snag a table once your order is ready. The clam chowder isn't necessarily a standout, but it's good for anyone who doesn't like soups that are too fishy. Like any good fish-and-chips joint, J's serves food in flimsy baskets lined with waxy paper and with sides of slaw and creamy tartar sauce.

Most entrées at the **Blackfish Café** (2733 U.S. 101, 541/996-1007, www.blackfishcafe.com, 11:30am-3pm and 5pm-11pm Wed.-Mon., $13-26) are some kind of seafood: local rockfish or Pacific swordfish, or a cioppino made from a collection of shellfish. The vibe is homey, not too fancy, but the dinners themselves have more preparation than the casual surroundings. Many dishes use locally sourced ingredients. The most popular desserts are the homemade Ding Dongs, chocolate pastries topped with a berry sauce and whipped cream—much better than the kind you can buy at a gas station.

ACCOMMODATIONS

Under $150

Siletz Bay Lodge (1012 SW 51st St., 541/996-6111, www.siletzbaylodgelincolncity.com, $138-158) is located right on Siletz Bay, a giant tidal marsh that is a wildlife refuge for waterfowl and small aquatic mammals. Many rooms have balconies, and all have views of the bay and ocean. But the hotel does, in places, seem stuck in the past: flowered bedspreads, generic wall art, and no air-conditioning, which can be a pain in the warmest summer months. The free continental breakfast is limited but includes some hot items. There's a hot tub and the nearby beach, perfect for evening bonfires.

The wood-sided **Looking Glass Inn** (861 SW 51st St., 541/996-3996, www.lookingglass-inn.com, $114-159) is the classic beach hotel. Some rooms have jetted tubs and fireplaces, and it's right on the water. Laundry facilities are available to guests, along with an outdoor picnic table and grill. Hoping to catch some crab for your dinner? There's an outdoor crab-cooking station. Some suites have kitchens, and pet-friendly packages include dog bowls, towels, treats, and waste bags. Some of the furniture is dated, but the hotel's location on the north end of Siletz Bay is nearly unbeatable.

The waterfront **Pelican Shores Inn** (2645 NW Inlet Ave., 541/994-2134, www.pelicanshores.com, $109-199) is practically on the sand, so the ground-floor rooms on the ocean have patios overlooking the waves. The indoor pool has an angled glass ceiling, so it feels something like swimming in a greenhouse. The hotel is somewhat small, with only 33 rooms, decorated with Pelican Shores life preservers. Some suites have a small kitchen or sleeper sofa; all have at least a refrigerator and microwave. The inn has a free continental breakfast. The cheapest rooms don't have a view.

The multicolored **Ashley Inn and Suites** (3430 U.S. 101, 541/996-7500, www.ashley-innlincolncity.com, $89-164) is a few blocks from the beach, but closer than most highway-side hotels. The lobby often smells of chocolate chip cookies (not as a tease, but as a freebie for guests). Some spa rooms have large two-person jetted tubs. The beds all have downy pillows and comfortable mattresses, and the somber decor is more subdued than the starfish-and-buoy motels that populate the Oregon Coast. Couches and multiroom suites are available.

$150-250

All 120 rooms at the ★ **Inn at Spanish Head** (4009 U.S. 101, 541/996-2161, www.spanishhead.com, $205-225) have ocean views. Many have kitchens and balconies, and all can access the pool, saunas, and spa. The outdoor heated pool almost has better views than the rooms themselves. The 10 stories are like a giant flight of stairs right on the beach, though the inland side, oddly, has a northern Italian vibe with its red roof and arches. Rooms and furnishings are adequate but not luxurious.

The three-floor **Inn at Wecoma** (2945 U.S. 101, 541/994-2984, www.innatwecoma.com, $148-219) is convenient to the highway but several blocks from the ocean. Some rooms have fireplaces or balconies, and there's an indoor pool and hot tub. The hotel rents bicycles, and the outdoor recreation area has grills and shuffleboard. The decor is modern and less beachy than some other hotels in the area. The free breakfast includes hot items like pancakes and biscuits and gravy.

Over $250

In a town of beachfront motels, **Salishan Spa & Golf Resort** (7760 U.S. 101, 541/764-3600, www.salishan.com, $259-289) is a different kind of beast—a golf and spa resort. Some rooms have sleeper sofas and fireplaces. The spa has whirlpools and saunas, and the resort has a large pool, tennis courts, and five restaurants, including a casual grill and a lounge with live music performances and balcony. Outdoors, play on the bocce courts or jungle gym, or stay inside with the video games in the entertainment center. For anyone who can't handle the regular golf links, try the 18-hole putting course. Although it's on the inland side of U.S. 101, many rooms have views of the south end of Siletz Bay.

Camping

At **Devil's Lake State Recreation Area** (1452 NE 6th Dr., 800/452-5687, www.reserveamerica.com) are 50 tent sites ($21), several walk-in sites for hikers and bikers ($6), and 25 RV sites with full hookups ($29-31). The flush toilets and hot showers mean that you barely have to rough it. The park also has 10 yurts ($45) available to rent—though you'll need your own bedding. Any campsite, yurt, or boat moorage spot ($10) can be reserved online. This is an especially good destination for campers looking for disabled access because the trail to the lake has a hard surface, and two campsites and two yurts are ADA accessible.

GETTING THERE

Lincoln City is about 44 miles south of Tillamook and 25 miles north of Newport, an easy drive on U.S. 101 from either starting point. The closest connection to Portland is Highway 18, which heads east from U.S. 101 at the small town of Otis. The Salmon River Highway, as Highway 18 is known, passes through the town of McMinnville before slogging through Portland suburbs as Highway 99 West. The drive from Lincoln City to Portland is about two hours under the best traffic conditions, but delays are common.

Depoe Bay

Just how tiny is little Depoe Bay? Signs proudly claim its little harbor is the world's smallest. The town also promotes itself as a whale-watching mecca, though it's also a good spot to wander a short downtown stretch within view of the ocean.

WHALE-WATCHING

The state-run **Whale Watching Center** (119 SW U.S. 101, 541/765-3304, www.oregonstateparks.org, 10am-4pm daily Memorial Day-Labor Day, 10am-4pm Wed.-Sun. Labor Day-Memorial Day, free) is informational, with whalebones and maps spread around the seafront space and binoculars for public use. Volunteers are on hand during busy times to explain where and when to see whales. The most popular animals are the gray whales whose migrations pass the spot twice a year, once in spring and once in winter, but the only times that whales aren't commonly seen in the area are November-early December and mid-January to mid-March. Other species seen include humpback, blue, and sperm whales, as well as orcas. Maps show the best shore spots for whale-watching. A whiteboard also tracks how many whales have been spotted that day, month, and year.

If peering through binoculars on land doesn't score you a whale sighting, head to the seas. **Whale Research EcoExcursions** (Ellingson St. and U.S. 101, 541/912-6734, www.oregonwhales.com, $40 adults, $32 children 2-12) advertises that its trips are done with a marine biologist, Carrie Newell, on board. Trips leave from the **Whale, Sealife & Shark Museum** (www.oregonwhales.com, 10am-4pm daily summer, 10am-4pm Fri.-Sun. winter, $5 adults, $3 children 4-12, children under 4 free), a cramped private museum whose exhibits—a crowded wall of shark jaws, models of seabirds—are best viewed only on the rainiest of days, or in conjunction with one of the trips. But Newell has been known to show off the body of a shark caught in the area in the parking lot. Her whale-watching trips are crammed with info, and they have a high sighting success rate.

The Whale's Tail (270 Coast Guard Dr., 541/921-1323, www.whalestaildepoebay.com,

the coast at Depoe Bay

Mar.-Sept., $30-40) was one of the first to perform approved whale-watching trips in Zodiac boats on the Oregon Coast. There are no stairs to access the boats, so it's a better choice for anyone with mobility issues (call for information). Look for the yellow signs for Dockside Charters. The boat only carries six passengers, so trips are intimate. They claim that they get fewer seasick riders because of the smaller boat's low center of gravity and lack of diesel fumes.

FOOD

★ **Restaurant Beck** (541/765-3220, www.restaurantbeck.com, 5pm-10pm daily, Wed.-Sun. only winter, $18-34), a fine-dining spot located in the Whale Cove Inn, is one of the best spots to eat on the coast, with breathtaking views of Whale Cove and an outdoor patio. Dishes are made from locally sourced ingredients by a chef—he prefers local fish and game meats like wild boar and duck—recognized by the James Beard Foundation. The beer and wine lists include some local standouts. Reservations are highly recommended.

Don't begrudge the name at **Gracie's Sea Hag** (58 U.S. 101, 541/765-2734, www.theseahag.com, 7am-9:30pm daily, $19-26)—the eatery and staff are anything but hag-like, and the joint's central location makes it one of the most popular spots in town. The lengthy menu has a little bit of everything, from shrimp cocktail to steak sandwiches to prime rib with Yorkshire pudding on Saturday nights. Gracie, the spot's namesake, still appears behind the bar. There's a bar and live music, but the feel is that of a very casual, small-town family restaurant. The menu includes a nine-ounce filet mignon, but this kind of joint calls for the fish-and-chips, or maybe the combination plate of deep-fried local seafood catches.

ACCOMMODATIONS

The **Whale Cove Inn** (2345 U.S. 101, 541/765-4300, www.whalecoveinn.com, $455-795) feels separate from everything else on the busy Oregon Coast. It's just north of Rocky Point State Park, south of Depoe Bay, and has a fairly unassuming edifice on the road. On the other side, however, the hotel looks down on Whale Cove, and inside the lobby is a large vertical water feature. It's a boutique hotel with a luxury feel and amenities, so the few rooms (only nine) are priced much higher than other hotels in the area. Beds are comfortable memory foam, and all rooms have fireplaces and bay views. They also have private balconies with personal outdoor Jacuzzis. A premier suite has three bedrooms. The Whale Cove Inn is where to stay when money's no object and privacy and luxury are desired.

GETTING THERE

Depoe Bay is about halfway between Lincoln City and Newport on U.S. 101, and about 12 miles from both. The town is located directly on the water, and a narrow bridge over the bay entrance goes through the middle of town. Parking on the main drag—since it's both the busy U.S. 101 and the town's busiest commercial street—can be difficult to find, but there are small lots and street parking uphill.

Otter Rock

The town of Otter Rock, 5 miles south of Depoe Bay, has **Mo's West** (122 1st St., 541/765-2442, www.moschowder.com, 11am-8pm daily, $9-12), one of the smallest outposts of the chain—there since 1972—and with a great view. It's the most charming way to take in a bowl of Mo's chowder. Next door, the **Flying Dutchman Winery** (915 1st St., 541/765-2553, www.dutchmanwinery.com, 11am-6pm daily June-Sept., 11am-5pm daily Oct.-May, $5 tasting fee) has regular tastings of their boutique wines. Of course, the grapes are grown inland, as they wouldn't thrive on this salty, windy coast.

DEVIL'S PUNCH BOWL STATE NATURAL AREA

You just know that the Devil would spike the punch. At **Devil's Punch Bowl State Natural Area** (851 1st St., 541/265-4560, www.oregonstateparks.org, free), a giant rock formation near the shore, the water churns in and out like a good frothy punch being stirred. It was formed when the roofs of some sea caves collapsed and water continued to dig out a space in the rock. There are tide pools just north of the formation. Catch a view from the end of the road in the small town of Otter Rock, 8 miles north of Newport and accessed from Otter Creek Loop just off U.S. 101. Picnic tables, fire pits, and restroom facilities can be found on the bluff above.

BEVERLY BEACH STATE PARK

Seven miles north of Newport, **Beverly Beach State Park** (NE Beverly Dr. and U.S. 101, 541/265-9278, www.oregonstateparks.org) is one of the most popular parks in the area. Parking is on the inland side of U.S. 101, but a walkway travels under and to the wide sandy beach. A visitors center has registration information for the campground as well as a small store. **Camping** is available in tent ($21), full hookup ($29-31), and hike-in ($6) sites, as well as group sites ($78). The yurts ($45-55) can be reserved online as well. There are play structures and picnic facilities.

Newport

One of the biggest towns on the Oregon Coast, Newport still retains a working waterfront that is as productive as it is touristy.

SIGHTS

Hatfield Marine Science Center

Less massive than the nearby aquarium, the **Hatfield Marine Science Center** (2030 SE Marine Science Dr., 541/867-0100, www.hmsc.oregonstate.edu, 10am-5pm daily Memorial Day-Labor Day, 10am-4pm Thurs.-Mon. Labor Day-Memorial Day, $5 suggested donation) is still a sizable sea-themed destination, albeit one that's more popular with the younger set. The building was originally a marine laboratory for Oregon State University and still hosts marine research of all kinds. A visitors center takes education to a direct level with touch tanks, water displays, and a resident octopus, plus tours of scientific research equipment (submarines) parked outside. Just how different is the center from the Oregon Coast Aquarium? It's been known to offer free events in which a biologist performs a necropsy on a river otter to explain how the animals live (and die)—you won't find that at more conventional science centers.

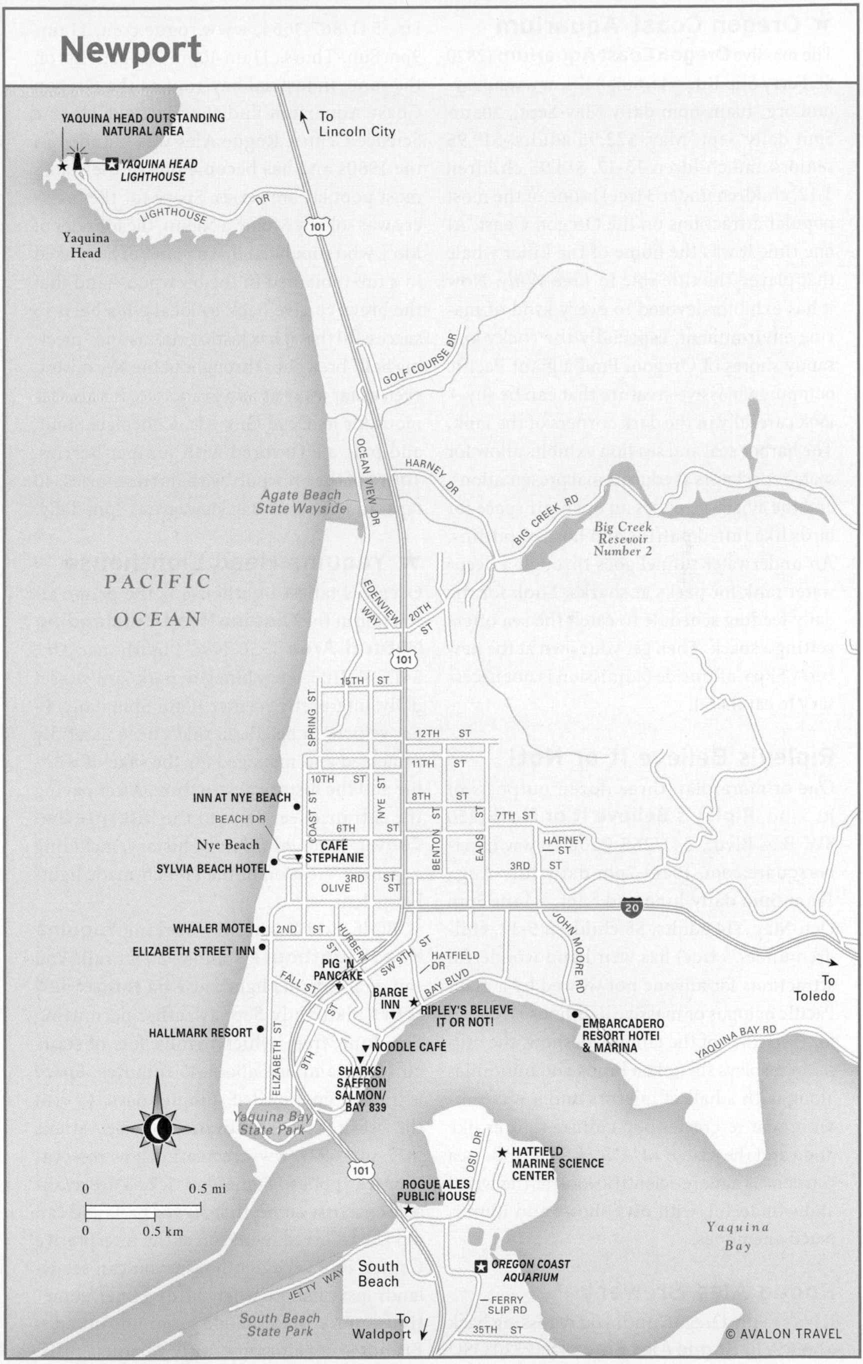
Newport
YAQUINA HEAD OUTSTANDING NATURAL AREA
YAQUINA HEAD LIGHTHOUSE
To Lincoln City
LIGHTHOUSE DR
101
Yaquina Head
GOLF COURSE DR
OCEAN VIEW DR
HARNEY DR
Agate Beach State Wayside
BIG CREEK RD
Big Creek Resevoir Number 2
PACIFIC OCEAN
EDENVIEW WAY
20TH ST
15TH ST
SPRING ST
12TH ST
11TH ST
10TH ST
NYE ST
8TH ST
7TH ST
INN AT NYE BEACH
BEACH DR
6TH ST
COAST ST
BENTON ST
EADS ST
Nye Beach
CAFÉ STEPHANIE
HARNEY ST
SYLVIA BEACH HOTEL
3RD ST
OLIVE ST
20
JOHN MOORE RD
WHALER MOTEL
2ND ST
ELIZABETH STREET INN
HURBERT ST
SW 9TH ST
HATFIELD DR
FALL ST
PIG 'N PANCAKE
BAY BLVD
To Toledo
BARGE INN
RIPLEY'S BELIEVE IT OR NOT!
HALLMARK RESORT
EMBARCADERO RESORT HOTEL & MARINA
YAQUINA BAY RD
ELIZABETH ST
9TH ST
NOODLE CAFÉ
SHARKS/ SAFFRON SALMON/ BAY 839
Yaquina Bay State Park
OSU DR
HATFIELD MARINE SCIENCE CENTER
0 0.5 mi
0 0.5 km
ROGUE ALES PUBLIC HOUSE
Yaquina Bay
South Beach
OREGON COAST AQUARIUM
JETTY WAY
FERRY SLIP RD
South Beach State Park
To Waldport
35TH ST
© AVALON TRAVEL

★ Oregon Coast Aquarium

The massive **Oregon Coast Aquarium** (2820 SE Ferry Slip Rd., 541/867-3474, www.aquarium.org, 10am-6pm daily May-Sept., 10am-5pm daily Sept.-May, $22.95 adults, $19.95 seniors and children 13-17, $14.95 children 3-12, children under 3 free) is one of the most popular attractions on the Oregon Coast. At one time it was the home of the killer whale that played the title role in *Free Willy.* Now it has exhibits devoted to every kind of marine environment, especially the rocky and sandy shores of Oregon. Find a giant Pacific octopus, a massive creature that can be shy—look carefully in the dark corners of the tank. The harbor seal and sea lion exhibits allow for seated spectators at educational presentations, and the aviary provides an open-air space for birds like tufted puffins and horned puffins. An underwater tunnel goes through a deep-water tank for peeks at sharks. Look for the daily feeding schedule to catch the sea otters getting a snack. Then get your own at the new Ferry Slip Café inside (admission is not necessary to eat there).

Ripley's Believe It or Not!

One of more than three dozen outposts of its kind, **Ripley's Believe It or Not!** (250 SW Bay Blvd., 541/265-2206, www.marinersquare.com, 10am-7pm daily July-Aug., 10am-5pm daily June and Sept., 11am-5pm Oct.-May, $14 adults, $8 children 5-12, children under 5 free) has weird and wonderful attractions for anyone not wowed by a giant Pacific octopus or massive lighthouse. Named for the father of the circus sideshow, the museum displays shrunken heads and mummies along with a hall of mirrors and a wax museum that re-creates pop culture figures like Yoda and the cast of *M*A*S*H.* The Undersea Gardens is a more scientific look at the weird and wonderful, with dive shows and illuminated anemones.

Rogue Ales Brewery

It isn't really Oregon until you're tossing back a brew. The **Rogue Ales Brewery** (2320 OSU Dr., 541/867-3664, www.rogue.com, 11am-9pm Sun.-Thurs., 11am-10pm Fri.-Sat.) sits on the same industrial bayfront as the Oregon Coast Aquarium and the Hatfield Marine Science Center. Rogue Ales was founded in the 1980s and has become one of the state's most popular breweries. Space for the brewery was sold by Mohava Niemi, the founder of Mo's, who stipulated that a photo of her naked in a tub remained in the brewpub—and that the brewery give back to locals. It's been so successful that it has tasting rooms and "meeting hall" brewpubs throughout the Northwest, even as far away as San Francisco. It's also famous for its Dead Guy Ale, Chocolate Stout, and pale ale flavored with juniper berries. **Tours** of the brewpub, with its two stories, 40 taps, and Yaquina Bay view, are at 3pm daily.

★ Yaquina Head Lighthouse

Oregon's tallest lighthouse is the prime attraction at the **Yaquina Head Outstanding Natural Area** (750 NW Lighthouse Dr., 541/574-3100, www.blm.gov, park 7am-sunset daily, interpretive center 10am-5pm daily, $7 per vehicle), a headland that's been carefully protected and managed for the sake of wildlife and the historical structure. After paying the entrance fee, drive to the **Interpretive Center;** it contains lots of history, including a giant re-creation of the French-made lighthouse lens.

Built in 1872, the still-working **Yaquina Head Lighthouse** stands 93 feet tall. You can go inside the lighthouse on **ranger-led tours** (daily July-Sept., weather permitting Feb.-June, free), which involve lots of stair-climbing and last about 45 minutes. Space is limited on crowded summer days, so visit the website or call in advance for reservations (877/444-6777, www.recreation.gov, reservation fee applies). Same-day tickets are available on a first-come, first-served basis and can only be reserved in person at the Interpretive Center. From the lighthouse, you can see islands just offshore where birds gather, sometimes more than 65,000 common murres, Brandt's cormorants, and various gulls.

Pelicans, bald eagles, and turkey vultures soar by. Look for gray whales in the water beyond. A 0.5 mile walking trail leads around the headland and to the top of Salal Hill, with great views up and down the coast.

Yaquina Bay Lighthouse

Not to be confused with its larger cousin, this lighthouse at **Yaquina Bay State Recreation Site** (1100-1198 SW 9th St., 541/265-5679, www.oregonstateparks.org, year-round, free) is more like a combination of a historical home and a lighthouse. Located in the middle of Newport at the mouth of the Yaquina River, it's the oldest structure in town. An older structure was built in 1871 and decommissioned only three years later when the much bigger Yaquina Head Lighthouse was built. Then it served as a Coast Guard station. Today the living quarters re-create life on the coast a century ago. The surrounding park area has beach access, picnic facilities, and viewpoints.

Parks and Beaches

Three miles south of Newport is **South Beach State Park** (S Beach State Park Rd. and U.S. 101, 800/551-6949, www.oregonstateparks.org), which has views up to Newport's big Yaquina Bay Bridge. Grassy dunes lead down to the beach, and the park is nearly 500 acres. A bike path winds through the park, interpretive programs and guided hikes are held daily in summer, and kayak tours sometimes explore the inland waterways of the area, but visit the campground's hospitality center for schedule information.

FOOD

There are five **Pig 'n Pancake** (810 SW Alder St., 541/265-9065, www.pignpancake.com, 6am-3pm daily, $8-18) restaurants along the Oregon Coast. All serve the kind of casual family fare that a beach weekend deserves—chowder, burgers, and of course, pancakes and bacon. The chain is still family owned and run. The pancakes come in buttermilk, Swedish, sourdough, and French batter varieties. The restaurant is housed in a building that used to be Newport's city hall, built in the 1920s in a vaguely art deco style. The side now has a pig painting in front of Newport's bridge. Inside are booths, tables, and counter seats, with busy waitresses trying to keep up and waiting patrons browsing the gift shop for postcards and souvenirs.

Newport's bayfront is a strange mix of restaurants, stores, and working waterfront, so

Yaquina Head Lighthouse

a fine meal might be right next to a machine sorting fresh-caught shrimp. In the center is **Rogue Ales Public House** (748 SW Bay Blvd., 541/265-3188, www.rogue.com, 11am-midnight Sun.-Thurs., 11am-1am Fri.-Sat., $8-16), sister to the brewery that sits across the bay. This used to be the brewery itself, until it moved in 1992, but this spot is a full-on restaurant with a pool room called the Crustacean Station. There are 35 beers on tap and a menu of beer-friendly dishes like spinach and artichoke dip or Kobe beef meatballs stuffed with Oregon blue cheese. Kobe beef burgers come topped with local Applewood-smoked bacon or local oyster mushrooms. The lengthy offerings also include seafood, pizzas, tacos, and root beer floats, but as the menu points out, no beluga caviar or foie gras—so don't even ask. Brewery tours are not offered, but the rowdy, friendly restaurant does like to offer "free bathroom tours," even though the loos aren't anything special.

This close to the working fisheries, there has to be a greasy, slightly grungy place to grab a beer and a burger. The **Barge Inn** (358 SW Bay Blvd., 541/265-8051, 7am-9pm Sun.-Thurs., 7am-10pm Fri.-Sat., $5-8) is that local joint. The burger menu is on a Pepsi-themed readerboard above the bar, and two bar-to-ceiling poles (which might block your menu view) are labeled "North" and "South." The building is shaped like a barn and labeled "tavern," though a sign above the bar notes it's home to "winos, dingbats & riffraff." It looks like a generic dive bar from the front, with its pool tables and jukebox, but inside it's friendlier—and a little less boozy—than it first appears.

The salmon dinner at ★ **Saffron Salmon** (859 SW Bay Blvd., 541/265-8921, www.saffronsalmon.com, 5pm-8:30pm Mon.-Tues. and Thurs., 11:30am-2:30pm and 5pm-8:30pm Fri.-Sun., $14-34) isn't actually cooked with saffron, but the spicy seafood stew does include it; the wild salmon is paired with vegetables and basil-pine nut butter. The restaurant serves some of the finest meals available on the bayfront section of Newport, with views of fishing boats as they return and unload, and seals frolicking in the bay. The waiter may even be able to point out which ships catch the crab that appears on the table. The pier location has a modern, updated look, but the windows provide the best decoration.

Look for the bright yellow exterior of **Café Stephanie** (411 NW Coast St., 541/265-8082, 7:30am-2pm daily, $5-12), a good beacon when hangovers hit on the salty coast. Breakfasts are legendary and indulgent, from vanilla cinnamon French toast to a "potato tornado" topped with sour cream. Everything is refreshingly cheap and filling, and decorative painted tentacles grace the walls inside. The space is small, so there can be waits on weekends, and there's limited outdoor seating.

The bayfront's **Noodle Café** (837 SW Bay Blvd., 541/574-6688, www.noodlecafenewport.com, 11am-2:30pm and 4:30pm-9pm Mon.-Tues. and Thurs.-Sat., noon-2:30pm Sun., $11-16) is just a small restaurant, but it's popular with locals up and down the coast. With its bright green exterior, it's hard to miss, and it backs up to the water and an outdoor picnic table area. Stormy days on the coast are a perfect fit for the pho noodle soup, udon, or spicy seafood broth, while those occasional sunny days are better for wraps made of chicken or shrimp tempura. The Asian menu has a wide range of classics, like stir-fry and bulgogi, plus homemade dumplings—actually most items are made from scratch, and it shows.

ACCOMMODATIONS

$150-250

The darling ★ **Sylvia Beach Hotel** (267 NW Cliff St., 541/265-5428, www.sylviabeachhotel.com, $135-275) is a cozy, bookish treasure in a town of big hotels. It's a blue four-story house on a bluff overlooking the beach, and much quieter than the usual beach motel. There are no TVs in the rooms, no wireless Internet, no telephones; but there is a resident cat and a library. Each room is named for an author or book, so the Colette room has a French feel and the Hemingway room has goofy animal heads mounted above the bed. The bedframe in the retro-futuristic Jules Verne room has sprockets and gears. For all the book influences, the library is more a relaxing space than a book depository, but with puzzles and games. Dinner is family style in the **Tables of Content Restaurant** (seatings at 7pm daily summer, 6pm Sun.-Thurs. and 7pm Fri.-Sat. winter, $28); reservations are required. Saturday stays require a two-night purchase, and single guests receive a $10 discount. The stairs are steep, and there's no elevator.

The giant block of the **Elizabeth Street Inn** (232 SW Elizabeth St., 541/265-9400, www.elizabethstreetinn.com, $220-230) is situated to maximize the ocean views from every private balcony. All rooms have fireplaces, and the inn has a heated indoor pool with ocean views. Rooms have updated decor and plush robes for lounging in front of the fire, and once the weather turns chilly, the hotel serves smoked salmon chowder in the lobby. The free breakfast includes hot items such as eggs and waffles. From its top-of-the-bluff location, it's a very short walk down to the beach.

The **Whaler Motel** (155 SW Elizabeth St., 541/265-9261, www.whalernewport.com, $154-204) has an indoor pool, but the ocean views from every room all the way up to Yaquina Head Lighthouse are more impressive. Rooms have a traditional motel feel—flowered bedspreads and dated furniture, but some have gas fireplaces or sleeper sofas. All have private balconies, and the hotel is largely pet friendly. The free breakfast is limited, though popcorn is available in the lobby. The hotel also rents beach houses.

The sloping roofs of the **Embarcadero Resort Hotel and Marina** (1000 SE Bay Blvd., 541/265-8521, www.embarcadero-resort.com, $109-239) are shaped so that every unit has a view of the harbor and the boats just outside. Located inside Yaquina Bay, it's got calmer waters outside and an indoor swimming pool. Standard rooms have flat-screen TVs and comfortable, if mismatched, furniture, and specialty suites are decorated by theme, so the Lady Ruth suite resembles the inside of a boat, and the Sail Away suite has anchors and ship's wheels everywhere. Many rooms have jetted tubs. With views of the bay and Yaquina Bay Bridge, and stained-glass windows, the on-site **Waterfront Grille** serves breakfast, lunch, and dinner in a dining room, plus a special prime rib dinner on weekends. Boaters can park their boats just outside, and one section of dock is reserved for crabbing, right next to the crab cookers. But be warned, the seals also know that this is a crab spot, and they like to steal.

Over $250

Nye Beach is just north of Yaquina Bay in Newport, one of the more central neighborhoods in town. **Inn at Nye Beach** (729 NW Coast St., 541/265-2477, www.innatnyebeach.com, $250-276) bills itself as a boutique hotel, not a beachside motel, offering perks like rain showerheads in the bathrooms, free tea service and French press coffeemakers, and sleek linens and decor. Some rooms have fireplaces or Jacuzzi tubs; a two-bedroom kids' suite has a room with bunk beds. Wine and fresh cookies are served in the lobby, and breakfast is available with room service (fee). The wood-shingle sides of the hotel have that classic beach look, making this is a romantic escape right on the water but still close to town.

Like many hotels on the coast, **Hallmark Resort** (744 SW Elizabeth St., 888/448-4449, www.hallmarkinns.com, $256-399, two-night minimum stay) is a big, blocky building angled right at the water so every room has a private waterfront balcony. Some rooms have fireplaces and two-person tubs, and the hotel has an indoor saltwater pool, a spa, and a sauna. Partial-view rooms are cheaper and still have a taste of the ocean, but not the panorama that larger, more expensive rooms offer. Other suites have lofts or additional rooms for groups and families; two-night minimums may apply. There's an on-site restaurant, **Georgie's Beachside Grill**

(541/265-9800, www.georgiesbeachsidegrill.com, 7:30am-10pm Mon.-Sat., 7:30am-9pm Sun.), with casual dining and excellent views.

Camping

South Beach State Park (S Beach State Park Rd. and U.S. 101, 800/551-6949, www.oregonstateparks.org) offers camping in tents ($17-21), RV sites with electrical hookups ($29), and hike-in sites ($6), as well as yurts ($45-55). Amenities include restrooms, showers, picnic tables, and an RV dump station.

GETTING THERE

Newport lies on U.S. 101, 24 miles north of Yachats and about 13 miles south of Depoe Bay. From Newport, U.S. 20 provides access inland to I-5. At U.S. 101, follow U.S. 20 east for 50 miles to Corvallis. Turn right onto Highway 34 and follow it for 10 miles to I-5.

Yachats

Pronounce this small coastal town "Yah-hots," not "yachts." It's little more than a populated bend in the road, but its placement between Florence and Newport makes it a convenient overnight stop.

FOOD

The busy, quaint **Green Salmon Coffee Shop** (220 U.S. 101, 541/547-3077, www.thegreensalmon.com, 7:30am-2:30pm Tues.-Sun., $5-10) is a worthwhile stop, even if Yachats doesn't end up demanding any more of your time. The little red building is right in the middle of town. The menus of the expanded coffee shop are written on blackboards that take up nearly an entire wall; order at a counter before trying to score a table. Pastries are made in-house, and the berry toast is topped with local blackberries. Breakfast sandwiches are hot and layered with local eggs and veggies. The shop roasts its own coffee and is dedicated to using fair trade and sustainably grown ingredients. Even if you have no time to eat at the table, it's the best place for a hot coffee and gooey Danish.

The warm feeling that radiates throughout **Yachats Brewing and Farmstore** (348 U.S. 101, 541/547-3884, http://yachatsbrewing.com, 11:30am-8pm Mon.-Thurs., 11:30am-9pm Fri.-Sat., 10am-4pm Sun., $11-17) might be from all the gleaming blond Douglas fir wood that lines the wall and bar, which came from an old locomotive shop in Portland. Or it could come from the drinks pouring from the 30 taps—beers from the brewer, along with kombucha, mead, and ginger beer. The food menu is equally local, featuring pork belly cooked on alder planks and salads topped with locally grown nuts.

ACCOMMODATIONS

The retro feel of the **Yachats Inn** (331 U.S. 101, 541/547-3456, www.yachatsinn.com, $94-150) extends outside, where small decks have Adirondack chairs facing the ocean. Kitchens in the suites are limited, but there is outdoor space and a pond in the middle of the property. Regular rooms have dated furnishings, but some of the original suites have gas or wood fireplaces or even a woodstove. The inn also has a small indoor pool and hot tub. Stairs lead down to the beach, and the hotel is close to the center of Yachats.

Deane's Oceanfront Lodge (7365 U.S. 101, 541/547-3321, www.deaneslodge.com, $94-139), about 3.5 miles north of Yachats, isn't particularly near anything. Look either direction on the highway from the turnoff, and you'll see mostly driveways and mailboxes for private residences, not more hotels and eateries. For being only just off the busiest road in the region, it's a remarkably quiet motel, and fairly cheap. Indoors, the rooms have whitewashed cedar walls, adding to the seaside look, and oceanfront rooms have patios with grills and picnic tables. Some have fireplaces, and showers are retro glass-block style. Stairs on the back of the property lead directly to the beach, and the hotel is very pet friendly. Amenities here don't get much fancier than the puzzles in the lobby, but it's the epitome of a quiet waterfront hotel.

Just north of Yachats, ★ **Overleaf Lodge & Spa** (280 Overleaf Lodge Ln., 800/338-0507, www.overleaflodge.com, $221-429) is one of the only true luxury destinations in the area. Some rooms have jetted tubs overlooking the water and balconies with ocean views. Other rooms have patios. The spa has a soaking pool with ocean views and a hot tub, plus steam rooms and saunas—all included for guests. The spa also offers massage and facial services. The included breakfast is a healthy buffet with hot items, too. A trail leads into the center of Yachats, which isn't far from the hotel.

GETTING THERE

Yachats is 25 miles north of Florence and south of Newport on U.S. 101.

Florence

Just slightly inland, Florence is protected from the ocean by a solid line of sand dunes. The old downtown is situated on the Suislaw River, crossed by the 1936 Suislaw River Bridge. Fishing boats leave from the river marina every day, though the town is more geared toward tourism these days, thanks especially to the Three Rivers Casino with golf, slots, lodging, and dining. Restaurants line the historical Bay Street, and more hotels sit along U.S. 101 both north and south of the river.

SIGHTS

Cape Perpetua

Leave U.S. 101 about 2 miles south of Yachats to visit the **Cape Perpetua Visitor Center** (2400 U.S. 101, 541/547-3289, www.fs.usda.gov, 9:30am-4pm daily summer, 10am-4pm daily fall and spring, 10am-4pm Thurs.-Mon. winter, $5 per vehicle), a nature interpretive site located up above the highway and overlooking one of the area's little capes. Rangers lead guided walks and informational sessions in the building while a bookstore sells postcards and souvenirs. Visit during special Whale Watch weekends, or go explore the tide pools to see what lives among the rocks. A number of short trails leave from the center.

★ Heceta Head Lighthouse

The **Heceta Head Lighthouse** (U.S. 101, 0.5 mile north of the Sea Lion Caves, near mile marker 178, www.oregonstateparks.org, $5 per vehicle) isn't the biggest lighthouse on the Pacific Northwest coast, but it's one of the prettiest, and it has something most don't—a bed-and-breakfast inside the keeper's house. It also has one of the strongest lights, in the 56-foot tower built in 1894. Its light can be seen 21 miles from shore. The lighthouse is named after a Spanish navigator who came to the coast in the 18th century. A parking area leads to a sandy beach, viewpoint, and tide pools, but the trail to the lighthouse itself is short. Free tours of both the keeper's house and the lighthouse are available in summer, and a gift shop is in the old generator room.

Sea Lion Caves

The **Sea Lion Caves** (91560 U.S. 101, 541/547-3111, www.sealioncaves.com, 9am-7pm daily, $14 adults, $13 seniors, $8 children 5-12, children under 5 free) are a natural formation, but it takes a trip through a heavily marketed tourist attraction to get to them. The cliff-front building leads visitors downhill to an elevator that goes 200 feet down through solid rock to a giant sea cave, 12 stories high inside, favored by sea lions. It's the largest sea grotto in the country (and claims to be the largest sea cave in the world) and an impressive sight even when the brown Steller sea lions are basking on the basalt rocks inside. The shop upstairs is crammed with beach souvenirs and tchotchkes, and tour buses stop often and can crowd the lines. But the elevator is large, and there are viewpoints on top if you have to wait. The sea lion statue outside is a good spot for photos.

Old Town Park

The tiny **Old Town Park** (Laurel St. and Bay St., www.ci.florence.or.us/publicworks/old-town-park), located just off the main Bay Street in downtown Florence, has a cute small gazebo and overlooks that provide great views of the river and bridge. It's where to polish off an ice cream cone after dinner, when the docks up and down the river illuminate the water. Picnic tables and benches face the old pilings from when a ferry was needed to cross the river.

SPORTS AND RECREATION

Hiking

★ HOBBIT TRAIL

Distance: 1 mile round-trip
Duration: 45 minutes
Elevation gain: 200 feet
Effort: moderate
Trailhead: U.S. 101, near milepost 177
Directions: Look for a turnoff and a small sign for the valley trail, and then cross the highway to find the trailhead.

There are easier ways to get to the beach, but the Hobbit Trail is an almost magical route to the sand. The trailhead leaves from U.S. 101; parking is on the inland side of the road, but the trail begins on the ocean side. Immediately past the trailhead, the trail splits: Head right and wander about half a mile to the waterfront. It's called the Hobbit Trail because of the peculiar tree shapes, twisted by the wind and with a trail dug out deep between the gnarled roots. It looks like something out of a fantasy novel. Walk between mossy limbs to the secluded sandy beach, but remember that you have an uphill hike to get back to the car.

Heceta Head Lighthouse

DEVIL'S CHURN

Distance: 2.2 miles round-trip
Duration: 1.5 hours
Elevation gain: 360 feet
Effort: easy
Trailhead: Cape Perpetua Visitor Center

Take the time to wander to the water side of U.S. 101 from the visitors center, turning south just after crossing the highway for a quick loop along the jagged coastline on what's called the Captain Cook trail. When you return to the highway, follow the trail north and out a small promontory overlooking Devil's Churn. You'll look down on black rocks and the crashing waves that beat them endlessly. The loop here is called the Trail of the Restless Waters, and indeed the ocean never seems very calm in this tight chasm. Return the way you came to reach the visitors center.

ENTERTAINMENT AND EVENTS

Located on the Siuslaw River in Florence, **Three Rivers Casino** (5647 Hwy. 126,

877/374-8377, http://threeriverscasino.com, 24 hours daily, table gaming 10am-1am Sun.-Thurs., 10am-3am Fri.-Sat.) is owned by a confederation of local Native American tribes. The modern hotel and casino has a slew of table games like poker, roulette, and craps, as well as bingo and keno. The sports bar and tap room is open 24 hours daily, and the casino offers a smoke-free slots room.

SHOPPING

Outside the **Wood Wizard Gallery** (1431 Bay St., 541/997-4500, www.woodwizard-gallery.com, 11am-6pm Tues.-Sun.) stands a wizard painting with two holes for faces—it's the kind of cheesy photo-op you can't pass up. There's a touch of kitsch to the wooden wares inside, like the carved flutes and chainsaw art, which are blocks of wood carved into surprisingly delicate animal figures using a bulky power tool. Dozens of bears made by a local chainsaw carver are here. Some of the furniture is beautiful but hard to pack during a long trip. More portable are the delicate wooden watches.

FOOD

The charming ★ **Waterfront Depot** (1252 Bay St., 541/902-9100, www.thewaterfrontdepot.com, 4pm-10pm daily, $11-20) is the best eatery for miles. It's not too fancy but nice enough to feel like a reward after a long day of play. The building was the Mapleton Train Station, moved to this spot next to the Siuslaw River Bridge; it's decorated with photos of old movie stars and chic mirrors. The outdoor dining area is used in summer, and the small dining space indoors can mean a wait on busy weekends. The bartenders make some of their own mixings, and a bar seat can mean a friendly chat from locals and visitors sitting there, too. The food is mostly American—surf and turf, pasta jambalaya—with hints of global influence, like lamb riblets in a New Zealand style or toasted onion-battered green beans in a Thai style. The owner's Southeast Asian roots are celebrated every week with Singapore chicken curry night.

Traveler's Cove (1362 Bay St., 541/997-6845, 9am-9pm daily, $8-14) bills itself as a family restaurant, but there's a welcoming hometown bar feel to the neon-lit joint with a menu of burgers, salads, and tacos. On weekends, there's live music and dancing in the bar. The patio out back is known as the Margarita Deck, the perfect spot for a cold drink when the sun is shining. The food is saucy and unremarkable, but the salsa is homemade, the vibe is good, and there's rarely a wait.

The big, bustling **Bridgewater Fish House** (1297 Bay St., 541/997-1133, www.bridgewaterfishhouse.com, 11am-10pm Wed.-Mon. summer, 11am-9pm Wed.-Mon. winter, $17-36) is located on the main street in downtown Florence, and the menu celebrates every kind of seafood—tiger prawns, scallops, salmon, and lobster. The whole Dungeness crab is served with melted butter. The building is historical, dating back to 1901, but the interior of the restaurant is modern. The Zebra Lounge cocktail bar has a horseshoe bar and a separate menu, including an early-bird dinner for $17, plus complicated cocktails.

Everything's local at **Homegrown Public House** (294 Lauren St., 541/997-4886, www.homegrownpub.com, 11am-8pm Tues.-Thurs., 11am-9pm Fri.-Sat., $11-21), from the food to the owner. The fish-and-chips is from the water and soil nearby, and even the salad has a taste of the landscape with its fiddlehead ferns on top. A connected deli makes good sandwiches to-go for adventures, and the pub's tap house is small but carefully curated.

ACCOMMODATIONS

The **River House Inn** (1202 Bay St., 541/997-3933, www.riverhouseflorence.com, $129-199) is located right on the Siuslaw River, close to the small, historical waterfront downtown area of Florence. Cheaper rooms don't have a view, but some riverfront rooms have private spa tubs. The complimentary breakfast is underwhelming, and better eateries are within walking distance. The decor is up to date, making up for the somewhat small rooms. The location, however, can't be beat.

Across the river, facing downtown Florence, **Best Western Plus Pier Point Inn** (85625 U.S. 101, 800/435-6736, www.bwpierpointinn.com, $215-275) sits on a bluff above the water. All rooms have views, and sunsets or fog over downtown Florence can be very picturesque. The rooms are updated and comfortable, and some suites have a full kitchen. A heated indoor swimming pool offers views across the river, spa, and sauna. The **Bay View Restaurant and Bar** (3pm-10pm daily) serves American dishes and local beers, and on Saturday night the bar hosts karaoke. Breakfast includes a staffed omelet bar.

The Victorian keeper's house at **Heceta Head Lighthouse** (U.S. 101, near mile marker 178, 866/547-3696, www.hecetalighthouse.com, $215-410) has a bed-and-breakfast with six rooms (some with a shared bath) that includes a seven-course breakfast using local meats, produce, and cheeses. Those staying at the bed-and-breakfast can drive in through a separate entrance; directions are given when reservations are made.

Camping

The **Cape Perpetua Campground** (Cummins Peak Rd., 877/444-6777, www.reserveamerica.com, May-Sept., $24), just north of the Cape Perpetua Visitor Center, has 37 wooded campsites, but no electrical hookups. Amenities include water, a picnic area, and flush toilets.

GETTING THERE

Florence is 50 miles south of Newport along U.S. 101, or just 25 miles south from Yachats. To reach I-5 inland (and continue on to Portland or return to Seattle), take Highway 126 east for 60 miles to Eugene and I-5. It takes about 1.5 hours of driving through rural Oregon hills to reach Eugene.

★ OREGON DUNES NATIONAL RECREATION AREA

The sand dunes lining the Oregon Coast aren't just a handy place to store sandcastle materials. Dunes provide a buffer between beach and land that keeps erosion at bay. They're also a great place to play. The **Oregon Dunes National Recreation Area** (South Jetty Rd. and U.S. 101, www.fs.usda.gov) is a 40-mile-long protected area with spots for hiking, paddling, and OHVs (off-highway vehicles), better known as dune buggies. The closest access point to Florence is at South Jetty Road, which passes several OHV staging

Oregon Dunes National Recreation Area

areas—look to the left to see a slope like a ski hill where motorists play—before turning and passing several spots for beach access. At the north end of the road is a fishing and crabbing dock, far from where the motorized vehicles are allowed.

The **Oregon Dunes Visitor Information and Interpretive Center** (855 U.S. 101, Reedsport, 541/271-6000, 8am-4pm Mon.-Fri., free) is 23 miles farther south in the town of Reedsport, and has exhibits, restrooms, and a gift shop. If you didn't pack your own OHV, do a sand dunes tour with **Sand Dunes Frontier** (83960 U.S. 101, 541/997-3544, www.sanddunesfrontier.com, tours $14-35). They drive around in big purple buggies that resemble trucks, and smaller, more agile vehicles. They'll be as daring as the passengers can tolerate, spinning down the sands. Rentals are available on-site from **Torex ATV Rentals** (541/997-5363, www.torexatvrentals.com, 9am-6pm daily, $50-265 per hour). And as for the most famous dunes, those in the science fiction book *Dune*? They were inspired by these very hills on the Oregon Coast.

Getting There

The Oregon Dunes National Recreation Area is located south of Florence along U.S. 101. To access the South Jetty Dune, follow U.S. 101 south for 2 miles to South Jetty Road. Turn right (west) and follow the road, which becomes Sand Dunes Road as it begins to run parallel to the shore. A number of parking areas provide access to the sand.

To return to I-5 and continue to Portland, drive north on U.S. 101 for 2 miles and turn right (east) on Highway 126. Drive 55.5 miles east through rural Oregon; then turn north onto Highway 569. Follow Highway 569 northeast for 9.5 miles to I-5. From this point, it's 110 miles north to Portland. The drive from the coast to I-5 is windy and slow to navigate in the dark, but it maximizes your time on the interstate. It's also possible to reach I-5 from Newport by driving north for 49 miles, then turning right (east) onto U.S. 20, a more traveled east-west route. Follow U.S. 20 east for 50 miles to Corvallis, and then turn right on Highway 34. Highway 34 reaches I-5 in 10 miles.

Coos Bay

Located on an inland bay, Coos Bay is connected by waterway to the Pacific Ocean, lending it a calmer charm than some other towns on the Oregon Coast. As a deep port for ships, it once served as an important part of the shipping corridor up the Pacific Coast, and produces large amounts of crab and clams. Its downtown has a few walkable blocks of shops and restaurants, with a harborfront forming one side of the city core. Keep an eye out for a giant mural memorializing Steve Prefontaine, a legendary distance runner who grew up here. It makes a nice stop to catch your breath or break up a trip down the coast and a chance to see Oregon coastal life beyond the tourist taffy shops and hotel clusters you'll find elsewhere.

The inland bay makes a sharp bend, forming a triangle of land inside the curved waterway, at the tip of which is tiny North Bend, which has little character of its own but bleeds into Coos Bay from the north. Southwest of Coos Bay, past another inlet called South Slough, Charleston is a small settlement with a few bars and restaurants, near where the Pacific waves break on ocean beaches.

SIGHTS

Coos History Museum and Maritime Collection

The **Coos History Museum and Maritime Collection** (1210 N Front St., 541/756-6320, http://cooshistory.org, 10am-5pm Tues.-Sun., $7 adults, $3 children 5-17) is just north of town. Oregon is famous for its mountains and forests, agriculture and viticulture, so it can be easy to forget how crucial the fishing and shipping industries once were to the region; this modest but thoughtful museum is a chance to understand how the ocean once defined life for almost everyone here. The blue-and-white building, bearing "Coos History Museum" on its side, holds artifacts relating to the area's sailing and shipping history—anchors and ropes, even whole dinghies—as well as exhibits dedicated to the Native American inhabitants of the area and the shipwrecks that were once common on the wild Pacific coast.

Cape Arago Light

Cape Arago Light is located on Chief's Island, which is private land (rather than, as one might incorrectly guess, on Cape Arago in Cape Arago State Park). While it's not possible to visit it, views of the picturesque lighthouse are available from a vista point near Coos Bay. To reach it, turn west onto Newmark Street from U.S. 101 in the town of North Bend just north of Coos Bay, near the Mill Casino Hotel. Follow the road as it becomes Cape Arago Highway; after about 10 miles and a trip through the small town of Charleston, take a right on Lighthouse Way and look for the parking area. It's a short walk to an overlook with lighthouse views. With its red roof above a white exterior, and sharp cliffs below it, the lighthouse is one of the most beautiful on the coast and a great spot for a classic photo.

SPORTS AND RECREATION

Parks and Beaches

Three state parks sit in a row along the coast, starting about 10 miles southwest of Coos Bay, not far from Cape Arago Light. The road that runs through them is the Cape Arago Highway.

SUNSET BAY STATE PARK

The beaches of **Sunset Bay State Park** (89814 Cape Arago Hwy., 541/888-3778, www.oregonstateparks.org, free) are long and wide, set back in the bay so the waves don't get too big. Fittingly, sunsets are beautiful here. Midsummer, it's a great wading spot, and rangers are on hand at the **interpretive center** (9:15am-5pm Fri.-Sun. May-mid-June, 9:15am-5pm daily mid-June-mid-Sept.) to lead nature walks and tide pool explorations.

SHORE ACRES STATE PARK

Located south of Sunset Bay State Park, **Shore Acres State Park** (89039 Cape Arago Hwy., 541/888-3732, www.oregonstateparks.org, 8am-dusk daily, $5) is an unusual sight along the rugged coast: a beautiful manicured set of gardens. Wander through a formal garden, a Japanese garden, and two rose gardens. The 745-acre park, located on the former estate of a local timber baron, includes an observation platform just off the parking area with views of the shoreline. Look for gray whales, sometimes spotted off the coast. The park has a gift shop and, Thanksgiving-New Year's, hosts a holiday light display with more than 300,000 lights.

CAPE ARAGO STATE PARK

South of Shore Acres, at the end of Cape Arago Highway about 13 miles southwest of Coos Bay, **Cape Arago State Park** (800/551-6949, www.oregonstateparks.org, 8am-dusk daily, free) is the wildest of the three, with little more than parking spaces and picnic facilities. Paths lead to the shoreline, but there's little beach here. Drake Point, which juts off near the parking lot, is named for Sir Frances Drake, who is believed to have anchored here in the 16th century during his search for the Northwest Passage; a small monument commemorates the explorer. Visit for some peace and quiet on a rugged stretch of coastline.

Water Sports

Behind Shark's Bite Seafood Café, **Waxer's Surf Shop** (242 S Broadway, 541/266-9020, www.surfwaxers.com, 11am-6pm Mon.-Sat.) is a one-stop shop for all things related to water sports, from the surfboards on racks to the kayaks on the wall and T-shirts emblazoned with "The Best Coast." The store sells gear but also offers rentals, from $35 for a day surf package to individual wetsuits and tie-down straps for transporting a board. There are single and tandem kayaks, with rentals starting at $45 or $65, respectively, for a half day. Stand-up paddleboards are $15 a day, and there are also boogie boards and junior packages for kids, though beware that the Oregon surf is intense.

Kite Flying

Oregon beaches are prime kite-flying territory. **Remember When Toys** (115 Anderson Ave., 541/266-8697, 10:30am-5:30pm Tues.-Sat.) is a small shop full of playthings just off the Coos Bay main drag. Head past the puzzles, stuffed animals, and games to find a small rack of kites to take a turn of your own.

ENTERTAINMENT AND EVENTS

It's a simple dive bar, but **Captain's Cabin** (275 N Broadway, 541/267-7772, 7am-11pm Sat.-Thurs., 7am-midnight Fri.) represents the blue-collar heart of the Oregon Coast, right down to the cheap drinks and the grumbling locals that hang out all night. The food is simple and fried—but the french fries are solid—and the service is friendly.

Though the southern Oregon shore doesn't have quite the influx of beer-makers that the more populated areas of the state enjoy, **7 Devils Brewing Company** (247 S 2nd St., 541/808-3738, www.7devilsbrewery.com, 11am-9pm Sun.-Mon. and Wed.-Thurs., 11am-10pm Fri.-Sat.) represents with a session pale, a mocha stout, and of course a hoppy IPA. The public house often hosts live music and dishes hearty mac and cheese and a hot tuna melt. As a bonus, the bar stocks a selection of scotch, bourbon, and other whiskeys.

The town's signature movie palace sits on the busiest block downtown, and true to its name the **Egyptian Theatre** (229 S Broadway, 541/269-8650, http://egyptiantheatreoregon.com) is decorated with pharaoh statues and hieroglyphic columns, inspired by the Egyptian mania that was big when the theater was built in the 1920s. Today the original historical Wurlitzer organ is still used on occasion, and the theater hosts film festivals and holiday films, with varying and sometimes free admission.

FOOD

German food may not be what you'd expect in this small coastal town, but **Blue Heron Bistro** (100 Commercial Ave., 541/267-3933, www.blueheronbistro.net, 11am-9pm Mon.-Fri., 9am-9pm Sat., 9am-8pm Sun., $10-18) has been dishing bratwurst for more than 40 years. Look for the Bavarian-style wooden cross-hatching outside and pictures of old-world castles under the wooden beams inside. Spaetzle, a kind of German macaroni and cheese, is a highlight.

Head to the sign with a big blue shark for **Shark Bite's Seafood Cafe** (240 S Broadway, 541/269-7475, www.sharkbites.cafe, 11am-9pm Mon.-Thurs., 11am-9:30pm Fri.-Sat., $8-20), which boasts one room with a long wooden counter and stools, and the other crowded with tables. The menu leans toward food from the sea, of course, with local Dungeness crab cakes and tacos made from beer-battered cod. The oysters, too, are local, and the service is friendly.

The Alder Smokehouse (1055 Virginia Ave., North Bend, 541/756-9599, 11am-3pm Tues.-Fri., $8-12), just north of Coos Bay, keeps its aim narrow and clear: meat cooked over alder wood, with sides like carrot salad or garlic toast to match. There's pulled pork and tri-tip, and on Thursdays the smokehouse serves a half-pound burger coated in barbecue sauce. The dining space is small, with tiny tables to match, but plenty of people just order at the counter and take their food to go.

ACCOMMODATIONS

The **Itty Bitty Inn** (1504 Sherman Ave., North Bend, 541/756-6398, www.ittybittyinn.com, $69) has a strange history, unsurprising since the hotel has been around since 1950 and is just off busy U.S. 101. After it made the news for being the site of a well-reported crime, it changed hands and got a retro makeover. There are Atari video game players and record players available for guests. With only five rooms, located just north of Coos Bay, it's a low-key place to stay, and rooms are simple but with lots of midcentury vintage decor. The inn will even loan you a growler to fill at the beer spot across the street.

The front side of **Edgewater Inn Coos Bay** (275 E Johnson Ave., 541/267-0423, http://edgewaterinns.com, $90-125) isn't particularly exciting, facing a Fred Meyer and a Safeway, but the window side of most rooms looks out on the waterways leading into Coos Bay. Some rooms have full kitchens, while others have spa tubs right next to the beds. With a common indoor pool and hot tub, it's the liveliest hotel in town.

Camping

Sunset Bay State Park (89814 Cape Arago Highway, 541/888-3778, www.oregonstateparks.org) has more than 60 RV sites ($29-31), 65 tent sites ($7-19), and a group camping area ($73). Half of its eight yurts ($43-53) are pet-friendly. Sites are located along Big Creek, slightly inland from the beaches; it's about a five-minute walk to the sand.

INFORMATION AND SERVICES

Get coastal maps, along with information on how to best access the coast and beaches, at the **Visitor Information Center** (50 Central Ave, 541/269-0215, www.coosbay.org, 9am-5pm Mon.-Fri. and 10am-2pm Sat.-Sun. summer, 9am-5pm Mon.-Fri and 10am-2pm Sat. winter) in the center of Coos Bay. Look for a building with windowed walls and solar panels on the roof.

GETTING THERE

Coos Bay is a few miles inland on a coastal waterway, located on U.S. 101 about 50 miles south of Florence, about an hour's drive.

Bandon

In a region known for growing cranberries, Bandon—technically "Bandon By the Sea"—is a charming place, perhaps the most vacation-ready Oregon Coast town south of Florence. It has a tiny, walkable downtown and waterfront boardwalk—it sits at the confluence of the Coquille River and Pacific Ocean—making for a great spot to eat fish-and-chips and drink beer in a seaside setting. And don't forget to pack your nine-iron: The state's best golf links are nearby.

OLD TOWN

Downtown Bandon features a large arch proclaiming "Welcome to Old Town Bandon." Walk the waterfront settlement—along the Coquille River's mouth—between Alabama and Elmira Avenues, along 1st and 2nd Streets, and you'll find single and two-story buildings with a salt-air polish filled with sleepy general stores, fish shacks, and coffee shops. The cheerful little town is ideal for stretching one's legs and eating some chowder after a long coastal drive.

SPORTS AND RECREATION

Parks and Beaches

One of the prettiest and most accessible lighthouses on this section of Oregon coastline, Coquille River Lighthouse, is found at **Bullards Beach State Park** (52470 U.S. 101, 541/347-2209, 11am-5pm daily mid-May-Sept., free), just north of Bandon. Drive through the park via Bullards Beach Road to its end and take a free tour from volunteer interpreters if they're present; they don't adhere to a regular schedule but are often around on summer weekends. The lighthouse, which dates back to 1896, opened to the public in the 1970s and got a solar-powered light in the 1990s.

It's worth leaving the highway for a short drive to **Face Rock State Scenic Viewpoint** (Beach Loop Rd., www.oregonstateparks.org), a parking area with views of the broad Face Rock—though where the face might be found is up to each observer. The area is surrounded by other giant sea stacks in the crashing waves, and a well-maintained stairway leads down to the beach. Don't touch harbor seal pups you might spot here; marine mammals should never be disturbed. The viewpoint is a wonderful place to watch sunset, even if mobility issues prevent you from descending to the beach. To reach the viewpoint, take Seabird Drive west about a mile south of Bandon, and go 0.5 mile to where it dead-ends into Beach Loop Road. Go right; the viewpoint is about a half mile north on the left, overlooking the ocean.

Golf

Teeing up with a view of the crashing Pacific surf explains the appeal of **Bandon Dunes Golf** (57744 Round Lake Rd., 541/347-4380, www.bandondunesgolf.com, guest greens fees $135-295), three miles north of Bandon, based at a resort that boasts four courses and an 18-hole putting course that sprawls over 2.5 acres. One course, Pacific Dunes, is often ranked among the best in the country, and tournaments are held at the photogenic holes. Resort hotel guests get the full spread of the amenities—like access to the putting course and discounted greens fees—but access is open to anyone if booked in advance. There's also a 13-hole par-three course ($50-100), Bandon Preserve, where greens fees benefit an environmental conservation nonprofit that protects the native silvery phacelia plant, now endangered. This is the ideal destination for more casual golfers who still want great scenery.

Boating and Crabbing

Tony's Crab Shack (155 1st St. SE, 541/347-2875, www.tonyscrabshack.com, shop/rentals 6am-6pm daily) rents motorboats ($30 per hour) and crabbing gear ($12 per day). It also serves up simple seafood.

ENTERTAINMENT AND EVENTS

Located in the middle of Bandon's walkable downtown, **Arcade Tavern** (135 Alabama

Bandon

Ave. SE, 541/329-0526 10am-2am daily) has a wood-shingle exterior suggesting the New England seaside. Inside you'll find a simple bar with beer specials and weekly karaoke, and the pool tables stay busy. Expect stiff competition for a seat on bingo night.

Bandon Brewing (395 2nd St. SE, 541/347-3911, http://bandonbrewingco.com, 11am-8pm daily) serves beers and wood-fired pizza ($12-20) in a wood-paneled pub, with tables right next to the beer-making vats. A chalkboard offers a wide array of ingredients for a design-your-own pizza, and sometimes the space hosts live music.

With its wet, mild autumns, Bandon is a region known for growing cranberries—some 30 million pounds per year. In late summer, Bandon's **Cranberry Festival** (http://bandon.com/cranberry-festival, Sept.) celebrates the seaside fruit with cooking contests, a festival market, and live music, with a big dance party in the middle of town. Enter the eating contest at your own risk.

SHOPPING

To find the kind of souvenirs an Oregon beach vacation requires—homemade fudge, maybe a baseball cap with Sasquatch on it—head to **Big Wheel General Store** (130 Baltimore Ave. SE, 541/347-3719, 9am-5:30pm Mon.-Sat., 10am-5pm Sun.), a shop that tries to capture the breadth and hominess of the old Western general store with wooden walls and vintage decor. It's also a good place to find a sweatshirt or fleece if the Oregon shore proves to be chillier than you expected.

Cranberry Sweets (280 1st St. SE, 541/347-9475, http://cranberrysweets.com, 9:30am-6pm Mon.-Sat. and 9:30am-5:30pm Sun. summer, 10am-5pm Mon.-Sat. and 11am-4pm Sun. winter) sells locally made cranberry jelly treats that've been made the same way for more than 50 years, available in both regular and chocolate-covered varieties.

FOOD

Located at the edge of town and within sight of the Coquille River Lighthouse, **Edgewaters** (480 1st St. SW, 541/347-8500, www.edgewaters.net, 5pm-9:30pm Mon.-Thurs., 11:30am-3pm and 5pm-9:30pm Fri.-Sun. June-Sept., 5pm-9pm Tues.-Thurs., 11:30am-3pm and 5pm-9pm Fri.-Sun. Oct.-May, $15-26) has its own two-story building with a giant orca mural, and many tables have windows offering views. The menu includes hearty half-pound burgers and plenty of seafood, from a signature calamari to a seafood Romanesco, a

Coquille River Lighthouse at Bullards Beach State Park

stew crammed with shellfish and fish. No restaurant in town could truly be called "fancy," but this is the best place to go for a leisurely or celebratory meal.

Just off the boardwalk, **Tony's Crab Shack** (155 1st St. SE, 541/347-2875, www.tonyscrabshack.com, crab shack 10:30am-6pm daily, $7-17) dishes seafood mostly the simple way—grilled with a simple sauce or served with just lemon and cocktail sauce on the side. There are also a few pasta dishes. With its attached gift shop and boat and crabbing gear rentals, it's the whole experience of an Oregon Coast vacation in a single spot.

For fish-and-chips in every form, look for the blue **Bandon Fish Market** (249 1st St. SE, 541/347-4282, www.bandonfishmarket.com, 11am-7pm daily, $8-20), with tiny painted fish along its exterior. The menu also includes New England clam chowder and a Pacific salmon chowder, plus burgers and seafood cocktails. Though tiny, there's a small patio with outdoor seating and plenty of places to wander with fish-and-chips in hand.

ACCOMMODATIONS

Under $150

Located just across from Face Rock State Scenic Viewpoint, **Table Rock Motel** (840 Beach Loop Rd., 800/457-9141, www.tablerockmotel.com, $70-165) has eccentric style, its rooms decorated with seagoing knickknacks or elegant draperies, or decked out in countryside cottage motifs or bright florals evoking Hawaii. There aren't many amenities besides kitchenettes in some rooms and a few picnic tables outside, but the hotel has a wonderful location and a very chill vibe.

$150-250

Located south of Bandon, not far from the Face Rock State Scenic Viewpoint—about half a mile away and inland—**Best Western Inn at Face Rock** (3225 Beach Loop Dr. SW, 541/347-9441, www.innatfacerock.com, $161-170) offers homier touches than you'd expect from a chain hotel, like white wood headboards and plaid curtains. The hotel has an indoor pool and hot tub, and some rooms have whirlpool tubs, fireplaces, or balconies and ocean views. A breakfast buffet is included, and a path outside leads to the beach, a five-minute walk away.

With its wood-shingled exterior and sharp white trim, **Bandon Inn** (355 U.S. 101, 541/347-4417, www.bandoninn.com, $144-279) has a cozy vibe, but its bluff-top location overlooking the small town means its views and walkability are the biggest selling points. The hotel offers a free shuttle to the Bandon golf courses, and the hotel's espresso stand will deliver to the room. Some king rooms have whirlpool tubs, and there are a few two-room spa suites.

Over $250

Located with the famous links, **Bandon Dunes Golf Resort** (57744 Round Lake Rd., 541/347-4380, www.bandondunesgolf.com, inn $260-380, lodge $230-280) offers the closest to luxury-level accommodations you'll find on the southern Oregon coast. The lodge has 17 rooms, some with views of the golf course, dunes, or ocean, and all have furnishings in a light beachy wood. The inn, a little less central, has almost 40 rooms with a slightly more modern (and less lodge-y) look, many also with views. Guests have access to a bar and reading room with lofty exposed wood beams. Prices drop in the off-season, and the grounds have several dining options, from a full-service restaurant to a grill, a pub, and bars.

Camping

To camp near the area lighthouse, look to **Bullards Beach State Park** (52470 U.S. 101, 541/347-2209, www.oregonstateparks.org) for more than 100 full-hookup RV sites ($31) and another 80-plus with electricity and water ($29). The hiker/biker campsites ($7) even have solar-powered USB charging ports, and almost half of the 13 rentable yurts ($43-53) are pet-friendly.

INFORMATION AND SERVICES

Find the **Bandon Chamber of Commerce and Visitor Center Office** (300 2nd St., 541/347-9616, http://bandon.com, 10am-4pm daily) in the middle of town for help in locating services in the area. The bigger hotels in town will also have maps and information.

GETTING THERE

Bandon is located about a 30-minute drive, or 25 miles, south of Coos Bay, just below where the Coquille River pours into the Pacific. The downtown, dotted with stores and restaurants, is just west of the highway and often filled with pedestrian tourists.

Ashland and Southern Oregon

Look for ★ to find recommended sights, activities, dining, and lodging.

Highlights

★ **Lithia Park:** Southern Oregon's most welcoming town is built around this quaint park (page 421).

★ **White-Water Rafting Near Ashland:** Hold on tight for a rip-roaring trip down southern Oregon's surging white waters, or opt for a gentle float (page 423).

★ **Oregon Shakespeare Festival:** Great theater comes alive in an annual, months-long salute to the Bard (page 424).

★ **Wizard Island Boat Tour:** Climb aboard for a ranger-led tour and visit to the island in the middle of Crater Lake (page 432).

★ **Hiking in Crater Lake National Park:** The terrain surrounding the deepest lake in the country is best explored on foot (page 432).

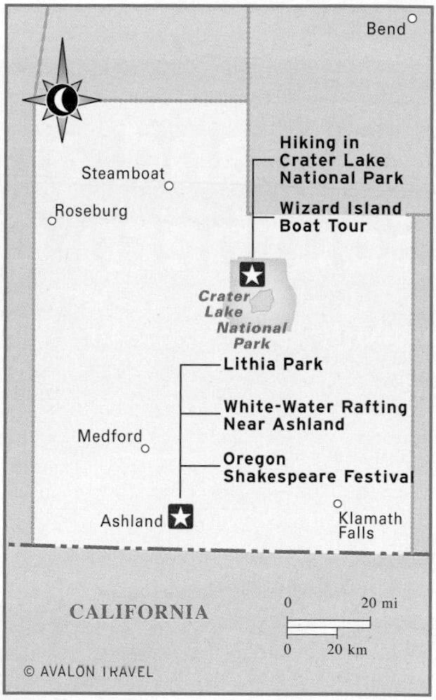

Located just a few miles north of the California border, the former mill town of Ashland is a cultural gem, famous for its quaint downtown and months-long Oregon Shakespeare Festival.

Standing out from the more agricultural cities of the region with its unhurried, artistic, hippie-friendly vibe, Ashland compels you to slow down and meet its pace, surrounded by farmlands and forests. There's a proud sense of style in every block here—48 of the town's buildings are on the National Register of Historic Places. Ashland's famous Shakespeare festival celebrates the Bard, sure, but salutes other playwrights as well, and crescendos in the summer. A highly walkable downtown is full of restaurants boasting the area's best dining.

Here in the Siskiyou Mountains, hills are low and rounded, covered with trees. Although Ashland is on the west side of the Cascades, it's not as rainy as most of Oregon's western side; the climate is a bit drier and a little sunnier, like a mix of the state's two sides. The Rogue and Klamath Rivers slice through the region, with Ashland up a low valley on one of the former's tributaries, offering recreational opportunities for white-water rafting.

Just a short drive away, the wild side of Oregon is on display at stunning Crater Lake National Park. A brilliant blue and formed by a volcanic eruption, Crater Lake is the deepest in the country and the state's only national park. The pace may be languid in southern Oregon, but there's much to discover.

PLANNING YOUR TIME

If you're visiting during Ashland's famous Shakespeare festival, which runs most of the year (Feb.-Oct.), book tickets to plays you might want to see in advance and build your time here around performances. For shows in the height of summer, book tickets in early spring; outside this high season, you can typically book tickets a few weeks in advance. The town itself can be seen in a day, but stay overnight if attending a night show.

A white-water rafting trip or an excursion

Previous: Lithia Park; Crater Lake. **Above:** the Oregon Shakespeare Festival.

Ashland and Southern Oregon

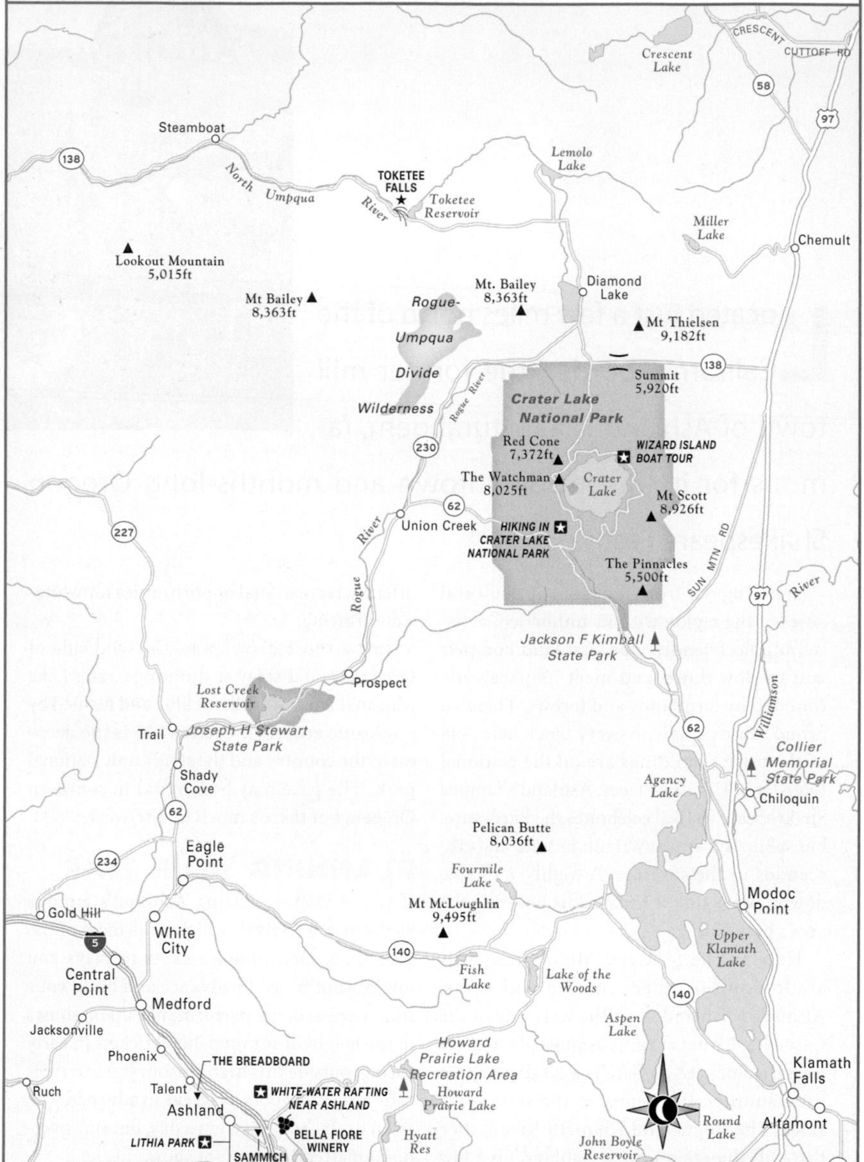

Crescent Lake
CRESCENT CUTTOFF RD
58
97
Steamboat
138
North Umpqua River
TOKETEE FALLS
Toketee Reservoir
Lemolo Lake
Miller Lake
Chemult
Lookout Mountain 5,015ft
Mt Bailey 8,363ft
Mt. Bailey 8,363ft
Diamond Lake
Rogue-Umpqua Divide Wilderness
Mt Thielsen 9,182ft
138
Summit 5,920ft
Crater Lake National Park
Rogue River
230
Red Cone 7,372ft
WIZARD ISLAND BOAT TOUR
The Watchman 8,025ft
Crater Lake
Mt Scott 8,926ft
62
Union Creek
HIKING IN CRATER LAKE NATIONAL PARK
227
SUN MTN RD
The Pinnacles 5,500ft
97
River
Rogue River
Jackson F Kimball State Park
Prospect
Lost Creek Reservoir
Williamson
Trail
Joseph H Stewart State Park
62
Collier Memorial State Park
Shady Cove
Agency Lake
Chiloquin
62
Pelican Butte 8,036ft
Eagle Point
234
Fourmile Lake
Modoc Point
Gold Hill
Mt McLoughlin 9,495ft
White City
5
Upper Klamath Lake
140
Central Point
Fish Lake
Lake of the Woods
Medford
140
Jacksonville
Aspen Lake
Phoenix
THE BREADBOARD
Howard Prairie Lake Recreation Area
Klamath Falls
Talent
Ruch
WHITE-WATER RAFTING NEAR ASHLAND
Howard Prairie Lake
Ashland
BELLA FIORE WINERY
Round Lake
Altamont
LITHIA PARK
SAMMICH
Hyatt Res
John Boyle Reservoir
OREGON SHAKESPEARE FESTIVAL
Emigrant Lake
0
10 mi
39
66
Pinehurst
0
10 km
River
Klamath
Mt Ashland 7,523ft
97
Siskiyou Summit 4,310ft

to Crater Lake National Park deserves at least an entire day each—don't try to mix them in with a Shakespeare day. Once off the interstate, travel can be slow on the small rural roads, so you'll want to build in plenty of time to get into the wilderness and then back out. In summer at Crater Lake, visitors can explore plentiful hiking options, drive the entire circumference of the lake via the Rim Drive, and take boat tours. In winter, there's snowshoeing and a meal at Crater Lake Lodge to fill the time.

Ashland

Ashland has a friendly vibe and just a touch of Oregon's signature hippie chill, and its walkable downtown and lovely park have all the charm of a Shakespeare comedy. The town is literally centered around its festival, radiating from where the theaters sit next to verdant Lithia Park. Many notable bars, restaurants, and hotels sit within a few blocks of this central location, and the downtown, in true Oregon form, is based around two one-way streets bisected by two-way streets. You can tell the locals from the visitors because the former are taking their time, in no rush to get around the quaint town. Despite all the festivalgoers, only on the busiest of summer weekends does it feel close to overrun with tourists.

SIGHTS

★ Lithia Park

Ashland's **Lithia Park** (N Main St. and Winburn Way, 541/488-5340, www.ashland.or.us/lithiaPark, dawn-11pm, free) occupies 93 acres of woodland around burbling Ashland Creek, which runs its length. Paved and dirt paths wind through the park and over quaint wooden pedestrian bridges. The park's trees and narrow shape make it feel cozy, like you're wandering a backyard garden that never ends. Its northern border begins at the western edge of downtown and stretches south about a mile. The Oregon Shakespeare Festival theaters are close by, making it an ideal place for a pre- or post-show ramble.

The park takes its name from a lithium-rich spring, which feeds a public fountain in

Lithia Park

Ashland

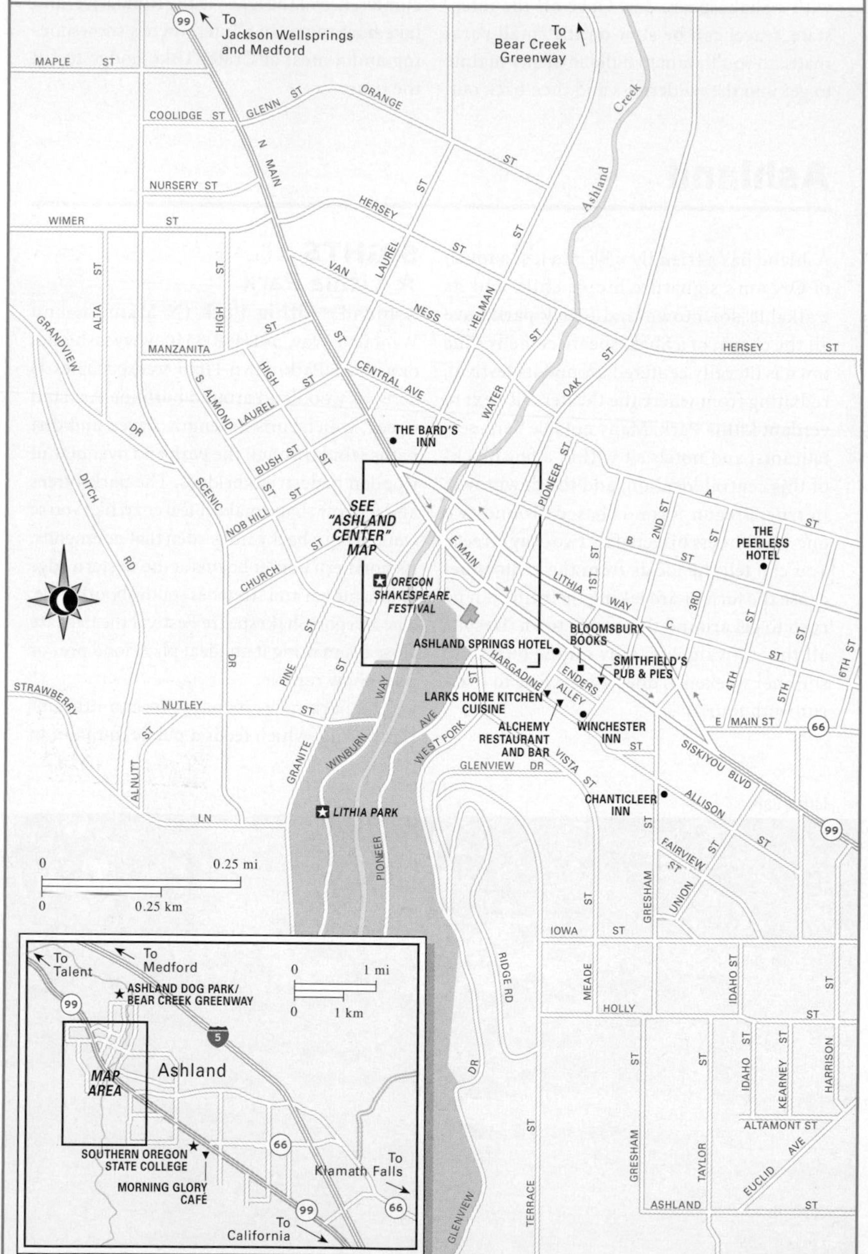

To Jackson Wellsprings and Medford
To Bear Creek Greenway
MAPLE ST
GLENN ST
ORANGE
COOLIDGE ST
N MAIN
NURSERY ST
HERSEY
WIMER ST
Ashland Creek
VAN NESS
LAUREL ST
HELMAN ST
ALTA ST
HIGH ST
GRANDVIEW
MANZANITA
HERSEY ST
S ALMOND
LAUREL
HIGH ST
CENTRAL AVE
WATER ST
OAK ST
SCENIC DR
DITCH RD
BUSH ST
NOB HILL ST
PIONEER ST
THE BARD'S INN
SEE "ASHLAND CENTER" MAP
E MAIN
A ST
B ST
2ND ST
1ST ST
3RD ST
CHURCH ST
LITHIA WAY
THE PEERLESS HOTEL
OREGON SHAKESPEARE FESTIVAL
C ST
BLOOMSBURY BOOKS
ASHLAND SPRINGS HOTEL
SMITHFIELD'S PUB & PIES
HARGADINE
ENDERS ALLEY
4TH ST
5TH ST
6TH ST
STRAWBERRY
NUTLEY ST
PINE ST
GRANITE ST
WINBURN WAY
LARKS HOME KITCHEN CUISINE
ALCHEMY RESTAURANT AND BAR
WINCHESTER INN
E MAIN ST
66
VISTA ST
WEST FORK
AVE
GLENVIEW DR
SISKIYOU BLVD
ALNUTT ST
LN
LITHIA PARK
CHANTICLEER INN
ALLISON ST
99
FAIRVIEW ST
GRESHAM ST
UNION
0 0.25 mi
0 0.25 km
IOWA ST
RIDGE RD
MEADE ST
HOLLY ST
IDAHO ST
KEARNEY ST
HARRISON ST
ALTAMONT ST
EUCLID AVE
TERRACE ST
GRESHAM
TAYLOR
ASHLAND ST
GLENVIEW DR
To Talent
To Medford
ASHLAND DOG PARK/ BEAR CREEK GREENWAY
0 1 mi
0 1 km
5
Ashland
MAP AREA
SOUTHERN OREGON STATE COLLEGE
MORNING GLORY CAFÉ
To Klamath Falls
To California
© AVALON TRAVEL

rafting the Rogue River

a small plaza near the northern end. Inside the park you'll find two duck ponds, a small playground, and the manicured Japanese Garden, as well as a bandshell where free concerts are held in the summer (7pm Thurs. mid-June-mid-Aug.). In winter there's an ice skating rink (100 Winburn Way, 541/488-9189, www.ashland.or.us/icerink, Nov.-Mar., admission and skate rental $4 adults, $3.50 children 5-13, free for children under 5).

Jackson Wellsprings

Ashland's mineral-rich waters have long been famous—touristed for its hot springs since the 1870s—and you can soak in them as well at **Jackson Wellsprings** (2253 Hwy. 99 N, 541/482-3776, www.jacksonwellsprings.com, 6pm-midnight Mon., 10am-midnight Tues.-Sun., day-use $10 adults, $8 seniors and students, $4 children), 2.5 miles northwest of downtown. Water from the region's hot springs are piped into an outdoor Olympic-sized soaking pool. The complex also has a steam room and a sauna, and private Jacuzzi tubs are available for an additional charge (1.25 hours, $30-40). A one-time $5 annual fee is charged first-time visitors on top of the day-use fees.

Tuesday-Sunday nights from sunset or 8pm (whichever comes first) are clothing optional. Spa services, including massages and facials ($80-135), are also available on-site and include a soak in the hot springs.

Belle Fiore Winery

Though wine is the star attraction at **Belle Fiore Winery** (100 Belle Fiore Ln., 541/552-4900, http://bellefiorewine.com, noon-7pm Sun. and Wed., noon-8pm Thurs.-Sat., $15-19 tasting fee), its gorgeous grounds are what makes it worth a trip. Modeled on a French chateau and with an Italian tasting room pavilion, the winery offers a little slice of Europe in the middle of the Rogue Valley. It's run by a winemaker who once worked at NASA and now produces a variety of red and white varietals. Tastings are held in a few different sites around the property. A tasting at the chateau itself includes some premium wines ($40-55 private tasting) and is by appointment only.

To get there, drive about five miles out of town, heading east on Main Street, merging onto Highway 66, and turning left onto Dead Indian Memorial Road, off which you'll find the winery. It's about a 15-minute drive.

SPORTS AND RECREATION

★ White-Water Rafting

Easily accessible from Ashland are the nearby Rogue and Klamath Rivers, offering copious opportunities for white-water rafting and floating adventures. A number of companies in the area run these trips, an exciting, athletic way to see the rugged landscape of southern Oregon as you make your way through beautiful, wild river miles, passing through gorges and forests.

Ashland's **Noah's River Adventures** (53 N Main St., 541/488-2811, http://noahsrafting.com) has standard half-day (three departures daily May.-Oct., $79-89,) and full-day

(May-Oct., $145) white-water trips on the Rogue River. A scenic float option (Mar.-Oct., $89) offers a calmer, half-day trip on the Rogue that's more focused on scenery, wildlife, and enjoying the sunshine. A full-day Upper Klamath River rapid trip (May-Oct., $175), on the other end of the spectrum, goes through 47 rapids in a single day. Some full-day trips include meals served riverside.

Rogue Rafting Company (404 2nd Ave., Gold Hill, 541/855-7080, www.roguerafting-company.com), based in the small town of Gold Hill north of Ashland, takes paddlers seven miles down a white-water section of the Rogue on a half-day trip ($85, two departures daily) and 14 miles on a full-day trip ($129). Some trips can be combined with a zip line and wine tasting.

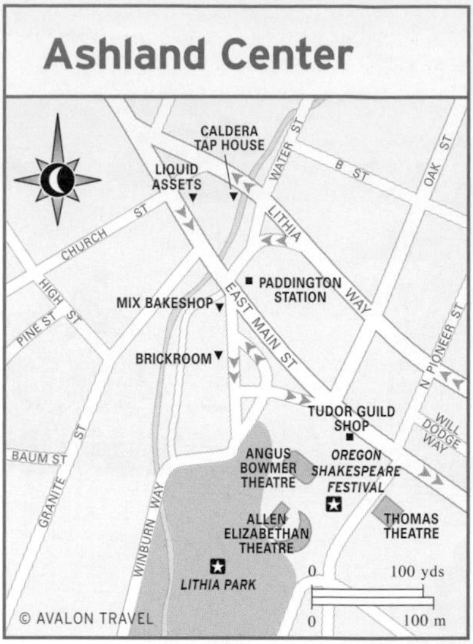

Biking

Ashland's fairly flat terrain makes for good biking. Cycling is done on roads with low traffic—and fortunately there are a lot of those around here—or on the **Bear Creek Greenway** (www.bearcreekgreenway.com), an 18-mile paved bike- and pedestrian-only path from Ashland that runs up north to the towns of Medford and Central Point. The **Ashland Loop** is a popular 28-mile ride that starts at Lithia Park and takes surface streets to a bikes-only road made of decomposed granite. Rent bikes and find maps at **Bear Creek Cycles** (1988 Hwy. 99, 541/488-4270, www.bearcreekbicycle.com, 9:30am-6pm Tues.-Sat., $15 per hour), located a mile northwest of downtown, near where the Bear Creek Greenway starts.

ENTERTAINMENT AND EVENTS

Nightlife

Liquid Assets (96 N Main St., 541/482-9463, www.liquidassetswinebar.com, 4pm-11pm Mon.-Thurs., 4pm-midnight Fri.- Sat.) focuses on wine, offering around two dozen varieties of red and white by the glass and hundreds more by the bottle. It also offers craft beer and cocktails, and the food menu ranges from truffled popcorn to coconut calamari. The space is warm, thanks to orange glass lighting and well-padded bar seats, and the walls are lined with art, with a focus on local artists and often including works from nature photographers and painters.

Caldera Tap House (31 Water St., 541/482-7468, www.calderabrewing.com, 2pm-9pm Mon.-Thurs., 11:30am-9pm Fri.-Sun.) is Caldera Brewing Company's downtown outpost (its brewing facilities and a restaurant are also located in Ashland, just off I-5). It claims to be the first West Coast brewery to can its own product. But at the tap room, the stars are obviously the drafts. Additionally, the pub has a three-tiered outdoor seating deck and a food menu offering burgers that pair well with a cold one. Children are welcome until well into the evening.

TOP EXPERIENCE

★ Oregon Shakespeare Festival

Southern Oregon is famous for Ashland's massive **Oregon Shakespeare Festival** (OSF, 15 S Pioneer St., 800/219-8161, www.osfashland.org, Feb.-Oct., $30-115), less of a singular event than a defining theater scene that runs through most of the year. It began in 1935, when a university teacher got $400 to start the festival; the first play was *Twelfth Night*.

Annually, about a half-million theatergoers come to watch a selection of Shakespeare and other plays. About half of the dozen or so shows put on each year are by the Bard, and each play has a different run length; some run through the bulk of the festival, while others only show for a month or so. Non-Shakespeare works might be recognizable to casual theater fans—a reimagining of Rodgers and Hammerstein's *Oklahoma!*, for example, or an adaption of a Jane Austen novel—or might be new or obscure works.

The two biggest venues, the **Angus Bowmer** and **Allen Elizabethan Theatres,** are right next to the courtyard entrance to the festival grounds, called Bricks, on Pioneer Street. A smaller indoor space, the **Thomas Theatre,** is just a block away. For the most classic Shakespeare experience, find a performance at the Allen Elizabethan Theatre, where plays take place in an open-air space, evoking the old British theater tradition. Backstage tours are also available some days ($20).

The Green Show (6:45pm Tues.-Sun. June.-Oct., free) takes place at the Bricks most days—a 45-minute program that may or may not have ties to the Shakespeare plays. Performances are always a surprise combination of dance, theater, and other arts. It's a very casual outdoor event that's become as integral to the festival as that Hamlet guy.

Other Festivals and Events

The late winter **Oregon Chocolate Festival** (www.oregonchocolatefestival.com, Mar., $20) takes place before the reliably nice summer weather kicks in; it's a good time to stay indoors for wine-and-chocolate pairing events and chef demos, and sneak out for a 5K walk or run to work off some of the sweets. Sculptures made of chocolate welcome attendees to the hotel-based event.

Though Shakespeare's plays are Ashland's calling card, the theater scene here also supports the **Ashland New Plays Festival** (www.ashlandnewplays.org, Oct.). The decades-old, five-day event features brand-new works in staged readings, letting audiences observe and be part of the workshopping process of creating new art. This flagship event takes place when the Oregon Shakespeare Festival plays are winding down for the year,

Oregon Shakespeare Festival

though the organization put on plays year-round. Ticket prices are modest, starting around $20.

SHOPPING

Of course there's a proper bookstore in such a bookish town. **Bloomsbury Books** (290 E Main St., 541/488-0029, www.bloomsbury-ashland.com, 8:30am-9pm Mon.-Fri., 9am-9pm Sat., 10am-6pm Sun.) is in a two-story space with plenty of reading nooks and a café between the rows of new books. The store's knowledgeable staff makes good recommendations. And, of course, there's a large drama section.

Whimsy abounds at **Paddington Station** (125 E Main St., 541/482-1343, http://paddingtonstationashland.com, 10am-5:30pm Sun.-Mon., 9:30am-8pm Tues.-Sat.), a gift shop made for browsing. Its wares stretch over three floors of a downtown building that dates back to 1904. Besides some Shakespeare-themed items, there's women's fashion, Oregon-made gifts, quirky artwork, and jewelry.

The official Oregon Shakespeare Festival gift store, **Tudor Guild Shop** (15 S Pioneer St., 541/482-0940, www.tudorguild.org, 11am-4pm Mon., 10am-8pm Tues.-Sat., 11am-8pm Sun. Feb.-Oct.), has hats and T-shirts with OSF logos and a whole range of Bard gifts, like a Yorick skull-shaped piggy bank and pot holders printed with Shakespearean insults. Find leather-bound books and costumes, finger puppets, and posters. The guild also operates the nearby **Brass Rubbing Center** (behind the Allen Elizabethan Theatre, 11am-3pm Wed.-Sat. summer, from $7), where visitors can create a rubbing of one of 73 replicas of historical English brass sculptures.

FOOD

American

The dreamy ★ **Alchemy Restaurant and Bar** (35 S 2nd St., 541/488-1115, www.alchemyashland.com, 5pm-8pm Wed.-Thurs. and Sun., 5pm-8:30pm Fri.-Sat., $16-26) has large windows facing the gardens of the Winchester Inn and towering rows of bottles behind the bar. Menu offerings—foie gras, stuffed endives, a stellar filet mignon—are presented with care, all picture-perfect with colorful garnishes or artful sauces. For all the restaurant's style, it doesn't feel too formal, just special.

Located in the central Ashland Springs Hotel downtown, **Larks Home Kitchen Cuisine** (212 E Main St., 541/488-5558, www.larksrestaurant.com, 11:30am-2pm and 5pm-8pm Mon.-Thurs., 11:30am-2pm and 5pm-9pm Fri., 11am-2pm and 5pm-9pm Sat., 11am-2pm and 5pm-8pm Sun., $25-42) has a vaguely old-fashioned-sounding name, but the bright dining room is modern and elegant, and the menu is crammed with locally sourced vegetables and dishes like rabbit cacciatore.

The 2nd-floor **Brickroom** (35 N Main St., 541/708-6030, http://brickroomashland.com, 8am-1am daily, $12-32) is a mix of modern and vintage, with dark wood furniture complementing the Edison bulbs and exposed brick walls. An artfully distressed leather couch sits by the fireplace, and a long bar runs through the middle of this very hip space. Meals are made up of brasserie classics and small plates that combine well. With style to spare, plus a Bloody Mary topped with a virtual vegetable garden on skewers, wait times can be long. Reservations are recommended, and note the bar also serves the full menu.

Sammich (424 Bridge St., 541/708-6055, http://sammichashland.com, 11am-6pm Mon.-Sat., 11am-4pm Sun., $7-14) is in a strip mall about a mile southeast of town. The counter-service interior is simple, but the massive Chicago-style sandwiches beckon with their piles of meat and veggies, classic pickle side, and knife that sits handle-out to help you tackle the beasts. Options include house-cured pastrami and tuna poached in-house, and are served with thick potato chips. Any sandwich can be made gluten-free. It's about a mile southeast of downtown, just past Morning Glory Cafe.

Breakfast

About a mile southeast of downtown, ★ **Morning Glory Cafe** (1149 Siskiyou Blvd., 541/488-8636, www.morningglorycafe.org, 7:30am-8pm daily, $12-20) is a sunny, ultracasual dining space with wall murals. It advertises a "giant cup of coffee" on the menu—only $3—and combos of greasy, hearty breakfast foods including piles of pancakes and waffles with delectable toppings, like berry compotes and lemon butter. It's a small space, so there may be a wait for breakfast. Sandwiches are on the menu for lunch, and the dinner menu includes classic fish and salad dishes, as well as extensive vegetarian and vegan options.

Breakfast is a leisure activity at **The Breadboard** (744 N Main St., 541/488-0295, www.breadboardashland.com, 7am-2pm daily, $9-13). For almost 40 years, it's been a staple in Ashland, and the owner has been known to serenade guests with his ukulele. Sourdough pancakes, numerous omelet options, and multigrain French toast are served. Muffins are baked fresh daily. The outdoor patio is popular, and lines form on weekends even though the spot is about a mile north of downtown.

Located in a strip mall about 1.5 miles southeast from downtown, **Little Shop of Bagels** (1644 Ashland St., 541/488-0718, 7am-3pm daily, $1-2) is a simple eatery populated with locals and home to a delicious everything bagel and a wide array of spreads. There are tables, but most comers grab a bite and take it to go.

Although **Mix Bakeshop** (57 N Main St., 541/488-9885, www.mixashland.com, 7am-8pm Sun.-Thurs., 7am-8:30pm Fri.-Sat., $3-8) sells pastries, the small café's coffee is probably its biggest draw. Located near the main entrance to Lithia Park and in the center of downtown, the Stumptown purveyor pours coffee to grateful tourists and locals all day, much of it topped with fancy patterns in the foam. Baked goods include chocolate confections and croissants.

British

A spin-off from Smithfields Restaurant and Bar across the street, **Smithfields Pub & Pies** (23 S 2nd St., 541/482-7437, http://smithfieldspubpies.com, 11:30am-midnight daily, $10-12) leans into the town's Shakespeare connection by serving British savory pies, pub food, and ales—plus it offers Guinness on a nitro tap. The menu is a throwback, but the tiled wall and decor are modern.

ACCOMMODATIONS

Under $150

Once an old motel, **The M Ashland** (145 Siskiyou Blvd., 541/482-2561, www.ashlandmotel.com, $100-135) was reborn as a boutique two-story property with a little more character than its first iteration. Super-mod decor spices up the boxy rooms, while futon-style couches and mini-fridges still lend a budget vibe. There's a swimming pool and free Wi-Fi. Some rooms have kitchenettes. The M is located about a mile southeast of downtown.

$150-250

Originally built atop a mineral spring, **Lithia Springs Resort** (2165 W Jackson Rd., 800/482-7128, http://lithiaspringsresort.com, $189-259 rooms, $269-289 suites) is a collection of 38 hotel rooms, studios, and bungalows, almost like a giant bed-and-breakfast, located a few miles north of downtown. The hot breakfast and afternoon tea spread are nice amenities, and there's a spa in a cottage among the gardens offering massages and other services. The mineral waters are known to be healing—not necessarily scientifically proven, but definitely relaxing. Soak in the spring water in the in-room tubs or in the swimming pool.

Easily walkable from downtown, **The Bard's Inn** (132 N Main St., 541/209-3015, http://bardsinn.com, $190-260) goes all in with its Shakespeare references: The four buildings that make up the inn are named Verona, Juliet, London, and Sonnet. The original 40 rooms at the London are the simplest and cheapest, with a pool onsite; Verona has a dozen higher-end, larger rooms; and Juliet and Sonnet appropriately offer more romantic and secluded options. Breakfast is included and hot, and the hotel is pet-friendly.

The six rooms that make up the **Chanticleer Inn** (120 Gresham St., 541/482-1919, http://chanticleerashland.com, $185-220) are all garden-themed, with floral linens and soft pastel walls, appropriate for a bed-and-breakfast surrounded by greenery and views of the valley. The house has a beautiful stone wall and is located in a quiet neighborhood, making it one of the more picturesque places to stay in town. Check the calendar to see when breakfast is included; winter rates are notably lower but may not include any meals.

The brick facade of **The Peerless Hotel** (243 4th St., 541/488-1082, http://peerlesshotel.com, $205-269 rooms, $289-305 suites), located a few blocks north of downtown, is a stately Victorian, originally a railworkers' boardinghouse but now a six-room boutique hotel. Rooms are unique; one has exposed brick and a wall mural, another has twin bathtubs. Suites are considerably larger. A two-course breakfast is served outside by a fountain when the weather is appropriate.

Over $250

Located downtown right next to the festival grounds and Lithia Park, ★ **Ashland Springs Hotel** (212 E Main St., 541/488-1700, www.ashlandspringshotel.com, $209-299) is the white tower in the town's center. Its exterior is decorated with stately columns and curlicues, and the 1925 interior—renovated in 2000—has a Mediterranean feel, right down to the palm trees. Rooms range from a simple king room to a parlor suite with a small living room. The hotel also has a spa, the Larks Home Kitchen Cuisine restaurant, and a small English garden, but its biggest draw is its incredible location.

The stately house that holds the **Winchester Inn** (35 S 2nd St., 541/488-1113, www.winchesterinn.com, $280 rooms, $365-455 suites) has a sophisticated vibe; four-poster beds in some rooms complete the look. Staff delivers pastries to rooms during turndown service in the evening, adding to the sense of luxury. With about two dozen rooms, it feels larger than a bed-and-breakfast—yes, breakfast is included—but smaller than a full hotel. Suites have multiple rooms and extra seating but maintain a cozy feel. Downtown is within walking distance and, on the 1st floor, Alchemy Restaurant and Bar dishes food that's as much of a treat as staying in the Winchester Inn.

Camping

Come for the hot springs, but stay for the tepees at **Jackson Wellsprings** (2253 Hwy. 99 N, 541/482-3776, www.jacksonwellsprings.com), several miles north of town near Lithia Springs Resort. Camping includes a soak in the mineral pool, and the tepees ($40 for first person) are a perfect place to sleep in Oregon's warm summers. Tents ($25 for first person) and RV sites ($35 for first person) are also available. It costs $15 for each additional person.

INFORMATION AND SERVICES

For more information about what to do in Ashland, visit the chamber of commerce's **information kiosk** (N Main St. and Winburn Way, 10am-5pm Mon.-Fri., 9am-6pm Sat.-Sun.) located in the plaza next to Lithia Park. You can also try the **Oregon Shakespeare Festival box office** (OSF, 15 S Pioneer St.) or the front desk of the **Ashland Springs Hotel** (212 E Main St.) for visitor information; staff at both are very knowledgeable.

GETTING THERE

The closest airport to Ashland is the **Rogue Valley International-Medford Airport** (MFR, 1000 Terminal Loop Pkwy., Medford, 541/772-8068, www.jacksoncountyor.org/airport) in Medford, about 16 miles away. **Crater**

Lake Taxi (541/333-3333, www.craterlaket-axi.com) serves the entire area, and a cab from the airport to Ashland is about a 30-minute drive and $45.

Ashland is just off I-5, not far from the Oregon-California border. From Portland in the north, take I-5 South for about 285 miles to exit 19, then turn right onto South Valley View Road. Make a left 0.25 mile later onto Highway 99. Stay on the highway for about three miles to downtown Ashland. The drive takes about five hours total.

Crater Lake National Park

Welcome to the deepest lake in the country, formed not so long ago—7,700 years in the past, when a volcanic eruption at Mount Mazama caused the mountain to collapse onto itself. The crater filled with rain and snow, creating a spectacular blue circle ringed by mountains. It became a national park in 1902, the only one in the state. Also home to one of the country's spectacular national park inns, Crater Lake is the jewel of southern Oregon.

VISITING THE PARK

Seasonal considerations are important in determining when to visit the park. In winter, Rim Village—where the Crater Lake Lodge is located—is the only part of the park you can access. It's only possible to drive the entire scenic loop around the lake, via the Rim Drive, in summer. Openings and closures depend on snowfall, but the whole road is typically open from July through October or November.

Entrance Stations

The main entryway to **Crater Lake National Park** (541/594-3000, www.nps.gov/crla) is the **south entrance station,** accessible via Highway 62. While this entrance is open year-round as weather permits, roads can close with little notice. Check with the park and the **Oregon Department of Transportation** (www.tripcheck.org) to make sure access roads are open on the day you plan to visit. The south entrance is near **Mazama Village,** a small area of services with a restaurant, gift shop, and hotel.

The less-used **north entrance station**

Crater Lake

Crater Lake National Park

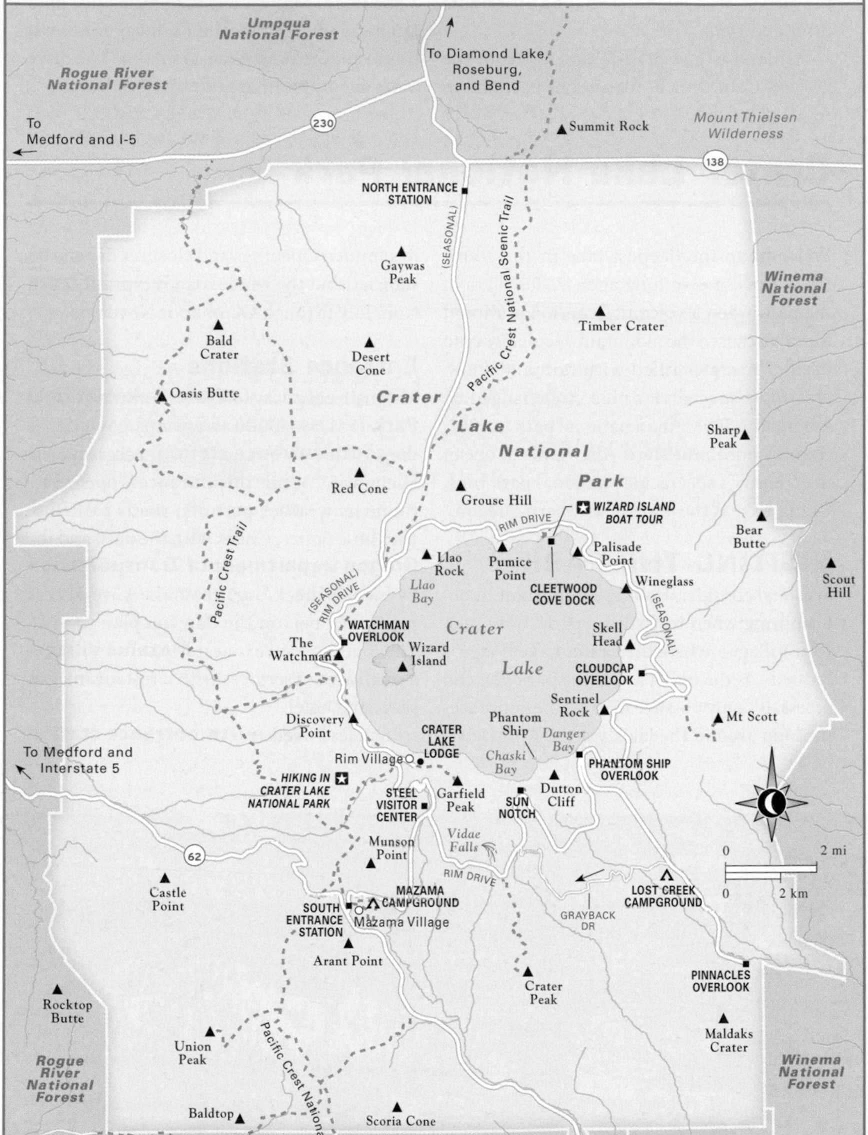
Umpqua National Forest
Rogue River National Forest
To Diamond Lake, Roseburg, and Bend
To Medford and I-5
230
Summit Rock
Mount Thielsen Wilderness
138
NORTH ENTRANCE STATION
(SEASONAL)
Pacific Crest National Scenic Trail
Gaywas Peak
Winema National Forest
Timber Crater
Bald Crater
Desert Cone
Oasis Butte
Crater Lake National Park
Sharp Peak
Red Cone
Grouse Hill
WIZARD ISLAND BOAT TOUR
RIM DRIVE
Bear Butte
Pacific Crest Trail
Llao Rock
Pumice Point
Palisade Point
Scout Hill
(SEASONAL) RIM DRIVE
Llao Bay
CLEETWOOD COVE DOCK
Wineglass
(SEASONAL)
Crater Lake
WATCHMAN OVERLOOK
Skell Head
The Watchman
Wizard Island
CLOUDCAP OVERLOOK
Sentinel Rock
Mt Scott
Discovery Point
Phantom Ship
Danger Bay
CRATER LAKE LODGE
To Medford and Interstate 5
Rim Village
Chaski Bay
PHANTOM SHIP OVERLOOK
HIKING IN CRATER LAKE NATIONAL PARK
STEEL VISITOR CENTER
Garfield Peak
SUN NOTCH
Dutton Cliff
Vidae Falls
Munson Point
62
RIM DRIVE
0
2 mi
0
2 km
Castle Point
MAZAMA CAMPGROUND
LOST CREEK CAMPGROUND
SOUTH ENTRANCE STATION
Mazama Village
GRAYBACK DR
Arant Point
PINNACLES OVERLOOK
Crater Peak
Rocktop Butte
Union Peak
Maldaks Crater
Rogue River National Forest
Winema National Forest
Baldtop
Scoria Cone
Goose Nest
Sky Lakes Wilderness
62
Sun Pass State Forest
Winema National Forest
Jerry Mountain
Tom Mountain
Goose Egg
To Klamath Falls
Sun Mountain
© AVALON TRAVEL

is only open in the summer, from about late June to late October or early November; dates change based on snowfall. This entrance is accessible via Highway 138. The national park website notes the current openings.

At the entrance stations, you'll pay a **fee** per vehicle: $25 per car and $20 per motorcycle mid-May-October and $10 per car or motorcycle November-mid-May. The bike- and walk-in fee is $12 year-round. Fees grant access for seven days.

Visitors Centers

The main indoor destination for day-trippers to Crater Lake is **Steel Visitor Center** (9am-5pm daily mid-Apr.-early Nov., 10am-4pm daily early Nov.-mid-Apr.), located at the park headquarters, four miles from the south entrance station. It's open every day but December 25, and it's chock-full of exhibits and information. A short film on the story of Crater Lake and the national park runs on a half-hour loop. You'll also find a gift and book shop here.

Rim Village, 6.5 miles from the south entrance station and overlooking the lake, is the heart of the national park. It's where you'll find the **Crater Lake Lodge** and **Rim Village Visitor Center** (9:30am-5pm daily late May-late Sept.), a summer destination with a gift shop and snack bar. Behind it, **Sinnott Memorial Overlook,** down a steep staircase, also holds exhibits and has an information desk. Buildings here are in classic national park style, with stone walls and steep wooden roofs that let snow slide off in the winter. Classic views of the lake can also be had here—relax in one of the row of chairs facing the lake just east of the lodge. Rim Village is a convenient spot to start the day here before venturing out on a hike, a scenic drive, or, in summer, a boat tour.

Rim Drive

Driving the 33-mile road circling Crater Lake, called Rim Drive, is one of the park's biggest attractions. Without stopping, the drive takes about 1.5 hours to complete, but given the winding road and scenic nature, it's best to take your time. More than 50 marked pullouts are on the route so you can stop for views and photo ops. Completing the full circuit is only possible in the summer, with snows closing the road for about half the year. The road is divided into two sections: the East Rim Drive and West Rim Drive. The West Rim Drive tends to open first, in May or June, while the East Rim Drive usually opens in July.

You can do the drive in either direction, but heading clockwise from Rim Village, one of the first lookouts you'll reach is **Discovery Point** (1.3 miles), where the first white man, John Hillman, "discovered" the lake in 1853 (of course, local Native American tribes had discovered it long before then). Continue on to **Watchman Overlook** (4 miles), one of the most popular for a reason; located on the side of a small peak called The Watchman, it offers views of the lake, with Wizard Island front and center, a classic postcard-perfect image. To the north you'll see Hillman Peak, the tallest peak on the rim.

Stop just 0.7 mile later for a lookout that does something different—it faces away from the lake, taking in the distinct shape of Mount Thielsen, another volcano. On a clear day, you may be able to spot the Three Sisters far behind it. A stop at **Llao Rock** (9.5 miles) gets you up close to a cliff that drops dramatically down to the water. Look across the lake and you'll see Sun Notch, a valley formed by glaciers.

At 10.7 miles, you'll reach the **Cleetwood Cove Trail,** where the parking lot and ticket booth mark the spot for boat tour departures. Even if you're not taking a boat tour, you can hike down the 1.1 miles to find the only spot where you can actually touch the lake. Swimming is allowed off the dock but keep in mind the water is frigid. At 17.5 miles, take a right turn to reach one of the few viewpoints not directly off the road; it's a short mile drive to **Cloudcap Outlook,** the highest elevation viewpoint in the park, where you'll get a view of the entire lake. Back on the main road, continue to just past mile 23 for the **Phantom Ship Overlook,** where you can peer down at the namesake rock formation poking out of the water.

Here is also the start of the road to the **Pinnacles Overlook;** drive six miles uphill, past Lost Creek Campground, to a viewpoint that takes in the Pinnacles, tall pointy formations that were formed by steam and hot gasses escaping the volcano. Return to Rim Drive and continue clockwise around the lake, stopping at **Vidae Falls** (28.5 miles) to see a small waterfall that sits among wildflowers. From here, it's about 4.5 miles back to Rim Village.

Boat Tours

In the summer, **boat tours** (www.craterlakelodges.com/activities, July-mid-Sept.) of Crater Lake are available, during which National Park Service rangers share information on the park's history and nature as the boat cruises around the lake. Because no roads lead down to the water's edge, this is your only chance to see Crater Lake from this beautiful inside perspective. The vessel is a simple open-air motorboat with no inside space, so bring sun protection.

Reservations can be made in advance for about half of the boat seats, with all bookable spots becoming available online in late spring. Boat tours can also be booked at kiosks in Mazama Village or in Crater Lake Lodge starting 24 hours before the boat ride up until two hours before the tour starts. Boat tours fill up in the summer, especially on weekends, but if you head to the ticket booth at Cleetwood Cove Trailhead about two hours before a departure, there are sometimes unclaimed tickets available. Children under two aren't allowed on the boat tours.

The boat tour parking lot is approximately 11 miles from Rim Village via the Rim Drive, and note that the dock is located down the steep 1.1-mile **Cleetwood Cove Trail,** which loses about 700 feet in elevation—and remember that you'll have to ascend this hill upon return—so the boat ride isn't a passive adventure. Make sure to budget 30-45 minutes to hike down to the dock.

LAKE CRUISE

There are six departures daily for the **Standard Lake Cruise** (9:30am, 10am, noon, 1:15pm, 3:30pm, and 3:45pm daily July-mid.-Sept., $42 adults, $28 children 3-12), one of the most popular activities in the park. The ranger-led boat tour cruises the lake for two hours.

★ WIZARD ISLAND BOAT TOUR

Although the standard boat tour passes near the lake's iconic island, only the **Wizard Island Boat Tour** (9:45am and 12:45pm daily July-mid.-Sept., $58 adults, $37 children 3-12) actually docks at the small formation jutting out of the lake. This five-hour, ranger-led tour includes some cruising time on the lake but leaves the largest portion—about three hours—for free time on the island. Upon drop-off at Wizard Island, you're on your own to explore, though a ranger is on hand to answer questions. You can spend those hours swimming (be prepared for icy water!), wandering the lakeshore, or hiking the single trail to the summit of the tiny island.

SHUTTLE

There's also a no-frills **boat shuttle** (8:30am and 11:30am daily July-mid.-Sept., $33 adults, $21 children 3-12) to Wizard Island, which offers drop-off, three hours of exploration on the island, and pick-up. The shuttle takes about 25 minutes to reach Wizard Island.

★ Hiking

DISCOVERY POINT

Distance: 2.2 miles round-trip
Duration: 1 hour
Elevation gain: 100 feet
Effort: easy
Trailhead: Rim Village Visitor Center parking area

From Rim Village, look for a trailhead on the lake side of the parking lot. Follow the out-and-back trail as it heads clockwise around the lake rim. Enjoy the shady lodgepole pine and hemlock trees as you stretch your leg on the easiest route from Rim Village that somehow manages to remain uncrowded. Trees block sight of the lake for much of the hike, but some small breaks in the pleasant forest afford private peeks at the lake. After about a mile of communing with the trees, you'll emerge at a viewpoint of the lake at Discovery Point.

GARFIELD PEAK

Distance: 3.4 miles round-trip
Duration: 3 hours
Elevation gain: 1,000 feet
Effort: moderate
Trailhead: east end of Crater Lake Lodge

Though the 8,054-foot Garfield Peak is right next to Rim Village, it takes some work to ascend the nearly 1,000 feet in a little over a mile and a half. Find the trailhead at the far end of Crater Lake Lodge, away from Rim Village. You'll immediately start gaining elevation in a traverse across a steep meadow. Continue to climb to the summit of Garfield Peak, which offers spectacular views down to the lake as well as the hilly terrain south of it. Here, it's easier to imagine what the landscape must've looked like during its wild volcanic history. In summer, the hike is a popular one and the trail gets crowded. Don't attempt the hike in heavy snow, or any snow without proper traction footwear; the steep climb can be slippery and dangerous.

MOUNT SCOTT

Distance: 5 miles round-trip
Duration: 4 hours
Elevation gain: 1,250 feet
Effort: strenuous
Trailhead: parking area on East Rim Drive, about 10 mlles counterclockwise from the Steel Visitor Center

Look for a large sign marking the popular trail to Mount Scott, the park's highest point. Follow the trail uphill for 2.5 miles, through open spaces with views of the lake. Despite the elevation gain, this hike doesn't have many steep drop-offs, but you should be comfortable with sustained uphill travel. Up top, a closed wildfire tower looks over the region and down at the lake, with Wizard Island in the distance. You can also spot Mount Thielsen from here; the pointy volcanic peak rises more than 9,000 feet in elevation, some 2,000 feet above the landscape around it, and it's easy to see why its nickname is Big Cowhorn. Bring layers; the wind can get brisk up top.

Crater Lake from Discovery Point

WIZARD ISLAND

Distance: 1 mile round-trip
Duration: 1 hour
Elevation gain: 700 feet
Effort: moderate
Trailhead: To get to Wizard Island, take the Wizard Island boat tour or shuttle. The trail departs from near the dock.

It takes some effort to reach Wizard Island, accessible only via boat tour or shuttle, so once you're here, make the effort to go all the way to the summit of the island's peak. Wizard Island is a volcanic cinder cone, and indeed looks like a mini volcano. Hike the dirt trail that rises as it rotates around the cone. At the top you're at the lip of the island's 90-foot crater—a crater inside a bigger crater. Look out and you're surrounded by lake views on every side, with the cliffs and mountains of Crater Lake's edges forming a spectacular fishbowl around you.

Keep in mind that getting to the boat dock to Wizard Island itself requires a hike down (and back up upon return) the 1.1-mile **Cleetwood Cove Trail.**

Winter Sports

In winter, when Crater Lake's ring road is buried under snow—43 feet in a typical winter—it's still possible to enjoy the scenery. Travel the snowy road or popular trails by snowshoe or cross-country skis. You can rent snowshoes at **Rim Village Gift Shop** (541/594-2255 ext. 3300, www.craterlakelodges.com, 10am-4pm Jan.-early Mar., 10am-5pm early Mar.-mid-May and Oct.-early Nov., 10am-6pm mid-May-early June and early Sept.-late Sept., 9am-8pm early June-early Sept., $16 adults, $12.50 children). They can be reserved in advance, which is recommended during holidays. No rentals for cross-country skiing are available in the park, so bring your own.

You can also join a **ranger-led snowshoe hike** (541/594-3100, www.nps.gov/crla, 1pm Sat.-Sun. Nov.-Apr., free). Tours start from Rim Village, last two hours, and come with free snowshoe rentals. No previous experience is necessary for the off-trail route, but reservations are required and must be booked over the phone; at least a week in advance is recommended to get a spot.

Food

The **Crater Lake Lodge Dining Room** (565 Rim Dr., 888/774-2728, www.craterlakelodges.com, 7am-10am, 11am-3pm, and 5pm-9:30pm daily mid-May-mid-Oct., $23-40)

Crater Lake Lodge

is appropriately grand, its windows facing a spectacular view of the lake. Giant log pillars—tree trunks, really—are interspersed between tables, and the sloped wood-beam roof affords the room a warm light, even though the walls are made of stone. The restaurant serves breakfast, lunch, and dinner daily in the park's busiest season, and reservations are available online and recommended, though walk-ins are accommodated when there's room. The menu includes Pacific Northwest favorites like clam chowder and pasta with Oregon mushrooms, a delicious reward after a hearty hike in the mountainous terrain. Hikers won't feel underdressed, especially at lunch, but it does feel like a moderately fancy meal considering it's in the middle of a national park.

Located in Mazama Village close to the south entrance, **Annie Lake Restaurant** (Crater Lake Hwy. and Munson Valley Rd., 541/594-2255, www.craterlakelodges.com, 11am-4pm and 5pm-8pm daily late May-mid-June, 7am-10:30am, 11am-4pm, and 5pm-9pm daily mid-June-Aug., 8am-10:30am, 11am-4pm, and 5pm-8pm daily Sept., $11-19) is a casual food spot with brick-oven pizzas and burgers, plus a nice spread of desserts.

Accommodations

At the 100-year-old **Crater Lake Lodge** (565 Rim Dr., 888/774-2728, www.craterlakelodges.com, mid-May-mid-Oct., $204-340), rooms are simple and a bit dated, though not as old as the hotel itself. But the real appeal is the entire building and the breathtaking views from lake-facing rooms. A few of the 71 rooms have lofts, and lakeside rooms are more expensive. Some rooms have bathtubs without showers, and none have phones or TVs. Enjoy the easy access to hikes and the Crater Lake Lodge Dining Room, or just hang out in the lobby, where a stone fireplace is surrounded by wood chairs and couches. Rocking chairs line a bluff outside, all with wonderful views. Reservations are available 13 months in advance; book for a summer weekend as soon as they're available.

The **Cabins at Mazama Village** (569 Mazama Village Dr., 541/594-2255, www.craterlakelodges.com, late May-late Sept., $169) is located seven miles from the lake's edge, but on the plus side the 40 cozy, cottage-style rooms are cheaper than at the lodge and may still be available when the lodge sells out (though reservations are still strongly recommended). All rooms have showers, but there's no air-conditioning (an important consideration in the middle of a hot Oregon summer). Rooms are hotel-style—don't expect a cabin to yourself—and rather sparse but serviceable. Reservations are available 13 months in advance; plan to book at least several months ahead of time.

Camping

The only reservable place to camp in the park, **Mazama Campground** (Mazama Village, 888/774-2728, www.craterlakelodges.com, $22-31), is near the south entrance station. Its 214 sites are open June-September, and the campground has tent and RV sites, flush toilets, and access to pay showers. Book in advance since the central location draws crowds in summer months; campsites become available six months in advance, though 25 percent of the sites are kept as first-come, first-served. Sites have a bear locker for storing food; use them not just for the rare bear but to keep smaller animals like chipmunks, raccoons, and mice from getting into food stores. The campground is fairly open, with sites visible to each other, but there's enough space that you won't feel too crowded.

Located more out of the way, the **Lost Creek Campground** (Pinnacles Rd., www.nps.gov, July-Oct., $10) is on a spur road four miles off the Rim Drive in the southeastern corner of the park. Its 16 campsites are more rustic than Mazama Camground's, with no running water, and all sites are first-come, first-served. Only tent camping is allowed.

To camp just outside the park, about 6.5 miles north of the north entrance, there's **Diamond Lake Campground** (Hwy. 230 near Hwy. 138, www.recreation.gov,

June-Sept., $16-27), operated by the forest service on the east bank of Diamond Lake. It's a large campground, with 145 sites, some of them on the lakeshore. Reservations are available up to six months in advance and are recommended, though there are also 95 sites designated as first-come, first-served. The campground also boasts a boat ramp and showers.

Getting There

To reach Crater Lake's south entrance station from Ashland, drive north on I-5 for about 10 miles to Medford, then take exit 30 and head northeast on Highway 62. Stay on Highway 62 for about 68 miles; look for national park signs. It takes about 1.75 hours.

To reach Crater Lake's north entrance from Portland, head south on I-5 for 111 miles to exit 188, just past Eugene. Jump on Highway 58 and follow it east 86 miles over the mountains. Merge onto U.S. 97 and continue 18 miles south. Turn right on Highway 138 and follow it 15 miles west. Turn left at signs for Crater Lake's north entrance; follow the entrance road about a mile to reach the pay station. The approximately 235-mile trip takes about 4 hours.

Vancouver

Look for ★ to find recommended sights, activities, dining, and lodging.

Highlights

★ **Stanley Park:** The forested acres of this massive downtown park are best seen from the seat of a bicycle (page 445).

★ **Vancouver Art Gallery:** Canadian treasures, including those by local standout Emily Carr, are displayed in a building from the province's most famous architect (page 448).

★ **Vancouver Police Museum:** Everything you wanted to know about Canadian crime prevention is here, plus some things you can't believe they let you see (page 450).

★ **Dr. Sun Yat-Sen Classical Chinese Garden:** More a historical manor house than a simple garden, this site is the jewel of Vancouver's Chinatown (page 451).

★ **Granville Island Public Market:** Shop for food, flowers, soaps, jewelry, or just about anything else you can imagine among the endless stalls (page 453).

★ **University of British Columbia Museum of Anthropology:** Totem poles receive a regal, light-filled display at this museum celebrating culture both at home and around the world (page 454).

★ **Grouse Mountain:** Ski in the winter, hike in the summer, and take in the mountaintop views year-round (page 456).

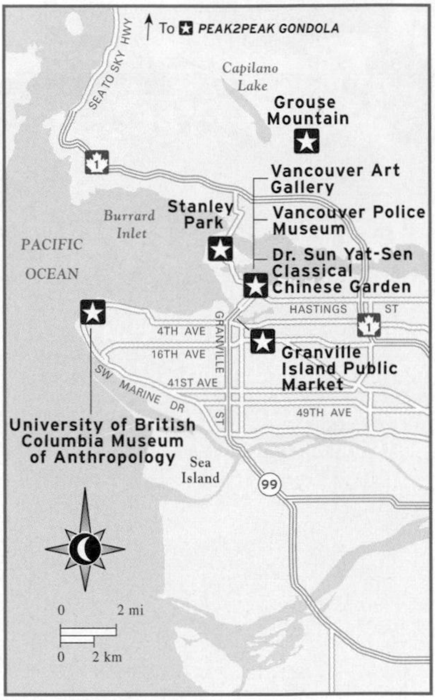

★ **Peak2Peak Gondola:** Fly through the skies—whether you're skiing or not—via this lift system linking Whistler's two giant mountains (page 484).

Has there ever been a city that can legitimately claim both the mountains and the water like Vancouver can?

Glass towers gleam with modern ambition, while deep forest gorges and mountains topped with ski resorts sit within city neighborhoods. Vancouver's downtown is almost an island, bordered on three sides by False Creek, English Bay, and Vancouver Harbour. Shops crowd the Robson and Granville Streets, while the renovated neighborhoods of Yaletown and Gastown have become known for their culinary choices. Another reinvention, Granville Island, has turned a once-industrial site into a giant market, theater center, and shopping district.

And throughout the city, international flavors abound—crowds flock to the night market and exquisite gardens in Chinatown, and the most popular restaurant is an Indian joint hidden on an unassuming street outside the downtown core. Streets crowd with businessmen and ski bums, tourists and First Nations locals. Nowhere is the area's native history better recognized than at the Museum of Anthropology's glass-walled gallery of totem poles. Culturally rich with native history and international industry, Vancouver is one of the most cosmopolitan spots on the West Coast of North America, the business, recreation, and tourism jewel of Canada.

The outdoors is never far away, with waterfront areas, a spectacular city park, and mountains right next to downtown. The Stanley Park bike path takes pedal pushers past woods, beaches, and rocky shores, while just across the harbor is Grouse Mountain, with skiing or snowshoeing accessible by city bus. And just a short drive north, Whistler boasts what is arguably the best skiing in the world, under a gondola that soars across the mountains like an airplane.

Although Vancouver's population is slightly smaller than Seattle's, it feels bigger thanks to its great variety and modern, glassy architecture. Canadians show off their famously friendly disposition on the city streets, and even the mountains that tower over Vancouver feel welcoming.

PLANNING YOUR TIME

Canada's West Coast hub is a truly international city, with first-rate culture and dining, so at least two days is recommended,

Previous: Dr. Sun Yat-Sen Classical Chinese Garden; Vancouver at night. **Above:** Gastown's Steam Clock.

Vancouver

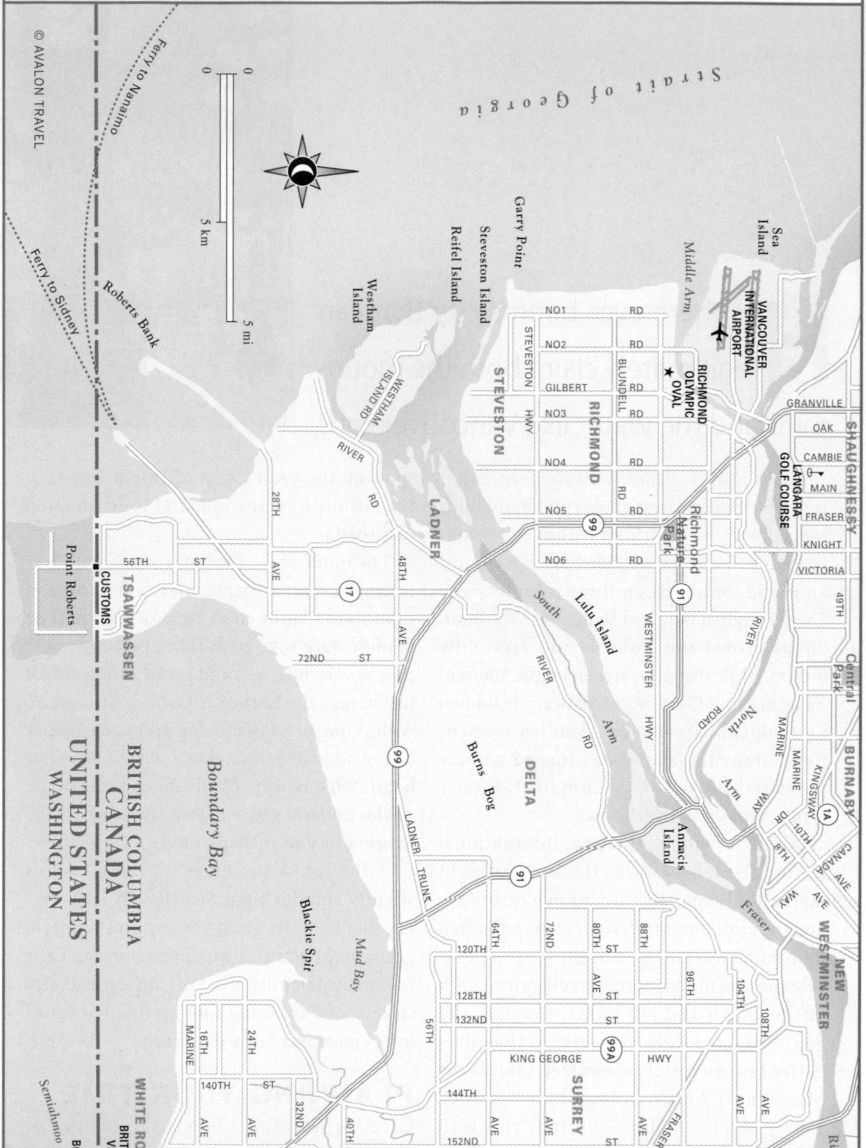

Strait of Georgia
Ferry to Nanaimo
Ferry to Sidney
Roberts Bank
0
5 mi
5 km
Sea Island
Middle Arm
VANCOUVER INTERNATIONAL AIRPORT
RICHMOND OLYMPIC OVAL
Garry Point
Steveston Island
Reifel Island
Westham Island
WESTHAM ISLAND RD
RIVER RD
STEVESTON
RICHMOND
LADNER
NO1 RD
NO2 RD
GILBERT RD
NO3 RD
NO4 RD
NO5 RD
NO6 RD
STEVESTON HWY
BLUNDELL RD
Richmond Nature Park
GRANVILLE
OAK
CAMBIE
MAIN
FRASER
KNIGHT
VICTORIA
49TH
LANGARA GOLF COURSE
SHAUGHNESSY
Central Park
BURNABY
NEW WESTMINSTER
56TH ST
28TH AVE
48TH AVE
72ND ST
CUSTOMS
TSAWWASSEN
Point Roberts
South Arm
Lulu Island
WESTMINSTER HWY
RIVER RD
North Arm
RIVER ROAD
MARINE WAY
MARINE DR
KINGSWAY
10TH AVE
8TH AVE
CANADA WAY
Burns Bog
DELTA
Annacis Island
Fraser River
LADNER TRUNK RD
BRITISH COLUMBIA
CANADA
UNITED STATES
WASHINGTON
Boundary Bay
Blackie Spit
Mud Bay
64TH AVE
72ND AVE
80TH ST
88TH AVE
96TH AVE
104TH AVE
108TH AVE
120TH ST
128TH ST
132ND ST
KING GEORGE HWY
144TH ST
152ND ST
154TH ST
158TH ST
158ND ST
140TH ST
MARINE DRIVE
16TH AVE
24TH AVE
32ND AVE
40TH AVE
56TH AVE
SURREY
CLOVERDALE
FRASER HWY
WHITE ROCK
Nicomekl River
8TH AVE
Semiahmoo Bay
BRITISH COLUMBIA VISITOR CENTRE
PEACE ARCH BORDER CROSSING
To Seattle
Douglas Island
99
17
91
99A
10
1A
1
© AVALON TRAVEL

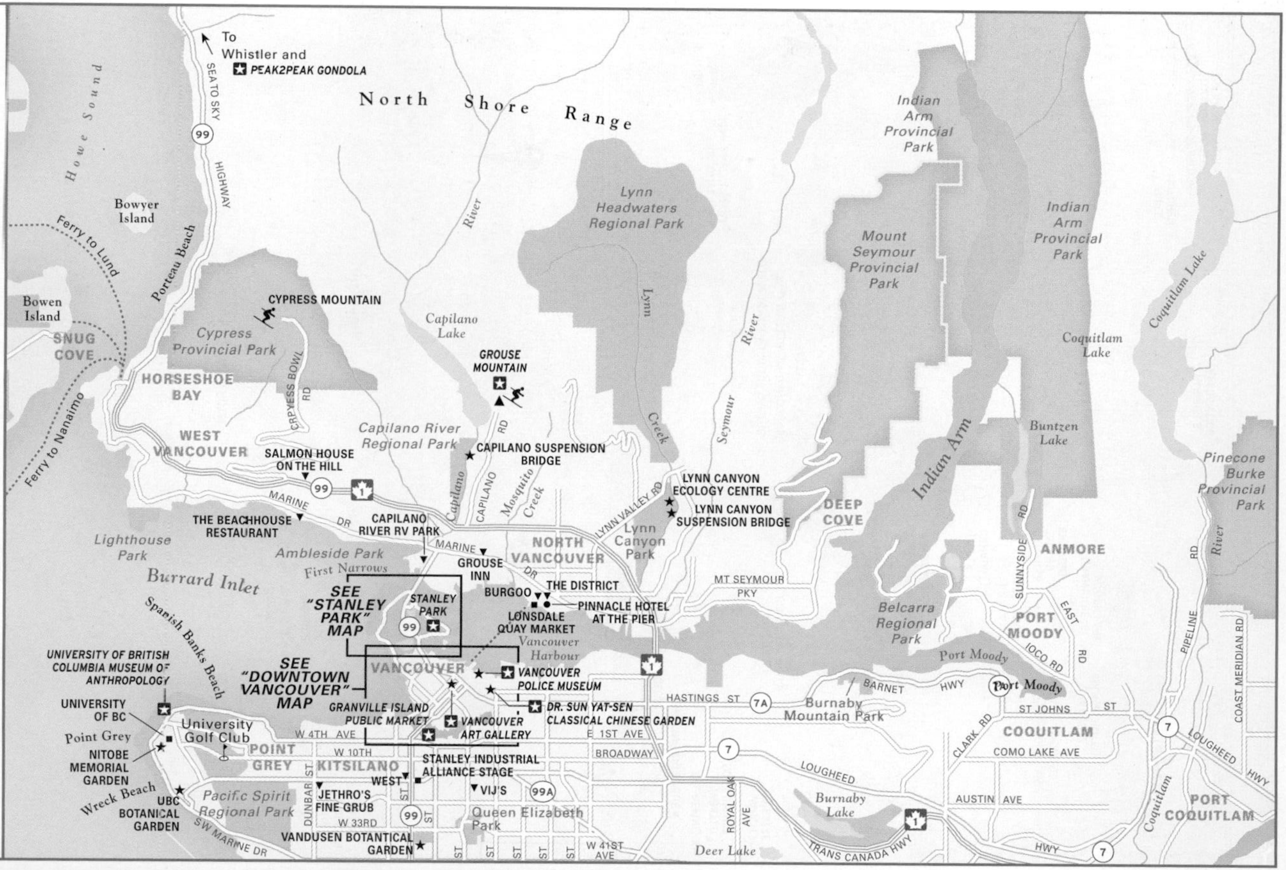
To Whistler and
PEAK2PEAK GONDOLA
SEA TO SKY HIGHWAY
99
North Shore Range
Howe Sound
Bowyer Island
Ferry to Lund
Porteau Beach
Bowen Island
SNUG COVE
HORSESHOE BAY
Ferry to Nanaimo
CYPRESS MOUNTAIN
Cypress Provincial Park
CRPYESS BOWL RD
WEST VANCOUVER
SALMON HOUSE ON THE HILL
MARINE DR
THE BEACHHOUSE RESTAURANT
CAPILANO RIVER RV PARK
Lighthouse Park
Ambleside Park
First Narrows
Burrard Inlet
Spanish Banks Beach
Capilano Lake
River
GROUSE MOUNTAIN
Capilano River Regional Park
CAPILANO SUSPENSION BRIDGE
Capilano
CAPILANO RD
Mosquito Creek
Lynn Headwaters Regional Park
Lynn Creek
Seymour River
LYNN VALLEY RD
LYNN CANYON ECOLOGY CENTRE
LYNN CANYON SUSPENSION BRIDGE
Lynn Canyon Park
NORTH VANCOUVER
GROUSE INN
BURGOO
THE DISTRICT
PINNACLE HOTEL AT THE PIER
LONSDALE QUAY MARKET
Vancouver Harbour
MT SEYMOUR PKY
SEE "STANLEY PARK" MAP
STANLEY PARK
SEE "DOWNTOWN VANCOUVER" MAP
VANCOUVER
VANCOUVER POLICE MUSEUM
DR. SUN YAT-SEN CLASSICAL CHINESE GARDEN
GRANVILLE ISLAND PUBLIC MARKET
VANCOUVER ART GALLERY
UNIVERSITY OF BRITISH COLUMBIA MUSEUM OF ANTHROPOLOGY
UNIVERSITY OF BC
Point Grey
University Golf Club
NITOBE MEMORIAL GARDEN
POINT GREY
KITSILANO
W 4TH AVE
W 10TH
E 1ST AVE
BROADWAY
STANLEY INDUSTRIAL ALLIANCE STAGE
WEST
VIJ'S
JETHRO'S FINE GRUB
DUNBAR ST
W 33RD
Wreck Beach
UBC BOTANICAL GARDEN
Pacific Spirit Regional Park
SW MARINE DR
VANDUSEN BOTANICAL GARDEN
Queen Elizabeth Park
W 41ST AVE
ST
99A
HASTINGS ST
7A
7
1
Burnaby Mountain Park
ROYAL OAK AVE
Deer Lake
Burnaby Lake
LOUGHEED
TRANS CANADA HWY
BARNET HWY
Port Moody
CLARK RD
ST JOHNS ST
COQUITLAM
COMO LAKE AVE
AUSTIN AVE
HWY
Indian Arm Provincial Park
Mount Seymour Provincial Park
DEEP COVE
Indian Arm
Belcarra Regional Park
Buntzen Lake
SUNNYSIDE RD
ANMORE
PORT MOODY
IOCO RD
EAST RD
Coquitlam Lake
Coquitlam Lake
Pinecone Burke Provincial Park
River
RD
PIPELINE RD
COAST MERIDIAN RD
LOUGHEED HWY
Coquitlam
PORT COQUITLAM

Downtown Vancouver

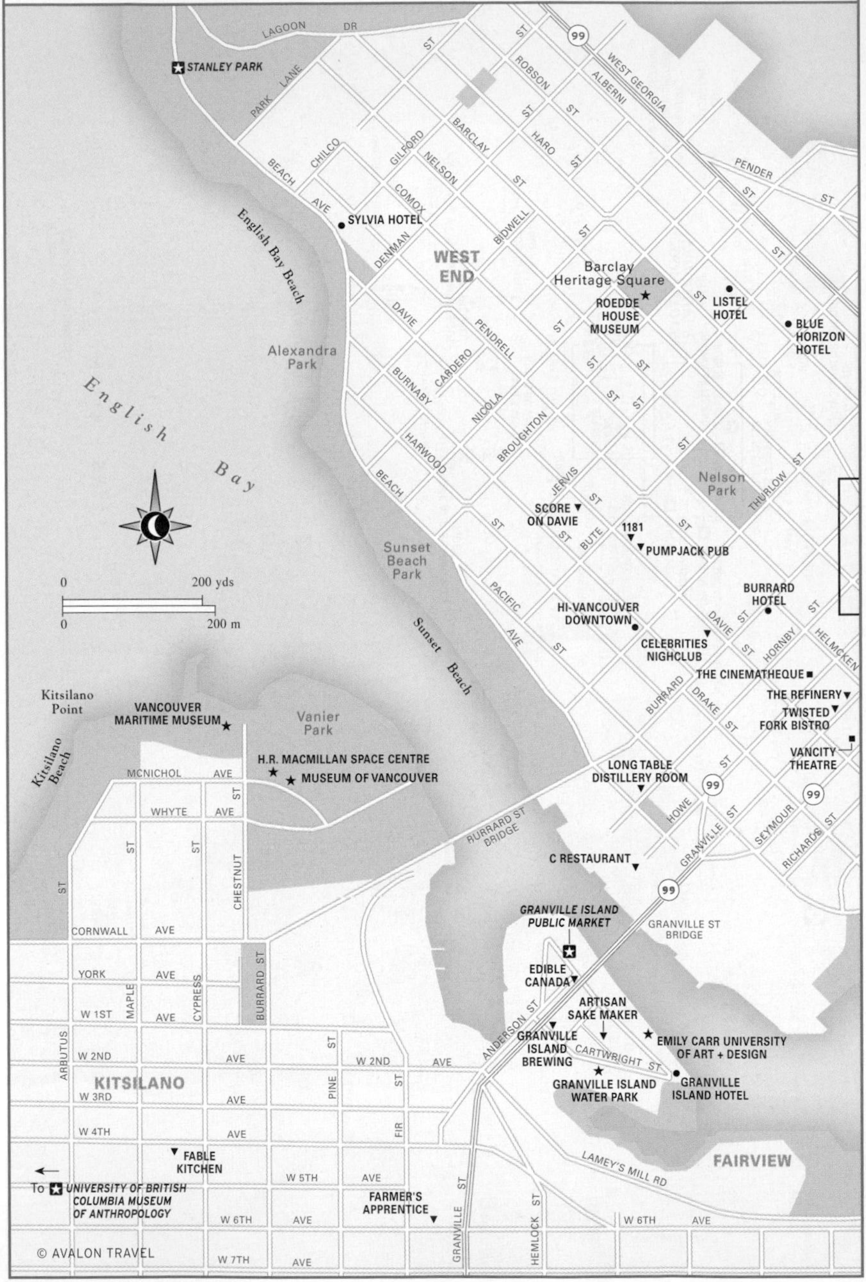

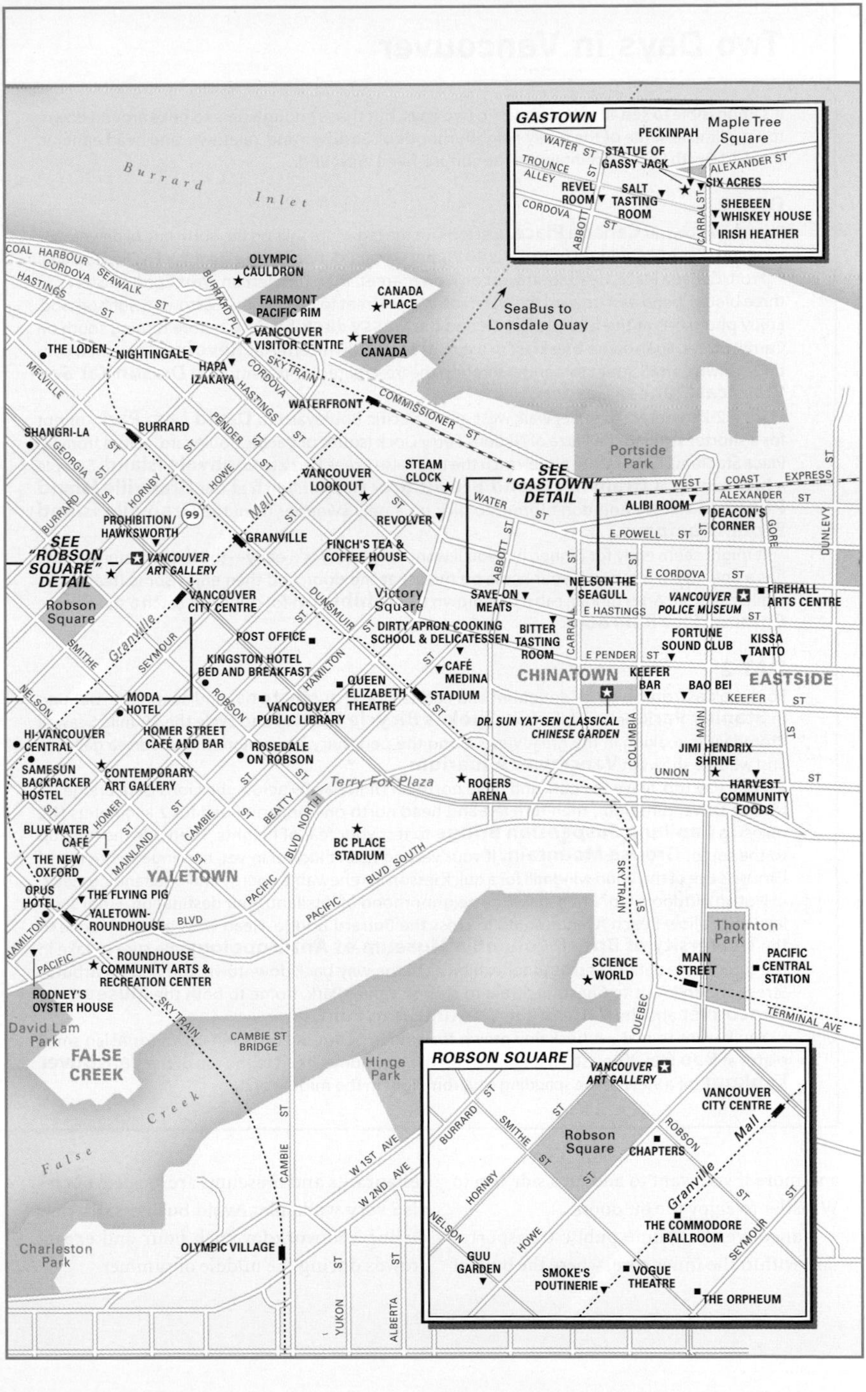
GASTOWN
PECKINPAH
Maple Tree Square
WATER ST
STATUE OF GASSY JACK
TROUNCE ALLEY
ALEXANDER ST
REVEL ROOM
SALT TASTING ROOM
SIX ACRES
SHEBEEN WHISKEY HOUSE
IRISH HEATHER
CORDOVA ST
ABBOTT ST
CARRALL ST
Burrard Inlet
COAL HARBOUR
CORDOVA
SEAWALK
HASTINGS ST
OLYMPIC CAULDRON
BURRARD PL
FAIRMONT PACIFIC RIM
CANADA PLACE
SeaBus to Lonsdale Quay
VANCOUVER VISITOR CENTRE
FLYOVER CANADA
THE LODEN
NIGHTINGALE
HAPA IZAKAYA
SKY TRAIN
CORDOVA
HASTINGS
MELVILLE
WATERFRONT
COMMISSIONER ST
SHANGRI-LA
BURRARD
PENDER ST
GEORGIA ST
HORNBY
HOWE
ST
Portside Park
STEAM CLOCK
VANCOUVER LOOKOUT
SEE "GASTOWN" DETAIL
WEST COAST EXPRESS
ALEXANDER ST
ALIBI ROOM
DEACON'S CORNER
BURRARD
99
Mall
PROHIBITION/ HAWKSWORTH
REVOLVER
WATER ST
ABBOTT ST
E POWELL ST
GORE
DUNLEVY
GRANVILLE
FINCH'S TEA & COFFEE HOUSE
SEE "ROBSON SQUARE" DETAIL
VANCOUVER ART GALLERY
E CORDOVA ST
NELSON THE SEAGULL
Robson Square
VANCOUVER CITY CENTRE
Victory Square
DUNSMUIR
SAVE-ON MEATS
VANCOUVER POLICE MUSEUM
FIREHALL ARTS CENTRE
E HASTINGS ST
Granville
SMITHE
SEYMOUR
POST OFFICE
DIRTY APRON COOKING SCHOOL & DELICATESSEN
BITTER TASTING ROOM
CARRALL
FORTUNE SOUND CLUB
KISSA TANTO
KINGSTON HOTEL BED AND BREAKFAST
HAMILTON
CAFÉ MEDINA
E PENDER ST
EASTSIDE
NELSON
ROBSON
QUEEN ELIZABETH THEATRE
CHINATOWN
KEEFER BAR
BAO BEI
KEEFER ST
MODA HOTEL
VANCOUVER PUBLIC LIBRARY
STADIUM
DR. SUN YAT-SEN CLASSICAL CHINESE GARDEN
HI-VANCOUVER CENTRAL
HOMER STREET CAFÉ AND BAR
COLUMBIA
MAIN
ROSEDALE ON ROBSON
JIMI HENDRIX SHRINE
SAMESUN BACKPACKER HOSTEL
CONTEMPORARY ART GALLERY
Terry Fox Plaza
ROGERS ARENA
UNION ST
HARVEST COMMUNITY FOODS
HOMER
CAMBIE
BEATTY
BLVD NORTH
BLUE WATER CAFÉ
MAINLAND
BC PLACE STADIUM
THE NEW OXFORD
BLVD SOUTH
YALETOWN
PACIFIC
SKYTRAIN
OPUS HOTEL
THE FLYING PIG
YALETOWN-ROUNDHOUSE
BLVD
HAMILTON
Thornton Park
ROUNDHOUSE COMMUNITY ARTS & RECREATION CENTER
SCIENCE WORLD
MAIN STREET
PACIFIC CENTRAL STATION
RODNEY'S OYSTER HOUSE
QUEBEC
TERMINAL AVE
David Lam Park
CAMBIE ST BRIDGE
FALSE CREEK
Hinge Park
False Creek
W 1ST AVE
W 2ND AVE
Charleston Park
OLYMPIC VILLAGE
YUKON
ALBERTA
ROBSON SQUARE
VANCOUVER ART GALLERY
VANCOUVER CITY CENTRE
BURRARD ST
SMITHE ST
Robson Square
CHAPTERS
ROBSON
Mall
Granville
HORNBY
ST
NELSON
HOWE
THE COMMODORE BALLROOM
SEYMOUR
GUU GARDEN
SMOKE'S POUTINERIE
VOGUE THEATRE
THE ORPHEUM

Two Days in Vancouver

It's impossible to see all of Vancouver in two days, but that's enough time to poke around downtown, glimpse some of the funky neighborhoods of Gastown and Yaletown, and head either to the wild North Shore mountains or the culture-filled West End.

DAY 1

Start downtown at **Canada Place.** Just look for the big white sails on the north end of downtown. View the Olympic Cauldron from the 2010 Winter Games, or ride a virtual flight at FlyOver Canada.

From Canada Place, head southwest on Howe Street, then turn left on West Cordova Street. In three blocks, bend east (toward the water) on Water Street to explore the Gastown neighborhood. Enjoy photo ops at the **Steam Clock** and the **Gassy Jack Statue** before turning south on Carrall Street. Grab some breakfast or a cup of Stumptown coffee at **Revolver,** and then continue down Carrall Street to wander through the (re-created) 15th century at **Dr. Sun Yat-Sen Classical Chinese Garden.**

It's a 2-kilometer (1.2-mile) walk west along Pacific Boulevard to **David Lam Park,** or opt for a shorter stroll to the Plaza of Nations Ferry Dock (south of Pacific Boulevard, across from BC Place Stadium). From either place, catch the tiny False Creek Ferry to **Granville Island.** Sample a beer tasting at **Granville Island Brewing,** or stop for lunch at the **Granville Island Public Market.** And don't forget to pick up a new sweeper from the **Granville Island Broom Company.**

It might seem early for dinner, but you'll want to get to **Vij's** early—the Indian eatery always has a line. Catch a cab, put your name on the list at the door, and then enjoy some free snacks while you wait. After dinner, cab it downtown to **Prohibition** for drinks, or catch a show at the **Commodore Ballroom.**

DAY 2

For breakfast, grab a quick doughnut and coffee at a **Tim Hortons,** and spend the morning in **Stanley Park.** Rent a bike from **Spokes Bicycle Rental** and cycle the 10-mile Seawall Promenade, soaking in the great views along the periphery. Or explore the undersea galleries and wildlife shows at **Vancouver Aquarium.**

For a day trip, leave the park and drive north on Highway 99 across the Lions Gate Bridge. At Marine Drive, turn right, then turn left and head north on Capilano Road for 2 kilometers (1.2 miles) to **Capilano Suspension Bridge** to test your fear of heights. Then ride the tram up to the top of **Grouse Mountain.** If your vertigo hasn't kicked in yet, continue to the top of Grouse's Eye of the Wind windmill for a quick lesson in renewable energy and outstanding views.

Not an outdoors fan? Then make the neighborhood of Kitsilano your destination. From Stanley Park, follow Beach Avenue south to cross the Burrard Bridge. Head west on 4th Avenue to the **University of British Columbia Museum of Anthropology.** Be sure to take in the totem pole gallery and outdoor exhibits. On the way back downtown, turn left on Arbutus Street and follow it to Chestnut Street to stop at Vanier Park, home to both the **Museum of Vancouver** and the **Vancouver Maritime Museum.**

You'll want to make it back downtown for dinner. Scoot over to Chinatown for Asian small plates at **Bao Bei.** If you still have energy on the way home, head to the top of the **Vancouver Lookout** for a view of the sparkling city from right in the middle of it.

and more if you want to add on a side trip to Whistler to enjoy the outdoors.

Vancouver has some public transportation within the inner core, where the bulk of restaurants and museums are located, but it's also very walkable. Avoid business districts during the workday rush hour and expect crowds during the middle of summer.

Sights

DOWNTOWN

The core of Vancouver almost feels like an island. It's surrounded by water on most sides—False Creek, English Bay, Burrard Inlet, and Vancouver Harbour. Only the area near Chinatown has a land connection to the rest of the city. Otherwise the main entrance points to downtown are over the Granville Bridge and over the Lions Gate Bridge near Stanley Park. In such limited space, the city packs row after row of shiny, tall apartment and commercial buildings, the windows almost blinding when the sunlight hits just right. The downtown area has one-way streets, bike lanes, water taxi and ferry terminals, and a SkyTrain (actually located underground), so leave some time for traffic and getting a little lost. The good news is that the city is very walkable, particularly between the downtown, Gastown, and Yaletown neighborhoods.

TOP EXPERIENCE

★ Stanley Park

Vancouver is proud of **Stanley Park** (604/257-8531, http://vancouver.ca) and rightfully so—its 1,000 acres are full of bike paths, beaches, viewpoints, tennis courts, and swimming pools. With half a million trees, it's even bigger than Central Park. It opened to the public in 1888, named for the Governor General of Canada, Lord Stanley.

The 8.8-kilometer (5.5-mile) **Seawall Promenade** that circles the park is perhaps its most popular attraction; the seawall itself extends around the city, but the park section is the most scenic. Two lanes are marked off, one for walkers and one for bikers and inline skaters, the latter traveling counterclockwise only. The promenade passes a number of statues including figures of *Harry Jerome,* a runner, and the *Girl in a Wetsuit* perched on a rock just offshore.

On a circular trip around the park, one of the first major stops is **Brockton Point,** where a collection of nine totem poles stands against the backdrop of Stanley Park greenery. Most are replicas of the originals, now in museums, but they are intricately carved and painted in bright colors.

totem poles at Stanley Park

Stanley Park

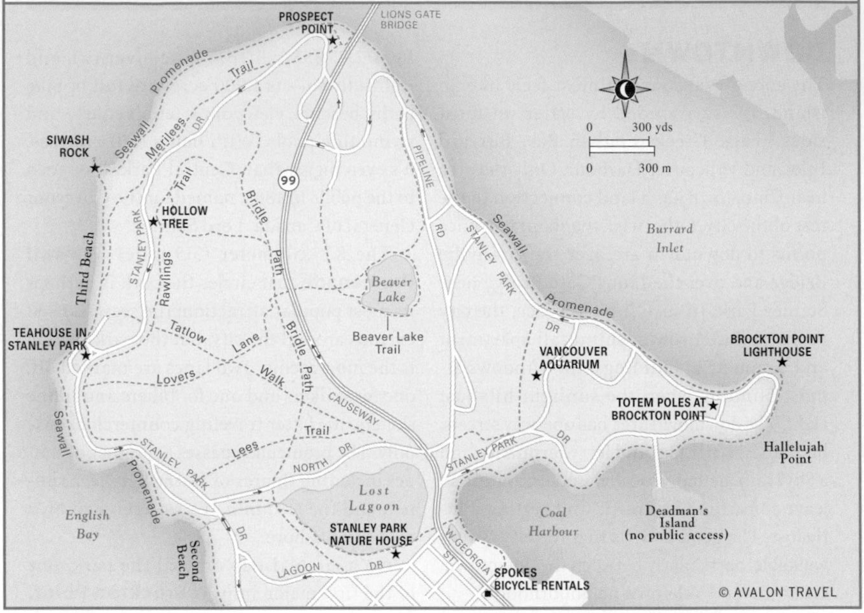

Other park attractions include the **Variety Kids Water Park** (next to the seawall at Lumbermen's Arc, 10am-6pm daily June-Sept., free), full of creative, large sprinklers, and the **Pitch & Putt** 18-hole golf course (604/681-8847, http://vancouver.ca, 8am-8pm daily mid-Mar. to mid-Oct., limited services and weather dependent mid-Oct. to mid-Mar., $14.25 adults, $10.50 seniors and children under 18). No trip to Vancouver is complete without a short trip to Stanley Park, even if it's just a quick drive through the Stanley Park Causeway and across the **Lions Gate Bridge** that travels to North Vancouver.

VANCOUVER AQUARIUM

Located near the center of Stanley Park, the **Vancouver Aquarium** (845 Avison Way, 604/659-3474, www.vanaqua.org, 10am-5pm daily, $39 adults, $30 seniors, students, and youth 13-18, $22 children 4-12, children under 4 free, discount with transit pass) is the wettest spot within its borders. More than 50,000 sea creatures are inside, including false killer whales, jellyfish, penguins, and harbor porpoises; the aquarium plan to bring beluga whales, a onetime central attraction, back in 2019. Outdoor seating and underground galleries allow for views above and below the water, and regular shows introduce the aquarium residents and educate visitors. A 4-D theater plays films about local wildlife, adding wind, mist, and scents to the experience. The aquarium also has a gift store and café.

STANLEY PARK MINIATURE TRAIN

Kids—and rail buffs—make a beeline to the **Stanley Park Miniature Train** (10am-4pm Sat.-Sun. May-June, 11am-4pm daily late June-early Sept., seasonal holiday hours Oct. and Dec., $6.80 adults, $4.86 youth 13-18 and seniors, $3.40 children under 13). The railway was built in a clearing that emerged after the 1964 Hurricane Frieda felled a number of trees in the park. The train itself is a replica of Canada's first transcontinental train, and the two-kilometer (1.2-mile) ride is supplemented on holidays with ghosts, Easter characters, native culture, or bright lights.

STANLEY PARK NATURE HOUSE

Located on the shores of Lost Lagoon, the **Stanley Park Nature House** (north end of Alberni St., 604/257-8544, http://stanleyparkecology.ca, 10am-4pm Sat.-Sun. Sept.-June, 10am-5pm Tues.-Sun. July-Aug., free) provides a peek at the natural side of the park. **Lost Lagoon** is a mudflat turned lake, formed when the Stanley Park causeway was created. It's now a sanctuary for birds, filled with rushes and grasses. The Nature House serves as a kind of ranger station where you can ask questions about the wildlife and check out interactive displays about the flora and fauna. The children's area has more exhibits and coloring. Birders will want to check for updates on the migrations of warblers, shorebirds, the area's four pairs of bald eagles, and the great blue heron colony.

PROSPECT POINT

Though a trip around the edge of Stanley Park hits a number of landmarks and attractions, you have to sweat—or drive—up an incline to get the best view. **Prospect Point** (5601 Stanley Park Dr., http://vancouver.ca, 11:30am-6pm daily), west of the Lions Gate Bridge, is the highest point in the park at 210 feet. Soak in the Lions Gate Bridge, Burrard Inlet, and the mountains that rise above North Vancouver. Stop for a bite at the **Prospect Point Bar and Grill** (604/669-2737, www.prospectpoint.ca, 9am-sunset daily), which reopened after renovations in summer 2017; there's also a café and ice cream counter.

SECOND AND THIRD BEACHES

Within Stanley Park, there are two major destinations that appeal to different kinds of beach lovers. **Second Beach** (8501 Stanley Park Dr., 604/681-8029, http://vancouver.ca) is located at Stanley Park Drive and North Lagoon Drive on the western shore near the golf course. This family-friendly area includes a giant, heated outdoor pool, a playground, washrooms, and pay parking nearby. **Third Beach** (Ferguson Point, http://vancouver.ca) is a bit harder to reach by car. Located farther north, it's more popular with cyclists and single adults. The beach faces directly into Burrard Inlet and even stretches up toward North Vancouver. Washrooms and pay parking are available.

sea otters at the Vancouver Aquarium

Roedde House Museum

The Victorian **Roedde House Museum** (1415 Barclay St., 604/684-7040, www.roeddehouse.org, 11am-4pm Tues.-Sat., 1pm-4pm Sun., $5 adults and children over 5, children under 5 free, Sunday tea $8), built in 1893 in the Queen Anne style, was the home of a bookbinder and is now a historical museum. Visitors can roam the rooms freely (no velvet-rope path) and touch some of the artifacts. On Sundays, the Tea and Tour includes a guided look at the house and a tea tasting. And unlike some preserved houses, this spot doesn't show off the lifestyles of the once rich and prosperous. Instead, it has been restored to show how the middle class lived in the late 19th century.

★ Vancouver Art Gallery

The 1906 building that holds downtown's **Vancouver Art Gallery** (750 Hornby St., 604/662-4700, www.vanartgallery.bc.ca, 10am-5pm Wed.-Mon., 10am-9pm Tues., $24 adults, $20 seniors, $18 students, $6 children 5-18, children under 5 free) was designed by British Columbia's most famous architect, Sir Francis Mawson Rattenbury, a British man who made his name designing major buildings in Vancouver and Victoria, like the landmark Empress Hotel. The gallery moved to the courthouse building in 1983, but the collection is much older, begun in 1931 and greatly expanded in the 1950s to include works by notable local artist Emily Carr. (A long-term plan to move the gallery to its own, new building elsewhere in Vancouver has been underway for years, but so far only preliminary designs exist.) Exhibits from the collection show off Canadian and specifically British Columbian artists, as well as 17th-century Dutch works and photos by the likes of Ansel Adams and Margaret Bourke-White. Vancouver Art Gallery also hosts touring exhibitions.

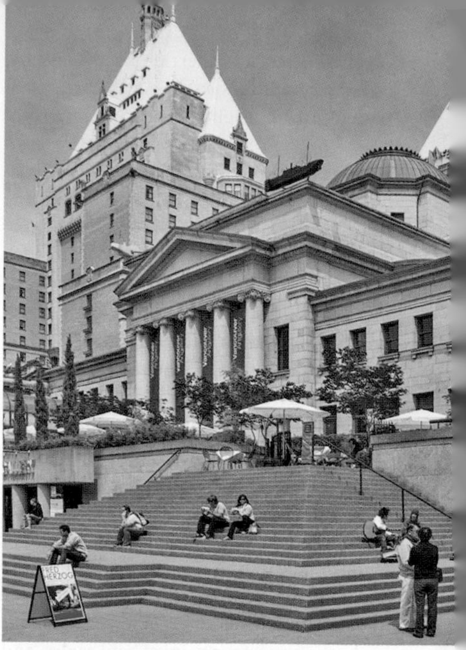

Vancouver Art Gallery

Vancouver Lookout

The round observatory of the **Vancouver Lookout** (555 W Hastings St., 604/689-0421, www.vancouverlookout.com, 8:30am-10:30pm daily summer, 9am-9:30pm daily winter, $17.50 adults, $14.50 seniors, $12.50 students and youth 13-18, $9.50 children 6-12, children under 6 free) pops above the Harbour Centre building like a jaunty hat. The glass elevators have as good a view as you'll get at the top (though you'll need a ticket to ride them), but the lookout isn't quite tall enough to tower over the city. Still, placards are well positioned to explain notable Vancouver buildings and the cities in the distance. No, the skyline you see a few miles away isn't Seattle, the signs announce. Daytime visitors can keep their tickets and return the same night.

Canada Place

The roof of the waterfront pavilion at **Canada Place** (999 Canada Pl., 604/665-9000, www.canadaplace.ca, free) resembles sails, or perhaps snow-topped mountains—you can see both from the outdoor walkways. Inside is a space built for Expo '86, the World's Fair held in Vancouver in 1986. It's the site of festivals, like the Aboriginal Spirit Celebration or Canada Day events, and cruise ships dock here before leaving for Alaska. Temporary exhibits highlight aspects of Vancouver's history, as well as the Canadian Trail path that leads to permanent installations about history, and at noon the Heritage Horns—giant aluminum horns that play at 115 decibels—sound the first four notes of Canadian national anthem "O Canada" at noon. Try the **FlyOver Canada** (604/620-8455, www.flyovercanada.com, 9:30am-10pm daily, $27 adults, $21 seniors, students, and youth 13-17, $17 children 4-12) simulation ride for an eight-minute "flight" over Canadian landscapes.

BC Place Stadium

The giant retractable roof over **BC Place Stadium** (777 Pacific Blvd., 604/669-2300, www.bcplacestadium.com) is the biggest of its kind on the world, something that was useful during the 2010 Winter Olympic Games, when the arena held the Opening and Closing Ceremonies. Now it's home to the **Vancouver Whitecaps FC** soccer team (604/669-9283, www.whitecapsfc.com) and the **BC Lions Football Club** (604/589-7627, www.bclions.com), which plays a sport similar to American football but not identical. It's also where the major music acts play in Vancouver; a U2 concert crowded the venue even more than the Olympics. A smaller interior roof can make the venue smaller for more intimate concerts (like ones with only 25,000 spectators), and a new LED light system decorates the interior.

Science World British Columbia

It's easy to spot **Science World British Columbia** (1455 Quebec St., 604/443-7440, www.scienceworld.ca, 10am-5pm Mon.-Fri., 10am-6pm Sat.-Sun. summer; 10am-5pm Tues.-Fri., 10am-6pm Sat.-Sun. winter; $22.50 adults, $18.50 seniors, students, and children 13-18, $15.25 children 3-12, children under 3 free), thanks to its giant geodesic dome—the one that looks like a big golf ball, made up of 766 triangles—which was made for Expo '86 and based on the famous design by R. Buckminster Fuller. Today it holds the OMNIMAX giant movie theater. Most of the center is a kid's paradise, with live hourly science shows, puzzles and interactive exhibits, and live animals. A *Bodyworks* gallery explains the inner workings of the human body, and a nature area includes a real beaver lodge, bear pelts, and the cast of a T. Rex. A sizable

Science World British Columbia

science store sells puzzles, lab kits, and models. A burger joint is also on-site.

GASTOWN AND CHINATOWN

Today it's home to hip bars, high-end shopping, and one weird clock. But Gastown was almost demolished to become a freeway, the pet project of mayor Tom Campbell in the 1960s. The buildings were mostly slums at the time, and the idea was that the route would be like Seattle's downtown waterfront freeway (now scheduled for removal). A community campaign halted the project, and businesses began buying up buildings. The neighborhood funded the construction of the Gastown Steam Clock, which is nowhere near as old as it looks—it was installed in 1977.

In a way, the story is similar to New York City's SoHo neighborhood, which had an influx of artists while a freeway project was slowly debated for the area. The road was never built and SoHo became the artist center of the city. Gastown, too, was spared a major demolition and is now one of the city's most popular neighborhoods.

Steam Clock

What do you get when you combine a locomotive and a timepiece? You get something like the **Steam Clock** (Cambie St. and Water St.) of Gastown, a street corner oddity that draws large groups of admirers. A miniature steam engine inside it is powered by steam from the downtown heating network. Even stranger is that it isn't as old as it looks—it was built in 1977 in an attempt to give Gastown a historical look (it even has electric fans inside). Clockmaker Ray Saunders basically guessed at how to make it, though he's made several other clocks since. The charming tower makes for a pretty picture, and the whistle and chimes mark the time at the quarter hour.

Gassy Jack Statue

Let the kids giggle. One Gastown attraction really is called **Gassy Jack Statue** (Alexander St. and Water St.), though not for any embarrassing personal habits. Captain John Deighton got the nickname for his tendency to speak at length—and he got the statue because he started one of the first establishments in Gastown, which was eventually named for him (and since that district later grew to become Vancouver, the entire metropolis could have ended up named for the endless talker). The original saloon served whiskey he brought in a barrel down the Fraser River—which is why Gassy Jack now poses on a barrel.

★ Vancouver Police Museum

You didn't misread it; the building that now holds the **Vancouver Police Museum** (240 E Cordova St., 604/665-3346, sinsofthecity.ca, 9am-5pm Tues.-Sat., $12 adults, $10 seniors, $8 students, children under 6 free) does indeed read "Coroner's Court." This used to be the city morgue, but you wouldn't know it from the front half of the second-story museum. Exhibits are charming, if dated and a bit cluttered. One traces the evolution of police uniforms for women; another pays tribute to canine cops. One con man's series of fake IDs takes up a whole wall, and a display of dangerous weapons confiscated by the police has everything from throwing stars to brass knuckles in the shape of a pair of lips. Not that the museum is living in the past; interactive exhibits invite visitors to examine a crime scene, and a computer offers the chance to re-create a perp's face using an automated sketch artist.

But where the museum gets really memorable is in the back (where it's obvious that the museum is not associated with the Vancouver Police Department). The sign that reads, "Exhibits beyond this point are graphic in nature" ain't kidding. The one-time morgue and autopsy suite are not for little children. Behind the rows of stainless steel morgue doors, the first room holds cases illustrating some of Vancouver's biggest murders—including replica skulls (the real skulls used to be in the case) and facial casts of two children

Dr. Sun Yat-Sen Classical Chinese Garden

killed in Stanley Park circa 1947 in an unsolved mystery.

The next room is tiled with two autopsy tables set up—the very room where the body of Errol Flynn was once examined (the erstwhile Robin Hood died of a heart attack while in town to buy a boat). Tissue samples, of flesh hit with bullets or brains wrecked by aneurysm, line the walls. The entire effect is grisly, but fascinating. Museum staff clearly approach the serious exhibits with a slight sense of humor—the doctor names on the old autopsy blackboard belong to *Harry Potter* and Shakespeare characters.

The museum is also the kicking-off point for **Sins of the City Walking Tours** ($18 adults, $14 students and seniors), which visit sites associated with the city's gangsters and biggest crimes. Tours last 90 minutes and focus on red-light districts (4pm-5:30pm Sat.) and opium dens (6pm-7:30pm Fri., 11am-12:30pm Sat.)—so the tours may not be appropriate for children. Book on the Vancouver Police Museum's website, or call.

★ Dr. Sun Yat-Sen Classical Chinese Garden

One of the first things tour guides at **Dr. Sun Yat-Sen Classical Chinese Garden** (578 Carrall St., 604/662-3207, http://vancouverchinesegarden.com, 10am-6pm daily May 1-June 14 and Sept., 9:30am-7pm daily June 15-Aug. 31, 10am-4:30pm daily Oct., 10am-4:30pm Tues.-Sun. Nov.-Apr., $14 adults, $11 seniors, $10 students, children under 5 free) explain is that the popular attraction isn't just a garden. It's more of a re-creation of a Ming Dynasty scholar's home, complete with courtyards, study, and yes, gardens. The 15th century is re-created in beautiful white and red architecture, and all materials came from China, even the rocks. Although the style is centuries old, it was built in the 1980s and named for a Chinese leader from the early 20th century who traveled the world to raise money for China's nationalist movement and was later named the Republic of China's first president. Hour-long tours of the grounds, free with admission, run 4-6 times a day and include hands-on activities like Chinese character drawing, and traditional tea is served.

Next door is the free **Dr. Sun Yat-Sen Park,** which has a similar feel to the Chinese Garden's grounds, but was built using more modern techniques (and American materials). Ironically, it has more of a garden feel than its next-door neighbor, with a few short paths to wander.

Jimi Hendrix Shrine

Though guitar god Jimi Hendrix hailed from Seattle, a **shrine** (206 Union St., 604/669-0377, noon-6pm Mon.-Sat., by donation) is set up in Chinatown where his grandmother lived and worked at a chicken shack that played host to famous black musicians like Louis Armstrong and Nat King Cole. The young Jimi was often left here with relatives. The small red shack and garden are open irregular hours, and the area smells strongly of marijuana. Still, music fans will enjoy the kitsch and Hendrix paraphernalia, and it's

Olympic Sites

For 17 days in February 2010, Vancouver hosted more than 2,500 athletes for the Winter Olympic Games. The region is still dotted with the venues and monuments of the games.

The most notable addition to Vancouver's landscape is the **Olympic Cauldron** (www.vancouverconventioncentre.com), located outside the Vancouver Convention Centre (1055 Canada Pl.), which served as the International Broadcast Centre during the games. The 10-meter (33-foot) sculpture is still lit occasionally for Canada Day. Inside the convention center is an Olympic Legacy display case full of medals and torches.

If you're really an Olympic nerd, you know the **Richmond Olympic Oval** (6111 River Rd., Richmond, 778/296-1400, www.richmondoval.ca, $19.50 adults, $13.70 seniors and youth 19-25, $11 children 13-18, $5 children 6-12, children under 6 free; rentals extra) was built especially for the games to host speed skating. Located about 20 minutes from downtown, the ice skating rink now has limited drop-in hours (children under 13 are required to wear a helmet). There's also a museum with sports simulators to re-create the feeling of doing a ski jump or riding a Paralympic sit-ski.

Cypress Mountain (6000 Cypress Bowl Rd., West Vancouver, 604/926-5612, www.cypressmountain.com, 9am-4pm daily Nov. to mid-Dec., 9am-10pm daily mid-Dec. to Mar., limited hours Apr.), located about 30 minutes from downtown Vancouver, was the site of the freestyle ski and snowboarding events. This is where Canada won its first Olympic medals on home snow when they scored the gold in men's moguls, women's snowboard cross, women's ski cross, and men's parallel giant slalom. In winter, you can ski the same slopes ($62 adults, $40 seniors, $46 children 13-18, $26 children 6-12, $8 children under 6) on six chairlifts, or the hit the snow-tube park ($18). During the summer, the area has disc golf and hiking trails through the yellow cypress fir trees, some of which are more than 1,000 years old, plus interactive displays in the Cypress Creek Lodge.

More skiing events took place in Whistler at the **Whistler Blackcomb** (4545 Blackcomb Way, 604/967-8950, www.whistlerblackcomb.com, two-day tickets: $176-206 adults, $147-181 seniors and children 13-18, $81-104 children 7-12, children under 7 free, $68 summer), a much larger ski mountain, and the **Whistler Sliding Centre** (4910 Glacier Ln., 604/964-0040, www.whistlerslidingcentre.com, 9am-5pm daily, rides $179, walking tours $10), where today visitors can climb into a bobsled or onto a skeleton luge and ride the same track the Olympic athletes did.

An epic final-medal hockey game, the Canadians versus the United States, was held at **Rogers Arena** (800 Griffiths Way, 604/899-7400, www.rogersarena.com). When Canada clinched the gold, a raucous celebration erupted in Vancouver's streets.

The logo for the Vancouver Olympics was the *inukshuk,* based on an Inuit rock symbol (though some Inuits were angered, saying that this version, a person-shaped *inukshuk,* was the sign that someone had died). A large *inukshuk* sculpture stands near **English Bay Beach** (Beach Ave., http://vancouver.ca), while nearby smaller handmade rock cairns, inspired by the form, line the beach.

a refreshingly undermanaged sight in a city that's otherwise quite polished.

YALETOWN

Located south of downtown, the Yaletown neighborhood sits between the busy commercial thoroughfare of Granville Street and the calm waters of False Creek. The streets used to be lined with warehouses, most of which are now home to upscale restaurants and shops—some even use the raised loading docks for outdoor patios. High-end condos rise above the once-utilitarian streets now filled with shoppers and tourists.

Roundhouse Community Arts & Recreation Center

Yaletown's **Roundhouse Community Arts & Recreation Center** (181 Roundhouse Mews, 604/713-1800, www.roundhouse.ca) sits in a building that used to service steam locomotives and once served as an exhibition hall for Expo '86. Now it has a performance center, exhibition hall, art studios, a gym, a café, and other rooms. The outdoor plaza has seating and a working crane that can be moved during performances. A schedule of what's playing at all the center's stages is online. The complex also houses the Engine 374 Pavilion, home to the engine that pulled the first transcontinental train into Vancouver. After getting rusted and weathered by the elements in Kitsilano Park, it was restored and now has an indoor home.

David Lam Park

Downtown the **David Lam Park** (1300 Pacific Blvd., http://vancouver.ca, 10am-dusk daily) is located along the seawall that borders False Creek—an ideal place for urban strolling—and its large lawns and playfields are often filled with Frisbee-throwers and soccer players. Stages are often set up in the park for major festivals, such as the Vancouver International Jazz Festival. The False Creek Ferries water taxi dock leads pedestrians to Granville Island or farther up False Creek.

Contemporary Art Gallery

The downtown **Contemporary Art Gallery** (555 Nelson St., 604/681-2700, www.contemporaryartgallery.ca, noon-6pm Tues.-Sun., free) is dedicated to visual art. Visiting exhibitions highlight photography, sculpture, video, and paintings by artists from around the world with a focus on Canadians. It also hosts gallery talks and family art-making days.

GRANVILLE ISLAND

Granville Island isn't an actual island. The original area was sandbars and tidal flats that were eventually reclaimed with fill to become an industrial area that's connected to the Fairview neighborhood. It was used for shipping, mining, and construction until it was no longer practical for modern industry, at which point it was converted to recreational and commercial use by the Canadian government. Some old tenants remain, like a concrete factory and a drill bit manufacturer.

In addition to the Granville Island Public Market, the area now includes the **Emily Carr University of Art and Design** and the Arts Club Theatre Company. The **Granville Island Water Park** (1318 Cartwright St., www.falsecreekcc.ca/waterpark.htm, 10am-6pm daily summer only, free) is the largest free water park in North America, and features a big yellow waterslide (though constant repairs to the waterslide mean it's not always open). There's also a great deal of shopping and many art studios, plus the Granville Island Brewing microbrewery.

To reach the area from downtown, you must cross the Granville Street Bridge and backtrack (the auto route soars above Granville Island before connecting with the Fairview neighborhood), or go by sea. Two boat services cross False Creek: **False Creek Ferries** (604/684-7781, www.granvilleisland-ferries.bc.ca, $3.50-6 adults, $2.25-4 seniors and children) has stops at Granville Island, Aquatic Center at the foot of Thurlow Street, the Maritime Museum, David Lam Park, Stamps Landing, Spyglass Place, Yaletown at Quayside Marina, Plaza of Nations, and Science World. The rainbow-colored **Aquabus** (604/689-5858, www.theaquabus.com, $3.50-5.50 adults, $1.75-3.75 seniors and children) goes to Granville Island, Hornby Street, David Lam Park, Stamps Landing, Spyglass Place, Yaletown at Quayside Marina, Plaza of Nations, and The Village, not far from Science World.

★ Granville Island Public Market

There's so much more than food at the **Granville Island Public Market** (1661 Duranleau St., 604/666-6477, www.granvilleisland.com, 9am-7pm daily). Booths in the covered structure—the building used to be a machine shop, evidence of Granville Island's previous life as an industrial center—sell jewelry, art, stained glass, and soap. And, yes, a good amount of local produce is available too, especially in the seasonal farmers market held just outside, in addition to goodies like jam, cured meats, and prepared foods. The candy and chocolate stalls are ideal for gift-buying. Grab bites or a carton of fresh berries to eat as you wander the aisles, or sit at one of the tables scattered throughout the indoor market space.

WEST SIDE

★ University of British Columbia Museum of Anthropology

It's worth the drive out to Vancouver's university area to visit the **University of British Columbia Museum of Anthropology** (6393 NW Marine Dr., 604/822-5087, www.moa.ubc.ca, 10am-5pm Wed.-Mon., 10am-9pm Tues., $18 adults, $16 students and seniors, children under 7 free), a world-class collection of local artifacts and cultural traces gathered worldwide. The indoor spotlight is a totem pole collection in the **Great Hall,** made by First Nation tribes like the Haida, Gitxsan, and Oweekeno. Though the structures, many more than 100 years old, are safely inside, they're lit by sunlight that pours through the ceiling-high windows. The building was designed in 1976 based on traditional structures. In the Bill Reid Rotunda, his wood sculpture called *The Raven and the First Men* gets center stage. If it looks familiar, that might be because the iconic shape also appears on the Canadian $20 bill.

Even though the carvings are reason enough to visit the museum, the Multiversity Galleries of more than 10,000 worldwide anthropological artifacts are equally intriguing. Chinese teacups, Mexican masks, Indonesian carvings—all get space behind glass, and you can pull open the drawers full of more treasures that sit under display cases. Touch-screen computers allow for virtual browsing. Outside is a **Haida House** exhibit, built in the 1950s and 1960s, resembling the villages that once populated Haida Gwaii (the Queen Charlotte Islands of British Columbia).

UBC Botanical Garden

The green grounds of the **UBC Botanical Garden** (6804 Marine Dr. SW, 604/822-4208, www.botanicalgarden.ubc.ca, 9:30am-4:30pm daily, $9-24 adults, $7-18 seniors, students, and children 13-17, $5-12 children 5-12, children under 5 free) contain a number of separate gardens, including a physics garden around a central sundial, containing plants used for drugs throughout early European history—plaques explain how and why doctors and apothecaries used them.

University of British Columbia Museum of Anthropology

Vancouver Maritime Museum

There are also alpine, rainforest, and food gardens. Fruits and vegetables harvested from the latter are donated to a soup kitchen downtown. Ticket prices vary depending on whether you want to incorporate specific attractions: The **Nitobe Memorial Garden** (9:30am-5pm daily Apr.-Oct., 10am-2pm Mon.-Fri. Nov.-Mar.) is a traditional Japanese garden, complete with a teahouse that is especially popular in spring when the cherry blossoms are in bloom, and the **Greenheart Canopy Walkway** (10am-4pm daily) tour climbs above the forest, crossing bridges 50 feet in the air. Guided tours last 45 minutes.

Museum of Vancouver

One goal of the **Museum of Vancouver** (1100 Chestnut St., 604/736-4431, www.museumofvancouver.ca, 10am-5pm Mon.-Wed. and Sun., 10am-8pm Thurs., 10am-9pm Fri.-Sat., $19 adults, $16 students and seniors, $9 youth 5-17, children under 5 free) in Vanier Park is to tell the story of the city from the 1900s to 1970s. The building is an impressive sight—the dome is meant to resemble the woven baskets made by First Nation people in the area. Outside is a stainless steel crab sculpture that stands more than six meters (20 feet) tall. Inside are permanent exhibits, many dedicated to individual decades in Vancouver's 20th-century history. (*Neon Vancouver, Ugly Vancouver* rescued the city's neon signs from junkyards and relit them to tell the story of Vancouver's urban transition.) The **H. R. MacMillan Space Centre** (www.spacecentre.ca, 10am-3pm Mon.-Fri., 10am-5pm Sat., noon-5pm Sun., $18 adults, $15 seniors and children 12-18, $13 children 5-11, children under 5 free) that shares the space is a planetarium with space-minded exhibits. Evening astronomy shows and open observatory times take place on Friday and Saturday nights, for a reduced admission charge.

Vancouver Maritime Museum

With so much of the city backing up onto waterfront, it's no wonder the city has the **Vancouver Maritime Museum** (1905 Ogden Ave., 604/257-8300, www.vancouvermaritimemuseum.com, 10am-5pm Fri.-Wed., 10am-8pm Thurs., $12.50 adults, $10 seniors, students, and children 6-18, children under 6 free) to tell the story of the city's ships and shipping. It's located right near the Museum of Vancouver in Vanier Park, and water taxis dock outside. The building is a tall A-frame structure that holds exhibits and model ships (including one made of bone by French prisoners of war), plus a children's center and a re-creation of the forecastle of George Vancouver's ship. The museum also has hand-drawn charts from Captain Cook's expedition and the Arctic exploration vessel *St. Roch*—the first ship to sail the Northwest Passage and the first to circumnavigate North America—but it's often undergoing renovations. Outside is the *Ben Franklin,* a NASA underwater vessel, plus the boiler of the first steamship in the region.

NORTH VANCOUVER

★ Grouse Mountain

The peaks behind North Vancouver are more than just a postcard backdrop. **Grouse Mountain** (6400 Nancy Greene Way, 604/980-9311, www.grousemountain.com, 8:45am-10pm daily, $45-59 adults, $40-55 seniors, $26-40 youth 13-18, $16 children 5-12, children under 5 free) is the easiest ski area to access from downtown Vancouver, though it's more than a one-season destination; the mountaintop complex also includes attractions and activities that are open year-round. It's accessed via the **Skyride** tram (every 15 min., 8:45am-10pm daily), which leaves from a spot within North Vancouver's residential streets and climbs a mile up to an area with a lodge, skating pond, trails, and ski area. Ticket prices vary depending on what you plan to do on Grouse Mountain, but all include the Skyride passage.

A turbine called **Eye of the Wind** generates some of the power that runs the compound, and visitors can go up the 20-story tower for an even better view of the mountains and city. The **Grouse Mountain Refuge for Endangered Wildlife** is home to two grizzly bears, both orphans found in British Columbia, and wolves retired from appearing in movies. Summer activity options include zip-lining, hiking, a lumberjack show, and paragliding. Truly brave souls can tackle the **Grouse Grind,** a hike from the tram's base to the top. Record holders do it in around 30 minutes, but you'll want to leave considerably longer unless you have thighs of steel.

In winter you can rent snowshoes ($20) to explore the woods surrounding the ski slopes, or sit back on a sleigh ride. Skiing is open during the day, but the night skiing is where Grouse Mountain truly shows off. The lights of Vancouver seem right at the base of each run on clear nights.

Year-round dining ranges from a casual coffee bar to an outdoor bistro and indoor fine dining at **The Observatory** (604/980-9311, 5pm-10pm daily, entrées $25-36, five-course prix fixe $130), which includes the cost of the tram ride up.

In summer, there's a free shuttle ride from downtown Vancouver, provided you've purchased a tram ticket, or you can take the SeaBus to Lonsdale Quay from downtown, then catch bus 236 to Grouse Mountain. To drive from downtown Vancouver, take Highway 99 through Stanley Park and across Lions Gate Bridge, then turn right on Marine

Grouse Mountain Skyride

Drive. Take the first left a hundred yards later onto Capilano Road, and follow it for six kilometers (3.7 miles); the road becomes Nancy Green Way along the way. The Grouse Mountain Skyride has a number of parking lots around the base; pay for parking at central kiosks.

Capilano Suspension Bridge Park

At one time it took a wilderness trek to reach the **Capilano Suspension Bridge** (3735 Capilano Rd., 604/985-7474, www.capbridge.com, daily: 9am-5pm Jan.-Feb and Oct.-Nov., 9am-6pm Mar. to mid-Apr. and Sept., 9am-7pm mid-Apr. to mid-May, 8:30am-8pm mid-May to Aug., 11am-9pm Dec.-Jan.; $43 adults, $39 seniors, $34 students, $27 children 13-16, $15 children 6-12, children under 6 free), but now it's a short drive from downtown, reachable by city bus. But the park is no less spectacular, still known for its signature bridge built in 1889. (Yes, it's safe. It was rebuilt in the 1950s, but you'll have trouble remembering that when you're 230 feet in the air above the Capilano River.)

On the other side of the forested canyon is a series of tree-to-tree bridges (not nearly so scary); come back across to where you started for the **Cliffwalk,** a narrow, cantilevered walkway overlooking the river. Very little here is appropriate for anyone afraid of heights, but it's all quite solid and an easy way to peek at British Columbia's signature nature. Drop into the Story Centre near the park entrance, next to its signature totem pole, for more history of the area.

Lynn Canyon Suspension Bridge

Though less popular than its Capilano cousin, the **Lynn Canyon Suspension Bridge** (3993 Peters Rd., www.lynncanyon.ca, 7am-9pm daily summer, 7am-7pm daily spring and fall, 7am-6pm daily winter) is no less dramatic—what's more, it's free. Built in 1912, it crosses more than 160 feet above Lynn Canyon and connects to walking trails in the heavily forested area. The **Lynn Canyon Ecology Centre** (3663 Park Rd., 604/990-3755, http://dnv.org/ecology, 10am-5pm Mon.-Fri., noon-4pm Sat.-Sun., $2 donation) has nature exhibits and puppet shows. Swimming holes are popular—well, in the summer, anyway.

Capilano Suspension Bridge

Entertainment and Events

NIGHTLIFE

Bars and Clubs

DOWNTOWN

There's nothing particularly new about the speakeasy bar, but **Prohibition** (801 W Georgia St, 604/673-7089, 7pm-1am Thurs., 7pm-2am Fri.-Sat., cover charge after 8pm) in the Rosewood Hotel Georgia manages to feel special and a bit elusive—just like good gin during the Prohibition era. Head toward the big wooden doors from the hotel lobby for the bar, where the dim room is brightened with teal stools and a lot of mirrors, as much'80s excess as '20s style. A beautiful ringed chandelier sets the fancy mood, and well-blended cocktails, small bites, and live music complete the decadent scene.

GASTOWN AND CHINATOWN

The cocktail menu at Gastown's **Revel Room** (238 Abbott St., 604/687-4088, www.revelroom.ca, 4pm-1am Tues.-Thurs., 4pm-2am Fri.-Sat., 4pm-midnight Sun.) is as much fun as a night out on the town—even during its "Sour Hour" (4pm-6pm Tues.-Sun.), a happy hour with sour drink specials. Seasonal offerings might include a Stay Puft S'more (it's a *Ghostbusters* reference, but yes, there are toasted marshmallows) or the Mother in Law (a bourbon-based tipple from New Orleans that's "perfect for settling arguments"). Food at the establishment is from the American South, hailing from the Southwest or New Orleans, and a house band plays jazz and blues every Sunday.

Menus at the **Six Acres** (203 Carrall St., 604/488-0110, www.sixacres.ca, 11:30am-11:30pm Sun.-Thurs., 11:30am-12:30am Fri.-Sat.) are bound in old children's books, but what's inside is decidedly grown-up. There is a rotating selection of bottled beers for the pickiest of beer nerds, and any nerd can enjoy the soundtracks playing in the bathroom—they rotate from radio plays to language tapes. The two-story bar is in the oldest brick building in the city and has an outdoor patio that faces one of the busiest intersections in Gastown. Still, the place has an intimate feel and is proud of the fact that it sits behind Gassy Jack's statue (and so patrons get to stare at his bronzed behind). Snacks include sliders and a very sharable plate of poutine with gravy made from St.-Ambroise stout. Happy hour is all day, every day, until 6pm.

The **Shebeen Whiskey House** (210 Carrall St., 604/688-9779, www.shebeen.ca, 5pm-midnight Tues.-Thurs., 5pm-2am Fri.-Sat.) isn't hidden, exactly, but you do have to walk through the Irish Heather Gastropub to find the bar. It's owned by the same guy, Sean Heather, who can't stop creating eateries in the area. Shebeen is one of his most modest, though the whiskey list doesn't hold back. The scotch menu separates the Scottish Isle of Islay selections from the Isla of Jura ones (wouldn't want to throw them all together), and even has whiskey selections from India and Japan. Bartenders aren't fussy, though, and the space is a bit less fussy than other Heather establishments.

Although **Salt Tasting Room** (45 Blood Alley Sq., 604/633-1912, www.salttastingroom.com, 4pm-11pm daily) is one of the more heavily designed spots run by Heather, it's earned its popularity. It sits on Blood Alley in Gastown, so named either for the refuse tossed by butchers onto the cobblestones, or for the crime that was committed in the area. The bar is decked out in brick and wood beams, with square metal stools and a wall-sized chalkboard that advertises the food offerings; it's mostly meat and cheese. Assemble a wine flight or nibble some snacks while the bartender selects a few two-ounce pours; personalized service is a stated goal, so don't be intimidated by the chic vibe.

Forget a wine list—the beer list at **Alibi**

Room (157 Alexander St., 604/623-3383, www.alibi.ca, 5pm-11pm Mon.-Thurs., 5pm-12:30am Fri., 10am-12:30am Sat., 10am-11:30pm Sun.) changes so frequently that it celebrated its 400th tap rotation after only about six years of operations. They're most proud of their selection of cask beers and rare microbrews, but the menu of upscale pub food is also popular.

The menu at **Darby's Gastown** (16 W Hastings St., 604/558-4658, www.darbysgastown.pub, 3pm-12:30am Sun.-Thurs., 3pm-1:30am Fri.-Sat.) is all about craft beers and local wines, specializing in Canadian flavors. There's an all-day breakfast wrap made with local veggies and Cajun chips, but the small bites—tacos, meatball sliders—pair well with the beers, or go for an elaborate wine and meat plate.

If a mad scientist decided to open a bar, it would look something like Chinatown's **The Keefer Bar** (135 Keefer St., 604/688-1961, http://thekeeferbar.com, 5pm-1am Sun.-Thurs., 5pm-2am Fri.-Sat.). There are vials and flasks in every corner, anatomical designs behind the bar, and bottles lit to look more like potions than simple spirits. But drinks are certainly potions of a sort, made carefully with bitters and fresh juices for a well-heeled, hip young crowd. The food selections are the strongest reminder of the neighborhood, including Peking duck sliders and shrimp miso shitake tacos, though drinks do use some Asian-inspired ingredients like dragon-fruit gin, sake, and syrup made from mushroom-infused tea.

In a space that used to be a Chinese restaurant, Chinatown's **Fortune Sound Club** (147 E Pender St., 604/569-1758, www.fortunesoundclub.com, hours vary) now blasts dance music. For a late-night club, it's very proud of its ecofriendly decor, including sustainable materials on the bar surface and a reclaimed-wood dance floor. A wall installation from street artist Shepard Fairey is in the front walkway. Inside, DJs and performers take turns in the DJ booth and stage.

YALETOWN

No need to be stuffy, old chap; **The New Oxford** (1144 Homer St, 604/609-0901, http://donnellygroup.ca/new-oxford, 11:30am-1am Mon.-Thurs., 11:30am-2am Fri., 11am-2am Sat., 11am-1am Sun.) is a British sports pub, sure, but it's hardly filled with cigar smoke and fuddy-duddies. The interior has a mix of comfy leather chairs and bright pop art, and the televisions showing sports manage to be somewhat unobtrusive among the wood-paneled and exposed-brick walls. Find a mix of local and British drafts (including Guinness, of course), plus a mix of house-made tonics and original cocktails.

The bright white and worn wood of **Rodney's Oyster House** (1228 Hamilton St., 604/609-0080, www.rodneysoysterhouse.com, 11:30am-11pm daily) recalls the boats where the food is caught; even the hooks on the walls look like they belong on a boat. Come for the clams, oysters, and "Oysters Rockerfellah," but stay for a drink called a Caesar—imagine a Bloody Mary, but one made with Clamato juice and topped with a big prawn. Canadians swear by them.

Just outside Yaletown, **Long Table Distillery Room** (1451 Hornby St., 604/266-0177, www.longtabledistillery.com, 1pm-6pm Wed.-Thurs., 1pm-9pm Fri.-Sat.) sits on a quiet street, claiming the title of the city's first microdistillery. Tastings of their gin and vodka are held in the space also occupied by shiny copper equipment and, yes, a big long table.

GRANVILLE ISLAND

If the Public Market is the crown jewel of Granville Island, then **Granville Island Brewing** (1441 Cartwright St., 604/687-2739, www.gib.ca, 11am-9pm daily) is its best ambassador. It began in the 1980s as the country's first microbrewery, though it is now owned by a subsidiary of Molson Coors and most of its beer is actually made in Kelowna, a city 320 kilometers (200 miles) inland. But the original taproom on Granville Island serves the beers that still bear the name of Vancouver neighborhoods and landmarks, plus small-batch brews not largely available. Tours ($9.75) include three 5-ounce tasters of beer, and the taproom serves 12.5-ounce servings.

Echoing the brewery's landmark establishment 30 years ago, **Artisan Sake Maker** (1339 Railspur Alley, 604/685-7253, www.artisansakemaker.com, 11:30am-6pm daily) has staked a claim as Canada's first fresh sake maker. The small space opens its garage door to welcome tasters and tour takers, showing off one variety that is made from organically grown rice harvested in the Fraser Valley. Larger servings of sake are also available, as well as a small menu of snacks.

WEST SIDE

Although it was known primarily as an LGBT spot when it opened a few decades ago, **Celebrities Nightclub** (1022 Davie St., 604/681-6180, www.celebritiesnightclub.com, 10pm-3am Tues. and Fri.-Sat.) is now a dance mecca for straight and gay crowds alike. It has a programmable light system, so some 20,000 LED lights flash in patterns in the large dance area, accompanied by a powerful sound system. Weekly parties are held, including karaoke Tuesdays and the long-running Stereotype Fridays, first launched to be proudly genre-free—not constrained to one type of music—and devoid of club culture clichés.

Gay and Lesbian

The vibe at **PumpJack Pub** (1167 Davie St., 604/685-3417, www.pumpjackpub.com, 1pm-2am daily) is a little less lavish than the party clubs of Vancouver; there are two pinball machines and cheap drinks. That doesn't mean there isn't a line, even on days other than Friday and Saturday. The joint is popular with the leather and bear communities, and there are often few women inside.

The small **1181** (1181 Davie St., 604/787-7130, www.1181.ca, 6pm-3am daily) is the watering hole for much of Vancouver's stylish, well-chiseled gay scene. It can get crowded but achieves more of an upscale lounge feel than its fellow gay bars. The good-looking bartenders are pretty friendly, and DJs spin even though there isn't much of a dance floor.

Score on Davie (1262 Davie St., 604/632-1646, www.scoreondavie.com, 11am-1am Mon.-Thurs., 11am-2am Fri., 10am-2am Sat., 10am-midnight Sun.) is a sports bar with a gay clientele, there to watch hockey or football. The bar serves all meals and has a 30-bottle beer list. Food is a step above normal fare—the burger comes on a brioche bun and has horseradish and Dijon aioli, and "handhelds" are fry cones with toppings. On Sunday mornings, the Bloody Caesars, topped with burgers, brownies, sandwiches, and more, are a meal unto themselves.

Live Music

Open since 1929, the **Commodore Ballroom** (868 Granville St., 604/739-4550, www.commodoreballroom.com) has a mix of the old and the new—pillars alongside the dance-floor-or-standing-room area, art deco wrought-iron handrails on the stairs, and complicated light shows from above. It has hosted everyone from Tom Waits to Tina Turner, David Bowie to Patti Smith. A neon sign outside calls it "The Fabulous Commodore Ballroom," and the big-name acts it gets help it live up to the moniker. Events are often for ages 19 and older and include Canadian and American rock, pop, and indie acts.

Even though it's best known as the home of the Vancouver Canucks hockey team, **Rogers Arena** (800 Griffiths Way, 604/899-7400, www.rogersarena.com) also hosts the city's major music shows. This is where Kanye and Beyonce perform when they're in town. It opened in 1995 with, what else, a Bryan Adams concert and was renamed Canada Hockey Place during the 2010 Olympics as it hosted the hockey matches, including the gold-medal game between Canada and the United States, considered to be one of the best hockey games in history (at least to the Canadians, who won).

The art deco-style **Vogue Theatre** (918

Granville St., 604/569-1144, www.voguetheatre.com) was originally an Odeon movie theater built by a bootlegger and opened in 1941. It's currently rumored to be inhabited by a ghost wearing a tuxedo (not the bootlegger, at least from what anyone can tell). The giant landmark sign out front has a neon figure of the Roman goddess Diana, and inside a recent restoration turned a once-crumbling relic back into a historical gem. A high-definition screen is available for film screenings. Otherwise the theater hosts bands, comics, and parts of the Vancouver International Jazz Festival and Vancouver International Film Festival.

THE ARTS

Classical Music, Opera, and Dance

Major folk and rock acts play the historical **Orpheum Theatre** (601 Smithe St., 604/665-3050, http://vancouver.ca), but it's also home to the **Vancouver Symphony Orchestra** (604/876-3434, www.vancouversymphony.ca), which plays more than 140 concerts per year as the country's largest performing-arts organization west of Ontario. The Orpheum also hosts the Vancouver Bach Choir, which has performed Bach and contemporary pieces since 1930, and the Vancouver Chamber Choir. The theater has an elegant scalloped backdrop, ornate ceiling, and red carpets in the elegant lobby. It dates back to 1927, when the Spanish baroque revival building was constructed to be a vaudeville house.

The lobby of the **Queen Elizabeth Theatre** (649 Cambie St., 604/665-3050, http://vancouver.ca) is hung with chandeliers that resemble snowflakes, a delicate juxtaposition to the mid-20th-century style of the building. The theater has been renovated several times since it was built in the 1950s and dedicated by Queen Elizabeth II. The theater hosts touring Broadway Across Canada shows, the Vancouver Christmas Market, and other touring productions. It's home to **Ballet British Columbia** (604/732-5003, www.balletbc.com) and the **Vancouver Opera** (604/683-0222, www.vancouveropera.ca), the country's second-largest opera company.

Theater

The buildings that house the **Firehall Arts Centre** (280 E Cordova St., 604/689-0926, www.firehallartscentre.ca) clearly used to be a fire station—actually the first motorized fire hall on the continent, built in 1906. From its place in a neighborhood underserved by the arts, the Firehall puts on plays, dance performances, art shows, and more. Art in the gallery sometimes links to the shows on stage, but not always. The campus also has an enclosed courtyard where audiences can hang between acts and get concessions.

The **Arts Club Theatre Company** (1585 Johnston St., 604/687-1644, www.artsclub.com) has put on 50 seasons of theater and is now performing at three theaters. One is on Granville Island, and the others are in the southeast end of the city. The **Granville Island Stage** (1585 Johnston St.) hosts popular plays and musicals, while the **BMO Theatre Centre** (162 W 1st Ave.) is not far, closer to the end of False Creek. The **Stanley Industrial Alliance Stage** (2750 Granville St.) is a longer trek from downtown but is the group's flagship theater, home to its biggest productions, often shows that premiered on Broadway.

CINEMA

Although membership is required to see films at **The Cinematheque** (1131 Howe St., 604/688-8202, www.thecinematheque.ca, $11-16 adults, $9-14 seniors and students), it's only an annual $3 fee. Plus, if you decide to stay for a double feature, you can upgrade to the double-bill price without buying a full second ticket. Not only that, but the concession stand sells popcorn and candy that won't actually cost more than a theater ticket. The movies are foreign and independent flicks, often part of film festivals and series.

Vancity Theatre (1181 Seymour St., 604/683-3456, www.viff.org/theatre) not only hosts the Vancouver International Film

Festival in September and October but also plays movies all year. Series include shorts programs and a BC spotlight, but all films are international, independent Canadian, documentary, or art movies. Beer and wine are sold at most films, but not flicks meant for kids—though few of the films even allow those under 18. Tickets include an annual $2 fee.

FESTIVALS AND EVENTS

The **PuSh International Performing Arts Festival** (www.pushfestival.ca, Jan.-Feb.) brings performances and parties to some otherwise quiet months in the city. Recent years have brought hundreds of artists from around the globe for 150 dance, theater, musical, and literary events. The overarching theme emphasizes contemporary expression and cutting-edge creativity. One event screened a movie that was filmed only an hour before the screening began. Parties and galas are also part of the series.

Held for more than 40 years, the Vancouver **Chinese New Year Parade** (Millennium Gate, www.cbavancouver.ca, Jan. or Feb.), also known as the Spring Festival Parade, celebrates the Lunar New Year and includes traditional lion dance teams, marching bands, and community groups in a colorful array of costumes, slowly winding their way through Chinatown.

Spring's prettiest celebration is the **Vancouver Cherry Blossom Festival** (www.vcbf.ca) in March or April, inspired by the Japanese Sakura festivals and starring the 40,000 ornamental cherry trees in the city, many of which came from Japan in the 1930s. Events include the Cherry Jam Downtown Concert, which starts with culinary demos, held at the Burrard Skytrain Station (Burrard and Dunsmir Sts., 604/953-3333, www.translink.ca), the Umbrella Dance near the Vancouver Art Gallery (750 Hornby St.), and the Sakura Days Japan Fair in the VanDusen Botanical Garden (5251 Oak St., 604/257-8335, http://vancouver.ca), located in a residential neighborhood. To experience the blooms without the crowds, find maps on the festival website with hundreds of locations of cherry trees, or find a walk held around the city.

On a day in early May, the **BC Spot Prawn Festival** (www.chefstablesociety.com/spotprawnfestival, May, $19.75) celebrates a local delicacy, a kind of shrimp—no, they're not actually prawns. The bash takes place at False Creek Fisherman's Wharf just west of Granville Island, near where West 1st Avenue meets Pennyfarthing Drive. Tickets get you entrance to a Spot Prawn Boil featuring the sweet, firm little creatures, plus the chance to see chef demonstrations and grab a few pounds to make them at home. A food tent also serves coffee, wine, and other bites. The season goes from May into early summer, and fresh catch is often sold at the False Creek Fisherman's Wharf.

About half a million people attend the **Vancouver International Jazz Festival** (www.coastaljazz.ca, June), made up off 300 concerts around the city in late June. Half of the concerts are free, and big names show up—the likes of Herbie Hancock and Esperanza Spalding. The Downtown Jazz Weekend, part of the festival, was relocated to the grounds of the Vancouver Art Gallery, where a free village of music and arts stages is set up alongside a family zone and artisan market, plus a dance party. It's been known to attract more than 150,000 over just two days.

The idea of Shakespeare performed al fresco is nothing new, but **Bard on the Beach** (604/737-0625, www.bardonthebeach.org, June-Sept.) takes it up a notch and moves the iambic pentameter to Vanier Park (1000 Chestnut St., http://vancouver.ca) in Kitsilano. Almost 90,000 people attend the festival, which produces four plays on two tented stages June-September. The bigger of the two has an open end, so the audience can see the water and mountains behind, while the smaller stage does lesser-known plays and unusual Shakespeare stagings. The Bard Village has concessions, bars, and a gift shop and also holds educational events.

What's better than fireworks? A fireworks competition. The **Celebration of Light** (http://hondacelebrationoflight.com, July) is a renowned international battle between three countries in the art of pyrotechnic. Spectators—almost half a million of them—head to the beaches of English Bay to watch over three nights in late July and early August. Entrants are judged on concept, color, and music correlation, but the event is more about 25-minute segments of nonstop dazzle.

November brings the **Eastside Culture Crawl** (www.eastsideculturecrawl.com, Nov.), a four-day arts festival attended by more than 30,000 people. Hundreds of artists show off their art in dozens of buildings within the bounds of Main Street, 1st Avenue, Victoria Drive, and the waterfront (so just east of Gastown and including some of Chinatown). Galleries hold special events and exhibits, but it's more fun to visit the studios open to the public for the day.

Shopping

There's an equal balance between large chain stores and artsy boutiques in Vancouver. The American and Canadian dollars are usually close in value, but consumer goods—clothing, electronics, and food—are mostly more expensive in Canada.

DOWNTOWN

Department Stores

Hudson's Bay (674 Granville St., 604/681-6211, www.thebay.com, 9:30am-9pm Mon.-Sat., 11am-7pm Sun.) department stores purport to be the oldest business in North America, and because they were trading for furs back in the 17th century, no one's challenging them for the title. The store in downtown Vancouver, a.k.a. The Bay, has come a long way since the days of bartering with First Nations people over blankets and beads. Now there's Lancôme and BCBG wares for sale in the downtown department store. But you can still purchase the Hudson's Bay Company signature multicolored striped wool blanket or Canada-labeled workout gear that's been sold since the 2010 Winter Olympics were held in Vancouver.

Fur used to matter in Canada because so many department stores were born of the fur trade. **Holt Renfrew** (737 Dunsmuir St., 604/681-3121, www.holtrenfrew.com, 10am-7pm Mon.-Tues., 10am-9pm Wed.-Fri., 10am-8pm Sat., 11am-7pm Sun.) emerged from a store that didn't collect them from trappers, but rather sold them to rich Europeans from Quebec City. Today the Vancouver store is a destination for shoppers of luxury brands like Armani, Gucci, and Valentino. The Holts Salon and Spa offers pampering if the gleaming white walls and skylights aren't calming enough.

Clothing and Shoes

If Canada had its own Gap, it would probably be **Le Château** (813 Burrard St., 604/682-3909, www.lechateau.com, 10am-7pm Sat.-Wed., 10am-9pm Thurs.-Fri.). The chain store has more than 200 outposts around Canada selling its midpriced casual wear and special-occasion outfits for both men and women. Styles are trendy but generally affordable.

Style is at a premium at **Aritzia** (1110 Robson St., 604/684-3251, www.aritzia.com, 10am-10pm Mon.-Sat., 10am-9pm Sun.), which was originally a single women's wear boutique in Vancouver. In 30 years it's grown into a chain with more than 50 stores, many in the United States. The store caters to the young set bent on looking effortlessly casual, even if it takes a little work and a little cash. The online website even includes a magazine full of style profiles and artist interviews.

Who cares what you wear to yoga? Everyone, ever since **Lululemon Athletica** (970 Robson St., 604/681-3118, www.

lululemon.com, 9am-10pm Mon.-Sat., 9am-9pm Sun.) turned om-wear into high fashion. Though the company began here in Vancouver in 1998, it took a good decade for its name to become synonymous with carefully cut tops, space-age fabric, and yes, yoga pants that can soar to over $100. But Eastern philosophy and stretching aren't the only philosophy linked to the workout togs—shopping bags are printed with the phrase "Who is John Galt?" a reference to the Ayn Rand book *Atlas Shrugged*.

Gourmet Goodies

Ladurée (1141 Robson St., 604/336-3030, www.laduree.fr/en, 10am-9pm Mon.-Sat., 11am-7pm Sun.) is a boutique—one that sells only cookies. The fancy French macarons are made in Europe and imported to Vancouver, and the multiple flavors are a rainbow behind the counter. The entire store feels like the inside of an elaborate birthday cake, and the delicate desserts make great gifts. A salon in back serves meals and sit-down treats; the surprisingly thorough menu features afternoon tea, sandwiches, and frothy desserts.

GASTOWN AND CHINATOWN

Clothing and Shoes

Welcome to the temple of **John Fluevog** (65 Water St., 604/688-6228, www.fluevog.com, 10am-7pm Mon.-Wed. and Sat., 10am-8pm Thurs.-Fri., noon-6pm Sun.), the shoe line's flagship store and workshop. The funky footwear is popular among celebrities (the brand is quick to point out that Madonna showed off a pair in her movie *Truth or Dare*). Fluevog, who began the store in Vancouver, still personally designs each shoe style in the open space of the second-story workshop, itself topped with multicolor glass skylights. Shoes often show off his sense of humor—one sole reports that it repels water, acid, and Satan.

The streets of Gastown are lined in high-end boutiques, but **Community Thrift and Vintage Frock Shoppe** (311 Carrall St., 604/682-8535, www.communitythriftandvintage.ca, 11am-7pm Mon.-Sat., noon-5pm Sun.) has markedly different stock—yet a similar look, with racks positioned artfully around a light-filled space. The shop calls its wares vintage clothing at thrift-shop prices. Most notably, it employs residents from the Downtown Eastside neighborhood, a poor area that directly borders the rejuvenated commercial center of Gastown, and donates all proceeds to charities that address local housing needs. There's also a unisex shop at 11 West Hastings Street.

The Chinatown street where boutique **Charlie & Lee** (223 Union St., 604/558-3030, www.charlieandlee.com, 11am-6pm Mon.-Sat., noon-5pm Sun.) sits is removed from the bustle of Gastown, but the fashion is no less up to date. Clothing pieces represent small designers from around the globe, but most are a casual retro style that would seem at home in Portland or Brooklyn—imagine a $90 chambray skinny tie. A dark den holds the menswear in the back, decorated with an arty axe on the wall.

Leatherworker **Erin Templeton** (511 Carrall St., 604/682-2451, www.erintempleton.com, 11am-5pm Mon.-Tues., 11am-6pm Wed.-Sat.) likes to work with recycled leather pieces, turning them into simple, bold bags and wallets, often in bright colors. She also sells vintage clothing out of her store and studio, located on a grubby corner of Chinatown.

Gift and Home

The good news is that **Secret Location** (1 Water St., 604/685-0090, www.secretlocation.ca, 11am-6pm Mon.-Sat., 11am-5pm Sun.) isn't as hard to locate as its name suggests. The real secret is what the real mission is here. A "concept" store out front has gifts and clothing in a wide space marked by tall concrete pillars and a pale wood floor.

You can be forgiven for thinking you took a wrong turn and ended up in Portland. No, you're just at **Old Faithful Shop** (320 W Cordova St., 778/327-9376, www.oldfaithfulshop.com, 11am-7pm Mon.-Fri., 10am-7pm

Sat., 11am-6pm Sun.), a home store that sells arty watering cans, artisanal relish, and retro canvas laundry carts (perfect for re-creating scenes from *Annie!*). The brick walls hark back to the owner's original inspiration, the general stores owned by his grandparents.

Gourmet Goodies

Save On Meats (43 W Hastings St., 604/569-3568, www.saveonmeats.ca, 10am-7pm Mon.-Thurs., 8am-10pm Fri.-Sat., 8am-7pm Sun.) isn't just a butcher shop—now it's a phenomenon, thanks to a reality show called *Gastown Gamble*. The owners reopened the once-shuttered neighborhood institution, saving the space from becoming a high-end condo, and relit the neon sign featuring a flying pig. Besides a long deli case full of raw meat, the spot also features a diner, cooking classes, and a sandwich counter. A token program is meant to address the number of hungry or itinerant people in the neighborhood. The $2.25 tokens, handed out individually or by the store's community partners, can be redeemed for hot breakfast sandwiches throughout the day, and a new clothing token system with $5 tokens was just launched.

YALETOWN

Gift and Home

The shelves at **Örling & Wu** (28 Water St., 604/568-6718, www.orlingandwu.com, 10am-6pm Mon.-Wed., 10am-7pm Thurs.-Sat., 11am-6pm Sun.) carry plates, clocks, glassware, and pillows from around the world, including Scandinavia and New York City. Many pieces represent a vintage look, and they're doing their part to bring wallpaper back into fashion.

Health and Beauty

Though not nearly as extensive as makeup emporium Sephora, **BeautyMark** (1268 Pacific Blvd., 604/642-2294, www.beautymark.ca, 10am-7pm Mon.-Sat., noon-5pm Sun.) excels at the lotions-and-lipstick trade while adding nail services and a smattering of hats and clothing in one corner. A more wide-ranging selection is on the store's website, but the bright shop on the edge of Yaletown offers personal consultations from staff, who like to hand out samples of recommended products.

GRANVILLE ISLAND

Arts and Crafts

Yes, you can wear the scarves made and sold at **Alarte Silks** (1369 Railspur Alley, 778/370-4304, www.alartesilks.com, 10am-6pm Mon.-Sat., 11am-6pm Sun.), but as the gallery-like space suggests, they're works of art. The pieces are painted by artist Izabela Sauer, whose textile work has won awards and who splits her time between the South Pacific and the Granville studio. Her Nuno collection includes Japanese-style felting, while the Shibori are creased into folds. None are cheap, but the wild-faced ceramic heads used as display mannequins are worth a peek even if you're not buying.

The Craft Council of British Columbia operates the show **Crafthouse** (1386 Cartwright St., 604/687-7270, www.craftcouncilbc.ca, 10am-6pm daily), and getting a piece on the shelves takes more than having a price sticker. Local artists must pass a Standards of Quality Jury, which judges the craftsmanship and picks product lines for the shop. Pieces include one-of-a-kind ceramic works, jewelry, and even cards, and staff members are adept at spelling out an artist's biography to interested shoppers.

Gift and Home

It doesn't matter if you already have a vacuum cleaner designed by NASA. The **Granville Island Broom Company** (1406 Old Bridge St., 604/629-1141, www.broomcompany.com, 10am-6pm daily) is a must-see on a trip around Granville Island. It's like entering the Wicked Witch of the West's fantasy closet, where broomcorn (a kind of sorghum) is handcrafted in a traditional Shaker style. Handles are made of eucalyptus, birch, or even locally forged iron. The sisters show off their broom making and even sell doll-like figures made from broom heads. They know you're not actually going to clean with these works of art.

Walking into **Ainsworth Custom Design** (1243 Cartwright St., 604/682-8838, www.ainsworthcustomdesign.com, 10am-6pm Mon. and Fri., noon-6pm Sat., noon-5pm Sun.) is like entering a birthday party already in full swing—brightly colored art pieces, wall hangings, and paper goods are for sale, all made by local Vancouver artists.

Rhinoceros Accessories (1551 Johnston St., No. 102, 604/684-3448, www.rhinostore.ca, 10am-6pm daily) is even more of an assault on the senses. The gift shop is crammed with hand-painted glassware, holiday decorations, and knickknacks. The store has been on the island for more than three decades, even opening a Gastown outpost in recent years. It's the kind of place where you go to buy a gift for someone you don't know too well.

Kids' Stuff

Though smaller than the food-and-arts Public Market on Granville Island, the nearby **Kids Market** (1496 Cartwright St., 604/689-8447, www.kidsmarket.ca, 10am-6pm daily) feels as big to the under-12 set. Two floors of 25 shops in an old factory building include a magic store, a kite and puppets emporium, and a kids-only hair salon where kids can get a trim while sitting in a Thomas the Tank Engine chair. Yes, kids only.

NORTH VANCOUVER

Gourmet Goodies

Located near where the SeaBus lands in North Vancouver, **Lonsdale Quay Market** (Lonsdale Ave. and Carrie Cates Ct., 604/985-6261, www.lonsdalequay.com, 9am-7pm daily) features individual shops hawking spices, candy treats, and flowers, plus full-service restaurants and cafés. There are also gifts of the scarf, jewelry, and handbag variety in the space, which opened during Expo '86. Climb to the top of the stairs in the Q Tower—literally a platform topped by a giant letter Q—for views of the city.

Sports and Recreation

PARKS

Portside Park

Follow Main Street all the way to the end, over the railroad tracks, and around a big curve to reach the waterfront **Portside Park** (101 E Waterfront Rd., http://vancouver.ca, dawn-dusk daily). The rocky beach has some of the best people-watching in the city, plus two playgrounds and a spray park for kids. The view takes in the more industrial side of Vancouver's waterfront plus the towering mountains behind Burrard Inlet. The full name is CRAB Park at Portside, CRAB standing for Create a Real Available Beach, the neighborhood group that supported the formation of the park. There's no crabbing to be done here, but a large lawn hosts arts performances in the summer.

Queen Elizabeth Park

Located a few kilometers south of downtown, **Queen Elizabeth Park** (4600 Cambie St., 604/873-7000, http://vancouver.ca) is one of the city's prettiest plots of land. Its peak, the 500-foot Little Mountain, is the highest spot in the city of Vancouver. It contains a garden built in a former quarry, sculptures, a rose garden, and an arboretum full of 1,500 trees from across the country. There's a pitch-and-putt golf course full of par-3 golf holes, tennis courts, and a lawn bowling area. The **Bloedel Conservatory** (33rd Ave. between Cambie and Main Sts., 10am-8pm daily summer, 10am-5pm daily winter, $6.50 adults, $4.35 seniors and children 13-18, $3.15 children 3-12, children under 3 free) opened in 1969. This geodesic dome is full of exotic birds, like macaws and African parrots, tropical plants, and a koi fish pond. Next door is the **Dancing Waters Fountain** with 70 jets of water.

BEACHES

The city's most popular beach is **English Bay Beach** (Beach Ave. between Gilford and Bidwell Sts., http://vancouver.ca), located southeast of Stanley Park and across from a busy neighborhood full of bars and shops. The beach has a long strip of sand with two volleyball courts (11:30am-8:30pm May-Sept.), lifeguards (May-Sept.), and a swimming dock with a slide. There are kayak rentals and a fenced off-leash dog park (Lagoon Dr., 7am-9pm). On New Year's Day, the Vancouver Polar Bear Swim Club takes a chilly dip in the water here. It started in 1920 with 10 brave souls and now more than 2,000 people take part. Washrooms, pay parking, and an outpost of the **Cactus Club Café** (1790 Beach Ave., 604/681-2582, www.cactusclubcafe.com, 11am-midnight Sun.-Thurs., 11am-1am Fri.-Sat., $23-40) are available.

The view from **Spanish Banks Beach Park** (4801 NW Marine Dr., 604/257-8400, http://vancouver.ca) is amazing. Where else can you sit in the sun on the sand and see snowcapped mountains and a cityscape? Spanish Banks East stretches toward Tolmie Street, offering volleyball courts and lifeguards (May-Sept.). Larger Spanish Banks West is designated as a "quiet beach" without stereos or other amplified sound. The park is located in Westside, between Kitsilano and the University of British Columbia. From downtown Vancouver, cross the Burrard or Granville Bridges and follow West 4th Avenue west to NW Marine Drive. Turn right onto NW Marine Drive and follow it for 1.8 kilometers (1.1 miles) to the park. Parking is free.

BIKING

Some of the best cycling in the city is inside **Stanley Park** (604/257-8531, http://vancouver.ca), but there are other places to pedal. Follow a seaside bike ride from **Vanier Park** (1000 Chestnut St., Kitsilano, http://vancouver.ca) along Kitsilano Beach, then on West 3rd Avenue until the road meets NW Marine Drive. Follow the bike lane to Spanish Banks Beach Park (4801 NW Marine Dr.) less than 6 kilometers (4 miles), or all the way to the Museum of Anthropology for a 9.6-kilometer (6-mile) cycle.

For mountain biking, try the North Shore's **Mount Seymour CBC Trail** (1700 Mount Seymour Rd., North Vancouver,

Grouse Grind

604/986-2261, www.mountseymour.com). It's not easy, but it is very popular and has a shuttle ($5) hauling bikes between endpoints of the trail.

Bike Rentals

To rent a bike near Stanley Park, head to the giant **Spokes Bicycle Rental** (1798 W Georgia St., 604/688-5141, www.spokesbicyclerentals.com, 8am-9pm daily summer, 9am-6:30pm daily winter, $7.82-10.48 per hour), where a well-oiled rental machine quickly gets tourists on a bike and headed toward the park on an easy cruiser and with a helmet and basket. The shop has existed in some form since 1938, so they know how to see Vancouver by bike.

For more specialized mountain bikes, try North Vancouver's **Endless Biking** (101-1467 Crown St., North Vancouver, 604/985-2519, www.endlessbiking.com/rentals, 9am-6pm daily summer, 10am-4pm daily fall, by appointment in winter, $35-65 for 4 hours). They have full suspension and hardtail bikes, and have packages that include pads, helmet, gloves, and armor—and maps. They also offer guided tours on North Shore trails.

HIKING

Grouse Grind

Distance: 2.9 kilometers (1.8 miles) one-way
Duration: 2 hours
Elevation gain: 853 meters (2,799 feet)
Effort: strenuous
Trailhead: Skyride Terminal (6400 Nancy Greene Way)

Grouse Grind has to be the city's hardest hike, an unforgiving slog up Grouse Mountain to the ski and recreation area on top. Leave from the Skyride Terminal and purchase a Grind Timer Card to track your time (the $20 ticket comes with free transfer for your bag to the top). The day's best times are logged on the website. It's a rough hike straight uphill, with steps that can exhaust even the most fit of hikers, but the trees offer nice shade for most of it. There are 2,830 stairs to tackle through thick, tall forest. Panting hikers rest on seat-like rocks on the side of the trail. But when you emerge up top, you'll behold vistas of the city sparkling below. Look west to see large freighter ships anchored just off Stanley Park. Hiking downhill isn't allowed for safety reasons, so you'll have to ride the Skyride ($10) back down.

Beacon Hill Trail

Distance: 1 kilometer (0.6 mile) round-trip
Duration: 50 minutes
Elevation gain: 100 feet
Effort: easy
Trailhead: access off Beacon Lane in Lighthouse Park

For an easy ramble, try Lighthouse Park in North Vancouver. The still-functioning lighthouse that gives the park its name dates back to the 1870s, and the park's trails wind next to cliffs and through forest. A short hike leads uphill on the Beacon Hill Trail to the lighthouse viewpoint and the knolls looking over Burrard Inlet and Howe Sound.

If you'd like to wander more, take a map at the trailhead to see the large network of trails—though don't worry too much about getting lost on this peninsula—and meander from one to the other, past first-growth Douglas fir trees. Routes head to coves and exposed points that offer more ocean views.

Food

This close to the Pacific Ocean it's not surprising that seafood has a firm hold in the Vancouver culinary scene. What *is* surprising is the huge variety (besides fish and clams), and that some of the most notable cuisine in town has Asian roots. As with the rest of the Northwest, local ingredients are highly coveted.

You can't go more than a few blocks in Vancouver, or any Canadian city for that matter, without coming across a **Tim Hortons** (www.timhortons.com). The doughnut and coffee chain is named for an NHL player who played professional hockey for 22 seasons and is known to have invented the slap shot. The restaurant he started is credited with inventing the apple fritter. Today Tim Hortons has more than 3,500 locations in Canada and sells fast-service coffee, doughnuts, and sandwiches, including breakfast sandwiches, and outside urban areas, many locations have drive-through service. The name Tim Hortons has become a cultural trademark, and while the fare may not be exciting cuisine, it is quintessentially Canadian.

DOWNTOWN

Canadian

Pretty much the entire menu at ★ **Smoke's Poutinerie** (942 Granville St., 604/669-2873, www.smokespoutinerie.com, 11am-11pm Mon.-Tues., 11am-3am Wed.-Thurs., 11am-4am Fri.-Sun., $7-10) is Canada's favorite dish, poutine. The counter-service spot has locations from Saskatchewan to Nova Scotia, and has even snuck down into the States. The menu has 30 combinations alone, plus a create-your-own option. The fry base is made from Canadian potatoes that are soaked, rinsed, and fried in canola oil (no trans fats, so it's almost healthy—yeah, right). They're seasoned before adding toppings, including gravy that comes in vegetarian, peppercorn, and signature Quebec styles; the cheese curds also hail from Quebec. Then come the extra toppings, like chipotle pulled pork, sautéed mushrooms, Italian sausage, caramelized onions—combine all four for the terrifying Hogtown poutine dish. Vegetable versions use vegetable gravy, and the meat averse can try the Rainbow poutine with sriracha. The

Hawksworth

space is ideal for food late at night, with stools, bright red lights, and takeout options.

The dining room at **Hawksworth** (801 W Georgia St., 604/673-7000, hawksworthrestaurant.com, 6:30am-10pm Mon.-Fri., 7am-10pm Sat.-Sun., $44-57) in the Rosewood Hotel Georgia is gleamingly white, but it's not oppressively fancy; locals gather beneath stark modern art pieces and give the restaurant a lively buzz. Head chef and namesake David Hawksworth is a celebrated Canadian chef, and his plates are as artistic as the walls. Lamb saddle is crusted with licorice, duck breast comes with a foie gras au jus, and every serving has its colorful toppings and garnishes placed just so. The same group also opened **Nightingale** (1017 W. Hastings St., 604/695-9500, http://hawknightingale.com, 11am-midnight daily, $15-28), a more casual dining spot downtown, to serve wood-fired pizzas and house-made pastas. That space is airier than the more formal Hawksworth, with bird motifs in a cavernous two-story space. The many seating options make it easy to have just the meal—casual, businesslike, or celebratory—that will fit your day. Don't miss the long list of vegetable dishes; they're not simple sides to be ignored.

Meat eaters shouldn't despair, **Botanist** (1038 Canada Pl., 604/695-5500, www.botanistrestaurant.com, 6:30am-10:30am, 11:30am-2pm, and 5pm-10pm Mon.-Fri.; 7am-2pm and 5pm-10pm Sat.-Sun., $22-38) doesn't only serve vegetables, even though its name calls to mind a greenery-only gardener. Located in the Fairmont Pacific Rim, a hotel inspired by the countries around the Pacific Ocean, the restaurant isn't an Asian spot but rather a local-first Canadian eatery serving picturesque fish, bird, and meat with a number of local vegetables. Tables sit under a trellis that holds dozens of local plants growing along it, and the champagne menu is extensive.

Asian

There are several Japanese Guu outposts around the city, but **Guu Garden** (888 Nelson St., 604/899-0855, www.guu-izakaya.com, 11:30am-2:30pm and 5:30pm-midnight Mon.-Thurs., 11:30am-2:30pm and 5:30pm-12:30am Fri., noon-3pm and 5:30pm-12:30am Sat., noon-3pm and 5:30pm-midnight Sun., $20-30) specializes in *oden,* a kind of Japanese hot pot that has roots in food cart cuisine but gets an upscale treatment here. The space has wood floors and ceilings, a small rock garden with a fountain out one side, and some outdoor seating. The menu also has *izakaya* classics and "carbohydrates": kimchi bibimbap and sushi dishes. The sake and *shochu* lists are matched by frozen cocktail specials and drinks made with lychee liqueur and Asian beers. "Guuing may be addictive" or "Guu is guuu'd" reads the chopstick packaging, and chopsticks don't lie.

Nightingale restaurant

★ **Hapa Izakaya** (909 W Cordova St., 604/420-4272, www.hapaizakaya.com, 11:30am-midnight Mon.-Fri., 5pm-midnight Sat.-Sun., $10-16) embraces the Japanese style of *izakaya*, a bar with bites. There are currently two Vancouver locations serving hot

Poutine: Canada's National Dish

The gourmands of Canada would probably insist that the national dish is some variety of carefully prepared fish, and coffee fiends would point to Tim Hortons coffee. But poutine is probably the best-recognized, unofficial national dish of Canada. It originated in Quebec but is easily found throughout all the provinces.

All poutine needs is three things: French fries, gravy, and cheese curds. (The latter are sometimes called "squeaky cheese" and are made without whey.) High-end restaurants will add pork belly or beef brisket, while others make it with mushroom gravy and different variations.

In downtown Vancouver, **Smoke's Poutinerie** has a version that will match almost any palate. At **The Flying Pig** the dish is served with pulled pork. The treat also comes in lowbrow versions at the drive-through: The Burger King chain in Canada serves a fast-food version of poutine, and Canadian chain Harvey's dishes up some with their skin-on French fries.

and cold tapas, plus a small smattering of rice and noodle dishes. The mini chain garners national awards and has been credited with helping popularize the restaurant style. The ultramodern decor of the downtown restaurant, in shades of tan and black, plus outdoor seating and plenty of sharable dishes attract a young and trendy crowd. The food is well regarded, but the scene and people-watching is even better. Reservations are recommended, and the happy hour (5pm-6pm daily and 9pm-close Sun.-Thurs.) has great deals.

Breakfast

It's not uncommon to see a line outside **Twisted Fork Bistro** (1147 Granville St., 604/568-0749, www.thetwistedfork.ca, 8am-3pm daily, $16.50) on weekend mornings, but here brunch happens every day, in a prix fixe mode. The frittatas, scrambles, and Benedicts are worth the queue, not to mention the six mimosa-like sparkling morning cocktails and more intense "hair of the dog" concoctions. The bistro has a French influence, but one need not know terms more complicated than "pâté" and "confit" to understand the menu. The wine and beer lists are pointedly local, including only British Columbia small wineries and microbreweries. Tables are smaller than the artwork on the deep red walls, and there isn't much seating in the narrow restaurant—so if you're in line for brunch, say yes to a counter seat.

GASTOWN AND CHINATOWN

Canadian

The popular ★ **Café Medina** (556 Beatty St., 604/879-3114, www.medinacafe.com, 8am-3pm Mon.-Fri., 9am-3pm Sat.-Sun., $12-19), located in a dark building with a black iron gate on the border of Chinatown, is surprisingly light and airy inside, with small tables and a few counter seats. The bistro has Belgian and Australian roots, which means venison burgers and Moroccan lamb-and-beef meatballs, plus handheld waffles covered in chocolate, pistachio rosewater, or berries. Brunch usually means a line, but you can fight hunger with drinks and waffles while you wait. Later in the day, wander next door to the **Dirty Apron Cooking School and Delicatessen** (540 Beatty St., 10:30am-6pm Mon.-Fri., 10:30am-5pm Sat.-Sun., $8.50-19), from the same owners, which offers cooking classes and has a store full of sandwiches, salads, and cheeses, plus canned goods and sauces. Courses teach cooking in French, Italian, seafood, or other styles, or for couples, singles, or kids.

Asian

The chic ★ **Bao Bei** (163 Keefer St., 604/688-0876, www.bao-bei.ca, 5:30pm-midnight Tues.-Sat., 5:30pm-10pm Sun., $14-25) has quickly become the place to see and be seen in Chinatown, an upscale brasserie that lives up to its name, which translates to "precious." Tables can be hard to come by on weekend evenings and particularly during the night market that invades Keefer Street during the summer. Tables are small and the lighting is low, barely enough to see the flowered wallpaper on one side and, on the other, the real knives and cleavers mounted on the wall, then painted over so they look like relief art. Culinary influences come from around China—Taiwan, the Sichuan province, and Shanghai—and the menu is largely made up of what they call "petits plats Chinois," sharable plates of salad and meat dishes. The "kick ass house fried rice" lives up to its name, and the octopus salad is a great fresh palate cleanser before the flavorful crispy pork belly. Reservations aren't taken, but it's easier to get a table now that it's been open a few years.

The unassuming **Harvest Community Foods** (243 Union St., 604/682-8851, ww.harvestunion.ca, 11am-8pm Mon.-Fri., 10am-7pm Sat.-Sun., $10-12) is so into fresh fruits and veggies, they operate a farm-share program out of the store, delivering boxes of produce to one-time or season-long members. For anyone not interested in hauling around a box of zucchini, there are hot Asian soups like udon and ramen, with ingredients rotating with the freshest crops of the week. Order from the counter in the small space and try to score one of the tables, or head outside to a sidewalk seat during warm months.

No one quite knew what to make of **Kissa Tanto** (263 E Pender St., 778/379-8078, www.kissatanto.com, 5:30pm-midnight Tues.-Sat., $18-46), an Italian-Japanese fusion restaurant in a small 2nd-floor space on an otherwise unremarkable block of Chinatown. But it was from the founder of Bao Bei, so it was no surprise when the unusual food began garnering rave reviews. Some single dishes combine both flavors—the chef's own lineage traces back to the two countries—like a lasagna with a miso béchamel sauce. The crudo is deservedly famous, and the fun interior recalls a 1930s club or train station. Reservations are necessary unless you want to show up midafternoon to wait for a table with other hopeful diners.

Bao Bei

Coffee

The very popular **Revolver** (325 Cambie St., 604/558-4444, 7:30am-6pm Mon.-Sat., $3-5) is all about the coffee, offering every variety of coffee preparation to java nerds drawn to the subtleties of the bean; you can even get a single coffee type prepared in three different ways to compare them. There isn't much to eat, just a small selection of pastries, but the energetic buzz from inside the brick-walled space comes from more than the caffeine.

The warm and darling ★ **Finch's Tea and Coffee House** (353 W Pender St., 604/899-4040, www.finchteahouse.com, 9am-5pm Mon.-Fri., 11am-4pm Sat., $5-9) is the perfect corner spot to relax over a cup of tea—or spend the day reading while you subsist on sandwiches and coffee (though don't rely on wireless access). The menu at the coffee joint is written on little chalkboards above the counter, and leafy plants hang from the ceiling.

Baguettes are topped with cheese, prosciutto, avocado, and free-range egg salad, and drinks include coffee, teas, and Italian sodas—everything delicate enough to match the cozy spot. A small table up by the window provides a great view of the Vancouver street, just beyond the white curtains.

Breakfast

You can smell **Nelson the Seagull** (315 Carrall St., 604/681-5776, www.nelsontheseagull.com, 8am-5pm Mon.-Fri., 9am-5pm Sat.-Sun., $5-12) before you get inside—the maddening aroma of bread wafts out to the street. Just "bread and coffee," announces the café, but they do a little more, dishing up salads, breakfast, and fresh-squeezed juices from the open kitchen. Breads and pastries are the real attraction, but it's not unusual for the bakery to sell out completely in the afternoon—so don't show up at closing with a baguette craving.

The breakfasts at **Deacon's Corner** (101 Main St., 604/684-1555, www.deaconscorner.ca, 8am-6pm Mon.-Fri., 9am-6pm Sat., 9am-5pm Sun., $8-14) are big and a little greasy, in a diner that resolutely rejects the hip, ecofriendly look so popular in modern Vancouver. It's meant to evoke a Manitoba truck stop: red walls, pies on pie stands, and stools in front of a long counter. These are the Southern-inspired dishes you use to treat a hangover or ravenous stomach: buttermilk pancakes served with pulled pork, chicken-fried steak, and eggs Benedict with truffle hollandaise sauce. Hash browns are seasoned and fried to a perfect brown. But what does all that have to do with a Canadian truck stop? Well, there are grits mixed with maple syrup, of course. Though breakfast is a highlight, there's also a lunch menu with the same philosophy—lots of flavor, lots of cheese, not a lot of delicacy.

Irish

Despite its very Irish name, **Irish Heather** (212 Carrall St., 604/688-9779, www.irishheather.com, 11:30am-midnight Sun.-Thurs., 11:30am-2am Fri.-Sat., $15-20) promises no green beer and no leprechauns. Its prime Gastown location makes it a kind of anchor for a collection of bars and restaurants owned by Sean Heather (who also created Shebeen Whiskey House and others). The menu has classic Irish dishes like soda bread and steak-and-ale pie, but it's more an upscale eatery than a beery pub. One side of the brick-walled restaurant has a 40-foot communal table that hosts a regular Long Table Series several nights a week with a prix fixe menu and a social atmosphere. Be sure to run to the loo, even if you haven't downed too many beer cocktails—famous quotes are beautifully displayed on the bathroom doors, so you can get a little culture even as you wait.

Southern

Gastown's **Peckinpah** (2 Water St., 604/681-5411, www.peckinpahbbq.com, 11:30am-11pm Sun.-Thurs., 11:30am-1am Fri.-Sat., $11-30) is dedicated to eastern North Carolina-style barbecue, even though its wood-fence decor and cattle-skull logo recall Texas. (Oh, and it's named for the California director known for his Texas cowboy films.) But don't linger over issues of authenticity. Peckinpah is located on a central corner of Gastown in a classic old red building that gets possibly more foot traffic than any spot in the city. Juicy ribs and mounds of coleslaw come in baskets lined with red-and-white wax paper, and the bourbon list is almost longer than the rest of the menu. Sauces include Carolina-style chili vinegar and a house mild sauce. The four-person banquet is almost $100. Lunch specials and occasional pig roasts are also offered.

YALETOWN

Canadian

The rotisserie at ★ **Homer Street Café and Bar** (898 Homer St., 604/428 4299, www.homerstreetcafebar.com, 11:30am-2:30pm and 5pm-10pm Mon.-Thurs., 11:30am-2:30pm and 5pm-11pm Fri., 10:30am-3pm and 5pm-midnight Sat., 10:30am-3pm Sun., $18-42) always has quarter, half, and whole chickens, along

Chinatown's Night Market

For years, Vancouver's Chinatown has hosted a **night market** (www.vancouver-chinatown.com) in the streets, allowing vendors to hawk arts, crafts, and food once the summer sun had set. But in 2013, the organizing committee decided that the market needed fresh blood, especially to differentiate the Vancouver version from the large night market in the nearby city of Richmond.

New acts and activities were brought in to the market stage: hip-hop karaoke, Chinatown Outdoor Cinema, and a Street Fighter II tournament. A Chinatown Night Market Ping Pong Club was formed. Food trucks park next to the stalls run by Chinatown businesses. The old standbys—booths selling socks, for instance—are still there, but crowds also gather for dim sum to go, art installations, and pieces of art.

The night market takes place on Keefer Street between Main Street and Columbia Street, 6pm-11pm every Friday, Saturday, and Sunday, May-September—and it happens regardless of the weather.

with the day's featured meat (beef, fish, lamb, or pork). Nothing's wasted—the chicken drippings flavor the roasted potatoes. The space, which spreads along the 1st floor of two historical buildings, was all kinds of factories before it became this chic Gastown spot. It's now farmhouse chic, decorated with delicately weathered fixtures and a black-and-white tile floor. It's a buzzy spot (the bar and multiple seating areas fill with Vancouver scenesters), but the eats are richer than those usually found in a destination dining spot. Before you leave, be sure to peek into the cockiest room in the place, the private dining area with reclaimed factory windows and row after row of rooster paintings.

Despite the name, **The Flying Pig** (1168 Hamilton St., 604/568-1344, www.theflyingpigvan.com, 11am-midnight Mon.-Fri., 10am-midnight Sat.-Sun., $21-36) by no means restricts its focus to pork. Entrées are sometimes served on wood planks and are as likely to include halibut, chicken, or veal, plus a bone marrow cheesy bread so rich the menu describes it as "OMG." Inside are bright red brick walls, glowing white barstools, and a young and attentive staff.

Seafood

It's clear that **Blue Water Cafe** (1095 Hamilton St., 604/688-8078, www.bluewatercafe.net, 4:30pm-1am daily, $17-44) serves seafood. From the name to the big plates of oysters being delivered to the blue water painting on the wall, it's no secret. But the massive restaurant is big enough to convince you that it serves all the seafood in Vancouver, especially in summer months when the outdoor seats on Yaletown's warehouse-like patio level are full. It's the first place people think of when considering fish dishes in the city. Its menu is crammed with sturgeon, sablefish, lingcod, and more. The raw bar serves sashimi and *nigiri* as well as familiar rolls. The two live tanks have lobster, clam, sea urchins, and the local delicacy geoduck (pronounced "gooey duck"), a large, slightly rubbery clam that's no challenge to most palates. While there may be individual dishes around the city that can beat Blue Water in terms of flavor, the breadth and sheer size of the joint keep it on top of the city's seafood dining scene.

GRANVILLE ISLAND

Canadian

Edible Canada (1596 Johnston St., 604/662-3606, www.ediblecanada.com, 10am-10pm Mon.-Fri., 9am-10pm Sat.-Sun., $18-32) doesn't sound great at first, billing itself as a "culinary tourism company." But besides a retail shop and tour base, it's a restaurant with excellent outdoor seating on Granville Island and a menu that makes the most of its proximity to the Granville Market. Fraser

Valley-raised meats and mussels from Salt Spring Island are served alongside duck fat fries and greens—plus a shot of whiskey is on the sides menu. Though it would be easy to make a restaurant in this location a tourist trap, there's real thought in the preparation and service, and it's not a bad place to get a quick survey of the area's cuisine. Lines move quickly.

WEST SIDE

Canadian

Though just across the bridge from downtown proper, **Farmer's Apprentice** (1535 W 6th Ave., 604/620-2070, http://farmersapprentice.ca, 5:30pm-10pm Mon., 11am-2pm and 5:30pm-10pm Tues.-Sun., $43-58) is a world away, a mimimalist space that almost looks like someone's crowded apartment. But here the menu is the star, changing nightly and served prix fixe. Both a vegetarian and an omnivore version are offered, but each focuses on what's fresh that day, and very little meat is used even on the latter.

The man behind **Fable Kitchen** (1944 W 4th Ave., 604/732-1322, www.fablekitchen.ca, 11:30am-2pm and 5pm-10pm Mon.-Fri., 10am-2pm and 5pm-10pm Sat.-Sun., $22-32) is something of a legend in Vancouver, having appeared on the TV cooking competition *Top Chef Canada*. He actually came up with the restaurant's concept and name while on the show. In a space decorated with reclaimed wood and exposed brick walls, the kitchen delivers sandwiches and salads for lunch and simple pleasures at dinner: steelhead trout, duck breast, and squash gnocchi. Despite its TV roots, the restaurant has a warm vibe. Desserts are good and brunch is even better.

Asian

People speak in reverent tones when they speak of ★ **Vij's** (3106 Cambie St., 604/736-6664, http://vijsrestaurant.ca, 5:30pm-10:30pm daily, $24-35). It's the kind of can't-miss meal you plan an entire night—or trip—around. The restaurant is in a fairly residential neighborhood south of downtown, but the line for the first serving at the Indian restaurant forms well before 5pm, and it's not unusual to find a two-hour wait for a table. What's more, it's not unusual to find diners happily waiting those two hours, getting cocktails or chai from Vij's tiny bar and snacks passed by the waitstaff.

Can dinner at Vij's really be worth all that trouble? In a word, absolutely. The space is fairly plain and diners aren't necessarily dressed in finery, but the food is tender, flavorful, mouthwatering Indian, inspired by all regions of the country. Dishes rotate seasonally, but the lamb popsicles (meat, not dessert) in fenugreek cream curry are a standby—the tender meat alone is worth the wait. Order some for the table, then add pork tenderloin, goat, or grilled fish. The restaurant makes its own ghee (clarified butter) and yogurt, and roasts and grinds its own spices.

Breakfast

Across from a Tim Hortons and a liquor store, **Jethro's Fine Grub** (3420 Dunbar St., 604/569-3441, www.jethrosfinegrub.com, 8am-4pm daily, $8-14) certainly captures the college vibe, making it a good stop for breakfast or lunch on the way to or from the University of British Columbia. Breakfast dishes are indulgent, with French toast made with chocolate-chip banana bread, apple cobbler, or Nutella; lunch includes sandwiches of the messy kind—a catfish po'boy, a Denver melt.

NORTH VANCOUVER

Canadian

Don't think too much of the name of the bistro **Burgoo** (3 Lonsdale Ave., 604/904-0933, www.burgoo.ca, 11am-10pm Mon.-Wed., 11am-11pm Thurs.-Sat., $10-18)? The owners dug the name out of a library book about stews (and a burgoo stew with lamb is even on the menu). The low-key restaurant has four locations across the city; this one is close to Lonsdale Quay in the busiest part of North Vancouver and right next to where the SeaBus docks. The menu is heavy on soups

Vij's Takes Over the World

When Vikram Vij and his wife Meeru Dhalwala started Vij's, a modest little Indian restaurant removed from downtown Vancouver's busy streets, they could never have imagined what it has become. Waits top two hours, and the *New York Times* called it "among the finest Indian restaurants in the world." Vij's first 14-seat diner opened in 1994, right around the same time he married Dhalwala. Eventually the restaurant began winning awards and moved to a (slightly) larger location. Food Network chefs began stopping by, and lines got longer and longer.

Vancouver locals have a strategy for Vij's—show up a little after 5pm, which gets you about 30 people back in line when the restaurant opens at 5:30pm, tell the hostess you want the second seating, and spend the next 1.5 hours noshing on free appetizers and sipping drinks from the bar. You'll get a table at an ideal dinner time, around 7pm.

Though Vij originated the recipes, it was Dhalwala who eventually took over the kitchen. Vij likes to wander the dining room every night. In 2016 the restaurant moved to a new space close by, expanding its seating capacity—but waits remain for the lamb popsicles and the rest of the menu.

Within Vancouver, there are ways to get Vij-inspired food besides waiting in line. There's **Rangoli** (1488 W 11th Ave., 604/736-5711, www.vijsrangoli.ca, 11am-midnight daily, $10-21) next door to the old restaurant, with a much shorter wait and lunch service. Menu items don't replicate what's served at Vij's but still represent a wide swath of Indian cuisine: curries, grilled fish, and spicy pulled pork. The market inside Rangoli has frozen packaged curries and chicken in Vij's masala, plus chutneys, spices, and rice pudding. And if getting out to the South Granville neighborhood is too much, track down Vij's food truck **Railway Express** (604/639-3335, www.vijsrailwayexpress.com, $9-12), which pops up on downtown streets and at farmers markets and serves yet another Indian fusion menu with choices like butter chicken and curried squash.

and salads, daily drink specials, and comfort dishes from around the world like jambalaya, ratatouille, and beef bourguignon. Biscuits ordered on the side are made with white cheddar and parsley.

The District Brasserie (13 Lonsdale Ave., 778/338-4938, www.thedistrictsocial.com, 3pm-11pm daily, $14-19), also near Lonsdale Quay, offers charcuterie, soups, and sharable frites in a variety of preparations, including an Amsterdam-inspired version with peanut sauce, mayo, and onions. Bigger plates include meats, mussels, and hearty burgers. The smallish restaurant fills quickly, so reservations are recommended; a small patio outside seats about 20 people.

Seafood

Although the "sea" section of the menu at **The Beachhouse Restaurant** (150 25th St., 604/922-1414, www.thebeachhouserestaurant.ca, 11:30am-10pm Mon.-Thurs., 11:30am-11pm Fri., 11am-11pm Sat., 11am-10pm Sun., $18-39) is longer than the "land" list, it's not totally a seafood restaurant. You can score a roast chicken or Angus beef filet if you're not up for a lobster roll or halibut from the Haida Gwaii (off the north coast of the province). The location at Dundrave Pier, however, is all about the water. Look across to Stanley Park or as far out as Vancouver Island. The patio is heated, so it doesn't shut down at the first sign of fall.

From its perch on the hills that rise in North Vancouver, **Salmon House on the Hill** (2229 Folkestone Way, 604/926-3212, www.salmonhouse.com, 5pm-9:30pm Mon.-Thurs., 5pm-10pm Fri., 10:30am-2:30pm and 5pm-10pm Sat., 10:30am-2:30pm and 5pm-9:30pm Sun., $29-45) has amazing views, including a look at the well-lit downtown once the sun goes down. It's been open for more than 40 years. The menu leans heavily toward seafood, like grilled sable fish with Thai curry potatoes and lobster tagliatelle pasta, but also has bison from the Peace River region and grilled lamb.

Accommodations

Downtown Vancouver has plenty of hotel rooms, partially thanks to the 2010 Olympics. Many midpriced hotels line Granville Street, which cuts through the city but can be a rowdy thoroughfare after dark. The Coal Harbor waterfront features shining towers with killer mountain views and is directly next to the cruise ships that depart for Alaska, while Yaletown properties tend to be fashionably reworked older buildings.

DOWNTOWN

Under $150

The stuffed bear and bar in the lobby of **SameSun Backpacker Hostel** (1018 Granville St., 604/682-8226, www.samesun.com, $38-51 dorms, $120-180 private rooms) says a lot about the place—on the looser and louder end of the spectrum. Breakfast, wireless Internet, and access to a Netflix-enabled TV comes with an overnight stay, and the hostel sells local sporting event tickets and advertises ski trips to Whistler.

Though **Hosteling International Vancouver Central** (1025 Granville St., 604/685-5335, www.hihostels.ca, $44-55 dorms, $114-160 private rooms) is right in the middle of bustling Granville Street, it retains a quaint charm with flower boxes in the windows. Stays include a free breakfast (the scones are particularly good) and free wireless Internet access. The kitchen has limited facilities: toaster yes, stove no. Both dorm beds and private rooms are available—some even have their own bathrooms. For a quieter stay, the **Hosteling International Vancouver Downtown** (1114 Burnaby St., 778/328.2220, www.hihostels.ca, $41-47 dorms, $108-173 private rooms) is located on a much quieter residential street and offers a roof deck and complete kitchen facilities, but the building has a distinct institutional vibe.

$150-250

The motor lodge past of the ★ **Burrard Hotel** (1100 Burrard St., 604/681-2331, http://theburrard.com, $149-389) is evident in the retro styling (stone walls in the lobby, yellow and blue hotel room doors). Cars are hidden below a central garden, where a courtyard area has seating, a big tree, and a giant Jenga game. Brooklyn Cruiser bicycles are available for guests to use for free, and the rooms themselves triumph in style even though they suffer from mid-20th-century standards for hotel room size.

Art is around every corner at ★ **Listel Hotel** (1300 Robson St., 604/684-8461, www.thelistelhotel.com, $220-407)—sometimes it's crouching next to the front desk, as is the case with a series of bright red statues. The boutique hotel is partnered with the Buschlen Mowatt Fine Art Gallery, which places more than $2 million worth of art around the building, including in individual rooms. Museum of Anthropology pieces also pop up around the property, and solar panels provide the power. For all the striking modern art, rooms have a surprisingly classic feel, but the unusual touches, like blood-red shower curtains, add personality to a space that could otherwise feel corporate.

The **Sylvia Hotel** (1154 Gilford St., 604/681-9321, www.sylviahotel.com, $169-289) harks back to a time of seaside retreats, when this eight-story building was the only thing standing on the English Bay beachfront. Much of the 1912 building is being swallowed by ivy that creeps up the brick facade, only adding to the charm. Inside, that charm and the killer views make up for the cramped rooms and basic amenities. The lobby has puzzling medieval touches—a coat of arms, a stained-glass window—but it's hard to wish a modern renovation on such a singular and affordable waterfront hotel. Select rooms and suites have kitchens.

There's a simplicity to the **Kingston Hotel Bed and Breakfast** (757 Richards St., 604/684-9024, www.kingstonhotelvancouver.com, $149-179 shared bath, $235-295 private bath), where rooms come with a single bed, a double bed, or two single beds; the latter come with private bath, and the former without. Furnishings are dated and floral, and the building dates back to 1910 but doesn't feel particularly historical. The fireplace lounge features a small but pretty rock chimney, and a continental breakfast is free. The location is central but not too loud. It's a good choice when on a budget.

Find a whole lotta blue at the **Blue Horizon Hotel** (1225 Robson St., 604/688-1411, www.bluehorizonhotel.com, $169-219), from the tiles in the lobby to the waters of the indoor swimming pool. With 214 rooms spread over 31 stories, the hotel is an impressive tower on Robson, especially because all the rooms have private balconies. Wireless Internet is free, parking is only $15 (not bad for downtown Vancouver), and the pool is joined by a whirlpool and sauna in the fitness center. The on-site **Abode Restaurant** (1223 Robson St., www.aboderestaurant.ca, 6:30am-10pm Sun.-Fri., 6:30am-10:30pm Sat.) serves breakfast, coffee, and cocktails as well as meals. The hotel shows some signs of age, but the location and amenities make up for it, and the price is a good deal.

Over $250

Close to some of the city's biggest and buzziest hotels, **The Loden** (1177 Melville St., 604/669-5060, www.theloden.com, $425-570) is tucked sideways on an unobtrusive block. The boutique hotel has high-end design touches, like giant tubs and sliding doors that open the space between bathroom and bedroom, and select rooms have patios next to a tiny water feature. Bikes are available for use, and two British taxi vehicles drive guests anywhere in the downtown core.

Although many hotels with the Fairmont name are historical properties—like the castle-shaped Fairmont Hotel Vancouver just a few blocks away—the ★ **Fairmont Pacific Rim** (1038 Canada Pl., 877/900-5350, www.fairmont.com, $594-738) is thoroughly modern, a luxury hotel with all the amenities (spa, rooftop pool, etc.). The decor is inspired by the Pacific Rim, and is mostly contemporary clean lines in neutral colors. Bathrooms on the north side of the hotel face the grassy roof of the convention center across the street, not to mention the striking North Vancouver mountains across the water. **The Lobby Lounge** (10am-1:30am Mon.-Sat., 10am-11pm Sun.) downstairs, with its fire element and high-end cocktails, attracts a buzzy, well-dressed crowd. The hotel is popular with celebrities, and a few luxury automobiles are usually parked outside by the valet stand. Got a lot of cash burning a hole in your pocket? The Chairman's Suite, inspired by a Balinese villa, is a two-story unit with two living rooms, a kitchen, a butler's pantry, and a rooftop patio—for only $10,000 per night.

Though the exterior of the ★ **Shangri-La Hotel** (1128 W Georgia St., 604/689-1120, www.shangri-la.com, $475-755) is a glassy tower much like the rest of Vancouver, it feels like a trip to Asia thanks to the lion statues outside and large art pieces inside. Rooms are decked out with luxury trappings—fine sheets and furnishings in warm, muted tones—and the spa has ultra-large rooms with private showers, an ideal spot for total relaxation when paired with the outdoor pool.

YALETOWN

$150-250

The exterior is white at the **Moda Hotel** (900 Seymour St., 604/683-4251, www.modahotel.ca, $129-199), but interior walls are apt to be black or even deep red, a calming design touch that nevertheless recalls the giant Staples store just across the street. Small bathrooms notwithstanding, this is the closest to a budget stay as you'll find this close to the tony blocks of Yaletown, complete with free wireless Internet and dog friendliness. Junior rooms have showers only and are as small as

150 square feet, while suites top out at 900 square feet.

The suites at **Rosedale on Robson** (838 Hamilton St., 604/689-8033, www.rosedaleonrobson.com, $149-249) fill up quickly—and the 200-plus rooms are all suites with galley kitchens, living rooms, and big windows. Amenities include an indoor pool and steam room and an outdoor garden terrace. Its proximity to the arenas that host football and hockey games inspire ticket packages offered by the hotel.

Over $250

The ★ **Opus Hotel** (322 Davie St., 604/642-6787, http://vancouver.opushotel.com, $380-456) has a signature scent, and rooms are designed around a series of imaginary guests (are you a Dede, a Pierre, or a Billy?). Still, the hotel isn't as loopy as its most notable touches, though very much on trend with solid-color walls, in-room iPads, and original artwork. Some rooms offer the use of a local cell phone with an unlimited data plan during the guest's stay. The central Yaletown location doesn't do anything to detract from the hip vibe of the hotel. It racks up awards, as does the Northern Italian eatery next to the lobby, **La Pentola della Quercia** (350 Davie St., 604/642-0557, www.lapentola.ca, 7am-10:30pm Mon.-Wed., 7am-11pm Thurs., 7am-midnight Fri.-Sat., 7am-10pm Sun., $9-18 breakfast, $12-19 lunch, $19-32 dinner).

GRANVILLE ISLAND

Over $250

Playing on Granville Island can fill an entire day or weekend. Staying there makes it a lot easier to enjoy the Public Market, boat rides, and shopping. The **Granville Island Hotel** (1253 Johnston St., 604/683-7373, www.granvilleislandhotel.com, $250-380) is the only place to stay in the tiny neighborhood and offers luxury amenities and waterfront views. Downstairs, the **Dockside Restaurant** (604/685-7070, www.docksidevancouver.com, 7am-10pm daily, $11-19 breakfast, $14-29 lunch, $26-37 dinner) is, as it sounds, a few feet away from the sailboats and yachts parked in False Creek. A 50-foot aquarium runs along the side of the kitchen, and a number of fireplaces warm the restaurant. Bikes are available to rent from the hotel, and the health center has a small hot tub covered by a glass ceiling.

NORTH VANCOUVER

Under $150

Just across Vancouver Harbour from downtown, **Grouse Inn** (1633 Capilano Rd., 604/988-7101, www.grouseinn.com, $105-225) is, like this North Vancouver neighborhood, a lot quieter. Its position near Highway 1 and Capilano Road gives travelers quick access to suspension-bridge or skiing day trips and lets anyone skip some traffic on the way to Whistler or the Victoria ferry at Horseshoe Bay. Standard rooms are clean but with few frills, and suites with sofa beds and kitchens are appealing to families.

Over $250

The **Pinnacle Hotel at the Pier** (138 Victory Ship Way, 604/986-7437, www.pinnaclepierhotel.com, $259-439) prominently faces downtown Vancouver, but you won't envy those across the harbor. Rooms have crisp linens, marble bathrooms, and cushy robes; the gym facilities include a swimming pool with a water view. The **Lobby Restaurant** (604/973-8000, www.pinnaclepierhotel.com, 6:30am-10pm Mon.-Fri., 7am-10pm Sat.-Sun., $8-16 breakfast, $9-19 lunch, $16-34 dinner) serves afternoon tea, complete with double Devonshire cream and finger sandwiches. And if all the peace and quiet is too much to bear, downtown is just a SeaBus ride away, as the passenger ferry docks nearby.

Information and Services

VISITOR INFORMATION

Located just across from Canada Place's big white sails, **Tourism Vancouver Visitor Centre** (200 Burrard St., 604/683-2000, www.tourismvancouver.com, 9am-5pm daily) is staffed with city experts who speak multiple languages and can hand out free maps and sightseeing ideas. The center is also where you can buy half-price theatre and sports tickets from Tickets Tonight (www.ticketstonight.ca), a vendor for reduced-price same-day tickets.

Library Square, home of the **Vancouver Public Library** (350 W Georgia St., 604/331-3603, www.vpl.ca, 10am-9pm Mon.-Thurs., 10am-6pm Fri.-Sat., 11am-6pm Sun.), is an entire block in downtown Vancouver. The library has the look of a Roman coliseum, with a curved concourse topped with a roof of glass surrounding one side of the building. Inside, the library offers public lockers and computers with Internet access.

MEDIA AND COMMUNICATIONS

The ***Vancouver Sun*** (www.vancouversun.com) broadsheet newspaper is a century old and provides daily news, sports, lifestyle, and arts coverage, but it isn't published on Sundays. It can be purchased from newsstands or newspaper boxes. Two free papers, ***Metro*** (www.metronews.ca) and ***24H*** (http://vancouver.24hrs.ca) are available on weekdays, often in boxes near transit stops. They cover news and arts and are meant to be read on a short commute.

For an alternative look at arts and culture, the weekly ***Georgia Straight*** (www.straight.com) is available in street boxes and has listings for live music along with political and lifestyle stories. The award-winning paper has been in existence since the counterculture 1960s and is proud of its history of being raided by police and hiring Bob Geldof.

SERVICES

The Vancouver **Main Post Office Retail Location** (495 W Georgia St., 866/607-6301, www.canadapost.ca, 9am-4pm Mon.-Fri.) offers stamps and package services.

There are no lockers at the Pacific Central Station, where Greyhound and Amtrak routes depart, but there is a baggage storage check. **C & N Backpackers Hostel** (927 Main St., 604/682-2441, www.cnnbackpackers.com), across the street, may take same-day baggage storage for a fee if they have room.

For urgent health care in the case of a nonemergency, try **Crossroad Clinics Vancouver** (507 W Broadway, 604/568-7229, www.crwalkin.com), though you may have to check if they accept citizens of other countries. In an emergency, call 911 or head to the emergency room at **St. Paul's Hospital** (1081 Burrard St., 604/682-2344, www.providencehealthcare.org).

Transportation

GETTING THERE

Air

Vancouver International Airport (YVR, 3211 Grant McConachie Way, Richmond, 604/207-7077, www.yvr.ca) is located on Sea Island, just 20 kilometers (12 miles) southwest of the city (technically in the suburb of Richmond). Canada's second-busiest airport sees daily arrivals from around the Pacific Rim. For **car rentals,** head to the ground floor of the airport terminal for a selection of rental companies. The drive into the center of Vancouver takes 20 minutes without traffic, longer during morning and evening rush hours.

A **taxi** from the airport to downtown Vancouver costs about $36. Alternatively, look for signs for the **Canada Line** (604/953-3333, http://thecanadaline.com, $9 adults, $7.75 seniors, students, and children 5-13, children under 5 free), a rapid rail link. The rail line takes 26 minutes to get to downtown Vancouver and ends at the Waterfront station (W Hastings St. between Howe St. and Seymour St.).

Train

Amtrak (800/872-7245, www.amtrak.com, $32-75) has two trains daily to Vancouver. The Cascades route departs King Street Station (303 S Jackson St.) in Seattle's Pioneer Square neighborhood with stops in Edmonds, Everett, Stanwood, Mount Vernon, and Bellingham, Washington. Arrival is at Vancouver's **Pacific Central Station** (1150 Station St., 604/683-8133, 5am-1am daily). Amtrak also has several bus departures between Seattle and Vancouver ($45).

Bus

The Greyhound-owned **BoltBus** (877/265-8287, www.boltbus.com) offers four daily Seattle-Vancouver trips, leaving Seattle at 5th Avenue South (at S King St.) and arriving in Vancouver at **Pacific Central Station** (1150 Station St., 604/683-8133, 4:45am-12:30am daily). Limited $1 fares are available online, but most trips cost about $24-28. The bus has wireless service, and most trips take a little over four hours.

The Seattle **Greyhound** station (800/231-2222, www.greyhound.ca, $15-32) is at 811 Stewart Street (206/628-5526, 7am-12:30am) and has three departures daily to Vancouver ($23, discounts for early and web bookings); the trip takes just over four hours.

Car

U.S.-CANADA BORDER CROSSING

It takes about three hours to drive from Seattle to Vancouver. The main route from Seattle is **I-5.** This multilane road is infamous for its traffic snarls, which are worst during early morning and late afternoon rush hours. The 8-mile-long express lanes, which change direction depending on where the bulk of cars are heading, can be a useful bypass. Traveling north, I-5 reaches the city of **Everett** 30 miles north of Seattle. From Everett, there's usually little to slow drivers until they reach the border crossing 80 miles north in **Blaine,** Washington.

Two options are available for crossing the border: the Peace Arch crossing at the end of **I-5** and the Pacific Highway crossing on **Highway 543.**

To reach the Peace Arch crossing, stay on I-5 north as it slowly funnels cars directly into the border-crossing lanes. The actual arch sits in a large green park between crossing stations. Take care when letting passengers out to explore the field while the driver waits in line because everyone will need to be back in the car well before the crossing station. Upon entering Canada, the route immediately becomes the **Canadian Highway 99.**

For the Pacific Highway Crossing (also called Truck Customs, for its use among commercial vehicles), take exit 275 off I-5. Follow Highway 543 for less than a mile before meeting the border. Once through the border crossing, follow **Canadian Highway 15** for several blocks, turn left on 8th Avenue, and then take a right at the roundabout at Highway 99. Though less scenic than the waterfront Peace Arch crossing, the Pacific Highway crossing often has a shorter wait.

FROM THE BORDER TO VANCOUVER

Highway 99, also called the Vancouver-Blaine Highway, swings north through the open plains that sit just south of Vancouver's suburbs. In about 30 kilometers (19 miles), Highway 99 passes through a tunnel under the Fraser River, emerging in the suburb of Richmond.

From Richmond, Highway 99 continues across the Oak Street Bridge. Turn left on West 70th Avenue and continue north on Highway 99/Granville Street for about 16 kilometers (10 miles) toward the Granville Bridge and downtown Vancouver. Although the route narrows from a highway to surface streets, traffic flows well into the downtown core.

After crossing the Granville Bridge, you'll arrive in the heart of Vancouver. Follow Seymour Street northeast to continue to the waterfront area and Gastown. Note that several downtown byways are one-way, so check all traffic signs before making any turns.

the Peace Arch at the U.S.-Canada border

Ferry

Two ferry routes travel between Victoria and Vancouver. The **Swartz Bay** (Hwy. 17, www.bcferries.com, $17.20 adults, $8.60 children 5-12, children under 5 free, vehicles $57.50, surcharges for fuel and large vehicles) route departs from the Saanich Peninsula, 32 kilometers (20 miles) north of Victoria at the end of Highway 17, just north of the town of Sidney. The boat travels to **Tsawwassen,** located south of the Vancouver-Blaine Highway, a 90-minute trip. From the Tsawwassen ferry terminal (1 Ferry Causeway, Delta), drive north on Highway 17A for 13 kilometers (8 miles), and then take Highway 99 north to Vancouver. The ferry travels 8-17 times per day in each direction. Reservations are recommended.

The second ferry departs from **Nanaimo** (www.bcferries.com, $17.20 adults, $8.60 children 5-12, children under 5 free, vehicles $57.50, surcharges for fuel and large vehicles), about 110 kilometers (68 miles) north of Victoria along Highway 1. Arrival is at **Horseshoe Bay** (6750 Keith Rd., West Vancouver), approximately 20 kilometers (12 miles) northwest of Vancouver. The trip lasts about one hour and 40 minutes; ferries run 7-12 times per day in each direction; reservations are recommended. From Horseshoe Bay, drive southeast on Highways 1 and 99 for 20 kilometers (12 miles) to North Vancouver. Highway 99 continues south across the Lions Gate Bridge into downtown Vancouver.

GETTING AROUND

Vancouver's downtown core is mostly walkable, and taxis are easy to find. The SkyTrain is less useful for tourists, but some trips can be simplified with the light rail trains. Visitors to Vancouver will best experience the city by foot or, for the slightly more daring, on a bike.

Car

Downtown Vancouver can be tricky to navigate because many streets are one-way and lanes through Stanley Park change direction according to the time of day. **Parking** downtown is also a challenge as parking meters accept both coins and credit cards and are connected to a pay-by-phone app (604/909-7275, http://vancouver.ca). Parking rates are $1-6 per hour and active 9am-10pm daily, and rates can change throughout the day. Parking on Granville Island can also be difficult, but some free spots can be used for up to three hours and pay lots offer rates from $3.50 per hour.

Vancouver's streets are crowded during **rush hour** (7am-9am and 4pm-6pm). Especially impacted are the Lions Gate Bridge, which connects Stanley Park and downtown to North Vancouver, and Highway 1, which runs east to west through North Vancouver.

Vancouver has no **toll roads,** but drivers looking to bypass downtown Vancouver on a trip from the U.S. border to Whistler should be aware that the Port Mann Bridge from Coquitlam to Surrey on Highway 1 requires a $3.15 toll for cars (plus an extra fee for vehicles not preregistered with the province's fee system). Drivers in Canada must have a valid driver's license from their home country (or an International Driving Permit for longer periods) and carry insurance.

CAR RENTALS

A number of car rental companies, including **Avis** (604/606-2847, www.avis.ca) and **Budget** (604/668-7000, www.budget.com), have rental facilities on the ground floor of Vancouver International Airport (3211 Grant McConachie Way, Richmond, 604/207-7077, www.yvr.ca). In downtown Vancouver, car rentals are at **Hertz Rent a Car** (1270 Granville St., 604/606-4711, http://hertz.com) and **Thrifty Car Rental** (413 Seymour St., 604/606-1666, http://thrifty.com). Or try a new kind of car share, **car2go** (855/454-1002, http://vancouver.car2go.com), where very small cars are rented by the minute (gas included) and can be picked up on the streets around the city or at the airport. Advance registration is required because users get a card that opens and activates their rental car.

Taxi

Don't rely on hailing a cab in Vancouver when you need one. Instead, call ahead to **Yellow Cab** (604/681-1111, www.yellowcabonline.com) or **MacLure's Cabs** (604/831-1111, www.maclurescabs.ca). Cabs are usually hybrid vehicles, and all drivers accept credit cards. Rates are $1.84 per kilometer, with an initial $3.20 fee.

RV

If driving an RV into Vancouver, head to West Vancouver's **Capilano River RV Park** (295 Tomahawk Ave., 604/987-4722, www.capilanoriverrvpark.com, $55-82), which has an outdoor pool and hot tub, plus laundry, a rec room, and Wi-Fi throughout the property. It's located just past the Lions Gate Bridge with easy access to both downtown Vancouver and the Capilano Suspension Bridge.

RV rentals are available from **CanaDream** (8223 92 St., Delta, 604/940-2171, www.canadream.com), a $42 cab ride from the airport in the town of Delta. Van campers and motorhomes that can hold up to six people are also available. In the town of Richmond, head to **Westcoast Mountain Campers** (150-11800 Voyageur Way, Richmond, 604/279-0550, www.wcmcampers.com), which has "vanconversion" rides and motorhomes, and offers transfers from the airport.

Public Transit

Public transportation is operated through **TransLink** (604/953-3333, www.translink.ca)

and includes bus, ferry, and light rail options. The bus system, which includes 12 NightBus routes, covers most of the city. The **SeaBus** is a passenger ferry that crosses from downtown to North Vancouver. The **SkyTrain** has three lines, including one that travels from downtown to the airport. Fares on the bus and train are determined by travel zones; there are three within the greater Vancouver area, though single-zone prices apply after 6:30pm everyday and all day on Saturdays and Sundays.

Within the downtown core, you'll only pay single-zone fares ($2.85 adults, $1.80 children 5-13 and seniors). To get to the airport from downtown requires a two-zone fare ($4.10 adults, $2.80 children and seniors). Buses require exact fare in cash. SeaBus and SkyTrain stations have vending machines. Compass Cards can be purchased at London Drug stores or SkyTrain and SeaBus stations, and can be pre-loaded with money. Day passes are also available for $10 ($7.75 for children and seniors) and are good across any TransLink transportation.

Whistler

Whistler isn't named for the slow "I'm impressed" whistle visitors make when they finally arrive at the mountain resort town (it got its moniker from the marmots that live in the rocks and make distinctive whistling sounds). Yet the area is undeniably dramatic, with some of the best skiing in the country, beautiful scenery, and a town full of restaurants, shops, and après-ski spots. High season is mid-December-mid-March, but the region is increasingly becoming a year-round destination, as summer sightseers can take the ski gondolas up to see the mountains in their green glory, and go hiking and mountain biking throughout the valley.

SIGHTS

★ Peak2Peak Gondola

Not a skier? That doesn't mean you have to miss the area's highlight, the **Peak2Peak Gondola** (4545 Blackcomb Way, 888/403-4727, www.whistlerblackcomb.com, 10:15am-5pm daily mid-May-mid-Sept., 10:15am-5pm Sat.-Sun. mid-Sept.-mid-Oct., 10am-5pm

Whistler Village

daily mid-Nov.-mid-Apr., $58.95 adults, $51.95 seniors and children 13-18, $29.95 children 7-12, free for children under 7), which connects Whistler and Blackcomb Mountains, making it easy for skiers as well as sightseers to experience both. At almost 460 meters (1,500 feet) high and more than 4 kilometers (2.5 miles) long, it's the highest and longest lift of its kind in the world. The experience can be a bit disconcerting for the height-averse, but the large, stable gondola cabins hold dozens and don't bob about even when it's windy. You'll feel like you're in a small plane soaring over the peaks, which are snow-coated year-round and seem to rise from every direction. In the summer, you can sometimes spot wildlife dotting the creek valley below. Sightseeing tickets include transportation up and down to the Peak2Peak via the Whistler Blackcomb resort's regular gondolas. It takes about two hours to do the entire loop—going up Whistler Mountain's gondola, riding on the Peak2Peak, and then heading down via Blackcomb Mountain's gondola to arrive back near your starting point. Be sure to check for seasonal hour adjustments or closures; the Peak2Peak shuts down in spring and fall for maintenance and, like so much in Whistler, exact time frames can depend on the year's snowfall. Advance tickets are available but not required; you can usually walk up and snag tickets.

Audain Art Museum

In a town devoted to activity and sport, **Audain Art Museum** (4350 Blackcomb Way, 604/962-0413, http://audainartmuseum.com, 10am-5pm Mon., Wed., and Sat.-Sun., 10am-7pm Thurs.-Fri., $18 adults, free for children under 17) is a welcome refuge of arts and culture. The museum is itself an architectural marvel, tucked between skier parking lots but still somehow in the trees, where cedar beams and glass hallways create a zen calm. The art, from the collection of a Vancouver philanthropist, is largely from British Columbia, including tribal First Nations masks and pastoral scenes from Canada's Emily Carr. Escape from the Whistler buzz to walk slowly through the small but well-designed museum.

Squamish Lil'wat Cultural Centre

Before this corner of Canada was famous for the Olympics and skiing, it was First Nations land and supported a number of tribes. At the **Squamish Lil'wat Cultural Centre** (4584 Blackcomb Way, 604/964-0990, http://slcc.ca, 10am-5pm Tues.-Sun., $18 adults, $13.50 college students, $5 children 6-18, free for children under 6), this history comes alive through film, exhibits, interactive displays, craft projects for kids, and lively tour guides. This isn't the kind of museum you wander yourself; admission comes with a tour that starts on the hour with a welcome song sung by museum staff, and the space also hosts a gift shop that specializes in unique local products, as well as a café. More in-depth tours and experiences ($65 adults, $25 children 6-12, free for children under 6) include First Nations meals and experiences and must be booked in advance; they generally take place at 6pm on Tuesday and Sunday evenings.

SPORTS AND RECREATION

Skiing

Whistler Blackcomb (4545 Blackcomb Way, 888/403-4727, www.whistlerblackcomb.com, 9am-3:30pm daily Nov.-Apr., two-day tickets: $158-210 adults, $142-189 seniors, $134-178 children 13-18, $80-106 children 7-12, free for children under 7) is a massive resort encompassing the two-mountain ski area with tons of everything—16 bowls, more than 8,000 acres of terrain, three glaciers, and hundreds of marked runs. This is, simply, some of the best skiing on the planet. The 37 lifts include gondolas, high-speed lifts, plus a few old-fashioned T-bars and triple chairs. Beginners and lesson-takers don't just get a small cordoned-off area; they get entire zones of easy slopes designed for instruction. Experts can hike into sidecountry surrounded by epic peaks and jagged rock, both above and below tree line. International visitors will stay and ski for weeks at a time. It's the rare resort that can continuously offer novel terrain, but this also means that lift lines can get long. A tip: Leave room for rest days, and take a lesson on weekends—instructors and students get to cut in line.

Whistler also offers Nordic skiing from its **Whistler Olympic Park** (5 Callaghan Valley Rd., 604/964-0060, www.whistlerolympicpark.com, Nordic skiing $16-27 adults, $9-16 children 7-18), with 27 trails for cross-country skiers and snowshoers. When in snowshoes, take care to stay out of groomed Nordic ski trails.

Hiking

While Whistler is primarily known as a ski area, it becomes a hiking mecca in summer.

ANCIENT CEDARS

Distance: 5 kilometers (3.1 miles) round-trip
Duration: 2 hours
Elevation gain: 152 meters (500 feet)
Effort: moderate
Trailhead: Head north on Highway 99 from Whistler for about eight kilometers (five miles) and turn left on Cougar Mountain Road. Follow it for 4.3 kilometers (2.7 miles) to the end of the road.

A short drive outside of Whistler proper, this trail feels far removed from the bustle of the ski area. Start near an old trapper's cabin at the parking lot and look for the well-signed trailhead. Follow the trail uphill. Stop at an overlook for Showh Lakes a few steps off the main trail, where views open up to a large valley. Return to the main trail and follow it until the trail meets a bridge and the start of a loop full of interpretive signs, a little more than 1.5 kilometers (1 mile) in. Take the short loop in either direction, reading about the old-growth trees that survived British Columbia's clearcuts here; some of the massive trees are 1,000 years old. Once you finish the loop, take the trail back to where you started.

TRAIN WRECK

Distance: 2 kilometers (1.2 miles) round-trip
Duration: 1 hours
Elevation gain: 30 meters (100 feet)
Effort: easy
Trailhead: across the road from the parking lot with signs that say "Train Wreck Parking"
Directions: Head south on Highway 99 from Whistler 7.7 kilometers (4.8 miles) and turn left on Cheakamus Lake Road. Follow it over the river and turn right on Jane Lake Road, about half a kilometer from the highway. Signed parking is on the left.

Whistler Blackcomb

There are more secrets than you'd ever guess in the woods around Whistler. Take this short trail through the woods on a gravel path (not the forest road that starts right next to it). There are a few other trails crisscrossing the area, but Train Wreck is well signed. For about a kilometer it winds through forest with few ups and downs. Then you descend to the Cheakamus River and cross a pedestrian suspension bridge over the rushing waters. On the other side of the river, walk up a boardwalk to find boxcars scattered in the trees; they've been here since a train crash in the 1950s, and since then have been spray painted and covered with mountain bike jumps. Wander the artful site before returning the way you came. Note that the hike is open in winter but heavily used, and the hardpacked snow quickly turns to slippery ice.

Mountain Biking

The slopes of Whistler and Blackcomb Mountains look different when the snow melts, but they're still a big playground. **Whistler Mountain Bike Park** (4545 Blackcomb Way, 888/403-4727, http://bike.whistlerblackcomb.com, 10am-8pm daily mid-May-Aug., 10am-5pm daily Sept.-mid-Oct., $69 adults, $61 seniors and children 13-18, $39 children 5-12) opens some ski runs to mountain bikers May-October. You can get a lift from the gondolas and chairlifts that already crisscross the mountains. Trails are marked by difficulty and guides can be hired to demystify the many routes. Rentals are available, but don't forget that true protective wear includes padding and coverage from head to foot.

Sliding Sports

When the Olympic Games came to Vancouver in 2010, many events took place in this mountain town rather than the big city. **Whistler Sliding Centre** (4910 Glacier Ln., 604/964-0030, www.whistlersportlegacies.com/venues/whistler-sliding-centre, 9am-5pm daily) hosted bobsled, luge, and skeleton racing, but the tracks weren't dismantled after the medals had been awarded. Today the venue hosts international competitions—there aren't that many tracks in the world, so it's popular—but also hosts public bobsled and skeleton rides (Dec.-Apr., $179). You'll slide in an Olympic-style vehicle as you coast down the same track the Olympians did—just going a lot slower. Book in advance, since spots fill up quickly, and don't let the summer weather discourage you, as bobsleds run on wheels, rather than ice, in warm months (June-Sept., $179). Sightseeing here is free.

Zip-Lining

Tie in and fly through the air at **Ziptrek** (Carleton Lodge, 4280 Mountain Square, 866/935-0001, http://whistler.ziptrek.com, $99-199 adults, $79-169 seniors and children), a zip-line park that operates year-round in an old-growth rainforest. The lines are long—even more than two kilometers (1.2 miles) for the epic Sasquatch, the longest zip line in North America. Fortunately, flyers don't have to operate the brakes or worry about their speed. Tours vary and include combos, so you can hit almost a dozen zip lines in a day.

Spas

Nothing feels better after a day of skiing than taking a dip in **Scandinave Spa** (8010 Mons Rd., 604/935-2424, www.scandinave.com/whistler, 10am-9pm daily, $70); in fact, it's also a pretty nice option to go for a soak in lieu of skiing or hiking. The sprawling spa campus has hot and warm pools outside, many fed by small water features, and indoor saunas and steam rooms. No talking is allowed in the pools, all the better to focus on relaxation. Spa services like massage are also available for extra fees. Bathing suits are required.

ENTERTAINMENT AND EVENTS

Nightlife

When the skiing—or hiking, or zip-lining—is done, it's time for après ski, or the afterparty—and **Garibaldi Lift Company** (GLC, 4165 Springs Ln., 604/905-2220, www.

whistlerblackcomb.com, 11am-1am daily) is the biggest party in town. Located at the base of the lifts in Whistler Village—actually atop one of the gondola buildings—the GLC is a series of indoor and outdoor tables crowded with partygoers celebrating the best runs or falls of the day. Expect to make friends as you go elbow-to-elbow for burgers and beers, but know that the craziness is a tradition. Things are busiest from early afternoon to early evening, before a pause and then the late-night fervor. Expect bands to play on the busiest weekends, with kids welcome at some tables before 8pm.

When you're in the mood for an actual club, not just drinks while you shimmy to whatever song's playing over the bar's speakers, **Garfinkel's** (4308 Main St., 604/932-2323, http://gibbonswhistler.com/garfinkels, 7pm-2am daily, cover varies) delivers in a giant underground space in Whistler. Music is of the popular and well-known top 40 variety; don't expect eclectic deep cuts. But the drinks flow freely and scenesters break out their best club wear once they shed heavy coats. This is a place to dance and shout, not sip quality cocktails; stick to simple requests at the bar.

Festivals and Events

Is it strange that the **World Ski and Snowboard Festival** (http://wssf.com, Apr.) is held in the spring? Not when you consider that it's really the cap to the ski season, a week of snow competitions to wrap up the ski year and a chance to listen to outdoor concerts. Several international ski competitions, including freeskiing and a Superpipe invitational, are serious events held around the still-snowy mountains, while a slush contest is more about staying up while skiing on a semi-frozen pond and wearing a good costume. Attendees get the chance to demo equipment for next year. Almost as big as the sports part of the event are the arts and film festivals that celebrate mountain culture with screenings and live music performances. Tickets ($10-40) are sold for individual films and a giant festival-ending party, but otherwise events are free to attend or observe.

The Whistler area is a haven for good produce. **Cornucopia** (http://whistlercornucopia.com, Nov.) in fall celebrates the food scene in the mountain town, with much of the fresh goods coming from nearby Pemberton. For about 10 days, the town fills with food-centric events in a variety of venues, from full-on meals to tasting tents with small bites. Book festival spots early for chef's table meals and drink seminars; tickets go on sale midsummer, and some events sell out a month or more in advance of the festival. The Grand Tasting brings together dozens of wineries. Ticket prices range from $10 to upwards of $200 for chef's table meals.

SHOPPING

Ski shops are all over the village, but **CAN-SKI** (CAN-SKI Village, Crystal Lodge, 4379 Lorimer Rd., 604/938-7137, www.whistlerblackcomb.com, 8am-8pm daily) is a reliable spot for tuning, boot fitting, and new ski gear. This being Whistler, it even offers a personal shopping experience. There are a number of CAN-SKI locations selling gear around the village, so you won't wander too far before seeing the familiar logo.

Both stylish and practical, the sweater is basically the Whistler uniform. **Amos & Andes Whistler Sweater Shop** (4321 Village Gate Blvd, 604/932-7202, http://whistlersweatershop.com, 10am-6pm daily) is part of a franchise that began in Nova Scotia, but this location has been open for 20 years—and let's face it, all of Canada knows something about good sweaters. Sweaters can run hundreds of dollars, but some are hand-knit on Vancouver Island and feature traditional Canadian designs; as the shop notes, they're wearable pieces of art.

FOOD

Canadian

Located in the high-end Nita Lake Lodge, **Aura** (2131 Lake Placid Rd., 604/966-5700, www.nitalakelodge.com, 6:30am-11am and

5:30pm-9:30pm Mon.-Sat., 6:30am-2pm and 5:30pm-9:30pm Sun., $24-38) has lakeside views and an aggressively local farm-to-table ethos. Much of the meat and produce comes from nearby Pemberton, and dishes are solid favorites like salmon or gnocchi, a good fit for traditionalists who want just a touch of imagination on the plate. Desserts and breakfasts are especially good.

Long considered one of the best restaurants in town, **Araxi** (4222 Village Square, 604/932-4540, www.araxi.com, 3pm-midnight daily, $28-42) has the confidence to keep the menu short but strong. A high-temp infrared grill cooks a solid beef tenderloin, while oyster bar offerings make a strange but somehow perfect match for the very mountainous landscape outside. Don't skip the cocktails, since they represent the best mixology in a village full of beers and après shots.

Seafood

Set apart from the hubbub of the village, ★ **Rimrock Café** (2117 Whistler Rd., 604/932-5565, http://rimrockcafe.com, 5:30pm-9:30pm daily, $34-52) is a Whistler standby. Somewhere just below ultra-fine dining, it's a refined way to end a busy day on the slopes. Exposed beams and a rock fireplace add atmosphere to the dining room, and the menu features seafood classics like salmon and oysters alongside turf standbys filet mignon and duck confit. Expect meals delivered with sophistication and competence.

Asian

You don't have to cook for yourself when you're on vacation, but at **Mongolie Grill** (4295 Blackcomb Way, 604/938-9416, www.mongoliegrill.com, 11:30am-9pm daily, $20 per pound) you can do the fun part by selecting ingredients for a stir-fry from a giant buffet before letting someone else do the work. It's an interactive meal that's fun for families but not particularly cheap; it's easy to weigh down your pay-by-the-pound plate quickly. Vegetarians will appreciate that they get separate grill space from the meat eaters—and even a discount at certain times of day.

Australian

Everything you could want, baked into a flaky crust—whether for breakfast, lunch, dinner, or dessert—can be found at **Peaked Pies** (4369 Main St. #105, 604/962-4115, www.peakedpies.com, 8am-9pm daily, $4-8). Run by an Australian and her Canadian partner, the counter-service café offers the perfect hot and portable meal for the ski slopes. It specializes in meat pies like the traditional Aussie (beef, onions, and gravy) but branches into Indian styles and even offers a ground kangaroo version. Dessert pies are more traditional, with mixed berries and apple crumble, but Australians will appreciate that the spot also offers Anzac biscuits, a type of cookie incorporating oats and coconut that used to be sent to soldiers serving abroad.

Breakfast

The lines that form outside **Southside Diner** (2102 Lake Placid Rd., 604/966-0668, http://southsidediner.ca, 7am-3pm daily, $11-16) before breakfast are just a sign that it offers one of the best morning plates in town: The brie French toast is richer than most of Whistler's high-end guests. The Creekside location—down the road a few minutes from Whistler Village proper—means it has the more relaxed vibe of a diner rather than a bistro. Read the "Rules of the House" printed on the placemats to learn just how to behave to get good service; essentially, don't be in a hurry and don't be a jerk.

French

The **Red Door Bistro** (2129 Lake Placid Rd., 604/962-6262, www.reddoorbistro.ca, 5pm-9pm daily, $25-38) calls itself "French at heart" with a "West Coast soul," and the menu certainly mixes the two, what with its West Coast bouillabaisse starring Dungeness crab. The small space and across-the-highway location lessens the crowded feel that can pervade Whistler, and the food is consistently ranked among the town's best. Service is attentive, making it a must-visit for many returning visitors.

Mexican

The bright **Tacos La Cantina** (4340 Lorimer Rd., 604/962-9950, http://tacoslacantina.ca, 11:30am-9pm Mon.-Thurs., 11am-9:30pm Fri.-Sun., $6-12) is a quick, fun spot for an affordable meal in an otherwise expensive area. Fill up on tacos topped with bright purple cabbage and electric-green veggies; a little good food goes a long way during an active vacation. The menu includes gluten-free and vegan options, plus a smattering of beers that pair well with giant burritos.

ACCOMMODATIONS

Don't expect to ski right out the door of **HI Whistler** (1035 Legacy Way, 604/962-0025, www.hihostels.com, dorm beds $42, private rooms $140); the chain hostel is about 10 kilometers (6.2 miles) from the center of Whistler Village. But there are plenty of mountain views and access to trails from the accommodations, which were originally part of the athlete's village in the 2010 Olympics. There's a café on-site and decks for hanging out and grilling food with other guests. Dorms have four beds and are separated by gender.

Located between the Creekside and the main Whistler Village lift centers, **Whistler Lodge Hostel** (2124 Nordic Dr., 604/932-6604, http://whistlerlodgehostel.com, dorm beds $45-50, private rooms $83) is more central than the HI, plus it boasts a hot tub and sauna. The hostel has two- and four-bed dorms, plus a ski waxing area and a large outdoor deck. Wood paneling gives it a lodge-like feel. This is the nicest cheap accommodations in town.

Tucked away on a lake that practically feels private, ★ **Nita Lake Lodge** (2131 Lake Placid Rd., 604/966-5700, www.nitalakelodge.com, $664-849) is a luxury destination that's somehow both walkable to the Creekside lifts while also seeming secluded and surrounded by nature. Rooms are spacious (and without kitchens, though the in-house restaurants are good enough for more than one meal a day), and the spa is one of the best in town. Sneak to one of the balcony hot tubs or take a walk around the lake.

Affordable lodging in Whistler is hard to come by during peak ski season, but **Whistler Village Inn and Suites** (4429 Sundial Pl., 604/932-4004, www.

Nita Lake Lodge

whistlervillageinnandsuites.com, $269-319) is one of the more affordable sets of condos near the city center. Condos are small and some have kitchenettes rather than kitchens, but there's a shared hot tub and easy accessibility to the slopes. The larger suites sleep up to six with a loft area. Some condos may have a two-night minimum.

It's impossible to miss the towering **Fairmont Chateau Whistler** (4599 Chateau Blvd., 604/938-8000, www.fairmont.com/whistler, $711-892), shaped like a European castle and dominating the Whistler skyline. With more than 500 hotel rooms, a spa, and multiple pools, it's the ultimate luxury destination right in the middle of Whistler Village. A ski valet keeps drippy equipment out of the rooms, and the six in-house restaurants offer plenty of variety, though the spread of all of Whistler's central dining is right outside the door. With sharp, deluxe trimmings, rooms are comfortable and the service is better, though anyone in town for more than a few nights might prefer a condo situation for kicking back after an active day.

As the sister property to a well-regarded Vancouver hotel, **The Listel Hotel** (4121 Village Green, 604/932-1133, http://listelhotel.com, $309-509) has a little more personality than most Whistler Village accommodations. Rooms are bright and welcoming, if not exactly luxurious, but there is a hot tub and sauna, and the central location make it walkable to almost everything. The lobby has bright art and a modern vibe, and a select few rooms are pet-friendly.

Camping

There's little camping close to Whistler, but **Riverside RV Resort & Campground** (8018 Mons Rd., 604/905-5533, www.parkbridge.com/en-ca/rv-cottages/riverside-resort) has sites in close proximity to Whistler Village (though not a walkable distance), with nice fire pits and clean facilities. RV sites ($55-58) are available, as are simple cabins and camping yurts ($125-230) that come with minimum stay requirements. Tent camping ($25) is only feasible about June-October given the weather, and the sites have lots of visibility of each other—not ideal for tent campers.

INFORMATION AND SERVICES

Find information and maps at the **Whistler Visitor Centre** (4230 Gateway Dr., 604/935-3357, www.whistler.com/whistler-visitor-centre, 9am-5pm daily Nov.-Dec. and May, 9am-6pm Sun.-Thurs., 9am-9pm Fri.-Sat. Jan.-Apr., 9am-6pm Sun.-Wed., 9am-9pm Thurs.-Sat. June-mid-Sept., 8am-8pm daily mid-Sept.-Oct.), located in the middle of the village in a round building with a Tim Hortons coffee shop inside it. Staff can help with transportation around town and information on parking—there are strict time limits for many of the spaces in town, so don't expect to ditch your car for a day or longer just anywhere.

Because there's little differentiation between Whistler the town and the Whistler Blackcomb resort, many questions can be answered by the resort itself (800/766-0449). Just don't forget that there is plenty to do, see, and eat beyond what the resort recommends.

TRANSPORTATION

Getting There

CAR

The closest international airport to Whistler is Vancouver International Airport. Whistler is an easy 90-minute drive north of Vancouver via **Highway 99,** known as the Sea-to-Sky Highway. From downtown Vancouver, take Highway 99 through Stanley Park and north to just past the Lions Gate Bridge to where it intersects with the Trans-Canada Highway, or Highway 1. Highway 99 joins Highway 1 for just a few kilometers (before the latter peters out at a ferry terminal), so follow the main road as it swings north along the coastline. Highway 99 continues about 120 kilometers (75 miles), through the town of Squamish and alongside breathtaking scenery, before arriving in Whistler. Even though the infamously dangerous highway got safer during upgrades for the 2010 Olympics, remember that it is still a winding road that gets a lot of rough weather—drive carefully. Look for the main Whistler Village entrance, also called Village Gate Boulevard, a few kilometers past the Creekside area. It's well signed.

BUS

Several bus companies run services between Vancouver and Whistler, such as **Epic Rides** (http://epicrides.ca, $24 one-way, $35 round-trip), whose buses depart from **Burrard Skytrain Station** (635 Burrard St.) in downtown Vancouver and the **Gateway Bus Loop** (4230 Gateway Dr.), next to the Whistler Visitor Centre. As many as seven departures leave the city daily for the two-hour trip, and there's no charge for equipment like skis and bikes.

For a bus directly from the Vancouver airport, try **Pacific Coach Lines** (604/662-7575, www.pacificcoach.com, one-way $59 adults, $30 children). Tickets for its service to Whistler can be booked ahead online or at its ticket counter near the International Arrivals area, just past customs. Some large baggage may be charged a fee, but the buses will drop off and pick up from a number of central Whistler hotels. There are 4-6 departures a day for the 2.5-hour trip to Whistler.

Getting Around

Since there are so many condos and hotels packed in a tight space and so few parking spaces, most travel around Whistler Village is best done on foot. **Pedestrian-only streets** make up the very center of the village, next to the gondolas, and small parking lots appear the farther you get from the center.

Visitors staying in a central accommodations can simply park their car at their hotel and spend the rest of the trip on foot; those staying outside or on the fringe of Whistler Village can use the **Whistler Transit System bus** (http://bctransit.com/whistler, $2.50 adults, free for children under 5) to get around town. Paying adults can bring up to three children. Look for well-signed stops and be prepared to share the buses with skis and snowboards during winter mornings and afternoons; passengers don't move quickly when they're hauling gear and walking in boots.

If you need to find **parking** in Whistler Village, look for the Village Day Lots labeled 1-5 ($5-10 per day, free after 5pm, 24-hour limit) on Blackcomb Way between Lorimer Road and Village Gate Boulevard. Free day parking is available underground in Creekside, in the center of the London Lane loop; look for signs and entrances into the parking garage.

There are two taxi services operating in town, **Whistler Resort Cabs** (604/938-1515) and **Whistler Taxi** (604/932-3333). Be prepared for costly rides from both—about $3.50 to start plus around $2.50 per kilometer—though distances don't tend to be large in this small town.

Victoria and Vancouver Island

Look for ★ to find recommended sights, activities, dining, and lodging.

Highlights

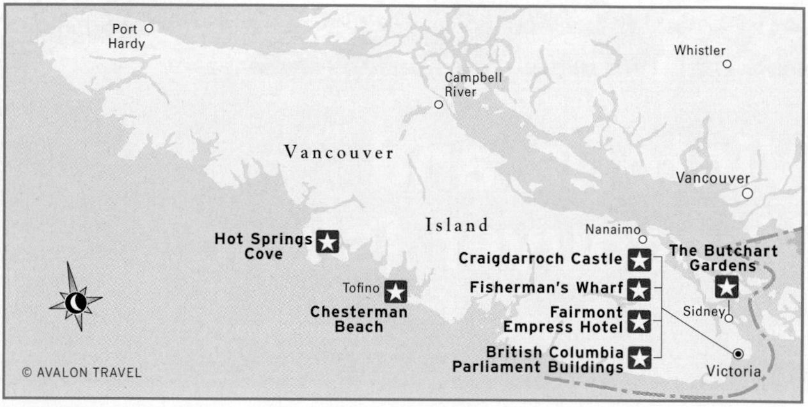

★ **Fairmont Empress Hotel:** This old castle of a hotel is home to a tea service that's worth raising a pinky (page 499).

★ **British Columbia Parliament Buildings:** Victoria's governmental buildings are one of the city's best architectural displays (page 499).

★ **Fisherman's Wharf:** The wharf's quaint floating homes provide a backdrop to waterfront food stands and great people- and wildlife-watching (page 502).

★ **Craigdarroch Castle:** The home of an industrial baron is now a historical site with dozens of original stained-glass windows (page 503).

★ **The Butchart Gardens:** An old quarry was transformed into a world-class garden (page 504).

★ **Hot Springs Cove:** Tucked between boulders, these remote hot springs are cooled by waves that lap up from the Pacific (page 519).

★ **Chesterman Beach:** Surf the waves or hike a sand spit to a small island at Tofino's signature beach (page 521).

With its stately old hotels and Parliament Buildings, Vancouver Island's little city may be a dead ringer for Britain, but it's no mere copycat—it's a bustling New World gem.

The city of Victoria is located at the very southeastern tip of Vancouver Island, a 280-mile bean-shaped landmass of small towns, pointed peaks, and rugged coastline.

Victoria is right across from Washington State's San Juan Island chain and is almost as close to Seattle as it is to Vancouver, but in truth the waterways have provided such a barrier to both that the city has grown its own unique character. The old-world architecture and afternoon tea tradition blends with a bustling harbor and windswept views. Visitors continue to squeeze themselves down narrow Fan Tan Alley in what was once North America's biggest Chinatown.

Although native Canadian tribes have lived in the area for centuries, Victoria's recent history began in 1843 when it became a Hudson's Bay Company trading post, grew as a port during the Fraser Valley gold rush on the mainland, and then gained an international flavor from its position as a busy seaport. As the province of British Columbia was formed, it was named the provincial capital.

As travel by sea diminished in the 20th century, the city of Victoria has lagged behind Vancouver when it comes to skyscrapers, keeping it a smaller, more historical city. Big mansions in Oak Bay and Rockland hark back to the city's boom years. A naval base, university, and fishing fleet regularly infuse the city with new influences. Float planes land every few minutes while ferries connect it to both the United States and the global hub of Vancouver.

But outside of Victoria, Vancouver Island feels like the end of the world—in a good way. This is a remote, wild corner of Canada. On the island's far western coast, beaches, trails, hot springs, and the Pacific Rim National Park Reserve beckon, and near the town of Tofino the waves of the Pacific deliver a world-class surf scene.

Previous: The Butchart Gardens; Fairmont Empress Hotel and the Victoria waterfront. **Above:** British Columbia Parliament Buildings.

Victoria and Vancouver Island

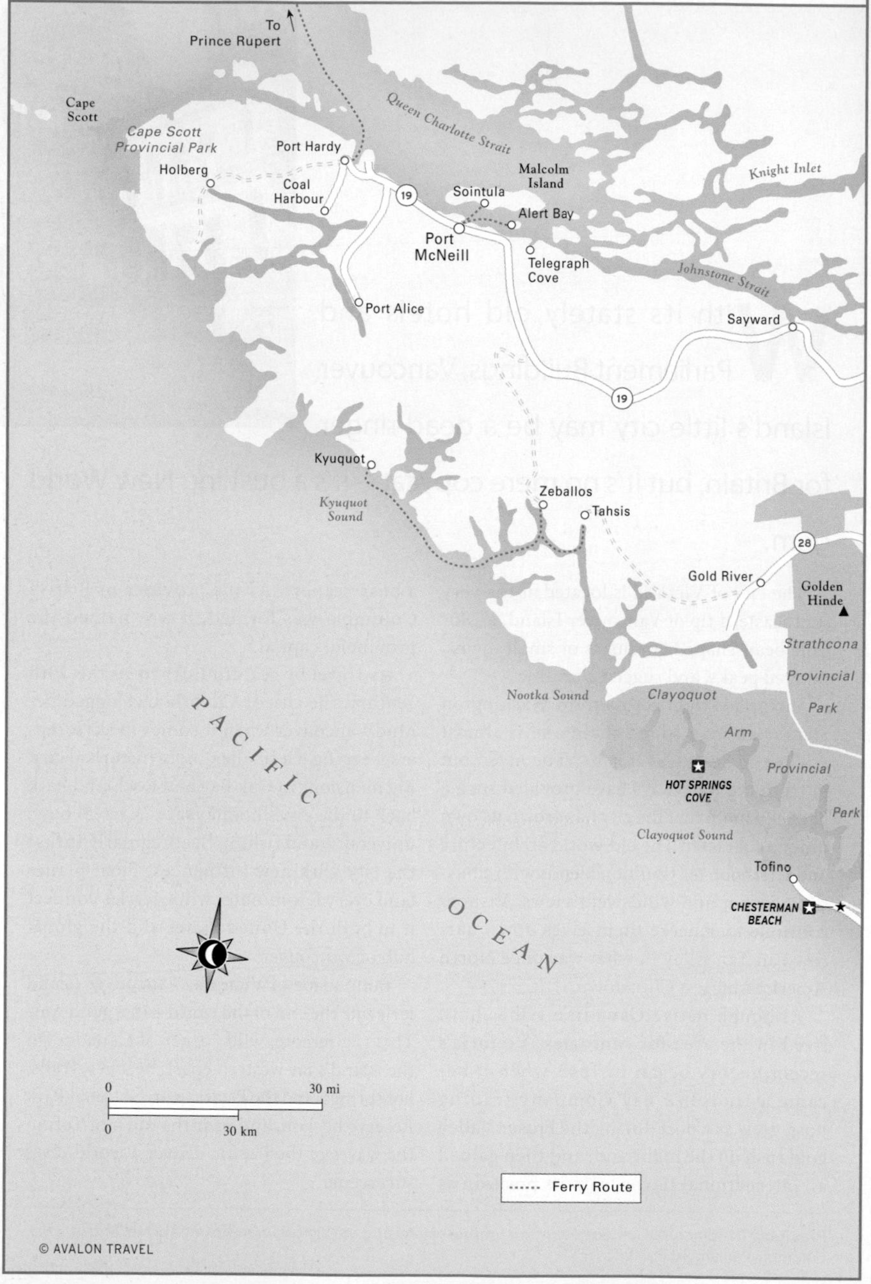
To Prince Rupert
Cape Scott
Cape Scott Provincial Park
Holberg
Port Hardy
Coal Harbour
Queen Charlotte Strait
Malcolm Island
Sointula
Alert Bay
19
Port McNeill
Telegraph Cove
Port Alice
Knight Inlet
Johnstone Strait
Sayward
19
Kyuquot
Kyuquot Sound
Zeballos
Tahsis
28
Gold River
Golden Hinde
Strathcona Provincial Park
Nootka Sound
Clayoquot Arm Provincial Park
HOT SPRINGS COVE
Clayoquot Sound
Tofino
CHESTERMAN BEACH
PACIFIC OCEAN
0
30 mi
0
30 km
Ferry Route
© AVALON TRAVEL

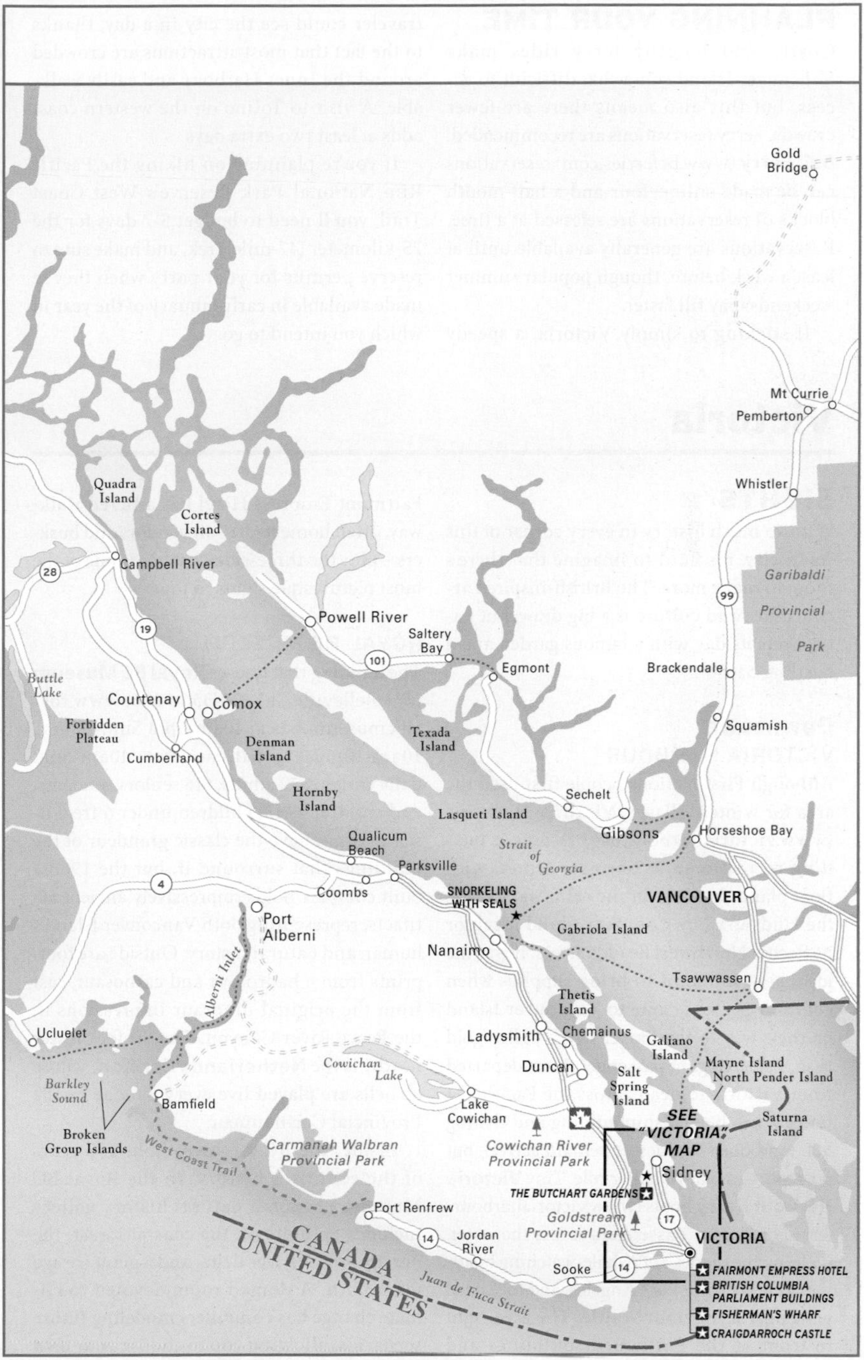

Gold Bridge
Mt Currie
Pemberton
Whistler
Garibaldi Provincial Park
99
Brackendale
Squamish
Quadra Island
Cortes Island
Campbell River
28
19
Powell River
Saltery Bay
101
Egmont
Buttle Lake
Courtenay
Comox
Forbidden Plateau
Cumberland
Denman Island
Texada Island
Hornby Island
Sechelt
Gibsons
Horseshoe Bay
Lasqueti Island
Qualicum Beach
Parksville
Strait of Georgia
4
Coombs
SNORKELING WITH SEALS
VANCOUVER
Port Alberni
Nanaimo
Gabriola Island
Alberni Inlet
Tsawwassen
Thetis Island
Ladysmith
Chemainus
Ucluelet
Cowichan Lake
Galiano Island
Mayne Island
North Pender Island
Duncan
Salt Spring Island
Barkley Sound
Bamfield
Lake Cowichan
1
SEE "VICTORIA" MAP
Saturna Island
Broken Group Islands
West Coast Trail
Carmanah Walbran Provincial Park
Cowichan River Provincial Park
Sidney
THE BUTCHART GARDENS
Port Renfrew
Goldstream Provincial Park
17
CANADA
UNITED STATES
14
Jordan River
VICTORIA
Sooke
Juan de Fuca Strait
FAIRMONT EMPRESS HOTEL
BRITISH COLUMBIA PARLIAMENT BUILDINGS
FISHERMAN'S WHARF
CRAIGDARROCH CASTLE

PLANNING YOUR TIME

Costly and lengthy ferry rides make Vancouver Island somewhat difficult to access, but this also means there are fewer crowds. Ferry reservations are recommended. **B.C. Ferry** (www.bcferries.com) reservations can be made online; four-and-a-half-month blocks of reservations are released at a time. Reservations are generally available until at least a week before, though popular summer weekends may fill faster.

If sticking to simply Victoria, a speedy traveler could see the city in a day, thanks to the fact that most attractions are crowded around the Inner Harbour and easily walkable. A visit to Tofino on the western coast adds at least two extra days.

If you're planning on hiking the Pacific Rim National Park Reserve's West Coast Trail, you'll need to budget 5-7 days for the 75-kilometer (47-mile) trek, and make sure to reserve permits for your party when they're made available in early January of the year in which you intend to go.

Victoria

SIGHTS

With so much history in every corner of this small city, it's hard to imagine that there's room to make more. The British-inspired architecture and culture is a big draw, but nature gets its day with a famous garden and a bustling harbor.

Downtown

VICTORIA HARBOUR

Although First Nations people first used the area for winter villages, **Victoria Harbour** (www.victoriaharbour.org) is now a bustling recreation and business center, with float planes landing in the calm waters that the Hudson's Bay Company found ideal for its Pacific Northwest headquarters. It was the ideal spot for ships to bring supplies when gold prospectors came to Vancouver Island on their way to the Fraser River Valley gold rush. Later, elegant passenger liners departed from Victoria to head across the Pacific. At times it has been a shipbuilding and fishing hub (and both businesses remain active), but now tourism plays a major role. Tiny **Victoria Harbour Ferry** boats (www.victoriaharbourferry.com) carry passengers across the water, dodging the planes and whale-watching boats, the car ferry from Port Angeles, and the speed passenger ferry from Seattle. The area right in front of the Parliament Buildings and Fairmont Empress Hotel has a tiered walkway, often home to artisan vendors and buskers—plus the three-sided harbor is one of the most picturesque sights in town.

ROYAL BC MUSEUM

The building that houses **Royal BC Museum** (675 Belleville St., 250/356-7226, www.royalbcmuseum.bc.ca, 10am-5pm Sun.-Thurs., 10am-10pm Fri.-Sat. summer; 10am-5pm daily winter, $22 adults, $16 seniors, students, and children 6-18, children under 6 free) itself may not have the classic grandeur of the buildings that surround it, but the 1960s-built complex holds impressively ancient artifacts, representing both Vancouver Island's human and natural history. Outside are footprints from a hadrosaur and carnosaur, cast from the original dinosaur impressions in the Peace River Canyon. The 90-foot tower nearby is the **Netherlands Carillon,** whose 62 bells are played live every Sunday by the Provincial Carillonneur.

Inside, the BC Archives hold 200 years of the country's history. In the Royal BC Museum proper, a natural history gallery includes exhibits on the coastal forest, the nearby Fraser River delta, and a giant ice age mammoth. A domed room devoted to climate change has computers modeling future scenarios, allowing you to choose your own

One Day in Victoria

Wake up in one of the city's quaint bed-and-breakfasts, like **Abbeymoore Manor,** to get a fresh, homemade meal, or grab a bite at the **Blue Fox Cafe.** Start a day of history at the **Royal BC Museum** and peruse the Haida carvings inside. Then walk west on Belleville Street to consider the city's architectural and governmental history during a free tour at the **British Columbia Parliament Buildings.**

Head across the street for the afternoon tea of cucumber sandwiches and scones at the **Fairmont Empress Hotel.** From the hotel, you can board a shuttle bus for **The Butchart Gardens,** 35 minutes north of downtown Victoria. Or it's just a 30-minute walk east along Fort Street to **Craigdarroch Castle,** where you can revel in the city's posh history.

Return downtown and head north up Government Street to the city's old Chinatown. Slip down super-skinny **Fan Tan Alley** and imagine life when opium dens instead of clothing stores lined the passageway.

End the day with an Italian meal around the corner at stately **Il Terrazzo Ristorante** before strolling the Inner Harbour again at night to see lights reflecting off the water.

adventure (or apocalypse). One floor up, the human history gallery holds a hall of totem poles and a collection of Haida carvings in argillite, a black shale found throughout the Haida Gwaii region. More modern exhibits show off a water wheel and cannery replica. Because the museum has so little room for its extensive collection—only 0.01 percent is on display—it hopes to expand in coming years. Visiting exhibitions are devoted to historical and artistic topics, sometimes premiering here before traveling across Canada or internationally.

The museum also boasts the largest IMAX screen in the province, showing educational films and Hollywood flicks on an 85-foot-wide screen.

★ FAIRMONT EMPRESS HOTEL

You don't have to stay at the **Fairmont Empress Hotel** (721 Government St., 800/441-1414, www.fairmont.com) to be impressed by Victoria's centerpiece. More than 800 people a day enter to enjoy afternoon tea at the **Lobby Lounge** (11am-6pm daily, $75), a tradition that requires both a reservation and a "casually elegant" dress code. Originally opened in 1908 as the Canadian Pacific Railway's Empress Hotel, it was almost torn down in 1965, when a campaign called "Operation Teacup" saved the hotel with a $4 million renovation. Notable guests have included celebrities, a few ghosts (allegedly, of course), and royals such as King George VI and Queen Elizabeth II.

The hotel has an artist in residence, whose pieces hang in the upper lobby and who often chats with visitors to the gallery. The lobby's design took its inspiration from the hotel's trademark William Edwards china (also sold in the lobby gift shop with the signature Empress Tea blend).

★ BRITISH COLUMBIA PARLIAMENT BUILDINGS

The **British Columbia Parliament Buildings** (501 Belleville St., 250/387-3046, www.leg.bc.ca, tours 9am-5pm daily summer, 9am-5pm Mon.-Fri. fall-spring, self-guided tours 8:30am-4:30pm Mon.-Fri.) are a reminder that Vancouver may have overtaken Victoria as western Canada's biggest city, but this is still the capital of British Columbia. The blue-domed buildings were designed in the late 19th century by a 25-year-old unknown named Francis Rattenbury. After entering a design competition using a pseudonym, he would go on to design major western Canadian Pacific Railway hotels, including the Empress Hotel and the courthouse that

Victoria

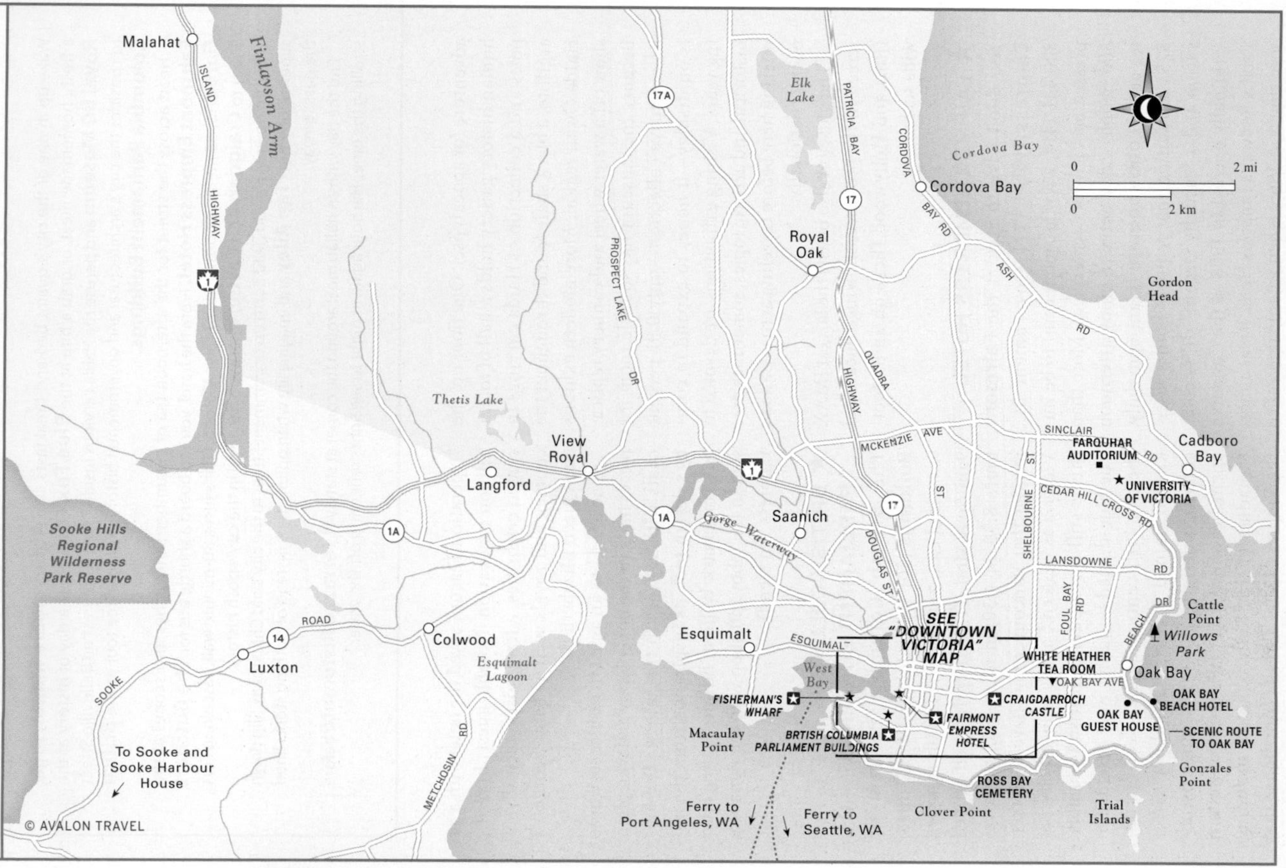

Malahat
ISLAND
HIGHWAY
Finlayson Arm
17A
Elk Lake
PATRICIA BAY
CORDOVA
Cordova Bay
Cordova Bay
BAY RD
17
Royal Oak
ASH
RD
Gordon Head
PROSPECT LAKE
DR
QUADRA
HIGHWAY
Thetis Lake
View Royal
Langford
1
1A
1A
Gorge Waterway
Saanich
MCKENZIE AVE
ST
SINCLAIR
FARQUHAR AUDITORIUM
RD
Cadboro Bay
UNIVERSITY OF VICTORIA
CEDAR HILL CROSS RD
SHELBOURNE ST
LANSDOWNE RD
DOUGLAS ST
Sooke Hills Regional Wilderness Park Reserve
14
ROAD
Luxton
Colwood
Esquimalt Lagoon
Esquimalt
ESQUIMALT
SEE "DOWNTOWN VICTORIA" MAP
FOUL BAY RD
BEACH DR
Cattle Point
Willows Park
WHITE HEATHER TEA ROOM
OAK BAY AVE
Oak Bay
West Bay
FISHERMAN'S WHARF
CRAIGDARROCH CASTLE
FAIRMONT EMPRESS HOTEL
OAK BAY BEACH HOTEL
OAK BAY GUEST HOUSE
SCENIC ROUTE TO OAK BAY
Macaulay Point
BRTISH COLUMBIA PARLIAMENT BUILDINGS
SOOKE
To Sooke and Sooke Harbour House
METCHOSIN RD
Gonzales Point
ROSS BAY CEMETERY
Trial Islands
Clover Point
Ferry to Port Angeles, WA
Ferry to Seattle, WA
© AVALON TRAVEL
0
2 mi
0
2 km

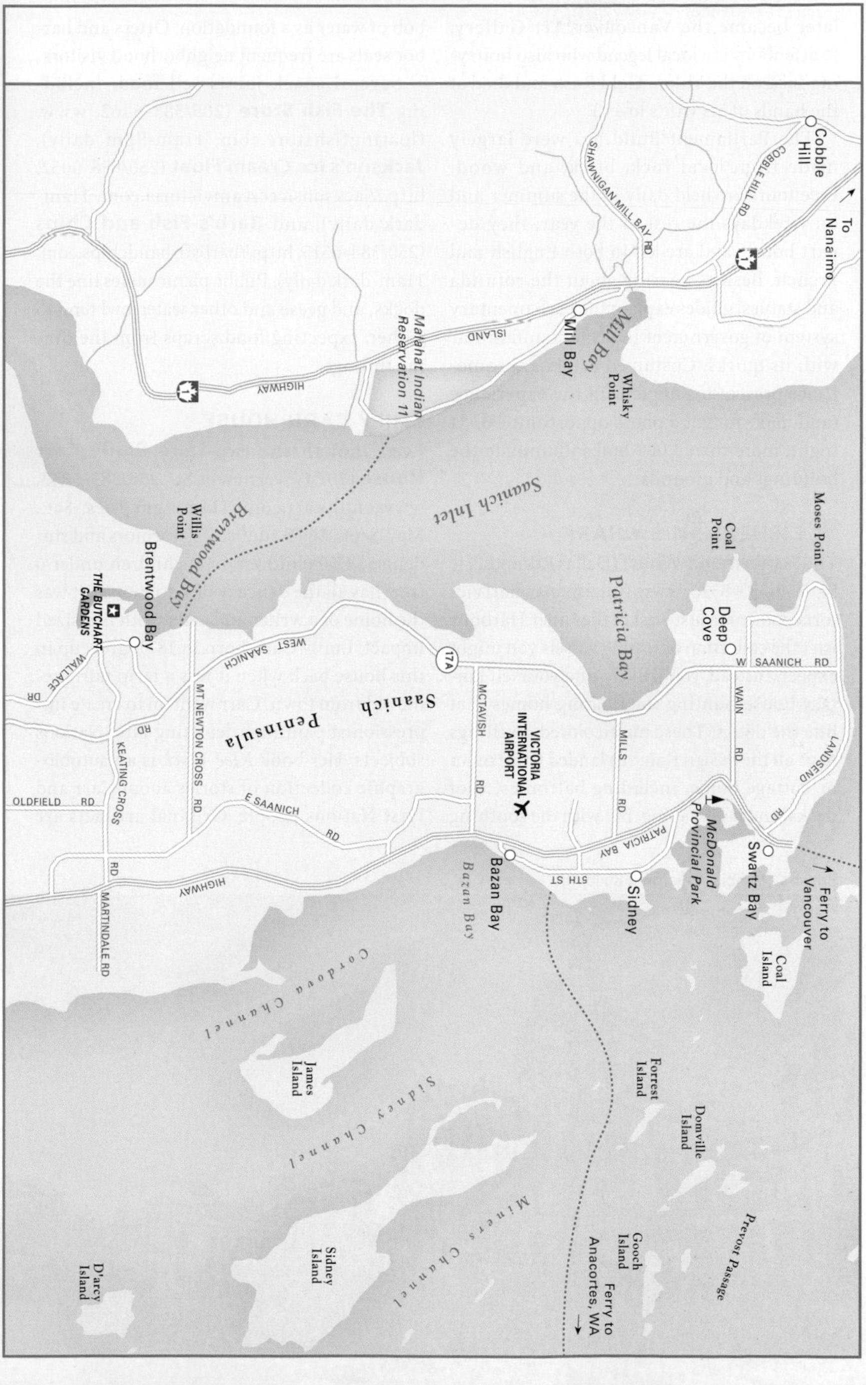
To Nanaimo
Cobble Hill
SHAWNIGAN MILL BAY RD
COBBLE HILL RD
Mill Bay
Mill Bay
Whisky Point
ISLAND
HIGHWAY
Malahat Indian Reservation 11
Saanich Inlet
Brentwood Bay
Willis Point
Brentwood Bay
THE BUTCHART GARDENS
WALLACE
DR
WEST SAANICH
RD
MT NEWTON CROSS RD
KEATING CROSS RD
OLDFIELD RD
MARTINDALE RD
HIGHWAY
E SAANICH RD
17A
Saanich Peninsula
MCTAVISH RD
VICTORIA INTERNATIONAL AIRPORT
Coal Point
Deep Cove
Patricia Bay
Moses Point
W SAANICH RD
WAIN RD
MILLS RD
LANDSEND RD
McDonald Provincial Park
PATRICIA BAY
5TH ST
Swartz Bay
Ferry to Vancouver
Sidney
Bazan Bay
Bazan Bay
Coal Island
Cordova Channel
James Island
Sidney Channel
Forrest Island
Domville Island
Miners Channel
Sidney Island
D'arcy Island
Gooch Island
Prevost Passage
Ferry to Anacortes, WA

later became the Vancouver Art Gallery. (Rattenbury is a local legend who also honeymooned on the Yukon Gold Rush and died at the hands of his wife's lover.)

The Parliament Buildings were largely made from local rock, brick, and wood. Free tours are held daily in the summer and on weekdays the rest of the year; they depart hourly and are led in both English and French. Besides hearing about the rotunda and statues, guides explain the parliamentary system of government to visitors unfamiliar with its quirks. Costumed actors are sometimes present to supplement the experience (and make for good photo opportunities). At night, more than 3,000 bulbs illuminate the buildings and grounds.

★ FISHERMAN'S WHARF

The **Fisherman's Wharf** (Dallas Rd. and Erie St., 250/383-8326, www.fishermanswharfvictoria.com) area just west of the Inner Harbour isn't the collection of fishing vessels you might expect. Instead, you'll likely find yourself fantasy house-hunting the floating homes that line the docks. These multicolored dwellings have all the design flair of a landed Craftsman or cottage home, including balconies, roof decks, and landscaping, but with the soothing bob of water as a foundation. Otters and harbor seals are frequent neighborhood visitors.

Several snack joints sell food, including **The Fish Store** (205/383-6462, www.floatingfishstore.com, 11am-9pm daily), **Jackson's Ice Cream Float** (250/858-0052, http://jacksonsicecreamvictoria.com, 11am-dark daily), and **Barb's Fish and Chips** (250/384-6515, http://barbsfishandchips.com, 11am-dark daily). Public picnic tables line the docks, and geese and other waterfowl tend to gather, expecting food scraps from the dining throngs.

EMILY CARR HOUSE

Even though the two-story **Emily Carr House** (207 Government St., 250/383-5843, www.emilycarr.com, 11am-4pm Tues.-Sat., May-Sept., $6.75 adults, $5.75 seniors and students, $4.50 children 6-18, children under 6 free) has all the delicacy of a dollhouse, it was the home of a writer and artist with life-sized impact. Emily Carr, born in 1871, grew up in this house back when it was a farm fairly removed from town. Carr went on to create impressionist paintings depicting First Nations subjects. Her book *Klee Wyck* is an autobiographic collection of stories about Carr and First Nations people. Original artifacts are

British Columbia Parliament Buildings

Craigdarroch Castle

gathered in one room, and the rest is restored with period-specific accuracy. The house is hung with Carr's work, but also serves as a gallery for new art exhibitions. Two cats, Misty and Whiskers, roam the grounds.

FAN TAN ALLEY

In Canada's oldest Chinatown, **Fan Tan Alley** (Fisgard St., between Stone St. and Government St.) is possibly the narrowest attraction in the province (in fact, it claims to be the narrowest street in the country). The ultrathin passage makes up in decoration what it lacks in width—old brick walls give way to doors and windows, and signs point to a barber shop and gift stores.

BEACON HILL PARK

At one time, **Beacon Hill Park** (100 Cook St., 250/361-0600, www.beaconhillpark.ca) was home to a series of beacons that warned sailors when they were maneuvering onto a dangerous sea ledge. Today the park has trails and ponds and is home to a number of waterfowl including herons and peacocks. It has a putting green and a children's petting zoo, the **Beacon Hill Children's Farm** (250/381-2532, http://beaconhillchildrensfarm.ca, 10am-5pm daily), which has goat stampedes twice a day. A totem pole towers more than 120 feet high, and in the summer live concerts take place in the park's band shell.

Greater Victoria

The fancy neighborhood of Rockland lies east of the Inner Harbour and southeast of downtown and used to be where the city's richest lived. The architecture today is evidence of the money they had to spend on their mansions. Farther afield is the Saanich Peninsula (the triangle-shaped outcropping of Vancouver Island that has Victoria at its base) with a handful of attractions for visitors, most notably the famous Butchart Gardens.

★ CRAIGDARROCH CASTLE

No, you've not stumbled into Scotland. **Craigdarroch Castle** (1050 Joan Crescent, Rockland, 250/592-5323, www.thecastle.ca, 9am-7pm daily summer, 10am-4:30pm daily fall-spring, $14.25 adults, $13.25 seniors, $9.25 students 13 and older, $5 children 6-12, children under 6 free) may be Scottish in style, but it's a Canadian "bonanza castle" built in the late 1800s by industrial baron Robert Dunsmuir. The estate has a colorful history of ownership; it was once sold in a raffle and later turned into a military hospital in World War I. Re-creations of its most vital era depend on a single photograph left from the early twentieth century. Visitors are asked to use an automatic shoe cleaner before exploring the four floors of renovated interiors, including a giant collection of 32 original stained-glass windows. The space has appeared in a number of movies, and the live arts use it as a stage in site-specific theatrical events.

ART GALLERY OF GREATER VICTORIA

The house that holds the **Art Gallery of Greater Victoria** (1040 Moss St., Rockland,

250/384-4171, www.aggv.ca, 10am-5pm Tues.-Wed. and Fri.-Sat., 10am-9pm Thurs., $13 adults, $11 students and seniors, $2.50 children 6-17, children under 6 free) is as much a work of art as everything inside. Built in 1889, the mansion was owned by the Spencer family, who needed not one, but two tennis courts. It now houses art collections focusing on Canadian and Asian artists, with permanent displays of books and paintings from Emily Carr. The Asian garden includes a Ming dynasty bell that was a gift to the city in 1903. Drop-in tours are free with admission and are held most weekends.

★ THE BUTCHART GARDENS

It's hard to imagine something as beautiful as **The Butchart Gardens** (800 Benvenuto Ave., Brentwood Bay, 250/652-4422, www.butchartgardens.com, daily: 9am-4pm Mar. and Oct., 9am-5pm Apr.-May, 8:45am-6pm June 1-15, 8:45am-10pm June 15-Sept. 2, 8:45am-9pm Sept. 3-15, 8:45am-5pm Sept. 16-30, 9am-3:30pm Nov. and Jan. 7-Feb., 9am-10pm Dec. 1-Jan. 6; $18.35-32.60 adults, $9.20-16.30 children 13-17, $2-3 children 5-12) started as an industrial limestone quarry and cement plant. After the deposits were taken from the area about 24 kilometers (15 miles) north of Victoria, the wife of the quarry owner, Jennie Butchart, brought in soil and turned it into the Sunken Garden. Later she added an Italian, Japanese, Mediterranean, and Rose Garden.

The **Rose Carousel** ($2) sits next to the **Concert Lawn,** which hosts open-air theater and music concerts (June-Sept.) as well as fireworks (Sat. evenings) in summer. In **Butchart Cove,** small boats (the *R.P.* and *Jennie B.* are named for the Butcharts) depart for **tours** ($11.80-18.80) of Tod Inlet. Winter brings fewer blooms but outdoor ice-skating ($3-5) and Christmas displays. The Butchart manor houses the **Coffee Shop** ($13-18), which offers to-go options, and the **Dining Room Restaurant** (250/652-4422, ext. 320), which serves an afternoon tea ($35.75), lunch ($19-19), and dinner ($29-41).

To reach The Butchart Gardens from Victoria, take Highway 17 north about 16 kilometers (10 miles), and then take a left at exit 18 onto Keating X Road. Keating X Road becomes Benvenuto Avenue, which leads into The Butchart Gardens. The drive can take up to half an hour. A **BC Transit** bus (250/382-6161, www.bctransit.com, $2.50) departs Victoria at Blanshard Street and Fairfield Road, just east of the Inner Harbour. Bus

The Butchart Gardens

packages from **CVS Tours** (877/578-5552, www.cvstours.com, $76.20 adults, $73.20 seniors, $55.24 children 12-17, $29.53 children 5-12, children under 5 free) include free hotel pickup, admission to the gardens, and narration from a guide during the bus trip, but you'll be on your own in the gardens; a visit to Victoria Butterfly Gardens follows.

To combine the gardens with something a bit more nautical, **Prince of Whales Whale Watching** (888/383-4884, princeofwhales.com/victoria-tours/the-whales-gardens, $150 adults, $125 youth 13-17, $100 children 5-12, children under 5 free) has a five-hour trip that goes in search of the orca whales that live nearby before docking at the Butchart private dock and offering guests a chance to wander the gardens.

ENTERTAINMENT AND EVENTS

Nightlife

The **Bard & Banker** (1022 Government St., 250/953-9993, www.bardandbanker.com, 11am-1am daily) looks like a posh bank on the outside. The name references Robert Service, a famous Canadian poet who once worked in the building as a bank teller. Inside are five fireplaces, a 50-foot polished bar, a second-level bar, two outdoor patios, and 30 beers on tap. (A fancy beverage system means the wine is also on tap.) The bar hosts live music every night and is incredibly popular; luckily there's enough square footage to handle all the comers.

Although located on the Inner Harbour, **Spinnakers Brewpub** (308 Catherine St., 877/838-2739, www.spinnakers.com, 8am-11pm daily) is out of the way on the north shore. The oldest brewpub in Canada, it serves its own ales and has a daily cask open during the week. The facility also makes malt vinegar.

The patio at **CANOE Brewpub** (450 Swift St., 250/361-1940, 11:30am-11pm Sun.-Wed., 11:30am-midnight Thurs., 11:30am-1am Fri.-Sat.) has waterfront views, and inside there's live music three nights a week. There's no cover, free parking, and kids are welcome at the 1894 brick-lined building until 9pm. The beer is made in house, and tours of the brewery are available for $10, though it's probably best just to experience the local craftsmanship with a Witbier at an outdoor table.

Victoria isn't known for its raging dance scene, but the **Distrikt** (919 Douglas St., 250/383-7137, www.strathconahotel.com, 10pm-2am Fri.-Sat.), located in the Strathcona Hotel, means serious business—it's tucked into the basement and pushes the bottle service scene during custom light shows and guest DJs.

Meanwhile **Upstairs Cabaret** (15 Bastion Sq., 250/385-5483, upstairscabaret.ca, 11am-3am Tues.-Thurs., 10am-2am Fri.-Sat.) has a dance floor for Top 40 and hip-hop music, plus a stage for local DJs and live music on Thursday nights.

Best known for its cheap drinks, **Paparazzi Nightclub** (642 Johnson St., 250/388-0505, www.paparazzinightclub.com, 4pm-2am daily) is gay friendly and popular by virtue of having little competition. Monday is karaoke night.

The Arts

The 1914 **McPherson Playhouse** (3 Centennial Sq., 888/717-6121, www.rmts.bc.ca/mcpherson) hosts family and music concerts amid beautiful interiors that were refurbished in the mid-20th century. Larger and closer to the Inner Harbour, the older **Royal Theatre** (805 Broughton St., 888/717-6121, www.rmts.bc.ca/royaltheatre) was built in 1913 and is home to classical groups like the **Pacific Opera Victoria** (250/385-0222, http://pov.bc.ca) and the **Victoria Symphony** (250/385-6515, www.victoriasymphony.ca), which is almost as old as the theater. The orchestral group hosts the annual Victoria Symphony Splash in the Inner Harbour in the summer and also performs at the **UVic Farquhar Auditorium** (University Centre, University of Victoria, 250/721-8480, www.uvic.ca/auditorium).

Downtown Victoria

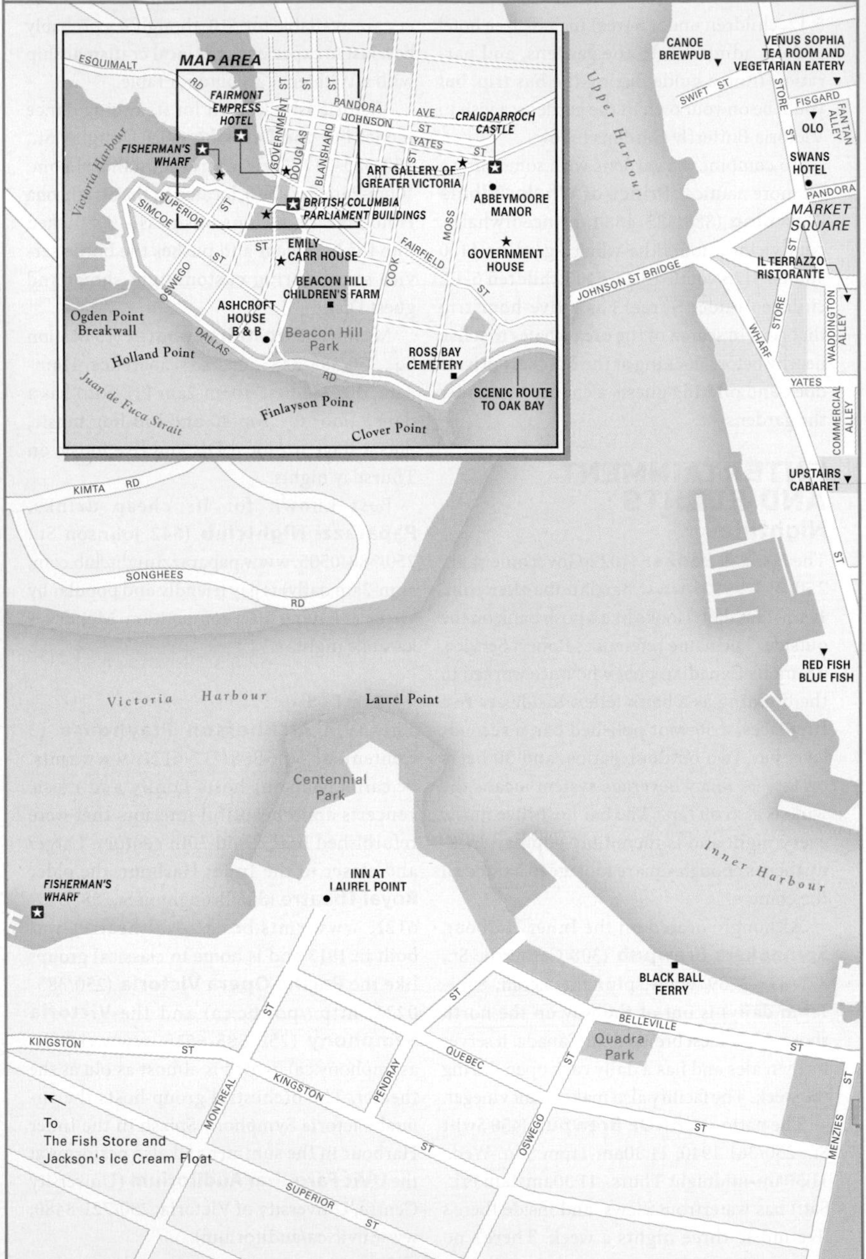
MAP AREA
ESQUIMALT RD
FAIRMONT EMPRESS HOTEL
FISHERMAN'S WHARF
Victoria Harbour
GOVERNMENT ST
DOUGLAS ST
BLANSHARD ST
PANDORA AVE
JOHNSON ST
YATES ST
COOK ST
CRAIGDARROCH CASTLE
ART GALLERY OF GREATER VICTORIA
BRITISH COLUMBIA PARLIAMENT BUILDINGS
ABBEYMOORE MANOR
SUPERIOR ST
SIMCOE ST
EMILY CARR HOUSE
MOSS ST
FAIRFIELD RD
GOVERNMENT HOUSE
OSWEGO
BEACON HILL CHILDREN'S FARM
Ogden Point Breakwall
ASHCROFT HOUSE B & B
Beacon Hill Park
Holland Point
DALLAS RD
ROSS BAY CEMETERY
SCENIC ROUTE TO OAK BAY
Juan de Fuca Strait
Finlayson Point
Clover Point
Upper Harbour
CANOE BREWPUB
VENUS SOPHIA TEA ROOM AND VEGETARIAN EATERY
SWIFT ST
STORE ST
FISGARD
FAN TAN ALLEY
OLO
SWANS HOTEL
PANDORA
MARKET SQUARE
JOHNSON ST BRIDGE
IL TERRAZZO RISTORANTE
WHARF
WADDINGTON ALLEY
YATES
COMMERCIAL ALLEY
UPSTAIRS CABARET
KIMTA RD
SONGHEES RD
RED FISH BLUE FISH
Victoria Harbour
Laurel Point
Centennial Park
Inner Harbour
FISHERMAN'S WHARF
INN AT LAUREL POINT
BLACK BALL FERRY
BELLEVILLE ST
Quadra Park
KINGSTON ST
QUEBEC ST
PENDRAY
MONTREAL ST
KINGSTON ST
OSWEGO ST
MENZIES ST
SUPERIOR ST
To The Fish Store and Jackson's Ice Cream Float

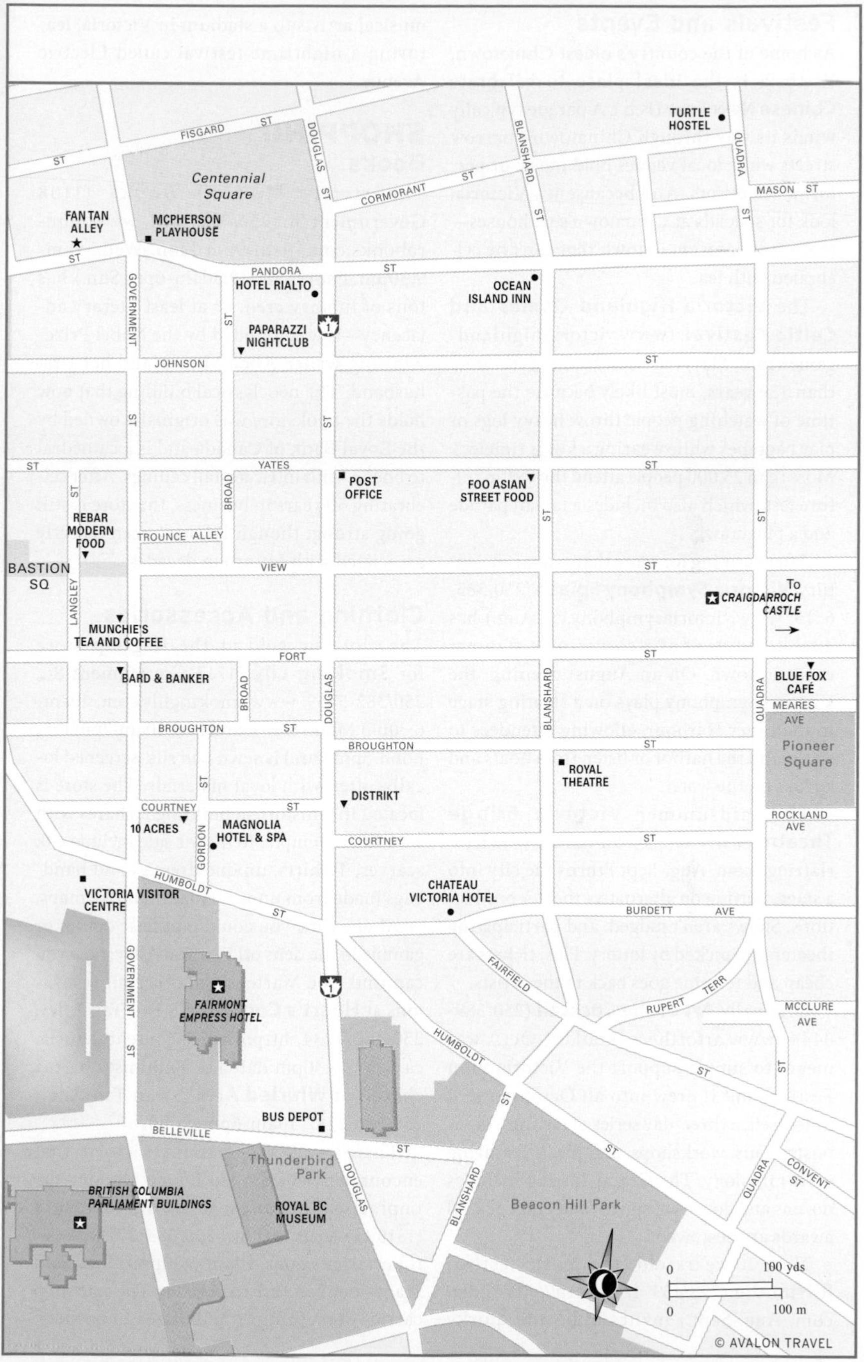
FISGARD ST
DOUGLAS ST
BLANSHARD ST
QUADRA ST
TURTLE HOSTEL
Centennial Square
CORMORANT ST
MASON ST
FAN TAN ALLEY
MCPHERSON PLAYHOUSE
PANDORA
GOVERNMENT ST
HOTEL RIALTO
OCEAN ISLAND INN
PAPARAZZI NIGHTCLUB
1
JOHNSON ST
YATES ST
POST OFFICE
FOO ASIAN STREET FOOD
BROAD
LANGLEY ST
REBAR MODERN FOOD
TROUNCE ALLEY
BASTION SQ
VIEW ST
To CRAIGDARROCH CASTLE
MUNCHIE'S TEA AND COFFEE
FORT ST
BARD & BANKER
BLUE FOX CAFÉ
MEARES AVE
BROUGHTON ST
Pioneer Square
ROYAL THEATRE
COURTNEY ST
DISTRIKT
ROCKLAND AVE
10 ACRES
GORDON ST
MAGNOLIA HOTEL & SPA
HUMBOLDT ST
VICTORIA VISITOR CENTRE
CHATEAU VICTORIA HOTEL
BURDETT AVE
FAIRFIELD
RUPERT TERR
MCCLURE AVE
FAIRMONT EMPRESS HOTEL
BUS DEPOT
BELLEVILLE
Thunderbird Park
CONVENT ST
BRITISH COLUMBIA PARLIAMENT BUILDINGS
ROYAL BC MUSEUM
Beacon Hill Park
0 100 yds
0 100 m
© AVALON TRAVEL

Festivals and Events

As home of the country's oldest Chinatown, Victoria is the ideal place to celebrate **Chinese New Year** (Feb.). A parade typically winds its way through Chinatown's narrow streets while local venues hold music or performance events. And because it's Victoria, look for specials at Chinatown's teahouses—there's no occasion in town that can't be celebrated with tea.

The **Victoria Highland Games and Celtic Festival** (www.victoriahighlandgames.com, May) has been running for more than 150 years, most likely because the pastime of watching people throw heavy logs or play bagpipes while wearing a kilt is timeless. More than 25,000 people attend the Celtic culture fest, which also includes a tartan parade and a pub crawl.

After running for more than a quarter century, **Victoria Symphony Splash** (250/385-6515, www.victoriasymphony.ca, Aug.) has established itself as a cornerstone summer event in town. On an August evening, the Victoria Symphony plays on a floating stage in the Inner Harbour, allowing attendees to sit around the harbor or listen from boats and kayaks on the water.

The midsummer **Victoria Fringe Theatre Festival** (250/590-6291, www.victoriafringe.com, Aug.-Sept.) turns the city into a stage, putting on alternative theater productions. Shows aren't judged, and participating theaters are picked by lottery. Plus, tickets are cheap and revenue goes back to the artists.

Originally **Art of the Cocktail** (250/389-0444, www.artofthecocktail.ca, Oct.) was meant to simply support the Victoria Film Festival, but it grew into an October event unto itself, a three-day series of tastings, demonstrations, workshops, and meals featuring craft mixology. The Grand Tasting includes dozens and dozens of spirits, and best cocktail awards are bestowed.

Now 10 years old, the music festival **Rifflandia** (778/433-4743, http://rifflandia.com, Aug.-Sept.) invites indie and quirky musical artists to a stadium in Victoria, featuring a nighttime festival called Electric Avenue.

SHOPPING

Books

The stately **Munro's Books** (1108 Government St., 250/382-2464, www.munrobooks.com, 9am-9pm Mon.-Wed., 9am-9:30pm Thurs.-Sat., 9:30am-6pm Sun.) has tons of literary cred, or at least literary adjacency—it was founded by the Nobel Prize-winning writer Alice Munro and her first husband. The neoclassical building that now holds the bookstore was originally owned by the Royal Bank of Canada and is a cathedral to books, with intricate, tall ceilings. After celebrating 50 years in business, the store is still going strong, though it hasn't been directly associated with Munro in decades.

Clothing and Accessories

The clothing sold at the flagship store for **Smoking Lily** (1713 Government St., 250/382-5459, www.smokinglily.com, 10am-6:30pm Mon.-Thurs. and Sat., 10am-7pm Fri., noon-5pm Sun.) is sewn and silk-screened locally, often with local materials. The store is located in a historical building it shares with a Buddhist temple. Items for sale include silk scarves, T-shirts, unique dresses, and handbags made from unusual materials like maps.

At one time you could purchase opium or gamble in the dens off Fan Tan Alley; now you can find Doc Martens and other punk fashions at **Heart's Content** (18 Fan Tan Alley, 250/380-1234, http://heartscontentvictoria.ca, 11am-5:30pm daily) or Buddhist dharma charms at **Whirled Arts** (3 Fan Tan Alley, 250/386-2787, 10am-6pm daily).

There's something about Victoria that encourages whimsy, so it's no wonder the impractical headwear at **Roberta's Hats** (1318 Government St., 250/384-2778, www.robertashats.com, 10am-5:30pm Mon.-Sat., 11am-5pm Sun.) are so popular. The cute shop carries everything from boaters to bowlers, and it can even suggest what to select based on your face and body shape.

Gourmet Goodies

Located in Chinatown, **Silk Road Tea** (1624 Government St., 250/382-0006, www.silkroadteastore.com, 10am-6pm Mon.-Wed., 10am-8pm Thurs.-Sat., 11am-5pm Sun.) goes further than the pastry-heavy afternoon tea rituals at nearby hotels and restaurants. The store sells Chinese tea blends and has a tea-tasting bar. The crisp, spacious destination is run by an owner who's been dubbed "Canada's Queen of Tea"—she even designed a teacup that won awards. Bath and body items are also for sale, and a spa is located in the store. Check the calendar for workshops, like the oh-so-educational free Sunday class on pairing tea with chocolate.

SPORTS AND RECREATION

Beaches

Although much of Victoria is on the water, there aren't many beaches. One exception is found in **Willows Beach** (Dalhousie St. and Beach Dr., www.oakbay.ca), which has a sandy beach on Oak Bay. It doesn't really have waves to speak of, just calm, lapping ripples in the very cold Haro Strait water. Changing rooms and picnic tables are available in the park, plus lawns and a children's play area. The neighborhood around the beach is residential, so the sand and walkway is often filled with locals.

Kayaking

Kelp Reef Kayaking Adventures (12 Erie St., 250/386-7333, www.kelpreef.com, $65-130) leads paddlers among the protected bays of Victoria or out of the Inner Harbour to visit kelp forests and view wildlife such as otters, herons, and eagles. Boats launch seasonally from Fisherman's Wharf, and trips depart in the morning, midday, or evening and last 2-3 hours. Morning trips include a picnic and the kayak-through snack options on Fisherman's Wharf.

Daily trips from **Victoria Kayak** (1006 Wharf St., 250/216-5646, www.victoriakayak.com, $59-149) explore the harbor, while the summer-sunset paddle ends at a pub for warm-up drinks. The outfitter also rents single and double kayaks (2 hours, $40-50), and the nighttime tour is ideal for spotting river otters.

Whale-Watching

Eagle Wing Tours (Fisherman's Wharf, 800/708-9488, www.eaglewingtours.com, $80-135) offers whale-watching tours that last 3-3.5 hours. The peak whale-watching season is May-October. An onboard naturalist will point out orcas and can sometimes even tell if they're from the resident killer whale pods that call the Strait of Juan de Fuca home. Bring warm clothing, binoculars, and sunscreen.

FOOD

The old Chinatown contributes a strong Asian culinary scene, while seafood is served up fast and fresh at Fisherman's Wharf.

Canadian

The dishes at **Olo** (509 Fisgard St., 250/590-8795, www.olorestaurant.com, 5pm-10pm Sun.-Thurs., 5pm-11pm Fri.-Sat., $19-35) are aggressively local, and its name is too—it comes from the Chinook jargon, a language used by First Nations people. (Fittingly, it means "hungry.") The farm-to-table Canadian fare leans heavily on vegetables, and one of the two prix fixe options ($45-55) is all-vegetarian. Still, there's plenty of meat, including ling cod, duck, and chicken. The farmhouse-style decor gives the restaurant a relaxed vibe, but it's one of the better dinners in Victoria.

Local ingredients are aggressively promoted at ★ **10 Acres** (611 Courtney St., 250/220-8008, www.bonrouge.ca, 11am-midnight Sun.-Thurs., 11am-1am Fri.-Sat., $19-32), which has its own farm to supply seasonal produce. The restaurant has a heated courtyard with an outdoor fireplace and metal art hanging above the diners, with rustic touches and wooden-block tables inside, a big change from when the place used to be painted red and called Bon Rouge. Daily lunch specials are often available, but all dishes usually feature something local, be it mussels or mushrooms. The free-range rotisserie chicken, served with pan-drip potatoes, is only offered during a short window in the dinner service.

Seafood

Try quoting some Dr. Seuss while you're in line at ★ **Red Fish Blue Fish** (1006 Wharf St., 250/298-6877, www.redfish-bluefish.com, 11am-9pm daily Feb.-Nov., $11-24), located in an old cargo container on a pier in the Inner Harbour. The fish-and-chip standbys are here in halibut, cod, or salmon, plus fish sandwiches like an "RFBF BLT" made with smoked albacore tuna belly and scallop burger. There's also spicy fish poutine and grilled oysters, and a number of creative sauces to flavor any dish. Counter seating is an option, but most people take food to go. Note that the restaurant operates seasonally, but if the weather's bad it may not open.

The Fish Store (1 Dallas Rd., 250/383-6462, www.floatingfishstore.com, 11am-9pm daily, $11-24) on Fisherman's Wharf is subject to the weather, which can affect its opening hours year-round. It processes fresh catch and will pack fresh seafood to go, but most people come for the ready-made food. The fish-and-chips come with homemade tartar sauce. Oysters come by the piece or by the dozen, fresh from local waters and a buck each in the late afternoon. Wait a little longer for steamed crab, which is picked from the live tank before being prepared. Around the Fisherman's Wharf area are picnic tables, shared by a few food stands, and geese and other waterfowl tend to gather, expecting food scraps from the dining throngs. Also try **Barb's Fish and Chips** (1 Dallas Rd., http://barbsfishandchips.com, 11am-dark daily Mar.-Oct., $11-24) for a classic take on one of the city's signature dishes: crisp-fried cod, sockeye, or halibut.

Asian

The theme at **Foo Food** (769 Yates St., 250/383-3111, www.foofood.ca, 11:30am-10pm Mon.-Sat., 11:30am-9pm Sun., $8-14) is "Asian street food," meaning it's inspired by a quick-serve stall despite being an actual brick-and-mortar restaurant. The chef once led the kitchen in Australia's Cambodian embassy and now pulls from around Southeast Asia and the subcontinent. The limited menu

a dish at 10 Acres

TOP EXPERIENCE

Victoria's Tea Tradition

Tea isn't a drink in Victoria, it's a meal. Famously served at the Fairmont Empress Hotel, afternoon tea is very different from high tea (a dinner meal for the working classes). The tradition was started by the Duchess of Bedford in the early 19th century as a filler meal between lunch and dinner, and it incorporated the invention by the Earl of Sandwich—a filling spread between two pieces of bread.

The **Fairmont Empress afternoon tea** (721 Government St., 800/441-1414, www.fairmont.com/empress-victoria, 11am-6pm daily, $75) is served in the Lobby Lounge, on tables made from the original wood floor, to almost 100,000 people per year. The pattern on the tea china was first used in Victoria during a visit by Queen Elizabeth. The tea itself is a proprietary blend that includes leaves from Kenya, Tanzania, South India, Assam, Sri Lanka, and China—and the experience comes with a free sample to take home. Bites come on a multilevel tray filled with cucumber sandwiches, scones, and shortbread. A dress code must be followed—hey, the waiters are wearing bow ties. Reservations for the mini-meal are recommended.

However, the Empress isn't the only tea game in town. **Murchie's Tea and Coffee** (1110 Government St., 250/383-3112, www.murchies.com, 7:30am-6pm Mon.-Sat., 8am-6pm Sun. $2-9) as a company dates back to 1894, but now has free wireless Internet and cheap scones. In Chinatown, **Venus Sophia Tea Room and Vegetarian Eatery** (540 Fisgard St., 250/590-3953, www.venussophia.com, 11am-6pm Wed.-Sun., $22-35) does a modern vegan or vegetarian twist on afternoon tea. **The White Heather Tea Room** (1885 Oak Bay Ave., 250/595-8020, www.whiteheather-tearoom.com, 10am-5pm Tues.-Sat., $23-68) in Oak Bay has sconewiches with pepper jelly and lots of homey charm. **The Butchart Gardens** (800 Benvenuto Ave., Brentwood Bay, 250/652-4422, www.butchartgardens.com, Apr.-Sept., $36) also offers a version of afternoon tea.

is printed on blackboards above the kitchen: banh mi, ramen soup, fried rice made with fresh pineapple, and butter chicken. Seating is on stools or available to go, and the Inner Harbour is not far for those who'd like to sit and watch the boats and seaplanes.

Breakfast

The bright colors of the **Blue Fox Cafe** (919 Fort St., 250/380-1683, www.thebluefoxcafe.com, 7:30am-4pm Mon.-Fri., 8am-3pm Sat.-Sun., $8-14) will wake you up if the menu doesn't—even the brick walls are covered in vivid art. The all-day breakfast is best paired with mango peach mimosas or the Bloody Caesar drink, a Canadian classic that's like a Bloody Mary made with Clamato juice. Sure, burgers, sandwiches, and other lunch items are on the menu, but it's hard to pass up the Moroccan chicken eggs Benedict or Apple Charlotte French Toast. While several Mexican-inspired dishes appear, the menu also has a touch of old Britain with bubble and squeak, a dish made with potato and vegetables.

French

Though much of Victoria salutes the very British roots of British Columbia, plus the deep First Nations culture that formed the region, **Brasserie L'ecole** (1715 Government St., 250/475-6260, http://lecole.ca, 5:30pm-11pm Tues.-Sat., $18-38) connects to Canada's French heritage. Red walls surround an intimate dining room whose wall mirrors do little to expand the space; expect to be cozy. The food is flavorful and the menu crammed with classics like French onion soup, mussels in a thick broth, and duck confit. Lines can form for the candlelit tables—no reservations taken—but that just leaves more time to think up excuses to order the crème brûlée.

Italian

Access ★ **Il Terrazzo Ristorante** (555 Johnson St., 250/361-0028, www.ilterrazzo.com, 11:30am-3pm and 5pm-9pm Mon.-Fri., 5pm-9pm Sat.-Sun., $16-42) from Waddington Alley downtown, and enter a covered courtyard that's more brick than anything else; it has six brick fireplaces around the dining area. The classic Northern Italian fare includes braised veal shank and a lamb dish, a wood oven roasts meats and pizza, and the pastas are homemade. The spot is incredibly popular, so the din of all the excited diners can be overwhelming, sometimes even ruining the romantic ambience.

Vegetarian

Inspired by a juice bar in Seattle, the chef behind **Rebar Modern Food** (50 Bastion Sq., 250/361-9223, www.rebarmodernfood.com, 11:30am-9pm Mon.-Fri., 9:30am-9pm Sat., 9:30am-8pm Sun., $13-21) is a full-fledged vegetarian restaurant with fresh salads and almond-vegetable burgers. A few fish-based dishes are served but no other meat, and several of the dishes are vegan. Juices and smoothies are made from local ingredients, including fruits and vegetables. The decor is aggressively funky, including an Elvis sculpture and copper jelly molds, and the walls are a stark chartreuse.

ACCOMMODATIONS

Downtown

UNDER $150

The cheerful, yellow house that holds **Turtle Hostel** (1608 Quadra St., 250/381-3210, www.turtlehostel.ca, $29-30 dorms, $38-62 private rooms) is several blocks inland from the Inner Harbour, but it's still walkable to Victoria's tourist attractions. Several small and mid-sized rooms have double beds, and dorm rooms have up to 10 bunks and bright murals on the walls. All share bathrooms. The hotel provides bed linens and towels. There's a fee for nearby parking.

Only a few blocks from Turtle Hostel but a little closer to the water is **Ocean Island Inn Hostel** (791 Pandora Ave., 888/888-4180, www.oceanisland.com, $35-43 dorms, $54-73 rooms with shared bath, $125-140 rooms with private bath), located in a utilitarian but large historical building. The rooms have the usual bright-wall hostel cheeriness, and dorms are both co-ed and single sex. Private rooms are barely big enough for the double beds; others have a pair of bunk beds. The shared kitchen is open 24 hours, and it offers laundry facilities. The hostel is decorated in Indonesian art. The hostel's lounge offers live music, along with open mic and quiz nights.

The rooms at the **Ashcroft House Bed and Breakfast** (670 Battery St., 250/385-4632, www.ashcrofthousebandb.com, $129-199) are in an 1898 house built by a globe-trotting Brit—inside the hotel, look for a photo of him on an elephant. The five rooms, some with fireplaces, have some classic touches but mostly bright, modern decor; some even have stark yellow walls. Breakfast is a grand procession of fresh scones, crepes, omelets, and pancakes. The James Bay location is a short walk from the Inner Harbour, close to Beacon Hill Park and the waterfront right on the Strait of Juan de Fuca.

$150-250

The downtown **Hotel Rialto** (653 Pandora Ave., 250/383-4157, www.hotelrialto.ca, $189-249) has a slight Italian theme, with fresco walls and marble touches, but rooms are sleek and modern. Bathrooms have heated floors, and rooms include plush linens. Some rooms have street noise from busy Douglas Street. To encourage sustainable environmental practices, the hotel gives a $10 restaurant credit for giving up maid service during a stay.

The **Swans Hotel** (506 Pandora Ave., 250/361-3310, www.swanshotel.com, $145-255) has only 30 units, all with full kitchens and homey touches like full couches and houseplants. Outside the 1913 building, a former warehouse, it's just as green, with flower boxes lining the glassed-off sunroom and a roof terrace with more greenery overlooking the city. Some rooms are located directly above the 1st-floor pub—home to nightly live music—and are not for light sleepers; other units are two stories. Bigger rooms have two bedrooms, and the penthouse has three levels, six balconies, and a wood-burning fireplace. The property also holds a brewery, bistro, and beer and wine shop. The hotel's name, the story goes, comes from the building's former "ugly duckling" status before it emerged with all the hospitality businesses.

Not quite as castle-like as the Empress Hotel located just adjacent, **Chateau Victoria Hotel** (740 Burdett Ave., 250/382-4221, www.chateauvictoria.com, $219-305) still has a great central location. Standard "traditional" rooms are located on the lower floors and are adequate, but not luxurious. Suites feature balconies and multiple flat-screen TVs, and a few include kitchens complete with a stove and an oven. Not all rooms have spectacular views though—some simply overlook the parking lot. The in-house bar, **Clive's Classic Lounge** (250/361-5684, www.clivesclassiclounge.com, 11:30am-midnight Mon.-Wed., 11:30am-1am Thurs.-Fri., 5pm-1am Sat., 5pm-midnight Sun.), focuses on classic and creative cocktails. It earned a nomination for World's Best Hotel Bar from the drinking expo Tales of the Cocktail.

OVER $250

The ★ **Inn at Laurel Point** (680 Montreal St., 250/386-8721, www.laurelpoint.com, $274-324) is not only located right on Victoria's Inner Harbour, it has its own tiny peninsula. Surrounded by Laurel Point Park, it's a 10-minute walk from the center of town and has a Japanese garden on the grounds—one that doesn't allow cell-phone use. The structure has two wings, the original Laurel wing of rooms with private balconies, and the newer Erickson wing with recently renovated suites. There's a small indoor pool and a collection of art pieces from Native American tribes and international cultures. The on-site restaurant, **Aura** (250/414-6739, www.aura-restaurant.ca, 7am-10pm daily) has a Pacific Rim menu, an outdoor patio and water views, and a monthly Sunday morning brunch with live music.

★ **The Magnolia Hotel and Spa** (623 Courtney St., 250/381-0999, www.magnolia-hotel.com, $219-429) is a refurbished deluxe hotel decked out in muted grays and creams. Some rooms have harbor views (as far across as the Parliament Buildings) and fireplaces or balconies. Bathrooms have big tubs and marble floors. The spacious on-site spa offers the usual massages, facials, and scrubs. The on-site **Catalano Restaurant & Cicchetti Bar** (250/480-1824, lunch and dinner daily, brunch Sat.-Sun.) has a Mediterranean angle and serves tapas-like dishes. All parking is valet, and breakfast is included (both hot and cold items).

The ★ **Fairmont Empress Hotel** (721 Government St., 800/441-1414, www.fairmont.com, $499-899) is more than a fancy hotel—it's the center of Victoria. Opened in 1908 and designed by Francis Rattenbury, the same person behind the Parliament Buildings, it's where royalty stays when they visit British Columbia. The stone-and-brick structure is built in what's called Chateau style, and the steep roofs, turrets, gables, and ivy-colored exterior are certainly castle-like. A major renovation in the 1980s added an indoor swimming pool. Shortly after the hotel's centennial, honeybee hives were added to make honey that's served at the hotel's famous afternoon tea. The 477 rooms are all slightly different, owing to the age of the building and various remodels and additions. Rooms look out at the city, the harbor, or the Inner Harbour. Some furnishings are fussy—flowered curtains, antique-style furniture—but consistently high-end. The hotel has a spa as well as several restaurants, including **Q at the Empress** (6:30am-11am, 11:30am-2:30pm, 5:30pm-9:30pm) and the **Lobby Lounge** for tea (11am-6pm daily).

Greater Victoria

UNDER $150

Oak Bay, about 5 kilometers (3 miles) east of the Inner Harbour, is a quiet, mostly residential neighborhood with a few choice accommodations. The **Oak Bay Guest House** (1052 Newport Ave., Oak Bay, 250/598-3812, www.oakbayguesthouse.com, $109-210) has been a hotel of some kind since 1922. Some of the nine rooms have dated four-poster beds while others have more cozy flowered curtains and simple beds. Not all rooms have tubs, but all have some kind of private bathroom, even if it is located across the hall. The bed-and-breakfast is the only one in the area, and the owners like to compare their hotel to *Fawlty Towers*. Breakfasts are a three-course affair, and the guesthouse is walking distance from the short commercial strip in Oak Bay.

$150-250

Abbeymoore Manor (1470 Rockland Ave., Rockland, 250/370-1470, www.abbeymoore.com, $149-259) is a few kilometers from the Inner Harbour, but close to Craigdarroch Castle and across the street from public gardens and the lieutenant governor's mansion. The bed-and-breakfast has a large porch and 2nd-floor balcony. The 1912 house is decorated in classic Victorian style, but rooms have flat-screen TVs, cable, and DVDs. Some have fold-out couches. Gourmet breakfasts are served in a sunny dining room. Some rooms have claw-foot tubs, deluxe showerheads, or gas fireplaces.

OVER $250

★ **Oak Bay Beach Hotel** (1175 Beach Dr., Oak Bay, 250/598-4556, www.oakbaybeachhotel.com, $312-869) is located in an area that used to be a seaside retreat and home to many Brits. The hotel overlooks the water, and a series of pools and hot tubs sit right next to the rocky shore. Some rooms have fireplaces, and all have oversized tubs and heated floors in the bathrooms. The vast on-site amenities include a spa offering diamond-dust facials and a Rolls Royce and driver available for pickups at the seaplane docks. This is the kind of hotel that can get you a tee time at an exclusive local course. The **Snug Pub** (11am-midnight Sun.-Wed., 11am-1am Thurs.-Sat.) serves beer and wine amid carefully salvaged wood beams and light fixtures, while the **David Foster Theatre** pairs dinner with a show ($30 theatre tickets support a local charitable foundation).

It's a 40-kilometer (25-mile) drive to **Sooke Harbour House** (528 Whiffin Spit Rd., Sooke, 250/642-3421, www.sookeharbourhouse.com, $329-525), located on the

Fairmont Empress Hotel

south shore of Vancouver Island. Rooms feature wood-burning fireplaces, jetted tubs, and private balconies or terraces; each comes complete with a complementary bottle of port. The hotel also has an art gallery, gardens filled with hundreds of edible plants, and a restaurant with a 2,000-bottle wine cellar. The views stretch across the strait to Washington State and the Olympic Mountains. The area is very quiet and secluded, even quainter than the town of Victoria.

INFORMATION AND SERVICES

Visitor Information

The **Victoria Visitor Centre** (812 Wharf St., 800/663-3883, www.tourismvictoria.com, 8:30am-8:30pm daily May-Sept., 9am-5pm daily Sept.-Apr.) is located right on the Inner Harbour. Maps are available, and the staff can recommend tours and accommodations, and they also tweet recommendations on Twitter (@victoriavisitor).

Media and Communications

The newspaper tradition in Victoria goes back to 1858, and today's ***Times Colonist*** (www.timescolonist.com, Tues.-Sun.) is a combination of two of the city's longtime papers. For music and event listings, visit the website of the weekly-turned-monthly ***Monday Magazine*** (www.mondaymag.com).

Services

Victoria's main post office is the downtown **Canada Post** (709 Yates St., 9am-5pm Mon.-Fri.), which offers stamps and international shipping services.

The Victoria **Greyhound** station (721 Douglas St., 250/388-5248, www.greyhound.ca, 7am-8pm daily) has no luggage lockers, but ticketed passengers can store a piece of luggage for 24 hours.

In the case of a medical emergency, call 911. Emergency rooms are located at **Royal Jubilee Hospital** (1952 Bay St., 250/370-8000, www.viha.ca), east of downtown, and at **Victoria General Hospital** (1 Hospital Way, 250/727-4212, www.viha.ca), northwest of the Inner Harbour.

TRANSPORTATION

Getting There

SEAPLANE

There's no way around it—getting to Victoria takes a while. The fastest route is by seaplane, at less than an hour from Seattle's Lake Union right to Victoria's Inner Harbour on **Kenmore Air** (866/435-9524, www.kenmoreair.com, $155-165). International customs are performed on the Canadian side, where there are none of the long lines that clog the highway border crossings and the large airport passport control. Though some Kenmore flights are seasonal, the Seattle-to-Victoria route is year-round, and despite the planes being small, they can fly through almost all weather, save extreme fog.

Departures from Seattle leave from the Kenmore terminals on Lake Washington (6321 NE 175th St., Kenmore) and Lake Union (950 Westlake Ave. N), in the South Lake Union neighborhood right next to the Museum of History and Industry. The trip includes spectacular vistas of Puget Sound and its wooded islands from above. The pilot may even point out specific towns, mountains, and islands during the flight; ask to sit in the front seat for the best views.

FERRY

The **Victoria Clipper** (800/888-2535, www.clippervacations.com, $95-109 adults, $47.50-54.50 children) is a passenger-only ferry that leaves from downtown Seattle and takes about three hours to reach the terminal in Victoria (254 Belleville St.). The ferry terminal is located on the south side of the Inner Harbour, between the Black Ball Ferry Terminal and Laurel Point Park, and is within easy walking distance of many hotels, including the central Fairmont Empress Hotel, and the Parliament Buildings. Ferry service between Seattle and Victoria runs year-round, with 1-2 ferries daily (though occasional blackout dates occur). The views from the boat as it passes through the San Juan Islands are gorgeous. The ride can double as a whale-watching trip when Puget Sound's resident and visiting orcas are visible.

CAR FERRY

Two vehicle ferries run between the greater Vancouver area and the Victoria end of Vancouver Island. Reservations are recommended for both routes. The **B.C. Ferry** (888/223-3779, www.bcferries.com, $17.20 adults, $8.60 children 5-12, children under 5 free, $57.50 vehicles, surcharges for fuel and large vehicles) departs Tsawwassen (1 Ferry Causeway, Delta), south of Vancouver, arriving in Swartz Bay north of Victoria. The ferry crossing is about 90 minutes. From Swartz Bay, follow Highway 17 south for 32 kilometers (20 miles) to reach Victoria. Ferry frequency can range from 8 crossings a day to as many as 16.

Another **B.C. Ferry** (888/223-3779, www.bcferries.com, $17.20 adults, $8.60 children 5-12, children under 5 free, $57.50 vehicles, surcharges for fuel and large vehicles) departs from Horseshoe Bay (6750 Keith Rd., West Vancouver), about 20 kilometers (12 miles) north of downtown Vancouver. The ferry arrives in the town of Nanaimo on Vancouver Island, and the trip takes about 1.7 hours. From Nanaimo, follow Canada Highway 1 south for 115 kilometers (71 miles) to reach Victoria. Ferrics run 7-12 times daily in each direction.

To take a car from Seattle via a single ferry, there is one option. About 80 miles north of Seattle, the **Washington State Ferry** (888/808-7977, www.wsdot.com/ferries, adults US$19.45, US$9.70 seniors and children, US$54.20-67 vehicle and driver plus surcharge for larger vehicles) offers a car ferry that departs from the Anacortes ferry dock for Sidney, BC, 25 kilometers (15.5 miles) north of Victoria. The ferry can take almost three hours to reach Sidney, and not every departure goes all the way to Canada. Besides, it may make as little as one trip a day in the off-season between October and April. International customs is on the Canadian end and can add time to the trip. To get to the ferry from Seattle, drive north on I-5 to exit 230 in Burlington, and then follow Highway 20 to the Anacortes ferry dock, a drive of about an hour and a half. Between the drive and the ferry, your total travel time could be almost five hours. Advance reservations are recommended.

Getting Around

CAR

A car can be helpful reaching some neighborhoods or attractions, or if coming into town by way of the road rather than by air or water. However, the streets around the Inner Harbour and the bulk of Victoria's main attractions are small and narrow, and most hotels and restaurants are within walking distance.

Rush hour isn't as intense here as in, say, Vancouver. Highway 1 and Route 17 (known as Douglas Street and Blanchard Street downtown, respectively) are busy in the morning and late afternoon on weekdays. Street **parking** (8am-6pm Mon.-Sat.) is available, and pay stations accept credit cards. Some stores offer coupons for an hour of free parking to the five city-run parking garages downtown, which otherwise require fees at all times.

Drivers in Canada must have a valid driver's license from their home country (or an International Driving Permit for longer periods) and carry insurance.

A rental car may be useful for travel to Oak Bay, The Butchart Gardens, or the Vancouver ferries. Downtown outposts for **Budget Car and Truck Rental** (757 Douglas St., 800/668-9833, www.budgetvictoria.com, 7am-7pm daily) and **Avis** (1001 Douglas St., 250/386-8468, www.avis.com, 7:30am-6pm Mon.-Fri., 8am-4pm Sat., 9am-4pm Sun.) are walkable from the Inner Harbour where the Port Angeles ferry and Seattle float plane flights arrive. Slightly farther away, **Island Rent-A-Car** (850 Johnson St., 250/384-4881, http://islandrentacar.ca, 9am-6pm Mon.-Sat., 10am-5pm Sun.) offers lower rates, but imposes more rules.

TAXI

The **Victoria Taxi** (250/383-7111, http://victoriataxi.com) cars are bright green, and the company offers an app that will hail cabs. **Yellow Cab of Victoria** (250/381-2222, www.yellowcabvictoria.com) vehicles are the more expected color. Both companies pride themselves on using hybrid vehicles. Rates within Victoria are $1.88 per kilometer with an initial $3.30 charge.

RV

Travel by RV is not ideal unless a trip to other destinations on Vancouver Island is in the cards. Otherwise, renting in Vancouver or Port Angeles is preferable. RV rentals are available at **RV Rent Victoria** (250/812-4610, www.rvrentvictoria.com, $735-910 per week). RVers can park their rig at **Fort Victoria RV Park** (340 Island Hwy., 250/479-8112, www.fortvictoria.ca, $50), about 7.25 kilometers (4.5 miles) from downtown.

PUBLIC TRANSIT

Victoria Harbour Ferry and **H20 Water Taxi** (250/708-0201, www.victoriaharbourferry.com) provide service around the Inner Harbour, Upper Harbour, and Outer Harbour. The water taxi has 11 stops, including Fisherman's Wharf and the Empress Hotel. Pay the captain of the tiny, passenger-only vessel ($6, more for trips outside the Inner Harbour), or purchase a 10-hop card for $51. The company also offers a 45-minute harbor tour ($26 adults, $24 seniors and students, $14 children 13 and under), and the fleet performs a coordinated 20-minute "ballet" on the Inner Harbour waters at 10:45am Sunday mornings (May-Sept.), a 20-year tradition.

For ground service, look to **BC Transit** (250/382-6161, www.bctransit.com, $2.50 adults, children under 6 free, $5 day pass) for regional service around Victoria, Sidney, and Sooke.

Vancouver Island

Victoria is just one small part of vast Vancouver Island, which is larger than the state of Massachusetts. Some of its corners are among the most remote lands in the province, with a handful of small towns—such as charming Tofino on the western coast, known for its great beaches and surf breaks—and few roads reaching into its many inlets and forests, including Pacific Rim National Park Reserve, preserving some of the region's best coastline and wilderness.

VICTORIA TO TOFINO

The highway from Victoria to the port town of Nanaimo is mostly suburban; expect adequate services and residential neighborhoods scattered along the way. Turning west at Nanaimo, the route starts to climb into the island's more mountainous center as you arrive at the small industrial town of Port Alberni. The last leg of the drive, from Port Alberni to Tofino, has even more hairpin turns past towering Douglas fir trees draped in moss. When you finally reach the beaches of Tofino, the mainland starts to feel very, very far away. The difficulty of reaching the town, a favorite hidden spot, is part of its charm.

Nanaimo

Nanaimo, the second-biggest city on the island, is a hub, a crossroads on an island that doesn't have many roads that connect points directly. Located on the east coast, it's also where many ferries from mainland British Columbia dock. But even as a hub, it's not that big, about 80,000 people, with the waterfront downtown dwarfed by the island's mountains that rise behind it. Though famous for a dessert, there's little reason to stop and hang out in Nanaimo for anything more than refueling.

Nanaimo's Famous Bar

Nanaimo is famous for one thing most of all: the **Nanaimo bar,** a confectionary made of a wafer base, custard filling, and chocolate ganache, like a brownie that doesn't require baking. The rich treat is available in bakeries around the city, and there's even a 16-stop **Nanaimo Bar Trail** (www.nanaimo.ca/docs/about-nanaimo/nanaimobartrail.pdf), a self-guided tour that includes stops at venues—you'll find Nanaimo bars most often at coffee shops—offering the bars, as well as stops for a cocktail and pedicure inspired by them.

Javawocky Coffee Shop (90 Front St., 250/753-1688, 7am-5pm Mon.-Fri., 8am-5pm Sat.-Sun., $3-7) on the waterfront offers a classic version of the bar. Or go all-in for a deep-fried Nanaimo bar, with cinnamon-flavored batter and served with ice cream, at **Pirate Chips** (75 Front St., 250/753-2447, http://piratechips.ca, 11am-9pm Tues.-Thurs., 11am-10pm Fri.-Sat., 11am-8pm Sun., $13-19), a restaurant that also serves good burgers topped with peanut butter, fish-and-chips, and various iterations of poutine. South of town is **Hearthstone Artisan Bakery** (50 Tenth St., 250/591-9944, www.hearthstonebakery.ca, 8am-6pm Mon.-Sat., $2-5), which has a peanut butter crunch version of the treat.

SIGHTS

Nanaimo Museum (100 Museum Way, 250/753-1821, http://nanaimomuseum.ca, 10am-5pm daily summer, 10am-5pm Mon.-Sat. winter, $2 adults, $1.75 students and seniors, $0.75 children 5-12, free for children under 5) has a smattering of local history exhibits and an optional tour to an 1890 miner's cottage and a restored locomotive ($10). It's a good stop when the weather's bad. Alternatively, visit the **Old City Quarter** (281 Fraser St., www.oldcityquarter.com), a collection of more than 70 shops and restaurants in the center of Nanaimo.

FOOD

Gabriel's Cafe (39 Commercial St., 250/714-0271, www.gabrielscafe.ca, 8am-7pm daily, $7-15) has counter service and a beautiful interior illuminated by jar-shaped lights made of glass. Sit on a bench made of burlap sacks and enjoy a rice bowl or wrap. Breakfasts, served into the afternoon, are farmhouse style and locally famous; expect a line.

The menu at **Firehouse Grill** (7 Victoria Rd., 250/716-0323, www.firehousegrillnanaimo.com, 11am-9pm Mon.-Thurs.,11am-10pm Fri.-Sat., 10am-9pm Sun., $11-25) is a bit of a head-scratcher: pulled pork sandwich and crab-topped burgers on one page, jambalaya on another, sushi rolls on yet another. But the restaurant does it all fairly well, though the sushi is definitely creative—made from beer-battered cod or fruit salsa—rather than authentic Japanese. The dining room is busy, but the service is good.

Port Alberni

The route from Victoria to Tofino means passing by the small sawmill town of Port Alberni on your way from east coast to west coast. Port Alberni seems a strange name for a destination in the middle of a landmass until you notice it's at the end of a deep inlet, the Alberni Inlet, which reaches all the way from the Pacific Ocean, nearly cutting the island into two. Its downtown, a few walkable blocks, is on the waterfront, and towering Mount Arrowsmith hovers over it. Don't plan for a lengthy stop, but it's a nice little town with a few options for a midday rest on the beautiful drive through the island.

SIGHTS

Need to stretch your legs? Walk **Harbour Quay** (5440 Argyle St.), a portion of the town's working waterfront with parks, shops, and historical markers next to a few benches. For a longer break in the area, you can ride the **Alberni Pacific Railway** (3100 Kingsway,

250/723-6161, www.alberniheritage.com/alberni-pacific-railway, $36 adults, $25 students, free for first child under 12, $20 per additional child), a historical train pulled by a restored locomotive from a classic train depot in town, which goes through thick forests to a historic mill site, all in cars with open sides. The ride is 35 minutes each way.

FOOD

Stopping for a bite? **Boomerangs Cafe** (4833 Johnston Rd., 250/724-5794, www.boomerangscafe.com, 6:30am-8pm Sun.-Thurs., 6am-9pm Fri.-Sat., $11-21) in downtown Port Alberni has Australian-inspired sandwiches and wraps (and yes, they have Vegemite). There's a substantial breakfast menu, including eight kinds of eggs Benedict; the chipotle maple waffle version might be pushing the definition of a Benedict, but it's delicious.

A waterfront town in the middle of the forest means great inland seafood. **The Clam Bucket** (4479 Victoria Quay, 250/723-1315, www.clambucket.ca, 11am-9pm daily, $10-18) isn't quite as casual as the goofy sign out front. Food is served on actual plates, not paper-lined baskets, and rich pastas and poutines are served along with a signature clam chowder. There's also a nice outdoor patio.

INFORMATION AND SERVICES

The town's most useful stop is the **Port Alberni Visitor Centre** (2533 Port Alberni Hwy., 250/724-6535, www.albernichamber.ca, 9am-5pm daily mid-May-June, 9am-6pm daily July-mid-Aug., 9am-5pm Mon.-Fri. and 10am-2pm Sat. mid-Aug.-mid-May), located right off the highway. It offers maps, brochures, seating, Internet access, and beautiful views of Mount Arrowsmith in the distance.

TOFINO

One of this seaside town's nicknames is Tough City, but only the wave breaks are punishing. The surf-happy spot is laid-back and beautiful—situated at the tip of a peninsula—and its best hotel is perhaps Canada's fanciest, while the town's best food is served out of a truck. Outdoor enthusiasts will appreciate the easy access to Vancouver Island's wild places, and families will like the slow pace and kid-friendly activities. Tofino's two main areas of activity are its small downtown near the boat docks, and along the Pacific Rim Highway running south to Ucluelet, full of shops and hotels and closer to the region's famous beaches.

Sights

★ HOT SPRINGS COVE

Located north of Tofino in a provincial park unconnected to the road system, **Hot Springs Cove** is one of the region's treasures. A visit involves a boat ride and then a hike to reach the natural hot springs, which are wedged between waterfront boulders. From afar, it just looks like a few tide pools in a rocky shoreline, occasionally splashed by waves—but then you see the touch of steam rising. The natural springs feed the pools from beneath while cold ocean waves lap in and keep the temperature from getting too hot.

Because the springs are only accessible by boat, they tend to remain serene, though a full tour's worth of people—12-15 travelers—pretty much fills up the tiny pools. Take care on the rocks; they get very slippery.

Full-day trips are offered through many whale-watching outfitters and include the $3 fee to access Maquinna Marine Provincial Park, which controls this wilderness spot. **Ocean Outfitters** (368 Main St., 250/725-2866, www.oceanoutfitters.bc.ca, $139 adults, $129 seniors and children 13-19, $99 children 4-12, free for children under 4) makes trips with boat captains who try to add whale or bear sightings to the 1.5-hour ride out to the remote dock. The unguided hike to the cove itself from the dock is 1.5 kilometers (0.9 mile) through the forest on a worn boardwalk, about a half-hour's walk each way. Trips are six hours long total and offered daily year-round, with an additional daily departure in the summertime.

Tofino

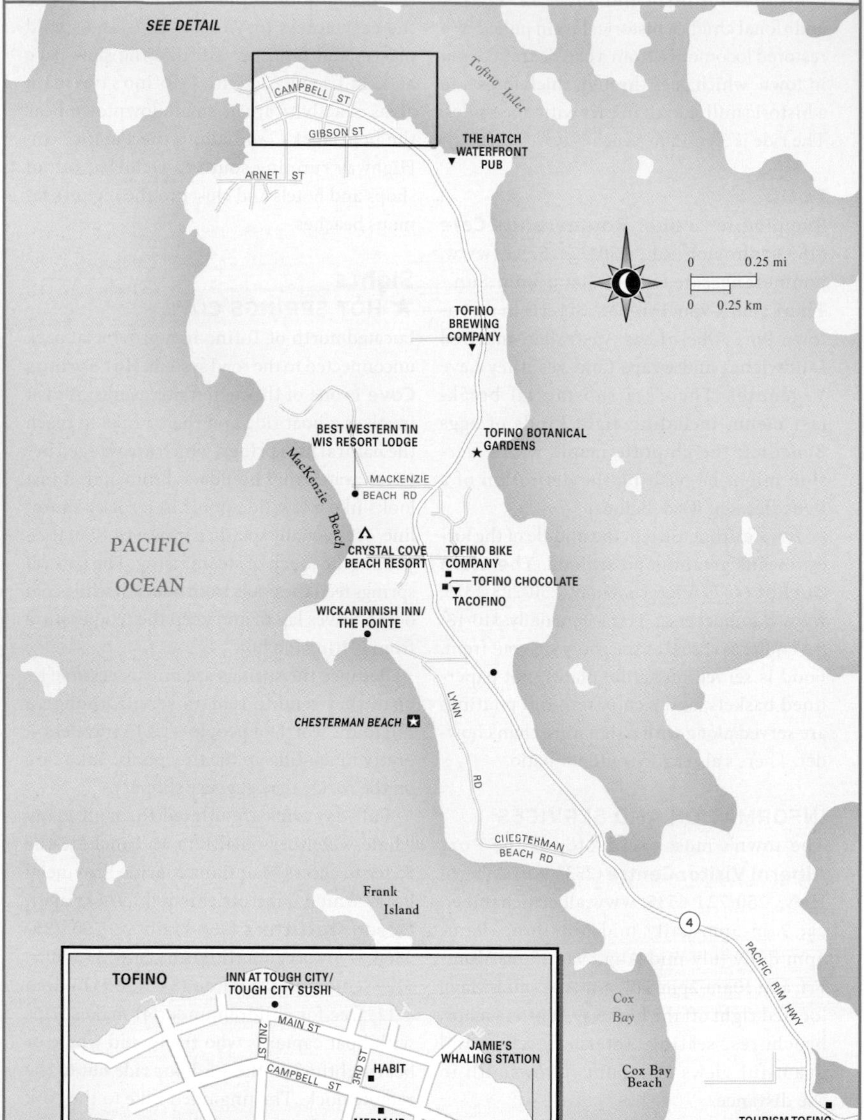
SEE DETAIL
CAMPBELL ST
GIBSON ST
ARNET ST
Tofino Inlet
THE HATCH WATERFRONT PUB
0 0.25 mi
0 0.25 km
TOFINO BREWING COMPANY
BEST WESTERN TIN WIS RESORT LODGE
TOFINO BOTANICAL GARDENS
MACKENZIE BEACH RD
MacKenzie Beach
PACIFIC OCEAN
CRYSTAL COVE BEACH RESORT
TOFINO BIKE COMPANY
TOFINO CHOCOLATE
TACOFINO
WICKANINNISH INN/ THE POINTE
LYNN RD
CHESTERMAN BEACH
CHESTERMAN BEACH RD
Frank Island
4
PACIFIC RIM HWY
Cox Bay
Cox Bay Beach
TOURISM TOFINO INFORMATION CENTRE
TOFINO
INN AT TOUGH CITY/ TOUGH CITY SUSHI
MAIN ST
2ND ST
3RD ST
CAMPBELL ST
HABIT
JAMIE'S WHALING STATION
MERMAID TALES
NEILL ST
WOLF IN THE FOG
TOFINO GENERAL HOSPITAL
1ST ST
4TH ST
SHELTER
GIBSON ST

the trail to Hot Springs Cove

TOFINO BOTANICAL GARDENS

In keeping with the region's wild nature, **Tofino Botanical Gardens** (1084 Pacific Rim Hwy., 250/725-1220, www.tbgf.org, sunrise-dusk daily, $12 adults, $10 seniors, $8 students, free for children under 13) isn't overly ordered or manicured. The 12 acres of gardens include art sculptures and fairytale-like structures made by a local driftwood artist, as well as trails and boardwalks through thick trees and colorful flower beds. The red lodge at the entrance hosts a café.

Parks and Beaches

★ CHESTERMAN BEACH

Tofino has many beaches, but **Chesterman Beach** (1377 Chesterman Beach Rd.) is the classic. It's 2.7 kilometers (1.7 miles) long, with the Wickaninnish Inn on one end and scenic bluffs on the other. In the middle, a sand spit emerges at low tide and allows access to small Frank Island, a 10-minute walk on the spit. If you walk out, be sure to head back to shore before the tide comes in, and give a wide berth to the one private residence on the tiny island. Tide pools also emerge at low tide. Surfers ride the waves here regularly, and it's not unusual to see local professionals catching a few rides before work in the morning.

OTHER BEACHES

Tonquin Beach (Arnet Rd.) is named for a fur-trading ship owned by John Jacob Astor that wrecked nearby in 1811. The remains of the ship were never found and are a favorite mystery among local divers. You can reach it via a short trail from town; it's a nice sunset spot. **MacKenzie Beach** (Hellesen Rd. and Pacific Rim Hwy.) has calm surf, making it popular with families and paddleboarders. **Cox Bay Beach** (Maltby Rd. and Pacific Rim Hwy.) has the most consistent surf and is often home to surf competitions. The north end of the beach has caves that emerge at low tide, full of marine animals like sea stars.

Surfing

It can be hard to imagine that the wild, often chilly western edge of Canada could be a surfing hot spot. But with the right wetsuit, the Pacific waters are surfable year-round. Because the sport can be dangerous, lessons are recommended for newbies (plus it helps to have someone assure you that no, you won't freeze once you have your suit on). **Surf Sister Surf School** (625 Campbell St., 250/725-4456, www.surfsister.com, summer lessons 9:30am and 1:30pm daily, winter lessons 11am daily, $89 group lessons, $109-179 pp private lessons) is a female-run company with a good reputation for introducing people—men and women both—to the sport. Supportive instructors have clients practice popping up on the sand before taking to the water. Most people manage a pop-up—standing on the board, or close to it, and riding a wave—by the end of a half-day lesson. **Tofino Surf School** (381 Main St., 250/522-0189, www.tofinosurfschool.ca, summer lessons 8am, noon, and 4pm daily; winter lessons by appointment, $70 group lessons, $95-140 pp private lessons) calls its teaching style a "four-step secret recipe" and gives discounts to college students with IDs.

Wildlife-Watching

The vast Pacific holds all kinds of marine wildlife, none as magnificent as the gray whales traveling past on their migration route. No surprise that whale-watching is one of the region's most popular activities. **Jamie's Whaling Station Tofino** (606 Campbell St., 250/725-3919, www.jamies.com, $109 adults, $99 seniors, students, and children 13-18, $79 children under 13) is so confident it can track the gray whales that any trip that doesn't spot a whale offers a ticket for another tour, free. Tours run early March-October via a variety of boats, from uncovered Zodiacs to larger vessels with indoor seating, and there are 4-6 departures daily. Tours generally last 2-3 hours, and boats hold 12-39 passengers.

The company also uses its fleet for **black bear-watching tours** ($109 adults, $99 seniors, students, and children 13-18, $79 children 4-12, free for children under 4) April-October, and gives the same sightseeing guarantee. The bear-watching tours depart 1-2 times a day, last 2-3 hours, and involve riding the boat to secluded coves and beaches on the islands around Tofino in hopes of spotting bears hanging out in the open. Captains are adept at finding the favorite feeding spots of the animals. Tours often spot other wildlife too, like seals, herons, and eagles.

Biking

The **Tofino Multi-Use Path** (www.tofino.ca/trails) is a paved trail that runs right next to the Pacific Rim Highway south from Tofino for six kilometers (3.7 miles). Find the northern terminus just north of the intersection of 4th Street and Campbell Street. The path currently ends at the Tofino visitors center near Cox Bay, but government funding should soon extend it farther south to Pacific Rim National Park Reserve, and someday even to Ucluelet.

Didn't pack a bike? Find rentals at **Tofino Bike Company** (1180 Pacific Rim Hwy., 250/266-7655, www.tofinobike.com, 10am-5pm Mon.-Fri., 9am-5pm Sat.-Sun., $35-75). Rentals come with a helmet, lock, and local bike map. Tandems, child seats, and surfboard racks are available, and the shop is just off the Tofino Multi-Use Path.

Hiking

TONQUIN BEACH TRAIL

Distance: 1.6-3.2 kilometers (1-2 miles) round-trip

Chesterman Beach

Duration: 0.5-1 hour
Elevation gain: 30 meters (100 feet)
Effort: easy
Trailhead: Arnet Road parking lot

Entering this forest trail, you'll cross a ravine via boardwalk and walk along a dirt path until you reach a set of stairs. Note that the steps can be wet and slippery after rains. Climb down to reach protected Tonquin Beach, which has milder waves than many of the others in the area and is a great spot for sunset. Return the way you came for a 1.6-kilometer out-and-back, or take a right shortly after reascending the stairs from the beach. The trail hits an overlook before it reaches a short spur down to Second Beach, a tiny stretch of sand, while straight ahead it links down to Middle Beach. To do the longest combination of these trails, hike from your car to Tonquin Beach and then to Middle Beach and back.

Entertainment and Events

NIGHTLIFE

Taps at **The Hatch Waterfront Pub** (634 Campbell St., 250/726-6122, http://tofinoresortandmarina.com, 11am-1am daily) curl around the bar like giant unfurled flower petals, pouring a slew of local beers. Located in the marina, it's a good hangout spot after a boat trip to watch whales or soak in the hot springs, and there are plenty of tables outside on the deck facing the water. In a town without many bars, it's a popular joint. Kids are welcome until 10pm.

Gleaming tanks of brewing beer are visible at **Tofino Brewing Company** (691 Industrial Way, 250/725-2899, http://tofinobrewingco.com, 11am-10pm daily). Beers are made with strong hops and, in one case, local kelp (unusual, but tasty), and the beermakers themselves are often hanging out. But this is a place to taste, not linger; there's a limit of one flight ($6) per person per day.

FESTIVALS AND EVENTS

The annual **Pacific Rim Whale Festival** (www.pacificrimwhalefestival.com, Mar.), held for more than 30 years, is a two-week celebration of the gray whales that pass by the region on their journey from Alaska to Mexico and back again. Events are held across Tofino and nearby Ucluelet, with signature happenings including a parade in Tofino and a chowder chow down at the Ucluelet Community Centre. A $5 button buys entrance to most events, while tickets for select marquee events cost $30.

The three weeks of **Feast Tofino** (http://feasttofino.com, Apr.-May, $45-135) include every form of food event, most saluting the seafood industry around town, with guest chefs, a long-table dinner, restaurant specials, and a festival with food samples. Forget farm-to-table; this is boat-to-table.

The magical **Tofino Lantern Festival** (Tofino Botanical Gardens, 1084 Pacific Rim Hwy., www.raincoasteducation.org, Aug., $15 adults, free for children under 12) illuminates the summer with handmade lights. The fundraising event supports the Raincoast Education Society, which also holds lantern-making workshops in the week leading up to it. The nighttime fest is popular with kids, who especially appreciate the magic of a lantern-lit garden. Tickets are cash-only.

Shopping

Though not a shopping destination, Tofino has a few small, friendly boutiques like **Habit** (430 Campbell St., 250/725-2906, 10am-6pm daily). The clothing store specializes in women's wear in the relaxed Tofino style, including fun statement shirts like one that says "Fries Before Guys." A part of each purchase goes toward an environmental nonprofit that plants trees.

Mermaid Tales (455 Campbell St., 250/725-2125, http://mermaidbooks.ca, 11am-5pm daily) is a small bookstore with a nice selection and friendly staff, plus a selection of toys and kites—an ideal addition to a day at the Tofino beaches. A cute courtyard out front has a few tables.

Tofino Chocolate (1180A Pacific Rim Hwy., 250/725-2526, www.chocolatetofino.com, 10am-6pm daily) offers rich handmade treats, using local flavors like lavender and wildflower honey. You'll also find gelato here, and it comes in more than a dozen flavors, scooped onto handmade waffle cones. The shop smells delightful.

Food

SEAFOOD

Located in the center of Tofino, on the 2nd floor of a chic, rustic building matched to the restaurant's style, ★ **Wolf in the Fog** (150 4th St., 250/725-9653, www.wolfinthefog.com, 5pm-10pm, $19-55) got national attention when it opened at this far end of Canada. With an emphasis on locally fished and foraged food, the menu shifts with the seasons. (What's always on the menu: an option to buy a six-pack of beer for the kitchen staff for $10.) With dramatic, cloud-like light structures and a soaring ceiling, this is a destination dinner, but the shared tables keep it on the casual side of fine dining. The downstairs bar (there's also one upstairs) offers small bites to anyone who failed to make a reservation on a busy night.

Even in terrible weather, **Shelter** (601 Campbell St., 250/725-3353, www.shelterrestaurant.com, 11am-midnight daily, $12-22) offers, well, shelter for semi-outdoor dining with its covered patio. Inside are two levels filled with tables, and on offer is local seafood, including oysters and a chowder made from local salmon. Great food, lovely views of docked fishing boats along the shore and green islands dotting the dark waters, a casual vibe, and fire pits—a perfect encapsulation of Tofino.

The dining room at the Wickaninnish Inn, **The Pointe** (500 Osprey Ln., 250/725-3106, 8am-9:30pm daily, www.wickinn.com, $32-58) is round and has nearly uninterrupted windows, with views of the cliffs below and the Pacific Ocean. Tables surround a central fireplace with a copper chimney. Food is high-end and artfully presented, with an emphasis on local seafood. A sommelier offers wine suggestions, and desserts like the house-made doughnuts are worth saving room for.

ASIAN

When near the sea, eat from the sea. **Tough City Sushi** (350 Main St., 250/725-2021, http://toughcity.com, 4pm-9pm daily Mar.-Nov., $9-16), located in the base of a small hotel downtown, serves classic rolls in a cozy space filled with Japanese memorabilia and model boats and planes. Don't be surprised if Crazy Ron, the owner, pops by to chat and talk about how he repurposes materials from around the world to build his business.

MEXICAN

While not Tofino's fanciest dining option, ★ **Tacofino** (1184 Pacific Rim Hwy., 250/726-8288, www.tacofino.com, 11am-6pm daily, $6-13) might be its most famous: The taco truck now has outposts around Vancouver and Victoria. But the original is here, parked behind a small shopping complex next to a few tables, and usually with a line of barefoot, wetsuited locals. Tacos are made with ling cod, albacore, beef, or beans, and hot tortilla soup is also available. On warm days, the icy slushies are popular.

Accommodations

$150-250

In the high season of summer, the limited accommodations can get expensive in Tofino. Downtown's ★ **Inn at Tough City** (350 Main St., 250/725-2021, http://toughcity.com, $169-249), attached to a sushi restaurant, is affordable and quirky, with different colored walls and fun art in each of the eight rooms. All rooms have balconies or decks, and it's one of the truly walkable hotels in town.

One of the few chain hotels in town, **Best Western Tin Wis Resort Lodge** (1119 Pacific Rim Hwy., 250/725-4445, www.tinwis.com, $221-239 rooms, $266 suites) doesn't have the usual monotonous beige design and forgettable interiors. There's an outdoor fire pit and indoor hot tubs, and some of the 85 rooms have patios and balconies that open onto MacKenzie Beach.

OVER $250

Run by a company that offers whale-watching tours, **Jamie's Rainforest Inn** (1258 Pacific Rim Hwy., 855/433-2323, http://tofinorainforestinn.com, $249-289 private rooms, $45 dorms) is located on four acres across the highway from the Wickaninnish Inn, next to a bird sanctuary. Here the 38 rooms mostly have views of the forest, though a few face the water, a strait between Tofino and Meares Island. Some rooms have fireplaces and jetted tubs. Dorms include five bunk beds in each room and are cramped but clean.

Regularly appearing on best-of lists for Canada, sometimes at the very top, the ★ **Wickaninnish Inn** (500 Osprey Ln., 250/725-3100, www.wickinn.com, $340-840 rooms, $460-1,800 suites) is a memorable high-end hotel with sumptuous waterfront views from its position on a rocky promontory. Some rooms have deluxe soaking tubs next to giant windows, offering views as nice as what you'll find from the balconies, and service is top-notch. "The Wick" and its 75 rooms make up one of the most luxurious getaways on the island.

CAMPING

Crystal Cove Beach Resort (1165 Cedarwood Pl., 250/725-4213, www.crystalcove.ca) is one of the nicest spots on the Tofino peninsula, across the highway from a small shopping complex (and Tacofino) and right on the southern end of MacKenzie Beach. It offers RV sites ($55-70), which are very private, shielded from each other by tall trees, and cabins ($315-540). It also offers spacious 30- to 40-foot RV sites ($245-270) with private fire pits and barbecues.

Information and Services

Look for a VW van bearing the town's name with surfboards on top. It's parked outside the **Tofino visitors center** (1426 Pacific Rim Hwy., 250/725-3414, http://tourismtofino.com, 9am-5pm daily June-Sept., 10am-5pm daily Oct.-May), which offers personalized accommodations advice and maps. It also has a small shop.

Getting There

To drive to Tofino from Victoria, head north on Highway 1 for about 106 kilometers (66 miles). In Nanaimo, make a right onto Highway 19. After 50 kilometers (31 miles), take exit 60 for Highway 4. Continue on Highway 4 for 128 kilometers (80 miles), heading west and passing by the small city of Port Alberni. Follow Highway 4 as it makes a sharp right turn and becomes the Pacific Rim Highway. Continue northwest on the highway for 32 kilometers (20 miles) to Tofino. The drive takes about 4.5 hours.

A faster way to reach the remote little town is to fly via small plane from Vancouver. The 45-minute flights into tiny **Tofino Long Beach Airport** (188 Airport Rd., 250/720-2700, www.tofinoairport.com) run about $109-220 and make the trip once or twice a day.

To travel via bus, reserve spots on **Tofino Bus** (346 Campbell St., 866/986-3466, www.tofinobus.com, $69), which goes from Victoria to Tofino, with stops in Nanaimo, Port Alberni, and Ucluelet. It's a 6.75-hour trip with two departures per day.

PACIFIC RIM NATIONAL PARK RESERVE

Pacific Rim National Park Reserve is a multipart entity that stretches across southern Vancouver Island. There are three units, unconnected geographically. The entire park is more than 500 square kilometers and includes beaches, rugged coastline, and temperate rainforests, much of it difficult to access. From Tofino, the Long Beach Unit, so named for the 10-kilometer (6.2-mile) stretch of beach it encompasses, along with others, is the most accessible and welcoming, with beautiful stretches just meters from the roads. Even if you're not surfing the waves, you'll appreciate strolling the sands. The other two units are the Broken Group Islands, located off the coast of Ucluelet and popular with kayakers, and the 75-kilometer (47-mile) West Coast Trail.

Visiting the Park

The beaches of the Long Beach Unit are accessible year-round. The Broken Group Islands are almost exclusively visited in summer and accessible via sea vessel only, and the West Coast Trail is only open May-September, with trailhead offices at both ends in Port Renfrew and Bamfield.

Visitors Centers

Find information about the whole park at **Kwisitis Visitor Centre** (485 Wick Rd., Ucluelet, 10am-4:30pm daily May-mid-Oct., 11am-3pm Fri.-Sun. mid.-Oct.-Apr.), near the southern end of Long Beach. It's chock-full of nature exhibits and hands-on activities on the natural and human history of the area. **Pacific Rim Visitor Centre** (2791 Pacific Rim Hwy., Ucluelet, 250/726-4600, www.pacificrimvisitor.ca, 10am-4:30pm daily May-late June, 9am-7pm daily late June-early Sept., 10am-4:30pm daily early Sept.-mid-Oct.) has tourist information and a gift shop.

Entrances

Pacific Rim National Park Reserve doesn't have entrance stations. You'll find self-pay parking stations ($4.90 adults, $4.30 seniors, free for children) at the Long Beach Unit.

The Broken Group Islands are accessible via boat only, by experienced kayakers or with a tour guide.

Hikers for the West Coast Trail usually travel northwest, starting at Port Renfrew and heading to the small town of Bamfield; trailhead offices are at either end. Permits for the West Coast Trail become available in early January and sell out quickly. They cost $127.50 per person, plus a reservation fee of $24.50.

Long Beach Unit

BEACHES

Long Beach (Airport Rd. and Pacific Rim Hwy.) is, appropriately, the longest beach in the Tofino area, at more than 10 kilometers (6.2 miles) in length, ideal for walks or runs. The large stone that rises at the beach's center is known as Incinerator Rock and can be climbed. Cycling is also allowed on Long Beach at low tide on the hard-packed sand.

Wickaninnish Beach (Wick Rd. and Ocean Terrace Rd.) has lots of driftwood and dunes, and is named for a local First Nations chief from the 18th century. Note that the Wickaninnish Inn does not sit on Wickaninnish Beach; it's farther north, though named for the same figure.

NUU-CHAH-NULTH TRAIL

Most hiking in the Long Beach Unit of the park consists of beach strolls, but there are a few trails in the unit, mostly short walks of less than a kilometer. The Nuu-chah-nulth Trail is the unit's longest.

Distance: 5 kilometers (3.1 miles) round-trip
Duration: 1.5 hours
Elevation gain: 46 meters (150 feet)
Effort: moderate
Trailhead: Kwisitis Visitor Centre

Follow the trail along Long Beach and into the trees. You'll quickly come to a fork; head straight for about 90 meters or so for a stop at South Beach, then backtrack to the junction and continue east. The trail quickly becomes a boardwalk, with more than 200 stairs, and is dotted with interpretive signs. Greenery crowds the trail from both sides, making it feel like a secret passage through the woods. Travel over the boardwalk and through a wetland until the path becomes dirt again. At 2.5 kilometers (1.6 miles) from the visitors center, walk down the stairs to reach Florencia Beach, named for a ship that sank here in the early 20th century; look for the memorial plaque. Return the way you came.

CAMPING

For camping close to the beach, try the park's **Green Point Campground** (Pacific Rim Hwy., Ucluelet, 877/737-3783, www.pc.gc.ca, Mar.-early Oct., $27.40-32.30), 18 kilometers (11 miles) south of Tofino. It has 94 drive-in sites and 20 walk-in sites that are more forested. Reservations can be made online and are recommended for May-September; reservations for the whole summer become available in early January. The campsites are walking distance to Long Beach but in the trees; some have beach views.

GETTING THERE

To reach the Long Beach Unit from Tofino, head south on the Pacific Rim Highway for 26 kilometers (16 miles) and turn right on Wick Road. Follow it for three kilometers (1.9 miles) to the Kwisitis Visitor Centre. There are also other Long Beach parking lots directly off the Pacific Rim Highway.

Broken Group Islands

The Broken Group Islands, a chain of more than 100 tiny islands—the bits of green and dark rock break up the very blue waters of Barkley Sound—is a separate unit of the park, located southeast of Ucluelet. They're popular with kayakers. Reaching the islands requires either significant sea kayaking experience or a guide. **Majestic Ocean Kayaking** (1167 Helen Rd., Ucluelet, 800/889-7644, www.oceankayaking.com, $1,299) offers four-day guided overnight tours. Trips depart once a week April-September. The ferry **MV Frances Barkley** (5425 Argyle St., Port Alberni, 250/723-8313, www.ladyrosemarine.com, $33) takes paddlers and their kayaks or canoes to the edge of the island chain from Ucluelet or Port Alberni June-mid-September, with once daily departures Monday, Wednesday, and Friday. Service from Port Alberni only is available once daily on Sundays in season. Some islands have **campsites** ($9.80).

West Coast Trail

One of Canada's signature hikes is the **West Coast Trail** (May-Sept.). It runs through the national park, from the town of Port Renfrew to the village of Bamfield. The hike traces the coast of Vancouver Island, around remote inlets and overlooking the rough ocean seas that have claimed ships for centuries. It involves not just trekking over rugged terrain but wading through creeks, climbing ladders, and soaring in a hand-operated cable car. It's a once-in-a-lifetime experience but requires extensive backpacking and wilderness experience.

Hiking the 75-kilometer (47-mile) West Coast Trail generally takes 5-7 days and requires an **advance permit** (877/737-3783, www.pc.gc.ca, $127.50 pp plus $24.50 reservation fee), reservable online or by phone. Reservations open in January and usually fill quickly. Hikers can depart from either Port Renfrew—closer to Victoria and more accessible—or Bamfield; visitors centers are at both ends of the trail, and this is where permit-holders can check in and undergo a required orientation.

For the West Coast Trailhead at Port Renfrew, follow Highway 1 west from Victoria for 15 kilometers (9 miles) to Westshore Parkway. Turn left and follow the parkway for 20 kilometers (12 miles) to where it dead-ends; turn right here for Highway 14. Follow it 71 kilometers (44 miles) to the town of Port Renfrew. The drive takes about two hours.

Reaching the Bamfield trailhead involves a return to Port Alberni and then driving more than 77 kilometers (48 miles) of gravel road not advised for rental cars. The **MV Frances Barkley ferry** (5425 Argyle St., Port Alberni, 250/723-8313, www.ladyrosemarine.com, $42) travels between Port Alberni and Bamfield year-round via the Alberni Inlet, with once daily departures Tuesday, Thursday, and Sunday June-mid-September.

UCLUELET

The small town of Ucluelet, 40 kilometers (25 miles) southeast of Tofino on the Pacific Rim Highway, is similar in nature but lower key. Many of the region's cheaper accommodations are here, and rooms don't book up as quickly. While Tofino can sometimes feel like a tourist town, with more visitors than residents, Ucluelet feels like a working, locals' town.

Sights

The town's biggest attraction is the **Ucluelet Aquarium** (180 Main St., 250/726-2782, http://uclueletaquarium.org, 10am-5pm daily mid-Mar.-late Nov., $14 adults, $10 students and seniors, $7 children 4-17, free for children under 4), a bright blue building hanging over the water. The child-friendly space is full of touch tanks and aquariums full of local marinelife; a "catch-and-release" policy means the fish are returned to the ocean after a stay in the aquarium.

The tip of the small peninsula that holds the town of Ucluelet is topped by the **Amphitrite Lighthouse** (Coast Guard Dr. and Peninsula Rd.), named for the mythological wife of Poseidon. Dating back to 1918, the squat lighthouse was constructed after a massive shipwreck took place nearby. It's a short walk from the parking lot and also the start of a short trail, part of Ucluelet's Wild Pacific Trail.

Hiking

Ucluelet's **Wild Pacific Trail** (www.wildpacifictrail.com), not to be confused with the Pacific Rim National Park Reserve's much longer West Coast Trail, is a local route perfect for day hiking. It's composed of two parts, a shorter Lighthouse Loop and a longer out-and-back section along the water. Some people make a large loop by returning through the streets of Ucluelet, but staying on the scenic coastline is more rewarding.

WILD PACIFIC TRAIL

Distance: 10 kilometers (6.2 miles) round-trip
Duration: 3 hours
Elevation gain: 76 meters (250 feet)
Effort: moderate
Trailhead: Brown's Beach parking (748 Odyssey Ln.)

This longer section of the Wild Pacific Trail starts at Brown's Beach and heads along the water. Take every left turn; right turns lead to small spur trails through the forest, but most rejoin the main trail. After about 2.4 kilometers (1.5 miles), you'll spot viewing decks that reach out over the water. Just past them, take the right at a junction for a brief loop through ancient cedars, before rejoining the main trail to head out through rocky bluffs. Look down at the wild waves below, but don't try to descend to the water. Return the way you came, this time taking every right at junctions.

After you've returned to your starting point, you can continue a bit farther south along Marine Drive, through Black Rock Oceanfront Resort or along the sands of Big Beach. You'll see an old shipwreck and interpretive signs describing it. Return the way you came; it'll add about 1.6 kilometers (1 mile) to your trip.

LIGHTHOUSE LOOP

Distance: 2.6 kilometers (1.6 miles) round-trip
Duration: 1 hour
Elevation gain: 15 meters (50 feet)
Effort: easy
Trailhead: Amphitrite Lighthouse parking lot
Directions: From Ucluelet, follow Peninsula Road south about two kilometers (1.2 miles), and turn right on Coast Guard Drive.

This section of the Wild Pacific Trail is ideal for young children or travelers with a short window for hiking. It loops from Amphitrite Lighthouse along the bluffs overlooking Barkley Sound, then continues through some of the peninsula's woods. The flat trail has several benches. About halfway through the circular loop, there's a short spur trail near a parking lot to the Terrace Beach Interpretive Trail—which adds little length to the trip, maybe 100 meters—with signs discussing First Nations canoe building.

Food and Accommodations

Tiny **Norwoods Restaurant** (1714 Peninsula Rd., 250/726-7001, www.norwoods.ca, 6pm-9pm Fri.-Tues., $14-48) brings international preparations to a local menu, often utilizing local seafood. The menu is highly seasonal, and wine pairings are important; a whole wall of the sparse space is taken up by bottles, and the menu lists appropriate drinks for each dish. The high-top tables keep the vibe casual, but the plates are works of art.

The dramatic **Black Rock Oceanfront Resort** (596 Marine Dr., 250/726-4800, http://blackrockresort.com, $314-660) is Ucluelet's nod to luxury, a curved building that faces the crashing waves over, of course, black rocks. Its 133 rooms are chic and modern, with less of the woodsy intent you see in much of the region's decor. Some have kitchenettes, others have giant tubs, gas fireplaces, and balconies, and all have oversized windows with nature views. The outdoor pool and hot tub are on a beautiful patio overlooking the rocky coast.

Located on Ucluelet's protected harbor, **Canadian Princess Fishing Lodge** (1943 Peninsula Rd., 250/726-7771, www.canadianprincess.com, $209-219 rooms, $259 suites) has low-key accommodations within walking distance to town. The cheery green buildings have balconies facing the marina, and many rooms are two-level suites with extra beds. Some have fireplaces. With just under 50 rooms, it's a mid-sized hotel that falls squarely between motel and high-end resort.

Getting There

To drive to Ucluelet from Victoria, head north on Highway 1 for about 106 kilometers (66 miles). In Nanaimo, make a right onto Highway 19. After 50 kilometers (31 miles), take exit 60 for Highway 4. Continue on Highway 4 for 128 kilometers (80 miles), heading west and passing by the small city of Port Alberni. Turn left onto the Tofino-Ucluelet Highway and continue on the road for about 8 kilometers (5 miles) into Ucluelet. The drive takes about 4.5 hours.

From Tofino, head southeast on the Pacific Rim Highway for 30 kilometers (19 miles), proceeding straight onto the Tofino-Ucluelet Highway and continuing 8 more kilometers (5 miles) into Ucluelet. The drive takes about 40 minutes. You can also take the **Tofino Bus** (1738 Peninsula Rd., 866/986-3466, www.tofinobus.com, $17) between the towns; it makes two departures in each direction daily, a 50-minute trip.

Background

The Landscape

GEOGRAPHY

The Pacific Northwest encompasses the states of Washington and Oregon in the United States and the province of British Columbia in Canada, though generally only the southern part of the Canadian province is considered part of the region, including Vancouver Island, a 285-mile mass of land just west of the mainland.

While the Pacific Ocean is the defining characteristic of the region, the Salish Sea—which includes Puget Sound, the Strait of Juan de Fuca, and the Strait of Georgia—may be the true heart of the Pacific Northwest, outlining the Olympic Peninsula, containing the San Juan Islands, connecting Seattle and Vancouver to the Pacific, and separating Vancouver Island from the mainland.

The Cascade Mountains are the region's spine, beginning in Canada and continuing south for more than 700 miles through Oregon and into California. A partially volcanic range, the Cascades were formed by geothermic activity millions of years ago. Remnants of the explosive action are evident in the volcanoes, some still active, that line the Cascade crest. The most prominent of these is Mount Rainier, but the lineup of volcanoes also includes Washington's Mount Baker and Mount St. Helens, which famously erupted in 1980, and Oregon's Mount Hood and Three Sisters. Other notable mountain ranges in the Pacific Northwest include the Coast Mountains, rising on the western end of lower British Columbia, and the Olympic Mountains, which form a circular cluster on the Olympic Peninsula in Washington.

Temperatures tend to be milder on the western side of the Cascade divide, with moderate amounts of rain feeding a green, lush landscape, including a temperate rainforest—the Olympic Peninsula's famed Hoh Rain Forest. In the higher elevations, wooded forest gives way to the alpine, where trees thin out to wide meadows and barren peaks. On the eastern side of the Cascades, where weather is starker, you'll find arid deserts, rolling hills—often sectioned into agricultural lands—and sprawling grasslands in between.

A couple of major rivers carve through the landscape, including British Columbia's Fraser River, the province's longest river at more than 1,367 kilometers (850 miles). The Columbia River's headwaters are in British Columbia, and it empties into the Pacific Ocean at Astoria, Oregon, 805 kilometers (500 miles) away. The Columbia is fed by the Snake and Willamette Rivers and forms much of the state border between Oregon and Washington.

CLIMATE

West of the Cascades

It doesn't always rain in the Pacific Northwest, no matter what you see in the movies. Clouds off the Pacific Ocean do bring rain, plus snow to higher elevations, but precipitation isn't as pronounced as many believe since it primarily takes the form of a light drizzle. Seattle, for example, gets about 37 inches of rain a year—less than New York City. Seattle and Portland both see about 155 rainy days per year, but rarely does more than an inch fall in a day. Vancouver is a bit wetter, with closer to 45 inches of rain per year spread over more than 160 days.

Rainfall is heaviest November-January. Seattle and Vancouver receive little snow, while Portland, slightly inland, sees a few inches a year. Winter temperatures in the

Previous: a ship passing through Seattle's Ballard Locks; Ross Lake in the North Cascades.

cities generally stay above freezing. Summers in Portland are warmest, topping out with averages in the low 80s in August, while Seattle typically experiences mid-70s and Vancouver low 70s. Although the summer boasts the warmest, driest averages of the year, there's a reason Pacific Northwesterners speak ruefully of "Juneuary": Sometimes June feels more like January.

East of the Cascades

The east side of the mountain range is much drier than its western counterpart, since precipitous clouds typically unleash as they cross the Cascades. For comparison, while Seattle receives 37 average inches of rainfall a year, the state's biggest urban center on the east side, Spokane, averages just 16 inches. Oregon's Bend receives about 11 inches to Portland's mid-30s. Temperatures in summer are also generally higher east of the mountains—Bend, for example, is about 2-3 degrees warmer mid-August than Portland—and fall a bit lower in winter.

Mountains 2,000 feet above sea level on either side of the Cascades receive snow late fall-spring, though levels can vary drastically year to year. Skiers will appreciate that the northern Cascades and the Coast Mountains generally receive significant snowfall, while the southern Cascades in Oregon see more sunny days but a smaller snowpack.

ENVIRONMENTAL ISSUES

The Pacific Northwest is known for its prizing of nature. Symbols of the region—on license plates, logos, and T-shirts—often include trees, mountains, whales, and birds. Portland and Seattle especially are known for their "green" ethos and environmentally friendly practices. But the first industries to thrive here were based on resource extraction—logging and fishing, primarily, but also power generation drawing upon natural resources.

Logging was a major industry in the Pacific Northwest in the 19th and into the 20th century. Operations were established in western Oregon, Washington, and British Columbia, including on Vancouver Island. By the late 20th century concerns about wildlife habitat and forest health shook the industry. In the 1990s, the spotted owl became a symbol of the battle between the timber industry and environmentalists, with the latter blaming logging for the owl's population decline. Today timber companies replant forests after harvest, and clear-cutting—removing all vegetation from a section of forest—is rarer.

The fishing industry has also long been significant in the Pacific Northwest, with salmon, shrimp, oysters, and more harvested from the region's waters. Washington fisheries took in more than 350 million pounds of seafood in 2015, as did British Columbia, and Oregon took in about 200 million. But water pollution, dams, and acidification have threatened the region's fisheries in the 20th century and limited salmon spawning habitat, causing population levels to fall. This has effects across the board, with Washington State's signature orca whales now threatened due to reduced salmon numbers, one of their primary food sources.

Plants and Animals

TREES

The signature tree of the Pacific Northwest is the evergreen, or conifer. In the western forests of the Cascades, Douglas firs grow to towering heights. Western hemlock, with smaller and fewer needles, are similar, and both are sought for timber harvest. On the east side of the Cascades, the brushy, lighter green ponderosa pine is widespread in areas such as the high desert of Bend; you can spot it by looking for its reddish trunk, much lighter in color than a fir tree's bark. Also found here is the fragrant juniper tree.

In the lowland rainforests, western red cedars can be found. These huge specimens can grow hundreds of feet tall, and some here are more than 1,000 years old. In North America, they're second only to redwoods in size. You can identify cedars by looking for their flat fan of needles, less brushy than fir. The bark of the western red cedar was used by coastal Native American and First Nations tribes in Washington and British Columbia for canoes as well as mats and baskets.

A rare but well-loved tree in the Pacific Northwest is the western larch, which looks like an evergreen in summer, but in autumn bursts into brilliant shades of yellow and orange before its needles fall off.

Much of the forest in the Pacific Northwest has been logged at one point or another, but there are still old-growth forests of western hemlocks and Douglas firs more than 500 years old. Naturalists estimate that less than 13 percent of the original woodlands of the Pacific Northwest remain old-growth. You can find old-growth forests in protected wilderness areas including Mount Rainier National Park and Olympic National Park, or around Mount Hood and in remote stretches of Vancouver Island.

While evergreens take center stage in this region, there are also plenty of leafy trees, including alder, maple, and oak, scattered on both sides of the Cascades.

PLANTS

In the rainforests and more temperate western forests of the Cascades, deer fern and bracken fern are common. Another common groundcover plant, salal, is found in coastal forests and often collected for use in floral arrangements. Hundreds of species of mosses are also found across western British Columbia, Washington, and Oregon, responsible for much of the lush feel of the western Pacific Northwest. On the east side of the Cascade crest, notable plants include bunchgrass, sagebrush, and brittle root.

MUSHROOMS

The dark forests of the Pacific Northwest are havens for many kinds of fungi. Smaller mushrooms tucked into wet soil west of the Cascades include delicate fairy ring mushrooms and squat boletes. Many locals enjoy foraging for edible mushrooms, with chanterelles and morels (and occasionally truffles) prevalent in Pacific Northwest forests. Note that eating wild mushrooms is unadvisable unless you are 100 percent sure of what you've found, since some can cause illness or death.

FLOWERS

Oregon is known for its roses, Washington for its rhododendrons and tulips, and British Columbia for its dogwood flowers. But the forests and grasslands of the Pacific Northwest are also known for their stunning wildflowers, of which there are hundreds of varieties. Wildflowers bloom from spring through late summer around the Pacific Northwest, starting with famously large swaths of yellow balsamroot along the Columbia River Gorge in early April. On the east side of the Cascades, flowers like phlox and larkspur pop up in the dry grasslands. In southwest Oregon you'll find the western azalea, a pinkish flower. Three-pointed trilliums grow in deep forests below 6,000 feet.

Alpine slopes near the timberline in the Cascades erupt into color around late July, depending on the weather. Meadows around Paradise at Washington's Mount Rainier and above Timberline Lodge on Mount Hood in Oregon are especially known for their displays. Common wildflowers found around the Cascades include lupine, which has purplish blue petals, and the fiery orange Indian paintbrush. Avalanche lilies, delicate white and yellow flowers, often appear right after the snowmelt.

LAND MAMMALS

The Pacific Northwest forests and plains are full of land mammals, and even species that were once hunted to near extinction in the region—like wolves—have managed to make comebacks. Urban areas see more raccoons and coyotes, plus countless deer, which have learned to adapt to the human population boom. Take note while driving at night; everything from a possum to an elk might cause a driver to swerve.

Bears

Black bears roam the forests of Washington, Oregon, and British Columbia, typically in coastal rainforests and high-elevation alpine zones. The species is smaller than grizzly bears, and their diet consists of grasses, horsetail, ants, grubs, and berries. They'll also eat the carcasses of larger animals killed by other species. Some go into a kind of hibernation in dens in the winter, though not all do. Black bears are not innately dangerous to humans, but once these scavengers discover human food they will continue to seek it out, upturning trash cans and raiding campsites in areas where human presence abuts the wilderness. In the absence of a food source, black bears are aggressive to humans only in the case of vulnerable cubs; if you encounter a black bear on a hiking trail, make lots of noise and wave your arms, and they'll generally run away. Do not approach black bears or cubs under any circumstances, and never feed or make food available to bears.

Only a handful of grizzly bears remain in Washington's North Cascades, with many more in the forests of British Columbia, though typically far removed from the Vancouver area. Grizzlies were hunted throughout the Cascades as trophies, and conservation efforts are under way to bring the population back to its historic levels.

Elk

The North American elk is present throughout Washington, Oregon, and British Columbia, roaming high meadows in the summer and returning to the lowlands for the rest of the year. In colder seasons, they're light brown in color, but can become a brilliant reddish brown by midsummer. Males have large, multipoint antlers that they shed in late winter. Elk largely avoid human interactions, but herds may move through areas near roads, and their size—males can weigh up to 1,000 pounds—makes them a dangerous road hazard.

The Olympic National Park area is known for its Roosevelt elk, the largest subspecies in North America. In fall, their mating season is marked by the sound of bugling, a distinctive shriek that serves as a mating call.

Cougars

Cougars, or mountain lions, are a type of large wildcat that lives across the Pacific Northwest. They are predators capable of taking down an elk or a moose, animals significantly larger than they are. Cougars in the region tend to weigh around 100-150 pounds. They're found in large swaths of forest in the Cascades, Olympics, Coast Mountains, and coastal hills of Oregon. While the giant cats are known for their ability to attack, they rarely target humans; unleashed small pets in regions where residential areas border the forest are the more common victims. If you encounter a cougar, back away calmly and do not run; like most wildlife, the animals generally avoid humans and are not considered a serious risk for outdoor recreationists in the Pacific Northwest.

Beavers

Beavers appear in waterways across the Pacific Northwest and are one of Oregon's signature animals. They grow to about 40-60 pounds, making them the largest rodents in North America. Once trapped for their thick pelts, the animals live near water and, using their sharp front teeth, cut down trees and build dams to create ponds, then lodges, or dens, near the pond surface. They can sometimes be spotted swimming, their large, flat tails distinguishing them from the similar muskrat. Beavers can get aggressive when cornered, and sometimes slap their tails on the water in warning.

Other Land Mammals

Hundreds of other mammals live in the Pacific Northwest, from mice to moose. Mountain goats live in remote, rocky, mountainous areas, including the Olympic Mountains—these aren't native to the area, but rather were brought in by hunters in the 19th century. Cascade goats, however, are native. Pacific Northwest forests are also home to wolverines, white-tailed deer, and gray foxes. In the high mountains, small furry creatures like pikas and marmots hide in alpine meadows—listen for the high whistle made by the latter. Some people even say Sasquatch, a mythical creature, lives in the Pacific Northwest woods, but no one's ever been able to prove it.

SEALIFE

Orcas

Killer whales, or orcas, are a signature Pacific Northwest animal, long revered by Native American tribes and beloved by current area residents. The black-and-white sea creatures are actually members of the dolphin family, and despite their name are not dangerous to humans. Long known to be a highly intelligent and trainable animal, killer whales have been attractions in marine theme park performance shows for years, and many of the country's captive whales came from the resident pods of Puget Sound. Whale-watching is a popular activity in the communities around the Salish Sea: the San Juan Islands, Victoria, and other parts of Vancouver Island. Spotters look for black dorsal fins moving through the water. You can sometimes see the whales poke their noses out of the water in what's called a "spy hop."

Three resident pods live in Puget Sound, spending much of the year around the San Juan Islands before heading out to the Pacific to feed along the coast south to California. Whale experts know each resident by sight, thanks to unique markings on their bodies and tails, and each one is given a number designation and a name. The matriarch of one pod lived to be more than 100 years old before dying in the mid-2010s. Sometimes orcas are even spotted off Seattle's waterfront or playing alongside commuter ferries in Elliott Bay. These whales, about 75 in total, primarily eat salmon, so the strength of the salmon population in Pacific Northwest rivers is crucial to their survival. Other transient groups of orcas also pass through the region, often with a broader diet of seals and sea lions in addition to fish.

Gray Whales

Gray whales are also a common sight in the region. They're larger than killer whales at almost 50 feet long and are filter feeders—rather than using teeth to eat, they sieve ocean sediment using a horny substance in their upper jaw called baleen to catch small crustaceans. Gray whales are recognized by their long, curved backs, which pop out of the water as they exhale through their blowholes. They travel annually between Alaska's Bering Sea south to the Sea of Cortez near Mexico, passing through the Pacific Northwest's waters twice a year, sometimes traveling 75 miles per day. They most often show up off the Pacific coast in Oregon or the western coast of Vancouver Island.

Salmon

Long a food staple of Native American tribes, salmon is the signature fish of the Pacific Northwest. There are several types of salmon, including coho, pink, and sockeye, but the most beloved is the chinook, or king salmon, which are about 10-15 pounds each, though historically have grown to more than 100 pounds in this region. The chinook are born in the giant rivers of the Pacific Northwest, including the Columbia and Snake Rivers in Washington and the Fraser River in British Columbia. They travel out to the Pacific Ocean to feed before returning to their birthplace to spawn, or reproduce. Since the major rivers of the region are dammed and as the ocean and river waters have been polluted by human industry, salmon levels have declined. Historically, up to 16 million salmon came back to the Columbia River every year to spawn, but the current average is around half a million annually. Salmon is also farmed, controversially, in spots around Vancouver Island.

Other Sealife

Sea otters and harbor seals swim in the shallow coastal waters off Washington and Oregon. Sea lions, a larger animal that breeds in California and Mexico, flock to the Oregon Coast in spring to feed, often affecting fish populations. You can spot them on docks in harbor towns, such as Oregon's Astoria and Newport; when they show up by the hundreds, whole marinas can be unusable for weeks. The waters of the Pacific Ocean and Salish Sea also teem with kelp and eelgrass, making it a rich habitat for a plethora of fish. Shellfish including oysters and mussels are farmed in the shallow tidal flats of Puget Sound and other small bays and inlets. Whidbey Island is particularly known for its Penn Cove mussels, and the Long Beach area of southwestern Washington is known for its oysters. Perhaps the most mysterious creature in the Salish Sea is the giant Pacific octopus, which lives underwater and may be the largest form of octopus alive, reaching up to 150 pounds. Its arms can have a 20-foot span, and it can change color based on mood and activity. Divers in Puget Sound, where they're commonly found, used to find them and wrestle them for sport.

BIRDS

The skies of the Pacific Northwest are teeming—Oregon alone is home to more than 400 bird species. The region's best-known bird is the bald eagle, which clings to treetops in Washington near the Canadian border. Bald eagles have wingspans of up to eight feet, with adults sporting the memorable white head and dark brown body. The biggest birds are female, and they often nest in the very tops of trees near bays, rivers, and estuaries, close to their food source, fish. While they're spotted across the Pacific Northwest, the Skagit River area, near Anacortes, is a popular place to see the birds.

Other raptors in the area include small hawks, such as the Cooper's hawk in southern Oregon and the red-shouldered hawk in the Rogue and Willamette river valleys, known for its rust-colored shoulder patches. Osprey, which sport black-and-white heads on a brown body, are prominent west of the Cascades throughout the Pacific Northwest and sometimes show up east of the crest. Peregrine falcons, which have been measured traveling more than 200 miles an hour as they spot prey and scoop it up, migrate throughout the region, and prairie falcons show up east of the Cascades.

Go to any seaside area in British Columbia, Washington, or Oregon and you'll find seagulls. Other shorebirds include great blue herons, whose wingspans reach up to six feet. The crane-like birds are found around the Pacific Northwest except in grasslands and high forests. They stay very still before striking their prey.

Owls are present throughout the region in wooded areas, including the great horned owl with its yellow eyes and tufted ears. They're largely found west of the Cascades, particularly in Oregon. The northern spotted owl is rarer, and is a mottled brown and white. They're famously unafraid of humans. Because they live in old-growth forests in Oregon, Washington, and British Columbia, protecting their habitat has become a controversial topic in the logging industry.

REPTILES

Snakes are found throughout the Pacific Northwest, but many are harmless. Parts of eastern Washington and Oregon are home to the western rattlesnake, the only venomous reptile indigenous to the area. Hikers should take care in those regions, though injurious bites on humans are rare, and even less often deadly. Other local reptiles include native small turtles, including the painted turtle found in western Washington and Oregon, often sunning itself on logs in ponds. The western pond turtle was once prevalent but has largely disappeared from its lowland habitat in western Oregon, and has been the subject of a repopulation effort by conservationists. The northern alligator lizard is about four inches long and lives on the Pacific coast, eating everything from crickets to snails.

ARACHNIDS

Black widows are found on the eastern side of the region, and while their bites can be serious, they're a rare occurrence. Female black widows have a distinctive red hourglass pattern on their belly. Black widows are found in dark places such as woodpiles, crawl spaces, and garages.

AMPHIBIANS

The lakes and waterways of the region are rich with frogs and a wide range of salamanders, including the coastal giant salamander, one of the largest found anywhere. They only live in the Cascade Mountains and the hills of southwest Washington, living under rocks in cold mountain streams, and can grow up to a foot long.

History

EARLY HISTORY

Humans first arrived in the Pacific Northwest more than 13,000 years ago, thought to have migrated from Asia across the ice sheets that linked the continents. They reached a region that had been shaped by the Glacial Lake Missoula, and settled throughout the Americas, ancestors of Native Americans and First Nations peoples.

Various indigenous hunter-gatherer tribes lived in the Pacific Northwest over the centuries before contact with white settlers. Coastal communities, including the Haida, Nuu-chah-nulth, Squamish, Skokomish, Klallam, Muckleshoot, Quileute, Quinault, Makah, and Tillamook peoples, relied heavily on the ocean's rich marinelife—salmon and whale specifically. Many of these tribes lived in wooden longhouses. Western red cedar trees were a major resource, their trunks used for homes, canoes, and fishing structures. The trees' strong, supple bark was used to weave baskets as well as clothing. Many of the coastal communities' art forms—such as paintings as well as totem and story poles—depicted the area's wildlife, such as the orca.

Inland lived the people of the Northwest Plateau. Many of these communities were centered around the region's great rivers. In British Columbia, the Lillooet and Nlaka'pamux people lived around the Fraser River, while the Okanogan people lived farther east. In what's now Washington State, the Columbia Plateau and Yakama tribes based themselves on the eastern side of the Cascades. Molalla, Klamath, and Umatilla peoples lived in Oregon. In the grasslands, prairies, and high desert, these communities hunted bison, birds, and deer, as well as fished for salmon in the rivers, foraged for roots and berries, and traded with other tribes. Willow and sagebrush were used for weaving.

COLONIALISM

White colonialists first came to the region in a very small trickle. By sea, white explorers reached the region looking for a "Northwest Passage" that would quickly link trade between Europe and Asia. Along the Pacific Northwest coast, ships would pop into bays and rivers in hopes of finding the mythical water route, then leave after naming a few mountains and rivers. Britain's George Vancouver, a naval officer and explorer in the 18th century, was perhaps the most notable.

By land, fur traders flocked here for the abundant wildlife, particularly the beaver and its warm, silky pelts. Spanish, American, British, and Russian settlements were established from present-day Alaska down to Oregon. Hudson's Bay Company had trading posts around the region, and Native Americans and First Nations people participated in the trading. Relations between the groups were generally peaceful on a large scale, though disagreements did occur.

Lewis and Clark Expedition

In the early 19th century, while the fur trade was still making its way west, U.S. President Thomas Jefferson directed two American explorers, Meriwether Lewis and William Clark, to explore the mid-continent Louisiana Purchase and beyond to the Pacific coast. The expedition was intended to document the unknown region with maps and records of its wildlife and native populations. At the time, the U.S. government had its eye on claiming territory from other European nations vying for it. Over the course of two and a half years, the expedition traveled about 8,000 miles, from St. Louis, Missouri, to the mouth of the Columbia River and back.

In their travels, the explorers met with dozens of tribes, and throughout the journey tribal assistance and guidance was key to the party's survival. In present-day North Dakota, the group added a fur trapper and his Native American wife, Sacagawea, to their numbers; she had been captured from a tribe to the west, and her interpretive skills turned out to be a huge boon to the expedition. She traveled with the party all the way to the coast.

The Oregon Trail

In the mid-19th century, the Oregon Trail popularized movement to the Pacific Northwest. With American territories established in modern-day Washington and Oregon, word got out that there was room for pioneers to settle in the rich farmlands. The route comprised approximately 2,000 miles of interwoven roads and trails between the Missouri and Willamette Rivers. Many settled in the Willamette Valley, with others peeling off to California or present-day Washington.

The expensive, arduous journey took several months. People walked alongside their few belongings and supplies, pulled in wagons by oxen. The harsh weather and disease took a large toll. Native Americans, many of whom traded with white settlements at the time, started to feel pressure as more and more easterners showed up to claim land. While violent interactions with native groups were rare, an infamous incident involved one of the Oregon Trail's early pioneers, Marcus Whitman. He and his wife settled near today's Walla Walla and built a religious mission; they were killed by local Cayuse Indians, whose population suffered from a measles outbreak that was blamed on the Whitmans. Nearly a half-million people eventually worked their way west on the Oregon Trail by the time railways replaced it.

STATEHOOD

In the second half of the 19th century, Oregon and Washington territories converted to statehood, and the colony of British Columbia joined Canada as a province.

In the 1850s, while the United States teetered on the brink of civil war, Oregon Territory was contested between slave-owning and non-slave-owning states. Delegates from around the territory gathered for a constitutional convention and voted against slavery as well as against allowing free African Americans to live in the brand-new state. Oregon became the 33rd state in 1859.

North of the Columbia River, Washington Territory was long contested between the United States and Great Britain. Eventually the two parties agreed on the 49th parallel as the border, though the American Civil War put a pause on the formation of new states for a time. In 1889, Washington became a state along with several others—Montana and the Dakotas—making it the 42nd in the union.

The fur trading region north of Washington Territory was British-controlled but had few settlers in the mid-19th century, although after the 49th parallel border was established, the Hudson's Bay Company moved its regional trading headquarters from its location near the Columbia River to Victoria on Vancouver Island. In the 1850s the rumor of gold in Fraser Canyon started a gold rush, and settlers quickly filled the mainland. The area built up through a second rush, the Cariboo gold rush, and in 1866 several British colonies and trading districts, including Vancouver Island, became a colony of British Columbia. Though settlers there considered joining the United States, which would have linked the American territories of modern-day Washington and Alaska, the region elected to join the Canadian Confederation.

Native American tribes in Washington and Oregon signed treaties with the U.S. government, which relegated some to separate reservation lands and granted many limited fishing rights. Canadian First Nations tribes signed fewer treaties, and many tribes hold reserves of land.

WORLD WAR II

During World War II, the Pacific Northwest, and Washington in particular, became a focus given the region's position on the West Coast. Puget Sound held a naval base and a submarine base, and was a strategic Japan-facing port. Seattle-based airplane maker Boeing hid its factories from possible Japanese air raids by disguising them as neighborhoods with fake grass, streets, and houses on their roofs.

Following the attack on Pearl Harbor in Hawaii, then a U.S. territory, the federal government instituted a discriminatory policy of Japanese American internment, forcing 120,000 citizens on the West Coast to relocate to centralized camps in California, Idaho, and farther inland. Japanese Americans on Bainbridge Island near Seattle were the first to be moved in 1942. Thriving Japanese American communities in Seattle and Portland were forced out, leaving businesses and homes behind. Reparations were eventually paid to surviving detainees in the 1980s, and President George H.W. Bush made a formal apology on behalf of the U.S. government.

CONTEMPORARY TIMES

Post-war, Washington, Oregon, and British Columbia thrived economically, the forests fueling a logging industry that had begun in the 19th century and grew to become a powerhouse in the early 20th. Logging was at its height first during the 1920s, then again through the 1970s. But by the turn of the 21st century, as conservation and declining demand hit the timber companies, the industry sank in the Pacific Northwest. Other sectors took over, from aerospace to, especially, technology. Boeing was already one of the world's most prominent airplane manufacturers, and the computers were coming.

Microsoft moved to Seattle in 1986, the same year it went public, and Portland-based Intel rose to prominence in the 1990s. Microsoft made software and Intel designed the microprocessor chips that made personal computing possible; the companies came to define the tech character of the Pacific Northwest. Today each company employs more than 100,000 people, and smaller tech companies have emerged in the region as well. The 21st century brought a new player to Seattle: Amazon. What started as a bookselling operation in 1994 grew to become an online giant—a general retailer and tech company—that's reshaped Seattle.

Meanwhile, Vancouver became Canada's third-largest city thanks to its seaport, a crossroads for the area's lumber that needed to be shipped elsewhere. As Canada's West Coast hub, it's also the ideal location to import and export goods to Asia. While agriculture and fishing are important industries in the entire province, the Vancouver area has become known for tourism—especially ecotourism—some international banking, and manufacturing. The city is also a center for Canadian (and some American) film and television production.

The Pacific Northwest is also known for its outdoor recreation brands. Sports giant Nike started in Oregon as a running shoemaker in the 1970s. Seattle boasts hiking and camping retailer REI. Dozens of smaller companies making gear for outdoor sports are also based here, including Oregon's Columbia Sportswear, Seattle's Outdoor Research, and Vancouver's Arc'teryx. Tourism is also a huge industry for the area, with visitors spending more than $30 billion per year in Washington and Oregon alone, and British Columbia pulling in about another $75 billion. The entire corridor from Vancouver to Portland is known for its recent rapid population growth, going up about 5 percent between 2012 and 2017 according to censuses.

Local Culture

DIVERSITY

According to the U.S. Census Bureau's 2017 population estimates, 69.5 percent of people in Washington identify as white, 8.6 percent Asian, 4.1 percent African American, 1.9 percent American Indian, and 12.4 percent Hispanic or Latino. In Oregon, 76.4 percent of the population identify as white, 4.5 percent Asian, 2.1 percent as African American, 1.8 percent American Indian, and 12.8 percent Hispanic or Latino.

The Canadian Census Program reports that in 2016, 30 percent of British Columbia's population is reported as a "visible minority," or non-white—most of Asian heritage—while First Nations people account for about 6 percent.

INDIGENOUS CULTURES

Washington State is home to 39 federally recognized tribes, and Oregon is home to 9. Some reservation lands are held by individual tribes or confederations of tribes. Reservation holdings vary, from small towns to rural lands to centralized businesses such as casinos. Other Native American groups have little or no separate lands. In Canada, some First Nations groups live on reserves across the province; there are more than 300 of them in Canada, with British Columbia home to 198 First Nations groups.

RELIGION

Christian religions are the most prominently represented in the region, though the Pacific Northwest is known for being secular. According to a 2014 survey done by the Pew Research Center, 61 percent of the adult population of Washington identifies as Christian (compared to about 70 percent nationally), with 25 percent evangelical Protestant and 17 percent Catholic. Muslim and Jewish faiths each make up about 1 percent. The same survey found that 61 percent of the adult population of Oregon identifies as Christian, with 29 percent evangelical Protestant and 12 percent Catholic. About 2 percent are Jewish and 1 percent Muslim. Both Oregon and Washington had over 30 percent of adults reporting as unaffiliated, well over the national average of 23 percent.

In British Columbia, the 2001 Canadian Census reported that the province was about 55 percent Christian. The region is 31 percent Protestant, 17 percent Catholic, and about 36 percent unaffiliated.

LITERATURE

The Pacific Northwest has a rich literary history. In Seattle, poet Theodore Roethke won the Pulitzer Prize for his works, many of which reference the natural world. Oregon's Beverly Cleary is a young adult genre giant, having written classics including her Ramona series. Oregon-based fiction writer and countercultural icon Ken Kesey became famous for *One Flew Over the Cuckoo's Nest.* Ursula K. Le Guin, writer of landmark science fiction and fantasy with a psychological bent, and Katherine Dunn of *Geek Love* fame made Portland their homes. Novelist Chuck Palahniuk also lives in Portland, writing dark, thoughtful books including the famous *Fight Club.*

Raymond Carver, renowned for his short stories, hailed from Oregon and was raised in Yakima; his stories about the brutal realities of midcentury American life are famous for their sparse style. In the mid-20th century, several Beat poets headed north from California to live and work in fire lookouts in the North Cascades, later writing about their lonely summers spent atop mountains. Gary Snyder worked on Sourdough Mountain Lookout and wrote several poems about the experience, many collected in his book *Look Out.* Jack Kerouac staffed the Desolation Peak Lookout and later wrote the novel *Desolation Angels* based on a diary of his time there.

VISUAL ARTS

Independent art icon Miranda July—known for her art installations and projects, fiction, and film—is originally from Oregon. Painter Chuck Close, famous for his large-scale abstract-realist pieces, works out of New York City but was born and raised in Washington and is a graduate of the University of Washington.

Glass artist Dale Chihuly, one of the most celebrated glass artists in the country, lives and works in Seattle. His glassblown sculptures appear in museums and businesses around the world. The Pacific Northwest is a central hub for glassmaking and glass art, partially thanks to the Pilchick Glass School he founded.

British Columbia's most famous artist was Emily Carr, who painted landscapes and modernist works. She was also a writer and focused on First Nations and nature themes in her paintings.

Gus Van Sant, a filmmaker known for prestigious indie movies including *My Own Private Idaho, Good Will Hunting,* and *Milk,* lives in Portland, as does director Todd Haynes, who has chronicled queer and outsider issues in movies like *Far From Heaven* and *Carol.* In Seattle, director Lynn Shelton works to capture the quirky, soulful, and sometimes humorous side of the Pacific Northwest in movies like *Your Sister's Sister* and *Humpday.*

MUSIC AND DANCE

In the 1990s, the Pacific Northwest was synonymous with grunge music, largely thanks to Nirvana, Pearl Jam, and the music label Sub Pop. But the region also has a history of jazz. The Central District was home to Seattle's black community in the early 20th century and became a hub for jazz clubs by the 1920s. Jackson Street held several performance spots, legal and not, and though the Depression of the 1930s wiped many of them out, the scene persisted into the 1940s. Today, Dimitriou's Jazz Alley is the center of the Seattle jazz performance world. In the 2010s, Seattle rapper Macklemore hit it big on the music charts, soon defined by his hits "Thrift Shop" and "Same Love" about gay marriage. He wasn't the only hip-hop artist to emerge out of Seattle, though, with rap pioneer Sir Mix-a-Lot before him and the experimental Shabazz Palaces after him. Punk act Sleater-Kinney started in Olympia before moving to Portland. Olympia is one of the smaller hubs for progressive live music in the Pacific Northwest, joined by college towns Eugene and Bellingham.

Back in the 1960s, Portland's Kingsmen earned fame for "Louie Louie." Now the city is largely known as a hub for indie rock, including the late Elliott Smith, The Decemberists, Modest Mouse, and the Shins. Woody Guthrie, one of the country's most famous singers of the genre, was once hired by the Bonneville Power Administration on the Columbia River to write songs about their dams and waterways; he penned works like "Roll On, Columbia."

Vancouver had its own little wing of the grunge scene in the 1990s, while at the same time local crooner Sarah McLachlan found international success with her languid ballads and created the female-centered Lilith Fair during a time when summer music festival rosters were largely dominated by men. In the 21st century the city became known for producing indie pop act The New Pornographers and pop singers Carly Rae Jepsen and Michael Buble.

FOOD

When people talk about Pacific Northwest cuisine, they're largely referring to two things: seafood and seasonality. Seafood is popular across the region for good reason; salmon, oysters, and mussels are all pulled from local waters. Harking back to how Native American tribes ate centuries ago, salmon cooked on a cedar plank is considered a classic. Apples from Washington and pears from Oregon are signature crops. The area's general environmental ethos and proximity to rich agricultural regions have fueled the affection for seasonality and sustainability, and farm-to-table restaurants flourish across the Pacific Northwest.

Thanks to the region's proximity to Asia and a relatively strong Asian population, Vietnamese and Japanese cuisines are popular as well, and Pacific Islander foods are lately appearing in everything from food trucks to high-end restaurants.

Coffee has long been identified with the Pacific Northwest, with Starbucks based in Seattle, but the region is full of indie coffee shops and roasters where you can relax, chat, and work with a strong cup.

In Washington and Oregon, enterprises that serve alcohol must also make some form of food available, so the line between a bar and a restaurant is often fuzzy and sometimes nonexistent. In general, expect to have food options at any drinking establishment, except perhaps a brewery or winery, as tap rooms operate under different guidelines. Also notable is that Portland and Seattle in particular tend to have good happy hour deals—sometimes twice a day, early in the evening and late at night—on food as well as drink.

Essentials

Transportation

AIR

Seattle

There is no "Seattle Airport." When approaching the Emerald City, flights land at the **Sea-Tac International Airport** (SEA, 17801 International Blvd., 800/544-1965, www.portseattle.org/sea-tac), so named because it sits between the cities of Seattle and Tacoma. Although its name is half and half, it's undeniably the Seattle airport and lies about 15 miles south of the city.

The vast majority of visitors who fly to the Seattle area come to Sea-Tac. A few flights from Boeing Field (a mostly private airport near downtown) go to San Juan Island, Orcas Island, and Port Angeles on the Olympic Peninsula through **Kenmore Air** (866/435-9524, www.kenmoreair.com). Kenmore also runs floatplane trips that leave from Lake Union to Victoria, Port Angeles, and spots all around the San Juan Islands. In Everett, north of Seattle, commercial flights from **Paine Field** (3220 100th St. SW, www.painefield.com) began in 2018 to Portland, Los Angeles, Las Vegas, and more.

The **Bellingham International Airport** (BLI, 4255 Mitchell Way, www.portofbellingham.com) is just 20 miles south of the Canadian border and about 95 miles north of Seattle. It's generally thought of as a regional option for those living in the area and a low-cost option for travelers from Vancouver and Seattle who don't mind the extra drive.

AIRPORT TRANSPORTATION

To reach downtown Seattle from the airport via public transportation, take the **Central Link light rail** (888/889-6368, www.soundtransit.org). The train runs to Westlake Center in downtown Seattle with stops in neighborhoods like Columbia City, Rainier Beach, the International District, and the stadium area; it then continues on to Capitol Hill and the University of Washington. The trip from the airport to Westlake is about 40 minutes, and passengers can buy tickets ($3 each way for a full trip) at the station before boarding. (Don't try to board without a ticket because fare enforcement staff will regularly board the train to make sure everyone has a valid ticket.) Trains arrive every 7-15 minutes and operate 5am-1am Monday-Saturday and 6am-midnight Sunday. The station is located across from the main airport terminal; exit on the mezzanine level to the parking garage and follow signs for the Link Light Rail.

Taxis depart Sea-Tac airport on the third level of the parking garage; look for a row of yellow cabs. A dispatcher is usually managing the line. A set fare of $40 covers trips from the downtown Seattle district to the airport; the trip from the airport to downtown is not set, but will cost about the same. Ride-sharing services like **Uber** (www.uber.com) and **Lyft** (www.lyft.com) will pick up from the airport in a designated area of the 3rd floor of the parking garage; look for signs. Cabs are subject to the same traffic considerations as private cars, and congestion on I-5 can be intense. Trips from the airport to downtown Seattle can take as little as 20 minutes or over an hour during rush hour.

Shuttle vans can also take travelers to downtown Seattle or throughout the city. **Shuttle Express** (425/981-7000, http://shuttleexpress.hudsonltd.net, $18) organizes trips to hotels or the convention center in downtown Seattle. Advance reservations are not required but are recommended, especially during peak travel times.

Previous: Portland Streetcar; a bridge on the Oregon Coast.

CAR RENTALS

The **car rental center** (3150 S. 160th St., www.portseattle.org/sea-tac) is separate from the main airport, accessible via regular shuttles that leave outside the baggage-claim area. The energy-efficient facility holds 13 different car rental companies, and shuttles run 24 hours a day.

Portland

Although Portland is the smallest of the Pacific Northwest's major cities, the **Portland International Airport** (PDX, 7000 NE Airport Way, 503/460-4234, www.pdx.com) remains a thriving airport, located 12 miles northeast of the city near the Columbia River. Flights depart for Asia, Europe, and U.S. destinations including Hawaii and Alaska. Nonstop service within Oregon is available to North Bend, Medford, Eugene, Klamath Falls, Redmond, and Pendleton.

AIRPORT TRANSPORTATION

The **TriMet/MAX Light Rail** (503/238-7433, www.trimet.org) Red Line trains reach downtown Portland from the airport in less than 40 minutes. Trains run 4:45am-11:45pm daily, and the adult fare costs $2.50. **White Van Shuttle** (503/774-9755, www.whitevanshuttle.com) provides daily shuttle service from the airport to locations within Portland. Reservations are required and can be made online; extra people are only $5 each.

Taxis are also available at the airport, and trips between the airport and downtown Portland run about $35. Many hotels offer courtesy shuttles downtown; for a list, visit www.portofportland.com. Ride-sharing services like **Uber** (www.uber.com) and **Lyft** (www.lyft.com) can also pick you up from the airport.

CAR RENTALS

Car rental companies are located at the airport across from the baggage-claim area. More are located just off the airport grounds, accessible by pickup vans on the airport's lower roadway.

Vancouver

The large **Vancouver International Airport** (YVR, 3211 Grant McConachie Way, Richmond, 604/207-7077, www.yvr.ca) is located in the city of Richmond, just 11 kilometers southwest of Vancouver. As Canada's westernmost major airport, it provides service to Australia, New Zealand, Asia, and Europe, as well as much of North America.

If you're stuck at the airport or miss your flight, the **Fairmont Vancouver Airport** (3111 Grant McConachie Way, 604/207-5200, www.fairmont.com/vancouver-airport-richmond) is walkable from the terminal and has nearly 400 rooms with airport and runway views.

AIRPORT TRANSPORTATION

The **Canada Line** (604/953-3333, www.translink.bc.ca) is a rapid-transit rail system that takes travelers from the airport to downtown Vancouver in less than 30 minutes. Service runs 5am-1am daily, and adult tickets cost $4.10 (plus $5 for the Canada Line YVR AddFare).

Long-distance buses leave from the airport to Whistler, Victoria, and around Washington State. **Pacific Coach Lines** (800/661-1725, www.pacificcoach.com) provides service to Whistler and Victoria; tickets are available in the International terminal on Level 2. **QuickShuttle** (800/665-2122, www.quickcoach.com) connects to U.S. cities such as Bellingham and Seattle; reservations can be made online.

Taxis from the airport to downtown Vancouver cost about $35. A number of downtown Vancouver hotels also run courtesy shuttles.

CAR RENTALS

Most car rentals at the airport are located within the terminal on the ground floor. The drive to downtown Vancouver takes about 20 minutes when there's no traffic, but longer during morning and evening rush hours.

TRAIN

Several major **Amtrak** (800/872-7245, www.amtrak.com) lines run through the Pacific Northwest. Most trains offer wireless Internet access and bistro cars that serve a limited menu and drinks.

- **Cascades:** Travels from Vancouver, BC, to Eugene in central Oregon with stops in Seattle and Portland. (Business Class seats on the Cascades trains offer more room.)
- **Coast Starlight:** Travels from Seattle to Portland continuing on to Los Angeles. For longer trips, sleeper cars offer "roomettes" with simple bunk beds and larger rooms with private bathrooms.
- **Empire Builder:** This east-west line connects both Portland and Seattle to Chicago and Milwaukee; it has sleeper accommodations, but no wireless Internet.

BUS

Greyhound (800/231-2222, www.greyhound.com) operates routes between Vancouver, Portland, and Seattle, as well as Olympic Peninsula destinations such as Port Angeles, Sequim, and Port Townsend, and Oregon Coast spots such as Cannon Beach, Florence, and Astoria. However, service outside of major cities may not be common, and public transportation within those regions is limited. Travelers without cars in those areas may find it difficult to reach sights and services.

Although owned by Greyhound, **BoltBus** (877/265-8287, www.boltbus.com) is more popular with younger travelers. Buses travel from central train stations in Vancouver, Seattle, and Portland, and continue down to major cities in California. Fares start low, as little as $1 for a trip, but those deals sell out quickly. Buses offer plug-ins and wireless Internet, as well as reserved seating.

CAR

When driving around the Pacific Northwest, orient yourself using **I-5,** the major interstate highway that runs north to south, parallel (but far inland) from the Pacific coast. It's by far the quickest route from Portland to Seattle and Seattle to Vancouver, though it stops at the U.S.-Canada border. Running east to west across the United States is **I-90,** which crosses the country from Seattle all the way to Chicago and Boston. In Oregon, **I-84** travels northwest from Salt Lake City to Portland. In Canada, **Highway 1,** or the Trans-Canada Highway, runs east-west, making it less useful for a traveler adding Vancouver to a Washington and Oregon trip.

Interstate highways generally have speed limits of 60 or 70 miles per hour and are the fastest, but not the most scenic route—though mountain passes are beautiful no matter the size of the road. Interstates are also prone to traffic congestion near cities, especially in mornings and late afternoons when business commuters are on the roads.

Closer to the coast, **U.S. 101** curves around the top of the Olympic Peninsula and then continues south near the Pacific coast all the way to the Oregon-California border and beyond. In some places it's a scenic wonder on the very edge of the rocky cliffs; at other times, the road travels far inland to the rural Pacific Northwest. Much of that stretch is a single lane in each direction, which requires careful attention from drivers. Slow down around curves and keep an eye out for cyclists on the small shoulders.

Car and RV Rentals

Seattle, Portland, and Vancouver airports have car rental counters from a variety of companies, including **Avis** (888/583-6369, www.avis.com), **Dollar** (800/800-5252, www.dollar.com), **Hertz** (800/654-3131, www.hertz.com), and **National** (www.nationalcar.com), with other companies represented in nearby off-airport locations. Cars can be booked online directly from the car rental company or through a reputable travel website such as **Expedia** (www.expedia.com) or **Kayak** (www.kayak.com). Prices can fluctuate wildly throughout the year, spiking during summer travel season, winter holidays, and large conventions, but generally a weekend car rental in

Seattle runs about $25-40 per day, Vancouver $14-30 per day (in U.S. dollars), and Portland $17-40 per day.

While prices and requirements vary, you'll generally need a credit card and driver's license, and must be over the age of 25. The age requirement may be waived if you have plane tickets to and from the local airport. Drivers with licenses issued in a language other than English may be required to show an International Driver's License in addition to their own. If you plan to drop your rental car at a location other than where you picked it up, there may be additional fees involved, particularly if you cross the border into Canada, and requirements may differ for citizens of different countries.

The narrow, winding roads of the Pacific Northwest mountains and coastal areas may be difficult to navigate in a large RV, while the bigger cities have few campgrounds nearby with RV-ready services. Nevertheless, RVs can be a handy way to explore the far-flung regions of the Northwest. RV rentals may include mileage charges, required additional insurance, charges for generator use while the vehicle is off, and one-way fees. Operating a smaller RV may not be more difficult than operating a normal large SUV or truck, but larger recreational vehicles take some practice—and drivers need to remember that they won't fit in many drive-through windows, tunnels, and parking garages. Companies like **Cruise America** (www.cruiseamerica.com) do rentals in Seattle, Portland, and Vancouver; **Campervan North America** (www.campervannorthamerica.com) rents out of Seattle; and **RV Northwest** (www.rvnorthwest.com) rents out of Portland. Few RV rental agencies are close to the airport, though many will provide airport pickups and drop-offs by request.

Driving Rules and Tips

Seat belts are required in Oregon, Washington, and British Columbia for every passenger in a car, with special **child seats** and booster seats required for children under the age of 8 or less than 40 pounds. Children must also ride in the backseat if less than 13 years of age in Washington. **Texting and cell phone use** is strongly prohibited in both states and British Columbia, and drivers can be cited even if fiddling with a phone for directions while behind the wheel.

In Washington and British Columbia, **tolls** are usually automatically billed rather than collected at a stationary toll booth—a camera takes a photo of your license plate, and you later receive a bill; if you're in a rental car, expect your rental company to bill you. Cash for tolls is generally only necessary on the toll bridges between Oregon and Washington, all located on the Columbia River far east of Portland. In Washington, some **HOV** (high-occupancy vehicle) lanes can be used by a single driver if a toll is paid, while British Columbia sometimes allow single drivers in electric-powered vehicles to travel HOV lanes.

In British Columbia, speeds are listed in **kilometers per hour** rather than miles per hour. A **flashing green light** signifies that the intersection may have a pedestrian crossing, and the driver must give the right-of-way before turning. International drivers can use their **international license** for only 90 days before they are required to get a Canadian one.

Although **cannabis** is now legal for recreational use in Washington, Oregon, and British Columbia, driving under its influence is illegal, and crossing state lines with it is against federal law. It's also against the law to cross the Canadian border in possession of the substance.

Motorcyclists are required to hold a special license and drive with a helmet, and may be subject to requirements on lights and sound levels. **Lane-splitting** is prohibited in Washington, Oregon, and British Columbia. Washington motorcyclists must have eye protection. Although **bicyclists** are subject to the same rules as car drivers, their much more vulnerable state means extra care needs to be taken in areas with bike traffic. Slow down when coming up behind a bicyclist and pass on the left only when oncoming traffic allows.

It's best to use **headlights even during the day** to appear visible to approaching vehicles. Also take care to watch for animals on the road, because hitting a deer at high speeds can be lethal to the driver as well as the deer. Passing is discouraged except in very open areas, and on roads that travel uphill there are often passing lanes built in to keep drivers safer.

Take note of your gas-tank level on all roads other than interstates, though **large regions without services** are often signed. In the Pacific Northwest, it's very important to have working **windshield wipers**—you'll encounter rain in every season here, and driving is impossible without them. Also locate your **bright lights** in advance of needing them, as they may be necessary in cases of fog or on rural highways without streetlights.

Note that in Oregon, only gas station attendants are allowed to pump gas in most places; as a general rule, there's **no self-service,** so sit in the car and wait for an attendant to approach the window. In 2018, a caveat to this law took effect, allowing **rural gas stations**—in counties with less than 40,000 people—to allow self-service at any time in some counties and at night only (6pm-6am) in others.

ROAD CONDITIONS

Mountain roads are prone to seasonal closures, and it's illegal to forgo **snow chains** when requirements are posted. However, this is only an issue on roads that climb to high elevations and isn't a problem on I-5 or coastal roads. To prepare for a trip in the winter months, check the official departments of transportation websites: the **Washington State Department of Transportation** (www.wsdot.wa.gov), **Oregon Department of Transportation** (www.oregon.gov/odot), and **British Columbia Ministry of Transportation** (www.drivebc.ca). Pass cameras, which show live feeds of snow and ice levels, backups, and accidents on Oregon roads are at **TripCheck** (www.tripcheck.com).

In Washington and Oregon, drivers can call 511 from a phone to get recordings of major **traffic information.** In British Columbia, the number is 800/550-4997. In the case of a **roadside emergency,** drivers should call 911 (in both the U.S. and Canada) to reach police and emergency services. For non-emergency cases, like a breakdown or flat tire, Americans can prepay for services from **AAA** (800/222-4357, www.aaa.com); in Canada it's **CAA** (888/268-2222, www.caa.ca). Subscriptions are required.

Crossing the Border

There are two vehicle border crossings between the United States and Canada. The primary crossing is the **Peace Arch** (noncommercial vehicles, 24 hours daily), located at the end of I-5. Peace Arch is a state park on the U.S. side and a provincial park on the Canada side. The buildings are surrounded by manicured lawns, sculptures, and a giant white arch to mark the border.

A few miles away is the **Pacific Highway Crossing** (commercial vehicles, 24 hours daily), also known informally as Truck Customs. The terminus is located off I-5 at Exit 275, where U.S. Highway 543 meets Canadian Highway 15. This crossing is less scenic than the Peace Arch but is often faster. Readerboards on either side will note the wait times for each crossing.

Americans traveling into Canada need proof of citizenship, typically a passport. Likewise, a passport or equivalent documentation (such as military orders or a permanent resident card) is required to enter the United States. Canadians can reenter Canada with a birth certificate and photo identification, but a passport is recommended.

Border officials may ask for vehicle registration papers. For rental cars, the appropriate paperwork from the rental agency should suffice. Be sure to check with the rental company that international travel is approved for your vehicle. For U.S. rental cars brought into

Canada, drivers may need a Canadian Non-Resident Insurance Card, issued by the rental company. For Canadians renting cars and crossing the border, there may be limits on how much time they can spend outside the country. Drivers are required to show proof of insurance in both countries. Frequent travelers can preregister with programs like NEXUS, SENTRI, or FAST (www.cbp.gov) for faster service.

Travel Tips

VISAS AND OFFICIALDOM

Passports and Visas

When visiting the United States or Canada from another country, a valid passport is required. Depending upon your country of origin, a visa may also be required when visiting the United States. For a complete list of countries exempt from U.S. visa requirements, visit http://travel.state.gov/visa.

Canadian citizens can visit the United States without a visa, but must show a passport or enhanced driver's license at the border. All car, train, and bus crossings may require questioning from border-control agents about the purpose of the visit, destination (including hotel address), and purchases made while in the country. To protect the agricultural industries of each country from the spread of pests and disease, the transportation of fresh fruit and plants may be prohibited. More information on crossing into the United States can be found at www.cbp.gov.

American citizens and permanent residents must show identification such as a passport or a U.S. Permanent Resident Card when crossing the border into Canada. A list of countries whose passport holders do not require a visa to visit Canada is available at www.cic.gc.ca/english/visit. There is a limit on the amount of alcohol and tobacco visitors can bring into each country.

Embassies

When traveling to the United States or Canada from another country, the embassy from your home country can help in the event of a lost passport or unexpected troubles. Embassies for many countries can be found in Vancouver, Seattle, and Portland. To find an embassy within the United States, visit www.state.gov/s/cpr/rls. For an embassy in Canada, visit www.international.gc.ca.

Customs

When entering the United States or Canada by plane, you will have to fill out a customs form. Be sure to have handy the information on your destination—name, address, and phone number. There are limits on the gifts you can bring into the country as well as the amount of tobacco and alcohol you can bring.

If you take prescription medications, bring documentation for your medicines. Medicines that require the use of syringes should be packed in checked luggage along with proper documentation. Find exact regulations on customs and duties for the United States online at www.cbp.gov; for Canada, visit http://caen-keepexploring.canada.travel/travel-info/customs-and-duty.

TRAVELING WITH CHILDREN

The Pacific Northwest is a wonderful destination for families because of its affordability, relaxed pace, and large number of activities for children. Most of the region's cities have parks, zoos, children's museums, and aquariums that cater especially to kids, as well as educational destinations such as Portland's OMSI and Seattle's Pacific Science Center. Look for family rates at museums and at gardens that require admission.

When traveling with children in the Pacific Northwest, be sure to make plans that include indoor stops. Kids can get stir-crazy in the event of a rainy day, which is common in the area. But there is also a prevalence of creative transportation options in the region: Rides on ferries, trams, and light-rail trains can be exciting for travelers of any age. Most hotels will happily accept children and can offer rooms away from noisy bars or events. Be sure to check before booking a bed-and-breakfast room, as some establishments may limit guests to adults only.

When visiting the beaches of Washington, Oregon, and British Columbia, take care with small children around the water. Pacific Ocean waves are very strong, and the cold water and undertow can be deadly for even experienced swimmers—most beaches in Washington and Oregon are for strolling, not swimming. Tides can come in quickly, stranding slow walkers or even erasing a beach. On shores with beautiful rocks to explore, the footholds around tidal pools are slippery. Avoid climbing rocks unless necessary, both to protect the wildlife and to avoid deadly injuries.

SENIOR TRAVELERS

Many older travelers will find discounts at bars, restaurants, museums, and transportation options around the Pacific Northwest. Age requirements vary and go by different names: For instance, the MAX light rail in Portland calls riders over 65 "Honored Citizens," and they pay less than half a normal adult fare. At hotels, ask for senior rates when booking. American travelers can also get discounts with membership in the AARP.

GAY AND LESBIAN TRAVELERS

The Pacific Northwest in both the United States and Canada is generally very friendly to gay and lesbian travelers. That warmth is sometimes less evident, but by no means absent, in smaller towns and more rural areas. The three large cities—Vancouver, Seattle, and Portland—hold annual pride parades.

Seattle hosts the **LGBT Visitors Center** (614 Broadway E, www.thegsba.org) at a small information stand inside a bank on Capitol Hill, which distributes maps of the area.

Gay marriage is legal in Canada and across the United States, but early adoption in Washington State brought an influx of LGBT destination weddings to the area. Check local city hall websites for more about the process of obtaining a wedding license.

HEALTH AND SAFETY

In both the United States and Canada, emergency services can be reached by dialing 911 from any phone. Although help is likely to be slower to arrive in rural areas, most of western Washington and Oregon, as well as southwestern British Columbia, is well saturated with hospitals and other emergency resources.

When hiking or doing outdoor activities, be sure to note the conditions before attempting an outing. Cell phone service may be spotty or nonexistent, so go in prepared to handle any conditions, and inform others of your plan before you depart. Stop by visitors centers or park offices to ask about regulations and advisories. Ticks, which are known carries of bacterium that causes Lyme Disease, are present in the Pacific Northwest, more commonly east of the Cascades. Hikers can use insect repellents with DEET to deter them. Check for ticks on your clothing and body during and after possible exposure. If you find a tick, remove it promptly with tweezers and clean the bite with an antiseptic ointment.

DRINKING AND SMOKING

The **drinking age** in the United States is 21 years old, and most bars and restaurants will ask for identification for anyone who looks close to that age. Almost all grocery stores and liquor stores will require identification as well.

Bars in Seattle stay open until about 2am and often close earlier on weeknights. Laws regarding when alcohol can last be served are very strict, but some dance clubs will stay open later after their bars have stopped serving alcohol. In the rest of Washington, select bars may stay open late, but many close at midnight or 1am. Oregon has a similar pattern, with bars in Portland serving drinks until 2:30am, but establishments elsewhere close earlier. The drinking age in British Columbia—the province that holds Vancouver and Victoria—is 19 years old. Bars can serve alcohol until 3am, though many bars have earlier closing times.

Smoking in bars, restaurants, and indoor places is prohibited. Some towns and state parks prohibit smoking in outdoor public places, including many in the Seattle area. Cigarettes are not sold to anyone under the age of 18, and identification is required. Canada has many of the same restrictions for smoking as the United States; for example, it is illegal to smoke in Vancouver parks and beaches.

In 2012, possession of **cannabis** for recreational use became legal in Washington State, and Oregon followed suit in 2015. That doesn't mean it's a free-for-all, however. Adults age 21 or older can possess up to one ounce of marijuana, but cannot smoke in a public place. Stores selling marijuana are slowly becoming a reality as the state works out regulations and taxation. However, marijuana is still illegal on federal lands, and it's also illegal to cross state lines in possession of it. Use of cannabis for recreational use was legalized in British Columbia in 2018, but it cannot be carried across the border.

INFORMATION AND SERVICES

Money

All businesses in Washington and Oregon accept the U.S. dollar ($), and most businesses, including taxi cabs, will accept major credit cards like Visa and MasterCard. Other cards, such as American Express and Discover, are often accepted as well. Currency exchange businesses are available in most airports, downtown areas of major cities, and in banks around the region. ATMs are prevalent.

The Canadian dollar (C$) is not interchangeable with the U.S. dollar; check currency exchange businesses or online for the current exchange rate. A limited number of businesses in downtown Vancouver and Victoria or near the U.S. border may accept U.S. currency, often returning change in Canadian money. However, it's best not to rely on that, and you may not get the best exchange rate. Note that banks may charge fees for using credit cards in countries other than where they were issued.

Travelers will be pleased to discover that the State of Oregon does not charge a general sales tax.

Maps and Tourist Information

When planning a trip to the Pacific Northwest, come prepared with a number of maps. City maps of Vancouver, Seattle, Victoria, and Portland are ideal for navigating the often-confusing waterfront cities. Routes to the Oregon Coast and Olympic Peninsula will require state maps of Washington and Oregon; the best versions are available at a book or travel store, or from **AAA** (www.aaa.com). What's more, the drive through Canada to Vancouver, while not difficult, can be stressful for drivers without a map to reassure them.

For travelers expecting to use GPS or cell phone route-finding, note that the service may not be available in rural areas of the coast and Olympic Peninsula, or in Canada with some service plans. Many towns have visitors centers with some form of free map, but reliable highway maps are a must to pack for a road trip in the area.

Resources

Suggested Reading

FICTION

Copeland, Douglas. *Microserfs*. New York: Harper Perennial, 2008. This British Columbia author captures the early absurdities of the tech boom.

Dunn, Katherine. *Geek Love*. New York: Knopf, 1989. Dunn's classic focuses on a family of sideshow performers and shows a wilder side of the Pacific Northwest.

Guterson, David. *Snow Falling on Cedars*. San Diego: Harcourt Brace, 1994. Guterson imagines a Puget Sound island shaken by Japanese internment in World War II.

Le Guin, Ursula K. *The Lathe of Heaven*. New York: Avon, 1971. The famous sci-fi novelist renders a Portland even stranger than reality, where dreams have real-world effects.

Semple, Maria. *Where'd You Go, Bernadette: A Novel*. New York: Little, Brown and Company, 2012. Everything from the weather to local manners is satirized in a hilarious novel that invites Seattleites to laugh at themselves.

NONFICTION

Brown, Daniel James. *The Boys in the Boat*. New York: Penguin, 2013. Brown's classic Seattle sports story is really about the city during the Great Depression.

Dillard, Annie. *Teaching a Stone to Talk*. New York: Harper and Row, 1982. This collection of Dillard's narrative essays includes one about a life-changing Northwest eclipse.

Egan, Timothy. *The Good Rain: Across Time and Terrain in the Pacific Northwest*. New York: Vintage, 1990. One of the region's best-known writers presents thoughtful essays about the modern Pacific Northwest.

Egan, Timothy. *Short Nights of the Shadow Catcher*. Boston: Mariner, 2013. Egan profiles photographer Edward Curtis and his relationship to the battered Native American population of the West.

Palahniuk, Chuck. *Fugitives and Refugees: A Walk in Portland, Oregon*. New York: Crown Journeys, 2003. Palahniuk presents an unusual travelogue of Portland, itself already an unusual city.

Taylor, Quintard. *The Forging of a Black Community: Seattle's Central District from 1870 through the Civil Rights Era*. Seattle: University of Washington Press, 1994. University of Washington professor Quintard Taylor tells the story of Seattle's black community.

Wolff, Tobias. *This Boy's Life*. New York: Atlantic, 1989. A writer partially raised in a small rural town in Washington chronicles his difficult childhood.

Internet Resources

WASHINGTON

Experience WA

www.experiencewa.com

Find travel resources for the entire state and access to the Washington State Visitors' Guide.

Mount Rainier National Park

www.nps.gov/mora

The national park's official site has information on park opening hours, road conditions, permits, and activities.

North Cascades National Park

www.nps.gov/noca

The national park's official site has information on visitors center opening hours and campgrounds, as well as maps.

Olympic National Park

www.nps.gov/olym

The national park's official site has campground information, maps, and suggestions on approaching the sprawling park.

Olympic Peninsula

www.olympicpeninsula.org

This travel website for the region has activity ideas and photo galleries.

Visit Rainier

www.visitrainier.com

This tourism website has listings for businesses, campgrounds, and activities around Mount Rainier National Park.

Visit Seattle

www.visitseattle.org

Seattle's official tourism site has maps, listings, trip ideas, and ticket deals.

Washington Department of Transportation

www.wsdot.wa.gov

The state's official transportation website has information on road conditions and planned closures, traffic updates, and cameras, plus information on ferry times, waits, and fares.

OREGON

Crater Lake National Park

www.nps.gov/crla

The national park's official site has road closure information, visitors center and hotel opening hours, and trail suggestions.

Travel Oregon

www.traveloregon.com

Oregon's official tourism site has trip ideas and listings, but its beautiful design is best suited to inspiration during planning.

Travel Portland

www.travelportland.com

Portland's official travel website offers accommodation listings and itinerary ideas, plus promotions and access to the visitors' guide.

TripCheck

www.tripcheck.com

The traveler's wing of the Oregon Department of Transportation offers an easy-to-use map of traffic cameras and construction alerts.

CANADA

Destination British Columbia

www.hellobc.com

The official website for the province has event calendars, itinerary ideas, and hotel listings.

Tourism Vancouver

www.tourismvancouver.com

Vancouver's official travel site has listings, itineraries, neighborhood descriptions, and promotional deals.

Tourism Victoria

www.tourismvictoria.com

The city's official website shares museum listings and featured events.

Index

A

B

C

D

E

H

I

J

K

P

QR

S

INDEX

T

U

V

W

XYZ

List of Maps

Photo Credits

Title page photo: alptraum | dreamstime.com;
all photos © allison williams except the following:
page 5 © mirekdeml | dreamstime; page 6 © (top left) hattanas kumchai/123rf.com; page 7 © (top) jackbluee | dreamstime.com; (bottom left) jbrichter | dreamstime.com; (bottom right) hannamariah | dreamstime.com; page 8 © chanowski | dreamstime.com; page 10 © (bottom) qwntm | dreamstime.com; page 11 © cascoly | dreamstime.com; page 13 © (top) irina88w | dreamstime.com; (bottom) f11photo | dreamstime.com; page 14 © the inn at abeja; page 15 © (top) artyooran | dreamstime.com; (bottom) cestes001 | dreamstime.com; page 17 © (top) oregon shakespeare festival / t charles erickson; (bottom) shamil1 | dreamstime.com; page 22 © nita lake lodge; page 23 © (left) neil fisher/vancouver aquarium; 24 © canbalci | dreamstime.com; page 26 © (right) omsi; page 27 © jbrichter | dreamstime.com; page 28 © josemaria toscano/123rf.com; page 32 © rcphoto | dreamstime.com; page 35 © j(top) ml12nan | Dreamstime.com; (bottom) alpegor | dreamstime.com; page 37 © kit anderson; page 40 © tashka | dreamstime.com; page 45 © jackbluee | dreamstime.com; page 46 © f11photo | dreamstime.com; page 49 © silivonochka | dreamstime.com; page 50 © rruntsch | dreamstime.com; page 55 © ted huetter/the museum of flight; page 65 © holyhikaru/123rf; page 80 © serrnovik | dreamstime; page 85 © (top) grant roush; (bottom) bpperry | dreamstime.com; page 94 © grant roush; page 97 © svetlana55 | dreamstime.com; page 98 © nadik25 | dreamstime.com; page 100 © michaelversprill | dreamstime.com; page 103 © svetlana55 | dreamstime.com; page 113 © william perry/123rf.com; page 115 © crackerclips | dreamstime.com; page 119 © grant roush; page 122 © grant roush; page 123 © kamchatka | dreamstime.com; page 125 © grant roush; page 126 © bpperry | dreamstime.com; page 129 © wellywelly/shutterstock; page 134 © edcorey | dreamstime.com; 141 © aquamarine4 | dreamstime.com;page 145 © (top) curtwill7 | dreamstime.com; (bottom) rodchron | dreamstime.com; page 147 © soundcontent | dreamstime.com; page 173 © stanislav moroz | dreamstime; page 187 © cathy williams; page 191 © (top) sclowe | dreamstime.com; (bottom) edbob1 | dreamstime.com; page 193 © rosario resort and spa; page 196 © paulandjudy | dreamstime.com; page 200 © tom956 | dreamstime.com; page 205 © friday harbor house/kip beelman; page 206 © shelley campbell bogaert; page 214 © sarah natasha horowitz; page 216 © rosario resort and spa; page 221 © nova askue; page 223 © (top) bpperry | dreamstime.com; (bottom) the inn at abeja; page 25 © jeffclimer | dreamstime.com; page 230 © kevnotesong | dreamstime.com; page 233 © the marcus whitman hotel; page 238 © michelle baumbach/shutterstock; page 242 © pixelsoft films; page 243 © 14 hands winery; page 247 © (top) jpldesigns | dreamstime.com; (bottom) groovysoup | dreamstime.com; page 253 © deebrowning | dreamstime.com; page 256 © portland art museum; page 259 © svetlana55 | dreamstime.com; page 260 © davidgn | dreamstime; page 262 © omsi; page 278 © deebrowning | dreamstime.com; page 279 © jit lim/123rf.com; page 298 © grant roush; page 299 © lwilk | dreamstime.com; page 310 © jkraft5 | dreamstime.com;page 311 © jeanneprovost | dreamstime.com; page 315 © (top) rcphoto | dreamstime.com; (bottom) michelejames | dreamstime.com; page 317 © jpldesigns | dreamstime.com; page 319 © deebrowning | dreamstime.com; page 323 © the allison inn and spa; page 325 © davidkrug/123rf; page 326 © pngstudio | dreamstime.com; page 330 © svetlana55 | dreamstime.com; page 332 © ron cooper; page 333 © joshuaraineyphotography | dreamstime.com; page 337 © joshuaraineyphotography | dreamstime.com; page 341 © jamiehooper | dreamstime.com; page 347 © (top) jkraft5 | dreamstime.com; (bottom) aiisha | dreamstime.com; page 349 © deebrowning | dreamstime.com; page 352 © toynutz | dreamstime.com; page 356 © grant roush; page 357 © toynutz | dreamstime.com; page 361 © crux fermentation project; page 368 © timstirling | dreamstime.com; page 371 © (top) bsdphotos | dreamstime.com; (bottom) slklimk | dreamstime.com; page 373 © suzyqbrown49 | dreamstime.com; page 377 © knowlesgallery | dreamstime.com; page 382 © cathy williams; page 388 © kit anderson; page 396 © john bailey/123rf.com; page 401 © zigzagmtart/123rf.com; page 406 © kit anderson; page 408 © kit andreson; page 417 © (top) viviansviews | dreamstime.com; (bottom) bpperry | dreamstime.com; page 419 © oregon shakespeare festival/t charles erickson; page 421 © akstp | dreamstime.com; page 423 © jade banson, rogue rafting co.; page 425 © oregon shakespeare festival/jenny graham; page 433 © gnagel | dreamstime.com; page 437 © (bottom) danbreckwoldt | dreamstime.com; page 445 © andrej blagojević | dreamstime; page 447 © vancouver aquarium; page 448 © deymos | dreamstime.com;

page 449 © leighton collins/123rf.com; page 456 © justek16 | dreamstime.com; page 457 © sergey breev/123rf.com; page 467 © lijuan guo | dreamstime; page 469 © hawksworth; page 470 © nightingale; page 484 © reefer | dreamstime.com; page 486 © outdoorsman | dreamstime.com; page 490 © nita lake lodge; page 493 © (top) philip bird/123rf.com; (bottom) jonghyunkim | dreamstime.com; page 502 © jakobradlgruber/123rf.com; page 504 © cybernesco | dreamstime.com; page 510 © belinda fontes photography; page 514 © jakobradlgruber/123rf.com; page 521 © vladthefool | dreamstime.com; page 522 © hsandler | dreamstime.com; page 530 © (bottom) grant roush; page 543 © (top) svitlana imnadze | dreamstime

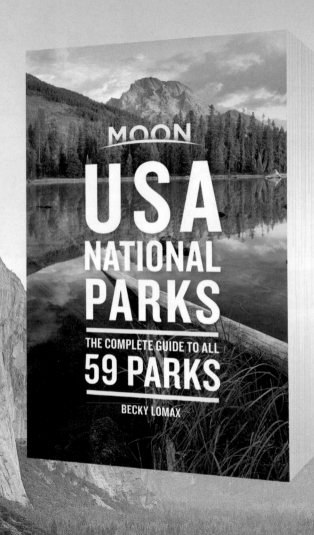

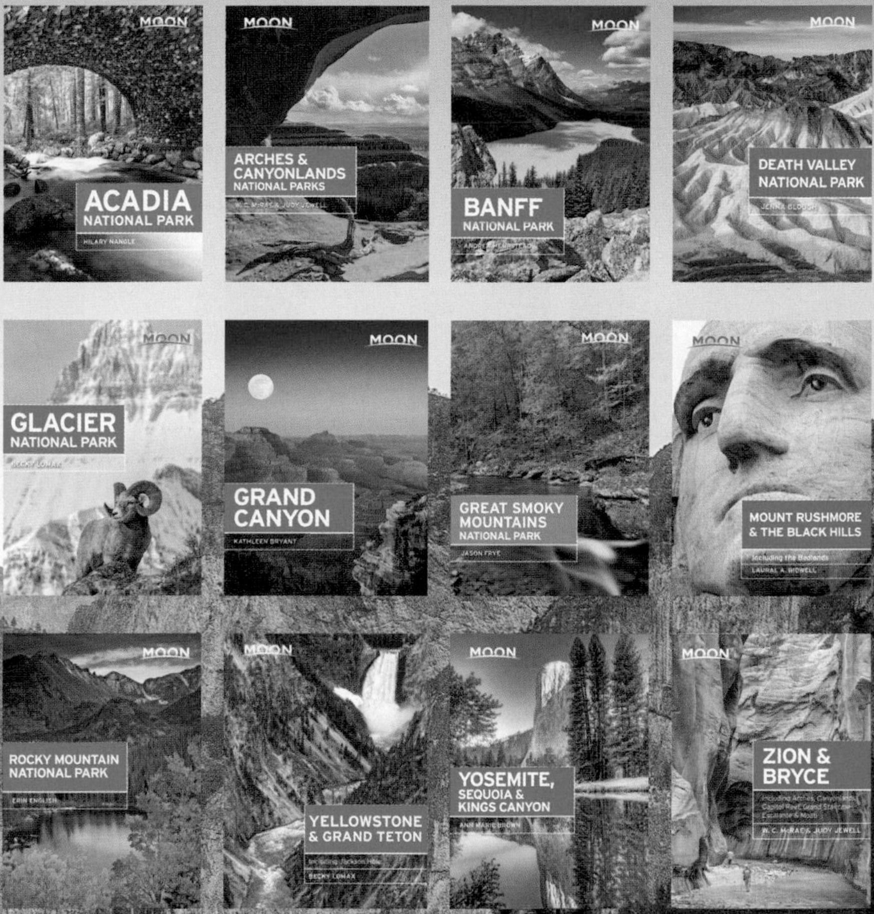
MOON
ACADIA NATIONAL PARK
HILARY NANGLE
MOON
ARCHES & CANYONLANDS NATIONAL PARKS
W. C. McRAE & JUDY JEWELL
MOON
BANFF NATIONAL PARK
MOON
DEATH VALLEY NATIONAL PARK
JENNA BLOUGH
MOON
GLACIER NATIONAL PARK
BECKY LOMAX
MOON
GRAND CANYON
KATHLEEN BRYANT
MOON
GREAT SMOKY MOUNTAINS NATIONAL PARK
JASON FRYE
MOON
MOUNT RUSHMORE & THE BLACK HILLS
Including the Badlands
LAURA K. BIDWELL
MOON
ROCKY MOUNTAIN NATIONAL PARK
ERIN ENGLISH
MOON
YELLOWSTONE & GRAND TETON
BECKY LOMAX
MOON
YOSEMITE, SEQUOIA & KINGS CANYON
ANN MARIE BROWN
MOON
ZION & BRYCE
W. C. McRAE & JUDY JEWELL

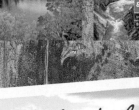

MOON ROAD TRIP GUIDES

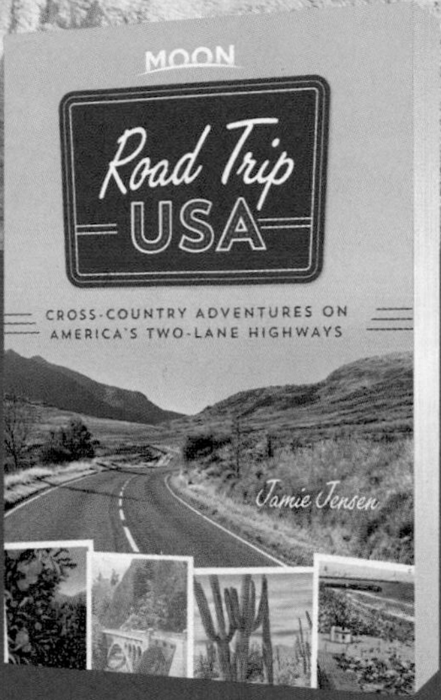

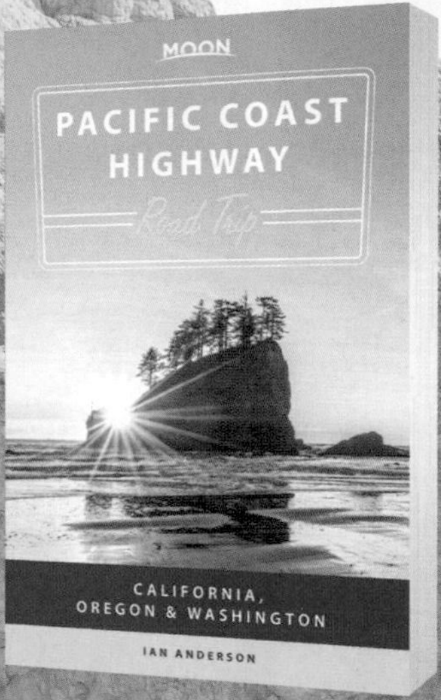

Road Trip USA

Criss-cross the country on America's classic two-lane highways with the newest edition of *Road Trip USA!*

Packed with over 125 detailed driving maps (covering more than 35,000 miles), colorful photos and illustrations of America both then and now, and mile-by-mile highlights

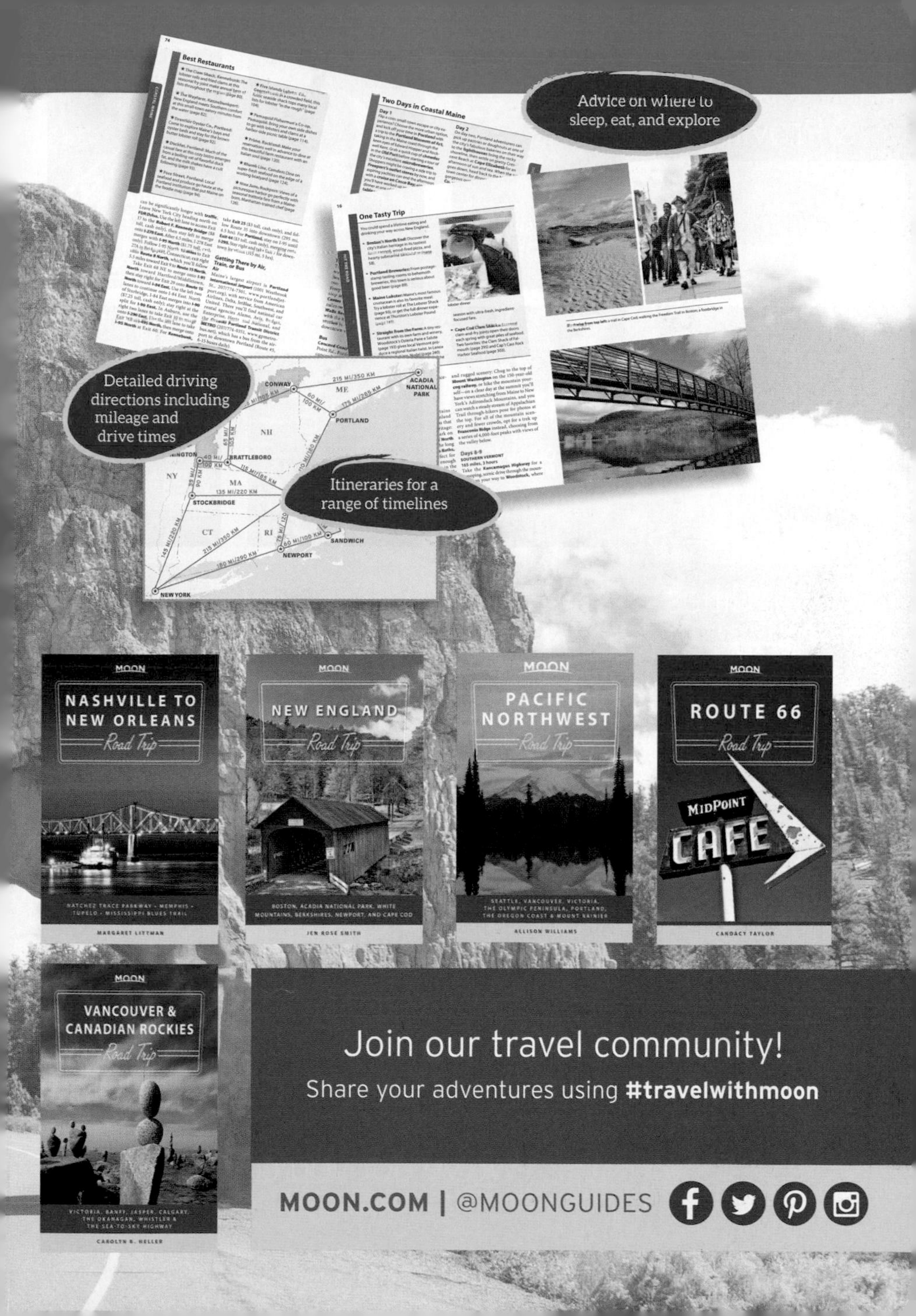
Advice on where to sleep, eat, and explore
Detailed driving directions including mileage and drive times
Itineraries for a range of timelines
MOON
NASHVILLE TO NEW ORLEANS
Road Trip
NATCHEZ TRACE PARKWAY · MEMPHIS · TUPELO · MISSISSIPPI BLUES TRAIL
MARGARET LITTMAN
MOON
NEW ENGLAND
Road Trip
BOSTON, ACADIA NATIONAL PARK, WHITE MOUNTAINS, BERKSHIRES, NEWPORT, AND CAPE COD
JEN ROSE SMITH
MOON
PACIFIC NORTHWEST
Road Trip
SEATTLE, VANCOUVER, VICTORIA, THE OLYMPIC PENINSULA, PORTLAND, THE OREGON COAST & MOUNT RAINIER
ALLISON WILLIAMS
MOON
ROUTE 66
Road Trip
MIDPOINT CAFE
CANDACY TAYLOR
MOON
VANCOUVER & CANADIAN ROCKIES
Road Trip
VICTORIA, BANFF, JASPER, CALGARY, THE OKANAGAN, WHISTLER & THE SEA-TO-SKY HIGHWAY
CAROLYN B. HELLER
Join our travel community!
Share your adventures using #travelwithmoon
MOON.COM | @MOONGUIDES

States
& Provinces
MOON
WASHINGTON
MATTHEW LOMBARDI
MOON
OREGON
JUDY JEWELL & W. C. McRAE
MOON
BRITISH COLUMBIA
Regions
& Getaways
MOON
OLYMPIC PENINSULA
MOON
COASTAL OREGON
W. C. McRAE & JUDY JEWELL
MOON
VICTORIA & VANCOUVER ISLAND
ANDREW HEMPSTEAD
Cities
COLOR FOLDOUT MAP
MOON
SEATTLE
MOON
PORTLAND
MOON
VANCOUVER
CAROLYN B. HELLER
Road Trips
& Outdoors
MOON
75 GREAT HIKES
SEATTLE
MOON
OREGON CAMPING
The Complete Guide to Tent and RV Camping
TOM STIENSTRA
MOON
PACIFIC NORTHWEST
Road Trip
SEATTLE, VANCOUVER, VICTORIA, THE OLYMPIC PENINSULA, PORTLAND, THE OREGON COAST & MOUNT RAINIER
ALLISON WILLIAMS
We've got you covered, PNW!

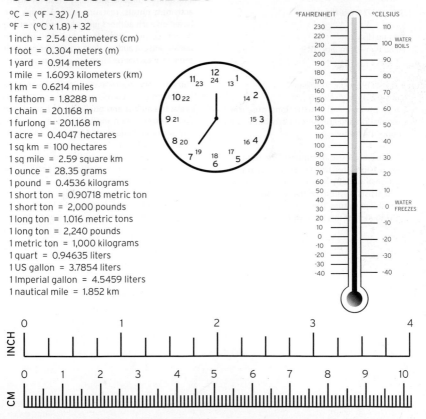

MAP SYMBOLS

- Expressway
- Primary Road
- Secondary Road
- Unpaved Road
- Feature Trail
- Other Trail
- Ferry
- Pedestrian Walkway
- Stairs

- ○ City/Town
- ⊙ State Capital
- ⊛ National Capital
- ★ Point of Interest
- • Accommodation
- ▼ Restaurant/Bar
- ■ Other Location
- Λ Campground

- Airport
- Airfield
- ▲ Mountain
- ✦ Unique Natural Feature
- Waterfall
- Park
- Trailhead
- Skiing Area

- Golf Course
- Parking Area
- Archaeological Site
- Church
- Gas Station
- Glacier
- Mangrove
- Reef
- Swamp

CONVERSION TABLES

°C = (°F - 32) / 1.8
°F = (°C x 1.8) + 32
1 inch = 2.54 centimeters (cm)
1 foot = 0.304 meters (m)
1 yard = 0.914 meters
1 mile = 1.6093 kilometers (km)
1 km = 0.6214 miles
1 fathom = 1.8288 m
1 chain = 20.1168 m
1 furlong = 201.168 m
1 acre = 0.4047 hectares
1 sq km = 100 hectares
1 sq mile = 2.59 square km
1 ounce = 28.35 grams
1 pound = 0.4536 kilograms
1 short ton = 0.90718 metric ton
1 short ton = 2,000 pounds
1 long ton = 1.016 metric tons
1 long ton = 2,240 pounds
1 metric ton = 1,000 kilograms
1 quart = 0.94635 liters
1 US gallon = 3.7854 liters
1 Imperial gallon = 4.5459 liters
1 nautical mile = 1.852 km

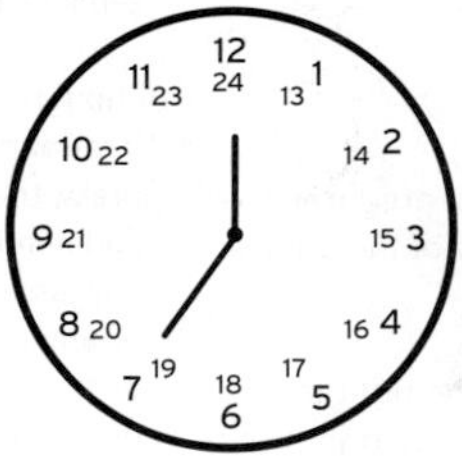

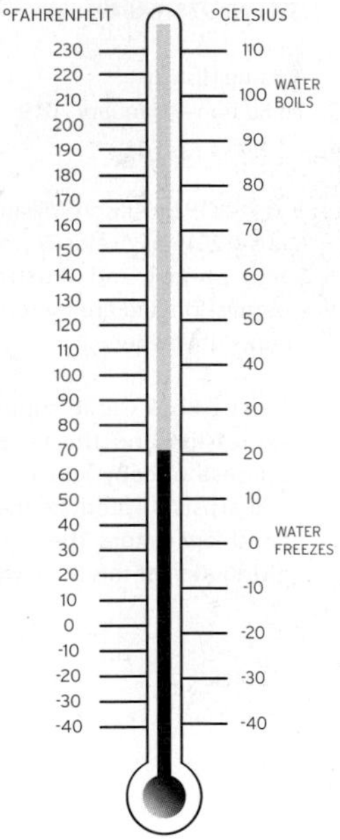

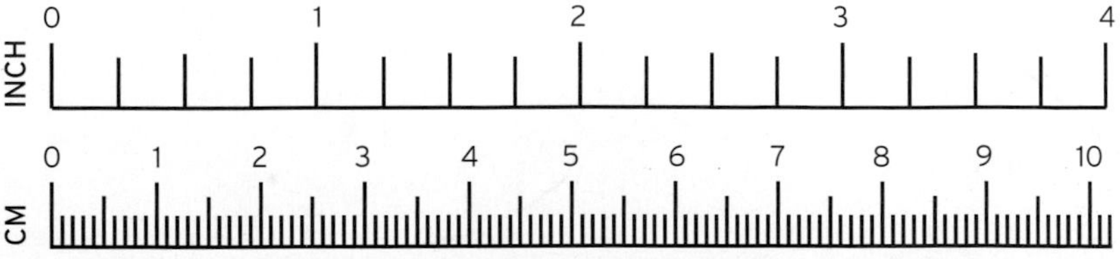

MOON PACIFIC NORTHWEST
Avalon Travel
Hachette Book Group
1700 Fourth Street
Berkeley, CA 94710, USA
www.moon.com

Editor: Kristi Mitsuda
Series Manager: Kathryn Ettinger
Copy Editor: Ann Seifert
Production and Graphics Coordinator: Krista Anderson
Cover Design: Faceout Studios, Charles Brock
Interior Design: Domini Dragoone
Moon Logo: Tim McGrath
Map Editor: Albert Angulo
Cartographers: Albert Angulo, Karin Dahl, Brian Shotwell
Indexer: Greg Jewett

ISBN-13: 9781640491625

Printing History
1st Edition — January 2019
5 4 3 2 1

Front cover photo: Pacific Northwest forest aerial view © franckreporter/Getty Images

Back cover photo: Heceta Head Lighthouse, Oregon © Thomas Lozinski/Dreamstime.com

Printed in China by RR Donnelley